## DATE DUE

| | | | |
|---|---|---|---|
| | | | |
| | | | |
| | | | |
| | | | |
| | | | |
| | | | |
| | | | |
| | | | |
| | | | |
| | | | |
| | | | |

PRINTED IN U.S.A.

# Guide to Gale Literary Criticism Series

| For criticism on | Consult these Gale series |
|---|---|
| Authors now living or who died after December 31, 1959 | *CONTEMPORARY LITERARY CRITICISM (CLC)* |
| Authors who died between 1900 and 1959 | *TWENTIETH-CENTURY LITERARY CRITICISM (TCLC)* |
| Authors who died between 1800 and 1899 | *NINETEENTH-CENTURY LITERATURE CRITICISM (NCLC)* |
| Authors who died between 1400 and 1799 | *LITERATURE CRITICISM FROM 1400 TO 1800 (LC)*<br><br>*SHAKESPEAREAN CRITICISM (SC)* |
| Authors who died before 1400 | *CLASSICAL AND MEDIEVAL LITERATURE CRITICISM (CMLC)* |
| Authors of books for children and young adults | *CHILDREN'S LITERATURE REVIEW (CLR)* |
| Dramatists | *DRAMA CRITICISM (DC)* |
| Poets | *POETRY CRITICISM (PC)* |
| Short story writers | *SHORT STORY CRITICISM (SSC)* |
| Black writers of the past two hundred years | *BLACK LITERATURE CRITICISM (BLC)* |
| Hispanic writers of the late nineteenth and twentieth centuries | *HISPANIC LITERATURE CRITICISM (HLC)* |
| Native North American writers and orators of the eighteenth, nineteenth, and twentieth centuries | *NATIVE NORTH AMERICAN LITERATURE (NNAL)* |
| Major authors from the Renaissance to the present | *WORLD LITERATURE CRITICISM, 1500 TO THE PRESENT (WLC)* |

# CLASSICAL AND MEDIEVAL LITERATURE CRITICISM

ISSN 0896-0011

Volume 34

# CLASSICAL AND MEDIEVAL LITERATURE CRITICISM

Excerpts from Criticism of the Works of World
Authors from Classical Antiquity through the
Fourteenth Century, from the First Appraisals
to Current Evaluations

**Jelena O. Krstović**
Editor

*GALE GROUP*

*Detroit*
*San Francisco*
*London*
*Boston*
*Woodbridge, CT*

**STAFF**

Jelena Krstović, *Editor*
Elisabeth Gellert, *Associate Editor*
Janet Witalec, *Managing Editor*

Maria Franklin, *Permissions Manager*
Kimberly F. Smilay, *Permissions Specialist*
Kelly A. Quin, *Permissions Associate*
Erin Bealmear, Sandy Gore, *Permissions Assistants*

Victoria B. Cariappa, *Research Manager*
Patricia T. Ballard, Wendy Festerling, Tracie A. Richardson, Corrine Boland, *Research Associates*
Phyllis Blackman, *Research Assistant*

Dorothy Maki, *Manufacturing Manager*
Cindy Range, *Buyer*

Pamela A. Reed, *Imaging Coordinator*
Randy Bassett, *Image Database Supervisor*
Robert Duncan, Michael Logusz, *Imaging Specialists*
Christine O'Bryan, *Desktop Publisher*

This book is printed on acid-free paper that meets the minimum requirements of American National Standard for Information Sciences—Permanence Paper for Printed Library materials, ANSI Z39.48-1984.

Library of Congress Catalog Card Number 88-658021
ISBN 0-7876-3256-2
ISSN 0896-0011
Printed in the United States of America

10 9 8 7 6 5 4 3 2 1

# Contents

# Preface

Since its inception in 1988, *Classical and Medieval Literature Criticism* has been a valuable resource for students and librarians seeking critical commentary on the writers and works of these periods in world history. Major reviewing sources have assessed *CMLC* as "useful" and "extremely convenient," noting that it "adds to our understanding of the rich legacy left by the ancient period and the Middle Ages," and praising its "general excellence in the presentation of an inherently interesting subject." No other single reference source has surveyed the critical reaction to classical and medieval literature as thoroughly as *CMLC*.

## Scope of the Series

*CMLC* is designed to serve as an introduction for students and advanced readers of the works and authors of antiquity through the fourteenth century. The great poets, prose writers, dramatists, and philosophers of this period form the basis of most humanities curricula, so that virtually every student will encounter many of these works during the course of a high school and college education. By organizing and reprinting an enormous amount of commentary written on classical and medieval authors and works, *CMLC* helps students develop valuable insight into literary history, promotes a better understanding of the texts, and sparks ideas for papers and assignments. Each entry in *CMLC* presents a comprehensive survey of an author's career, an individual work of literature, or a literary topic, and provides the user with a multiplicity of interpretations and assessments. Such variety allows students to pursue their own interests; furthermore, it fosters an awareness that literature is dynamic and responsive to many different opinions.

*CMLC* continues the survey of criticism of world literature begun by Gale's *Contemporary Literary Criticism (CLC)*, *Twentieth-Century Literary Criticism (TCLC)*, *Nineteenth-Century Literature Criticism (NCLC)*, *Literature Criticism from 1400 to 1800 (LC)*, and *Shakespearean Criticism (SC)*. For additional information about these and Gale's other criticism series, users should consult the Guide to Gale Literary Criticism Series preceding the title page in this volume.

## Coverage

Each volume of *CMLC* is carefully compiled to present:

- criticism of authors, works, and topics which represent a variety of genres, time periods, and nationalities

- both major and lesser-known writers and works of the period (such as non-Western authors and literature, increasingly read by today's students)

- 4-6 authors, works, or topics per volume

- individual entries that survey the critical response to each author, work, or topic, including early criticism, later criticism (to represent any rise or decline in reputation), and current retrospective analyses. The length of each author, work, or topic entry also indicates relative importance, reflecting the amount of critical attention the author, work, or topic has received from critics writing in English, and from foreign criticism in translation.

An author may appear more than once in the series if his or her writings have been the subject of a substantial amount of criticism; in these instances, specific works or groups of works by the author will be covered in separate entries. For example, Homer will be represented by three entries, one devoted to the *Iliad*, one to the *Odyssey*, and one to the Homeric Hymns.

Starting with Volume 10, *CMLC* will also occasionally include entries devoted to literary topics. For example, *CMLC*-10 focuses on Arthurian Legend and includes general criticism on that subject as well as individual entries on writers or works central to that topic—Chrétien de Troyes, Gottfried von Strassburg, Layamon, and the Alliterative *Morte Arthure*. Presocratic Philosophy is the focus of *CMLC*-22, which includes general criticism as well as essays on Greek philosophers Anaximander, Heraclitus, Parmenides, and Pythagoras.

# Organization of the Book

An author entry consists of the following elements: author heading, biographical and critical introduction, principal works, principal English translations or editions, excerpts of criticism (each preceded by a bibliographic citation and an annotation), and a bibliography of further reading.

- The **Author Heading** consists of the author's most commonly used name, followed by birth and death dates. If the entry is devoted to a work, the heading will consist of the most common form of the title in English translation (if applicable), and the original date of composition. Located at the beginning of the introduction are any name or title variations.

- A **Portrait** of the author is included when available. Many entries also feature illustrations of materials pertinent to the author or work, including manuscript pages, book illustrations, and representations of people, places, and events important to a study of the author or work.

- The **Biographical and Critical Introduction** contains background information that concisely introduces the reader to the author, work, or topic.

- The list of **Principal Works** and **English Translations** or **Editions** is chronological by date of first publication and is included as an aid to the student seeking translated versions or editions of these works for study. The list will focus primarily on twentieth-century translations, selecting those works most commonly considered the best by critics.

- **Criticism** is arranged chronologically in each entry to provide a useful perspective on changes in critical evaluation over the years. All titles by the author featured in the critical entry are printed in boldface type to enable the user to ascertain without difficulty the works being discussed. Also for purposes of easier identification, the critic's name and the publication date of the essay are given at the beginning of each piece of criticism. Anonymous criticism is preceded by the title of the journal in which it appeared. Publication information (such as publisher names and book prices) and parenthetical numerical references (such as footnotes or page and line references to specific editions of works) have been deleted at the editors' discretion to provide smoother reading of the text. Many critical entries in *CMLC* also contain translations to aid the users. Footnotes that appear with previously published pieces of criticism are reprinted at the end of each essay or excerpt. In the case of excerpted criticism, only those footnotes that pertain to the excerpted text are included.

- A complete **Bibliographic Citation** provides original publication information for each piece of criticism.

- Critical excerpts are also prefaced by **Annotations** providing the reader with information about both the critic and the criticism, the scope of the excerpt, the growth of critical controversy, or changes in critical trends regarding an author or work. In some cases, these notes include cross-references to excerpts by critics who discuss each other's commentary. Dates in parentheses within the annotation refer to a book publication date when they follow a book title, and to an essay date when they follow a critic's name.

- An annotated bibliography of **Further Reading** appears at the end of each entry and lists additional secondary sources on the author or work. In some cases it includes essays for which the editors could not obtain reprint rights. When applicable, the Further Reading is followed by references to additional entries on the author in other literary reference series published by Gale.

**Topic Entries** are subdivided into several thematic rubrics in which criticism appears in order of descending scope.

# Cumulative Indexes

Each volume of *CMLC* includes a cumulative **author index** listing all authors who have appeared in Gale's Literary Criticism Series, along with cross references to such biographical series as *Contemporary Authors* and *Dictionary of Literary Biography.* For readers' convenience, a complete list of Gale titles included appears on the page prior to the author index. Useful for locating an author within the various series, this index is particularly valuable for those authors who are identified with a certain period but who, because of their death date, are placed in another, or for those authors whose careers span two periods. For example, Geoffrey Chaucer, who is usually considered a medieval author, is found in *Literature Criticism from 1400 to 1800* because he died after 1399.

Beginning with the tenth volume, *CMLC* includes a cumulative index listing all topic entries that have appeared in the Gale Literary Criticism Series *Classical and Medieval Literature Criticism, Contemporary Literary Criticism, Literature Criticism from 1400 to 1800, Nineteenth-Century Literature Criticism,* and *Twentieth-Century Literary Criticism.*

Beginning with the second volume, *CMLC* also includes a cumulative nationality index. Authors and/or works are grouped by nationality, and the volume in which criticism on them may be found is indicated.

# Title Index

Each volume of *CMLC* also includes an index listing the titles of all literary works discussed in the series. Foreign language titles that have been translated are followed by the titles of the translations—for example, *Slovo o polku Igorove (The Song of Igor's Campaign).* Page numbers following these translated titles refer to all pages on which any form of the title, either foreign language or translated, appears. Titles of novels, dramas, nonfiction books, and poetry, short story, or essay collections are printed in italics, while those of all individual poems, short stories, and essays are printed in roman type within quotation marks. In cases where the same title is used by different authors, the author's name or surname is given in parentheses after the title, e.g. *Collected Poems* (Horace) and *Collected Poems* (Sappho).

# Critic Index

An index to critics, which cumulates with the second volume, is another useful feature of *CMLC.* Under each critic's name are listed the authors and/or works on whom the critic has written and the volume and page number where criticism may be found.

# A Note to the Reader

When writing papers, students who quote directly from any volume in the Literary Criticism Series may use the following general forms to footnote reprinted criticism. The first example pertains to material drawn from a periodical, the second to material reprinted from books.

> Rollo May, "The Therapist and the Journey into Hell," *Michigan Quarterly Review,* XXV, No. 4 (Fall 1986), 629-41; excerpted and reprinted in *Classical and Medieval Literature Criticism,* Vol. 3, ed. Jelena O. Krstovic (Detroit: Gale Research, 1989), pp. 154-58.

> Dana Ferrin Sutton, *Self and Society in Aristophanes* (University of Press of America, 1980); excerpted and reprinted in *Classical and Medieval Literature Criticism,* Vol. 4, ed. Jelena O. Krstovic (Detroit: Gale Research, 1990), pp. 162-69.

**Suggestions Are Welcome**

Readers who wish to make suggestions for future volumes, or who have other comments regarding the series, are cordially invited to write or call the editors (1-800-347-GALE; Fax: (248) 699-8049).

# Acknowledgments

The editors wish to thank the copyright holders of the excerpted criticism included in this volume and the permissions managers of many book and magazine publishing companies for assisting us in securing reproduction rights. We are also grateful to the staffs of the Detroit Public Library, the Library of Congress, the University of Detroit Mercy Library, Wayne State University Purdy/Kresge Library Complex, and the University of Michigan Libraries for making their resources available to us. Following is a list of the copyright holders who have granted us permission to reproduce material in this volume of *CMLC*. Every effort has been made to trace copyright, but if omissions have been made, please let us know.

**COPYRIGHTED EXCERPTS IN *CMLC*, VOLUME 34, WERE REPRODUCED FROM THE FOLLOWING PERIODICALS:**

*Anglia*, v. 95, 1977. © Max Niemeyer Tübingen 1977. Reproduced by permission of the publisher.–*The Chaucer Review*, v. 6, Fall, 1971. Copyright © 1971 The Pennsylvania State University, University Park, PA. Reproduced by permission.–*Classica et Mediaevalia*, v. XXXV, 1984. Reproduced by permission of Museum Tusculanum Press, University of Copenhagen.–*The Classical Bulletin*, v. 45, February, 1969. Copyright © 1969 The Classical Bulletin. All rights reserved. Reproduced by permission of the publisher via Copyright Clearance Center, Inc.–*Classical Philology*, v. LXVIII, April, 1973 for "The Sexual Episodes in the 'Satyricon'" by Christopher Gill. © 1973 by The University of Chicago. Reproduced by permission of the publisher and the author.–*Der Islam*, v. 51, 1974 for "The Unity of the Ghazals of Hafiz" by Von R. M. Rehder.–*Islamic Culture*, v. XX, April, 1946 – July, 1946 for "Hafiz and His English Translators" by A. J. Arberry. Reproduced by permission of the Literary Estate for A. J. Arberry.–*Journal of Near Eastern Studies*, v. 31, January, 1972 for "Hafez and Poetic Unity Through Verse Rhythms" by Michael Craig Hillman. © 1972 by The University of Chicago Press. All rights reserved. Reproduced by permission of the University of Chicago Press and the author.–*Medium Aevum*, v. XXXVI, 1967. Reproduced by permission.–*The Phoenix*, v. II, 1954; v. XVIII, Spring, 1964; v. XXVII, Spring, 1973. All reproduced by permission.–*Speculum: A Journal of Medieval Studies*, v. XLIV, April, 1969; v. LI, October, 1976. Both reproduced by permission.–*Studies in Philology*, v. LXIV, July, 1967. Copyright © 1967 by the University of North Carolina Press. Used by permission of the publisher.–*Transactions and Proceedings of the American Philological Association*, v. 102, 1971. Reproduced by permission of the American Philological Association.

**COPYRIGHTED EXCERPTS IN *CMLC*, VOLUME 34, WERE REPRODUCED FROM THE FOLLOWING BOOKS:**

Barron, W. R. J. From *English Medieval Romance*. Longman, 1987. © Longman Group UK Limited 1987. All rights reserved. Reproduced by permission of Pearson Education Limited.–Bürgel, J. Christoph. From "Ambiguity: A Study in the Use of Religious Terminology in the Poetry of Hafiz" in *Intoxication, Earthly and Heavenly: Seven Studies on the Poet Hafiz of Shiraz*. Edited by Michael Glünz and J. Christoph Bürgel. Peter Lang, 1991. © Peter Lang, Inc. 1991. All rights reserved. Reproduced by permission.–Delany, Sheila. From *Medieval Literary Politics*. Manchester University Press, 1990. Copyright © Sheila Delany 1990. Reproduced by permission of the author.–Ganim, John M. From *Style and Consciousness in Middle English Narrative*. Princeton University Press, 1983. Copyright © 1983 by Princeton University Press. All rights reserved. Reproduced by permission.–Glünz, Michael. From "The Poet's Heart: A Polyfunctional Object in the Poetic System of the Ghazal" in *Intoxication, Earthly and Heavenly: Seven Studies on the Poet Hafiz of Shiraz*. Edited by Michael Glünz and J. Christoph Bürgel. Peter Lang, 1991. © Peter Lang, Inc. 1991. All rights reserved. Reproduced by permission.–Grube, G. M. A. From an introduction to *A Greek Critic: Demetrius On Style*. University of Toronto Press, 1961. Copyright, Canada, 1961, by University of Toronto Press. All rights reserved. Reproduced by permission of Hackett Publishing Co., Inc. for the Literary Estate of G. M. A. Grube.–Grube, G. M. A. From *The Greek and Roman Critics*. University of Toronto Press, 1965. © G. M. A. Grube 1965. All rights reserved. Reproduced by permission of Hackett Publishing Co., Inc. for the Literary Estate of G. M. A. Grube.–Mehl, Dieter. From *The Middle English Romances of the Thirteenth and Fourteenth Centuries*. Barnes & Noble, Inc., 1969. (c) Dieter Mehl 1969. Reproduced by permission of Taylor

## PHOTOGRAPHS AND ILLUSTRATIONS APPEARING IN *CMLC,* VOLUME 34, WERE RECEIVED FROM THE FOLLOWING SOURCES:

# Demetrius

## Third century B.C.

Greek critic.

## INTRODUCTION

Demetrius is the author of *On Style*, a treatise on literary style and elocution very uncertainly dated to the third century B.C. If this date is correct, *On Style* is the sole surviving critical text from the time of Alexander the Great up into the first century B.C. Demetrius examines four kinds of style—plain, grand, elegant, and forceful; he is also the first known writer to thoroughly discuss epistolary style. Demetrius's work not only served as a foundation for other theories on letter writing and style, but continues to be valid today.

## Biographical Information

Nothing is known about Demetrius except that he was not the same person as Demetrius of Phalerum. Demetrius of Phalerum was traditionally credited with writing *On Style*, but studies of content and style have conclusively suggested a later date for the work than would have been possible for the man from Phalerum. Demetrius was not an uncommon name and to differentiate him from others with the same name, some critics refer to him as Demetrius the Stylist.

## Major Works

Critics also refer to *On Style* by its Latin title, *De Elocutione*. *On Style* is generally favored because the work concerns itself with more than public speaking. It consists of 303 numbered paragraphs, divided into five sections. First is the introduction, in which Demetrius outlines his general premises, defines terms, and discusses the colon, comma, and period. This is followed by sections on four different styles or manners of writing: plain, grand, elegant, and forceful. In turn, each of these styles is further examined in terms of choice of words, arrangement of words, and subject matter. Common faults are also briefly considered. Among the subjects covered by Demetrius are the use of such stylistic devices as the hiatus, metaphor and simile, witticism, affectation, and quoted material. Demetrius uses illustrative examples throughout. Critics have noted that he was clearly influenced by Aristotle, particularly the third book of the *Rhetoric*, but that he is not overly respectful; instead, Demetrius uses Aristotle to meet his own ends and does not hesitate to correct or make changes to Aristotle's words when he feels it beneficial to do so.

Scholars have also pointed out that Demetrius was influenced by the Greek philosopher and scientist Theophrastus.

## Critical Reception

*On Style* has generally been praised by critics. Scholar G. M. A. Grube has credited Demetrius with the gift of the striking phrase, a discerning eye, dry humor, and independence of mind. He is sometimes criticized for not being systematic enough and for digressing too much, although these charges have been easily refuted. Much scholarly focus has been aimed at trying to determine the composition date of *On Style*, particularly through studies of diction and internal references. Grube has argued for a date of approximately 270 B.C. The acceptance of an origin in the second century B.C. has also been advocated, and other critics have speculated that the date could be as much as three hundred years later. Datable references in the text are frustratingly ambiguous and there will be no complete agreement among scholars concerning the time of composition unless conclusive new evidence presents itself.

---

## PRINCIPAL WORK

*On Style* [*De Elocutione*] (essay) third century B.C.?

---

## PRINCIPAL ENGLISH TRANSLATIONS

*A Greek Critic: Demetrius on Style* [edited and translated by G. M. A. Grube] 1961

*Demetrius on Style* [edited by W. R. Connor] 1979

*Demetrius on Style* [edited and translated by Doreen C. Innes, based on translation by W. Rhys Roberts] 1995

---

## CRITICISM

### G. M. A. Grube (essay date 1961)

SOURCE: An introduction to *A Greek Critic: Demetrius On Style*, University of Toronto Press, 1961, pp. 3-56.

*[In the following essay, Grube offers background on the philosophical and rhetorical traditions of Greek*

*literary criticism, examines the content, nature, and structure of* On Style, *and considers the problems of determining the authorship and date of composition of the work.*]

## The Background

Greek criticism of literature was derived from two distinct and independent sources, the philosophical and the rhetorical. The philosophers were first in the field. As early as 500 B.C. we find Xenophanes and Heraclitus vigorously censuring Homer for his immoral and untrue stories about the gods.[1] Thus started what Plato was to call the ancient quarrel between poetry and philosophy, in which the philosophers stressed the social responsibility of the poet, and the importance they attached to this reflects the vital place of poetry in the life of Classical Greece. Formal education consisted, as is well known, mainly of physical training, music, and poetry, especially Homer. The Olympian gods cared little for the conduct of their worshippers; except for a very few traditional requirements such as the sanctity of an oath, respect for parents, and the laws of hospitality, they insisted only on the performance of due ritual. There was no preaching in the temples, and men turned to the poets for guidance in the art of living. Hence the deep-rooted feeling that the poets were the teachers of men; we find this point of view first clearly formulated in Aristophanes, but it is, as a feeling if not a theory, very much older. This moral responsibility might well have surprised Homer, but Hesiod would have accepted it, so would most of the lyric poets, and by the time of the great tragedians it was well established. In any case, where poetry is a vital force in society, it cannot live in an ivory tower. Art for art's sake is a theory which does not arise until poetry has retired to the study and music to the studio. It was therefore very natural that criticism of literature—and this up to the third quarter of the fifth century meant criticism of poetry exclusively—should, particularly in Greece, have begun as moral criticism, as criticism of content rather than of form, and this philosophical approach was rarely absent in the better critics of antiquity.

From the middle of the fifth century, however, a quite different approach to literature was being developed by the teachers of rhetoric. First in Sicily, then in Athens, with the growth of democracy, the art of swaying assemblies and juries was the road to political power, and this was clearly recognized by the ambitious. Teachers of rhetoric were in great demand, and the Sophistic movement arose to fill this demand, for, in spite of their individual differences, the Sophists all had an interest in language in common.

When Gorgias of Leontini came to Athens in 427 B.C. and brought with him from Sicily all the tricks of his rhetorical trade, he is said to have taken Athens by storm. Certainly, the Athenians were predisposed to appreciate the new art of speech: their education had endowed them with a sensitive appreciation of poetry; they eagerly discussed the works of the great dramatists; they had applauded Pericles and other orators in the assembly. Indeed it may well be argued that they were already thoroughly familiar, in practice, with Gorgias' antitheses, homoioteleuta, balanced clauses, and so forth, and it is probable that the direct influence of Gorgias on the style of the great writers of the time, Euripides and Thucydides for example, has been exaggerated by both ancient and modern critics. Nevertheless, as the first *theorists* of the art of language, the Sophists did have a very great influence on the development of Greek style.

When Gorgias praised the power of Logos, the spoken word, he was claiming for prose a place by the side of poetry as a sister art and he clearly wakened the Athenians to a new awareness of the art of speech. Indeed, when Aristotle speaks of the old simple style of writing,[2] he means writers before the time of Gorgias, including Herodotus. As a theoretical innovator, however, Gorgias went too far, and it was easy for Aristotle and later critics to ridicule his poetic diction, his farfetched metaphors, his too neatly-balanced clauses, his word-jingles, rhymes, and the rest. Indeed his fragments fully deserve their censures.

Gorgias and the other teachers of rhetoric were interested only in the art of persuasion, in rhetorical tricks to arouse the emotions of an audience, and Plato was no doubt right when he maintained that they felt no moral responsibility whatever. "The word" said Gorgias "is a mighty power; . . . it can end fear, remove pain, bring joy, and increase pity." He went on to extol the power of words to play upon human emotions, and to show how a speech (*logos*) can delight and persuade a great crowd "not because it is spoken with truth but because it is skilfully composed." Gorgias may be regarded as the first conscious technician of the art of speech in continental Greece; he brought with him an already well-developed technical vocabulary. From him ultimately derives that tendency to analyze figures of speech and thought which, in the rhetorical works of later criticism, often looks upon literature, from Homer down, as a mere treasure-house of rhetorical devices.

This emphasis on the means of persuasion and on rousing the emotions, fear and pity in particular, without regard for morality or truth, naturally went hand in hand with scepticism, with a questioning of all accepted values. The new teachers undoubtedly helped to undermine the traditional education of Athens and the traditional social morality. Because of this they aroused the anger and resentment of conservative Athenians, whose spokesman was Aristophanes, the great comic poet (*ca.* 450-385 B.C.).

The comedies of Aristophanes bear convincing witness to the important place which poetry—tragedy in particular but not tragedy only—held in Athenian life. They are full of literary allusions, parodies, and criticisms which he expected his audience, the people of Athens, to appreciate and enjoy. His hatred of the new education and the new scepticism is especially clear in the *Clouds* (423 B.C.), where Socrates is his chief butt. For twenty years he attacked Euripides as the exponent of the modern spirit. But Aristophanes' greatest contribution to literary criticism is the famous contest in the *Frogs* between Euripides and Aeschylus for the Chair of Tragedy in Hades. The comedy was produced in 405 B.C., soon after Euripides' death. Aeschylus had been in his grave for fifty years, and he stands here as the defender of tradition. Euripides is attacked for his immoral subjects and evil influence, but there is also much criticism that is purely aesthetic, where the younger poet is censured for his realism, his innovations in metre and music, his use of a narrative prologue, his excessive use of lyric monodies, his prosaic everyday language. The whole debate puts before us two different views of drama, and of literature generally, which are perennial and irreconcilable. The differences can in part be explained historically: the tempo of Aeschylean tragedy was already archaic in 405 B.C. and so was a good deal of its language; the more "sophistic" techniques of Euripides are also partly due to his date. Essentially, however, the conflict goes very much deeper, for it is the conflict between the romantic and the realist, the former believing that many true things are better ignored, the latter that truth, the whole truth, will make men free. The grand manner of Aeschylus requires the grand style and impressive language; the realism of Euripides inevitably requires a simpler diction. Aristophanes' sympathies were all with Aeschylus, but the criticisms of him which he puts in the mouth of Euripides also neatly hit the mark, and in the end he refuses to judge between them as dramatists or as poets. The contest is one of the most vivid pieces of literary criticism in ancient literature, as well as the most amusing. For all his dislike of the new techniques, Aristophanes was clearly thoroughly familiar with them.

So was Plato (who was growing to manhood at this time) in spite of all the bitter things he said against the Sophists and rhetoricians in his dialogues. In practice he was a most careful stylist, and one likes to remember the story told by Dionysius of Halicarnassus that, when Plato died, tablets found among his belongings showed how he had tried many different word-orders for that simple, easy-flowing sentence with which he begins his *Republic*.[3] His style takes its place in the history of fourth-century Greek prose as the superb culmination of that process of development which Gorgias and the rhetoricians had started about the time of Plato's birth. But Plato was a philosopher, the disciple of Socrates. He knew, better than Aristophanes, that Socrates had laboured for a much deeper, more philosophic education than that of the Sophists, an education which aimed at philosophic inquiry into the nature of reality by way of painful self-knowledge and self-criticism. When, a teacher himself and the spiritual heir of Socrates, Plato opened his Academy in the eighties of the fourth century, it was natural that he should examine critically the claims of those other teachers old and new, the poets and the rhetoricians. It is thus that he approaches rhetoric in the *Gorgias*, and poetry in the *Republic*. What are their claims to knowledge and what is it they can claim to teach? The world of literature has never forgiven Plato for banishing the poets, or at any rate most of them, from his ideal republic, but that banishment is essentially a challenge to the poets to recognize their social responsibility, a challenge which has never been completely answered. Every civilized state except ancient Athens has adopted Plato's theory of censorship—the subordination of the artist to the legislator, in some form or other. Nor have they waited, before doing so, for the establishment of the ideal republic or the rule of the philosopher-king! Plato was deeply convinced that poetry, music, and the arts had a tremendous influence upon the formation of character, and he was terribly afraid of an uncritical emotional response to that influence, especially in drama where impersonation makes the response more immediate and more complete, both for the actor and for the audience. Hence the vigour of his attack, and his forbidding the impersonation of any evil at all upon the stage.

His theory of art as imitation of life does not mean, of course, that the best painting is a coloured photograph or the best drama a mere record of actual conversations, though it must be confessed that his ironically emphatic language almost seems to say so at times. It does mean, however, that the artist, and especially the dramatist, must draw his material from life and be true to life. This is, to him, an accepted truism[4] rather than an original theory, and, after it had been more calmly stated and more fully worked out by Aristotle, it was never challenged in antiquity. Moreover, when he insisted that the poet could not directly imitate or represent the eternal verities that are the Platonic Forms, but could do so only indirectly as they are mirrored in actual life, was he not right at least to the extent that drama must be represented through individuals, and that a drama of pure ideas is not drama, or indeed poetry, at all?

The *Phaedrus* is a corrective of the too intellectual and social approach of the *Republic* with its apparent attack upon passion and emotion. The myth of the *Phaedrus* is a superb vindication of passion and inspiration, but the inspiration must come from the gods. This, translated into philosophical terms, means that the passion of the poet must be directed towards beauty and truth, and directed by reason.

The second part of the *Phaedrus* is written in a calmer mood. It sets out to discover how to write well, whether in prose or verse, and it contains a statement of basic critical principles. Plato states clearly, for the first time, the difference between criticism of form and of content.[5] He insists that the writer must know his subject and adds ironically that he will find this useful even if his aim is only to deceive. He must define his subject. Every *logos*, every work of prose or poetry, should have a definite structure, with a place and function for each part, like a living organism, with a beginning, middle, and end, and with every part in its proper place, in its proper relation to the whole. The technique of writing or speaking are a preliminary requirement, but technique is not art. Plato dwells on this last point at some length: the man who knows the notes of the musical scale but cannot relate them to each other is no musician; the man who knows the effects of drugs but not when to use them is no doctor; the man who can make speeches, long or short, to arouse pity or fear, but knows not *when* to make them, is no tragic poet. Sophocles and Euripides would laugh at his pretensions "knowing well that the art of tragedy is no other than the interrelating of these elements in a manner fitting to each other and to the whole work." And Plato goes on to pour ridicule upon the rhetoricians' boast that they can arouse and calm emotions at will, as also upon their ever more complex technical vocabulary and their neglect of the fundamentals of their own craft.[6]

Plato discussed poetry and music once more, in the second book of the *Laws*, the work of his old age. *Mousikê*, which includes both, is a gift of the gods with two functions: the training of the emotions in youth and the recreation of emotional stability at all ages. Poetry and music have their roots in primary human needs and instincts, in the natural need for motion and utterance. As the random movements of the infant, gradually brought to orderly control by the human sense of harmony and rhythm, culminate in the dance, so the same sense of rhythm and meaning brings under control the infant's random cries until this process culminates in reasoned speech and ultimately in poetry. We all speak and move; we are all to some extent poets and musicians.

There are, in the *Laws*, three criteria by which art must be judged: one of these is still the moral criterion; the second is pleasure, even though Plato insists that it must be the pleasure of the educated and that art must not be judged, as we might put it, by box-office receipts. The third criterion is artistic or aesthetic, even though the formulation of it is rather rudimentary, that is, the "correctness" of the imitation. Both pleasure and artistic perfection are thus recognized as criteria. We are further told that the poet need not be the judge of the moral values of his work but he must, in that case, accept the judgment of the legislator who in turn must, in order to give an adequate judgment, understand the aim of the artist.[7]

The *Poetics* of Aristotle continues the philosophic approach to literature and at many points tries to answer Plato. It is important to realize that Aristotle accepts, in the main, the moral approach of Plato and his philosophic predecessors. This is quite clear from the *Politics*, the only place where he discusses the function of *mousikê* in society. Even in the *Poetics* tragedy is "the imitation of a morally good action."[8] He accepts the principle of censorship, and the place of poetry and music in both education and recreation. He accepts, too, Plato's theory of art as "imitation," *mimêsis*, though he adds that the poet may imitate or represent things as they are, as they were, as they were thought to be, or as they ought to be, thus making it clear that the Greek *mimêsis* does not mean copying. He modifies the moral criterion to the extent that any evil act or speech in a play must be judged not in itself but in relation to the effect of the play as a whole, and in relation to the character concerned. His theory of catharsis: "tragedy . . . by means of pity and fear achieves the purgation (catharsis) of such emotions" is now generally accepted as a medical metaphor. The effect, as he explains in the *Politics*, is the same as that of orgiastic music which through exciting emotions to a crisis has an ultimately calming effect. And he answers Plato by suggesting that "the more vulgar parts of an audience, mechanics and general labourers . . . whose souls are perverted from their natural state" and in a state of over-excitement, need this catharsis to recreate emotional stability and that this kind of dramatic performance should therefore be allowed. The passage makes it abundantly clear that the cathartic effect of drama is mainly restricted to these weaker types. The Aristotelian philosopher, who has perfect emotional control, presumably remains unaffected. Even Aristotle's theory of the tragic hero as neither villain nor saint, but a man with some flaw in his character and therefore more "like ourselves," recognizes the need at least for weaker men, if not for himself, of that emotional identification which Plato so greatly feared. Moreover, where he insists upon the unity of plot (the only kind of unity he does insist on) and explains how one incident should follow the other as inevitable or at least probable, with the end emerging from the plot itself, he is elaborating upon the Platonic conception of the unity of a work of art as an organism. He adds important suggestions of his own: the preference for an unhappy ending, the importance of *peripeteia* or the sudden change of direction toward misfortune, and of recognition and discovery. The *Poetics* is a triumph of unemotional analysis; it is extraordinarily suggestive in detail; some of its limitations are due, however, precisely to the fact that the author's emotions are nowhere engaged.

What we have called the philosophic, as against the rhetorical, approach to literature thus began with moral criticism and continued to insist upon the writer's responsibility to society, but in Plato and Aristotle it also developed a considerable body of literary theory. Of this approach in its purer form the *Poetics* is our last extant example.

During the century between the famous visit of Gorgias to Athens and the publication of Aristotle's *Rhetoric*, textbooks on rhetoric multiplied, and it is these which both Plato and Aristotle regard with contempt. Most of them, undoubtedly, were purely technical and amoral. Of this considerable literature very little remains. We know that Thrasymachus of Chalcedon, a contemporary of Gorgias, was an adept at arousing and again calming the passions of his audiences, that he paid some attention to rhythm, wrote in short rhythmical clauses, and affected the use of paeonic feet. He seems to have been able to arrange his material clearly, to express his thoughts with succinct compactness, and to have developed a kind of prose diction that was neither too poetical, like that of Gorgias, nor lacking in distinction.[9] We have a short essay of another rhetorician, Alcidamas, on the necessity for an orator to speak extempore.

But if rhetoric finally established itself as *the* higher education from the fourth century B.C. onward—and to this place of rhetoric in education the rhetorical nature of our later critical texts is largely due—the credit or discredit for this should be given mainly to Isocrates (436-338 B.C.). Several years older than Plato, he died at the time of the battle of Chaeronea which established Philip's supremacy over Greece. He was the teacher of most of the great Athenians of his day. He called himself a philosopher, though neither Plato nor Aristotle would have conceded him the title. He had little respect for "useless" knowledge; he was the apostle of general education, which for him consisted in being able to speak well on great subjects—and this also meant to be able to write. He rejected, however, the amorality of the rhetorical technicians; he insisted that you cannot speak well on noble subjects without practical knowledge of them, and, furthermore, since an orator (or writer) must make a good impression on his audience, he will desire to be a good man: "To speak well is the greatest sign of intelligence; a truthful, lawful, just speech is the outward image of a good and loyal soul."[10] The later theory of Cicero and Quintilian, that the good orator is a good man *vir bonus dicendi peritus*, as old Cato put it[11]—ultimately derives from Isocrates' theories of education, superficial as these obviously were.

It may be added that Isocrates, though included in the later canon of the Ten Attic Orators, was prevented from public speaking by a physical handicap; he published his speeches as pamphlets, and *logos* obviously means, to him, both the written and the spoken word. Of poetry he says very little. He was a pupil of Gorgias and a very careful stylist: antitheses and balanced clauses follow one another in carefully constructed periods, and he avoids any hiatus like the plague. His patriotism was sincere, but it never caused him to write an inelegant sentence, and the total effect—we have a considerable number of his "speeches"—is one of deadly monotony. His contemporary influence however was very great (greater than that of the Academy or the Lyceum); his posthumous influence was no less—we can trace it clearly in the texts we possess, in Cicero, Dionysius, and Quintilian.

Although Isocrates was a teacher of the art of speech, he was hardly a rhetorician in the strict sense; he did try to communicate to his pupils a general philosophic outlook. For an example of the more strictly rhetorical approach at this time we have to go to a treatise preserved for us among the works of Aristotle, the *Rhetorica ad Alexandrum*. The dedication, a letter from Aristotle to Alexander the Great, is an obvious forgery. The work itself, however, is definitely dated in the fourth century B.C. and often thought to be the work of a contemporary of Aristotle, the rhetorician and historian Anaximenes. It is, at any rate, our sole remaining example of the more sophistical treatises of the period. It displays the completely cynical, amoral attitude which was so repugnant to Plato; it is concerned exclusively with the question: what kind of arguments will, in particular kinds of cases, be convincing? These are listed, named, and described at considerable length and with great precision. Even if this particular work was not written before Aristotle's *Rhetoric*, there can be no doubt that many works of the type were in existence, and it is against this kind of background that the *Rhetoric* of Aristotle must be judged.

Unlike the *Poetics*, the *Rhetoric* had an immediate and lasting influence in antiquity. It is very different kind of book, for here Aristotle meets the rhetoricians on their own ground. He writes the kind of book which should be written about their craft. Indeed, it might well be said that he establishes the art, and even Isocrates' theory of education, on a much more solid philosophic foundation. Aristotle himself, in the *Poetics*, refers us to the *Rhetoric* for all that concerns the expression of thought in words, be it in poetry or prose. For we should never forget that *rhêtorikê* was the art of expression as a whole, even if oratory was the art of expression par excellence. And in part Aristotle is still, as so often, answering Plato: he sets forth in the first two books the kind of knowledge of politics and psychology which an orator should have, and which can suffice, the kinds of arguments and proofs based on probability, which he should employ. The first twelve chapters of the third book then deal with style, and concern us closely; we shall see that the author of our treatise *On Style* is thoroughly familiar with them, and much indebted to them. Many of the later critical and rhetorical formulae of the schools appear here for the first time, at least for us.

Among these are the statement that the diction of poetry is necessarily different from that of prose; the division of rhetoric into three kinds: the forensic, the deliberative, and the epideictic; the division of style into diction (or the choice of words) and the arrangement of the words thus chosen; the further division of word-arrangement into the running or strung-along style of the "ancient" writers and the periodic structure. Here too are the divisions of a speech into proem or introduction, narrative, proofs, and epilogue. Aristotle will allow only these four; he would prefer two only, statement and proof, and he mentions with Platonic contempt the over-subtle subdivisions affected by contemporary rhetoricians. Prose must have rhythm but not metre, a statement repeated for centuries by Greek and Roman critics.

Aristotle recognizes only one "virtue" of style, lucidity. This is most easily attained by the use of current, everyday language, but men like the strange and the new, so we must introduce a certain number of unusual words and a degree of ornamentation, in order to strike a happy mean, always making our style suitable and fitting. . . to the occasion, the audience, and the speaker. Aristotle deals at length with metaphor, the chief ornament he allows in prose; it is also the one thing that cannot be learned from others for it involves a capacity to see similarities in things. Like every Greek, Aristotle is well aware of the importance of semantics, of whether, as he puts it, you call Orestes his mother's murderer or the avenger of his father. The discussion of style ends with an attempt to analyze the reasons for successful sayings: their success is related to man's delight in learning something new—a delight that can be derived from a good metaphor, a particularly apt word, a clever antithesis or argument. All these gain from brevity, for example, Pericles' famous remark after many young Athenians had been lost in battle that "the year had lost its spring." Vividness, riddles or half-riddles, similes, proverbs, hyperboles, all these can contribute to success. Moreover, there is not one perfect style suited to all occasions; each kind of rhetoric has its own appropriate style. The style of written work is not that of debate; it is more precise, less histrionic. Nor will Aristotle accept brevity as necessarily a good thing: one should be neither too concise nor too verbose, but seek the right mean.

The rest of the book is more definitely concerned with rhetoric in the more restricted sense: it deals in turn with the aim and purpose of each of the four parts of a discourse and how the speaker should deal with each part (13-17). This section is also much drier and more technical in style. If Aristotle shared Plato's contempt for the technicalities of the rhetoricians, he had a good deal more patience in dealing with them.[13]

From the time of Aristotle to the first century B.C. we have no extent critical texts, unless indeed it be our treatise **On Style**. We know that Theophrastus, the disciple and successor of Aristotle, wrote a book on style. . . . The references to this work in later writers, who usually mention him along with Aristotle, are scrappy and tantalizing. Scholars have attempted to reconstruct his critical theories, but the evidence is insufficient. On the whole it would seem that he did not depart very far from his master's theories which he expanded and explained.[14]

During the third and second centuries B.C., Alexandria developed a school of literary scholarship rather than of rhetoric or literary criticism. The scholars of the Museum edited, with commentary, all the great classical writers. The catalogues of the great library formed the basis of the first histories of literature, while the commentaries did evolve some critical principles, notably those of Aristarchus (*ca.* 217-143 B.C.). He stated that Homer must be interpreted in the light of the social customs of his day and not those of a later age; that any statement must be judged by reference to the character who makes it or, as he put it, "all that is said in Homer is not said by Homer"; that poets must be given some licence in dealing with historical facts: they need not tell us every detail of what happens but may leave certain things to the reader's imagination. Aristarchus championed the unity of Homer and he may have defended the artistic unity of the *Iliad* and the *Odyssey*.[15]

We know that the so-called Asiatic style developed rapidly as the Greek language spread over Asia Minor and that Hegesias of Magnesia (*fl.* 250 B.C.) was criticized by Dionysius and Cicero as the great exponent of that florid, over-rhythmical, artificial manner. In the next century Hermagoras revived rhetorical studies and seems to have written a great work in which he classified all the possible kinds of court cases, the different kinds of issues and how each should be dealt with. It must have been during this period too that the various formulae which we find in the Roman rhetorical writers of the first century B.C. were developed: that of the three main styles, for example, or that of a specific number of rhetorical virtues, but we cannot trace the origin of either for lack of evidence. Nor did the philosophers, as far as we can make out, make any further substantial contribution. While the Peripatetics probably continued in the tradition of the *Rhetoric* to analyze style and to use both prose and poetry to illustrate the points they made, the Stoics seem to have concentrated on allegorizing Homer so as to make a Stoic of him, and on pure linguistics. Their main contribution seems to have been to add "brevity" to whatever list of rhetorical "virtues" then came into fashion, and though brevity is often to be commended it is not in itself, as Aristotle knew, necessarily a virtue.[16] But the Stoics seem to have despised all conscious stylistic effort, and the Epicureans, by and large, seem to have taken little interest in literature of any kind.

When we come to the first century B.C., however, we again have a large number of texts, partly Latin and partly Greek. As we are here primarily concerned with a Greek treatise, it will not be necessary to follow, in any detail, the development of Roman rhetoric or criticism, for the Greek rhetoricians hardly ever mention a Latin writer or a Latin theorist. This is not primarily due to arrogance, or to discretion, but to the simple fact that they had no need to mention them. They were concerned with Greek literature and with Greek style; they took their illustrations from the Greek authors of the classical age and, to a lesser extent, from those of Alexandria. Nor could they be required to mention Roman critics or rhetoricians, for the Romans took their theories from the Greeks. There were, to be sure, specifically Latin or Roman problems such as, for example, the quarrel between the champions of the ancient Latin writers and those "moderns" who took the Greek classics as their models, but these were of no concern to a Greek writer.

Suffice it to say, therefore, that in the Roman tradition there is nothing to correspond to what we have called the purely philosophical approach. The ancient quarrel between poetry and philosophy was long forgotten, and in any case Rome produced no original philosophers. The approach was therefore rhetorical, but of two kinds: the strictly rhetorical on the one hand, and on the other what may well be called the Isocratean, that more general approach which, though still rooted in rhetorical training, nevertheless stood for a more cultivated outlook and a general interest in human affairs. Our first Latin text, the *Rhetorica ad Herennium*, is of the first, more professionally rhetorical kind. It is preserved among the works of Cicero; it was most probably not written by him, but was in any case written at the time when he was a very young man, probably between 86 and 82 B.C.[17]

The *Ad Herennium* is of considerable interest as the first extant attempt to Latinize the Greek rhetorical vocabulary, and, although the author is impatient of the over-elaborate subtleties of the Greek rhetoricians, all the formulae are carefully set down: the three kinds of rhetoric which we saw in Aristotle; the main formula, also used by Cicero, of the capacities the orator must possess: he must be able to think of what he should say (*inventio . . .*), to order his material (*dispositio . . .*), he must have style (*elocutio . . .*), memory, and a good delivery (*actio . . .*). Each part of a speech, of which the author recognizes six,[18] is discussed; we then proceed to *inventio* in relation to the types of argument to be used in each type of case, and so with the other parts of the main formula. The fourth and last book discusses the three styles, the plain, the grand, and the intermediate, all of which the good orator should be able to use at the right moment, and various kinds of qualities, ornaments, and figures (sixty-four of these altogether).

The more technical of Cicero's rhetorical works are of much the same type—the *De Inventione*, the *Topica*,

the *Partitiones Oratoriae*. He shows the same impatience with Greek subtleties and the same inability to shake them off, a greater virtuosity in the translation of technical terms, and an occasional purple patch, usually the introduction. His more general works, however, take a broader, more Isocratean view; in them the technical formulae take second place. The *Brutus* is largely a history of Roman oratory introduced by a brief sketch of Greek oratory. It also, however, contains many passages of more general interest. Cicero wrote very quickly and he is extremely careless in the use of technical terms, but his main concern, as in the three books of the *De Oratore* and in the *Orator*, is to rescue rhetoric from the study of mere techniques, to insist that oratory is an art which must be solidly rooted in a general education in philosophy, history, and jurisprudence, an education in the liberal arts which will ensure a moral education as well. He goes into a good deal of detail but he never forgets his main purpose: the general education of the orator. In spite of his own predilection for the grand manner, he recognizes that the orator must instruct (*docere*) and entertain (*delectare*) as well as rouse the emotions (*movere*) and he must therefore be able to use each of the three styles at the right time (*apte*). His lists of "virtues" of style vary from one work to the other but purity of language (*Latinitas*), lucidity (*dilucide*), appropriateness (*decorum*) and stylistic ornament (*ornatum*) are the most frequent.

When we turn from Cicero to Dionysius of Halicarnassus, who settled in Rome about twelve years after Cicero's death, we find ourselves in a world still dominated by the rhetorical education but definitely more literary than oratorical. Dionysius never mentions Cicero, nor Horace whose contemporary he was; yet, as we know from his history and from the introduction to his work on the orators, he was extremely well-disposed to the Romans. It was to the cultured Romans of his day that he gave the credit for stamping out, as he thought, the plague of Asianism in style. We have a considerable bulk of his critical writings. One of them . . . , *On Composition* or *Word-Arrangement,* is a masterpiece. It deals with the collocation of words from the point of view of sound, the music of language which results from the sound of letters in combination, from rhythm and pitch and stress. The Greeks were extremely sensitive to this music of language even in prose; Dionysius pursues its aesthetic appeal to its very elements and discusses the sound of each letter and its contribution to the total effect, incidentally giving us a good deal of information about the correct pronunciation of Greek. When dealing with rhythm he tries to prove too much, for he reduces his examples to metrical feet whereas, in prose, it is the total effect that matters, as Theophrastus seems to have realised.[19] Dionysius insists that there must be variety, and that the language-music must be appropriate to the matter, the occasion, and the emotions which the speaker or writer wishes to arouse.

Dionysius recognizes three main styles of word-arrangement, the dry or austere . . ., the flowery . . ., and the intermediate. The first is the severe style of Thucydides: the words stand apart and cannot be run together, harsh collocations are deliberately used, with an abundance of broad syllables; the rhythms are impressive, the clauses not balanced equally. Sense and sentence-structure do not correspond, smoothness of every kind is avoided and even grammatical sequence at times disregarded. The other extreme is the flowery, elegant word-arrangement of Isocrates, and there the words are run together in flowing continuity, and only the periods come to a definite and distinct end. The clauses are carefully balanced, the rhythms neither too heavy nor too light, all harsh collocations are avoided, as is any hiatus between words. The general effect is like that of a painting where light and shade everywhere merge into one another. The intermediate type, which uses the effects of both extremes at the appropriate time, is the composition or word-arrangement which we find in Homer, Sophocles, Plato, and Demosthenes.[20]

Dionysius' other extant works include fragments of a work on *mimêsis* or emulation, separate studies on the style of Lysias, Isocrates, Demosthenes, and Thucydides, and three short treatises known as the Three Literary Letters. The work on Emulation consisted of brief critical valuations of classical authors much in the manner of Quintilian's historical sketch of Greek and Roman writers in the tenth book of his *Institutio Oratoria*; indeed Dionysius may have been one of Quintilian's sources, but of course only for the Greeks. Dionysius' enthusiasm for Isocrates is for a practitioner of the true practical philosophy, an educator who made his pupils "not only clever speakers but men of good moral character, men who served their house, their city, and the whole of Greece."[21] This is akin to the liberal education of the orator as understood by Cicero and Quintilian, but with more emphasis on rhetoric and less on general education.

Dionysius is unique among our extant critics in that he uses his critical-rhetorical formulae as a means of evaluating the style of an author, and not his authors merely to illustrate the formulae. He quotes freely from their writings and discusses certain passages at considerable length; he compares them with passages from others. This method of comparative criticism seems to have been characteristic of Greek criticism, at least in Rome, in his day, for we know that his contemporary and friend Caecilius of Calacte wrote critical essays on Lysias, whom he preferred to Plato, and attempted comparative valuations of Cicero and Demosthenes, of Demosthenes and Aeschines.[22]

Dionysius has certain weaknesses: he is somewhat naïve and lacking in imagination, as in his strictures on Plato's diction; his moral earnestness betrays him into an unbounded admiration for Isocrates and condemnation of Thucydides as unpatriotic, or as inferior to Herodotus in his choice of subject: "one war, which was neither noble nor fortunate, which had much better not have happened, and, when it had, should have been left to silence and oblivion, and ignored by posterity."[23] It is only fair to add that this kind of nonsense is quietly dropped in his later essay on the historian. The moral earnestness itself, however, shows him to be more a man of letters than a rhetorician in the stricter sense, even though Demosthenes, for him as for Cicero, is the greatest of all writers.

Horace's letter to the Pisos on the *Art of Poetry* is, as already mentioned, contemporary with Dionysius. There is little in this informal, delightfully phrased advice that is original. We may note, however, that Horace is, in a sense, trying to do for poetry what Cicero attempted to do for prose: he insists that his poet must understand life and man, and that his work must be true to that knowledge. He emphasizes the need for unity and appropriateness, the need for talent and training, the importance of the choice of subject, of the choice of words, of structure, and so on; behind the deliberate informality of the epistle we can easily trace a thorough knowledge of the critical-rhetorical formulae of the day. But Horace is also concerned with specifically Roman problems, as for example, the controversy between the "ancients" and the "moderns."

After Horace we find ourselves in the world of the rhetorical schools, where the practice of *declamatio* was becoming increasingly fashionable and almost superseding every other method of teaching. Declamations were of two kinds: the *suasoria* in which the pupil had to imagine himself in some historical dilemma—should Alexander, for example, cross the Indus?—and devise a speech appropriate to the occasion; and the *controversia*, where he had to speak in an imaginary, often highly artificial and improbable, law-suit. The masters of rhetoric themselves gave display declamations of both kinds before an admiring public. The elder Seneca published a curious collection of such *suasoriae* and *controversiae* for the benefit of his sons, in which he records the adroit and clever things said by the rhetoricians of the Principate. His book is extant, and from it we gain a better understanding of how this practice, which put all the emphasis on ingenuity and clever epigram—for the same subjects were dealt with again and again—affected silver Latin style. The dangers of declamations and of their increasing artificiality are vigorously denounced throughout the first century by the elder Seneca himself, by Petronius, by Persius, by Tacitus, and at the close of the century by the great Quintilian, but they flourished in spite of them all.[24] It was in the last years of the century that Quintilian published his massive work in twelve books on the education of the orator, the *Institutio Oratoria*. Quintilian was Professor of Rhetoric by imperial appointment, and his book, complete, authoritative, lucid, sensible, not too original and at times more than a little dull, is an almost perfect pattern of what a professorial work should be. We find in it, in proper historical perspective, all the best thought of Rome on education, literature, criticism, and rhetoric.

We have no critical or rhetorical texts in Greek for this period, though it is fashionable among scholars today to assign to the first century A.D. both our Demetrius' treatise **On Style**, about the date of which more will be said later, and the famous short treatise *On the Sublime* which tradition attributed to Longinus in the third century A.D. In the second century A.D., however, we have the considerable works of Hermogenes on various qualities of style and forms of argument. They are purely rhetorical text books, dry and over-subtle in distinctions and classifications. We note that the theory of styles is now quite abandoned, and that Demosthenes is solidly established as the one supreme model for the young. The works of Hermogenes continued to be edited, commented on, and studied for the next ten centuries, but no really original mind appears in the vast collection of rhetorical writings which we still possess from that millennium.

Something more needs to be said, however, about the short and fragmentary treatise known as "Longinus on the Sublime."[25] Whatever its date it is a work of original genius. The author knows and uses many of the usual rhetorical formulae, but he remains their master, they never master him. It is not a work on the grand style or any other particular style, indeed the theory of particular styles is completely absent. Rather the author seeks to find the secret of the kind of great writing which suddenly sweeps one off one's feet. He traces it to five sources: vigour of mental conception, strong and inspired emotion, the skilful use of figures, noble diction or the proper choice of words, and dignified and spirited word-arrangement. The first, vigour of mental conception, implies nobility of mind, the power of grasping great ideas, and undoubtedly a certain grandeur. This, however, does not mean grand words; indeed it sometimes requires no words at all, as when Homer makes Ajax stride away in silence when Odysseus addresses him in the underworld, or the simplest of words, as in Ajax' famous prayer to Zeus to clear away the mist from the battlefield "that we may die in daylight." It does imply, however, the capacity to select the significant details and to weld them into a meaningful picture, and of this quality Longinus gives as an example the famous ode of Sappho, preserved here only, which begins ". . . [*phaimetai moi keinòs isos theoisi*]."

The treatment of passion is lost. To illustrate the proper use of figures—a favourite subject in rhetorical critics who usually discuss it with great care and dullness— "Longinus" first gives a full and brilliant analysis of one sentence of Demosthenes, the famous Marathon oath in his speech *On the Crown*, and then gives ex-

amples of other figures to show how "as dimmer lights are lost in the surrounding sunshine, so pervading greatness all around hides the presence of rhetorical devices." Of the treatment of diction much is lost; what remains shows Longinus to be fully aware of the importance of the choice of words which "endows the subject matter with a speaking soul." He very properly allows vulgarisms in the right places, and insists that there is no limit to the number of metaphors that may be used in a passage provided that successfully conveyed passion can make them convincing.

As for composition, that is, word-arrangement and sentence structure, he glorifies the music of language in poetry and prose, a music allied with meaning and thus making a powerful appeal to the soul and mind of man. Like all the critics, he rejects both metrical, as against rhythmical, prose, and also broken, hurried, or monotonous rhythms. He insists that the anatomy of the sentence must be such that each part fits into the whole like the parts of a living organism.

"Longinus" sees the dangers of attempting greatness, and he names four vices into which the attempt may fall: turgidity, puerility ("the thinking of the schools which ends in frigidity through over-elaboration"), misplaced or artificial passion which leaves the reader unaffected, and frigidity which is often due to strange conceits. Faults and virtues are both illustrated from the greatest writers, and not even Homer is spared criticism. Indeed one of the most striking passages is where he argues that greatness is always accompanied by faults, for genius is careless, but it is always to be preferred to flawless mediocrity. The whole work is full of quotable passages such as the famous comparison of Cicero and Demosthenes: "The greatness of Demosthenes is for the most part abrupt, that of Cicero is like a flood. Our man is violent, swift, strong, intense; he may be compared to a lightning-bolt which burns and ravages. Cicero is like a spreading conflagration which rolls and ranges far and wide. . . ."

With "Longinus"—whether we place him before or after Hermogenes in time—the living stream of Greek criticism reaches its end. We saw that the philosophers of the fifth and fourth centuries posed the problem of literature's social function and responsibility, and built up the beginnings of literary theory. The contemporary development of rhetoric led to a study of style and stylistic devices as such, and it is this approach which triumphs after Aristotle. A continuous output of rhetorical textbooks was published throughout the centuries, but the more responsibly-minded men of letters, while they remain in the stylistic tradition of the rhetoricians, yet have absorbed from Isocrates and the philosophers a sense of the social function of literature, and it is upon literature as a whole, of which oratory is only a part, that they direct their attention. That the Roman rhetorical and literary theories remain derivative, while the Greeks still retained some originality, is proved by Dionysius and, gloriously so, by "Longinus" at the very end. Where, in this general line of development should we place the work known as "Demetrius on Style"?

### The Treatise on Style

The author of our treatise obviously belongs to the rhetorical, not the philosophic tradition. Moreover, the moral concern for the character and education of the orator—the good man skilled in speech—which we have traced from Isocrates through Cicero to Quintilian, is totally absent. "Demetrius" is concerned with style exclusively. There is in his work no comparative criticism such as we have noted in Dionysius. His approach is quite objective: the theoretical framework is stated and illustrated from great and less great writers. On the other hand, he seems to be a man of letters rather than a professional rhetorician: he says nothing about types of cases, arguments, or issues, about ways of convincing a jury, or about methods of handling the different parts of a speech. His interests are obviously literary rather than rhetorical in the strict sense: the orators are frequently quoted, but only as practitioners of one kind of literature among many. We have here an example of literary criticism from a cultured man with a very good knowledge of Classical and early Alexandrian Greek literature, a man rhetorically trained, but not a mere rhetorician. The work is in many ways unique, the more so if it belongs to Hellenistic times, as it was traditionally thought to do, for we have no other extant critical text from this period.

The date of the work is, however, uncertain, and modern scholars have argued for various dates from the late third century B.C. to the middle of the second century A.D., but they have all but unanimously rejected the manuscript tradition which gives the author as Demetrius of Phalerum.[26] This Demetrius was the pupil and friend of Theophrastus, a distinguished man of letters and a voluminous writer. He ruled Athens from 317 to 307 B.C. on behalf of Cassander, the king of Macedon. He then fled from Athens to Thebes and later, after the death of Cassander, to Alexandria, where he enjoyed the patronage and friendship of Ptolemy Soter. Nothing is known of his later life or the time of his death except what we are told by Diogenes Laertius (5.78):

> Hermippus says that, after the death of Cassander, in fear of Antigonus, he made his way to Ptolemy Soter. There he stayed a considerable time, and advised Ptolemy, among other things, to hand on the kingly power to his children by Eurydice. The king did not take his advice but passed on the diadem to his son by Berenice (Ptolemy Philadelphus) who, after the death of his father, decided to have Demetrius kept under guard in the country, until he decided what to do with him. There Demet-

rius lived in discouragement. He was somehow bitten in the hand by an asp while he was asleep, and died. . . .

Diogenes (or Hermippus?) does not directly connect the death of Demetrius with the king's displeasure, though he may seem to imply it, but Cicero, in his speech against Rabirius Postumus (9.23) quotes the case of Demetrius as one of those who owed their death to the enmity of a despot, and clearly suggests that he was murdered (*aspide ad corpus admota*). Ptolemy Soter died in 283/2 B.C.

Before we consider the evidence, internal and external, for both date and author, however, let us first consider the content and nature of our treatise, and, to avoid awkward circumlocutions, we may as well call the author Demetrius without assuming him to be Demetrius of Phalerum.

### Nature and Structure of the Work

It falls into five sections. The first, which is also the shortest (1-35), is introductory and deals with different kinds of sentence structure, while the other four discuss four different "styles" or manners of writing, the grand, the plain, the elegant, and the forceful.

It is natural enough that the treatment of sentence structure should form a general introduction, since, with some exceptions to be mentioned later, different kinds of sentences can be used in all four "styles," and Demetrius begins with the general advice that the structure of the sentence must correspond to the structure of the thought. This correspondence must apply also to the clauses (the *kôla*, the basic units in prose as the verses are in poetry) and even to the shorter phrases or *kommata*. After he has repeated, but in his own terms, the Aristotelian distinction between the periodic style and the looser, non-periodic sentence structure, he differentiates three kinds of periods (a formula not found elsewhere).

At one extreme is the involved, Demosthenic period which he calls rhetorical; at the other extreme the looser, simpler, apparently effortless period of dialogue or conversation, which approaches the loose, non-periodic style; intermediate between these is the period he calls historical. There are some further remarks on different kinds of clauses, on the relation of sentence to sense, and a correction of Aristotle's definition of a clause (34).

After these general remarks, Demetrius proceeds to a description of what he considers the four main manners or styles of writing. This is his notorious theory of four "styles." But the word "style" is misleading, first because we think of style as something peculiar to the individual writer whereas the ancients thought of it more objectively, but mainly because, in ancient criticism, we associate the word [*kharacter*] mostly with the formula of the "three styles" which is found in later and mostly Latin writers.[27] There we find three separate styles rigidly differentiated, and while an orator is supposed to be able to use each of the three as the occasion demands, only one style can be used at a particular time.[28] But the Greek term [*kharacter*] is very general in meaning, and Demetrius' use of it is much less rigid. His "styles" can, with the exception of the plain and the grand, be mixed, that is, used at the same time. One can be elegant and forcible, plain and elegant, forcible and plain. The same word [*kharacter*], which is applied to these four "styles," is also applied to the faults to which each of them is prone; and Demetrius speaks of the "frigid style," "the affected style," and so on. He also speaks of the "epistolary style." The point is of some importance if we are to understand his intention: he is not drawing up a list of four styles by which you may judge this author or that, or different writings. He believes that there are four main elements of style, four qualities or manners of writing or speaking, and he examines how these are to be practised.

Each "style" is analyzed under three aspects: diction or the choice of words, composition or the arrangement of words, and subject-matter. On this last he has least to say.[29] And, somewhat irregularly under one heading or the other, he also brings in the figures of speech or thought that are most appropriate to each style.

The distinction between content and style is, as we have seen, found in Plato, and may be older. The subdivision of style into diction and word-arrangement is, if not explicitly formulated, certainly implicit in Aristotle, for chapters 2-7 of the third book of his *Rhetoric* deal with diction, while 8-9 deal with word-arrangement. The formula may have been clarified by Theophrastus.

It is important to realize that these subdivisions do not quite correspond to modern categories. Diction, which was later more precisely termed the choice of words, includes not only the choice of current or unusual terms, of rare or newly-coined words, but also words which express passion and character (an angry man uses different words from those he uses when sorrowful), different forms of the same roots, and so on. Further, diction also includes the use of loaded words, of metaphors and similes.[30] It includes all this in Aristotle as well as in later critics. We have already seen that the Greeks were shrewdly aware of the importance of semantics, illustrated in Aristotle by the story of Simonides who refused to write an ode on the victors in a mule race, "half-asses" as he contemptuously called them, but when the fee was increased he wrote the poem beginning: "Hail, ye daughters of storm-footed steeds, . . ." but, the phi-

losopher comments, they were still the daughters of asses.[31] Diction then includes in part the expression of emotion as well as the writing in character, in so far as these follow from the use of certain words.

*Synthesis*, or the arrangement of words once chosen, ("composition" though etymologically correct, is a misleading translation) has three things in view: the structure of the sentence, the sound of the words in collocation, and rhythm. The first of these Demetrius has already discussed in the introductory section. The second (much neglected today) is part of that music of language to which we have seen that the Greeks were extraordinarily sensitive. It too has a part to play in the expression of emotion, for, though we are less aware of this, an angry man uses harsh, guttural sounds where a lover or a suppliant quite unconsciously will use mutes and labials. It is still true that words that can be run into one another, without pauses between, are softer than those that willy-nilly make us stop. No one, however hard he tries, can (meaning apart) put the same emotional tone into two phrases such as "You accursed crooked cur" on the one hand and "My lovely angel sweetheart" on the other. The third point, closely connected with the other two, is rhythm, and this, in Greek prose as in Greek poetry (except when it was set to music) has nothing to do with stress or pitch, but only with the length or shortness of syllables. Here Demetrius, like all ancient critics, repeats the Aristotelian dictum that prose must be rhythmical but not metrical, that is, its rhythms must be more varied and never repeated regularly. It is then with these three things in view—word-arrangement, diction, and content—that Demetrius discusses each "style."

"Neighbouring" each successful style or manner is a particular vice or faulty style into which an unsuccessful attempt will fall. An unsuccessful attempt at grandeur or impressiveness is apt to fall into frigidity, attempted elegance into affectation, simplicity into dryness or aridity, and forcefulness will become bad taste. This theory of the "neighbouring vice" is found in other critics too—we know it best in Horace and Longinus[32]—but whether Demetrius was the first to put it forward we cannot tell. As in so many things, our opinion will depend upon our view of his date. He does not claim to be original at this point.

*Structure of the Work*

This general plan is quite simple and clear. It is also carried out more systematically than is often alleged, and what appears at first sight to be a digression or repetition seems to be reasonably well placed in the work as a whole. Demetrius does, however, seek variety, and he deliberately begins one section with subject-matter, another with diction, and so on. Certainly there are repetitions: a figure of speech may in one place be said to contribute to elegance, for example, while later we find it contributing to forcefulness. There are many such cases, and this seems at first sight confusing, but is Demetrius not essentially right? Is it not true that the same way of putting things has, in different contexts, a different effect? We will take one example which is found in the discussions of three of our "styles," namely *anaphora* or the repetition of words at the beginning of consecutive clauses.

In 61 we have the passage on Nireus in the Homeric catalogue of ships. Demetrius says that Homer makes this one mention of Nireus, who led only three ships to Troy and is never heard of again, much more impressive by the use of anaphora. This is the passage (*Iliad* 2.671-674):

> Nireus from Syma brought three curved ships,
> Nireus, son of Aglaïa and of Charopus,
> Nireus, most beautiful of all the Greeks
> Who came to Ilium, save Achilles only.

Here, surely, Demetrius is right. In 141 he is discussing the elegant charm of a poem of Sappho, of which he quotes:

> O Evening Star, all things you bring;
> You bring the sheep, you bring the goat,
> You bring the child to its mother.

Dimly through this inadequate translation, and much more clearly in the Greek of Sappho (see note on 141), we can see that the same figure of speech has a quite different effect from that in the Nireus passage, that the effect here is one of charm, not of grandeur or impressiveness. Then we find anaphora once again in 268, from the great speech of Aeschines against Demosthenes: "You call him as a witness, a witness against yourself, a witness against the laws, a witness against the democracy."[33]

Here again Demetrius is right. The effect of the repetition in this passage is like a series of blows, it is forceful, certainly not charming! The fact that these effects are so different may raise doubts as to the soundness of Demetrius' basic categories but, given these, the discussion of the same figure in different sections is justified, and Demetrius is the better critic for having seen that figures of speech depend for their effect on other factors. Not all his repetitions can be justified in this way, and we shall note them as we read the text, but some of them can be, and the point should be kept in mind.

Demetrius has also been criticized for digressions. Rhys Roberts (pp. 28-31) listed no less than fifteen "subsidiary topics" of this kind, in fact every passage where Demetrius ventures upon some general description or explanation which is perhaps not immediately required by his present purpose. Of the nine so listed in the discussion of the grand style, only one is of any length and worth mentioning here; all the others seem perfectly natural where they occur. It is the discussion of metaphors and similes (78-90), a subject which Aristotle had discussed at some length and regarded as the main ornament allowed in prose. Now metaphor is appropriate in a discussion of impressiveness, but not only there, and it is a general discussion of the subject which we find at this point. It is an extremely interesting passage, in which Demetrius discusses, where it first comes up in a natural way (there are several references to impressiveness in the passage), the whole subject of metaphor. And he does not discuss it again, although, obviously, a metaphor can be elegant or forcible!

The digression found under the plain style are clearly due to a change of plan in this section. Demetrius deals mainly with the *qualities* which the plain style should have, namely lucidity, persuasiveness, and vividness, and he tells us how to achieve these by means which may concern both diction and word-arrangement. Hence, after a very brief statement (190-191) on simple subject-matter and diction, he says that lucidity is here the chief aim, and proceeds to tell us how this lucidity is to be attained (192-203). He then goes on to word-arrangement (200-208); we are told that vividness and persuasiveness are most acceptable to the plain style and we proceed to deal with these two qualities (209-220 and 221-222). After this comes one of his best passages, on the style of letter-writing: this too should be in the plain style (222-235).

Thus the treatment of the plain style follows a different plan. Perhaps Demetrius felt that all that could be said about plain diction and composition was that they should be plain, and that it would be both more profitable and more interesting to discuss the main qualities which this style strove to attain. He may also have welcomed the opportunity for a variation in his approach. It is true that these qualities are not the exclusive possession of the plain style; and it is true that in the discussion of these three qualities, lucidity, vividness, and persuasiveness (especially the last two), he goes beyond the bounds of the plain style. He does not deal with them again.

The discussion of the proper style for writing letters (223-235) can hardly be called a digression since it is a particular application of the simple style and is discussed under that heading. Demetrius may at first sight seem to contradict himself when, after saying that letters require the simple style, he concludes the discussion by saying that it needs to be a mixture of the simple and the elegant. This, however, is not really the case. He begins by disagreeing with Artemon who said that a letter should be regarded as one side of a dialogue. Dialogue as a literary genre tries to reproduce the style of actual conversation, but Demetrius feels that a letter is something more than that. While it is true that the subject and the style should both be simple, a letter is also an expression of friendship, a "gift" from the writer to the recipient; hence it deserves more care (though not too obvious care) on the part of the writer, whose character it inevitably reflects; it must not, on the other hand, become a treatise. Such treatises, it is true, are often addressed to a correspondent, but they are essentially quite another genre. The proper epistolary style, then, is basically simple, but there should be a certain admixture of elegance, and the letter may be said to require a mixture of the simple and the elegant styles.

This is the first discussion of letter-writing in ancient texts and as such of considerable historical importance. The principles it expresses are found reflected in all later theorists on epistolography.[34]

Finally, in the section on the forceful style, there are two alleged digressions, the treatment of "figured language" (287-298) and that of the hiatus (299-300). The second of these is very brief and, since hiatus is said to contribute to forcefulness, it is no digression at all but a further reference to a subject already more fully discussed under impressiveness (68-74).

The first is more important and more interesting for the light it throws upon our author's method. After treating of the peculiar force of Demades, he is led to mention a figure, much misused (presumably to attain forcefulness) by contemporary orators (287), which he calls . . . not so much "figured language" as allusiveness or innuendo. This can properly be used for reasons of good taste or discretion. In the first case it is forceful, as is shown by an example from Plato (288-289); then the cases of discretion are explained: the figure is used when addressing a despot, an all-powerful populace, and the like (292-295). The subject of this figure arises naturally in a discussion of forcefulness, to which it often contributes, and, as it is of some interest, its other uses are then added, even though they are not strictly relevant. At this point comes a true digression (296-298) on the different forms in which a thought may be expressed—statement, advice, question, and so on. This arises very naturally from the different effect of allusiveness and bluntness, but it is irrelevant to the subject under discussion, to which we then quickly return.[35]

From this brief survey of supposed digressions we may conclude that Demetrius does here and there allow himself to pursue for a moment a particular point which has come up naturally, and to do so at greater length than strict relevance would demand. He also varies his method, particularly in the section on plain style where he deals more with the qualities at which it aims than with the means of attaining it, but he does not seriously transgress the scheme he has set himself. Whether

we blame or praise him for these near-digressions will depend upon the rigidity of our own minds.

*Elegance or Wit?*

A much more serious flaw in our treatise, one of ideas rather than of structure, seems to have escaped attention. It is a basic confusion in Demetrius' account of . . . the elegant or polished manner (128-189). This "style" does not, like the others, express one clear basic idea, and the confusion is reflected in the terminology. The word . . . by which it is described in contrast to the others, is almost immediately replaced by . . . charm or grace, and is thereafter little used in the discussion.

At the very beginning (128) we are told that elegant language may be described as a gay playfulness of expression. The charm is then said to be of two kinds: on the one hand the graceful poetic charm of such passages as Homer's description of Nausicaa playing among her handmaidens; and, on the other hand, witticisms. The difficulty is that too much is included under the second: the witticisms quoted at the very beginning (e.g. the old woman's teeth are sooner counted than her fingers) have no trace of charm, or indeed of elegance or grace. Moreover, this is true of many other jests quoted; for example, the grim humour of the Cyclops (130) and Xenophon's jest (134) about the hard-headed Persian from whom it would be easier to strike fire than laughter.[38] When Demetrius calls this the most effective charm . . . (135) he is straining the meaning of that word beyond all bearing. He seems to have included all witticisms, whether gracious or crude, under his second kind of [kharis], and to believe that, because they could all be called [kharientismos], a word that could be applied to any kind of witticism, he could use the root word [kharis] to apply to them also, although in all its usages elsewhere the word implies what we would call charm or grace or graciousness. Even if it could be so used—and no doubt it is presumptuous to challenge the Greek usages of a Greek— the ideas he deals with have nothing in common with each other except a certain cleverness in the handling of words, which is not enough to class them together under one and the same manner of writing. Homer's description of Nausicaa has grace and charm in plenty, but no wit; Sophron's remark about the rascal who made as many drachmas as he deserved strokes of the lash is very witty but by no stretch of imagination can it be called charming or gracious. It is a [kharientismos] but it has no [kharis]. It seems more than a matter of taste, which notoriously varies in different places and ages. Demetrius may well have considered the cruder witticisms he quotes as in good taste—and here lies another verbal confusion for he later uses the word [akhari], bad taste, for the vice neighbouring on forcefulness (302). He might therefore have considered these witticisms as [enkhari] (he uses that term as nearly equivalent to [kharieis] in 156), but witticisms can be

in good taste without having grace or charm. The confusion of words implies a confusion of thought.

Demetrius seems to have realized something of this
when he, at a later stage in this discussion (163), draws
a definite distinction between the charming . . . and the
ridiculous . . ., but only for a moment, for we find that
this becomes only a repetition of his former distinction
between poetic grace and jest. The section is confused
(163-169) both in thought and language since up to
this point he had called *both* divisions . . . charming.

This confusion is a serious flaw in the discussion of
the elegant style. True, elegant playfulness of language
can be divided into charming grace on the one hand
and gracious wit on the other. The mistake is to include all witticisms, even the grimmest and the merely
witty, under the second head, and not to have excluded
here, as he should have done, those grim and satiric
jests which he himself later includes under the peculiar
forcefulness of Demades (282-286). He does not there
draw attention to their wit; yet a comparison with 130-
131 will show that they are essentially of the same
kind, and that he was aware that a relationship existed
between wit and forcefulness.

However, where he is dealing with the elegant and
charming properly so-called, he has a great deal to say
that is worthy of our attention.

### Demetrius and Aristotle

Another feature of our treatise is its peculiar, indeed
in many ways unique, relationship to Aristotle. It is
obvious, and universally admitted, that much of what
Demetrius says can be traced back to the *Rhetoric* of
Aristotle. It is also clear that this dependence is far
more pronounced in certain sections of the book than
in others. But there is more than that: our author seems
to use Aristotle in a manner unparalleled in other
critical texts. Sometimes he corrects what Aristotle
says and improves on him; at other times he changes
the Aristotelian terms in what seems a deliberate
manner, now and again making them simpler and
clearer. In a word, he uses Aristotle for his own ends.
The question is whether such changes as he makes
should be attributed to unknown intermediate sources
or whether they argue personal knowledge of the
*Rhetoric* and, further, whether his attitude to Aristotle
is more likely at an early date such as the early third
century. Certainly no parallel can be adduced from
Roman times.

The introductory section makes use of Aristotle at every
turn; that on the grand manner makes use of him on
particular subjects such as rhythm (38-43), metaphor
(78-90), and frigidity (116), and there are frequent
Aristotelian echoes, particularly at 58, 77, and 93-115.
The discussion of the elegant style has very little that

is Aristotelian, though his writings are three times used
in illustration (144, 154, 157). On the simple style there
are a few Aristotelian echoes (190-194) and references
to his letters in the section on letter-writing. The section on forcefulness has practically nothing that recalls
him. Demetrius' scheme of four styles is of course
quite un-Aristotelian, for to Aristotle there was only
one right way of saying a particular thing at a particular time; moreover he recognized only one virtue or
*aretê* of speech, namely lucidity.

As the greatest use of Aristotle is made in the discussion of sentence structure the peculiar nature of the
relationship will emerge most clearly if we deal with
it first (1-35). We may note at the outset that the very
title . . . already seems to betray a careful use of
words. . . .

Any reader who will glance at the first five sections of
the ninth chapter of the third book of Aristotle's *Rhetoric* will see at once how much Demetrius' discussion of
sentence structure derives from it. All the main ideas are
there, but they are mostly applied with a difference.
Aristotle says the period limits the sense, should end
with it, and that this is the main difference between the
periodic and the loose or unperiodic structure. A period
should also be capable of being uttered in one breath.
All this is in Demetrius, but he goes further: he applies
the correspondence with the thought also to clauses (1-
3) which to him are the basic unit; they too must be of
reasonable length (4-7, cp. *Rhet.* 3.9.6). He associates
brief clauses—and here he brings in the even smaller
division, the phrase or *komma*—with maxims and lacon-
isms (cp. *Rhet.* 2.21.13). He then quotes Aristotle's
definition of the period, but he quotes it only in part,
and expands this with the image of runners who have
their goal in view (11, cp. *Rhet.* 3.9.2-3), using his own
words and adding the etymology of the word [*periodos*]
which Aristotle does not mention.

There are interesting changes in terminology. Aristotle's
term for the periodic style is [*leksis katestrammene*],
Demetrius keeps the adjective but changes the noun to
[*ermeneia*]; Aristotle's term for the looser, non-periodic style is [*legis eiromene*], a rather difficult phrase—
the "strung-along" style. This Demetrius changes to
the simpler . . . "the disconnected style"—an adjective
which Aristotle used for a period of which the clauses
are not in antithesis (3.9.7). Both writers note the loose
style of the older writers (*Rhet.* 3.9.1 . . .) but Demetrius
quotes Hecataeus instead of Herodotus. He ignores at
this point Aristotle's division of periods into those with
one and those with more clauses, but later (19) replaces it by a tripartite division of his own into rhetorical, historical, and conversational periods. . . .   He
then uses as an example of this single-clause *period*
the sentence of Herodotus which Aristotle used as an
example of the *non*-periodic, and which Demetrius there
replaced by an example from Hecataeus.

In 15 Demetrius says, with emphasis on the first person singular, "I consider" that a discourse should not consist of a series of periods. There is no such statement in Aristotle, but it is a commonplace in Dionysius of Halicarnassus and in Cicero. The advice to avoid monotony is Aristotelian in other contexts (e.g. on rhythm, 3.8.1). Nor is there anything in Aristotle to correspond to the requirement (18) that the final clause of the period should be the longest.

At 22-24 we come to antithesis, also discussed by Aristotle (3.9.7) who does not distinguish between antithesis of thought and of words (a doubtful distinction). He does, however, also condemn the fake verbal antithesis (3.9.10) and Demetrius uses his example of it, adding a comment of his own.

At 25 there is another change of terminology. Where Aristotle (3.9.9) restricts *paromoiôsis* to similarities of words or sounds at the beginning or the end of consecutive clauses, and uses *parisôsis* for balanced clauses of equal length, Demetrius uses the adjective XXX to cover both—a more natural use since the word simply means similar—but he uses XXX, a much more expressive word, to refer to balanced clauses. Of his three examples, the first comes directly from Aristotle in this passage, the second is used by the philosopher in another connection (3.9.7); the third is not found in the *Rhetoric*. Neither is Demetrius' comment that the use of these studied devices is inadvisable in forceful or emotional passages, but he illustrates his point by examples from a lost work of Aristotle.

The definition of the enthymeme (30-33) is Aristotelian (*Rhet.* 1.2.8) and Demetrius' insistence on the difference between it and the period is in accord with that meaning.[40]

The last references in this section are the most interesting. Demetrius quotes (in his own words) the Aristotelian definition of a clause as "one of the two parts of a period" and naturally complains that this contradicts the existence of the one-clause period. He then quotes and accepts the correction of one Archedemus into: "a clause is either a simple period or a part of a composite period" and he ends his discussion of sentence structure by another statement (35) about Archedemus: that he *seems* to imply that a period may consist not only of one or two, but of three or more clauses. Demetrius had already stated (16) that he considered four clauses the advisable limit. Let us be quite clear that Archedemus (whoever he was) is quoted only for his definition, with a comment that this definition *appears to imply* that Archedemus established no limit to the number of clauses.[41] I am at a loss to understand the position taken by Roberts (and others), when he says (p. 218) that this reference to Archedemus "is of such a nature as to suggest that the author of the [*Peri*] may have drawn a good deal of his doctrine from him."

In the other sections the dependence on Aristotle is less constant. When Demetrius begins his discussion of the impressive style with a discussion of rhythm, he is obviously making use of *Rhet.* 3.8.4-6. But the way he uses it should warn us to be cautious in the use we make of such alleged quotations where we do not have the original text before us. Demetrius' words are: "A paeonic arrangement is, *as Aristotle says* . . .,[42] impressive" (38). Occurring as this does in a discussion of the grand manner, it might be thought to imply that Aristotle said that the paeonic rhythm was appropriate to the impressive style, and one might well deduce from this that the theory of several styles goes back to Aristotle. Fortunately we have Aristotle's text, and he says nothing of the kind. His discussion of rhythm has nothing whatever to do with any theory of styles, nor does he use the adjective [*megaloprepes*], grand or impressive. What he does say in his discussion of rhythm is that one should aim at dignity and take the hearer out of himself . . ., and he then goes on to advise the use of the paeonic metre at the beginning and end of clauses, presumably as having this effect. Since both dignity and passion belong, for Demetrius, to the impressive style, he is quite justified in saying that, as Aristotle says, the paeonic is impressive, for what Aristotle says does fit in with the description of the grand manner. There is no intention to deceive, only to use Aristotle for his own purposes. He then goes on (41) to use Theophrastus to improve on Aristotle. Even if we cannot have paeons exactly at the beginning and the end of a clause, we can still have a general paeonic effect, *"and this is what Aristotle, it would seem, recommends,"* and he gives an example of his general paeonic rhythm from Theophrastus. But Aristotle did not say so, and probably did *not* mean this.

Sometimes our author obviously has a passage of Aristotle in mind, but does not mention him. Aristotle said that connectives . . . should correspond exactly (*Rhet.* 3.5.2) but Demetrius says they should not, at least in the grand style (53), and gives an example from Antiphon.

The discussion of metaphors and similes (78-90) is full of Aristotelian echoes. A number of the same examples are used. There are also several things which Aristotle does not say: that a metaphor is sometimes more lucid and precise than the specific term (82), and that the transference should, at least in the grand style, be from the greater to the less, not *vice versa* (83), that in metaphors from one species to another, the transference does not always work both ways, so that you can say the foot of a mountain but not the slope of a man (79). These are good points, not in Aristotle.

The treatment of similes in the two authors is perhaps the most interesting of all. Demetrius says that when the metaphor is too bold we should convert it into a simile, and similes are safer in prose (80); the examples he gives conform to Aristotle's classic distinction between the two (*Rhet.* 3.4.1), namely that "Achilles leapt *like* a lion" is a simile, while "A lion, he leapt" is a metaphor. But when Aristotle goes on to say that "the simile is useful in prose, but rarely, for it is poetical" while he allows metaphor as *the* ornament in prose (3.2.8-15), we are confused, for it is simply not true that "Achilles, a lion, leapt" is less poetical than "Achilles leapt like a lion." This strange advice is almost certainly due to Aristotle's having the extended Homeric simile in mind, but the core fusion remains. Demetrius clarifies all this: to him the simile, as stated above, is safer, but he adds that the simile must be brief (89); if it is extended it becomes a "poetic comparison" ( . . . i.e. a Homeric simile) and this can only be used in prose with the greatest caution (90). There can be no doubt that Demetrius is improving on Aristotle.

Enough has been said to show that our author's relation to Aristotle is unique in extant critical texts. It might be described as respect falling short of veneration, and he does not hesitate to improve upon the master. He is quite ready to give credit to others, as when he quotes Theophrastus always very aptly, but he does seem to be himself quite familiar with Aristotle. He may be quoting from memory, and this may account for some inaccuracies, but it would not seem to account for his changes in terminology which impress one as purposeful. The use he makes of Aristotle is everywhere subordinated to his own categories.[43] This way of using Aristotle cannot be paralleled in any other critic whether Greek or Roman, in the first century B.C. or later, and it seems unlikely that it derives from one or more intermediate sources.[44] I am again at a loss to understand Rhys Roberts' view (p. 249) that "the relation . . . of the [*peri hermeneias*] to Aristotle suggests a follower far removed in time." As far as it goes, it suggests to me the exact opposite.

We cannot prove, of course, that this or that point was not derived from an intermediate source, but we must not automatically assume that this applied to everything Demetrius says where no sign of such sources is found in our text and we have no evidence elsewhere that the opinions found here were held by anyone else. Our author's attitude as a whole seems to be far more easily explained as that of a man who had read Aristotle himself, and used him independently. Such a man is much more likely to have lived in the late fourth or early third century than at a much later date.

### Theophrastus

Next in importance to Aristotle himself comes Theophrastus. He is quoted four times in all, each time on a specific topic, and each time he was well worth quoting. Curiously enough, the particular theories attributed to him here are not found elsewhere. At 41, Theophrastus' example of a paeonic clause which does not begin or end with a paeon leads to the improve-

ment already noted on Aristotle's conception of prose-rhythm, and for this improvement Theophrastus was probably responsible, though the improvement may have been implicit rather than explicitly stated in Theophrastus. At 114 a general definition of frigidity from Theophrastus precedes quotation of Aristotle's analysis of frigidity of *diction* into four kinds (116). At 173-174, Theophrastus' analysis of the causes of beauty in words is quoted in preference to Aristotle's remarks on the subject (*Rhet.* 3.2.13, in the discussion of metaphors, of which Demetrius makes use elsewhere), probably because his terminology was clearer and because he dealt with the subject specifically. Finally, at 222 we have Theophrastus' suggestion that some things should be left to the imagination of the reader; to this there is no parallel in Aristotle.

This seems to imply that Demetrius knew his Theophrastus as well as his Aristotle. If he were quoting from an (unknown) intermediate source, it is unlikely that he would have restricted himself to these four cases or that, in each case, the reference would have been so apt; it seems very much simpler to conclude that Demetrius made his own selection. Nor do I see any supporting evidence for the suggestion that "Theophrastus is probably followed in many other places." It may be so, but it is at least as likely that Demetrius took Aristotle as his primary guide in certain sections, and quoted Theophrastus when he found something particularly good in his works.

### The Question of Date

References to Aristotle and Theophrastus do not, in themselves, affect the question of date, though the manner of them may, if we believe it to indicate considerable familiarity and a freer use of them than is found in writings of Graeco-Roman times. References to later writers, however, may well affect the date of our treatise. We will now examine further references which have been considered incompatible not only with the authorship of the Phalerean Demetrius but also with an early Hellenistic date.

1. *References to persons.* One unusual feature of our treatise is the large number of references to, and quotations from, persons who are known to have lived in the late fourth and early third centuries. These are interesting in themselves; moreover, they would seem at least as compatible with an earlier as with a later date.

There is, first of all, Demetrius of Phalerum himself. Words spoken by him about Craterus are quoted as an example of innuendo at 289. As long ago as 1594 Victorius took this as a proof of the authorship of that Demetrius, which it obviously is not. On the other hand, Rhys Roberts expresses the view now generally accepted when he says: "No literary reference throughout the *De Elocutione* is so damaging to the traditional view as this," presumably on the assumption that such a self-revelation is in impossibly bad taste. But that is not true either. Plato and Xenophon, for example, do mention themselves in their works. All we can be sure of is that if our author did tell a story about himself, he would certainly have told it, as it is told, in the third person. The story itself is no evidence one way or the other. One interesting point about it, however, is that it is a late fourth-century anecdote told by no one else.

At 193 where Demetrius has been speaking of disconnected sentences as more appropriate for oral delivery, he continues: "That is why Menander, whose style lacks connectives, is mostly acted, while Philemon is read." Menander's date is 342-291, and Philemon's 361-262. This way of referring to them, we are told, "seems to be the judgment of *posterity*" (Rhys Roberts, p. 53). But is it? There is a parallel in Aristotle where he too is discussing the difference between oral and written style, a passage which our author most probably had in mind.[45] Aristotle says: "Poets who write to be read are in everybody's hands, like Chaeremon . . . or Licymnius. . . ." Licymnius lived a generation or two before Aristotle, but Chaeremon, the tragic poet, was certainly his contemporary. Aristotle never hesitates to mention contemporaries where appropriate. Our author need not avoid doing so. His reference to Menander and Philemon does not prove them contemporaries, of course, but neither is there any reason to consider this "the judgment of posterity." In fact the passage proves nothing at all, except that the treatise cannot have been written *before* Menander and Philemon were well known to their contemporaries, but then they both were well known before the end of the fourth century!

The lengthy reference to Ctesias (212-216), whom others criticized for prolixity while Demetrius defends him as being vivid, offers no difficulty of dating, since he was writing at the end of the *fifth* century, and it is difficult to see the point of Roberts' remark that he was "not yet a classic" in the time of Demetrius of Phalerum. He had been dead over a hundred years by the early third century and could, whether a "classic" or not, be the subject of literary controversy.

A sentence is quoted at 182 from Dicaearchus, a contemporary of Theophrastus, and Nicias, the painter, is quoted at 76: (*fl.* 340 to after 306). We cannot build much on the tense of these various references, though "Nicias *used to say* that the choice of subject was no smaller part of the art of the painter" is at least as compatible with personal knowledge or oral tradition as with quotation from another intermediate source.[46]

The three references latest in time seem to be Clitarchus who is criticized for bad taste in 304; Praxiphanes, who is quoted in 57 as a literary critic, and Sotades referred to in 189. Clitarchus' exact date is uncertain. Roberts puts his *floruit* at 300 B.C., the *Oxford Classical Dictionary* speaks of him as writing some time

after 280 B.C. Praxiphanes cannot be dated exactly; he is said to have been a pupil of Theophrastus, and Callimachus (305-240 B.C.) wrote a book against him. Sotades was a contemporary of Ptolemy Philadelphus and seems to have been old enough to object to that king's marriage in 289.[47] All three seem to have belonged to the first half of the third century, and indeed to have been active in the first quarter. Sotades was notorious later for his broken and soft verses, known as Sotadeans. Roberts says: "the use of the term 'Sotadean' for feeble and affected rhythms is probably of still later date." We might reply that the term need not have been in general use when it was used for the first time, but it is more profitable to reflect that the Alexandria of, say, the second quarter of the third century was a highly sophisticated literary society where reputations were quickly made (and unmade). We know that there was a great deal of literary controversy among contemporaries. The literary war between Callimachus and Apollonius of Rhodes is famous enough; the book of Callimachus *Against Praxiphanes* has already been mentioned. In that kind of atmosphere references to contemporaries (in a work like ours) would be very natural, and even the term "Sotadeans" might well be current during the lifetime of Sotades.

This does not prove that our author was writing in Alexandria at that time, but not one of these references is incompatible with this assumption, nor are they evidence of a "later" date. And if we ask at what time these unusually frequent references to writers of the later fourth and early third centuries are most likely, we may well answer that they would be much more likely in the first half of the third century than at the "later date," such as the first century B.C. or A.D., to which our treatise is now commonly assigned. Indeed it would be hard to find any author in those centuries as familiar with the late fourth century and early third as our Demetrius seems to be.

The references to the orator Demades (*fl.* 350-319 B.C.) as an exponent of forcefulness where he gets a brief section all to himself (282-286) is also significant. The works of Demades were, according to Quintilian (2.17.13), not committed to writing, so that they were not extant in Roman times. We may, if we wish, suppose that the examples given here were taken from a "collection" of his sayings, which would then have to have been made shortly after his death and survived. We have no evidence of such a collection, nor is he often quoted by later writers. It is at least as likely that these very striking sayings were remembered in oral tradition at the time of our treatise; they would certainly live on for some time. And we are reminded that Theophrastus valued Demades more highly than he did Demosthenes.[48]

I have not so far mentioned the unknown three, Archedemus (34-5), Artemon (233) and the mysterious

Gadereus (237), because we know nothing about them. Archedemus corrected Aristotle's definition of a *kôlon* or clause: there is no reason whatsoever to connect him with a Stoic philosopher of that name who *may* have lived as late as 130 B.C., except that they have the same name. Nor do we know anything about Artemon except what we are told here; true, we know of several other men of that name, one of whom also *may* have been living in 130 B.C., but there is no reason to identify him with our Artemon.[49] However, the real display of ingenuity is . . .: "as Gadêreus wrote (in trivial fashion) about the battle of Salamis." This improbable name is likely to be a corruption, and editors have amended it to . . . "the man from Gadara." This Gadarene is then identified with Theodorus of Gadara, the famous rhetorician and tutor of Tiberius, but if he wrote on the battle of Salamis, trivially or otherwise, we have no record of it. The identification is then used as evidence for a later date, and so is the manner of referring to him by the name of his city, a later practice. When scholars thus argue on the basis of their own conjectures as evidence, it might be salutary to remember that we teach students to respect Socrates because he knew he did not know what he did not know. The truth is that we have no means of knowing who the mysterious "Gadereus" is intended to be, just as we are quite unable to identify either Archedemus or Artemon. These three unknown names provide no evidence at all.

2. *Other "late" references.* As far as references to persons in our treatise are concerned, the unusual familiarity with many who lived in the late fourth and early third century would seem to favour an early date, in fact one almost contemporary or at least within the reach of oral tradition; on the other hand the references to Clitarchus, Praxiphanes, and Sotades would seem to make the first quarter of the century improbable but offer no difficulty if we assume a date about 270 B.C. or later. However, the absence of references to later authors is no argument for an early date, for it was the practice of even later critics to draw their illustrations from the writers of Classical Greece and Alexandria. Nor would it be safe to draw any conclusion from the absence of references to later critics, though we may well feel that in a later work we might expect some reference to Hegesias (250 B.C.) and to the Asiatic style in general, for both were universally condemned by critics from the time of Cicero on, and these references would have been especially apt in connection with the affected style. Indeed it has been suggested that some examples of it, such as "a Centaur riding himself" and the pun on Olympias (187) are typical of Asianism and may well be derived from Asiatic writers of the third century.[50] But if we remember that Hegesias' *floruit* was the middle of that century, a taste for affectation obviously developed before his day, and our author may well be quoting from writers with "Asiatic" tendencies earlier in the century, before the name of Asianism or the reputation of

Hegesias had developed. Nor need we regard historical inaccuracies (at 238 Aristides is reproached for not being present at Salamis) or excessive hyperboles as betraying clear traces of the artificiality of the rhetorical exercises of Roman times. Even Isocrates was careless of historical truth and some pretty wild hyperboles are quoted by Aristotle.[51]

Our author mentions certain characteristics of rhetoric in his day. He tells us that his contemporaries are apt to confuse grandeur with eloquence itself (38); that forcefulness is in fashion (245); that the term [*kakozelos*] was commonly applied to affectation or preciosity (186) and this was apparently a recent coinage (239), which, in word-arrangement, was applied to broken rhythms (189) like those of Sotades; finally, that such affectation when combined with aridity of thought was called [*kserokakozelia*] (189 and 239). We are told also that the orators of the day did not know how to use innuendo without making it ridiculous (287). These are all faults of taste; they are quite insufficient to give any clear indication of date, but they seem quite appropriate to the early Hellenistic period when Cicero tells us the fatty or corpulent Asiatic style came into fashion.[52] Certainly these faults are not particularly characteristic of *Greek* style from 100 B.C. to 100 A.D., and in so far as they were current then, they were certainly not new.

Certain specific phrases are also supposed to betray a late date. For example, Demetrius' use of the expression [*oi arkhaion*], the old writers or the ancients, to designate the Classical writers. This, we are told, is a late usage. The word is used three times: in 12, the adjective is applied to the loose, unperiodic sentence-structure; we have the same contrast in 244 and we are told again that "ancient" writing is unperiodic because "the ancients were simple men." Obviously, this does *not* mean the Classical writers but those who wrote before periodic structure came into fashion. Aristotle uses the word in exactly the same sense (*Rhet.* 3.9.1) and in the same context, and gives, as an example of the "ancient" manner, a sentence from Herodotus. Indeed Aristotle goes further, for in the previous sentence he compares the period to "the antistrophes of the ancient poets," . . . which must include at least Pindar, and probably the three fifth-century tragedians as well. The truth is that [*arkhaios*] is a very elastic term, like our own word "old," and, if Aristotle could apply it to fifth-century poets, we should not be surprised if a couple of generations later it could include Demosthenes in the one place (67) where Demetrius uses it of the Classical writers as against those of his own day: "the old writers use many figures but they use them so skilfully that they seem less artificial than those who use none." The contrast between old and contemporary writers is there, but such expressions may mean no more than half a century. Modern critics of the twenties and thirties certainly used such expressions to contrast their contemporaries with the writers of even the late nineteenth century.

In 204, Demetrius says that "the new comedy" uses shorter verses. We are told that "the triple division of comedy is Alexandrian and this suggests a later date than Demetrius of Phalerum." How much later? Does the expression "the new comedy" really imply a tripartite division? Aristotle already used a very similar expression when he said the difference between crude and polished wit is seen in "comedies old and new."[53]

In 181, prose of a general rhythmical nature is said to be practised by Plato, Xenophon, and "the Peripatetics." The objection is that only "later" writers would thus have referred collectively to the school of Aristotle and to writers of that school. Perhaps, but we do not know when the Aristotelians became Peripatetics (*LSF* traces it back to about 200 B.C.). Is it not the kind of nickname that should be almost contemporary with the first two heads of the school?

The expression [*hoi Attikoi*] to designate the inhabitants of Attica, where Attic dialect is contrasted with Doric at 175-177, is even less significant. The adjective is, of course, quite Classical and Aristotle uses the phrase [*hoi Attikoi hretores*] for the Attic orators (*Rhet.* 3.11.16). There is no reason to consider this a gloss, but in any case Plato speaks of "the Attic speech" and "the old Attic speech."[54]

There is one other phrase the meaning of which presents a pretty problem. In 108, Demetrius says "altogether, ornamental addition . . . may be compared to those external displays of riches, (ornamented) cornices and triglyphs and broad purples. . . ." The meaning of this last phrase is very obscure, but the context requires some ornament used to display wealth, almost certainly in connection with buildings, probably awnings or drapes of some kind. The fact that Lucian in the second century A.D.[55] uses a somewhat similar expression to refer to the *laticlavus*, that is, the broad purple band which Roman senators wore on their toga, is hardly enough to see a reference to it here. In any case the senatorial purple was not a sign of wealth but of caste and prestige, nor did *mere* wealth entitle one to it, certainly not in the first century B.C. or A.D.

Finally, the citing of 172 as a proof of a later date by Roberts, Radermacher, and others seems a good example of faulty logic. Demetrius tells us that certain jibes may be allowed, and he clearly implies that they are allowed because their frequent use . . . has blunted their sting. The two examples he gives are that a tall dark man is called "an Egyptian clematis" and that a fool on the water (whether rowing or swimming is not clear) is called "a sheep at sea," the word "sheep" . . . being common parlance for a stupid fellow also in other contexts. Now we are told by Seneca (*De Constantia* 17) that Chry-

sippus (280-207 B.C.) mentioned someone who was indignant because he was called a sheep at sea, *vervex marinus*; and from Diogenes Laertius (7.1.2) we learn that in a work on proverbs or saws Chrysippus said that Zeno, who was tall and dark, was called an Egyptian clematis. As both expressions are traced to Chrysippus, this proves, we are told, that Demetrius is extracting them from Chrysippus' collection of proverbs. It surely proves nothing of the kind: it is in no way surprising that two jibes quoted by Demetrius as in frequent use should reappear in a collection of such proverbial sayings by Chrysippus one or two generations later. Proverbs hardly find their way into a collection until they have been in use for a considerable time.[56]

*Language and Vocabulary*

Both Radermacher and Roberts, and indeed all those who have argued that **On Style** must have been written much later than the traditional date, have put a good deal of emphasis upon the language of the treatise. It is one of their main arguments, at times their chief argument. The fullest study of the language of Demetrius is that of Dahl, and most of his arguments will be found in Rhys Roberts' edition. In this question of language we are admittedly on very slippery ground, for we have no third-century prose works to give us a standard of comparison. We know that linguistic habits were changing by the second half of the fourth century. The number of word-forms, apart from technical terms, which appear for the first time in Aristotle and Theophrastus is very considerable. The *Rhetorica ad Alexandrum* is of special interest in this respect, for it is a fourth-century text and, being a rhetorical work, it is roughly of the same kind as **On Style**. Even a superficial study of its language and vocabulary makes quite evident that it contains a substantial number of words, expressions, and constructions which would certainly have been condemned as "late" if the date of the treatise had not been so firmly established.[57]

At the end of the fourth century, Greek spread rapidly all over the Near East until it became the common language, the *Koinê* of the Eastern Mediterranean world. All our later authorities agree that this was the time when the florid, over-rhythmic Asiatic style was born; all of them associate this style with the name of Hegesias whom they unanimously condemn, and the *floruit* of Hegesias was as early as 250 B.C. Clearly the degeneration was rapid. Obviously, many changes took place before then.

What kind of Greek, then, would be written in Alexandria in the first half of the third century, and written by the scholars of the Museum who had been attracted there by the patronage of the Ptolemies from all over the Greek world? They studied and edited all the great Classics, they were students of *all* dialects. They wrote Greek, but it is pretty well established that they did *not* write Attic Greek, nor any particular dialect, unless indeed a particular type of Greek was required by convention for a particular genre of poetry. One would expect to find Attic and Ionian, poetic and prose forms appearing cheek by jowl with colloquialisms we know only in Aristophanes; it would be a mixture of the old and the new, and a more heterogeneous mixture than either the later *Koinê* of the New Testament, or the deliberate Atticism of Roman times. We should not be surprised, therefore, to find in a scholarly text of that period both forms and constructions that are specifically Attic, . . . and even an occasional use of the dual, which we know had almost disappeared. We should also expect a relaxation of that grammatical precision which is so characteristic of the best Classical authors (the beginnings of this process too we can trace in Aristotle), for example, a less exact use of prepositions, a slackness in the use of [an] with the optative, in short an erratic kind of inconsistency. And this is precisely what we do find.

As for the words themselves, we should always remember that our evidence is incomplete for any period. Unless the method of word-formation is itself late, when we call a word "late" it only means that it does not appear *in our extant texts* before a later period. Even where the manner of derivation is late, we cannot be sure, for the Greeks always formed words very easily, especially compounds. There is surprisingly a large number of words that occur only once in extant literature. Our treatise has sixteen such words.[58]

Where the form is regularly derived from a word in common use in Classical times—when, for example, the verb and the adjective are used in Classical writers but the noun is not, or *vice versa*,—there seems very little point in considering such forms as "late."[59] It is true that later Greek shows a tendency to use compounds, and double compounds (verbs formed with two or even more prepositions) carelessly, where the simple word would do just as well, while the Classical writers are, with occasional lapses, more careful. This tendency too began in the fourth century. Our Demetrius, however, is here, at least on a number of occasions, on the side of precision. He uses double compounds with each preposition having its full meaning so that the double compound is fully justified.[60]

In fact, Demetrius has a tendency to be precise also in his technical terms. We have already seen that he on occasion changes the technical terms of Aristotle, even where he follows him closely, from an apparent desire to simplify. We are very ignorant of the technical rhetorical vocabulary which, by the end of the fourth century, had been developing for well over a century. Plato quotes a few such terms in the *Phaedrus* in order to ridicule them; Aristotle gives us more, but his attitude to rhetorical subtleties is not very different.[61] There are some more rhetorical terms in the *Rhetorica ad*

*Alexandrum*; of Theophrastus we have only a few uncertain fragments on matters of style. Yet, clearly, the vocabulary of rhetoric and criticism had, by this time, reached considerable proportions. Most of these terms are, for us, inevitably "late." Moreover, even in the first generation after the foundation of the Museum, the learned men of Alexandria were no doubt adding technical terms of their own. We must therefore expect some "new" and some "late" technical words in Demetrius in any case. There are altogether about twenty. It would be very surprising if there were fewer.[62] These terms do not appear again till the first century, but then we have no extant critical or rhetorical works in which they could appear.

It is perhaps more surprising that some words that are very common in later criticism do not appear in Demetrius at all. The most obvious of these are [tropos] in the sense of "trope," [apheles], later applied to the simple style, a word also used by Aristotle for the "simple" period, which Demetrius avoids, as he seems to avoid or not to know the phrase [eklage onumaton], the choice of words, meaning diction. Moreover, Demetrius uses a number of terms in a sense closer to the Classical than to the later meaning.[63]

If we carefully review all the words and expressions suspected of being "late," (as is done in Appendix I), we shall, I believe, conclude that the evidence for a date much later than the traditional one is, as far as language goes at any rate, not convincing. It is true that the effect of such suspicious words is cumulative; if enough words are listed as suspect, the reader is tempted to believe that there must be something in the argument, but we should not forget the truism that poor arguments, however numerous, do not lead to sound conclusions. There are a half-dozen Classical forms used in a "non-Classical" sense. Of the fifty or so words said to be "late" in form, most could pass anywhere and the exceptions are less than a dozen. There are some deviations from the Classical usage in the use of adverbs, prepositions, and syntactical constructions. All this is, I believe, quite consistent with an early third-century date.

Is it, however, consistent with the traditional author? It is true that Cicero regards Demetrius of Phalerum as the best Greek exponent of the middle style, yet sharply marks him off from the Classical writers and regards him as an exponent of a less vigorous, softer style. Quintilian says his style is more suitable for display than for the struggle of the courts. We know from other sources that he was very affected and easy-living as a young man. Cicero actually links him with the later "Asiatics," at a time when he was more kindly disposed to the latter than he was in his later years.[64] We may conclude that his affectations did lead him to new ways of style. How would such a man write after some years in Alexandria? How far does an expatriate scholar adopt the ways of speech of his adopted country and of the community in which he lives? The question is hard to answer, especially in the case of a man like Demetrius. We may be quite sure that some non-Attic forms would slip in; yet he was an Athenian, a contemporary of Theophrastus and Menander, and we may well feel it hard to believe that he would write in this somewhat medley mixture of Attic and non-Attic. While other aspects of the treatise, its relationship to Aristotle and Theophrastus for example, would suit Demetrius very well, the language of the treatise may well be felt to be a strong argument against his authorship.

*General Critical Views*

To infer from the occurrence of the four "styles" here that "the writer lived at a time, considerably later than Aristotle, when the doctrine of the types of style had undergone many developments"[65] is to confuse our author's scheme of four main manners of writing which can all be used together (except that the plain and the grand do not mix) with the far more rigid formula of the separate and distinct three styles which we first meet in the *Ad Herennium,* and then in Cicero, but in no earlier Greek extant texts. The "styles" of Demetrius are much more like qualities of style than [kharakteres] in this more rigid sense,[66] and they seem rather to belong to a time when the three-style formula had *not* become current.

As for the general standpoint of our author, it does not seem to be "that of the Graeco-Roman period, earlier than Hermogenes and (possibly) later than Dionysius."[67] Demetrius does *not* seem to share either the point of view or the concerns of Cicero, Dionysius, Horace, or their successors. They are deeply concerned to restore rhetoric to its Isocratean place as the true philosophy based on a general education, and they insist that the writer, poet, or orator must know life and imitate it. Cicero and Dionysius are vehement in their condemnation of Asianism. There is not a word about all this in our treatise. There is no such comparative criticism as was the fashion in the circle of Dionysius and Caecilius. Demosthenes is not for Demetrius, as he was for Dionysius and Hermogenes, *the* supreme model; even [deinotes] is not his above all others, for he shares it with others as well as Demades. Demetrius is aware of the basic formula which differentiates matter from style and subdivides the latter into diction and word-arrangement, but the far more elaborate critical formulae of Dionysius do not appear. There is no trace of the rhetorical *mimêsis* or emulation so important to Cicero, Dionysius, and Quintilian. The whole apparatus of criticism seems very much simpler.

We do not know what the Greek critics of the first century A.D. were concerned with; for the schools of Theodorus of Gadara and Apollonius seem to have concentrated on matters purely rhetorical.[68] We do know, however, that the Romans were extremely concerned with the evil results of declamations and the decay of eloquence. Indeed the treatise *On the Sublime* has been dated in the first century largely on the strength of its concluding chapter on this latter subject. There is nothing of all this in Demetrius, nor of the more specifically Roman controversies between the "moderns" and the "ancients," any more than about Asianism vs. Atticism, Analogism vs. Anomalism, or any other topical question of that period. It is hard to see in what respect our Demetrius can be said to share the standpoint of Graeco-Roman times.

As for the place where our treatise was written, the concern with literature in general rather than with rhetoric would suit Alexandria very well, and the apparent familiarity with Egypt would tend to confirm an Alexandrian origin.[69]

*External Evidence*

There are a few somewhat uncertain references to our treatise in much later authors. There are also one or two references in Philodemus which deserve more attention than has been paid to them. Also, the references to, and fragments of, Demetrius of Phalerum himself, which have recently been collected by Wehrli,[70] should be examined anew to see what light they throw on his possible authorship.

These last are somewhat disappointing. The [peri hermeneias] does not occur in the list of his works in Diogenes Laertius (early third century A.D.).[71] The list is not very long, as compared for example with the works of Theophrastus, though Diogenes tells us that he wrote more than any contemporary Peripatetic. He also says that Demetrius wrote rhetorical works, but the only clearly rhetorical title is a *Rhetoric* in two books. There are, however, some other titles that may be rhetorical: the [peri pisteos], [peri kharitos], and [peri kairon] may well have been *On Proof, On Elegance,* and *On Good Taste*[72] in the rhetorical sense, rather than *On Faith, On Favour,* and *On Opportunity* in general.[73] The word [kharis] is used by our Demetrius as one of the terms to describe the elegant style, and Radermacher even suggests (p. 95) that our author may have owed a good deal to this work of the Phalerean. It is, at any rate, a point of contact between the two, if a slight one.

Both Plutarch and Stobaeus[74] tell us that Demetrius of Phalerum advised Ptolemy to read books on kingship as he would find written there the advice his friends did not dare to give him, which may remind us of *On Style* (292-293) on how despots have to be addressed with care. More directly reminiscent of that whole section is a passage in Philodemus,[75] who says that

Demetrius, together with the Sophistic kind of speeches, added to the deliberative and forensic kinds of rhetoric . . ., that is, the speech which knows how to address all audiences and obtain favour with all. Philodemus seems to mean that Demetrius included this under "sophistic" (which in Philodemus means epideictic) rather than that he made it a fourth kind of rhetoric, but, in any case, he obviously attached great importance to methods of addressing, in particular, popular assemblies and ruling princes. This subject may also have been treated in the . . . (how to speak as an ambassador?)[76] which is listed among his works by Diogenes. . . . Now this . . . is highly reminiscent of what our Demetrius says about innuendo, which he too specifically links with princes and assemblies (289-293). Here again we have a distinct point of contact between the two Demetrii.

There is another interesting sentence in Philodemus, where he says that "long periods are bad for delivery, as we read also in Demetrius about those of Isocrates. . . ."[78] We should note that the name "Demetrius" is uncertain, though the restoration has been generally accepted, and some commentators have admitted this as a reference to our treatise. The sentence occurs in a discussion of delivery in which just before "the Phalerean" (that name is quite clear) was said to have disliked the delivery of Demosthenes.[79] If the name "Demetrius" is correct in the sentence quoted, there is therefore no doubt that it refers to Demetrius of Phalerum, and if the reference is to our treatise, then Philodemus, *in the first century* B.C., already believed the author of our treatise to be Demetrius of Phalerum.

What Philodemus says of the long periods of Isocrates does accord very well with what we find in our section on forcefulness. From the very beginning of that section we are told that the forceful style requires short phrases rather than clauses (241-242), brevity and lack of smoothness (241-244), vehemence (246), the avoidance of the antitheses and balanced clauses found in Theopompus, the pupil of Isocrates (247). We may have periods but they should be short (252); forcefulness favours harsh sounds and abrupt endings (255-256), but not smoothness or regularly connected clauses (258, 269). Moreover, dramatic delivery is clearly related very closely to forcefulness, indeed at one point all but identified with it (271, and compare 193, where the disjointed word-order is said to be histrionic . . .). Returning to forcible word-arrangement at 299, we are there told that "smooth word-order, *as practised most by the school of Isocrates*" is not suited to forcefulness; it is better to do without connectives (301) and a little later (303) *long, continuous periods* are said to be unpleasant and tiresome in this style. We also remember that our author said (12) that he disliked a style which is entirely periodic like that of Isocrates.

In view of the specific mention of Isocrates at 299, of Theopompus at 247, of the emphasis throughout this section on characteristics of Isocrates' style which are undesirable in the forceful style, and the all but identification of the forceful style with that of delivery and debate, it would seem that Philodemus is indeed referring to our treatise when he says that it is "stated in Demetrius" that the long periods of Isocrates are not suited to delivery, even though where Isocrates is specifically mentioned Demetrius refers to the smoothness of Isocrates' periods rather than to their length. In Isocrates certainly the two went together. It seems, therefore, more than probable that Philodemus believed Demetrius of Phalerum to be the author of our treatise; in any case, we have here a very close similarity of viewpoint between the two Demetrii.

There is one other matter of interest in connection with Demetrius of Phalerum. We are told that, in common with Theophrastus and other cultured Athenians, he was very critical of Demosthenes' delivery; they considered it to lack dignity and simplicity, and they disliked his boldness and violence.[80] Now the attitude to Demosthenes in our treatise is unusual. He is quoted fourteen times in the section on forcefulness, usually with approval though he is once (250) condemned. No other style is illustrated by a quotation from him. At 80 a metaphor of his is quoted to illustrate the difference between a metaphor and a simile. The other three references are illustrations of periods in the first section. In other words Demetrius regards forcefulness as characteristic of the orator, *and that style only*. And even that section he shares not only with Demades but with seventeen illustrations from other writers.

How very different from the picture of Demosthenes which we find in Cicero, Dionysius, and Hermogenes! The [*deinotes*] attributed to him by all the writers of these later centuries is no longer the one quality of forcefulness but an over-all excellence in every kind of style, at times including force but not restricted to it.[81] In our treatise Demosthenes has not reached that supremacy. Not only is he used to illustrate one style only, but other writers are both more frequently quoted and illustrate various styles. As against the eighteen references to Demosthenes, there are thirty-seven references to Homer, twenty to Xenophon, nineteen to Plato, eighteen also to Aristotle, and twelve to Thucydides. Altogether, Demetrius' attitude to Demosthenes is almost as unlike that of later critical texts[82] as his attitude to Aristotle.

There are no other references to our treatise in writers of the Classical period. Ammonius, the commentator on Aristotle (*ca.* 500 A.D.) does refer to the [*peri hermeneias*] of "Demetrius" and explains that Aristotle's work of the same name dealt with a different subject.[83] True, he does not add "of Phalerum" but Demetrius of Phalerum is by far the most natural reference in such a Peripatetic context. One feels that if he had not meant the friend and pupil of Theophrastus he would certainly have said so. Specific references to the author as Demetrius of Phalerum do occur in the eleventh century and later, but these are of little value except in so far as they support the tradition of the manuscripts.[84]

*Conclusion*

None of the arguments in favour of a date much later than the traditional one seem to me at all compelling. On the other hand, our author's familiarity with Aristotle and the way he uses him, his attitude to Demosthenes, his unusual familiarity with people living in the late fourth and early third centuries about whom he gives us a good deal of information not found elsewhere, his general critical outlook, his remarks on contemporary oratory and his silence about later controversies—all these things seem to point to a quite early date. The use of some technical terms in a Classical or near-Classical sense while often ignoring later meanings seems to point in the same direction. There are some references to Alexandrine personalities, on the other hand, which make a date before 270 unlikely. Certainty in such matters is of course impossible to attain, but I incline to the view that our treatise was written about 270 B.C., or not very much later.

As for the author, we have seen that, as far as critical ideas are concerned, there are several points of contact with Demetrius of Phalerum. It must also, I think, be admitted that Ammonius (*ca.* 500 A.D.) regarded him as the author. Far more important, it seems highly probable that Philodemus, in the first century B.C., also attributed our treatise to him. On the other hand, the un-Attic nature of the language does not seem to suit the Phalerean. Moreover, if we accept the evidence of Cicero and Diogenes Laertius quoted above[85]—and in the absence of any evidence to the contrary it seems that we must accept it—Demetrius of Phalerum most probably died shortly after the death of Ptolemy Soter in 283/2 B.C. He cannot then have been the author of our treatise.

This leaves us with a treatise **On Style** probably written in Alexandria not much later than 270 B.C. by an unknown author. This author must, obviously, have had strong Peripatetic connections, and to some extent have shared the critical ideas of Demetrius of Phalerum, whom he had probably known, and with whose writings, as with those of Aristotle and Theophrastus on rhetoric and style, he was no doubt familiar. If his name was also Demetrius—for it was a common enough name—this might help to account for confusion between the two even at an early date.

### Notes

[1] H. Diels, *Die Fragmente der Vorsokratiker*[6] (Berlin 1951), Xenophanes fragments 1 and 11, also 14, 15, 32, and 34. Heraclitus fragments 40 and 42.

[2] *Rhetoric* 3.9.1-2. For Gorgias' praise of Logos see Diels, 2. 290.

[3] *On Composition,* ch. 25. Diogenes Laertius (3.37) tells the same story and attributes it to Euphorion and Panaetius.

[4] *Laws* 2. 668b-c.

[5] At 236a. . . .

[6] *Phaedrus* 255-267. Plato selects a few technical terms for mention. . . . This casual selection of technical terms, some of which do not recur elsewhere, obviously from a far larger number, is a salutary reminder of how little we know of the rhetorical vocabulary of the fourth century. Some of these elaborate compounds are of the kind we often consider as "later" because we do not come across them again till Roman times.

[7] *Laws* 2.653-673. For full references and a discussion of Plato's views on poetry and rhetoric see my *Plato's Thought* (London 1935 and Boston 1958) 179-215.

[8] . . . See my *Aristotle on Poetry and Style* (New York 1958) xxi-xxii and xiv-xvii for *mousikê* in the last chapters of the *Politics.* For another view see S. H. Butcher, *Aristotle's Theory of Poetry and Fine Art* (republ. Dover Publications 1951) 198-214.

[9] For Thrasymachus' capacity to rouse the emotions see Plato, *Phaedrus* 267c and Aristotle, *Rhetoric* 3.1.7. Also *Rhet.* 3.8.4 for his use of paeonic rhythms. His short rhythmic clauses are mentioned by Cicero, who contrasts them with the rounded periods of Isocrates (*Orator* 39-40). Dionysius of Halicarnassus, in *Lysias* ch. 6, credits him and Lysias with a virtue of style. . . . This I believe to mean the capacity to express thoughts succinctly and compactly. . . . For a full discussion of these interpretations see my "Thrasymachus, Theophrastus and Dionysius of Halicarnassus" *AJP* 73 (1952) 251-267. See also G. A. Kennedy's "Theophrastus and Stylistic Distinctions" in *Harvard Studies in Classical Philology* 72 (1957). He agrees that "the stylistic distinctions of Dionysius of Halicarnassus (i.e., in the first seven sections of the *Demosthenes*) are made on the basis of diction" (p. 101).

[10] *Nicocles* 7. See also *Antidosis* 184, 207, 271-272, 344.

[11] Seneca Rhetor, *Controversiae* 1. Praef. 9; cp. Quintilian 1. Praef. 9. . . .

[13] Aristotle (*Rhet.* 3.13) would, as a philosopher, prefer to recognize only two necessary parts of a speech, the statement . . . and the proofs. . . . However, he compromises by accepting four: the introduction . . ., the statement or narrative . . ., the proofs, and the epilogue

or peroration. . . . He notes and discards as ridiculous further subdivisions such as (contrast), (recapitulation). From Theodorus of Byzantium, he quotes (supplementary narrative), (preliminary narrative), (refutation), (supplementary refutation), and, from Licymnius (improving one's case, lit. wafting along), (digressions, lit. wanderings) and (ramifications).

[14] In particular, scholars have attempted to trace back to Theophrastus the formula of three styles and that of four virtues . . . of style. See H. Rabe, *De Theophrasti libris* . . . (Bonn 1890); A. Mayer, *Theophrasti . . . Fragmenta* (Leipzig 1910); and J. Stroux, *De Theophrasti Virtutibus Dicendi* (Leipzig 1912). See also G. L. Hendrickson, "The Peripatetic Mean of Style and The Three Stylistic Characters," in *AFP* 25 (1904) 125-146, and my "Theophrastus as a Literary Critic," in *TAPA* 83 (1952) 172-183. The controversy is in any case somewhat academic, as most of the ideas involved, apart from the actual formulae, were doubtless discussed by Theophrastus, as they were by Aristotle.

[15] See A. Roemer, *Aristarchs Athetezen in der Homerkritik* (Leipzig 1912) and *Die Homerexegese Aristarchs* (Paderborn 1924); A. Severyns, *Le Cycle épique dans l'école d' Aristarque* (Liège 1928).

[16] *Rhet.* 3.16.4. For the Stoics see Karl Barwick, *Probleme der stoischen Sprachlehre und Rhetorik* (Berlin 1957).

[17] See H. Caplan's edition in the Loeb Library (1954), especially the introduction.

[18] The six parts of a speech are (1.3 (4)) *exordium, narratio, divisio, confirmatio, confutatio,* and *conclusio.*

[19] See Demetrius 41, below.

[20] The three styles of word-arrangement are described by Dionysius in his *Camposition,* chs. 22-24.

[21] *Isocrates* 4-7 (543).

[22] See J. W. H. Atkins, *Literary Criticism in Antiquity* (London 1952) 2. 106-108 for references.

[23] *Letter to Pompey,* ch. 3. For a full account of Dionysius' criticism of Thucydides see my "Dionysius of Halicarnassus on Thucydides," in *Phoenix* 4 (1950) 95-110.

[24] See S. F. Bonner, *Roman Declamation in the Late Republic and Early Empire* (Liverpool 1949) and H. Bornecque, *Les Déclamations et les déclamateurs d'après Senèque le Père* (Lille 1902).

[25] See my translation *Longinus on Great Writing* (New York 1957) and Rhys Roberts' *Longinus On The Subline* (Cambridge 1907).

[26] The two standard editions of our treatise were published almost simultaneously: L. Radermacher's *Demetrii Phalerei qui dicitur de elocutione libellus* (Leipzig 1901) and W. Rhys Roberts' *Demetrius on Style* (Cambridge 1902). Roberts' text and translation were reissued, with a brief introduction in the Loeb Library in 1927, reprinted in 1953.

Both editors agree in rejecting the manuscript tradition which attributes the treatise to Demetrius of Phalerum, and would date the work between Dionysius of Halicarnassus and Hermogenes, that is, in the first century A.D. or early in the second. This was the generally accepted view at the end of the last century; see in particular the monographs of R. Altschul, *De Demetrii rhetoris aetate* (Leipzig 1889), F. Beheim-Schwarzbach, *Libellus . . . qui Demetrii nomine inscriptus est* (Kiel 1890), and K. Dahl, whose *Demetrius . . .* (Zweibrücken 1894) contains the fullest study of the language of the treatise. Some, like Dahl, and Hugo Rabe in *De Theophrasti libris . . .* (Bonn 1890) 19, favoured the second century A.D. because they thought that the language was that of the period of strict Atticism, while others favoured the first century. The last defender of the Phalerean authorship was Hugo Liers in his *De aetate et scriptore libri qui fertur Demetrii Phalerei . . .* (Bratislava 1881), while some, notably C. Hammer in his *Demetrius . . .* (Landshut 1883), continued to favour an earlier date, about 100 B.C.

This last opinion has more recently been supported by F. Boll in *Hermes* 72 (1917) 25-33; more recently still, F. Kroll in his article on rhetoric in *RE,* Suppl. 7 (Stuttgart 1940) 1078-9, has argued for an earlier date, namely the end of the third century B.C. It is clear that the arguments, based on both language and content, which were thought to have settled the matter at the beginning of this century are not as definitive as they then appeared.

[27] Dionysius of Halicarnassus does indeed have three styles of composition in his *Composition,* and he classes authors in accordance with these; he also has three styles or types of diction, but the two formulae cannot be telescoped. Isocrates, for example, whose composition is flowery . . . uses the mean or mixed type of diction. See note 9 (above).

[28] See, for example, *Ad Herennium* 4.16 (ch. 11) and Cicero, *Orator* 69.

[29] Radermacher (p. xii) suggests that the poverty of the treatment of subject-matter is due to the fact that this heading was not dealt with in the books . . . which our author had before him, and in particular in that of Theophrastus. As we have no knowledge of these "sources" the suggestion cannot be disproved. The poorer treatment may also be due, however, to the fact that the category is not a very sound one, even though

it might be traced to Aristotle's dictum that different genres of imitation imitate different objects (*Poetics* ch. 3.5).

[30] For the weakness of this approach to metaphor, which is common to all Greek critics, see W. B. Stanford's stimulating little book, *Greek Metaphor* (Oxford 1936), especially pp. 6-9.

[31] *Rhet.* 3.2.14.

[32] *On the Sublime* ch. 3; Horace, *On the Art of Poetry* 25-31; also *Ad Herennium* 4.15 (ch. 10).

[33] The translation given here is different from that in the text because there are other figures involved in the Greek passage, which must also be rendered. Here, however, it seemed better to translate the *anaphora* only, as the other figures are not relevant.

[34] See on this point H. Koskennieni's "Studien zur Idee und Phraseologie des griechischen Briefes bis 400 n. Chr." in *Annales Academiae Scientiarum Fennicae,* B 102 (Helsinki 1956) 18-47. On the general subject of ancient letter-writing see J. Sykutris, "Epistolographie" in *RE* Suppl. 5 (1931) 185-220. Neither the references to Aristotle's letters nor to one of Thucydides in section 264 (which latter is not likely to have been genuine) should be used as evidence for a later date. The writing of letters in the person of famous men became a literary genre which is often said to have begun in the second century B.C., but for this date there is no evidence. Sykutris suggests that the practice began in the fourth century and points out that there may have been many motives for such writing, quite apart from any intention to deceive. One may add that this would be especially true at a time when the introduction of historical and nearly contemporary personages into dialogues was a well-accepted literary convention. See also, on this point, Ernst Howald's *Die Briefe Platons* (Zürich 1923) 14-15; J. Harward, *The Platonic Epistles* (Cambridge 1932) 65-78.

[35] Demetrius passes, we might say, from the use of the particular figure of innuendo for a particular purpose (forcefulness) to other uses of it which are not strictly relevant in a discussion of forcefulness, and then from the use of a particular form or figure of speech to different forms in which the same thought may be cast. . . . A modern writer would avoid the charge of irrelevance by using footnotes. . . .

[38] It is significant that Demetrius himself, perhaps unconsciously, uses the term "forceful" and "forcefulness," in describing the effect of such witticism at 130 and 131.

[40] See note on section 30 of the translation and Appendix I, A. . . .

[41] Demetrius seems to have misunderstood Aristotle. The reference is *Rhet.* 3.9.5. Aristotle has been criticizing a period he attributes to Sophocles as improperly divided (he seems to take the lines as equivalent to *kôla*): . . .

> (This country, Calydon, of Pelops' land,
> The opposite shore, fertile and happy plains.)

Aristotle's criticism is that if we stop at the end of the first line, the division is haphazard, and does not correspond to sense. He tells us that a complex period must not be divided in this manner. . . . Aristotle commits himself to periods of two [*kola*] only. On the other hand, if it refers to the sentence quoted in part, that is, "a colon is either part of *this* sentence" (which is grammatically preferable), we hardly have the general definition which we should expect. Modern editors seem to gloss over this difficulty (see Frese's Loeb translation p. 289, Cope and Sandys, 3. 97-98, Voilquin and Capelle's Budé edition, p. 343) and generally agree with Demetrius who boldly replaces [*tantes*] by [*phesi*]. It is not certain whether Archedemus interpreted the passage as Demetrius does. Even if he did, this does not prove that Demetrius did not have the *Rhetoric* before him. Modern editors certainly do.

[42] It may be worth noting that [*phesi*] does not introduce a direct quotation. As we have the controlling text of Aristotle, no harm is done. But we do not have the text of Theophrastus, for example, and this kind of semi-quotation only too often has been built on excessively.

[43] There is an excellent article by Alfred Kappelmacher in *Wiener Studien* 24 (1902) 452-456, on "Die Aristotelzitate im der Schrift der Pseudo-Demetrius" which shows how Demetrius reproduces the sense rather than the words of Aristotle. In 116 on frigidity, as Kappelmacher points out, the parallel with *Rhet.* 3.3 is so close that we can with certainty fill in the sense of the lacuna; and yet Demetrius gives the four causes of frigidity in a different order with only one example of each (Aristotle gives many) and one of his examples is not in Aristotle. Kappelmacher also deals with Demetrius 11 and 34 (see note 41) and the "misleading" quotation in 38 (see above pp. 36-37). Even from such an incomplete survey the conclusion is convincingly established.

[44] As is supposed by F. Solmsen in *Hermes* 66 (1931) 241-267. Solmsen tries to link the four "styles" of Demetrius with the four virtues of style attributed to Theophrastus, but this too is a conjectural reconstruction of modern scholars, and based on doubtful evidence. See *TAPA* 83 (1952) 179-181. Solmsen's article, however, contains a useful discussion of Demetrius' indebtedness to Aristotle. Solmsen is right when he says that the four styles of Demetrius are more like qualities than "styles."

We know of course that a number of works on style were written by Peripatetics, but the insistence on intermediate "sources" at all costs seems to assume that no Greek or Roman critic can ever have quoted directly from Aristotle, and that known parallels are always due to some unknown intermediate source. These persistent attempts to explain the known by the unknown seem to me in the present case quite unnecessary.

[45] *Rhet.* 3.12.2. And there are interesting verbal parallels. . . .

[46] It is interesting to note a close parallel to this use of the imperfect in the treatise *On the Sublime* 3.5, where the author discusses the vice of false enthusiasm "which Theodorus used to call parenthyrsos"— . . . and that scholars have *there* argued from the imperfect that "Longinus" must have heard Theodorus and was indeed a younger disciple. See for references my "Theodorus of Gadara" in *AJP* 80 (1959) 360.

[47] See *OCD*, *s.v.* Sotades and Ptolemy Philadelphus.

[48] Plutarch, *Demosthenes* 10. See below, p. 54-55.

[49] See H. Koskenniemi's "Studien zur Idee und Phraseologie des griechischen Briefes" in *Annales Academiae Scientiarum Fennicae*, B.102 (Helsinki 1956) 25. He points out that in view of the early collections of the letters of other philosophers, that is, Plato and Epicurus, it is very unlikely that the letters of Aristotle remained unpublished until the second century, and suggests that the Artemon mentioned by Demetrius may well have been a contemporary of Theophrastus.

[50] By Norden, *Kunstprosa* 1.148 note 1 (quoted by Roberts). We may remember in this connection that Quintilian tells us that "fictitious themes in imitation of lawsuits and of deliberative speeches" began in the time of Demetrius of Phalerum, even if these were not as artificial as the Roman type of declamation which he seems to regard as of more recent origin (cp. Quint. 2.4.41 and 2.10.1).

[51] At *Rhet.* 3.11.15-16. The specific passages said to bear clear traces of the later rhetorical schools (Roberts, p. 251 and Radermacher, pp. 91 and 112) are: the rock of the Cyclops at 115, the Amazon's girdle at 138, the Centaur and the pun on Olympias at 187, the reproach to Aristides at 238, and the obscure phrase . . . at 239. Radermacher also considers the advice on how to address despots at 292-293 to smack of later declamations, though one would have thought it quite as topical in the third century B.C. Alexander was certainly a frequent topic for *suasoriae* and the rock of the Cyclops (but not this phrase) is found in Seneca, *Suas.* 1.12. These were perennial subjects.

[52] *Adipata dictio, Orator* 25.

[53] *Nic. Ethics* 1128a 22. . . .

[54] *Cratylus* 398d. We may also remember Aristophanes' phrase "the Attic look" in *Clouds* 1176. . . . The verb is found in the comic writers of the fifth and fourth centuries.

[55] Lucian, *Demonax* 41: "Seeing one of the grandees taking pride in the width of his purple . . .

[56] We may add one more reference. At 158 Demetrius refers to a legend that "cats grow fatter and thinner as the moon waxes and wanes," and quotes a further elaboration by an unknown writer. Now Plutarch (*Isis and Osiris* 63, 376f) gives a different version, namely that a cat's *pupils* grow larger at the full moon. As it seems established that this and other Egyptian tales were first told in the West by Apion in the first century A.D. and that this is Plutarch's source, Demetrius, Radermacher asserts, must have got it indirectly from the same source and got it wrong. But no one suggests that Apion invented the legend, and if our author was writing in Alexandria, or indeed had been in Egypt at all, he might have heard it from anyone, correctly or incorrectly, and so could anyone else. Such arguments surely have little force. I understand from my colleague Professor R. J. Williams that the story is not found in native Egyptian sources.

[57] See Appendix II.

[58] As given by Rhys Roberts p. 57.

[59] Examples will be found in Appendix I. . . .

[60] See Appendix I. . . . Rhys Roberts (p. 229) himself says there are comparatively few such double compounds in our treatise. . . .

[61] See notes 6 and 13 above.

[62] See Appendix I, A, where 20 are listed, but some might be added, from other sections, which contain at least semi-technical words.

[63] See Appendix I. . . .

[64] On the style of Demetrius of Phalerum see Cicero *De Oratore* 2.95, *Orator* 92, *Brutus* 37, and Quintilian 10.1.33 and 80.

[65] Roberts p. 59; this view seems to be generally accepted.

[66] As is indeed pointed out by Altschul (p. 31, note 21) but he rather surprisingly takes this as evidence of a later date. It should be noted that Solmsen links the four styles with the four virtues which he traces back to Theophrastus (note 44 above). We first meet the

formula of the three styles in the *Ad Herennium* 4.8-11. It is there clearly stated (ch. 11, 16) that every orator must use all styles. So in Cicero (e.g. *Orator* 20-21, 75-99) who links the three styles with the three *officia oratoris* (*ibid. 69: subtitle in probando, modicum in delectando, vehemens in flectendo*).

Dionysius has three kinds . . . of diction and three kinds of word-arrangement, but these do not correspond (see *AJP* 73 [1952] 261-267). We do, however, have a passage of Aulus Gellius (6.14) which not only speaks of the three styles and their corresponding vices, but further states that Varro said that Pacuvius was an example of *ubertas*, Lucilius of *gracilitas*, and Terence of *mediocritas*, that is, of the grand, the plain, and the intermediate respectively. As Gellius, however, calls them *virtues* as well as *genera dicendi*, this need not imply any classification according to "styles" in Varro; he may have given these authors as examples of particular qualities only.

The earliest Greek classification by three styles seems to be a doubtful passage in Tryphon. . . . He gives Thucydides and Antiphon as examples of the first, Demosthenes, Hyperides, Demarchus, and Lycurgus as examples of the intermediate, and Aeschines, Isocrates, Lysias, Andocides, and Isaeus as examples of the simple style. The passage is quite irrelevant where it stands, the classification contrary to that of critics like Dionysius; Spengel brackets it.

67 Roberts, p. 59. See also note 26 above.

68 See my "Theodorus of Gadara" in *AJP* 80 (1959) 337-365. . . . In any case the main preoccupations of "Longinus" are quite different from those of Demetrius.

69 See sections 77, 158, 172. We may add 97, for Boll (*Rhein. Mus.* 72 [1917] 27-28) gives good reason to think that the word [*skafites*] is of Egyptian origin.

70 See Fritz Wehrli, *Demetrius von Phalerum, Die Schule des Aristoteles* 4 (Basle 1949).

71 Diogenes Laertius 5.80-81 = Wehrli 74.

72 The meaning of [*kairos*] and [*kairios*] in criticism comes very close to that of [*prepon*], that is, appropriateness to the occasion. Dionysius complains in *Composition* 12 that no rhetorician or philosopher has written a treatise on the subject since Gorgias first dealt with it. For an interesting, if somewhat fanciful, discussion of [*kairos*] in Gorgias see W. Vollgraff, *L'Oraison funèbre de Gorgias* (Leiden 1952) 21-27.

73 As R. D. Hicks translates these titles in his Loeb version of Diogenes.

74 Plutarch, *Reg. et Imp. Apopth.* 189d, Stobaeus 4.7.27 = Wehrli 63.

75 *Rhetorica* IV, Col. XIᵃ. . . . There can be little doubt that Philodemus is referring to Demetrius of Phalerum, as Wehrli and others have taken him to be.

76 So Hubbell, "The Rhetorica of Philodemus," *Trans. Connecticut Acad. Arts and Sciences* 23 (1920) 304, note. "Obtaining favor with all" is Hubbell's translation. . . .

78 *Rhetorica* IV. Col. XVIᵃ. . . .

79 The point seems to have escaped Roberts who says (p. 60): "it is to be noticed that Philodemus speaks vaguely of 'Demetrius' without any addition, and so may, or may not, have Demetrius Phalereus in mind." Hammer (p. 60) admits the reference is to our treatise which was therefore known to Philodemus, but he does not make the connection with Phalereus. A look at Sudhaus' text makes clear that there is no possible doubt that the two passages go together.

80 Besides the passage just referred to from Philodemus, see also Plutarch, *Demosthenes* 9 and 11 and other references in Wehrli 162-169.

81 See Appendix I, A. . . .

82 It is true that "Longinus," *On the Sublime* (33-35), recognises that Demosthenes lacks many virtues which Hyperides possesses, but this is meant to show that those he does possess are by far more important, in a passage which insists that faulty genius is to be preferred to flawless mediocrity.

83 *In Arist. de Interpretatione,* Berlin edition, 4. 4-5, 966-997a. See Appendix I, A. . . .

84 Quoted by Rhys Roberts, pp. 60-61.

85 P. 23.

## G. P. Goold (essay date 1961)

SOURCE: "A Greek Professorial Circle at Rome," *Transactions and Proceedings of the American Philological Association,* Vol. XCII, 1961, pp. 168-92.

*[In the following essay, Goold explores what can be determined about the author of* On Style *and its date of composition, arguing against some of G. M. A. Grube's positions (see previous excerpt).]*

To establish beyond a shadow of doubt the date and authorship of the tractates *On the Sublime* and *On Style* is a task which has long defied—and in all probability will continue to defy—the best endeavors of scholarship. But the seeker after truth is a detective, not a magistrate; and like a detective, he will often feel satisfied that he has solved a case, though fully aware that the evidence is highly circumstantial and will not convince all of the jury. Of such a nature is the present inquiry. Nevertheless, the matter has been recently brought into court and argued at length by two eminent advocates;[1] and rightly so, since keeping an open mind is a poor excuse for remaining in the dark. Yet in the dark I fear they will have us stay, for neither has mentioned the solution which falls least short of certainty and throws most light on what was before obscure. The following plea is therefore tendered on behalf of a Greek professorial circle at Rome—*indocti discant, et ament meminisse periti*—before the tribunal of the learned retires to consider its verdict. . . .

## II. Demetrius *On Style*

Now that G. M. A. Grube[21] has assigned the tractate *On Style* to the early reign of Ptolemy Philadelphus, the orthodox opinion which puts it three hundred years later is confronted with a challenge long overdue; and in an introduction replete with learning Grube has no difficulty in exposing much argument to which scholars had clung in their unhappy incertitude as inconclusive, for example, that "broad purples" in 108 refers to the senatorial laticlave, or as most improbable, for example, that the corrupt name in 237 (of a writer alluding to the battle of Salamis . . .) is that of the rhetorician Theodorus of Gadara. Yet the fresh interest which Grube's vigorous study will stimulate is likely to reveal the paradox that his carefully argued conclusions are less securely based than the perfunctory ones which he opposes. His position is fundamentally a cautious one, characterized by a disinclination to abandon the authorship and hence the date dubiously indicated by the chief manuscript; and his ascription of the work to about 270 B.C. is not so much a safe arrival in port as a reluctance to navigate in the darkness. But, alas, the quest for truth is always dangerous, and caution can prove as fatal as daring. *Ond' io per lo tuo me' penso e discerno / Che tu mi segui, e io sarò tua guida.*

To begin with the external evidence: the Codex Parisinus 1741, the archetype of the other manuscripts, exhibits the title [*Demetriou Phalereos peri hermeneias ho esti*] and the colophon [*Demetriou peri hermeneias*] The latter preserves all that is genuine. The last four words of the title, which have all the marks of a gloss, appear to have been added by way of explanation, and to indicate that [*Phalereos*],which word constitutes the *whole* of the evidence for the Phalerean's authorship, is a fellow impostor, possibly transferred by some sciolist from 289. This section, in which Demetrius of Phalerum is quoted by name, all but proves that our Demetrius is not the Phalerean, for, whilst many writers ancient and modern have referred to themselves in the third person, such a practice in a teacher of style is sham modesty and would never be limited to a single

instance. Moreover, Demetrius of Phalerum, an Attic orator of distinction and good enough for comparison with the best, certainly wrote in Attic. Demetrius the Stylist, if I may so call him, certainly does not. Finally, no treatise entitled [*Peri hermeneias*] is attributed to him by Diogenes Laertius in the latter's register of his works (5.5.9). The case against his authorship is conclusive.

We possess no reference to Demetrius the Stylist before the Christian era. The alleged citation in Philodemus is a mirage which vanishes at our approach. Philodemus[22] declares that "long periods are awkward to deliver, a criticism Demetrius brings against those of Isocrates." Look for such a criticism in the tractate *On Style*, and you will look in vain. It is not there. Our Demetrius mentions Isocrates three times, once (12) to cite him with Gorgias and Alcidamas as an example of periodic writing, and twice (68, 299) to comment on his avoidance of hiatus. One cannot infer from our Demetrius that he disapproved of the length of Isocrates' periods, or even regarded them as "long" at all. When our Demetrius in 303 briefly warns against "periods which are continuous and long, and make a speaker run out of breath," he does not bring this as a criticism against anybody; no orator is mentioned by name or implication. Only by joining together what our Demetrius has put asunder and imputing to him something which he does not expressly say has Grube[23] been able to refer Philodemus' statement to him and so claim that he ante-dates the latter, who flourished between 70 and 40 B.C. There is a simple explanation: Philodemus is not citing our Demetrius at all, but Demetrius of Phalerum, whom he has mentioned elsewhere and to whose [*Peri hretorikes*] he twice[24] makes explicit reference.

The one sure piece of external evidence is furnished by the fifth-century Syrianus in his prolegomena to Hermogenes' *De ideis*,[25] where he proffers the following opinion: "The critics who ventured to enumerate and define the various styles embarked on a futile task. For Dionysius there are three: the plain, the middle, the grand. Hipparchus adds the graphic and the florid, whilst Demetrius rejects the graphic and is satisfied with four." That Dionysius of Halicarnassus and Demetrius the Stylist are designated here is not open to doubt. Dionysius opens his appreciation of Demosthenes[26] with a survey of precisely the three styles mentioned by Syrianus, and later tells us that whereas other eminent Greek writers are to be regarded as representative of one or another, Demosthenes achieves excellence in all three. And Demetrius' work is distinguished from all others by precisely such a fourfold division of styles as Syrianus attributes to him, three roughly corresponding to those of Dionysius, together with a fourth, largely designed to put the overpraised Demosthenes in his place. Do I hear someone object that Syrianus implies that Demetrius' fourth style is *anthêros* and not *deinos*?

And that Demetrius' "style" has a different significance from Dionysius'? He takes the words from my mouth. But Syrianus' explicit assertion that Demetrius preaches a classification of four styles, from which the graphic is excluded, is unchallengeable. As for implications, he did not intend any; an unbeliever scoffing at articles of doctrine does not pick his words with a view to elucidating the catechism. Syrianus, however, has not been called to the witness-box as a technical expert; he is subpoenaed solely as a lay witness to a point of time. His testimony, associating Demetrius with the Graeco-Roman period of literary theory, enables us to assign the tractate **On Style** to an age contemporary with or not far removed from that of Dionysius of Halicarnassus, who flourished at Rome in the first thirty years of the principate; since he mentions before and not after Demetrius the unknown Hipparchus whose system embraced five styles, it rather looks as if Syrianus has named the three critics in chronological order, as if, that is to say, Demetrius' work is later than Dionysius'.

No safe argument can be built on the dates of the authors quoted or mentioned by Demetrius. They cover a period from Homer to Sotades (early third-century B.C.) and permit the opinion, to which my other arguments compel me, that Demetrius regards them as "classical" authors. We encounter a similar range of authors, a similar recognition of a "classical" period, and a similar silence about the contemporary scene in other rhetorical works, in Dionysius' *De compositione verborum*, for example, which is of the Augustan period. Grube maintains that references to writers of the later fourth and early third centuries are "unusually frequent."[27] They have not seemed so to any other scholar. None of these writers, with the exception of Menander, is mentioned more than once, and Menander is only mentioned twice; Sappho is referred to more times than all put together. I do not count Theophrastus and his disciple Praxiphanes, whom Demetrius cites as technical authorities. Nor do I count Archedemus and Artemon, two more technical authorities cited in 34 and 223 respectively. Apart from these two, all writers named by Demetrius have been identified with persons otherwise known, and this circumstance has led to the plausible conjectures that here are mentioned Archedemus of Tarsus and Artemon of Cassandria, who are generally assigned to the second half of the second century B.C. Two proverbial sayings quoted by Demetrius in 172 are also quoted by Seneca and Diogenes Laertius, who name Chrysippus (second half of the third century B.C.) as their source; hence the plausible conjecture that Chrysippus has been used by Demetrius also as a source.[28] If any one of these three conjectures is true, Grube's date would be refuted at a blow. We should not assume that, because confirmation of these conjectures is precluded by our lack of knowledge, they are false and the possibility of them being true may be safely disregarded.

I digress to consider a special passage. In 193 Demetrius remarks that a disjointed style is appropriate to the stage, and "for this reason Menander, whose style is for the most part broken, is acted, whereas Philemon is read." This statement is most readily referred to a period subsequent to the careers of those writers; when Demetrius wrote, Philemon's plays were no longer acted; and Philemon did not die till 262 B.C. But the passage is chiefly interesting for the singularity of the comparison. It was Philemon and not Menander who was preferred by contemporary theatre-goers; and it is no rash inference from Plautine *Quellenforschung* to assert that Philemon held his own on the stage for at least the rest of the century. Only with the activity of Terence is it clear that Menander has been awarded posterity's accolade. Even then Philemon was not pushed off the boards at once. Performances of his pieces took place as late as the second century of our era, when a statue commemorating him was erected at Athens. How then could Demetrius take for granted a ready acceptance of his statement? Only, I think, if he was writing long after the age of Plautus, yet at a time when Philemon was still quoted, that is, was still frequently read. The turn of the millennium is the time which would best accord with our professor's remarks; and it should be noted that Rome is a likely place, where the plays of Menander were often performed.[29]

The evidence of language and style has been fully set forth by Roberts and Grube in their editions,[30] and there is no need for another tabulation. Grube, who is obliged to prove that Demetrius is not writing a prose which became current only three centuries after his death, has attempted a thorough rebuttal of all the evidence adduced by Roberts in support of a late date. Yet, even if we accept as proved the contention that Demetrius' prose *could* have been written in 270 B.C., it is highly improbable that it was then penned by a teacher of style. By Grube's account Demetrius was a younger contemporary of Theophrastus and Menander; his teachers had listened to Demosthenes and Aristotle; he himself aspired to become the Strunk of his age. Such a man was bound to employ an Attic pure to the point of pedantry. We do not expect in a manual on style the unproved fashions of up-to-date language; H. W. Fowler does not write like P. G. Wodehouse. We expect a syntax, diction, and discipline sanctioned as authoritative by the best usage of the preceding age, and unmarked by the novelties of the rising generation. In this regard the variegated *koinê* of Demetrius must be held to favor a date distinctly later than that maintained by Grube.

Nor should it escape notice that in his assessment of the lexicographical evidence Grube has frequent recourse to the argument of analogy. If a word in Demetrius is of a type or formation analogous to that of a word found in the classical period, there is no reason—Grube maintains—why Demetrius' word could not have been current in the classical period, even though it is not attested until much later. Accordingly, since *philophronoumai* is found in Herodotus, Xenophon, and Plato, Grube considers *philophronêsis* "natural enough"[31] for 270 B.C., even though it is not found "again" until Dionysius of Halicarnassus, Josephus, and Plutarch. Usage, however, is not determined by analogy, but by an infinite number of usually undiscoverable factors; caprice and not reason is the final arbiter. The words *dread*, *dreadful*, *dreadfully*; *peace*, *peaceful*, *peacefully* are attested in written English by 1300. So are the words *force* and *help*; yet *forcefully* is not attested until 1774, and *helpfully* not until 1832. *Strengthful* and *sleepful* occur before 1400; their adverbs have yet to make their début; and it is not through lack of written English that these words are not found from Chaucer to Hemingway. The lesson taught by these facts is that in order to date a literary work by its vocabulary we must proceed empirically, treating each word—no matter how closely related to or modeled upon another word it may be—as a separate entity. No exception can be taken to Grube's statement[32] that Demetrius's *cacophônia* ("ill-sounding-ness") is a perfectly natural formation from Aristotle's *cacophônos*. But the question is: when did this perfectly natural formation acquire an actual as opposed to a potential existence? For we must not assume that *cacophônos* was bound to give birth to a noun. *Strengthful* did not give birth to *strengthfully*, though it had a start of two hundred years on *forceful*. Again, *cacophônos* might just as naturally have produced *calophônos*, but the word is not recorded. Since our source-material is necessarily incomplete, and particularly so for the Hellenistic period, it is not possible to draw a reliable conclusion from a single word. But when we find that not one word, but a second, and then another, and then yet more, lack attestation before Graeco-Roman times, and when we find Grube resorting on each occasion to the argument of analogy to maintain his defence of an early date, then such a defence draws upon it greater and ever greater suspicion, until finally it is no defence but a self-indictment.

Aristotle (*Rhet.* 3.2.1404b) had taught that the ideal style (*lexis*) is a lucid mean, capable of embracing simplicity on the one hand and elevation on the other; and if Theophrastus preserved this teaching unchanged in his [*Peri lexeos*],[33] his words at any rate seem to have misled Dionysius[34] into thinking otherwise, and may have led ultimately to the tripartite classification of styles (Middle, flanked by Plain and Grand) first attested in the *Rhetorica ad Herennium*, ca. 85 B.C. At first sight the four styles of Demetrius have no relationship to this tripartite classification. The *charactêres* are not for Demetrius, as they are for Dionysius, separate personalities, of which a writer may possess only one; they are rather suits of clothes in his wardrobe, each available for wear on the appropriate occasion. Yet a close look shows that, whatever his conception of them, Demetrius'

styles are, in origin, of the same nature as the styles of Cicero and Dionysius. Grube[35] is rightly suspicious of Solmsen's[36] attempt to link them to the four Theophrastean virtues. To record that Demetrius' styles are *elevated*, *elegant*, *plain*, *forcible* and Theophrastus' virtues *correctness*, *lucidity*, *propriety*, *ornamentation* is refutation enough. Of Demetrius' styles the *plain* (*ischnos*) is the same as the *plain* (*litos*) of Dionysius; the *elegant* (*glaphyros*), though not identical with the *middle* (*mesos*) of Dionysius, is closely connected with the *middle* of Philodemus and Cicero;[37] the *elevated* (*megaloprepês*) is the same as the *elevated* or *grand* (*hypsêlos*) of Dionysius. When Cicero[38] represents the *plain* and the *grand* as two extremes, and Demetrius ( 36) says that the *plain* and the *elevated* stand in irreconcilable opposition and contrast, we are justified in concluding that Demetrius had after all points of contact with the orthodox Graeco-Roman school, and that Syrianus[39] knew what he was talking about. I have already indicated why Demetrius added a fourth style, the *forcible* (*deinos*). I think he objected, as Longinus objected, to the perpetual hosannas which were everywhere raised at the name of Demosthenes. Merely to show that the orator variously employed the three available styles would be to add color to the Dionysian dogma that the greatness of Demosthenes transcended the limitations of other Greek stylists. By associating Demosthenes with a fourth style, indeed by practically demoting him to it, our author fashioned an effective weapon against the teaching of the Dionysians. The perspicacious will notice that increasing the number of styles from three to four necessitates changing the name of the old *middle* style, for the second of four is obviously not *mesos*. It is possible that it was Hipparchus and not Demetrius who was responsible for the innovation. There are, however, obstacles in the way of placing Demetrius either before or after Dionysius. Had Demetrius' four-fold classification been propounded before the time of Dionysius, it is strange that the latter should nowhere have thought fit to criticize it. *On Style* cannot be ante-Dionysian. But it cannot be later either.   179, wherein Demetrius states that no earlier critic had treated of "elegant word-order," strongly suggests that *On Style* was written before Dionysius' *De compositione verborum*. It seems best to regard the two men as contemporaries. In any case unprofitable wrangling over the stylistic classification of authors soon discredited this section of rhetorical teaching; in Dionysius' own lifetime Longinus abandoned it, and in the succeeding age we look in vain for further disputation. Henceforth Greek and Roman literary theorists turn to the practical field of oratory. Technical considerations prescribe for Demetrius's *On Style* a late Augustan date.

It is important to bear in mind that Demetrius "must have had strong Peripatetic connections," and that his attitude towards Aristotle "might be described as respect falling short of veneration." But when Grube, whose words these are,[40] suggests that the relationship between Demetrius and Aristotle is that of two critics not far removed in time,[41] some remonstration is called for. The relationship is, on the contrary, similar to that which might exist between a modern Roman Catholic theologian and Thomas Aquinas. On fundamental matters a chronological proximity might appear to be indicated, but differences of emphasis in the application of doctrine and a greater precision in technical minutiae, not to mention general linguistic discrepancies, would reveal the lapse of the centuries between them. So it is with Aristotle and Demetrius. . . . Demetrius seemingly disputes an appraisal of Demosthenes not formulated till the time of Cicero and Dionysius, and this in a chapter which "has practically nothing that recalls Aristotle."[43] "That our author's relation to Aristotle is unique in extant critical texts"[44] is but another way of saying that the text of Demetrius the Stylist is the only literary treatise we possess written by a confirmed Peripatetic.

Now, if we search the Augustan age for a literary professor who had strong Peripatetic connections, who thoroughly knew his Aristotle, and who opposed the Dionysian idolatry of Demosthenes and taught that attention to Aristotelian precepts was more important than Demosthenic *mimêsis*, we shall sooner or later alight on a letter of Dionysius in which such a literary professor is mentioned, though unfortunately not named. He answers so closely to the description of the missing man as to warrant the conjecture that he is Demetrius himself, the author of **On Style**. I quote the passage in full in Roberts's translation.[45]

> You said that a certain Peripatetic philosopher, in his desire to do all homage to Aristotle the founder of his school, undertook to demonstrate that it was from him that Demosthenes learnt the rules of rhetoric which he applied in his own speeches, and that it was through conformity to the Aristotelian precepts that he became the foremost of all orators. Now my first impression was that this bold disputant was a person of no consequence, and I advised you not to pay heed to every chance paradox. But when on hearing his name I found him to be a man whom I respect on account of his high personal qualities and his literary merits, I did not know what to think.

Notice that the words "on account of his high personal qualities" . . . permit the possibility of personal acquaintance, and this is placed beyond doubt by the concluding words of the paragraph: "I wished therefore . . . to induce the person who has adopted this view, and is prepared to put it in writing, to change it before giving his treatise to the world." So the Peripatetic teacher of rhetoric is accessible to Dionysius' demurs, and has actually announced a forthcoming treatise!

At last I see land. But perhaps there are some who are unconvinced that we are making for shore? They dispute the identification and will not assent until they find Demetrius' actual name in Dionysius' text. Let them turn to Dion. Hal., *Ep. ad Pompeium* 3, Roberts 104, lines 8-11: "You wished also to learn my view with regard to Herodotus and Xenophon, and you wished me to write about them. This I have done in the essays I have addressed to Demetrius[46] on the subject of imitation." This Demetrius was a teacher of Greek literary criticism like Dionysius himself. That much is guaranteed by the context. Dionysius addressed his works either to Roman patrons (doubtless students and friends as well) like Quintus Aelius Tubero and Melitius Rufus or to professional associates like Gnaeus Pompeius Geminus, the author of *The Sublime*. With a name like Demetrius, the addressee of a treatise must have belonged to the second category. Observe that elsewhere[47] in this letter to Pompeius (or Longinus, as the world will continue to call him) Dionysius names Demetrius of Phalerum in full as [*Demetrios ho Phalereus*], whilst the professional associate is referred to quite simply as Demetrius. It follows that Longinus knew Demetrius, at least by name, and they may have enjoyed closer acquaintanceship.

Grube further urges as supporting his position: "There is no trace [in the tractate **On Style**] of the rhetorical *mimêsis* or emulation so important to Cicero, Dionysius, and Quintilian."[48] This I should explain by asserting that Demetrius is a staunch Peripatetic whose relationship with Cicero, Dionysius, and what I may call the orthodox Roman school may be likened to that of a Roman Catholic theologian with Protestant ones. There is no reason why contemporary literary critics at Rome should have differed any less than Christian thinkers do. And no less than these did the former find themselves at variance with each other. Longinus, we saw, had ventured to disagree with Dionysius on the matter of Plato's style; and an elaborate reply duly reached him. . . . It would hardly be surprising if Dionysius found fault with the absence of *mimêsis* from Demetrius' teaching, and labored to persuade his fellow-professor to include it in his syllabus. Nor, *scio quod dico*, if he herein labored in vain.

Further external evidence about the author of **On Style** does not seem to exist. Many Demetriuses find place in the vast mass of material which antiquity has bequeathed to us. One would like to know more of that Demetrius unflatteringly immortalized in the tenth satire of Horace's first book; and of the Peripatetic Demetrius (Plut. *Cat. Min.* 65, 67 ff.) who attended the Younger Cato in the extremity of his fortunes. Some, discerning in our Demetrius an "apparent familiarity with Egypt,"[49] have suspected that Alexandria rather than Rome was the place of composition; and others besides Muretus have deemed this suspicion confirmed by Diogenes Laertius, who, in his list of twenty celebrated Demetriuses, records (5.5.11) that "the eighth is the professor who resided at Alexandria, the author of rhetorical treatises." This cannot, however, be our man: whether or not Diogenes took over his biographical material from Demetrius of Magnesia (*fl.* 50 B.C.), his list seems to adhere to a general chronological sequence, and this necessitates placing Diogenes' Demetrius who lived at Alexandria and compiled rhetorical treatises in the second century B.C.

It is not possible to determine with precision the date at which our Demetrius issued his tractate. We are restricted to a rough estimate based on the activity of Dionysius, the only dates of whose life known to us are 30 B.C., when he came to Rome, and 8 B.C., when he wrote the preface to his *Antiquitates Romanae.* We have no notion how old he was on either occasion, nor when the literary treatises were written. As Longinus had corresponded with Dionysius, and *The Sublime* has been fixed at A.D. 12, the probability is that some at least of Dionysius' critical work was written later than 8 B.C. I therefore suggest that, since the contents of Demetrius' tractate are not discussed anywhere in Dionysius, but a work by Demetrius is heralded in the *First Letter to Ammaeus,* the year A.D. 1 as the approximate date of **On Style** cannot be far out.

### III. Greek Professors in Rome

> Possibly, if our information were not so scanty, we might find that men like Caecilius and the other friends of Dionysius, like Theodorus of Gadara, like the author of the [*Peri hypsous*], like the author of the [*Peri hermeneias*], and even like Manilius . . ., had this in common that they belonged to the age of Augustus . . ., and further resembled each other (in some instances) in being freedmen or sons of freedmen attached to the great Roman houses such as that of Pompey, and in having an Eastern or Jewish origin.[50]

It is a pity that Rhys Roberts, to whom every student of Greek literary theory is deeply indebted, should in his search for the authors of our two tractates have later indulged in improbable hypotheses when he might without absurdity have amplified his statement above. This amplification I have now endeavored to supply, claiming that it merits priority over all other theories, for even the protestation that the author of *The Sublime* is unknown is essentially a conjecture—no less audacious than mine—that the name of the author occurs nowhere in ancient records.

The association of Dionysius, Longinus, and Demetrius enables us to appraise more accurately the aims and methods of higher education and more particularly the position of the Greek language in early imperial Rome. Their circle was not a literary, but a professorial one; they had no connection with and showed no awareness of. Roman poets and Roman literature. Manilius is Romaic rather than Roman. The sole reference to Cicero (*De subl.* 12.4-5) makes of

the greatest wielder of the Latin language only an illustrative footnote. The Dionysians were not mere *grammatici.* Their courses were not "Greek without tears" or even Greek courses at all; their works presume in those they taught—and these must have been Romans—a complete mastery of Greek and a wide acquaintance with the Greek classics. They were Professors of Literature, which meant Greek literature, since they had not the faintest idea that Latin—and not Greek—was to become the common tongue of Western Europe and was already pregnant with the speech of modern civilization; they were Professors of Classics, like ourselves, with their attention focused on the genius of an age long since passed; and their writings contain no direct reference to the times in which they lived. To judge from their apparent ease of movement and communication, they enjoyed the privileged life of university men, for Dionysius could send junior colleagues with offprints of his work, as it were, to Longinus and Demetrius, whilst Longinus had heard Theodorus of Gadara in Rhodes[51] and had secured a copy of Caecilius' dissertation as soon as it came on the market.

Their methods of teaching literary style suffer from the misconception, exposed as such by the very language they wrote, but still prevalent two thousand years later,[52] that classical Attic was the absolute standard for Greek; imitation of Demosthenes was in the age of Augustus a counsel, not of perfection, but of impossibility. Our Greek professors recognized of course that certain virtues of style are independent of a particular language, but this makes all the more significant their failure to consider Latin. It is very probable that Greek was much more widespread in ancient Italy than we commonly suppose; and that many in Augustan Rome, including our Greek professors, entertained hopes that Greece would take her captor captive in the matter of language.

True bilingualism in a nation (as opposed to bilingualism in marginal areas like Alsace-Lorraine) is a very rare phenomenon; man is by nature unilingual. In bilingual environments the struggle of one language against another, even within the personality of a single individual, rages unceasingly; equality may be attainable under favorable circumstances, but equilibrium never. The greater the communicative power of a language is felt to be, the less able are its speakers to feel and exploit the power of another (or, if you like, the less ready they are to learn another). Few speakers of English do not feel its communicative power to be absolute; hence the vast majority of English-speakers are unilingual; of the total number of bilingual persons to be found, for example, in Canada or South Africa or Wales, the vast majority speak as their mother tongue French or Afrikaans or Welsh. In the Augustan age Greek and not Latin probably enjoyed the greater communicative power.[53] It was the Romans who were eager to learn Greek from their slaves, not the slaves Latin from the Romans. Outside Italy Greek was still entrenched at Massilia and Syracuse, whilst beyond the Adriatic—with the curious exception of Dacia—Latin hardly secured any foothold, not even later when, surrounded by grandees of church and state, Roman emperors held court in the cities of the Eastern Empire. In Italy and in Rome itself, the Greek-speaking population, though servile, fell not far short of the Roman; most books—and most of the classics—were Greek, and yet we never hear of "Loebs" or literal translations; Strabo was writing his *Geography* in Greek, and Diodorus Siculus his *Historical Library*; commerce with abroad was conducted, medicine practised, and the sciences investigated in Greek. Small wonder that Romans generally exhibit an extraordinarily fluent knowledge of Greek; it was no school-Greek, to be compared with the school-French of English-speakers, in which eminent Romans from Gracchan to imperial times addressed Greek audiences, wrote letters—tragedies, even—or in their leisure moments conversed at dinner-parties.[54]

Such is the conception of Greek entertained by Dionysius, Longinus, Demetrius, and, we may be sure, many an ancient professor besides. Greek was for them the chief language of the empire and the world, and they probably hoped that it would one day reign supreme in Rome itself. That their hopes were blighted by the march of history does not necessarily mean that their conception of Greek was unnatural or unjustified at the time. The practical fruit of their labors matured a century later in the widespread and lasting return of literary aspirants to an artificial Attic. Their real achievement, however, securely based on a tasteful appreciation and genuine love of all that was good and beautiful and effective in speech and writing, was their preservation of the living voice of Hellas. And Time's stern, searching judgment, from which there is neither dissent nor appeal, has upheld their teaching of the classics by preserving their voice, too.

### Notes

[1] Eduard Norden "Das Genesiszitat in der Schrift vom Erhabenen," *Abh. der berl. Ak., Kl. f. Sprachen,* etc., 1954 (Berlin 1959) Nr. 1. G. M. A. Grube, *A Greek Critic: Demetrius On Style* (Toronto 1961) 39-56. . . .

[21] *Op. cit.* (above, note 1).

[22] *Rhet.* 1.198.9 f., ed. Sudhaus.

[23] *Op. cit.* (above, note 1) 53, and 56, "highly probable."

[24] *Rhet.* 1.274.4; 1.346.1, ed. Sudhaus.

[25] *Rhet. Gr.* 7.93, ed. Walz. Writing about A.D. 500 the Aristotelian commentator Ammonius (*Comm. Arist.*

*Berl.* 4.996-97) also mentions Demetrius the Stylist, but furnishes no information bearing on his date.

[26] *De Dem.* . 1-7.

[27] *Op. cit.* (above, note 1) 41, bottom.

[28] Seneca, *De const. sap.* 17; Diogenes Laertius 7.1,2; quoted by W. Rhys Roberts, Demetrius *On Style* (Cambridge 1902), note on 150, 15, page 241.

[29] See, for example, *Anth. Pal.* 9.513; Quintilian, *IO* 11.3.91; and Cassius Dio 60.29 (Book 61, Boissevain, vol. 4, page 1), who quotes, as from the same poet, *Epitrep.* 157 and Kock, *FCG* 3, *Adesp.* 487, evidently overlooked by Koerte in the Teubner Menander, vol. 2.

[30] Roberts, *op. cit.* (above, note 28) 55-59; Grube, *op. cit.* (above, note 1) 46-50, 133-55.

[31] *Op. cit.* (above, note 1) 152.

[32] *Op. cit.* (above, note 1) 141.

[33] See G. L. Hendrickson, *AFP* 25 (1904) 125-46.

[34] Dionysius (*De Dem.* 3) implies that Theophrastus considered Thrasymachus a representative of the *middle* style. For the sake of clarity I do not discuss in this paper Dionysius' complete system of tripartite classification, which contains three styles of *diction* as well as three styles of *composition.*

[35] *Op. cit.* (above, note 1) 50, note 66.

[36] *Hermes* 66 (1931) 241-67.

[37] Of the *middle* style Cicero says (*Or.* 96): "Est enim quoddam etiam insigne et florens orationis genus pictum et expolitum in quo omnes verborum, omnes sententiarum illigantur lepores." This is identical with Demetrius' *glaphyros.* Similarly Quintilian (*IO* 12.10.58): "Tertium alii medium ex duobus, alii floridum (namque id *anthêron* appellant) addiderunt." The relevant sentence in Philodemus (*Rhet.* 1.165, IV 2-5, ed. Sudhaus) is unfortunately mutilated, but is restored by Radermacher . . ., rightly interpreted by Hubbell (*Trans. Connecticut Acad.* 23 [1920] 297-98) as "*plasma* refers to the distinction between grand and plain and middle or smooth style," since one cannot have a *middle* style of four styles. . . .

[38] *Brutus* 201, with Hendrickson's note in the Loeb edition (1939) 172 f.; *Orator* 20.196-97.

[39] See above, note 25.

[40] *Op. cit.* (above, note 1) 56 and 37.

[41] *Op. cit.* (above, note 1) 38, line 7. . . .

[43] Grube, *op. cit.* (above, note 1) 33.

[44] Grube, *op. cit.* (above, note 1) 37.

[45] Dion. Hal., *Ep. ad Ammaeum* 1.1, Roberts (above, note 9) 52 f.

[46] This Demetrius as the author of *On Style* was tentatively considered by W. Rhys Roberts, *CR* 14 (1900) 440b.

[47] Dion. Hal., *Ep. ad Pompeium* 2, Roberts (above, note 9) 98, line 23.

[48] *Op. cit.* (above, note 1) 51.

[49] Grube, *op. cit.* (above, note 1) 52. In identifying Demetrius as a member of a Roman professorial circle, I am not to be held as rejecting the possibility that his origin and even his literary training may have been Alexandrian.

[50] W. Rhys Roberts, *CR* 14 (1900) 440 f.

[51] *De Subl.* 3.5. If Longinus did not hear Theodorus (the natural interpretation in view of the chronology involved), he must have studied Theodorus' works during the latter's lifetime. I am thus not troubled by Grube's doubts, *op. cit.* (above, note 1) 41, note 46.

[52] See above, note 18.

[53] Bilingualism in ancient Rome is discussed in his *Stranger at the Gate*[2] (Oxford 1948) 309-26 by T. J. Haarhoff.

[54] It was surely in Greek that Pontius Pilate (though "eminent" is hardly *le mot juste* for him) cross-examined Jesus Christ; none of the gospels makes mention of interpreters at the trial.

## J. M. Rist (essay date 1964)

SOURCE: "Demetrius the Stylist and Artemon the Compiler," *The Phoenix*, Vol. XVIII, No. 1, Spring, 1964, pp. 2-8.

[*In the following essay, Rist attempts to determine the date of composition of* On Style *by investigating Artemon, an editor of Aristotle's* Letters *mentioned by Demetrius.*]

The appearance of G.M.A. Grube's book[1] on Demetrius the Stylist has revived interest in the date of his work. Grube dates it at about 270 B.C. whereas G. P. Goold holds[2] that it was written in the Augustan Age. Such a discrepancy is disturbing; two hundred and fifty to three hundred years is a wide margin of error. This note therefore is intended to reduce the gap by an investigation of the Artemon who is described by Demetrius (223) as the editor of Aristotle's *Letters*. It seems that some progress may be possible here, although the matter has been quickly passed over by both Grube[3] and Goold.[4] More in fact can be discovered about the date of Artemon than either of these scholars has indicated. To attain such knowledge, it is necessary to examine the traditional accounts of the contents of the Aristotelian corpus.

There are three basic lists surviving of the Aristotelian writings. The first is that of Diogenes Laertius (3.22-27); the second is by an unknown hand and is often associated with Hesychius;[5] the third, not preserved in Greek, derives from the list of a certain Ptolemy. Versions of this appear in the writings of two thirteenth-century Arabic scholars: al-Qifti and ibn abi Useibia.[6] Of the general nature of these catalogues little need be said here. The information is readily available in the works of Moraux and Düring.[7] Well-grounded opinion exists that the list of Ptolemy, which differs considerably from the others, is the direct representative of a list of the Aristotelian writings compiled by Andronicus of Rhodes in the first century B.C.[8] Andronicus, according to Porphyry,[9] arranged Aristotle's works according to subject-matter. The lists of Ps.-Hesychius and Diogenes Laertius, which are derived ultimately from a common source, differ greatly from that of Ptolemy. They are in places affected by the work of Andronicus, but their origin is very much older and is attributed by the vast majority of modern scholars to Hermippus, the pupil of Callimachus.[10] Moraux, who dissents from this view, proposes Ariston,[11] the head of the Lyceum after the death of Lycon in 226 B.C. His arguments however have been successfully countered by Düring,[12] and it can be safely assumed that Hermippus is the source of the lists as we have them. For our present purposes, however, it is not important whether Ariston or Hermippus is the source, provided that one of them is. The two men were more or less contemporary. The list must have been composed in the last quarter of the third century B.C.

Let us now consider certain entries on the lists that we have. Almost at the end of Diogenes' version (5.27), we find a group of Aristotle's letters listed as follows: letters to Philip about Selymbrians;[13] to Alexander, 4 books; to Antipater, 9 books; to Mentor, 1 book; to Ariston, 1 book; to Olympias, 1 book; to Hephaestion, 1 book; to Themistagoras, 1 book; to Philoxenus, 1 book; to Democritus, 1 book. We are not told how many books were written to Philip, but the total of the others is twenty books. Thus if we were to attempt to reconstruct the list of Hermippus from Diogenes only, we might suppose he knew of twenty books of letters and a number of extras.

Let us now turn to Ps.-Hesychius. His list contains a reference to letters in twenty books (p. 16 Rose). Thus if we compare Ps.-Hesychius and Diogenes, we find that they both know twenty books of letters, and that Diogenes has some knowledge of a further group, though he does not seem to know how many letters this group contained. What is the most likely deduction from this? Surely that the common source of Diogenes and Ps.-Hesychius knew the twenty-book collection and no more. Thus it was a twenty-book collection which was in circulation about 200 B.C.

We can now turn to our third list of Aristotle's writings—that preserved by Qifti and Useibia from the [pinakes] of Ptolemy and Andronicus. The version of the relevant part of the list that is given below is taken from the text of Qifti.[14] Relevant alternative readings of Useibia are added in square brackets, additions in pointed brackets.

> The books which were found in the library of a man called Apellikon. Namely the following books.
>
> A book in which a man named Artemon collected a number of letters by Aristotle in eight parts (*juz '*).
>
> [a large book, a compendium containing a number of letters in eight parts.]
>
> A book by him (Aristotle) on the ways of cities. . . . Two discourses (*maq la*).
>
> And other letters which Andronicus found in twenty parts.
>
> And writings in which there are memoranda such that men cannot discover their number.
>
> And the earlier parts ("names," Useibia) of them are to be found in the fifth discourse of the book of Andronicus in the index of the books of Aristotle.

Here we find two collections of the letters of Aristotle: one by Artemon in eight parts, the other "found" by Andronicus in twenty. Even the numbers are significant. The twenty-part collection "found" by Andronicus can hardly be other than the twenty books known to Ps.-Hesychius, Diogenes, and their source, Hermippus. What then about the eight-part collection of Artemon? These could be the same as the unnumbered group which appears in Diogenes, namely the letters to Philip. Some confirmation of this may be found in the Aristotelian commentator Elias.[15] Elias is describing those writings of Aristotle that deal with a specific concrete topic and are addressed [pros hena]. Such writings are called [merika] and letters are an example of them. By "letters" here we must assume that Elias means Artemon's collection, for he writes: "The letters which a certain Artemon, who lived after Aristotle, collected in eight

books, . . . were written [pros hena]." [Pros hena] in these two passages could mean either "to one single person" or "to individuals." Grube, in a letter to me, takes the latter interpretation. If the former is possible, however, we could guess, by comparing the passage of Diogenes, that the single person was Philip. We should recall in addition that, as in Qifti, the number eight is associated with Artemon's collection.

Elias' passage is closely paralleled and probably much influenced by the work of Olympiodorus on the same theme.[16] Olympiodorus brackets Andronicus and Artemon (in that order) together as compilers of Aristotle's letters. He too is analyzing Aristotle's work. He too marks off a class of writings as [merikon]. Such a class contains "everything written privately to certain individuals such as were the letters which Andronicus and Artemon compiled." There is an obvious difference between this text and that of Elias. Elias, speaking only of Artemon's collection, says that the letters were written [pros hena]; Olympiodorus, referring to the collections of both Artemon and Andronicus, says that they were written to *certain individuals.* . . . Is it not possible that knowing that Artemon's collection of letters were all written to one single individual, namely Philip, Elias gave up Olympiodorus' [pros tinas] and substituted [pros hena]? However it must be admitted that the identification of the eight-book collection with the letters to Philip is only a conjecture.

Since the source of the Arabic writers is ultimately Andronicus, we must assume that Andronicus knows of two collections: his own in twenty parts, and the eight-part volume of Artemon. Now Diogenes and Ps.-Hesychius are basically dependent on Hermippus, but Diogenes was aware not only of the twenty-book collection, but of other letters as well. We cannot tell where this further information comes from, but since it does not include the number of books, it can hardly come directly from Andronicus' [pinakes]. Now Ps.-Hesychius does not use any additional Andronican material, but rather sticks to the original list of Hermippus. We must repeat that it is the twenty books of Hesychius that Diogenes knows in more detail and that this fact suggests that the common source spoke of twenty books and twenty only.

So far then we can say that Artemon's collection of letters was not known to Hermippus (or for that matter to Ariston) in the late third century B.C. At that time the catalogue of Aristotelian works contained no mention of Artemon. May we not conclude that in 225 B.C. Artemon's collection had not been made?

It is now time to look at the Arab list derived from Ptolemy in more detail. As we have seen, a number of works are there listed as coming from the library of Apellikon. There is, fortunately, a good deal of evidence about the nature of this collection. It seems that on the death of Theophrastus (288 B.C.) his books, together with the writings of Aristotle himself, which had passed into his possession, were left to Neleus of Skepsis.[17] Neleus may have sold some of these books to Ptolemy Philadelphus,[18] but the rest were handed on to his descendants, who took little care of them and later hid them in a cave to prevent their falling into the hands of the bibliophile Attalids of Pergamum. In the late second century B.C. they were sold, in bad condition, to Apellikon of Teos, who had them copied and published, though still inadequately restored and full of errors. Apellikon's library was at Athens, and its owner was raised to high estate in that city by Aristion, the general of Mithradates VI of Pontus. On the capture of Athens by Sulla in 86 B.C., Apellikon's library was seized and taken to Rome. Here Tyrannio worked on it. Later Andronicus acquired copies of the books from Tyrannio, which he published along with the [*pinakes*] of Aristotle's writings which were circulating in the time of Plutarch.[19]

Now we know from Ptolemy through Qifti and Useibia that there is some connection between Artemon and Andronicus, and the library of Apellikon. The two collections of letters are given as among the contents of the library. Have we therefore any means of dating Artemon more precisely? We have already concluded that he is unknown ca. 225 B.C., the time of Hermippus. Can we bring him down later still? The entries in Qifti's list relevant to Artemon and Andronicus are, we recall: (*a*) a book in which a man called Artemon collected a number of letters by Aristotle in eight parts; and (*b*) and other letters which Andronicus found in twenty parts. At first sight we might suppose that the names of Artemon and Andronicus were to be found with their respective groups of letters in Apellikon's library when he first acquired it. We cannot say at the moment whether this was true of Artemon; we can be certain, however, that it was not true of Andronicus, for Andronicus (as we have observed above) had no connection with Apellikon's library until the middle of the first century B.C.,[20] that is, until long after Apellikon was dead and his books had passed into the hands of Tyrannio. Consequently since, despite what seems an obvious interpretation of Qifti, Apellikon's library could not have *originally* contained a volume of Aristotle's letters edited by Andronicus, it is not at all unreasonable to doubt whether it contained a book in eight parts edited by Artemon. A possible, and, as we shall see, likely explanation of the text of Qifti is that when Andronicus published the Aristotelian letters (as part of his new edition of the Aristotelian corpus) he associated the name of Artemon, which *he had found* attached to an eight-book collection of letters, with a part of the work. This would mean that people who knew of Artemon's collection of letters derived their knowledge from Andronicus' great edition of Aristotle and from the [*pinakes*] he compiled to go with it. Artemon would, on this reasoning, be a man who lived

sometime between the original acquiring of Neleus' library by Apellikon and its eventual publication by Andronicus.

There is a minor problem which should be cleared up before we proceed further. If the letters in twenty books of Diogenes and Ps.-Hesychius are the same as those in the edition of Andronicus, why do the texts of Qifti and Useibia say that Andronicus *found* these letters and imply that knowledge of them derives from him alone? It would seem rather that they were already available to Hermippus—a fact which Andronicus would have known. The explanation of this is probably quite simple and was suggested to me by Rose's attempt to restore the original Greek of Ptolemy. Rose's Greek version runs: [*epistolai allai ais enetukhen Anbronikos*]. The Arabic word which he renders [*enetuchen*] is *wajada*, he ordinary word for "find." If [*enetukhen*] therefore was the reading of Ptolemy, we should expect to find *wajada* as an Arabic equivalent if the original Syriac translator took [*enetukhen*] in its normal sense of "found."[21] Yet there is a less common but well-attested extended meaning for [*enetukhen*], which could easily have eluded the translator. This is simply "read."[22] By keeping this in mind, we can free ourselves of difficulties. Andronicus recorded on his [*pinax*] that he *read* a twenty-part collection of letters in Apellikon's library. These letters, however, were not those collected by Artemon, which Andronicus had already listed, but the group known to Diogenes, to Ps.-Hesychius, and to their source Hermippus. This twenty-part collection was then not only known by Hermippus but was familiar to one of the original owners of Apellikon's library, that is either to Neleus or to Theophrastus himself. Thus Koskenniemi's view[23] that there was a collection of Aristotelian letters current in the time of Theophrastus may well be correct. This collection, however, was not the compilation of Artemon, but the well known twenty-book collection of Diogenes, Ps.-Hesychius, and Andronicus.

Although it has already been demonstrated that Artemon, on the evidence of Ptolemy, *need* not be earlier than Apellikon (since Andronicus is certainly later) there still remains the possibility that he *might* have been earlier. Could Apellikon have procured for his library a volume of Aristotelian letters already labelled with Artemon's name? The answer to this question must be No. First, Artemon's collection is apparently unknown to Hermippus. This is of very considerable importance, since Hermippus made use of the library at Alexandria. (If the source of Diogenes is Ariston, the position is the same. Then it would be the head of Aristotle's own Lyceum who is unaware of Artemon's work.) Secondly, if there was a collection made by Artemon, when in fact could it have been compiled? It seems that before the publication of Apellikon's library this collection was unknown. Therefore if Artemon lived before Apellikon and later than Neleus, he must have worked with certain letters which were uncopied and eventually passed into Apellikon's hands.

We know the history of Apellikon's library. It was in the hands of the descendants of Neleus, who neglected the books. Such careless individuals could hardly have included a compiler of letters. Earlier owners were Neleus himself and Theophrastus. If either of these had known Artemon, their knowledge must have been quite common knowledge since they were both members of the Peripatetic school. And had the knowledge been public, we should hardly know about *these particular* letters *merely* through Apellikon's library. We are driven to suppose that Artemon himself lived long after Neleus and Theophrastus, and that his collection of letters is either a new find, unknown even to the earliest followers of Aristotle, or a later forgery. In any case it was added to the original collection some time between the acquiring of Theophrastus' books by Apel-likon and their publication by Andronicus. If the library of Neleus, say, contained both the eight- and the twenty-part collection, how could it come about both that these collections were separate in the library, and that one was widely known while the other was known to no one? Reason cries out that before the time of Apellikon no one knew anything about either Artemon or his collection.

We must therefore conclude that Artemon cannot be dated before the late second century B.C. at the earliest, and that Demetrius the Stylist, who refers to him, must certainly be later than ca. 100 B.C. and probably later than the publication of Andronicus' Aristotle at Rome in the years between 40 and 20 B.C.[24] We should observe that Demetrius not only refers to Artemon but also quotes letters other than those in Artemon's collection of letters to Philip. In section 225, for example, he refers to a letter to Antipater. Thus Demetrius probably knew both the eight- and the twenty-book collections. It is likely that he read them in that place where they were to be found side by side, namely the edition of Andronicus.

So far the discussion has been limited to Artemon, the compiler of Aristotle's letters. This is as far as we can go with certainty. Nevertheless it seems quite likely that the view which identifies our Artemon with Artemon of Cassandreia (probably late second century B.C.) is correct. Our Artemon clearly worked on the books from Apellikon's library. Such a man may well have been a bibliophile. Artemon of Cassandreia wrote two works which look like the products of a bibliophile.[25] . . .

### Notes

[1] G. M. A. Grube, *A Greek Critic: Demetrius on Style* (Toronto 1961).

[2] G. P. Goold, "A Greek Professorial Circle at Rome," *TAPA* 92 (1961) 168-192.

[3] Grube (note 1), who on p. 111 writes that nothing is known of the Artemon who edited Aristotle's letters, mentions on p. 42 the suggestion of H. Koskenniemi, "Studien zur Idee und Phraseologie des griechischen Briefes," *Annales Academiae Scientiarum Fennicae* B.102 (Helsinki 1956), that the Artemon mentioned by Demetrius may have been a contemporary of Theophrastus.

[4] Goold (note 2) 181.

[5] For bibliography on the authorship of this anonymous catalogue (which I shall refer to as "Pseudo-Hesychius") see P. Moraux, *Les Listes Anciennes des Ouvrages d' Aristote* (Louvain 1951) 195. The text is printed in V. Rose's *Aristotelis Fragmenta* (Leipzig 1886) 9-18 and (with discussion) in I. Düring's *Aristotle in the Biographical Tradition* (Göteborg 1957) 82-93.

[6] Rose has given us a "version" of the Greek of Ptolemy, compiled by an amalgamation of the evidence of the two Arabic sources (pp. 19-22). He is not very accurate. For the whole problem see Düring (note 5) 208-246 and Moraux (note 5) 288-309. On the Arabic evidence (or lack of evidence) about Ptolemy himself, see Düring 208. I am grateful to Professor G. M. Wickens of the Department of Islamic Studies of the University of Toronto for examining the texts of Qifti and Useibia.

[7] See note 5.

[8] Moraux (see note 5) 306-309. For the date of Andronicus' arrival in Rome (50-40 B.C.), see Düring (note 5) 421.

[9] *Vita Plotini* 24. Cf. Düring (note 5) 414-416.

[10] Cf. Moraux (note 5) 215.

[11] Moraux, *ibid.* 237-247.

[12] I. Düring, "Ariston or Hermippus?" *Classica et Mediaevalia* 17 (1956) 11-21.

[13] For the correctness of this emended text see Düring (note 5) 50 and (note 11) 16.

[14] Cf. Düring (note 5) 230. Professor Wickens has very kindly translated the passages of Qifti and Useibia.

[15] Elias, *In Cat.* 113. 25-26 Busse.

[16] Olympiodorus, *Prol. et in Cat.* 6.12 Busse.

[17] D. L. 5.52.

[18] The evidence for the fate of the books derives basically from Strabo 13, 608-609, whose account, with some variations and reductions, reappears in Plutarch,

*Sulla* 26 and Athenaeus 3AB, 214A-F. We should recall, as testimony to Strabo's accuracy, that he was himself a pupil of Tyrannio (12.548). This should be borne in mind when considering the justice or injustice of Moraux's suspicions about the story (note 5, 312-313). For what is probably the best account of the affair, see R. Shute, *On the History of the Process by which the Aristotelian Writings Arrived at their present Form* (Oxford 1888) 29-34.

[19] Plutarch, *Sulla* 26.

[20] For the dating of Andronicus' work on Aristotle (40-20 B.C.) see Düring (note 5) 421.

[21] That Ptolemy's writings, like many other Greek philosophical works, passed through a Syriac stage before reaching Arabic, is almost certain. Cf. Moraux (note 5) 291, Düring (note 5) 184-185.

[22] Cf. Plutarch, *Sulla* 26; Plato, *Lysis* 214 AB, *Symp.* 177B; Strabo 1.1 etc. . . .

[23] H. Koskenniemi (note 3).

[24] See Düring (note 5) 420-421.

[25] I would particularly like to thank Professor G. M. A. Grube for his detailed comments on the original draft of this paper. Our views of course differ widely but without his help this paper would be very much more unpolished than it is.

## G. M. A. Grube (essay date 1964)

SOURCE: "The Date of *Demetrius on Style*," *The Phoenix*, Vol. XVIII, No. 4, Winter, 1964, pp. 294-302.

[*In the following essay, Grube reasserts his position regarding the date of* On Style, *responding to opposing arguments made by Goold and Rist (see two previous excerpts).*]

Since the publication of my *A Greek Critic, Demetrius on Style*,[1] two of my Toronto colleagues have published articles challenging my dating of the treatise in 270 B.C. or not much later; both G. P. Goold's "A Greek Professorial Circle at Rome," *TAPA* 92 (1961) 168-192 and J. M. Rist's "Demetrius the Stylist and Artemon the Compiler" in *Phoenix* 18 (1964) 2-8, argue for a much later date.

I

Goold has a double aim: he seeks to reinforce the view that Demetrius was a contemporary of Dionysius of Halicarnassus in the first century B.C. in Rome, and

then to identify him with the Peripatetic philosopher whose contention (that Demosthenes learned his rhetorical art from Aristotle) Dionysius disproves in the first letter to Ammaeus, *and also* with the Demetrius to whom Dionysius had sent an essay on Imitation, as he tells us in the letter to Pompey (chapter 3 *ad init.*). Pompeius himself is then further identified with the author of *On the Sublime*, but that does not concern us at present.

Goold writes well, but I fear that attractive rhetorical phrases not infrequently take the place of argument. Like Horace, he says what others have said before but says it better. These parts of the article I must ignore, for I cannot here repeat all I have already said in many pages. To give one example: I showed that there are in the treatise an unusually large number of references to and quotations from persons who are known to have lived in the late fourth and early third centuries, and I listed and discussed these. Goold replies (p. 181) that "they have not seemed so to any other scholar," which proves nothing. Indeed it was my reason for pointing this out. That kind of argument I must ignore, and try to restrict myself to points that are new, or where something is added.

Nor am I a lone objector to "the orthodox opinion which puts it three hundred years later." This was the orthodox view sixty years ago, but a number of scholars have more recently argued for earlier dates, varying from the late third century to 100 B.C.[2]

I agree that the passage in Philodemus' *Rhetoric*[3] which states that "long periods are bad for delivery, as we read in Demetrius about those of Isocrates . . ." refers to Demetrius of Phalerum. In fact I pointed this out. My argument was and is that Philodemus is clearly referring to the Phalerean, and that *if* the reference is to our treatise (which Hammer believed and Rhys Roberts thought possible) then, obviously, Philodemus thought the Phalerean to be its author. Goold maintains there is no such criticism of Isocrates in the treatise **On Style**, that "one cannot infer from our Demetrius that he disapproved of Isocrates' periods or even regarded them as long at all" (p. 179). This is not quite Philodemus' point, but Goold is too hasty when he says that "Isocrates is mentioned only three times, once (12) to cite him with Gorgias and Alcidamas as an example of the periodic style, and twice to comment on his avoidance of the hiatus." At 12 Demetrius goes on to say that "in their work" (i.e., the work of Isocrates, Gorgias, and Alcidamas) "one period follows another just as surely as one hexameter follows another in Homer" and 15 proves this to be adverse criticism since it says that no *logos* should consist of a string of periods; 16 adds that no period should have more than four clauses. And then, at 25-28, quotations from Isocrates and Theopompus, among others, are followed by strong comments that the rhetorical devices of their style are incompatible with force or passion and are bad art . . . .

But Philodemus' "bad for delivery" would naturally refer to the section on the forcible style . . . (240-303) since this depends on delivery more than any other. We have already been told (193) that the style which omits connectives is more suited to debate, more histrionic . . .; at 271 forcefulness is all but equated with the disconnected style (the opposite of the Isocratean). Then we find that the forceful style requires short phrases (241), brevity (242), avoids antitheses and balanced clauses (247, where an example of these is given from Theopompus, the famous pupil of Isocrates); if one uses periods, they must be short (252); connectives should often be omitted (269); and again (299): "smoothness in the arrangement of words, *as affected by the school of Isocrates . . .* with its avoidance of hiatus, is not suited to forceful speech." Finally we are told (303), that "long, continuous periods, which make the speaker pant for breath, not only surfeit but repel him."

It is crystal clear that Demetrius did dislike the long, balanced, antithetic periodic style of Isocrates and his school. In fact he condemns it in no uncertain terms, both in his introductory discussion and especially in connection with delivery and the forceful style. The precise words of Philodemus are not found in any particular section, but the idea is expressed several times. Even if Isocrates' name were not mentioned at all, every one of the above passages would be understood by any reader acquainted with rhetoric to refer to him and his school, and there is in my opinion a strong probability that Philodemus is referring to our treatise.

There is another passage of Philodemus which I did not use because, as always, the text is very doubtful, but Goold uses it to prove that Philodemus knew only of a three-style formula (185, n. 37); but not of any four-style formula such as we find in Demetrius. On the contrary, the most probable interpretation of the sentence seems to prove that Philodemus at least knew a four-style formula. . . .

However, modern scholars did not like the idea that Philodemus knew of a four-style formula, and so Radermacher proposed [mesoteta] instead of [megesthos].[4] This is legitimate, since only the is certain; but this reading requires us to take the third XXX in a completely different sense from the other two; it signifies equivalence where the other two are enumerative; you cannot, of course, have a mean style in a four-style formula. I find this reading quite unconvincing. Goold himself suggests (185, n. 37) [mesen tina] which avoids the difficulty of the third [e], which it deletes. But this use of [tina], i.e., [mesen tina giaphuroteta] "or (thirdly) a kind of in-

termediate elegance," is very awkward and unusual in a general description of the different kinds of [plasma]. As is the case with Radermacher's, the only purpose of this restoration is to make the text conform to the preconception that Philodemus must be referring to three styles. I think that Sudhaus' restoration, [megethos e] is much more likely, and that Philodemus is referring to a formula of four styles. And if we can take [hadrographia] in the sense of forcefulness, a natural meaning, though later critics use [hadron] as a synonym for the grand style (here [megethas]), then these are indeed the four styles of Demetrius. However, I did not, and do not, press this argument, for the text is much too fragmentary. It may be noted, however, that Wilamowitz also thought that Philodemus here refers to four styles (*Hermes* 35 [1900] 30, n. 4).

Goold (p. 180) makes much of a reference in Syrianus (c. 400 A.D.) who is speaking of formulae of styles:[5]

> One of these is Dionysius, for he says that there are three styles: the simple, the mean, and the grand. Hipparchus adds the picturesque and the flowery. Demetrius rejects the picturesque, being satisfied with four.

We are told that Syrianus must be referring to these three critics in chronological order. Demetrius is therefore later than Dionysius and the unknown Hipparchus. This, however, is far from certain, especially so with the use of the present tense. Dionysius, moreover, did not use [grand] for the grand style, and Demetrius is left with four styles with a mean! I do not think much importance can be attached to this late and somewhat confused passage.

On the language of Demetrius, Goold indulges in a false analogy (pp. 183-184): he says quite rightly that very often perfectly normal derivatives do not appear for a long time, and he illustrates this by English examples; whereas "help" and "force" are attested in 1300, yet "forcefully" does not appear till 1774 and "helpfully" till 1832. He then adds: "it is not through lack of written English" that we can be sure that certain adverbs are not found "from Chaucer to Hemingway." But therein lies precisely the falsity of his analogy. My point was and is that we do *not* have written texts (and no other critical text) which would enable us to determine whether certain forms were or were not in use in the third century B.C. And we do have an earlier critical text, the *Rhetorica ad Alexandrum,* firmly dated in the late fourth century where we find quite a number of expressions and constructions which are also "late."[6]

There are two other difficulties which Goold has to face: he admits that Demetrius' attitude to Demosthenes is very different from that of later critics: to them the great orator was a paragon of all the virtues and styles; Demetrius uses him only to illustrate forcefulness. So Goold has to imagine his Demetrius as objecting "to the perpetual hosannas everywhere raised at the name of Demosthenes" in the first century, and then further as inventing a forceful style specifically in order to be able to "demote" the orator into it, thus fashioning "an effective weapon against the teaching of Dionysius" (p. 185). This fanciful picture is not supported by any evidence; indeed, the whole tone of **On Style** is against it. It is not in the least polemical, and shows no hostility whatever against Demosthenes, nor does the orator in any way monopolize the chapter on forcefulness. The absence of any reference to oratorical *mimêsis* or emulation in our treatise is explained by a similar imaginative flight: Demetrius, as a "staunch Peripatetic" is here also in conscious opposition to Dionysius (p. 187).

But the description of Demetrius as a staunch Peripatetic is somewhat startling. I discussed at some length (pp. 32-38) the unusual attitude of our author to Aristotle, whose works on rhetoric he obviously knew and used for his purposes, simplifying his terminology at times, sometimes improving on him, in a way unparalleled in later times. This is Goold's only reply (186):

> The relationship is, on the contrary, similar to that which might exist between a Roman Catholic theologian and Thomas Aquinas. On fundamental matters a chronological proximity might appear indicated, but differences of emphasis in the application of doctrine and a greater precision of technical minutiae, not to mention general linguistic discrepancies, would reveal the lapse of centuries between them.

My knowledge of theology is inadequate to enable me to appreciate the nature of the relationship here indicated, but the simile does not apply to Demetrius and Aristotle, for the differences between them are in essential matters as well as in details—the whole basis and structure of the treatise is un-Aristotelian: the four styles, distinguished by difference of subject-matter, diction, word-arrangement, figures, and the rest. Demetrius has none of Aristotle's philosophical approach and logical distinctions. Whatever Demetrius may have been, he was no staunch Aristotelian.

I shall but briefly refer to Goold's identifications of Demetrius in the first century. He looks for a "literary professor" who is "a Peripatetic teacher of rhetoric." He finds the anonymous Peripatetic *philosopher* of the letter to Ammaeus and promptly identifies them, though one doubts that any rhetorician would have said that Demosthenes owed his art to Aristotle (who never mentions him). Goold then finds that Dionysius says he addressed essays on Imitation to one Demetrius

(a common enough name) and declares this Demetrius to be the same man. As we know nothing more about either of these men the identification can certainly not be disproved. But this is pure play of fancy—a pleasant fancy if we are sure on other grounds that Demetrius wrote in Rome in the time of Dionysius; it makes no contribution whatever to the problem of date.

II

I will now deal with Rist's article on Artemon, whom Demetrius (223) mentions as the editor of Aristotle's letters. This is a very thorough and careful hypothetical structure which concludes that Artemon cannot have lived before the end of the second century B.C.—so that Demetrius should not be dated till 100 B.C. and probably later. I am not convinced, for two reasons: first, because in this type of structure where each hypothesis serves as a basis for the next, the degree of probability is obviously less at each step, and, moreover, a quite different conclusion can be drawn from the same evidence.

Rist's case may fairly be summarized as follows: We have three lists of Aristotle's works. The first two, that of Diogenes Laertius and the second, usually connected with Hesychius, are generally believed to derive either from Hermippus or Ariston, who both lived in the late third century, so either will do for our purpose. Now Hesychius mentions twenty books of Aristotle's letters, while Diogenes knows a number of books which add up to twenty but also some other letters to Philip about the Selymbrians. It follows that only twenty books were known to their common source, whether Hermippus or Ariston.

The third list is preserved only in Arabic, in two versions of the 13th century. These are generally believed to be ultimately derived from the compilation of Andronicus of Rhodes who, we know, worked on the Aristotelian works of the library of Apellikon which Sulla brought to Rome early in the first century. This library of Apellikon contained most of the library of Neleus, who, as the well known story of Strabo tells us, had received the library of Theophrastus at his death.[7]

The Arab versions speak of the library of Apellikon as containing two lots of letters. The first lot is described in one version as (I quote from Rist's article, p. 4): "a book in which a man named Artemon collected a number of letters by Aristotle in eight books"; and the other version says: "a large book, a compendium containing a number of letters in eight parts." The second lot is described in both Arab lists as: "other letters which Andronicus found in twenty parts." From this Rist makes the following deductions: the twenty books of letters are the twenty books mentioned by both Diogenes and Hesychius, and these were known to their third-century source, be it Hermippus or Ariston. The eight books could then be the same as Diogenes' letters to Philip. In this connection, Rist notes some confirmation in that Elias, among works of Aristotle on concrete topics speaks of "the letters which a certain Artemon, *who lived after Aristotle* (my italics), collected in eight books," and which "were written [*pros hera*]." These must, Rist believes, be the letters to Philip.[8] Olympiodorus speaks of Andronicus and Artemon *in that order* as compilers of Aristotle's letters (my italics: the chronological order again), and he speaks of letters [*pros tinas idia*], which describes *both* their compilations. Elias means the letters to Philip (as in Diogenes), Olympiodorus all those to individuals, including the collection of Andronicus.

So we have twenty books throughout, and eight books, the collection of Artemon, unknown in the late third century, but appearing in Diogenes (from somewhere) and in the Arab version. As Artemon's collection was not known in the third century, it cannot have been in the original collection of Apellikon. The Arabs may have got his name from Andronicus, and he would then at best, be "a man who lived some time between the original acquiring of the library by Apellikon and its eventual publication by Andronicus," i.e., between the late second century B.C. and the second half of the first. And so Demetrius cannot be earlier than 100 B.C., since he knows the collection of Artemon (i.e., the letters to Philip) as well as other letters.

This longish summary was necessary if the following criticisms were to be intelligible.

1. It is true that Hermippus is often accepted as the common source of the lists in Diogenes and Hesychius. Moraux does not accept Hermippus but plumps for Ariston.[9] But it need be neither one nor the other. Let us remember that Diogenes Laertius wrote about the beginning of the third century A.D., Hesychius in the fifth (when the actual compiler of the second list wrote is totally unknown). Diogenes at least does *not* (*pace* Düring, p. 79) say Hermippus is his main source, and does *not* mention him in connection with the list. These exercises in *Quellensuche* are very uncertain, even those that are generally accepted.

2. That both Diogenes and Hesychius mention twenty books, and that one of them mentioned other letters as well, does not really mean that their source knew only the twenty books. Even if Hesychius is generally believed to be more faithful to his source, in this case it might be Diogenes, especially as he is more detailed about the twenty books also. Yet Rist's reasoning leans strongly on his assumption that Hermippus (or Ariston) did not know Artemon's collection.

3. Rist speaks of the extra letters in Diogenes as "letters to Philip about the Selymbrians," but the text actually is [*epistolai pros Phillippon Selumbrion epistolai pros Alexandrou epistolai d'*] . . . . By putting a stop after the first [*epistolai*] and inserting [*peri*] before [*Selumbrion*], Düring gets this: "Letters: Letters to Philip about the Selymbrians . . .," but this use of the first [*epistolai*] as a heading is unique in the list. A much more natural translation is: Letters to Philip; Letters of (or about) the Selymbrians; i.e. two different lots of letters. Then Rist's identification of Elias' letters [*pros hera*] (to one person) with the Letters to Philip loses all its force, and so does the identification of the extra letters with Artemon's collection as being to Philip only. The result is confusion, but Aristotle's correspondence seems to have been precisely in that state till Andronicus, except for Artemon's collection.

4. From the Arabic versions above, which mention both Artemon and Andronicus by name, Rist suggests that it looks at first sight as if these two men's collections were in the original library of Apellikon. As this is obviously impossible for Andronicus, "it is not at all unreasonable to doubt whether it contained a book in eight parts edited by Artemon" (p. 6). But even at first sight one surely sees that in the Arabic version, as quoted by Rist himself, what is said of the two men is not at all the same thing. It is categorically stated that there was in the library a collection of eight books of letters edited by Artemon (a large collection, the other version says) and then also twenty parts or books "which Andronicus found" (or read) and these were no doubt the material on which his own edition was based. It does not say or imply that Andronicus' name was connected with these letters before he worked on the library about the middle of the first century. This is the obvious meaning.

However, one might accept all Rist's evidence and most of his assumptions (except those mentioned in the last paragraph) and draw from them quite different conclusions, as follows. The Arab version specifically states that Artemon's collection *was* in Apellikon's library, and since we have no evidence to the contrary, the natural assumption is that it was there when he acquired it, that it therefore came from Neleus' library and ultimately from that of Theophrastus when he died. In that case the collection must have been made soon after Aristotle's death and before that of Theophrastus (i.e., between 322 and c. 285). This gets slight support from Elias' reference to Artemon "who was born after Aristotle," i.e., a younger contemporary, for it would be a singularly otiose thing to say if he lived a century or so later.[10] Obviously no editor of Aristotle's letters could have lived before him! These were probably letters to individuals, some of them to Philip. . . . If this collection was unknown to Hermippus and/or Ariston, and generally at the end of the third century B.C., it can only be because this collection was among the books which Strabo tells us went to Neleus and were lost even to the Lyceum.

How does this situation affect Demetrius? He knows Artemon (223) as the man who edited Aristotle's letters . . . and it is a fair inference that this is the only collection he knows. The quotation from a letter to Antipater which follows immediately shows that the collection contained letters to others than Philip. Demetrius in fact shows an unusual familiarity with Aristotle's correspondence which most probably derived from Artemon's collection, of which he may have possessed a copy. It was, we know from the Arab version, a "large book." Now if, as we have shown, the collection disappeared into Neleus' library, it follows that Demetrius must have known it before Theophrastus' death. He clearly knew and had read Artemon whose views he also quotes on the right epistolary style generally (223-224). This does not mean that all the letters included in Artemon's collection were necessarily lost. He no doubt had copies made for his edition: the originals or other copies may have remained in the Lyceum, been collected in Alexandria, and may even have found their way also into Apellikon's library. The edition of Artemon and the twenty books or bundles no doubt overlapped— but the particular collection of Artemon with his name on it as editor was hidden away with the other Aristotelian manuscripts by the successors of Neleus till Apellikon came along and bought them two generations later.

All these assumptions being taken as fact, "reason cries out" (if I may borrow a phrase from both my colleagues) that Demetrius cannot have written his treatise "**On Style**" much after 270 B.C.

To prevent misunderstanding, however, let me hasten to make clear that there are far too many uncertainties in this last piece of argumentation of my own for me to attach much weight to it, but its degree of probability is at least as great as that of the conclusions of Professors Rist and Goold. And if I have stated as fact what is only assumption, this of course is one of the rigid rules of the genre.

*Notes*

1 University of Toronto Press, 1961.

2 See *A Greek Critic,* p. 22, n. 26; also G. A. Kennedy, *The Art of Persuasion in Greece* (Princeton 1963) 285-286 and H. Gärtner's review in *Gymnasium* 70 (1963) 61-63.

3 S. Sudhaus, *Philodemi Volumina Rhetorica* (Leipzig 1892) vol. 1, p. 198. . . .

4 In *RhMus* 54 (1899) 361, n. 1.

5 Syrianus *In Hermogeni Commentaria,* ed. H. Rabe (Leipzig 1892) vol. 1, p. 99, 18.

6 These are listed in the second appendix of *A Greek Critic,* pp. 159-163.

7 See Strabo 13.54 (608-609) and Plutarch *Sulla* 26. The story is discussed by P. Moraux, *Les Listes anciennes des ouvrages d'Aristote* (Louvain 1951), who views it somewhat sceptically, see especially pp. 1-6, 311-321.

8 Elias *In Cat. Prooemium,* Berlin edition of Commentaries on Aristotle, vol. 18, ed. Busse (1900) p. 113, 25-26. . . .

9 Moraux, 221-233 and 245. Cp. I. Düring, *Aristotle in the ancient bibliographical Tradition* (Göteborg 1957) 67-68.

10 See note 8.

---

## FURTHER READING

Denniston, J. D. "Notes on Demetrius, *De Elocutione.*" *The Classical Quarterly* XXIII, No. 1 (January 1929): 7-10.

Provides emendations and interpretations of particular lines from *On Style.*

_____. "Demetrius, *De Elocutione.*" *The Classical Quarterly* XXIV, No. 1 (January 1930): 42-3.

Answers criticisms by J. F. Lockwood regarding earlier emendations and interpretations.

Grube, G. M. A. "Demetrius on Style." In his *The Greek and Roman Critics,* pp. 110-21. London: Methuen & Co Ltd, 1965.

Overview of *On Style* that includes examination of what Demetrius meant by "style" and his various approaches to conveying his subject matter.

Lockwood, J. F. "Demetrius, *De Elocutione.*" *The Classical Quarterly* XXIII, No. 2 (April 1929): 105-08.

Criticizes J. D. Denniston's conclusions about the meaning of assorted passages in *On Style.*

_____. "Notes on Demetrius, *De Elocutione.*" *The Classical Quarterly* XXXIII, No. 1 (January 1939): 41-7.

Attempts to clarify difficult lines from *On Style* and examines how various translators have dealt with particular lines in their editions.

Roberts, W. Rhys. "Milton and Demetrius, *De Elocutione*." *The Classical Review* 15 (1901): 453-54.
   Contends that Milton was acquainted with *On Style*.

Schenkeveld, Dirk Marie. *Studies in "Demetrius On Style."* Amsterdam: Adolf M. Hakkert, 1964, 186p.
   Compares Demetrius's treatment of style, metaphor, and neologisms to the treatments found in other rhetorical writings of antiquity.

# Hafiz

## c. 1326-1389/90

(Full name Shamsoddin Mohammad Hafiz of Shiraz.) Persian poet.

### INTRODUCTION

Acclaimed as the supreme lyric poet of Persia, Hafiz is best known for his *Divan* (believed to have been compiled in around 1368), a collection of more than five hundred of his ghazals, or short lyric poems. The poems celebrate conventional subjects such as love and its pleasures and pains, and the drinking of wine, but Hafiz's subtlety has endeared him to scholars and the general public alike. Using simple, unaffected language, Hafiz took traditional themes and, with skill and artistry, arranged them in such a way that his work has never been bettered in Persion literature. He is credited with inventing the technique of combining two or more themes, sometimes incongruous ones, into a harmonious whole that can be read literally or metaphorically. His technical innovations allowed him to make mystery the focal point of many of his poems–mystery related to what A. J. Arberry has termed Hafiz's "doctrine of intellectual nihilism." In times past the poems' mystical element—Hafiz practiced Sufuism—dominated discussion of his works, but a more literal reading now prevails.

### Biographical Information

Little verifiable information is known concerning Hafiz's life. Shamsoddin Mohammad, Hafiz's given name, was born in Shiraz, in what is now Iran, to a merchant father who died when the boy was young. Hafiz was educated in the Arabic language, studied the *Koran* ("Hafiz" means one who has memorized the *Koran*), all the Muslim sciences taught at the time, and literature. Hafiz later worked as a teacher and a copyist of manuscripts. Once his own poems became recognized and admired, Hafiz acquired wealthy patrons. It appears likely that Hafiz lived some years at the court of Shah Mensour as an official poet. Although legend has it that Hafiz left Shiraz only once in his lifetime, there is some indication that he journeyed out of the immediate area on a few occasions. Nevertheless, Hafiz was devoted to Shiraz and refused offers from assorted sultans and princes to leave his land and practice his craft elsewhere.

### Major Works

Hafiz's work, consisting of more than five hundred poems, is collected under the title of *Divan*. According to tradition Hafiz prepared his own edition in about 1368. This manuscript, if it existed, is not the source of the thousands of extant variant transcriptions; they seem to derive from a posthumous edition published by Hafiz's friend Muhammad Gulandam. Editors have been plagued with doubtful or spurious poems attributed to Hafiz, because placing Hafiz's name with another's poem was an easy way to ensure a large readership. It is sometimes very difficult for scholars to decide which of Hafiz's poems are incontrovertibly genuine. The poems of Hafiz have received tremendous acclaim and have been translated into many languages. For example, Johann Gottfried von Goethe loosely rendered some of them into German. Translators have had some difficulty in doing justice rendering Hafiz's work in English. Arberry writes that it is generally agreed "that it is a mistake to attempt to reproduce in English the monorhyme which is so characteristic a feature of the original." Richard Le Gallienne writes that "so distasteful to English ideas are the metrical devices and adornments pleasing in a Persian ear that the attempt to reproduce them in English can only result in the most tiresome literary antics, a mirthless buffoonery of verse. . . . Rhythms which in Persian, doubtless, make the sweetest chiming, fitted with English words, become mere vulgar and ludicrous jingle." To combat this translators favor being faithful to the original idea and not concerning themselves with imitating rhymes or having the same number of lines.

### Critical Reception

Arberry asserts that "Hafiz is as highly esteemed by his countrymen as Shakespeare by us, and deserves as serious consideration." Much scholarly effort has been directed towards interpretation. J. Christoph Bürgel has summarized the problem: "The difficulty of understanding Hafiz correctly does not lie in his lexicon or grammar. He does not use rare or difficult words and his phraseology is simple and very clear. There is hardly any single verse of Hafiz posing a problem in itself. However, there is also hardly a ghazal not posing a problem of meaning and, consequently, of interpretation. In other words, the obfuscation of meaning is created by the juxtaposition of verses that seem to contradict each other, be it by their moral implications or by their belonging to different ontological layers." While some early critics went so far as to claim that Hafiz's poems are incoherent and lack unity, such comments can often be traced to faulty translations and cultural misunderstandings.

## PRINCIPAL WORK

*Divan* (poetry) compiled 1368?

## PRINCIPAL ENGLISH EDITIONS

*The Poems of Shemseddin Mohammed Hafiz Of Shiraz.* 3 vols. [translated by John Payne] 1901

*Fifty Poems* [edited by Arthur J. Arberry] 1953

*The Divan-i-Hafiz* [translated by H. Wilberforce Clarke] 1997

## CRITICISM

### John Payne (essay date 1901)

SOURCE: An introduction to *The Poems of Shemseddin Mohammed Hafiz of Shiraz*, E.J. Brill, Leyden, 1901, pp. xi-xxix.

[*In the following essay, Payne discusses the limitations of various biographies of Hafiz before providing his own sketch of the poet's life which emphasizes his lack of religious belief.*]

I

There are many so-called lives of the greatest of Persian poets; but they are all, without exception, mere collections of pointless and irrelevant anecdotes, mostly bearing manifest signs of ex post facto fabrication and often treating of matters completely foreign to the nominal subject[1], and carefully refrain from touching upon the essential points of Hafiz's history. For instance, in none of these insipid compilations are we vouchsafed any particulars as to his family and extraction, nor is even the date of his birth stated; and indeed the only real biographical information, such as it is, which is to be gleaned from their jejune and wearisome pages, is that the poet was born and lived all his life at Shiraz and that there he died at some date, towards the end of the fourteenth century of our era, variously stated as from A.D. 1384 to A.D. 1393. In this absence of official record, the only trustworthy data at our disposal, respecting the life and career of Hafiz, are those to be gathered from the study of his poems and from such painstaking and authoritative commentaries upon the latter as that of the Turkish seventeenth century writer Soudi. Pursuing this line of research, with the primary object of establishing some probable date as approximately that of our poet's birth, the ear-

liest landmark which offers itself to us is the mention, as a prince contemporary with himself, of Sultan Shah Mesoud, (Emir Jelaleddin Mesoud Injou), Viceroy or Sultan of Fars, A.D. 1335—6, to whom he, in Ode DXCII, addresses a petition on the subject of his mule, which had apparently been stolen from him and hidden in the royal stables, and complains that all the substance, which he had, in three years' space, amassed by the munificence of the king and his minister, had been ravished from him by malignant Fortune. From this latter statement it is evident that Hafiz must have been established at the court of Shiraz, in high favour with the reigning prince and his ministers and probably in some official character, such as court-poet, at least as far back as A.D. 1333, which would bring us to the later years of the viceroyalty of Mesoud's father, Mehmoudshah Injou. It may fairly be supposed that, at this date (1333), the poet had at least reached man's estate, or he would hardly have attained the position which he seems to have held at Shiraz; and this supposition is corroborated by the fact that, as the commentators tell us, he had, in his youth, followed the regular collegiate course of education, necessary to fit the Muslim aspirant for any kind of public career, and had taken the theological degree of *Hafiz* (whence his sobriquet)[2], which after enabled him to fill the chair of Koranic exegesis founded for his benefit by a later patron. We are, therefore, entitled to assume that he must have been at least twenty years old in 1333, and this assumption would fix his birth as having occurred in 1313 at the latest, a postulate to which there seems to be no reasonable objection, as the latest estimate of the date of his death would not thus attribute to him an age of more than eighty years. Shiraz, the poet's birthplace and life-long residence, is a town of considerable size, pleasantly and picturesquely situated in a small but beautiful and fertile plain surrounded by a chain of lofty hills, in the heart of the great South-Western mountain-system of Coelo-Persia. It is the capital of the great province of Fars or Persia Proper and was, in Hafiz's time, a place of more than its present importance, being the seat of a Sultan and possessing, in all probability, at least double its present population. It is, however, still a thriving town of some forty or fifty thousand inhabitants and is (as in the Middle Ages) celebrated for the production of wine and rosewater, of which it exports considerable quantities to all parts of the East. In addition to the pleasance-place of Musella, in which Hafiz's grave is situated, some two miles without the walls, Shiraz possesses numerous beautiful pleasure-gardens and is famous for its orchards and rose-fields. The climate is, however, not altogether congenial, the cold being severe in winter, and the country is said to be malarious in the hot season. The province of Fars formed part of the vast dominions of the Khalifate; but, after the fall of Baghdad in 1258, it passed under the sway of the new dynasty founded by the Mongol conqueror Hulagou (or Holagou) upon the ruins of the Abbaside power, the seat of government of

*Tomb of Hafiz in Shiraz, Iran.*

which continued to be the ancient capital of the Khalifs on the Tigris and which was styled the Ilkhani or Tribal dynasty, as being nominally subject to the suzerainty of the Khacans or Mongol emperors of China and Tartary. The last effectual ruler of Hulagou's house was Abou Said, the eighth Sultan in succession from the conqueror of Baghdad, upon whose death, in 1335, the Persian portion of the Ilkhani empire, although continuing to be nominally ruled, first, by a succession of puppet princes of the same family and later by the powerful Emirs of the Jelayir house, (who also assumed the title of Ilkhani, as claiming kinship with the original founder), was, until the irruption of Tamerlane (Timour-i-Leng) at the end of the century, divided among a number of petty princes, who, although professedly viceroys and vassals of the suzerain Sultans of Baghdad, were, in all but name, independent rulers. The principality of Fars, with its capital Shiraz, fell to the lot of Abou Said's former Grand Vizier, Mehmoudshah Injou before-mentioned, who appears to have, during the last years of that monarch's reign, acted as viceroy of the province and survived his master but a few months. He was succeeded by his son, Sultan Shah Mesoud, who died in 1336 and left the throne of Fars to his brother, Shah Sheikh Abou Ishac. Hafiz's position at the court of Shiraz was unaffected by the accession of Abou Ishac, with whom (probably owing to the fact that they had both been members, in youth, of the same Soufi order,) he remained in high favour during the whole of his reign, and the new prince's Grand Vizier, Hajji Kiwameddin Hassan, so often mentioned and eulogized by Hafiz, was the latter's constant friend and patron and appears to have befriended and supported him on every occasion until his own death, which occurred in 1353. It is he who is said to have founded, for the poet's benefit, a professorship of Koranic exegesis, the duties of which (according to Soudi) Hafiz actually performed, at all events, from time to time, during his benefactor's lifetime, signalizing his occupation of the chair by annotating the *Keshf-ul-Keshshaf*, Ez Zemekhsheri's famous Commentary on the Koran, and the *Miftah-ul-Uloum* (Key of the Sciences or Encyclopædia) of Sekkaki, copies of which two works, with marginal glosses in the poet's handwriting, are stated by Soudi to have been still extant at Shiraz in his own time. Shah Sheikh Abou Ishac was, in 1353, ousted from Shiraz and afterwards, in 1357, from Ispahan, where he lost his life, by the robber prince, Mubarizeddin Muhemmed el Muzeffer, Sultan of Yezd and Kirman, and the Muzefferi dynasty replaced that of Injou on the throne of Fars and Persian Irac. Hafiz does not seem to have in any way suffered by the change of dynasty, being apparently confirmed in his official position by the new sovereign, whose Vizier, Khwajeh Kiwameddin-w'ed-daulet Sahib Eyar,[3] became his patron and continued to protect and befriend him until his own death, ten years later; and he appears to have enjoyed the consistent favour and protection of the succeeding princes of the house of Muzeffer (all of

whom, with the exception of Zein-ul-abidin, 1384-7, are mentioned and eulogized by him,) until their final overthrow and expulsion by Timour in 1393. A well-known anecdote represents the Tartar conqueror as having, on his entry into Shiraz, summoned the famous Persian lyrist to his presence and reproached him, with grim jocularity, for the affront which he had put upon his (Timour's) two famous cities of Bokhara and Samarcand, in presuming to promise them as an equivalent for such a trifle as the mole or beauty-spot upon his mistress's cheek; to which Hafiz is said to have replied that it was the practice of such extravagant acts of generosity which had reduced him to his present state of indigence or (according to another version of the story) by asking how the gifts of the slave (himself) could impoverish the lord (Timour). The poet's ready reply is said to have at once established him in the favour of the rough soldier of fortune; but it is doubtful whether the interview in question ever took place, as there is no certain record of Timour having personally visited Shiraz during Hafiz's lifetime. It seems, at all events, certain that Hafiz was not molested by the Tartar invaders[4] and was allowed by them to end his days in peace at Shiraz, where, according to the *tarikh* or chronogram on his tomb, which is still extant at Musella aforesaid, he died in 1389. There is, however, as has already been remarked, no consensus of opinion as to the actual date of his death, some authorities holding that he died as early as 1384, whilst others prolong his life till 1393, the year of the definitive defeat and slaughter by Timour of Shah Mensour, the last Muzefferi Sultan of Fars. Nor is this last opinion without some basis of probability. Hafiz repeatedly mentions and eulogizes Shah Mensour as the regnant king and it is therefore evident that he survived till some time after that prince's accession in 1388. Indeed, to judge from the fact that the name of no other contemporary sovereign occurs with such frequency in his poems[5], it is probable that he lived for several years at Shah Mensour's court, in the exercise of his functions as poet-royal, and it is even possible that he may have survived till 1393 and so have come in contact with Timour, in accordance with the legend. However, had this been the case, it is difficult to account for the absence, in his poems, of any mention of the catastrophe which deprived him of so staunch a patron as the last Muzefferi Sultan of Fars and for the fact that no reference of any kind is made by him to the Tartar conqueror, although he[6] bestows an elaborate eulogy upon the latter's most troublesome and persistent antagonist, Sultan Ahmed, the last Jelayir sovereign of Baghdad, who was incessantly at war with Timour and his successors, now losing and now regaining his capital, from his accession in 1382 till his death in 1410[7]. Despite the continual complaints which he makes of the inappreciative and curmudgeonly character and behaviour of his fellow-countrymen and the chronic neglect and closefistedness which he attributes to the royal and noble patrons upon whom he depended for the means of subsistence, Hafiz appears, on the whole, (as he himself acknowledges in such poems as Odes CCCCVII and CCCCXLI) to have led a fairly comfortable life at Shiraz, under the protection of the various kings and viziers of his time. The continual intestine wars, which devastated the country, do not seem to have occasioned him any considerable inconvenience, as the various robber chieftains, who succeeded each other in the occupation of the province, appear not only to have respected his person and property, but to have treated him, as far as we can judge, with distinguished consideration and even munificence; and his situation, therefore, will compare not unfavourably with that of the other poets and scholars of his day. He seems, at any rate, to have been passionately attached to the land of his birth, and no promises or inducements, such as were, according to contemporary chronicle, not lacking on the part of the Sultans of Baghdad and the other princes of Persia and even India, appear to have availed to persuade him permanently to abandon those waters of Ruknabad and that earth and air of Musella of which he speaks with such fondness. Indeed, he is said by several of his biographers to have left Shiraz on but one occasion, that of the expedition, of whose ill results he speaks with such bitterness, to Yezd, in South-West Khorasan, then a town of some fifty or sixty thousand inhabitants and the seat of an independent Sultan, situate about 185 miles, as the crow flies, and 245 or 250 miles, by road, to the North-East of Shiraz. Nevertheless, it appears certain, on the evidence of his own poems,[8] that he made one or more journeys to Ispahan, the capital of Persian Irac, a town about 300 miles North-East of Shiraz, and even resided there awhile. It is also probable that he, at some time or other, (possibly in the reign of Sheikh Uweis or that of Sultan Ahmed, both patrons of his,) visited Baghdad, the seat of the suzerain power and the residence of his intimate friend and fellow-poet Selman Sewaji, and he seems, indeed, to have retained so favourable a memory of his stay there and of the local wine that he was apparently only prevented from returning thither by want of means.[9] He appears, also, to have received at least two royal invitations to visit India, one (according to Ferishteh, the seventeenth century historian of the Mohammedan dynasties of the Peninsula) from Mehmoudshah Behmani I (A.D. 1378-97), King of the Deccan, and another from Ghiyatheddin Purbi, King of Bengal, to whom[10] he had addressed an eulogistic poem, which is not extant; and he is said to have actually travelled to Hurmouz or some other port on the Persian Gulf, with the intention of taking ship for India, but abandoned his purpose on being reminded, by the sight of the stormy sea, of the perils and hardships of the voyage. These scanty particulars represent all that can, with any certainty, be predicated as to the essential points of Hafiz's career; and the task of gleaning and winnowing these scattered grains of fact from the mass of his verse is much increased in difficulty and incertitude by the whimsical Oriental habit (already mentioned in the Introduction to my Translation of the Quatrains of Omar Kheyyam) of arranging the collected poems of an author, not in the order of their composition or according to the nature of their contents, or indeed in any other logical order, but after an arbitrary and unmeaning fashion, in the alphabetical sequence of the end-letters of their rhyme-words.

II

None of the Persian poets has been more strenuously and more persistently claimed as an affiliate and co-religionist by the mystical fraternity, known as the Soufis or Wool-wearers, than Hafiz; and none, to my mind, with less colour of reason. Of the followers of this curious religious sect (whose tenets are a sort of bastard offshoot of Vedantic pessimism, awkwardly grafted upon the alien stem of Semitic optimism, and who, for their insinuating persistence and their skill in adapting and fashioning to their own ends the most opposite of influences and currents of opinion and circumstance, may not inaptly be styled the Jesuits of the East,) and of their habit of claiming to interpret the writings of the most obviously unmystical and indeed anti-religious authors in a formal symbolical sense, in correspondence with their own theosophical doctrines, I have already spoken in the Introduction to my Translation of the Quatrains of Omar Kheyyam, where I have so fully stated the considerations, which seem to me to negative the theory of the Soufism of such poets as Kheyyam and Hafiz, that it is unnecessary to repeat them here. It need only be noted, in addition, that the anti-Soufi case is, in my judgment, much stronger with respect to Hafiz than to Kheyyam, as the later poet was certainly, in youth, a member of some Soufi community and tells us again and again, in his poems, that the insight, which his early connection with the sect had given him into the hypocrisy and insincerity with which the whole order was tainted and the scandalous system of falsehood and imposture, by which the Soufis and their like contrived to hoodwink the world and to exploit the credulity of the folk for their own mean purposes, had for ever disgusted him with the theosophists, and indeed with professional pietists and religionists generally, and had caused him to become a toper and an amorist, in the confidence that winebibbing and loverhood were venial sins, compared with the unpardonable crime of hypocrisy, which, with all its attendant and consequent vices, he is never tired of ascribing to his former associates. Moreover, it is abundantly evident to those who have studied the history, literary and general, of the Mohammedan East, that the adoption by the pietists of the Epicurean poet of Shiraz as a symbolical writer, conveying abstract theosophical doctrines in poetical form and under the guise of sensuous exhortations to pleasure and gallantry, as well as the pretention to claim him as a secret affiliate of the Soufi order, whose dithyrambic effusions were to be construed, according to a set formula peculiar to that sect, as in reality hymning the praises of a personal God and inculcating the tenets of an anthromorphic cult, mystically sublimated after the regular theosophical recipe, was an afterthought, neither conceived nor acted upon until long after the poet's death and forced upon the adopters by irresistible stress of circumstance. Nothing, for instance, can be more obvious than the fact that Hafiz was, during his lifetime, generally regarded by the professors of religion as an enemy of the orthodox faith and that it was solely to the abiding favour in which his exquisite literary gift and the charm of his personality had established him with the easygoing monarchs and ministers, who ruled the land of his birth, that he owed his exemption from persecution and punishment at the hands of the pietists and zealots; whilst he himself continually tells us that the Soufis, in particular, were never weary of calumniating and backbiting him and endeavouring to compass his disgrace and ruin. Nor did their enmity cease with his life; no sooner had the breath left his body than the orthodox party with one voice denounced the dead man as a notorious unbeliever, evil liver and enemy of the Faith and protested against the concession to his remains of the customary rites of decent burial; and it was not until his friends, by a happy stroke of luck or skill, extracted from his own works a *Sors* or oracular declaration,[11] in favour of his acceptance with the heavenly powers, that the superstitious deference of the Oriental to anything in the shape of a fatidical pronouncement from the Unseen World overrode the opposition of the poet's foes and he was suffered to be buried in peace. The pietists, silenced, but not convinced, soon recovered from their temporary defeat and continued to rail at the dead poet and to oppose, by all means in their power, the circulation of his poems, which were duly collected and made public, in Divan-form, by his friends and disciples and at once became popular throughout Persia, whence their reputation rapidly spread all over the Muslim East. In short, Hafiz quickly became the favourite poet of the Persian-speaking peoples of India and Asia generally, amongst whom he still holds much the same position as that of Shakspeare with ourselves; and in Turkey, in particular, the knowledge of his poems was so wide-spread and their popularity so great with all classes of the population as to raise to the highest pitch the alarm and indignation of the orthodox party, who, making a supreme effort to compass the defeat of the heretical influence, endeavoured to obtain a virtual decree of excommunication against the memory of the bard of Shiraz, in the shape of a canonical declaration that his poems were unfit, by reason of their immoral and unorthodox tendencies, for the perusal of the Faithful. Their machinations were, however, defeated by the common sense and impartiality of Abou Suoud, the Chief Mufti, or supreme authority on canonical jurisprudence, of the time, who, on the case being submitted to his decision, issued a *fetwa* or formal judicial pronouncement, to the effect that every one was at liberty to use his own judgment

in the matter of the meaning to be assigned to Hafiz's poems and that, in fine, to the pure all things were pure. Thus baffled in their hopes of securing the help of the canonical authorities for the suppression of the obnoxious writings, the Soufis and other zealots of the orthodox camp executed a complete change of front and finding that they could not succeed in ousting the love and admiration of Hafiz from the popular intelligence, determined, with characteristic flexibility, to adopt him as one of themselves and so convert their deadliest foe into an actual auxiliary. To this end, they applied themselves to insist that the Shirazi poet was, in reality, although in secret, an affiliate of the Soufi order and that his apparent abuse of the Soufis was only to be held to apply to those false members of the brotherhood who perverted its forms and doctrines to hypocritical and egotistical uses; that his (apparently) dissolute and erotic verse was to be construed solely in a symbolic and mystical sense, according to a formula constructed to harmonize with the tenets of the sect; that, when he spoke of wine and intoxication, he was to be understood as meaning the love of God and the ecstasy of spiritual communion with the Deity; that the Beloved was only a symbolical name for the Supreme Being; that by the often-mentioned cupbearer and wine-seller the *Murshid* or spiritual teacher and the *Pir* or Elder of the sect were in reality meant, and so on, in accordance with a regular vocabulary drawn up for the purpose; and this course they pursued with such consummate skill, persistence and success that the opinion of the Mohammedan world is still divided upon the point, the majority of men of culture, indeed, especially in India, inclining, to this day, (incredible, in view of the uncompromising thoroughness with which the poet contrives to dissemble any sneaking kindness he may have secretly cherished for the Soufis and their fashions and opinions, as it may seem to the European student of his works, who does not bear in mind the absorbing passion, well illustrated in such treatises as that of Gobineau on Oriental letter-magic and talismancy,[12] of the Eastern theologian and general reader for the extortion of an esoteric meaning from phrases and writings, the exoteric sense of which is obvious and sufficient,) to the belief that Hafiz's verse is only rightly to be understood, when paraphrased in the terminology of a cut-and-dried symbolical system of interpretation, which might, in the judgment of the unprejudiced critic, be applied with equal fitness and success to the Bab Ballads or L'Imitation de Notre Dame la Lune.[13]

### III

It is evident to the impartial student of his poems that Hafiz was no mystic, except as every true poet is a mystic, in the sense that he sees life and the world through a haze of imaginative glamour, which invests them with a glory and a significance invisible and incomprehensible to the common herd. The unmistakable fragrance of personal goodness exhales from his verse; but otherwise there is nothing to show that he held any religious sentiments, in the ordinary meaning of the word, or that he professed any religious belief other than that of the poet, whose gospel is the worship of beauty, truth and righteousness and whose observance is to do justly and love mercy and to keep himself unspotted from the world.

To his tenure of this creed his poems bear ample witness; but, beyond this, there is nothing to show that he in any way concerned himself with the forms and dogmas of technical religion. He appears, indeed, to have taken life and its problems altogether more lightly than his great predecessor, Kheyyam. Lacking the Indian and Greek culture of the latter, his attitude towards revealed religion was rather that of the tolerant man of the world than of the uncompromising philosopher who refuses to allow that the wise and the just should be deluded in a world such as ours.[14] If religion would leave him in peace, he was content to do likewise, to live and let live; and beyond the general insistance on the right of the poet to drink and make merry, to avail himself of such passing compensations as might offer for the toils and troubles of this sorry sublunary existence, and the bitter contempt with which he branded the sacrilegious pretenders to piety, we find little in his poems to account for the accusations of heresy and impiety with which he was pursued, both in his lifetime and after his death, by the orthodox party. The whole question, upon which the debate of religion turned, was manifestly without significance for his Olympian view and the matters in dispute were too trivial and too ill-defined for him to risk the spoliation of the rare sweet hours of life by the courting of unnecessary martyrdom for the sake of opinions which were, at bottom, indifferent to him. Hafiz was no Leopardi, no heaven-born "empêcheur de danser en rond", cast in the midst of the contemporary revel of inanity and impurity; no *desdichado de la vida*, divorced from all delight, like Heine; no eternal exile, like Lamennais, brow-branded with the Cain-mark of a divine despair,[15] whose stern soul refused to compromise with the brutalities and meannesses of life and who was incapable of solacing his Titanic miseries with its trivial pleasures. Though free from the coarseness of moral fibre and the ignoble weaknesses of the two French poets, he had this in common with Hugo and de Musset that "du pain, du vin et la première venue" sufficed for his satisfaction at those unirradiated hours when the angels forbore to warble to him from the battlements of heaven, reminding him of his celestial origin and of the obligations in which it involved him. There were two men in him; one the celestial poet, whose lips burned with the live coals of inspiration and whose soul was consumed with contempt for all that was not the "blauen Blumen" of the fields of heaven, whose eyes were blinded to the sights of this sublunary sphere by the visions of the viewless world and whose ears deafened to the sounds of life by the spheral harmonies of the Ideal; and another (the Div, to use his own language, who entered in, when the Angel departed from his soul,) the careless Epicurean, for whom life was sweet and who was unconcerned to quarrel with a world in which wine and women, praise and pleasure, were to be purchased at the cost of a trifling song or a set of laudatory verses addressed to some king or man of wealth and liberality. His Epicureanism was that of the child of nature, who knows not, in his unclouded hours, of evil and is as incapable as Hawthorne's Donatello of forbearing to rejoice in the natural pleasures of unharassed existence, in the intoxication of the Spring's rebirth and the calmer, if fuller, joys of the Summer splendours, that of the poet rather than that of the voluptuary, and his needs and the satisfactions which he sought for them were rather moral than material. He was of the race of his own "Calenders of debauchery," the dreamers who, with "brick beneath the head for pillow and foot upon the Seven Stars," give and take away, at will, the diadems of kingship and the realms of night and day. It was little that he needed for the establishment of his own heaven here on earth; it was enough for him to sit at the willow-foot, to drink the bitter wine of Bihisht and listen to the chirp of the rebeck and the wail of the reed-pipe, by the marge of the rill, the silver lapse of whose waters recalled to him, with no unpleasing admonition, the fleeting character of those goods of life and the world which he was content to barter for the darling and less deceptive illusions of dreamland. Here, under the spell of the heart-kindling moonlight, the charm of the night-exhaled rose-breath and the music-making stress of the rivulet's ripple, he was fain to forget the sorrows and miseries, the gauds and glories of existence, and to dream away the hours in an Armida's garden of his own creation, for whose evocation there sufficed him a cup of wine and a handful of roses in blossom. The modest subsidies, upon which the man of letters, in a time when learning and literary and artistic ability of all kinds looked entirely to the patronage and too often the caprice of the rich and great for their reward, depended for the means of life and comfort, were often, it is true, hard to come by, capriciously or corruptly withheld or delayed; but, the necessary funds once forthcoming, the troubles of the time of straitness were quickly forgotten and the poet hastened to provide himself with the simple elements of mirth, "the gear of pleasance," as he calls it, roses and wine, a cupbearer and a minstrel and a fair-faced light of love to share and poetize the frugal debauch. These granted, life had yet sweet hours for Hafiz. When the rose-bride came once more to the festival of Spring, when the sweet bird had brought its dulcet pipe at Summer's sign and the tulips overran the April meadows with their red-raimented hosts, the loveling of youth's sweet season tarried not to return to the visions of the bard of Shiraz and he was content for awhile to dream the dreams of the lover and the poet in the banqueting-hall of the cornfields, overshaded by the canopy of the clouds. Who shall blame him? Who will not rather, in these our days of stress and storm, when the old naïve remedies suffice us no longer against the culminating agonies of the Weltschmerz, look back with indulgence and sympathy upon the sweet singer of Fars and envy him his ableness to conjure from his path, by such simple spells, the troubles and wearinesses of life? Who would not wish that he could himself exorcise, at so cheap a rate, the giant phantoms that squeak and gibber in the streets of the city of our life, in this our eleventh hour of the night? Let us take Hafiz as he was; Epicurean and idealist, courtier (in the sense of Boccaccio and Baltasar Gracian) and poet; in his one shape, admirable and immortal, and in the other, surely not destitute of claim to our sympathy and our affection. We of these latter days, belated wayfarers wandering distractedly in the goblin-haunted mazes of our nightmare-dream of universal democracy, are apt to forget that Nature, in her eternal character of the most aristocratic of all institutions, still produces (as she has always produced and will forever continue to produce, until that supreme moment when this our distracted globe, "défonçant sa "vieille et misérable écorce, Ira fertiliser de ses restes immondes Les sillons "de l'espace où fermentent les mondes,") certain creatures of election, not alone distinguished above their fellows, but differing toto coelo from the rank and file of humanity, in that they are not to be appraised by the ordinary rules of criticism and that the laws of social conduct and the canons of everyday morality show, when applied to the appreciation of their actions and characteristics, but as the idlest of fables agreed upon. Exiled Sun-Gods, tending the Admetus-herds of an unappreciative contemporaneity, falcons-royal of the Empyrean, winged for the travel of the plains of heaven, they are among us, but not of us; their joys and sorrows are other than ours. The splendour of their celestial origin shines in their faces; the heavenly ichor that floods their veins is untroubled by the puzzles and perplexities that stir our sluggish blood. Unbound by our laws and unfettered by our prescriptions, above our approof and beyond our blame, such as Hafiz are not to be tried by our standards or condemned by our limitations; they have an inalienable title to the privilege which forms the foundation of our English judicial system; they can only be judged by their peers. Like Shakspeare, like Socrates, like Mendelssohn, Hafiz was of the children of the bridechamber, who mourn not, for the bridegroom is with them. Happy, thrice happy those rare elect ones among the servants of the Ideal, to whom it is given, through shower and sunshine and without default against their august vocation, to cull the rose of hilarity from the storm-swept meads of life, who are gifted to respire with impunity the intoxicating breath of the lilies and jessamines of love and joy, unconstrained by iron necessity to sate the burning longings of their souls with the hueless and scentless blossoms of the plant of Sad Content,

that austere flowerage of renouncement which is the common portion of those who seek the things of the spirit, the one stern solace which the Gods vouchsafe to the majority of their servants! These are the Parthenogeniti of life; they need no purification, as do those who have come out of great tribulation and have made white their robes in the blood of the Lamb; intemerate and free were they born, as the flowers of the field, and pure and incontaminable shall they abide for ever. Like Ben Jonson's lily of a day, they are the plants and flowers of light; they toil not neither do they spin; yet eternity is full of their glory.

*Notes*

[1] E. g. the lengthy account of Sultan Ahmed, the last Jelayir sovereign of Baghdad, and his struggles with Timour-i-Leng, which occupies a full quarter of Dauletshah's so-called Life of Hafiz.

[2] His own name was Shemseddin Mohammed. His family name is not known.

[3] In the note to Ode CLXVI, 1, the name "Hajji Kiwameddin Hassan" should read "Khwajeh Kiwameddin". The mistake is that of Soudi, who constantly confounds the two Kiwameddins with each other and with another Vizier of the Ilkhani Sultans bearing the same name. The second Kiwameddin, the Vizier of Mubarizeddin and of his son Shah Shejaa, is stated by some biographers to have been the patron who founded for Hafiz the chair of Koranic exegesis before-mentioned; but Soudi asserts Hajji Kiwameddin Hassan to have been the benefactor in question and (as the Orientals say) "God [alone] is most (i. e. all) knowing!" It may here also be conveniently explained (in replacement of an accidentally omitted note) that these and other Viziers are styled by Hafiz the "*Asefs* of the time" in a complimentary sense, as likening them to Solomon's famous but mythical Vizier, Asef ben Berkhiya, who is the Muslim type of good government.

[4] A fact which testifies to the comparatively high culture and esteem for poetry and poets of the people of mediæval Asia and one which it would be difficult to match in our ruder days. One cannot, for instance, imagine any special consideration being shown to Mr. Swinburne, as the greatest of living poets, by French, Russian or even Prussian invaders of London.

[5] See Odes CLXVII, CCLXXVI, CCLXXVII, CCCLXXX, CCCCXVIII, CCCCXXXVIII, CCCCLIII, CCCCLVI, DLXXVIII and Skinker-Rime, also Odes DXIII and DXXII, in which Mensour's Finance Minister, Imadeddin, is mentioned.

[6] Ode CCCCXCVII.

[7] Five years after that of Timour.

[8] See Odes CCLIII, CCLXX, CCCXCI etc.

[9] See Odes CCXIV, CCCCXCVII, etc.

[10] See Ode CLVIII.

[11] According to the biographers, such of the (as yet uncollected) poems of Hafiz as were accessible were cut up into slips, each containing a single couplet, and thrown into an urn, from which a young child was deputed to draw a slip at random. The couplet drawn was the last of Ode LX, i. e. "Withhold not the foot from the funeral of Hafiz; For, though he be drowned in sin, he fareth to heaven"; which, of course, formed a victorious answer to the poet's traducers. The story is probably apocryphal; but the custom of using the Divan of Hafiz for bibliomantic purposes, after the fashion of the Sortes Coranicae, Virgilianae, Biblicae etc., has long been established in the East.

[12] See Traité des Écritures Cunéiformes par le Comte A. de Gobineau.

[13] In this connection it may be interesting to note a fact which has been overlooked by the translators and commentators of Hafiz, to wit, that Soufism, which is now (like Agnosticism with us) a mere abstract opinion, its place as an active religious force having been, to a great extent, taken by Bâbism, appears, on the evidence of his poems, to have been, in Hafiz's time, a regular *business*, the affiliates of the sect forming, it would seem, an ordinary mendicant order, like the Dervishes, Fakirs and Calenders of the present day, the members of which, like the latter, contrived, under colour of religious enthusiasm and on pretence of the practice of extreme asceticism, to fare royally at the expense of the credulous and wealthy of the day, putting in action by anticipation the doctrine of the Sage of Wapping; "Them as has plenty money and no brains is meant for them as has plenty brains and no money." It will be seen that Hafiz, in many passages of his poems, accuses the Soufis of his day of being, not only hypocrites and impostors, but thieves and "oppressors", i.e. reprobates and malefactors, of the deepest dye.

[14] v. Kheyyam, Q. 296.

[15] "Celui que Dieu a touché est toujours un être à part; il est, quoiqu'il fasse, déplacé parmi les hommes; on le reconnait à un signe. Il n'a point de compagnon parmi ceux de son age; pour lui les jeunes filles n'ont point de sourire".—*Renan.* "L'exilé partout est seul".—*Paroles d'un Croyant.*

## A. J. Arberry (essay date 1946)

SOURCE: "Hafiz and His English Translators," in *Islamic Culture*, Vol. XX, No. 2 and 3, April, 1946 and July, 1946, pp. 111-28, 229-49.

[*In the following essay, Arberry, who has himself translated Hafiz's works, traces the history of English translations of the poems of Hafiz.*]

I

A century and a half ago, when the East India Company had but recently stumbled into a great Imperial inheritance in Bengal, and its servants were concerned to equip themselves linguistically for the onerous responsibilities that had settled upon their shoulders, it was a mark of polite culture in the brilliant society of Calcutta to be able to illustrate a point or adorn an argument with quotations from the Persian poets. War-ren Hastings was himself an early convert to the fashion, which continued well into the nineteenth century, until in fact Persian ceased to be the common medium of politics and business in the ruined Mughal Empire, and Macaulay was pleased to condemn the scholars of India because they were ignorant of Greek and Latin. In this interval the vogue of Persian poetry spread rapidly from India to England, and from England to the Continent. This was the background against which Edward Fitzgerald grew up; otherwise it could hardly have occurred to him to spend his time and convert his genius translating the quatrains of Omar Khayyam. Of the many Persian poets whose words were on the lips of these enthusiastic orientalists, none enjoyed greater esteem and admiration than Hafiz of Shiraz. It was a devotion that persisted through three generations, bridging the years that separate Sir William Jones from Gertrude Bell. A book could be written about all the Englishmen and Englishwomen who have worshipped at the shrine of Hafiz: this article only touches the fringe of the matter, in accordance with the Arabic saying that what cannot be entirely attained need not therefore be entirely abandoned.

Travellers in Persia during the seventeenth century, among them Sir Thomas Herbert, did not fail to report on the esteem in which Hafiz was held by his fellow-countrymen. But, so far as can be traced, the first English scholar to translate any of the poems of Hafiz was Thomas Hyde (1636-1703), a Cambridge scholar who succeeded Edward Pococke the Elder as Laudian Professor of Arabic at Oxford; and is best known for his remarkably learned treatise on the religion of the Ancient Persians (*Historia Riligionis Veterum Persanem,* Oxford, 1700), and his edition and translation (Oxford, 1665) of the astronomical tables (*Zij*) of Ulugh Beg, the grandson of Tamerlane. Hyde was an adventurous scholar, and made the most of his opportunities as Bodley's librarian to indulge a Catholic taste for linguistics; but it is not necessary for us here to follow him in his easy progress through Samaritan, Ethiopic, Syriac, Pahlawi, Singhalese, Telugu, Tartar and Chinese. It was probably about the year 1690 that he transcribed the first Ghazal of Hafiz and rendered it into Latin, with the aid of a Turkish commentary: This trifle was ultimately printed in 1767, in the second volume of Gregory Sharp's edition of Hyde's miscellanea.

It happened that Hyde's halting attempt first came before the public at a time when a far greater oriental scholar, in the first fresh enthusiasm of youthful erudition, discovered for himself that Persian poetry was a rich and yet unexplored mine of glittering jewels, and Hafiz the brightest among them. Sir William Jones (1746-1794), newly a fellow of University College, Oxford, had just begun work on his remarkable thesis on Asiatic poetry (though the *Poeseos Asiatical Commentarionem Libri Sex* were not published until 1774), and was already familiar with the Persian Language. Early in 1768 he met Count Reviczki, a Polish diplomat who was a true fellow-spirit: the new friends were inexpressibly delighted to find they shared a boundless admiration for Persian poetry. Reviczki was especially interested in Hafiz, and from time to time sent Jones 'une de mes dernières traductions. . . . dont je n'amuse qudque fois quand J'ai du loisir': he published a small selection of the odes with a Latin translation at Vienna in 1771. But Jones had already preceded him in the mission of introducing the Nightingale of Shiraz to the cultured society of Europe. Being commissioned by King Christian VII of Denmark to prepare a French translation of a Persian biography of Nadir Shah, he improved the occasion by publishing as an appendix (1770) French verse-translations of thirteen Ghazals of Hafiz. Thus the first poetical translation of Hafiz ever to be printed by an Englishman were actually done in French, and that of excellent quality. A single example will perhaps be sufficient illustration . . .

O toi, léger & doux Zéphire,
Quand tu passes par le séjour
Où l'objet de mon tendre amour
Entousé des grâces respire,
Fais qu'au retour, selon mes vocux.
Ton habine soit parfumée
De cette senteur embaumée
Qu'épand l'ambre se ses cheveux.
Que de son souffle favorable
Mon être seroit ranimé,
Si par toi de mon bien-aimé
J'avois un message agréable!
Si trop foible tu ne peux pas
Porter ce poids, à ma prière
Jette sur moi de la poussière,
Que tu recueilles sous ses pas.

Mon âme languit dans l'attente
De son retour si désiré,
Ah! quand ce visage adoré
Viendra-t-il la rendre contente?
Le pin put moins haut que mon cœur,
A présent au saule semblable,

Pour cet objet incomparable
Il tremble d'amoureuse ardeur.

Quoique celui que mon cœur aime,
Pour ma tendresse ait peu d'égards,
Hélas! pour unde ses regards
Je donnerois l'univers même.
Que ce seroit un bien pour moi,
Puisqu' à ses pieds le sort m'enchaine,
De n'avoir d'autre soin ni peine,
De ne vivre que pour mon Roi.

We see in this rendering a characteristic that marks a far more famous version of Hafiz which Jones published in the following year in his *Grammar of the Persian Language*, namely, the expansion of the original Persian to something like one and a half times its length. This feature, which has appeared in many translations by other hands—though seldom to so great an extent—has often been discussed, and the conclusion has generally been reached that it is inevitable: having regard to the fact that many of the ideas and figures used by Hafiz are unfamiliar to a Western reader not versed in the religious, literary and historical background of the Persian poet, it seems beyond hope to achieve the same pregnant brevity and concise felicity of phrase in any other language if the richness and variety of Hafiz style are in any way to be reproduced. The celebrated version now to be quoted scored a remarkable success immediately upon publication, and has remained a firm favourite ever since: in fact, until outshone by the brilliancy of Fitzgerald's *Rubáiyát*, it *was* Persian poetry for the vast majority of English readers not familiar with the Persian language. . . .

Sweet maid, if thou would'st charm my sight,
And bid these arms thy neck infold;
That rosy cheek, that lily hand
Would give thy poet more delight
Than all Bocara's vaunted gold,
Than all the gems of Samarcand.

Boy, let yon liquid ruby flow,
And bid thy pensive heart be glad,
Whate'er the frowning zealots say:
Tell them, their Eden cannot show
A stream so clear as Rocnabad,
A bower so sweet as Mosellay.

O! when these fair perfidious maids,
Whose eyes our secret haunts infest,
Their dear destructive charms display;
Each glance my tender breast invades,
And robe my wounded soul of rest,
As Tartars seize their destin'd prey.

In vain with love our bosoms glow:
Can all our tears, can all our sighs,
New lustre to those charms impart?

Can cheeks, where living roses blow,
Where nature spreads her richest dyes,
Require the borrow'd gloss of art?

Speak not of fate: Oh! Change the theme,
And talk of odours, talk of wine,
Talk of the flowers that round us bloom:
'Tis all a cloud, 'tis all a dream;
To love and joy thy thoughts confine,
Nor hope to pierce the sacred gloom.

Beauty has such resistless power,
That ever the chaste Egyptian dame
Sigh'd for the blooming Hebrew boy!
For her how fatal was the hour,
When to the banks of Nilus came
A youth so lovely and so coy!

But oh! sweet maid, my counsel hear
(Youth should attend when those advise
Whom long experience renders sage):
While music charms the ravish'd ear;
While sparkling cups delight our eyes,
Be gay; and scorn the frowns of age.

What cruel answer have I heard!
And yet, by heaven, I love thee still:
Can aught be cruel from thy lip?
Yet say, how fell that bitter word
From lips which streams of sweetness fill,
Which nought but drops of honey sip?

Go boldly forth, my simple lay,
Whose accents flow with artless ease,
Like orient pearls at random strung:
Thy notes are sweet, the damsels say;
But O! far sweeter, if they please
The nymph for whom these notes are sung.

'As a translation the *song* is open to serious criticism,' writes Professor R. M. Hewitt in a recent issue of *English Studies*. 'The rhyme system and the stanza are remote from those of the original, and there is no approach to the rhythm. The matter of the poem has been inflated by exactly a half.' These comments are very true; though as regards rhythm it is worth pointing out that Jones's octosyllables are not so very far short of exactly reproducing the *Hazaj* of Hafiz. But there are other more fundamental issues raised by this version than those mentioned by Professor Hewitt. Several translators have made the attempt to put Hafiz into English in the exact metres and rhyme-schemes of the original; of these experiments more will be said later; but Jones is at least equal in boldness to any who have not feared, where it took their fancy, to substitute an English for a Persian figure, and even to introduce wholly original images that lack all justification if strict fidelity is to be the criterion of poetic translations. But is this to be the criterion? Let Richard Le Gallienne,

who in his own way is at least as bold as Jones, argue the case for the defence. Surely the only service of a translation is to make the foreign poet a poet of one's own country not to present him as a half-Anglicized foreigner speaking neither his own language nor our own! It is beyond dispute that many of the versifiers who have tried to produce 'faithful' versions of Hafiz have only succeeded in robbing him of every poetic quality. Jones's *Persian Song* is not Hafiz, and Fitzgerald's *Rubáiyát* is certainly not Omar Khayyam, but both give the uninitiated English reader a good opinion of Persian poetry, and that may be regarded as a great compensation for any lack of verbal or rhythmic fidelity. Jones writes in the authentic manner of his age, the age of Pope and Gray and Goldsmith; it would have been an unparalleled literary miracle if he had not; but his writing has the enduring quality of the true classic, and gives pleasure even today. Finally, the *Persian Song* encouraged many in Jones's day and later to take up the study of Persian; and that in itself is a sufficient testimonial to its merit. For it must be remembered that Jones, in pleading the cause of Persian poetry, was in his day a pioneer of pioneers; and, like all pioneers, he found himself confronted by a solid wall of conservative prejudice. Literary criticism was still the handmaid of the classical tradition, and it savoured almost of blasphemy for a man to suggest that Hafiz the Persian was at least as worthy of study and imitation as Anacreon the Greek and Horace the Roman. So Jones was obliged to apologise for his boldness. 'I must request, that, in bestowing these praises on the writings of *Asia*, I may not be thought to derogate from the merit of the *Greek* and *Latin* poems, which have justly been admired in every age; yet I cannot but think that our *European* poetry has subsisted too long on the perpetual repetition of the same images, and incessant allusions to the same fables: and it has been my endeavour for several years to inculcate this truth, that, if the principal writings of the *Asiatics*, which are deposited in our public libraries, were pointed out with the usual advantage of notes and illustrations, and if the languages of the *Eastern* nations were studied in our great seminaries of learning, where every other branch of useful knowledge is taught to perfection, a new and ample field would be opened for speculation; we should have a more extensive insight into the history of the human mind; we should be furnished with a new set of images and similitudes; and a number of excellent compositions would be brought to light, which future scholars might explain, and future poets might imitate.'

Before leaving Sir William Jones, who certainly did more than any other European scholar, before or since his time, to establish in the West a true appreciation of Persian poetry, it will not be without interest to furnish two further illustrations of his astonishing virtuosity, this time in the form of a Latin verse translation of an ode of Hafiz, first published in his volume of *Poems*

(1772), and a Greek rendering of another in the style of Theocritus, printed in his *Poeteos Adsiaticæ Commentari* (1774). . . .

Jam rosa purpureum caput explicat. Adsit, amici,
    Sauvis voluptatum cohors:
        sic monûere senes.

Nunc laeti sumus: at citiùs laeta avolat ætas.
    Quin sacra permutem mero
        Scragula nectareo?

Dulcè gemit zephyrus. Ridentem mitte puellam,
    Quan molli in amplexu tenens
        Pocula laeta biban.

Tange chelyn. Sævit fortuna; at mitte querelas.
    Cur non canoros barbiti
        Elicimus modulos?

Ea! florum regina nitet rosa. Fundite vini,
    Quod Amoris extinguat facem,
        Rectareos latices.

Suavè loquens Philomela vocor: Quî fiat ut umbrâ
    Tectus rosarum nexili
        (Veris avis) taceam? . . .

## II

Three years after Jones and Reviczki published their first versions of Hafiz, a colleague of Jones at the Temple, John Richardson (1741-1811), fired by this double example, and animated with the desire to provide servants of the East India Company with materials for their Persian studies, produced a small volume containing the text, literal and verse translations, and detailed analysis of three odes of Hafiz. Richardson is best known for his Persian-Arabic-English dictionary which, founded on the earlier publication of Meninski, and later revised by Francis Johnson and Sir Charles Wilkins, served three generations as a standard work of reference, until in fact it was displaced by Steingass. His methods as a translator were closely similar to those of Jones, and his versions are marked by a polished elegance which gives cause for regret that he did not attempt more. For example, two stanzas from his rendering of Hafiz' first ode, the same which Hyde did into Latin: we give Hyde's translation for purpose of comparison . . .

Agedum, O Pincema, circunmitte poculam & præbe illud:
Amor enim poimò facilio videatur, sed accidunt tamen difficilia.

Propter odorem Moschothecæ, quam subsolani extremitas ex illis
    antiis aperit;

Propter crispaturam cincinnorum ejus suaveoleutium,
    quantus incidit cordibus ardor!

Fill, fill the cup with sparkling wine,
Deep let me drink the juice divine,
    To soothe my tortured heart:
For love, who seemed at first so mild,
So gently looked, so gaily smil'd,
    Here deep has plunged the dart.

When, sweeter than the damask rose,
From Leila's locks the Zephyr blows,
    How glows my keen dèsire!
I chide the wanton gale's delay,
I'm jealous of his am'rous play,
    And all my soul's on fire.

In order to follow the chronological sequence of Hafiz's English translators it is now necessary to transport ourselves, as Jones had done in 1783, from London to Calcutta, where we find Francis Gladwin (d. *circa* 1813), sometime officer in the Bengal Army, and encouraged by Warren Hastings to continue his Persian studies, sponsoring in 1785 and 1786 the two volumes of the short-lived *Asiatick Miscellany*. This ill-fated periodical during its brief career permitted the publication of a number of versions from Hafiz by several hands. Jones himself contributed many articles on Persian and Sanskrit subjects to the *Miscellany*; a good number of these are unsigned; and the second volume contains two anonymous versions of Hafiz, one over the initial H and the other subscribed HH, which have the unmistakable timber of this great scholar's work: the attribution is strengthened by the fact that H also stands below a quatrain whose ascription to Jones is attested by his biographer Lord Teignmouth as well as the *Thraliana,* and which is printed under his name in *The Oxford Book of English Verse*; the little poem has had a great vogue, and it will not be without interest to supply its original in Persian. . . .

On parent knees, a naked new-born child,
Weeping thou sat'st, when all around thee smil'd:
So live, that, sinking in thy last long sleep,
Calm thou may'st smile, when all around thee weep.

The version of Hafiz, initialled H, is a rendering of the well-known *Mukhammas* whose authenticity is now generally rejected by Persian editors: the poem does not occur in the oldest manuscripts of the Diwan. An extract will suffice to prove the translation's charm. . . .

Blest idol, view, absorb'd in Love,
    Thy helpless victim's fate.

In thee alone I live and move,
    Ah! see my wretched state.

Yet, should a thousand lives renew my soul,
At thy dear feet I sacrifice the whole.

When shall kind fortune be my friend?
    When shall thy pitying breast

Permit thy suppliant to attend,
    And urge his heart's request?

O when, bright tow'ring eagle, will thou deign
To grace his nest, and hear his plaintive
    strain?

Is cruelty familiar grown,
    Yet from its ways depart:

Delight in misery disown—
    Thou hast no iron heart;

O come, my love, pass o'er thy votary's head,
Which prostrate o'er thy threshold's dust is
    laid.

The other verse translations of Hafiz contained in the *Asiatick Miscellany* are the work of 'the late Capt. Thomas Ford' and of Thomas Law. The former is of a poem which is certainly not genuine, and therefore hardly merits attention. The latter deserves less summary treatment, if only for the sake of its translator. Thomas Law (1759-1834), seventh son of a bishop of Carlisle, went to India in 1773, and resigned from the Company's service in 1791 on the customary grounds of ill-health. Perhaps under Jones's influence, he conceived an admiration for the young republic on the other side of the Atlantic, and spent the latter part of his life in the United States, where he made a name and lost a fortune by interesting himself in American Currency questions: his second wife was a granddaughter of Mrs. Curtis, whose second husband was George Washington; he was one of the chief mourners at Washington's funeral. His 'imitation' of Hafiz is sufficiently pedestrian, but here it is, with its value as a curiosity . . .

My bosom grac'd with each gay flow'r,
    I grasp the bowl, my nymph in glee;
The monarch of the world that hour,
    Is but a slave compar'd to me.

Intrude not with the taper's light,
    My social friends, with beaming eyes;
Trundle around a starry night,
    And lo! my nymph the moon supplies.

Away, thy sprinkling odours spare,
    Be not officiously thus kind,
The waving ringlets of my Fair,
    Shed perfume to the fainting wind.

My ears th' enlivening notes inspire,
    As luta or harp alternate sound;
My eyes those ruby lips admire,
    Or catch the glasses sparkling round.

Then let no moments steal away,
    Without thy mistress and thy wine;
The spring flowers blossom to decay,
    And youth but glows to own decline.

From Calcutta we now return to London and the most ambitious enterprise yet: seventeen *Select Odes* edited and translated into English verse. This volume was a product of the fluent pen of John Nott (1751-1825), a noted scholar in his day. Originally trained as a physician, he travelled out to China in 1783 as surgeon of an East Indiaman, and turned three years' absence from home to good account by learning Persian; these translations of Hafiz were the first and solitary fruits of his excursion into orientalism. Thereafter he roved over a wide field of studies; translated Latin, Greek and Italian classics; established himself as an authority on Elizabethan poetry; but wrote such long and tedious annotations on George Wither as to provoke the disgust of Charles Lamb and the subsequent sarcasm of Swinburne. He was also renowned as a conversationalist, which presumably means that he talked as readily and variedly as he wrote. His versions of Hafiz are quite pleasing in the eighteenth century manner, and he courteously acknowledged his debt to Reviczki, Richard-son and Jones. The specimen which follows is characteristic of his style . . .

Go, friendly Zephyr! whisp'ring great
Yon gentle fawn with slender feet;
Say that in quest of her I rove
The dangerous steeps, the wilds of love.

Thou merchant who dost sweetness vend
(Long may kind heav'n thy life defend!)
Ah, why unfriendly thus forget
Thy am'rous sweet-billed parroquet?

Is it, O rose! thy beauty's pride
That casts affection far aside,
Forbidding thee to court the tale
Of thy fond mate, the nightingale?

I know not why 'tis rare to see
The colour of sincerity
In nymphs who boast majestic grace,
Dark eyes, and silver-beaming face.

What tho' that face be angel fair,
One fault does all its beauty mar;

Nor faith, nor constancy adorn
Thy charms, which else might shame the
 moon.

By gentle manner we controul
The wise, the sense-illumin'd soul:
No idle lure, no glitt'ring bait
Th' experienc'd bird will captivate.

What wonder, Hafiz, that thy strain,
Whose sounds inchant the etherial plain,
Should tempt each graver star to move
In dances with the star of love?

### III

All the preceding translators had laboured under the handicap of having to establish their text of Hafiz on the authority of manuscripts, often faulty, always inflated, for no poet has suffered more than the Nightingale of Shiraz from the felonious attentions of later versifiers' ambitions to win currency for their own creations by signing them with his name. The first printed edition of Hafiz came from Upjohn's Calcutta Press in 1791, set up in the *Nasta'liq* types designed and cast by Sir Charles Wilkins: the book never had a very wide circulation, and few copies came to this country; it is now a great rarity. The text of Upjohn's edition leaves much to be desired, but at all events it was a step in the right direction, and a material help to students in India. John Haddon Hindley (1765-1827), the next to make a volume of Hafiz, was not able to use the 1791 edition, but had good manuscripts at his disposal in the Chatham Library at Manchester, which was in his charge when his **Persian Lyrics** (London, 1800) appeared. Hindley, like Richardson, never went East, but his work—he also did the *Pand-Namah* of 'Attar—is none the worse for that. He was the first to discuss at length and in detail the problems involved in translating Hafiz, and his remarks are still memorable. 'To give a literal or perfect translation of our author metrically, or even prosaically, into *English*, may be confidently pronounced impossible. An obvious proof of this assertion will be found, on considering for a moment those oppugnancies, which occur so generally in the idiomatic construction of the languages of England and Iran, and which must ever most effectually militate against such closeness of version. Whatever might be looked for from favourable analogies, the frequent and varied allusions from words of similar sound and formation, though generally of exactly opposite signification, as well as the lively and often recondite *lusus verborum*, so common in the *Arabic* and *Persian*, and which, though strange, if not trifling, to a *European* ear, are, to the habitual feelings of the *Asiatic*, both choice and exquisite. These obstacles, I say, must alone render every chance of translative imitation in this case completely hopeless." Hindley

next passes to another obstacle—the frequent use of compound words in Persian poetry, impossible to reproduce in elegant English. He also refers pertinently to the problems raised by Hafiz's habitual use of Sufi imagery. The next point which calls for comment is the very construction of the Persian ode, with its repetitive monorhyme: here Hindley's comments are indeed worth pondering by all who may even yet be unconvinced, despite the palpable failure of previous experiments that the form of the Ghazal cannot be imitated in English. 'The constant recurrence of the same rhyme. . . . is not suited to our language, which, as has been often observed by critics, will not bear reiterated monotonies. In such cases, then, he (the translator) may surely dispense with the minutiæ of punctilious imitation, 'provided he strictly confine himself to the prominent ideas of his original, where no eccentricities oppose him.' In this remarkable preface Hindley also discusses a further point of great interest even yet, namely, the criticism levelled against the Persian ode that it consists of a string of unconnected and incoherent ideas. This charge is still brought from time to time, as in the recent paper *Harmonious Jones* by Professor Hewitt from which we have already quoted: 'This particular ode of Hafiz,' writes the critic, referring to the original of Jones's **Persian Song**, 'is more than usually incoherent, and what unity it possesses comes from the rhyme which is the same throughout and occurs ten times.' Later in this paper we shall return to this criticism: for the present it is instructive to see how Hindley in his day answered the same charge. He maintains that Hafiz is in fact far less guilty of the alleged incoherency than most of his compatriots, and that what looseness and variety of images do occur in his poems can be readily condoned in a lyric poet. Besides, 'if we attend only to the time, the place, the object, the intention and the imagery of each *Ghazal,* the ideas for the most part appear to flow naturally, and without any absurd or harsh transition: and surely in these lighter rhapsodies, the coruscations of wit, the effusions of tenderness, and the luxuriant sallies of an unrestrained and impassioned imagination, may be fairly presumed to have been aided by the delicious wines, by the joyous symposiacs, and by the instructive and delightful *Macamat* of *Shiraz,* just as similar poetical beauties are reported to have arisen from similarly stimulating and exhilarating causes in that truly *Hafizian* poetry so immediately present to classical recollection, which sings the praises of *Teios, Mitylene and Falemum.* Under these circumstances, therefore, the translator will only have to allow our author, what he finds in the Grecian and Roman lyric poets, and what we should be willing to allow any poet of our own, the liberty of glancing with the frenzied eye of inspiration from earth to heaven, from heaven to earth, in search of objects adopted to the subject of his composition; and, after attending to the minute turns of the versification, we suspect, it will be his own fault, if he finds an unsurmountable difficulty in explaining his author's meaning in a manner so perceptibly connected as to avoid exciting disgust in an English reader.' One last counsel Hindley adds. The Persian language, he reminds his readers, is still only imperfectly and rarely understood in England, though the situation is improving; Persian poetry is as yet exotic fare; therefore, do not serve up too much of it at a time, for 'by attempting too much, we may disgust, instead of pleasing.' How salutary a warning, even for the present day! Hindley himself heeded it, by only translating eleven odes; we again confine ourselves to a single illustration of his methods, choosing for the purpose his version of the poem which we selected as characterising Sir William Jones's still as a versifier in French:

Zephyr, should'st thou chance to rove
By the mansion of my love,
From her locks ambrosial bring
Choicest odours on thy wing.

Could'st thou waft me from her breast
Tender sighs to say I'm blest,
As she lives! my soul would be
Sprinkl'd o'er with ecstasy.

But if Heav'n the boon deny,
Round her stately footsteps fly,
With the dust that thence may rise,
Stop the tears which bathe these eyes.

Lost, poor mendicant! I roam
Begging, craving she would come:
Where shall I thy phantom see,
Where, dear nymph, a glimpse of thee?

Like the mind-tost reed my breast
Fann'd with hope is ne'er at rest,
Throbbing, longing to excess
Her fair figure to caress.

Yes, my charmer, tho' I see
Thy heart courts no love with me,
Not for worlds, could they be mine,
Would I give a hair of thine.

Why, O care! shall I in vain
Strive to shun thy galling chain,
When these strains still fail to save,
And make Hafiz more a slave.

Hindley dedicated his volume to Sir William Ouseley, 'an able and zealous restorer of oriental literature in Great Britain at the close of the Eighteenth Century.' Sir William had himself published a number of prose-translations of Hafiz in his *Persian Miscellanies* (London, 1795) and *Oriental Collections* (London, 1797-1800); but as the subject of prose renderings of Hafiz in general falls outside the scope of this paper, further reference to these attempts would be superfluous. Simi-

larly we do not propose to comment on the prose-versions offered by Sir Gore Ouseley (1770-1844) in his *Biographical Notices of Persian Poets* (London, 1846), but will only quote his estimate of Hafiz that 'his style is clear, unaffected, and harmonious, displaying at the same time great learning, matured science, and intimate knowledge of the hidden as well as the apparent nature of things; but, above all, a certain fascination of expression unequalled by any other poet.'

IV

The generation of Sir William Jones had thus paid no mean tribute to the greatest lyric poet of Persia: if the versions produced during those thirty years exhibit a marked uniformity of style and spirit, the matter is easily explained on two scores—the still strong influence of the classical tradition in English poetry, not yet demolished by the Romantics, and the overwhelming personal authority of Jones himself, unchallenged in his lifetime and undisputed for many years after his premature death. But while the inspiration of these versions of a Persian poet now began to work itself out ever more widely in the English poetry and verse of the nineteenth century, Hafiz himself, like all his compatriots, presently suffered the same neglect in this country which befell all oriental studies. While the German von Hammer (Tübingen 1812) and Rozenzweigschwannau (Vienna 1856-1864) translated the entire Diwan, the latter into creditable verse interleaved with a sumptuous though inflated edition of the text, and H. Brockhaus (Leipzig 1854-1856) printed the first eighty odes with a Turkish commentary, it was not until 1875 that the next volume of English verse-translations appeared, though two years earlier S. Robinson published *A Century of Ghazals in Prose*. Credit for this belated revival of Hafiz studies belongs to Herman Bicknell (1830-1875), a remarkable character: having studied medicine, he joined the army as a surgeon, saw service in India, China, Kashmir and Tibet, and in 1862, taking the name of Muhammad 'Abd al-Wahid, made the pilgrimage to Mecca undisguised. Bicknell spent many years with his Hafiz, and went so far as to live for a time at Shiraz 'with the object of clearing up doubtful points, and of becoming personally acquainted with the localities mentioned by the poet.' The appearance of his production was a result of brotherly piety, for Bicknell died before he could see his volume through the press: C. E. Wilson gave a helping hand in getting the book into proper shape. It is an ornate work, florid after the bastard Persian style of the mid-Victorian period to which it belongs: it contains versified translations of no fewer than 189 odes, as well as numerous other pieces. E. G. Browne names Bicknell as one of the three most successful English translators of Hafiz, and in his *Literary History of Persia* quotes two of his renderings, only to establish their inferiority to Miss Gertrude Bell's. To rank Bicknell third in the imposing concourse of Hafiz-worshippers is to pay him too much honour, though quantitively his work is certainly considerable: yet in quality his versions are not wholly lacking in merit, their chief fault being that they aim at too strict a literalness to be truly poetic. Here we give a typical specimen, rather pedestrian, very workmanlike, and still smelling of the midnight oil: the joyous rapture of the original is almost wholly vanished . . .

> In blossom is the crimson rose, and the rapt
> *bulbul* trills his song;
> A summons that to revel calls you, O Sufis,
> wine-adoring throng!
>
> The fabric of my contrite fervour appeared
> upon a rock to bide;
> Yet see how by a crystal goblet it hath been
> shattered in its pride.
>
> Bring wine; for to a lofty spirit, should they at
> its tribunal be,
> What were the sentry, what the Sultan, the
> toper or the foe of glee?
>
> Forth from this hostel of two portals as finally
> thou needst must go.
> What if the porch and arch of Being be of
> high span or meanly low?
>
> To bliss's goal we gain not access, if sorrow
> has been tasted not;
> Yea, with *Alastu's* pact was coupled the
> sentence of our baleful lot.
>
> At Being and Not-being fret not, but either
> with calm temper see:
> Not-being is the term appointed for the most
> lovely things that be.
>
> Asaf's display, the airy courser, the language
> which the birds employed
> The wind has swept; and their possessor no
> profit from his wealth
> enjoyed.
> Oh! fly not from thy pathway upward, for the
> winged shaft that
> quits the bow
> A moment to the air has taken, to settle in the
> dust below.
>
> What words of gratitude, O Hafiz,
> Shall thy reed's tongue express anon,
> As its choice gems of composition
> From hands to other hands pass on?

In 1877 E. H. Palmer (1840-1882) published his *Song of the Reed*, a collection of verses original and translated. Palmer was a competent Persian scholar and a good draftsman, and his tragic early death cut short a career of great promise still largely unfulfilled. His six versions from Hafiz contained in this volume are pleasing after the mid-Victorian manner, not at all like the polished classical style of Jones, quiet reading for the heavily-curtained drawing-room, with little inspiration but sound scholarship and good taste. We again choose one of Hafiz's most popular lyrics to illustrate; though its authenticity is highly questionable . . .

> O minstrel! sing thy lay divine,
> Freshly fresh and newly new!
> Bring me the heart-expanding wine,
> Freshly fresh and newly new!
>
> Seated beside a maiden fair,
> I gaze with a loving and raptured view,
> And I sip her lip and caress her hair,
> Freshly fresh and newly new!
>
> Who of the fruit of life can share,
> Yet scorn to drink of the grapes's sweet
> dew?
> Then drain a cut to thy mistress fair,
> Freshly fresh and newly new!
>
> She who has stolen my heart away
> Heightens her beauty's rosy hue,
> Decketh herself in rich array,
> Freshly fresh and newly new!
>
> Balmy breath of the western gale,
> Waft to her ears my love-song true;
> Tell her poor love-lorn Hafiz's tale,
> Freshly fresh and newly new!

## V

Twenty years passed over Palmer's little-remembered volume of verses, and then was published what by general consent takes rank as the most successful attempt so far made to translate Hafiz, body and soul, into the English idiom. In *Poems from the Divan of Hafiz* (1897) Gertrude Bell (1867-1926) made her first bow to the world of letters: it is a brilliant and remarkable performance, one that makes every lover of Persian poetry regret that the unusual talents there displayed should never again have been employed in the same direction. Of these translations, 43 in all, E. G. Browne has written that they 'are true poetry of a very high order and, with perhaps the single exception of Fitzgerald's paraphrase of the Quatrains of 'Umar Khayyam are probably the finest and most truly poetical renderings of any Persian poet in the English language.' Miss Bell turned her back on the Bicknell school, that is the translators who conceive it to be their task to make their versions as literal as the bondage of verse-form permits, and equal in length to the original and went back to the older tradition of Jones.

E. G. Browne, who appears to have been somewhat allurgic to Jones, wrote of his versions that they 'are pretty enough,' but 'can hardly be dignified by the name of poetry, and are, moreover, so free that they can scarcely be called translations'; yet of Miss Bell's he wrote that 'though rather free, they are in my opinion by far the most artistic, and, so far as the spirit of Hafiz is concerned, the most faithful renderings of his poetry.' This praise of a contemporary worker was undoubtedly fully merited, but the verdict on a great predecessor is surely unjust: both Jones and Gertrude Bell were true children of their environment, and a true comparison between their productions must take into account other factors than fidelity and impassionedness—it must be based on the criteria of English literary history. Moreover, while judgments involving what is called the spirit of an original and its reproduction in the version are necessarily tenures, it is not without interest to recall that Miss Bell herself confessed, 'I am very conscious that my appreciation of the poet is that of the Western. Exactly on what grounds he is appreciated in the East it is difficult to determine, and what his compatriots make of his teaching it is perhaps impossible to understand.' That is at first reading a startling statement, but no doubt allowance should be made for a very great degree of modesty, natural and becoming enough in a young scholar taking the stage for the first time. At all events, let us turn for the present from these abstractions and consider our concrete materials, the versions themselves; and, since comparisons though odious are always instructive and sometimes illuminating, let us examine what Gertrude Bell made of one or two poems which had already exercised her predecessors. First, her idea of Jones's ***Persian Song***:

> Oh Turkish maid of Shiraz! in thy hand
> If thou'st take my heart, for the mole on thy
>   cheek
> I would barter Bokhara and Samarkand.
> Bring, Cup-bearer all that is left of the wine!
> In the Garden of Paradise vainly thou'lt seek
> The lip of the fountain of Ruknabad,
> And the bowers of Mosalla where roses twine.
> They have filled the city with blood and broil,
> Those soft-voiced Lulis for whom we sigh;
> As Turkish robbers fall on their spoil,
> They have robbed and plundered the peace of
>   my heart.
> Dowered is my mistress, a beggar am I;
> What shall I bring her? a beautiful face
> Needs nor jewel nor mole nor the tiring-
>   maid's art.
>
> Brave tales of singers and wine relate,
> The key to the Hidden 'twere vain to seek;
> No wisdom of ours has unlocked that gate,
> And locked to our wisdom it still shall be.
> But of Joseph's beauty the lute shall speak;

> And the minstrel knows that Zuleika came
>   forth,
> Love parting the curtains of modesty.
>
> When thou spokest ill of thy servant 'twas
>   well—
> God pardon thee! for thy words were sweet;
> Not unwelcomed the bitterest answer fell
> From lips where the ruby and sugar lay.
> But, fair Love, let good counsel direct thy
>   feet,
> Far dearer to youth than dear life itself
> Are the warnings of one grown wise—and
>   grey!
> The song is sung and the pearl is strung;
> Come hither, Oh Hafiz, and sing again!
> And the listening Heavens above thee hung
> Shall loose o'er thy verse the Pleiades' chain.

This version is unquestionably more faithful than Jones's and it is also shorter, in fact, roughly equal to the original in length: but its style is equally unquestionably less mature, and it contains few memorable lines or phrases. Nevertheless, it is both competent and attractive: yet it is by no means the translator's best.

Secondly, Miss Bell's rendering of Palmer's pleasant verses.

> Singer, sweet singer, fresh notes strew,
>   Fresh and afresh and new and new!
> Heart-gladdening wine thy lips imbrue,
>   Fresh and afresh and new and new!
>
> Saki, thy radiant feet I hail;
> Flush with red wine the goblets pale,
> Flush our pale cheeks to drunken hue,
>   Fresh and afresh and new and new!
>
> Then with thy love to toy with thee
> Rest thee, Oh, rest! when none can see;
> Seek thy delight, for kisses sue,
>   Fresh and afresh and new and new!
>
> Here round thy life thy vine is twined;
> Drink! for elsewhere what wine wild find?
> Drink to her name, to hours that flew,
>   Hours ever fresh and new and new!
>
> She that has stolen my heart from me,
> How does she wield her empery?
> Paints and adorns and scents her too,
>   Fresh and afresh and new and new!
>
> Wind of the dawn that passest by,
> Swift to the street of my fairy hie,
> Whisper the tale of Hafiz true,
>   Fresh and afresh and new and new!

This is a notable achievement, for with a minimum of extraneous comment the translator has brilliantly succeeded in reproducing the true form of the original Persian, even including the internal rhyme; and her verses have a lilt and a pace which put them far above Palmer's in poetic fervour, while at least equalling his in fidelity.

Thirdly, what is one of Miss Bell's finest renderings, which to compare with Bicknell's is to establish the interval that separates fine poetry from flat verse:

> The rose has fleshed red, the bud has burst,
> And drunk with joy is the nightingale—
> Hail Sufis! lovers of wine, all had!
> For wine is proclaimed to a world thirst.
> Like a rock your repentance seemed to you;
> Behold the marvel! of what avail
> Was your rock, for a goblet has cleft it in
> two!
>
> Bring wine for the king and the slave at the
> gate!
> Alike for all is the banquet spread,
> And drunk and sober are warmed and fed.
> When the feast is done and the night grows
> late,
> And the second door of the tavern gapes
> wide,
> The low and the mighty must bow the head
> 'Neath the archway of life, to meet what. . . .
> outside?
>
> Except thy road through affliction pass,
> None may reach the halting-station of mirth;
> God's treaty: Am I not Lord of the earth?
> Man sealed with a sigh: Ah yes, alas!
> Nor with Is nor Is Not let thy mind contend;
> Rest assured all perfection of mortal birth
> In the great Is Not at the last shall end.
>
> For Asaf's pomp, and the steeds of the wind,
> And the speech of birds, down the wind have
> fled,
> And he that was lord of them all is dead;
> Of his mastery nothing remains behind.
> Shoot not thy feathered arrow astray!
> A bow-shot's length through the air it has
> sped,
> And then. . . . dropped down in the dusty
> way.
>
> But to thee, Oh Hafiz, to thee, Oh Tongue
> That speaks through the mouth of the slender
> reed,
> What thanks to thee when thy verses speed
> From lip to lip, and the song thou hast sung?

Two further examples must be all we have space to include here to illustrate Gertrude Bell's methods. The first is her version of the opening Ghazal in the *Diwan*. . . .

> Arise, Oh Cup-bearer, rise! and bring
> To lips that are thirsting the bowl they praise,
> For it seemed that love was an easy thing,
> But my feet have fallen on difficult ways.
> I have prayed the wind o'er my heart to fling
> The fragrance of musk in her hair that
> sleeps—
> In the night of her hair—yet no fragrance
> stays
> The tears of my heart's blood my sad heart
> weeps.
> Hear the Tavern-keeper who counsels you:
> "With wine, with red-wine your prayer carpet
> dye!
> There was never a traveller like him but knew
> The ways of the road and the hostelry.
>
> Where shall I rest, when the still night
> through,
> Beyond thy gateway, Oh Heart of my heart,
> The bells of the camels lament and cry:
> "Bind up thy burden again and depart!"
>
> The waves run high, night is clouded with
> fears,
> And eddying whirlpools clash and roar;
> How shall my drowning voice strike their ears
> Whose light-frighted vessels have reached the
> shore?
>
> I sought mine own; the unsparing years
> Have brought me mine own, a dishonoured
> name.
> What cloak shall cover my misery o'er
> When each jesting mouth has rehearsed my
> shame!
>
> Oh Hafiz, seeking an end to strife,
> Hold fast in thy mind what the wise have
> writ:
> 'If at last thou attain the desire of thy life,
> Cast the world aside, yea, abandon it!'

The second (and final) specimen is the rendering of the poem carved on Hafiz's tomb. . . .

> What are the tidings of union? that I may
> arise—
> Forth from the dust I will rise up to welcome
> thee!
> My soul, like a homing bird, yearing for
> Paradise,
> Shall arise and soar, from the snares of the
> world set free.
> When the voice of thy love shall call me to
> be thy slave,
> I shall rise to a greater far than the mastery
> Of life and the living, time and the mortal
> span:

Pour down, oh Lord! from the clouds of thy
    guiding grace,
The rain of a mercy that quickeneth on my
    grave.
Before, like dust that the wind bears from
    place to place,
I arise and flee beyond the knowledge of man.
When to my grave thou turnest thy blessed
    feet,
Wine and the lute thou shalt bring in thine
    hand to me,
Thy voice shall ring through the folds of my
    winding-sheet,
And I will arise and dance to thy minstrelsy.
Though I be old, clasp me one night to thy
    breast,
And I, when the dawn shall come to awaken
    me,
With the flush of youth on my cheek from thy
    bosom will rise.
Rise up! let mine eyes delight in thy stately
    grace!
Thou art the goal to which all men's
    endeavour has pressed,
And thou the idol of Hafiz's worship; thy face
From the world and life shall bid him come
    forth and arise!

## VI

While Gertrude Bell was still engaged in compiling her choice volume, Walter Leaf (1852-1927), the great Homeric scholar, was similarly employing himself, bringing to bear on Persian poetry a mind and a taste refined by long study of the classics: his *Version from Hafiz* came out in 1898. Whereas Miss Bell had deliberately thrown off the restraint of scrupulous fidelity to form and metre, Leaf had other views of the translator's duties. "Those who want them have not far to seek for translations of Hafiz. . . . They may scent in our Western winds the aroma from his Eastern garden, perfumed with musk of Tartary; they may gaze on the flame of rose and tulip, or taste of the tart and heady Persian wine, and wind their fingers in the ringlets of the beloved. But to the fifth sense of hearing not one, I think, has attempted to appeal, and the song of the Bulbul of Shiraz has fallen upon European ears only in measures transformed at best, often only in the wingless words of prose. But for Hafiz, at least as much as for any poet, form is of the essence of his poetry. More indeed than for the poets whom we know best. We have learnt from our Greek masters to seek the unity of a poet in thought or mood developed in it. Whether sensuous or intellectual, the unity is internal and essential. To a Persian poet this is not so; and that is a hard lesson which we must learn before we can do full justice to Eastern art. In the Persian ode we find a succession of couplets often startling in their independence, in their giddy transitions from grave to gay, from thought to mood. . . . It is from the common metre and common rhyme alone that an ode gains a formal unity. . . . For all these reasons it seems worthwhile to make an attempt, however poor, to give English readers some idea of this most intimate and indissoluble bond of spirit and form in Hafiz. And with it all, one must try to convey some faint reminder of the fact that Hafiz is, as few poets have been, a master of words and rhythms.' And so Walter Leaf made his heroic and not wholly unsuccessful experiment of translating 18 of the odes into English verse, monorhymed and metred in conformity with their originals. The first is one of the best, a new version of the poem that attracted both Palmer and Gertrude Bell (the latter, as we have seen, uncommonly faithful to the Persian), it is to be noted that this ode is of doubtful authenticity, and has been rejected by Hafiz's latest and most learned Persian editors.

Minstrel, awake the sound of glee, joyous and
    eager, fresh and free;
Fill me a bumper bounteously, joyous and
    eager, fresh and free.

O for a bower and one beside, delicate,
    dainty, there to hide;
Kisses at will to seize and be joyous and
    eager, fresh and free.

Sweet is my dear, a thief of hearts; bravery,
    beauty, saucy arts,
Odours and unguents, all for me, joyous and
    eager, fresh and free.

How shall the fruit of life be thine, if thou
    refuse the fruitful vine?
Drink of the vine and pledge with me, joyous
    and eager, fresh and
    free.

Call me my Saki silver-limbed, bring me my
    goblet silver-rimmed;
Fain would I fill and drink to thee, joyous and
    eager, fresh and free.

Wind of the West, if e'er thou roam, pass on
    the way my fairy's home;
Whisper of Hafiz am'rously, joyous and eager,
    fresh and free.

Jones's *Persian Song* comes out thus in Leaf:

An if you Turk of Shiraz land this heart
    would take to hold in fee,
Bokhara town and Samarcand to that black
    mole my dower should be.

Ho, Saki, pour the wine-flask dry; in Eden's
    bowers we ne'er shall find

Musallas' rosy bed, nor streams of Ruknabad's
  delightsome lea.

Alack, these saucy Lulis, dear beguilers that
  the town embroil,
The wantons tear the heart-strings as the Turks
  their plunder-
    banquetry.

On our frail love the loved One's pure
  perfection no dependence
    knows;
Can unguent, powder, paint and patch
  embellish faces fair, pardie?

Be wine and minstrel all thy theme; beware,
  nor plumb the deeps
    of fate;
For none hath found, nor e'er shall find by
  wit, that great enigma's
    key.

Of that fair favour Joseph wore, to make more
  fair the day, we know;
For him love bade Zulaikha tear apart her veil
  of pudency.
Thy words were hard, yet I submit; forgive
  thee God! Thy words
    were good;

The tart response beseemeth well the honeyed
  ruby lips of thee.

Give ear, my life! Perpend my words; for
  more dear e'en than life
    itself

To youth, so blest of Fortune, speaks the sage
  advice of ancientry.

The ode is made, the pearls are strung; go,
  Hafiz, sweetly sing thy
    lay;

With jewels from the Pleiad crown doth
  Heav'n engem thy minstrelsy.

Ingenious, but not poetry; the body of Hafiz, but
not his soul; does not this type of literary exercise
remind one of the set pieces that are written so
cleverly by so many entrants for the competitions
promoted by the weekly reviews, or done impromptu
at Christmas parties? We add one more example, a
bad one, to show how easily this technique of translation degenerates into parody, and to prove that
Homer's editor, like Homer himself, sometimes
nods. . . .

All bounds my heart is breaking; friends, haste
  to my salvation!
Woe's me! My secret hidden cries loud for
  proclamation.

'Mid reefs my bark is grounded; blow fair, O
  breeze of mercy;
Mayhap we win the Friend yet, Love's goal of
  navigation.

This ten-day smile of heaven swift passes like
  a tale told!
Be gracious while thou mayest, brook not
  procrastination.

That glass of Alexander naught save the bowl
  of wine was;
See all Darius' kingdom spread there in
  revelation.

Go to, thou lord of power, do thanks for
  fortune's dower,
Seek out the poor unfriended, raise up the
  lowly station.

All peace within the two worlds, two words
  alone assure it,
"Tow'rd lovers loving-kindness, tow'rd foes
  dissimulation."

Ringed round with wine and roses, sweet sang
  the bulbul yestreen,
"Bring quick the morning goblet; friends,
  watch in expectation."

All entry men forbid me inside the gate of
  virtue;
So, sir, and wilt thou scorn me? Go, change
  predestination!

More sweet to me than kisses, more soft than
  maiden's cheeks are,
That bitter named of Sufis "Dam of
  abomination."

When comes the hour of sadness, turn thou to
  wine and gladness;
Karuns of beggars maketh wine's chemic
  transmutation.

Wine-flecked is Hafiz' cassock, yet not of
  choice he dons it;
Ah, Shaikh of hem unspotted, hear thou my
  exculpation!

It seems a fairly safe guess that this translation has
given pleasure to nobody but the translator; certainly it
presents Hafiz in a particularly unfavourable guise; and
matters are not helped by the fact that Leaf was work-

ing from a text which has set the order of lines in the poem completely awry.

## VII

Walter Leaf was not long in finding a convert to his theory. In 1901, printed for the Villon society for private circulation, in three elegant white-bound volumes came **The Poems of Shemseddin Mohammed Hafiz of Shiraz**, with a title-page proclaiming them 'now first completely done into English verse from the Persian, in accordance with the original forms.' The translator was John Payne, who had previously exercised his ingenuity in making versions of Francois Villon, Boccaccio's *Decameron*, *The Arabian Nights*, Omar Khayyam, etc. That was the kind of man he was: after his death, a John Payne Society sought to keep alive his name. Undeniably he had remarkable qualities and a rare gift of rhyming; but his versions of Hafiz suggest that he had little literary taste, and no powers of self-criticism, for a more wearisome and turgid collection it would be difficult to find. To parody Richard le Gallienne, "Is it good translation to turn what is such pleasure for the East into positive Payne for the West?" In a preliminary discourse Payne argues verbosely the case for excluding all mysticism from the interpretation of Hafiz: his concluding summary of the poet's character perhaps best illustrates his view-point. "Unbound by our laws and unfettered by our prescriptions, above our approof and beyond our blame, such as Hafiz are not to be tried by our standards or condemned by our limitations; they have an inalienable title to the privilege which forms the foundation of our English judicial system; they can only be judged by their peers. Like Shakespeare, like Socrates, like Mendelsohn, Hafiz was one of the children of the bridechamber, who mourn not, for the bridegroom is with them. Happy, thrice happy those rare elect ones among the servants of the Ideal, to whom it is given, through shower and sunshine and without default against their august vocation, to cull the rose of hilarity from the storm-swept meads of life, who are gifted to respire with impurity the intoxicating breath of the lilies and jessamines of love and joy. . . . These are the Parthemogeniti of life; they need no purification, as do those who have come out of great tribulation and have made white their robes in the blood of the Lamb; intemerate and free were they born, as the flowers of the field, and pure and incontaminable shall they abide for ever. Like Ben Jonson's lily of a day, they are the plants and flowers of light; they toil not, neither do they spin; yet eternity is full of their glory." Hafiz would be surprised at such a tribute!

There, in three volumes, is the whole of Hafiz and pseudo-Hafiz, done to death by John Payne, a literary crime as monstrous as murder: it is more than a little shocking to find Edward Burne-Jones named as the principal accessory before the act, to him being dedi-

cated "this book which owed its completion to his urgent instance." How much Persian did Payne really know? It is difficult to answer this question: for he had available to him, as others have unfortunately had, the extraordinary complete prose-rendering of Henry Wilberforce Clarke (Calcutta, 1891), with its odd critical and explanatory notes," and all that he needed to do was to use this as a hazardous crib, rejecting, as suited his taste, all Clarke's ingenious mystical interpretations. On the whole, it seems inevitable to condemn John Payne for the not uncommon offence of plagiarising the pundits. Fortunately, the small circulation to which he condemned his book has limited the damage it has done to Hafiz' reputation. We quote three typical specimens: first, Jones's **Persian Song** is yet another key.

Lo but that Turk of Shiraz take My heart
   within her hand of snow,
Bokhara, ay, and Samarcand On her black
   mole will I bestow.

Give, cupbearer, the wine that's left; For
   thou'lt not find in Paradise
The banks of Ruknabad nor yet Musella's
   rosegarths all a-glow.

Alack, these saucy sweet-sellers, These town-
   perturbing gipsy maids!
They ravish patience from the heart, As
   Turkmans plunder from the
   foe.

The beauty of the Friend of love Imperfect
   independent is;
What need of patch and pencilling And paint
   have lovely faces, trow?

The tale of wine and minstrel tell Nor after
   heaven's secrets seek;
For this enigma to resolve None ever knew
   nor yet shall know.

For that still-waxing loveliness That Joseph
   had, too well I knew
That love would cause Zuleikha forth The veil
   of continence to go.
Thou spak'st me ill; Yet I'm content. God
   pardon thee! Thou
   spakest well;
For bitter answers well on lips Of sugar-
   dropping ruby show.
To admonition lend thine ear, O soul; for
   dearer than the soul
To happy youths the counsels are Which from
   wise elders' lips do
   flow.
Songs thou hast made and jewels strung.
   Come, Hafiz, and recite
   them well,

So heaven on thy string of pearls The
    clustered Pleiades may strow.

That is undoubtedly one of Payne's least offensive
efforts. The following version runs truer to form . . .

For our pain no cure, ywis, is. Help! oh help!
For our woes no end in bliss is. Help! oh
    help!
Faith and heart they've ta'en and threaten now
    the soul:
'Gainst these cruel cockatrices. Help! oh help!
Help, against the heart-enslavers pitiless,
Souls who seek in price of kisses! Help! oh
    help!
See, our blood they drink, these stony-hearted
    trulls!
Muslims, say, what cure for this is? Help! oh
    help!
Day and night, I fare distracted, weep and
    burn,
As the wont of me, Hafiz, is. Help! oh help!

This rendering writes its own epitaph: it is equally
appropriate to the next. . . .

When my Beloved the cup in hand taketh
The market of lovely ones slack demand
    taketh.
I, like a fish, in the ocean am fallen,
Till me with the hook yonder Friend to land
    taketh.

Every one saith, who her tipsy eye seeth,
"Where is a shrieve, that this fair firebrand
    taketh?"

Ho, at her feet in lament am I fallen,
Till the Beloved me by the hand taketh.

Happy his heart who, like Hafiz, a goblet
Of wine of the Prime Fore-eternal's brand
    taketh.

Can it be seriously maintained that this kind of translation is either Hafiz or poetry?

## VIII

It is small wonder that so excellent a critic as Richard
le Gallienne, when he came to the task of putting
Hafiz into English, revolted against John Payne's
theory and practice, and found it expedient to enun-
ciate principles of translation whose validity can hardly
be questioned. "Surely the only service of translation
is to make the foreign poet a poet of one's own country—not to present him as a half-Anglicized foreigner
speaking neither his own language nor our own. . . .
no translation, however learned, is of any value that

does not give at least some of the joy to the reader
that was given by its original. Hafiz has for centuries
been one of the great literary joys of the Orient. Is it
good translation to turn what is such pleasure for the
East into positive pain for the West?" le Gallienne
was the first to address himself to the task of translating Hafiz while admittedly possessing no knowledge whatsoever of the Persian language; and it is
highly interesting to read his defence. "I feel myself
justified in thinking that in their translations (*i.e.*, those
of Wilberforce Clarke and Payne) I have as trustworthy, if not more trustworthy, material for the making
of an English rendering than if I had studied Persian
for myself for ten years. Were I to make such original
studies, I should arrive in the end no nearer to the
poet's meaning than the previous labours of Colonel
Clarke or Mr. Payne enable me to do by the comparatively right study of their translations. It is true that
I should have formed some notion for myself of the
metrical music of Hafiz. . . . but to have heard that
music would, I feel sure, more than ever have convinced me of the futility of any attempt to reproduce
it in English." On the attempts to copy Persian rhymes
and metres in English he writes, "so distasteful to
English ideas are the metrical devices and adornments
pleasing to a Persian ear that the attempt to reproduce
them in English can only result in the most tiresome
literary antics, a mirth-less buffoonery of verse compared with which Browning at his grotesquest is endurable. Rhythms, which in Persian, doubtless, make
the sweetest chiming, fitted with English words, become mere vulgar and ludicrous jingle." On another
cardinal point, the alleged incoherence of Hafiz, le
Gallienne has something instructive to say: "The difficulty of inconsequence I have endeavoured to overcome, partly by choosing those poems that were least
inconsequent, partly by supplying links of my own,
and partly by selecting and developing the most important motive out of the two or three different motives which one frequently finds in the same ode!"
Finally, his purpose in what he did. "My aim has
been to make English poetry—rather than a joyless
shadow of a great classic. I offer this rendering, in
the first place as poetry, in the second as translation;
but, at the same time, my aim has been, as faithfully
as in me lies, truly to interpret the great Persian poet
to English readers, so that the total result of my endeavour is really—if not literally Hafiz."

There are one hundred le Gallienne translations for
those to analyse who may wish to make an extended
study of his methods, and the total volume of his contribution to the interpretation of Hafiz. In this essay we
will confine ourselves to a handful of examples based
on well-known originals. Here is part of the opening
poem of the ***Diwan***:

Saki, for God's love, come and fill my glass;
    Wine for a breaking heart, O Saki, bring!

For this strange love which seemed at first,
  alas!
    So simple and so innocent a thing,

How difficult, how difficult it is!
    Because the night-wind kissed the scented
curl
    On the white brow of a capricious girl,

And, passing, gave me half the stolen kiss,
    Who would have thought one's heart could
bleed and break

For such a very little thing as this?
    Wine, Saki, wine—red wine, for pity's
sake!

O Saki, would to God that I might die!
    Would that this moment I might hear the
bell
      That bids the traveller for the road
prepare,
      Be the next stopping-place heaven or hell!

Strange caravan of death—no fears have I
    Of the dark journey, gladly would I dare

The fearful river and the whirling pools;
    Ah! they that dwell upon the other side,
    What know they of the burdens that we
bear?
      With lit-up happy faces having died,
    What know they of love's bitter mystery,
    The love that makes so sad a fool of me?
A fool of Hafiz!—Yea, a fool of fools.

This version is of course very free; it expands and inserts considerably; but in the end it comes out faithful enough to the spirit of Hafiz, in spite of a number of features ("With lit-up happy faced having died") which are purely English and characteristically le Gallienne; and it has a pleasing dignity. This translation, then, can be safely pronounced successful after its kind, though not by any means perfect. The tale of the **Persian Song** is somewhat different.

You little Turk of Shiraz-town,
    Freebooter of the hearts of men,
As beautiful, as says renown,
    Are your freebooting Turcomen;
Dear Turco-maid—a plunderer too—
    Here is my heart, and there your hand:
If you'll exchange, I'll give to you
    Bokhara—yes! and Samarcand.
    Indeed, I'd give them for the mole
Upon your cheek, and add thereto,
    Even my body and my soul.

Come, bearer of the shining cup,
    Bring the red grape into the sun,
That we may drink, and drink it up,
    Before our little day is done;
    For Ruknabad shall run and run,
And each year, punctual as spring,
The new-born nightingale shall sing
Unto Musella's new-born rose;
But we shall not know anything,
Nor laugh, nor weap, nor anywise
Listen or speak, fast closed our eyes
And shut our ears—in Paradise!

You little robber-woman, you
    That turn the heads of Shiraz-town,
With sugar-talk and sugar-walk
    And all your little sugar-ways,—
Into the sweet-shop of your eyes
    I innocently gaze and gaze,
    While, like your brethren of renown,
O little Turk of Shiraz, you
Plunder me of my patience too.

Yet all too well the lover knows
    The loved one needs no lover's praise;
What other perfume needs the rose?
Perfection needs no words of ours
    Nor heeds what any song-bird says—
Sufficient unto flowers are flowers.

Nay, give it up! nor try to probe
    Secret of her, or any heaven;
It is a most distracting globe—
    Seven the stars, our sins are seven;
Above no answer, nor below:
Let's call the Saki—he may know;
Yes, who knows, HE may know.

O love, that was not very kind!
    That answer that you gave to me;
Nay, I mistook, you spoke me well!
    For you to speak at all to me
    Is unforeseen felicity;
Yea, bitter on your lips grows sweet
    And soft your hardest words to me.

Sweetheart, if you would hearken me,
    I am a very wise old thing,
And it were wise of you to hear.
My little Turk, my cypress dear,
    So wise the wisdom that I sing
    That some day on a shining string
High up in heaven, tear by tear,
    As star by star, these songs shall hang
At evening on the vested sky,
    These little songs that Hafiz sang,
    To one that heard not on his knees:
So well I sang them—even I—
    That, listening to them, Heaven's Lord

Tossed me from heaven as reward
The small change of the Pleiades!—
These little songs that Hafiz sang
To one that heard not on his knees.

However this version may strike an English reader
unaware of Persian, to those who are familiar with the
original Hafiz its inadequacies and misrepresentations
are all too apparent; it is altogether too girlish for Hafiz;
and there are some terrible arch touches that only the
Edwardian age for which le Gallienne was then writing could fully appreciate. As with Jones, so with le
Gallienne, time and environment played their part; and
unhappily the pleasantry of one generation has a way
of becoming the slang of the next, and the very acme
of triteness to the following. Jones has his 'blooming
Hebrew boy' to make us snigger; and le Gallienne his
'you little robber-woman, you' and his 'wise old thing'
to make us shiver; and the significant fact about all
this is that there is nothing in the poetry of Hafiz that
the years have soured or current speech debased. The
unhappy mixture of good and bad, felicitous and un-
felicitous, which mars le Gallienne's version of the
*Persian Song* is seen again in this third and final example, an ode which Jones in his day made into very
fair French. . . .

Shiraz, city of the heart,
    God preserve thee!
Pearl of capitals thou art,
    Ah! to serve thee.

Ruknabad, of thee I dream,
    Fairy river:
Whoso drinks thy running stream
    Lives for ever.

Wind that blows from Ispahan,
    Whence thy sweetness?
Flowers ran with thee as thou ran
    With such fleetness.

Flowers from Jafarabad,
    Made of flowers;
Thou for half-way house hast had
    Musalla's bowers.

Right through Shiraz the path goes
    Of perfection;
Anyone in Shiraz knows
    Its direction.

Spend not on Egyptian sweets
    Shiraz money;
Sweet enough in Shiraz streets
    Shiraz honey.

East Wind, hast thou aught to tell
    Of my gipsy?

Was she happy? Was she well?
    Was she tipsy?

Wake me not, I pray thee, friend,
    From my sleeping;
Soon my little dream must end;
    Waking's weeping.

Hafiz, though his blood she spill,
    Right he thinks it;
Like mother's milk 'tis his will
    That she drinks it.

What a pity, that so pleasant a poem is spoiled by the
false note of 'Was she tipsy'!

IX

Nothing further happened to Hafiz in English after
le Gallienne in 1905, until in 1921 the Oxford University Press published Elizabeth Bridges' **Sonnets
from Hafiz & Other Verses**, in its own way and
within its all too limited scope a most interesting
and significant contribution. "The last fifteen pieces
in this book," writes the late Laureate's daughter,
"are not translations. Their aim is rather to convey
if possible something of the original spirit than to
give a faithful rendering of either thought or form;
and I have not scrupled to omit, insert, alter or even
deliberately to pervert the idea as fancy or feeling
dictated. Some of the poems follow the Persian fairly
closely. . . . others are merely founded on or suggested, by one or two couplets!" This introduces a
new technique, admittedly more revolutionary even
than le Gallienne's; but it is a technique which may
well have a greater following in the future. Here is
an example of the less literal versions, obviously
based on Ode of the **Diwan**.

Arise, O cup-bearer, and bring
Fresh wine for our enrapturing!
O minstrel, of our sorrow sing
'O joy of whose delight we dreamed,
'O love that erst so easy seemed,
'What toil is in thy travelling!'

How in the loved one's tent can I
Have any rest or gaiety?
Ever anon the horsemen cry,
'O lingering lover, fare thee well!'
Ever I hear the jingling bell
Of waiting steed and hornessry.

O seeker who wouldst surely bring
To happy end thy wandering,
O learner who wouldst truly know,
Let not earth's loves arrest thee. Go!
Mad thee with heaven's pure wine, and fling
To those clear skies thy rapturing.

In one version Elizabeth Bridges imitates metre and monorhyme. . . .

> Where is the pious doer? and I, the estray'd
>     one, where?
> Behold how far the distance, from his safe
>     home to here!
>
> Dark is the stony desert, trackless and vast
>     and dim,
> Where is hope's guiding lantern? Where is
>     faith's star so fair?
>
> My heart fled from the cloister, and chant of
>     monkish hymn,
> What can avail me sainthood, fasting and
>     punctual prayer?
>
> Wht is the truth shall light me to heaven's
>     strait thoroughfare?
> Whither, O heart, thou hastest? Arrest thee,
>     and beware!
>
> See what a lone adventure is thine unending
>     guest!
> Fraught with what deadly danger! Set with
>     what unseen snare!
>
> Say not, O friend, to Hafiz, 'Quiet thee now
>     and rest!'
> Calm and content, what are they? Patience and
>     peace O where?

Unfortunately fifteen pieces are not enough to satisfy: even less sufficient are the few examples which R. A. Nicholson has published in translation of Hafiz; and much could have been expected from his pen, which has represented the mystical lyrics of Rumi so superbly well. His method, in the specimens published in *Eastern Poetry and Prose* (Cambridge, 1922), is very similar to that of Miss Bridges: "Some," he writes, "are pieced together from verses which occur in different odes, while others are free or fairly literal translations of passages in the same ode," adding in another place, "in a few from Hafiz. I have taken the same kind of liberty which Fitzgerald used in his version of Omar Khayyam." His version of the first ode is fairly complete.

> Saki, pass the cup and pour,
> Pour me out the balmy drink!
> Love, who seemed so light of yore,
> Underneath his load I sink.
> Quoth mine ancient Guide, who knows
> Every inn upon the way:
> "Well for you if purple flows
> O'er the carpet as ye pray!"
> Zephyr, quick! blow loose the knot
> Of my sweetheart's tangled hair!
> 'Tis the heart of all the plot

> Laid against my life, I swear.
> Sea and storm and dead of night,
> Midst the whirlpool's ghastly roar:
> Ah, what know they of our plight,
> Happy loiterers on the shore?
> In this mansion of Farewell
> Pleasure, ere it comes, is gone,
> Where a never silent bell
> Tolls "Arise and journey on!"
> Hafiz, tired of blame and praise,
> If thy spirit longs for rest,
> Leave the world and all its ways,
> Clasp the Loved One to thy breast!

Three verses from a single ode inspire a truly poetic version. . . .

> Mortals never won to view thee,
> Yet a thousand lovers woo thee;
> Not a nightingale but knows
> In the rosebud sleeps the rose.
>
> Love is where the glory falls
> Off thy face: on convent walls
> Or on tavern floors the same
> Unextinguishable flame.
>
> Where the turban'd anchorite
> Chanteth Allah day and night,
> Churchbells ring the call to prayer,
> And the Cross of Christ is there.

And a couplet provides the original of verses which are in the true tradition of English metaphysical poetry. . . .

> The calm circumference of life
> When I would fain have kept,
> Time caught me in the tide of strife
> And to the centre swept.
>
> Of this fierce glow which love and you
> Within my breast inspire,
> The Sun is but a spark that flew
> And set the heavens afire!

To complete this review of the English verse-translations of Hafiz it only remains to mention P. L. Stallard's thirty-three *Renderings from the Dewan of Khwaja Shamsu'ddin Mahammad Hafiz Shirazi* (Basil Blackwell, Oxford (1937). This book, which, if it is not the best, at least is not the worst that has been published on Hafiz, brings nothing new to the general problem; but it may be interesting to cite these latest versions of two old favourites.

First, Ode 1.

> Pour, pour the wine, Ha! Saki: aye, and
>     speed!
> For love seemed easy once that now is hard!

At length, though breezes bring the breath of
  nard
From her dark tress, in its glint hearts must
  bleed!

See! If the ancient Magian bid thee so,
With wine thy prayer-mat tincture thou: for,
  say,
Shall he that travelled by the path not know
The road's each stage and fashion of the way?

Here in Love's inn what solace mine, or rest,
While still complain the camel-bells a-chime
Ceaseless, and call that now, and now, 'tis
  time
We bound our litters to new bournes addrest?

Fear of the mounting sea, mirk of the night,
Right horror of the whirlpool, all our state
How should they know, who with their burden
  light
To the far shore have passed the sundering
  strait?

I thought my works to prosper in self-will,
And all, thereby, in ill-repute have end!
Where lies inviolate that secret still
The which the companies of saints perpend?

Would'st thou gain to His presence, Hafiz? So
Go not about thyself from Him to hide.
But, reaching thither, cleave thou to His side,
And for the Loved let all the World's pride
  go!

Second, the *Persian Song:*

  Should that little chit of Shiraz
    Bear my heart within her hand,
  For her cheek's swart mole I'd barter
    Bukhara and Samarcand!

  Bring me wine, boy, all remaining;
    For in Paradise no flowers
  Fledge the Ruknabad, nor blossom
    Roses in Musalla's bowers.

  But, ah! as the Turk his plunder,
    So my heart's ease have they ta'en
  All these wantons and these fair ones,
    Wrecking cities in their train.

  Yet, for love as lame as mine is,
    Is my darling's scorn the meed
  As for patches, paints, and potions,
    Stands what perfect face in need?

  Bring a tale of wine and minstrels:
    Leave Time's secret where it lies;

  None have yet, nor shall, unravel
    Mysteries that transcend the wise.

  Well I know how Yusuf's beauty,
    Shining as an ampler day,
  Rent Zulaikha's veil, and rending
    Stole her chastity away.

  Yet lean ear to counsel, darling:
    Youths who'd prosper ever hold,
  Dearer than the breath within them,
    By the wisdom of the old!

  Didst thou twit me? God forgive thee!
    Spak'st me fair? But then we know
  Tart words ill become that ruby
    Lip of thine, that sugared bow!

  Hafiz, come! Thou'st done thy rhyming,
    Strung thy pearls; the Pleiads throng
  To shed splendour from the chiming
    Circles on thy well-tuned song!

It seems a pity about chit and twit, and it is a pity that Longfellow should have spoken of mournful numbers in this particular metre, but there it is. And these, for the present, ends the long catalogue of those who have occupied their time and wit putting Hafiz of Shiraz into English rhyme.

## Eric Schroeder (essay date 1948)

SOURCE: "Verse and Translation and Hafiz," in *Journal of Near Eastern Studies*, Vol. VII, No. 4, October, 1948, pp. 209-22.

[*In the following essay, Schroeder discusses translations of the works of Hafiz, focusing on the importance of rhythm, repetition, and extensive annotation, and criticizing the rendering of Hafiz's poems by A. J. Arberry.*]

Amodest book generally arouses gratitude and respect, and these are among the feelings with which one lays down Professor Arberry's selection from the works of Hafiz and his fifteen English translators. His explicit purposes—to provide a textbook for those beginning to read Persian poetry and to exhibit the variety of Hafiz' work and the variety of its translation by different hands—are accomplished. His Introduction contains a summary of the facts of Hafiz' life and times, a brief discussion of the *Divan* text, its variants, and the causes of corruption, two Persian appreciations, an outline of the history of the *ghazal*, and a most interesting provisional analysis of Hafiz' development as a poet. The texts of fifty poems are given cleared of interpolation; and the verse translations include nine eighteenth-century versions, others in similar style by

Bicknell and Palmer, more modern versions by Bell, Le Gallienne, Leaf, and others, and sixteen new poetical translations by Professor Arberry himself. The notes give variants and some guidance to the symbolism and reference of the texts.

Possibly the circumstances of Hafiz' life might have been illuminated by some description of the working of Mongol feudalism, some images of the intercourse between the alien military caste in their exotic dress and arms and the Persian subjects who furnished not only a peasantry but a bureaucracy and urban luxury, arts, and culture. And some more pictorial vision of the poet's town, its streams and gardens and mountain crown, and the wine-growing villages about it, might have been more informative than so intricate a history of the town's political vicissitudes, to which Hafiz was deliberately indifferent. Such changes probably affected him less, for instance, than the architectural transformation inaugurated in his lifetime, the development of brilliantly colored *kashi* ornament. Of the two eminent Persian critics whom Professor Arberry's modesty puts forward as spokesmen for that native appreciation to which foreigners must remain foreign, the second occupies rather more space than he enlivens. One has to summarize in order to grasp any substance; and, although the selections may be inserted with some art and some little irony as specimens of the oriental preface, they do not perhaps suggest any very fruitful approach to the poet on the part of the Western novice. This reviewer personally would have preferred larger type for the Persian text. And he would have liked a literal prose translation of at least one poem to have been incorporated in the notes. On this subject there is more to be said, but even in the volume as it stands some such translation would have made more of the literary artifices employed by the poet perceptible to the reader who knows no Persian.

The selection does justice to Hafiz' greatness, inclining to a large inclusion of his more philosophic poetry and a diminished proportion of poems to which his verbal felicity is essential. Apart from the new translations, it is the fifth section of the Introduction (pp. 28-33)—in which Professor Arberry sums up the poet's philosophy and characterizes, by content and technique, three periods in his work—that makes this the most valuable introduction to the poet which has hitherto appeared in English. It is the product of a deep study. To me personally it has been an "opener of doors." When I add that, of all the translators represented, Professor Arberry comes nearest to combining fidelity with poetic quality, I hope it will be clear that I regard his achievement as no mean one. And if we are still dissatisfied with the relationship between Hafiz and his Western reader, there can be no doubt that Professor Arberry feels something of the same dissatisfaction.

There is no discontent with the manner in which he has fulfilled his stated aims. The dissatisfaction which I wish to examine is rather with the modesty of his program. What remains in question after reading this **Hafiz** is really the appropriateness of modesty to the performance of the task which introducing Hafiz implies.

An adequate introduction should persuade the reader of the poet's greatness. It is a translation to which there are two parties: the introducer and the reader. In the case of some readers it may be hopeless. To persuade one whose poetic taste calls for Milton or Dryden, for Wordsworth or Kipling—one for whom meaning must be explicitly stated—that a poet whose more serious meaning is abstruse from its visible symbols is a great poet cannot be easy. For Hafiz' beautiful verbal surface is too complex to retain the felicity of poetry when fully rendered into English. The acoustic structure of English equivalents, it is superfluous to say, could never echo the flawless music of the Persian words. Occasionally, as in Nos. 34, 44, and 47, the translator (in these cases Professor Arberry himself) rises to something of the unembarrassed force of real poetry while remaining largely faithful to his text; this is an effective, though not ultimately the most truthful, means toward the persuasion of Hafiz' greatness. Readers of this volume will generally be persons who know a little Persian and others who know none. Even the former class will for the most part be comparative novices in the world of Persian art and thought and prone to accept the standard of interpretation here set. And, although it is to them that the book is ostensibly addressed, Professor Arberry at once suggests that Hafiz "can still teach useful lessons to all who are interested in the evolution of poetic expression" and that "Hafiz' technique can by modified imitation inspire new developments in Western poetry." Heartily indorsing these views, I now propose to consider the volume not as a beginner's textbook but as a representation to those who care for poetry of Persia's greatest poet.

It is plain that the author shares Richard Le Gallienne's opinion that "the only service of translation is to make the foreign poet a poet of one's own country." English-speaking Orientalists are peculiarly exposed to this conviction by the success, which they alone can appreciate, of FitzGerald's Omar Khayyám. The service to which they aspire, however, requires that they shall be true English poets. And, further, if FitzGerald's Omar be compared, for instance, with Dryden's Horace, it is soon clear that even a fine English poem which conveys the meaning of a foreign poem is not always wholly satisfactory as a translation. For *FitzGerald's versions have much the same poetic impact as their originals*, and Dryden's versions have not. The simplest way of putting the case is to say, for the moment vaguely, that FitzGerald seems to have been in some way a Persian poet as well as an English one. This explains the unique popular success of the *Rubáiyát*: FitzGerald provided the English with what is essentially Persian poetry. His exploit is hardly intelligible without·reference to the man himself. Free alike from the competitive ambition, the moral vehemence, the conventionality, or the materialism of his various fellow-Englishmen, choosing the unhurried practice of his art, the unambitious cares of a garden, and the complete idleness which can be had in the Western world only on a yacht, he exemplified Persian rather than Western culture.

But such a phenomenon as FitzGerald is so rare that few translators can hope that their own achievement may resemble his. Scott-Moncrieff's *Beowulf* is a comparable even if less astonishing success; and it is the only one which comes readily to mind. Both writers are true translators and true poets; but, beside these gifts, they both possess another no less important to their task—a taste for and a mastery of certain *technical* devices characteristic of their originals. FitzGerald uses with apparent ease, first, the rhymed quatrain (in wisely chosen iambics, to an English ear both definitely poetical and poetically neutral); second, the recurrent symbolic convention which he happily proclaims by capitalization; and, third, a very Persian economy of poetical phraseology which enables him to reproduce the cool and occasionally colloquial tone of Omar. Scott-Moncrieff "attempted to make the sort of lines that an Englishman of the Heptarchy would recognize as metrical," and mastery let him (in his noble dedicatory poem) express in such lines his own thought and passion. He had become an Old English poet. An Englishman may make himself perhaps more easily an Old Englishman than a Persian; Scott-Moncrieff was exploiting certain acoustic preferences which have been constants in the English ear. But the capacity to embody certain emotionally or intellectually necessary elements of an alien technique as well as alien meaning is as vital to satisfactory verse translation as it is rare.

If the translator commands it, the force of his translation is increased many fold. But how if he have it not? In that case, abandoning the attempt to produce poetry, either he may furnish the meaning and the imagery in a literal prose translation or, fitting the translated meaning and imagery to his personal poetic technique, he may produce a new poem. It may be "a very pretty poem—but you must not call it Homer." The style is the man; and technique is a thing of the soul. Moreover, liking and disliking are so absolute in poetry that the verse translator risks the precious meaning and imagery in a frail vessel. If the flavor, the vocabulary and rhythm, of the poetical translation are not to our taste, they rouse actual disgust. At best, the additional words, laden with association, which are constantly necessary in adjusting the translated matter to its new verse form, will alter emphasis. At worst, they will poison the poem.

All these objections Professor Arberry has undoubtedly weighed. His valuable article on the particular problem of Hafiz' case[2] shows what concessions he thinks necessary, though he sometimes prefers the opinions of others. Expansion of Hafiz' length is inevitable: "It seems beyond hope to achieve the same pregnant brevity." And the repetitive monorhyme of the *ghazal* is abandoned under cover of J. H. Hindley's dictum: "The constant recurrence of the same rhyme is not suited to a language which, as has been often observed by critics, will not bear reiterated monotonies." In a word, for Professor Arberry, as for most of his predecessors, "Hafiz cannot be translated"; and "to make the foreign poet a poet of one's own country" is all that remains.

It may be as well to say, even here and prematurely, that Hafiz' pregnant brevity will keep in English well enough, so long as the translator is not afraid of seeming uncouth, and to point out that in the first half of the seventeenth century, when its use was understood at least as well as in Hindley's time or ours, the English language supported reiterated monotonies with powerful effect.

But for the moment let us follow Professor Arberry and see where we are led. The question is: What kind of an English poet shall we make of Hafiz? A sentimental one? Sir William Jones's versions in his own time were popular and influential; but few readers of this book will think his or Nott's worth repeated reading. Hafiz in them is no longer Hafiz but simply Akenside, or Beattie, or Shenstone—some hedonistic eighteenth-century Englishman of taste. His voice is the unmistakable voice of a polite rational materialist; and, as spokesman for the poetic and philosophic personality of Hafiz, it is absolutely false.

What worse horrors can befall the attempt to make an English poet of Hafiz the unlucky Le Gallienne has himself most ignominiously shown. His version of the famous "Shirazi Turk" *ghazal* (reprinted and criticized in Professor Arberry's article) contains such lines as:

You little robber-woman, you!

and

O love, that was not very kind!

"It is altogether too girlish for Hafiz," says Professor Arberry, "and there are some terrible arch touches." So terrible, indeed, that we wonder whether making an Edwardian poet of Hafiz did him any service at all. To make a modern poet out of him, in the style of the Arab poets recently translated by Howarth and Shukrullah in *Images from the Arab World*, might insure him some enthusiasm, if not a just appreciation, for a few years. But when that mode too has gone by, how shall we feel about modern mannerisms?

We know well enough: We shall feel embarrassed by them. Poetical mannerism brings out the snob in all of us. Clothes which can establish a man in one company will ruin him in another. Words and phrases which have once acted as incantations will startle another and a later reader away. Such a phrase, for example, as "Love's passionate red wine" might proclaim a line as poetry forty years ago; today it marks it as verse of a certain age. To call verse which so affects us "uninspired" or "tame" may be correct, for the creative excitement necessary to powerful rhyme is irrational, sudden, rich, and deep-seated. As poets know, writing a poem is the release in comparatively few selected words of a whole inner world of meaningful images, of reminiscent and musical notions, so entangled in the words selected that the very soul seems to issue in them. Only after the forgetting of a poem one has written does a rereading show how much of that inner composition was actualized. Now, translation, the arrangement of already selected matter, rouses far less energy. There is less "head" to the flow. A. E. Housman illustrates how relaxed or enfeebled, both critically and creatively, is a poet translating when compared with himself composing. The Muse is not in presence.

The fact might be explained by supposing that the amount of energy still available in translated matter is in direct ratio to the translator's power of self-negation. The discipline is rare in minor poets, who generally develop power by self-specialization. When we come to ask why a feebleness or an error in taste is fatal to the effect of poetry, why our snobbery is unashamed and ruthless, we must risk a ponderous answer which would be inappropriate to the review of a modest book had not that book covered, with the authority of high and original scholarship and the company of some quite beautiful and fairly faithful renderings, a number of what, seriously considered, are misrepresentations of a very great poet. Such a version as No. 41, for instance, is little better than a travesty.

Two of the foremost Western minds needed little persuasion of the value of the poet. Emerson was one, and the other Goethe. The latter is of particular interest, not only because of the characteristically prophetic or universal quality of his understanding, but because of the clarity of his introspection. "I had to protect myself against Hafiz by composing," he wrote; "otherwise I should not have held my ground against the mighty presence." As with FitzGerald, a Persian genius possessed him, at least for a while; and though little of Goethe's *West-Eastern Divan* is actual translation, there are to be found in that display of lyric skill manipulations of some of the more intractable technical peculiarities of Hafiz—colloquialism and the monorhyme. Goethe, like FitzGerald, fearlessly wedded his own soul

to strangeness; and he, too, had his reward. Such courage in embracing the conventionally uncouth is like the kissing of the "Loathly Bride":

> Her breath was strang, her hair was lang
> And twisted thrice about the tree;
> And with a swing she came about:
> "Come to the craig and kiss with me!"

The kisser must be a hero, a "kingis son"; but when such a one "steppit in, gave her a kiss,"

> Her breath was sweet, her hair grew short
> And twisted nane about the tree;
> And smilingly she came about,
> As fair a woman as fair could be.

The myth contains something very material to the problem of translation—the fact that fear is an evil counselor. The apprehension that English readers may not like, for example, so much repetition as Hafiz liked is fear that they may not like Hafiz. A more perfect love for the poet would cast out that fear; and a fearless translator would give *all that could be given in the translator's tongue.* Persian music may be untranslatable into English music; but for a reader who wants the Persian poet no amount of English music will compensate the loss or clouding or adulteration of the Persian meaning.

On this point Goethe has something to say which should be heard in the recollection that it is a great poet who speaks: "I revere the rhythm as well as the rhyme, by which poetry first becomes poetry; but that which is really, deeply, and fundamentally effective—what is really permanent and furthering—is what remains of the poet when he is translated into prose. Then remains the pure perfect substance, of which a brilliant surface often has the effect of exhibiting the false semblance when the real thing is not there, and which, when it is there, such a surface often has the effect of concealing. I therefore consider prose translations more advantageous than poetical ones. . . . Those critical translations which vie with the original seem really to be only for the private delectation of the learned."

Of this statement I would emphasize the phrase "permanent and furthering" as an indication of what matters in poetry. Poetry, considered not *in vacuo* but in its relation to life, has a well-defined level of operation. Its theater is the *soul,* that feeling, feminine person of our triunity which may be damned or blest by ignorance or by knowledge of her proper Bridegroom. The soul is never quite free from a sense of its ultimate or proper destiny. Though all loveliness (I use this term as distinguished from "beauty" by Dr. Coomaraswamy) may be seductive to the immature, and though great loveliness is always seductive, the soul is increasingly aware of a station beyond the lovely, for which it is bound; and this sense of destination is what makes us so merciless to loveliness not great enough to be seductive. Poetry in any case does not as a rule exert so strong a compulsion on our appetites as do physical things. It is easier for the intellectual will (of scholastic psychology) to determine our reaction. And so it is easy for us, as we begin to ripen, to reject infantile or fleshly poetry. This easy rejection is the snobbery of poetical taste. The normal Poet's Progress (both in the poet and in his reader) is from "The Rose" to "The Winding Stair," from "The Prelude" to "The Excursion," from *Romeo* to *The Tempest*. It is a progress from the beauty of the world to the beauty of the underlying, and often an ascent from verbal beauty to intellectual beauty precipitated in words, with some loss of verbal loveliness, as if understanding held the lovely and the loathly in a harmony of its own. Poetry which rouses the snob in us is embarrassing because it appeals to feeling at a level of this psychic ascent which we wish to be past.

In poetry the progress may be marked by certain changes in poetic technique, in vocabulary and phrasing, imagery and rhythm. As English poets ascend, the vocabulary relies less on gorgeous or precious association, more on the distillate of everyday and wide experience. The phrasing is bolder, does not shrink from hard effects, has less fear of the banal. The imagery is less crowded and less highly colored. The rhythm, less songlike, takes on a more unmistakable *beat*, insistent, though in English iambic verse often highly irregular. There is in general a growing fearlessness and at the same time a growing thrift. For the sake of having simple labels (too simple to be just), we might say that feeling, the censor of poetry, is at first "soft" and later "hard." One or two very great English poets, the myriad-minded ones—Shakespeare and Joyce—retain even at a "late" stage the power of writing in an "early" style, much as Beethoven could vary the Alpine sublimity of his last quartets and sonatas with movements of warm romantic feeling. In Joyce's *Pomes Penyeach*, for example, "Alone" and "Tutto e Sciolto" are "soft" poems, uttered through a romantic or adolescent *persona*, while "Tilly" and "A Memory of the Players" are in every way "mature" or "hard."

Hafiz' verse, like all Persian verse, is more intoned than English. But, making allowance for this difference, a comparison of it with various types of English verse will show that most of the *ghazals* belong, in vocabulary and imagery, to the "late" or "hard" level of poetry. Consequently, if it is proposed to turn Hafiz into English verse, the verse should be pitched right; the translator should model himself on English poetry of like timbre.

The translations assembled by Professor Arberry vary in technique and in quality; and some of the later versions are considerably more like Hafiz than the eigh-

teenth-century lyrics of which I have spoken above. The influence of FitzGerald can be seen in practically all subsequent translators, and in lines where it is strongest, as in Gertrude Bell's

> Last night I dreamed that angels stood
>   without
> The tavern-door, and knocked in vain,

the result is pleasing. FitzGeraldese is a very good English equivalent for Persian, so far as it goes, no doubt; but it will not stretch far enough. Omar is a much simpler poet than Hafiz, and FitzGerald affords no guidance in preserving the compact mystery of such a *ghazal*, for example, as *Dil-i Shayda*. Professor Arberry was wise to give his own versions of the wonderful later odes, for he is most free from FitzGerald, and an eclectic of wide poetical reading. But even he is comparatively "soft" in poetical technique when set beside his original, "hard" though he seems when set beside Richardson or Leaf or Bell.

As an epitome of "softness" I choose Leaf's rendering of Hafiz' *khuy kardeh*, "sweating," by "cheek beflushed." Whose voice says, "Only animals sweat: gentlemen perspire, and young ladies are all in a glow"? It is not the voice of Hafiz, certainly—not even the voice of my grandmother, but the voice of my grandmother's governess. Professor Arberry himself can turn *kujai*, "Where are you?" into "Whither fled?" But I will waste none of my rotten eggs on him; I want them for the others. Many passages of Hafiz are turned by him with an elegance I can only admire; but his associates lapse into the worst sentimentalities of the "fleshly school" of the latter nineteenth century. "I say prayer, and praise I send thee" becomes "What whispered prayers and what full meed of praise I send to thee."

Hafiz is not so soft or precious; and his rhetoric depends less on the raised or the plaintive tone than on a kind of intellectual involvement. His apostrophes and questions are those of common Persian speech; "O ask not whom!" and so on (in No. 26) is quite wrong for his "Don't ask!"

It may be questioned whether any English poet of any period has enough in common with Hafiz to serve as guide in these technical difficulties. Perhaps Donne comes closest. In his poetry, as in the *Divan* of Hafiz, there is a changing relation and a constant connection between the erotic and the metaphysical: even in youth his erotic is not sentimental but charged with physical reality and an incipient metaphysical penetration which allows of a strange and wide-flung rhetoric in which the bodily and the cosmic lie together entangled. When he writes:

> The hair a Forest is of Ambushes
> Of springes, snares, fetters, and man-
>   acles. . . .

or

> The nose (like to the first Meridian) runs
> Not 'twixt an East and West, but 'twixt
>     two suns . . .

or

> Let every Jewel be a glorious Starre
> Yet starres are not so pure as their
>     spheares are . . .

we seem to hear the celebration of the Saqi's lovelock, eyes, or girdle. The closely folded assonances of both sound (glor-, Starre, pure, spheares) and concealed meaning (hair, forest, am*bush*) are devices loved by the Persian. Donne, too like Hafiz, can make us see the Cosmic Face, or God as Face:

> Though thou with clouds of anger do dis-
>     guise
> Thy face; yet through that mask I know
>     those eyes,
> Which, though they turn away sometimes,
> They never will despise.

And Donne, too, though occasionally and late (as in certain of the "Holy Sonnets" or in the "Hymne to God the Father"), uses—like Hafiz—a repetitive or "percussive" technique, a spondaic music of meaning and of sound, which moves at a Persian pace, though heavily.

The resemblance, however, is far indeed from complete. Donne's breath is autumnal and stormy, Hafiz' of a more flowery season. Hafiz' art is on the whole a *gay* art, however serious his purpose. And that makes it no easier, for there has been no great gay poet in English since Spenser.

All this sounds like perfectionism, for a translator who shall be both Donne and Spenser, and a chastened scholar to boot, is a tall order. But there is an appropriate level for the verse translation of any poet, below which even the comparatively good is not good enough, and in the case of Hafiz that level is, so far as I can see, a very high one. And I have faith that no scholar will in the full consciousness of what he is doing degrade so great a poet into verse too minor. The responsibility of making new verse out of a poet like Hafiz is a perfectly grave one. To reprint Jones's or Le Gallienne's versions implies (although Professor Arberry does not say so) that they are in a sense held up as possible models. And with this implication my quarrel is mortal. To deviate from a modest fidelity (of which every scholar is capable, and which makes Professor Nicholson's Rumi a treasure beyond price) into literary self-indulgence is a sin which I shall be rude enough to call by its true name.

And now, to confess the suspicion which has been strong enough to give these remarks a tone mounting, I am afraid, to indignation, I believe that although Professor Arberry's own interest in Hafiz' meaning is evidently profound, this volume exhibits and condones indifference to it. And I believe Hafiz' thought to be so rich as to be worth the having in a stammering ungraceful speech if no smoother is to be had.

As to the prime significance of the poet, I would agree that Hafiz was probably passionate and voluptuous, that he drank and sang the wine of the grape and hungered and thirsted after the flesh. But I am also sure that he was increasingly possessed by the need of an absolute relationship with God, and that sexual desire, insatiable as it is, and drunkenness, in which bliss a sense of insight does actually expel the impious cares of reason, were perhaps always and without doubt increasingly types of religious experience, for him as for other Sufis. The one contemporary reference to him· cited by Browne indicates a man too occupied with the metaphysics of the Koran and with the philosophy of rhetoric to collect his own poems. His **Divan** is permeated with Sufism; and the meaning of his life and work is primarily religious or metaphysical. Even an aesthetic critique of his verse which fails to show the intricacy of his metaphysical reference is aesthetically shallow, since much of his art itself is precisely the calculated weaving of multiple meaning.

The meaning of any particular *ghazal*, that notion of which the orderly development holds the words and images together, that piece of Hafiz' thought, is both temporally and psychologically prior to the words. The words even of a long monorhyme are not suggested by a rhyming dictionary only, in the case of a great poet. They receive sanction from a nonverbal scheme. That is what makes real translation possible. "When we read a book in a foreign language, we suppose that an English version of it would be a transfusion of it into our own consciousness. But take Coleridge or Bacon, or many an English book besides, and you immediately feel that the English is a language also, and that a book writ in that tongue is yet very far from you— from being transfused into your own consciousness. There is every degree of remoteness from the line of things in the line of words. By and by comes a word true and closely embracing the thing. That is not Latin, nor English, nor any language but *thought*. The aim of the author is not to tell truth—that he cannot do, but to suggest it. He has only approximated it himself and hence his cumbrous, embarrassed speech; he uses many words, hoping that one, if not another, will bring you as near to the fact as he is. For language itself is young and unformed. In heaven, it will be one with things. Now, there are many things that refuse to be recorded— perhaps the larger half. The unsaid part is the best of every discourse."[3]

A good translation of a *ghazal* will not pull the "line of words" further from the "line of things" than is inevitable. The translator, it follows, must make out the "line of things" as clearly as he can. In Hafiz' work the things that matter are approximated as a rule by symbols, limited in number, but mostly very rich in reference, with a good deal of which his audience was already familiar.

By way of example, we may take the lovely ode printed as No. 44, "**Rose and Nightingale,**" Professor Arberry's version of which has considerable beauty. It is one of the very best renderings in the book. The poet, coming to the garden to pluck a rose, suddenly hears a nightingale, whose love song for the rose assails his ear, then his mind, then his heart, and the last unbearably. The ode might profitably be expounded word by word; but our present purpose can only be to find its central thought, the "line of things," as a preliminary to showing how the requirements of poetic form have pulled the "line of words" away from it even in this fine rendering. Hafiz' audience, it need hardly be said, understood the Nightingale as a reference to the poet as turner into music of his unsatisfied longing for self-sufficient beauty (the Rose), and also as a reference to God as Lover (Lover of Souls, a Catholic might say). In the poem the Nightingale is actualized in the following terms: the voice or *solo* of his song; needy; and entangled or involved; the gurgling sound of his song, as of wine being poured; wedded or equivalent to Love (as contrasted in the same line with the Rose, which is the companion or sweetheart merely of Beauty); no change in it. There is a curious precision in these words—a precision of almost theological cast. Unless it is accidental, we must see the pre-verbal thought closely pressing the words. . . .

There is a wavering in this English version of a "line of words" which in the Persian ran straight and close to the "line of things." Hafiz' choice was delicately adjusted to the divine symbolism; and it is the mounting force of what is symbolically present which changes the eager poet of the first couplet to the philosopher of the last. For the poem ends in an austere couplet where the close beauty of the garden landscape is exchanged for something wide and cold, the Wheel of Heaven: this circumferential World is as ruthless as the Rose. . . . The poem's development is only acceptable under the presidency of its meaning: if all the fuss is about a garden nightingale, it is sentimental, and its development improbable.

Now these central notions—of the concomitance of beauty and pain and of world pain as the pouring-out of God's longing for souls, which, once felt, transmutes the lust for individual possession of individual beauty—are surely of sufficient importance to call for the most respectful preservation in any English rendering. Without them, Hafiz' poem is merely charming; embodying them, it sinks deep in the mind. Had Professor Arberry contented himself with a prose rendering, his scholarship and his taste would have insured the safe-conduct of Hafiz' intention. But in verse, to which his literary gift has given a charm of its own, that intention is obscured.

It would be ungrateful, when Professor Arberry has given us so interesting an Introduction, and such good verse as his translations of Nos. 15, 30, 34, 44, 46, 47, Leaf's No. 28, and the pleasant songs in English classical style, to criticize these versions so relentlessly as representatives of Hafiz without saying what kind of a translation I think due.

It will be appropriate here to quote Arthur Waley's introductory note on his method of translation from the Chinese. He writes:

> I have aimed at literal translation, not paraphrase. . . . . Above all, considering imagery to be the soul of poetry, I have avoided either adding images of my own or suppressing those of the original. . . . Translating literally, without thinking about the metre of the version, one finds that about two lines out of three have a very definite swing similar to that of the Chinese lines. The remaining lines are just too short or too long, a circumstance very irritating to the reader, whose ear expects the rhythm to continue. I have therefore tried to produce regular rhythmic effects similar to those of the original. Each character (word) in the Chinese is represented by a stress in the English, but between the stresses unstressed syllables are of course interposed.[4]

This method, in Waley's hands, produced versions which have persuaded innumerable readers of the quality of their Chinese originals. And the question springs to mind: May this method, or an adaptation of it, be applied to the translation of Hafiz?

By way of experiment, I chose more or less at random a *ghazal* (No. 24 in this collection) of which the translation given (Gertrude Bell's) displeased me and tried to make a literal translation, preserving the monorhyme at the end of each couplet at the cost of natural word order. It then appeared that comparatively little manipulation was necessary to produce a version which could be read in the rhythm of the original. It certainly lacked the *music* of the original, and the meter not being an English one, the result is not really English verse at all. However, although I failed to translate the ambiguity of the third couplet, it proved possible to preserve, in awkward words, much of the system of verbal echoes and permutations which were so remarkable in the Persian.

Gertrude Bell's version of the lines, cleared of interpolation by Professor Arberry, runs as follows:

> I cease not from desire till my desire
> Is satisfied; or let my mouth attain

My love's red mouth, or let my soul expire,
Sighed from those lips that sought her lips
    in vain.
When I am dead, open my grave and see
The cloud of smoke that rises round thy
    feet;
In my dead heart the fire still burns for
    thee;
Yea, the smoke rises from my winding
    sheet!
Reveal thy face! that the whole world
    may be
Bewildered by thy radiant loveliness;
The cry of man and woman comes to thee,
Open thy lips and comfort their distress.
My soul is on my lips ready to fly,
But grief beats in my heart and will not
    cease,
Because not once, not once before I die,
Will her sweet lips give all my longing
    peace.
My breath is narrowed down to one long
    sigh
For a red mouth that burns my thoughts
    like fire:
When will that mouth draw near and
    make reply
To one whose life is straitened with de-
    sire?
Yet when sad lovers meet and tell their
    sighs,
Not without praise shall Hafiz' name be
    said,
Not without tears, in those pale companies
Where joy has been forgot and hope has
    fled.

The literal version runs as follows:

This Hand from Begging I'll not hold till
    my Seeking be come;
Or Body come to Soul's-love, or Soul from
    Body let come.
Open my Burial-place after my death,
    and you'll see
From Fire of What's-within-me sighing
    Smoke from the Shroud come.
Unveil the Face! that a Creation go crazed
    and wildered;
Open the Lips! that the Cry from Man
    and Woman may come.
Soul at the Lips; in the Heart—pining,
    that forth from those Lips,
Nothing of all its Seeking clasped, Soul
    from Body must come.
By pining after His Mouth my Soul is
    come to the Pinch—
Self-seeking of the Pinched Hand: when
    from that Mouth should it come?

Speak they his Good in the Troop of the
    Gamblers-for-Love
Where'er the name of Hafiz into the Com-
    pany come.

It will be noticed that the commonplace metaphor "smoke/sigh," to which Professor Arberry draws attention in his note, is incorporated in the phrase "sighing Smoke." . . .

The two versions, unsigned, were submitted in typescript to a number of good-natured persons, taken at random and without narrower selection than was implied in my supposing that they occasionally read poetry. All were asked which version they found the more interesting. A substantial majority (thirteen to seven) preferred the literal to the poetical translation.

What the experiment seems to indicate is that Hafiz' meaning and imagery are more interesting than minor English verse, even without any annotation or key to the reference. Of the awkwardness of my version no one is more uncomfortably aware than myself. A verbal surface which should be smooth and firm is gnarled and corky. It seems that its superior attraction owes little to literary charm, and everything to the preservation of much of Hafiz' design. That element, design both verbal and ideal, is paramount in the great odes. Here it consists in the disposition of certain verbal motifs . . . and the various words meaning "mouth" and "lips," along a line of changing or developing feeling. The development reaches its crisis . . . which solves the intellectual stress of the poet's despair and permits the elegiac or "disembodied" return to earthly company in the final couplet. This contains an important play on words . . . suggesting "soldier," literally "one who stakes his head"; and the poem thus ends on a note of wit and self-possession very different from the "lovers' litany" atmosphere of Gertrude Bell's translation of it.

In point of design the lyric is such a masterpiece that the translator's most obligatory duty is surely to indicate it. However awkward it may be to use "seeking" . . . it must be done for the sake of the lead to "self-seeking," in which the poet sees himself, among others, diminished by the vast illumination of the third couplet, in which ("Face") floats like a suddenly unclouded moon (an inevitable suggestion in Persian commonplace), the unclouding hinted by the "Smoke" of the preceding line. We have seen the whole world as landscape permeated with the longing which had in the first couplet been personal and as selfish as a beggar's begging.

This intricacy of design is what gives the little lyric its seedlike power of growth in the mind. *Here* is what makes Hafiz worth an English poet's study—a music of meaning beyond the music of the words, a richness of which Emerson was aware when he called Hafiz a "fact-book which all geniuses prize as raw material and as antidote to verbiage and false poetry."

In order to render the design perceptible, proper translation must be annotated; and for novices I would have it more fully annotated than the present volume. Certainly I would have any translation of so orderly a poet as neat as may be; the constant interpolation in his very text of didactic interpretation is to me a hardly pardonable fault in the prose translations by Wilberforce Clarke. But the reader has not really read Hafiz until something like the full reach of association and reference has opened out from the words. For example, it seems to me essential to the understanding of the mysterious *mathnawi* "**Wild Deer**," No. 47 of this selection, that the Khizr mythology should be given more fully, that the resemblance between the poem's structure and the structure of a *qasida* be pointed out and the desert background of the *qasida* sketched, and that the story of Majnun be told. (I cannot believe that there is any lack of learning or failure on Professor Arberry's part to recognize that the figure of the poet calling to the wild deer is the figure of Majnun.) The substance of the poem is a kind of wondering change from seeing the world of bereavement as the desert of Majnun's despair to seeing it as the land of shadows in which Khizr found the water of life, running in counterpoint with a change from the quest of a distant heaven to the recognition of heaven as an eternal aspect of the here and now. Fish and reed are water creatures—but they are creatures of the water of life itself. The reference at the poem's resolution to Koran 68:1, supplied by Professor Arberry, must be extended to verse 2: "By the grace of your Lord you are not mad (*majnun*)." The poem as a whole appears to be a mystical exposition of Koran 21:31 ("The Heavens and the Earth were closed up; but We have opened them; and We have made of water everything living"). The earthly way ambushed before and behind of the second line, the heavenly way unmarked of line 15, and the varying returns to water as tears and so forth, leading to the growing "seed" of the resolution, seem to make this certain. I would have the novice's attention drawn to this framework, and also to the zoölogical knowledge of Hafiz' time which makes the references to deer, musk, Cathay, so rich in the poem. Am I rash in also supposing an important implication of disease and cure in the poem? In contemporary pharmacology the musk of the deer is hot and dry to the third degree. It is therefore a drug and not a food. It turns the complexion yellow (like worldly love); it is antidote against actual poisons (like worldly love); and it makes visible the breath of the mouth (in sighs and poetry, like love). Its own pernicious effects are removed by camphor (in which to any *hafiz* would emerge a reference to Koran 76:5, interpreted by the commentators as the extinction of worldly love in those who drink the cup of Love). The "mixing" of line 25 may refer to the koranic phrase.

To supply a modern Western reader with these implied meanings must be a cumbrous procedure; but the weaving of them was a vital part of Hafiz' art. And *it can be done in English*.

For the right literal rendering, the translator must risk, where there is a choice, words and phrases capable of bearing (even if they stagger under) the references and connections which are the tissue of the poem. Of most of the odes the aftereffect is of something which has come and gone swiftly, and of a superficially precise statement which, once past, leaves an enigmatic echo in the mind. This precise textural effect is largely achieved by the system of interrelations, an interlocking of sounds, images, and meanings; at the same time a certain sense of mystery arises from the crowding of varied recurrences upon already established associations, from puns, from the deliberate ambiguity of occasional ambivalent words and parenthetic phrasing, and from the definitely hypnotic effect of monorhyme.

The monorhyme word, where it occurs, and which translation impoverishes itself in avoiding, is of equal importance as a constant element in Hafiz' method of design with the significant commonplace (the Rose, the Cup, the Cypress, the Wind, and the rest). It demands special care. Translations 12, 14, and 26 of this volume preserve it in diluted form. "Recall" in No. 14 is too literary in English flavor and too weak in sound to convey the longing in the Persian spondee: "bring back" would have served better. The version of No. 26 by H.H. gives a series of slight variations ("Ask me not how, O ask not whom," etc.) . . . Apart from the sentimental ring of such phrases in English, the variation of the last word of the phrase qualifies what was in Hafiz absolute. "Don't ask" or " . . . that you'd better not ask" sound colloquial, but that very quality may correspond usefully with the abruptness of the Persian phrase. Often in translating Hafiz will the dilemma arise: one English phrasing poetizes, another is too prosaic. In general, since a literal translation will inevitably be more prosaic than its original, the translator can count on preserving some consistency in choosing the more accurate correspondence in meaning and flavor, even when he chooses a phrasing more prosaic than he would wish.

Commonplace and monorhyme matter not only because Hafiz loved and chose a form to which they are essential but because both are eloquent paradigms of the Persian philosophy of life and art. Rhythmic repetition has been a constant principle of composition in Persian art because its basis lies deep in the mind. Medieval Persia saw in repetitiveness the principle of order in a time-extended cosmos; and this vision of cosmic manifestation as cumulative repetitive variation broods over her art and literature from the age of Firdawsi onward. At the center in which the coil began and will end is Allah, no doubt; but there is no other escape from the turning wheel which rules worldly affairs. It is no accident, but a proof of historical necessity, that the doctrine of the Wheel appeared in its clear Hurufi form in the Persia of Hafiz' lifetime. The Persian conned these odes as he conned life itself. Repetition informs not only the technique of the *ghazal* but its poetic substance. The reappearing commonplaces Cup and Wind, "rhyme in the mind"; and the process—one of recognition followed by the revival of old and the discovery of new connotation—is the psychological process of consciousness itself.

To understand any Persian artistic exploit, one must discard the notion that the repetitive is wholly wearisome. Its life in memory, after all, is mother to the Muses, and is the half of beauty; all music and all rhyme derive from it. That the Persians valued it more highly than we have lately done both in philosophy and in art does not necessarily mean that they are shallower than we. The idea of progress is probably exactly as deep and exactly as shallow as the idea that history repeats itself.

The Persians essayed to complete the mental structure inwardly. The self-contained *intricacy* which is so characteristic of Hafiz' art, as of the visual arts of his and the next age, is fundamentally an exploration of intensive or nonextensive variety. To Persian wisdom, all the wilds of our pilgrimage are within and the heart is the true horizon.

There should be no fear that Hafiz will be uninteresting in a translation which exposes what a Persian draftsman would call the "bones" of his composition. Annotation may be laborious; but it is, so far as I can see, the only substitute for a thorough Persian and Sufi education. And, once the references and internal structure of an ode are understood, its hidden perfections emerge and its far-reaching intellectual vistas open up so startlingly that one can hardly wonder if Hafiz has rivaled the Koran as a popular source of omens and prognostications. When a *ghazal* can mean so much, the superstitious may be forgiven for supposing that any sentence means everything, future as well as past.

So if we are offered translation from Hafiz, let it be fearless; and let what Persia has loved remain.

Reading over this vehement judgment, I half repent of it. Professor Arberry's book not only occasioned the intensified interest in the poet which caused me to write it but supplied the very framework of my notions of his development. It will be good for me to confess that I was so ignorant of Hafiz as never to have read (because it is printed so late in the long **Divan**) the "**Wild Deer**" *mathnawi*. Now it has become for me perhaps the greatest of all Hafiz' poems, and surely one of the greatest poems in any language. And although Professor Arberry's translation does not satisfy me (any more

than, I feel sure, it satisfies him), all the greatness was not lost in it. I owe to him the impulse to make my own translation of the poem and the discovery that that too does not satisfy me. Hence I return even to the poetical paraphrases with a humbler intolerance and to the rest of the book with increase of gratitude and with very real respect.

*Notes*

[1] A review of Arthur J. Arberry, *Fifty Poems of Hafiz* (Cambridge: At the University Press; New York: Macmillan Co., 1947).

[2] "Hafiz and His English Translators," *Islamic Culture*, XX, Nos. 2 and 3 (April and July, 1946).

[3] Emerson, *Journals*.

[4] *170 Chinese Poems* (New York, 1938), p. 33.

**Alessandro Bausani (essay date 1958)**

SOURCE: "A Way to a Better Understanding of the Structure of Western Poetry," *East and West*, Vol. 9, No. 1-2, March-June, 1958, pp. 145-53.

[*In the following essay, Bausani analyzes the text of many Persian verses, including those of Hafiz, discussing the styles and techniques displayed in the lyrics of seventh-century Iran.*]

The scientific study of style in both European and Oriental lyrics is a comparatively recent conquest of our literary criticism. Unfortunately, the student of the form and historical developments of European, "Western", literary style does not have at his disposal sufficient materials for stylistic comparisons. "A thing is better known through its contrary" says an old Muslim tradition. One of the causes of the rather complicated and somewhat obscure language of many Western studies dealing with problems of stylistics lies, in my opinion, in the lack of comparing possibilities. Our critics considered the world of Western lyrics as *the world* of Lyrics, thus assuming a colonialistic attitude, which, strangely enough, they often succeeded in forcing upon some modern Asian critics as well. Dislike for the alleged "euphuism" and baroque form of Muslim classical art, absolute appreciation of the "natural", the "passionate directness" of Western literary style are attitudes often taken even by contemporary Oriental littérateurs: one of these was for instance the famous Urdu poet Hali (d. 1914), not to speak of some modern Persian writers.

A better understanding of the form of classical Muslim lyrics (the most perfect example of which is, probably, the Persian *ghazal*) would help—I think—modern European critics to a deeper insight into the structure of *our* lyrics. Persian lyrical style offers—to this purpose—an especially favourable field of study. It started from a point of departure not too far from that of our medieval "traditional" lyrics of the troubadours, but it afterwards developed on quite different lines.

My purpose in this article is to introduce the reader, to whom the Persian language—perhaps the richest poetical instrument of the Near and Middle East—is unknown, into the labyrinthine forms of the lyrics of "modern" Iran, that is to say the Iran of the 7th century after the Islamic conquest. As I am addressing a reader to whom I presume the language is unknown, I must have recourse to a rather laborious analysis of some texts belonging to a lyrical tradition that uses materials other than those familiar to us, and this will require of the reader the closest *attention*—in the etymological meaning of that word—and for this I apologise in advance.

Those who know Persian poetry through translations are led to one of two conclusions. They will either conceive for it an ingenuous admiration, reminiscent of the 19th century enthusiasms of Platen or Fitzgerald, admiring something which is not, strictly speaking, Persian poetry at all; or they will be bored and confirmed in their belief that the said poetry is nothing but a tiresome series of verbal acrobatics, a poor replica of European euphuism. Thus the well-known and widespread impression that our Western tradition alone has produced, in this field as in others, something really "living" and vital will be confirmed and the reader will be led once more to limit himself to the philological and cautious cultural provincialism of the West. Both these conclusions are alike discouraging for the Orientalist who believes that the subjects he deals with are of more than scientific importance and that it is his mission to enable large circles of the educated public—acquainted in our case with the culture of the West—to appreciate as fully and accurately as possible the spiritual "structures" of another type of culture.

Unfortunately, both the special difficulties of the task when lyric style is the subject dealt with, and the general tendency of European orientalism to restrict its field to that of philological science, have reduced to very small proportions studies devoted to the style and technique of Persian poetry. I do not think I exaggerate when I say that were it not for the very noteworthy names of Ritter who, in a youthful work of his of 1927 (2) made a truly fine study of the imagery used by Nizami, and for that of the Czech, Rypka (3), author of a masterly analysis of Turkish and Persian lyrical forms, were it not for these two writers who have both studied Persian poetry from the inside, the field with which we are dealing would be practically unexplored. In any case we may say that the *history* of the several styles and the study of the variations of Persian lyrical forms, which are not so uniformly monotonous as some believe, is practically untrodden ground. As we shall see, in the course of time at least five different styles have been used successively.

And now as an introduction to our subject, let us begin by reading a free translation of a famous lyric by Hafiz (14th century), the Prince of Persian poets, to which we will add a more detailed analysis. It will clearly show that in this field more than in any other, and often without his being at fault, the translator is necessarily a traitor. The general atmosphere of this ghazal is vaguely "the return of the Spring".

1 - Once more the age of youth has returned to the garden—and the sweet-singing nightingale receives the good news of the Flower.

2 - Oh, gentle breeze! should you once more reach the budding plants in the meadow, give my greetings to the Basil, the Rose, the Cypress tree.

3 - The young Son of the Magi, the Vintner, appears before me in such charming motions that I am ready to sweep with my eyebrows the dust of the Tavern.

4 - Oh, thou who coverest with purest amber the face of the Moon, do not perturb yet more this man perplexed by love.

5 - I greatly fear that those who laugh at wine-bibbers may at last make a tavern of their Faith in God.

6 - But mayest thou remain a friend of the Holy Men, for in the Ship of Noah there is still a handful of Mud that knows how to defy the Deluge.

7 - Go out from this Dwelling, that has the Heavens for roof, and do not ask it for Food, for that Vile One at the end shamelessly kills her Guest.

8 - And say to those whose last resting-place will be a handful of Dust: "Friend, what avails it to raise high palaces to the Skies?"

9 - Oh, moon of Canaan! The throne of Egypt has been allotted thee; it is now high time that thou shouldst say farewell to the Prison!

10 - Oh Hafiz, drink wine, and be a libertine, and live joyfully, but take care, not, as others do, to make a snare of the Book of God!

We have here an excellent example—the poem has been chosen almost by chance—of many features characteristic of the style of Persian lyrical poetry of the golden age. Let us list, first of all, the several motifs: of the images indeed none, without exception, are original, though they may strike a Western ear as such.

1. - Nightingale-Rose (Flower). It may seem strange, but this motif, perhaps the one that occurs most frequently in Persian lyrics, has never been the object of historical research (4). It appears in the most ancient Persian lyrics of the 10th century. In the maturer lyrical forms (Hafiz) it contains the following meanings:

The rose is beauty aware of itself, the supreme, inaccessible symbol of the divine *istighna*; often the rose disdainfully derides the nightingale but as soon as it blossoms it dies. This is the cause of the twofold sadness of the nightingale, which mourns over the rapid death of the rose and its disdainful rejection of union. But between the two there is a kind of mysterious connection: the Bird of Dawn (an epithet very frequently applied to the nightingale) alone understands the secret language of the rose. The nightingale sings in *Arabic*—the sacred language—invitations to partake of the mystic wine. Inebriated with the perfume of the rose it fears to end as did the magic-angel, Marut. As in the traditions (Cfr. Qur'an, XVII, 78) the prayer offered at dawn is of special value and has special power, so the lament of the nightingale is the auroral prayer. But it is a dolesome prayer, offered to something inaccessible, for, as Muqaddasi says in his charming book translated in the middle of last century by Garcin de Tassy (5) "my song is a song of grief and not of joy . . . Each time that I flutter over a garden I warble of the affliction that will soon replace the gaiety that reigns there". In an Indian Moslem allegory, the romance of the *Rose of Bakawali* (6) the inaccessible Rose, so difficult to find, is the only remedy that can restore the sight of King Zainu'l-Muluk, etc. The God-Rose identity in the famous preface of the *Golestan* of Sadi can be clearly seen when the Mystic who travels in the transcendental world is unable to bring back any gift from his travels because: "I had in mind that when I reached the Rose tree I would fill my lap with roses as gifts for my friends, but when I reached it I was so inebriated with the perfume of the Rose that the hem of my robe slipped from my hand". (7)

The enthusiastic pan-iranist, Pizzi, has endeavoured, but without adequate evidence, to show influence of the Persian Rose motif in the mediaeval *Roman de la Rose*, whose symbolism is reminiscent of this (8). But in the absence of definite documentary evidence and of preparatory studies we cannot exclude the opposite hypothesis which is that a Hellenistic motif may have penetrated into both cultures, derived from that civilisation which in various ways and forms fertilised them both, *i.e.* the late Hellenistic symbolism. The reader should, however, bear in mind that what we refer to is a *motif* and not *an emotional and original perception* by Hafiz of the "romantic" and vivid reality of the Spring and the flowers. As we shall see, the "originality" of a Persian poet must be sought in other directions.

2. - And here we have another "personage", the *saba*, "the zephir", the spring-time breeze, generally held to be—and not for the first time by Hafiz but by innumerable poets before and after him—the Messenger *par excellence*. The breeze also is personified in a bird, more especially the hoopoe. Why? because with a very slight change in the transcription, the pronunciation of its name is identical to that of the famous region of *Saba* (Sheba) whose Queen, we read in the Qur'an, sent a hoopoe as her messenger to King Solomon. Thus the "secondary images" aroused in the mind of the listener by the word *saba* are quite other than those awakened in us by the word "zephir", now ineradicably associated in our minds with Metastasio and Watteau. *Saba* is a sound that reverberates with a rich symbolism which can be traced back historically and clearly to a "gnostic" world. Basil (*raihan*), mentioned soon after, which to us suggests little more than the idea of "perfume", is instead a word quoted in the Qur'an. The fragrance of basil is one of the chief components of the olfactory joys of the Islamic paradise (cfr. Qur'an, LVI, 89), and, singularly enough, of the Zoroastrian paradise also (cfr. *Menoke Xrat*, chpt. VII). On the other hand, the Cypress, familiar to all amateur collectors of Persian carpets and miniatures, in its charming conventionalised shapes, is the sacred tree of Zoroaster. It is identified with the Prophet himself who planted a specially memorable cypress (that of Kashmar) just at the time when the ecstatic-prophetic experience first thrilled him (9). It is a motif that seems to have come straight from a Central Asian spiritual area: the Shaman, indeed, plants a tree when starting on his "prophetic" career (10). Thus, even if in the case in point the words are not always intentionally and knowingly symbolical, they are not merely descriptive but are related to verbal-psychological cycles with which they have no connection in our languages.

3. - In the springtime scenery summoned before us, the nightingale, the rose, the zephir, the cypress, basil and the "young" (plants) of the meadow are playing a part in a scene which, even from our descriptive standpoint might acquire a certain unity. But now there enters a character who to our eyes may seem truly extraneous. He is the young Magian (*moghba è*), the vintner, and the *Tavern*. Elsewhere (11) I have shown that the "Zoroastrian" character of the images connected with wine, with the *Superior* of the Magi, and with the Young Magian (all images—the reader may be sure—not invented by Hafiz, for the connection between inebriety and forbidden practices with the Zoroastrian belief dates back to *Daqiqi* (12) of the 10th century) are but words used to summon up the idea of that which is forbidden, of sacred impiety. Poets ancient and modern, to evoke this idea use indiscriminately the words *Magian Christian, temple of fire* or *church*. Sa'di (13th century) although the differences were known to him, uses indiscriminately the words "priest", "bishop", "Brahmin" "Magian", "temple of fire", "church", "mon-

astery" in the same poem (13). The ideas that these lyrical-symbolic images summon up are not something precisely and theologically Zoroastrian (wine indeed is only a secondary element in the Zoroastrian ritual); they serve as signs indicating an esoteric rite. As lyrical poetry was traditionally condemned both by Islam and by Zoroastrianism, the motif of *self-abasement* is added to this intricate image-motif. The poet, the Initiate, is willing even to wipe with his face the door of the tavern-temple where the Young Magian reigns. Here is summed up the material inherited from the frankly libertine poetry of the Arab *neoteroi* (14) (wine-Christian Convent, already found in pre-Islamic Arab poetry) with the mystical gnostic motif of a Rite of the Wine which, even if, as Massignon would have it (15), it is already found in the Qur'anic symbolism of Paradise (*yaum-i mazid*), is nevertheless of more ancient sincretic-gnostic origin.

4. - And now, as in a filiform succession of images, the Young Magian takes on the ambiguous appearance of a boy-girl. Our aesthetic taste compels us sometimes to translate in the feminine what perhaps—and I say *perhaps* because the feminine gender is unknown to Persian grammar—was masculine. The fourth verse should more accurately be translated as: "Oh thou, who drawest across the moon a polo-stick (*chaugan*) of the purest amber, do not make me, whose head whirls (like a polo ball) yet more confused". And we must then add that the game of polo, which is of Persian origin, supplies a wealth of images to this lyric. The polo stick, with its characteristic hooked shape, is the *zolf*, the long whisp of hair, black as the night, and the moon is no other than the face (the roundness of the face is traditionally greatly admired in this lyric). The Child-Magian who is also the Beloved of the Poet (or his *Initiator*, or *God*, for even if Hafiz does not consciously wish it, tradition wills it thus) has the brilliant and round face of the moon. By mischievously half-veiling it with his black curl, shaped like a polo stick, he only makes the already confused head of the poet whirl like a polo-ball. And here the reader should be warned of a feature of this poetry, a rule of style studied by Ritter, which, I have suggested elsewhere (16), should be called the law of the *formal harmony of comparison*. In other words, the objects compared must have the same *shape*. The Persian poet does not create new poetic images but creates skilful, and if possible new *relations between objects*. In Persian poetry there are no mythological characters; things retain their natural shape: the wizardry of the poet consists in his skilful treatment of objects while respecting their shapes (moon=face, curl=polo-stick).

5. - In this verse the poet introduces another motif: he upbraids the *doctors of the law*, the *othodox*. And here, let me repeat, Hafiz must not for this be taken for an "anticlerical", a "progressive". There may be cases in the traditional poetry of Persia of *mullas* who, when

indulging in this literary style, are obeying its conventions in abusing . . . themselves as a class. This motif can only have arisen from the fact that this kind of poetry gave a gnostic-neo-platonic interpretation to materials—derived from the Arabian Abbasid libertine poetry—quite heterogeneous to Islamic orthodoxy. The result was a strange combination of libertinism and mysticism that confers on it a special kind of style of its own.

6. - The verse that follows contains a transparent allusion to the superiority of the Saint (the man of God) over the Doctor of the Law, very skilfully expressed. Noah's ship is the human race, the handful of mud that it contains, possessing however the supreme faculty of overcoming any deluge, is the Perfect Man. the Saint, the mystic Master. He is "earth", mud indeed, but one which—as the original puts it—*be-abi nakharad tufanra*, that is to say "would not buy the deluge for a drop of water", i.e. gives no importance to external "deluges" (and here note the word-play water-deluge-earth). We should therefore be friends of those Masters and not of the doctors of the law.

7-8. - The ethnical-mystical warning continues. But, be it always remembered, without undue personal tension. The world is seen as a house, an "old dilapidated convent". But the world—in Arabic a word of feminine gender,—is also often compared by the Persian poets to a malicious, faithless old woman. Here the word we have translated by "Vile One" is *siyah-kasè*, "of the black pot", also "miserly" "despicable"; hence the play of words "food"- "pot".

9. - The following verse contains a metaphor which may be familiar to the Westerner also Joseph the Jew, the symbol of perfect beauty, or of the Soul, for whom the therone of Egypt is prepared, but who yet groans in prison (a classic neo-Platonic metaphor). The last verse reiterates the traditional accusation of hypocrisy addressed to the *mullas*.

The reader unaccustomed to this kind of poetry will have noted a rather disconcerting feature it displays. Each verse forms a closed unit, only slightly interconnected with the others. Some modern scholars (17) to explain them have invoked the "psychology of depth" to show that there is unity, but an *unconscious* one, in the *ghazal*. However this may be, external incongruity would seem to be a real rule in classic Persian poetry. We are in the presence of a bunch of motifs only lightly tied together.

Now, is this lyrical style so monotous and invariable, as many have said? We think it is not, and we shall try to show the direction in which changes have come about, taking as our starting point the most important stylistic theme, the lyric of the golden age to which we have been introducing the reader.

The brief composition I shall now present is one of the most ancient specimens of Persian literature; it is by Daqiqi and dates back to the 10th century.

1 - A cloud from Paradise, oh my Idol, has clothed the earth in the gala raiment of April,

2 - And the rose garden looks like the paradise of Eden, with trees garlanded with flowers like the houris of heaven.

3 - So changed is the world that you would say that the tiger leaps on the kid only for a harmless scuffle,

4 - And you would say that the world has become like a peacock, here rough and uneven, there soft and smooth.

5 - The earth looks like a brocade spotted with blood, and the wind seems a hand wrapped in fragrant musk,

6 - A gracious hand that outlines on the meadow the image of the beloved in lines of wine and musk.

7 - An *idol* with ruby-coloured cheeks, a wine red as a garment sparkling in the *temple*.

8 - And from the dust rises a perfume as of rose-water, and you would think that roses were kneeded in the mud.

9 - But the good Daqiqi of the innumerable things of this world has chosen four, of all the good and the evil, four charming virtues:

10 - A lip that looks like a ruby, and the tender lament of the lute, and wine the colour of blood, *and the faith of Zoroaster*!

We have already referred to the religious images in Persian poetry and to the mysticallibertine cipher of Zoroastrianism. Here we should note not only the antiquity of these religious images—in the above brief poem there are at least *four or five*—but also that, in the first place, they have not yet succeeded in permeating the whole style, and in the second place that the technique of the image and of the comparison, while it does not reject word-play (*gil-gul*, etc.), has not yet been codified in those supremely harmonious but monotonous lyrical forms of the golden age. For instance, the wind compared to *a hand wrapped in musk* is, for instance, an idea which perhaps already differs from those which will become the traditional canons of the imagery; while the *description*—of which we shall have many lengthy examples in the later lyrics—is more vivid and at the same time less rich in resonances and in that mystical background which we have found in Hafiz. Here we see the "religious" features still bare and in a process of fusion: the houri-trees, the beloved-

idol, the paradisiac cloud, wine and libertinage explicitly connected with the religion of Zoroaster. The several component parts are not yet throughly fused, and for this reason congruity of the verses is greater: the whole is nothing but a description of the Spring. So in the lyric poetry of this period, which we may call preclassic or archaic, we come often across *descriptive* poems, such as the description of old age ascribed to Rudagi, or long dialogues between the poet and his beloved like the famous one of Onsori, descriptions of love scenes as that by Farrokhi, etc.

The passage from this style to that of the golden classic age is characterised above all by the penetration of gnostic-mystical features (whose advent was already *terminologically* prepared) into the heart of the lyrical composition, a penetration which shatters the harmony of the composition and gives rise to that typical feature of the classic *ghazal*, the conceptual independence of the several verses, one of which may deal with love, another with spring, another again with the mystic wine while yet another will contain an ethical warning. It was above all in the 12th century that the classic *ghazal* arose, as Mirzoev (18) has well seen, though he refused to recognize the notable influence that mysticism had in bringing this change about, an influence which, far from being disproved, is justified by having been already to some extent terminologically prepared by the more ancient poetry. It thus happens that mysticism uses, on the one hand, the language of love while on the other the language of love is enriched by mystical under-tones. It should be noted how Khaqani (12th century), who was not a mystic, describes his success in resisting the temptations offered by a beautiful girl (or beautiful boy): "When I saw that she had celebrated the-Feast of *Sadè* like the Magi, and that *fire* was flowing from her tulip petals ( = her face) and that her tangled amber curls formed a Cross,

"Then I understood that it was the Fire which is adored by Zoroaster and his Festival: I saw that from afar, and I would not draw near.

"I who at the Kaaba had celebrated the festival (Kaaba= *earth*) and had tasted the *water* of *Zamzam*,

"How could I have tasted, like sugar cane, her moist *Fire* ( = the lips)? (19)".

We here see that a non-mystic like Khaqani, when he wishes to speak of love and of "amusement", not to say dissipation, *inevitably uses religious images*. This shows that in his time the fusion of the two realities had been already brought about in literary style.

This first *variation on the theme* in the history of Persian lyric poetry, a variation, which, as we have said, consists in replacing a *natural description* by an *allusive* one, accompanied by a notable conceptual independence of the several verses of the composition on the one hand and by a more definite formulation of the technique of the images, in what we termed above the *formal harmony*, on the other, is followed in the history of Persian poetry by another change which occurred in the 16th-17th century. As this variation, originating in Persia, was transplanted in India where, for various reasons, it found a favorable soil and where it acquired its most perfect forms, it has been called the "Indian style" (*sabk-i hindi*).

One of the best known representatives of this style, not then yet *Indian* properly speaking, was the Persian Sa'ib of Tabriz, in the 17th century ( + 1677). Let us read a *ghazal* of his, picked out by chance (20):

1 - In vain we cast the seed of our hope in the house of the world, in vain we sowed our grain in saltish soil.

2 - The pure earth of the eye was the place of the pearl of Warning, and we, with childish wantonness, cast there the seed of desire.

3 - Each one cast his grain in the earth, and we, foolishly, sowed the seed of chains in the midst of the desert.

4 - Like beings bearing light weight, we shall not pass the scales on the Day of Judgement for from one end to the other we have sown them with dents and notches.

5 - In the soil of the heart, the seat of Passion, of the fiery seal of love, our faulty nature has led us to sow the seed of Longing.

6 - The tie that binds us to the beauty-spot at the corner of that mouth is not of today, We sowed the seed of our love of her in the deepest heart of hearts.

7 - And every seed that we sowed here in the world, oh Sa'ib, has grown into the ear of repentance, except the seed of tears.

For the purpose I have in view I have endeavoured to translate this poem of Sa'ib as literally as possible. Here are a few preliminary remarks to assure an understanding of it, even if only on the outside.

V. 4. According to Moslem eschatology, all human actions on the Day of Judgement will be weighed on great scales.

V. 6. The heart of hearts is the *suvaida-e qalb* of the psychological-anatomical Hellenistic-Arabic-Persian tradition. It means literally "the blackness of the heart", the black spot of the heart. *Formaliter*, for its blackness and smallness, it may be compared to a mole or beauty-spot.

Now, those who are accustomed to read the *divans* of the classic period, that of Sadi and of Hafiz, feel that in a *ghazal* of this type there is a dissonance. In an article of a more technical character (21) I have shown that in defining the "Indian style" the following features must be taken into special consideration:

(a) As we go forward in time and penetrate geographically into the Indian world, the shattering of the law of *formal harmony*, of which we have spoken, becomes more marked.

(b) The tendency to give tangible shape to abstractions. Hence the number of comparable objects increases, and this gives rise to a richer terminology. Things even apparently commonplace or "vulgar", become subjects of poetry and, moreover, the entering of a great mass of abstract ideas into the play of images gives rise to a pseudo-philosophic tendency that is often tortuous and intricate.

For instance, "the pearl of warning" in the "earth" of the eye, in the poem just quoted, is an image which it would perhaps be difficult to find in a classic. The eye is formally too different from the earth. The "seed of chains" requires a special explanation. Tradition speaks of the flight in the desert of the unfortunate lover *Majnun*, the "madman". Chains are of course used to fetter madmen. *To sow the seed of chains in the desert* now becomes intelligible but the expression is not grotesque to our ears only, but probably also to those of a classical Persian. But it does not strike a classical Persian as grotesque that the lover's curl should be "a polo-stick that makes the ball of the lover's head whirl swiftly". One must therefore be careful not to interpret *grotesque* too precisely and too much in its European meaning. The image taken from the game of polo is quite consistent in its several features, as understood by the law of formal harmony (the curl can quite well be compared to the polostick and the ball to the head). On the other hand, the image drawn by Sa'ib, which we are studying, has, from the standpoint of classic criticism, at least two defects: one is that it offers a comparison whose terms are irreversible (it would hardly come into one's head, that is to say, to compare the link of a chain to a seed), the other is that, *considered dynamically*, there is also formal incongruity (the idea of the chain growing from seeds of chain), for while one of the terms of the comparison, a seed, does grow if planted, the other does not. As you see, the Persian traditional classic critic is anything but indulgent to creative imagination; in some of its aspects, the variation introduced into the classic technique by the "Indian style" brings it nearer to the "arbitrary creativeness" of the modern Western artists. The same remark holds good also to the "dents of the scales", and so forth.

It is curious to note that in this variant of Sa'ib greater congruence is obtained in a certain sense between the several verses of the composition. This is accounted for partly by the fact that the creators of this style attached great importance to that technical device known as *radif*, that consists in repeating at the end of each line one or more identical words or even a whole expression (in the case in point *kashtim*, *"we sowed"*) thus forcing the poet to observe greater unity. But other reasons also contribute to confer greater unity on the composition, among which, last but not least, the *conceptualism*, the *pseudo-philosophy*, the tendency to loiter over ideas and turn them over and squeeze out all their possible contents.

At the end of the 18th century, coinciding more or less with the rise of the dynasty of the Qajar, another variation occurs in the style of Persian poetry, a variation which might be called neo-archaism, if we continue to assign to the poets of the pre-Sadi and pre-Hafiz period the far from correct term of "archaic". But it is in no sense a mere return to the antique. The refinement introduced by mysticism, the melody of Hafiz, the use of terminology taken from the notions and facts of every-day life, which characterised the Indian style, were features that could not easily be set aside.

We will now give an ode characteristic of the greatest of these poets, the most melodious, Qa'ani (+ 1853). It is a joyous hymn celebrating the Persian New Year festival, the *Nauruz*, when tradition requires that seven objects be brought together, all beginning with the letter *sin* (s), *i.e.* the hyacinth (*sunbul*), the apple (*sib*), lilies (*susan*), silver (*sim*), garlic (*sir*), vinegar (*serkè*), and rue (*sepand*). But a single *sin* is enough for Qa'ani, that of the *saghar* (wine-cup).

"The festival has arrived, come, oh cupbearer, and carry round the cup, and give a kick to the revolving globe and to the passing of time!

"The *sin* of the cup suffices me, oh fine Turk, for the day of the festival: jolly good fellows who love wine have no need of seven *sins*!

"They are all talking now of new clothes, but I, lip to lip, seek the glass in which old and flavorsome wine is clothed.

"All are now putting sugar on the table and reciting prayers and exchanging wishes; I prefer to listen to the insults from your sugary lip.

"Today all have in hand silver and augural grain, but I desire only the grain of thy beauty-spot, oh thou whose body is of silver!

"The people have a superabundance of garlic (*sir*) on the table, while I am satiated (*sir*) with life if I have not the lovely Joy who has stolen my joy!

"Pistachio and almonds are the sweet food of *Nauruz*, but I need neither pistachio nor almonds for I have your eye and your lip!

"The festive guests burn aloe and I, deprived of my idol, burn like aloe, for with her beauty-spot, black as a Hindu, she plunders the hearts of the Moslems.

"They all kiss one another today, and I torture myself, dying, and think: "why is that sweet charming mouth to be kissed by another?".

"Vinegar is on the table of all, and like vinegar my friend turns to me acid and surly her rose-coloured face!

"The Festival lasts one day in the year for all; but looking at that royal face the festival is for me the year and the month and the week and every dawn and every evening!

"Indeed this special festival of mine (may its power and glory be eternal) conquers and defeats all the festivals of the common herd! (22)".

Here the images are still those of the classic type; the efforts based on the Indian style have been abandoned (and I know not whether this is a good thing or not). What has remained of that style is above all a richer terminology applied to the objects of poetry. The gnostic mystical element of the classic style has been abandoned, leaving behind it only its formal framework. Once more natural phenomena and objects have reacquired their natural appearance, even if they be sung with more charm and sometimes in a more mannered style. It may seem strange that this return to a more natural style should have coincided with what is universally considered to be a period of decadence in the political history of Persia. In reality, it was a reaction, a return to former days, to a *reflected* naturalness. The poets were weary of experimenting with new styles.

And it was at this time in the evolution of Persian poetry that the European experience was violently introduced (23).

The space at my disposal has only allowed me to give very few examples of this traditional style. But I hope I may have succeeded in making two things clear. *One is the great variety* of this Persian poetry of the *ghazal*, one of the most refined products of the age-old Iranian civilisation, and which,—strange as it may seem in view of its hermetic forms—has had an incredibly wide and deep influence on the literatures of Asia. From the shores of the Ionian Sea, only a few miles from Italy, where, until a few dozen years ago poems were written in the Albanian language imitating the Persian *ghazal* (for instance, those of Nezim, a famous Albanian *ghazal* writer of the 18th century) (24) as far as the Malay

Archipelago, where the Persian *ghazal* had many imitators, from the steppes of Central Asia, one of the centres where the Indian style prospered greatly, to the tropical Deccan whose forests, as far back as the 15th-16th century, began to resound to the mystical *ghazal*, that "short yet spacious lay" provided the chief instrument for poetic expression for the most widely differing peoples in the most varied languages.

The *other* is the power of assimilation of the Iranian race, which has succeeded in its poetry in combining harmoniously motifs coming from the most diverse civilisations, forming a real bridge between Semitic Asia Minor, Babylonia, Islam, and the world of the ancient Aryas whose name is proudly borne by the land of *Iran* itself. The ancient cosmic vision of light and darkness, the world of angels and of the transcendent hypostases, the grandiose conception of Divine Time and of the sacred transparency of human time, typical of Iranian religious thought; the robust antimythological sense of Islamic monotheism; the refinements of neo-platonic Hellenistic philosophy, provide the background, of diverse origin yet miraculously unitarian, on which this lyric poetry has grown.

I should like to close these remarks by reading the translation of a lyrical fragment by a great poet-philosopher who succeeded in a very remarkable way in fusing in himself both Iran and Islam, the philosophy of the Greek *falasifa* and of the Moslem *ilahiyun*. I refer to Naser-e Khosrov, of the 11th century, the period of transition in which the pre-classic lyric was shaped into the classic.

The shades of evening are falling on the soul of the poet and on the world: Persian pessimism, with which you are all familiar as powerfully expressed by a Khayyam, seems to be taking possession of the poet. But in the very depth of night the Iranian faith in the victory of Light over Darkness, of Heaven over Earth, reasserts itself. The stars begin to shine, the ancient *Nahid* (Venus), the goddess of fertility and of the waters, the Milky Way, the Pleiades, victorious lights, angelic powers which will at last defeat the Satanic powers of despondency and evil. And may this voice from Iran be not only to us but also to the friendly sister people and to the whole world, now so close to the Ahrimanic darkness, an augury and a symbol of resurrection (25).

"Look at the branch of the tree, bent like the back of the *dal* (26), look at the leaf shrivelled like a wasted face.

"The cloud of sadness has come and with its damp breath has watered everything, gardens and even deserted ruins.

"Beneath the dark cloud the disk of the sun . . . looks like thick dust on an ancient vase of gold.

"And when the autumn wind had clothed with garments of dark clouds the vault of heaven,

"The sun from the meridian heights hastened towards the low lying bed of the sea to cleanse its face from the black dust.

"When the fair-haired sovereign is defeated, the fierce Ethiopian prince will revenge himself on us (and it is perhaps for this that each night such an armed array of stars gathers in the heaven).

"Yester evening my eye was powerless to penetrate in meditation what a cruel fate wanted of me:

"Black was the sky, dark the heavens, I an ant; dust and earth whirling in a pitchblack box!

"And when half the night had passed I exclaimed: 'It is perhaps the omnipresent Time that has opened its black mouth!'.

"In the sky (a minute ago the blackest of bodies) only the planet Venus glowed, a shining beauty-spot of certainty on the black face of doubt.

"Then there appeared, little by little, the light of the Milky Way, like white milk spilt on an azure table,

"And then the Pleiades, like the last streaks of light on the nape of the neck of Ahriman left after the strong grasp of the Angel's fingers:

"Now the hosts of heaven were arming themselves with light, while in despair the soldiers of the earth were draping themselves in a shroud of pitch!'.

*Notes*

[1] This article is the re-elaboration of a lecture entitled "Thought and Form in Persian Poetry" delivered at IsMEO, May 7, 1958. The lecture deals more especially with the most important Persian lyrical form, that of the *ghazal* or ode.

[2] H. Ritter. *Ueber die Bildersprache Nizami's*. Berlin-Leipzig, 1927.

[3] Notable above all from this standpoint are his works: *Beiträge zur Biographie, Charakteristik und Interpretation des türkischen Dichters Sabit*. Praha, 1926, and more recently the full "Persian Literary History" *Dejiny perské a tádicke literatury*. Praha, 1956.

[4] Also in Ritter's recent, large-scale work (*Das Meer der Seele*, Leiden, 1955) which, whilst dealing more especially with the poetical world of F. Attar (12th century). contains a rich collection of very many mo-

tifs of Persian mystical lyrics in general, this motif is not studied historically.

[5] In his still useful *Allégories, récits poétiques et chants populaires traduits de l'arabe, du persan, de l'hindoustani et du turc*, Paris, 1876², pp. 25-26.

[6] Ibid, pp. 307 et seq.

[7] *Golestan*, Furughi ed., p. 3.

[8] I. Pizzi. *Storia della poesia persiana*. Turin, 1894, Vol. II, pp. 450-51.

[9] Daqiqi ( 952) speaks of it in his epic fragments inserted in the *Shahnama* of Firdausi. For a further collection of material on the "cypress of Kashmar" see the very beautiful work in Persian by M. Moin *Mazdayasna va ta'sir-e an dar adabiyat-e farsi*. Teheran, 1326 (= 1948), pp. 339 et seq.

[10] Cfr. M. Eliade. *Manuale di Storia delle Religioni* (Italian ed.), Turin, 1954, p. 318.

[11] In a recent communication in the "International Islamic Colloquium" at Lahore (Dec.-Jan. 1957-58) entitled *"Can we speak of Muslim Poetry?"* published in an abbreviated form in "Pakistan Quarterly" (Vol. VII, n. 4, 1957), pp. 38 et seq.

[12] On the presumed "Zoroastrianism" of Daqiqi see the acute article by H. H. Schaeder, *War Daqiqi Zoroastrier?* in "Festschrift G. Jacob". Leipzig, 1932, pp. 288-303.

[13] The text can be found in the *Bustan* (Furughi ed., pp. 215 et seq.) in an episode concerning the Hindu temple of Somnath. The essentially non-Islamic character of many of the features and motifs that form the complex picture of traditional lyrical poetry is sometimes clearly realised by the poets themselves. Thus the great Urdu and Persian poet Ghalib (d. 1869) of Delhi, says:

> *farman-rava na-gasht musalman ba-hich asr*
>
> *gar raft mogh zi-maikada tarsa furu girift!*

"The Moslem has never dominated in any century; as soon as the Magian leaves the tavern, the Christian enters!" (*Intikhab-i Ghalib*, Bombay, 1942, p. 57).

[14] See, for instance, the verses quoted by Gabrieli in his *Storia della Letteratura Araba*, Milan, 1952, p. 127.

[15] L. Massignon. *Essai sur le lexique technique de la mystique musulmane*, Paris, 1922, p. 89.

[16] See my article *Contributo a una definizione dello "stile indiano" della poesia persiana* in "Annali dell'Istituto Univ. Orientale", Naples, N. S., Vol. VII, 1958, pp. 167 et seq.

[17] For instance, in Pakistan, Dr. Abu'l-Lais Siddiqi, on page 37 et seq. of his critical study in Urdu *Ghazal aur mutaghazzalin*, Karachi, 1954. He disagrees with oversimplified attacks made on the traditional *ghazal* started by the great Urdu critic, Hali (1914). Hali's ideas on *ghazal* are set forth and discussed in my article *Altaf Husain Hali's ideas on ghazal* in "*Charisteria Orientalia*" Praha, 1956, pp 38 et seq.

[18] Abdu 'l-Ghani Mirzoev. *Rudagi va inkishaf-i ghazal dar asr-ha-ye X-XV*, Stalinabad, 1957.

[19] Text quoted in Moin op. cit., p. 482.

[20] I am translating from the lithographed Nawalkhishore edition, Lucknow, 1880, p. 559.

[21] Already quoted in Note 16.

[22] Persian text in Browne, *A Literary History of Persia*, Cambridge, 1953, Vol. IV, pp. 333-34.

[23] Another article will deal with a study of the style of Persian poetry subsequent to European influence.

[24] See on this matter E. Rossi: *Notizia su un manoscritto del canzoniere di Nezim . . .* In RSO, XXI, pp. 219 et seq.

[25] Only part of the text of this long poem has been translated. It is not, technically speaking, a *ghazal,* but a *qasida*, of ethical-religious content, but the vigour of the expression and the beauty of this fragment—lyrical from our point of view—have led me to select it to close this very brief summary of the history of the style of the Iranian lyric poetry. I translate from the edition of the canzoniere of Naser-e Khosrov by Nasrullah Taqavi, with an introduction by Hasan Taqi-zadè, Teheran, 1307 (= 1929), p. 332.

[26] The Arab letter *dal* has a curved shape.

**Michael Craig Hillman (essay date 1972)**

SOURCE: "Hafez and Poetic Unity through Verse Rhythms," *Journal of Near Eastern Studies*, Vol. 31, No. 1, January, 1972, pp. 1-10.

*[In the following essay, Hillman attempts to explain the musical elements of Hafiz's verse, contending that it is the inability of translators to adequately capture these rhythms in English that makes their work unsatisfying.]*

The following is an impressionistic translation of a poem by Hafez (fourteenth century A.D.), the premier lyric poet in the Persian language:

> (1) Your entwined tresses,
> I'm ever drunk with the brought breeze of
> them.
> Your sorcerer's eyes,
> I'm ever lost to self because of them.
> (2) My long vigil—lord—oh,
> Will it raise a night time vision
> Of your brows, my vigil shrine,
> Before which the candles of my eyes glow—
> (3) Their black orbs I hold dear:
> Mirrors of your midnight Hindu mole.
> (4) The world is yours to immortalize:
> Bid the breeze blow aside your veil.
> (5) The world is yours to eternalize:
> Pray the breeze rain down
> Life down from among your hair.
> (6) The breeze and I are one,
> Homelessly blown about.
> Drunk with your hair's fragrance
> Is the breeze,
> I with your sorcerer's eyes.
> (7) Hafez's lofty love be lauded—
> His lot here and hereafter
> That his eye cherish threshold dust
> And no more.[2]

This rendering of a typical Hafezian lyric poem[3] departs further, in terms of conventional verse aspects of the original, from the Persian than do Edward Fitz-Gerald's quatrains from the Khayyamic *robais* from which FitzGerald drew inspiration; yet, it is closer in spirit and tone to Hafez's original than is Matthew Arnold's *Sohrab and Rustum* to Ferdowsi's *Sohrab*.[4] However, the fact remains that FitzGerald and Arnold composed successful poems in English, thus—as has not been done with Hafez's poems—bringing to readers of English poetry a taste of Persian *robai* and literary epic traditions at their best.

That Hafez has not survived translation at the hands of the dozen or more scholars and lovers of medieval Persian poetry who have published versions of Hafez's poems in English may be less the result of the fact that no one as talented as FitzGerald and Arnold has tried his hand at it,[5] than of the fact that there is inherent in the verse form employed by Hafez an emphasis on the musical potentiality of words, phrases, and verse lines that resists translation. In fact, in some of Hafez's poems, the patterns of verbal rhythm seem to be a basic organizing principle, the plain sense of the poetic statements complementing the verbal music.

A partial elucidation of this asserted emphasis or reliance by Hafez on the unifying power of musical elements of verse is the aim of this paper, the thrust being not to determine how, in terms of it, Hafez ought to be translated, but rather to demonstrate that the poetics which can be deduced from Hafezian poems such as Q95 seems quite different from the poetics of lyric poetry in the English language.[6]

To this end, the following literally translated version of Q95, freely rendered above in an attempt to convey something of the integrity and intensity of the speaker's feeling and tone, is presented. The literal version, while losing all the life of the original, at the same time preserves its images, metaphors, and plain sense with exactitude (words in parentheses are explanatory, indicating synonyms, connotations, or ordinary second denotations):

(1) The breeze (fragrance) from (of) the lock(s, curls) of your hair intoxicates me continually (wine). The deceit of your magician's (sorcerer's) eye(s) destroys (annihilates, brings to loss of awareness of self) me continuously (time and time again, second by second; i.e. look by look).

(2) After all this endurance (patience, perseverance), oh lord, will (can) one see (envision) an evening on which I light (my) candle-(like) eye(s) in the *mehrab* (prayer-niche or alcove in a mosque, i.e., the direction in which people pray, facing the *mehrab*) of your eyebrow(s) (to which the curved upper edge of the *mehrab* is similar in shape).

(3) The blackness of the surface of my eye's pupil(s) I hold dear (preserve) because it is a memento (written copy) for my soul of the picture (image) of your Indian mole (which is, thus, reflected in the lover's pupils which function as a mirror).

(4) If you want to adorn the world wholly (completely) with immortality, tell the breeze to blow aside for a moment (time) the veil from your face;

(5) and, if you wish to abrogate the law (destroy the custom) of impermanence (transience, mortality) from the world, shake (your head) till (so that) from each (strand of) hair thousands of spirits (souls, life) fall (pour) to the ground (down).

(6) The breeze and I (are) two destitute (musk-bearing) and perplexed (wandering, aimless) (creatures), (our efforts) fruitless; I (am) intoxicated by the sorcery of your eye(s); and he (the breeze) is (drunk) with the fragrance of your hair.

(7) Praise be (how wondrous is) the ambition Hafez has: in this world and in the next nothing will be cherished by his eye(s) except for the dirt (dust) at your threshold.[7]

The two translations taken together reveal, first, a consistency of tone. The speaker's attitude toward the beloved and toward his own plight *vis-à-vis* the beloved is one throughout the poem. Secondly, the images in the poem are of a piece. The lover's state is that of a worshiper, a petitioner, the beloved, by virtue of her perfection, effecting in him the conditions of intoxication, perhaps spiritual, and the loss of awareness of self, analogous to spiritual absorption. Thirdly, a single theme runs through the whole poem. The beloved is a subjectively ideal and unattainable beauty, in the service of whose love the speaker worshipfully and fruitlessly remains faithful. Whether or not the poem thematically oscillates between a subjective idealization of the love for a woman and the possible use of the image of a woman to represent the condition of man's love for his creator is a moot point, Hafez's possibly intentional ambivalence in this regard in no way affecting the integration of the tone, images, and theme, but merely offering another level upon which the poetic materials may be felt to operate.[8]

However, whatever can be said for the consistency of tone, theme, and imagery in this poem, nothing about Hafez's use of a particular tone, theme, and images persuades a reader that the poet's ordering of his statements (numbered in both translations above) is inevitable or final. For example, nothing evidenced by the literal translation above prevents a reader from rearranging the numbered statements as follows:

       1, 6, 4, 5, 2, 3, 7
       1, 6, 2, 3, 4, 5, 7
       4, 5, 1, 6, 2, 3, 7
       2, 3, 1, 6, 4, 5, 7

To be sure, these suggested reorderings indicate some limitations in the capacity of Hafez's poem to submit to rearrangement. For example, the seventh statement is, in terms of its content, a concluding note. The third statement continues the image and sense of the second; and, the coordinating conjunction at the beginning of the fifth statement links it to the fourth. . . .

This capacity of Hafez's poem, and many others in the collected poems of Hafez,[9] to submit to a hypothetical rearrangement of its several statements without violation of the tone, theme, or patterning of images seems to set much medieval Persian lyric poetry apart, as a species, from lyric poetry in English and prompts many readers of poems such as Q95 to judge medieval Persian lyric poetry defective (i.e., in terms of so-called organic unity) in comparison with lyric poetry in English.[10]

In any case, it is obvious that if Hafez's Q95 is a poem, that is, is a single, whole poetic statement ordered through means proper to poetry, the principles of its organization must lie in the words and statements of the poem as seen other than as aspects of the plain sense, tone and theme. . . .

From this transliteration, it is seen that the poem contains fourteen verses with a rhyme scheme of *a,a,b,a,c,a,d,a,e,a,f,a,g,a.* The rhyme scheme itself reveals three facts. First, the second verse of every pair of verses exhibits a feminine rhyme in -*úyat* (-*at* = "your . . . ," "of you"), the capacity for such a monorhyme in Persian where the rhyme strikes a hearer as neither forced nor monotonous quite unparalleled in English verse. And, if perchance an English poet succeeds once or twice in using such a monorhyme, then let the limit be raised to a hundred such pairs of verses, which some medieval Persian panegyrics contain, or let the rhyme be expanded to seven syllables (i.e., six repeated syllables following a syllable of masculine rhyme), as Hafez himself employs in Q75.

Secondly, in structural terms, the rhyme scheme bears out the previous observations on the endstopped nature of the poem's several statements, each statement now seen to be a pair of verses, and on the lack of inevitability or finality in the arrangement of these pairs of verses. For, if the traditional sonnet rhyme schemes *abba, abba, cdecde* and *abab, cdcd, efef, gg* generally reflect the divisions or aspects of thoughts, feelings, images, and statements in that verse form, the rhyme scheme in Hafez's poem implies that each pair of verses is coordinate to the other pairs, there not being a more lengthy or comprehensive rhyme-thought-syntactic unit than one pair.

Thirdly, the first pair of verses consists of two rhymed verses (-*súyat,* -*dúyat*), which gives this pair special aural emphasis. That being so, this pair of verses naturally deserves a place of special emphasis in the poem, either at the beginning or at the end, those being the usual two places of special emphasis in discourse. But, this rhymed pair of verses cannot occupy the final slot because the seventh pair of verses, as observed above, very obviously constitutes a concluding note to the poem, part of its force as such the effect of the use of the *nom de plume*, Hafez, in that pair. Therefore, the *aa* pair naturally occupies the first place in the poem, its internal rhyme a means of arousing reader interest and creating in an auditor an expectation of the repetition of the rhyme *a* in later verses.

If the above is a fair analysis, the pattern of the poem is seen finally to be:

         2, 3
     1 + 4, 5 + 7
         6

the arrangement of 2-3, 4-5, and 6 with respect to each other still arbitrary. This deduced pattern: first pair (rhymed) + x-number of pairs + last pair (*nom de plume*) represents, in fact, the limits of any traditional definition of the Persian verse form called *ghazal* of which

Hafez's Q95 is a typical example. For instance, in Alessandro Bausani's words, a Persian *ghazal*

> . . . consists of a few *bayts* (verses, or distichs), generally not less than five and no more than twelve, with a single rhyme (often accompanied by a *radif*); in the first *bayt*, called *matla*, both hemistichs too [*sic*] rhyme together; the last *bayt*, called *makta*, contains the nom-de-plume (*takhallus*) of the author; the contents of the *ghazal* are descriptions of the emotions of the poet in front of [*sic*] love, spring, wine, God, etc., often inextricably connected.[13]

Thus, if a principle of organization exists in the Persian *ghazals* which, like Hafez's Q95, are not ordered on the basis of theme or its manner of presentation, images or their patterning, or the tone of the poetic speaker, the conventions of the *ghazal* verse form do not provide a clue either. On the other hand, there is no question that a critical reader of *ghazals*, such as Q95, senses in the original a singleness of impression and a completeness and integrity of poetic statement, in short, the same sense that he experiences in reading good lyric poems in English.

What accounts for this sense seems, very simply, to be the existence in such Persian *ghazals* of a set of rhythmic patterns so basic, pervasive, and subtly intertwined as to weld the non-rhythmic aspects of the *bayts* together and to help create the effects called poetic.[14] Thus, in Q95 not only does it seem impossible to determine the arrangement of the three sets of couplets 2-3, 4-5, and 6, but it seems unnecessary as well insofar as the obligation of the groups of *bayt*s is to make contextual sense and their function, beyond that, to provide the raw materials for the resultant patterns of rhythm.

Vocabulary in some Persian *ghazal*s is seen to be manipulated as are musical notes and chords. The pervasiveness of end rhyme in medieval Persian poetry (deriving from) the anterior, causative facility for rhyme inherent in Persian) is one piece of evidence for this assertion. A stronger piece of evidence is the often observed fact[15] that a poet such as Hafez employs a totally conventional poetic direction which flourished from four centuries before Hafez and that is employed even today by some poets. In other words, there is no vocabulary item in Q95 that does not appear, and in the same context, in the lyric poems of countless Persian poets before Hafez's time and countless times in his own poetry. For the reader of English poetry who does not know Persian any attempt at verbalization of this fact partakes of understatement because the capacity of a reader of English poetry to conceive of fresh and effective poetic statement involving a word, an image, a *bayt*, or a whole *ghazal* that five or six poets have previously made use of is experientially limited. But, the freshness and effectiveness of Q95, in which

the word "breeze," for example, appears for about the two hundredth time in the course of Hafez's collected poems, one hundred fifty of these occasions in similar terms and contexts, is a fact. And, such poetic freshness, if it is often in Hafez a matter of "what oft was thought but ne'r so well expressed," nevertheless owes most to the verbal music that conventional vocabulary, images, metaphors, sequences of images, and conventional themes serve to create, this music creating the distinctiveness of individual poems which employ conventional vocabulary and figures of speech. . . .

Because the Persian language, like English, is characterized by patterns of syllable stress in words and phrases, and does not feature syllables long or short by nature or position, the adoption of the Arabic *ilm al-arud* (science of prosody) by the early Persian poets of the Islamic era obliged these poets and later prosodists to formulate strictly Persian *zahaf* (deviations from a basic or "regular" metric foot) in using Arabic meters, to make greater use of some more suitable, "regular" meters infrequently employed in Arabic, and to conventionalize metrical fictions in the use of even the most basic and suitable Arabic meters.[17] . . .

In any case, even such a fiction is regularly observed, the result being that, although the rhythmic quality of a poem such as Q95 in a standard Arabic meter is far different from the quality of an Arabic poem in the same meter, in which the quantity of a syllable (i.e., a long syllable takes twice as long to pronounce as a short syllable) takes precedence over word and rhetorical stress patterns, Q95 can be read in metronomic fashion according to the *hazaj* meter.[19] And, unquestionably, the *hazaj* rhythm emerges in any natural reading of the poem, even if read by a person unaware of the existence of the Arabic meter employed. A reader incapable of scanning Q95 quantitatively might immediately sense any imperfection or deviation from the *hazaj* meter if such an imperfection existed.

But, the *hazaj* meter in Q95 lies behind a stronger accentual pattern of rhytham . . . , according to which every verse exhibits five stressed syllables *vis-à-vis* differing numbers of unstressed syllables (each verse has fifteen to seventeen syllables). Other readings of Q95 are possible; but each would seem to fall into an accentual pentameter pattern. This pattern, of course, corresponds to the nature of the Persian language which, as mentioned above, is characterized by patterns of syllable stress in single words and phrases. What the most basic verse rhythm in Persian may be or what the most natural foot is composed of, that is, analogous to the consideration of the iamb in English verse, this writer does not know, there existing no discussions of Persian meters in terms of stress patterns or accents in Persian literature studies.[20] It is possible that a basic Persian foot, reflecting the most elemental accent patterns of multisyllabic Persian words and Persian phrases in converation does not exist as such, because of a difference in effect between the accentual rhythm that is at the core of medieval Persian poetry and that which a poet in English might compose in. The difference is that the regular number of stressed syllables in a Persian verse tends to drown out the unstressed syllables so that a hearer is not conscious of irregular amounts of space, in terms of the number of pronounced unstressed syllables, between each stressed syllable; whereas, the very term "sprung rhythm" in English seems to imply a sort of leaping out of a stressed syllable in the face of unstressed syllables, their relative number varying and recognized as being varied. In short, the basic aural effect of this sprung rhythm in Persian is a sense of strong lilt and regularity that would, in fact, border on singsong, did not the less natural and native, yet better understood and appreciated, quantitative meters, such as the *hazaj* meter observable in Q95, exist, rising contrapuntally to the surface, especially in groups of unstressed syllables (some of which are bound to be conventionally long in quantity) that occur between stresses.

In conclusion, it would seem that Hafez's Q95, according to any formalistic criticism, is a composition in which three statements, i.e., 2-3, 4-5, and 6, are free to move about within the framework of the opening *a a* couplet and the concluding couplet featuring the *nom de plume*.[21] The effects of the monorhyme, marked alliteration and assonance patterns, and euphony of the composition, which embodies a single theme, tone, and consistency of imagery, is to lend an external or superficial unity to the composition. But, it is the combination of the *hazaj* quantitative tetrameter superimposed on the sprung rhythm pentameter of syllable stress that effects the inner or organic integration and oneness and pleasure that is common to poetry. When T. S. Eliot observes that, "It is the immediate favorable impression of rhythm and diction which disposes us to accept a poem, encourages us to give it further attention and to discover other reasons for liking it,"[22] he hits the mark, but from the opposite side of the target. For, his experience with Western poetry teaches him to look for something, usually meaning, beyond the music; whereas in Q95 it is the music beyond the meaning that is to be looked for. On a first reading, Q95 appeals to a reader because of its plain sense and images and promises him that there is more aurally to be discovered in further readings, in which the warp and woof of the patterns of rhythm gradually communicate themselves.

It is this writer's contention that Q95, and others like it in Hafez's **Divan**, is a poem, and a successful one, by virtue of its interwoven patterns of rhythm, an aspect of its character that wholly resists transmission in translation and that, perhaps, has resisted transmission in the foregoing description of it. In any case, the re-

alization that very different means were at Hafez's disposal to achieve the same ends and effects achieved by lyric poets in English may prompt new critical approaches through which medicval Persian lyric poetry can be better understood and appreciated and through which a fuller sense of Persian originals can be transmitted by scholars who try their hand at producing English translations.

*Notes*

[1] Several ideas in this paper were first aired in a paper read at the First Iranology Congress of the University of Tehran (September 1970), the text of that paper subsequently printed in *Ayandegan* 3 (1970-71), No. 857 (October 15, 1970), p. 4, and No. 858 (October 18, 1970), pp. 4 and 7. I wish hereby to thank Professors Hosayn Nasr and Iraj Afshar for allowing me to address the "Iranian Literature—Islamic Period" Section of the Congress.

[2] Mohammad Qazvini and Qasem Ghani, eds., *Divan-e . . . Hafez* (Tehran: Zavvar, 1941), No. 95, p. 66. The variant recorded in this edition, based upon the oldest complete MS of Hafez's poems yet published in Iran (Khalkhali MS, dated 827 A.H.), corresponds exactly in number and order of verses with that recorded in an MS selection of Hafez's poems, dated 813 and 814 A.H., edited and published by Parviz Natel Khanlari, *Ghazalha-ye . . . Hafez Shirazi* (Tehran: Sokhan, 1958), p. 30. The significance of this correspondence of variants in the criticism of Hafez's poems, considered by M. C. Hillmann, "Naqd-e Adabi va Divan-e Hafez," *Rahnema-ye Ketab* 13 (1970-71): 44-45, lies in the fact that, because Hafez apparently did not prepare or approve an edition of his poems, only those poems the variant texts of which correspond in the oldest MSS in terms of number and order of verses are ready for critical scrutiny.

[3] Mohammad Ali Eslami, "Taamol dar Hafez," *Yaghma* 16 (1963-64): 218, observes that, although " . . . it is one of Hafez's simpler *ghazals*, without any complicated philosophical or mystical subject matter, . . . it is one of those *ghazals* that can well serve as a demonstration of Hafez's thought and poetic craft." This essay, reprinted in Eslami's *Jam-e Jahan-bin*, 3d ed. (Tehran: Ebn-e Sina, 1971), pp. 261-80, has been translated by M. C. Hillmann in an article called "Sound and Sense in a *Ghazal* of Hafez," *The Muslim World* 61 (April 1971): 111-21.

[4] An examination of wherein essentially Arnold's poem differs from Ferdowsi's is the subject of an article by M. C. Hillmann entitled "Rostam: A Study of Probability in Ferdowsi and Arnold," to appear in *Iran-Shinasi* 3 (1971), No. 1. In any case, Arnold never read any of Ferdowsi's *Shahnameh*, even in translation.

[5] A. J. Arberry, "Hafiz and his English Translators," *Islamic Culture* 20 (1946): 111-28 and 229-49, entertains the merits and defects of extant English translations of Hafez, as does part of Arberry's "Orient Pearls at Random Strung," *Bulletin of the School of Oriental and African Studies* 11 (1946): 699-712. A list of Hafez translators is included in Arberry's compilation, *Fifty Poems of Hafez* (Cambridge: University Press, 1962), p. 62, to which list must be added Peter W. Avery and John Heath-Stubbs, *Hafiz of Shiraz: Thirty Poems* (London: John Murray, 1952) and Robert Rehder's versions in *Anthology of Islamic Literature* (New York: Mentor, 1966), edited by James Kritzeck.

[6] As Elder Olson argues in "Sailing to Byzantium: Prolegomena to a Poetics of the Lyric," reprinted in Wilbur Scott, ed., *Five Approaches of Literary Criticism* (New York: Collier Books, 1962), pp. 216-17, the question is properly one of the poetics of individual lyric poems, their "scrutiny" being "the beginning of the critical enterprise" which inquires "what form has been imposed upon the medium of words." Such inductive openmindedness is especially necessary in comparative literature study where the greater familiarity of a critic with his native poetic tradition may tend to lead him unwittingly to employ the limits of that tradition as a criterion in the study of other poetic traditions.

[7] This interpretation differs slightly, for textual reasons (cf. note 12 below), from those by Eslami, "Taamol" pp. 275 ff. and by the Turkish Sudi (sixteenth century A.D.), Hafez's most famous commentator, in *Sharh-e Sudi bar Hafez*, vol. 1, translated by Esmat Sattarzadeh (Tehran: Rangin, 1963), No. 100, pp. 583-87.

[8] According to Mahmud Human, with Esmail Khui, *Hafez,* 2d ed. (Tehran: Tahuri, 1968), pp. 110, 117-18, and 351-52, Q95 is an example of the first period of Hafez's development as a poet and thinker, a period in which the poet, in Human's view, is primarily concerned with secular love, *rendi* ("nonconformist abandon"), and *nazarbazi* ("ocular flirtation").

[9] Within the spectrum of Hafez's collected poems, viewed in terms of formal or organic unity, Q95 seems to lie about half-way between a poem such as Q26 (translated in Arberry, *Fifty Poems*, p. 90f., which submits to no transposition of its several statements, and the Western favorite, Q3 (translated in Arberry, ibid., pp. 85-86), which gives voice to three or four distinct themes in its nine statements. On the basis of a consideration of poems such as Q3, Arberry, in "Orient Pearls," p. 704 f., asserts that Hafez "constructs each lyric poem upon the basis of a limited number of themes selected from a repertory which is itself definitely restricted, and to a great extent conventional," the arrangement of the selected themes giving the key to an understanding of the poem's form. In the case of a poem such as Q95, which embodies a single tone, one theme, and consistent imagery, yet submits to a hypothetical transposition of its several statements, Arberry's explanation does not apply and, perhaps, *a fortiori*, does not apply to poems embodying several distinct themes.

[10] Ali Akbar Dehkhoda, "Ghazal," *Loghat Nameh,* No. 62 (Tehran: University Press, 1961), p. 209, asserts that the thematic independence of each *bayt* (pair of verses) in a *ghazal* (the verse form exemplified by Hafez's lyric poems) is a technical flaw inherent in the verse form. Walter Leaf, as quoted in Arberry, "Orient Pearls," p. 704, remarks: "In the Persian ode (*ghazal*) we find a succession of couplets often startling in their independence, in their giddy transitions from grave to gay, from thought to mood. To the Persian each couplet is a whole in itself, a *nokteh* or point, sufficiently beautiful if it be adequately expressed, and not of necessity owing anything or adding anything to that which comes before or after. It is from the common metre and common rhyme alone that the ode gains a formal unity. . . . " Leaf's insinuations are (1) that rhyme and meter are practices with the same purposes and effects regardless of the nature of the language in the poetry of which they may be employed; (2) that a "common metre and common rhyme alone" are not enough to effect real formal unity; and (3) that, owing to the supposed independence of individual couplets in some medieval Persian lyric poems, the whole poem can be assumed to have only that effect which is the sum of the several effects of the couplets read individually. . . .

[13] Alessandro Bausani, "Ghazal," *Encyclopedia of Islam:* New Edition (London: Luzac, 1965), p. 1033, in which essay Bausani asserts that a conceptual incongruity among the statements in a single poem seems to be a formal characteristic of the technical *ghazal* form: this, however, begs the question.

[14] What these effects are seems unamenable to definition, although a reader of poetry recognizes them experientially. As T. S. Eliot, *On Poetry and Poets*, p. 6, puts it, " . . . poetry has to give pleasure. If you ask me what kind of pleasure then I can only answer, the kind of pleasure that poetry gives."

[15] Shebli Nomani, *Sher al-Ajam,* vol. 2, 2d ed., translated by Mohammad Taqi Fakhr Gilani (Tehran: Ebn-e Sina, 1950), pp. 204 and 211; E. G. Browne, *A Literary History of Persia*, vol. 2 (Cambridge: University Press, 1956), p. 84.

[16] Gotthold Weil, "Arud," *Encyclopedia of Islam,* New Edition, pp. 667-77, is the most comprehensive description of Arabic prosody available in English. The available English translations of medieval studies of Arabic prosody as adapted by Persian prosodists and

poets include: H. Blochmann, *The Prosody of the Persians* (Calcutta: Lewis, 1872) and G. S. Ranking, *The Elements of Arabic and Persian Prosody* (Bombay: Education Society's Press, 1885), both books containing a translation of Sayfi's "Essay on Prosody," Blochmann's study including, as well, a translation of Jami's "Essay on Rhyme."

[17] The existence of some *zahaf* is, as Mahdi Hamidi, in *Aruz-e Hamidi* (Tehran: Haydari, 1963), pp. 7-27, sardonically exhibits, no more than the admission that the metrical facts of classical Persian verse are different from or more comprehensive than the conventional Arabic molds which are supposed to account for all the possibilities. In other words, the conventional classification of meters in *ilm al-arud* does not represent some possible and natural Persian metrical patterns (aside from the fact that these meters do not reflect the nature of Persian verse as essentially accentual). Q95, however, was chosen for discussion partly because it exhibits *salem* (i.e., sound or regular) *hazaj* feet. P. N. Khanlari describes the inapplicability of Arabic *arud* to classical Persian verse in greater detail in the second chapter of *Vazn-e Sher-e Farsi* (Tehran: Bonyad-e Farhang-e Iran, 1966), pp. 93-108. Khanlari's study is the first comprehensive attempt to derive a valid theoretical explanation of what are the bases and kinds of classical Persian meters. Unfortunately, the attempt is marred by linguistic inaccuracies and imprecision, as, for example, the author's failure to consider the differences between word, rhetorical, and metrical accents. Also, in his consideration of the quantitative meters that may operate in classical Persian verse (i.e., not the theoretically applicable meters of Arabic origin, but the ones actually employed), Khanlari arbitrarily chooses all the mathematical possibilities, save one, of combining so-called long and short syllables in dimeter and trimeter feet (p. 161) to represent the basic patterns, rather than to conduct an inductive analysis of poetic practice. . . .

[19] Meredith-Owens, loc. cit., observes: "The most outstanding feature of the *Arud* system as adopted by the Persians is the emphasis laid on quantity, which gives to Persian verse a lilt and swing which can be more readily appreciated by ears to which the more subtle rhythms of Arabic verse are unfamiliar." What Meredith-Owens fails to recognize is that "the lilt and swing" probably owes nothing to the adoption of Arabic meters by Persian poets; but, it is rather the natural, accentual pattern of the Persian language, described below in relation to Q95, emerging as the basic rhythm upon which the Arabic quantitative meters are superimposed. Also, the subtlety of Arabic verse rhythms unquestioned, that of Persian, insofar as subtlety is related to complexity, ought to be tentatively established by its description in this essay.

[20] Both Hamidi, *Aruz-e*, and Khanlari, *Vazn-e Sher*, loc. cit., by demonstrating the inadequacies of the Arabic *arud* system as a description of medieval Persian poetic practice, bring the investigation of medieval Persian prosody to the point where the question of stress patterns should naturally present itself. However, to this writer's knowledge, the question has not heretofore been discussed, despite the fact that it may be the single, most important critical problem in the study of medieval Persian technical *ghazals* insofar as no feature or aspect of many *ghazals* can account for the reader's sense that they are poems except for the patterning of rhythms.

[21] Of course, the statements are not "free to move about" in the sense that an editor may determine their order according to his own taste, because, whatever the reason, conscious or intuitive, Hafez ordered Q95 in a particular way. William K. Sumner rightly asks whether musical movement beyond the two verse patterns might not make the order of 2-3, 4-5, and 6 even hypothetically unchangeable. However there does not seem to be any musical movement beyond individual verses and couplets, although, in line with T. S. Eliot's observation, in his *On Poetry and Poets*, p. 30, that "the music of verses is not a line by line matter but a question of the whole poem," the rhythms in Q95 have a developing, cumulative effect.

[22] Ibid., p. 191.

## Von R. M. Rehder (essay date 1974)

SOURCE: "The Unity of the Ghazals of Hafiz," *Der Islam*, Vol. 51, 1974, pp. 55-96.

[*In the following essay, Rehder critiques A. J. Arberry's analysis* (see Further Reading) *of the unity of Hafiz's ghazals and discusses his own conclusions on the subject.*]

The study of the poetry of Hafiz is important not only in its own right and for the understanding of Persian (and Islamic) literature, but also for what it contributes to poetics, to the understanding of all poetry. Persian literature has only very rarely been looked at as literature, and this is true of Hafiz's poems as well, but one subject which has attracted some attention is the problem of the unity of his ghazals. The first discussion in any detail of this subject is A. J. Arberry's 'Orient Pearls at Random Strung,' *Bulletin of the School of Oriental and African Studies* [BSOAS], xi (1946), 699-712, and I will take this article as my point of departure. I will (I) analyze Arberry's conclusions about the unity of the ghazals of Hafiz, (II) discuss the text of the poem he uses as an example (the famous and beautiful poem beginning: *Agar an Turk-i Shirazi* . . . ), (III) examine Arberry's specific comments on this poem, and (IV) analyze the poem myself and make some general statements about the unity of the ghazals of Hafiz.

## I

The following summary statement is made by Arberry: 'Hafiz' technique is fundamentally thematic; by which is meant, that he constructs each lyric upon the basis of a limited number of themes selected from a repertory which is itself definitely restricted, and to a great extent conventional. Having chosen his themes—as a rule not more than two or three whole themes, with fragments of others so familiar as to be immediately recognisable—he then proceeds to work out his pattern. It is supremely important to understand how vital and inevitable pattern is to the Persian poet: a people which produced craftsmen of unsurpassed skill in the arts of line and colour might indeed have been expected to throw up men of equal parts in the marshalling of verbal images and sounds; and it was natural that they should work their materials into forms essentially similar to those invented by their fellow-craftsmen, the creators of mosaics and miniature paintings. So it is as a mosaic of sounds and symbols that the Hafizian lyric is to be appreciated; and its artistry, including its unity, is to be understood as being of the order of artistic unity that is found in the finest mosaic pattern.' (Orient Pearls, 704-705).

Arberry's statement as to how Hafiz constructed each lyric has no historical evidence to support it. In the oldest sources for the biography of Hafiz (those texts composed or copied within about 140 years of his death) there is neither any reference to his habits of composition nor anything which clearly indicates his attitude to his poems.[1] There is nothing to suggest that Hafiz conceived of a *ghazal* as a presentation of, or as a variation on, several themes, or that he first chose his themes and then worked out his pattern. What for Arberry is two or three themes may have been for Hafiz one subject, but there is nothing in the biographical evidence to prove that Hafiz saw disunity or unity in his poetry.

The oldest manuscripts reveal neither the genesis nor the development of the poems. There are some variant readings which seem to represent different versions, or corrections made by Hafiz. An example is the two final bayts preserved for QG 440, but there is not enough in what is known at present even to begin to document a description of how Hafiz composed his ghazals.[2]

Arberry also speaks 'of the complete works of dozens of poets certainly studied by Hafiz in his formative period and always kept by him close at hand.'[3] The anonymous old Preface to the **Divan-i Hafiz** states that the poet spent time in 'scrutiny of the works of the Arab poets (*tajassus-i davanin-i arab*),' and the *Tadhkirat al-shuara* asserts that Kamal Khujandi was a friend of Hafiz and that they exchanged poems.[4] This is all that is known from the biographical sources about Hafiz's reading of poetry. There is no evidence that all the poets he alludes to, or makes use of, in his works were read at the same time early in his life in any 'formative period,' and nothing suggests that he composed with certain books 'always kept by him close at hand.'[5] From his *laqab, hafiz,* and the importance of rote learning in his culture, one assumes that he probably had many poems and bayts in his memory, but the sources do not help us beyond this point. There is also the textual problem of whether the *bayts* and *misras* which contain these literary allusions are authentic.

That Hafiz's poems are traditional and conventional is clear when they are read in conjunction with the poets who preceded him, but Hafiz's exact place in the tradition of Persian lyric poetry is still obscure and careful study of the poems themselves may only provide a limited amount of illumination.[6] That 'Hafiz was understandably most ambitious to surpass' Sadi cannot be proven, however interesting it may be as an hypothesis.[7] The fact of an allusion is usually not enough to describe the attitude of the poet making the allusion. To show that Hafiz echoed Sadi's poems, as Arberry has, is important, but it is not the same thing as showing that Hafiz was 'most ambitious to surpass' him. In addition, this idea must be considered side by side with the sense of superiority and the great confidence in his own work which Hafiz expresses at the end of many of his ghazals.[8]

A number of serious criticisms must be made of the statement that 'Hafiz's technique is fundamentally thematic.' There is the problem as to what Arberry means by *theme*. How does one decide where one theme ends and another theme begins? The opening *bayt* of the first poem in the Qazvini-Ghani edition may be translated:

> Hey, *saqi,* pass the cup and hand it on,
> For love first seemed easy, but difficulties
> 　　appeared.

Is this to be identified as the theme of "drinking" or as "the difficulties of love," or as "drinking to forget love's difficulties"? Is part of the *bayt* to be considered the theme and the remainder the fragment of another theme? The address to the *saqi* and the circulation of the wine-cup are extremely common in Persian poetry. In this context are they whole themes or fragmentary themes? This raises the question of how much space a theme may take up and stay a theme. If the first *misra* read:

> Hey, let us drink until the daybreak,

would the number or names of the themes and theme fragments in the *bayt* be changed, that is, does the definition of a theme depend on the general idea expressed or on the specific images or language in which it is expressed, or both?

However one deals with these questions, the effect of Arberry's analysis is to shift the attention from the poem to the analysis itself, from the words of the poet to the words of the critic. The definite and particular language of the poem is subsumed to alien and abstract categories. The poems of Hafiz, like all poems, should be described in common language, as simply as possible, and should be analyzed in their own terms and in the terms of their author. To show that they are conventional and traditional one does not need the category of *themes*, one has only to list the apposite parallels with other poets, as Arberry himself has done when he cites *bayts* in the *Ghazaliyat* of Sadi which appear to have been echoed in QG 3, in what is the most valuable part of his article (Orient Pearls, 707-709).

In speaking of 'how vital and inevitable pattern is to *the* [my italics] Persian poet' Arberry glosses over the fact that not all Persian poets have the same attitude to pattern and form. The short lyric poems of Rudaki, Khayyam, Rumi and Hafiz, for example, differ in this respect. At the same time Arberry does not distinguish the peculiarities of Persian practice from that of other poets. Inevitably pattern is vital to all poets, and to assert this fact does not bring us very much closer to Hafiz.

Similarly, to consider Hafiz's ghazals primarily in terms of their themes stereotypes them unnecessarily, and fragments them so that there is a tendency to look more at the affiliations of parts of a poem with parts of other poems *by other poets*, and less at the relationships and functions of the parts within the poem, and at the poem as a whole. Such an emphasis substitutes a simple historical labour for the more complex process of understanding the poem as a poem, as the unique creation of a unique individual.

Thus Arberry writes: 'No complete understanding and appreciation of this poem [his example, QG 3] is attainable, as we have already indicated, until all prior treatments of the themes have been examined, and all images and verbal pictures drawn by earlier poets have been compared.'[9] If one does not quibble on the word *complete*, this judgement denies that an individual poem has any significant existence by itself, which certainly goes against the grain of experience, and mistakes the nature of poetry. Are the only satisfactory interpretors of a poem those scholars who have examined 'all prior treatments of the themes' it contains? Do we understand and appreciate Shakespeare when we have not read all his predecessors? Overlooking the obvious limitations of human life and memory, I would prefer to say that good poems are usually those which can be understood and appreciated by themselves.

There is also a curious historical problem in all this. Hafiz himself was probably not aware of 'all prior treat-ments of the themes' which he took up. How then is one to assess the influence upon him of that of which he was ignorant? There is the further problem of distinguishing between those prior treatments of which he was conscious and those of which he was unconscious, and among those of which he was aware, to distinguish those which intrigued him from those in which he took no interest. The question dissolves into myriad shadows and abysses such that no analysis worthy of the name can make the accumulation of parallels its major purpose.

Analogies between the arts are sometimes very interesting, and they are necessary if one is to form any good idea of a culture as a whole, but extreme care must be taken in making them, and it cannot be forgotten that they are only analogies, suggestions of partial, putative, and commonly unessential, similarity. Painting and poetry, for example, are so different in their ways and means, in the modes of the mind which they engage, that the more one is concerned with the essential aspects of one of them, the less the help which is provided by analogies with the other. The paintings of Turner do not explain the poems of Wordsworth, and the more one tries to describe the essential and characteristic qualities of either artist the more it is necessary to forsake any analogy, and to deal with the given work or the given art on its own terms.[10] The most interesting problems: meaning, style, form, unity, development, are radically different in the different arts. The patterns and forms of mosaic making and miniature painting cannot help us very much in understanding the unity of the ghazals of Hafiz, or what they are as poems. Literary problems must be solved in literary terms.

Furthermore, there is no reason to believe that 'a people which produced craftsmen of unsurpassed skill in the arts of line and colour might indeed have been expected to throw up men of equal parts in the marshalling of verbal images and sounds.' This assumes a correspondence between painting (and/or craftsmanship) and literature which does not exist. The great period of Dutch painting in the seventeenth century threw up no poets or writers at all comparable to the painters. English history is unusually rich in great poets but comparatively poor in great painters, and the best English poets do not regularly appear in the periods of the best painters. The ancient Egyptian culture 'which produced people of unsurpassed skill in the arts of line and colour' never produced a literature commensurate with its art. The archaic Arabic poetry appears in a culture in which there seems to have been no painting and very little art work.

As I have already stated above it is virtually impossible, because of the different ways, means and modes of the different arts, for poems to be made 'into forms essentially similar' to those 'of mosaics and miniature paintings.' It would be difficult enough, perhaps impossible, to show that Persian mosaics exhibit 'forms essentially similar' to those of Persian miniature painting. The majority of mosaics are geometric designs, while the majority of miniatures are representations of human and animal figures. Consequently, they very often have a center, a subject, and a meaning to which there is nothing comparable in most mosaics, where the principle of composition is commonly the repetition of a geometric or calligraphic form. There are also great differences in size, colour and quality of design between the two arts.

With mosaics and paintings we usually behold the form or pattern at a glance. There is a sense of unity inherent in the very act of vision which is absent when we hear or read a poem. The form of the *ghazal* is primarily determined by meter, monorhyme, the *bayt*, and the system of rhetorical figures. They have no counterparts in mosaics and miniature paintings. Are all the instances of the colour blue in a design to be said to *rhyme*? If so, then how can an analogy be made between the single rhyme of the *ghazal* and designs in which there are several colours? Are the outlines which the miniature painters filled in to be compared to the *bayts*, although they are, unlike the *bayts*, of different shapes and sizes? Or is a *bayt* to be compared to a brick or a tile? Also does 'pattern' refer to the transformation and combination of ideas within the *ghazal* or to the formal elements which I have listed above? The more one thinks about different works of art the more their individuality becomes apparent. As for calling Hafiz's poetry a 'mosaic of sounds and symbols,' this, in so far as it has any meaning, could be said not only of all poetry but of all literature and all speech.

So far I have followed Arberry's usage of *mosaic* even though it is not a very satisfactory term to use for Iranian art. It suggests to a European or American St. Vitale in Ravenna or Aya Sofya and the Church of the Chora in Istanbul, and while there are similar mosaics in the Umayyad mosque in Damascus, there are none, as far as I know, in Iran. It is necessary to distinguish between the architectural designs made with plain bricks laid in different directions, or indented or set-out from the surface of a building, and designs in coloured bricks (which may also incorporate direction and surface irregularity). Both of these are different from the so-called faience mosaics where the pieces are coloured and of different sizes and shapes (unlike the more-or-less uniform modules of most Byzantine mosaics). They must not be confused with the designs composed of painted tiles. There are also the more modern mirror mosaics, as well as the inlay work known as *khatam-kari*. All of these techniques may be said to produce *mosaics*, and it is questionable whether they, compared to each other, display the same sense of pattern or essentially similar forms.

'The creators of mosaics and miniature paintings' are from the same hypothetical, hypostatic, and ahistorical realm as 'the Persian poet.' Just as all 'the arts of line and colour' cannot be run together, the Isfahan of Shah 'Abbas cannot be used to gloss the Shiraz of Hafiz. The buildings of the Seljuqs are not like those of the Timurids, nor do Bihzad's illustrations for Sadi's *Bustan* (dated 894/1489) resemble the miniature paintings of the Tabriz school (dated to the end of the fourteenth century) in the Kevorkian MS of Rashid al-din's *Jami al-tavarikh*.[11] These disparate things may be compared, and ought to be compared, but particular care must be taken to appreciate their individuality and to understand the uniqueness of their historical context. This cannot be done by the wave of a hand or the flourish of a phrase.

If one wants to assume that artists of different kinds share certain inarticulate notions or are informed by the same spirit, the easiest and simplest place to begin is with contemporaries in a given culture. This possibility is passed over completely by Arberry. Unfortunately, the art of fourteenth century Shiraz, or for that matter, of Iran, has not been studied in anything approaching detail.[12]

Arberry, however, seems to postulate more a *Kulturgeist* than a *Zeitgeist*, a Persian Islamic spirit which is the genii and genius of the whole historical existence of the culture. It is, as he states it, a variation of the familiar description of Islamic civilization as *atomistic*. Bernard Lewis, for example, sees atomism as one of the four major features of medieval Islamic civilization. 'By this is meant the tendency to view life and the universe as a series of static, concrete and disjunct entities loosely linked in a sort of mechanical or even casual association by circumstances or the mind of an individual, but having no organic interrelation of their own . . . Arabic literature, devoid of epic or drama, achieves its effects by a series of separate observations or characterisations, minute and vivid, but fragmentary, linked by the subjective associations of author and reader, rarely by an overriding plan. The Arabic poem is a set of separate and detachable lines, strung pearls that are perfect in themselves, usually interchangeable. . . . Arabic art—mainly applied and decorative—is distinguished by its minuteness and perfection of detail rather than by composition or perspective. The historians and biographers, like the fiction writers, present their narrative as a series of loosely connected incidents. Even the individual is drawn as a sum of attributes, often listed, as a recent writer remarks, like the description of a passport.'[13]

Kowalski refers to the 'molecular structure' of Arabic and Persian poetry, and Rypka writes, 'Thus, a Persian poem should be read in a different manner from that customary to the European, less as a whole, more as filigree work, for it is full of finely-wrought details, with no strictly logical sequence of verses in any given poem as is common in the West. It is as if the poets exhausted themselves to such an extent by giving form to such refinement that the fitting together as a whole escaped them.'[14]

I do not propose here to discuss all the difficulties inherent in these statements, but as far as the atomism of Islamic poetry is concerned it is important to note that the *atom* is different for each author. For Arberry it is the theme which is the fundamental unit, for Lewis it is the line (does he mean *misra* or *bayt*?), for Rypka it is the individual detail or point (*nuktah*), although I would say the two are not synonymous.

The atomism of Islamic literature appears to be more a matter of emphases than of essences.[15] Some of Lewis' observations are true, but they misrepresent the subject as a whole. There is unity in the longevity and vitality of forms such as the *qasidah* and the *ghazal*, and in the nature of the literary tradition. Men for hundreds of years wrote ghazals not out of mere habit, but because the *ghazal* expressed what they wanted to say in a way which pleased them. The many conventions, the common store of ideas and subjects, the repeated images, the many allusions to the work of other poets, as they testify to the power of the literary tradition they testify to its unity. That so many historians, even if their interest was in recent or contemporary history, began their works with the creation and the early history of the world, and then commonly went through all the periods of Islamic history, bespeaks their sense of the wholeness of the past and of their own culture. Chronological order, the order of virtually all Arabic and Persian histories, is a logical sequence, and possesses an obvious and simple unity. Thus the histories can be used as illustrations of atomistic thinking *and* of a feeling of wholeness, which suggests certainly that the best summary is one which gives up the dichotomy and includes both aspects.

Islamic philosophical writing exhibits unity in that it can all be said to be the elaboration and exploration of one philosophy, a body of thought permeated and transformed by Greek ideas. Wolfson has described the Hebrew, Latin and Arabic philosophical literatures to which Spinoza was the heir as 'a common tradition.' 'They were all based upon Greek philosophy, at the centre of which stood Aristotle. The same Greek terminology lay behind the Arabic, Hebrew, and Latin terminology, and the same scientific and philosophical conceptions formed the intellectual background of all those who philosophized in Arabic, Hebrew, or Latin. The three philosophic literatures were in fact one philosophy expressed in different languages, translatable almost literally into one another.'[16] This unity has its literary expression in that many native speakers of Persian and Turkish felt obliged to write in Arabic when they wrote on philosophical subjects. Very often

their works are in the same form and they take up not only the same problems but discuss them in the same order, dividing the question, and arguing the points in a similar manner. As in the case of history, an overriding plan is clearly visible. That original work was presented in the form of commentaries on the works of others, and that so many commentaries were written, is good evidence that the authors felt the unity of the tradition and the continuity of the problems.

Finally, Islamic literature abounds in encyclopaedias, epitomes, anthologies, handbooks and surveys. How does one explain this number and this variety of general and comprehensive works as the expression of an *atomistic* spirit?

Atomism, then, is not a satisfactory theory of Islamic culture, and theories of culture, such as atomism, the notions of a *Kulturgeist* and a *Zeitgeist*, and analogies between various arts, neither explain the unity of Hafiz's ghazals nor illuminate the beauty of his style.

II

Criticism of a literary work can proceed only after the state of the text has been considered. This means only that textual problems must be taken into account, because in many cases they cannot be solved. It appears that the text of the **Divan-i Hafiz** will never be absolutely fixed. The student, therefore, has no choice but to deal with probabilities, possibilities, hypotheses and conjectures instead of certainties.[17]

Qazvini has shown how the number of poems in the **Divan-i Hafiz** began to increase rapidly after the ninth century A.H., and Rempis has demonstrated the existence of spurious poems in two Hafiz MSS of the early part of the ninth century A.H. (Muzaffar Husayn MS 87 dated 810 A.H. and the New Delhi MS dated 818 A.H.).[18] A comparison of old and new MSS and editions reveals that as the number of poems in the **Divan** increased, individual poems became longer, and the order of the *bayts* was sometimes changed.[19] The preface to a recension of the **Divan** made in Harat in 907/ 1502-1503 proves that the text was thought of as corrupt at that time. The statement 'many ghazals . . . which because of the indolence and misapplication of the copyist have remained forsaken and unknown on the page of time were put in order (*dar silk rabt dar amad*)' suggests that the order of the *bayts* was considered a problem. In the next phrase this process is spoken of as *tanqih*, *cleaning* or *purging*, so it may be that the problem was seen as the addition of spurious *bayts*. My guess is that both problems were recognized, but in either case it shows that the integrity of individual poems was in doubt.[20]

To illustrate his remarks on Hafiz, Arberry employs the *ghazal* beginning *Agar an Turk-i Shirazi* . . . (QG

3). Since the Qazvini-Ghani edition is easily available (and as Arberry reproduces the text of the poem from that edition), I will give the text as it appears in Aya Sofya 3945 (without changing the orthography) and then collate it with the other old MSS available to me:[21]

Akar an Turk-i Shirazi ba-dast aradh dil-i ma-
ra
　Ba-khal-i Hindu-yash bakhsham Samarqand
u Bukhara-ra
Bi-dih saqi may baqi kih dar jannat nakhvahi
[y]aft
　Kanar-i ab-i Ruknabadh va kulkasht-i
Musalla-ra
Fighan k-in luliyan-i shukh-i shir[i]n-kar-i
shahr-ashub
　Chunan burdand sabr az dil kih Turkan
khvan-i yaghma-ra
Man az an husn-i ruz-afzun kih Yusuf dasht
danastam
　Kih ashq az pardah-yi ismat birun arad
Zulaykha-ra
Bad-am kufti va khursandam afaka Allah niku
kufti
　Javab-i talkh mizibad lab-i la l-i shakar-
kha-ra
Nasihat kush kun jana kih az jan dusttar
darand
　Javanan-i sa adatmand pand-i pir-i dana-ra
Ghazal kufti va dur sufti biya va khush ba-
khvan Hafiz
　Kih bar nazm-i tu afshanad falak aqd-i
surayya-ra

Aya Sofya 3945 is the oldest, largest known Hafiz MS, dated 813/14 A.H., and copied in Shiraz. Of it Ritter declared: 'Dieser älteste, nur 22 Jahre nach des Dichters Tode in seiner Vaterstadt für den damaligen Herrscher dieser Stadt geschriebene Textzeuge darf sicherlich die höchste Autorität beanspruchen.'[22]

I do not have very detailed information on all the known MSS which are possibly older than the Khalkhali MS, but on the basis of what is available to me, this poem does not appear in the Mujam MS, the Isfahan Munici-pal Library MS, in British Museum 261/27 or in the Tarbiyat MS. In addition to Aya Sofya 3945, it appears in the New Delhi MS, Saray Revan Kösk 947 (dated 822 A.H.; f. 1b-2a) Nuru Osmaniye 3822 (dated 825 A.H.; f. 2b), and in the Stalinabad MS.[23] . . .

There are not very many variant readings. In her list of the first lines of the poems in the Stalinabad MS Galimova omits the, between Samarqand and Bukhara in the first *bayt,* but this is likely to be an error either in transcription or printing.[24] In the second *bayt* Saray Revan Kösk 947 reads *may-yi safi* and *nakhvahi did* (although some letters are effaced in this MS), and in

the fourth *bayt* it reads *ruy* instead of *rang.* The major difference between QG and the older MSS is in the first *misra* of *bayt* six. Kamaliyan reports a reading identical to the one in Aya Sofya 3945 as the only significant variant *from QG* for this poem in the New Delhi MS.[25]

Saray Revan Kösk 947 has:

Bad-am kufti va khursandam jazaka Allah
niku kufti

Nuru Osmaniye 3822 reads:

Bad-am kufti va khursandam niku kardi va
khvush kufti

It is interesting to note that these variations, important as they are, do not represent a change either in the purport of the *bayt* or in its images, and consequently do not affect in any significant way the discussion of the unity of the poem. The only other variant reading is in the first *misra* of *bayt* nine where Saray Revan Kösk 947 has *kuy* and *kuy* in place of *gu* and *ju.*

On the basis of the evidence the text of the first *misra* of *bayt* six should be emended so as to adopt the read-ing of Aya Sofya 3945 and the New Delhi MS. There is also the possibility that one or both of *bayts* four and eight are spurious, and if eight is genuine there re-mains a question as to its place in the sequence of the poem.

### III

To show how his theory of thematic technique and unity can be applied to a specific text, Arberry makes the following comments on the poem, *Agar an Turk-i Shirazi . . .* :

> The principal theme—is the fair charmer, beautiful, proud, unapproachable, the human, this-worldly reflection of the immortal loveliness of the Divine spirit. This theme is stated in line 1; lines 3, 4, 5 and 6 develop it, introducing variations in the form of fragments and reminiscences of other themes from the general stock-in-trade: the tumult of love (line 3), the unworthiness of the lover and the self-sufficiency of the beloved (line 4), the story of Yusuf and Zalikha as a myth of divine and profane love (line 5), and the sweet-bitter tongue of the beloved, symbolizing the pleasure and pain of loving (line 6). Restriction of space prevents the quoting of parallel passages from Hafiz' other lyrics; but all familar with the **Divan** will have no difficulty in recognising these themes as favourites of the poet.

> The subsidiary theme is—wine (and music) are the sole consolation of the lover, to compensate his sorrow over the incapacity of his love, and the

transitory nature of mundane affairs, and to enable him to solve those mysteries of the spirit which baffle and defeat the reason. Line 2 introduces the theme; it is developed in line 7 (listen to the advice of the old man of experience who knows the way by having trodden it) and line 8. This is perhaps the most important and characteristic of all the themes used by Hafiz: it expresses supremely well his theory of the "intoxicated" lover (who has in his hand the Mirror of Alexander, the Cup of Jamshid), and symbolizes his rejection of all formal, "sober" life, whether it be the life of the cloistered Sufi, the orthodox theologian, or the philosopher.

The foregoing analysis, brief and inadequate as it is, demonstrates the superb skill and artistry with which Hafiz treats two typical themes separately and in close integration; it is a fair example of the technique which informs all his poetry, though it should be added that in this poem he is being comparatively simple and straightforward.

These eight lines complete the statement and development of the chosen themes, to the evident and not unjustified satisfaction of the poet: it only remains therefore to sign the poem. Hafiz has a number of different devices for appending his signature, and a close study of his final lines brings its reward in an increased appreciation of his poetic artistry. The "clasp" theme here used is a very common one, but its present treatment is scarcely surpassed for beauty in the whole **Divan**. The poet looks upon his handiwork and finds it very good: it is deserving of praise and reward.[26]

That Arberry himself feels the difficulties (discussed in the first part of this essay) of delimiting individual themes is demonstrated by his remark that 'the principal theme' is developed and varied 'in the form of fragments and reminiscences of other themes.' The reasonably clear and coherent picture of the beloved's character is thus broken up into a rubble of subjects. These difficulties are compounded by the problem of deciding upon a 'principal,' 'subsidiary' and 'clasp' theme. In the poem the poet drinks wine because of the behaviour of his beloved. The two things are related. To say that one is 'subsidiary' to the other is to misrepresent the poem. He creates an hierarchy which is not in the poem. The distinction, moreover, appears to be merely one of space. The poem in QG has nine *bayts*; the principal theme fills five, the subsidiary, three, and the clasp theme, one. Any consideration of the force, beauty, or function of the *bayts* is excluded, except in the case of the so-called clasp theme which is defined on a different standard from the principal and subsidiary themes. Its position and function are considered, although Arberry does not note that it shares with *bayt* eight the subject of song and an allusion to a knot, and is, therefore, more than a mere appendage.

Thematic analysis is not subtle enough for connections of this kind. In addition, while perhaps one may speak of a clasp theme in a poem like this, where the poet names himself in the final *bayt* and makes a statement which does not seem to be explicitly tied to, or derived from, the rest of the poem, there are poems by Hafiz where this is not the case. In QG 1, QG 30 and QG 341, for example, the poet's name appears in the last *bayt* but that last *bayt* follows obviously from the rest of the poem. What, then, is the clasp theme? The final *bayt* of QG 20 is continuous with the rest of the poem, but nowhere in the poem does the poet's name appear. Is there a clasp theme? The meaning of the last *bayt* of QG 319 may be said to be different from those immediately preceding it, (although there are ideas in the last *bayt*, such as the poet's servitude and his obedience to the great, which echo other bayts in the poem) but its second *misra* imitates the first *misra* of the first *bayt* with words of the same form in the same syntactical order. The poet's name occurs in the next-to-the-last *bayt*. I do not think the idea of a clasp theme can be applied here.

Another shortcoming of thematic analysis can be seen in the statement that the principal theme is 'the fair charmer' herself, and not anything which she does or is in the poem.[27] The description, 'beautiful, proud, unapproachable,' is so general as to fit many very different poems. In this way all the particularities in the poem, the specific nature of the character of the Turk, of the mood of the poet, of their relationship, are glossed over. This is particularly damaging because the unity of Hafiz's poems depends in part upon these specifics, upon, in this case, for example, the several Turkish allusions. That the Turk's beauty is said to be the 'thiswordly reflection . . . of the Divine spirit' reveals the tendency of thematic criticism to amalgamate elements (and again to ignore everything which is unique about a poem). There is nothing in this poem to cause us to believe that this is a religious or *Sufi* poem, or that the beloved is in any way divine. In fact, the capricious and ruthless behaviour of the Turk, the blasphemous statement in *bayt* two, and the way in which the poet invokes God's help for the Turk, and the absence of any contrary evidence, suggest that this is a secular love lyric. It is worth noting that Sudi not only identifies the Turk as one of the descendents of the Turkish soldiers of Hulaku Khan who settled in Shiraz (the historicity of this story does not affect its value as evidence here), but makes a point of declaring that the Shirazi Turk is not to be understood in a metaphorical sense.[28] Similarly, the story of Yusuf and Zulaykha is in some contexts, 'a myth of divine and profane love,' but there is nothing in the poem to indicate that that is its meaning here.

There is no question that Persian poetry is very conventional, and that a limited number of conventions are used over and over. This, however, does not make all ghazals interchangeable. What is interesting is that *within these narrow limits* some poems seem artificial, trivial and insipid while others generate great power and beauty, and that whatever their quality there is a great variety of poems. It is very important to discriminate between the different ways in which a given poet made use of the tradition. That the story of Yusuf and Zulaykha was used to speak of divine love, that Hafiz was aware of the tradition (as he doubtless was), does not immediately establish what it means in this poem. The context of a word or phrase is probably more important than its history in determining its meaning. Thematic criticism, as it is usually practiced, ignores or takes very inadequate note of the context in which words appear. These problems can only be untangled by detailed analyses of individual poems and comparative studies of poems and poets. This is the most important work which students of Persian literature can perform at this time.

Also, in this poem there is no sign of 'the Mirror of Alexander, the Cup of Jamshid.' Wine provides the poet with consolation for his troubles, not with any glimpse of the future. It does not 'enable him to solve those mysteries of the spirit which baffle and defeat the reason.' He is uncertain of what the behaviour of the Turk will be, and the point of *bayt* eight is that a man cannot know his fate or understand the nature of things. It is certainly wrong to attribute a 'theory of the "intoxicated" lover' to Hafiz. Literature is the enemy of theory. Men whose major concern is theory rarely find self-expression in writing poetry, or prose stories. Here it is indeed all formal, sober life which the poet is rejecting. *Hikmat*, philosophy, theoretical speculation, is rejected by name, but one theory is not exchanged for another. Furthermore, *intoxicated* should not be in italics. It is real wine that the poet is drinking.

IV

The unity of any particular *ghazal* is dependant on what the *ghazal* is as a form. The essential unit of the *ghazal* is the *bayt* and each *bayt* is composed of two *misraat*. There is nothing in English poetry which corresponds to these units. Neither *bayt* nor *misra* may be correctly translated by *line*. Each *ghazal* is metrically regular, but a number of meters are used for ghazals. Every *misra* (and consequently every *bayt*) in a given *ghazal* is metrically identical. In QG 3 the same foot, / - - -, is repeated throughout the poem, but the meter is said to be: / - - -| / - - -| / - - -| / - - - which comprises one *misra*. Usually a *ghazal* meter is made up of different feet. In QG 2 the meter is: / - / -| / / - - | / - / -| / / / - which again comprises one *misra*. The meter, then, is defined in terms of the *misra*. From these two examples it can be seen that the *bayts* of one *ghazal* may be of a different length than those of another *ghazal*. Also, because two short syllables may be

substituted for a long syllable (and vice versa), within a single *ghazal* some *bayts* may have one or two more syllables than the others, although they are metrically of equal length. In most ghazals such substitutions, if they occur at all, do not occur more than a few times. Frequently they are confined to a single foot in the meter. These small modulations, meters composed of different feet, and the slight irregularity in the number of syllables in combination with metrical regularity (as well as other things, such as that many syllables may be either long or short depending on the demands of the meter), help to preserve the *ghazal* from monotony. The meter is, nevertheless, one of the forces which holds the *ghazal* together and unifies it.

In a *ghazal* the end of every *bayt* rhymes in the same rhyme, and in the first *bayt*, the end of the first *misra* rhymes in this same rhyme with the end of the second *misra*. As a result the *ghazal* has not only the unity provided by a regular rhyme scheme, but a special cohesiveness because only one rhyme is used, and this rhyme is repeated twice in the first *bayt*, as if to clearly establish it, and then once in every subsequent *bayt*. This monorhyme is another aspect of the *ghazal* which has no counterpart in English poetry. In Persian it does not sound peculiar, ridiculous or forced as it does in English, when it is possible. One reason for this is that the rhymes are further apart in Persian than they are in English. In English it is difficult to successfully sustain a line which is regularly more than ten syllables. The units of the *ghazal* are much longer. In the examples above, in QG 2 each *misra* is fourteen or fifteen syllables and each *bayt* is between twenty-eight and thirty syllables. In QG 3 each *misra* has sixteen syllables and each *bayt* thirty-two. A rhyme at the end of thirty-two syllables is very different from a rhyme at the end of ten syllables.

The monorhyme of the *ghazal* is also a unifying factor in that it sets up a certain syntactical regularity within the poem. QG 3 is a good example. The rhyme is -*a-ra* in which the -*ra* is the suffix which denotes what may be called the object of attention in a sentence, commonly the definite direct object. It can also be used in a dative construction. The choice of -*ra* as part of the rhyme causes Hafiz in QG 3 to place a noun or noun with modifiers at the end of each *bayt*, and in all the *bayts* but one (QG 3/5b where the dative construction is employed) the noun is the definite direct object of the sentence. The first person singular of the past tense of the verb *kardan* (to do or make) forms the final part of the rhyme in QG 319 'which makes the poem a succession of assertions and heaps up a whole series of completed past actions.'[29] Ibn Khaldun (1332—1406), who was perhaps Hafiz's greatest contemporary in the Islamic world, understood the power of rhyme as an organizing force in a poem. In giving directions to poets, he recommends: '(The poet) should have the rhyme (in mind), when the verse is first given shape and form. He should set it down and build (his) speech on it all the way through to the end, because if the poet neglects to have the rhyme (in mind) when he makes a verse, it may be difficult for him to get the rhyme into its proper place, for it often is loose and unstable.'[30]

The *ghazal* is always a short poem, which in itself causes it to be felt as a whole, but it does not have to be a fixed length. Browne says that the *ghazal* 'seldom exceeds ten or a dozen *bayts'* and Rypka defines it as having from 'five to fifteen' bayts.[31] Kamal Khujandi, a contemporary of Hafiz who died probably in 803/ 1400—1401, declared that he made a point of writing ghazals of seven *bayts*. This is presumably what he had in mind when he wrote in one of his ghazals: 'For the form of the *ghazal* Hafiz does not ride along with us,' as Hafiz's ghazals are usually more than seven *bayts*.[32]

In the last *bayt* of a *ghazal* the poet very often mentions his own name or pen name. This does not happen invariably (although it is the ordinary case in Hafiz's ghazals), and appears to be a later development in the history of the form. Browne comments, 'In later days (but not, I think, before the Mongol Invasion) it became customary for the poet to introduce his *takhallus*, nom de guerre, or "pen-name" in the last *bayt* or *maqta*, of the ghazal which is not done in the *qasida*.'[33] Rypka states that 'this custom came into more general use only later (6th/12th century), though sporadically, it is true, at the end of a lyrical song as early as Daqiqi,' but that 'when it occurs in Rudaki it is certainly a forgery' (Rudaki died in 329/940-941 and Daqiqi between 366/976 and 370/981).[34] With the *takhallus* as with length there is flexibility possible in the form of the *ghazal*, but by the period of Hafiz, and in the work of Hafiz, the *takhallus* appears in the final *bayt* often enough that one may say that there was a sense of the *ghazal* as a form having both a beginning (the *matla* or initial *bayt* with its double rhyme) and an end (the *takhallus*). Any criticism of disunity in Hafiz must recognise this sense of the *ghazal* as a formal whole.

It is also true that each *bayt* in a *ghazal* is usually a syntactical whole and a complete thought. A *misra* is commonly a distinct syntactical unit, such as a clause, and it may even be able to stand as a complete sentence, although in the context of the poem it may not be the complete thought (a good example of this is QG 3/4a). That the *misra* is the basic unit for the meter, and that the *bayt* is the basic unit for the syntax and meaning is one of the things which makes the *ghazal* an interesting poetic form. Beyond being a complete sentence and a complete thought, each *bayt* is expected to have a particular point and beauty of its own. Ordinarily, the meaning is expressed epigrammatically and in the form of a rhetorical figure. The *bayt* has an independence which in some ways suggests an English

stanza. This is an independence of form and imagery which is only in some contexts an independence of meaning.

*Bayts* three, five, and six in QG 3, for example, are all about the same subject, the relationship between the poet and his beloved, and they all may be said to express the same general meaning: the cruel behaviour of the beloved does not diminish the poet's passion.[35] If they seem unconnected, it is because in each *bayt* the thought is expressed in different images: the mischief-making and banditry of *luliyan* and *Turkan* in *bayt* three, the love story of Yusuf and Zulaykha in *bayt* five, and the sweetness of even bitter words from the beloved in *bayt* six. It is also because there are no connecting particles, or any other explicit connections to link the *bayts*. The lack of transitions and connectives, however, is not necessarily incoherence or disunity. What is absent is any explicit or obvious logical sequence: *bayt* five may precede *bayt* three or follow *bayt* six without substantially altering the meaning or the style of the *ghazal*, which is obviously another very interesting characteristic of the form. In addition, it should be noted that there is nothing illogical about any sequence in which these three *bayts* may be arranged, and no reason, beyond the change of imagery (which is, I would say, a small change in this context), to feel a *jump* from one to another. In a poem as short as the *ghazal* the number of changes of imagery alone is important. Many such changes can give the impression of disunity where there has been no change of subject or meaning.

How important the context is can be illustrated by Shakespeare's ninety-fourth sonnet:

> 6 They are the Lords and owners of their
>  faces,
>  Others, but stewards of their excellence:
>
> 8 The sommers flowre is to the sommer
>  sweet,
>  Though to it selfe, it onely liue and die,[36]

If each pair of lines is thought of, momentarily, as a *bayt* one can feel here the same absence of any transition or explicit connection that one feels in the excerpt from Hafiz, especially if the colon is forgotten. The colon connects the lines in a way which was not available to Hafiz as his language had no punctuation marks. When the lines are restored to their context, one can see that the *jump* between lines seven and eight is the only one of its kind in the poem, and that it is, in terms of the whole poem, less of a jump not only because it is unique, but also because lines 1-8 develop the same idea in the same terms, and lines 6-14 present a similar unity, *and* because the second image, of the summer with its flowers and weeds, is developed so as to be analogous, and suggest parallels, with them 'that haue powre to hurt, and will doe none.' Between Hafiz and Shakespeare there is not so much a difference in essential technique as a difference in the way techniques are employed.

The *ghazal* is also defined by certain limitations as to subject matter. The *Kitab al-mujam*, one of the most important Persian books on prosody, rhyme and rhetoric, (which was begun in Marv in 614/1217 and completed in Shiraz in 630/1232-1233) states that: 'Any poem which has as its purpose the ways of love, the description of the curl and the mole, "and the story of union and separation, and the manifestation of passion by the mention of sweet-smelling herbs and flowers," and the winds and the rains, and the description of the traces of habitation and ruins, is called a *ghazal*. Originally the word *ghazal* meant evening conversation with girls and stories about them, and amorous, flattering talk with women. One says: a man is a *ghazil*, that is, a man is a gallant and one who enjoys listening. Consequently, the commentary on the states of the lover and the description of the beauty of the beloved is called a *ghazal*.[37] The *ghazal*, then, is a love lyric by definition, and this concentration on the single subject of love cannot but give unity to individual ghazals and it is, in part, why so many of them seem all of a piece. Here, as elsewhere, the sonnet offers many analogies. The ghazals which are religious poems and panegyrics nevertheless remain within the terms of the love lyric. They refer to 'the curl and the mole,' tell 'the story of union and separation,' comment 'on the states of the lover,' and describe 'the beauty of the beloved.'

The subject matter of the *ghazal* is restricted further in practice. It is very difficult to recover references to specific events, of any kind, from a poet's ghazals or even to distinguish personal experience. This is not to say that they may not contain many such references and represent the poet's experience, but that the facts have been transmuted by the poem, usually beyond recognition. This is particularly striking in love poems. As a love lyric the *ghazal* is both personal and impersonal. There is intimacy without autobiography. As a group, ghazals are ahistorical, which is not the case with either qasidahs or qitahs. The difficulties which Ghani had in dating Hafiz's ghazals (see his book cited in footnote 5) make this clear. This aspect of the *ghazal* as a form is tacitly noted by Browne when he remarks of Hafiz's contemporary, Kamal Khujandi: 'As is so often the case with Persian poets, Kamal's fragments [*qitat*] are much more intimate and personal, and contain more allusions to contemporary events and persons (though for lack of fuller knowledge these allusions must often remain obscure) than his odes [*ghazaliyat*] . . . '[38] This absence of historical detail from the *ghazal* has meant that it has been filled instead with emotion, genuine or spurious, and because of its shortness there was no room for complicated patterns or elaborate rhetoric.

They are associated with the *qasidah*.[39] Love of rhetoric usually finds expression in long speeches and long poems, and a short poem can sustain emotion in a way a long poem cannot. Compression means exerting pressure. It must intensify and, to a certain degree, simplify. Mere shortness in a poem makes every aspect of it more conspicuous, if not more significant. English haiku furnish an interesting illustration of this phenomenon (the more so because the form is simplified by its removal from its cultural context). The limitations of length *and* subject matter appear to have operated so as to make many ghazals bland and dull, but in the ghazals of Hafiz they have contributed to the depth and sharpness of the feelings.

In order to understand the *ghazal* as a form it is necessary to think of all these things together, the *bayt* and *misra*, the regular meter, the monorhyme, the syntactical regularity set up by the rhyme and the epigrammatic nature of the *bayt*, the rhetorical figures, the *takhallus*, the restrictions of length and of subject matter, and the body of conventional images and allusions. When they are all considered together, it can be seen that the *ghazal* is a very rigorous form. The uniformity, such as it is, of so many ghazals, the conformity of so many poets to this pattern, demonstrates that this definition of the form was understood and accepted. Moreover, poems such as this do not happen by themselves. There is no spontaneous poetic generation. Each part and every aspect of the poem is the result of a decision by the poet, although they all may not have been highly conscious or meditated decisions. The poet, furthermore, has the opportunity to revise his work after he has composed it, and revisions, like the decisions not to revise, are made in terms of some sense or ideal of what the poem ought to be. The greater the poet the stronger that sense of the ideal is likely to be.

If the *ghazal* is seen as a deliberate and deliberated creation, the question of its unity is seen in a new light. The poet must select a meter and words to fit it. He must decide whether to change the subject or the imagery. He must choose an order for the *bayts* and establish a length for the poem. If one *bayt* follows another, it is because he has so arranged it. If the poem has nine *bayts*, it is because he had decided that his poem demanded it and that his purposes could not be accomplished in eight. Each *ghazal* has the unity of the form, of being a *ghazal*, and of being the particular poem which it is, the result of countless definite decisions by a given poet. This does not mean that the reader or scholar, or even the poet himself, can recover all or most of these decisions, much less the order and atmosphere in which they were made. The texts of most Persian poems are such that we shall probably be permanently uncertain as to whether they are as their authors left them. Similarly, there does not seem to be any possibility of describing or reconstructing the process of composition for any of the older Persian poets. Any detailed biographical criticism is extremely difficult, if not next to impossible, because the biographical information about most Persian poets is at least as dubious and problematical as the texts, as well as, in most cases, very sparse.

That there was a sense of a poem (and of the *ghazal*) as an aesthetic whole can be seen in a number of old texts. In the final *bayt* of QG 3 the poet expresses consciousness of having completed his poem: 'You have spoken a *ghazal* and bored the pearls come and sweetly sing, Hafiz . . . ' The metaphor appears to be that the *ghazal* is a string of pearls with each *bayt* probably corresponding to a pearl, each unit a unity, but all of a uniform colour, size and quality—with a hint of a vision of the whole as a necklace. The craftsman's skill which is emphasized is that of drilling holes in pearls, not, as Arberry says, sorting and grading. Furthermore, Arberry apparently understands *durr sufti* as 'the pearls are strung' which is incorrect.[40] In the poem it is almost as if the singing, the performance of the *ghazal*, strings the pearls. The metaphor of the pearls is continued in the play on *nazm* which means both *verse* and, according to Steingass, 'Joining (pearls) in a row' and 'a string (of pearls),' and is subtly echoed in the image of 'the knot of the Pleiades.' This constellation may be said to resemble a small handful of pearls ready for stringing (although this cannot definitely be said to be in the poem), and in the poem the stars are to be scattered, like a broken necklace. Images of the Pleiades have a long history in Islamic poetry and that this particular idea is present in the tradition is proved by Ibn al-Tazriyyah's *bayt*: 'When the Pleiades were in the sky as though they were pearls scattered from their (broken) string.'[41] The image of the necklace is extremely common in Islamic literature. The anonymous friend of Hafiz who is the author of the old Preface to the **Divan-i Hafiz** there compares each poem to a pearl and all of them to a necklace.[42]

Ibn Khaldun's discussion of poetry, although he is primarily concerned with the *qasidah*, may be used as a gloss here. He clearly asserts the independence of each *bayt*, but at the same time is very concerned with transitions, and behind his discussion is a notion of the poem as a whole ('the whole complex') which can be damaged by poor transitions or sharp contrasts: 'The whole complex is called a "poem" (*qasidah* or *kalimah*). Each verse, with its combinations of words, is by itself a meaningful unit. *In a way*, it is a statement by itself, and independent of what precedes and what follows. By itself it makes perfect sense, either as a laudatory or an erotic (statement), or as an elegy. It is the intention of the poet to give each verse an independent meaning. Then, in the next verse, he starts anew, *in the same way*, with some other (matter). *He changes over from one (poetical) type to another, and from one topic to another, by preparing the first topic and the ideas*

*expressing it in such a way that it becomes related to the next topic. Sharp contrasts are kept out of the poem.* From a description of the desert and the traces of abandoned camps, he changes over to a description of camels on the march, or horses, or apparitions (of the beloved in a dream). From a description of the person to be praised, he changes over to a description of his people and his army. From (an expression of) grief and condolence in elegies, he changes over to praise of the deceased, and so on.'[43]

A little further on he repeats himself, but with greater emphasis on the harmony that must exist between all the *bayts*: 'A poet must produce (a verse that) stands alone, and then make another verse in the same way, and again another, and thus go *through all the different topics suitable to the thing he wants to express. Then, he establishes harmony among the verses as they follow upon each other in accordance with the different topics occurring in the poem.*'[44] This argues a standard for the appropriateness of topics within a given subject matter, and for a stylistic 'harmony' between *bayts* based on their meaning. How 'they follow upon each other' is important to the poet. A sense of the poem as a whole appears very clearly when Ibn Khaldun states: 'If a verse is satisfactory but does not fit in its context, (the poet) should save it for a place more fitting to it.'[45] Throughout this discussion by Ibn Khaldun, as in the books of rhetoric, the making of a poem is a matter of craftsmanship and knowledge. The 'intention' of the poet is stressed. The decisions involved are thought of as conscious and deliberate.

The Harat preface of 907 A.H. (cited in footnote 20) is evidence that the order of the *bayts* in the ghazals of Hafiz was felt to be important. It is, in fact, the reason given for the new recension, and vehement invective is used against those responsible for the disorder. That *cleaning* or *purging* of the ghazals was necessary suggests that the members of the court of Faridun Husayn Khan who engaged in this task had a sense of each *ghazal* as a whole, as I suspect that this process was accomplished more by literary than by textual criticism.

Khvandamir, in his account of Shah Mansur's arrival in Shiraz, introduces into the narrative two *bayts* from a *ghazal* by Hafiz. On that occasion, he says Hafiz 'arranged a *ghazal* on the thread of style (*ghazali dar silk-i insha intizam dad*).'[46] This conventional phrase may indicate that Khvandamir had a sense of 'context' or 'harmony' similar to that of Ibn Khaldun, and that he felt that Hafiz's ghazals were unified by style. A theory cannot be built on a single example such as this, but together with the other evidence it is important, and it helps to show that the ideas and feelings which form the thinking about poetry in a culture (and in the Islamic culture for the period of Hafiz) are not always fully articulated.

This appreciation of the form and nature of the ghazal does enable us to see that it is not necessary to read ghazals, or any Persian poem, in any way radically different from the way in which we read sonnets, or any European poem, or any other poems. The *ghazal* must be read differently than a European poem in so far as it is part of a different culture, but as a poem it must be read in the same way. We see also, that the lack of an explicit logical sequence similar to that in certain European poems is not the same thing as disunity, incoherence, or a total want of logic. It becomes clear that it is not correct to assert of this lack of explicit logical sequence in the *ghazal*, that, 'It is as if the poets exhausted themselves to such an extent by giving form to such refinement that the fitting together as a whole escaped them.'[47] This is incorrect, not only because in many instances it is not true, and in other instances other techniques of order and 'fitting together' are to be found, but also because it is unreasonable to assume that great poets capable of solving the formal problems of the *ghazal* could not have successfully put their *bayts* in an explicit logical sequence if they had wanted to. This notion of them exhausting their abilities and energies suggests Yeats' 'Three Movements':

> Shakespearean fish swam the sea, far away
>     from land;
> Romantic fish swam in nets coming to the
>     hand;
> What are all those fish that lie gasping on the
>     strand?

but those that 'lie gasping on the strand' are more often the critics than the poets, and many of the charges of disunity in the *ghazal* must be dismissed as failures of analysis and understanding.

When one considers the rigorousness of the *ghazal* as a form and the strength of the literary tradition of which it was a part, it seems more reasonable to assume that many explicit logical connections were not made because they were not felt to be necessary, and that they were not felt to be necessary because the plot, logic and connections were provided (in varying degrees depending on the poem) by the tradition, by the many conventions. In writing ghazals the Persian poets may have taken for granted much of what a European lyric poet would have felt obliged to spell out. Or it may be that what is now sometimes felt as disorder and disunity is merely the expression of their individuality, that the very rigorousness of the *ghazal* created a desire for freedom and innovation, or a certain impatience with what was customary, which was satisfied *within the tradition* by including more subjects in a single poem, by glossing over or ignoring transitions, and by making tacit and allusive connections between the *bayts*. By the time of Hafiz it would have been difficult to write ghazals *and* to do anything new within the limits of the conventions in any other way. That

Hafiz may have felt something of all this is suggested not only by his ghazals, but also by the story referred to above in the first footnote in the *Tarikh-i habib al-siyar.*

If Khvandamir is to be trusted, one day Shah Shuja, in a faultfinding mood, said to Hafiz: 'The *bayts*—not one—in your ghazals, from the opening to the closing, do not happen to be of one kind, instead in each *ghazal* there are three or four *bayts* about wine and two or three *bayts* about sufism and one or two *bayts* about the characteristics of the beloved. The changeableness of each *ghazal* is contrary to the way of the eloquent. The Khavajah said: That which the blessed tongue of the Shah discerns is the essence of truth and of unalloyed accuracy; however, the poetry of Hafiz has found consummate fame in all regions of the world and the verse of his various rivals has not set foot beyond the gate of Shiraz.' Even allowing for the situation and the temper of the two speakers it is interesting that Hafiz completely accepts the truth of Shuja's criticism. This criticism, that the ghazals of Hafiz contain too many different subjects (however they may be connected?!), depends upon an idea of the *ghazal* as a whole. The objection to many subjects is presumably that they destroy the unity which tradition ('the way of the eloquent') demanded in the *ghazal*. Shuja thinks of the *ghazal* as having between six and nine *bayts*, and of three distinct subjects, even if treated in two or three *bayts* each as too many for one *ghazal*. It would seem that he means each subject is treated in consecutive *bayts,* but this is not absolutely clear.[48]) The views of Shuja are similar to those of Ibn Khaldun cited above. He, too, evidently feels that sharp contrasts should be kept out of a poem, and that a harmony should be established among the *bayts* of a poem.[49]) Thus, the evidence suggests that the ghazals of Hafiz were seen by his contemporaries as a departure from tradition, and that the poet himself knew very well what he was doing.

Arberry cites the following remarks by William Leaf: 'We have learnt from our Greek masters to seek the unity of a poem in the thought or mood developed in it. Whether sensuous or intellectual, the unity is internal and essential. To a Persian poet this is not so; and that is a hard lesson which we must learn before we can do full justice to Eastern art. In the Persian ode we find a succession of couplets often startling in their independence, in their giddy transitions from grave to gay, from thought to mood. To the Persian each couplet is a whole in itself, a *nukta*, or "point," sufficiently beautiful if it be adequately expressed, and not of necessity owing anything or adding anything to that which comes before or after. It is from the common metre and common rhyme alone that the ode gains a formal unity . . . The lyric poetry of Persia is indeed a reflection of the minds of those who sang it—sensual, mystic, recalling the voluptuous dreams of Hash-

ish, the flashes of intuition wherein the Godhead reveals himself in moments of blinding visions to the
ecstatic drunk with wine, be it of Heaven or of Earth.'[50]
Leaf is attacking the unity of Hafiz's ghazals, but when
this passage is put side-by-side with QG 3, one can see
that the poem does exhibit an obvious unity of thought
and mood.

In the poem, the poet declares his passion for the Shirazi
Turk and the cruelty of the Turk in not requiting his
passion causes him to reflect on the meaning of life.
The unexpressed logic of the poem seems to be that
the Turk in being difficult, capricious and incalculable
suggests to the poet that every man is treated by life as
he is treated by the Shirazi Turk. Nevertheless, it is too
much to say that the poet discovers in his love of the
Turk an image of every man's predicament, because
the two ideas are not explicitly connected and the
particular occasion is not merely an excuse for a general lesson. The poem is neither allegorical nor an
example of simple moralizing, nor an account of how
the poet has become wise. Its beauty derives from its
elegance and subtlety, from the fact that these connections are suggested and not directly stated. In a sense,
the first *bayt* states the situation or problem and the
second *bayt*, the solution, and the whole poem may be
seen as a development of those two statements, but
this, as will be seen, ignores the other ways in which
the *bayts* are connected. Then, too, this successful
parataxis cannot be called disunity if the first two *bayts*
are recognised as the statement and resolution of a
single problem.

Despite the troubles which are mentioned the mood of
the poem is joyous. The extravagance of the first *bayt*
is matched by the last. The Shirazi Turk may not return his love, but the poet is drinking wine and singing, two activities on which in the poem he places the
highest value, and he is in Shiraz, which he obviously
considers the best place to be. The hard words of the
beloved satisfy him and make the beloved seem sweeter.
The poet says he must sing sweetly (not sadly), and
there are no sighs, tears or lamentations, all of which
are common in Hafiz's poems. The inscrutable and
knotted problems of life cause him to think of the beauty
of the Pleiades, the immortality of his work, and that
he should be well paid for his art. Thus, the poem is
of a single mood and the character of the poet in the
poem does not vary. None of his feelings and thoughts
are incongruous in this context. Similarly, the character of the beloved is a unified and consistent whole.
The Shirazi Turk does not share the poet's passion, but
is compared to the flirtatious, trouble-making *luliyan*
and the raiding, plundering Turks of Central Asia. The
Turk is more beautiful every day, with lips as red as
rubies and as sweet as sugar, and the bitter reply which
those lips make to the poet is said to be completely in
character. Everything in the poem suggests that the
Turk will not change.

There is a further unity to this poem in that, like so
many of Hafiz's ghazals, it is the discourse of a single
speaker. Those ghazals which are not the discourse of
a single speaker are usually dialogues. The poet is
speaking, but his call to the *saqi* for the last of the
wine gives the poem the effect of conversation rather
than an interior monologue. *Bayt* two, consequently,
should be understood as an aside in his speech instead
of the beginning of a new and disconnected subject. It
indicates the setting of the poem, revealing indirectly
that the poet is drinking in a wine-house. The successive imperatives in the three final *bayts* also strengthen
the impression that the poem is being spoken aloud or
sung, as does the statement that the poet would like his
poem crowned with stars, which contains a hint to a
patron that the poet would like money as a reward for
his labour. This hint makes sense only if the *ghazal* is
addressed to an audience other than the poet himself.
There is perhaps a slight problem as to who is speaking in *bayt* eight, which is the advice of the *pir-i dana*.
In *bayt* seven the poet asks his soul to listen to the
advice of the *pir*, which is a good reason for thinking
that the poet and the *pir* are two different persons,
although *jana* is a simple vocative without a possessive pronoun and may be understood as directed to the
poet's audience. The poem as a whole causes me to
believe that the poet is speaking to himself, as well as
his audience, and that he is repeating the advice he has
heard from the *pir*, the immediacy and applicability of
which he now feels very keenly.

This *ghazal* is the embodiment of the poet's emotion.
Hafiz is not describing something which he *sees* either
in his mind or around him. The beloved is no more
than a beautiful Turk with red lips and a black mole.
The emphasis is on the beloved's behaviour and the
poet's reaction to it. There is no precise or specific
visual description, no concentration on the uniqueness
of things. Definite places are named, but the name is
left to conjure up by itself the qualities of the place.
Nothing distracts the attention from the poet's feelings, but this generality is neither vague nor abstract.
The emotion is personal and particular. Yusuf and
Zulaykha, and the *luliyan* and *Turkan*, are as specific
as Samarqand and Bukhara or the Pleiades, and even
the *pir-i dana* and the *javanan-i saadatmand* must count
here as specific and definite.

Emotion is, of course, more a matter of mood than of
a necessary sequence, and a certain discontinuity or
illogicity of thought in its literary representation may
be the most accurate way to render it. A rush of feeling
does not have or need a plot, except perhaps its place
in the plot which is every man's life. Here there is
nothing which can be identified as autobiographical or
historical. How the Shirazi Turk actually fitted into the
poet's life is unknown. There is no story or anecdote.
Beloved and lover confront each other in what may
barely be called a situation and they can barely be said

to act out their parts. There are two characters and one mood. The whole poem is the brief testimony of only one witness. The philosophy, if it may be called that, in the eighth *bayt* has the quality of emotion. Wisdom is a better name for it, and wisdom is often felt to be virtually spontaneous and in many ways like emotion. It is significant that in the poem the advice of the *pir* is opposed to philosophy as a formal study (*hikmat*) and presented as a result of experience and old age. The advice is a simple assertion. There is no reasoning and no argument.

The pleasure which the poet takes in his own emotions is expressed in the extravagant statements which open the *ghazal*. If his beloved will accept his love, the poet will give away Samarqand and Bukhara, two of the richest and most famous cities in the whole Iranian world, in order to possess the mole on his beloved's face. That the poet does not possess the cities and cannot in any sense give them away is part of the extravagance (and humour) of this declaration. The gesture was such as to capture the imagination of Timur and of many of Hafiz's biographers.[51] The second *bayt* is identical to the first in its extravagance, for in it the poet clearly implies that Shiraz is better than Paradise, and that the pleasures of this world are better than those of the next. *May-yi baqi* probably refers to the *durd*, the lees or dregs of the wine (the *durdkashan* or dregs-drinkers are often met with in the **Divan-i Hafiz**, see, for example, QG 9/5, QG 26/5, QG 110/6, and QG 131/6) so the poet is not only celebrating the drinking of wine, prohibited by Islam, but also suggesting that the dregs of the wine of this world may be superior to anything to be enjoyed in Paradise. All this is blasphemous and even dangerous in an intolerant, religiously orthodox society, and is more than rhetorical daring.[52] Orthodoxy is challenged and mocked again in the poem with the same spirit in *bayt* eight when the poet refers to the *hadis* of music and wine. He appears to enjoy allowing his emotion to carry him away. This pitch of feeling is maintained either by grammatical forms, such as vocatives and imperatives, or by the subject matter: by the imperative, *bidih*, to the *saqi* (*bayt* 2), by the vocative *fighan* (*bayt* 3), and by the vocative *jana*, and the imperatives, *gush kun* (*bayt* 7), *qu* and *ju* (*bayt* 8) and *biya* and *bikhvan* (*bayt* 9), as well as by the *luliyan* stirring up trouble and the Turkan plundering (*bayt* 3) and Zulaykha forsaking the veil of chastity (*bayt* 5). That uncontrollable emotion is expressed in a rigorously controlled form is not felt at all to be a paradox in Hafiz, it seems rather to be a purpose of poetry.

This *ghazal* of Hafiz, like his other ghazals, shows a further form of unity in the rhetorical figures which may be traced throughout the poem. These have sometimes been seen as fragmenting the *ghazal*, but it must also be understood that because each *bayt* embodies one or more rhetorical figures, the whole *ghazal* is a single poetic texture. The figures are a poetic algebra in which a whole range of values may be substituted in essential forms. In Islamic literature they are not an adjunct to poetry, but of its substance. One feels in Hafiz that their use might be barely conscious, that they are a mode of his mind and moulds of his thought. The unobtrusiveness of his figures as figures is a reason for the greatness of his poetry, its smoothness and elegance. They shape the discourse and participate in it without interrupting it.

Form and meaning (content is something more) are two points of view from which a poem may be considered. In poetry both aspects must be considered together. There is no meaning without words and there are no words without form. A thorough knowledge of rhetorical figures would be a pressure on the poet not only to compose in figures, but also to vary his figures—to play on all the keys of the repertory. The demand to cast each *bayt* as a new and separate figure might also force a change of subject. There is, however, no need to have a certain number of figures or to have any particular figure, or have them in any particular order. They determine neither the length nor the order of the poem. The figures, as is the case with meter, both inhibit and inspire the poet. They might limit him, or serve as a store of ready possibilities, or give his thought a particular bias and momentum. . . .

That a poem can be described in terms of rhetorical figures is not, of course, proof that the system was known to the poet. Because rhetorical, like grammatical, analysis can be used for all language, such proof cannot consist merely of the fact that figures can be *discovered* in a poem. It must mean an analysis of the figures and of the way in which they figure in a poem, *and* historical evidence about the poet and the literary culture of the period of the poem. Everything about this poem causes one to think that Hafiz was familiar with the system of rhetorical figures, and this is confirmed by the statement in the old Preface that Hafiz studied the *Miftah al-'ulum* of Sakkaki and by the variety of evidence which indicates that he was a learned man.[54]

That identifying the figures is not enough to describe the way in which they are employed can be shown by a single example. *Mutadadd* does not denote the complexities of the relationship of the *Turk-i Shirazi* and the *khal-i Hindu*. Essentially the antithesis is between black and white, although no colour is named and no abstract, general words are used. (In a similar way the antithesis in *bayt* two is essentially between heaven and earth. Both cases offer examples of the specificity and definiteness mentioned above.) The two terms are not equal, a part is opposed to the whole. There is perhaps a similarity in shape: the circular moon-face of the Turk and the small black circle of the mole, and both are thought to be beautiful. Two contrasting forms of beauty, however, are present. The traditional idea is expressed by Kay Kaus in the *Qabus-namah*: 'It is known to all that their [Turkish] and Indian [*Hindu*] beauty and ugliness are opposite. Look, for example, at the Turk in detail—the large head, wide face, narrow eyes, flat nose, and inelegant lips and mouth—although when you look in detail he is not beautiful, nevertheless consider everything and see it together and he is beautiful. The Indian face is the opposite of this. When one by one you examine its features, each in and of itself appears beautiful, but when you look at the whole it does not appear like a Turkish face. First, the Turk has a natural freshness and clearness of complexion which the Indian does not. The Turks have surpassed all races in freshness.'[55] Interestingly, in the poem the whole is Turkish and the individual feature is Indian. The adjective *Shirazi* does not enter into any of the antitheses generated by the two terms. *Turk* is set off against both *khal* and *Hindu*. *Turk* and *Hindu* not only stand for colours and for two types of beauty, but they represent geographical extremes and styles of civilization: the nomadic culture of the north and the settled culture of the south. *Turk* also belongs to the group of Turkish references which give a distinctive quality to the opening of the poem, while *Shirazi* fits with Bukhara and Samarqand, and with Ruknabad and Musalla. The proliferation of subdivisions and subtypes within the classification of figures represents the efforts of the rhetoricians to capture what they felt was eluding them.

The lesson of the rhetorical figures is what they suggest in the way of forms and poetic techniques. To compose poetry with the system of rhetorical figures in mind, consciously or half-consciously, means producing poetry of a particular kind. The enumeration above illustrates how the presence of many rhetorical figures creates a single poetic texture (a form of unity), and helps to make clear some of the effects which Hafiz sought as well as the nature of his control over the poem. The texture, the effects and the control are all complex because of the disparate natures of the rhetorical figures. *Mutadadd*, for example, is a matter of meaning, while *muzdavaj* depends only upon the repetition of sounds. Both may be contrasted to the three forms of *mubalaghah*, classified according to their truth-value, as possible, improbable and impossible.[56] Their mixed quality as a group is embodied in the terminology of the rhetoricians which is an amalgam of grammar, philosophy, and an attempt to describe in abstract terms the play of meaning and connotation in all possible poems. By means of the rhetorical figures, notions of form and meaning are tangled up together in the theory of Islamic poetry. There are, moreover, other forms and techniques in the poem which are not, in the terms of Hafiz and his contemporaries, rhetorical figures, but which may be said to be analogous to them. It is difficult to describe and classify them, because their effect is in their combination and, like the rhetorical figures, they are a mixed and disparate group.

The most common figure in the poem is *mutadadd* (antithesis). The *bayt*, as a poetic unit composed of two equal parts each long enough to contain a statement, lends itself easily to antithesis, and indeed promotes it. (There are reasons for supposing that this binary form may be a vestige of oral poetic composition.) The binary aspect of the *bayt* may also promote the many symmetries and correspondences of grammatical forms, the pairings and balancings, which help to unify the ghazals of Hafiz and which seem analogous to antithesis but in no way the figure *mutadadd*. The continuity of a long literary tradition can be felt here as the same ends and means can be observed in ancient Near Eastern texts, in Gilgamesh and in the poetry of the Old Testament. It is part of Hafiz's skill that he uses these symmetries and correspondences to complicate the structure of his ghazals and to prevent them from resolving into simple bipartite forms.

The first *bayt* is a conditional sentence where the first *misra* is the protasis and the second *misra* the apodosis. (The fourth, fifth, sixth and eighth *bayts*, although not conditional, have the same structure. The ninth *bayt* is similar except that the first *misra* is made up of short sentences.) The syntax of the first *misra*, however, cannot be said to be parallel with that of the second, although there are many correspondences between the two *misraat*. There is one verb in each half of the *bayt*. They are in a similar position and each is followed only by its direct object. That they are opposite in meaning is a further correspondence. The antithesis acts as a bond. *Bukhara* and *Samarqand* balance each other *and* are set off against *Shirazi* while *dil-i ma* is set off against *khal-i . . . ash*, *Turk* against *Hindu*. Almost every word or phrase in the first *misra* of the first *bayt* has one or more counterparts (of some kind) in the second *misra*. The correspondence is sometimes of linguistic form, sometimes of meaning, and not infrequently involves both. A word may be balanced by a phrase, a noun by an adjective and the corresponding words are arranged in different orders within their respective *misra*.

Correspondences such as these can be discovered between the first and second *misra* of every *bayt* in this poem, but, more important for the unity of the *ghazal*, they also exist between *bayts*. The whole second *misra* of the second *bayt* can be said to be parallel to *Samarqand u Bukhara-ra*. Each unit contains two proper nouns (both place names) joined by the conjunction *va*, and is the direct object of its respective sentence (and *bayt*). The members of each pair of place names are congruous. Samarqand and Bukhara are comparable cities in Turkestan, the banks of the Ruknabad and the gardens of Musalla are two comparable pleasances in Shiraz. This same combination of Turkestan and Shiraz exists in the name of the beloved *Turk-i Shirazi*, and also between *Turk-i Shirazi* and *Samarqand u Bukhara*. There are probably more correspondences of this order between the first two *bayts* than any other two *bayts* in this poem, and some other *bayts* (for example, three and four, or three and five) are not strongly connected *in this way* at all.

Antitheses established by the poem cannot be classed as examples of *mutadadd*. Every *bayt* except perhaps the ninth is built on such antithesis. The whole poem, in fact, is an expression of the antithesis between the Shirazi Turk and the poet.

What may be called groups of references and allusions are another aspect of the unity of the ghazals of Hafiz. I am not certain that this phenomenon can be delimited by any clear, comprehensive, abstract definition. I do believe that it can be defined by example and that this definition can be applied by analogy. I have attempted, therefore, to elucidate this aspect of the poem without insisting upon any classification or terminology.

There are five Turkish references in the first three *bayts* of QG 3. In the first *bayt* there is the Shirazi Turk, and Bukhara and Samarqand, the names of two famous cities of Turkestan. Hafiz in another *ghazal* speaks of 'the Turks of Samarqand.'[57] The third *bayt* refers to the *Turkan* at the *khvan-i yaghma. Yaghma* is both the name of a Turkish tribe of Turkestan and a word meaning *plunder.*[58] This double meaning conveys clearly the reputation of the Turks. Under *yaghma*, Steingass records that it is the 'name of a city in Turkistan celebrated for the beauty of its inhabitants.' The phrase may be translated either as 'the feast of the Yaghma' or 'the feast of the plunder.'[59] I am uncertain as to which sense Hafiz intends or whether he is playing on both. In any case, *yaghma* is a Turkish reference, and particularly apt in this poem as some of the qualities the Yaghma Turks were reputed to possess are those of the Shirazi Turk.

This repetition of meaning and connotation has its effect like the repetition of phrases and words, sounds (assonance, consonance—and their special cases, alliteration and rhyme) and meter. The Turkish references, and the other groups like this one in the poem, help hold the *ghazal* together. They do not form any special pattern or occur with any fixed frequency. The bond which they supply does not depend on any order or sequence. There is no mention of the Turks in the second *bayt*, but the allusions in the other two *bayts* contribute to making a whole of the initial four or five *bayts*. Other arrangements of the five Turkish references would give analogous effects, for example, transferring one of the two references in *bayt* three to *bayt* four or five. Neither as a group nor individually are they necessary to the action, ideas or mood of the poem, although the poem would, of course, change if they were changed. They are not *themes* in any sense of the word, and not all of them are traditional. As far as I know, there is no convention for alluding to the *khvan-i yaghma*, or mentioning Samarqand and Bukhara in the same poem with either Shiraz or the Yaghma.

Other groups of references knit this *ghazal* together. Three cities are named in the first *bayt* and the *luliyan* are described as city-disturbing (*shahr-ashub*) in the third *bayt*. Shiraz is referred to in the first *bayt* and two places in Shiraz are mentioned in the second *bayt*. These groups can be described as reinforcing the Turkish allusions in that they connect the same *bayts* with different words and meanings, and in different combinations. The fourth and fifth bayts do not share in any groups of this order.[60] The beloved's lips are mentioned in the sixth *bayt*, and emphasized by two strong adjectives. This glimpse of the beloved's face forms a weak but palpable connection with the opening *bayt*, the only other *bayt* in the poem in which the Turk's features are described.

The advice of the wise man forms the subject matter of the seventh and eighth bayts. *Hadis* and *hikmat*, as traditional forms of learning, help to join *bayt* eight with seven (which also contains two words for wisdom: *nasihat* and *pand*) even though they are antithetical in terms of the meaning of the poem. This group of words for knowledge (*nasihat, pand, hadis* and *hikmat*) is not of the same order as the Turkish references, and does not function in the *ghazal* in exactly the same way. Although both are unifying factors, the latter group is integral to the poem in a way the former is not. Criticism can, perhaps, go no further than this. The point is delicate and important. The descriptive phrases of a distinction such as this should not be used as categories.

The interconnections of the final three *bayts* are particularly subtle. The various forms of knowledge are seen as embodying different attitudes or *solutions* to the problem of fate, which is first described as *raz-i dahr*, the secret or mystery of time, and then as in *mu'amma,* this enigma, riddle or puzzle. In combination with the verbs (*na-gushavad u na-gushayad*) with their sense of *to loosen* as well as *to open* and *to resolve*, there is a hint here of the image of the knot and the necklace which is so clear in the final *bayt*. The bored pearls, the thread of verse and the knot of the Pleiades (as has been already pointed out) all suggest the image of a necklace. Furthermore, the knot of the Pleiades may be about to be opened and the stars scattered, and the pearls of the poem may be seen as loose and ready to be strung. *Aqd* is thereby related to *raz* and *muamma*, but *surayyara*, too, has its connection with *dahr*. The sky is an old metaphor in Persian poetry for fate.[61] The Pleiades are in the sky and in the final *bayt* it is the sky (*falak*) which is virtually personified as a cosmic power able to disperse them—at the prompting of the poet. Thus the poet can succeed where the philosopher failed. Hafiz has made a knot of the ideas of *fate, sky, puzzle* and *necklace*.

*Bayt* eight then can be taken as the advice promised in *bayt* seven, and Hafiz in *bayt* nine appears to obey the command in *bayt* eight to sing a story or *hadis* of music and wine. *Bayt* nine is not only joined to *bayt* eight by the reference to music but also to *bayt* two, as making music and drinking wine are the activities of the wine-house. Moreover, the reference is at the same time to the *ghazal* as a whole. The whole poem is Hafiz's song.[62] It should be noted that *bayts* eight and nine evoke the scene of the wine house set in *bayt* two in a way similar to the manner in which *bayt* six brings back the picture of the beloved's face. I have also discussed above how the poet's reflections on fate are related to his passion for the Shirazi Turk. The close of the *ghazal* is, in a variety of ways, a true conclusion to the poem as a whole.

I do not wish to exaggerate the unity of the ghazals of Hafiz. That there are forces which hold his poems together does not mean that there are not others which, simultaneously, tug them apart, and certainly all his ghazals do not possess the same degree of unity. Each *ghazal*, nevertheless, must be considered as a whole, and Hafiz's ghazals cannot be described as 'a bunch of motifs only lightly tied together.'[63] As a rigorous poetic form in a conventional, slowlychanging literature, the *ghazal* had a formal unity apart from whatever meaning it expressed, and what it was *as a form* included matters of content. Analysis of *Agar an Turk-i Shirazi* (a representative *ghazal* by Hafiz) reveals the web of interrelationships which exist within the poem—beyond its unity as a *ghazal*. It exhibits a unity of mood and thought, which might be expected of a single speech on a given occasion, and demonstrates that changes of images do not invariably mean a change of subject matter or of the basic idea in a poem, and that the lack of a necessary logical sequence is not the same thing as disunity and need not make a poem illogical. The unity of the *ghazal* is created also by patterns of grammatical form and of meaning which are necessary neither to the subject nor to the mood of the poem, although they are essential to the fabric of the poem and a characteristic of the ghazals of Hafiz. That they are random, partial patterns, which are more-or-less independent of each other, and not total patterns, does not make them any the less unifying factors, and in the poem they belong at the same time, to other patterns of different orders. The distinctions of analysis should not be confused with the indivisible whole which is the poem, a whole greater than the sum of its parts.[64]

### Notes

[1] These texts are translated and analyzed in my book *Hafiz: An Introduction* [Hafiz] which I hope will be published in the near future. The Roman numerals in the references to this work refer to the chapters. There is one passage in the *Tarikh-i habib al-siyar* (Tihran, 1333 A.H.S.; iii, 315-316) which gives us a hint of Hafiz's attitude (see Hafiz, iii, for a translation and for an analysis), but it is only a hint and even then the story may not be authentic. Moreover, the text is late. Hafiz died in 792 A.H. and Khvandamir wrote his book between 927 and 930 A.H. Arberry did not consider this passage; see *loc. cit.*

[2] Hafiz, iii; for an inventory of the oldest, known MSS, see ii. QG stands for the edition by M. Qazvini and Q. Ghani, Tihran, 1320 A.H.S. of the *Divan-i Khvajah-yi . . . Hafiz Shirazi*. Thus, QG 440/8a refers to the first *misra* of the eighth *bayt* of *ghazal* 440 in QG.

[3] Orient Pearls, 705.

[4] QG, *qu*. See Hafiz, iii, for a discussion of the authenticity of the Preface, a translation, and an analysis of its biographical value. Dawlatshah, *Tadhkirat al-shuara*, edited by M. Abbasi (Tihran, 1337 A.H.S.), 365-366. The references to Hafiz in the *Divan-i Kamal Khujandi* are discussed in Hafiz, iii, as is the linkage of the names of Kamal and Hafiz in Jami's *Baharistan*.

[5] This idea of a 'formative period' in Hafiz's life when he was influenced by other poets, especially Sadi, is developed by Arberry in his *Fifty Poems of Hafiz* (Cambridge, 1962), 28-33. This book was first published in 1947, a year after 'Orient Pearls at Random Strung.' The problems presented by this periodization are discussed in Hafiz, Bibliographical Note [BN]. Despite the excellent and fundamental work of Ghani in his *Bahs dar asar va afkar va ahval-i Hafiz*, i (Tihran, 1321 A.H.S.), the chronology of Hafiz's poems is still largely problematical. Rypka's statement 'that important progress has been made which has led to the chronological determination of a considerable number of the poems' is too optimistic; J. Rypka, *History of Iranian Literature* (Dordrecht, Holland, 1968), 266. Lescot's article, 'Essai d'une Chronologie de l'œuvre de Hafiz,' *Bulletin d'études orientales*, x (1944), 57-100, as is not always noticed, is a review of Ghani's book (and others), and much of his reasoning is extremely tenuous; cf. Hafiz, BN.

[6] The Arabic and Persian *tadmin* of Hafiz are discussed by Qazvini in 'Badi-yi tadminha-yi Hafiz,' *Yadgar*, i/5 (1323 A.H.S.), 67-72; i/6, 62-71; i/8, 60-71 and i/g, 65-78. *Tadmin*, as Arberry understands (Orient Pearls, 706, n. 1), is only a small part of what is traditional and of what is borrowed or echoed in Hafiz.

[7] Orient Pearls, 706.

[8] See, for example, QG 4/8, QG 42/7, QG 233/6, QG 319/10, and QG 447/7, and the passage in the *Tarikh-i habib al-siyar* referred to above.

[9] Orient Pearls, 707.

[10] Wordsworth (1770-1850) and Turner (1775-1851), although almost exact contemporaries, do not seem to have taken any notice of each other, which is especially curious as poetry was very important to Turner. He both read a considerable amount of poetry and wrote poetry. Wordsworth and Turner were the greatest English artists of their time and great innovators. Each achieved a large body of work. They shared a taste for ordinary life and a deep love of the countryside. Nature was the subject of their best work and both turned to it for similar reasons and both felt in it a suspernatural power. The comparison is extremely interesting, so much so that it is surprising that no one has written on it, nevertheless, the detailed study of the works of Wordsworth does not help very much with the detailed study of the works of Turner and *vice versa*.

Jack Lindsay in his very good book, *J. M. W. Turner, His Life and Work* (London, 1966), uses Turner's own poems and his reading of other poets to help explain his development. This is, of course, a different case than the one discussed above in the text as Turner himself, his mind and character, is usually the subject, and not style or a particular painting. Even when paintings are involved the poetic parallels help us most with meaning and least with the style, form, unity and colour, that is, with those aspects which distinguish them as paintings. Turner's writing and reading, in so far as they can be recovered, are a gloss on what he was thinking at the time he was doing a painting, and, therefore, only indirectly, upon the painting itself. The book makes the limitations of such evidence as clear as its uses. The assumption that every fact we know about an artist aids us in understanding his works must be applied with intelligence and caution. That Dr. Johnson put orange peels in his pocket (*Boswell's Life of Johnson*, Oxford Standard Authors edition, 1960, 602-603, and 1222) does not advance us much in understanding his greatness. This same assumption extended, *by analogy*, that every fact we know about a culture reveals its personality is more radically problematical, even if one accepts the idea that cultures have a personality or character. As one moves from the study of a man to the study of a culture the problems change their nature as well as increase in number and difficulty.

[11] Compare plates 886 and 887 with plates 847, 848 and 849 in A. U. Pope, *A Survey of Persian Art*, (London and New York, 1964-1965), ix.

[12] See, for example, J. D. Pearson, *Index Islamicus 1906-1955*, (Cambridge, 1958), and his *Index Islamicus Supplement 1956-1960* (Cambridge, 1962). Under the heading of 'FINE ART: LOCAL FORMS' for Iran there is nothing specifically on the fourteenth century in either volume, nor is there anything on the period's 'MOSAICS.' Under 'ARCHITECTURE' in the two volumes there is only: M. E. Crane, 'A fourteenth-century mihrab from Isfahan,' *Ars Islamica,* 7 (1940), 96-100. 'MINIATURE PAINTING' is better represented. In the *Index* in twelve double-column pages there are ten items whose titles indicate that they are about miniature painting in Iran in the fourteenth century. Most of them are short notices of new discoveries rather than long studies. There is one item in the *Supplement* on this subject: R. Ettinghausen, 'Persian ascension miniatures of the fourteenth century,' *Convengno di scienze morali, storiche e filologiche* (1956), 360-383. Judging from the titles of the various items, which are somewhat deceptive, the lives and thoughts of the artists themselves, in any period, have rarely been a subject of study. The study of these arts is, of course, limited by what has survived. There is, as I remember, only one major surviving building in Shiraz which Hafiz may be assumed to have seen. This is the Masjid-i Jumah, which like so many of its kind, is a composite of many periods, and it has often been repaired, altered and restored since his death.

O. Grabar in his survey, 'The Visual Arts 1050-1350,' writes that 'the disastrous lack of proper monographic studies—except in the case of a very few objects and buildings—makes any generalization somewhat hazardous,' and that 'it is, at this stage of our research, still almost impossible to co-ordinate properly the monuments with the events of the time; and often in trying to explain the monuments one misses the human and spiritual context in which they were made and used.' He goes on to say that, 'almost no attempt has yet been made by archaeologists or historians to separate pan-Iranian trends from local ones or to assess the exact character of any one provincial development;' *The Cambridge History of Iran*, (Cambridge, 1968), v, 627-628.

[13] B. Lewis, *The Arabs in History* (London, Grey Arrow edition, 1958), 141-142. The book was first published in 1950. The whole relevant passage is 139-143. Lewis makes atomism an Arab rather than a Persian phenomenon, but the distinction between what is Arabic and what is Islamic is sometimes blurred in the chapter. There is also the problem of whether, 'The atomistic outlook on life received its complete expression in the scholastic theology of Al-Ashari . . . ' (142).

[14] T. Kowalski, *Na sz akach Islamu*, (Kraków, 1935), 109 as quoted by Rypka, *op. cit.*, 102; and Rypka, *ibid.*, 102; see also 99-100.

[15] By literature I mean everything written, with a special emphasis on the best writing. I believe it distorts the forms, values and ideas of the culture to refuse or fail to consider history and philosophy as literature, or to isolate, as is often done, certain works as *belles-lettres*, (which always carries with it at least a slightly pejorative sense) or to impose any foreign and artificial classification. It is a characteristic of Islamic lit-

erature that there are many works composed of alternate passages of prose and poetry. There are Arabic and Persian philological works wholly in rhyme, and there are histories written in an elaborate style akin to that of the *maqamat* and others written as *masnaviyat*, while books of stories, like the *Gulistan*, are stylistically similar to the *tadhkirat*. The *masnaviyat* of Attar, like many of the poems of Mawlana, must be considered both as philosophy and as poetry. That most of the best Persian poets were learned men and the learned nature of much of Persian poetry has not been fully appreciated. For a discussion of Hafiz's learning see Hafiz, iii.

[16] Harry Austryn Wolfson, *The Philosophy of Spinoza* (New York, 1960), i, 10. See also the whole first chapter, 3-31 and the opening of the same author's *Philo* (Harvard, 1947), 2v.

[17] This point is made in my 'New Material for the Text of Hafiz,' *Iran*, viii (1965), 114, and again with a fuller explanation in Hafiz, ii. For a history of the text of the *Divan* and an inventory of the known MSS older than the Khalkhali MS (dated 827/1424), the base MS of QG, and on QG as a basis for literary criticism, see Hafiz, ii.

[18] QG, *kt-lh* and C. Rempis, 'Beiträge zur Hayyam-Forschung,' *Abhandlungen für die Kunde des Morgenlandes*, xxii (1, 1937), 126-127. On the two MSS see Hafiz, ii.

[19] Hafiz, ii.

[20] Istanbul University MS F87, f. 99b—100a. I have used the facsimile published at the end of H. R. Roemer's *Staatsschreiben der Timuridenzeit*, (Wiesbaden, 1952). On the recension see also Hafiz, ii.

[21] Aya Sofya 3945, f. 402a.

[22] H. Ritter, 'Philologika XI: Maulana Galaladdin Rumi und sein Kreis (Fortsetzung und Schluß),' *Der Islam*, xxvi (1942), 239. See also Hafiz, ii.

[23] On the various MSS, see Hafiz, ii.

[24] G. Galimova, 'The Oldest Manuscript of the Poems of Hafiz,' [in Russian] *Sovetskoe Vostokovedeniye* (1959), 109. Unfortunately the first line of QG 3 is all she gives in her article. This undated MS is not 'the oldest manuscript.' For a full discussion of its date, see my 'New Material for the Text of Hafiz,' *op. cit.*, or Hafiz, ii where the discussion is repeated with some proofreader's corrections.

[25] Mahdi Kamaliyan, 'Nuskhah-yi badalha-yi Divan-i Hafiz,' *Farhang-i Iran Zamin*, vi (1337 A.H.S.), 206. Unfortunately Kamaliyan in his collection of the New

Delhi MS with QG does not give the order of the bayts and reports only those variants which he believes have value and merit (*'vajid-i maziyat va rujhan'*); 204.

[26] Orient Pearls, 706—707. When he says *line* he means *bayt*. The Persian *bayt* and the English *line* are not commensurate.

[27] Sudi refers to the Turk as *mahbubah* rather than *mahbub;* Sudi, *Sharh-i Sudi bar Hafiz* (Tihran, 1341 A.H.S.), i, 25, but compare E. Yarshater, 'The Theme of Wine-drinking and the Concept of the Beloved in Early Persian Poetry,' *Studia Islamica*, xiii (1960), 43—53.

[28] *ibid.*, i, 24.

[29] Hafiz, iv, where the whole poem is discussed.

[30] Ibn Khaldun, *The Muqaddimah*, translated by F. Rosenthal (New York, 1958), iii, 385. It is worth noting that he also wrote some poetry, although he did not have a very high opinion of his own efforts; see iii, 396, and also i; xliii, xlv.

[31] E. G. Browne, *A Literary History of Persia*, (Cambridge, 1951), ii, 27; Rypka, *op. cit.*, 95.

[32] Hafiz, iii. For the poem see Aziz Dawlatabadi's edition of the *Divan-i Kamal* (Tihran, 1337 A.H.S.), 160-161. The poem imitates QG 167.

[33] Browne, *op. cit.*, ii, 27.

[34] Rypka, *op. cit.*, 99 and 124, n. 94 and 96; for the death dates see 144 and 167, n. 16 and 153. In another place (123, n. 75), Rypka writes that the regular insertion of the *takhallus* in the last *bayt* of a *ghazal* is a 'custom being first introduced by Hafiz.' The context is not absolutely clear here, instead of giving his own view he may be summarizing A. M. Mirzoyev, *Abu Abdullo Rudaki*, (Stalinabad, 1958). There were two editions of this work, one in Russian, the other in Arabic characters.

[35] As noted above, throughout this essay I have referred to the *bayts* by number according to their order in QG (as Arberry also does). In considering here *bayts* three, five and six as a sequence I am, of course, following, for this example, the text of Aya Sofya 3945. The point of *bayt* four is not very different from that of the others. The poet's love is said to be incomplete and his beloved is independent of his feelings. The poet is as unnecessary to the beloved as cosmetics. The detachment and aloofness of the beautiful one is made clear in both *bayts* four and five. In *bayts* three and six the beloved appears directly concerned with the poet. In *bayt* four, the poet does not assert his enduring passion,

and less action is depicted. It is abstract, general and bland in a way the other *bayts* are not.

[36] *Shake-Speares Sonnets* (London, 1609), Scholar Press facsimile (Menston, Yorkshire, 1970). This sonnet is a hybrid in form, both Shakespearean and Italian. By the rhyme scheme it divides into three quatrains and a couplet, by subject matter and imagery it divides into an octave and sestet.

[37] Shams al-din Muhammad al-Razi, *Kitab al-mujam fi maayir-i ashar al-ajam*, edited by Qazvini and Mudarris-i Radavi (Tihran, n.d.), t-y, 201-202, compare also 413-414.

[38] Browne, *op. cit.*, iii, 330.

[39] *ibid.*, ii. 84.

[40] Orient Pearls, 703. Arberry also speaks of 'the double string' of pearls which is in no way suggested by the poem.

[41] G. von Grunebaum, *A Tenth-Century Document of Arabic Literary Theory and Criticism* (Chicago, 1950), 75. This citation from Ibn al-Tazriyyah was widely circulated. Von Grunebaum refers to eight Arabic books in which it occurs. See also Hafiz, iii.

[42] QG, p. qi.

[43] Ibn Khaldun, *op. cit.*, iii, 373-374 (my italics).

[44] *ibid.*, iii, 375 (my italics).

[45] *ibid.*, iii, 385.

[46] Khvandamir, *op. cit.*, iii, 321. The metaphor of the necklace is present not only in *silk* (thread) but in *intizam* which according to Steingass also means 'strung in a line,' and is from the same root as *nazm* mentioned above. In another passage about Hafiz, Khvandamir employs the phrase: *ghazali dar silk-i nazm kashidah*; *ibid.*, iii, 316. These metaphors, with their sense that the *ghazal* is *linear*, help to show the untenableness of Wicken's idea of 'radial symmetry;' see his two articles, BSOAS, xiv (1952), 239-243 and xv (1952), 627-638.

[47] Rypka, *ibid.*, 102.

[48] For a detailed analysis of the whole passage, see Hafiz, iii.

[49] Ibn Khaldun (*op. cit.*, iii, 385-386) warns against 'putting too many ideas into one verse . . . If there are many ideas, the verse becomes crowded. The mind examines the (ideas) and is distracted. As a result, (the listener's literary) taste is prevented from fully under-

standing, as it should, the eloquence (of the verse). A poem is easy only when its ideas are more quickly grasped by the mind than its words. Thus our *shaykhs* used to criticize the poetry of the poet of eastern Spain, [Abu Bakr] b. Khafajah, for crowding too many ideas into one verse.' Abu Bakr's dates are given by F. Rosenthal as c. 451/1059-1060-533/1139.

[50] W. Leaf, *Versions from Hafiz*, 5—6, as cited in Orient Pearls, 703—704. Arberry properly calls Leaf's comments 'high-flown nonsense,' but does not refute their main point.

[51] Hafiz, iii. The story of Timur's comment on this *bayt* appears in the *Anis al-nas*, *Tadhkirah al-shuara* and *Lataif al-tavaif*.

[52] Ibn Battutah speaks of the piety of the inhabitants of Shiraz; *The Travels of Ibn Battutah*, edited by H. A. R. Gibb (Cambridge, 1962), ii, 300. The rule of Mubariz al-din is described in terms of oppressive orthodoxy by the *Matla al-sadayn* and the *Tarikh-i al-i Muzaffar*. Hafiz's feelings on this 'time of abstinence' are expressed in QG 41. On the dating of this poem, see the section on the *Matla al-sadayn* in Hafiz, iii. Shuja, whatever his motives, persecuted Hafiz on the grounds of his religious views according to the *Tarikh-i habib-al-siyar*; Hafiz, iii. . . .

[54] QG p. qv; Hafiz, iii. Ibn Khaldun (*op. cit.*, iii, 337) records that: 'Contemporary Easterners are more concerned with commenting on and teaching (the *Miftah*) than any other (work).'

[55] Kay Kaus, *The Nasihat-Nama known as Qabus-Nama . . .* , edited by R. Levy (London, 1951), 64. This text is also evidence of a sense of an aesthetic whole independent of, or greater than, its parts.

[56] E. G. Browne, *op. cit.* ii, 69.

[57] QG 440/8. The text of this *bayt* is discussed by Qazvini in his footnotes, and also in Hafiz, iii.

[58] On the Yaghma Turks, see *Hudud al-Alam*, translated and explained by V. Minorsky (London, 1937), 95-98. Compare Kay Kaus, *op. cit.*, 64.

[59] Sudi (*op. cit.*, i, 27) understands it as 'the feast of the Yaghma,' food spread out for the Yaghma on holidays and important occasions. The dictionaries do not preserve any hint of it being a particular occasion or ceremony. Steingass defines it as 'A public feast to which all are invited, an open table,' and Redhouse, in his *Turkish-English Lexicon*, as 'one's board, a tray of food set out for the poor to scramble for.'

[60] For this discussion I am following, as can be seen, the text of QG. Because the text of Hafiz is not fixed,

I have deliberately moved back and forth between Aya Sofya 3945 and QG in this essay so as to try and take account of as many probable textual variations as possible, so that the analysis and conclusions do not depend upon a single version of the text. I believe this way of working is necessary in cases of this kind.

61 Helmer Ringgren, 'Fatalism in Persian Epics,' *Uppsala Universitets Årsskrift* (1952), 1—134.

62 Because of the close connection of *bayt* eight to bayts seven and nine, and the easy and simple way in which the three *can* be seen to form a sequence, I prefer the sequence of QG for the final three bayts. For these reasons *bayt* eight seems out of place in Saray Revan Kösk 947 and Nuru Osmaniye 3822. The unifying network of references is changed, not destroyed, by these alternate sequences.

63 A. Bausani, 'Ghazal: ii—In Persian Literature,' NEI, ii, 1036.

64 I wish to express my gratitude to the American Philosophical Society and the National Endowment for the Humanities, with whose support I have finished this essay.

## J. Christoph Bürgel (essay date 1991)

SOURCE: "Ambiguity: A Study in the Use of Religious Terminology in the Poetry of Hafiz," in *Intoxication, Earthly and Heavenly: Seven Studies on the Poet Hafiz of Shiraz*, edited by Michael Glunz and J. Christoph Burgel, Peter Lang, Inc., 1991, pp. 8-39.

[*In the following essay, Bürgel argues that Hafiz's ghazals resist an easy understanding and must be examined as part of a large, complex, and ambiguous context.*]

I. The difficulty of understanding Hafiz correctly does not lie in his lexicon or his grammar. He does not use rare or difficult words and his phraseology is simple and very clear. There is hardly any single verse of Hafiz posing a problem in itself. However, there is also hardly a ghazal not posing a problem of meaning and, consequently, of interpretation. In other words, the obfuscation of meaning is created by the juxtaposition of verses that seem to contradict each other, be it by their moral implications or by their belonging to different ontological layers.

What makes Hafiz so difficult, then, is the complexity of his poetic universe. What is the message of this poet? We hardly face this problem when reading, say, Sa'di or 'Umar Khayyam, 'Attar or Rumi, even though

they count among the main forerunners of Hafiz, and Hafiz' poetry bears many traits that can be traced back to the works of those predecessors.

Let us give just one striking example for the obfuscation of a seemingly clear meaning through juxtaposition. The following verse seems to convey a clear Islamic message, concerned with the ritual water, or perhaps mystical wine:

> There is a difference between the water of Khizr, which is in the darkness,
> And our water, the source of which is Allahu akbar.
>
> (KH 40,9)

Allahu akbar—"God is the greatest!" is the Islamic battle-cry. The water springing from it could thus even refer to the blood of martyrs of the Holy War or, at any rate, Islamic values ranging above the "Water of Life" which is hidden in darkness and guarded by Khizr (in other verses, Hafiz calls his poetry "Water of Life," which shows the problem of elucidating one verse by another of his verses). At any rate, the religious message of the verse seems to be indisputable. Yet, it is totally put into question by the preceding verse of the ghazal:

> Shiraz and the water of Ruknabad and the pleasant zephir-
> Don't blame it, it is the mole in the face of the seven climates!

Here, the atmosphere is that of an outing in the vicinity of Shiraz with implications blameworthy in the eyes of the addressee, whom we may easily imagine to be the "ascetic" or a preacher in the mosque (see below). Furthermore, the verse immediately reminds the reader of the famous verse in the "Fair Turk" ghazal, where a similar scene is described, with wine this time expressly mentioned:

> Cup-bearer, bring the remaining wine, since in Paradise you'll not find
> the banks of Ruknabad's stream or Musalla's rose garden.
>
> (KH 3,2)

But it must also be mentioned that the Persian word translated here by "remaining" is ambiguous and could be rendered—this is the official reading—by "everlasting" or "eternal," even though this meaning seems to contradict the context.

The question of what was the intrinsic meaning of his poetry apparently already intrigued his contemporaries and it has continued to be an issue throughout the centuries up to the present day.[1] There are, at least, two opposite schools, one that takes his verses at face value, which makes him predominantly an advocate of enjoying life and love, the other that reads his poetry as the enciphered message of a mystic or a gnostic.

The mystical or "gnostic" (*'irfani*) reading was, and still is the one mainly propagated in Persia; today, it is even the official interpretation of the ruling class;[2] and this is understandable, for it is by such exegesis that one takes the edge off Hafiz' attacks on the representatives of exoteric Islam, i.e. the mollahs, the influential class of Hafiz' time and ruling class of present-day Iran and other Islamic states.

The non-mystical interpretation was favoured in sober Sunnite Turkey, its outstanding protagonist being the Turkish-writing Bosnian scholar Sudi whose commentary influenced the Viennese orientalist Hammer-Purgstall in his German rendering of the divan.[3]

This, again, was to unleash Goethe's enthusiasm for the "Holy Hafiz," his Eastern "twin," as he labelled him in one of his poems.[4] With this first and complete translation of Hafiz' ghazals into a European language, the poet's name became known to Occidental intellectuals and the problem of how to read him, how to define his message, started being discussed at least among some Western orientalists.

Goethe perceived the element of insincerity in the mystical exegesis of verses talking of wine and drunkenness, the tavern and the cup-bearer, the beautiful lad who would rob the heart of every beholder, if all this was to refer to religious truths, if the cup-bearer was to be a metaphor for Muhammad and the wine for Islamic gnosis. He discussed the problem in two poems of his "Westöstlicher Divan." In the poem "Offenbar Geheimnis" ("Open Secret") Goethe rejected the reduction of meaning to the mystical sphere as a dubious trick, without however denying that there is a true mystical dimension in Hafiz' poetry:

> They have called you, o holy Hafiz,
> The mystical tongue.
> And have not recognized, these scholars of the
>     word,
> The value of the word.
> They call you mystical, because reading you
> They think foolish things,
> Pouring out in your name
> Their impure wine.
>
>                . . .
>
> You, however, are mystically pure,
> While they don't understand you.
> For, without being pious, you are redeemed.
>
> This is what they don't want to admit.

In the next poem, "Wink" ("Hint"), Goethe corrected himself by emphasizing that poetical language is never single-layered:

> And yet, they are right, those whom I scold,
> For that a word is not a simple ("onefold")
>     value,
> Should go without saying . . .

Friedrich Rückert, the German poet and orientalist and one of the most illustrious translators of oriental poetry ever to have lived followed Goethe in this view. Using an ingenious pun he described the nature of Hafiz' poetry as evoking "something metaphysical" (übersinnliches) when he talks "about something sensual" (über Sinnliches) and vice versa, so that the secret of its poetry is "unübersinnlich"—one of Rückert's many word-coinings meaning something like "inextricable by thought."[5]

Goethe and Rückert, and, in their wake, Hans Heinrich Schaeder, who found that Hafiz' style was marked by an intentional oscillation,[6] were thus closer to the kernel of the problem of Hafiz' poetry than were later authors, who often fell victim to the temptation of simplifying its meaning or reducing it to one particular layer. This holds true for some minor German poets of the past such as Daumer and Bethge who imitated Hafiz and reduced his message to shallow hedonism, as well as for some Iranists of this century who pigeonholed him instead of admitting his problematical in-between.

Thus, Lescot believed that, basically, Hafiz' poetry was panegyrical and that occasional mystical overtones were hardly more than a tribute to the taste of his time.[7] Two other scholars, Hillmann and Rehder, denied that there was a mystical element, at all.[8] Braginskiy, a Soviet Iranist of the Marxist school, stylized Hafiz into a revolutionary poet.[9]

Much more differentiated is what Arberry wrote in the introduction to his Hafiz anthology. He sees the gist of Hafiz' message in a "philosophy of unreason," a "doctrine of intellectual nihilism," even though this latter term does not really reflect Arberry's decription of Hafiz' spiritual attitude, which includes "precious moments of unveiled vision," in which man "will perceive the truth that resolves all vexing problems."[10]

Incidentally, again under the influence of Marxism, together with structuralism, Hafiz' message was reduced to actual nihilism by the Polish scholar Skalmowski (now Louvain), who arrived at the strange conclusion that the poet's epithet "the Tongue of the Invisible" (*lisan ul-ghayb*) actually meant "the Tongue of Nothingness" (Die Zunge des Nichts). Furthermore, Skalmowski holds the Beloved in Hafiz' poetry to be a metaphor for the reader and adjusts the meaning of the rest to this central constellation, a hardly plausible idea.[11]

H. Broms' effort to illuminate our poet by aligning him with the European symbolists seems to me similarly unsuccessful, since the obscurity in Hafiz does not result from the invention of new, unheard-of metaphors, but from the arbitrary play on, and mixing of, various generic traditions.[12]

Hafiz' fan-like oscillation led—or rather misled—Wickens, a scholar whose merit is usually indisputable, to perceive ten different layers of meaning in one single poem, the famous ghazal about the "Fair Turk."[13] Strangely enough, however, he overlooked the most important and evident meaning of the poem, the message of love; this provoked a caustic criticism from another British Iranist.[14] On the other hand, some fruitful new departures were made in recent times in order to cope with the many contradictions in Hafiz' poetry. Julie Meisami pointed out the various addressees and different speakers or "voices" in Hafiz' ghazals; through this stratagem, as in a ritual, the main types of a medieval (and, to a large extent, still contemporary) Muslim society were put on stage.[15]

Claire Kappler looked for code-words or principle verses in a poem to which the remaining verses then would have to be subordinated and interpreted accordingly. She proposes to apply this method also on the larger scale of the whole divan. This is an interesting idea that is, however, not devoid of a certain arbitrariness.[16]

The present writer has made various attempts to come closer to a true understanding of Hafiz' poetry, emphasizing amongst others the opposition of Reason and Love[17] and the importance of the concept of *rind*. Even though its original meaning is something like "rogue" or "scoundrel," this term has a totally positive connotation in Hafiz: it refers to a character opposed to the hypocrisy of the clergy, somebody who "does not care" (*la ubali*) what people say about him, who drinks wine, but does not harm anybody.[18]

I also pointed out that, apart from the hedonistic, mystical, and panegyrical layers of meaning there exists a poetological one. More than once, Hafiz uses "wine" as a metaphor for poetry, which opens a new dimension in a number of verses, e.g. those in which the image of the friend appears in the wine-cup. The Friend/Beloved might here be understood——not as the reader, but rather as the male muse, whom our poet addresses alternatively as *hatif* ("the inner voice"), as Surush (a Zoroastrian angel), and as Hafiz, when this name is given to a figure separate from the lyrical I, the alter ego of the poet. There are even some lines in which he compares his poetry to a beautiful bride, whom he, as her wooer, unveils. To present a long epical poem to a prince as a well-bred virgin was a common device in Persian poetic tradition. However, these aspects are rather like momentary flashes and cannot be extended to the whole of Hafiz' poetry; they are not a general clue for decoding his message.[19]

In what follows I shall approach the problem from a somewhat new angle, I shall proceed from the tension between the sacred and the profane, the frequent and quite particular use of a religious terminology, trying to lay bare the "message" implied in this linguistic stratagem.[20]

II. Hafiz does not, I think, advance any radically new idea. Traces of all his main conceptions can be found in his predecessors. The cult of love, one of his major topics, may be followed back to early Arabic poetry and ultimately to Neoplatonic and Christian thought. Efforts to sacralize love occur already in poets of the so-called 'Udhri school. Minstrels like al-'Abbas ibn al-Ahnaf or Bashshar ibn Burd used religious language to express their feelings (see below).

On the other hand, love had become a central notion in Islamic mysticism. The love of the "friend" appeared in mystical poetry, at the latest since Sana'i. The "friend" is usually seen as a symbol for God. But in the case of Djalal ud-Din Rumi he is of flesh and blood. Rumi does not refrain from singing his praise in the language of—surely sublime, but nevertheless unmistakably sensual—erotic poetry.[21] On the other hand great mystics like al-Halladj and Ibn 'Arabi propagated the idea that love is the central secret, the very substance of any religion, manifesting itself not only in the love of God or an earthly relection of it, but in social behaviour, human relations in general.

Let us quote just a few verses from various periods in order to highlight this tradition of sacred love or use of sacred language in speaking of love: Djamil, one of the outstanding early 'Udhrite poets, sang of his beloved Buthaina:[22]

> She is the full moon and the (other) ladies are
>   stars,
> And how great is the difference between full
>   moon and stars!
> She excels mankind in beauty just as
> "The night of Power" excels a thousand
>   months.[23]

This is a clear allusion to Sura 97: the Night of Power in which the first revelation of the Koran was sent down "is better than a thousand months."

In the 3./9. century al-'Abbas ibn al-Ahnaf, the minstrel at the court of Harun al-Rashid used many religious references in his praise of his beloved fauz:[24]

> O you who ask about Fauz and her shape!
> Look up to the moon, if you don't see her!
> It is as if the Paradise was her abode,
>   and she came to mankind as a divine sign and
>   example.
> God did not create the like of her on earth.
> I don't reckon her to be a human creature.[25]

If the beloved being is so celestial, it is small wonder that the act of loving her should be regarded as a kind of adoration or even religion itself. Several Arabic poets have made this point in various ways. Ibn Hazm, the author of the famous *"Necklace of the Dove,"* the gracious manual on courtly love, drew the parallel between monotheism and true love:

> I love you with a love that knows no waning,
> whereas some of men's loves are midday
>   mirages.
> I bear for you a pure, sincere love, and in
>   [my] heart
> there is a clear picture and an inscription
>   [declaring] my love for you.
> Moreover, if my soul were filled by anything
>   but you, I would pluck it
> out. .[26]

And again, in another poem, he emphasizes:

> He who claims to love two lyingly commits
>   perjury,
> just as Mani is belied by his principles.
> In the heart there is no room for two
>   beloveds,
> nor is the most recent of things always the
>   second.
> Just as reason is one, not recognizing
> any creator than the One, the Clement,
> Likewise the heart is one and loves only one,
> though he should put you off or draw you to
>   him.[27]

Another Andalusian poet, al-A'ma at-Tutili ("The Blind Man of Toledo"), compares his beloved to the Kaaba in one of his *muwashshahat*:[28]

> Oh Kaaba to which all hearts journey forth!

And he proposes that his tears should serve as pebbles (for the ceremony at Mina, the so-called stoning of the Devil), his heart as victim (for the *'id al-adha*, the "sacrificial feast"), in other words, he proclaims his readiness to sacrifice his life, if necessary, and die the death of love, thus enacting the old 'Udhrite attitude of total love in a new Islamicized guise.[29]

The absoluteness of love claimed in these and similar verses could easily take on heretical overtones, e.g. in the following verse of Bashshar ibn Burd addressed to his beloved 'Abda:

> I had no Lord except God, o 'Abda,
> until your face became my Lord![30]

The emphasis on true love being the love of one man for one woman conveys an implicit criticism of Islamic sex morals is, at any rate, totally at variance

with the *hadith* (utterance of Muhammad): "The best of my community are those with the biggest number of wives."[31]

The "religion of love" itself in such verses could thus be understood as something like a counter-movement, a counter-religion to orthodox Islam. Likewise, it furnished arguments and metaphors for Islamic mysticism, in which, however, absolute love was no longer the love of a human being, but of God, even though it could be experienced on a preliminary level; in other words, human love could be interpreted as a symbol, or a prelude of, "the bridge" leading to the heavenly love,[32] with carnal union foreshadowing the mystical union; a mystical "friend" could, as Shams ud-Din from Tabriz did for Djalal ud-Din Rumi, represent the manifestation of the divine in a human body.

III. All these potential developments of the idea of love had taken place and shape and entered Persian poetry long before Hafiz. The same holds true for other concepts, all more or less linked with the religious sphere, that we meet in his poetry.

One is the recourse to Zoroastrianism as an escape from asceticism, the legal aspects of orthodox Islam. This is, of course, rather an Iranian element. We find a pristine vestige of it in one of the earliest remnants of new Persian poetry, a line attributed to the poet Daqiqi, one of the forerunners of Firdawsi. At the end of a bacchic poem, he confesses having chosen four things of the world: ruby lips, the sound of the harp, purple-coloured wine, and the religion of Zoroaster.[33]

The strange neighbourhood of hedonism and the Zoroastrian religion can be explained by the social fact that, like in Christian cloisters, wine was available also in the *dayr-i mughan*, the convent of the Magians. Those who drank wine in an Islamic society would, of course, arouse the suspicion of the pious. They were given unfriendly names such as "ruffian," scoundrel" (*qalandar, 'ayyar, awbash, qallash*) or the already mentioned "rogue" (*rind*).[34] Yet, instead of being ashamed they "did not care"[35] and they even adopted these names as honourable epithets and boasted of their *rindi*, their qalandardom. Actually, *qalandari* became the name of a mystical order, and great mystical poets like Sana'i or Djalal ud-Din Rumi did not hesitate to call themselves *rind* and *qalandar*.[36]

Here are some typical lines by Sana'i showing the mixture of these elements:[37]

> Saqi, give wine, since nothing but wine breaks
>   fasting,
> So I may rid myself for some time of that
>   delusive asceticism!
> The riches of the family of man do not have
>   any value,

The kingdom of Parvez must be regarded as
  the road's dust.
The religion of Zoroaster and the rule of
  qalandardom
Should now and then be made the provisions
  of the lover's journey.
Throw all the (earthly) means into the fire and
  sit gaily down!
*rindi* and not-having are the best things for
  the Day of Resurrection![38]

Similar verses occur in the divan and the *Mukhtarnama*,
a collection of quatrains, by the mystical poet 'Attar,
particularly in a section entitled "Qalandar and Wine
Poems," where one finds e.g. the following quatrain:

In my love of you, I shall change my religion,
I shall become a disciple of Christendom,[39]
I shall take on the fourfold girdle (*zunnar*) of
  the Zoroastrians,
I shall leave my (Islamic) turban as a pawn at
  the tavern.[40]

If the religion of Zoroaster could serve as an escape
from the yoke of the Islamic *shari'a*, another form of
escapism, developed in mystical circles, was labelled
*malamatiya*, meaning the "people of reproach," those
who, intentionally, behaved in an improper, objectionable way, in order, so they argued, to avoid hypocrisy.[41]

Another element that has to be mentioned is the coming in use of wine imagery in mystical language. It is
certainly a strange phenomenon that the forbidden wine
should have become the symbol for mystical intoxication in an Islamic environment. And we must remind
the reader that, before this imagery developed with
Persian mystics, Arabic tavern poets like Abu Nuwas[42]
had made a totally unholy use of religious allusions,
desacralizing Koranic language and Islamic notions and,
as it were, sacralizing their bacchanalian debaucheries,
in verses that sometimes sound like the frivolous litur-
gies of a religion of wine and homosexual pleasures.[43]

I permit the prohibited beaker, for I am rich.
But I shall renounce it, as soon as I am poor.
If my riches soared as high as my pleasure,
I would cause connaisseurs like Cesar and
  Khusraw to fall into oblivion.
Putting my confidence in God, who pardons
  every Muslim,
I do not detach myself from the golden drop,
  as long as I live!
Nor from the pretty eyes of the lustful one,
  who appears to you like as a
basil-stalk, swaying and green,
Girdled in a *zunnar* and with sick lids over
  his eye-balls,
And lips that are sugar for whoever should
  suck them.

A blind man on whom he, awake or asleep,
  bestows his nearness, will
become seeing.
He falls down, drunken and prostrate before
  the pure one in the chalice,
blessing it, when they mix it, and saying "God
  is great!"[44]

In using the imagery of the tavern for their religious
experiences the mystics could thus, at least partly, make
use of that language by just reversing its polarity. It was
due to their "mightiness" that they were able to do that.[45]
They would, however, usually take care to underscore
the purely spiritual quality of their wine and their intoxication. Nevertheless, the linguistic stratagem was certainly not without ambiguity. And the same ambiguity is
palpable when divine love is described with the language of sensual love. But both procedures had, so to
speak, their model in the Koranic descriptions of the
paradise. These heavenly pleasures, including maidens
and boys and wine, must certainly surpass their earthly
counterparts, but the Koran, obviously in lack of an
adequate, truly celestial language, describes them with
earthly speech, thus secularizing the Heaven and enno-
bling the earthly pleasures of the flesh with a divine
bliss. Furthermore, we should not forget that the Koran
itself introduced the notion of ambiguity in grouping
two kinds of verses in the divine revelation, those that
are "firm" or univocal (*muhkam*) and others that are
"ambiguous" (*mutashabih*) (Sura 3,7).

IV. If we ask what Hafiz added to these elements, the
answer is probably that, rather than enhancing the inherited traditions by new concepts, he refined them, playing
on them with graceful images; he intertwined them so as
to weave an ingenious network of allusive relations between these various layers, producing a rich intertextuality,
and appealing to the reader's ability to discern his message through the oscillating veil of ambiguous metaphors,
puns, allusions, double-entendres. Modifying one of his
favorite metaphors we might say that Hafiz invites the
reader to behold his smiling face as it appears and fades
in the sparkling wine, the water-of-life of his poetry.

We shall now present and, where nescessary, discuss a
few of Hafiz' verses in which religious terms are used,
an undertaking which has of late become an easy task
thanks to the extremely helpful index prepared by Dr.
Daniela Meneghini.[46]

Of the 230 verses in which the poet speaks of love we
shall for the moment quote only the following:

The temple of Love has a higher portal than
  that of reason,
  he kisses its threshold who has his soul in his
  sleeve (is ready to give it
  away for the beloved).

(KH 117,2)

We need only confront this with one or two of those verses in which Hafiz praises his beloved in a totally wordly way, to become aware of the difference, the gap between two apparently incompatible poles:

> My idol, who did not go to school nor learn
> to write,
> became the "problem-instructor" of a hundred
> teachers by one twinkling.
>
> (KH 163,2)

> Wine of two years and a sweetheart of
> fourteen,
> this is enough for my commerce with small
> and big.
>
> (KH 251,9)

The official commentators of Hafiz have no problems in pinpointing the religious meaning of such verses. Thus, according to them, the former refers to Muhammad's *ummiya*, his illiteracy, which, according to Muslim tradition, makes the miracle of his prophecy all the more remarkable.

However this may be, it is clear that, in the one case, Hafiz himself uses religious language, whereas in the other he moves in a totally wordly sphere.

The above line (KH 117,2), even though it uses *harim* for "temple," does not sound particularly Islamic; other verses do; they allude to the main Islamic rites of ablution, prayer, fasting, and the pilgrimage. Like Sa'di and others before him, Hafiz declares his love to be his religion (*din*).

> It is a long time that the passion for idols is
> my religion,
> My grieved heart is enlivened by this grief.
>
> (KH 53,1)

This religion of love is clearly opposed to the religion of the ascetic, which figure, in turn, is only a symbol for orthodox, legalistic Islam. In Hafiz' poetry, the Islamic rites are either discarded or given a new function. First of all, the state of purity is no longer achieved by the ritual ablution, but by the ablution of love:

> I used tears for the ritual washing (*ghusl*), for
> the adherents of the path say:
> First become pure, and then direct your look
> upon the pure one.
>
> (KH 258,7)

> The moment I made the ablution (*wuzu*) from
> the source of love,
> I spoke four Allahu akbar over all that exists.
>
> (KH 21,2)

> When a lover does not make his ablution with
> his heart's blood,

> His love is not sincere, says the Mufti of
> Love.
>
> (KH 254,4)

In one ghazal, the question of ritual purity is the dominating motif, occurring in three of the six verses of the poem. However, here tears and blood are enhanced by a new and very different element:

> The gnostic made his ablution (*taharat kard*)
> with the clear liquid of wine,
> since, in the morning, he went to the tavern.
> Blessed be the prayer and the poverty of those
> who achieved purity
> (*taharat*) from headache by their tears and
> their heart-blood.
> Should the Imam of the community ask,
> tell him, Hafiz made the ablution (*taharat
> kard*) with wine.
>
> (KH 128,1,3,6)

If this would seem to sound offensive in the ears of an orthodox muslim (Persian readers became, however, soon accustomed to this kind of speech), it is offensive only because of the hearer's value system, since there is no open contumely in the words used. This is typical of Hafiz' criticism of exoteric Islam, as many of the following examples will confirm.

Ritual purity is the precondition for the correct execution of any ritual act in Islam. No wonder, therefore, that Hafiz extends his playful use of the religious sphere also to prayer and pilgrimage. Let us first consider some verses dealing—and often rather doing away—with prayer. Apart from ablution, they usually concern one of the three other prerequisites of Islamic prayer: the *qibla* or direction of Mecca, into which worshippers have to turn their faces during prayer, the *mihrab*, which, in a mosque, indicates this direction, and the *sadjdjada* or prayer-carpet used by the worshipper to be on clean ground, if he is not in a mosque. All three elements will, as we may easily now predict, either be substituted or receive a new function in Hafiz' religion of love. Most frequent is his concern with the erotic *mihrab*, the eye-brows of his beloved, a substitution based on a poetic comparison: the eye-brows resemble the vault of the prayer-niche.

> Those who have made the ablution with their
> heart-blood,
> Will pray before those vaulted *mihrab*-like
> eye-brows.
>
> (KH 127,4)

> The eye-brows of the friend are the *mihrab* of
> happiness.
> Do rub your face there and ask your wish
> from him.
>
> (KH 405,2)

Hafiz, go and prostrate yourself before his
    mibrab-like eyebrow!
For you will never make a true prayer except
    there.

                  (KH 471)

There is no other *mihrab* for Hafiz' heart
    than your eye-brow;
In our religion it's not possible to obey
    anybody save you!

             (KH 133,10)

It is befitting that Hafiz should long for your
    eye-brow;
The people of the word sit down in the
    corner of the *mihrab*.

             (KH 304,9)

The "people of the word" (*ahl-i kalam*) are the theologians to whom Hafiz himself belonged. But the reference here is rather to his being a poet. The verse is one of the many examples for a certain pseudo-logical structure that is favoured by Hafiz and other Persian poets and reminds one of the *enthymeme*, this central figure in Aristotle's rhetoric and in the whole tradition following after it; but it is also an instance of the much discussed definition of poetry as a logical procedure operating with false or untrue premises.[47] Hafiz argues here that since his beloved's eye-brow is a *mihrab*, and the people of the word, to whom he himself belongs, usually assemble before a *mihrab*, why should be not long to sit there? It is a fine example also of that intended, often playful ambiguity lurking everywhere in his poetry. The playful tone can have an element of irony or even sarcasm:

You heathen-heart leaving your tresses
    unveiled, I fear,
The bend of that heart-robbing eye-brow will
    turn away my *mihrab*.

             (KH 404,7)

I'm afraid of my belief being destroyed, for
    the *mihrab*
Of your eye-brow robs the peace of my
    prayer.

             (KH 392,7)

Other verses speaking of ritual prayer contain open attacks on exoteric Islam, as e.g. the following one:

Devout man! Since nothing springs from your
    prayer,—
(Better is) nightly carousal, my secret and my
    longing!

             (KH 392,2)

Some very poignant verses concern the prayer-carpet:

There is no generosity in anyone, and time
    for pleasure passes.

The only choice is selling the prayer-carpet
    for wine.

             (KH 369,2)

In the lane of the wine-shopkeepers, they
    don't accept it for one cup,—
what a prayer-carpet, that is not worth one
    tumbler!

             (KH 147,2)

May the wine-shopkeeper take the frock and
    the prayer-carpet of Hafiz,
If the wine comes from the palm of that
    moon-faced cup-bearer!

             (KH 155,7)

Suppose even I'd lay my prayer-carpet on my
    shoulders like a lily,
With the colour of wine on my frock like a
    rose,—would I be a Muslim?!

             (KH 213,3)

The motif of the wine-coloured carpet is struck up in the very first ghazal of the divan, and there it is linked with that mysterious figure, the Prior of the Magians, who will occupy our thoughts in a later section of this paper.

The third element belonging to the topic of prayer is the *qibla* or direction of Mecca to which the prayers have to turn their faces. It goes without saying that it is the beloved who indicates this direction and not the Kaaba or Mecca. The topic of the *qibla* is thus tightly linked with the Kaaba. The term *qibla* occurs, however, only twice in the divan of Hafiz, probably because it offered less possibilities of variation than the much more concrete objects *"mihrab"* and "carpet." In turning to the *qibla* we thus now turn to the Kaaba.

Whoever comes to the Kaaba in your lane,
Finds himself in the middle of prayer, thanks
    to the *qibla* of your eye-brow.

             (KH 41,8)

Where there is no purity, Kaaba and pagan
    temple are the same;
There is no good in a house where there is
    no innocence.

             (KH 213,6)

Similar ideas are developed concerning the pilgrimage, particularly its final stage, when, approaching the Kaaba, the pilgrim has to enter the sacred state (*ihram*) by putting on the two white towels and renouncing washing, shaving, having sexual intercourse until the ceremonies of the *hadjdj*—among these are the circumambulation of the Kaaba and the ritual course (*sa'y*) between the two places Safa and Marwa on a street in Mecca, both of which have to be executed seven times—are over.

> Hafiz, whoever did not strive for love and
> union,
> Has entered the *ihram* for the
> circumambulation of the heart's Kaaba
> without ablution.
>
> (KH 32,7)

Religious ceremonies are useless if love is absent. Hafiz expresses this idea in ever new ways, often with graceful puns.

> Why should we take upon us the ihram, if
> that *qibla* isn't there?
> Why should we labour at the *sa'y,* if Safa is
> absent from the Kaaba?
>
> (KH 82,7)

Here, it is important to know that Safa is not only the name of one of the two places mentioned above,— "Safa and Marwa are among the waymarks of God," says the Koran (Sura 2,158)—but also a word of the Persian language, and one of the code-words of Hafiz' universe at that, meaning "sincerity," or "purity (of the heart)." The meaning thus operates on two levels: Safa is absent from the Kaaba, because the true Kaaba is where the friend is, and purety (*safa*) is absent from the Kaaba because its guardians, or those performing the ceremonies there, do not have a pure heart.[48]

> The heart that after circumambulating the
> Kaaba in your lane came to a "standstill,"[49]
> Its longing for that temple is so great, it does
> not want to go to the Hijaz.
>
> (KH 255,6)

> Nobody will receive the recompense of
> fasting and of pilgrimage,
> save those who visit the dust of the tavern of
> love.
>
> (KH 127,2)

But as in the case of the carpet, Hafiz did not refrain from connecting even the Kaaba with the idea of wine in a most provocative way:

> Around the Holy Temple of the wine-cask,
> Hafiz
> will circumambulate until he dies.
>
> (KH 256,7)

V. As the reader will have noticed, practically all of these verses, if taken at face-value, betray a sometimes sublime, sometimes rude disrespect of what is sacred for the Muslim believer. Certainly, the value of the rites is questioned, but this is done at various

grades, ranging from sheer libertinage to an engagement for something considered of higher value than the performance of these rites.

On reading such verses, one gets the impression of facing something like a counter-religion. It is confirmed by further features of Hafiz' poetry. Thus, there are quite a number of verses in which he attacks the representatives of the religious establishment for not being sincere. More than 30 verses mention the ascetic (*zahid*), make a mock of him or criticize his hypocrisy, very often in a personal address.

The ascetic is a "surface-adorer" (*zahir-parast*), a representative of religious legalism and exoteric Islam.

> The surface-adoring ascetic is not aware of
> our state;
> Nothing he says about us is objectionable.
>
> (KH 72,1)

> Do not scold the "rogues" (*rindan*), o pure-
> natured ascetic!
> For the sins of others will not be written
> down on your account.
>
> (KH 87,1)

> The ascetic craves for the wine from (the
> stream) Kawthar (in Paradise),
> Hafiz for the (earthly) beaker. Let us see
> what God has decreed!
>
> (KH 66,8)

> If the ascetic does not betake himself to the
> *rinds,* he is excused.
> Love is a work that rests on (spiritual)
> guidance.
>
> (KH 154,3)

Other figures from the same quarter are the shaykh, the preacher (*wa'iz*) and the *faqih*, the judge (*qa i*), the mufti (one who gives fetwas or religious opinions on legal and moral issues), the public inspector (*muhtasib*) and the imam. Only one of these figures is ambiguous: the shaykh appears also as *shaykh-i djam*, "the elder of the cup" (KH 7,8).

All of them "catch it," even though with various frequency; the judge e.g. is mentioned only once. Again, some of these verses are very witty and particularly aggressive:

> Go after your own business, oh preacher!.
> What is this shouting?!
> From me my heart has fallen (out of love);
> what has fallen from you?
>
> (KH 36,1)

Learn about love from Hafiz, not from the
    preacher,
Even though he displays much artistry in his
    rhetoric!

(KH 127,7)

Even though this word may not please the
    preacher of the town:
As long as he practices hypocrisy and deceit,
    he is not a Muslim!

(KH 220,)

Since the preacher of the town chose the
    love of the king and the police,
What harm is there in my choosing the love
    of the idol?

(KH 222,4)

The preachers who make such a show on the
    pulpit and by the prayer-niche,
make that other thing, as soon as they are in
    their privacy.

(KH 194,1)

I fear it won't bring any advantage on the
    day of resurrection,
the licit bread of the shaykh over our illicit
    liquid!

(KH 11,5)

Yesterday, the *faqih* of the madrasah was
    drunk and gave this fetwa:
Wine is forbidden but better than (to enrich
    oneself by) *waqf* money.

(KH 45,4)

Sometimes, Hafiz tries to persuade this party to tread
in his steps:

When the faqih advises you not to play the
    play of love,
give him a cup and tell him to moisten his
    brain!

(KH 389,6)

You inhibit me from loving, oh mufti of the
    time!
But I consider you excused, for you haven't
    seen Him yet!

(KH 420,4)

All this adds up to a clear refusal of exoteric Islam.
Does this mean that Hafiz was a Sufi and his verses
have to be interpreted as we interpret Rumi? I don't
think so. Rumi makes it quite clear that he speaks of
mystical wine in verses like the following:

The drunkenness of this world vanishes after
    one night's slumber.

The drunkenness of the beaker of God
    accompanies you into the tomb.[50]

Similar declarations are to be found in other poets. It
does not mean that their poetry is void of ambiguity.
But the ambiguity is certainly much stronger, and intentionally so, in the poetry of Hafiz than in that of
others. Neither his wine nor his beloved are reducible
to their usual mystical connotations, unless we deny
the obvious meaning. And what is more, Hafiz occasionally also attacks the Sufis for their hypocrisy, thus
placing them in the corner of the religious establishment.

Hafiz' "religion," confession, or order thus hovers
above, or beyond, not only exoteric Islam but also
above Islamic mysticism.

We already know some definitions of this order: it is
an order of love, an order of wine, both taken in a
oscillating and ambiguous sense. In order to see clearer,
we should now turn our attention to the head of that
order as presented by Hafiz in many confessional verses,
the *pir-i mughan*, "the Prior of the Magians" or "Head
of the Zoroastrians."

VI. As I already mentioned, the Prior of the Magians
enters the scene in the very first poem of Hafiz' divan, and what he stands for, becomes perfectly clear
from the shocking words he could be expected to say:

Colour your prayer-carpet with wine, if the
    Prior of the Magians says so!
The pilgrim should not be unaware of the
    customs and ceremonies of the
    stations of the path!

In another famous ghazal, the prior is portrayed as a
timeless authority who initiates our poet:

Yesterday, I brought my problems to the
    Prior of the Magians, who would solve any
    enigma by his enlightened insight.
I found him cheerful, smiling, the wine-cup
    in his hand,
In the mirror of which he perceived hundred
    visions.
I said: this world-viewing cup, when did the
    Wise one (God) give it you?
He said: The day He built this azure vault!

(KH 136,3-5)

Yet, it is not only the solution of his problems what
Hafiz obtains from that guru, it is a handful of other
graces he hardly ever receives from the beloved: acceptance, fidelity, favor, consolation.

If grief opens an ambush in a corner of your
    heart,

The temple of the Prior of the Magians
suffices as shelter.

(KH 263,4)

Hafiz, the court of the Prior of the Magians
is a safe place of fidelity.
Read the lessons of love before him and hear
them from him.

(KH 398,7)

In this tumult, where nobody cares for
another,
I received the favor of the Prior of the
Magians

(KH 324,6)

The almost holy dimensions of this figure are high-
lighted time and again:

I am the slave of the Prior of the Magians
who freed me from ignorance,
Everything our Prior does is sheer saintliness
(*'ayn-i vilayat*).

(KH 154,4)

More than once our poet confesses to his being the
disciple of that saintly figure:

If the Prior of the Magians has become my
spiritual guide, what's the difference?
In nobody's head is a secret that is not from
God.

(KH 70,9)

The door of (deep, inner) sense was opened
before my heart on the day
I joined the inhabitants of the abode of the
Prior of the Magians.

(KH 317,6)

I am the disciple of the Prior of the Magians.
Don't worry, oh shaykh!
Why? Because you promised, but He
fulfilled!

(KH 141,8)

My cloister is a corner in the tavern;
The blessing of the Prior of the Magians is
my morning prayer.

(KH 262,3)

A fine spiritualized reference to the Zoroastrian fire-
worship is made in the following verse:

They hold me dear in the cloister of the
Magians.
Because in my breast there is the fire that
never dies.

(KH 26,8)

A wonderful ambiguity is operating in the following
verse:

I have a fetwa of the Prior of the Magians
and it's an ancient word:
Wine is forbidden wherever the boon
companion is not the friend.

(KH 360,1)

Which means likewise: wherever wine is forbidden,
there the friend and everything he represents is absent.

This leads us back to the other aspect of the Prior of
the Magians, who, as Lord of the Tavern, is also the
Lord of the *rinds*, even though the two notions are
never used in one and the same verse, which means
that, despite their mutual relationship, they belong to
two slightly different conceptual systems.

Nevertheless the *pir-i mughan* remains a symbol of
the *rind* ideology and therewith an ambiguous figure
oscillating between the sacred and the pagan, as is
evident from the following verse:

Look at the kindness of the Prior of the
Magians! Whatever we
bad drunkards do, it is beautiful to his
benevolent eyes.

(KH 192,2)

Here, as in many other cases, Hafiz seems to speak of
real wine, the intoxicating liquid made of grapes; but
in many other verses, he clearly speaks of something
different which he himself occasionally calls the wine
of "the Day of *Alast*," a reference to the Koranic tale
how God asked the souls, "am I not your Lord" (*a-
lastu bi-rabbikum*), and they answered "Certainly!"
(Sura 7,172). But to avoid any confusion with the
expectations inspired by the Koran, Hafiz draws a
precise borderline between his wine and that of Paradise:

Go, o ascetic, and do not cavil at those who
drain the cup to the dregs,
For we were given no other present on the
Day of Alast.
We drank what He poured into our beaker.
No matter whether it was the wine (*khamr*)
of Paradise or the intoxicating wine (*bada-i
mast*)!
The laughter of the wine-glass and the
knotted tresses of the idol,
how many conversions like the one of Hafiz
have they turned over!

(KH 22,5-7)

VII. The question now arises whether Hafiz' "counter-
religion" is more than a highly sophisticated mas-

querade for the libertine escapades of intellectuals, something like a poetical carnival? Many Muslims, and particularly those belonging to the party attacked in his poetry, would give an affirmative answer. In recent times, both a Marxist Iranian thinker, Ahmad Kasrawi,[51] and an outstanding Muslim reformist, Muhammad Iqbal,[52] have pointed out the moral dangers involved in these verses.

On the other hand, Hafiz sees himself as the representative of sincerity as against hypocrisy. If his religion of love and wine were nothing but a refined hoodwinking, his pretence of sincerity would be doubly insincere, or, at least, "sincerity" (*safa*) would mean no more than to admit one's sinfulness, to indulge openly in one's vices and boast of one's moral "ruin," the Hafizian *kharabi*.[53] Here, too, an element of ambiguity remains.

There is, however, an additional message that surpasses the mere pretence of sincerity or frankness, even though it is palpable only in a very small number of verses. Yet its importance is not diminished by this limited evidence. It is the engagement for non-violence that we meet also e.g. in the work of Nizami[54] and which seems to have belonged to the moral codex of—at least some—*qalandars*.[55] In a religion where killing in the name of God was—and is—part of the divine law, this element merits our attention. Several times, Hafiz stresses the harmlessness of drinking wine, particularly if it is compared to religiously sanctioned violence; and the issue of violence is implicitly touched upon wherever Hafiz and other Islamic poets talked of wine, wine being one of the great sins that was punished by eighty lashes:

> For one sip, resulting in nobody's injury,
> How much trouble I risk,- don't ask!
>
> > (KH 266,3)

> Do you know what harp and lute are
>    pronouncing:
> Drink wine in secret, for (otherwise) they'll
>    punish (you)![56]
> What harm does it cause, if I and you drink
>    some cups of wine?
> Wine is from the blood of grapes, not from
>    your blood!
>
> > (KH 25,7)

> I am very thankful to my arm that
> I don't have the power to torment people!
>
> > (KH 318,5)

> We conquered the kingdom of (inner) welfare
>    not by armies,
> We erected the Throne of (spiritual)
>    sovereignty not by violence.
>
> > (KH 357,4)

This, then, is a concrete unequivocal appeal.

VIII. What remains to be discussed is Hafiz' self-allotted role within what we called his "counter-religion." He does not pretend to be a prophet. He has no programmatic lines praising the mutual closeness of prophecy and of poetry, as they exist in the opening section of Nizami's first epos.[57] Yet, the idea certainly was not altogether strange to him. In his usual playful manner, he gives himself those dimensions of a cosmic man, that would belong to a prophet according to the Islamic doctrines of the time: a primordial existence, and a power of speech that is timeless and space-pervading.[58]

He also stresses that his *rindi* was not his free choice but his lot from all eternity:

> On the first day (of creation) I was ordered
>    nothing but *rindi*.
>
> > (KH 145,3)

Something that has still to be clarified is the relation of Hafiz' message to the message of Islam. One could argue, and Muslim defenders of Hafiz will do so, that what he criticizes is the pretenders of Islam, not Islam itself. A very small number of verses could be cited in favour of that view: e.g. the one quoted above, which says that, as long as the preacher practices hypocrisy, he is not going to be a Muslim.

On the other hand, it strikes the reader of Hafiz that there is so little truly Islamic in his poetry, and almost no trace of unblurred Islamic piety. The name of Muhammad does not appear throughout his divan, except once in the adjective *Mustafawi*, which here is juxtaposed with *Abu-Lahabi*, referring to Abu Lahab, the opponent of Muhammad mentioned in the Koran, in Sura 111. The verse runs as follows:

> In the meadow, nobody ever plucked a rose
>    without thorn.
> Oh yes, the lamp of Mustafa goes always
>    together with the sparks of Abu Lahab.
>
> > (KH 65,4)

This absence of the Prophet is all the more striking when compared with his presence in the works of other Persian poets of renown. Nizami commenced each of his five epic poems with long panegyrics of Muhammad and his ascension, and so did 'Attar. Rumi's divan is rich in glowing praise of the prophet, Sa'di's opens with a hymn, each line of which echoes the name of Muhammad. Instead, Hafiz' divan begins with the provocative appearance of the *pir-imughan*.

Another striking fact is that Hafiz does speak of other, pre-Islamic prophets including Adam, Noah, Solomon and Jesus, giving them certain, mainly traditional features which enhance our picture of his religious views. The most remarkable of these features are the following: Adam is the one whose clay was kneaded with wine by the angels in the tavern of love[59] and whose soul-bird was lured by the seed of beauty, so he left Heaven and settled on Earth;[60] Noah is the captain of the ark, under whose patronage one need not fear the flood—however, at least in one case, the "ship of Noah" is evidently a metaphor for the wine-glass—;[61] Moses is the prophet, to whom God spoke from the burning bush, a scene which repeats itself for Hafiz in the fire of the rose and the song of the nightingale in spring-time;[62] he is the prophet who asked God "Let me see you!"—one of the rare Koranic quotations in Hafiz' poetry, and with whom God made a covenant.[63] Solomon, whose name allowed panegyrical allusions to contemporary patrons,[64] is the mighty king in possession of the world-ruling ring;[65] his bird, the hoopoe, is Hafiz' guide to the realm of the mysterious *'Anqa* (= Simurgh), a symbol of God.[66] But as an earthly ruler, he is also the symbol of transi-toriness. His command over the wind referred to in the Koran is reversed into a metaphor for illusion.[67] David is referred to in two places as the musician whose tune the birds sing.[68] Jesus, the Messiah, is the prophet, whose breath raised the dead,[69] who wrought his miracles through the emanation of the Holy Spirit,[70] and who ascended to the fourth sphere of the sky, where the sun receives the light of his lamp.[71] Together with Venus, he is enraptured to dancing by the poetry of Hafiz,[72] a verse which points to the two main elements of Hafiz' poetry: earthly love including music, and wine-drinking, and divine love including peacefulness and non-violence.

The result hardly differs if we examine the role of the words Islam and Koran in Hafiz' divan. Islam occurs only twice. One of the two lines is again full of playful irony:

> The cup-bearer's twinkling so much waylays
>   Islam that the Little Red One[73]
> will perhaps renounce the Red One (wine).
>
>                                   (KH 183,4)

The other line, part of a panegyric, praises the patron as the protector of Islam.[74] Islam is after all the official religion. But again, it strikes one as unusual that despite the many panegyrical ghazals this aspect, normally of the highest importance, should be so marginal in Hafiz' divan.

Even more striking are the few lines mentioning the Koran. The word is used either playfully or in an ambiguous way. There is actually only one verse in which the Holy Scripture is spoken of in a way a pious man would deem proper:

> Hafiz, as long as in the corner of poverty
>   and the privacy of dark nights

> your prayer is blessings and your reading is
>   the Koran, don't grieve!
>
>                                   (KH 250,10)

In the following verse, the Koran is the object of imposture of those pious hypocrites Hafiz attacks in his poems:

> O Hafiz! Drink wine and behave as a *rind*
>   and enjoy life! But
> Don't use the Koran as a trap of imposture
>   as the others do!
>
>                                   (KH 9,10)

In two cases, the Koran appears as of little avail in matters of love:

> Love comes to your help, even if you, like
>   Hafiz,
> recite the Koran in its fourteen versions.
>
>                                   (KH 93,10)

In other words, despite your reciting the Koran so well and knowing by heart its fourteen variant readings, you will be in need of love's help. The same idea is corroborated by the following verse:

> How often I recited the Fatiha, the Yemenite
>   spell, and blew the *Surat*
> *al-ikhlas* behind him (i.e. the friend), he went
>   away.
>
>                                   (KH 85,3)

In the rest of cases, the lyrical I swears by the Koran in a more or less ambiguous way:

> Hafiz, by the Koran, turn away from deceit
>   and hypocrisy!
> It must be possible to beat the ball of
>   pleasure in this world!
>
>                                   (KH 150,8)

> I have not seen anything more pleasant than
>   your poetry, Hafiz,
> By the Koran, that you have in your breast!
>
>                                   (KH 438,7)

The Koran the wine-drinker Hafiz has in his breast is rather a heretical book than the Koran of the pious.

> If the ascetic does not understand the *rindi*
>   of Hafiz, what does it matter?
> The demon (*diw*) flees from those people
>   who read the Koran.
>
>                                   (KH 188,11)

IX. The verse quoted at the end of the previous section has the character of a picture-puzzle, the meaning of which changes according to the angle from which one looks upon it. At first glance, the div would seem to be the ascetic, and Hafiz one of those who read the Koran. After all, Hafiz' name means "he who knows by heart (the Koran)." On the other hand, the ascetic is the one who can claim that his ethics are based on the Koran, whereas the wine-drinking *rind* certainly cannot. This verse of Hafiz' is therefore one of those in which the ambiguity is, on purpose, driven to its extreme. The same ambiguity obtains again in the following verse:

> The wine-casks are all in ebullition and
>   gurgling from intoxication;
> And the wine that is there, is reality, not
>   metaphor!
>
> (KH 41,2)

At first reading, the meaning seems to be univocal. Yet, if we look at the text in the light of the mystical tradition, its meaning is reversed. For in mystical texts, this world is a metaphor, whereas reality is the invisible, metaphysical world. And again this ambiguity is being consciously evoked by the poet.

Thus, in the poetical universe of Hafiz, one verse contradicts the other, one interpretation is belied by another and this by a third one, all of which can point to a number of verses in their support. The longer we read Hafiz and the better we know him and the literary traditions on which he plays, the more we feel this ambiguity. We even arrive at the conclusion that perhaps this very ambiguity is his message. For is not life ambiguous? Is not religion ambiguous? Is not love ambiguous? Hafiz seems to confirm this interpretation:

> Our existence is an enigma, Hafiz,
>   which, when studied, remains but a spell and
>   a fairy-tale.
>
> (KH 418,9)

Certainly, in his poetical universe there is a certain consistency in the antagonism between the fair world of the Prior of the Magians and the gloomy world of the religious hypocrites.

But even if his message should not go beyond ambiguity and a helpless shoulder-shrugging in the face of life's riddles it would still be opposed to that of the ruling religion, which, of course, claims to be univocal and to have answers for every problem. Hafiz' message, however, certainly goes beyond that ambiguity. His general answer is to enjoy life without hypocrisy, life on all its levels, and make love the dominant, many-faceted theme of one's existence, but with an ultimate reference to that "religion of love" whose advocates are the Prior of the Magians and Hafiz himself.

X. Let us add another word about the Prior of the Magians, or rather the place of Zoroastrianism in Islamic society. The general image of this religion certainly was quite negative, if we take the dark figures representing it in the *Thousand and One Nights* tales as an indication. Again, in Nizami's *Iskandarnama*, the long epic poem on Alexander the Great, Alexander's main task consists in destroying the temples of the Persian fire-worshippers, i.e. the Zoroastrians, after having defeated Darius of Iran—an unexpected turn after so much pleading for non-violence in Nizami's previous writings[75] But there is also the famous story of the Jew and the Zoroastrian, written down by the Arabic bel-esprit at-Tawhidi in the 10th century, in which the former represents a legalist whose religion tells him to fight against non-Jews, whereas the latter is a person whose religion tells him to love man irrespective of his race or religion, and both act accordingly. In other words, the Jewish religion here stands for fanaticism, whereas Zoroastrianism stands for religious tolerance.[76]

But if the Achaemenians inspired by Zoroastrianism seem, in fact, to have been the first rulers to have practiced tolerance towards other religions in the countries they had conquered, Hafiz and his time hardly knew anything about this old Iranian principle of foreign policy.[77] Nevertheless, Tawhidi's image of Zoroastrian corresponds with Hafiz' *pir-i mughan*. In other words, the Prior of the Magians is not simply part of a reversed value system in the universe of the ghazal; he also echoes contemporary reality and concrete experience or expectations, as would his opponents in the ghazal.

Thus, what Hafiz pleads for in the following verse might imply more than just a juggling with religious traditions:

> Renew the cult of the religion of Zarathustra
>   in the garden,
> Now that the tulip kindled the fire of
>   Nimrud!
>
> (KH 198,8)

Our poet's tolerance seems also to vibrate in the following verses:

> In this business, Arabic and Turkish are one
>   and the same:
> Hafiz, tell the story of love in the language
>   you know.
>
> (KH 467,7)

There is no difference between the love of the cloister and that of the tavern:

> Wherever there is the radiance of the friend's
>   face, there is love.
>
> (KH 64,5)

The sober ones no less than the intoxicated,
   they all seek to find (or: are disciples of)
   the friend,
Everywhere is the house of love, be it a
   mosque or a church.

                              (KH 78,3)

This message had already been promulgated by al-Halladj that "all religions are God's,"[78] the same Halladj who was totally aware of the ambiguity of appearances.[79] One might say that by denying the univocality of one particular religion, Islam, it became possible to attribute a relative value to every religion and at the same time postulate the existence of a higher form of religion of which only irregular flashes appeared in the visible world and whose common denominator was love.

XI. Hafiz' poetry comes about by the refined super-imposing of those various levels of life, combining colour-ful facets as in a carpet where several ornamental systems are superimposed. His poetical technique might, however, also be compared to a musical procedure. The clashes between various ontological levels remind one of dissonances, in other words they have also an aesthetic function. But since dissonance and solution presuppose the existence of chords which were (and are) absent in Persian traditional music, we should rather talk of modulation, in particular because this musical metaphor was used by Hafiz himself, as in the following verse:

From where is this musician who played in
   the tune of Iraq and then
modulated in the mode of Hijaz?[80]

It is exactly thanks to this technique that Hafiz has so many answers, that he became the oracle of his people, gradually taking on the function of a counter-prophet without ever even having pretended to be a saint. Thus, what he prophesied became true:

They bless his memory, the host of lovers,
Wherever the name of Hafiz comes up in a
   circle.

                              (KH 229,7)

And his advice is still looked for and fulfilled, be it on the practical or on a metaphorical level:

If you pass at my tomb, ask me for mental
   support (*himmat*),
For it will be a place of pilgrimage
   (*ziyaratgah*) for the *rinds* from all over
   the world.

                              (KH 201,3)

Hafiz plays with language, plays with literary and even with spiritual traditions, and, by doing so, lays bare the ambiguity of language, perception and thought. Something similar had already been done by the authors of the *Maqamat*, al-Hamadhani and al-Hariri. Hafiz did it on a much more sophisticated, more generalized and at the same time more specific level. His poetry may be understood as a questioning of the authenticity of religious language and revealed speech, which is all the more remarkable since it happened in a period when the Islamization of thought, science, art, in short, of every cultural phenomenon had almost reached its peak.[81] At the same time, however, this poetry admits that human reason cannot reach beyond such doubt. Poetry, however, can do more, it can play with the universe of ideas and thereby make the world light and transparent. Poetry can become a world-viewing wine-glass, can conjure up the friend's image in the wine. Who is the friend? The reader, each single reader, will have to decide, and their answers will be different according to their particular visions.

*Notes*

[1] An excellent survey is given by A. Schimmel, "Hafiz und seine Kritiker," in: *Spektrum Iran* 1/1988,5-24, apart from some disputable judgment I don't share.

[2] One typical example is R. Feiz, "L'amour, l'amant, l'aimé," in: *Luqman* 5/1988-89, 15-20.

[3] On this scholar see the fundamental book by I. H. Solbrig, *Hammer-Purgstall und Goethe*, Bern-Frankfurt 1973.

[4] On Goethe and Hafiz see H. H. Schaeder, *Goethes Erlebnis des Ostens*, Leipzig 1938; J C. Bürgel, "Goethe und Hafis," in: Bürgel, *Drei Hafis-Studien* (Europ. Hochschulschriften I, 113), Bern 1975, 5-42; id. "'Wie du zu lieben und zu trinken'-Zum Hafis-Verständnis Goethes," in: A. Mahler (ed.), *J. W. Goethe. Fünf Studien zum Werk* (Kasseler Arbeiten zur Sprache und Literatur 15), Bern and Frankfurt 1983, 115-41; id. "Goethe et Hafiz. Quelques réflexions," in: *Luqman* 5/1989, 87-104.

[5] Cf. A. Schimmel, *Friedrich Rückert. Lebensbild und Einführung in sein Werk* (Herder Taschenbuch 1371), Freiburg i. Br. 1987; Bürgel, "Kommt Freunde, Schönheitsmarkt ist! Bemerkungen zu Rückerts Hafis-Übertragungen," in: W. D. Fischer (ed.) *Friedrich Rückert. Dichter und Sprachgelehrter in Erlangen* (Schriften des Zentralinstituts für Fränkische Landeskunde und allgemeine Religionalforschung an der Universität Erlangen-Nürnberg 29), Neustadt 1990, 13-146.

[6] Schaeder, l.c.

[7] R. Lescot, *Essai d'une chronologie de l'oeuvre de Hafiz*, (Bulletin d'études orientales 10) Beirut 1944.

[8] M.Hillmann, *Unity in the Ghazals of Hafez* (Studies in Middle Eastern Literatures 6) Minneapolis & Chicago 1976; R. M. Rehder, "The Unity of the Ghazals of Hafiz," in: *Der Islam* 51/1974, 55-96; cf. my review "Der Schöne Türke, immer noch mißverstanden. Zu neuer Hafis-Literatur," in: *Orientalistische Literaturzeitung* 75/1980, 105-111.

[9] I. Braginskiy/D. Komissarov, *Persidskaya literatura. Kratkiy ocerk*, Moscow 1963. 52f; Braginskiy, who wrote the part on classical poetry, speaks of his "revolutionary existence", his "revolutionary thought".

[10] *Fifty Poems of Hafiz*, Text and Translations collected and made, introduced and annotated, Cambridge 1970, 31f.

[11] W. Skalmowski, "The Meaning of the Persian Ghazal," in: *Orientalia Lovanensia Periodica* 18/1987, 141-162.

[12] Broms, H. *Two Studies in the Relations of Hafiz and the West* (Studia Orientalia - Societas Orientalis Fennica 34), Helsinki 1938.

[13] Wickens, G. M., "An Analysis of Primary and Secondary Significations in the Third Ghazal of Hafiz," in: *BSOAS* 14/1952, 627-638.

[14] Boyce, M., "A Novel Interpretation of Hafiz," in: *BSOAS* 15/1952.

[15] J. S. Meisami, "Persona and Generic Conventions in Medieval Persian Lyric," in: *Comparative Criticism* 12/1990, 125-52.

[16] C. Kappler, "De la forme au sens: la lecture de Hafez comme méditation," in: *Luqman* 6/1989-90, 39-48.

[17] Cf. "Verstand und Liebe bei Hafis," in J.C. Bürgel, *Drei Hafis-Studien*, 43-54.

[18] Reysner, M.L., "Predvaritel'nie soobrazhenia o soderzhanii termina rind v literature na farsi XI-XIV vv. Sootnoshenie literaturnogo i istoricheskogo aspektov," in: *Iran - Istoria i kul'tura v shrednie veka i novoe vremya*, Moscow 1980, 168-75.

[19] Cf. Bürgel, "Le poète et la poésie dans l'oeuvre de Hafez," in: *Convegno Internazionale sulla poesia di Hafez* (Roma, 30-31 Marzo 1976), Rome 1979, 73-98.

[20] Cf. Bürgel, "Profane und sakrale Sprache," in: *Fück-Symposium*.

[21] See A. Schimmel, *The Triumphal Sun: A Study of the Works of Jalaloddin Rumi*, London and The Hague 1978.

[22] On Djamil see F. Gabrieli, " amil al-'Udhri. Studio critico e raccolta dei frammenti," in: *RSO* 17/1937, 40-71; 132-72; "Contributo alla interpretazione di amil," in: *RSO* 18/1938, 173-98.

[23] *Kitab al-Aghani* (Turathuna) Cairo, undated, VIII, 15 1

[24] On 'Abbas see B. Hell, "Al-'Abbas ibn al-Ahnaf, der Minnesänger am Hofe Harun al-Rašids," in: *Islamica* 2/1926, 271-307.

[25] *Dīwan*, Beirut, Dar Sadir 1965, 165.

[26] J.T. Monroe, *Hispano-Arabic Poetry. A Student Anthology*, Berkeley 1974, 170.

[27] Ibid., 172.

[28] On al-A'ma śee H. Pérès, *La poésie andalouse en arabe classique au X^ème siècle*, Paris 1953, Index, s.v. L'aveugle de Tolède.

[29] Monroe, l.c. 248.

[30] A. Roman, *Baššar et son expérience courtoise*, Beirut 1972, 15,13.

[31] al-Ghazali, *Ihya' 'ulum ad-din* II,38

[32] Djami, *Haft Awrang*, ed. M. Gilani, Teheran 1337, 594.

[33] Cf. Dh. Safa, *Tarikh-i adabiyat dar Iran*, Tehran 1965, vol. I, 409.

[34] Cf. Bürgel, "The Pious Rogue. A Study in the Meaning of qalandar and rend in the Poetry of Muhammad Iqbal," in: *Edebiyat* 4/1979,43-64.

[35] The present writer intends to write an article on the history of the "I don't care" (*la ubali*) attitude which has roots even in the *hadith*.

[36] On *qalandari* cf. H. Ritter, *Das Meer der Seele. Mensch, Welt und Gott in den Geschichten des Fariduddin 'Attar*, Leiden 1978², index, s.v. Qalandariya; F. Meier, *Abu Sa'id-i Abu l-Hayr (357-440 / 967-1049)— Wirklichkeit und Legende* (Acta Iranica 11), Leiden-Téhéran 1976, 494-516.

[37] On Sana'i see J.T.P. De Bruijn, *Of Piety and Poetry. The Interaction of Religion and Literature in the Life and Works of Hakim Sana'i of Ghazna* (Publication of the "De Goeje Fund" No. XXV), Leiden 1983.

[38] *Diwan-i Sana'i*, ed. M. Razawi, no 6.

[39] *tarsa'i*, Ritter's translation "feuerkult" is a lapsus calami.

40 Ritter, l.c. 490.

41 On Malamatiya see A. Schimmel, *Mystical Dimensions of Islam*, Chapel Hill 1975, 86f.

42 On this poet see E. Wagner, *Abu Nuwas. Eine Studie zur arabischen Literaturgeschichte der frühen 'Abbasidenzeit* (Ak. d. Wiss. u.d. Lit. Veröff. d. Or. Komm. Band 17), Wiesbaden 1965.

43 Cf. the chapters "Profanisierung sakraler Sprache" and "Sakralisierung profaner Sprache" in my forthcoming book *Allmacht und Mächtigkeit*, München 1991.

44 Abu Nuwas, *Diwan*, Beirut, Dar Sadir, 276.

45 On the concept of "mightiness" see Bürgel, *The Feather of Simurgh—The 'Licit Magic' of the Arts in Medieval Islam*, New York 1988 and also *Allmacht und Mächtigkeit* (mentioned above, note 43).

46 D. Meneghini Correale, *The Ghazals of Hafez—Concordance and Vocabulary*, Rome 1988.

47 Cf. B. Reinert, *Haqani als Dichter. Poetische Logik und Phantasie* (Studien zur Sprache, Geschichte und Kultur des islamischen Orients Neue Folge 4), Berlin 1972.

48 A variant reading has: "when Safa has left Marwa." Now, the letters of *Marwa* are identical with *muruwa* = "virtue," which is immediately insinuated to the reader, even though the prosody here only allows Marwa. Nevertheless, the double-entendre is certainly intended. Both versions remind the attentive reader that *safa*, one of the key-words of Hafiz' poetry, is absent from the Koran.

49 *Wuquf* is a part of the ceremonies at 'Arafat, outside Mecca.

50 *Diwan-i Shams-i Tabriz*, ed. Furuzanfar, Nr. 537.

51 A. Kasravi, *Hafiz chi miguyad*, Kitabhay-i mah, 4th ed. Teheran 1335.

52 Cf. Bürgel, "Die griechische Ziege und das Schaf von Schiras. Bemerkungen zu Gedanken Muhammad Iqbals über Plato und Hafis," in: H.R. Roemer/A. Noth (edd.), *Studien zur Geschichte und Kultur des Vorderen Orients*, Leiden 1981, 12-27.

53 Over 80 occurrences according to Meneghini.

54 Cf. Bürgel, "L'idée de la non-violence dans l'Islam—Quelques reflexions et quelques examples," in: III^ème *rencontre Islamo-Chrêtienne. Droits de l'homme*. CERES, Série Études Islamiques 9, Tunis 1985, 229 - 233.

55 Meier, l.c. 510.

56 *Diwan*, edd. Qazwini/Ghani 200,1; a variant reading has *takfir mikunand* instead of *ta'zir mikunand*: "they'll anathematize you/declare you to be infidels" (implying capital punishment).

57 See Bürgel, "Nizami über Sprache und Dichtung," in: R. Gramlich (ed.) *Islamwissenschaftliche Abhandlungen Fritz Meier zum sechzigsten Geburtstag*, Wiesbaden 1974, 9-28.

58 See Bürgel, "Le poète et la poésie," (above, note 19).

59 KH 191,1; 194,6 etc.

60 KH 59,3; 310, 1-03 etc.

61 KH 250,5 etc.; KH 19,97.

62 KH 235,3; 477,1-2.

63 KH 366,4.

64 KH 198,9 etc.

65 KH 59,2; 117,3 etc.

66 KH 312,2.

67 KH 21,7; 88,6.

68 KH 170,2; 198,7.

69 KH 71,6.

70 KH 136,7.

71 KH 399,3.

72 KH 4,8.

73 *Suhaib* (lit.: the little red one) is the name of a companion of the Prophet celebrated for his abstemiousness.

74 KH 298,2.

75 *Sharafnama*, ed. Dastgirdi, 238ff.

76 at-Tawhidi, *al-Imta' wal-mu'anasa*, edd. Amin & Zain, II, 157.

77 Cf. W. Hinz, *Darius und die Perser—Eine Kulturgeschichte der Achaemeniden*, Baden-Baden 1976, 228; W. Knauth, *Das altiranische Fürstenideal von Xenophon bis Ferdousi*, Wiesbaden 1975, 45ff.

78 *Akhbar al-Halladj*, Texte ancien relatif à la prédication et au supplice du mystique musulman al-Hosayn

b. Mansour al-Hallaj, publié, annoté et traduit par L. Massignon et Paul Kraus, Paris 1936, No. 45.

[79] L. Massignon, *La passion d'al-Hosayn ibn Mansour Al-Hallaj, martyr mystique de l'Islam,* vol. III: *La doctrine de Hallaj,* 2nd ed. Paris 1975, 329.

[80] KH 129,4; the verse contains a pun, based on the ambiguity of a number of words which are used as musical terms. Thus 'Iraq and Hijaz are not only toponyms, but also names of musical modes or tunes; *rah* means way and musical mode, etc. The verse could thus also be translated as follows:

> From where is the musician who prepared the journey to 'Iraq and then decided to return on the way to Hijaz.

[81] On this phemonenon cf. my forthcoming book *Allmacht und Mächtigkeit,* (above, note 43).

## Michael Glünz (essay date 1991)

SOURCE: "The Poet's Heart: A Polyfunctional Object in the Poetic System of the Ghazal," in *Intoxication, Earthly and Heavenly: Seven Studies on the Poet Hafiz of Shiraz,* edited by Michael Glünz and J. Christoph Burgel, Peter Lang, Inc., 1991, pp. 53-68.

[*In the following essay, Glünz explores the many metaphorical meanings and functions Hafiz derives from the word "heart."*]

*Introductory remarks*

When we look at the frequency-list of lexical items in Hafiz' divan[1] we find that the item *'dil'* (heart) ranks 19th in a field of 4810 items and is far ahead of any other noun. This alone would justify an inquiry into the special function or functions the heart fulfills in the type of poetry that has reached its perfection in the **Diwan-i Hafiz**, i.e. the ghazal.

For the purpose of our inquiry it would be enough to take examples from Hafiz only. I have, however, included examples taken from other poets writing either in Persian or Ottoman or Chaghatay Turkish. By doing so I wanted to illustrate my thesis that the ghazal in post-mongol Persian literature and in the literatures derived from it, is much more than just an outward form into which individual poets cast their own thoughts and feelings; it forms a whole system of poetic expression, it establishes a close-meshed network of interrelations, and it determines to a very large extent the kind of thoughts and feelings that can be conveyed through the medium of lyric poetry.

The poetic system of the ghazal can, in my opinion, be regarded as a superset of a number of subsets distributed on different hierarchical levels, with the individual poet's work on the lowest level, the abstract—or prototype—ghazal on the highest, and the Persian, Turkish, or Urdu ghazal or the ghazal of different periods and geographical regions on intermediate levels. There is a high degree of compatibility between these subsystems that allows us to take the ghazal poetry of post-mongol times on the whole as a macrotext into which individual poems and lines of poetry (*bayts*) are embedded.

1 The heart has two qualities that allow for its integration into the world view of medieval Islamic mysticism: on the one hand, it is a vessel, and on the other, it is regarded as the center of the human body. As a physical vessel it contains what is most precious for the body—its lifeblood. In analogy to the heart as a physical organ, mystical doctrine postulates a spiritual organ located at the core of man's spiritual being and containing the most precious content of all—the Self, Reality, the Godhead. The ultimate goal of the mystic path, therefore, lies not in the outside world but within man's own being, it is what is enclosed in the heart.

In a famous verse, Hafiz uses the image of the mythical Cup of Djamshid to express this notion:

> Over years the heart demanded the Cup of Djamshid from us; what it possessed itself it demanded from a stranger.[2]

Another Persian poet, Khiyali of Bukhara, says:

> As long as those who tread the path have not arrived at the sanctuary of the heart, they have not reached one station in the valley of the ultimate goal.[3]

Technically speaking, the poet in this line uses the figure *mura'at un-nazir*; he does so by choosing the words *'haram'* (sanctuary), *'manzil'* (station), and *'wadi'* (valley) from the vocabulary of the Islamic pilgrimage. But he also links the poetic element "heart" to the concept of the *hadjdj* which itself is used as an image for the mystic quest.

The analogy of the heart and the Kaaba is quite evident: the Kaaba is usually called "The House of God" and the heart can be said to be a vessel for the Deity. As an often cited *hadith qudsi* goes:

> My heaven and my earth contain me not, but the heart of my faithful servant contains me.[4]

Islamic mystics, especially the school of Ibn 'Arabi, have established a fairly elaborate network of correspondences between the heart, the Kaaba, and various other elements of their mystical and cosmological doctrines. For the purpose of the present inquiry, however, there is no need to go deeper into that. We only have to note that the close connection between "heart" and "Kaaba" has made the expression *'ka'ba-i dil'* one of the stock-metaphors of Persian, Turkish, and Indian poets.

Gada'i, for example, who lived in the 15<sup>th</sup> century in Central Asia and wrote in Chaghatay Turkish, says:

> The Kaaba of my heart has been ruined by the plundering of your eyes; this kind of cruel injustice has never come from the hand of any infidel.[5]

He combines both the language of erotic poetry and the vocabulary of religion. Read as a line of love poetry the verse says: "My heart has been destroyed by the coquetry of your charming eyes; your behaviour towards me is most cruel." A mystical reading of the verse, on the other hand, would have to take into account that the word "eyes," too, has a corresponding element in the system of mystical doctrine which is, however, not mentioned here. If we look it up in one of the glossaries of mystical symbolism, we find:

> Eraqi [i.e. Fakhr ud-Din-i 'Iraqi, d. 1289] states that the eye "is said to express the mystery of the Divine Vision" . . . Since the Divine Vision does things that are beyond our comprehension and the scope of our understanding, we are ruined by the eyes of the Beloved . . . [6]

Thus, a mystical interpretation of the verse would be: "The vessel of my real Self has been destroyed by the Divine Vision; Thou art indeed a powerful and cruel God."

The poet achieves a high degree of complexity in his poetic utterance by combining elements from different levels of language as well as from different conceptual systems. Apart from the two readings of this verse mentioned above——each of them integrating a number of semantic elements into a coherent structure——we find the previously mentioned figure *'mura'at un-nazir'* ("heart," "eyes," "hand") and the antithesis of "Islam" (represented by the Kaaba) vs. "heathendom."

Sayf-i Farghani, a poet of the 13<sup>th</sup> century who had emigrated from Transoxania to Anatolia, uses the metaphor "Kaaba of the heart" in another way. He builds a dual structure contrasting the inner world of mystical experience, represented by the hearts of the mystical lovers, with the outside world of Islamic beliefs and observances, represented by the two cities of the Prophet of Islam, Mecca and Medina. The term

"Kaaba" serves as a means to bridge the gap between the two domains.

> Know that in the two worlds [i.e. our world and the hereafter] the Kaaba of the hearts of the lovers prides itself with [possession of] the Friend, like the Two Holy Cities with the Elected One [i.e. Muhammad].[7]

The dual metaphor "Kaaba of the heart" is not the only way of linking the heart to the *hadjdj*. Nedim (1681 - 1730), the famous poet of the "Tulip Age" of Ottoman culture, says:

> Amongst (or: in the middle of) the pilgrims toward His quarter the heart is coming along like the lamp of the caravan, burning with desire.[8]

The heart has a somewhat ambiguous position in this verse: on the one hand it appears to be personified as one of the pilgrims that are drawn toward the Friend by their spiritual desire, and on the other hand it is compared to a burning lamp. We will have to explore both aspects.

Starting with the comparison between the heart and a lamp, we can consult 'Abd ar-Razzaq al-Qashani's glossary of mystical terms and find under the heading "heart":

> The heart is a pure luminous essence.[9]

The author then draws our attention to the simile in sura 24,35 of the Koran which reads:

> God is the Light of the heavens and the earth; the likeness of His Light is as a niche wherein is a lamp (the lamp in a glass, the glass as it were a glittering star) kindled from a Blessed Tree, an olive that is neither of the East nor of the West whose oil wellnigh would shine, even if no fire touched it; Light upon Light . . . [10]

Khayali Bey (d. 1556), another Ottoman poet, uses "lamp" as a metaphor for "heart" and alludes to the same Koranic text; he does not mention the *hadjdj*, however. In a ghazal that describes the beauty of the beloved and the devotion of the lover, he says:

> The more the tears of my eye flow the more intense is the burning within the heart, it seems as if the tears of my eyes were the oil of that lamp.[11]

The poet establishes a causal nexus—which is empirically not tenable—between the shedding of tears and the burning of desire in the lover's heart by mapping the relationship between the elements "oil," "fire" (represented by "burning") and "lamp" to the elements "tears" and "heart" (containing "desire").

With "lamp" and "oil," however, the Verse of Light (Koran 24,35) is alluded to and thus the erotic level of meaning is linked to the mystical.

In a line by Qabuli, a Persian poet who was attached to the court of the Ottoman sultan Mehmet the Conqueror, this linkage is more obvious:

> The blood of my liver burns in my heart like oil in a glass, for never would the lamp have brightness without oil.[12]

While Khayali Bey uses *'chiragh'* and *'yagh'* to denote "lamp" and "oil," Qabuli takes two of his words directly from the Koran: he uses *'zudjadj'* for "glass" and *'siradj'* for "lamp"; for "oil," on the other hand, he has the Persian *'rawghan'*.

Qabuli's statement would make sense even if we were unaware of its reference to the Koran; we could just take it as a line of love poetry saying: pain (for which the blood of the liver stands metonymically) is the oil that makes the light of love shine brightly in the heart of the lover. By taking into account the sub-text provided by a mystical interpretation of Koran 24,35, we will not change its meaning, but rather deepen it and arrive at the insight that the heart of the mystical lover is the place where human suffering is transformed into the shining light of Divine love.

The examples we have examined so far show clearly that the semantic value of "heart" depends not only on the immediate context of the expression, verse, or poem it is found in, but also on various sub-texts provided by the semantic system of mystical doctrine (*'irfan*).

Seen from the point of view of semiotics, "heart" is a sign and as such belongs to a system of signs—or "semion-symbol system" to use a concept first introduced by Floyd Merell.

While it is very difficult, and in many cases even impossible, to connect elements of the semion-symbol system of ghazal poetry to external referents in the "world of objects, acts, and events,"[13] it is quite easy to find referents in other semion-symbol systems. There are three such systems that are commonly used as systems of reference for ghazal poetry, namely mysticism (*'irfan*), love, and power/authority.[14] Apart from topical references that may or may not be there in a given line of a ghazal, the meaning of the line in question, and probably that of the whole ghazal it is part of, is to a greater or lesser degree determined by one, two, or all of the three systems of reference. By providing sub-texts suitable for a broad variety of poetical utterances these systems of reference play an important role in the organization of the macro-text of ghazal poetry, and in the establishment of intertextual relationships.

The importance of mysticism as a system of reference for a single line and at the same time for the whole poem becomes obvious in an example taken from the divan of Na'ili-i qadim (d. 1666), the most prominent figure of the "Indian style" in Ottoman poetry. The opening line of ghazal 177 reads:

> The heart who is an/the infidel in the monastery of *'alast'* has gazed upon your beauty and become a worshipper of faces/outward appearances/icons.[15]

An erotic-anachreontic reading of this text would yield the meaning: the (personified) heart that rejects the formal prescripts of the Islamic religion and is a regular visitor of the Christian monastery——where among others wine is served or sold——has fallen in love at the sight of your (i.e. a boy's or girl's) beauty and is now devoted to the worship of your beatiful face. The word *'alast'*, however, leaves no doubt that we have to look for a mystical sub-text and and revise our first reading of the verse. The sub-text this word alludes to has at its core Koran 7,172:

> And when thy Lord took from the Children of Adam, from their loins, their seed, and made them testify against themselves [saying], 'Am I not your Lord?' They said, 'Yes, we testify'——lest you should say on the Day of Resurrection, 'As for us, we were heedless of this,'[16] . . .

God's question "Am I not your Lord?" (*a-lastu bi-rabbikum?*) and the answer "Yes, we testify!" is known in Islamic mysticism as "the covenant of *alast.*" The "monastery of *alast*" then has to be the place where that covenant was made and the "infidel" the person who rejected it. The consequence of his rejection is that he does not embrace monotheism but remains a worshipper of idols or icons (which are likely to be found in any Greek monastery).

But, if we take the person referred to by the "you" in "your beauty" as being God, then how can God's beauty be the cause for remaining a worshipper of idols? The answer to this may be found in a text that deals on one level of its meaning with the relationship between absolute or Divine beauty and its reflection in the created world. This text is Djami's *mathnawi Yusuf u Zulaikha*. In Djami's version of the story, Zulaykha, the allegory of the human soul, falls in love with Yusuf, the allegory of Divine beauty. Her infatuation with Yusuf, however, keeps her for a very long time from converting to monotheism until, after a period of intense suffering, towards the end of her life she smashes her idol—a statue made of stone—and prays to the one and only God, whereupon she finally attains union with her beloved.

Zulaikha's inability to proceed from the reflection of God's beauty in the phenomenal world, to the true origin of all beauty, keeps her entangled in this world with all its deceptions, disappointments, and sufferings. The same thing happens to the heart in the opening line of Naili's ghazal. And in the same ghazal the poet says:

> In this place of attachment [to earthly things] which is full of snares, the royal falcon of [our spiritual] existence remains tied by the legs in spite of his hope for release.[17]

To close this part of our inquiry I would like to quote Halûk Ipekten's characterization of Na'ili's poetry, since to my mind, it is also valid for many—but not all!—of the other ghazal poets:

> " . . . for a great number of his verses it is impossible to find a meaning at first sight; only after having been explained in terms of mystical thinking do they make sense."[18]

2 As a system of signs, ghazal poetry is defined not only by its relationships to the outside world or other systems of signs its elements and structures might refer to, but also, and even more so, by its internal organization. The ghazal is a world of its own, governed by the laws of language and poetical imagination. Seen from the viewpoint of logic, poetical statements are in many, if not most, cases neither valid, nor consistent, nor sound; a statement like the line by Qabuli cited above is, when taken as a non-poetic statement, sheer nonsense, or, if judged morally, a lie.

Our analysis should, however, not stop there. In order to describe the internal organization of ghazal poetry as a system, we have to examine the rules that make statements poetically valid, consistent, and sound, even if they appear to be nonsensical in terms of ordinary reason. One of the basic rules of poetical logic—as opposed to normal logic—allows statements of the type "A is B" to be true in cases where A and B only have one thing in common, but are neither the same nor does B include A (as in "a lion is an animal").

Of the different ways this equation can be formulated in the ghazal we will consider two, with "heart" in the place of A. The first way is the explicit statement "the heart is B" or the corresponding *i afat*-construct *'B-i dil'*. This equation allows the poet to introduce A ("heart") into a context where it would not occur normally and to combine elements in ways not admissible or trivial under normal circumstances. How would we, for instance, combine "heart," "sugar," and "air" in a normal sentence? We could, maybe, say: "My heart rejoices when I throw sugar into the air." This and most of the other sentences we could form would be rather trivial, if not ridiculous. But, speaking as a poet, Hafiz can say:

> Hold my heart (A) in esteem! For this is the fly (B) that flies to the sugar. Ever since it has begun to *soar in the air of* (or: *long for*) you [who are sweet as sugar] it has the charisma of [the mythical bird] Huma.[19]

By embedding "heart" into a new and unusual context, the poet's imagination transforms what is normally considered to be a part of man's physical or spiritual organism into a new and different entity. The semantic category this new entity belongs to, is determined by the semantic value of B. As the scope of this paper does not allow an enumeration of all the occurences of such categories in ghazal poetry, I will select only a few in order to demonstrate this process of transformation.

In the line by Hafiz we just quoted, B belongs to the category of animate beings that have wings and can fly. In another poem Hafiz says:

> How could I unfold my wings in the air of union when the bird (B) of my heart (A) has lost its feathers in the nest of separation.[20]

Birds such as the nightingale[21] or the falcon[22] are most probably equated with the heart because birds are traditional and very old symbols for the human soul.

Among the categories of inanimate objects, there is the category of vessels, comprising elements such as cups, glasses, bottles, houses etc., which is chosen for obvious reasons (cf. part 1 of this paper). A category closely related to this is the category of objects with a flat and polished surface such as a slate of marble or a mirror. In the system of *'irfan*, the mirror is a symbol for man's ability to reflect the Divine Beauty and as such it is very often identified with the mirror of Alexander and is akin to the Cup of Djamshid.[23]

> Even if the body would turn into ashes, the secrets of your tresses would remain hidden in the mirror (B) of the heart (A) like the luster [of its polished surface].[24]

A quite different category is that of topographical structures such as landscapes, the sea, or a city:

> The affliction you cause me (lit.: your affliction) is a palm-tree that grows anew whenever I, who have no heart, pluck it out of the river-bank (B) of the heart (A).[25]

> Does it appear as strange when we become upset by our continuous sighing? With the strength of the wind (lit.: breath) the deep sea (B) of the heart (A) becomes wildly agitated.[26]

In order to burn my existence, love has thrown fire into the city (B) of the heart (A).[27]

It is not quite clear why the category of topographical structures is selected; a probable reason could be that the concept of physical space is used as a metaphor for inner (i.e. psychological or spiritual) space associated with the heart.

Such metaphors put "heart" into contexts where it does not occur in normal language—or we could also say: where it does not belong to—; their effect is to objectify the heart, to separate it from the human body and the person that owns it. The heart as an object of the world of the ghazal enjoys great autonomy. As a result of the process of personification, it is transformed into an independent figure, one of the actors on the stage of the ghazal's drama.

Personification can be achieved by using the equation "A is B," with the heart as A and a human being as B, as is the case in Na'ili 177, 1. In most cases, however, this equation is not made explicitly by saying "the heart is B" or by using the expression 'B-i dil,' but implicitly.

Implicit personification can be achieved in two different ways: either by referring to the heart in the 2nd person or in the 3rd. Where the heart is referred to in the 2nd person, we usually find the vocative 'ay dil' or 'dila' (oh, heart!), as for instance in:

The path of love is filled with turmoil and trouble, oh heart, anyone who proceeds on this road in a hurry will fall down![28]

As the receiver of the message sent by the speaker (the lyrical I) of the ghazal, the heart occupies the place that is normally attributed to the listener. The listener on the other hand assumes the role of an audience that follows the dialogues of a play. In an example such as the following, also taken from Hafiz, we can very well imagine a stage where the main actor turns away from the person he has been speaking to and addresses the audience:

The crazy heart has stopped listening to good advice, maybe I should put it in chains [made] from the tips of [the beloved's] curls.[29]

The role the speaker usually plays is that of a man well versed in the art of love and knowing all its secrets and dangers, or a wise man detached from all its troubles and turmoils, whereas the heart appears as a person driven by his desires, defying reason and well-meant advice, unaware of or indifferent to mortal danger. In the drama of love the heart most often ends up a captive in the "dungeon of the beloved's dimple," entagled in his black curls, or exiled in the "China of his tresses" (*chin-i zulf-i u*).[30] The speaker warns it, not to set out on the dangerous path of love, but the heart does not pay heed and runs away. That is why the lover (the original owner of the heart) in the ghazal calls himself "heartless" or "the man without a heart" (*bidil*).

While the "heartless" lover has to exist as a being deprived of one of its vital organs, the heart—as an independent and autonomous inhabitant of the world of the ghazal—has won a body and organs of its own. This transformation of the heart into an imaginary entity——be it a pseudo-human figure, an animal, a plant, or some inanimate object——ss one of the numerous transformational processes that are essential to the creation of a ghazal's inner world. What is true or false in that world cannot be determined by the laws of common logic but by the rules of poetry alone. Once transformed by application of the formula 'A (in our case: the heart) is B', A acquires all the properties of B and whatever holds true for B, does so for A as well. Thus, if B is a human person and if it is true that a human person has eyes, hands, feet, a liver etc., it is poetically valid to speak of "the eyes/hands/feet/liver . . . of the heart" and there is no need to look for anything in the outside world to which an expression such as "the liver of the heart" might refer.

3 The semantic structure of the poetic system of the ghazal is—by its very nature as a structure—determined by its syntagmatic and paradigmatic relationships. In order to create a line of ghazal poetry we have to select elements from certain repertories (in the paradigmatic dimension) and combine them (in the syntagmatic dimension) in a well-formed statement.

The global repertory from which selections can be made is not a simple list or set of elements, but rather a complex structure. Its elements are divided into a number of sub-repertories and a great variety of categories, and linked to other elements on different levels and in different parts of the whole.

Certain elements are linked together to form—more or less independent and complete—fields of meaning. We can call these frames. There is, for example the frame '*bazm*' (banquet) with its actors (host, guests, cup-bearer, musicians, dancers etc.), food (meat, sweetmeats, fruit), drink (wine), utensils (musical instruments such as the lute, the drum, the flute etc., the censer and incense, bottles with rose-water . . . ), and emotional content (joy, gaiety). Or the frame "garden" with flowers (rose, lily, violet, narcissus . . . ), birds (nightingale, crow), winds (morning wind, zephyr, storm), seasons (spring, autumn, and winter; rarely summer), the gardener, and so on.

For a line of ghazal poetry to be successful it sometimes is enough just to take one of these frames out of the repertory and combine its elements in a way that fits the metre of the poem and produces a pleasant melody of speech.

In most cases, however, elements of a given frame are combined with elements that do not belong to that frame, by way of metaphorical embedding.

In the following line by Manuchihri the main elements of the "banquet"-frame are simply enumerated:

> At the banquet (A) of free men you need three things and not more: wine (B), the *rebab* (C) and roast meat (D).[31]

Helaki, an Ottoman poet of the 10th/16th century, takes this line and combines it with the "torments of love"-frame:

> My tears(B') are the wine (B) and my crying (C') the *rebab* (C) and the liver (D') is the roast meat (D); at the banquet of grief (A') this kind of joy and pleasure (A) is enough for me.[32]

The "torment of love"-frame is composed of the categories "pain" (suffering, despair), "cause of pain" (love, separation), "organs afflicted by pain" (body, breast, eyes, heart, liver), and "effects of pain" (wounds, sighs, tears, blood).

When the two frames "torment of love" (frame t) and "banquet" (frame b) are combined with each other, the pairing of elements is not rigidly fixed, and any element of t can be paired with any element of b provided they are poetically equivalent.

> Strike the lute and play; if there is no aloe-wood, don't complain! Take as my fire (A) love (A'), my heart (B') as the aloe-wood (B), and my body (C') as the censer (C)![33]

> Since my liver (D') has been roasted (meat, D) by the fire (A) of separation (A') from that idol, my eye (E') has become a goblet (E) filled with wine (F) from the blood (F') of my heart (no correspon-ding element in this verse).[34]

The three elements "eye," "heart," and "liver" of frame t are very closely connected because the three of them are vessels containing fluids (water and/or blood). When one of them occurs in a verse, it is highly probable that the two others, or at least one of them will also occur, regardless of any other frames involved.

> Do not, like the torrent of tears, run out of the eye, for you have filled my heart with blood, oh

you, who are my heart, lungs and liver (*djigar-band*)![35]

It is up to the poet to decide if he wants to use only one frame, or two; or even more of them. 'Amri, for instance, combines the three frames "torment of love," "garden," and "banquet":

> Since your eye has thrown fire (A) from the face of the rose (A') into my heart, the nightingale (B') of the heart (B") has been roasted and grilled (meat, B) by pain (A").[36]

Bidil combines the "torment of love," "banquet," and "craziness" frames; the following rather complicated statement is easier to understand when we are aware of this fact:

> When does the bottle (A) cross the cup (B) without the (wine C, substituted by:) blood (C') of the liver (A')? My amazement-stricken eye (A') is the blister (A") of the foot of the heart (B').[37]

In the second hemistich the heart is personified as a madman who roams the desert and whose feet develop blisters. The blister filled with water and blood resembles the eye of the crazy lover and the eye resembles the bottle filled with wine which is analogous to the blood of the liver. The first hemistich appears to be coherent: whenever the bottle crosses the rim of the cup in order to fill it, wine gushes forth and this wine looks like the blood of the liver flooding the lover's heart. In the second hemistich there is a dissociation between the speaker (the poetical I) and the heart, both of which are characterized as madmen or crazy lovers. What brings them together again is the resemblance between the stuporous eye of the one and the blister of the foot of the other, as well as the formal link of an antithesis between "up" (the eye as a part of the head) and "down" (the foot). What makes the whole verse somehow awkward is the lack of symmetry between the two hemistichs; they seem to be connected only by the analogies between "blister," "eye," and "bottle" on the one hand, and "cup" and "heart" on the other hand.

*Conclusion*

As an element in the poetic system of the ghazal, "heart" performs different functions on different levels of the text.

On the level of textual reference, it serves as a link between the fundamental domains of reference of the ghazal. The heart, which occupies prominent places in both the psycho-physiology of earthly love and the doctrine of man's spiritual existence, is located at one of the nodes that bind together the conceptual networks of erotic and mystical discourse. At such nodes in the text of the ghazal, transitions from one network to the other could quite easily take place, and in the process of decoding the text, one should always consider the possibility of shifts in the domain of reference or intertextual references.

On another level of the text, on the "stage" where its drama is enacted and stories are told, the heart is separated from the physical body it would belong to; it undergoes various transformations and appears in the form of animate as well as inanimate beings. Its main function on this level, however, is that of an independent actor in the play of love and longing, and in most cases it appears as a double of the poetical I of the poem.[38]

On a third level of the text, the semantic structure of its individual lines (bayts), the element "heart" can be described as one of the items that are bound together by pre-determined semantic frames. Its functions in the structure of the micro-text of the bayt are dependent on the overall functions of the given frame. In cases where a certain frame is selected from the global repertory to be combined with one or more other frames, its individual items enter into two-, or three-place relations with corresponding items of the other frame(s).

*Notes*

[1] Daniela Meneghini Correale, *The Ghazals of Hafez—Concordance and Vocabulary*, Roma: Cultural Institute of the Islamic Republic of Iran in Italy, 1988, p. 847.

[2] KH 136,1; all translations, unless indicated otherwise, are my own.

[3] *Diwan-i Khiyali-i Bukharayi*, ed. 'A. Dawlatabadi, Tabriz: Danishkada-i Adabiyat wa 'Ulum-i Insani, 1973, 200, 1.

[4] Javad Nurbakhsh, *Traditions of the Prophet*, New York: Khaniqahi-Nimatullahi Publications, 1981, p. 25.

[5] *The Divan of Gada'i*, ed. Janos Eckmann, Blooming-ton: Indiana University; The Hague: Mouton, 1971 (Latin script & facsimile of the MS), 181, 5.

[6] Javad Nurbakhsh, *What the Sufis Say*, New York: Khaniqahi-Nimatullahi Publications, 1980, p. 68.

[7] *Diwan-i Sayf ud-Din Muhammad-i Farghani*, ed. Dhabihullah-i Safa, Tehran: Danishgah, 1962, 55,9.

[8] *Nedim Diwani*, ed. Khalil Nihad, Istanbul 1919-21 (Arabic script), p. 144, bayt 13.

[9] Kamal ad-Din 'Abd ar-Razzaq al-Qashani, *Istilahat as-sufiya*, Cairo: al-Hay'a al-Misriya al-'Amma li-l-Kitab, 1981, p. 145.

[10] Trl. taken from Arberry, *The Koran Interpreted*, London: Oxford University Press, 1964, pp. 356f.

[11] *Hayâlî Bey Dîvâni*, ed. A. Nihat Tarlan, Istanbul: Üniversite, 1945 (Latin script), p. 190, no. 137,2.

[12] *Külliyyât-i Dîvân-i Kabulî*, ed. I.H. Ertaylan, Istanbul: Üniversite, 1948 (Facsimile of the MS), p. 254, bayt 2.

[13] Floyd Merell, *A Semiotic Theory of Texts*, Berlin etc.: Mouton de Gruyter, 1985, p. 27.

[14] Cf. Walter C. Andrews, *Poetry's Voice, Society's Song—Ottoman Lyric Poetry*, Seattle, London: University of Washington Press, 1985, chapters 4-6.

[15] *Nâ'ilî-i Kadîm Divâni*, ed. H. Ipektén, Istanbul: Millî E itim Basimevi, s.d. (Latin script), 177,1.

[16] Arberry, *The Koran . . .* , p. 164; Arberry's expression "touching themselves" has been replaced by "against themselves".

[17] Na'ili 177,6.

[18] Halûk pekten, "Gazel erhi Örnekleri II," in: *Türk Dili* No.s 415-17, 1986, p. 276.

[19] KH 119,4.

[20] KH 291,5.

[21] Eg. Nedim p. 134, bayt 14.

[22] Eg. Khiyali 176,1.

[23] Cf. KH 136,1, cited above.

[24] Nedim, p. 138, bayt 1.

[25] Khiyali 245,3.

[26] Na'ili 132,3.

[27] Amrî, *Dîvan,* ed. M. Çavusosslu, Istanbul: Üniversite, 1979 (Latin script), 45,2, 1st hemistich.

[28] KH 216,4.

[29] KH 339,2.

[30] E.g. KH 187,4; *'chin-i zulf* normally means "the folds of the tresses," but the context of the verse requires the reading "China" for *'chin';* the figure is called *'iham'* (amphiboly).

[31] *Diwan-i Manuchihri-i Damghani*, ed. Muhammad-i Dabir-i Siyaqi, p.7.

[32] Helâkî, *Dîvan*, ed. M. Çavu o lu, Istanbul: Üniversite, 1982 (Latin script), 41,2.

[33] KH 252,4.

[34] Qabuli p. 265, apu.

[35] Khiyali 191,4.

[36] 'Amri 44,3.

[37] *Diwan-i Mawlana 'Abd ul-Qadir-i Bidil-i Dihlawi*, ed. Kh. Khalili, Kabul: Da Pohanai Wizarat, 1962 (Reprint Tehran: Nashr-i Bayn ul-Milal, 1984, vol. 1, p. 306, bayt 14.

[38] Cf. also Michael Glünz, "Dichter und dichterisches 'ich' bei Qabuli," in: *XXIV. Deutscher Orientalistentag—Ausgewählte Vorträge*, Stuttgart: Steiner, pp. 205-210.

## Julie Scott Meisami (essay date 1991)

SOURCE: "The Ghazal as Fiction: Implied Speakers and Implied Audience in Hafiz's Ghazals," in *Intoxication, Earthly and Heavenly: Seven Studies on the Poet Hafiz of Shiraz*, edited by Michael Glünz and J. Christoph Burgel, Peter Lang, Inc., 1991, pp. 89-103.

[*In the following essay, Meisami argues for taking a literary—as opposed to a biographical or allegorical—approach to studying the relationship between speaker and audience in Hafiz's poetry.*]

Since Roger Lescot called attention to the plurality of the object or addressee of Hafiz's ghazals, it has become commonplace to speak of parallelism between the *ma'shuq, mamduh* and *ma'bud*.[1] While Lescot was primarily interested in the correlation between the ghazal's addressee and actual individuals, others, notably Gilbert Lazard, have discussed the problem in connection with the "symbolic meaning" of the ghazals. On the basis of the triad of potential addressees Lazard posited three "degrees" of Hafiz's use of language, one literal, according to which the ghazal may be taken at face value, and two metaphorical, in which the ghazal contains a panegyric or mystical subtext; although these three interrelated fields of meaning may be present simultaneously within a given poem, one will usually be dominant.[2]

These discussions are valuable as far as they go; but they do not go far enough, as they do not delve deeply enough into the literary world of the ghazal. Their focus is typically on the identification of the literal, or actual, addressee in a particular ghazal. Less attention has been paid to the existence of yet other addressees who exist in some relationship to the poem's speaker, or to the fact that changes in addressee are often accompanied by a change in speaking voice as well. This, it seems to me, is because behind most readings of the ghazals, whether as secular, mystical, or panegyric, lies the assumption that the speaking voice is always that of the poet, and that the sentiments conveyed are his own, even though they may be rhetorically "dressed up" to appear otherwise (a tendency exemplified by Lescot's reduction of mystical imagery and allusions to a mere rhetorical strategy).[3] Further testimony to this assumption is the endless series of discussions of Hafiz's "philosophy" with which we are all familiar.

Jan Rypka voiced the typical Orientalist view of the relationship between the lyric poet and his poems when he observed, "It is indeed not easy to say to what extent lyric poetry consists of a masterly variation on conventional themes and where actual experience begins."[4] This assumes a dichotomy between convention and reality and equates "true poetry" with the expression of personal experience. Yet, as we know, Persian poetry is highly conventional; could it have flourished as such for many centuries if poets found its conventions cumbersome and intolerably restricting? As Robert Rehder points out, "Men for hundreds of years wrote ghazals not out of mere habit but because the ghazal expressed what they wanted to say in a way which pleased them,"[5] and stresses that "as a love lyric the ghazal is both personal and impersonal. There is intimacy without autobiography."[6]

To what extent is it appropriate to equate the statements of any poet, but especially a medieval poet working in a highly conventional craft, with his own views, as is routinely done in the case of Hafiz? One result of this legacy of Romantic theories of poetry (arguably inapplicable even to Romantic poets) is that the inconsistencies perceived in a poet's oeuvre, which violate the Romantic criterion of "sincerity", must be rationalized by recourse to a variety of pseudo-explanations: the exigencies of patronage, a chronogical development of the poet's "ideas" in which different views represent different stages, the corruptions introduced by scribes, and, especially in the case of Hafiz (but not limited to him), an all-encompassing mystical allegoresis which absorbs inconsistencies by interpreting all statements according to a predetermined code. None of these approaches has been of great utility in the study of Hafiz, and they have often created more problems than they have solved. For this reason I would like to suggest a different approach to reading Hafiz (and by extension other Eastern poets), one which is literary rather than biographical or allegorical, and which has been utilized in the study of other pre-modern poets.

Over forty years ago Leo Spitzer, in an article which was to have a major impact on literary theory, warned against confusing between what he called "the *poetic* and the *empirical* I."

> In the Middle Ages [wrote Spitzer], the 'poetic I' had more freedom and more breadth than it has today: at that time the concept of intellectual property did not exist because literature dealt not with the individual but with mankind: the *'ut in pluribus'* was an accepted standard . . . And we must assume that the medieval public saw in the 'poetic I' a representative of mankind, that it was interested only in this representative role of the poet.[7]

Discussing the example of Dante, he continues,

> All the modern misunderstandings on the part of commentators of the 'biographical approach' school are due to their confusion of the 'poetic I' with the empirical or pragmatical 'I' of the poet—who, in the very first lines of his poem, has taken care to present his 'poetic I' as representative of humanity: *'Nel mezzo del cammin di nostra vita / Mi ritrovai per una selva oscura . . . '* At the same time, however, Dante does not allow us to forget that his empirical personality (his feeling, speaking, gesticulating personality) is also included in this 'I' . . . For the story that Dante had to tell, both aspects of his composite 'I' were necessary: on the one hand, he must transcend the limitations of individuality in order to gain an experience of universal experience; on the other, an individual eye is necessary to perceive and to fix the matter of experience.[8]

In other words, while the poet may incorporate recognizable biographical details into his work (just as he incorporates recognizable reality items drawn from the world around him), they are transformed by this inclusion into literary materials, and must henceforth be considered with respect to their literary function. Although he did not use the term himself, Spitzer's article greatly influenced what soon came to be known as persona criticism. The notion of the literary persona is not a new one; it was recognized to some extent at least by Plato and Aristotle,[9] and we should not forget that among the "proofs" of classical rhetoric is that by character, or *ethos*, which involves convincing the audience, or jury, that the speaker arguing (for example) a legal case is of a certain character.[10] But this important critical concept has remained virtually ignored in the study of Near Eastern literatures, despite its clear potential for the illumination of many critical issues.

Persona criticism makes a distinction between the implied author (or speaker) in a work and the real-life author of that work; the implied speaker is a fictional creation whose chief function is to provide the norms which inform the world presented in the work. "The degree to which the implied author reveals himself and the nature of the norms that he espouses are dictated by the effects that the author wishes his work to have . . . Considerations of the sincerity of the author and the degree to which the implied author does or does not represent the norms of the real-life author are relegated to biography."[11]

Classicists have applied the concept of the persona to the study of the Roman elegiac poets. As Robert Elliott observes,

> Classical literary doctrine assumed no necessary connection between the most intense personal poems and the lives or personalities of their authors. The Roman elegists . . . write of their mistresses with memorable passion; to our ears the poems seem openly confessional, "sincere"; yet modern scholars have shown the folly of reading [such poems] as autobiographical documents. Despite its personal form, erotic poetry cannot be taken to reflect the true feelings or conduct of the writer. There are conventions for love poetry as for other forms of artistic expression, and the poets themselves insist on the distinction between art and life . . . For [these poets] sincerity is a function of style, involving a relationship between the artist and the public; it has to do with the presentation of a self appropriate to the kind of verse being written, to the genre, not with the personality of the poet.[12]

Similar obervations have been made for medieval lyric: Peter Dronke notes that the term "personal" "implies not (or not necessarily) the revelation of private experience, but rather the realisation of a *persona*, that is, the attainment of a certain objectivity . . . The authenticity lies in . . . the strength of the imaginative projection."[13] The notion of persona is also central, if implicit, in Frederick Goldin's discussion of varying perspectives in the courtly lyric.[14] Of particular importance is Martin Stevens' modification of the notion of persona to a theory of the "performing self" to which attention is called by the poet's self-referential statements in his poem.[15]

Conventionally the ghazal is univocal: that is, each poem typically features a single speaker who remains consistent throughout. Different types of ghazal, however, present different speakers, a fact which becomes apparent when we discard the notion that the speaker in any ghazal is the poet himself. The characters and roles of the ghazal's various speakers are conventional and determined by generic considerations; many such "speaking voices" can be traced back to earlier

Arabic poetry, in particular that of the early Abbasid period, which saw the development of specialized types of poem such as the *khamriya*, the independent love poem, and the *zuhdiya* or homiletic poem, each characterized by a distinctive speaking voice. In the *zuhdiya* the speaker is the sage, contemptuous of the world and its deceits, who exhorts to abandonment of worldly concerns and enjoins a life of piety in preparation for the Hereafter. In the love poem it is the lover, who complains of separation from his beloved and of her cruelty and protests his undying dedication. In the *khamriya* the speaker is the libertine who boasts of his exploits in the tavern and praises the wine which is, to him, the only worthy object of devotion. Other voices inform other types of poetry, encomium, satire, *mudjun* poetry, and so on; moreover, as a poet moves from one genre to another, so does the implied speaker make a corresponding shift.

In the *qasida* various speaking voices may be combined; though they complement each other, all are implicitly subsumed under the dominant generic persona of the encomiast. A contrast is sometimes established between private and public aspects of the persona; for example, the love relationship described in the *nasib* parallels or contrasts with the poet-patron relationship in the *madih*. But in the short poem—the Arabic *qit'a* or "short *qasida*", as al-Djahiz termed the independent, single-topic poem, or the various brief Persian lyric forms—the implied speaker is, conventionally, consistent throughout the poem. In the ghazal, which is *par excellence* a love poem, this speaker is a lover, the addressee or dedicatee his beloved, and the poem is sung to gain the favour of this implied addressee.

But not all ghazals are love poems; and not all love poems deal with secular love. In the mystical ghazal the implied speaker is the mystical aspirant, a questing lover on the path of divine union. In wine poems (both secular and mystical) we often hear echoes of Abu Nuwas's libertine persona, revived in that of the *rind* who prefers honest sin to hypocritical piety and who (in contrast to his generic adversary the *zahid*) enjoins his listener to "seize the day". With the development of mystical poetry and the frequent overlapping of the language of mystical and courtly ghazal the persona of the *rind* comes to encompass not only that of the lover but also that of the sage, especially when, with poets such as Sa'di, the Sufi sage takes on the generic, as well as the actual, function of advisor to princes, and becomes a fixture in the courtly as well as the mystical world of the ghazal. Each of these personae is conventional and each has a long tradition behind it; thus the implied speaker of any poem would have been instantly recognizable to its hearers, as would the subtlest variation on any of its conventions.

The speaker of a given poem exists in relation to his audience, which is represented in the world of the poem and which, like the speaker, combines reality with fiction. It is the audience, and the different elements within it, which determines the role assumed in any poem—and in different portions of a single poem—by its speaker. As Frederick Goldin notes,

> The courtly community is represented in the lyric by the audience; the directions that love may take, by the different kinds of persons in that audience and the conflicting impulses of the 'I', the courtly lover, in the lyric . . . The lyric audience consists of friends and enemies who are so designated by the singer as he responds to them in the course of his song.[16]

Goldin's remarks are of particular importance because he emphasizes the performance context of the lyric, a context often conveniently forgotten by those who equate poetic statements with personal opinions and who overlook the fact that medieval poetry is not, in terms of its production, either confession or private meditation, but public performance. Goldin suggests a method of reading such lyrics, central to which is the notion of the "basic fiction" of the courtly lyric.

> . . . This fiction is fragmented, analyzed into a fixed register of episodes, moods, and postures, from which the poet draws in order to arrange a certain nonnarrative pattern . . . The courtly audience knew this fiction thoroughly, and once it heard the opening lines it would place each lyric at a specific point in the round of courtly love . . . The opening lines, like the opening moves of a game, determine the possibilities that can follow . . . Once the audience located the lyric, it would know ex-actly what to expect, and the poet would go on to satisfy or astonish his listeners.[17]

It is scarcely necessary to review the basic conventions of courtly love: the inaccessibility, or cruelty, of the beloved, the lover's single-minded devotion, his joy at the least favour shown him, his despair at separation or at obstacles to the realization of his love. Nor is it necessary to dwell on the ethical dimensions of this fiction: that "Courtly love . . . is the love of courtliness, of the refinement that distinguishes a class, of an ideal fulfilled in a person whom everyone recognizes," and who is concretely embodied in the singer of the poem, "the performer who stands before the audience in the role of a courtly lover," and whose song has at one and the same time "a universal and an individualized significance: the singer reveals to the audience its own idealized image and at the same time proves his right to belong to the courtly class."[18] Essential to this ideal of courtliness was the maintenance of the fiction; for what could be more absurd (as romance writers East and West have shown) than taking literally the fiction of courtly love, which "as a literary theme . . . is an ameliorating and unifying influence, but as the basis of an actual relation between flesh-and-blood lovers . . . is simply ridiculous."[19] It is this—and not biography—which accounts for the remoteness, the unattainability of the love object (whether real or spiritualized), a remoteness parodied by the bacchic poets who, like Abu Nuwas, sing of a real, accessible beloved rather than the ephemeral Laylis and Hinds of the love poet.

The speaker may at times identify himself with the hostile elements in his audience: the slanderers, spies, hypocrites, false lovers, false poets, vulgar people, and, in Persian ghazal in particular, the ascetics and their ilk, who condemn his love and wish to discredit it;[20] he may criticize their lack of perception, or adopt their viewpoint momentarily only to reject it. He thus addresses varied elements in his audience, friends and enemies alike, moving from one to the other in his poem. The structure of the poem, the order it observes, are determined by this movement, "by the singer's successive awareness of the various segments in his audience during the performance of the song."[21]

This technique—which Goldin terms "the technique of playing through the perspectives of an audience, the technique of the performed song"[22]—is characteristic of the ghazal. It accounts for the change of acting persons within a single poem first commented on by Joseph von Hammer, who noted that "the poet may, in one and the same poem, speak now in the first person, now in the second, now in the third," and saw this as contributing to the ghazal's lack of unity.[23] This feature reflects the interaction of the speaker with different segments of his audience, who represent different perspectives on, or responses to, his poem;[24] while yet more shifts in perspective are provided by the *takhallus*, also frequently seen as another cause of the ghazal's incoherence.

Reading the lyric as performance, as the dramatisation, so to speak of an accepted and familiar fiction, sheds light on many of Hafiz's ghazals, for example the famous "Shiraz Turk" ghazal (P3)[25], over which more ink has been spilled (and to less point) than any other.[26]

> 1 Should that Turk of Shiraz take my heart into his hand, I'd give up, for his Hindu mole, all Samarqand and Bukhara.
>
> 2 Saqi, bring the last of the wine, for you'll not find in Paradise the banks of Ruknabad's stream, or the rosegarden of Musalla.
>
> 3 Alas! those jesting gypsies, so graceful and disturbing, have robbed my heart of patience, as Turks plunder the feast.

> 4 Of our imperfect love the beloved's beauty has no need: what need for paint, for mole and down, has the beauteous face?
>
> 5 From that daily-growing beauty which was Joseph's I knew that love would bring Zulaikha out from the veil of chastity.
>
> 6 Though you revile and curse me, yet I will pray for you, for bitter answers well become sugared, ruby lips.
>
> 7 Listen to this advice, my love, for better than life itself do the fortunate young love the counsel of wise elders:
>
> 8 Talk of the minstrel and of wine; seek less the secret of Time, for no one has solved, or will, through wisdom that enigma.
>
> 9 You have sung a ghazal and threaded pearls; come, sing sweetly, Hafiz, that the sphere may scatter the Pleiads' necklace upon your verse.

The speaker begins by addressing the friends in his audience, confiding to them his despair in love, and his willingness to give all for a sign of favour. Despairing of success, he seeks solace in wine and the pleasures of the present company because, as he says, he can endure no more of this torment. This is typical *hasb-i hal* material, and it is not necessary to see in *may-i baqi* any more than this literal sense (his willingness to drink whatever remains of the wine reinforces the lover's desperation). Then follow those lines which have excited mystical interpretation for generations, as the speaker ponders the perfection of his beloved—a beauty which, like that of Joseph, would drive anyone to distraction—and his own imperfect state, both givens of the fiction of courtly love. Even those who avow purity, says he (casting a sidelong glance at the enemies in his audience, the critics of his excess), would be putty in the hands of such a beauty; but while they might criticize the beloved's ill-treatment of the lover, he forgives it, "for bitter answers well become sugared ruby lips." He continues to address his beloved (implicitly among the audience) with advice meant to incense the ascetic enemies: talk only of wine and music, for who can understand love's mysteries? The implication is that he will go on with his obsession, despite the grief it brings and the danger of ridicule from others, because this is, after all, the lover's role. The final cap demonstrates the artificiality of all this, plus the fact that it is a performance and not a "slice of life": the singer's poem is so excellent, so well constructed and adorned, that the heavens will bestow on him the "Pleiads' necklace" in reward.

This is perhaps an oversimplified reading; but it has the advantage of dispensing with glosses, explications and commentaries relying on items which are not in the text itself, and which can only be put there with a considerable amount of strain. The *takhallus* line, moreover, calls attention to the fact that the ghazal which has preceded it is a fiction, and stresses the role of the poet as creator and performer of that fiction. The various forms of self-reference in the *takhal-lus*, paradoxically, both emphasize the named poet as author of the text, and distance him from that text. Often (as in the "Shiraz Turk") the speaker stands back from the poem to admire it; at other times he refers to it as if it were the work of another; he sometimes addresses himself, at other times a member or members of his audience, at others he may refer obliquely to a specific segment of that audience. Such strategies may establish a distinction between the speaker of the ghazal itself and the speaker of the *takhallus*; or they may create an identity, a community of sentiment, between the implied speaker and one segment of the audience (the friends, the patron) or an opposition between the speaker and the values he represents and another segment of the audience (the enemies, the detractors).

The technique of representing a variety of perspectives through shifts in speaking voices or through changes in acting persons is not distinctive to Hafiz's ghazal; there are precedents in earlier ghazal, both courtly and mystical, as there are for other strategies, such as the multiplicity of speakers in dialogue poems, or in poems which contain passages of discourse either reported by the speaker or directed to him by another person in the fictional world of the poem. But Hafiz varies these familiar techniques in a number of ghazals in which we find a plurality of implied speakers within the body of the poem, a plurality of personae each of whom informs a particular segment of the ghazal. Overtones of this are present in the "Shiraz Turk" ghazal, in the advice addressed to the beloved, where the speaker moves briefly from the role of lover to that of sage: "Listen to this advice, my love, for better than life itself do the fortunate young love the counsel of wise elders." In this context the implied addressee correspondingly shifts from beloved to prince, who are thereby conflated. These voices are also combined in my second example (P8),[27] which was discussed by A. Bausani as an example of "formal incoherence" in Hafiz's ghazals,[28] and which recalls Shah Shudja''s famous (if perhaps apocryphal) criticism of Hafiz for mingling verses on wine, Sufism and love in a single poem.

> 1 The brilliance of youth's time has returned to the garden; news of the rose has reached the sweet-singing nightingale.

> 2 Saba, if you pass by the youths of the meadow, carry my regards to cypress, rose and basil.

> 3 If the wine-selling Magian child displays himself so, I will sweep the threshhold of the wineshop with my eyelids.

> 4 O you who draw over the moon a polo-stick of pure amber, do not cause me, a bewildered wanderer, distress.

> 5 I fear that those people who laugh at the drinkers of dregs will place faith at the disposal of the tavern.

> 6 Be the companion of the men of God; for in Noah's ship is earth which gives not a drop for the tempest.

> 7 Go out of this turning dwelling, and do not ask for bread, for that much-visited host in the end kills its guest.

> 8 The last resting-place of everyone is a handful of earth; say, what need then to raise a palace to the skies?

> 9 O my Moon of Canaan, the throne of Egypt is yours; it is time for you to bid farewell to your prison.

> 10 Hafiz, drink wine, practice *rindi*, and be happy; but do not, like others, make the Koran a snare of hypocrisy.

The ghazal begins (lines 1-2) with a description of spring (*wasf-i bahar*), a characteristic prelude to love poems, wine poems, and panegyrics, and suggests that the speaker is elsewhere than in the garden described. Lines 3-4 identify his whereabouts as the wineshop, where he sings for a less formal gathering, and where the beauty of the "wineselling Magian child" threatens to rob him of his wits. With lines 5-8 the tone shifts abruptly from a lover's complaint to admonition, in which the speaker offers sententious advice; the segment remains linked to the previous one, however, by the motifs of wine, tavern and saqi. Yet the voice of the speaker is a different, sterner one: that of the *rind* in his incarnation as sage, who exhorts to sincere piety as opposed to hypocrisy, and warns of the transience of this world. The two final lines recapitulate, in the same order, these two voices: the lover apostrophizes his beloved, the sage *rind* exhorts himself to eschew hypocrisy. Line 9 employs a topic of ghazal, the anticipated appearance of the beloved, now given courtly overtones; the final line combines an *invitatio* (invitation to drink) with a further warning against hypocrisy.

That the generic dominant in this poem is not ghazal, or love poetry, but admonition, is clear from the central position and the amount of space devoted to that genre, and from its linkage with other elements which provide supporting evidence for the unspoken thesis that contentment with life's simple joys is superior to material aspirations thinly veiled by hypocritical piety. The poem's homiletic character makes irrelevant the glossing of the rose as "the supreme, inaccessible symbol of the divine *istighna*;" in ghazal the rose is the beloved, in panegyric the prince, in homiletic poetry an emblem of the transience of beauty and power; a mystical interpretation is extraneous to the ghazal itself. The over-interpretation of such figures as the *mughbacha*, the rose and the nightingale—who in this poem at least is not singing "invitations to partake of the mystic wine"—stems from the view that "tradition" imposes meanings on topics and images that the poet "does not consciously wish;" in fact, the poet selects the areas of meaning he wishes to stress, chooses his images and topics accordingly, and places them in the mouth of an appropriate speaker.

This pre-determined reading, moreover, misses an important field of meaning that the poet has deliberately built into this ghazal: the courtly one. We may assume that the ghazal was composed for, and performed before, a courtly audience in a courtly setting. The garden of the opening lines is a courtly garden, its inhabitants—cypress, rose and basil—all emblems of royalty. That the speaker is not present in that garden, that he asks the lovers' messenger (the *Saba*) to convey his greetings there, and that he is troubled by his beloved's cruelty, suggest, in this courtly context, that he is out of favor, has lost his place in the courtly garden. This suggestion is strengthened by the homiletic segment, where the speaker turns on the hypocrites, accusing them of false piety and reminding them that the last resting place of all is in the earth: what good are lofty palaces then? The sudden apostrophe to the beloved, with the allusion to Joseph, freed from prison to become ruler of Egypt, suggests not a mystical but a topical reference to the prince (perhaps alluding to his restoration as ruler of Shiraz in 1366). Beneath the voices of lover and of *rind* lies that of the encomiast, the court poet who combines in his person two complementary sets of values, two stances—dedication to love and to virtue—traditionally held up for emulation by the audience. Both audience and dedicatee are invited to displace themselves into the persona of the speaker, to occupy either, or both, of these stances and thus to distinguish themselves from the enemies, who scoff at the drinkers and who make the Koran "a snare for hypocrisy."

Another type of poem, to which I have referred to elsewhere as Hafiz's microcosmic ghazal,[29] features both reported discourse by a substitute speaker or speakers as well as a plurality of implied speakers. This type is represented by the two final examples, which exhibit remarkably parallel structures. The first (P48)[30] begins with the dialogue of nightingale and rose.

1 At dawn the bird of the meadow said to the new-risen rose, "Less coquetry! for many like you have flowered in this garden."

2 The rose laughed: "Indeed, the truth does not disturb us; but no lover ever spoke a harsh word to his beloved.

3 "If you desire to drink the ruby wine from that bejewelled cup, many a pearl must you string with the tips of your eyelashes.

4 "The scent of love will never come to the nostrils of one who does not sweep the sill of the wineshop with his forehead."

5 Last night in Iram's Garden, when, with the gentle air, the hyacinth's curls were stirred by the dawn breeze,

6 I said, "O Throne of Djamshid, where is your world-seeing Cup?" It answered, "Alas, that waking fortune slept."

7 The words of love are not those which come to the tongue: Saqi, bring wine, and cut short all this talk.

8 Hafiz's tears have cast wisdom and patience into the sea. What can he do? the burning of love's grief cannot be hidden.

In the opening dialogue (1-4) the nightingale is a substitute speaker for the lover; the rose represents the beloved, replying as such a person might. The second segment (5-6) shifts to the voice of the court poet as sage, who questions the personified throne of Djamshid and receives in answer the type of sentitious statement normally expressed in the voice of the sage himself. In the third segment (7-8) the distressed lover addresses the *saqi* with a typical complaint (the *saqi* is customarily not required to reply, but merely to pour the wine, and we must envisage a real *saqi* among the assembly doing just that); the final cap suggests the reason for the complaint (as if in reply to a hostile criticism) which by extension relates to the entire poem: love carries with it, paradoxically, not only the obligation of "concealing the secret," but of speaking out, of communicating lived experience, or sentitious wisdom, to others in order that they may learn from it, so taht they may more perfectly identify with the roles to which they aspire.

The final example (P468)[31] presents the same set of speakers in a slightly different combination which involves recapitulation as well as alternation.

1 The nightingale, from the cypress branch, to a Pahlavi air, sang last night the lesson of spiritual stations:

2 "Come, for Moses' fire has put forth a rose, that you may hear from the tree the subtle sentence of Unity."

3 The birds of the garden are all poets and wits, that the lord may drink wine to the sound of Pahlavi songs.

4 Djamshid bore nought from this world but the tale of the Cup: beware! set not your heart on worldly things.

5 How pleasant is the beggar's mat and secure sleep; this life is not within the grasp of the royal throne.

6 Hear this strange tale of upside-down fortune: my beloved has slain me with his life-giving breath.

7 Your eyes have, with a glance, destroyed men's homes; may you suffer no headache, who walk so gracefully drunken.

8 How well the ancient Gardener put it to the Youth: "O light of my eyes, you shall reap nought but what you sow."

9 Did the Saqi give Hafiz more than his share, that the end of his divine's turban has become disarrayed?

The first segment (1-2) presents the nightingale (substituting for the court poet) and announces his lesson, that of the meaning of divine Unity, implicitly contained in the conceits of the poem which follows. Line 3 establishes the courtly setting in which the ghazal is performed. In lines 4 and 5 the speaker, as sage, delivers his own lesson: that of contentment with life's simple pleasures, a "station" which cannot be gained by those who, like kings, concern themselves only with worldly things. In lines 6 and 7 the speaker, now in the role of lover (yet still, implicitly, the admonishing court poet), addresses his beloved, complains of his cruelty, and conveys another piece of advice: the warning not to be too proud. The eighth line is a *sententia* which glosses both the nightingale's lesson and that of the sage: as ye sow so shall ye reap; the "Unity" which emerges from this lesson is that of sincere dedication to an ethical ideal, what Hafiz calls in other contexts *ya-krangi*, matching deeds to principles, being virtuous in fact

as well in aspiration. The final cap puts us directly back into the courtly gathering, as a somewhat hostile listener, probably bored with this combination of lyricism and moralizing, asks whether the poem itself is motivated by ethical intent or by more mundane causes: is it not because he has received more than his share of the wine that Hafiz (the poet-figure within which are subsumed the various identities of the persona) is carrying on this way? Such effusions, it is suggested, are unbecoming to a divine—that class of which Hafiz is in fact a member, but from which he dissociates himself in much of his poetry.

It is thus not merely "themes" (as Shah Shudja', and many others since him, have supposed) which are mingled in Hafiz's ghazals, but voices as well; and it is with reference to these voices that various segments of their implied audience, as well as the addressee, can be established, their identities contingent on that of the implied speaker. It is the voice of the *rind* (in his manifestation of lover or of sage) who criticizes the *mudda'i*, the *zahid*, the *muhtasib*, the hypocritical Sufi; it is the voice of the sage (conflating lover and *rind*) who proffers advice, whether directly or indirectly, to the prince (who may be depicted as an inexperienced lover, a cruel beloved, an arrogant rose). Such persons constitute the dramatis personae of the fictive world of the ghazal, a world which mirrors, but is not co-extensive with, the real world in which the poet lives.

*Notes*

[1] Roger Lescot, "Essai d'une chronologie de l'oeuvre de Hâfiz," *BEO* 19 (1944), pp. 57-100.

[2] Gilbert Lazard, "Le langage symbolique du ghazal," *Poesia di Hâfez* (Rome: Accademia Nazionale dei Lincei, 1978), pp. 59-71.

[3] Lescot, "Essai," pp. 96-97.

[4] Jan Rypka, *History of Iranian Literature* (Dordrecht: D. Reidel, 1968), p. 86.

[5] Robert Rehder, "Unity in the Ghazals of Hafiz," *Der Islam* 51 (1974), p. 65.

[6] Ibid., p. 78.

[7] Leo Spitzer, "Note on the Poetic and the Empirical 'I' in Medieval Authors," *Traditio* 4 (1946), pp. 415-16.

[8] Ibid., p. 415.

[9] "Persona," *Princeton Encyclopedia of Poetry and Poetics* (=PEPP), ed. Alex Preminger, enlarged ed. (Princeton: Princeton University Press, 1975), p. 959.

[10] Aristotle, *Rhetoric*, I.ii.3-6.

[11] *PEPP,* p. 960.

[12] Robert C. Elliott, *The Literary Persona* (Chicago: University of Chicago Press, 1982), p. 43.

[13] Peter Dronke, *The Medieval Lyric* (London: 1968), p. 93.

[14] See Frederick Goldin, "The Array of Perspectives in the Early Courtly Love Lyric," in: *In Pursuit of Perfection*, ed. J. Ferrante and G. Economou (Port Washington, NY: Kennikat Press, 1975), pp. 51-100.

[15] Martin Stevens, "The Performing Self in Twelfth-Century Culture," *Viator* 9 (1978), pp. 193-212.

[16] Goldin, "Array of Perspectives," p. 51.

[17] Ibid., pp. 52-53.

[18] Ibid., pp. 54-55.

[19] Ibid., p. 57.

[20] Ibid., p. 58.

[21] Ibid., pp. 67-68.

[22] Ibid., p. 68.

[23] *Der Diwan,* ed. J. von Hammer (Stuttgart: 1812; rept. Hildesheim, 1973), 1:vii; cf. Annemarie Schimmel, "Hâfiz and His Critics," *Studies in Islam* 16 (1979), p. 15.

[24] Goldin, "Array of Perspectives," pp. 76-78.

[25] KH 3; see Appendix.

[26] All texts cited are from the *Diwan,* ed. H. Pizhman, Tehran 1318/1939 (=P); translations, unless otherwise indicated, are the author's.

[27] KH 9; see Appendix; for a French translation see Mme Kappler's article, p. 73

[28] Alessandro Bausani, "The Development of Form in Persian Lyrics: A Way to a Better Understanding of the Structure of Western Poetry," *East and West,* n.s., 9 (1958), pp. 145-53; see also *EI²*, s.v. "ghazal". The translation is Bausani's.

[29] See J.S. Meisami, *Medieval Persian Court Poetry* (Princeton: 1987), pp. 285-98.

[30] KH 81; see Appendix.

[31] KH 477; see Appendix.

## FURTHER READING

Ahmad, Nazir. "A Very Old Source of Hafiz's Ghazals." *Indo-Iranica* XVIII, No. 1 (March 1965): 35-47.
> Explores an early manuscript containing 126 ghazals of Hafiz, some of which have not generally been anthologized.

Arberry, A. J. "Orient Pearls at Random Strung." *Bulletin of The School of Oriental and African Studies, University of London.* XI, No. 4 (1946): 699-712.
> Examination of William Jones's classic *A Persian Song* that considers how faithful it is to Hafiz's strongly thematic original. Also describes the difficulties peculiar to translating Persian into English.

———. Introduction to *Fifty Poems of Hafiz,* edited and translated by Arthur J. Arberry, pp. 1-34. Cambridge: The University Press, 1970.
> Includes a biographical sketch, descriptions of extant manuscripts and possible models used by Hafiz, and assesses his overall contributions to literature.

Bashiri, Iraj. "Hafiz and the Sufic *Ghazal.*" *Studies in Islam,* No. 1 (January 1979): 34-67.
> Detailed study of two ghazals that attempts to provide evidence that Hafiz's poems are "unified pieces, composed around preconceived themes and written within the confines of predetermined structural descriptions."

Boyce, Mary. "A Novel Interpretation of Hafiz." *Bulletin of the School of Oriental and African Studies,* University of London XV, No. 2 (1953): 279-88.
> Attacks G. M. Wickens's view that Hafiz's written words contain extensive and deliberate ambiguities because of their association with other words that look similar.

Hillman, Michael Craig. "Sound and Sense in a *Ghazal* of Hafiz." *The Muslim World* LXI, No. 2 (April 1971): 111-21.
> Decries a lack of Hafiz studies which consider his poems in their entirety and as poems.

Schimmel, Annemarie. "Hafiz and His Critics." *Studies in Islam,* No. 1 (January 1979): 1-33.
> Surveys interest in Hafiz's work through the centuries, particularly Western studies and interpretations.

Wickens, G. M. "An Analysis of Primary and Secondary Significations in the Third *Ghazal* of Hafiz." *Bulletin of The School of Oriental and African Studies, University of London* XIV, No. 3 (1952): 627-38.

Analysis of a particular poem that seeks to demonstrate that Hafiz made use of words which gain in allusive meaning by virtue of their etymological roots.

# Havelok the Dane

## c. Twelfth-thirteenth century

English verse romance.

### INTRODUCTION

*Havelok the Dane* is one of the oldest Middle English romances, generally considered to have been written around the thirteenth century, and consisting of some 3000 lines of rhymed octosyllabic couplets. In addition to being an exciting and vigorous tale in its own right, *Havelok the Dane* provides the first glimpse of the lives of common people after the Norman Conquest. Written in a Lincolnshire dialect, *Havelok the Dane* offers local color and insight into the diverse people inhabiting England, championing their humble lifestyle. It is also an important historical source for the understanding of political and legal procedures of the time. The work has been praised by critics for its narrative style and gritty realism.

### Textual History

*Havelok the Dane* exists in only one manuscript, positioned towards the end of a collection of saints' lives and immediately before the verse romance *King Horn* (circa 1225). *Havelok*'s inclusion in this collection perhaps reflects Havelok's vaguely divine status in the tale. While the English romance version is the longest of the various forms of the Havelok tale, the basic story exists in several other guises. Its first known telling was around 1135-40 in Geffrei Gaimar's *L'Estoire des Engles*. It was on this work that the 1112-line Old French (or Anglo-Norman) version, *Le Lai d'Haveloc* (1190-1220) was based. Robert Mannyng's *Chronicle of England,* commonly called the Lambeth Interpolation, contains a concise rendition of Havelok's story in eighty-two long lines. Scholars continue to debate to what degree one version is indebted to others and to what extent common, mythical elements are incorporated.

### Plot and Major Characters

The Havelok tale begins in England, where the beloved Christian King, Æthelwood, has died, leaving his daughter, Goldboro, sole heir to the throne. She is entrusted to her guardian, Earl Godrich of Cornwall, who sets up an oppressive rule and imprisons Goldboro in a tower, denying her the kingdom. She is told she can marry no one but the "highest" man in England. Shifting to another plot, the reader learns of Birkabeyne, the dying King of Denmark. The King entrusts his son, Havelok, and Havelok's two sisters into the protection of their guardian, Earl Godard. Wishing to assume rule himself, Godard slits the young girls' throats and orders his serf, Grim, to drown the Prince in return for Grim's freedom. Before Grim can carry out his order a blazing light leaps from Havelok's mouth, indicating his kingly origin and divine mission. Further, Grim sees a "king-mark" on Havelok, a birthmark in the shape of a cross. Grim spares the boy, adopts him, and flees with his family and Havelok to England, where they take up residence in Lincolnshire. Here Havelok works tirelessly and cheerfully in a series of menial jobs. The work helps Havelok grow strong and through his participation in sports he gains skill and agility. Eventually he becomes employed as a cook's helper in Godrich's household. Godrich, thinking Havelok of common origin, marries him to Goldboro. One night the beam of light again appears from Havelok's mouth and is witnessed by Goldboro, who realizes her husband is a prince. An angel speaks to Goldboro and tells her of her husband's destiny. Havelok, Goldboro, and Grim and his family travel to Denmark. Havelok raises an army, defeats and hangs Godard, then goes back to England and defeats Godrich, who is burned at the stake. Havelok unites the kingdoms of Denmark and England and he and Goldboro rule the countries and have fifteen children who become kings and queens themselves.

### Major Themes

Thematically, *Havelok the Dane* is concerned with the triumph of good over evil, the importance of the rule of law, and the protection of God for good men, who may be used as his instruments. It deals with a man who rises to his rightful seat on the throne not solely by virtue of his birth, but also through his Christian qualities, personal abilities, and hard work. Some critics have also made the case that the work sought to demonstrate the legitimacy of Danish rule over England.

### Critical Reception

Scholars have praised *Havelok the Dane* for stylistic sophistication not generally found in its time. It is dual-plotted and the author appears to be aware of his narrative skill: he neatly inserts himself at times between the action and the audience and is adept at rendering transitions, sometimes of numerous years. The work has also been acclaimed for its liveliness; for its treatment of characters, even minor ones, as individuals rather than types; for its realistic, natural style; and for its inclusion of legal facts and procedures. Critics have contrasted it with French tales of the time, noting that, while they emphasize an idealized aristocracy, *Havelok the Dane* focuses on the peasant class. Source studies of the Havelok tales are of particular interest to scholars. Extensive research has yielded much information and much contention over such matters as derivation of words and names, sequence, correspondences, and references. There is no disagreement that the Gaimar version, *Le Lai d'Haveloc,* and the Lambeth Interpolation are heavily related; however, scholars debate the source of the English version. Some believe *Havelok the Dane* to be based on the French tale, others believe it is the source of the French. A common source for all versions is not ascertainable, but many believe that this conjectured original was of Scandinavian origin. Scholars have also devoted much effort to trying to determine the date of composition of *Havelok.* Herlint Meyer-Lindenberg has contended that *Havelok* must have been composed between 1203 and 1216, advancing several arguments to support the thesis. George B. Jack has taken issue with each of these conclusions and has insisted that the date of composition cannot be determined any more precisely than from the late twelfth century to around 1272. Concerning the derivations and interrelations of the various Havelok tales, G. V. Smithers has written that "finality has not been reached and is hardly possible."

---

## PRINCIPAL ENGLISH EDITIONS

*The Lay of Havelok the Dane* [translated by W. W. Skeat; revised by K. Sisam] 1973

*Medieval English Romances*, Vol. I [edited by A. V. C. Schmidt and N. Jacobs] 1980

*Havelok* [translated by G. V. Smithers] 1987

---

## CRITICISM

### Edward Kirby Putnam (essay date 1900)

SOURCE: "The Lambeth Version of *Havelok,*" *Publications of the Modern Language Association of America*, Vol. XV, No. 1, 1900, pp. 1-16.

[*In the following essay, Putnam examines the version of* Havelok the Dane *found in the Lambeth manuscript and considers its origin, pointing out possible debts to both French and English sources, omissions of supernatural and clearly fictitious elements, and its unusual sequence.*]

Of the several abridgments of the Havelok story in the chronicles of the fourteenth and fifteenth centuries, that which is interpolated in the Lambeth MS. of Robert Mannyng of Brunne's translation of Peter de Langtoft, is the longest and in many respects the most noteworthy.[1] It has, however, not received the attention it merits. Madden attributes it to the scribe, who, he says, has made other changes in the MS. He describes it as "an abridged outline of the story itself, copied apparently from the French chronicle of Gaimar," but presents no arguments to support his contention. Skeat simply copies Madden. Kupferschmidt,[2] in his extremely valuable discussion of the relations of the various versions of Havelok one to another, accepts without investigation Madden's statement that the Interpolation is based on Gaimar. In view of the great interest attaching to the romance of Havelok a more careful investigation of this Interpolation may be of some service.

The Interpolation consists of 82 lines in rimed pairs. The meter is generally of six feet, but is not very regular. The language is such as might have been written at the end of the fourteenth century. The style is marked by extreme condensation, an entire incident often being told in a single line. As a result the story appears in a surprisingly complete form, as will be seen from the following analysis:

Gounter (the Danish king who has been fighting with Alfred and who has been baptized) goes with all his folk to Denmark (1). He has a war with a Breton king who came "out of Ingeland" to demand from Denmark the tribute "that Arthur whylom nam" (2-4). The Danes say they would rather fight (5-6). They are defeated and Gounter is killed (7-8). When he is dead the victors plan to bring his blood to shame (9). Gounter's wife was Eleyne, daughter of King Gatfere (10-11). With difficulty she escapes to the sea with her child Havelok (11-13). At the haven she meets Grym, "a wel god marinere," who knows her and promises to take her out of the land that night (14-16). On the sea they are attacked by outlaws and the queen is killed, but Grym, Havelok and five others escape (17-21). They arrive at the haven of Grymesby (22). Havelok is brought up by Grym and his wife as their own child; men do not know otherwise (23-24). He becomes large and strong and a "man of mykel cost," so that "for his grete sustinaunce, nedly serve he most" (25-26). He takes leave of Grym and Seburc "as of his sire & dame" (27-28). He goes northward to the court of King Edelsy, who holds the kingdom of Lyndeseye from the Humber to Rotland (29-30). Edelsy, who is "of Breton kynde," has married his sister Orewayn to Egelbright, a Dane, king of Northfolk, who holds the land from Colchestre to Holland. They have a daughter Argill (31-36). Egelbright and Orewayn die and therefore Edelsy is joyful. He takes "in hande" Argill and the kingdom "al at his owene will" (37-40). Havelok serves there as "quistron" and is called Coraunt (41). He is large, strong as a

THE

ANCIENT ENGLISH ROMANCE

OF

# Havelok the Dane;

ACCOMPANIED BY

THE FRENCH TEXT:

WITH

AN INTRODUCTION, NOTES, AND A GLOSSARY,

BY FREDERICK MADDEN, ESQ.

F. A. S. F. R. S. L.

SUB-KEEPER OF THE MSS. IN THE BRITISH MUSEUM.

PRINTED FOR THE

# Roxburghe Club.

LONDON.

W. NICOL, SHAKSPEARE PRESS, MDCCCXXVIII.

*Title page of the 1828 translation of* Havelok.

giant, bold, courteous, free, fair, and "god of manere." All the folk love him (42-44). The king, from a desire to disinherit Argill and because of a "chere" which he has seen her make to Coraunt, arrays them simply and weds them, although many are wroth (45-48). For a while they dwell at court in poor degree. Argill has shame and sorrow. She asks her master about his father, kin and friends. She says she would rather lead a poor life without shame than be a queen with shame (49-54). They go to Grymesby "al by his wyves red" (55). They find Grym and his wife dead (56). They find Aunger, Grym's cousin, whom Grym and his wife had told about Havelok (57-59). They[3] tell Havelok who he is and advise him to go to his own country to see what grace he may find among his friends. They will arrange for the shipping (60-62). Aunger ships them and they sail for Denmark (63-64). He finds there "sire Sykar," who had been high steward of his father's property (65-66) Sykar is glad of his coming and promises to help him recover his heritage from King Edulf (67-68). They assemble great folk of his relatives and friends (69). King Edulf gathers his power, but he and his army are overcome in the battle (70-71). Havelok conquers his heritage (72). He prepares great power to go to England to win his wife's kingdom (73-74). The king of Lyndeseye hears that he has come on the coast and gathers a great host (75-76). Edelsy is beaten in the battle and by treaty gives Argill (here called Argentille) her heritage (77-78). As she is next of blood he gives her Lyndeseye after his day and makes her his heir (79-80). At the last both Northfolk and Lyndeseye fall into the hands of Havelok (81-82).

It is obvious that both the names and the incidents in the Lambeth Interpolation are closer to the French versions of the romance than to the English. Grim and Havelok are the only names common to this and to both the English and the French versions. The names in the Interpolation, however, agree very well with those in Gaimar. Thus Gounter corresponds with Gunter, Gatfere with Gaifer, Seburc with Saburc, Edelsy with Edelsi, Orewayn with Orwain, Edelbright with Adelbrict, Aunger with Alger, Sykar with Sigar, and Edulf with Edulf. Argill appears once as Argentille, the form used by Gaimar. It will be seen too that when the names in the French versions vary, the Interpolation is closer to Gaimar than to the Lay, which has the forms Alsi, Ekenbright and Hodulf, while Gaifer and Alger are not found in the Lay. The names therefore show that the Interpolation cannot be derived from the English romance and that it is closer to Gaimar than to the Lay.

The most noteworthy thing discovered by a comparison of incidents is the omission in the Interpolation of everything supernatural or extravagantly fictitious. There is no flame from Havelok's mouth, no dream, no throwing of stones from the church tower, no magic horn, no setting up of bodies on stakes to represent living men, all of which incidents are found in the French versions

and the flame also in the English. Otherwise the incidents in the Interpolation agree fairly well with those which are common to Gaimar and the Lay as opposed to the English romance. Thus there is an invasion of Denmark on account of a tribute dating back to the time of Arthur. Gunter is killed, and the queen, who does not appear in the English romance, flees with Havelok. There is an attack by pirates in which the queen is killed. Instead of a king over all England and a usurping earl, as in the English version, there are two kings, one ruling over Lincoln and the other over Norfolk. Havelok is called Coraunt (Cuaran), a name which does not occur in the English romance. Havelok returns to Grimsby by his wife's advice. He does not know who he is, until told by Grim's relative. Edelsi submits after fighting and gives Argentille her heritage. In addition to the omissions noted above, the Interpolation says nothing about Grim's being a fisherman and salt merchant in Grimsby, about Cuaran's being a juggler or fool at the court, about the attack on Havelok and his bride by the six youths, nor about Havelok's fear when led into the hall before Sigar. None of these omissions need cause any surprise. It was almost inevitable that the more extraordinary incidents should be cut down by a matter-of-fact writer, such as this interpolator seems to have been, while the other omissions resulted naturally from the attempt to condense. When these allowances are made, it is evident that the general outline of the story is the same in Gaimar, the Lay and the Interpolation.

A more detailed examination reveals the following points in which the Interpolation is closer to Gaimar than to the Lay: (1) The invasion of Denmark is for tribute which had been withheld (Lamb. 2-4, Gaimar 410-411).[4] In the Lay it is to demand tribute (lines 27-30). (2) Grim in both appears as a mariner, whereas in the Lay he is a baron (Lamb. 14, Gaimar 423, Lay 57). (3) Edulf is defeated in a general battle and not as in the Lay in a single combat (Lamb. 70-72, Gaimar 739-742, Lay 940-970). In all three cases the agreement between Gaimar and the Interpolation seems to point to an earlier form of the story than that contained in the Lay. Grim certainly has no right to be a baron. That this is a modification made by the rather late writer of the Lay is almost self-evident, but is made certain by the slip in line 135 of the Lay where we are told that Grim, when he reached Grimsby, went fishing "as he was accustomed to do."[5] The writer forgot that he had transformed the fisherman or sailor into a baron. The change is due to the fact that the Lay has throughout a more courtly and knightly tone, approaching the form of fiction in vogue during the thirteenth century. The Interpolation, on the other hand, is simpler, and in this respect resembles Gaimar, both these versions preserving what must have been the spirit of the original.

Additional evidence for the close relationship between Gaimar and the Interpolation is furnished by the agreement in geographical details. In both, for instance, Edelsi's kingdom extends from the Humber to Rutland,[6] and Adelbrict's from Colchester to Holland.[7] For the first of these pairs the Lay has Rutland and Stanford, while the second is replaced by "vers les Surois," Surrey being probably intended.[8]

So far nothing has been presented to disprove Madden's assertion that the Lambeth Interpolation was derived from Gaimar. In fact the evidence has all pointed that way. But there are differences between the two which must not be overlooked or ignored. Most prominent perhaps is the fact that the order in which the events are related is not the same. Gaimar's narrative opens in England. There is no direct relation of the early events in Denmark and at Grimsby, these being recapitulated very briefly by Kelloc and others.[9] The allusions to the early part of the story are so scattered and incoherent that they give the impression that they are echoes of a more complete original which Gaimar modified for the sake of condensation or, perhaps, to secure a sort of epic unity by plunging *in medias res*. The Interpolation, on the other hand, opens in Denmark and the early parts of the story are related in consecutive order. This order might be made up from the allusions in Gaimar, but that would require more skill and pains than could be expected in a scribe, even though he were clever enough to be an interpolator. The natural thing for a man of his capacity to do is to follow the order of events in his original. This alone would not prove that the Interpolation had a different original from Gaimar, but it raises a question which must be met. The matter is made the more noteworthy from the fact that the order of events is exactly the same in the Interpolation and in the Lay. For this to be accidental is possible but not very likely. Other matters being left out of consideration, it would be reasonable in such a case to suppose some sort of relation between the Interpolation and the Lay independent of Gaimar.

This relationship between the Interpolation and the Lay is made the more evident by certain details which the two have in common, but which are not found in Gaimar, such as the following: (1) Gunter's enemies plan shame for his relatives (Lamb. 9, Lay 79-82). (2) Edelsi, instead of being called merely "Breton," as in Gaimar (line 61), is said to be "of Breton kynde" (Lamb. 31) or "Bret par lignage" (Lay 200). (3) In Gaimar Edelsi forces Cuaran and Argentille to lie together without a formal marriage (lines 167-176), while in the other versions there is a marriage (Lamb. 47, Lay 377-380). (4) The Interpolation says that he brings about the marriage, though many are wroth, which seems to correspond with the account given in the Lay of the anger of the barons at the king's violation of his oath (Lamb. 48, Lay 279-376). (5) In Gaimar there is no description whatever of Havelok's departure from Grimsby for Lincoln and the only allusion to it is the statement of Havelok to Kelloc that he departed from Grimsby when Grim was dead

(line 371). In both the Interpolation and the Lay Grim is alive when Havelok departs, and dead when he returns with his bride (Lamb. 27, 56; Lay 157-192, 565). (6) Gaimar introduces the fight rather abruptly after Havelok's return to England (line 767). The Interpolation and the Lay mention the gathering of a host by Edelsi (Lamb. 75-76, Lay 1007-1026). It is difficult to imagine that all these resemblances are accidental. The first two and the last might be so, but the others seem to point to details in a source common to both the Interpolation and the Lay. This common source cannot be Gaimar, because in these points Gaimar differs. Moreover, in all three points Gaimar, rather than the other versions, seems to show a change from what must have been the original form of the story. It seems reasonable to suppose that there was a marriage, that Argentille's friends should become angry at her disgrace and the seizing of the kingdom by a usurper, and that there should be some more definite statement about Havelok's departure from Grimsby. The number of important details common to the Interpolation and the Lay and the exact agreement in the order of the narrative establish a close relationship between the two and a common source independent of Gaimar. It becomes evident, therefore, that the traditional view, hitherto held without question, that the Interpolation is "copied" from Gaimar, must from now on be rejected.

In looking for the source of the Lambeth Interpolation it may be well to set aside at the outset any notion that it may be derived from a combination of two or more versions. Such a combination would of course explain anything except itself. An interpolating scribe, for the sake of inserting into a chronicle an episode of less than a hundred lines, is not likely to take the trouble to compare varying versions of a romance, perhaps in more than one language, and to make out of them a consistent whole. It was hard enough in those days for the most skilful writer of chronicles or romances to make such a combination without revealing the artifice by a botch or confusion.[10] The Lambeth Interpolation tells a straightforward, consistent story, and any lack of clearness is due to nothing more than the extreme condensation. There is every reason to believe that it had a single source.

It has already been shown that this source of the Interpolation could not have been either Gaimar or the Lay. The source, however, must have been closely related to both Gaimar and the Lay, and the probabilities are all in favor of its having been in French. There is evidence for this in the fact that Havelok is called "quistron" instead of scullion. Though it is now lost there must have existed at some time a French version of the romance distinct from Gaimar and the Lay. That such a version did exist and was the common source of both Gaimar and the Lay has been effectively proved by Kupferschmidt.[11] As the Lambeth Interpolation cannot be derived directly or indirectly from Gaimar or the Lay, about the only possible arrangement that remains is to derive it from this lost French version. This explains all the points which the Interpolation has in common with both Gaimar and the Lay. It accounts for those points in which the Interpolation agrees with one of the French versions in opposition to the other, in which case an agreement with either Gaimar or the Lay would establish the form of the romance taken in any incident by the lost French original. This arrangement further makes possible the preservation in the Interpolation of elements lacking in both Gaimar and the Lay, but which may have existed in the lost French version, or even in still earlier forms of the romance. Inasmuch as this arrangement clears up old difficulties and presents no new ones, it may be regarded as settled that the Interpolation goes back to the lost French version which was also the source of Gaimar and the Lay.

So far the Lambeth Interpolation has been examined in its relation with the French versions of *Havelok*. It has, however, one or more incidents in common with the English romance, while in other details it differs from all other extant forms of the story. The most striking point in common with the English romance in opposition to the French is the reason assigned for Havelok's leaving Grimsby and going to Lincoln. It will be remembered that Gaimar passes over this portion of the story and merely makes Havelok say that he left home when Grim was dead (line 371). In the Lay, Grim, believing that the boy would still regain his heritage, tells Havelok to go to the court in order to hear instruction and learn sense (lines 157-187). This sounds very much like the custom common in the romances of chivalry of sending a youth to court to learn knightly accomplishments. The Lambeth Interpolation, however, gives a different reason. It says that Havelok was brought up by Grim and his wife as their own child

Til he was mykel & mighti, and man of mykel cost,
That for his grete sustinaunce, nedly serue he most.

Lambeth, 25-26.

The next line says he took his leave and went to the court. The passage is not in itself very clear, but it certainly seems to mean that he became large and strong, that it required so much to sustain him that he must work for his living and that on this account he left Grim. The interpolator did not find any suggestion of this in Gaimar or the Lay. The incident, however, corresponds remarkably with the English version. The English writer makes constant reference to Havelok's great appetite. The boy thinks he eats too much and determines to go to work (lines 788-810). When the famine arises so that Grim does not have enough to eat for himself and his family, he advises Havelok to go to Lincoln and find work (824-852). As it is extremely improbable that the interpolator had more than one source, and as it is likewise improbable that this agreement with the English romance is accidental, it seems to be clear that this must have been an element of the story in an early form, and its preservation in the Interpolation shows that it was also found in the lost French version. Gaimar omitted it in his condensation, the Lay changed it in giving the romance its courtly tone, while the English version and the Interpolation have preserved the original.[12] It is also to be noted that in several details in which the Interpolation agrees with one of the French versions in opposition to the other, it agrees also with the English romance. Such are the humble position of Grim and the defeat of the Danish usurper in general battle, common to Gaimar, the English romance and Lambeth; and the marriage of Havelok, the finding of Grim dead, and the calling out of the host, common to the Lay, the English romance and Lambeth. This agreement with the English makes all the more positive the derivation of the Lambeth Interpolation from the common source of Gaimar and the Lay which was evident from a comparison of the French versions. Incidentally it shows the difficulties in the way of any attempt to derive the English romance from either of the extant French versions.

There are several details in which the Lambeth Interpolation is unique. (1) Gunter, Havelok's father, is identified with the Guthrun or Gormo who fought against Alfred in the ninth century, the only allusion to Arthur being the statement that the invasion of Denmark was to collect tribute which he had formerly taken. It is not safe to make much of this for the story is interpolated at this point in the chronicle merely because Langtoft, by confusion of names perhaps, called Gunter the father of Havelok. An interesting question is involved as to the historical basis of the Havelok legend, which, however, need not be discussed here. (2) When the Danish king is killed, his queen escapes to the sea with Havelok and meets Grim on the shore (lines 12-16). There is reason for believing this to be a feature going back to the original form of the story. There is nothing in Gaimar's condensed account of the early Danish events to contradict the assumption. The Lay makes an unquestionable modification here in that it calls Grim a baron, and has the queen and child entrusted to him in a castle (lines 53-68). The English version, too, shows an entire modification of the early Danish events in order to carry out an extended duplication of the English part of the story.[13] Thus in both England and Denmark the king knows he is going to die, he summons his barons, and he entrusts his kingdom and infant heir to an earl who takes an oath and afterwards usurps the kingdom. Of the two series of events that in England must have been the original because it is also found in the French Lay. There is, therefore, little or nothing in the English romance to show what its original had to say about the early Danish part of the story. (3) The Lambeth Interpolation states definitely that Havelok was brought up by Grim and his wife as their own child and regarded himself as such (lines 23-24). This is implied in both Gaimar and the Lay, in both of which Havelok does not know who he is until told by Grim's relatives. In the English romance Havelok is apparently at all times conscious of his position, though it may be hard to reconcile this with his inaction and indifference. In this the Lambeth version seems to represent best the original form of the story. (4) The king is influenced in marrying Argentille by a "chere" which he has seen her make to Coraunt (line 46). This touch is probably an addition on the part of the scribe. (5) Edelsi, after his defeat, voluntarily makes Argentille heir to Lyndeseye (lines 79-80). These details, some of them significant, add to the importance of the Lambeth version in the discussion of *Havelok*, for it must be borne in mind that it is possible for this brief analysis of the story, interpolated in a late manuscript of a chronicle, to preserve elements belonging to the original legend.

This agreement with the English romance in certain details and the preservation in others of traces of a lost original make all the more conclusive the observation that the Lambeth Interpolation is derived from a form of the story earlier than Gaimar or the Lay, for in no other way could these incidents have come down to the interpolating scribe. That this early form of the story was identical with the lost source of Gaimar and the Lay has already been shown. The present investigation, therefore, may be regarded as giving the Lambeth Interpolation, for the first time, its proper place in the development of the romance.

Of the more general results obtained by the investigation the most noteworthy is the additional light thrown on the lost French version in octosyllabic rimed couplets,—the common source of Gaimar and the Lay. With merely Gaimar and the Lay to work with,[14] it is not always possible to determine accurately what form of any particular incident was taken by this lost version. It is frequently evident, where the two differ, that one of the extant French versions represents the original better than the other, but to a certain extent this is inference and not proof. A third version, however, such as the Lambeth Interpolation has been shown to be, furnishes an invaluable check. Any incident common to any two of the three versions, Gaimar, the Lay and the Interpolation, may now be regarded with almost certainty as belonging to the lost French romance. It is possible, therefore, to reconstruct with considerable accuracy the form of the story that served as a source for these three writers.

With the existence established of this lost French form of the romance, the question may be asked, Was it not also the source of the English *Havelok*? It was certainly more likely to be so than either Gaimar or the Lay, and its existence is a strong opposing argument to

any attempt to derive the English romance in whole or in part from the extant French versions.[15] But it seems extremely improbable that this lost French version could have been the source of the English. For this there are numerous and significant reasons, among which may be mentioned the complete dissimilarity of names, the fact that the English has no mention whatever of Arthur, the great variation in even the more important incidents, the difference in tone, the fact that the English appears to be closer to tradition, and the lack of convincing evidence to show that the English is a translation from the French. Against these arguments can be alleged the general presumption that every Middle English romance was translated from the French, a presumption which does not hold for *Horn*[16] and which lacks proof in the case of *Havelok*. It seems likely, therefore, that the lost French version and the English romance both go back to an earlier source or sources. Into the question, however, of the original form of the story, it is not the function of the present investigation to go. Before plunging into theory it is well to make sure of what firm ground is within reach. In confirming the existence of the lost French version of *Havelok* and in determining the probable form of its story, one step, at least, seems to have been taken in the direction of explaining the development of the romance. Toward this step the hitherto neglected Lambeth Interpolation has rendered material aid.

*Notes*

The present paper has grown out of a report made by the writer to the course on Early English Metrical Romances, given at Harvard University in the spring of 1899 by Professor George Lyman Kittredge, to whom thanks are due for valuable suggestions and advice.

[1] The Lambeth version, frequently referred to as the Interpolation, is printed by Madden in his edition of *Havelok* for the Roxburghe Club, London, 1828, pp. xvii-xix, and again by Skeat in his reprint for the Early English Text Society, London, 1868, pp. xi-xiii. In neither case are the lines numbered, but the passage is so short that the references to lines need cause no trouble. A description of the rather interesting variations in the allusions to Havelok contained in Langtoft and Mannyng will be found in Madden, pp. xi-xix, and in Skeat, pp. v, ix-xiii. See also H. L. D. Ward, *Catalogue of Romances*, Vol. I, London, 1883, pp. 442-443.

[2] Max Kupferschmidt: "Die Haveloksage bei Gaimar und ihr Verhältniss zum Lai d'Havelok," in Böhmer's *Romanische Studien*, Vol. IV, pp. 411-430 (1880). On page 430, he says: "Dass die Interpolation in der Lambeth copy der Uebersetzung von Peter von Langtofts Chronik durch Robert of Brunne aus Gaimars Darstellung der Haveloksage geschöpft ist, hat schon Sir Fr. Madden gezeigt."

[3] There is a slight confusion here, there being no antecedent for the pronoun "they." A comparison with the other versions shows that Aunger and his wife are probably meant.

[4] References to the French versions of *Havelok* are to the edition of Gaimar in the Rolls Series, London, 1888.

[5] "Pescher aloit si com il soloit."—Lay, 135.

[6] Lamb. 30, Gaimar 51.

[7] Lamb. 34, Gaimar 75.

[8] Lay 198, 201.

[9] Gaimar 359-454, 575-628. Lines 505-528 are related by the author, but merely as an incidental explanation.

[10] An example of such confusion occurs in the abridgment of *Havelok* in Thomas Gray's *Scala Cronica*, the passage being reprinted in Madden, pp. xxxiv-xxxv. Gray failed to recognize that Havelok and Cuaran were the same person.

[11] Kupferschmidt's investigation, already referred to, must be regarded as settling the fact that Gaimar and the Lay had a common source written in French octosyllabic rimed couplets. Ward appears not to have read Kupferschmidt. His attempt to derive the Lay directly from Gaimar cannot be accepted. Every one of his six arguments can be used with equal force in favor of a common source for Gaimar and the Lay. Ward, *Catalogue of Romances*, Vol. 1, 437-440. With the exception of Madden, who thought Gaimar had merely abridged the Lay, and of Ward, practically every investigator has concluded that the two extant French versions had a common source. The early writers assumed this to have been a "Breton lay;" but the later ones have realized that this source must have been a lost French version.

It would be very hard to defend the possibility that the lost French version was derived from Gaimar, and became in turn the source of both the Lay and the Interpolation. There are too many points in which the Lay and the Interpolation, one or both, point back to a form of the story earlier than Gaimar. Kupferschmidt has mentioned some of these and might have added the narration of the early events in Denmark and Grimsby, the marriage of Cuaran and Argentille, and the opposition thereto, and Havelok's finding Grim and his wife dead when he returns with his bride. Gaimar constantly gives the impression of having been condensed from an original, and in one instance at least this seems to have resulted in confusion. Sigar, in reassuring Havelok the morning after the attack by the six youths, says:

Kore vus aim plus ke ne fis hier
Quant vus asis a mon manger.
                                        Gaimar, 669-670.

"I love you now more than I did yesterday when I placed you at my table." But Gaimar makes no mention whatever of Sigar's placing Havelok at his table the preceding day and the allusion cannot well be explained unless it is assumed that Gaimar had an original in which there was some such mention. The Lay (lines 675-694) does tell about the entertainment of Havelok at dinner on the preceding day, an incident also found in the English romance (lines 1660-1745). This is additional evidence for the lost original of Gaimar and the Lay, and for a relationship between this lost version and the English romance.

Dr. W. H. Schofield suggests that the probable date of this lost version seems to be established by the references to Arthur in Gaimar, the Lay and the Interpolation. In each case the reference stands in connection with an invasion of Denmark to demand or collect tribute. This must have been in the lost version, which therefore could not have been written before Geoffrey of Monmouth's history, and which must have been written before Gaimar. This leaves 1136 and 1150 as the outside dates, with the probabilities in favor of a middle point, somewhere between 1140 and 1145. This mention of Arthur furnishes new evidence for the immediate popularity of Geoffrey.

[12] There are also two minor points in which the Interpolation agrees with the English romance. (1) It is said in the Interpolation that while Havelok is at the court all the folk love him (line 44). The English writer says that knights, children, young and old, all love him (lines 955-958). (2) According to the Lambeth version Edelsi hears that Havelok has come to the coast (line 75). In the English, Godrich hears that Havelok has come into England (lines 2531-2547). In the French versions nothing is said about the usurper's hearing of the return of Havelok before he sends his defiance.

[13] This duplication of events was suggested by G. Wittenbrink, in a dissertation, *Zur Kritik und Rhythmik des altenglischen Lais von Havelok dem Dänem*, Burgsteinfurt, 1891, p. 5.

[14] As Kupferschmidt has suggested, additional light may be thrown on the lost version, by the Havelok episode in the *Brute*, but in view of the possible contamination with the English version, indicated by the name Birkabeyn, it is not here considered.

[15] The tradition that the English version is derived from the Lay goes back to Madden, but even Madden seems to admit the possibility that an earlier form of the story was used as a source by both the Lay and the English romance.—Madden, p. viii. Ward (*Catalogue of Ro-*

*mances*, p. 440) says the English romance represents a popular development of the legend, but that its writer must have been acquainted with the Lay. This last statement is made necessary by Ward's unsatisfactory attempt to prove that the Lay is nothing but an expansion of Gaimar. See also ten Brink, *History of English Literature, to Wyclif*, translated by Kennedy, New York, 1883, pp. 150, 181, 232-234; Kupferschmidt, *Romanische Studien*, Vol. IV, 430; Gaston Paris, *Romania*, IX, 480; Körting, *Grundriss der Geschichte der Eng. Lit.*, 2nd edition, pp. 98-99; Wohlfeil, *The Lay of Havelok the Dane*, a dissertation, Leipsic, 1890, p. 12.

[16] Child, *Ballads*, Vol. I, 187; Ward, *Catalogue of Romances*, Vol. I, pp. 447-467.

## Harald E. Heyman (essay date 1903)

SOURCE: "Historical Allusions," *Studies on the "Havelok-Tale,"* Upsala, 1903, pp. 64-91.

[*In the following excerpt, Heyman attempts to trace many historical allusions in* Havelok the Dane *to their sources.*]

After his short analysis of the English Romance ten Brink says: "Im Havelok haben wir festen geographischen Boden unter uns;[1] doch fehlt auch hier die Brücke, die von den Personen und Ereignissen der Fabel zur Geschichte oder zur älterer Volkssage hinüberführte—zum wenigsten fehlt eine Brücke, die wir uns ohne Gefahr anvertrauen könnten."[2]

This is true not only of this English version of the tale but of all the versions.

The question of the basis of the folk-traditions, on which the Havelok-tale is built up, is one which is rendered rather difficult, partly on account of the late records extant, and partly because none of the versions are of a very original character.—The interpretation of the various versions, and—as far as historical and pseudo-historical elements go—the endeavour to trace the statements of the legend to historical facts, are both impeded by the vagueness of the allusions. These latter, moreover, differ widely in the various versions, as we have seen from the analyses given.

The variations are, however, not so great as to throw the least doubt on the identity of the tale in all the versions. The chief episodes and, above all, the leading idea, viz. Havelok's becoming king of Denmark and England or part of it reappear unmistakably in them all.—It is true that only two names, Havelok and Grim (cf. p. 16), are common to all the versions. The change of personal names in mediæval tales is, however, a common phenomenon. This variation may depend on the insertion of various episodes at various

times, when the tale was told or written down, or on the influence exercised by reminiscences from other tales known to the gleemen or others, who handed down the tradition.

The variety of the elements or motives, of which the Havelok-tale consists, has already (p. 13) been alluded to, and a classification of these motives ventured under the chief headings: "pseudo-historical" and purely "imaginative" or "fabulous". To the first class we assign Havelok-Cuaran[3] in his capacity as an exiled Danish prince, who reconquers Denmark and becomes king of that country and later also of all England, as in the English lay, or of only a part of it, as in the two Anglo-Norman versions and the Lambeth interpolation. This is the framework of the Havelok-tale, but at the same time the central idea of the whole story—the purpose of it, so to say.

All the other episodes are of secondary importance, and consist of renderings of more or less common legendary motives, frequent in mediæval tales. To the latter class of motives we count those of Havelok's marriage, of his being a kitchenboy, of the flame and the cross, of the horn, of the visions, etc.

The principles, on which the Havelok-tale is built up, are evidently the general ones on which popular tales with an historical basis are formed. Popular imagination is aroused either directly, by reality itself in the shape of some extraordinary person, event or deed, or by a tradition, based on this reality. Both have a lively effect upon the imagination, and are capable of inspiring the patriotic or poetical feelings of the tale-tellers or song-singers with enthusiasm. What is more natural under such circumstances and in a romantic period, than that the hero is credited with supernatural features, and has deeds ascribed to him, which he never committed, or adventures, in which he never took part?[4]

The question is: which historically known events form the basis of the Havelok-tale—or to which persons or events, stated by history really to have existed or to have taken place, may the pseudo-historical episodes of the tale be referred?

One point is self-evident from the beginning. The pseudo-historical and romanticized folk-traditions, that form the frame in which the legendary and fabulous adventures of the Havelok-tale are inserted, are in some way connected with Anglo-Danish relations.[5] From the reappearance in all the versions of the scene where the tale plays, the conclusion has been arrived at that the tradition was current among the Danes of the Danelaw (cf. p. 58 sqq.). The final form[6] in which we know the tale, as extant in the various versions, must, no doubt, be referred to the time in which the Danes were powerful in England.[7]

The whole story is, as it were, a song of praise to the honour of some Danish or, perhaps rather, Anglo-Danish hero, whose great exploit is the union of Denmark and England (or part of it) in the hands of one king.

If, consequently, the events of the last period of the Scandinavian invasion[8] may be presumed to have excercised a decisive influence on the development of the Anglo-Danish heroic legend of Havelok—for Havelok is in all the versions made king of Denmark—the *first* origin of the Havelok-Cuaran character seems with equal probability to date back to a still earlier period. Although there are sufficient reasons to justify the view expressed that the Havelok-tale is an *Anglo-Danish* legend, it will be seen that the hero himself is of *Norwegian (-Irish)* descent.

The time in which the traditions originated has above (p. 14) been assigned to the middle of the 10th century. This assertion involves that the Havelok-traditions developed in proportion as the political relations of the Scandinavians and the Anglo-Saxons developed from minor invasions to the ultimate Anglo-Danish union.[9]

It seems as if the hero of the Havelok-legend originally was connected not with this union, which is the greatest event in the beginning of the 11th century, but with an earlier conquest of the Danelaw by an originally Norwegian viking, who at different periods was king of Dublin and of parts of England.[10]

These two facts: that the Havelok-story brings us in connection with the Norwegian invaders, who came from Ireland in the middle of the 10th century, and that the same story expressly points to the time of the Anglo-Danish union, make it probable that a contamination of two traditions has taken place, or, perhaps rather, that the Havelok-story only by degrees developed into the form, which we have in the English lay.

There are especially three circumstances, from which evidence can be drawn in favour of this view. The chief reason, on which the assertion of Havelok's Norwegian origin may be based, is the occurence of the name Cuaran[11] in three of the four versions of the tale. As far as we know, this name is applied only to the historical *Olaf Cuaran* and to the poetical *Havelok Cuaran*.

The second reason to suppose that an Olaf was the prototype of Havelok is, that there is a kind of linguistic connection between the names Olaf and Havelok.[12]

The third reason to assume that the Havelok-tale was composed of elements from various historical periods, is connected with the extension of Havelok's kingdom in England. In the very same texts—the two Anglo-Norman versions and the Lambeth interpola-tion—in which Havelok is surnamed Cuaran, he is made king of but a part of England. Thus he represents an earlier stage of the Scandinavian invasion than the Havelok of the English lay (who is not called Cuaran) and is made king of all England, thus representing a decidedly later stage of the invasion, viz. the Anglo-Danish union.

The word *Cuaran* is of Irish origin (Irish cuarán) and signifies a shoe, a sock, a sandal, "a shoe fastened with thongs" (Todd), "a brogue of untanned leather or skin, commonly worn with the hairy side outwards" (Skeat).[13]

I have remarked above (p. 68) that, from a linguistic point of view, the name Havelok is connected with the name Olaf. This question has been touched on by several scholars,[14] but there are still some points that require an explanation.

The Northern hypothetical and original form is *AnulaitaR*.[15] In a period, when this word had been reduced to *AnlaitR*,[16] from which the later Óláfr is derived, it was borrowed by the Anglo-Saxons, who pronounced it *Anláf*, and by the Irish; in Irish it is recorded as *Amhlaibh, Amlaf* etc.[17] In the Welsh language the name *Abloyc (Abloec, Abloc)* occurs as an Irish loanword. Before the year 1000 all Irish spirants were reduced to one sound. It is uncertain whether the Welsh spelling 'c' became current in Wales through literature, or if the final Irish sound conveyed to Welsh ears a sound which was spelt 'c'. When the Normans adopted this word they either rendered it with the Welsh spelling, or heard a 'g'- or 'k'-sound which they spelt 'c'.— The 'm' of Amhlaibh was in Irish pronounced as a bilabial sound, which, having lost its nasal character, approached the sound of 'w', and was in the Welsh language spelt 'b'.[18] That the sound kept its bilabial character is evident from the Norman 'u' (v).—The Irish 'ai' was according to a Welsh sound-law rendered by 'oi', which later was reduced to 'o'. This gives us the Welsh *Abloc* and the Anglo-Norman *(H)av(e)lok*.

The name Havelok is consequently a normalized (and anglicized) Irish loanword in the Welsh language; the Irish word is, in its turn, an early Northern loanword, emanating from the some source as Olaf.

In the Icelandic sagas[19] *Oláfr kvaran* or *kuoran* occurs several times. I give a few instances.

*"Olaf Tryggvason's saga"* tells us of the Norwegian king, Olaf Tryggvason, that he married Gyda, who is usually represented as the sister of Olaf Cuaran, and only occasionally as his daughter.[20] The text runs as follows: "En þar fór um landit þingboð nokkut ok allir menn skyldu til þings koma; en er þing var sett, þá kom þar drótning ein, er Gyða var nefnd, systir Olafs kvárans, er konungr var a Irlandi í Dyflinni."[21]

Some chapters below: "Síðan fór þorir vester til Írlandz til Dyflinnar ok spurði þar til Ala; var hann þar med Oláfi konungi kváran, mági sinum."[22]

In the *"Landnámabók"* an Icelandic poet is said to have visited Olaf Cuaran in Dublin: "þorbjörn het maðr————; hans son var þorvarðr, er átti þórunni————; þeirra synir voru þeir þórarinn blindi ok þorgils orraskáld, er var med Oláfi kváran í Dyflinni."[23]

In the *"Gunnlaugssaga"* Cuaran is alluded to in the following way: "Nú siglir Gunnlaugr of Englandi norþr til Dyflinnar. Þá réþ þar fyrir Sigtryggr konungr, son Oláfs kvárans ok Kormlaþar dróttningar."[24]

In the English records I have found the famous Anlaf mentioned once by the name of Cuaran in the form "Cwiran", viz. in the *Anglo-Saxon Chronicle* in the entry for the year 949: "Her com Anlaf Cwiran on Norðhymbraland."[25]

This entry is apparently copied by Gaimar in the *"Estorie des Engles"*:

"Quant il[26] regnout el secund an
Idunckes vint Anlas Quiran"

(ll. 3549 sq.).[27]

Olaf Cuaran is mentioned by his Irish name in the Irish chronicle *"Chronicon Scotorum"* in the entry for the year 968. The translation of this text runs: "Cennanus was plundered by Amhlaib Cuaran————."[28]

The name is said to occur in the *"Ulster Annals"* under the years 944 and 946, and further in the *"Four Masters"*.[29]

In the two Welsh chronicles, which I have quoted, the name Abloyc, Abloec occurs as follows:—

In the *"Annales Cambriæ"* the death of Olaf Cuaran's cousin, Olaf Godfreyson,[30] is recorded in the entry for the year 942: "Abloyc rex moritur".[31]

In the *"Brut y Tywysogion"* (The Chronicle of the princes) the death of this king is mentioned in the entry for the year 940: "Nine hundred and forty was the year of Christ, when king Abloyc died."[32]

In the following entries Olaf Cuaran himself is concerned. Under 959: "And the sons of Abloec devastate Caer Gybi and Lleyn."[33]

Under 988: "And then Glumaen, son of Abloec, was killed."[34]

Under 1013: "And than Brian, king of all Ireland————————and many other kings were stirred up against Dublin, where Sitruc, son of Abloec, was king."[35]

With few and unimportant exceptions the dates referring to Cuaran (either called Oláfr kváran as in the Icelandic sagas, or Anlaf Cwiran as in the A. S. Chronicle and the Estorie des Engles, or An(a)laphus, Onlaf etc. as in the latin chronicles, or Amhlaibh Cuaran as in the Irish chronicles, or Abloyc, Abloec, as in the Welsh chronicles) coincide in almost all the records extant.

It seems advisable to give a short sketch of Olaf Cuaran's adventurous life and to note the most important events of it. No doubt he was one of the most famous vikings who warred in Ireland and England in the middle of the 10th century. It seems fairly possible that his life, so full of vicissitudes, should be remembered and glorified in the tales and romances of later times.

Olaf Cuarans father was *Sitric*,[36] who two years before his death was married to a sister of Athelstan.[37] He was king of Dublin and Northumberland, and died in 927.[38] His brother, *Godfrey*, passed over to Northumberland in order to secure his succession to the throne.[39] Already at this time Olaf Cuaran seems to have made efforts to the same effect, but both men were expelled by Aethelstan.[40] Godfrey returned to Dublin, and Olaf Cuaran went to Scotland, where Constantin III was king.[41] Cuaran married his daughter.[42] In 934 Aethelstan ravaged Scotland.[43] Godfrey died in Dublin in the same year, and his son, *Olaf Godfreyson*, succeeded to the throne in Dublin.[44] Both cousins, Olaf Godfreyson and Olaf Cuaran, the latter aided by Constantin, his father-in-law, made great efforts to reconquer Northumberland from Aethelstan. Olaf Cuaran entered into an alliance with several Scandinvian chieftains, and Olaf Godfreyson came from Dublin with reinforcements.[45] In 937 Olaf Cuaran sailed with a large fleet up the Humber and conquered York.[46] Soon after followed the famous battle of Brunnanburgh.[47] It will be enough to say that the Scandinavians, as is well known, were entirely defeated; Olaf Cuaran, who fled from the country, seems to have taken part in ravages in Ireland during the following years.[48] When in 940 Aethelstan died, and was succeeded by Edmund, Olaf Cuaran returned to York from Dublin.[49] The Northumbrians made him king, and great numbers of the Scandinavian settlers joined him. According to a treaty between Edmund and Olaf Cuaran, the latter was to rule the country north of Watlingastræt, and Edmund the country south of this boundary.[50] In the same year, 943, Olaf Cuaran was baptized.[51] Olaf Godfreyson, who had also taken part in this expedition, had been killed one or two years before this time (cf. the quotations above, p. 73). His brother *Ragnvald*, who is recorded as joint king north of Watlingastræt, was baptized too.[52] The peace was, however, of short duration, for in 944 king Edmund expelled the two kings.[53] According to the Irish annalists Olaf Cuaran returned to Dublin, and warred there.[54]

In 946 Edmund died and Edred became king of the Anglo-Saxons. In the Northern Scandinavian territories one Erik had in the mean-time been made king of York.[55] In 949 Olaf Cuaran once more appeared as claimant of the Northumbrian throne, and was supported by the Scots and his Dubliners.[56] (Cf. above the entries of the A. S. Chr. and the Estorie des Engles, referring to Anlaf Cwiran). He conquered the whole of Bernicia, but, having been expelled a few years later, he again returned to Dublin,[57] and in 953 he is again recorded as king of Dublin and as leader of ravaging expeditions in Ireland.[58] His last great attempt was the battle at Tara in 980.[59] Having lost this battle he went on a pilgrimage to Iona, where he died in 981.[60]

From this brief outline of Olaf Cuaran's life, compared with the account given of the Havelok-tale, it is evident that there is no *close* connection between his history and the saga. There are in the Havelok-Cuaran story no details, with exception of the names Cuaran and Havelok, that suggest any striking resemblances between this saga and Cuaran's history.

Gaimar offers a few details from which the conclusion may be drawn, that some of his authorities identified the historical with the poetical hero, to a certain extent at least.

Following the fashion of the time in which he wrote, and influenced by Geoffrey of Monmouth, whose "Historia Regum Britanniæ" he was one of the first to translate in the first, now lost, part of his work, the "Estorie des Bretuns",[61] Gaimar connects the Havelok-tale with the Arthurian cycle. In line 41 he quotes Gildas:

> "Si co est veir ke Gilde dist
> En la geste, trova escrit
> Ke dous reis out ja en Bretaigne
> Quant *Costentin* estait chevetaigne;
> Cil Costentin li nies Arthur,
> Ki out lespee Caliburc"
>
> (ll. 41 sqq.)[62]

Constantin occurs in Geoffrey of Monmouth's "Historia" as Arthur's successor,[63] and in the "Epistola Gildæ."[64] But as in the latter of these works there is not the least mention of any other of the persons concerned in the Havelok-tale, we may assume that Gaimar's reference to the "geste" of Gildas goes back to some work of his, now lost to us.[65]

Though the name Constantin is here taken from the "Historia Regum Britanniæ"[66] or from Gildas, it certainly brings King Constantin of Scotland to our minds (cf. above p. 75). The remarks made by Ward seem to draw the only conclusion that is possible from this coincidence. If Gaimar found right at the beginning of the version of the Havelok-tale, to which he owes the interpolation in the "Estorie", a reference to a

King Constantin, this might perhaps have referred to Olaf Cuarans father-in-law, though "Gaimar, with his head full of the Brut, would naturally understand it to mean the Constantine who succeeded king Arthur".[67] Gaimar never mentions the Scotch king, and seems to be ignorant of the part he played in Olaf Cuaran's history. This helps to prove that it was perfectly natural for Gaimar to think of the Constantin that Monmouth or Gildas suggested to him, and by connecting the Havelok-tale with this king, to transfer it to the sixth century.

This combination of Gaimar's proves, consequently, that he was ignorant of the connection between Olaf Cuaran and Havelok, which was suggested to some of his authorities by the identity of the nicknames. For there is in the "Estorie des Engles" another point of departure from which the conclusion may be drawn that there existed among the authorities, from which Gaimar compiled his work,[68] some one, to whom the relation between Olaf Cuaran and Havelok Cuaran was not quite unknown. Many passages of the "Estorie des Engles" correspond closely with the Anglo-Saxon Chronicle.[69] When Gaimar reaches the year 871 his narrative of the battle of Ash-down closely follows the words of the Chronicle: "þær wearð *Sidroc* eorl ofslæзen se ealda & *Sidroc* sезeonзa".[70] The corresponding passage of the "Estorie" runs as follows:

> "*Sydroc* le veil ki ferir sout
> E od lui le iouene *Sydroc*
> *Ki fu parent le rei Hevelok*"
>
> (ll. 2986 sqq.).[71]

We have seen above that Olaf Cuaran's father was named Sitric, and this was also the name of one of his sons.[72] It seems utterly improbable that the older Sydroc here stands for Olaf Cuaran's father, and it *is* absolutely impossible that his son can be meant. The fact remains, nevertheless, that Havelok is connected with a name which was common in Olaf Cuaran's family, and it is evident that the chroniclers had formed a notion of a kind of connection between the two heroes. This notion must however have been very vague. For when Gaimar reaches the year 949, and inserts in his "Estorie" the name Cwiran, given by the A. S. Chronicle, he omits to make references of any kind to his former entry.[73]

According to Storm's opinion the etymological connection between the names Olaf and Havelok is sufficient proof for the *identity* of the two heroes. He adds: The true history of Olave Cuaran in England cannot but confirm these conclusions".[14]

It seems, however, as if the relation of the two names, and the attaching of the name Cuaran to both, do not justify more than the conclusion that there was a certain, limited connection between the two heroes. At all events a comparison between Olaf Cuaran's history and the pseudo-historical elements of the Havelok-tale does not prove their identity.

It is true that the name Havelok is nothing but a normanized form of the Welsh Abloyc, and that the nickname is attached to both Olaf and Havelok. But this proves nothing else than that Olaf Cuaran must have enjoyed a great popularity among the population of the northern Scandinavian provinces of England. His name must have been exceedingly well fitted for that of a hero in a Scandinavian legend, who acts against the native Anglo-Saxon population. The historical folk-traditions that were current in these provinces were likely to concentrate round a name so famous as that of Olaf Cuaran, even although, as is decidedly the case with the Havelok-traditions, these were inspired chiefly by the events of later times. The two Anglo-Norman versions and, following them, the Lambeth interpolation, are the versions which should reflect most closely the episodes in Olaf Cuaran's history. In these versions Havelok is made king of only the Danelaw, and it is a fact that Olaf Cuaran was no more than that. But also in these versions Havelok is made king of Denmark. In order to find a parallel to this fact in Olaf Cuáran's history, it would be necessary to assume that those who handed down the tradition so radically altered it as to change a *Norwegian king in Ireland* into a *Danish king of Denmark*—which is very improbable.

An identification of Olaf Cuaran and Havelok is by no means justified by the fact that Olaf Cuaran succeeded in making himself king of the Danelaw, nor by the single striking resemblance that lies in the identity of the nicknames. We believe that Olaf Cuaran's name, that was connected with so many fights between the Scandinavians and the Anglo-Saxons, became the one to which the deeds of a later Scandinavian hero were attached. Olaf Cuaran's exploits may have been the foundation of a series of traditions which were absorbed in the Havelok-traditions. His deeds were, however, forgotten in the important events that took place in the last decade of the 10th and in the beginning of the 11th century. These have played a much greater part in the formation of the Havelok-traditions than the events of the middle of the 10th century. The latter were forgotten, but the famous name of Olaf Cuaran remained. It seems, consequently, as if the supposed identity of the two heroes, the historical and the poetical, might be reduced to an *identity of names*.

Not only traditions which were connected with the history of Olaf Cuaran have in the course of time been confused with the Havelok-saga. Those who handed down the Havelok-traditions confounded them also with other pseudo-historical elements.—Gaimar, the Lai d'Haveloc and the Lambeth interpolation all make Havelok the son of the Danish king Gunter. This name cannot have been taken from Geoffrey of

Monmouth, in whose "Historia" no Danish king of this name occurs.[75] Gunter is connected with Arthur, who goes to his land and conquers it, and this would, as we have seen above (p. 78), transfer the Havelok-tale to the sixth century. The whole of this passage is of course due to confusion on the part of the chroniclers. It will be seen, that the occurrence of Gunter in the Havelok-tale is to be ascribed to a similar tradition as that which Gaimar follows in his "Estorie", when he connects Havelok with the Sitric who fought in the battle of Ashdown.

When *Pierre de Langtoft* in his "Chronicle" reaches the year 871, and treats of the fights of King Alfred with the Danish invader, *Guthrum*, he says:

> "Tant cum vers le north Alfred est allez,
> *Gountere le pere Havelok de Danays ray*
>    *clamex*
> Of grant chuvalerye est Engleterre entrez
> Destrut ad les viles et arses les citez."[76]

*Robert Manning of Brunne* following Langtoft, translates the line in question thus:

> "Havelok fader he was, Gunter was his
>    name."[77]

This Gountere or Gunter of the quoted texts is easily recognized as the historical Danish invader and king of East Anglia, Guþrum (Goþrum, Goþorm, Guþram), who was baptized by King Alfred, and assumed the name of Aethelstan.[78] The northern name Guþorm was in England mixed up with Guþere, which name to the ears of the Anglo-Norman chronicler conveyed another form of the same word, Gountere, which was familiar to him.[79] Since he connects him with Arthur, it is evident that Gaimar was ignorant of the fact that his Gunter and the historical king Guþrum, were identical. When he reaches the time of King Alfred he calls the Danish king by his two usual names.

From what source the original of the three mentioned versions drew the conclusion that Havelok was the son of king Gunter, it is impossible to say, and the whole passage seems very hard to explain. It is possible that the fact, that king Guþrum (or Gunter) once had been king of an essentially Danish province, gave rise to the tradition of Havelok's being his son. With reference to Munch, Ward suggests that Guþrum (often shortened into Gorm) was identical with "Gormo Auglicus" and "Gorm the Old", and, if this be true, it would account for king Gunter being "styled king of Denmark".[80]— At all events Havelok's connection with Gunter did not originate with Langtoft, who wrote in the beginning of the 14th century.[81] It seems likely that his insertion of Havelok in his "Chronicle" is due to some version of the Havelok-tale itself.

How confused the view was which the old chroniclers held about Havelok and the traditions connected with his life, is clearly seen from the introduction in the Havelok-tale of Guþrum-Gunter, who, as we have seen, belongs to the time of king Alfred; and further, by the occurence in the same versions, in which Gunter is made father of Havelok, of the name Cuaran, which, in its turn, brings the story in connection with the events of the middle of the 10th century.

Another proof of this confusion lies in the view Gaimar held on the time when the Danes first came to England. We have already touched on the reference to Havelok, made by Gaimar in his "Estorie", when he comes to the battle of Ashdown in the latter part of the 9th century. In two other places in the "Estorie" Havelok's name occurs in a connection from which the conclusion may be drawn, that, according to Gaimar's opinion, Danes had been rulers of Britain long before the Saxons came to the country, and that Havelok was one of the kings of these early Danes.

In the introduction of the "Estorie des Engles" we are told that the Saxons under Cerdic and Cynric took possession of England, although they were much hated *by the Danes* (l. 37). Consequently the Danes, according to Gaimar, must have been in the country already then, *i. e.* before the middle of the 6th century. In the narrative of these events,[82] which corresponds with the entries of the Anglo-Saxon Chronicle for the years 495-556, the Havelok-tale is inserted, and some lines further on we find another statement referring to the Danes and to Havelok:

> "En Norfolc erent les Daneis
> Del tens ke *Havelok* fu reis:
> Si defendeient cel pais
> E cel ki fu al reis *Edelsis*"
>
> (ll. 897 sqq.).[83]

Another allusion to the same effect occurs in the "Estorie" when the compiler comes to the events told by the Anglo-Saxon Chronicle under the year 787. The Chronicle says, that in the days when Beorhtric took Eadburgh, the daughter of king Offa, to wife, "comon ærest III scipu Norðmanna————þæt wæron þa ærestan scipu Deniscra manna þe Anʒelcynnes land ʒesohtan".[84] Gaimar alludes to this entry, but adds with regard to the Danes, though it is hard to say on what he bases his information:

> "Car entrels eurent regarde
> E dit ke co est lur herite,
> E mulz homes de lur linage
> Urent le regne en heritage.
> Ainceis ke Engleis i entrast
> Ne home de Sessoigne i habitast:
> Li reis Danes[85] tint le regnez
> Ki de Denemarche fu nez,

> Si fist *Ailbrith* e *Havelok*
> E plus en nomerent ovoc."
>
> (ll. 2077 sqq.)[86]

There is another passage in the "Estorie" illustrating the view Gaimar held on the age of the Danish rule in England.[87]

—The two kings in England, named by Gaimar *Adelbrict* and *Edelsi,* cannot be identified. The corresponding English names are, however, common in the chronicles.[88] The French spelling of Adelbrict corresponds with an English *Aepelbryht* or *Aepelberht,* while Edelsi stands for *Aepelsize.*[89] In l. 2085 of the "Estorie" Gaimar writes *Ailbrith,* which name probably is to be derived from *Ezelbryht.* On coins from the time of Aepelred (978-1017) this name occurs alternating with that of Aezelbryht, although the two names are of different etymological origin.[90]—In the Lai d'Haveloc the kings are called *Ekenbright* and *Alsi,* whereas the Lambeth interpolation writes *Egelbright* and *Edelsy.* Ekenbright is perhaps the same name as the English *Ecgbryht* (cf. the spellings *Achebrit* of mss. D. & L. of the "Estorie des Engles" and *Echebrit* of ms. P. of the Lai d'Haveloc.)—Alsi occurs alternating with *Aelfsize.*[91]

For these two kings the English lay has substituted *Athelwold,* and made him king of all England. He cannot be identified.—*Birkabeyn* is in this version the name of Havelok's father, the king of Denmark. This name has originally nothing at all to do with the Havelok-traditions. It could not have been known in England before the end of the 12th century. The name *"Birke-beinar"* means in English "birch-legged fellows".[92] In 1174 it was given by Norwegian peasants to a set of outlaws who formed a political party in Norway,[93] and who later on chose Sverre Sigurdson for their leader. The "Birkebeinar" made him their king, and in the succeeding years he conquered all Norway with their help. In 1184 he was acknowledged as sole king of the country.[94] The Latin Chronicle "Gesta Henrici II et Richardi I", composed in England towards the end of the 12th century, and commonly attributed to *Benedict of Peterborough,* contains some particulars with regard to Sverre's wars and his accession to the throne.[95] In a somewhat different shape this chronicle forms a part of *Roger de Hoveden's* big Latin "Chronica",[96] which was composed not long after Benedict's "Gesta". In Hoveden the name of Sverre also occurs, but the author calls him *Swerus Birkebain.*[97] It is, as Storm[98] and Ward[99] suggest, very probable that the name owes its occurrence in the Havelok-tale to Hoveden's chronicle. It may be supposed that the Latin chroniclers did not understand the word; the English poet or poets who handed down the Havelok-traditions evidently did not do so, but they may have known that it was originally a Scandinavian name, and therefore they called Havelok's father Birkabeyn.

We have now touched on all the chief points but one with regard to the formation of the historical frame of the Havelok-tale. Our investigation has led to the result, that there is, among all these historical allusions in the tale, none from which a full and thorough historical parallel may be drawn.—The remaining allusions refer especially to Havelok in his capacity of a *Danish king* who conquers England.

From the end of the 10th century onwards the Scandinavian invasions display a thorough change of character. Having consisted up to this time chiefly of minor ravaging expeditions, they now develop into a great political conquest. The idea of a united kingdom on both sides of the North Sea did not originate until the time when the Scandinavians were exceedingly strong in England. The man who first realized this idea of a united kingdom was the Danish king Sven Tveskæg; the completion of the scheme was left to his successor, Cnut. It seems quite natural to refer the definite formation of the Havelok-tale to this time. The popular fancy of the Danes in England would scarcely have been able, before this time, to imagine a conqueror who was not only made king of the Danelaw, or, as in the English lay, of all England, but at the same time *king of Denmark,* as in *all* the versions.

The history of *Sven Tveskæg* cannot but confirm these conclusions. It contains some details that to some extent remind one of the most important events of Havelok's life: his expulsion from his own country, and his two big conquering exploits:[100] that of Denmark and that of England. Sven Tveskæg was, as we know, expelled from Denmark, and went to England.[101] In 988 he returned to Denmark, and, after gaining a battle, he succeeded his father as king of this country.[102] He now swore to conquer England.[103] It is too well known to require further comment, how after years of strife and hardship Sven Tveskæg in 1013 became king of England, thus for the first time uniting England and Denmark in the hands of one king.

With exception of these few facts, referring to Sven Tveskæg, to which the frame of the Havelok-tale renders a parallel, it is fairly evident that we have no right to consider Sven as the only prototype of the Havelok of the legend. On the other hand it seems as if the events that took place in England and Denmark during his time, rather than those of Olaf Cuaran's time, had influenced the formation of the Havelok-story, even if, as we know, the hero in some versions bears Cuaran's name.

Here we may insert a few words with regard to Storm's opinion on the relation between the Havelok-story and the romance of Guy of Warwick. Olaf Cuaran was, as we know, defeated at Brunnanburgh, but in all the versions of the Havelok-tale Danish sympathies are clearly marked and there is no mention made of any defeat of the Danes. "The open space", says Storm, "is filled up by an *English* tale, which represents Aveloc as the declared foe of the English people", viz. by the tale of the fight between Guy of Warwick and the heathen giant Colebrand. Storm owes this suggestion to the occurrence of the name *Avelocke* instead of Anlaf in the Percy Folio Ms. version of "Guy and Colebrande".[104] It is, however, hard to accept this suggestion of Storm's, for this "Auelocke" cannot, any more than the "Hauelok" of the Metrical Chronicle of England (cf. above, p. 68, note 2), be the same as our Havelok. "Auelocke is the declared foe of the English", it is true; but at the same time it must be born in mind, that he is forced to flee back to Denmark. This is the very contrary to what Havelok does—when *he* comes to England as Danish king he conquers the English, and remains in the country. We believe that the remark made by Furnivall[105] is quite correct: "the change here [of Auelocke for Anlaf] is, no doubt, due to the Romance of **Havelok the Dane**".

We are of the opinion that Havelok may, from an historical point of view, be considered as an expression of Scandinavianism in England, and that it is impossible to prove that the character of the Danish prince is copied exclusively from one single person. Havelok's nickname suggests his connection with the Norwegian viking Olaf Cuaran; his being the son of a Danish king in Denmark, his becoming king of Denmark, his conquest of England and the friendly relations between the two countries, all these facts remind one of Sven Tveskæg; and when, as in the English lay, he goes to *London* to be crowned, this circumstance points to the time of Cnut.[106]

*Notes*

[1] Cf. above, p. 57 sqq.

[2] Gesch. I, p. 292.

[3] Concerning the various forms of the word "Cuaran" cf. the list of names on p. 16.

[4] Cf. Ahlström, Lais-Litt., p. 121 sq.

[5] T. Brink, Gesch. I, p. 187.

[6] T. Brink, Gesch. I, pp. 187, 292.

[7] Wülker, Gesch., p. 97, points out the fact that in the English lay (l. 158) Winchester and not London is the capital of Athelwold. Havelok goes to London, however, to be crowned (ll. 2941 sqq.).

[8] Worsaae, Erobring, pp. 237 sqq., 263 sqq.—Steenstrup III, p. 217.—Loanwords II, p. 279.

[9] Cf. Storm, Bidrag, p. 87.

[10] Cf. A. Bugge, Norsemen in Ireland I, pp. 1 sqq., 9, 11 sqq. The aim of this essay is to prove—against Zimmer—that the early Scandinavian invaders of Ireland and kings of Dublin were *Norwegians* and not *Danes*. Danes were of course also to a certain extent concerned in the wars and settlements in Ireland—much as the Norweigians in the Danelaw. Cf. p. 11, note 3 of Bugge's treatise.

[11] Cf. p. 16.

[12] It is not absolutely impossible that this connection was felt to a certain extent by the early chroniclers. One proof in favour of this suggestion is, that Olaf Tryggvason in the Metrical Chronicle of England (Metrical Romances II, p. 270) is called Havelok. Cf. C. R. I, pp. 436, 464, 472 sq.

[13] Todd, Gaedhill, pp. CI, note 1, 280(5).—Revue Celtique III, p. 189.—Storm, Bidrag, p. 175.—C. R. I, p. 430, note.—Ahlström, Lais-Litt., p. 123, note 4 suggests a possibility "that some misunderstood northern epithet of the famous viking is concealed in the word." I have found no proof in support of this suggestion.—Bugge, Bidrag, p. 131.—Skeat, Cl. Pr., p. XXXVII, esp. notes 1 and 2.

[14] Todd, Gaedhill, passim; esp. pp. LXX, note 1, C, CI, note 1, 280(5) points out the fact that the bearers of the Irish name Amblaib, Amlaif etc. are identical with the northern Olafs. But he never states expressly that the names are derived from the same root.—Concerning the connection between the Irish name and the Welsh Abloyc, Abloec, Todd's explanation, p. 283, note 4, is hardly intelligible: "c for f as usual in the Welsh dialect of Celtic."—Köster, Havelok Danske, p. 78 (cf. above, p. 5) gives no philological reasons for his suggestions with regard to the connection between the names Olaf, Abloec and Havelok.—Storm, Havelok Kvaran, p. 3 sets forth briefly the etymological correspondance between the Northern, Irish and Welsh forms of the name, and adds that "Aveloc—in later English Havelok—must be the Anglo-Norman pronouciation of Abloc".—Ward in C. R. I, p. 413 sq. quotes Köster and Todd; to Todd's statements regarding the interdependance of the Irish and Welsh names he adds evidence from another authority, Prof. John Rhys, at Oxford, and says: "Professor Rhys informs us that this note is not strictly correct, but he does not question the main fact that the Irish Amlaeibh (or Amhlaeibh) is here [Annales Cambriæ; see below] and elsewhere in Welsh Chronicles represented by Abloyc."—Cf. Ahlström, Lais-Litt., pp. 32, 123.—Skeat, Cl. Pr., p. XXXVI.—Max Förster in Anglia, Beiblatt XIV, No. 1, p. 13 criticizes Skeat's interpretation of Storm's statements, and adds: "Ich wenigstens habe Storm immer so verstanden, dass Anleifr, ein echt nordischer name, in keltischem munde die formen ir. Amlaib (oder wohl besser Amhlaibh) und kymr. Abloyc angenommen habe. Ob dies freilich richtig ist, ist eine offene frage, da, wie mir prof. Sommer freundlichst bestätigt, der gleichsetzung der drei namen Anleifr, Amlaib und Abloc grosse lautliche schwierigkeiten im wege stehen".

[15] Cf. Noreen, Grammat. p. 52.

[16] Cf. Zimmer in Z. f. d. Altherthum, N. F. XX, p. 264, note 1.

[17] Cf. Noreen in Paul's Grundr. I², pp. 524, 557, 566.

[18] Cf. the transscript by Storm, Havelok Kvaran, p. 3.—Steenstrup III, p. 88, note 3.

[19] Cf. Steenstrup III, p. 144.—Bugge, Bidrag, p. 132.

[20] It seems more natural that Gyda should be represented as the daughter of Cuaran than as his sister. In Heimskringla I, p. 313 (chap. 32) she is said to be "ung kona ok frió", and it is known that Olof Cuaran died of old age in 981, (cf. Bugge, Bidrag, l. c.), and that Olaf Tryggvason was in England about 994. Cf. the quotations below: in the latter one it is said that Olaf Tryggvason visited Olaf Cuaran, which is in itself impossible (cf. Steenstrup III, p. 243)—and it seems to be in harmony with the whole passage to interpret the word "márg" as father-in-law. Cf. Storm, Snorre Sturlason, p. 159, note.—Todd, Gaedhill, p. 287(6).—Worsaae, Erobring, p. 247.

[21] Heimskringla I, p. 311 sq. (chap. 32).—Cf. Flateyarbok I, p. 150.

[22] Heimskringla I, p. 345 (chap. 47).—Cf. Flateyarbok I, p. 218.

[23] Landnámabók, p. 139.—Cf. Steenstrup, l. c., note 1.

[24] Gunnlaugssaga Ormstungu, p. 13 (chap. 7). Cf. also on the same page the following verses:

> "Kann'k máls of skil
> hvern'k mæra vil
> konongmanna kon:
> hann's Kvarans son
> etc."

[25] A. S. Chron. I, p. 215.

[26] Edred.

[27] Gaimar I, p. 149.

[28] Chron. Scot., p. 218 sq.

[29] Cf. Mon. hist. Brit. I, p. 388, note a.—A. S. Chr. II, p. 89, note 3.—Todd, Gaedhill, p. CI, note I: "This Olaf is called Cuaran, or Olaf of the *Sandal*, by the

Irish Annalists". Further p. 282, where Todd remarks that the "Four Masters" under 944 "distinctly mention Olaf Cuaran".—Steenstrup III, p. 79, note 1.

[30] Cf. Todd, Gaedhill, pp. 278, 287(8).

[31] Ann. Cambr. p. 17.

[32] Brut y Tyvysog., pp. 20, 21.

[33] Ibid., pp. 24, 25.—Cf. C. R. I, p. 431.

[34] Brut y Tywysog., pp. 30, 31.—Cf. Todd, Gaedhill, pp. 278, 288. C. R. I, l. c. sq.

[35] Brut y Tywysog., pp. 34, 35.—Cf. C. R. I, l. c.

[36] This name is the same as the Icelandic Sigtryggr. Cf. Zimmer in Z. f. d. Alterthum, N. F. XX, p. 266, note 1.

[37] Cf. Steenstrup III, pp. 26, 64.

[38] Cf. Steenstrup III, p. 64.

[39] Cf. Todd, Gaedhill, p. 280.

[40] Cf. Todd, Gaedhill, p. 281.—Steenstrup III, p. 65.

[41] Cf. Steenstrup III, p. 257.

[42] Cf. Steenstrup III, p. 70, 87.—His intimate connection with the Scots is probably the reason why the "Egilssaga", p. 266 (Ch. 51), calls Olaf Cuaran (Olafr Raudi) "Konúngr a Scotlandi", and adds that he was "Skozkr a faudr-kyni". Cf. the expression "Oláfr Skotakonúngr in Ch. 52, p. 269.

[43] Cf. Steenstrup III, p. 70 sq.—Bugge, Bidrag, p. 131: "Ethelred" seems to be a slip of the pen for Aethelstan.

[44] Cf. Todd, Gaedhill, p. 281.

[45] Cf. Todd, Gaedhill, pp. 281, 282.—Steenstrup III, p. 72.

[46] Cf. Steenstrup, l. c.

[47] Cf. Steenstrup III, p. 73 sqq.

[48] Cf. Todd, Gaedhill, p. 282.—Steenstrup III, p. 73.

[49] Cf. Steenstrup III, p. 79.

[50] Ibid.

[51] Ibid.

[52] Cf. Steenstrup III, p. 81.

[53] Ibid.

[54] Cf. Todd, Gaedhill, p. 284 sq.

[55] Cf. Steenstrup III, p. 86.

[56] Cf. Steenstrup III, p. 87.

[57] Cf. Steenstrup III, p. 88.

[58] Cf. Todd, Gaedhill, p. 285 sq.—Steenstrup III, p. 143 sqq.

[59] Cf. Todd, Gaedhill, p. 286.—Steenstrup III, p. 146.

[60] Cf. Steenstrup III, p. 147.—Bugge, Bidrag, p. 132,

[61] Hist. Littéraire XIII, p. 63 sqq.—De La Rue, Essais II, p. 104 sqq.—T. Brink, Gesch. I, p. 174.—Suchier-Birch-Hirschfeld, p. 113.—Gröber's Grundr. II: 1, p. 472 sq.

[62] Gaimar I, p. 3. Cf. l, 4, p. 1.—Wendeburg, G. von Monmouth, p. 16.

[63] Lib. XI, c. 2, 3, 4, 5.

[64] Mon. Hist. Brit. I, p. 16, C, D.

[65] Cf. Gaimar II, p. XX.

[66] Cf. Gaimar II, p. XVII.

[67] C. R. I, p. 426.

[68] Cf. Gaimar II, p. XVII sq.—C. R. I, p. 425.

[69] Gaimar II, pp. XIX sqq., XXIII sqq.

[70] A. S. Chr. I, p. 139.

[71] Gaimar I, p. 124.

[72] Todd, Gaedhill, p. 278.

[73] Cf. C. R. I, p. 430.

[74] Storm, Havelok Kvaran, p. 3.

[75] Cf. Gaimar I, p. 22, l. 524. King "Aschis" mentioned here is evidently taken from Geoffrey of Monmouth, Lib. XI, chap. 2, where he is called Aschillius of Dacia.

[76] Langtoft I, p. 318.

[77] Hearne, Langtoft-Brunne I, p. 25.

[78] Cf. Steenstrup II, p. 74.

[79] C. R. I, p. 442. Stephens, King Waldere's lay, p. 21 (3).

[80] Cf. C. R. I, p. 443 sq.—Munch, N. F. H. I: 1, p. 628 sq.

[81] Cf. Körting, p. 124.—Langtoft, I, p. XII.—T. Brink I, p. 357.

[82] Cf. C. R. I, p. 424 sq.—Mon. Hist. Brit. I, p. 775, note d.—Gaimar II, p. 27, note.

[83] Gaimar I, p. 37.

[84] A. S. Chr. I, p. 96.—Cf. Loanwords II, p. 262 sq.

[85] Cf. Saxo, Lib. I.

[86] Gimar I, p. 83.

[87] This passage, in which there is no direct reference to Havelok, is contained in the narrative of the meeting of Cnut and Edmond Ironside in 1016. Gaimar makes Cnut say (Gaimar I, p. 183):

"E bien sachez, loigtenement
Lurent Daneis, nostre parent,
Pres de mil anz lout Dane anceis
Ke unc i entrast Certiz li reis"

(ll. 4315 sqq.).

This idea of Gaimar's, represented by the three last quotations, is not without parallels in other mediæval compilations. The "Ynglingasaga" claims the same for the northern hero, Ivar Vidfamne, viz. that he conquered a part of England (Heimskringla I, p. 74; chap. 41).—Saxo (Lib. II, p. 46 sq.) makes King Frode defeat Britons and Scots; Hamlet (Lib. IV, p. 104 sq.) wars with the Britons, and a second king Frode (Lib. V, pp. 166, 168 sq.) with the Britons and the Irish.—Cf. Steenstrup I, p. 12 sq.

[88] Cf. Ahlström, Lais-Litt., p. 123 sq.

[89] Searle, Onomast., p. 222.

[90] Cf. Björkman in Herrig's Arch. f. d. n. Spr., Bd. 101, 1898, p. 393.—Morsbach, King Horn, p. 305 is of a somewhat different opinion.

[91] Searle, Onomast., p. 20 sq.

[92] C. R. I, p. 440.

[93] Munch, N. F. H. III, p. 45 sq.

[94] Munch, N. F. H. III, p. 180 sq.

[95] Bened. of Peterb. I, pp. 266 sqq., 320.

[96] Rog. de Hoveden I, p. LI.

[97] Rog. de Hoveden II, pp. 214 sqq., 290; III, p. 270 sqq.; IV, pp. 25, 162.

[98] Storm, Havelok Kvaran, p. 4.

[99] C. R. I, p. 440.

[100] Cf. Madden, p. XXXVIII.

[101] Maurer, Bekehrung I, p. 256 sq.—Worsaae, Erobring, p. 240 sq.

[102] Worsaae, Erobring, p. 244.

[103] Worsaae, Erobring, p. 245.

[104] P. Fol. Ms. II, p. 509, sq. This change of names occurs also in the edition printed by Copland. Cf. P. Fol. Ms. II, p. 511.—Tanner, Guy von Warwick, p. 53.—Körting, p. 100.—C. R. I, pp. 473, 500.

[105] P. Fol. Ms. II, p. 528, note 2.

[106] Steenstrup III, p. 287.—Cf. T. Brink, p. 292.

## *Works Cited*

A. Bugge, *Norsemen in Ireland* = Contributions to the History of the Norsemen in Ireland by *Alexander Bugge*. I. II. Christiania 1900. Videnskabsselskabets skrifter. II. Historisk-filosofisk Klasse No. 4, 5.

Ahlström, Lais-Litt. = Studier i den fornfranska lais-litteraturen. Akad. Afhandl. af *Axel Ahlström*. Upsala 1892.

Aiol, N. R. = Aiol . . . p. p. *Jacques Normand* et *Gaston Raynaud*. Société des anciens textes francais. Paris 1877.

Ann. Cambr. = Annales Cambriae. Edited by *John William ab Ithel*. London 1860. Rerum Britannicarum medii ævi scriptores, or Chronicles and Memorials of Great Britain and Ireland during the Middle Ages, No 20. [In the following references shortened to: *Chron. and memor.*]

A. S. Chr. = The Anglo-Saxon Chronicle. Edited, with a translation by *Benjamin Thorpe*. Vol. I. Original Texts. Vol. II. Translation. London 1861. Chron. and Memor. 23.

Bartsch-Horning = La langue et la littérature francaises . . par *Karl Bartsch* et *Adolf Horning*. Paris 1887.

Behrens, Beiträge = Beiträge zur Geschichte der französischen sprache in England von *Dietrich Behrens.* Französische Studien. Hrsgg. von *G. Körting* und *E. Koschwitx.* V. Bd. 2 Heft. Heilbronn 1886.

Bened. of Peterb. = Gesta regis Henrici Secundi Benedicti abbatis. Ed. by *William Stubbs.* Vols. I-II. London 1867. Chron. and Memor. 49.

Bibl. Normannica = Bibliotheca Normannica . . . hrsgg. von *Hermann Suchier.* VII: Der anglonormannische Boeve de Haumtone . . . von *Albert Stimming.* Halle 1899.

Brut y Tywysog. = Brut y Tywysogion or The Chronicle of the Princes. Edited by *John William ab Ithel.* London 1860. Chron. and Memor. 17.

Bugge, Bidrag = Bidrag til den ælste skaldedigtnings historie. Af *Sophus Bugge.* Christiania 1894.

Camden, Britannia = Britannia sive florentissimorum regnorum Angliæ, Scotiæ, Hiberniæ . . . authore *Guilielmo Camdeno.* Londini 1600.

Chaucer = The poetical works of *Geoffrey Chaucer.* With an essay on his language and versification . . . By *Thomas Tyrwhitt.* London 1871.

Chron Scot. = Chronicum Scotorum. A chronicle of Irish affairs . . . Ed. by *William M. Hennessy.* London 1866. Chron. and Memor. 46.

C. R. = Catalogue of Romances in the Dept of Mss. in the British Museum. By *H. L. D. Ward.* Vols. I, II. London 1883, 1893.

De la Rue, Essais = Essais historiques sur les bardes . . . par l'Abbé *De la Rue.* Vols. I-III. Caen 1834.

Descript. Catal. = Descriptive Catalogue of Materials relating to the History of Great Britain and Ireland . . . by *Sir Thomas Duffus Hardy.* Vols. I-III. London 1862-1871. Chron. and Memor. 26.

Egilssaga = Egils-Saga sive Egilli Skallagrimii vita . . . Havniæ 1809.

Flateyarbók = Flateyarbok. En samling af Norske Kongesagaer . . . I-III. Christiania 1860-68.

Foerster, Erec und Enide = Kristian von Troyes Erec und Enide . . . Hrsgg. von *Wendelin Foerster.* Romanische Bibliothek VIII. Halle a. S. 1896.

Foerster, R. L. B. = Richars li Biaus z. e. m. hrsgg. von *Wendelin Foerster.* Wien 1874.

Furnivall, Rob. of Brunne = The story of England by *Robert Manning of Brunne* . . . Ed. by *Frederick J. Furnivall.* Vols. I, II. London 1887. Chron. and Memor. 87.

Gaimar = Lestorie des Engles solum la translacion Meistre *Geffrei Gaimar.* Ed. by *Sir Thomas Duffus Hardy* and *Charles Trice Martin.* Vols. I, II. London 1888-89. Chron. and Memor. 91.

Gautier, Epopées = Les epopées franccaises par *Léon Gautier.* Vols. I-IV. 2e édit. Paris 1878-94.

G. G. A. = Göttingiche Gelehrte Anzeigen. Göttingen 1890.

Grimm, Heldensage = Die deutsche Heldensage von *Wilhelm Grimm.* Göttingen 1829.

Grüninger = Herpin. Der weis Ritter wie er so, getruwlich bei stund ritter Leuwen, des Hertzogen sun von Burges, das er zu letst ein Künigreich besass. Grüninger, Strassburg, 1514.

Grässe, Sagenkreise = Die grossen Sagenkreise des Mittelatters . . . von *J. G. Th. Grässe.* Dresden und Leipzig 1842.

Gröber's Grundr. = Grundriss der romanischen Philologie. Hrsgg. von *Gustav Gröber.* II: 1. Strassburg 1902.

Gunnlaugssaga Ormstungu = Gunnlaugssaga Ormstungu . . . hrsgg. von *E. Mogk.* Halle a. S. 1886. Altnordische Texte hrsgg. von E. Mogk, I.

Hagen, Gesammtabenteuer = Gesammtabenteuer . . . hrsgg. von *F. H. von der Hagen.* I—IV. Stuttgart und Tübingen 1850.

Hearne, Langtoft-Brunne = Peter Langtoft's Chronicle illustrated and improv'd by *Robert of Brunne.*—Transcribed . . . from a ms. in the Inner Temple Library by *Thomas Hearne.* Vols. I, II. Oxford 1725. The works of Thomas Hearne, vols. III, IV.

Heimskringla = Heimskringla. Nóregs Konungasogur af *Snorri Sturluson.* Udgivne . . . ved *Finnur Jónsson.* I—IV. Kjöbenhavn 1893—1900.

Hist. Littéraire = Histoire littéraire de la France. Vols. XIII, XVIII, XX, XXII, XXVII. Paris 1814—1877.

Holthausen, Havelok = Havelok. Edited by *F. Holthausen.* London, New York and Heidelberg 1902. Old and Middle English texts. Edited by L. Morsbach and F. Holthausen. Vol. I.

Jonckbloet, Guill. D'Orange = Guillaume d'Orange . . . p. p. *M. W. J. A. Jonckbloet.* Vols. I, II. La Haye 1854.

Junker, Grundr. der Franz. Litt. = Grundriss der Geschichte der französischen Litteratur von ihren Anfängen bis zur Genenwart von *Heinrich Junker*. 2. Aufl. Münster i W. 1894. Sammlung von Kompendien für das Studium und die Praxis. I. Serie. 2.

Krit. Jahresb. = Kritischer Jahresbericht über die Fortschritte der Romanischen Philologie . . . hrsgg. von *Karl Vollmöller* . . . I—III, 1890—1894, München, Erlangen, 1892—1897.

Körting = Grundriss der Geschichte der Englischen Litteratur von ihren Anfängen bis zur Genenwart von *Gustaf Körting*. 2. Aufl. Münster i W. 1893. Sammlung von Kompendien für das Studium und die Praxis I. Serie 1.

Köster, Havelok Danske = Sagnet om Havelok Danske. Fortalt af *Kristian Köster*. Kjöbenhavn 1868.

Landnámabók = Landnámabók. Udg. af det Kongl. Nordiske Oldskriftselskab. Kjöbenhavn 1900.

Langtoft = The Chronicle of *Pierre de Langtoft* in French verse . . . Edited by *Thomas Wright*. Vols. I, II. London 1866, 1868. Chron. and Memor. 47.

Leland, Collectanea = *Joannis Lelandi* Antiquarii de Rebus Britannicis Collectanea. Ed. *Thomas Hearne*. Vols. I—VI. London 1774.

Liebrecht, Volkskunde = Zur Volkskunde. Alte und neue Aufsätze von *Felix Liebrecht*. Heilbronn 1879.

Livy = Titi Livi ab Urbe condita. Stockholm 1893.

Loanwords = Scandinavian Loanwords in Middle English I; II (Studien zur Englischen Philologie, hrsgg. von Lorenz Morsbach XI). Halle a. S. 1900, 1902.

Madden: The ancient English Romance of Havelok the Dane, accompanied by the French text . . . by *Frederick Madden*. Printed for the Roxburghe Club, London . . . 1828.

Maurer, Bekehrung. Die Bekehrung des Norwegischen Stammes zum Christenthume . . . von *Konrad Maurer*. I, II. München 1855, 56.

Metrical Romances = Ancient Engleish Metrical Romanceës, selected . . . by *Joseph Ritson*. Vols. I—III. London 1802.

Michelant, Guill. de Palerne = Guillaume de Palerne, p. p. *Henri Michelant*. Paris 1876.

Michel, Havelok = Le lai d'Havelok le Danois, p. p. *Francois Michel*. Paris 1833.

Mon. Hist. Brit. = Monumenta Historica Britannica or Materials for the History of Britain . . . Vol. 1. Edited by *Henry Petrie* and *John Sharpe*. London 1848.

Morris and Skeat, Specimens = Specimens of Early English . . . by *Richard Morris* and *Walter W. Skeat*. Part II. Oxford 1879.

Morsbach, King Horn = Die Angebliche Originalität des frühmittelenglischen "King Horn" . . . von *Lorenz Morsbach*. Sonderabzug aus: Beiträge zur romanischen und englischen Philologie. Festschrift für Wendelin Foerster. Halle a. S. 1902.

Munch, N. F. H. = Det norske folks historie af *P. A. Munch*. Vols. I-III, Christiania 1852-57.

Nord. Myt. = Nordens Mythologi eller Sindbilled Sprog . . . af *Nik. Fred. Sev. Grundtvig*. Kiöbenhavn 1832.

Noreen, Grammat. = Altnordische Grammatik von *Adolf Noreen*. I. 2. Aufl. Halle 1892.

Norw. Saga þidriks af Bern = Saga þidriks Konungs af Bern . . . Udgivet af *C. R. Unger*. Christiania 1853.

Nyrop, Heltedigtning = Den oldfranske Heltedigtning by *Kristoffer Nyrop*. Kjøbenhavn, Heilbronn, Paris 1883.

Olrik, Sakses Oldhistorie = Kilderne til Sakses Oldhistorie. En litteratur-historisk undersögelse af *Axel Olrik*. I, II. Köbenhavn 1892, 94. ·

Paris, Manuel = Manuel d'ancien français. La Littérature française au Moyen Age par *Gaston Paris*. 2ᵉ. éd. Paris 1890.

Paul's Grundr. = Grundriss der germanischen Philologie . . . hrsgg. von *Hermann Paul*. II¹. Strassburg 1889-1893.

Percy, Reliques = Reliques of Ancient English poetry . . . by *Thomas Percy*. Ed. by *J. V. Prichard*. Vols. I, II. London 1876.

P. Fol. Ms. = Bishop Percy's Folio Manuscript. Ballads and Romances. Edited by *John W. Hales* and *Frederick Furnivall*. Vol. I-IV. London 1867-68.

P. Meyer, Bulletin 1878 = De quelques chroniques anglo-normandes qui ont porté le nom de *Brut* par *Paul Meyer*. Bulletin de la Société des anciens textes français, 1878, No. 3. Paris 1878.

P. Paris, Mscr. = Les manuscripts françois . . . par *Paulin Paris*. III. Paris 1840.

Putnam, Lambeth = The Lambeth version of Havelok . . . by *Edward Kirby Putnam*. Publications of the

Modern Language Association of America 1900. Ed. by *James W. Bright*. Vol. XV: 1, New Series, Vol. VIII: 1. Baltimore 1900.

Raimbert, Ogier. La Chevalerie Ogier de Danemarche par *Raimbert de Paris*. I, II. Paris 1842. (Ed. *J. Barrois*). Romans des douze pairs de France. VIII, IX.

Reiffenberg, le Chev. au Cygne = Le chevalier au cygne et Godefroid de Bouillon p. p. *F. A. F. Th. Reiffenberg*. Vol. II, Bruxelles 1848. Vol. III par *A. Borgnet*. Bruxelles 1854.

Revue Celtique = Revue Celtique publiée . . . par *H. Gaidoz*. I, III. London 1870-72; 1876-78.

Rog. de Hoveden = Chronica *Magistri Rogeri de Houedene*. Ed. by *William Stubbs*. Vols. I-IV, London 1868-71. Chron. and Memor. 51.

Rom. Stud. IV = Die Haveloksage bei Gaimar und ihr Verhältniss zum Lai d'Havelok von *Max Kupferschmidt*. Romanische Studien, hrsgg. von *Eduard Boehmer*. Vierter Band 1879—80. Bonn 1880.

Saxo = Saxonis Grammatici Gesta Danorum. Hrsgg. von *Alfred Holder*. Strassburg 1886.

Schmidt, zur Heimatbestimmung = Zur Heimatbestimmung des Havelok. Diss. (Göttingen) von *Friedrich Schmidt*. Göttingen 1900.

Searle, Onomast. = Onomasticon Anglosaxonicum by *W. G. Searle*. Cambridge 1897.

Skeat, Cl. Pr. = The lay of Havelok the Dane . . . by *Walter W. Skeat*. Oxford, Clarendon Press 1902.

Skeat, E. E. T. S. = The lay of Havelok the Dane . . . by *Walter W. Skeat*. Early English Text Society. Extra Series. No. IV. London 1868.

Steenstrup = Normannerne. Af *Johannes Steenstrup*. I—IV. Kjöbenhavn 1876—1882.

Stephens, King Waldere's Lay = Two Leaves of King Waldere's lay . . . by *George Stephens*. Cheapinghaven, London 1860.

Storm, Bidrag = Kritiske bidrag til Vikingetidens Historie. (I. Ragnar Lodbrok og Gange-Rolv). Af *Gustav Storm*. Kristiania 1878.

Storm, Havelok Kvaran = Havelok the Dane and the Norse king Olaf Kuaran. By *Gustav Storm*. Christiania Videnskabsselskabs Forhandlinger 1879. No. 10. Christiania 1880.

Storm, Snorre Sturlason = Snorre Sturlason, Kongesagaer.

Oversat at *Gustav Storm*. Nationaludgave. 2:den udgave. Kristiania 1900.

Suchier, Beaumanoir = Oeuvres poétiques de *Philippe de Remi Sire de Beaumanior* p. p. *Herman Suchier*. Vol. I. Paris 1884.

Suchier-Birch-Hirschfeld = Geschichte der französischen Litteratur . . . von *Hermann Suchier* and *Adolf Birch-Hirschfeld*. Leipzig und Wien 1900.

Swed. Didrik af Bern = Sagan om Didrik af Bern . . . utgifven af *Gunnar Olof Hyltén-Cavallius*. Stockholm 1850. Samlingar utgifna af Svenska Fornskrift-Sällskapet. Femte delen.

Tanner, Guy von Warwick = Die Sage von Guy von Warwick . . . Diss. (Heidelberg) von *A. Tanner*. Bonn 1877.

T. Brink, Gesch. = Geschichte der englischen Litteratur von *Bernhard ten Brink*. I, Berlin 1877. II, hrsgg. von *Alois Brandl*. Strassburg 1893.

Todd, Gaedhill = The war of the Gaedhill with the Gaill . . . Ed. by *James Henthorn Todd*. London 1867. Chron. and Memor. 48.

Wace's Brut = Le Roman de Brut par *Wace* . . . publié . . . par *Le Roux de Lincy*. I, II. Rouen 1836—38.

Warton, H. E. P. = History of English poetry . . . by *Thomas Warton*. Ed. by *W. Carew Haxlitt*. Vols. I—IV. London 1871.

Wendeburg, Gottfried von Monmouth = Ueber die Bearbeitung von Gottfried von Monmouth's Historia Regum Britanniæ in der Hs. Brit. Mus. Harl. 1605. Dissert. (Erlingen) von *Otto Wendeburg*. Braunschweig 1881.

Wilhelmi, Lion de Bourges = Studien über die Chanson de Lion de Bourges. Dissert. (Marburg) von *Heinrich Wilhelmi*. Marburg 1894.

Vising, Dissert. = Étude sur le dialecte anglo-normand du XII[e] siecle par *Johan Vising*. Dissert. (Upsala). Upsala 1882.

Vising, Franska Språket = Franska Språket i England af *Johan Vising*. I, II. Göteborg 1900, 1901.

Wolf, Hofman, Prim. y Flor de Rom. = Primavera y Flor de Romances . . . publ. por *Fernando José Wolf y Conrado Hofman*. Vols. I, II. Berlin 1856.

Worsaae, Erobring = Den danske Erobring af England og Normandiet ved *J. J. A. Worsaae*. Kjøbenhavn 1863.

Worsaae, Minder = Minder om de Danske og Nordmændene i England, Skotland og Irland af *J. J. A. Worsaae*. Kjöbenhavn 1851.

Wright, Gaimar = The Anglo-Norman Metrical Chronicle of *Geoffrey Gaimar*. Ed. by *Thomas Wright*. Publications of the Caxton Society 2. London 1850.

Wülker, Gesch. = Geschichte der englischen Litteratur . . . von *Richard Wülker*. Leipzig und Wien 1896.

Z. F. D. Alterthum N. F. XX = Zeitschrift für deutsches Alterthum und deutsche Litteratur. Hrsgg. von *Elias Steinmeyer*. Bd. 32. Neue Folge 20. Berlin 1888.

**Alexander Bell (essay date 1923)**

SOURCE: "The Single Combat in the *L'ai d'Havelok*," in *Modern Language Review*, Vol. XIII, No. 1, January, 1923, pp. 22-8.

[*In the following essay, Bell discusses the relationship of the* L'ai d'Haveloc *to Gaimar's account of the story, particularly concerning the battle between Haveloc and Odulf.*]

The suggestion has been made in a recent number of this *Review*[1] that the account of the meeting of Canute and Edmund Ironside at Olney, given by Henry of Huntingdon and others, is not due primarily to a simple misunderstanding of the phrase 'comon togædere' of the A.S. Chr. s.a. 1016; that a tradition of an earlier and equally decisive single combat was a predisposing factor in the choice of the hostile rather than the friendly sense of the phrase; and that this tradition is to be sought amongst those which had gathered round the historical and romantic figure of Anlaf-Haveloc. Though the evidence there (*l.c.* pp. 119 ff.) adduced from a consideration of the battles of Brunanburh and Vinheith renders the existence of such a tradition possible, it is on a passage in the *Lai d'Haveloc*—and apparently on that alone—that the conclusion is reached: 'there is no good reason to doubt that the single combat formed part of the original story' (*l. c.* p. 118). When, however, this is based on the statement that 'the earliest version of the Haveloc story which has come down to us appears to be that of the French *Lai d'Aveloc*, which probably belongs to the first half of the twelfth century' (*l. c.* p. 116), there seems to be some confusion between the extant version of the *Lai* and the earlier one from which it and Gaimar's account have been supposed to derive.

In the course of my work on the *Estoire des Engleis* I have been led to review the whole question of the relations between Gaimar and the *Lai*, and, as a result of a detailed investigation which I hope soon to publish, I very much doubt whether the passage in the *Lai*

*d'Haveloc* cited by Miss Ashdown has quite the evidential value she ascribes to it.

In the first place it is not correct to say that the existing *Lai d'Haveloc* is the earliest version of the story, for that honour belongs to the one of which Gaimar is the author. The exceptional regularity of the language and the absence of dialectical features make it extremely difficult to date the *Lai* on linguistic grounds alone, but, so far as this evidence goes, it points to a period later than Gaimar, i.e. in the second half of the twelfth century. This result was arrived at long ago by Kupferschmidt[2], though the phenomenon on which he chiefly relied—the use of -*eit* in imperfects of the first conjugation—is shown by a critical study of the text to have been unknown to the author. The date is supported, and defined more closely, by other considerations: the rule of the couplet is no longer strictly observed, and not only is the technique of the 'lai' adopted, but there has been some measure of direct influence by those of Marie de France; and the nature of the local allusions suggests the period of the revival of the Scandinavian trade in Lincolnshire and the consequent rivalry of the seaports of that county—say *c.* 1200—as the date of composition.

Secondly, as the single combat is related neither in Gaimar nor in the English **Havelok** but only in the *Lai d'Haveloc*, which is not the earliest version, it becomes essential to determine the position of the latter in the Haveloc tradition. If—which is the generally accepted view—it and Gaimar are both derived independently from an earlier French poem of the first half of the twelfth century, then it is conceivable that the former retained and the latter omitted the account of the combat, and there is thus some justification for the assumption that such a combat originally formed part of the Haveloc story. If, on the other hand (which is the conclusion I have arrived at), the *Lai* is derived, entirely or in the main, from the Haveloc episode in Gaimar, then this passage must be carefully scrutinised before it is taken as evidence that the incident belongs to the Haveloc story.

Premising that my results are based on a study of both MSS. of the *Lai d'Haveloc*, whereas the printed editions follow one only, and that the later of the two, my grounds for asserting the dependence of the *Lai* on Gaimar are, briefly stated, as follows:

(i) At least one reading of the *Lai* seems incompatible with the existence of the common source, and two of the names in the *Lai*—'Achebrit' and 'Sigar l'Estal'—seem to derive from the text of Gaimar.

(ii) Of the numerous parallel passages in the two texts, a marked proportion are confined to two sections of the narrative which are peculiar to the French versions—Argentille's dream and the battle between Haveloc and

Edelsi—and their differences of expression seem to be due to the author of the *Lai* rather than to Gaimar.

(iii) Since the later text is written in the form of a 'lai,' there must necessarily be some changes in the order of the narrative, and reasons of technique are sufficient to account for the varying explanations of Haveloc's presence at Edelsi's court, and the only difference which could be held to prove the independence of the *Lai* is its use of the 'strongest man' motive[3], which is also found in the English version. Careful study of the text of Gaimar suggests that this motive was unknown to him and could not have been omitted by him, but that it is probably a later development of the story in local tradition.

(iv) One difference appears to be due directly to a misunderstanding of Gaimar's text. On two occasions in the French versions Haveloc makes use of an axe in self-defence. In Gaimar, after his arrival in Denmark and appeal for protection to the Danish lord, Sigar, he is attacked in his lodging by some of the latter's servants who abduct his wife; he seizes an axe which he finds hanging up in the house, rushes out into the street, rescues his wife and kills most of the assailants; later, when he is to be presented to an assembly in Sigar's hall, he is apprehensive of punishment and seizes an axe from one of the bystanders in order to defend himself if necessary. In the *Lai* the ambush takes place in the street and the axe is there seized from one of the assailants, but, in Sigar's hall, Haveloc passes undisturbed through the bystanders and, still unhindered, takes down an axe from the wall. I suggest that the author of the *Lai*, misunderstanding the phrase 'dans la ruelle' used by Gaimar with reference to the scene, not of the abduction but of the subsequent rescue, imagined the whole affair as taking place in the street, adopted the second of the two methods of obtaining an axe as more suitable and, consequently, had to do the best he could with the other when he came to the scene in Sigar's hall.

(v) There are four features peculiar to the French versions which, as they fit in with Gaimar's sources of knowledge and methods of composition, appear to have been introduced into the story by him. They are:

(*a*) Argentille's dream. This is made the turning point of the first part of the story, is quite different from the English account, seems reminiscent of Iseult's dream in the Forest of Morrois and has evidently been composed with the finish of the French versions in view. As there is some evidence from the *Estoire des Engleis* that Gaimar was acquainted with the Tristan story, the innovation may be due to him.

(*b*) The Capture by 'outlaws.' In the English **Havelok** Grim and his companions are driven by an unexpected storm to England; in the French he is a regular travel-ler between Denmark and England, and is attacked by 'outlaws.' As these do not appear to have been familiar to the author of the *Lai*, whereas there is ample evidence that Gaimar was well acquainted with their existence, it would seem that he is responsible for their introduction.

(*c*) The Geography of the poems. In Gaimar the two kingdoms concerned—of Edelsi and of Adelbrit—are very definitely in East Anglia, and the bounds of the former agree very closely with those of the Southumbrian realm subsequently described by him in his *Estoire*. In the *Lai*, though the author does not appear to have a very clear conception of the relations of the kingdoms with which he has to deal, to each other and to England as a whole, yet Edelsi's kingdom is described in the same detail as in Gaimar. It seems probable that this does not represent the original state of affairs and that Gaimar is responsible for their reduction in status from national to local sovereigns, though residence in Lincolnshire most likely accounts for the greater detail in describing Edelsi's realm, as opposed to Adelbrit's, noticeable in the *Lai*.

(*d*) The Chronology of the poems. Both in Gaimar and the *Lai* the events are ascribed to the period following the death of Arthur, and, though a general reference to that monarch might not be out of place in a 'lai,' actually he is referred to in the *Lai* in the same terms—historical rather than romantic—as in Gaimar, but with no obvious purpose. As there is in Gaimar a clear intention of linking up the events of the story with that period in order to provide a basis for the subsequent Danish claim to have reigned in England prior to the arrival of the English, and as his appeal to Gildas (v. 41) appears to be not entirely a mere literary device for securing credence, it is highly probable that he is responsible for attaching the story to this period.

If these features have been introduced by Gaimar—the arguments only have been outlined and no attempt has been made here to adduce evidence in their support—and if they are also found, as they in fact are, in the *Lai,* it follows that the latter must have derived them from the former. Consequently, in view of these and other points in which the *Lai* has been shown dependent on Gaimar and of the lack of proof to the contrary, it can no longer be regarded as representing an independent version of the Haveloc story, and the presence of an incident in the *Lai* cannot be accepted as proof of its occurrence in the original unless other evidence is forthcoming in support.

Thirdly, a distinction must be made between the motive for the combat and the combat itself. Of the former Miss Ashdown remarks (*l. c.* p. 117): 'the humanitarian note is curious, and one might be inclined to see in it the refining tendency of French romance'; but, holding, as she does, that the *Lai* is older than Gaimar, she rejects this possibility and seems thereby to regard the motive as well as the combat as part of the original Haveloc story. There does not appear to be any compelling need to do this, for, in her own words (*l.c.* p. 124, n. 3), 'the fact that a certain motive is suggested in the version which has come down to us does not destroy the possibility that the original version implied a different motive'; and the mere fact that the story has been rewritten as a 'lai,' and has been influenced by their technique, renders it *a priori* probable that the motive is derived from French romance rather than from Scandinavian tradition. Moreover, the concern for the common people attributed to Haveloc by the author of the *Lai* seems to me to have been introduced by him partly from the same literary considerations as the additional touches whereby he makes of Edelsi a model leader, who goes out on personal reconnaissance before calling on his followers to do battle, and to suggest that no adequate motive for the combat was offered by the form of the story from which he derived his account.

If we turn to Gaimar's description of the battle between Haveloc and Odulf, we are at once struck by the fact that there is no explicit mention of the latter's fate and that it is uncertain whether he was killed or pardoned, though Gaimar's language—'Li reis Odulf fud dune vencuz Kar Haveloc si se cuntint Il sul en ocist plus de vint' (vv. 742-4)—seems rather to imply the former. On the other hand, Gaimar lays considerable stress on Haveloc's elemency after the battle; he pardons two .enemy princes—apparently Gaimar's own invention—and 'del pais la menue gent Vindrent a merci ensement E Haveloc lur fist parduns Par le cunseil de ses baruns' (vv. 749-52). As he usually evinces some interest in the outcome of the battles he describes, even to the extent of turning an indecisive into a decisive engagement (e.g. vv. 1417 ff.), it seems reasonable to assume that a single combat between the two monarchs did not figure in the story as Gaimar knew it. Neither does it appear probable, in this case, that the author of the *Lai* developed the combat from the uncertain data at his disposal in Gaimar's text, though, if he knew in addition another form of the story in which such a combat figured, Haveloc's elemency in Gaimar would supply him with a motive for it.

That he was acquainted with the tradition in some other form than Gaimar—very possibly oral—is shown especially by his treatment of Sigar's recognition of Haveloc. In Gaimar, Sigar first sees Haveloc when besieged in the church tower, and his resemblance to the late king—his father—is so great that the Danish lord grants him a truce, takes him to his hall, learns his name and story, in consequence of which he has him watched in expectation of the mystic flame, and this convinces him of Haveloc's identity. In the *Lai*, the same events, in slightly different order, lead up to the same conclusion, but even more stress is laid on the

physical resemblance. Yet, in spite of this being so great that it strikes Sigar in the conflict round the church tower, when, a short time before, Haveloc had sat as an honoured guest at his table, the resemblance passes unnoticed. In the English **Havelok**, the recognition depends entirely on the mystic flame, there is no question of resemblance, and consequently Haveloc attracts no special attention when at the Danish lord's hall prior to the attack on his lodging. These agreements show that the *Lai* is combining Gaimar's account with one derived from some other source; for, just as he sought to provide a motive for his introduction of Argentille's visit to the hermit, so he provides one for Haveloc's visit to Sigar in view of a version of the recognition which he does not adopt.

In favour of this suggestion, that the author of the *Lai* found mention of a single combat in his second source, it may be urged that, whilst he has throughout shown a decided tendency—under the influence, as I believe, of the *Lai des deux amants* of Marie de France—to make Argentille play a more important part in the story and to make Haveloc more than ever disinclined to act save at the instance of others, in this case he is made to show unwonted decision of character in proposing the single combat with Odulf entirely on his own initiative.

We have seen that this combat was probably unknown to the tradition used by Gaimar, but as probably known to that used by the author of the *Lai* to supplement the former's account, and the problem arises: was this combat an original feature of the story or is it an addition made in the later twelfth century? The evidence collected by Miss Ashdown seems, as far as I can judge, to render it likely that such a combat did figure in the Anlaf-Haveloc traditions; but, in seeking to link it up with that related in the *Lai*, is it not possible that she has overlooked one consideration? Assuming the correctness of her deductions from Brunanburh and Vinheith, we should expect the combat, which is to decide the fate of a kingdom and of which Anlaf-Haveloc is a protagonist,. to take place in *England*, but the one thing clear about the battle between Haveloc and Odulf is that it occurs in *Denmark*. In the English **Havelok**, however, though no single combat in the sense of this discussion takes place, yet, because 'Havelok saw his folk so brittene' (v. 2700), he makes for his opponent, Godrich, fights and captures him; the details are in full accord with the boisterous nature of this poem and its rough-and-tumble hero, but there is also the suggestion of a single combat and the battle takes place in England.

It is well known that the conclusion of the story in the French version is very different, involving as it does the account of the dead men set up on stakes to personate the living, but it has not, to my knowledge, been ascertained—I have been concerned only with the two French texts and not with the wider problems of the Haveloc tradition—which of the two versions represents more closely the original ending, though I cannot be sure, in my own mind, that the ruse of the dead men was not introduced into the story by Gaimar. There can be little doubt that, in addition to his interest in the Haveloc story for its own sake, he had in mind its importance for strengthening the Danish claim of prior possession of England put forward, in his account, by Canute at his celebrated meeting with Edmund Ironside; and that claim would be strengthened if Haveloc obtained Edelsi's kingdom by the latter's free gift rather than by right of conquest. Also, if the ending underlying that of the English *Havelok* be the original one, the outcome of the combat was probably fatal to Haveloc's opponent.

Therefore, if Gaimar knew the dead men ruse from another source—and he was not unacquainted with Danish traditions—it would, with his purpose in view, supply him with a better and more striking ending, and, to judge by his methods on other occasions, he would not have scrupled to adopt it instead of the original combat ending. Further, when both Gaimar and the second source conflict, the author of the *Lai* seems to prefer the former but likes to make use as well of any additional features from the latter. Hence, assuming that the single combat figured in his second source—here representing the original tradition—he would have a very striking incident at his disposal, after deciding to adopt the ruse ending from Gaimar, which he could use to good purpose in the, as yet, rather colourless Haveloc-Odulf incident.

Thus, though I have taken away from Miss Ashdown with the one hand in showing that this passage of the *Lai* cannot safely be used as direct proof of her contention, yet I have returned her somewhat with the other, and, should it be possible to substantiate the hypothesis of the preceding paragraph, it may be that she will consider herself the gainer, rather than the loser, by the exchange.

### Notes

[1] M. Ashdown, 'The single combat in certain cycles of English and Scandinavian tradition and romance.' *Mod. Lang. Rev.* XVII, p. 113.

[2] M. Kupferschmidt, *Die Haveloksage bei Gaimar. Rom. Studien*, IV, p. 411.

[3] Edelsi promises his dying brother-in-law to protect Argentille, then an infant, and, when she is of fit age, to marry her 'al plus fort home' in his kingdom; in order to deprive her of her inheritance, he adheres to the letter of his promise by giving her to his scullion, Haveloc, because of his prowess in wrestling and other feats of strength.

### Robert W. Hanning (essay date 1967)

SOURCE: "*Havelok the Dane*: Structure, Symbols, Meaning," *Studies in Philology*, Vol. LXIV, No. 4, July, 1967, pp. 586-605.

[*In the following excerpt, Hanning praises* Havelok the Dane *for its unified structure and consistent symbolism which work together to clarify and support the main meaning of the work.*]

The so-called Matter of England romances—the middle English romances whose stories are drawn from the sagas and traditions of pre- and post-conquest England—[1] have yet to receive their due share of attention from critics of medieval literature. Earlier investigators of *King Horn*, *Havelok*, *Athelston*,[2] *Richard the Lion Hearted*, *Guy of Warwick*, *Bevis of Hampton*, and *Gamelyn*, concentrating mainly on sources and analogues, on the priority of the various saga versions, and on folklore parallels and basic story patterns,[3] showed little inclination to discuss questions of literary worth. Despite major shifts in critical emphasis, little has been done in recent years to redress the balance in favor of a literary analysis of the Matter of England romances through a systematic study of structure, symbols, and central concerns. J. M. Hill's reconsideration of *King Horn*,[4] a happy exception to the general neglect, has established beyond doubt the need for such study, and it is the intention of the present discussion to follow Hill's lead by re-examining the romance of *Havelok the Dane*.[5] I hope to show that *Havelok*, for all its popular quality and its roughhewn versifying, is nevertheless deserving of commendation for its unified structure, for its consistent use of central symbolic acts and devices, and for the way in which structure and symbols cooperate to establish and clarify the work's central meanings.

There are several versions of the Havelok story, of which *Havelok the Dane* is the earliest extant English version.[6] The basic story concerns a young crown prince of Denmark who, while still a child, is deprived of his inheritance and almost of his life. He flees to England and grows up a commoner. After a series of adventures, and marriage to the analogously dispossessed heiress to an English kingdom, Havelok, by now fully grown, returns to Denmark and regains his throne. The story ends with Havelok's return to England to punish those who had denied his wife her inheritance, and with the inauguration of a joint rule over both kingdoms by Havelok and his wife.

This farfetched plot has, it will be granted, a popular ring to it.[7] It also has important similarities to the plot of *King Horn*, which, as Hill has shown, is basically the story of a hero's coming of age.[8] In both *Horn* and the Havelok story, the young prince, having attained adulthood, regains his royal patrimony, and in the process marries a princess whose land he will also rule after he has recovered his own kingdom. Nor do similarities cease with the respective heroes. The heroine of the Havelok story (Goldeboru in *Havelok the Dane*, Argentille in the earlier versions of Gaimar and the Anglo-Norman *lai d'Avelok*) is, like Rimenid, heroine of *Horn*, the daughter of a king, and is married against her will. In the case of Goldeboru (to give her the name she has in the version here under discussion), her unwilling marriage to the unrecognized Havelok is preceded by years of imprisonment in a castle, thanks to the wicked guardian who wishes to usurp her throne.

The parallels just outlined are not unique to *Havelok* and *Horn*; rather, they represent three common elements of romance plots, medieval and non-medieval, which may be characterized as follows: (1) the hero's movement from loss to recovery.[9] This movement is often linked with (2) his development from immaturity or faultiness toward maturity or perfection.[10] The process of development, in turn, often involves (3) a love relationship which unites the hero (in his deprived and/ or developing state) and a heroine who has also been the victim of deprivation or other injustice.[11]

Hill has suggested that these themes, so closely bound together in *Horn,* serve there to reflect the process of growth taking place within the hero. In his view, the various betrayals and forced marriages which form the climaxes of the romance represent a symbolic *psychomachia* between Horn's desire to excel in deeds of prowess and his desire for the love of Rimenild.[12] It is Horn's immaturity and indecisiveness which cause, and are reflected in, the trials of the heroine.

The psycho-symbolism which Hill proposes as the key to the meaning, and to the thematic complexes which determine the meaning, of *King Horn* is not, however, a suitable key to *Havelok the Dane*. This becomes clear at the very beginning of the latter work, where we see that the heroine's misadventures, far from being introduced as reflections of the hero's state of emotional immaturity, form the opening episode of the story. Goldeboru's perilous predicament—her father, king Athelwold, dies and she is left in the protection of earl Godrich, who betrays her and wishes the throne for himself—comes at a time when we have as yet heard nothing of Havelok, and when, as we soon learn, he is himself a helpless child undergoing the process of being orphaned, betrayed, and deprived of his inheritance.[13] If, however, the interacting plot elements of *Havelok the Dane* are not susceptible of explanation in the same way as the analogous parts of *King Horn*, this is not to say that the *Havelok* poet has failed to impress any unified artistic design upon his largely inherited narrative fabric. I believe it possible to demonstrate that *Havelok* has a structure capable of supporting a consistent meaning and that the structural

skeleton is garbed in the firm flesh of artistically convincing and emotionally fitting incidents.

The first clue to the ability and intent of the poet is provided by those opening scenes of the poem to which allusion has just been made. Havelok and Goldeboru are subjected to exactly parallel introductory calamities: each is the juvenile heir of a good king struck down by disease while still in his prime;[14] each child-monarch is then entrusted to a baron of the realm who betrays his trust and oppresses the helpless protagonist to satisfy his own greed and ambition.[15] The elaborate parallelism of these incidents is a noteworthy peculiarity of this version of the Havelok story. In the earlier versions found in Gaimar's *Estoire des Engleis* and the Anglo-Norman *lai d'Avelok*,[16] the heroine's situation is much as we find it in the English romance,[17] but Havelok's misfortunes stem from King Arthur's conquest of Denmark, which unseats and destroys the king and establishes a traitor on the throne, forcing a loyal noble, Grim, to flee the country with the endangered child.[18] In short, this earlier form of the Havelok story includes political and historical elements which the poet of *Havelok the Dane* removes, preferring in their place a double statement of the process by which a helpless child is stripped of his rights, and therefore of his future, by a strong and wicked adult.[19] The poet's restatement of these hard facts reinforces our impression of the helplessness of youth and the contrasting power of adulthood; there are no political or pseudo-historical considerations to divert our attention from this central, stark contrast. Why the poet should wish to emphasize the contrast becomes apparent when we recall that the central movements of the Havelok story are from loss to recovery and, complementarily, from youth to maturity. By linking youth and loss twice in quick succession without other complications, *Havelok the Dane* unmistakably announces the thematic interests which control its narrative progress.

The narrative begins by examining royal power, and then proceeds to portray a double transfer of royal power, underscoring in the process the crucial relationship between power and human destiny. It is important to note that royal power is two-fold in nature: there is the personal power which allows the king to maintain possession of his throne, and there is the social power which keeps his kingdom in a state of order and peace. The latter, social power of the king is stressed in the encomium on Athelwold which opens the poem:

> It was a king bi are dawes,
> þat in his time were gode lawes:
> He dede maken an ful wel holden; . . .
> Wreieres and wrobberes made he falle,
> And hated hem so man doth galle;
> Vtlawes and theues made he bynde,
> Alle that he micthe fynde,
> And heye hengen on galwe-tre; . . .

And wo dide widuen wrong,
Were he neure knicth so strong
þat he ne made him sone kesten
In feteres, and ful faste festen, . . .

(27-82)[20]

although his personal power is not ignored:

Of knith ne hauede he neuere drede, . . .
And oþer he refte him hors or wede,
Or made him sone handes sprede,
And "Louerd, merci!" loude grede.

(90-96)

When death threatens the king, his first worry is that his offspring is too young and weak to wield the personal power necessary to survive in the royal office:

"Crist, wat shal y don?
Louerd, what shal me to rede?
I woth ful wel ich haue mi mede:
Hw shal nou mi douhter fare? . . .
Sho ne kan speke, ne sho kan go.
Yif scho couþe on horse ride,
And a thousande men bi hire syde,
And sho were comen intil helde,
And Engelond sho couþe welde,
And don of hem that hire were queme,
And hire bodi couþe yeme,
Ne wolde me neuere iuele like,
Ne þou ich were in heuene-riche!"

(117-33)

The king's fears are justified: the rightful heir falls an easy prey to the treacherous baron, who usurps and misapplies the royal power in order to keep the country for himself and his heirs.

þe riche erl [Godrich] ne foryat nouth
þat he ne dede al Engelond
Sone sayse intil his hond; . . .
Soþlike, in a lite þrawe,
Al Engelond of him stod awe;
Al Engelond was of him adrad
So his þe beste fro þe gad. . . .
þo bigan Godrich to sike,
And seyde, "Weþer [Goldeboru] sholde be
Quen and leuedi ouer me? . . .
Sholde ic yeue a fol, a þerne,
Engelond, þou sho it yerne? . . .
Ich haue a sone, a ful fayr knaue:
He shal Engelond al haue!

(249-309)[21]

The first five hundred lines of *Havelok the Dane* recount the stripping away of all the legitimate rights and expectations of Goldeboru and Havelok; this equals one-sixth of the entire poem, and brings us to the low point of the narrative. That point, I suggest, comes not when Grim is preparing to kill Havelok at Godard's command,[22] but earlier, at line 484. There the child Havelok, after watching the fiendish Godard slaughter his two sisters, kneels before the usurper and surrenders his inherited sovereignty, saying:

Manrede, louerd, biddi you![23]

The medieval ceremony of offering homage, here portrayed in stark simplicity, symbolized the establishment or reaffirmation of a special relationship between the lord and his vassal. Coming at this moment in *Havelok the Dane*, the hero's act of homage takes on additional significance, for by offering homage to Godard, Havelok is symbolically denying his identity as king and lord of Denmark. The loss of social identity implicit in Havelok's surrender of sovereignty determines and prefigures his subsequent, explicit loss of personal identity in leaving Denmark to grow up as a fisherman's son in England.

In addition to serving the functions mentioned so far, line 484 also provides an important clue to the overall construction of *Havelok the Dane*. By recognizing the line (and the situation it describes) as the low point of the story, we are enabled to perceive the relationship carefully established by the poet between Havelok's moment of loss and his moment of recovery, and thus to gain a new appreciation of the poem's structural symmetry. The moment of recovery occurs after Ubbe, the powerful earl of Denmark, has recognized Havelok by the latter's birth—or "destiny-marks."[24] Realizing that Havelok is the rightful heir to the throne on which Godard still sits, Ubbe calls together his men and, falling on his knees before the astonished Havelok, cries,

Manred, louerd, bede y þe.

(2172)

The almost literal duplication of the earlier line is surely no accident; Havelok has regained all that he lost years before in kneeling to Godard. The pattern is neat and decisive: Havelok surrenders his sovereignty; loses his identity; regains his identity; recovers his sovereignty. At line 2172 the main action of *Havelok the Dane* is fulfilled; what remains is Havelok's firm establishment on the throne by the destruction of Godard, and the overthrow of Godrich, the corresponding villain in England.[25]

The progression from loss of power to recovery of power is thus clearly marked in the structure of *Havelok*. So is the other central thematic progression, that of development from helpless youth to capable adulthood. It is, of course, the second, developmental progression which makes possible the completion of the first pattern, while it is the onset of adversity (the first part of the loss-recovery pattern) which determines the mold into which the maturation process is to be cast.[26] Since the process of development or growth must, unlike the loss-recovery movement, be gradual, it is represented in the narrative not by a symbolic beginning and ending (such as line 484 repeated at line 2172), but by a *series* of repeating symbols, the recurrences of which mark stages in the hero's journey toward maturity.[27] I have discovered three main repeating symbols in *Havelok*, none of which, to my knowledge, have been previously recognized for what they are. They include: (1) feasts; (2) feats of strength; and (3) discovery of Havelok's birth- or "destiny-marks." Such symbolic moments and events in *Havelok the Dane* reflect the poet's ability to manipulate his main themes with skill and effectiveness.

Feasts often occupy an important place in the narrative of medieval romances, where they possess a special ritual or symbolic value over and above their nutritional function. Examples which come to mind at once are the Grail feast in the Grail romances, and the Whitsun feast at Arthur's court which often serves as the starting point for an adventure involving one or more of the knights of the Round Table.[28] In *Havelok the Dane*, no less than six eating occasions are described in 3000 lines.[29] Each feast is more important than the one before, though all come at crucial moments in the story, and signal important stages in Havelok's development. Of special note is that the first two feasts have nothing of the social ritual about them; they serve to revive Havelok at times when he has been without food for days.

The first meal takes place in Grim's hut in Denmark. The bondsman has received Havelok from Godard with orders to throw the child into the sea. He takes the child home to his cottage, binds and gags him, and leaves him on the floor. When Grim and his wife arise in the middle of the night to prepare for the murder, they see the flame which plays around Havelok's mouth and discover the cross-mark on his shoulder which indicates his royalty. These revelations save his life; Grim asks mercy and promises obedience to Havelok. The text continues,

> þo was Haueloc a bliþe knaue;
> He sat him up and crauede bred,
> And seide, "Ich am ney ded,
> Hwat for hunger, wat for bondes
> þat þu leidest on min hondes."
>
>                                    (632-36)

Grim's wife responds,

> "Wel is me þat þu mayth hete!
> Goddoth!" quath Leue, "y shal þe fete
> Bred an chese, butere and milk,
> Pastees and flaunes; al with suilk

> Shole we sone the wel fede,
> Louerd, in þis mikel nede."
>
>                                    (641-46)

Havelok eats all that is placed before him with great gusto:

> þanne sho hauede brouth þe mete,
> Haueloc anon bigan to ete
> Grundlike, and was ful bliþe;
> Couþe he nouth his hunger miþe.
> A lof he het, y woth and more,
> For him hungrede swiþe sore.
> þre dayes þer-biforn, i wene,
> Et he no mete, þat was wel sene.
>
>                                    (649-56)

The poet stresses the variety of homely fare, and Havelok's great need of it. The humble feast is the first concrete sign that Havelok has stepped back from the brink of death, and since it also acts to restore his famished body, it aptly typifies the course of the narrative at this point.

The second meal in *Havelok*, like the first, breaks a fast for the hero. Havelok, now a young man in England, has left the home of his putative father because of a famine which has ravaged the land and made it impossible for Grim to feed his large family.[30] He arrives at the town of Lincoln, barefoot, clad in a suit made from an old sail, friendless, and hungry.

> Hwan he kam per, he was ful wil:
> Ne hauede he no frend to gangen til;
> Two dayes þer fastinde he yede,
> Pat non for his werk wolde him fede.
>
>                                    (863-66)

On the third day, he finds work carrying baskets of fish for the earl's cook, and after carrying prodigious loads on two consecutive days, he is hired on a regular basis as the cook's apprentice. The cook tells him,

> Go pu yunder [to the castle] and sit pore,
> And y shal yeue the ful fair bred,
> And make the broys in the led.
> Sit now doun and et ful yerne:
> Dapeit hwo the mete werne!
>
>                                    (922-26)

This quite satisfies Havelok, who has just told the cook,

>               . . . leue sire,
> Bidde ich you non oper hire:
> But yeuep me inow to ete. . . . .
>
>                                    (909-11)

Again, obtaining nourishment becomes an important symbolic act, this time of Havelok's first independent and competitive steps in the world.[31]

The third occasion for a meal is also the first in which the prime motive is not the assuaging of violent hunger. After Havelok and Goldeboru have been married at the command of Godrich—and much to the chagrin of the princess, who thinks she has been forced to marry a churl—Havelok, fearful for his safety and for the virtue of his bride in Lincoln, rushes her off to Grimsby—only to discover that Grim is dead.[32] His children are still there, however, and are overjoyed to see Havelok:

> On knes ful fayre he hem setten
> And Hauelok swipe fayre gretten,
> And seyden, "Welkome, louerd dere!
> And welkome be pi fayre fere! . . .
> Pou mipe us bope yeue and selle,
> With pat pou wilt here dwelle. . . .
> We hauen shep, we hauen swin;
> Bileue her, louerd, and al be pin!
> Pou shalt ben louerd, pou shalt ben syre,
> And we sholen seruen pe and hire."
>
> (1211-30)

These lines describe the turning over of Grims' household, its goods and inhabitants, to Havelok in terms which suggest the bondsman's surrender of himself and his property to his lord ("pou mithe us bope yeue and selle. . . . pou shalt ben louerd, pou shalt ben syre,/ And we sholen seruen pe and hire"). Grim himself had used similar words to the helpless Havelok when the latter's identity was first revealed to him.[33] Havelok has returned to his home, which has also become his "kingdom" now that Grim is gone. It is the first moment in which Havelok's majesty accords at all with his situation—he has also wed a princess—and the contrast between the hero's stage of growth at this time and the stage at which Grim first offered him service is sharply etched by means of two feasts, the first of which, in Grim's cottage, has already been mentioned. As opposed to that humble repast, the present meal is an elaborately prepared, joyfully consumed banquet, serving not so much to fill empty stomachs as to celebrate Havelok's i stallation as head of Grim's household. Seen in this light, the dinner also prefigures Havelok's final coronation feast; it thus looks both forward and backward along the arc of the hero's development:

> Hwan he pis ioie haueden maked,
> Sipen stikes broken and kraked,
> And pe fir brouth on brenne;
> Ne was ther spared gos ne henne,
> Ne pe hende ne pe drake:
> Mete he deden plenté make;
> Ne wanted pere no god mete,
> Wyn and ale deden he fete,
> And hem made glade and blipe,
> Wesseyl ledden he fele sipe.
>
> (1237-46)

The fourth feast is even grander and more sumptuous. It is prepared for the disguised Havelok on his arrival in Denmark with Goldeboru and the three sons of Grim. Ubbe, a noble who had been a staunch friend of Havelok's father, King Birkabeyn, takes an immediate liking to the strong, handsome stranger who seems more than the merchant he claims to be.[34] Ubbe invites the newcomers to dinner, where

> Biforn hem com the beste mete
> þat king or cayser wolde ete:
> Kranes, swannes, ueneysun,
> Lax, lampreys, and god sturgun,
> Pyment to drinke, and god claré,
> Win hwit and red, ful god plenté.
>
> (1724-29)

The near-royal fare and the joyful occasion with its many toasts ("And fele siþes haueden wosseyled") underscores the importance of the moment: Havelok is back in his own land and is on the threshold of the victory toward which he has been maturing and developing since the very first night—and meal—in Grim's house.

The fifth feast crowns the series. It is Havelok's coronation feast, and is preceded by games and tournaments, songs and minstrelsy.[35] Of the meal itself the poet says,

> þere was swiþe gode metes;
> And of wyn þat men fer fetes,
> Rith al so mikel and gret plenté
> So it were water of þe se.
> The feste fourti dawes sat;
> So riche was neuere non so þat.
>
> (2340-45)

Significantly, it is only after the festivities are over that Havelok dispatches his knights to apprehend Godard. Havelok's coming of age and his recovery of what he had earlier lost are treated as self-enclosed thematic movements; just as the political and historical considerations of the French versions are excised from the beginning of *Havelok the Dane*, so at the end the obvious revenge motif and scenes are isolated from the story's main thematic concerns, and provide a spectacularly gory "sideshow" to the central action.[36]

Why did the *Havelok* poet choose eating and feasting as a symbolic action marking off stages in Havelok's development? The answer is not far to seek: all human strength and growth depend upon sufficient nourishment, and therefore repeated feasts accord well with the poet's constant interest in Havelok's progress from an impotent child to a strong adult.[37] Moreover, the feasts in *Havelok* are closely related to the next symbolic device I propose to discuss, viz., Havelok's feats of strength. Havelok himself alludes to the interrelationship of food, growth, strength, and destiny just before his return to Denmark and recovery, when he tells Grim's sons of his real lineage and heritage, and commends Grim's loyalty in saving his life years before in the face of Godard's evil schemes:

> For-þi fro Denemark hider [Grim] fledde,
> And me ful fayre and ful wel fedde,
> So þat vn-to þis day
> Haue ich ben fed and fostred ay.
> But nou ich am up to þat helde
> Cumen, that ich may wepne welde,
> And y may grete dintes yeue,
> Shal i neuere hwil ich lyue
> Ben glad, til that ich Denemark se.
>
> (1431-39)

Havelok is repeatedly referred to as a strong man;[38] on three occasions he performs a prodigy of strength which has important consequences for his development. The first is actually a two-fold feat: Havelok overpowers all his competitors for a job as basket-carrier to the earl's cook in Lincoln, and carries an incredible load of fish by himself. This display wins Havelok food (his second feast) and a steady job. It is closely related by the poet to the first appearance in Havelok of social, royal qualities—gentleness, generosity, justice—which complement his personal might.[39] Shortly thereafter, the cook orders Havelok to compete in the games at Lincoln, to which young champions have come from all over England. Despite his ignorance of the game, Havelok puts the shot further than any other contestant. This feat of strength wins the hero great fame,[40] and earl Godrich, hearing of the prodigy, decides to marry the imprisoned Goldeboru to the supposed servant, ostensibly to fulfill his promise to the dying Athelwold,[41] actually to disgrace the princess beyond recovery. Ultimately, then, Havelok's heroic shotput wins him a wife.[42]

The third occasion in which Havelok's strength manifests itself combines the greatest display yet of personal power with clear indications of the social uses of that power, and thus prepares the audience for the hero's imminent accession to kingship, where both personal and social power are essential.[43] Like the fourth feast, the third feat of strength comes after Havelok's return to Denmark, but before the final recognition and recovery. Havelok beats off almost single-handedly a band of seventy robbers who besiege the house of Bernard Brun, a retainer of Ubbe with whom Havelok is staying the night following Ubbe's feast. The fight is a gory affair, recounted with gusto; by morning, the house is surrounded by bleeding bodies and battered limbs.[44] When the incident is made known to Ubbe, stress is laid on Havelok's success in saving Bernard's life and goods, and on the common danger from which Havelok has delivered the area in destroying the brigands.[45] No such social consequences attend the fight analogous to

this one in the earlier versions of the story; there Havelok saves his wife from the brutal attentions of six retainers of the earl himself.[46] As presented in *Havelok the Dane*, the incident rather looks back to the poet's introductory praise of the good king Athelwold, whose social power freed the land from thieves so effectively that a man would walk from one end of England to the other laden with gold, without fear for his treasure or his safety.[47]

The result of Havelok's powerful and socially benevolent deed is that Ubbe houses him in his own castle and is therefore able that night to discover Havelok's real identity, thanks to the fiery breath and the cross-mark, and finally to offer him the climactic "manred," the homage which marks the hero's full recovery. It should be clear, then, that Havelok's great strength in *Havelok the Dane* is not simply a folk tradition, exploited at random for sensational effects, but is closely integrated into the total scheme of Havelok's growth into kingship.[48]

The fiery breath and cross-mark just mentioned form together the third symbolic device of the poem. In the story the two marks which distinguish Havelok are always employed together; discovery of the fact that Havelok emits fire from his mouth while he sleeps leads to a revelation of the "kyne-mark" (604) on his right shoulder, a cross which identifies Havelok as of royal stock. The distinguishing birth-mark, a common romance device, always serves the same purpose in romances, *i. e.*, to emphasize the uniqueness and the special destiny of each individual, despite all outward changes of state due to fortune or malice.[49] In Havelok's case, the marks of his birth and destiny reappear periodically in the narrative, coming each time as a surprise to their discoverers. The repeated shock of disclosure and recognition reminds us of the discrepancy between Havelok's current situation and his final destiny, a discrepancy which will disappear only when he becomes king. At the same time, like the feasts and feats of strength, recognition of the marks measures and advances Havelok's progress.

The earlier versions of the Havelok story make their first use of the flaming breath after Havelok's marriage. The union does not begin happily, since the princess is mortified at being forced to marry a man of low station, while Havelok knows that he is only a pawn in the game of Argentille's wicked guardian. Eventually, however, the partners overcome their mutual dislike and consummate their marriage. That night, Argentille has a marvellous dream and, awakening in perplexity over its meaning, sees Havelok's flame for the first time, which compounds her confusion. The lovers decide to go to Grimsby, where they discover Havelok's identity.[50]

The flame enters the story again in the French versions when Sigar (*i.e.*, Ubbe) of Denmark, suspecting Havelok's true identity, confirms his suspicion by arranging to spy on the sleeping merchant in order to see the flame. In both these cases, the use of the device is anticlimactic. The consummation of the marriage, which prefigures and assures the eventual union of Denmark and England, takes precedence in the first episode, while Havelok's defense of his wife against the earl's men, which all but convinces the earl of the stranger's royalty, removes all suspense from the second.

*Havelok the Dane* adds a third instance, and presents all three so that the appearance of the fiery breath is the central and unexpected fact of the episode, creating in the process considerable suspense and tension. The first discovery has already been mentioned: as Grim prepares to carry out his assignment to kill Havelok in the middle of the night, his wife, Leve,

> saw þerinne a lith ful shir,
> Also brith so it were day,
> Aboute the knaue þer he lay.
> Of hise mouth it stod a stem
> Als it were a sunnebem:
> Also lith was it þer-inne
> So þer brenden cerges inne.
>
> (588-94)

She calls Grim, the two undress the child, find his mark, and realize who he is. The flame has unexpectedly saved Havelok's life at the last moment.

No more is said of the marks until Havelok and Goldeboru go to bed after the feast prepared for them by Grim's children.

> On þe nith, als Goldeborw lay,
> Sory and sorwful was she ay,
> For she wende she were biswike
> þat she were yeuen un-kyndelike.
> O nith saw she þer-inne a lith,
> A swiþe fayr, a swiþe bryth,
> Al so brith, al so shir,
> So it were a blase of fir.
> She lokede norþ, and ek south,
> And saw it commen ut of his mouth
> That lay bi hire in þe bed.
>
> (1247-57)

The princess' reaction is swift and to the point:

> þouthe she, "Wat may this bimene?
> He beth heymen yet, als y wene:
> He beth heyman er he be ded!"
>
> (1259-1261)

She then sees the cross-mark and immediately hears an angel prophesy Havelok's future as king of Denmark and England. Goldeboru awakens Havelok, who tells

her of a prophetic dream he has had; she interprets the dream and advises him to return at once to Denmark.

It is immediately clear that a major turning point in the story, which in the French versions is spread out over several events (the marriage, the consummation, the dream, the trip to Grimsby, the revelation of Havelok's identity), is here reorganized and constricted to take place in one bedroom scene, where the order of events makes for maximum cumulative effect. The consummation of the marriage is omitted, so that the discovery of Havelok's destiny by Goldeboru becomes the sole determining factor in cementing the relationship of hero and heroine. Moreover, instead of Goldeboru's having a dream which Havelok misinterprets, as he does in the other versions,[51] Havelok has the dream, and Goldeboru, prompted by the prophetic voice which only she has heard,[52] interprets it, and offers sound advice to fulfill it. The reason for these changes is evident: the poet wishes to emphasize at this crucial moment the role of love in Havelok's development. As soon as Goldeboru accepts Havelok, she becomes a valuable counsellor. The third plot element of the three enumerated earlier in this discussion is thereby closely integrated with the development theme, completing the interdependence of all the main narrative movements.[53]

The final instance of the flaming breath again differs from its analogues in other versions of the Havelok story, and again has been reordered for maximum effect. Elsewhere, as has been mentioned, the Danish noble arranges to see Havelok asleep to confirm an already strong suspicion that he is the lost king. Neither Sigar nor the reader is surprised by the flame.[54] In *Havelok the Dane*, Ubbe invites Havelok into his home without any inkling that he is accommodating his lord. Ubbe awakens in the middle of the night, sees an eerie glow emanating from the next room, and investigates.[55] Startled by the flame, he calls his retainers, who rush to the scene to behold the hero and heroine asleep in each other's arms, and to note the cross-mark which reveals his identity. Wild joy and excitement break loose, Havelok awakens, and Ubbe climatically swears fealty. The entire scene traverses a curve of mounting excitement, from Ubbe's awakening, through his discovery, to his declaration. Once again, the poet has demonstrated his deft touch in the effective presentation of his material.[56]

This brief consideration of some of the narrative and structural devices employed in *Havelok the Dane* has aimed at defending the poem's integrity and worth in the face of generations of critical indifference and patronization. If I have been able to indicate that *Havelok* is carefully constructed, that the various stages of the story are clearly marked, and that the recurring incidents clarify and buttress the work's central meaning, then my efforts have been gratifyingly successful. The meaning itself, as I understand it, is no less impressive for being presented in a popular rather than a courtly garb: the hero and heroine, stripped of their rights at the beginning of the poem by powerful and evil antagonists, recover their losses and fulfill their destinies as a result of the natural process of growth into capable adulthood. *Havelok the Dane* celebrates human development, and shows that love has a privileged role to play in the combined process of maturation and recovery. In so doing, the poem affirms its romance preoccupations with a degree of capability and originality that should prompt us to revise the dominant opinion of its worth, and incidentally to reappraise our general estimate of the Matter of England romances.

### Notes

[1] The standard studies of saga traditions in the Old and Middle English periods are C. E. Wright, *The Cultivation of Saga in Anglo-Saxon England* (Edinburgh, 1939), and R. M. Wilson, *The Lost Literature of Medieval England* (London, 1952), pp. 27-64, 123-32. Evidence collected by Wright and Wilson indicates that many more sagas were current throughout the medieval period than are extant as connected narratives; accordingly, there were undoubtedly more Matter of England romances than those we now possess.

[2] A. McI. Trounce, in the introduction to his edition of *Athelston* (*EETS* 224, 1951, repr. 1957), argues convincingly for *Athelston's* kinship to and dependence upon the *chanson de geste* tradition. See especially pp. 4-25.

[3] A typical and standard example of earlier scholarship is M. Deutschbein, *Studien zur Sagengeschichte Englands* (Cöthen, 1906). An exhaustive bibliography of early studies is to be found in L. A. Hibbard (Mrs. L. H. Loomis), *Medieval Romance in England* (New York, 1924, new ed. 1960), *passim*.

[4] "An Interpretation of King Horn," *Anglia*, LXXV (1957), 157-72.

[5] All references to the text of *Havelok the Dane* (hereafter *HD*) follow the edition of the poem in W. H. French and C. B. Hale, *Middle English Metrical Romances* (New York, 1920), pp. 71-176. This edition adopts the line numbering and much of the commentary of W. W. Skeat's edition (*EETS, ES* 4, 1868; rev. K. Sisam, Oxford, 1915).

[6] For an account of the various versions and their relative chronology see Hibbard, pp. 103-5. French and Hale posit a date of "about 1285" for the dialect of the only complete MS of *HD*.

[7] H. H. Creek, "The Author of *Havelok the Dane*," *Englische Studien*, XLVIII (1914-15), 193-212, exam-

ines closely the various popular features, and the details of town and peasant life, in *HD*. The elaborate minstrel's preface (ll. 1-26) is another indication of popular origin.

[8] Hill, p. 161.

[9] This is the most common element of the romance plot. Well-known examples occur in the *Odyssey*, in Shakespeare's final romances, and, in the medieval period, in *Sir Orfeo*, *King Horn*, Chrétien's *Yvain*, Marie's *Guigemar*, *etc*. Romances of separated families and lovers, or of the discovery of "real identity," are built around this device.

[10] Stories of castaways or foundlings tend to fall into this pattern, and stories where education is an important factor, *e. g.*, the Telemachus subplot of the *Odyssey*, and the various versions of the Perceval story.

[11] Marie's *Guigemar* relies on a modified form of this motif, as do the Gahmuret-Belakane and Parzival-Condwiramurs relationships of *Parzival*.

[12] Hill, pp. 161-62.

[13] *Cf. HD*, ll. 110-327 and 364-446.

[14] *Cf. HD*, ll. 114 and 352-57.

[15] *Cf. HD*, ll. 286-327 and 408-46.

[16] Both versions are edited with a translation by J. D. Hardy and C. J. Martin (Rolls Series 91, pts. 1 and 2, London, 1888-89).

[17] *Estoire*, ll. 65-104; *lai,* ll. 193-234, 281-338.

[18] *Estoire*, ll. 400-32, 511-16; *lai,* ll. 25-109. The versions differ in some respects; the *lai*, for example, stresses Grim's rank. The Queen, unmentioned in *HD*, plays an active role in saving Havelok in both versions, and is then killed by pirates. The idea for the episode comes from Geoffrey of Monmouth's world-conquering Arthur. *Cf. Historia regum Britanniae* ix. 11 (ed. Griscom, pp. 446-51).

[19] It can be argued, of course, that Arthur and his war on Denmark were already missing from the sources which the *HD* poet used. Lacking intermediary versions of the story, we can only guess at its evolution from the French versions to its form in *HD,* and only assess *HD*'s structure and art *vis-à-vis* the *Estoire* and the *lai*. The resulting critical judgments are valid in any case; if the *HD* poet is not to be commended for the effectiveness of his work, then someone else is. The poet's changes in the early part of *HD* are noted by Creek (see footnote 7, above), p. 199. Creek also points out some of the inconsistencies in the poet's

exposition (pp. 200-2), especially on the matter of Havelok's awareness of his royal birth at various moments in the story. Creek's article is not primarily concerned with the poet's art, but with his moral purposes and his station in life.

[20] One might compare these lines and their sentiments with the briefer portrait of the good heroic king and his social power at the beginning of *Beowulf* (ll. 1-11). The *Beowulf* poet's estimate of Scyld Scefing could equally apply to Athelwold: "That waes god cyning!"

[21] Godrich's term of contempt for Goldeboru—*þerne* (serving maid)—is indicative of the close relationship between power and rank in *HD*.

[22] Ll. 575-85.

[23] *Manred* is the term for the homage which a vassal offers his lord. See *NED, s. v. manred,* 1.

[24] See below, pp. 601-2.

[25] There is no equivalent of these lines in either French version. The *lai* describes the general act of homage to Havelok after his return to Denmark (ll. 915-21), but no one speaks these essential words.

[26] The interrelationship of the two thematic progressions is elsewhere apparent in, e. g., Chrétien's *Yvain* and in *The Winter's Tale*. See the following note.

[27] There is a remarkable parallel between the interplay of theme and structure in *HD* and that of *Sir Gawain and the Green Knight*, which is also built around an act (the "beheading game") performed at the beginning of the story and repeated at the end, and uses a series of repeated symbolic moments (the hunts and bedroom scenes) to portray the hero's changing state. On the latter progression in *Gawain*, see H. L. Savage, *The "Gawain"-Poet* (Chapel Hill, 1956), pp. 31-48.

[28] See, *e.g., Yvain*, ll. 1-6, 723 ff. The source for the Whitsun feast as a quintessential moment of Arthurian splendor, and hence an apt starting point for adventures which will test the worth of the court or of one of its best knights, is Geoffrey's *Historia* ix. 13 ff., where the crown-wearing celebrations (themselves patterned on Anglo-Norman royal practice) form the context of the Roman challenge to Arthur's imperial rule. *Sir Gawain and the Green Knight*, in which feasts also mark important points in the story, changes the time of the opening feast to New Year's day, and adds feasts before Gawain's departure from the court and after his arrival at Bertilak's castle.

[29] The sixth, Havelok's coronation feast in England, is anti-climactic, and the poet dismisses it in three lines (2948-50), without details. My discussion will treat the fifth as the last important feast, in keeping with what seems to be the poet's intent.

[30] Ll. 824 ff. There is no mention of this famine in either of the French versions; the *Estoire* says that Havelok left Grimsby when Grim died, and the *lai,* after describing Grim's sadness that Havelok has grown up in surroundings not fitting to his birth, has Grim counsel the young man to go to England and attach himself to the court, as a servant, in order to rise in it.

[31] Havelok's method for gaining employment involves knocking over all the other claimants for the job. See also ll. 785-810, in which Havelok first resolves to go out and work for his food, since he eats more than Grim and his children, and has now grown up enough so that "Swinken ich wolde for mi mete" (798). *Cf.* the juxtaposition of growth, food, and the hero's purposeful activity cited on pp. 599-601 below.

[32] Ll. 1189-1203.

[33] *Cf.* ll. 617-20, 627-31.

[34] See ll. 1645-54; Ubbe exclaims, "Deus! qui ne were he knith?" (1650).

[35] Ll. 2320-29.

[36] See p. 590, above. Godard's death by torture is described in ll. 2488 ff., Godrich's by burning in ll. 2838 ff. Havelok himself takes no part in Goddard's capture, though he battles Godrich personally in England, as Goldeboru's champion.

[37] There is no series of feasts in either French version, though in both, Havelok interprets Argentille's prophetic dream as referring to a royal feast.

[38] See, *e. g.,* ll. 987-90, and the passage just quoted in the text.

[39] Ll. 930-44 describe Havelok's strength, and ll. 945-58 his meekness, cheerfulness, and generosity. The description closes with the significant lines, "All him loueden þat him sowen,/ Boþen heye men and lowe." *Cf.* ll. 30-34, in the description of good king Athelwold: "Him louede yung, him louede holde, . . . / And al for hise gode werkes." There are similar descriptions of Havelok in the *Estoire,* ll. 105 ff., and the *lai,* ll. 241 ff., but they do not occur after a specific feat of strength; there is no specific line which states the universal love for Havelok, nor, of course, is there a parallel with the Athelwold passage. In fact, in the *lai,* Havelok's qualities seem to be more those of a simple-minded, goodhearted fool than of a future king. See especially l. 256.

[40] See ll. 1059-66.

[41] Ll. 198-201.

[42] Godrich's reasoning appears in one of the few trenchantly ironic passages in the poem: "þoru þis knaue/ Shal ich Engelond al haue,/ And mi sone after me;/ For so i wile þat it be" (1073-76). The irony is two-fold, for not only is Gildeboru's "disgraceful" marriage not disgraceful, but Godrich is actually giving Havelok in Goldeboru an important aid to his development toward kingship. See p. 603, below.

[43] See above, pp. 590-91.

[44] Ll. 1899-1906, 1920-25.

[45] See ll. 1974-75, 2002-5, 2016-23, and, on the bandits' danger to "burgmen and knithes," 2044-51.

[46] *Estoire*, ll. 533 ff.; *lai*, ll. 695 ff. There may be a reminiscence of the earlier version in *HD*, ll. 1926-29, 1934-35.

[47] See ll. 45-50.

[48] Havelok, in his prophetic dream at Grimsby (ll. 1285-1312), sees himself grasping all Denmark in a strong embrace, and later gathering England into one hand and giving it to Goldeboru. The dream is different in the French versions (see pp. 603-4 and note 51, below); in *HD*, its images of physical strength and power effectively prefigure the advent of Havelok's kingly power and provide another reinforcement of the poem's unity.

[49] Odysseus' scar in *Odyssey* xviii (not strictly a birthmark, but serving the same function) and Ascanius' fiery hair in *Aeneid* ii (a divine indication of his destiny which persuades Anchises and Aeneas to leave the doomed Troy) are classical examples of the device. In the French versions of the Havelok story, only the fiery breath appears.

[50] *Estoire*, ll. 181 ff.; *lai*, ll. 381 ff. In the *Estoire*, Grim's daughter Kelloc reveals Havelok's true origins to him without the poet's preparing his audience for the revelation; in the *lai*, Goldeboru visits a holy hermit who tells her she will learn of her husband' birth and destiny by taking him to Grimsby.

[51] The dream is an animal allegory of a kind familiar in the *chanson de geste* tradition (*cf. Chanson de Roland*, ll. 725-36, 2555-69). Havelok interprets it as referring to a royal banquet on the following day. See *Estoire*, ll. 195-290; *lai*, ll. 397-484.

[52] This device replaces the much less effective visit to the holy hermit (see note 50, above), which diffuses the impact of the discovery, especially as Goldeboru only goes because she is advised to do so by a sympathetic chamberlain who makes no other appearance in the *lai*.

[53] There is a suggestion for *HD*'s portrayal of Goldeboru the counsellor in the other versions, where Argentille advises Havelok on the eve of his final battle with Edelsi to set up the bodies of dead soldiers on stakes and thus terrify the enemy by means of an apparently huge army (*Estoire*, ll. 773 ff.; *lai*, ll. 1047 ff.). The poet of *HD* transforms his sources by moving the Queen's advice to a central, climactic position in the story, and by making her counsel at once more intimate and more appropriate to a wife.

[54] In fact, the earl goes back to sleep and only reveals his discovery the next morning.

[55] The suspense is ironically heightened by Ubbe's grumbling that at this time of knight only evil men are up and about. See ll. 2096-105, and compare the similar effect achieved in dramatic and operatic "discoveries," *e.g.*, in *The Spanish Tragedy* and *Don Giovanni*.

[56] Ll. 2106-72. The passage also exploits the tension by humorous touches at l. 2135 (the knights thought that staring at the naked, sleeping lovers was "god gamen") and ll. 2162-64 (Havelok is awakened by the knights kissing his feet, including his toes and toenails!).

## M. Mills (essay date 1967)

SOURCE: "Havelok and the Brutal Fisherman," *Medium Aevum*, Vol. XXXVI, No. 3, 1967, pp. 219-30.

[*In the following essay, Mills concentrates on the characterization of Grim and compares him to earlier examples of the brutal fisherman type.*]

When Havelok first meets with the sons of Grim the fisherman, he gives them a vivid account of his early sufferings at the hands of Earl Godard, the regent into whose hands he had been committed. In this he lays particular stress on the fact that Grim had refused to carry out Godard's command that he should drown the boy:

> 'Deplike dede he him swere
> On boke, þat he sholde me bere
> Unto þe se and drenchen inne,
> And wolde taken on him þe sinne.
> But Grim was wis and swiþe hende,
> Wolde he nouht his soule shende:
> Leuere was him, to be for-sworen,
> Þan drenchen me and ben for-loren;
> But sone bigan he forto fle
> Fro Denemark, forto berwen me.'
>
> (1417-26)[1]

This places Grim in a wholly admirable light, making him comparable in virtue with his namesake in the

French versions of the story,[2] and perfectly typical of the 'good fisherman' of folk-tale and romance—the humble character who is the means of saving the hero's life when this is threatened by seemingly irresistible forces.[3] But the lines quoted above, while true as far as they go, are by no means the whole truth about Grim, and for this we must go back to the author's own narrative of the same events in lines 526-656 of *Havelok* (H):

> Grim is told by Godard (whose man he is) that he will be granted his freedom and made wealthy if he will murder Havelok for him. Grim ties up the lad, takes him to his hut, and there gives him into the charge of his wife Leve (who, like Grim, treats him very roughly). In the middle of the night, just as he is getting ready to put to sea with the boy to drown him, he sees that the hut is flooded with a miraculous light. This he finds proceeds from Havelok's mouth; he and his wife untie him and as they are stripping off his clothes discover a birthmark that puts his royal status beyond doubt. The fisherman at once transfers his loyalty from Godard to Havelok, and Leve brings food to the starving hero.

That Havelok, in his own later account of the scene, should leave out all mention of Grim's brutality is hardly surprising. By this point in the story the fisherman is quite firmly on the side of the angels, and it would serve no useful purpose to recall his less engaging characteristics either to his own sons (who seem never to have known of them) or to the wider audience of the romance (which may by now have forgotten all about them).[4] But however much Havelok and the reader may forgive or forget as the story unfolds, the split down the middle of Grim's rôle is sufficiently curious to demand some kind of explanation. It has not often received attention in the past. Neither Holthausen nor Skeat[5] discuss the matter in their editions, while W. H. French and C. B. Hale content themselves with referring the fisherman's sudden change of heart to the popular belief in the sanctity of the king's person.[6] Only H. L. S. Creek seems to have found Grim's behaviour in any way surprising, and he finds the vital clue to it in the English author's desire to provide his hero with an early history as unhappy as that of his wife-to-be. In other words, since, in both the French and the English versions Edelsi (Godrich H) has the power of life and death over Argentille (Goldeboru H), Havelok must in the same way become Godard's prisoner (as Haveloc never is that of Odulf). Then, since godard does not wish to bear direct responsibility for the boy's death, Grim is forced to play a 'cruel and unnatural part . . . inconsistent with the fidelity and generosity which [he] later displays'.[7] This does not stand up to very close scrutiny—the Godrich-Goldeboru episode will not in fact account for the most striking peculiarities of its Danish counterpart—and the mode of argument as a whole seems to suffer from two weaknesses. First, a tendency (hardly surprising in an admirer of Bédier's)[8] to ascribe too much importance to the inventive powers of a single redactor; second, the assumption that the traditional character-types of romance literature were always simple in their earliest manifestations and only became complex or confused at some later stage. To redress the balance I should like to suggest that 'brutal fishermen' whose characters and actions strikingly parallel those of Grim are to be found in texts considerably earlier in date than H, so that the English author, far from being perversely original in his conduct of the scene, was actually keeping with some fidelity to an established pattern. Furthermore, a careful study of the French texts suggests that the character of Grim may not, in any case, have ever been totally above reproach.

I

The most important evidence for the previous existence of the 'brutal fisherman' as an established character-type is offered by the *Gregorius* (G) of Hartmann von Aue,[9] and the *Wigalois* (W) of Wirnt von Gravenberc.[10] Wolfram's *Parzival*[11] contains a fisherman who resembles Grim in being both ill-mannered and covetous, but who does not go to the extreme of being prepared to kill the hero—or to let him die—in the hope of enriching himself. As presented by Hartmann the scene runs as follows:

> Gregorius comes to the fisherman's house on his quest for a desert place in which to do penance for his unwitting marriage with his mother.[12] On hearing of his mission, his host—who has from the beginning treated him with contempt and suspicion—is very sceptical of the firmness of his resolve, but promises to take him to a barren rock surrounded by water where he can at once enter upon his life of atonement. He makes him lodge that night in a hovel; next morning, when it proves difficult to rouse Gregorius, he loses patience and prepares to go off in his boat without him. But the hero is wakened just in time by the fisherman's wife, and is taken to the rock; in his haste, however, he leaves behind him a tablet on which the circumstances of his birth had been recorded, and which he had carefully kept with him since setting out in the world. Once on the rock, he is fettered and the key thrown into the water—only when it comes to light again will his sins have been forgiven. Seventeen years later emissaries from Rome are searching for Gregorius, who has been revealed in a vision as their next pope. They come to the fisherman's house, and are served with a large fish as their evening meal. In its belly is found the key to the fetters; the fisherman violently repents his earlier treatment of Gregorius and next day takes the messengers to the rock. There they find a naked and almost unrecognizable figure who, in his shame, tries to run away from them. The fisherman begs his forgiveness, and they take him back to the mainland. Before leaving for Rome he recovers the tablet from the ruins of the hut in which he had been lodged. (G 2751-3740).

In W, on the other hand, it assumes the following form:

> After his battle with the dragon Pfetan, Wigalois is lying unconscious at the edge of a lake. Here he is found by a poor fisherman and his wife, who strip him of his armour and also take from him a magical girdle which has the power of protecting the life of its wearer. When he seems to be coming to his senses, the wife tries to drown him, but is restrained from doing so by her husband. She is in any case shortly afterwards moved to pity by the beauty of his naked body. The pair make off with their booty, but are observed by a maiden who subsequently conducts her mistress and companions to the fisherman's hut. The mistress (whose husband had been rescued from the dragon by Wigalois) promises the fisherman a rich reward if he will take them to the knight he has robbed. He does this; when the ladies arrive Wigalois at first flees for shame but is at length persuaded to go back with them. (W 5123-954)[13]

At first glance the two episodes offer very different points of contact with H. Hartmann's contains a rough and unsympathetic fisherman (= Grim), Wirnt's, a violently-disposed wife (= Leve); Hartmann stands closer to the English romance in locating an important part of the scene in the fisherman's own hut, Wirnt, in threatening his hero with drowning, having his body stripped, and recording a complete change of heart on the part of the wife. But a more detailed scrutiny of the three episodes reveals that all three preserve a very similar sequence of events, although the significance of individual parts of it may have been obscured by the need of accommodating it to the very different demands of the stories into which it has been introduced. We may set out the essential common features under the headings of the character of the fisherman and the treatment of the hero.

(I) *The character of the fisherman*

(*a*) A dominant motive is his desire to enrich himself. This is most sympathetically presented by Wirnt, who lays heavy stress on his poverty in W 5292-318 and 5687-95; this is not clearly presented in either H or G, but Grim undertakes the murder in the expectation of being made *riche* as well as *fre* (H 530 f.), while the *vischære* is described as *schazgîre* in G 3294.

(*b*) He is prepared to connive at the hero's death in some way or another. Grim is most direct in this (*i shal drenchen him* (H 583), but Hartmann's villain is quite as callous in the pleasure which he takes in abandoning Gregorius on a barren rock on which, it seems, he must infallibly perish. Even in W, where he earns from Wirnt the approving label of *der vil getriuwe man* (W 5378) as the result of hindering his wife's murderous intentions, he is still quite prepared to leave Wigalois in a helpless state, feeling that he is bound to die before long (*er doch niht genesen kan* (W 5379); com-

pare G 3350-7, where the fisherman tells the messengers from Rome that it is pointless to seek Gregorius on the rock as he must long since have died of exposure).

(*c*) He is impatient to get on with his principal business and as such is sharply contrasted with his wife. The contrast is made most explicit in W, where the husband lacks all sympathy with the woman's sudden concern with reviving Wigalois, and tells her to help him carry off their booty (W 5458-61).[14] In G his determination to put to sea without wasting a moment is immediately followed by his wife's sympathetic rousing of the hero so that he may not miss his chance of entering upon the life of penance that he so greatly desires. Leve also helps to get Havelok ready for his 'fatal' journey in H 575-85, but the distinction between her actions and those of Grim is in other ways closer to the situation in W. For Grim's first words to his wife at this point:

> 'Ne þenkeste nowht of mine oþes,
> þat ich haue mi louerd sworen?'

have a violence that could suggest slowness or reluctance on her part. If so the wife's behaviour would follow a very similar pattern (moving from initial brutality to final sympathy) in these two texts.

(2) *The treatment of the hero*

(*a*) In both H and G he has a great deal to put up with. Havelok is tied up and gagged by Grim (H 545 f.), Gregorius put in fetters by the *vischære* (G 3088 f.); Havelok spends a very uncomfortable few hours on the floor of Grim's cottage (H 567-75), Gregorius is forced to spend the night

> in ein sô armez hiuselîn
> daz ez niht armer enmöhte sîn
>
> (G 3033 f.)

In W details of this kind are quite lacking. The man hides his ill-gotten gains in his hut, but Wigalois is never brought inside it; furthermore, since he is already more dead than alive when he is found there can be no question of tying him up. These developments follow on naturally from the fact that the scene came directly after the fight with the dragon in the common source of W and *Le Chevalier du Papegau*.

(*b*) Both Havelok and Wigalois are stripped by their captors. Such an action would most logically precede an attempt to drown the hero, as in W, but with a more definite causal connexion established between the two (Wigalois is stripped because the fisherman wants his armour, and the wife does not conceive the idea of drowning him until afterwards (W 5331-44 and 5383-6)). In H, too, the undressing of the hero does not come at quite the expected point; it seems to have been motivated by the sight of the *stem* which issues from his mouth (H 599-603) and as such could only be given real significance by supposing that Grim had known that there were two tokens by which the heir to the throne might be recognized, and that having seen one of them he at once started searching for the other (the cruciform birthmark on the boy's shoulder).[15] As for Gregorius, although he is not actually naked when left on the rock by the fisherman—presumably because a penitential garment (*ein barîn hemede* (G 3112)) must now play a part in the scene—he is completely *nacket unde blôz* when he is found by the messengers from Rome (G 3410).

(*c*) As we have noted, the stripping of Havelok reveals the *kyne-merk* which establishes his identity. In W the same process reveals an equally marvellous token in the *gürtel* of W 5349, but the significance of this is too esoteric for it to move the wife (who alone sees and pockets it) to compassion.[16] What does affect her is the beauty of the hero's body and not any mark or talisman found about it.[17] But very shortly after her change of heart she is led to acknowledge the princely rank of Wigalois by the magnificence of his armour (W 5451-3), which therefore—in spite of its relatively commonplace nature as a status-symbol—serves very much the same function as the birthmark had done in H. In G the vital issue at this point in the story is not the identity or the rank of Gregorius, but his spiritual state, while in any case the physical distance between him and the fisherman makes it impossible for the latter to find any token of any kind about his body. And so the function performed by the *kyne-merk* is taken over, in part at least, by the key to the fetters, which had been thrown into the sea with the chilling words:

> daz weiz ich âne wân,
> swenne ich den slüzzel vunden hân
> ûz der tiefen ünde
> sô bist dû âne sünde
> und wol ein heilic man.
>
> (G 3095-9)[18]

But the key is not the only token in G that has affinities with the birthmark of Havelok and the girdle and armour of Wigalois; also noteworthy is the *tavel* which had recorded the incestuous birth of Gregorius. Like the *gürtel*, this was bequeathed to the hero by his mother and kept closely hidden by him (G 747 ff. and 2277-87; W 1364-77); moreover, in spite of the grief which it causes him it finally becomes something of a talisman in itself, in that it lightens his burden of sin rather than adds to it. Certainly its supposed loss causes him great distress while he is on the rock (G 3682-93; compare the lamentation of Wigalois for the loss of his protective talisman in W 5992-6000). It also serves as a recognition token of a very precise kind at an earlier point in the tale, when it reveals his identity to his

mother (G 2471-85), and duplicates the key as an index of his hard-won sanctity by its unblemished condition when found again at the end of the seventeen years (G 3730-40).

(*d*) In both H and G the fisherman's reaction to the sight of one of the tokens is immediate and violent:

> 'Goddot', quath Grim, 'þis ure eir,
> þat shal ben louerd of Denemark!
> He shal ben king, strong and stark.
>
> (H 606-8)

> dô erkande er sich zehant
> wie er getobet hâte
> und vie sich alsô drâte
> mit beiden handen in daz hâr.
>
> (G 3306-9)

In W, as we have seen, a comparable change of heart (this time in the wife) is less explicitly related to either token, but is still placed quite close to the mention of the second of these (the armour). In all three texts the wife brings food and/or water to the hero. In W she merely tries to rouse him with the second of these (W 5454-7), but in both H and G she offers him a great deal more, Leve promising to bring

> 'Bred and chese, butere and milk,
> Pastees and flaunes,'
>
> (H 643 f.)

the wife of the *vischare, ir aller besten spîse* (G 2889), although in the sequel Gregorius will accept only water and *ein ranft von haberbrôte* (G 2892) and Havelok is represented as eating only *a lof . . . and more* (H 653).

As often happens with cognate episodes of this type, no single version of those surviving presents all the common features in the most convincing way. But it can hardly be doubted that behind all three of them there must have existed very much the same basic sequence of incident, in which a fisherman and his wife who at first treat the hero very roughly undergo a complete change of heart after catching sight of some (miraculous) token which serves to establish his identity. It is, of course, quite possible that even in its early (twelfth-century) form, variant versions of some of its features had been developed—now the man, now the woman, may have constituted the principal threat to the hero's life. But what is more surprising than the variation in individual detail is the tenacity of the ensemble, and never more so than in Hartmann's poem. Here the pressures of the pious legend as a whole have modified the contours of the primitive episode much less than might have been expected. With his external circumstances changed beyond recognition the *vischære* yet remains constant to his old ways. He is not afflicted with poverty or by any servile status, but he is still covetous; he is now supposedly an agent of the Divine Providence that leads the sinner to salvation, but no gloss of sanctity has rubbed off upon him.[19] On the contrary, he develops a sadistic turn of irony that makes him more purely evil than Grim,[20] and the gap of seventeen years which separates the first part of his story from the second is not used to make plausible any creeping sense of remorse on his part; he admits later that he had dismissed Gregorius from his mind as soon as he had left him on the rock (G 3648 f.) and he is clearly his old and obnoxious self when the messengers from Rome appear. This has the effect of making his 'conversion' as sudden and unexpected as that of Grim, or of the wife of the fisherman in W. All in all, the legend seems to have upset the primitive structure of the episode much less than the episode has upset that of the legend, and the malice of the fisherman is stressed to a degree that makes it difficult to hold firmly to the notion that the sufferings of Gregorius are altogether the result of God's anger at his sins (see G 2678 f.) and not, to some extent at least, the work of the man

> der den sælderîchen
> sô ungezogenlîchen
> in sînen dürften emphie
> und die übele an im begie
> daz er in durch sînen haz
> sazte, dâ er noch saz,
> ûf den dürren wilden stein
> und im dâ sîniu bein
> slôz in die îsenhalten.
>
> (G 3241-9)

## II

No such tension exists in H between the traditional characterization of the fisherman and his function in the story; indeed, with one important exception, the English version seems likely to stand closer to the primitive scene than either of the German examples had done. This exception concerns the relationship of Grim to Godard. The English fisherman does not—impelled by a mixture of economic necessity and original sin—act on his own behalf, but as the instrument of an evil master, and this modification brings him to some degree within the orbit of the much better-known character-type of the hired assassin who fails, through pity, to carry out his orders. The two types have some obvious features in common[21] and it is thus not surprising that Grim should sometimes have been regarded as an example of the second. Creek compared his dealings with Godard with those of Saber with the mother of Bevis of Hamtoune,[22] while G. Bordman has lately rejected Stith Thompson's view of Grim as a benevolent fisherman[23] in favour of seeing him as a compassionate executioner.[24] But Grim is still set apart from most other examples of this character by the whole-

heartedness with which he complies with Godard's wishes, and this characteristic seems a legacy from the story of the brutal fisherman. Nor does it entirely disappear after H 606 ff., since when he returns to Godard to announce his 'success', he enters into the part with rather disquieting relish:

> 'Louerd, don ich haue
> þat þou me bede of þe knaue:
> He is drenched in þe flod,
> Abouten his hals an anker god;
> He is witer-like ded,
> Eteth he neure more bred;
> He liþ drenched in þe se.
> Yif me gold and oþer fe,
> þat y mowe riche be,
> And with þi chartre make me fre,
> For þu ful wel bi-hetet me,
> þanne i last spak with þe!'
>
> (H 667-78)

From one point of view the assertiveness of the first half of this passage is reasonable enough. Executioners who turn compassionate in a watery rather than a woodland setting cannot in the nature of things produce the heart of an animal or some garment soaked in an animal's blood as proof of their efficiency, and so Grim, in spelling out his message so carefully (what he tells Godard four times is true) may simply be trying to make good this lack. But lines 674 ff. seem more gratuitous, and the total effect of the passage is to resurrect the figure of the brutal and venal fisherman that should really have passed from the scene with the discovery of the *kyne-merk*. Because of this a certain ambiguity clings to the lines which describe Grim's flight from Godard after the latter has taken up an unexpectedly moral stance (*þou haues don a wicke dede* (H 688)) and repudiated him:

> Grim þouchte to late, þat he ran
> Fro þat traytour, þat wicke man,
>
> (H 691 f.)

since *traytour* might here have the sense of 'one who betrays any person that trusts him' (the first of those recorded for the noun in *OED*) rather than 'one who is false to his allegiance to his sovereign' (the second). In other words, Godard's lack of reliability as an employer may just as well have been uppermost in Grim's mind (and that of the author) at this point as his treachery towards Havelok. But if so this is the last point at which we are reminded of the fisherman's earlier character; after H 692 he settles down firmly into the groove of helpful virtue and never again leaves it.

He had never really left it at all in the French versions of the story, where he has no personal contact of any kind with Odulf, Godard's counterpart.[25] But at the same time he *is* connected with a group of characters who are very far from respectable, and who prove as fatal to Haveloc's mother and retainers as Godard was to be to his sisters. These are the *uthlages* met with by the Danish fugitives on their way to England. In Gaimar's version they are mentioned twice: first when Kelloc, Grim's daughter, tells Haveloc of their earlier escape from Denmark; second when Haveloc, in his turn, relates the same events to Sigar the Danish earl.[26] In the first passage we learn that everyone in the boat apart from Grim, his wife, and the children, was drowned by pirates who attacked them on their crossing, and that the survivors owed their lives to the fact that the fisherman was known to the attackers

> 'Mis pere esteit lur cunuissant,
> Pur co garirent li enfant—
> E jo e vus e mi dui frere—
> Par la preiere de mun pere.

(Gaimar 431-4)

In Haveloc's later version of this exactly the same facts are given, but the hero seems to have forgotten just why he had been spared (*jo gari, se sai en quel guise* (584)). This difference in precision corresponds in miniature to that noted at the beginning of this article between the ME author's account of Grim's treatment of Havelok and Havelok's own. The distance which separates the English Grim's willingness to drown Havelok and the French Grim's failure to prevent the pirates from drowning his mother is, of course, very considerable, but it should not blind us to the essential similarity of pattern between the two versions:

(1) Grim is the friend or willing accomplice of ruthless and powerful associates.

(2) These murder one or more of Havelok's blood-relations.

(3) Grim, who had been unable to prevent this crime, is yet able to preserve the boy's life.

It is much easier to perceive these similarities than to establish which version of the common elements stands closest to that of the *Ur-Havelok*, but it at least seems unlikely that Gaimar would have developed his own version directly from one resembling the English account.[27] Our poet's conception of Grim and of his relationship with Godard is surely too detailed and vivid to have been removed without leaving more trace than the three points of contact listed above. It would certainly seem more likely that a terse and rather colourless account such as that of Gaimar should have been elaborated to produce something more lively. But there is in any case no reason why there should not have existed an intermediate (or supplementary) version that would have provided a more tangible springboard for both departures, and if we wish to indulge our fancy it would not be difficult to construct one such with the help of stories such as those of Tristan,

Apollonius and Octavian, which in other episodes show points of similarity with our story:[28] Havelok might, for example, have been sold to merchants or kidnapped by outlaws, and subsequently rescued by Grim. But if the relative 'authenticity' of the English and French poems must remain a matter of dispute there is nothing vague or obscure about their different effectiveness as literature. Like much else in the English romance, the character and conduct of Grim may be 'honeycombed with inconsistencies and difficulties'[29] when judged by limited and *a priori* notions of what constitutes plausible human behaviour, but the self-consistency of his opposite number in the *Lai* and in Gaimar seems a very tepid virtue when set against the excitement generated by his own less predictable behaviour. And in helping to produce this excitement the story of the brutal fisherman has played a vital part.

*Notes*

[1] *Havelok (Alt- und Mittelenglische Texte* I) ed. F. Holthausen 'Heidelberg 1928'.

[2] *Le Lai d'Haveloc* and the Haveloc episode in Gaimar's *Estorie des Engleis*, both of which are given in A. Bell's edition of the *Lai* (Manchester 1925).

[3] See for example the representatives of the type found in the stories of Guy of Warwick and Apollonius of Tyre (lines 9806-45 of the Caius MS. of *Guy* and 634-65 of the eighth book of the *Confessio Amantis*). This simplified view of Grim was accepted by Stith Thompson, who listed the episode under his type R 131.4 ('Fisherman rescues abandoned child') in his *Motif-Index of Folk Literature* (Copenhagen 1955-8).

[4] In a still later description of the same events, Ubbe, the Danish earl, sticks rather more closely to the facts:

> Hwan Grim saw, þat he was so fayr,
> And wiste, he was þe rihte eir,
> Fro Denemark ful sone he fledde

(H 2234-6)

It is true that the primary account had made no mention of the impact of Havelok's beauty on his captors, but this motif is of importance in at least one other version of the episode; see below n[17].

[5] *The Lay of Havelok the Dane* ed. W. W. Skeat, rev. K. Sisam (Oxford 1950).

[6] *Middle English Metrical Romances* (New York 1930), p. 98.

[7] 'The Author of "Havelok the Dane"' *Englische Studien* XLVIII (1914-15) 201.

[8] Ibid. 194.

[9] ed. F. Neumann (*Deutsche Klassiker des Mittelalters*, N.F. II) (Wiesbaden 1958). In what concerns the fisherman as in other parts of the legend, Hartmann's treatment is more elaborate than that of either of the French versions. For the relation of these to G, see H. Schottmann 'Gregorius und Grégoire' *Zeitschrift für Deutsches Altertum und Deutsche Literatur* XCIV (1965) 81-3; for Hartmann's additions to the episode discussed in the pages which follow, ibid., 91 f. and the notes to lines 2821 ff., 3055 ff. and 3095-9 in Neumann's edition.

[10] ed. J. M. N. Kapteyn (Bonn 1926). Reference must also be made to the fifteenth-century romance of *Le Chevalier du Papegau* which, cognate with W for much of its length but not derived from it, has often preserved the material common to both in more authentic form; see Saran 'Ueber Wirnt von Gravenberg und den Wigalois' *Beiträge zur Geschichte der Deutschen Sprache und Literatur* XXI (1896) 336 ff.

[11] ed. A. Leitzmann (*Altdeutsche Textbibliothek* XII) (Halle 1955), 142.11-144.16.

[12] He is himself the child of her incestuous union with her brother.

[13] A much abbreviated version of the same scene is found in *Le Chevalier du Papegau* p. 68 f. (see n. 10 above); it must therefore have been already present in Wirnt's source. But some of the detail of W could well have been taken directly from G, both from the episode under consideration and the earlier scene in which two fishermen discover the infant Gregorius after he has been committed to the sea (G 939-1216). Hartmann's *Iwein* was certainly laid under contribution for such later details as the discovery of the hero by a group of ladies and his lamentation on recovering his senses (*Iwein* 3359-593; for a discussion of these borrowings see R. Bethge *Wirnt von Gravenberg* (Berlin 1881) p. 59 ff.).

[14] The same contrast is implied by what we are allowed to hear of the conversation between the fisherman and his wife after the robbery in *Le Chevalier du Papegau* (the scene itself is never described by the author).

[15] Like Sigar the Danish earl (= Ubbe H) in the French versions. Here twofold proof of royal birth is provided by the miraculous flame (Gaimar 633-40, *Lai* 833-40) and by the ability to sound a horn that had belonged to Haveloc's father, King Guntier (Gaimar 670-724, *Lai* 879-914).

[16] Wirnt has not mentioned it since the hero's departure from his mother's home. At the beginning of W it had figured chiefly as a protective talisman (W 610-12), but by the time it is given to Wigalois by his mother it may also have been meant to serve as a token

by which he and his father Gawain could recognize each other (W 1367-75).

[17] Compare G 2835 f. in which we are told (at the very beginning of the episode)

> Des übelen vischæres wîp
> erbarmte sich über sînen lîp.

[18] For the widespread diffusion of this motif independently of the story of the fisherman, see K. H. Jackson *The International Popular Tale and Early Welsh Tradition* (Cardiff 1961) pp. 25-9.

[19] In this he contrasts sharply with his counterpart in the related story of Martinian; see H. W. J. Kroes 'Die Gregorlegende' *Neophilologus* XXXVIII (1954) 170.

[20] In his tardy confession of his sins to Gregorius he admits

> darnâch volcte ich iuwer bete
> wan daz ich ez in hônschaft tete.

> (G 3643 f.)

[21] In making the effective cause of the wife's compassion the beauty of the hero's body (instead of the perception of some talisman or token of rank), Wirnt has made the overlapping of the two types more obvious than ever. Compare lines 85-7 of *King Horn*:

> Payns him wolde slen,
> Oþer al quic flen,
> ȝef his fairnesse nere.

[22] 'Character in the "Matter of England" Romances' *JEGP* X (1911) 432.

[23] See n.3 above.

[24] *Motif-Index of the English Metrical Romances* (Helsinki 1963) pp. 10 and 53 (where the episode is listed under *K 512.8).

[25] Odulf is responsible for the death of Guntier, Haveloc's father, and persecutes all those who had supported him (*Lai* 81 f.), but his act of regicide is so briefly presented (*Odulf l'oscist par traïsun* (*Lai* 35, 603)) as to have much less impact than Godard's murder of Havelok's sisters in H 465-80.

[26] Lines 424-34 and 580-6. The corresponding passages in the *Lai* are lines 609-14 and 782-6, but these are preceded by another more detailed version, narrated by the author himself (lines 110-22).

[27] French and Hale boldly declare that 'the French poets replace this episode [H 519 ff.] with an attack by pirates, after which Grim saves Havelok from the sea.'

(op. cit., p. 94), but unfortunately produce no supporting evidence for their belief (they do not even indicate the points that the English and French episodes have in common).

[28] For the relationship of the first and second of these to the story see A. Bell, op. cit., pp. 47-9 and H. Newstead 'The Enfances of Tristan and English Tradition' *Studies in Medieval Literature in Honor of A. C. Baugh* (Philadelphia 1961) pp. 169-85.

[29] *ES* XLVIII (1914-15) 199.

## Judith Weiss (essay date 1969)

SOURCE: "Structure and Characterisation in *Havelok the Dane*," *Speculum: A Journal of Mediaeval Studies*, Vol. XLIV, No. 2, April, 1969, pp. 247-57.

[*In the following essay, Weiss credits* Havelok the Dane *with subtle structure and strong characterizations of not only its hero, but also its villains and minor characters.*]

There are three principal versions of the tale of Havelok extant: the "Haveloc episode" in Gaimar's *Estoire des Engleis*,[1] the *Lai d'Haveloc*,[2] and the romance of *Havelok the Dane*.[3] Of the three, the English poem is the longest and the most literary treatment. It is possible that its author knew the Anglo-Norman accounts and may have taken ideas from them, but he chose to impose a far more formal and complex pattern on a story which in their hands had stayed relatively short and simple.[4]

The tale of Havelok shows the union of a Danish prince, whose kingdom is usurped by a treacherous nobleman, and an East Anglian princess, whose guardian attempts to deprive her of her inheritance. Both Gaimar and the author of the *Lai* must have seen the resemblances between the situations of Haveloc and Argentille, but they did not develop them. The English poet, on the other hand, takes care not only to emphasise these parallels but to create still more, making England and Denmark almost exact counterparts. He presents Goldeborw (the equivalent of Argentille) as inheriting not merely East Anglia[5] but *all* England: she is thus heir to a whole nation, as Havelok is, and the concept of the *whole* country and its possession is as vital to the action in England as it is in Denmark.[6] Each land is first depicted as ruled by a just and much-loved king—Athelwold, Birkabein—who, before he dies, summons his barons in order to make them choose a guardian for his child/children till they come of age. This situation is described in Denmark at less length than the one in England, for it is England the writer is more interested in; besides, to have two such scenes of equal detail would be an artistic fault; but the episodes nevertheless echo each other down to the words used. The king

is "hosled" and "shriuen" (212, 362-364), makes his "quiste" (218-219, 365); and obliges the appointed guardian to swear to keep his oath on the "messe-bok" and the "messe-gere" (186-188, 389-391). The guardians have almost identical names, they are both chosen because they are thought to be trustworthy and honest, and they betray the trust—each "let his oth al ouer-go" (314, 2220). They put the children in castles where they are poorly fed, scantily clad, and where 'non ne mihte hem comen to' (320-327, 412-414). These parallels already also compel us to notice the difference between the two traitors—Godard being more villainous than Godrich—and prepare us for their trials, when they are eventually brought to justice: they are both judged by an assembly drawn from all classes in the land, but Godard's punishment is crueller, and his agony is described at length.

But the structure of **Havelok the Dane** is not confined to these rather artificial patterns that the writer has created. He uses the story to support and give prominence to a number of themes that interest him. The first and perhaps the most obvious of these is the idea of a pattern of good which continues to operate despite all attempts to thwart it. Athelwold wishes Goldeborw to be married to:

> þe [hexte] man þat mihte liue,
> þe beste, fayreste, the strangest ok . . .
> (199-200),

the most eminent man in the kingdom. Godrich, ironically repeating Athelwold's words (1080-1), imagines he is foiling Athelwold's purpose and securing the kingdom for himself by giving Goldeborw to a scullion who suits the requirements superficially; yet Havelok *is* 'the best man,' not only physically but morally and by virtue of his unknown rank. Evil appears to have been decided on, but is about to reinforce the original good.

The action is interspersed with the appeals of the poet to a God depicted primarily as revenger of the innocent and helper of the helpless, who is thus behind the workings of the pattern:

> Iesu Crist, that Lazarun
> To liue brouhte fro dede bondes,
> He lese hire with hise hondes;
> And leue sho mo[te] him y-se
> Heye hangen on galwe-tre,
> þat hire haued in sorwe brouht,
> So as sho ne misdede nouht!
> (331-337)

> Iesu Crist, þat makede go
> þe halte, and þe doumbe speke,
> Hauelok, þe of Godard wreke!
> (542-544)

Ubbe (the Danish nobleman who helps Havelok regain his throne) attributes Havelok's escape from Godard to the pity of God (2226-29); and Havelok knows that Godard cannot avoid judgement since "God is angry with him in every way" (2469).

A religious bias also colours the theme of trust, and betrayal of trust, running through the poem. Godard and Godrich belie the faith placed in them and are both compared to Judas, the archetypal traitor (319, 425). By contrast, the fisherman Grim and his family, the humble people, keep faith with Havelok throughout his fortunes: "Ne weren he neuere ayeyn hem fikel" (1210).

The centre of the writer's concern, however, is a subject that could be entitled 'the land and its rulers.' The theme appears at the very beginning of the romance, when Goldeborw's father Athelwold establishes an ideal of the perfect Christian king. He protects the helpless and innocent (75-86), punishes evil-doers, maintains peace and justice. He observes his religious duties but is also a man of action (87-96); and though he properly consults his vassals on matters of moment, he knows how to control their behaviour (90-2, 77, 80): he rules constitutionally but firmly. This saintly king, "Engelondes blome" (63), is adored by his people:

> Him louede yung, him loueden olde,
> Erl and barun, dreng and thayn,
> Kniht, [and] bondeman, and swain,
> Wydues, maydnes, prestes and clerkes . . .
>
> (30-33)

At the opening of the poem, therefore, we have a king who rules by love. He is quickly supplanted by one who rules by fear. Athelwold and Godrich are contrasted in everything except their control over the land, and the contrast is emphasised by religious overtones. Athelwold lives and dies in an exemplary Christian manner; Godrich (like Godard) is twice called "worse than Satan" (1100, 1134). He governs by force, not just for the principle of justice but to strengthen his own grip on the country (266-273), and reaps the result: the intimidated people obey but fear him:

> Soþlike, in a litel þrawe,
> Al Engelond of him stod awe;
> Al Engelond was of him adrad,
> So is þe beste fro þe gad.
>
> (276-279. See also 2568-69)

The striking image crystallises the feeling of the people towards the usurper. Godard follows the same course as Godrich, though it is described in less detail (437-442); and the images expressing the relation between governor and governed, absent here, recur, interestingly enough, when Ubbe presents Havelok to the Danes as their legitimate king. The figure of Ubbe is drawn with some subtlety. He appears to be the effective ruler of Denmark, despite the early description of Godard's seizure of power; and perhaps the missing leaf in the MS of 180 lines, that must have described Havelok's arrival in his native land, told us why. At any rate, Ubbe is depicted as wielding considerable power over the country; and when he summons both his immediate vassals and, later, the people of Denmark to his presence, to acknowledge Havelok, several comments indicate the nature of their obedience:

> His bode ne durste he non at-sitte
> þat he ne neme, for to wite
> Sone, hwat wolde þe iustise . . .
>
> (2200-02)

> Of hem ne wolde neuere on dwelle,
> þat he ne come sone plattinde,
> Hwo hors ne hauede, com gangande.
> So þat with-inne a fourteniht,
> In al Denmark ne was no kniht,
> Ne conestable, ne shiréue,
> þat com of Adam and of Eue,
> þat he ne com biforn sire Ubbe:
> *He dredden him so þef doth clubbe.*
>
> (2281-89)

> He weren for Ubbe swiþe adrad,
> And dide sone al þat he bad . . .
>
> (2304-05)

Ubbe wields his authority for good, not ill, but he is nevertheless no more the rightful ruler of Denmark than Godard, and once again a suggestive image—"He dredden him so þef doth clubbe"—implies that his relationship with the people cannot conform to the ideal.

The romance closes, as it began, with a picture of the right king in power, punishing wrong-doers (2809-41), suitably rewarding his followers (2897-2927), conciliating his former adversaries (2858-83), and consulting his people on important issues (2808-17). This consultation, the mark of constitutional monarchy, is emphasised by the writer, and is one of his most striking additions to the Havelok story.[7] Whereas the *Lai d'Haveloc* shows Edelsi in some measure obliged to concede to the demands of his barons (291-374), the author of ***Havelok*** cuts out all mention of any baronial pressure on Godrich, Edelsi's counterpart, or of his consulting anyone on Goldeborw's marriage (1073-99): he acts despotically. But the English poet evidently believes that the people are almost as important as the ruler; they have their part to play in government and should be allowed it. Furthermore this part is allowed to all classes and all ages.

The people, in turn, bear a collective responsibility when their decisions produce an unfortunate result.

Ubbe uses one of the Danes' wrong decisions to persuade them to acknowledge Havelok:

> A þing ich wile you here shauwe,
> þat [ye] alle ful wel knawe.
> *Ye witen wel* þat al þis lond
> Was in Birkabeynes hond,
> þe day þat he was quic and ded;
> And how þat he, *bi youre red,*
> Bitauhte hise children þre
> Godard to yeme, and al his fe . . .
> *Alle herden ye* him swere . . .
>
> (2206-16)

The English people admit to Goldeborw that they shirked their responsibility to set the kingdom to rights:

> Is non of us, [ne] yung ne old,
> þat [he] ne wot, þat Athelwold
> Was king of [al] þis kunerike,
> And ye his eyr, and þat þe swike
> Haues it halden with mikel wronge . . .
>
> (2802-06)

The author of **Havelok** is profoundly concerned with the problems and ideals of government, the relation between ruler and people; but beyond this, he feels for the land itself. "Al Denemark," "al Engelond," constantly remind us of the specific identity of a country and its completeness, its totality (277, 278, 264, 294, 309, 386, 485, 516, etc.); and the concept is continually evoked by the usurpers who long to possess what they are not entitled to. Godard's intense possessive love of the country he rules by force is expressed in his determination to deprive Havelok and Goldeborw of the very earth of her inheritance:

> Ne shulde he hauen of Engellond
> Onlepi forw in his hond.
>
> (1093-94)

This feeling for the land is most beautifully evoked by Havelok's dream, which gives symbolical expression to a central theme. The English poet does not take over the rather wooden and lifeless images of the visions in Gaimar and the *Lai* but replaces them by a simpler and more poetic idea: Havelok dreams that, sitting on the highest hill in Denmark, he embraces and possesses the whole kingdom, which clings to his arms:

> I gan Denmark for to awe,
> þe borwes and þe castles stronge;
> And mine armes weren so longe,
> That i fadmede, al at ones,
> Denmark, with mine longe bones;
> And þanne y wolde mine armes drawe
> Til me, and [þouhte hem] for to [awe],

> Al that euere in Denemark liueden
> On mine armes faste clyueden . . .
>
> (1292-1300)

He then imagines he comes to England and "al closede it intil min hond" (1310). Here the metaphor of possession in "hauen in hond" is specifically linked with its physical origins.

The poet is, naturally enough, more involved with the situation of England than Denmark; and **Havelok** shows a patriotic attitude,[8] a feeling for national unity, that reflects the emergence of English nationalism in the thirteenth century. The poem's preoccupation with the nature of the ideal ruler and, to a lesser extent, with the nature of government also seems natural against the background of the baronial struggles for reform, a movement which affected high and low alike. It was a century of "parlements"—the word came into vogue in the 1240's[9]—assembled from representatives of many classes, such as the one of 1244 in London which drew up a scheme of reform and forced the king to accept it, or Richard of Cornwall's Parliament of 1254, to which were summoned two knights elected from each shire, or de Montfort's Parliament of 1264.[10] The general interest in how England should be governed and by what sort of ruler is epitomised in the short treatise Grosseteste, Bishop of Lincoln, wrote for de Montfort around 1252, called "The Principles of Kingship and Tyranny,"[11] and in the Latin poem on the battle of Lewes, which discusses the ideal of a prince who rules by law, justice and the consultation of his subjects.[12] It is more than probable that this national interest in the nature of an ideal governor influenced the author of *Havelok* to shape his material round a political theme.

The conception of the characters in **Havelok** is inevitably closely connected with the poem's central theme of a country and its rulers. Havelok himself must be seen to be a worthy successor to Athelwold, and thus not only must he show himself to be a constitutional monarch, when he achieves power, but he must also be obviously a man of action and decision. Now the portraits of Haveloc in Gaimar's *Estoire* and the *Lai d'Haveloc*, though not especially detailed, continually suggest that he is an amiable but weak-minded figure, to a great extent dominated by others. Naive, sexually ignorant (*Estoire* 175-178), strong but curiously passive, Haveloc often takes second place to his wife Argentille, who initiates action, makes decisions, and gives proof of much more resource. Such a conception of Havelok did not suit the English poet, who firmly restores him as the active centre of the romance. It is Havelok who has the prophetic dream, not Goldeborw, as in Gaimar and the *Lai*. From the beginning of the poem he is lively and "sumdel bold" (450), protesting against his captivity (450-464), protesting against his marriage (1136 ff.) His "Hwat sholde ich with wiue do?" seems like a clever modification of Gaimar's "Cil ne saveit que femme esteit/Ne qu'il faire ne li deveit" (*Estoire* 175-176); Havelok does not know what to do, not from sexual ignorance but for practical reasons:

> I ne may hire fede, ne cloþe, ne sho.
> Hwider sholde ich wimman bringe?
> I ne haue none kinnes þinge . . .
>
> (1138-40)

He makes his own decisions, whether to work for Grim, to leave for Grimsby, in case his wife is humiliated at Lincoln (1189-93). By his own spirit and initiative he forces himself upon the notice of Godrich's cook, knocking down all his competitors (871 ff.). Instead of the passive, bewildered figure of the *Estoire* and the *Lai*, the English writer creates a character with a conscience, aware of his actions and their consequences, accepted, significantly, within his environment—the Danish citizens support his stand against the thieves who have attacked him, instead of pursuing him as in the Anglo-Norman poems—because only a man like this can properly take over the rule of the kingdoms of England and Denmark.

But the ruler should also obviously be the *best* man in the kingdom, and throughout **Havelok** the hero's uniqueness is constantly emphasised. The poet adapts a motif from the *Lai* for this purpose. Achebrit makes Edelsi promise to marry Argentille "al plus fort home . . . K'en la terre trover poreit" (227-228), understanding "fort" in the sense of "powerful," "eminent"; Athelwold, on the other hand, specifically stresses the physical superiority of the man Goldeborw must marry: "þe [hexte] man þat mihte liue,/þe beste, fayreste, the strangest ok" (199-200, 1080-81). Havelok's *height*, above all, is his distinguishing physical characteristic: it is described in images which at the same time express the smaller stature of lesser folk:

> þo stod Hauelok als a lowe
> Aboven [þo] þat þer-inne wore,
> Riht al bi þe heued more
> þanne ani þat þer-inne stod.
>
> (1699-1702)

> Hauelok stod ouer hem als a mast.
>
> (986)

Havelok's visible superiority of height, strength, and beauty is the outward expression of his moral superiority: "In Engelond [was] non hise per" (989), either for strength, or humility, and the Christian virtues. When all England is agog with the stories of this man who is by nature intended to rule, what superb irony that Godard should hear them only to decide: "þoru þis knaue /Shal ich Engelond al haue" (1073-74)!

Yet the English poet keeps some of the traits of the Anglo-Norman Haveloc in that, though he enhances

his hero's role, he does not make him aristocratic or courtly. The ideal of "knighthood" Havelok represents is one primarily of strength,[13] secondly, perhaps, of respect for religion. It is totally unrelated to the service of woman or any concept of *fine amour*. As in the Anglo-Norman poems, Havelok does not choose his wife, and he is reluctant to marry. His affection and concern for Goldeborw are carefully established (1189-93, 1668-73), and there is little doubt the poet intends his final description of their happy life together to represent an ideal of marital love (2967 ff.), but passionate love plays no part at all in the story.[14] For the greater part of the tale Havelok is still a peasant, and he uses a peasant's weapons; his longest and most interesting fight is against a gang of thieves whom he brains with the bar of a door. This, and not the battles to regain Denmark and England, is the true "epic" struggle of the poem, when Havelok is one against sixty, like a bear surrounded by dogs (1838-39), and performs heroic feats:

> He broken armes, he broken knes,
> He broken shankes, he broken thes . . .
> He maden here backes al-so bloute
> Als here wombes, and made hem rowte
> Als he weren kradelbarnes . . .
>
> (1902-12)

Havelok's uncourtly nature, his easy absorption into and acceptance of peasant life,[15] emphasises by contrast Goldeborw's shame at her social degradation. The poet's sympathy for his heroine is never more obvious than on her arrival at Grimsby. Grim's sons and daughters joyfully greet Havelok with a rustic feast, but what is familiar and pleasing to him is uncouth and strange to his wife, and their conviviality is sharply juxtaposed to her misery:

> Hwan he þis ioie haueden maked,
> Sithen stikes broken and kraked,
> And þe fir brouht on brenne,
> Ne was þer spared gos ne henne,
> Ne þe ende, ne þe drake,
> Mete he deden plenté make;
> Ne wantede þere no god mete,
> Wyn and ale deden he fete,
> And maden hem [ful] glade and bliþe,
> Wesseyl he ledden fele siþe.
>
> On þe niht, also Goldeborw lay,
> Sory and sorwful was she ay,
> For she wende she were bi-swike,
> þat she were yeuen un-kyndelike.
>
> (1237-50)

Goldeborw's condition is often depicted and commented on with sympathy. Her helpless position as a young child (112-113), her bitter resignation to the fact that as a woman she can be treated like a chattel (1163-68), reflect the writer's warmth of feeling towards her. He represents her as a woman of spirit and intelligence: she protests as strongly as Havelok against the marriage (1111-16); she interprets the dream, and she takes over the role of Kelloc, Grim's daughter, in the *Estoire* and the *Lai*, in that she urges Havelok to go to Denmark, as strongly and as positively as she can: "I wot so wel so ich it sowe . . . Haue þou nouht þer-of [no] doute/Nouht þe worth of one noute" (1323, 1331-32), supporting her advice with the authority of proverbs (1338, 1352).

Her importance in the romance is nevertheless, to a certain extent, reduced. Inevitably, if Havelok plays the central role, Goldeborw must take second place. The writer's wish to diminish her part may well explain the contradictory and confused motivation given for the attack on Havelok by the thieves.[16] The ruse of the dead men used to simulate the living, that wins the battle against Edelsi in both Gaimar and the *Lai*, is omitted in **Havelok**, partly perhaps because it is the princess's idea. The defeated Godrich is placed in Goldeborw's charge, and the English barons recognise her as their rightful queen, but these scenes are due more to the poet's sense of what is appropriate to the ending of the story than to any wish to specially enhance her role.

It is not only Havelok and Goldeborw whose roles and personalities are carefully delineated. One of the most striking features of **Havelok the Dane** is the characterisation of the two villains of the story, which is very much more extended and subtle than in the Anglo-Norman poems. Though their positions and actions run parallel, a careful distinction is made: Godard is the worse of the two. Not only is he chosen as a trustworthy man to guard Birkabeyn's family, but he is also "þe kinges oune frende" (375), which makes his betrayal of trust worse. He not only mistreats the heir to the throne, but kills his two sisters, apparently on impulse, before his eyes and tries to have him drowned. He refuses to keep his promises to Grim, threatens and abuses him, and, though he once swore to assume all responsibility himself for the killing of Havelok (536), now tries to shift the blame to him:

> Go hom swiþe, fule drit-cherl;
> Go heþen, and be euere-more
> þral and cherl, also þou er wore.
> Shaltu haue non oþer mede;
> For litel [shal] i do þe lede
> To þe galues, so God me rede!
> For þou haues don a wicke dede . . .
>
> (682-88)

The writer curses him more vehemently and at greater length than Godrich. He is appropriately given worse and longer punishment: first he is humiliated by being led on a scabby mare to Havelok, before his trial (2449

ff.), whereas, by Havelok's command, Godrich is spared the ordeal (2762-65). Next, he is judged to be flayed alive, and this cruel process is described with particular relish (2493-2503). Godrich only shares with him the final ride, facing the tail of a mare, to execution. The portrait of villainy is almost entirely unredeemed, though the writer does insert a speech of Godard's, rallying his fleeing knights (2416-25), that momentarily enlists our sympathy for his situation.

Godrich, on the other hand, is more ambivalently portrayed. His character is built up little by little, hinted at before fully revealed—a process worth considering in more detail since it is typical of the poet's gift for indirect description. The first mention of his name, as guardian for Goldeborw, is accompanied by ominous praise: "men haueden of him mikel drede" (181). He takes possession legally of England, after Athelwold's death, and only an ironic turn of phrase suggests his eagerness to do so: "þe riche erl ne foryat nouht,/þat he ne dede al Engelond/Sone sayse intil his hond" (249-251). His methods of establishing his authority are above reproach, but the motivation behind it is double and suspect:

> Schiréues he sette, bedels and greyues,
> Grith-sergeans, with longe gleyues,
> To yemen wilde wodes and paþes
> Fro wicke men, þat wolde don scaþes;
> And forto hauen alle at his cri,
> At his wille, at his merci . . .
>
> (266-271)

Finally, the image of England, fearing him like the beast the goad (279), sums up the tight, intimidating grip he has acquired over the land, and prepares us for the next stage in the action, when Godrich's wickedness is fully revealed. This happens only when the issue of the inheritance is forced upon him by Goldeborw nearing maturity:

> Quanne þe Erl Godrich him herde
> Of þat mayden, hu wel she ferde;
> Hu wis sho was, hu chaste, hu fayr,
> And þat sho was þe rihte eyr
> Of Engelond, of al þe rike;-
> þo bigan Godrich to sike . . .
>
> (286-291)

The style well captures Godrich's increasing distress as the facts come home to him: Goldeborw is proving worthy to rule the kingdom she has by right. The gradual manner in which aspects of Godrich's character have been indicated, and the way in which, only now, he appears to consciously realise the possessive love of England that motivated him to control it so firmly, suggest the insidious corruption by power of an originally good man. The beginning of Godrich's monologue inclines us sympathetically to his resentment at having to submit to the rule of a girl (291-295), even if his later decisions turn us against him. More space is given to showing his feelings and his decisions, his pride and his courage in battle. He makes an admirably clever speech to incite his followers against the "foreign invaders," Havelok's troops, and persuade them that their cause and his cause are the same (2595). A traitor, but a traitor of some distinction.

The English poet introduces many more minor characters into his romance than are to be found in the Anglo-Norman poems. Most of these come from the less well-to-do ranks of society: Gunnild, Leuiue, Grim's three sons, Bernard Brun. The writer's sympathetic interest in them is patent, especially in his portrayal of Grim's family. Their qualities of generosity and fidelity merit their elevation to the aristocracy: Havelok's descriptions of Gunnild and Leuiue seem to assert they are natural aristocrats (2874-77, 2916-21). But the elevation is also humorously envisaged; the three sons, Roberd the Red, William Wendut, and Huwe Raven, freshly-dubbed knights, formerly accustomed to wielding staves and door-bars, are patently eager to use their new swords in the field:

> Roberd saw þat dint so hende,
> Wolde he neuere þeþen wende,
> Til þat he hauede anoþer slawen
> With þe swerd he held ut-drawen.
> William Wendut his swerd vt-drow,
> And þe þredde so sore he slow . . .
> Huwe Rauen ne forgat nouht
> þe swerd he hauede þider brouht . . .
>
> (2628-37)

Both the humour and the affection are characteristic of the English poet's attitude to his protagonists: he sees them as people, not lay figures, tries to present them in as realistic and lively a way as possible, and is involved with his own creations, in that he attempts to enlist sympathy for them from his audience far more energetically than many romance-writers.

*Havelok the Dane* represents a considerable expansion on what in Gaimar's *Estoire* and the *Lai d'Haveloc* is still a very bare and unelaborated tale. The English poet has given it a far more subtle structure than a mere chronological framework, and he has filled it with carefully drawn, often complex, characters. I think it unlikely that all this can be attributed to a lost source. That *Havelok* did draw on sources unknown to us—besides possibly using Gaimar and the *Lai*[17]—is obvious, but these need have been no longer than the Anglo-Norman poems. The expansions and elaborations of the English romance are such as one man might impose on a story in order to shape it to his own conceptions. The writer of *Havelok* who, judging from his exuberant use of every kind of rhetorical device, was a consciously literary man, is the most likely to be fully responsible for its attractive content and form.

*Notes*

[1] Written between 1135 and 1140. The edition of the *Estoire* referred to is by A. Bell (Oxford, 1960). Havelok's name is spelt with a "c" in the *Estoire* and the *Lai*, and so I have retained this spelling when referring to them.

[2] Late twelfth or early thirteenth century; based on Gaimar's "Haveloc episode." Edited by A. Bell (Manchester, 1925).

[3] Thirteenth century. Edited by W. W. Skeat, 2nd ed. rev. K. Sisam (Oxford, 1915), whose bracketed emendations or insertions I reproduce. For other editions, and a general bibliography, of *Havelok, A Manual of the Writings in Middle English, 1050-1500* ed., J. B. Severs (New Haven, 1967), should be consulted.

[4] Since writing this article, my attention has been drawn to Dieter Mehl's recent book, *Die mittelenglischen Romanzen des 13. und 14. Jahrhunderts* (Heidelberg, 1967). Some of my observations on *Havelok* are substantially the same as his, but were independently arrived at.

[5] In Gaimar and the *Lai*, Argentille's father Achebrit dies and leaves her the kingdom of Norfolk, which is administered for her during her minority by her uncle Edelsi, king of Lindesey. Eventually she inherits both kingdoms.

[6] It has been argued that, in depicting all England ruled under one king, Athelwold, *Havelok the Dane* shows its descent from an older form of the story than that known to Gaimar and the *Lai*, because it must be portraying the reign of Alfred (A. Bell, "Gaimar's early 'Danish' kings, *PMLA*, [LXV], [1950], 635; *Lai d'Haveloc*, 45-46). But in describing the division of East Anglia into two kingdoms, of which Lindesey is ruled by a Briton (*Estoire* 59, *Lai* 202), Gaimar and the *Lai* appear to reflect the historical fact of a line of East Anglian kings, who took over the separate kingdom of Lindesey from the British—at a period long before Alfred. Saxons and British seem to have coexisted there peacefully enough, perhaps even intermarried (see F. M. Stenton, "Lindesey and its kings," *Essays in history presented to R. L. Poole* (Oxford, 1927); J. W. F. Hill, *Medieval Lincoln* [Cambridge, 1948], p. 15); this is possibly reflected in the friendship and family ties between Argentille's father and the British Edelsi in Gaimar and the *Lai*. The Anglo-Norman poems thus seem to represent a setting and situation older than those in *Havelok* (see, for a similar view, H. L. Creek, "The author of *Havelok the Dane*," *Englische Studien*, XLVIII [1914-15], 198), which may, in any case, be

due more to the English author's shaping of the tale than to any historical reminiscences.

[7] The idea may have been suggested by the role the barons play in the *Lai*; see E. Fahnestock, *A Study of the sources and composition of the Old French "Lai d'Haveloc"* (New York, 1915), pp. 53-55.

[8] Note how Godrich plays on the hatred of foreign invaders in his address to his army, ll. 2574-2601.

[9] F. S. Stevenson, *Robert Grosseteste* (London, 1899), p. 220.

[10] Stevenson, *Grosseteste*, pp. 220-21; N. Denholm-Young, *Richard of Cornwall* (Oxford, 1947), pp. 78-79; Hill, *Medieval Lincoln*, p. 209.

[11] Stevenson, *Grosseteste*, pp. 269-270; *Monumenta Franciscana*, ed., J. S. Brewer (London, 1858), p. 110. We only know of the treatise from a letter of Adam Marsh to Grosseteste: Remitto dominationi vestrae abbreviationem illam quam scripsistis de principatu regni et tyrannidis, sicut misistis signatam signo comitis Leycestriae.

[12] *The Political Songs of England*, ed., T. Wright (London, 1839), p. 94 ff.

[13] Ubbe's words make this plain:

> Hauelok bi-held he swipe wel,
> Hu he was wel of bones maked,
> Brod in þe sholdres, ful wel schaped,
> þicke in þe brest, of bodi long;
> He semede wel to ben wel strong.
> 'Deus!' quath Ubbe, 'qui ne were he kniht?'
>
> (1645-50)

[14] We are particularly told, ll. 995-98, that Havelok is chaste and avoids contact with women.

[15] "Havelok's qualities—his instinct for survival, opportunism, modesty, industry, lack of sentiment, practical good sense, love of children—are the virtues of common people." D. Pearsall, "The Development of Middle English Romance," *Medieval Studies*, XXVII (1965), 98.

[16] The motivation appears to be two-fold. Since both Ubbe (1741-44) and Havelok fear harm and "shame" to Goldeborw, it might be supposed that the English poet intended to use the reasons for the attack given in the *Lai*—the retainers of Sigar (= Ubbe) desire Argentille and follow her. But in fact all such lustful intentions are left unmentioned. We do not discover that the thieves *are* Ubbe's retainers till some time after the incident (1928-29). During the fight they never mention Goldeborw, yet Huwe Raven assumes they

have come on her account (1869-70). Bernard Brun and the townsfolk impute the attack to robbery (1956 ff., 2016 ff.) The poet was obviously confused as to what reason to give, but he has apparently tried to minimise the sexual motivation and the role played by Goldeborw.

[17] Gaimar and the author of the *Lai* both wrote in Lincolnshire, probably (in Gaimar's case, certainly) for local patrons, and their poems were still being used by Lincolnshire writers in the fourteenth century for their accounts of Havelok. (See *The Chronicle of Pierre de Langtoft*, ed., T. Wright, Rolls Series, 2 vols. [London, 1866-68], vol. I, and *Peter Langtoft's chronicle as illustrated and improved by Robert of Brunne*, ed., T. Hearne, 2 vols. [Oxford, 1725], vol. I.) As *Havelok the Dane* also seems to have been written in Lincolnshire, it is not unlikely that its author knew the two Anglo-Norman poems.

### Dieter Mehl (essay date 1969)

SOURCE: "*Havelok the Dane*," in *The Middle English Romances of the Thirteenth and Fourteenth Centuries*, Barnes & Noble, Inc., 1969, pp. 161-72.

[*In the following excerpt, Mehl praises* Havelok the Dane *for its emphasis on direct speech, its vivid and elaborate descriptions, its use of a narrator as an intermediary between story and reader, and for its ambitious structure and unity of theme.*]

. . . It seems at first sight as if **Havelok the Dane** and *King Horn* are only slightly different variations of the same type of tale and they are therefore often grouped together in literary histories. They are both among the earliest Middle English romances, are preserved side by side in the same manuscript (Laud Misc. 108), and have several story-motifs in common. On closer inspection, however, it appears that in structure, theme and narrative technique the two poems are very different from each other and this is why they are discussed in different chapters here. *King Horn* is obviously the condensed version of a story which, as the Anglo-Norman version shows, could be treated equally well in the form of a long novel, whereas **Havelok** seems to be by far the longest of all the early versions of the saga; the two French versions are both much shorter.[5] For once it was the English adapter who deliberately embellished his story-material and made something like a brief novel out of it.

The author's tendency to expand the story and to slow down the narrative tempo can be seen in the description of individual episodes as well as in the structure of the whole poem. One of the first things that strike the reader of this poem is the extensive use of direct speech even where the action does not demand dialogue, and brief summary might be thought to fulfil the same purpose. The author's preference for direct speech is apparent in his use of dramatic dialogue, like the vivid scene between Godard and Grim (ll. 663-90) in which Grim is told that his services will not be rewarded, in several revealing soliloquies, like that of Godard (ll. 507-22) in which he reasons with himself as to whether he should let Havelok live (see also Godrich's similar monologue, ll. 291-311), and, particularly, in formal orations, addressing some larger assembly, as the dying speeches of Athelwold and Birkabeyn (ll. 166-75 and 384-96) and Ubbe's long address to the Danes (ll. 2204-51; see also Godrich's speech to his knights, ll. 2576-2605). Ubbe's account is also an example of the frequent use of recapitulation in this poem. Some important parts of the plot are thus deliberately impressed on the memory of the hearers. Other instances are Havelok's prayer (ll. 1359-84) and his address to Grim's children (ll. 1400-44). It is possible that such recapitulations were inserted with particular regard to the situation in which the poem would be read and that they were meant as a help to newcomers or less attentive listeners, but this is only a fanciful surmise. At any rate, the technique clearly contributes to an accentuation of the story and to the epic quality of the poem. The use of recapitulation is also related to the device of parallelism in the structure of the plot to which I shall return and it clearly shows that the poem, despite its apparently simple structure, was carefully planned and designed.

Apart from his preference for long speeches, the author of *Havelok* devoted particular artistry to the description of often brief, but vivid scenes. Not only the more important stages of the story, the two death-scenes at the beginning, Havelok's marriage and the raid on Barnard's house are depicted in some detail, but also less decisive events are presented in the form of colourful scenes, like Havelok's successful attempt to earn his keep as a porter (ll. 863 ff.). Some scenes are given a particularly dramatic and at the same time spatial quality by the immediate reaction of one of the characters, as when Havelok has to watch the slaughter of his two sisters:

þer was sorwe, hwo so it sawe,
Hwan þe children bi þe wawe
Leyen and sprauleden in þe blod:
Hauelok it saw, and þer-bi stod.
Ful sori was þat seli knaue,
Mikel dred he mouhte haue;
For at hise herte he saw a knif,
For to reuen him hise lyf.

(ll. 473-80)

Havelok's horror and fear are effectively portrayed and the scene gives a vivid picture of the injury done to the young prince. Twice in the course of the action Havelok recalls the scene in very similar words (ll. 1364-8 and ll. 1411-16) as a concrete image of his sufferings.

The three miraculous lights by which Havelok's royal birth is disclosed, are also described in the way they appear to the beholders. The effect of the miracles on those around the prince helps to focus our attention on the hero and his exceptional fate and at the same time contributes to the development of the action. The first miracle saves Havelok's life and provides him with an invaluable ally (ll. 586 ff.); the second reveals to Goldeboru that her husband, like herself, is of royal blood and thus the two strands of the action are finally united (ll. 1247 ff.); the third convinces Ubbe, and he and his men do homage to Havelok who can now regin his inheritance (ll. 2092 ff.). This is not a case of simple repetition, as in some other romances, but an obvious attempt to give more shape to the story and to bring out the central theme of the poem. The three scenes also show that the author was not at all concerned with condensing his story, but aimed at a certain breadth in the narrative and made use of the time-honoured devices of the epic poet, parallelism and repetition. Thus the events do not pass swiftly before the reader's eyes, as, for instance, in *King Horn*, but there is a carefully designed dramatic development and a deliberately graded sequence of episodes building up the tension towards the final climax.

Another way of embellishing the story, frequently found in *Havelok*, is the elaborate description of situations and events, enriching the action with apparently superfluous detail. This is another point of difference between this poem and *King Horn* where the rapid flow of the narrative allows of no pauses. It is interesting to see that all the more extensive descriptions in *Havelok* refer to rather homely and uncourtly subjects. In one place where there would have been an opportunity of enlarging on a more courtly entertainment, the poet passes it over with a revealing *occupatio:*

Of þe mete forto telle,
Ne of þe win bidde i nouht dwelle;
þat is þe storie for to lenge,
It wolde anuye þis fayre genge.

(ll. 1732-5)

This does not at all mean, however, that the style of the poem is simple and artless. Though the subjects described are often ordinary enough, the method of description clearly betrays the poet's familiarity with the art of rhetoric. Impressive instances are the picture of an ideal commonwealth under Athelwold (ll. 27-105), the feast of Havelok's knighting (ll. 2266-353), or the elaborate catalogue of Grim's prey:

Grim was fishere swiþe god,
And mikel couþe on the flod;
Mani god fish þer-inne he tok,
Boe with net, and ek with hok.
He tok þe sturgiun, and þe qual,

And þe turbut, and lax with-al,
He tok þe sele, and ek þe el;
He spedde ofte swiþe wel:
Keling he tok, and tumberel,
Hering, and þe makerel,
þe butte, þe schulle, þe þornbake:

(ll. 749-59)

The modern reader is inclined to notice here above all the 'realistic' detail which is indeed remarkable, but such descriptions are at the same time rhetorical devices and products of a very conscious art. Their homely content does in no way detract from their literary character. Indeed, it is this remarkable mixture of an ornamented style and very plain subject-matter that makes *Havelok* such an intriguing poem. Notwithstanding many statements to the contrary, the style of the poem is anything but 'popular'; it reveals an astonishing degree of sophistication, although the poet is clearly anxious to achieve popular appeal. The descriptions are not arbitrary digressions or signs of garrulousness, but are indispensable to the unassuming and yet ceremonious tone of the poem and have an important function in the whole design. Thus the rhymed tirade on Athelwold's government, which at first sight seems only an elaborate but slightly irrelevant rhetorical set-piece, is, as we shall see, a vital part of the exposition of the theme (ll. 87-105).

The poet's thorough acquaintance with rhetorical devices can be seen not only in his use of description, but throughout the poem. There is abundant use of alliteration, anaphora, formulaic patterns, and other comparatively simple ornaments of style, belonging with the *ornatus facilis*.[6] Often such repetitions sound like the primitive mannerisms of an oral style, and this may in some cases be true, but they also belong to a rhetorical tradition and show a degree of conscious artistry which accords very little with the picture, often drawn, of a popular minstrel entertaining a group of illiterate peasants in a market-place or a tavern.

A particularly elaborate passage, illustrating various stylistic devices, is the speech in which Grim's children express their homage to Havelok:

'Welkome, louerd dere!
And welkome be þi fayre fere!
Blessed be þat ilke þrawe
þat þou hire toke in Godes lawe!
Wel is us we sen þe on lyue,
þou maght us boþe selle and yeue;
þou maght us hoþe yeue and selle,
With-þat þou wilt here dwelle.
We hauen, louerd, alle gode,
Hors, and net, and ship on flode,
Gold, and siluer, and michel auhte,
þat Grim ure fader us bitawhte.
Gold, and siluer, and oþer fe

Bad he us bi-taken þe.
We hauen shep, we hauen swin,
Bi-leue her, louerd, and al be þin!
þou shalt ben louerd, þou shalt ben syre,
And we sholen seruen þe and hire;
And ure sistres sholen do
Al that euere biddes sho;
He sholen hire cloþes washen and wringen,
And to hondes water bringen;
He sholen bedden hire and þe,
For leuedi wile we þat she be.'

(ll. 1213-36)

Only ignorance of medieval rhetorical traditions could lead one to mistake this highly stylized rhetoric for the primitive product of an unlearned minstrel. Undoubtedly, the poet knew that such simple patterns would be particularly effective in recitation, but this applies, with varying degrees of sophistication, to all medieval rhetoric. The fact that he mainly uses rather uncomplicated *colores* does not necessarily mean that he was unfamiliar with more sophisticated language or that he did not know what he was doing. He evidently aimed at suiting his style to the story and to his audience. This can also be seen from his particularly vivid comparisons which often give picturesque glimpses of everyday experience and never take their material from the world of courtly refinement. Thus, the thieves that invade Bernard's house are soundly beaten:

He maden here backes al-so bloute
Als here wombes, and made hem rowte
Als he weren kradelbarnes:
So dos þe child þat moder þarnes.

(ll. 1910-13)

Of the bright cross that appears miraculously on Havelok's back during the night, we are told:

It sparkede, and ful brihte shon
So doth þe gode charbucle-ston,
þat men se mouhte, by þe liht,
A peni chesen, so it was briht.

(ll. 2144-7)[7]

There is no doubt that the poem is addressed not to a courtly, but to a middle-class audience, with the intention of appealing to a great variety of tastes. There is no indication in the text, however, that illiterate peasants or labourers were the chief listeners, and from the little we know about the living-conditions of those people, this appears very unlikely. It can safely be assumed that 'a cuppe of ful god ale' which the narrator asks for at the beginning (l. 14) was available not only in a market-place or a tavern, but in any bourgeois household throughout the country. We cannot tell, of course, whether the author had a more extensive knowledge of courtly manners or not, but it is clear that he did not want to give detailed descriptions of things his audience would not be interested in and that he made a very conscious effort to popularize his material. This is why we get circumstantial accounts of Grim's fishing, Havelok's endeavours to find a job for himself, his extraordinary feats at the country games and his heroic thrashing of the thieves. The poem is rich in descriptions of native or even local customs, like the popular games (ll. 980 ff., 1007 ff., 2320 ff.), the table-manners (ll. 1722 ff.), the wedding-ceremony (ll. 1169 ff.) and the gruesome details of the traitor's execution (ll. 2488 ff.). Another mark of this deliberately popular style is the great number of proverbial expressions and generalizing aphorisms (see, for instance, ll. 307, 600, 1338, 1352, 1693, 1712-3, 2461, 2813, 2983). By such expressions of popular wisdom rather than by direct moralizing, the author draws attention to the general applicability of his story. There is no doubt that he was familiar with the life and the customs of his audience.

Another device to heighten the effect of the poem in recitation is the emphasis on the rôle of the narrator as an intermediary between the story and the audience. In **Havelok**, this is more consistently employed than in most other English romances. Thus, the prologue is particularly extensive, and it has been suggested that it was interpolated,[8] but there is no need for this assumption, because the first 26 lines of the poem successfully evoke an atmosphere of conviviality and establish a certain personal contact between the narrator and the audience. Often in the course of the story, the narrator intrudes in order to show his personal involvement in it. In most cases he makes use of traditional formulas, such as can be found in many romances and in Old French epic literature, but they are here employed with particular gusto and with an assured sense of dramatic effect. Very striking are the repeated curses on the two traitors, Godard and Godrich (e.g. ll. 422-36, 446, 542-4, 1100-2, 1157-8, 2447, 2511), which also emphasize the partiality of the narrator. In one passage, the brief curse is extended into a rhetorical incantation:

> þanne Godard was sikerlike
> Vnder God þe moste swike,
> þat eure in erþe shaped was,
> With-uten on, þe wike Iudas.
> Haue he þe malisun to-day
> Of alle þat eure speken may!
> Of patriarke, and of pope,
> And of prest with loken kope,
> Of monekes and hermites boþe! . . .
> And of þe leue holi rode
> (þar) God him-selue ran on blode!
> Crist him warie with his mouth!
> Waried wurthe he of norþ and suþ!
> Of alle men, þat speken kunne,
> Of Crist, þat made mone and sunne!
>
> (ll. 422-36)

Sometimes such malediction is combined with a prayer for one of the main characters, as in the passage quoted in Chapter I above (p. 27, ll. 331-7), or in the short prayer:

> Iesu Crist, þat makede go
> þe halte, and þe doumbe speke,
> Hauelok, þe of Godard wreke!
>
> (ll. 542-4)

There are a number of similar blessings in the poem (e.g. ll. 403-7) and also several transitional or explanatory formulas which remind us of the narrator's presence (ll. 328-30, 338, 731-2, 2369).

Thus the poet enlivens the story and heightens the dramatic tension. In spite of the stylistic embellishment, there is no lack of narrative tempo and suspense. The author's craftsmanship is not, however, confined to rhetorical devices and vivid scenes, but the whole structure of the poem reveals careful planning and conscious artistry. As the use of recapitulation shows, the poet was anxious to present the action of the poem as a coherent and meaningful whole and to point to inner correspondences between the episode. The simplest correspondence is that between treason and punishment, between innocent suffering and final happiness. The repeated references to the scene in which Godard threatened Havelok's life (cf. ll. 1364-8, 1411-16, 2222-9) not only keep this episode in our minds, but also bring home the justice of Godard's terrible fate. Havelok's kingship, impressively confirmed by the three miraculous light-appearances, can only be usurped temporarily by Godard's treason, but triumphantly asserts itself in the end. Goldeboru's very similar fate serves as a commentary on the story of Havelok and points to its exemplary character. Like Havelok, she is the legitimate heir to a kingdom, bereft of her rightful inheritance until, by the grace of God, she is fully reinstated in all she has lost. In contrast to the French versions, where Havelok's story is presented on its own, and Goldeboru's similar fate is only briefly summarized later, the English poet emphasizes the resemblances by devoting practically the same amount of space to both strands of the narrative. This contributes to the symmetrical structure of the poem: first we are told about Athelwold's death and Godrich's treason, then, in very similar words, about Birkabeyn's death and Godard's crime. The central section of the poem tells of the union of the two disinherited children, their journey together to Denmark, and, as a preparation for the last part, Havelok's glorious defeat of the robbers. The two victories over Godard and Godrich and the execution of the two traitors correspond exactly to the first parts of the poem and herald a return to the blissful state of law and order described at the beginning. Poetic justice even extends to a minor figure like Bertram the cook, who is royally rewarded for his kindness towards Havelok in his misery (ll. 2896 ff.).

This doubling of plots is a means of intensifying the drama and underlining its significance. It was a particularly successful stroke of the author to begin the poem with Goldeboru's youth and Godrich's treason. Only after her story has been told so far is Havelok himself introduced. His fate appears even harder, and Godard's treachery more abhorrent than Godrich's. A comparison of these parallel episodes shows that the author stresses the common features, but at the same time avoids monotony by skilful variation in detail (Birkabeyn's death is described more briefly than Athelwold's, but Godard's villainy is related more circumstantially than Godrich's). The two strands meet when Havelok is forced to marry Goldeboru. This seems to be the lowest point in their fortunes and is meant as the crowning humiliation of Goldeboru. Both the royal children feel that it is the end of their hopes, but the reader can already detect the working of God's providence in Godrich's wicked plan. The subtle irony of the episode lies in the fact that Godrich means to be true to his oath and yet to avoid the consequences of Athelwold's last will by this literal fulfilling of his promise to marry Goldeboru to the strongest and best man that can be found (ll. 198-200, 1077 ff.), but by his very treachery he unintentionally acts according to Athelston's dying wish and helps to bring about the happy turn of events. Thus the prosperous end is foreshadowed at a very early point in the story. The almost pyramidal structure of the poem is also underlined by the three miraculous lights which, as we have seen, introduce three new phases of the action and clearly accentuate the story of Havelok's recovery of his inheritance.

Even a brief outline of the action reveals that the unity of the poem lies just as much in its theme as in its plot. Behind the exciting story of treason, exile, trial and return there is the concept of an ideal government which upholds peace and prosperity for all, whereas the usurper can rule only by force and injustice. The raid on Bernard's house, which is described at such length, stands in pointed contrast to the vivid picture of a well-governed commonwealth at the beginning of the poem (ll. 51 ff.) where we are told that nobody had to be in fear of robbers. Both passages could at first sight appear to be unnecessary digressions, but they are essential to the intention of the poem. The fighting in Bernard's house illustrates the lawlessness that has spread under Godard's rule and presents Havelok as the champion of law and order, whereas the long introductory description of Athelwold's just government sets the standard by which all the following events are to be judged. This remarkable passage is quite unique in Middle English romance; in no other poem do we find such an extensive and concrete exposition of a well-ordered state, not an idealized Utopia, but a very realistic expression of any citizen's longings and, at the same time, of the poem's 'message'. After this introduction, the treason of Godrich and Godard is bound to appear the more revolting, a contrast which is heightened by the narrator's curses on the traitor. Both are repeatedly compared with the arch-traitor Judas and with the devil himself (see ll. 319, 425, 482, 1100-1, 1133-4, 1411, 2512); this illustrates that in the context of this poem, disloyalty and perjury are the greatest sins imaginable. The traitors' oaths of loyalty are repeatedly referred to (ll. 313-5, 419, 2216-19, 2708-15), and it is probably significant that Havelok cuts the traitor's hand off in the fight (ll. 2751-3). Surely we are meant to remember the false oath Godrich has sworn to Athelwold (ll. 184-203) at this point.[9] Only the legitimate King and heir can bring back peace and order. Thus *Havelok* presents the picture of an ideal government by a strong and rightful King and a severe warning against disloyalty and lawlessness. It also contains the portrait of a perfect ruler who combines royal birth and divine sanction with personal integrity and strength. Havelok's progress from Girm's cottage to the thrones of Denmark and England illustrates the maturing of an ideal King, not in any systematic educational process, but in an effective dramatic as well as thematic climax. It is characteristic of the particular appeal of the poem that Havelok does not prove his superiority by any marvellous feats of knighthood or in courtly surroundings, but by rather down-to-earth exploits, fighting for a job, carrying tremendous loads, and winning the prize in the unsophisticated country games. His triumph at 'putting the stone' is the uncourtly equivalent of the glorious victories in tournaments won by other heroes of romance. Without any help from others, Havelok earns by his strength, but also by his kindness and purity (ll. 991-8). When Godrich tells him to marry Godeboru, he wants to refuse because he is unable to support a wife (ll. 1136-46), whereas the girl's reason is much more aristocratic and shows that she is well aware of what is due to her (ll. 1111-16). When the two arrive in Denmark, Havelok again tries to earn his bread by a rather lowly occupation, until his victory over the robbers proves him worthy of knighthood. Then his rise to power begins; its visible climax is his defeat of Godrich. His regard for order and justice is illustrated by his honourable treatment of the traitor who has to be lawfully tried by his knights, not simply slain in battle (ll. 2754-65).

Havelok is thus a truly popular King who is not just surrounded by a group of select noblemen, but is intimately acquainted with the lower classes, their struggle for food and drink and their simple loyalty. Havelok's generosity towards Bertram the cook shows that class-distinctions are of no importance to him. Though the poet clearly enjoys telling a good story and embellishing it with picturesque detail, we should not overlook the exemplary if not didactic quality of the poem. *Havelok* is not a 'mirror for magistrates', but it obviously wants to glorify the blessings of a well-ordered commonwealth and of loyalty towards the legitimate ruler. Every character is judged by these standards. Grim and Ubbe are faithful to the legitimate King although they endanger themselves seriously by their loyalty, and Grim's children do homage to Havelok without any hope of reward. *Havelok* therefore belongs to a type of romance quite different from poems like *King Horn*. It does not relate miraculous adventures in the service of love or personal trials, passions and virtues, but above all tries to portray historical incidents as a model and a warning for the present. The person of the hero is less important than the political virtues he embodies and the ideas of law and order that are illustrated by his fate. The historical claim of the poem is enforced by its reference to the founding of Grimsby:

> And for þat Grim þat place auhte,
> þe stede of Grim þe name lauhte;
> So þat Grimesbi it calle
> He þat þer-of speken alle;
> And so shulen men it callen ay,
> Bituene þis and domesday.
>                    (ll. 743-8; see also 2528-9)

In its subject-matter the poem shows a marked resemblance to *Athelston*, where the authority of historical events and authentic scenery also help to bring home the moral, and loyalty, though in a different form, is extolled. Another interesting link is suggested by Raouf de Boun's chronicle *Petit Brut d'Angleterre* (c. 1310) where Guy of Warwick is connected with Havelok's son.[10]

*Havelok* does not seem to have enjoyed the same popularity as Horn, Guy or Beves of Hamtoun. It may be that the rather more sober tone of the poem did not appeal to later audiences as much as the romantic and often phantastic biographies of other romance-heroes. It is worth noting that in the manuscript *Havelok* is called a *vita*, not a very common term for the romances, but the poem certainly resembles the *vitae* of some Saints in that it presents models of human behaviour and provides instruction as well as entertainment, in a more specific sense than can be said of the shorter romances. There is no 'escapism' in this poem, unless we consider as escapism the genuine craving for a just and peaceful order of society which is so movingly expressed in this poem.[11] . . .

## Notes

. . .[5]See *Le Lai D'Havelok and Gaimar's Haveloc-Episode*, ed. A. Bell (Manchester, 1925), and L. A. Hibbard, pp. 103-14. See also the useful article by H. L. Creek, 'The Author of "Havelok the Dane"', *Englische Studien*, 48 (1914-15), 193-212, and the remarks by Pearsall, pp. 97-9.

[6] See Stemmler, *Die englischen Liebesgedichte*, pp. 59-61 and *passim*.

[7] See also ll. 1838-9, 1967, 2434-40.

[8] C. T. Onions, 'Comments and Speculations on the Texts of "Havelok"', *Philologica: the Malone Anniversary Studies*, ed. T. A. Kirby and H. B. Woolf (Baltimore, 1949), pp. 154-63; cf. also Schelp, p. 33.

[9] See also the specific references to Grim's oath of loyalty to Godard (ll. 578-9, 1423-4) which he breaks for the sake of Havelok.

[10] L. A. Hibbard, p. 104.

[11] See the thorough interpretation by Schelp, pp. 31-53, where the exemplary character of the poem is well treated. . . .

## John Halverson (essay date 1971)

SOURCE: "*Havelok the Dane* and Society," in *The Chaucer Review*, Vol. 6, No. 2, Fall, 1971, pp. 142-51.

[*In the following essay, Halverson compares and contrasts the French and English versions of the Havelok romance, contending that they reflect some large differences between French and English societies.*]

*Havelok the Dane* is one of a very small number of Middle English romances that still retain their charm. It is no monument of medieval literature, to be sure, but it endures; it is incomparably more readable than other popular romances such as *Guy of Warwick* or *Beves of Hamtoun*, which represent a vulgarization of the genre. *Havelok,* unlike these, is not, I think, a translation or adaptation of a French work, but an independent version of an older tale. Both the principal French rendering[1] and the English version apparently have their roots in Lincolnshire, but the latter poem seems to be more English than the language itself accounts for. I think this impression comes not only from language and locale, but also from the background of social class. The English poem suggests what I should call vaguely a "middle-class" milieu, while the French *Lai* implies an upper-class source. Stylistically, the latter is closer to the "courtly" tradition, the former to the "bourgeois."

The English story seems more English because the culture that produced it was more "bourgeois" than the French. In thirteenth and fourteenth century England, the social blending of lesser nobility, merchants and prosperous farmers in the parliamentary sphere was in sharp distinction to the separation of classes in contemporary France. And in England, the French language and the French literature of chivalry belong mainly to the upper nobility. (We recall Richard II's taste for French romance.) By comparing the two versions of the Havelok legend, it may be possible to come to a better understanding not only of the poems themselves but also of the socio-literary classifications "courtly" and "bourgeois."

Dating is quite uncertain, but a rough consensus places the French poem in the early thirteenth century, and the English one in the early fourteenth century. There is more scholarly confidence that both are of insular origin. The significant difference between them, however, is not in provenance, but in modes of consciousness: in what the writers are aware of, in what is important to them, in how they see their hero and his world. The characteristic tone of each is set in the opening lines:

> Volunters devreit l'um oïr
> E recunter e retenir
> Les nobles fez as ancïens
> E les pruësses e les bens,
> Essamples prendre e remembrer
> Pur les francs homes amender.
> Vilainies e mesprisuns:
> Co devreit estre li sermuns
> Dunt l'um les deust chastïer
> Kar mult i ad vilain mester.
> Chescuns s'en gart cume pur sei.
> L'aventure d'un riche rei
> E de plusurs altres baruns
> Dunt jo vus nomerai les nuns,
> Assez brefment la vus dirai,
> L'aventure vus cunterai.
>
> (1-16)[2]

> Herkneth to me, gode men,
> Wiues, maydnes, and alle men,
> Of a tale ich you wil tell,
> Hwo-so it wile here, and þer-to duelle.
> Þe tale of Hauelok is i-maked;
> Hwil he was litel, he yede ful naked.
> Hauelok was a ful god gome,
> He was ful god in eueri trome,
> He was þe wihtest man at nede
> Þat þurte riden on ani stede.
> Þat ye mowen nou y-here,
> And þe tale ye mowen y-lere,
> At þe beginning of vre tale,
> Fil me a cuppe of ful god ale;
> And y wile drinken, er y spelle,
> Þat Crist vs shilde all fro helle!
>
> (1-16)[3]

The French voice is that of a slightly didactic narrator, who is not really talking *to* anyone, but addressing himself rather indirectly to *francs homes*; for their edification he will tell an *aventure* of royalty and barons. The English voice is that of the minstrel, very much present, demanding attention and ale, speaking to *gode men* or "goodmen," or ordinary householders, and their wives and daughters. He will tell a *tale*, not an *aventure*[4]; and it is about a *god gome*—just a man, neither king nor lord. The simple piety of his exhortation continues in this passage and often recurs, in contrast to the French narrator, who rarely invokes the deity. The latter is also constrained to place the narrative in the time of King Arthur (of whom there is no mention in the English version) gratuitously, for the Arthurian connection is altogether superfluous to the story and meaningless to whatever historical context may be involved. But the Frenchman evidently feels bound by literary convention: for a literary person, a lay or romance of the past would be, more or less as a matter of course, Arthurian. And he is a literary person. His editor has found some parallels to his style in Marie de France which he believes to be in fact borrowings. To these one might add this echo of Chrétien:

> Le cor sona par tel aïr
> K'um le pot mult de loinz oïr.
>
> (*Lai*, 905-6)

> Erec le prant et si le sone;
> tote sa force i abandone
> si que molt loing an va l'oïe.
>
> (*Erec et Enide*, 6109-11)[5]

I fear that this is no more compelling than Mr. Bell's citations, but actual borrowings are of no great importance; the point is the stylistic matrix: the Frenchman has behind him the courtly romance tradition, as the Englishman does not. Another instance is the presence of the magic horn,

> Ke nuls hom ne poeit soner
> Si dreiz eir ne fust de linage
> Sur les Daneis par heritage.
>
> (48-50)

By easily sounding this horn, Haveloc eventually proves his royal identity (like young Arthur withdrawing the magic sword from the stone), and immediately produces a response of joy reminiscent of that when Erec blows the horn. It bespeaks a more literary influence than the birthmark of the English hero, a folk-tale ingredient. (The miraculous flame is common to both.)

The English minstrel takes up his tale with an encomium on King Athelwold, father of Havelok's future wife. An epitome of the good king, it has no parallel in the French. Athelwold was a good king because he made good laws for the good of all classes, and was no respecter of rank. Whoever wronged a widow was promptly cast into fetters "Were he neure kniht so strong." Therefore he was loved by all, young and old,

> Erl and barun, dreng and thayn,
> Kniht, and bondeman, and swain,

Wydues, maydnes, prestes and clerkes,
And al for hise gode werkes.

(31-34)

Such broad social consensus is absent from the French version, as indeed are the lower orders generally. Hierarchical lists like that above occur about five times in **Havelok**, three adding the *burgeys*.[6] The Frenchman's one list is purely military: *chevaler, Sergant, vallet, esquier* (887-88).

The rank of Grim, the hero's foster father, is completely different in the two versions. In the French he is a *barun, prudom* and *riches hom*, and keeper of the queen's castle; he has the same status as the lord Sigar. In the English story he is a *þral*. Not even a free man, he belongs to the evil Godard, who offers him his freedom—for which he yearns (629-31)—in return for killing the infant Havelok. Godard betrays his promise in haughty, class-conscious terms:

Wiltu nu ben erl?
Go hom swiþe, fule drit-cherl;
Go heþen, and be eure-more
Þral and cherl, als þou er wore.

(681-84)

The language curiously anticipates Richard II's betrayal of the English insurgents of 1381: "Rustici quidem fuistis et estis; in bondagio permanebitis. . . . "[7]

Earl Godard, usurper of the Danish throne, is particularly blood-thirsty, with a kind of sinister *Hausmärchen* wickedness about him. His murder of Havelok's child sisters is almost comically sadistic in the folktale manner:

Godard herde here wa,
Ther-of yaf he nouht a stra,
But tok þe maydnes bothe samen,
Al-so it were up-on his gamen;
Al-so he wolde with hem leyke,
Þat weren for hunger grene and bleike.
Of boþen he karf on-two here þrotes,
And siþen hem alto grotes.

(465-72)

The whole long episode of the infants' terrible treatment by Godard is fraught with the simple sadism and sentimentality of the unsophisticated mind. The picture of the hungry child asking for food reminds one irresistibly of Oliver Twist:

"For us hungreth swiþe sore,"
Seyden he, "We wolden more."

(454-55)

Of like quality is the bourgeois tone of Havelok's plea for his life, with the promise of fealty:

But þe knaue þat litel was,
He knelede bifore þat Iudas,
And seyde, "Louerd, merci nou!
Manrede, louerd, biddi you!"

(480-83)

This tone is to be found again in Chaucer, most notably in the *Prioress's Tale* (where, however, it seems to be quite consciously created and purposefully manipulated), but it is not a feature of what we usually regard as "courtly" literature. In the French *Lai*, this part of Havelok's history is absent altogether. Odulf (the French Godard) kills Haveloc's father *par traïsun*, but never sees the child, who is spirited off to England by Grim.

In both versions Grim makes his livelihood as a fisherman. This is a perfectly plausible occupation for the escaped *þral*
but it is most dissonant for the *barun*. The French writer shows no awareness of any inconsistency here; nor does he further on when he apparently contradicts himself regarding Haveloc's awareness of his real status. In lines 165-66, Haveloc wishes to improve himself:

Kar il quidot en sun corage
K'uncore avreit sun heritage.

But in 591 ff., he is altogether ignorant of his heritage, which he discovers from his foster-sister. These inconsistencies suggest that the English author is closer to original, no doubt onomastic, legends of Lincolnshire, and that his work is quite independent of the Frenchman's. The plot of the latter has been somewhat skewed by its resetting in a more courtly framework not completely appropriate to the story.

The English Grim's hard work and prosperity are spelled out in great detail in thirty-five lines or more, including a well-informed catalogue of marketable fish and the commodities of ordinary peasant life (749 ff.). The author is clearly familiar with such details, is interested in them, and praises Grim's enterprise. When Havelok decides to strike out on his own, it is because he is a burden to his foster-father:

Ich ete more, bi God on liue,
Þan Grim and hise children fiue!

(793-94)

And his attitude toward labor is positive:

Swinken ich wolde for mi mete.
It is no shame forto swinken.

(798-99)

The point of view is that of the prosperous, hard-working middle-class; there is something here of what has since been called "the protestant ethic." The French writer's point of view is quite different. Grim's success occupies only three very generalized lines (137-39). The writer knows nothing of the life in question or is not interested enough to say anything about it—or most probably both—and has no praise of honest work. His Haveloc shows no remorse at being provided for by another's labors; his only motive in leaving is self-improvement (161-64). Grim is in complete agreement, and refers rather disparagingly to the fisher folk (168-74). Haveloc sets out to make his fortune appareled in *novels dras* in contrast to the English hero's first crude garment of sail cloth. The minstrel returns frequently to Havelok's "nakedness" and inadequate clothing as if to emphasize not only his poverty but also his pristine beginnings in the social world: it is a rags-to-riches saga.

When the hero begins his first gainful employment, the difference of interest of the two writers is again very clear. The Frenchman is most perfunctory about Haveloc's duties; he is interested only in the demonstration of his great strength, that this should come quickly to the attention of the usurper Edelsi so that Edelsi's plot (and *the* plot) may proceed apace. The Englishman, on the other hand, evokes in robust and ballad-like diction the sights and sounds of work. One hears the cook calling: "Bermen, bermen, hider swiþe!" We see Havelok shouldering aside his competitors and eagerly taking up his tasks: "Sparede he neyþer tos ne heles." Concrete details of the life of the kitchen are given at length (909 ff.). Godrich calls a parliament of his earls and barons, but it is the ordinary people accompanying them who interest the writer:

> Champiouns, and starke laddes,
> Bondemen, with here gaddes,
> Als he comen fro þe plow.
>
> (1015-17)

Because of his proficiency at their great sport of putting the stone, certainly a village pastime, Havelok immediately becomes famous. Even the barons' *champiouns* belong to the folk, and are major participants in the village games.

The story progresses along parallel lines in the two versions, with the supposedly ignominious marriage of the rightful heiress of the English throne to Havelok, the cook's helper; the revelation of Havelok's royalty by signs and visions; and the journey to Denmark to reclaim the hero's throne. There a disaffected lord—Sigar Estal, Ubbe—is sought as an ally. In both versions, the great fight of the hero is in defense of his wife, who is lusted after by the lord's men. In the English story, Havelok poses as a merchant, and his wife, interestingly, seems to be considered fair game right from the beginning: Ubbe feels called upon to reassure Havelok about her:

> And haue þou of hire no drede.
> Shal hire no man shame bede.
>
> (1663-64)

When the fight actually comes, Havelok wreaks a great slaughter of sixty-one of Ubbe's *sergaunz*. And his sole weapon is a *dore-tre*, that is, a peasant's staff or club. Likewise his foster-brothers: "Roberd a staf grop, strong and gret, . . . And William Wendut grop a tre." In the French version, Haveloc fights with a battle-ax (*hache*), still not a knight's sword but a respectable weapon nevertheless, which subsequently Haveloc as a king uses against Odulf. It is another example of a minor awkwardness in elevating the social tone of the story. The English Havelok naturally enough seizes a heavy door-bar at hand, but this is, for the French poet, an unsuitable weapon, though he is at a loss to explain Haveloc's access to an ax:

> Mes Aveloc ad recovrée
> Une hache trenchant e dure—
> Ne sai par cumfete aventure
> Un de cels la tint e porta—
> Il li tolli e s'en venga.
>
> (696-700)

Not only is the Englishman perfectly comfortable with Havelok's choice of an unknightly weapon; but in the comparative degree of slaughter, there begins to be a suggestion of a certain class antagonism. The French hero kills only five, and wounds one.

It is in the concluding episodes, as the hero and heroine regain their heritage, that the most striking and significant differences occur between the two versions. The French story comes to an end with perfect decorum. Haveloc slays Odulf in knightly combat, and extracts an honorable surrender from Edelsi (who dies an apparently natural death within a fortnight). The new king and queen receive the homage of the barons and reign for twenty years. *Si finist Aveloc.*

But in the English story there now erupts what I think can best be called a peasant fantasy. The main focus of this is of course Havelok himself, utterly a peasant in every way, who is yet secretly a king. And in his rise, there ensues a train of transformations completely alien to the consciousness of the French story. The class structure is turned on its head in the way of wish-fulfillment as the three sons of Grim—sons, that is, of a thrall, the lowest of social ranks—are made knights and barons. The thrall's daughter, Gunnild, marries the Earl of Chester, who acquiesces to this *mésalliance* without demur. Bertram, the cook who had befriended Havelok, becomes the Earl of Cornwall. As this remarkable wheel turns, the two noble usurpers, conversely (and in striking contrast to the French story), fall to the most shameful and ignominious of deaths. Earl Godard is tied on a "scabbed mere, Hise nese went unto þe crice"; at last he is flayed alive and hanged. Earl Godrich is transported in like manner upon an ass's back—"His nose went unto þe stert"—and is burned alive. There is clearly great satisfaction taken in this brutal and scatalogical debasement. Not only Goldeboru is "ful bliþe," but the minstrel as well: "Daþeit hwo recke! he was fals." The earthy crudity of such revenge is at the very least unchivalric, and suggests a peasant mentality with overtones of class hostility. From the same kind of consciousness stem the simple ideals of individual life: a long life and a large family. Thus Gunnild and her earl produce five good sons; the cook-earl of Cornwall lives a hundred years and sires "mani children"; Havelok and Goldeboru rule for sixty years and have no fewer than fifteen children, "Hwarof þe sones were kinges alle, . . . And þe douhtres alle quenes."

The "bourgeois elements" of *Havelok the Dane* have not, of course, escaped notice till now.[8] But neither word of that phrase is quite satisfactory. "Bourgeois" inevitably suggests an urban background; and particularly since the work of Charles Muscatine,[9] both "bourgeois" and "courtly," referring to literary traditions, suggest certain genres (fabliau as opposed to romance, for instance), since that is the principal framework of Muscatine's approach. "Middle-class" might be a slightly preferable designation, referring to a wide social range including the villager and peasant at one end and powerful burgher and even petty nobility at the other. *Havelok* seems to emerge from the lower levels, the peasant stratum; whereas if an examination similar to the present one were undertaken of the Middle English *Floris and Blaunchflour*, I think it could be seen to belong to a higher and more urban level: there the king and queen have every indication of being the baker and his wife in disguise. As for genre, despite the fact that both Havelok stories belong to the same romance type, one is nevertheless distinctly "courtly" and the other "bourgeois."

To speak of bourgeois "elements" in *Havelok* may be misleading, for it suggests something like "coloring," something added, accidentally perhaps, to an original French story. Of such elements there is a great plenty: the colloquial, balladic style; the milieu of fisher folk, the village games, the kitchen; the conventional piety of both minstrel and characters; the middle-class ideals of honest work and the family; the unknightly hero; the sentimentality towards children. But when we come to the world-turned-upside-down of the conclusion, and as we compare the whole poem to its French counterpart, it becomes clear that *Havelok* is entirely and *essentially* middle-class—that it is, in fact, a peasant fantasy of class ambition and resentment. And the French *Lai* appears to be only a barely successful attempt to adapt and rehabilitate that fantasy by casting it into a chivalric mode.

The role of kingship in *Havelok* also reflects middle-class positions: both the varying but pervasive alliance between royalty and middle class in opposition to the lords common in the later Middle Ages, and the sentiment, or mystique, concerning the king. It was this sentiment that no doubt saved Richard II during the Peasants' Rebellion from the popular hostility directed toward the Lord Chancellor, the Treasurer, the Duke of Lancaster, the Earl of Derby, and others; indeed it enabled the boy-king to assert royal authority at Mile End and Smithfield. But it was, of course, a sentiment effective long before Richard's time. In *Havelok*, too, there is a transcendence about the king that sets him not only above but beyond the social hierarchy; this is expressed at the fantasy level in the person of Havelok himself, a true king despite his peasant rearing. And when he becomes king in fact, he shows a transcendent disregard for the established social order, as had, at a more rational level, the much-praised Athelwold. Usurping earls, conversely, *cannot* be true kings; Godard and Godrich are "fals" not only personally but, so to speak, ideally.

Quite similar is the social consciousness, anti-baronial and royalist, implied in the very English *Tale of Gamelyn*,[10] where the youngest son of a knight fights usurpation and unjust authority with his favorite weapon, a club; and his bloody revenge on sheriff and justice receives the sanction of the king. The Robin-Hood atmosphere and sentiment of the Tale seems, like the fantasy of *Havelok*, to be peculiarly English.

*Notes*

[1] The version of Gaimar is not under consideration here.

[2] *Le Lai d'Haveloc and Gaimar's Haveloc Episode*, ed. Alexander Bell (Manchester, 1925).

[3] *The Lay of Havelok the Dane*, ed. W. W. Skeat and K. Sisam (Oxford, 1915).

[4] In the courtly tradition, *aventure* is known to the nobility exclusively. Thus the *vilain* master of the beasts in *Yvain*: "D' 'avanture' ne sai je rien. N'onques mes n'an oï parler" (368-69).

[5] Ed. Mario Roques, CFMA (Paris, 1955).

[6] 1327-28, 2184-85, 2194-95, 2465-66.

[7] Thomas Walsingham, *Historia Anglicana*, ed. H. T. Riley (London, 1864), II, 156.

[8] Cf. A. C. Baugh, *A Literary History of England* (New York, 1948), I, 177.

[9] *Chaucer and the French Tradition* (Berkeley and Los Angeles, 1957).

[10] Ed. W. W. Skeat, *The Works of Geoffrey Chaucer* (Oxford, 1900), IV, 645-67.

## David Staines (essay date 1976)

SOURCE: "*Havelok the Dane*: A Thirteenth-Century Handbook for Princes," *Speculum: A Journal of Mediaeval Studies*, Vol. LI, No. 4, October, 1976, pp. 602-23.

[*In the following essay, Staines contends that* Havelok the Dane *is primarily an idealized biography of a ruler perfectly embodying the best kingly characteristics, and that the author's political motive in writing the tale was to advise the king of the wishes of his subjects.*]

The thirteenth-century English romance of **Havelok the Dane** is unique among the medieval accounts of Havelok's career because it is more than a retelling of Havelok's life. Whereas many romances rework traditional material to offer yet another episodic narration, the English romancer turns to the Havelok story because it offers interesting parallels to the contemporary political situation which he can develop in the course of his narration. Two earlier versions of the story, the account in Gaimar's *L'Estoire des Engleis* and the *Lai d'Haveloc*, do present straightforward narrations of Havelok's rise from banished heir to the Danish throne to king of Denmark and England. **Havelok the Dane**, however, adapts and expands its source material in order to create a portrait of the growth and education of the ideal king. By seeing the correspondences between the world of Havelok and Edward I's England and incorporating them into his version of the Havelok tale, the poet creates a romance which is a mirror of thirteenth-century political life and a portrait of the ideal king delineated from the point of view of the lower classes. This portrait emerges as a warning to the thirteenth-century English monarchy of the needs and the demands of the lower classes.

After the Norman Conquest the folk tradition of Havelok flourished in England. Here was a vivid example of the male Cinderella motif, the young orphan deprived of his kingdom and unaware of his regal parentage. When the English romancer came to employ the Havelok tradition, he found a story which had been the subject of frequent poetic reworkings. Before we can properly approach the remarkable portrait of the hero of the English romance, we need to survey the presentation of Havelok in the romance's analogues. Then we will be able to comprehend more fully the uniqueness of the English romancer's reworking of his material.

The earliest account of the Havelok story appears in Geffrei Gaimar's *L'Estoire des Engleis*, an Anglo-

Norman chronicle history written between 1135 and 1140. Gaimar was writing an Anglo-Norman translation of the *Anglo-Saxon Chronicle* as a sequel to his translation of Geoffrey of Monmouth. In the course of his translating, he moved to Lincolnshire where he became acquainted with the local legends concerning Havelok; unwilling to omit such an interesting story from his history, he placed it shortly after the death of Arthur. During the reign of Arthur's nephew Constantine, two British kings, Adelbert and Edelsie, strengthened their friendship through Adelbert's marriage to Orwain, Edelsie's sister. Adelbert's early death put his daughter Argentille in her uncle's power; in order to obtain Argentille's inheritance, Edelsie married her to Havelok, his lowly cook.[1]

Gaimar describes the young cook in detail. First of all, Havelok is physically attractive:

> Mes mult esteit bel vadletun;
> Bel vis aveit e beles mains,
> Cors eschiwid, süef e plains,
> Li suen semblanz ert tut tens liez,
> Beles jambes ot e bels piez.[2]
>
>                 (104-108)

(He was a very handsome young man. He had a fine face, good hands, a graceful body, sweet and smooth. His expression was always cheerful. He had fine legs and good feet.)

His exceptional strength complements his handsome physique; he can overpower and defeat any groom in the household. Gaimar notes that the cook never fights merely for the sake of victory; indeed, he is happiest when he and his opponent embrace in mutual esteem. Between the nobility and the cook exists an uncommon bond of respect:

> Pur ço qu'esteit si bien amez
> E si preisiez e si loez,
> N'aveit francs hum en la meisun,
> Si Cuaran en voleit dun,
> Ke ne lie dunast volentiers.
>
>                 (137-141)

(On account of this, he was so well loved, respected, and praised that there was no free man in the household who, if Cuaran wanted a gift, would not give it to him willingly.)

Havelok's generosity eclipses the kindness of the knights: "Quanqu'il aveit, trestut dunot / Mes nule rien ne demandot" (When he had anything, he gave it all away, but he never asked anyone for anything). In his employment, Havelok is assisted by his two supposed nephews, who are of a noticeably inferior rank. Though he is of low estate, the cook, according to Gaimar, comes of "gentil lif."

After the seemingly ignoble marriage of Argentille and Havelok, Gaimar focuses upon the naivete and immaturity of the protagonist. On their wedding night, Havelok did not know what to do; as soon as he came to bed, he fell asleep. During the night Argentille sees a flame in her husband's mouth and becomes frightened when Havelok is able to offer no explanation. Bewailing the dishonor in which they live at the court, she decides that they should visit his relatives. An always passive and obedient husband meekly replies: "Jo f[e]rai ço que vus volez, / La vus merrai, si vus loez" (I will act in whatever way you wish. I will take you there if you wish).

When the couple visits his relatives in Grimsby, Kelloc, the daughter of Grim, Havelok's supposed father, feels obliged to tell Havelok his true lineage; she fears, however, that if he learns it, he will also learn what great harm may come to him. Like Gaimar, Kelloc has serious reservations about his maturity: "Il nen est mie si savant, / Qu'il saced cuvrir sun talent" (He is not wise enough that he knows how to hide his desire). When Kelloc does disclose the truth, she advises him to return to Denmark; in addition, she prepares his provisions and arranges all the details for the journey. As he assumes the course of destiny his royal parentage demands of him, Havelok remains an almost wholly passive individual.

In Denmark, Havelok and his companions stay at the home of Sigar, the faithful steward of Havelok's father. In an attempted abduction of Argentille, Havelok shows his superior strength by killing two of his opponents, disabling three others, and cutting off the hand of the remaining villain. For their own protection, Havelok and his company flee to a nearby church where they defend themselves by hurling stones at the attackers. When Sigar arrives, he regards Havelok with amazement: "A sun seignur si resemblot / Que quant le vit, tel pitied ot / Qu'a mult grant paine pot parler" (He resembled his lord so much that when he saw him he took such pity on him that he could speak only with great difficulty). Because of the resemblance, Sigar stops the fighting and listens to Havelok's account of his lineage. The following night, he sees the flame in Havelok's mouth, a further proof of royal blood. One final test remains; Havelok must blow his father's horn, which can be sounded only by the Danish king or his rightful heir. A magic ring of infinite power awaits the man who can blow the horn. Declaring openly that he has never blown such an instrument, Havelok refuses even to make an attempt. Forcefully prodded by Sigar, he reluctantly agrees to try the horn; his immediate success leads to Sigar's acknowledgement of Havelok as his lord. In five days, forty thousand men are assembled to support the heir; the wicked king is soon defeated and Havelok is proclaimed king.

In the final episode of Gaimar's account, Havelok openly defies Edelsie to return to Argentille her proper possessions. Edelsie's refusal leads to war. In the subsequent battle, Havelok's success depends solely upon a clever military scheme devised by his wife. Fifteen days later Edelsie dies and the barons offer the English kingdom to Havelok, who rules for the next twenty years.

Gaimar's Havelok is a markedly royal figure whose nobility has been submerged but not destroyed by his lowly upbringing. Gaimar carefully observes a distinction between the nobility and the common people. At Edelsie's court, Havelok and his assistants are not of the same natural nobility; Havelok is united with the nobles in kindness and generosity. Even amid menial occupations true nobility asserts itself. In this early nascent rendition of the male Cinderella motif, Havelok's ignorance of his true identity complements the strain of passivity in his character to create a protagonist who never assumes active command of his own destiny.

In the latter half of the twelfth century an anonymous writer retold this story of a princely figure in a humble disguise. He may have reworked Gaimar or reworked Gaimar's lost source.[3] Whichever he did, his poem, the *Lai d'Haveloc*, follows the general pattern of Gaimar's story. But it imposes a courtly tone: the author adds courtly details and employs the Breton lai framework. And—what is most important for our purposes—he presents the hero in a different manner.

In this second Anglo-Norman version the background story, the tale which explains how a prince came to appear in the guise of a cook, is not left as a mystery to be discovered; it is introduced at the very beginning of the story. In the final days of his war with King Arthur, Gunter, Havelok's father, fears for the safety of the royal family and entrusts his wife and son to Grim, a baron. Aware of the ruthless ambitions of Gunter's enemies, Grim flees to England to protect the prince. During the sea voyage, a pirate attack leaves Havelok motherless. When the survivors reach England, the always wary Grim takes a final precaution: "Grim li ot fet changer sun nun / Ke par tant nel con[e]ust l'um" (Grim had made him change his name so that, because of this, no one would know his identity).[4]

The emphasis in the *Lai* falls on Havelok's role as heir to the throne. Not only does Grim depart from Denmark for Havelok's safety, but he sends him away from Grimsby because he believes the town is not the proper place for a prince's education. Grim's final exhortation attests to Havelok's kingly calling: "A tote gent te fai amer" (Make yourself beloved by all people).

Havelok's employment in Alsi's court leads to his marriage to Argentille, the king's niece. Havelok's strength is continually stressed because the union of Havelok and Argentille depends upon Alsi's oath to her dead father that she will marry the strongest man in the realm. Therefore, the poet reports Havelok's many feats of strength. Ten of the strongest men cannot withstand him; twelve men cannot lift the burdens Havelok alone can bear.

At the court, however, Havelok's kindness does not create a bond of friendship between Havelok and the nobility; because of his generosity the nobles "Le teneient entr'els a sot, / De lui feseient lur deduit" (thought him a fool and made fun of him). The English court is more wicked than its counterpart in Gaimar. Alsi is a more shameful villain; his manipulation of the marriage secures his own position and he takes a demonic delight in thinking of the shame Argentille will face as the "queen of kettles."

These details give the second Anglo-Norman version a more refined tone; in this courtly account the naive innocence of Gaimar's betrothed Havelok is absent. On their wedding night, Havelok and Argentille have great shame of each other, but the reason is now quite different; Havelok is ashamed of the flame in his mouth. In time they do come to love each other, though Havelok still remains ignorant about the meaning of the flame. In a scene absent from Gaimar's version, Argentille visits a hermit who explains the flame as a sign of Havelok's royal lineage; the hermit prophesies the great future that this young couple will have as king and queen. Consequently, Argentille insists that Havelok learn his true identity by returning to Grimsby; an acquiescent Havelok willingly obeys her request.

The narrative follows the general structure of Gaimar's account. Only in the final episode does the character of Havelok become more clearly defined. Here Havelok's concern for his men appears. In the campaign against Hodulf, the Danish ruler, Havelok takes pity on his supporters; lest they be killed in the fighting, he issues a personal challenge to his opponent. When Hodulf is killed, his people ask Havelok for mercy and the noble Havelok offers immediate pardon to all. The subsequent episode, Havelok's return to England, is now motivated only by Argentille's petitioning that her territories be recovered. In the battle against the English, Havelok becomes distressed about his men's safety:

> Aveloc fu mult irascuz
> Pur ses homes k'il ot perduz;
> Od ses Daneis s'en fust alez,
> E a sa navie returnez,
> Si la reïne li suffrist.
>
> (1055-1059)

(Havelok was very angry about the men he had lost. He would have gone back with his Danes and returned to his fleet if the queen would have allowed it.)

Grim sent Havelok into the world to "aprendre sens a aveir quere" (attain wisdom and seek profit); Havelok has become a mature individual capable of powerful action and selfless thinking. Less passive than his counterpart in Gaimar, he is now a regal figure whose education among the common people has made him aware of the obligations demanded of a monarch on behalf of his subjects. In the *Lai*, this awareness is reflected primarily, indeed solely, in the concern of Havelok as a military leader for the lives of his men.

Opening in Denmark instead of England, the *Lai* expands the roles of Havelok and Argentille into greater prominence than they received in Gaimar. Their new importance can be partially attributed to the natural difference between an historical chronicle and a Breton lai. In addition, however, Havelok has grown as a literary figure; he is now less passive, less naive, a prince showing evidence of understanding his own regal position.

Both versions of the Havelok tale seriously question the propriety of calling Havelok a hero. Though he does exhibit extraordinary strength, though he does perform deeds of strength and valor, though he does display fortitude and greatness of soul, he remains basically a passive individual. A hero is essentially a man who desires to accomplish some good deed, a man who conceives of himself as having a specific role to play in this world. Whatever qualifying traits apply to a hero, he must reveal some degree of activity, some degree of conscious commitment, in his attempt to accomplish his aspiration. Though there is a movement from Gaimar to the *Lai* whereby Havelok does become a more active individual, there still exists a strain of passivity in his character. If Grim had not had faith in Havelok's ultimate return to the Danish throne, Havelok might well have remained in Grimsby. Thus Grim's faith seems to substitute for Havelok's as yet undeveloped sense of responsibility and mission in life. This element of passivity is a trait which the English romancer must subsume within the total character of Havelok if his protagonist is to emerge as a hero.[5]

The thirteenth-century English version of the Havelok story differs markedly from these Anglo-Norman accounts. There are similarities in proper names, in physical descriptions, and in certain actions, yet the deliberate intention underlying the poet's reworking of the tale significantly alters the presentation of Havelok. The English romancer may have known the Anglo-Norman versions or he may have known only their ultimate source.[6] Whatever his source may have been, however, he employed the material to make the romance genre the vehicle for the depiction of an ideal king; more importantly, at the same time he made this depiction the vehicle for a critical overview of the contemporary political situation and the desires and complaints of the lower classes. For the moment, let us study the kinds of incidents and descriptions that now surround Havelok. Then, when we return to study Havelok within the full context of the poem, we will be able to see clearly the particular kind of hero the romancer is creating.

Havelok first appears in the fatal meeting with his protector Godard. In order to secure the throne for his own posterity, Godard decides to kill Havelok and his two sisters. Havelok's reactions to this treachery are those of any young boy in such a dilemma; horrified at the thought of his own death, he begs his assailant to spare his life. Havelok is quite clearly a "seli knaue." There is no trace of imposing regality in his pleading; his is the voiced desperation of a young boy who has already witnessed the brutal slaughter of his two sisters. His plea does momentarily affect Godard, who finds himself assenting to the boy's wishes: "þer was mirácle fair and god, / þat he þe knaue nought ne slou, / But for rewnesse him with-drow." Through active entreaty of his loathed enemy, Havelok saves his own life.

Godard's pity is short-lived. He commands Grim, a fisherman, to drown the child. Before the drowning can take place, however, Grim and his wife see the light in Havelok's mouth. The light is only the first revelation of his true identity. On his shoulder is a birthmark which indicates his royal lineage. In contrast with the preceding scene, Havelok's power is now inborn; his own person should and does command respect and submission. Whereas a pleading Havelok caused Godard to forego his slaughtering, Grim respects Havelok's identity:

> Þis ure eir
> Þat shal [ben] louerd of Denemark,
> He shal ben king, strong and stark;
> He shal hauen in his hand
> Al Denemark and Engeland.
>
> (606-610)

After Grim's family arrives in England, Havelok perceives the burden his presence adds to Grim's impoverished household. As soon as Havelok realizes that he must work for his livelihood, the poet begins to develop Havelok's innate nobility. A reasonable and responsible boy, Havelok displays a wholesome attitude to labor:

> It is no shame forto swinken;
> Þe man þat may wel eten and drinken
> [Þar] nouht ne haue but on swink long;
> To liggen at hom it is ful strong.
>
> (799-802)

Without any regard for his royal background, he joins Grim's family in their work and excels at every menial task he undertakes. Later, confronted with the possible starvation of his family, Grim advises Havelok to go to Lincoln to earn a living.

The poet carefully enumerates the many lowly jobs which Havelok willingly and successfully accomplishes in assisting Bertram, the earl's cook. The cook listens attentively to the distinctly lower-class occupations Havelok can perform (911-920); Havelok's extraordinary strength and his ingratiating personality gain him immediate employment. In his delineation of Havelok's abilities, the poet pauses to note his serene temperament:

> Of alle men was he mest meke,
> Lauhwinde ay, and bliþe of speke;
> Euere he was glad and bliþe,
> His sorwe he couþe ful wel miþe.
>
> (945-948)

In contrast to the situation in the *Lai* but similar to the episode in Gaimar, the people at the court do not think Havelok a fool; his generosity, his kindness, and his strength win their respect. The cook feels such pity for his assistant that he finds "cloþes, al spannewe" for him. The poet completes this portrait with his personal comment:

> It was neuere man þat yemede
> In kineriche, Þat so wel semede
> King or cayser forto be,
> Þan he was shrid, so semede he.
>
> (975-978)

In Lincoln as in Grimsby, Havelok continues to display his strength. He is taller than "Þe meste þat þer kem." In wrestling, he can overthrow any opponent. Yet for all his strength, he is "softe"; despite a man's cruelty to him, he "no hond on him with yuele leyde." Such physical excellence and self-control are surpassed only by his moral purity, a trait not mentioned in earlier versions of the story:

> Of bodi was he mayden clene;
> Neuere yete in game, ne in grene,
> With hire ne wolde [he] leyke ne lye,
> No more þan it were a strie.
>
> (995-998)

The English Havelok is a distinctly active and unselfish individual, not only the victim of certain situations, but also the instigator of many of the plot developments. Except for his departure from Grimsby, which is prompted by Grim, and his conveniently forced marriage to Goldeboru, Havelok is a free-thinking and self-motivated man. The journey back to Grimsby is prompted neither by a dream nor by wifely insistence.

In great detail, Havelok surveys his situation after his marriage; realizing their shameful plight at the court, he decides that they should go to Grimsby.

During their first night at Grimsby, Goldeboru sees the flame in her husband's mouth and the golden red cross on his shoulder. An angel's voice speaks a prophecy reminiscent of Grim's outburst: "He shal ben king, strong and stark, / Of Engelond and Denemark." Havelok's simultaneous dream of conquering all of England and Denmark also underlines the theme of the destined role that has fallen to Havelok. Goldeboru's eagerness to begin their trip to Denmark enkindles Havelok's nascent ambition. Yet before they embark, Havelok observes simple religious practices: he prays to God that he will avenge the murder of his sisters; he says the rosary; he leaves an offering on the altar. Havelok's religious piety is another trait mentioned only in this version of the tale.

From the time when Havelok reaches Denmark, the poet's emphasis falls not on Havelok as the strong man but on Havelok as the noble king. The entire episode at Ubbe's castle indicates this shift in stress. As always, Havelok excels at his vocation, which is now that of a merchant. Yet the noble Ubbe instinctively recognizes Havelok's worth: "Betere semede him to bere / Helm on heued, sheld and spere, / þanne to beye and selle ware." Reminiscent of the earlier scene in Grim's cottage, the episode is significant because no supernatural signs as yet inform Ubbe of Havelok's lineage; Ubbe is rightly puzzled that the merchant is so "hende." With the subsequent recognition through the flame and the birthmark, Ubbe displays proper loyalty to his prince by assuming the role of dutiful and helpful subject; he assembles all the barons from the surrounding areas to pay homage to their true lord.

With the restoration of Denmark to peace and harmony, Havelok returns with his forces to England to regain his wife's lawful possessions. Unlike the Anglo-Norman accounts, the English romance does not make Goldeboru's insistent pleas the basis for this final expedition. An actively zealous monarch capable of forming his own decisions and acting upon them, Havelok sets out to restore justice to his wife's homeland. In a further distinction from earlier versions, Havelok's battle with Godrich, the English usurper, includes his admiration for his opponent's manly prowess and strength; he appreciates those particular qualities the poet has already associated with Havelok himself. In a display of magnanimity, Havelok offers to pardon Godrich if the usurper restores the kingdom. Havelok's kindness has no effect on the thoroughly evil traitor.

The final episode of the poem is the description of the homage England pays to Havelok and Goldeboru. Since the country rightly belongs to his wife, Havelok refuses to pass judgment on Godrich; he surrenders his victim to his wife for sentencing. Moreover, he refuses to accept the fealty of the English people until they have accepted and acknowledged his wife as their lawful queen. As an exemplary leader of military forces, Havelok rewards his faithful followers and punishes his opponents. As an ideal ruler of the country, he makes the necessary arrangements for a good government. With such preliminary details ratified, he leaves for the coronation in London.

If this dissected view of the protagonist formed the entire extent of his characterization, the English romance's Havelok would emerge as a fuller delineation of his counterpart in the Anglo-Norman accounts, though with emphasis put on those qualities in his character which make him an ideal ruler. The poet, however, employs extensive character contrasts to deepen his presentation of Havelok as the ideal king.

The opening section of the poem (26-337) provides the proper frame for Havelok's introduction. The first part of the frame is an extended eulogy of Athelwold, Goldeboru's father. Though the poet does outline the peaceful conditions in England during Athelwold's reign, he is more explicitly concerned with the nature of the monarchy.[7] The harmony of the kingdom is a direct reflection of its ruler; the presentation of Athelwold is a portrait of a unique, indeed ideal, monarch. Athelwold receives the homage of all his subjects:

> Him louede yung, him loueden olde,
> Erl and barun, dreng and thayn,
> Kniht, [and] bondeman, and swain,
> Wydues, maydnes, prestes and clerkes,
> And al for his gode werkes.
>
> (30-34)

The love and respect all classes offer to Athelwold are the most important features of the portrait because they are the direct result of his actions as king. As a military leader, Athelwold is strong and fearless, exceptionally agile as a horseman and remarkably powerful in battle. As his country's political head, he is a stern and hard monarch; he is both the wise king who creates good laws and the strict monarch who enforces them. By his legislation, he returns his country to a state of prelapsarian perfection. Thieves and traitors meet their deaths through his fervent and faultless justice. England is cleansed to such a degree that merchants can travel freely throughout the country with no fear of robbery. Athelwold's justice and legislation are complemented by his generosity; to the poor and the needy his home is always open. Moreover, his generosity is an outgrowth of his religion: "He louede god with al his miht, / And holi kirke, and soth, and riht." For these reasons,

> þanne was Engelond at ayse;
> Michel was svich a king to preyse,

Þat held so Engelond in grith!
Krist of heuene was him with.
He was Engelondes blome.[8]

(59-63)

The portrait of Athelwold is an idealization which will be realized in the fully matured Havelok. As soon as Havelok is hired by Bertram, the poet echoes his initial praise of Athelwold by describing Havelok:

Him loueden alle, stille and bolde,
Knihtes, children, yunge and olde;
Alle him loueden þat him sowen,
Boþen heye men and lowe.

(955-958)

Like Athelwold, Havelok commands the homage of all classes. Furthermore, he merits the respect that is rightfully due to him. In every example of fealty to Havelok, his subjects pledge themselves willingly and happily, realizing that Havelok is not only their king but also a man worthy of the respect of his regal position. *Havelok the Dane* becomes, therefore, a study of the growth and development of Havelok into the kind of king Athelwold represents. Havelok's strength and generosity have already been discussed; indeed, he seems to have all the qualities of the ideal ruler. Like Athelwold, he is religious, selfless, and just to his subjects. Moreover, the final test of the good king is the state of his realm; the attitude of his subjects at the end of the romance is indicative of the national harmony Havelok creates for them.

The poet, then, reworked the Havelok tale to make his protagonist the embodiment of the ideal qualities of a good king. But he did this from a particular point of view and addressed himself to a particular audience: the lower classes.[9] The importance of the audience in this study cannot be underestimated: the delineation of Havelok is partially determined by the audience. Havelok is unmistakably a regal heir; he epitomizes nobility. His innate regality, however, is neither an exclusive nor an overbearing display of superiority. His rise to his rightful position is a journey through the life and ways of the lower classes exemplified by Grim and his family and by Bertram and his associates. Havelok becomes an able member of the mercantile class and of the servants of the court. In this respect, it is especially significant that the Havelok of the English romance, unlike his Anglo-Norman counterparts, is always aware of his true parentage. His knowledge does not lead him to lament his inferior surroundings nor does he disdain his lowly life. Apparently without hope of regaining his proper position, Havelok remains content to work amid the lower members of society. Only when fate offers the possibility of reclaiming his kingdom does Havelok rise to heroic stature in his clearly-defined mission.

When Havelok assumes his regal office, the poet looks at court society from the outside; there is no extended glimpse of court life, no description of the life of the nobility. Even the initial presentation of English royalty does not emphasize the life at court, but focuses attention on the peaceful country Athelwold provides for his people. Athelwold's selfless goodness wins the respect of all his subjects; he merits their obedience without demanding it by force. After his death Godrich transforms England into a terrified body of citizens subject to him and forever "at his cri, / At his wille, at his merci." Against this background of subjection the homage of Grim to Havelok is even more effective. As a member of the royal family, Havelok receives the kind of obedience Godrich attempts to obtain through force. And the poet emphasizes the love shown by Grim and his family to the prince. If this love were solely the consequence of his regal nature, the poet would have created an artistic plea for the doctrine of absolute monarchy and hereditary succession. The romance shows, however, that such love is justified by the character and by the actions of Havelok.

At the end of the romance, in a scene without parallel in the analogues, Havelok dispenses justice by suitably rewarding his faithful followers, the lowly characters who assisted him in his youth. Remembering the kindness of Grim and his family, he gives Gunild, Grim's daughter, to the Earl of Chester in marriage. Levive, Grim's other daughter, is betrothed to Bertram, the cook. And Bertram, who befriended Havelok when he left Grim's household, is knighted and presented with the earldom of Cornwall and all the land that Godrich held. Athelwold was "large, and no wiht gnede"; Havelok is now described as "large and nouht chiche." In this happy ending, the lower-class people receive high honors from their king. Yet even now Havelok remains basically the young, noble, generous lad whose strength they admired and whose character they respected. Though supernatural elements distinguish Havelok as a member of the royal family, the poet examines Havelok's personal claim to the honor his birth demands.

From the moment when he begs a cup of ale before beginning his tale, the romancer develops the portrait of a prince who is not isolated in his royal throne; Havelok becomes a king both of the people and for the people. His education makes him conscious of the needs and problems of his subjects. His accession to the throne heralds the return of a time when merchants wander freely, when the hungry receive food at the king's table, when the king recognizes his primary commitment to the needs of his people.

*Havelok the Dane* is not primarily an adventure nor a series of adventures; it is first and foremost an idealized biography cast in the form of a tale of action. The biography concentrates, not on the most exciting moments of Havelok's life, but rather on those episodes which delineate most clearly the poet's conception of the ideal king. His conception represents a concrete illustration of contemporary attitudes to the monarchy and the good qualities of a king which would win the admiration of the lower classes are strongly emphasized. The portrait of Havelok becomes an analogue to depictions of the proper ruler in political and legal treatises, in political songs, and in the chronicles.

The lower-class attitude to the monarchy, shaped by the general medieval concept of the true prince, finds full expression in John of Salisbury's *Policraticus*, the earliest detailed examination of politics in medieval England. Written in the middle of the twelfth century, the *Policraticus* "represents the purely mediaeval tradition unaffected by ideas newly borrowed from classical antiquity. It is the culmination, in their maturest form, of a body of doctrines which had developed in unbroken sequence from patristic literature in contact with the institutions of the earlier Middle Ages."[10] The discussion of the monarchy begins with an explicit contrast between a prince and a tyrant:

> Est ergo tiranni et principis haec differentia sola vel maxima, quod hic legi obtemperat et eius arbitrio populum regit cuius se credit ministrum, et in rei publicae muneribus exercendis et oneribus subeundis legis beneficio sibi primum vendicat locum.[11]

> (There is this single and major difference between a tyrant and a prince, that the latter obeys the law and rules his people by its judgment, seeing himself as its servant. Through the law he makes good his claim to the foremost and chief place in the operation of the state's affairs and in bearing its burden.)

The subsequent description of a prince corresponds to the presentation of Havelok in the English romance. A prince works for the welfare of his subjects[12]; he is the protector of the poor, the orphaned, and the widowed[13]; he is the provider for the lower classes.[14] Though the central concern of a prince is the welfare of his people, he must also know the proper manner of judgment. First of all, a prince must be a God-fearing individual, since the beginning of wisdom is fear of the Lord.[15] A good ruler must always be aware of wise counsel, since an effective ruler profits from the wisdom and the experience of his advisers.[16] Lastly, the ideal prince must temper his justice with mercy.[17]

As the traits of the ideal prince of the *Policraticus* conform closely to the poet's delineation of Havelok, John of Salisbury's discussion of a tyrant corresponds to the briefer sketches of Godard and Godrich; indeed, just as the **Havelok** poet places the two traitors in contrast with Havelok, so the *Policraticus* discusses the nature of a tyrant to show the contrast with its preceding discussion of a prince.[18] **Havelok the Dane**,

however, does not support the conclusion of the *Policraticus* that tyrannicide is a valid, often necessary, action by a tyrant's subjects.[19] Though the barons might well support John of Salisbury's arguments in favor of tyrannicide, the lower classes, the audience of the English romance, would tend to hate the possibility of tyrannicide which, for them, would mean further civil disruption.

Though written a century later than the *Policraticus*, Henry of Bracton's *De Legibus et Consuetudinis Angliae* follows closely John of Salisbury's treatment of the proper prince, though Henry's legal training asserts itself in the greater emphasis placed on the monarch as law-giver. In his analysis of the tyrant, however, Henry rejects the validity of tyrannicide; he believes that a tyrant's subjects must trust God who will eventually punish the tyrant and annihilate his rule.[20] The subjects of Godrich and Godard follow Henry's position in foregoing any revolutionary tactics against their wicked rulers; consequently, Havelok becomes the natural agent of God to end the tyrant's rule. The re-establishment of harmonious rule in both Denmark and England is a complete delineation of perfect rule by a proper prince which accords with the theories of John of Salisbury and Henry of Bracton.

The conception of the prince outlined in these legal and political treatises finds a further theoretical presentation in a popular song, *The Battle of Lewes*, written shortly after its titular event.[21] Though an elaborate presentation of the principles which stood behind the barons' opposition to Henry III, the song also sets forth a detailed statement of the popular conception of a good ruler. For the anonymous author, the ideal king must be a God-fearing man: "Omnis rex intelligat quod est servus Dei" (Let every king bear in mind that he is a servant of God). In the affairs of the realm, the king must be a servant and an administrator of the law.[22] As an administrator, the ruler must be merciful and compassionate; in this regard he must seek and heed the advice of his counsellors.[23] Such a delineation of the ideal ruler is exalted; the monarch, "Vir prudens and humilis" (a prudent and humble man), becomes a leader of outstanding wisdom, virtue, and understanding:

> Principis contere non est, sed tueri;
> Principis obprimere non est, sed mereri
> Multis beneficiis suorum favorem,
> Sicut Christus gratiis monium amorem.
> (725-728)

> (It is not the part of a prince to bruise, but to protect; neither is it the part of a prince to oppress, but rather to deserve the favor of his people by numerous benefits conferred upon them, as Christ by his grace has deserved the love of all.)

*The Battle of Lewes* emphasizes fear of God, respect for the law, mercy, and an abiding commitment to the welfare of the people as the most important qualities of the good ruler. It is significant, then, that this poem, a reflection of the anti-monarchical outlook of the mid-thirteenth century, embodies the same principles for the behavior of the ruler that are found in the more theoretical discussion of the monarchy. The poem becomes a testimony to the general acceptance and understanding of the principles enunciated in the more formal fashion of John of Salisbury and Henry of Bracton. And *Havelok the Dane* represents the kind of ruler who would be willingly and eagerly accepted by the pro-baronial author of *The Battle of Lewes*, even though the author of the romance has made his ideal king embody these principles in such a way that Havelok wins the respect, not only of the barons, but, more importantly, of the lower classes.

In their depiction of Edward I, the chronicles of the period presented a portrait of an ideal ruler who often becomes the personification of these same noble qualities of the good prince and, at the same time, a further analogue to the portrait of Havelok by the English poet. The social climate of the second half of the thirteenth century needed and demanded a popular hero who would restore peace and stability to the country. In the pages of the medieval chronicles, Edward became the popular ideal of the good king.[24]

At the time of the coronation of Edward I in 1274, England was suffering many of the social problems depicted in *Havelok the Dane* after Athelwold's death and prior to Havelok's accession to the throne. The country was full of thieves: "Rarus aut nullus in Anglia fuit tutus, eo quod terra visplionibus erat plena" (There were few or no places in England which were safe, because the whole country was filled with night robbers).[25] Laws seemed to favor the rich; the poor were always the oppressed.[26] The system of justice was corrupt; many royal officials violated the code of conduct they were supposed to represent. Immediately after his coronation, therefore, Edward began to correct the many abuses and injustices that had become part of his country's governing structure. He ordered a survey of every county to determine the degree to which the king's rights were being endangered by his subjects and to learn about all illegal activities of his royal officials. The result of the survey, the Hundred Rolls, presented a vivid and sorry account of the problems of the period and formed the basis of many of the statutes passed in succeeding years. In the Statutes of Westminster of 1275, Edward enunciated his purpose: "First the King willeth and commandeth, That the Peace of Holy Church and of the Land, be well kept and maintained in all points, and that common Right be done to all, as well Poor as Rich, without respect of Persons."[27] The Statutes imposed a series of penalties for royal officials who violated their authority. Despite Edward's

efforts, however, the corruption of officials seemed to continue into the fourteenth century.[28]

Such correspondences between the England of Edward I and Havelok's world are complemented by some striking similarities between the two rulers. Like Havelok, Edward was a prince of immense strength and physical prowess. One chronicler commended him as "magnae probitatis viro" (a man of great prowess) and "in armis strenuus et pulcherrimae juventutis" (a man mighty in arms and in the flower of youth).[29] As a warrior, Edward admired the manly virtues of courage and strength, even when they belonged to his enemies. On one occasion, he challenged Adam Gurdun to a single combat; the boldness and bravery of his opponent prompted the victorious Edward to apply cataplasms to Gurdun's wounds and to treat his defeated opponent as a friend.[30] Compassion and clemency became frequent attributes in the depictions of Edward. When describing the submission of John of Vesci to Edward in 1266, one chronicler depicted the prince "cujus inaestimabilis et universa semper contra transgressores extitit misericordia" (whose incalculable and general sympathy always extended towards wrongdoers).[31] In the following year, Edward attacked the plunderers in the Isle of Ely; "misericordia motus" (being moved by pity), he granted them peace, even though they were his enemies.[32] *The Chronicle of Bury St Edmunds* might well have been referring to Havelok when it called Edward "si alter Salomon in monibus agendis suis hactenus strenuus, magnificus et gloriosus" (up until this time, in all actions energetic, generous, and triumphant like another Solomon).[33]

In *Havelok the Dane*, the hero's humane understanding is a product of his religious piety. The medieval chronicles also draw attention to Edward's spirituality and his devotional practices. It was his habit to have masses offered as an expression of his gratitude for divine assistance in his military campaigns. He went to the Holy Land to fight the infidels. The chronicles testify again and again to his continual observance of feast days and other religious celebrations. Though his laws did tax the clergy with increasing severity, he always remained very generous in his contributions to the establishment and maintenance of religious edifices. Havelok vowed to establish "Al for Grim, of monekes blake / A priorie to seruen in ay / Iesu Crist til domesday"; Edward's most famous contribution was the founding of the Cistercian abbey of Vale Royal in fulfillment of his earlier vow to God for protection in a storm.[34]

Before becoming king, both Edward and Havelok experienced a long period of regal apprenticeship. As an exiled prince, Havelok has to win the respect of his former subjects and regain his rightful throne. As a young prince, Edward had to defend his father's monarchy against the barons. In the baronial wars during the sixties, Edward took command of the royal forces and defeated his opponents. Despite the fact that his father remained on the throne for another seven years after the barons' defeat, Edward seemed to be king in all matters except the title. He pursued the vestiges of the rebellion and restored the realm to peace. Only when England was restored to peace did Edward organize his crusade to the Holy Land. Before he came to the throne, he was a man of unlimited experience in military and political affairs; the turmoil of mid-thirteenth-century England offered him an education not dissimilar to the practical problems Havelok faced in his quest to regain his rights.

After becoming king, both Edward and Havelok revealed themselves to be intelligent and merciful kings; both were lawgivers who consulted parliament for its advice. Edward began the practice of calling parliament to assist him in his administrative and legislative decisions. From the time of his coronation until his departure for France in 1286, he summoned parliament at least twice every year and he continued this practice, except when wars prevented it, after his return in 1289. Moreover, he followed de Montfort's practice of admitting to parliament representatives of towns in addition to the lords, the major clergy, and the knights of the shire.

The final similarity between the world of the romance and Edward's career is the sternness of the kings as it asserts itself in their harsh treatment of traitors. Godard is flayed alive and hung; Godrich receives a more severe sentence:

> And demden, him to binden faste
> Vp-on an asse, swiþe un-wraste,
> Andelong, nouht ouer-þwert,
> His nose went unto þe stert,
> And so [un]-to Lincólne lede,
> Shamelike in wicke wede—
> And hwan he [come] un-to þe borw,
> Shamelike ben led þer-þoru,
> Bisouþe þe borw, un-to a grene—
> Þat þare is yete, als y wene—
> And þere be bunden til a stake,
> Abouten him ful gret fir make,
> And al to dust be brend riht þore.
>
> (2820-2832)

Though Derek Pearsall is correct in referring to "the scrupulously detailed punishment of the traitors at the end" as an example of the poet's respect for law and order,[35] it should be noted that the English romancer is singularly brief in this regard in contrast to the chroniclers' descriptions of similar punishments decreed by Edward. All contemporary chroniclers described Edward's severe treatment of inveterate traitors in his campaigns against the Welsh. Llewellyn, Prince of Wales, was beheaded; his head was taken to

London and placed on display at the top of the Tower of London.[36] A more severe judgment awaited his brother David. As a traitor to the king, David was drawn to his place of execution by horses; as a murderer, he was hung; as a consequence of his sacrilege in committing his crimes on Palm Sunday, he was disembowelled; as a consequence of plotting the death of the king, he was quartered. The manner of David's execution may have served as a basis for the treatment of Godrich. Moreover, Edward did not pass judgment on David; he summoned a parliament at Shrewsbury to judge the case and form a verdict. The sentence, as in the verdicts against Godard and Godrich, represented the agreement of the king and his advisers.[37] In contrast to the Anglo-Norman versions of the Havelok story where Odulf, the counterpart of Godard, dies in battle and Edelsie, Godrich's counterpart, dies shortly after Havelok's return without suffering any punishment, the English romancer introduces punishments for the two traitors similar in severity to the punishments Edward was bestowing on those leaders who were disturbing the peace of his country.

The chronicle accounts of Edward I and their similarities to the presentation of Havelok by the English poet suggest the true distinction of this Middle English romance. Though the portrait reflects discussions of the good ruler found in writings of the period, the originality of the English poet lies, not only in his imposition of the contemporary philosophy of kingship on the Havelok tale, but also in his adaptation of the story to the social climate of his time. The employment of the Havelok story, the continual focus on the nature of the king's governing power, the deliberate choice of a particular audience, such factors suggest that the English romancer turned to the Havelok story because it offered an interesting and valid analogue to governmental problems of the late thirteenth century. Aware of the affinities between events in the Havelok story and the contemporary political scene, he did not set out to create a political allegory; he did intend, however, to adapt the story according to the social problems of his generation. Out of this mixture of a local legend and the political reality of his time the poet created a portrait of the ideal king which is at the same time a subtle commentary on the late thirteenth century. The general similarities between the world of the romance and the late thirteenth century extend, finally, to the figure of their kings. The romancer saw the parallels that existed between Havelok's world and the world of Edward I and he created a portrait of the ideal king which becomes an analogue to the presentation of Edward in the chronicle accounts of his reign.

The chroniclers' presentation of the popular ideal of kingly virtue embodied in their figure of Edward I suffered a series of blemishes as the century drew to a close. Havelok is the ideal king who brings a lasting peace to his country in the world of romance; Edward is the king of a real country where Havelok's prelapsarian perfection can never reach its complete realization. The later years of Edward's reign were filled with severe personal and political disappointments for the king. In 1290, his wife died. The final decade of the century witnessed the beginning of the wars with Scotland, and the remaining years of Edward's kingship were an unending and futile attempt to impose a forced unity between England and Scotland. In addition, Edward began to see that the dissolute behavior of his son Edward did not bode well for the quality of the reign of Edward II.[38]

Even though the political turbulence of Edward's later years prevented his reign from assuming the perfect harmony of Havelok's united realm, both the Havelok poet and the chroniclers shared a similar conception of an ideal king: a man of intelligence and compassion, strictness and mercy, fear of God and love of the nation and its inhabitants. One final similarity relates the English Havelok to Edward I. The romance depicts its hero as a man of striking physical appearance and exceptional strength. When Ubbe first meets him, he notices "Hu he was wel of bones maked, / Brod in þe sholdres, ful wel schaped, / Þicke in þe brest, of bodi long." At Lincoln, Havelok towers over his peers:

Was Hauelok bi þe shuldren more
Þan þe meste þat þer kam:
In armes him noman [ne] nam
Þat he doune sone ne caste;
Hauelok stod ouer hem als a mast.
Als he was heie, al[s] he was long,
He was boþe stark and strong;
In Engelond [was] non hise per
Of strengþe þat euere kam him ner.

(982-990)

Edward I, nicknamed "longshanks" because of his long legs,[39] was a man of similar appearance and strength. One contemporary chronicler described him:

Elegantis erat formae, staturae procerae, qua ab humero et supra communi populo praeeminebat. . . . Brachiorum ad proportionem corporis flexibilis productio, quibus vivacitate nervica nulla erant ad usum gladii aptiora: pectus ventri praeeminebat, tibiarumque longa divisio, equorum nobilium cursu et saltu, sessoris firmitatem prohibuit infirmari.[40]

(He had a fine figure, tall in stature, by which he towered over the common people from his shoulder and above. .`. . The length of his arms was in the proper proportion to his body; no sinews were better fitted to the use of the sword. His breast projected forward from his stomach; the length of his legs kept him from being unseated when he raced or jumped noble horses.)

This point of close similarity, their unusual height, suggests, finally, that the romancer may have intended his portrait of the ideal king to be a reflection of and a compliment to his own monarch.[41]

The similarities between the romancer's presentation of Havelok and the chroniclers' depiction of the career of Edward I are a final indication of the romancer's conscious adaptation of the materials of the Havelok story to present a portrait of the ideal king modeled both on the Havelok of local legend and on the thirteenth-century understanding of the ideal king. Contemporary reality and legendary history unite in this late thirteenth-century account of the Havelok tale.[42]

*Havelok the Dane* is a unique treatment of the Havelok story and a significant employment of the romance genre. It reworks the materials of the Havelok tale, not to offer a further retelling, but to make Havelok's career the embodiment of the ideal king from the point of view of the lower classes. Havelok is an earlier version of Shakespeare's Prince Hal, though Shakespeare's hero undergoes his lower-class education by choice, not by necessity; for both Havelok and Hal, education outside the court offers an understanding of the problems of the king's lower-class subjects.

The romancer adapts the story so that Havelok is no longer the passive protagonist of the Anglo-Norman accounts; he is now a hero, the ideal king, the embodiment of those virtues designated by other writings of the period as the qualities of the true prince. By seeing the parallels between the world of Havelok and Edward I's England and incorporating and expanding them into his version of the Havelok tale, the poet creates a romance which is both a portrait of the ideal king and a mirror for princes offered from the point of view of the lower classes. The distinctly thirteenth-century portrait does become a handbook for princes, a guide to lower-class attitudes to the monarchy and a commentary on the interest and demands of this segment of society. As a reflection of the lower-class conception of the ideal king, the romance speaks ultimately to the king himself. By creating his romance for this particular audience, the poet focuses on the qualities of the good king which win the respect and love of the audience. As a consequence, the poem also stands as a guide for the proper behavior of the wise monarch, as a lesson for the king who is willing to heed it. Havelok stands as a servant of God and as a servant of his people. He is stern to the traitors who disturb the peace of his country; he is generous to all the members of the lower classes who support his kingship. Not isolated but a part of his people, not selfish and aloof, but compassionate and understanding, Havelok is the monarch as he should be.

The dissimilarities between Havelok's everlasting peace and Edward's beleagured later years are a painful reiteration of the ultimate difference between the world of **Havelok the Dane**, a romance, and the reality of late thirteenth-century England.

*Notes*

[1] In the two Anglo-Norman versions of the Havelok tale, Havelok is also called Cuaran; the second name does not appear in the Middle English romance. For a discussion of the significance of the alternate name, see Charles W. Dunn, "Havelok and Analf Cuaran," *Franciplegius: Medieval and Linguistic Studies in Honor of Francis Peabody Magoun, Jr*, ed. J. B. Bessinger, Jr., and R. P. Creed (New York, 1965), pp. 244-249. For consistency, I refer to the protagonist solely by his name of Havelok. Though both Anglo-Norman versions spell Havelok with a final 'c' instead of a 'k,' I follow the Middle English spelling with the final 'k.'

[2] All quotations from Gaimar are from Alexander Bell's edition of *L'Estoire des Engleis* (Oxford, 1960).

[3] H. E. Heyman, *Studies on the Havelok-Tale* (Upsala, 1903), concluded that the *Lai* represents another adaptation of the lost source of Gaimar's account. Edith Fahnestock, *Study of the Sources and Composition of the Lai d'Haveloc* (Jamaica, New York, 1915), concluded that the *Lai* was a carefully polished reworking of Gaimar. In his edition of *Le Lai d'Haveloc and Gaimar's Haveloc Episode* (Manchester, 1925), Alexander Bell developed Fahnestock's theory and concluded that the *Lai* is "undoubtedly derived in the main from Gaimar's version of the Havelok story" (p. 51).

[4] All quotations from the *Lai d'Haveloc* are from Bell's 1925 edition.

[5] The Lambeth Interpolation of the Havelok story need not be included here. This eighty-two line abridged outline of the story occurs only in the Lambeth MS of Robert of Brunne's translation of Peter de Langtoft's *Chronicle*. The Interpolation is a short, straightforward, and blunt description of Havelok's life; it offers no exceptional traits of character or of his life that separate him from his Anglo-Norman counterparts. In "The Lambeth Version of Havelok," *PMLA* 15 (1900), 1-16, E. W. Putnam showed that it is a third account derived, like the other two, from a lost French source. In addition, there are short accounts of the Havelok tale later in composition than the English romance and derived from the more complete versions found in Gaimar, the *Lai*, or the English romance; for a complete classification and discussion of them, see Heyman, *Studies*, pp. 109-138.

[6] In the first edition of the romance, *The Ancient English Romance of Havelok the Dane* (London, 1828), the editor, Sir Frederick Madden, dated the manuscript of the romance "about, or a few years previous to,

A.D. 1300" (p. lii) and suggested a date of composition between 1270 and 1290. In the most recent edition, the second revised edition of W. W. Skeat's edition (Oxford, 1963), the editor, K. Sisam, accepts Skeat's conclusion about the dating: "The first draft of the poem must surely have been composed earlier than 1300; but how much earlier it is impossible to say. That the dialect was, in the first instance, that of Lincolnshire, is consistent with the fact that we can still detect the characteristic suffix *-es* of the pres. s. indicative . . . and the pl. suffix *-e*" (p. xxv). Skeat's statement about the romance's source still holds true: "It is scarcely possible to determine the relation of the French versions to the English poem; nor, on the evidence of a single complete manuscript, can the earlier history of the English poem be demonstrated" (pp. xix-xx). All quotations from the romance are from Sisam's revised edition.

[7] In "Structure and Characterization in 'Havelok the Dane'," SPECULUM 44 (1969), 247-257, Judith Weiss sees the poet's central concern as "the land and its rulers." Though my study does not disagree with her article, I regard the poet's primary, indeed sole, concern as the nature of the ideal king.

[8] Another example of Athelwold's excellence is the subtle distinction between his death and the death of Birkabeyn. On his death-bed, Athelwold assembles his barons to obtain proper guidance regarding his young daughter and the future of the realm. In Denmark, when Birkabeyn realizes that he is about to die, he summons priests and monks to give him the sacraments; then he proceeds to take thought for his realm. In contrast, the "good" Athelwold assembles his barons and resolves the political implications of his death before he takes thought for himself.

[9] Among the features of the romance which suggest its lower-class audience are the complete absence of any love scenes between Havelok and Goldeboru, Havelok's practical fears regarding his marriage with the regal Goldeboru, the poet's enumeration of Grim's actions in preparing to set sail for England (699-713), the catalogue of fish (751-759), the enumeration of Havelok's menial occupations (911-920), and the poet's careful depiction of Havelok's final rewarding of his lowly companions and supporters.

[10] John Dickinson, "The Mediaeval Conception of Kingship and Some of its Limitations, as Developed in the 'Policraticus' of John of Salisbury," SPECULUM 1 (1926), 308. This article was incorporated into the long and thorough introduction to Dickinson's translation of the *Policraticus* (New York, 1927). Further discussion of John of Salisbury's theory of kingship may be found in R. W. and A. J. Carlyle, *A History of Mediaeval Political Theory in the West* (New York, 1950), 3:136-146; 4:330-341.

[11] *Policraticus* 4.1. All quotations are from C. C. J. Webb's two-volume edition, *Ioannis Saresberiensis Episcopi Carnotensis Policratici* (Oxford, 1909).

[12] *Policraticus* 4.3: "Se non sibi suam vitam sed aliis debere cognoscit, et eam illis ordinata caritate distribuit" (He knows that he owes his life not to himself and his own ends, but to others, and allots it to them in proper charity).

[13] *Policraticus* 5.6: "Eo, inquit, quod liberassem pauperem, pupillum, et periturum; et consolatus sum cor viduae. In his enim maxime principalis claret auctoritas quae a Domino instituta est ad iniurias propulsandas" (The reason, he says, is that I had set free the poor man, the orphan, and him who was about to die; and because I consoled the heart of the widow. For in such acts the nature of the authority of the prince reveals itself chiefly.)

[14] *Policraticus* 6.20: "Debent autem obsequium inferiora superioribus quae omnia eisdem vicissim debent necessarium subsidium providere. Unde Plutarchus ea dicit in omnibus exequenda quae humilioribus, id est multitudini, prosunt" (Superiors in their turn owe it to their inferiors to provide them with all things needful for their protection and succor. Therefore Plutarch says that that course is to be pursued in all things which is of advantage to the humbler classes, that is to say, the multitude).

[15] *Policraticus* 4.7: "Sapientia parit et firmat principatum; atqui initium sapientiae timor Domini" (Wisdom institutes and strengthens the government of a prince, and the beginning of wisdom is fear of the Lord).

[16] *Policraticus* 5.6: "Impossibile enim est ut salubriter disponat principatum qui non agitur consilio sapientum" (It is impossible for a prince to administer properly who does not act on the counsel of wise men).

[17] *Policraticus* 4.8: "Meditatur ergo iugiter sapientiam, et de ea sic iustitiam operatur, quod lex clementiae semper est in lingua eius; et sic clementiam temperat rigore iustitiae, quod lingua eius iudicium loquitur" (So he must ceaselessly ponder wisdom, and by its assistance he does justice in such a way that the law of mercy is always on his tongue. Thus he tempers mercy with strict justice so that his tongue speaks only justice).

[18] *Policraticus* 7.17: "Et quanto quis potentiae cupidior est, tanto eas facilius expendit. Cum vero potentiam nactus est, erigitur in tirannidem et aequitate contempta naturae et conditionis consortes inspiciente Deo deprimere non veretur. . . . Dicitur autem quia tirannus est qui violenta dominatione populum premit" (The more a man lusts after power, the more lavishly he spends for the sake of it. But when such a man does attain to power, he exalts himself into a tyrant, and, spurning equity, does not fear, in the sight of God, to humiliate the equals of his rank and nature. . . . It is said that a tyrant is one who oppresses a whole people by rulership based on force).

[19] *Policraticus* 3.15: "Porro tirannum occidere non modo licitum est sed aequum et iustum. Qui enim gladium accipit, gladio dignus est interire. Sed accipere intelligitur qui eum propria temeritate usurpat, non qui utendi eo accipit a Domino potestatem" (To kill a tyrant is not merely lawful but right and just. For whosoever takes up the sword deserves to perish by the sword. And he is understood to take up the sword who usurps it by his own rashness and who does not receive the power of using it from God).

[20] *De Legibus*, f. 5b-f. 6: "Igitur non debet esse maior eo in regni suo in exhibitione iuris, minimus autem esse debet, vel quasi, in iudicio suscipiendo si petat. Si autem ab eo petatur, cum breve non currat contra ipsum, locus erit supplicationi, quod factum suum corrigat et emendet, quod quidem si non fecerit, satis sufficit ei ad poenam, quod deum expectet ultorem. Nemo quidem de factis suis praesumat disputare, nec multo fortius contra factum suum venire" (There ought to be no one in his kingdom who surpasses him in the doing of justice, but he ought to be the last, or almost so, to receive it, when he is the plaintiff. If it is asked of him, since no writ runs against him, there will be opportunity for a petition, that he correct and amend his act; if he does not, it is punishment enough for him that he waits for God's vengeance. No one may presume to question his acts, much less contravene them). The quotation is from the four-volume text edited by George E. Woodbine (New Haven, 1915-1942) and the two-volume translation by Samuel E. Thorne (Cambridge, Mass., 1968). For a detailed analysis of Henry of Bracton's legal theory, see Ernst Kantorowicz, *The King's Two Bodies* (Princeton, 1957), pp. 143-192. In "Bracton on Kingship," *English Historical Review* 60 (1945), 136-176, Fritz Schulz studies Bracton's conception of a prince and notes the indebtedness to John of Salisbury.

[21] *The Political Songs of England*, ed. and trans. Thomas Wright (London, 1839), pp. 71-121.

[22] "Nam quid lege rectius qua cuncta reguntur, / Et quid jure verius quo res discernuntur?" (For what is more just than law, by which all things are ruled? and what more than justice, by which all things are administered?).

[23] "Ergo quales quaerat / Princeps, qui condoleant universitati, / Qui materne timeant regnum dura pati" (Let a prince seek such counsellors as may condole with the community, who have a motherly fear lest the kingdom should undergo any sufferings).

[24] With their tendency to see characters as either good or bad, the chronicles tended to exalt the figure of Edward I by removing some of the failings noted by other writers. "A Song of the Times," a song popular shortly after Edward's accession, finds injustice and poverty throughout the country (*The Political Songs of England*, pp. 133-136). Edward's foreign wars and his long battle with Scotland produced further songs against his reign (cf. "Song of the Husbandmen" and "Song on the Scottish Wars," *The Political Songs of England*, pp. 148-152, 160-179). Such signs of popular dissatisfaction with Edward's reign only show that his true character was more complicated than the accounts of the chronicles frequently suggest.

[25] Matthew of Westminster, *Flores Historiarum*, ed. H. R. Luard, Rolls Series (London, 1890), 3:10.

[26] In "Annales Prioratus de Dunstaplia," *Annales Monastici*, ed. H. R. Luard, Rolls Series (London, 1866), 3:251, the chronicler noted: "Proceres regni Angliae in pluribus locis, propter regis impotentiam, pauperes opprimebant; nec fuit ex parte regis qui justiciam faceret tribulatis" (The nobles of England, because of the king's weakness, were oppressing the poor in many places. There was no one to give justice to the oppressed in the king's name). In "A Song of the Times," *The Political Songs of England*, p. 47, the poet commented: "Omnes fere divites nimis sunt avari; / Pauper pausa possidens debet depilari, / Et ut ditet divitem rebus spoliari" (Almost all the rich men are too avaricious; the poor man, who possesses little, must be robbed and spoiled of his property to enrich the wealthy).

[27] *The Statutes of the Realm* (London, 1963), 1:26.

[28] In a popular song of the beginning of the fourteenth century, "A Song on the Times," *The Political Songs of England*, p. 197, the poet lamented the corruption of the king's officers: "Thos kingis ministris beth i-schend, / To ri3t and law that ssold tak hede, / And al the lond for t'amend, / Of thos thevis hi taketh mede. / Be the lafful man to deth i-bro3t, / And his catel awey y-nom; / Of his deth ne tellith hi no3t, / Bot of har prei hi hab som."

[29] Matthew of Westminster, 3:484; 3:19.

[30] For a complete account of the episode, see Matthew of Westminster, 3:10.

[31] "Chronicon Vulgo Dictum Chronicon Thomas Wykes," *Annales Monastici*, ed. H. R. Luard, Rolls Series (London, 1869), 4:198.

[32] Matthew of Westminster, 3:16.

[33] *The Chronicle of Bury St Edmunds*, ed. Antonia Gransden (London, 1964), p. 118.

[34] For an account of Edward's relationship with the Abbey, see *The Ledger-Book of Vale Royal Abbey*, ed. John Brownhill (Chester, 1914), pp. 2-8.

[35] Derek Pearsall, "The Development of Middle English Romance," *Mediaeval Studies* 27 (1965), 99.

[36] Accounts of Llewellyn's death may be found in Matthew of Westminster, 3:57; "Annales Prioratus de Dunstaplia" 3:292-293; Nicholas Trivet, *Annales*, ed. Thomas Hog (London, 1845), p. 305; Florence of Worcester, *Chronicon ex Chronicis*, ed. Benjamin Thorpe (London, 1849), 2:227; Bartholomew of Cotton, *Historia Anglicana*, ed. H. R. Luard, Rolls Series (London, 1859), p. 162; Henry Knighton, *Chronicon*, ed. J. R. Lumby, Rolls Series (London, 1889), 1:276-277; Walter of Guisborough, *Chronicle*, ed. Harry Rothwell (London, 1957), p. 221; *Chronicon de Lanercost*, ed. Joseph Stevenson (Edinburgh, 1839), p. 112.

[37] The fullest account of David's sentence and execution may be found in "Annales Prioratus de Dunstaplia," 3:293-294; other accounts include Matthew of Westminster, 3:58-59; Nicholas Trivet, p. 307; Florence of Worcester, 2:229-230; Bartholomew of Cotton, p. 164; Henry Knighton, 1:277; Walter of Guisborough, p. 221; *Chronicon de Lanercost*, pp. 112-113. In "Riding Backwards: Theme of Humiliation and Symbol of Evil," *Viator* 4 (1973), 153-176, Ruth Mellinkoff offers an interesting historical analysis of the treatment of traitors which includes a discussion of Godard and Godrich.

[38] I have restricted my discussion of Edward I to contemporary accounts of his career. Modern biographies also depict Edward in a manner which shows some of the affinities between his life and the career of Havelok. See Augustus Clifford, *The Life and Reign of Edward I* (London, 1872); T. F. Tout, *Edward the First* (London, 1893); John E. Morris, *The Welsh Wars of Edward I* (Oxford, 1901); F. M. Powicke, *King Henry III and Lord Edward*, 2 vols. (Oxford, 1947); L. F. Salzman, *Edward I* (London, 1968).

[39] The first recorded use of Edward's nickname is found in *The Chronicle of Pierre de Langtoft*, ed. Thomas Wright, Rolls Series (London, 1868), 2:284. It is significant that the English romance, alone of all the early versions of the Havelok story, describes Havelok as long-legged.

[40] Nicholas Trivet, pp. 281-282.

[41] The lower classes might well know very little about their king, though a detail such as unusual height would probably be a part of their limited knowledge.

[42] The similarity between Havelok and Edward suggests a further means of dating the poem. Since *Havelok the Dane* praises the happy marriage of Havelok

and Goldeboru, I would suggest that, in view of the possibility that the poem was intended as a compliment to Edward I, the poem was written no later than 1290, the year of the death of Edward's first queen. Furthermore, after David's execution, Edward traveled to Lincoln where he held a small parliament in February, 1284 ("Annales Prioratus de Dunstaplia," 3:305). Though this brief stay in Lincoln was not a full gathering of councillors and representatives, the two references to parliaments in the poem (1006, 1179) may refer to this previously unnoted parliament; in "Parliaments Held at Lincoln," *Englische Studien* 32 (1903), 319-320, W. van der Gaaf failed to include this meeting. Moreover, the manuscript in which the romance survives suggests that the poem was originally part of the repertory of a wandering minstrel: "The original manuscript from which Havelok was copied had twenty lines to the page (Zupitza in *Anglia*, vii. 155); the same may be inferred for this copy of Horn from the transposition of 0 1462-81. It is therefore probable that both poems were copied from the same manuscript, and that of a *format* such as a wandering minstrel would possess" (*King Horn*, ed. Joseph Hall [Oxford, 1901], p. ix). Thus *Havelok the Dane* may have originated as part of the festivities in Lincoln at the time of the 1284 parliament. Its lower-class audience may reflect its inclusion as entertainment for the townspeople or for some of the king's retinue. I would conclude that these considerations suggest that the poem was composed about 1284, a date in keeping with the linguistic evidence in the poem (see n.6 above).

## George B. Jack (essay date 1977)

SOURCE: "The Date of *Havelok*," *Anglia*, Vol. 95, 1977, pp. 20-33.

[*In the following essay, Jack takes issue with Herlint Meyer-Lindenberg's attempt to date* Havelok the Dane *more exactly, considering and rejecting all six of his arguments in turn.*]

Though it would generally be accepted that the Middle English romance **Havelok** must have been in existence before 1300, there has been little agreement on any very precise date of composition; and indeed an agnostic view of the matter was taken in the edition by Skeat and Sisam, who concluded that it was impossible to determine how much before 1300 the poem may have been composed[1]. Nevertheless, there has been one recent attempt to assign a much more exact date to the poem, for it has been argued by Herlint Meyer-Lindenberg that **Havelok** must have been composed between the years 1203 and 1216[2]. This has significant implications, as it provides a basis for the further conclusion that the English text was one of the sources of the French *Lai d'Haveloc*[3]; and it is bound to influence

our conception of the kind of poem that **Havelok** is, since the arguments used by Meyer-Lindenberg require us to see **Havelok** as a literary reshaping of early thirteenth-century events, intended to be recognised as such by a contemporary audience. It is therefore a matter of more than passing importance that the arguments for such a date should be sound; yet it seems to me that they are very much open to doubt, for they involve many difficulties.

The case for dating **Havelok** between 1203 and 1216 rests on three primary arguments and three secondary ones[4]. The primary arguments are (1) that in Havelok's misfortunes at the hands of Godard there is a reflection of the fate of Arthur of Brittany, who died in 1203, (2) that one theme in **Havelok** is that of the inviolability of strictly hereditary succession, a theme of special appropriateness during the reign of King John, and (3) that the portrait of Athelwold in lines 27-105 of the poem also has particular appropriateness to the reign of John. The first of these arguments is intended to show that the earliest possible date of composition is 1203, the year of Arthur's death; and the second and third arguments are designed to establish that the latest possible date of composition is 1216, the last year of John's reign. In addition to these primary arguments there are three secondary ones, depending on (1) the allusions to Roxburgh as marking the northern boundary of England (lines 139, 265), (2) the reference to the creation of itinerant justices (lines 263-5), and (3) the use of the name Birkabeyn for Havelok's father. None of these three points indicates so specific a time as 1203-16, but they all, in Meyer-Lindenberg's view, suggest a date in either the late twelfth century or the early thirteenth, and to that extent support the assumption of early thirteenth-century composition.

The view that **Havelok** cannot be earlier than 1203 rests, as we have just noted, on the supposition that there are significant parallels between the fate of Arthur of Brittany and the treatment of Havelok by Godard in the early part of the romance. On the death of Richard I in 1199 the succession was disputed: John was accepted in England and Normandy, Eleanor (the queen-mother) in Aquitaine, and Arthur of Brittany in Anjou, Maine, and Touraine. Then in 1202, at Mirabeau in Poitou, John captured Arthur and his sister and imprisoned them. What then happened to Arthur is not known with certainty, but the probability is that he was killed in 1203 by John himself[5]. Meyer-Lindenberg argues (pp. 92-6) that these historical events are reflected in the narrative of **Havelok**, forming the basis of the scene in which Godard imprisons Havelok and his two sisters, murders the sisters, and plans to have Havelok murdered by Grim (lines 408-544).

I find this implausible. It seems to me initially rather unlikely that the hero of a popular romance such as **Havelok** would be based on Arthur of Brittany, for

Arthur was not a popular hero in England[6]. There are also more particular difficulties, for the narrative of the romance is in various ways unlike the historical events concerning Arthur of Brittany, and such similarities as there are chiefly involve features that are recognised motifs of popular literature and are at least as likely to owe their presence in *Havelok* to that source as to be reflections of historical events. To begin with the first of these points, we may notice that there are considerable divergences between the historical events surrounding Arthur of Brittany and the narrative of *Havelok*. Havelok is a young child when imprisoned by Godard (according to line 417 he is less than three years old); but Arthur of Brittany was at the time of his capture by John between fifteen and sixteen years of age—in Powicke's words, nearly a man in those days[7]—and he was engaged in besieging his grandmother at Mirabeau castle, hardly the activity of a young child and certainly without any parallel in *Havelok*. More generally, the circumstances of the historical succession were unlike those in the romance. In the romance Godard is simply a usurper and Havelok unquestionably the true heir, since he is the king's son; but Arthur was not the king's son and was by no means unambiguously the rightful heir, for John too had a claim to the throne and was in fact named by Richard as his successor. The dispute between John and Arthur was chiefly concerned with the succession to the French provinces and followed a course bearing little resemblance to the romance narrative. Following Richard's death in 1199 there was a brief period of conflict in France, ended by the Treaty of Le Goulet in 1200, whereby John was recognised by Philip of France as Richard's lawful heir, though Arthur was to hold Brittany as John's vassal. Then in 1202 war broke out between John and Philip, who hoped to take Normandy and replace John by Arthur in the other French provinces, and it was in the course of this conflict that John captured Arthur. The dispute between John and Arthur was thus spread out over several years, was complicated by the intervention of Philip of France, and was mainly concerned with the succession to only part of Richard's realm. But in the romance events are different and simpler. Godard, though ostensibly Havelok's guardian, plans to murder Havelok and usurp the throne; the events take place swiftly, involve no complicating intervention from any figure corresponding to Philip of France, and are concerned with the succession to the whole kingdom, rather than only part of it. So the historical events concerning Arthur of Brittany are in many ways unlike the narrative of *Havelok*; the romance does not seem to match those events in a sufficiently detailed and accurate way to make it reasonable to assume that it is based on them.

It might be maintained, however, that no great weight should be attached to these differences between the romance and history. A romance, it might be said, is not a chronicle, and detailed historical fidelity is not to be expected; even an approximate resemblance in some essentials of the narrative may be enough to indicate a source in historical events and to alert an audience to an intended parallel to such events. This point may in principle be a fair one, but in the particular case of *Havelok* it is of doubtful importance, because the aspects of the poem that do resemble events concerning Arthur of Brittany mainly involve motifs of popular literature, and may with as much plausibility be derived from that source as from actual events. Thus imprisonment in a tower, the starvation of the captives, the intention to murder Havelok by drowning, and his rescue by a fisherman, all points cited by Meyer-Lindenberg (p. 96) as common to *Havelok* and to accounts of Arthur's fate that are found in thirteenth-century chronicles, are likewise all recognised motifs of folk-tale[8]. Moreover, there are other Middle English romances containing episodes that show resemblances to Godard's treatment of Havelok and his sisters. In *William of Palerne* a plot is hatched by which the king's brother, hoping to gain the throne, bribes two ladies to murder the true heir, the king's young son; but the child is carried off by a wolf and brought up in safety by a cowherd[9]. In *King Horn* the child Horn is set adrift on the open sea by Saracen pirates who have killed his father, the king, and seized the realm to which Horn is heir; and the pirates intend Horn to die[10]. In view of these parallels it seems likely that the comparable episode in *Havelok*, in which the usurper Godard attempts to kill the young heir to the throne, has its roots in a common story-pattern, rather than being a reflection of particular historical events. And in general the similarities that there are between *Havelok* and the events concerning Arthur of Brittany appear to me to be of little significance; they can so readily be explained as motifs of popular literature that it seems dangerous to rest any weight upon them as an indication of historicity in the romance.

I turn next to Meyer-Lindenberg's two arguments for 1216 as the latest possible date of composition of *Havelok*. One argument depends on the fact that *Havelok* asserts the principle of hereditary succession: Havelok and Goldborough, the hereditary rulers, recover their kingdoms, overthrowing the usurpers Godard and Godrich, and the poem gives some prominence to the theme of the rightful heir. Meyer-Lindenberg maintains (pp. 99-101) that this was intended by the poet to be a comment on contemporary events, and in particular that it was an assertion of the claims of strict heredity at a time—the reign of John—when the succession had been disputed. John's reign ended in 1216, and since the succession was not then disputed the theme of strictly hereditary succession would after 1216 no longer have immediate contemporary relevance. Therefore, Meyer-Lindenberg argues, 1216 is the latest possible date of composition for *Havelok*. This I find unconvincing, in part because the restoration of the rightful heir after the overthrow of a usurper is a narrative pattern that is found also in other Middle English romances: in *King Horn* Horn returns to his own kingdom, defeats the usurping Saracens, and regains his throne; in *Gamelyn* the inheritance properly due to Gamelyn is first appropriated by his eldest brother, then recovered by Gamelyn after the discomfiture of the brother; in *Generydes* the hero Generydes, heir to the kingdom of India, defeats the usurper Amelok and recovers his realm. The presence of a similar pattern in *Havelok* may therefore be explained as simply an example of a familiar narrative type; no special historical relevance need be assumed. Nor can it be accepted that the emphasis given in *Havelok* to the theme of the rightful heir indicates composition at a time when the succession had recently been disputed. This argument would be valid only if we were to assume that the poet's themes were a direct reflection of the time in which he lived, and that his work was shaped primarily by recent history. But if we allow, as surely we must, that literature need not be like this then the argument disappears, for an emphasis on the theme of the rightful heir can as easily be supposed to have its source in the poet's imagination as in his actual experience. It is surely possible to compose a poem asserting the claims of hereditary succession at a time when the succession does not happen to be in dispute.

Meyer-Lindenberg's other argument for 1216 as the latest possible date of composition is of a similar form; it depends on claiming (pp. 98-9) that the portrait of Athelwold in lines 27-105 must have been intended by the author to have special relevance to the reign of John, thus indicating that the poem must have been composed during John's reign, and therefore by 1216 at the latest. The argument involves three steps. (a) The portrait of Athelwold is disproportionately long, in view of his relatively small part in the narrative, and the only likely explanation of this is that the author was attempting to fit into his story a comment on his own times. (b) More particularly, in presenting a portrait of Athelwold as an ideal ruler the poet intended to give a measure of the deficiencies of the king reigning in his own time; therefore the poem was composed during troubled times. (c) This would suggest that the poem was composed either during the reign of John or at some time after 1234 in the reign of Henry III; and since for other reasons the reign of Henry III is unlikely as the time of composition, this implies a date at some point in the reign of John. There are several objections to this argument. Even if we accept that the portrait of Athelwold is disproportionately long, this may be explained in ways other than the one favoured by Meyer-Lindenberg: the poet may simply have been an erratic craftsman, who genuinely but mistakenly believed that the passage was appropriate in length; or he may just have liked composing passages in this vein. Simply from the premiss that the passage is dispropor-

tionately long we cannot reasonably deduce that it was intended as a tract for the times. Moreover, even if we did assume that the passage was intended to have specific contemporary relevance it would not follow that it must have relevance to a troubled reign; it seems at least as plausible to assume that it might be intended as a celebration of a just and peaceful reign[11]. And finally, it is by no means clear that the passage is indeed disproportionately long; a good case can be made for the view that the passage is a fitting expression of the values that will be overthrown by the usurpers Godard and Godrich and re-established by Havelok, and that it thus provides a moral framework for the subsequent action of the poem[12]. No sound argument for the dating of *Havelok* can be based on the portrait of Athelwold.

We may now consider the three secondary arguments presented by Meyer-Lindenberg (p. 99), arguments intended to show that the date of composition, though not necessarily in the precise period 1203-16, must fall at some point in the late twelfth century or the early thirteenth. The first of these arguments depends on the references at lines 139 and 265 to Roxburgh as marking the northern boundary of England. These were used in the past as a basis for dating the poem, but in view of the fact that Roxburgh castle first came into English hands in 1174 they have generally come to be seen as rather unhelpful, indicating only that the poem can hardly have been composed before that date[13]. Meyer-Lindenberg's argument, however, is based on the fact that Roxburgh castle, after passing to the English in 1174, was recovered by the Scots in 1189 and held by them from then until 1296. If we assume that a reference to Roxburgh as marking the northern boundary of England would be likely only at a time when the castle either was or had recently been in English hands, then this implies a date of composition either around the late twelfth century or at the very end of the thirteenth. Meyer-Lindenberg argues on other grounds (which I shall consider below) that *Havelok* certainly cannot be later than 1250; this therefore leaves a time around the late twelfth century as the most likely period for the composition of the poem, given the references to Roxburgh[14].

This is not a good argument, for the historical assumptions on which it is based seem to be faulty. There is no real justification for the view that the holding of Roxburgh castle by the English between 1174 and 1189 underlies the references to it in *Havelok* as marking the Anglo-Scottish frontier. By the Treaty of Falaise in 1174 William of Scotland became the feudal vassal of the English king and ceded five castles to England; Roxburgh was one, and the others were Berwick, Edinburgh, Jedburgh, and Stirling. The effect of the treaty was not to alter the boundary of the two countries so that Roxburgh became part of England instead of Scotland; what the treaty meant was that the whole of

Scotland was brought into subordination to England. Edinburgh castle was restored to Scotland in 1186; then in 1189 by a charter of quit-claim Richard I restored the castles of Berwick and Roxburgh to Scotland (Jedburgh and Stirling were not mentioned, and may in fact never have been garrisoned by the English)[15]. The importance of this is that it shows that when Roxburgh castle came into English hands it would not thereby have been seen as marking the northern boundary of England, for the whole Scottish kingdom was then in subjection to England, and Edinburgh, a castle much further north than Roxburgh, was also garrisoned by the English. Therefore there is no reason to suppose that the references to Roxburgh as marking the border of the kingdoms depend on the actual holding of the place by the English between 1174 and 1189. The correct explanation must be that the author of **Havelok** referred to Roxburgh as marking the border, not because it was (or had recently been) held by the English, but simply because it was a known town in the border area. It would be unrealistic to expect the author of **Havelok**, belonging (as the linguistic evidence shows) to the East Midlands of England, to have exact knowledge of the Anglo-Scottish border; there would certainly be no map available with the border conveniently inked in, and it is likely enough that he was relying on hearsay rather than first-hand knowledge. Moreover, Roxburgh is in fact very close to the border, for it is less than ten miles from the border that was effectively recognised in 1237 by the Treaty of York and had apparently been tacitly accepted for many years before then[16]; and so it would not be unreasonable to use Roxburgh to indicate more or less where the border lay. From this, however, it follows that no conclusion about the dating of **Havelok** can be based on the references to Roxburgh, for these would have been possible at any time in the thirteenth century or in the twelfth.

Before going on to the next of the secondary arguments we may consider Meyer-Lindenberg's reasons for thinking that, quite independently of any arguments for a date between 1203 and 1216, **Havelok** certainly cannot have been composed later than 1250. The basis for this assumption lies in the fact that there is a version of the Anglo-Norman *Brut* incorporating an an account of Havelok that displays certain features otherwise found only in the English **Havelok**[17]. As Meyer-Lindenberg suggests (p. 97), it is reasonable to assume that these features were in fact derived from the English **Havelok**. Meyer-Lindenberg also assumes, following Brie, that the features in question were incorporated first into a version of Wace's *Brut* and then taken from there into the version of the *Brut* in which they actually appear; and since Brie suggested that this presumed version of Wace cannot have been much later than 1250[18], this means that the English **Havelok** must have been in existence by that date. This appears to be too early.

Brie gave no reason for the date he ascribed to the version of Wace through which he assumed that the Havelok story reached the *Brut* with which we are concerned. All that can reasonably be concluded is that the English **Havelok**, since it was apparently the source of features in the *Brut* (either directly or through a version of Wace), was in existence by the time at which the text of the *Brut* in which these features actually appear was composed. The earliest manuscript of this version of the *Brut* (Paris, Bibliothèque Nationale, fonds français 14640) is *circa* 1300[19]. The chronicle contained in this manuscript continues to the year 1272[20] and was presumably composed around that date. On the assumption that this chronicle derived features from the English **Havelok**, this implies that **Havelok** was in existence by about 1272; but it does not support a *terminus ante quem* of 1250.

The next of Meyer-Lindenberg's secondary arguments arises from the mention in lines 263-5 of itinerant justices. In these lines Godrich is described as creating justices who will travel the length and breadth of England, and Meyer-Lindenberg sees this as reflecting the historical fact of the establishment of itinerant justices by Henry II. I take it that Meyer-Lindenberg is here thinking particularly of the Assize of Clarendon (1166). This is hardly a satisfactory argument. First, even if we agree that the lines in question are a reflection of the Assize of Clarendon (and this may be doubted) it is far from obvious that this provides support for the assumption that **Havelok** was composed between the years 1203 and 1216. An allusion to an event of 1166 would show only that the text could not have been composed before that date; it would not indicate how much after 1166 the poem might have been composed, and would in principle be consistent with a date either before or after 1203-16. Moreover, it is not in fact clear that lines 263-5 do allude to the Assize of Clarendon. The assumption that they do depends on interpreting *Iustises dede he maken newe* (line 263) as meaning 'he had justices of a new kind established'. But line 263 may mean rather 'he had new justices appointed'—that is, that the incumbents were new, not the office itself[21]. If this is the true meaning of line 263, then it removes the basis for claiming that **Havelok** shows knowledge of the *establishment* of itinerant justices. Lines 263-5 would then show only that the author knew of the *existence* of itinerant justices, and this would be compatible with a date of composition at almost any time from about 1130 onwards; for although the Assize of Clarendon gave instructions on which itinerant justices were to act, the practice of sending royal justices into the shires had existed before then, at least as early as 1130, and it continued during the thirteenth century[22]. For these reasons, then, lines 263-5 cannot be regarded as lending any firm support to the assumption of a date of composition between 1203 and 1216.

The last of Meyer-Lindenberg's secondary arguments depends on the name Birkabeyn, used of Havelok's father in the English text. This name is of Norse origin, evidently deriving from one applied to King Sverrir of Norway (1184-1202) and coming originally from the nickname *Birkibeinar* used of Sverrir's followers[23]. Meyer-Lindenberg takes the use of the name in *Havelok* to be an indication that the date of composition is likely to be during or not long after the reign of Sverrir. But this argument has no force, since we do not know the process by which the author of *Havelok* learned the name Birkabeyn and therefore cannot assume that his knowledge of the name indicates proximity in date to the reign of Sverrir. If the name came to England through the fame of Sverrir, it could well have remained in currency for some time before being used in *Havelok*. And in any case we do not know whether the name came to England in that way, for it was used of other Scandinavians in the thirteenth century[24] and may not have reached England until considerably after Sverrir's time. So the use of the name Birkabeyn indicates nothing more precise than that the date of composition cannot have been before the time of Sverrir, the earliest date at which the name could have reached England from Scandinavia.

I would therefore suggest that there are insuperable difficulties in the arguments for dating *Havelok* between 1203 and 1216. More generally, the evidence does not seem to be sufficient for any dating of the poem aiming at that degree of precision, and a less definite conclusion is all that can reasonably be expected. Clearly the poem must have been composed by the early fourteenth century, the date of the Laud MS.; and since the textual and linguistic character of *Havelok* indicates that the Laud version was not the first copy that had been made of the poem, it is at least plausible that a gap of some years separated composition from the production of the Laud version. As we have already noted, moreover, the presence in a thirteenth-century version of the *Brut* of features apparently deriving from the English *Havelok* implies a probable date of composition no later than about 1272; and the use of the name Birkabeyn suggests composition no earlier than the late twelfth century. Taking these points together, therefore, we arrive at a date of composition at some time between the late twelfth century and about 1272. It might also be argued that the references at lines 1006 and 1179 to a parliament held at Lincoln imply that the poem does not antedate 1226, when, it has been suggested, parliament first met there[25]. But this seems an unjustified conclusion. The poet could well have made parliament meet at Lincoln in his romance even though it had never done so in fact, for as Meyer-Lindenberg points out (p. 92) the narrative of *Havelok* requires Godrich to be at Lincoln and the holding of a parliament provides a convenient explanation of his presence there. We should not attach great weight to the particular term *parlement* used in *Havelok*, for it may simply mean 'council, assembly' rather than having any more technical sense. Certainly this more general meaning of the word 'parliament' is found in Middle English, as in Latin and French in the twelfth and thirteenth centuries[26]; and the context in *Havelok* indicates that by *parlement* is meant an assembly of barons and bishops summoned to meet in the king's presence, a council of a kind already in existence before the thirteenth century[27]. Such a council could meet in a variety of places[28], and it would be quite reasonable for the author of *Havelok* to depict one as meeting at Lincoln, whether or not he knew that it had done so in fact. From the evidence of datable references in the poem, therefore, the composition of *Havelok* cannot be more precisely fixed than within a time between the late twelfth century and *circa* 1272.

*Notes*

[1] W. W. Skeat and K. Sisam, *The Lay of Havelok the Dane*, 2nd ed., revised impression (Oxford, 1967), p. xxv. This also provides (pp. xxiii-xxv) a convenient summary of discussion of the date of *Havelok*. But it should be noted that Skeat and Sisam are in error when they state (p. xxiii) that Deutschbein "inclines to a date in the second half of the thirteenth century", for in fact Deutschbein suggests that the first version of *Havelok* was composed in the last quarter of the twelfth century (M. Deutschbein, *Studien zur Sagengeschichte Englands* [Cöthen, 1906], p. 165).

[2] "Zur Datierung des *Havelok*", *Anglia*, 86 (1968), 89-112.

[3] See Meyer-Lindenberg, op. cit., pp. 102-12.

[4] This division is my own.

[5] See A. L. Poole, *From Domesday Book to Magna Carta*, 2nd ed. (Oxford, 1955), pp. 378, 381-3.

[6] See F. M. Powicke, *The Loss of Normandy*, 2nd ed. (Manchester, 1961), p. 314.

[7] Powicke, op. cit., p. 310.

[8] See S. Thompson, *Motif-Index of Folk-Literature*, 2nd ed. (Bloomington and Copenhagen, 1955-58), motifs K958, R41.2, R51.1, R131.4.

[9] *William of Palerne*, ed. W. W. Skeat, EETS, ES 1 (London, 1867), pp. 1-12 (this includes an opening section taken from the French text, for the beginning of the English text is missing).

[10] *King Horn*, ed. J. Hall (Oxford, 1901), lines 1-116 (MS. C).

[11] This was in fact the assumption made by Deutschbein, who suggested (op. cit., p. 165) that if a historical basis were to be sought for the portrait of Athelwold it might reasonably be found in Henry II.

[12] For discussion see D. Mehl, *The Middle English Romances of the Thirteenth and Fourteenth Centuries* (London, 1968), p. 170, and J. Weiss, *Speculum*, 44 (1969), 249f.

[13] See Skeat and Sisam, op. cit., p. xxiii.

[14] In Meyer-Lindenberg's article the argument is not explicitly set out in this form; but this must, I think, be the reasoning lying behind the use of the references to Roxburgh.

[15] See W. Croft Dickinson, *Scotland from the Earliest Times to 1603*, 2nd ed. (London, 1965), p. 78; D. W. Hunter Marshall, *Scottish Historical Review*, 25 (1927-28), 20-23.

[16] See G. W. S. Barrow, *The Kingdom of the Scots* (London, 1973), ch. 4; this was earlier published in *Northern History*, 1 (1966), 21-42.

[17] See F. Brie, "Zum Fortleben der Haveloksage", *Englische Studien*, 35 (1905), 359-71.

[18] Brie, op. cit., p. 364.

[19] Brie, op. cit., pp. 361-2; J. Vising, *Anglo-Norman Language and Literature* (London, 1923), p. 98.

[20] Brie, op. cit., p. 360.

[21] The use of the verb *make* in the sense 'appoint' is recorded from the twelfth century; see the *Middle English Dictionary*, s. v. *maken*, v. 1, sense 6.

[22] See Poole, op. cit., pp. 399f. But see also W. T. Reedy, "The Origins of the General Eyre in the Reign of Henry I", *Speculum*, 41 (1966), 688-724, for discussion of differences between the practice during the reign of Henry I and that following the Assize of Clarendon.

[23] See L. A. Hibbard, *Mediaeval Romance in England*, 2nd ed. (New York, 1960), p. 104; E. Björkman, *Nordische Personennamen in England*, Studien zur englischen Philologie, 37 (Halle, 1910), s. v. *Birkabein*.

[24] See E. H. Lind, *Norsk-isländska personbinamn fran medeltiden* (Uppsala, 1920-21), s. v. *Birkibein*.

[25] See W. van der Gaaf, "Parliaments Held at Lincoln", *Englische Studien*, 32 (1903), 319-20. This assembly was not in fact officially referred to as a parliament; the earliest known official use of the term is in 1236, referring to an assembly that was to take place in 1237 (see H. G. Richardson and G. O. Sayles, "The Earliest Known Official Use of the Term 'Parliament'", *English Historical Review*, 82 [1967], 747-50).

[26] See *OED*, s. v. *parliament,* sb. 1, sense 2, and H. G. Richardson, "The Origins of Parliament", *Transactions of the Royal Historical Society*, 4th Series, 11 (1928), 137-83.

[27] See G. O. Sayles, *The King's Parliament of England* (London, 1975), ch. 2, esp. p. 32.

[28] In the reign of Henry II there were, for instance, meetings of council at Northampton, Winchester, and London (*Gesta Regis Henrici Secundi Benedicti Abbatis,* ed. W. W. Stubbs, Rolls Series, 49 (London, 1867), I, 107, 118-9, 138-9).

## John M. Ganim (essay date 1983)

SOURCE: "Community and Consciousness in Early Middle English Romance," in *Style and Consciousness in Middle English Narrative*, Princeton University Press, 1983, pp. 16-54.

[*In the following excerpt, Ganim describes a repeated pattern found in* Havelok the Dane *in which the epic gives way to the real—which in turn yields to comic synthesis. Ganim further explores the use of geography to evoke distinctions between social classes.*]

A number of scholars have described the change in society, sensibility, and form that surrounded the transformation of epic into romance.[1] Most studies, however, have concerned themselves with the elegant Old French productions of the twelfth century or have debated the degree of overlap and continuity between the two genres. The shift from heroic to chivalric values, from social struggle to individual quest, from concern with the survival of the entire community to concern with the perfection of specific class ideals, all these have been documented and explained. The road that takes us from the gloom of *Beowulf* to the glitter of Chrétien's romances crosses barriers of language, social structure, taste, and historical change, but it is a road that has been mapped in some detail.

One reason why the early Middle English romances have not as often been taken seriously is that in most respects they seem to represent a decline in literary history:

> *Beowulf* was composed for persons of quality, *Havelok* for the common people. Old English narrative poetry was, in its day, the best obtainable; English metrical romances were known by the authors, vendors and consumers of them to be inferior to the

best, i.e. to the French; and, consequently, there is a rustic, uncourtly air about them. Their demeanour is often lumbering, and they are sometimes conscious of it.[2]

I do think that the poets were often "conscious of it," even to the point of playing with an occasional sophisticated air and sometimes contrasting a rapid and deftly constructed narrative with details and phrases that, though they were perhaps striking, were also rustic and quaint. This is not to argue that the *Havelok*-poet was nearly as sophisticated as Chaucer in such a respect. But he thought he knew what he was good for, and he liked to show it.

From a broader point of view, this note of rusticity, even of naiveté, has a certain rhetorical function, and it is this function that I want to explain here. These romances announce potentially epic themes and then retreat from the implications of those themes. They seem to manifest a sense of history, growth, and change and suddenly retreat into a timeless utopian vision of existence. They sometimes represent the dimensions of physical and social reality in profoundly disturbing detail and then counter that sense of reality with comic or grotesque devices. The conceptions of time and space implicit in the narrative structure of these romances differ from such conceptions in either chivalric romance or in epic. They borrow the conventions of courtly romance but use those conventions to appeal to the reader in a radically different way.

There is no question that French courtly romance was the most characteristic genre of high medieval culture, in much the same way that Gothic architecture was the dominant architectural mode. But in twelfth-century France, romance had flourished in a rarefied atmosphere, that of court patronage, with an elite audience capable of comprehending an often esoteric code of social values. Indeed, the very source of courtly literature is in its insistence that its audience is exceptional and could understand things that a larger audience could not.[3] It was an art of delicate balance—on the one hand, hints and cues that serve as signs to the initiated; on the other, long and sometimes tiresome exploration of states of consciousness, fused in an action of fantastic adventure. In a totally different social and literary situation, that of thirteenth-century England, in which class distinctions, though clear, seemed to require less elaborate markings and in which, in comparison, the flowering of provincial courts had never advanced that far, this art was under strains that threatened to transform it beyond recognition. This is not merely to repeat the observation that English romances are less refined and therefore more popular than their French antecedents. Rather it is to describe an entirely different literary and rhetorical situation. Far from confirming the elite nature of a court audience, early Middle English romance speaks to a larger community, and

the narrating voice makes an attempt to include itself and its audience in that world. The "flaws" that result are only contradictions if we abide by whatever generic standards we draw from French romance. The result is a form in Middle English romance that borrows widely from many different genres in an attempt to establish its own authenticity and that moves towards a form less courtly and exclusive and more encyclopedic and inclusive, a combination that has considerable implications for the development of later Middle English poetry.

Not only does English romance borrow from a wide variety of genres, which in themselves each imply a specific audience, but it borrows from a wide spectrum of romances.[4] During the high point of Middle English romance, romance as a genre in France was already two hundred years old, and without too much exaggeration one could point not only to clearly aristocratic but also to popular romances, as well as to those that combined such elements. Often the earliest English romances have the quality of anthologies; consistency of tone is one of their problems. Elements that derive from lyric or epic, from delicate *lai*, from *chanson de geste*, from chivalric romance, are found together, as if jerked from their original historical context. But this problematic situation also leads to Middle English literature's greatest strengths—the multiplicity of perspective and wide appeal of such works as *The Canterbury Tales*—as well as to a kind of included criticism of an entire tradition that I, along with other critics, believe is found in *Sir Gawain and the Green Knight*.

As I argued in my Introduction, this inclusive but contradictory attitude towards the action is most clearly evidenced in those passages that create the sense of time and space in the poem. Hence the following description of *Havelok the Dane*, the most interesting of these early Middle English romances, concentrates on such transitional scenes. After some conclusions about the effect of these scenes I move to a discussion of *King Horn* in light of these conclusions, and then to an attempt to characterize the mentality of the early Middle English romances.

*Havelok the Dane* is based on a nicely merged dual plot. The king of Denmark dies, leaving his heir, Havelok, in the hands of one Earl Godard. Godard, not about to give up such power, imprisons the boy and his two sisters. He slits the throats of the two girls but spares the prince, ordering a fisherman, Grim, to drown the boy. Meanwhile, we are told of a similar situation in England, where a king has died, leaving his daughter, Goldboro, in the hands of an equally nefarious guardian, one Godrich. Godrich, who dislikes the idea of handing the country over to a mere girl, locks her up in a tower, and prevents her marriage to anyone save the strongest man in England in ironic loyalty to the oath he has sworn to her father. We return to the story of Havelok. Grim, converted by a magic flame that comes out of the hero's mouth, has spared the child, adopted him, and migrated to England. In time of want Havelok travels to Lincoln, where he works as a cook's helper, engages in sports, and establishes a reputation as the strongest man in England. Godrich, delighted that he can break Goldboro's claim to the throne by marrying her to such a commoner, forces the match. The marriage presumably lacks spark, until she too sees a magic flame shoot from the mouth of her husband, notes a magic birthmark, and recognizes by these signs his royal origins. At any rate, Havelok grows conscious of his position, gathers an army, which becomes larger and larger, overthrows both Godrich and Godard, unites England and Denmark, and settles down with Goldboro and their fifteen children, who all become kings and queens, to a long and happy reign. The action takes place in slightly over three thousand lines, which assumes a somewhat more leisurely pace than most early Middle English romances.

Whenever the narrator of *Havelok* shifts the scene of his action, he feels compelled to impress upon us the importance and seriousness of his theme, either through an elevation of style or through outright statement. His perspective is suddenly enlarged, and he comprehends units as large as miles and years:

> Fro londe woren he bote a mile—
> Ne were it neuere but ane hwile—
> That it ne bigan a wind to rise
> Out of the north—men calleth "bise"—
> And drof hem intil Engelond,
> That al was sithen in his hond—
> His, that Hauelok was the name—
> But or, he hauede michel shame,
> Michel sorwe, and michel tene,
> And yete he gat it al bidene;
> Als ye shulen nou forthward lere,
> Yf that ye wilen therto here.
>   In Humber Grim bigan to lende,
> In Lindeseye, rith at the north ende.
> Ther sat is ship upon the sond. . . .
>
>                     (721-735)[5]

This passage is a good starting point for a study of how the poet constructs and uses the "world"—the time, space, and scene—of his fiction and also of the anxiety the poet feels towards the attitude of his audience to this world, for at the same time that he exerts this effort to shift the locus of his action, he also reminds us that this story is about serious issues, which make a claim to be read as history.

In these few lines the narrator seems especially concerned with establishing a sense of place. He tells us exactly where the ship has gone. The fateful "bise" is more than an accident, for it takes Havelok to the

proper place at the proper time, a providence the poet calls to our attention. Yet his geography is schematic. This world is like a map, neither felt nor experienced, nor is it described in the easy and proficient style of the poet's most vibrant local scenes. He provides enough information here to avoid the sense of scene thrown against scene, but at best, the world between remains abstract, though with the convincing accuracy of an annal. More necessary to his narrative, especially a narrative about heroes and heroines growing up, with a theme of succession and a plot device of coincidence, is the establishment of time referents. Within the fairly limited compass of a hundred lines surrounding the passage quoted above, we are given three significant time indications. One deals with plot time, one with the narrator's and audience's sense of duration, and one with historical time. The last lines I have quoted above (728-732) return us abruptly and gravely to the time of the narrator and his audience, hence emphasizing the importance of this journey as a turning point in the narrative. However, we can also feel a qualified note in such narrative self-importance, which tells us a good deal about the relationship of poet to audience, as expressed in the somewhat apologetic line: "Yf that ye wilen therto here." Such humbleness comes, of course, precisely at the moment when the pieces of the narrative seem at their farthest point apart, yet also at the point when they are about to come together, and both author and audience know this. The shift to historical time is contained in those lines that have always attracted critics who praise *Havelok*'s realism:

> And for that Grim that place aute,
> The stede of Grim the name laute;
> So that Grimesbi calleth alle
> That theroffe speken alle;
> And so shulen men callen it ay,
> Bituene this and domesday.
>
>                     (743-748)

I do not think that these lines mean the poet of *Havelok* is a thirteenth-century precursor of local color and regional writing. First, the narrator's elevated perspective seems to work against an entirely local flavor. Second, the passage is part of the entirely conventional time indication, in this case putting all of us—characters, narrator, auditors, and Grimsby itself—into the framework of historical time. The narrator wants to emphasize the drama and importance of this journey for the plot. The brief reference to apocalyptic history is another distancing factor. It puts the story into a larger reality, just as the first time indicator "woke" us up from the fiction itself. Yet this epic appeal is suddenly reduced in the next few lines by the humble and local place names, which neither demand nor display such grandeur. Finally, the plot time indicator tells us that while all these distancing factors have taken up our attention, twelve years have passed, during which, while we have been floating around in history and rhetoric, Grim has been working:

> Thusgate Grim him fayre ledde:
> Him and his genge wel he fedde
> Wel twelf winter other more:
> Hauelok was war that Grim swank sore
> For his mete, and he lay at hom:
> He thouthe, "Ich am nou no grom. . . . "
>
> (785-790)

And while Grim has been working, Havelok has grown up. It is an important fact, though thrown out at us indirectly. The passage of those twelve years is not at all indicated to us by the wonderful scenes of Havelok eating and Grim fishing. They are indeed splendid scenes in their own right. But they are static and separable rather than dynamic parts of the narrative. The poet has to provide essential narrative information in scenes other than those in which he describes the most distinctive actions of his characters.

The smaller transitions are handled more deftly. An excellent example of the proficiency of the poet in these smaller units is the scene in which Havelok leaves Grim to go out on his own. Starving, barefoot, unemployed, it is his social nadir, the king as lumpenproletarian:

> He tok the sheres of the nayl,
> And made him a couel of the sayl,
> And Hauelok dide it sone on.
> Hauede he neyther hosen ne shon,
> Ne none kines other wede;
> To Lincolne barfot he yede.
> Hwan he kam ther, he was ful wil:
> Ne hauede he no frend to gangen til;
> Two dayes ther fastinde he yede,
> That non for his werk wolde him fede;
> The thridde day herde he calle:
> "Bermen, bermen, hider forth alle!"
> Poure that on fote yede
> Sprongen forth so sparke of glede.
> Hauelok shof dune nyne or ten
> Rith amidewarde the fen,
> And stirte forth to the kok,
> Ther the erles mete he tok
> That he bouthe at the brigge:
> The bermen let he alle ligge,
> And bar the mete to the castel,
> And gat him there a ferthing wastel.
>
> (857-878)

There is, I think, no need to emphasize the Christic paradigm of Havelok's ordeal. We could search through a thousand literatures and always find a heroic ordeal similar to Havelok's. As Auerbach has shown, Christianity, and the specifically devotional intensity of this period, allowed the mixture of the humblest details with the highest spiritual and literary aspirations.[6] All I would maintain at this point, however, is that the first half of this passage is clearly of a mythic dimension.

Our interest is in the way in which this passage, clearly a transition from Grimsby—on the road to Lincoln, to the town, over the Witham bridge, and on to the castle—organizes the space of the narrative for us. When Grim and his family migrated from Denmark, the journey was narrated in an almost epic conventional voice, from a distance, in a way that involved a good deal of strain on the poet's style. The shorter movement of Havelok to Lincoln in the first half of this passage is handled with a good deal more confidence, though it is an aspect of the mythic dimension of the story: the deposed king, barefoot, starving, alone, clad in the sail which Grim takes from his ship. He fasts for two days and is saved by a voice on the third, a time period that owes less allegiance to narrative realism than to mythic resonance. Suddenly, in a stylistic moment that reminds us of Langland, we are brought down to earth with a markedly earthly and unmistakably naturalistic cry: "Bermen, bermen, hider forth alle!" And we are in a world, and a specific street, filled with a social reality of great and almost poignant detail. That the cook who calls for help should be so rushed suggests the quite awful reality of famine, in an image that would not be all that exotic in some parts of the world today. And as Havelok bowls down his fellow workers, we wonder what happened to the aura of Christian humility that surrounded his journey to Lincoln.

The mythic sobriety of his journey in the first few lines of this passage disappears. The spatial organization of the second half is specific and moves us quickly along from city to bridge to castle. The tempo reflects Havelok's own energy, I suppose, his willingness to work, and the fact that his fortune has changed. In addition, we now know that the larger theme of union with Goldboro and revenge upon their usurpers has some realistic basis since Havelok is in the employ of Godard and has access to him. The bustle of the street is suggested but not described in detail. The careful "three days" of Havelok's starvation was mythic and otherworldly. But the carelessly accounted nine or ten battered porters are paradoxically more likely to convince us of the "reality" of the scene. Havelok, carrying the food to the castle, becomes more tangible then the figure who "To Lincolne barfot . . . yede." The movement to the castle is more comprehensible and more able to suggest literal life than Havelok's outlined journey to Lincoln.

Whenever the poem shifts its locus of action, it cannot help also shifting the social as well as the geographic surroundings. In fact, it tends to see geography and scenery almost in class terms. The fishing village, the town, the castle, correspond to different levels of society, of modes of life. But there is a limit to *Havelok*'s realism. True, we can learn a great deal about the poem's social milieu from the fact that the porters run so quickly to the cook and from the fact that it is the cook who is the contact between castle and town. However, such serious, problematic realism is quickly dispelled by the poet: "Alle made he dem dun falle." The poet defends himself, and perhaps his audience, from the texture of quite real social conflict behind all these entertaining details by a sort of zany cartoon hyperbole. It is classic depression comedy. Such caricature also distends our perception of a "realistic" street scene, confusing our spatial orientation, as if the poet were putting off the possibility of too many questions about the mimetic, social, and even moral intent of the story.

This pattern, we might note, is repeated throughout the poem: a static, almost epic background, suddenly filled with a remarkable sense of life, realism, local immediacy, then, before we can question the contradiction between these two stylistic tendencies, a comic synthesis of the two into a cartoonlike hyperbolic distortion. The same stylistic pattern and the same identification of geography with social class is found in the transition that takes Havelok and his new bride Goldboro back to the town of Grimsby. Havelok decides that the threat to his own life and the possibility that "men sholde don his leman shame" are too great in Lincoln:

> Forthi he token another red:
> That thei sholden thenne fle
> Til Grim, and til hise sones thre;
> Ther wenden he altherbest to spede,
> Hem forto clothe and for to fede.
> The lond he token under fote—
> Ne wisten he non other bote—
> And helden ay the rithe sti
> Til he komen to Grimesby.
> Thanne he komen there, thanne was Grim ded
>     . . .

(1194-1203)

Havelok discovers when he gets to Grimsby that Grim has died, but his children are still alive and they offer themselves and their possessions to the couple. We note again that the poet seems incapable of changing his scene without letting the facts of life intrude: "Hem forto clothe and for to fede." The locales have names, Lincoln and Grimsby, but the movement of the couple is recounted by means of the more economical cartographic perspective of the narrator.

That cartographic perspective also conditions the realism of the journey. Havelok and his wife move in the same mythical way that Havelok, barefoot and alone, came to Lincoln. We wonder in fact, what the "rithe [sti]" is. The line is unfortunately mangled. What does the direction indicate? To the right? The most direct route? A moral quality? It could easily be a desperate

rhyme. But why had Havelok not heard until now of Grim's death? How long has Grim been dead? And by extension, how long has Havelok been in Lincoln? On the one hand, these may be naive questions that we are not supposed to ask, but on the other hand, the poem does offer half answers. The poet is again straining his style, heightening it, in order to rearrange his characters into dramatic confrontations in which everyone— Havelok, Grim's family, Goldboro, the Angel—has set speeches. So perhaps all the spatial indications we need are stage directions. But the very ambiguity or absence of those indications and the fact that this transition hinges together two quite different scenes is also indicative of some larger patterns.[7]

In Lincoln we had a marriage, political plans, ambitions, class "conflicts," fear, a city. In Grimsby we have a group of loyal retainers, dreams, magic conversions, comfort, and despite the lower social standing of the inhabitants, a sense that they all recognize and respect "the right way," the natural order. Even the gap between rich lords and starving porters in Lincoln is resolved here in favor of a "middle" class, for Grim's sons, *nouveau riche* fish entrepreneurs, have done well for themselves. And significantly, it is in Grimsby that the political and social contradictions that arose in Lincoln—that Goldboro must marry a commoner, that the couple would starve, that their marriage would be uneasy—are all resolved by ordination, as if by magic. The road from Lincoln to Grimsby is not only a physical road.

Everyday life, though it bursts from every scene, is only uneasily integrated into the narrative. I have examined above, with a close eye to formal and narrative elements, the passage in which Havelok, under Grim's care, migrates to England. In that passage the poet was working with fairly conventional narrative elements, straining to achieve a flexibility and fluidity for which his style and immediate literary models are at this point historically unprepared. If we read the passage only with an eye to content, however, its variety of realistic themes is extraordinary. Within the compass of a few hundred lines we travel through social classes from kings to commoners, through economic periods from plenty to starvation, and in however stylized a way, we worry about politics, weather, food, clothing, travel directions, and business. So to some extent *Havelok the Dane* does demand for itself a special niche in the classification of romance, rebelling both against the strict class interest of romance and against its stylized and formal unreality. It might well belong to what we have come as common readers to consider a peculiarly "English" strain of literature, filled with God's plenty, genre scenes, robust and hearty details, looking life straight in the eye. But it must also be pointed out that the style of the narrative prevents this realism from crucially influencing the action of *Havelok*. All this life is recorded, to be sure, but it remains supplementary. The beginning and the end of *Havelok* sound very much like a verse chronicle.[8] The natural ground of *Havelok the Dane*, as we learn from both the introductory and concluding passages, is one of peace, order, and fecundity, and that which disturbs that peace is not only evil but unnatural and should be punished in kind. When Godrich is executed, when Havelok punishes his attackers, we can forget both balance and compassion. We are certain, with the poet and his audience, that such retribution is indeed the wrath of God and his earthly king, as we indeed know that any absorption in such nihilism and violence is a fairly safe business, for eventually we will return to a natural ground of stability.

Significantly, the poet uses a narrative style in both the opening passage, describing the life and death of the old kings, and in the concluding passage, describing the return of the kingdom to Havelok, which is very much like the style of an aristocratic chronicle. For all the mixing of classes in the poem, the normal state of things, in both the beginning and the end of the poem, is communicated in a style that suggests a rigid class order.

We are meant to compare the death of Aethelwold, dignified and peaceful, with that of Godrich, outrageous and unnatural. The lesson is that a man dies as he lives. Aethelwold, and a number of other good characters, are described time and again as the best that ever rode a horse. Godrich and Godard, however, at their death, also end up riding horses, though backwards, and face down, with their noses in the horses' "crich," an almost Dantesque suitability of punishment. But the contrast between good and evil characters goes further than that. We are told that except for his soul Aethelwold's greatest concern at his death is for the safety of his daughter. Godrich and Godard, on the other hand, are punished precisely because of the way in which they treat their charges. In the abstract, of course, their crime is usurpation, disloyalty, and treason to one's knightly oath. In the concrete, however, their villainy is communicated to us by the way in which they treat their charges, the children they have sworn to protect. It becomes a battle, not so much of political forces and dynasties, but of generations. In many romances we find such alignments between the hero and his disenfranchised followers against usurpers. Odysseus, disguised as a beggar, had to fight them in the form of his wife's suitors. Havelok, a peasant, fights against Godrich, who, we learn, is a propounder of a new order in law. Romance as a mode frequently pits the traditionalists and the young against the new men.

Towards the end of the story, when Havelok is finally able to command a following of warriors, he proceeds with dispatch to return and regain his land and punish his usurpers. It is at this point that the narrative be-

comes obsessed with feats of arms and the descriptions of the battle scenes reach the stage of the grotesque:

> Hauelok lifte up the dore-tre,
> And at a dint he slow hem thre;
> Was non of hem that his hernes
> Ne lay therute ageyn the sternes.
> The ferthe that he sithen mette,
> Wit the barre so he him grette
> Bifore the heued that the rith eye
> Vt of the hole made he fleye,
> And sithe clapte him on the crune
> So that he stan-ded fel thor dune.
> The fifte that he ouertok
> Gaf he a ful sor dint ok
> Bitwen the sholdres, ther he stod,
> That he spende his herte blod.
> The sixte wende for to fle,
> And he clapte him with the tre
> Rith in the fule necke so
> That he smot hise necke on to.
>
> (1806-1823)

We are meant to sense a turnabout in Havelok's fortunes in these explosions of violence and to realize that, having married and established a band of retainers, he is close to fulfilling his calling. The narration is no longer like love-romance. We are reading a *chanson de geste*.

Yet the political theme that such a change in fortune should suggest gets lost. The poet delves into the grotesque when the subject approaches the socially problematic. Similarly, the poet not only fails to resist the temptation of comedy but indulges in comedy at precisely those moments when either tenderness or piety threaten to overwhelm his narrative, or when the audience is about to be overwhelmed by magic. Havelok is awakened by his suddenly ecstatic wife after she discovers his "king-mark." Later Ubbe's men enjoy the sight of the half-naked couple when they investigate a light coming from the tower in which Havelok and Goldboro are bedded. Saved by a conversation between Grim and leue, the baby Havelok is dropped on a rock and wishes that he had never been born a king. After Havelok defeats the other participants in a shot-putting contest, they walk away muttering, "We dwellen her to longe!"

Even in the frequent scenes of violence in the poem the horror of what is being described is very often mitigated by an exaggerated scale and an enthusiastic, uncritical tone. Such a style allows a certain evasion. The peculiar moral climate of the poem, in which bloodshed is rendered downright entertaining, is not, I think, a remnant of a healthy paganism. Rather, the blood, gore, and torture of some of these scenes suggest to the audience not naturalism, but a rather naive fantasy world not unlike a modern cartoon or western. The battle scenes, which are meant as references to the battle scenes of epics and *chansons de geste*, are devoid of criticism, moral imperative, or martial excitement, for the vigor and frequent zaniness of the description tend to reduce either our delight at Havelok's revenge or our horror at a peaceful scene being destroyed. For the moment, we are drawn into a cheerful nihilism, by which destruction imposes its own effect, a holiday from morality, resembling comedy.

The poem ends on a utopian note that at the same time recalls the chronicle mode in which the poem opened, for we began as we end, with a perfect government. The poet becomes a recorder, and his record is truth, though one that we might only hope for were we the poet's contemporaries. The irony is that having seen how such a union and such a kingdom might come about, a medieval audience could well throw up its hands, for there is no human way to organize and will helpful angels, magic flames, and incredible coincidences. In a sense, then, the serious political advice, even the indirect criticism, that is contained in the prologue to the poem is compromised.[9]

The world of **Havelok** never seems particularly amenable to human will. Even the markedly realistic details for which it has so often been praised are communicated in such a qualified way that we are rarely impressed with the poem's handling of physical reality. Instead, the mind of the reader backslides, concentrating on miracles and gruesome or bizarre images. For the poet too the integration of epic themes with the genre scenes that he too is fond of is accomplished only at moments, and then, only with the aid of magic and dreams:

> Herkne nou hwat me haueth met!
> Me thouthe y was in Denemark set,
> But on on the moste hil
> That euere yete kam i til.
> It was so hey, that y wel mouthe
> Al the werd se, als me thouthe.
> Als i sat upon that lowe,
> I bigan Denemark for to awe,
> The borwes and the castles stronge;
> And mine armes weren so longe
> That i fadmede, al at ones,
> Denemark, with mine longe bones;
> And thanne y wolde mine armes drawe
> Til me, and hem for to haue,
> Al that euere in Denemark liueden
> On mine armes faste clyueden;
> And the stronge castles alle
> On knes bigunnen for to falle;
> The keyes fellen at mine fet.—
> Another drem dremede me ek:
> That ich fley ouer the salte se
> Til Engeland, and al with me
> That euere was in Denemark lyues

> But bondeman and here wiues;
> And that ich kom til Engelond,
> Al closede it intil min hond,
> And, Goldeborw, y gaf it the . . .

> (1285-1311)

Throughout the narrative we are aware of various patterns that seem at some points to dominate the story. There is the theme of political destiny. Then there are striking and successful localized pictures of domestic life, rare in medieval romance and therefore valued perhaps more by modern readers than the author might have intended. Finally there is the *Märchen*-like progress of the hero, which connects the story to fairy tale. But only at certain points in the narrative, which tend to be revelations, as in this dream, does the style rise to any great imaginative power and connect with ease the themes of magic, cabbages, and kings. The dream acts as a unifying device. We know, after Goldboro's commentary on Havelok's dream, not only what their destiny will be but also how the Cinderella theme is connected to the historical imperative, the union of Denmark and England.

In a series of delightfully linked wonders, all occurring on Havelok's and Goldboro's wedding night, Havelok's description of his dream stands out. To prevent Goldboro from having a claim to the throne, the wicked Godrich marries her to a commoner who has achieved renown in the land for his deeds of strength and kindness. Distraught by her new social position, surrounded by commoners with "hors and net, and ship on flode," who brag of their gold and silver, who promise to wash her clothes and bring her water, she lies awake at night, realizing that she has been deceived, when suddenly a beam of light blazes out of the mouth of her new husband. She is now, of course, more terrified than ever, but the voice of an angel tells her that this means her husband is king and she shall be queen after all. At this, with a change of heart, she embraces and kisses her comfortably sleeping mate, who awakes and tells her his dream.

As I have shown in detail above, the narrative has placed great emphasis on geography. But this dream shrinks the entire known world into a surrealistic, iconlike single scene. In this one dream Havelok as king stretches out his arms and, from the hill he imagines himself on, is able to embrace the castles and cities of Denmark. On the night of his actual marriage he also dreams of a mystical political marriage, of the king and his land.[10] As we learn from the second dream, in which Havelok flies to Denmark and brings back all of the land in his hand and gives it to Goldboro, she too plays a political as well as romantic role. Havelok's vision is as much a love song as it is a dream of empire. One reason why this dream is so fascinating is that it seems to have other medieval parallels. The geographic detail that the poet of **Havelok** imparts in the course of his story is touching and naive, but the fantastic scale of this dream is sophisticated and accomplished. The literary models for dream visions were no doubt more sophisticated than those for the representation of reality. The overarching perspective, the point of view of the dreamer from a height far above the world, is a common one in medieval dream tradition. The dream combines perspective, geography, prophecy, and apocalypse. In addition, the figure of the hero reaching halfway across the world, embracing oceans and cities, is not unlike those on icons of royalty in the visual arts. Finally, the delicate tone of Havelok's description resembles that of a love lyric:

> And, Goldeborw, I gaf it the:
> Deus! Lemman, hwat may this be?

Medieval love poetry often combines visual images in a similarly elusive fashion, but the combination is significant here because the poet assumes such an intimate style to communicate information of potentially monumental significance.

The fact remains that the style of this spatially fantastic dream is more accomplished and striking than the style used in presenting the realistic, localizing details for which the poet is so often praised. It is as if the narrator is more concerned with lifting Havelok out of the mire of day-to-day existence than he is in exploring the literary possibilities of that existence. The *Havelok*-poet is not a realist in the sense of dealing seriously with the everyday or the socially problematic. *Havelok* brings a touch of grace to the lives of fishermen, wrestlers, and merchants. It does not draw its grace from them.

Auerbach has conjectured that the breadth and sense of freedom of movement in the Germanic epics derived from the fact that their historical setting was in the period of tribal migrations, so that, compared to later narratives, "the spaces about the occurrences and the heaven above them are incomparably wider . . . and the structure of society is not so rigidly established."[11] Narratives such as the *Roland*, for their part, seem constricted, limited in their settings, with distinct, parceled scenes, resulting in a structure reflecting feudal political forces. What can such suggestions tell us about *Havelok*? True, the alignments of its characters might be seen as a "post-feudal" alliance of king and commons against the barons, but that does not explain its form and movement.[12] Rather, its uncertain locus of action and its backgrounds, which vary from the realistic to the schematic, indicate a wariness, perhaps unconscious, on the part of the poet as to where the weight of his action should lie. Neither the court nor the street seems powerful enough to sustain the presentation of the world by itself. The social forces that we can now identify in the poem—urbanization and mercantilization—seem to have crept into its structure almost by accident.

The poet's seriousness, or at least what he considers as potentially serious in his material, is made clear in the opening section describing the death of Aethelwold. The poet's comments are political and social, attempting to bring the poem into a kind of history. Although such themes are not immediately subverted by his narrative style, it is worth noting that although the poet can sustain a heightened tone when he wants to, he is a nervous entertainer. When he thinks his audience is tiring of high seriousness, or when he tires of it, he switches his tone in an alarmingly adroit, almost apologetic fashion. Similarly, the poem at first exhibits a well-planned structure. One could mark off divisions in the poem, using the frequent summaries of the plot that the poet includes, something like chapters or books; but gradually, we, and the narrator, lose sight of such ordering, and episode piles upon episode, climax upon climax. We lose the sense of history that the poet establishes at first and have only a denouement that reverses the trials of—how many?—years. I emphasize these structural patterns less to be critical than to underline the themes that the poet himself considered important. In fact, paying attention to such "epic" elements in *Havelok the Dane* corrects the excess attention critics have paid to the story's charm or "Cinderella" theme. That is what the poet does best. But it is not all he has tried to do, and it is not all he has done. The narrative pays due attention to epic and potentially tragic themes and aspires, however awkwardly, to some status as a monumental poem. That the miniature and the comic should be what we value the poem for is certainly not what the poet intended. Yet that disparity is part of *Havelok*'s fascination as a narrative.

The sensory realism in the scenes of Grim fishing, Grim's barnyard, and Havelok working in the streets of Lincoln (for the realism of the story is limited to this series of episodes) is energetic and exuberant, but that energy is explosive, and neither the poet nor the rhetorical means he has at hand have much idea what to do with it. We become conscious, on the one hand, of these images of real life. On the other hand, the actual narrative seems to be indulging in the machinery of monumental epic. Yet the poet seems to lack the means to integrate the two. However much we explain this distance in terms of medieval rhetoric or medieval "perspective," the fact remains that the poem is attempting to harness energies for which the literary means have not yet been perfected.

Only at moments of revelation, as we have seen, is there even an uneasy alliance between the marvelous, the epic, and the realistic elements of the poem. The coordination is possible because, as Dieter Mehl has pointed out in another context, the poet borrows more from the typical saint's life than he does from the typical romance.[13] Indeed, one could find the basis of Havelok's cartoonlike humor in any number of saints' lives. But it may also be that the saint's life illustrates in a similar way the workings of the supernatural in a setting that is entirely mundane. So indeed does the *Grettisaga*, and so, to some extent, do folk tales. The *Havelok*-poet's problem is the opposite: he must invest the everyday with a sense of wonder. It may well be that there is some stylistic or structural debt by the *Havelok*-poet to folk tales or saints' lives. But it may also be that such an artful contrast of the mundane and the miraculous is an obvious solution to a common medieval literary problem. The aesthetic result of such a narrative style is to reflect the light that comes from royalty or the supernatural onto the lives of fishermen, peasants, villagers, and the humble apparatus of works and days.

Although there is no character development as such in the narrative, there is a hint of growth, a step towards characters having some strength of their own outside simple narrative functions. Havelok does seem to undergo an education fit for a king, growing from child-like fear to strength and bravery and love.[14] He experiences the conditions of life of all the various social castes that he will rule. Reversals of loyalty are common. Godard and Godrich both turn against their sworn oaths and rationalize their actions in soliloquies. Goldboro, who grows from a baby to a rather haughty young princess, at first despises Havelok, then loves him, in a scene which displays at least as keen a sense of sexual comedy as Chaucer and Chrétien, when she discovers his royal origins. Grim and Leue, whose plight is first rationalized in sociological terms, also turn their allegiance from Godard to Havelok. Grim, Leue, and Goldboro, however, change their minds only when Havelok's mouth shoots its magic flame. And Havelok, no matter what his experience, will still be a king, for kings, in this poem, are born and marked, not made or taught. These attempts at character development, too brief to be convincing, represent an impulse on the part of the poet to invent psychological explanations for that which is already explained by destiny.

Nor is there the attention to tone we can find in a number of other medieval narratives, most specifically those of the alliterative school, but also such romances as *King Horn*. The *Havelok*-poet's art is closer to the art of the preacher, reaching here to the abstruse qualifications of theological speculation, there to the popular and coarse joke.[15] Indeed, the pulpit "stance" of the common preacher, explaining to an often unlettered following, and hence conscious of when the common or the abstract is heading too far in one direction, is analogous to the stance that *Havelok*'s narrator takes. The desire for both ale and salvation is thrown together in the final words of the poem, in a not entirely irreligious or parodic combination of the human and the eternal.

Thus it appears that the voice of the narrator, in however primitive a fashion, begins in *Havelok the Dane*

to take on far greater aesthetic importance than in most romances. It may well be that when romance as a narrative form broke beyond the class boundary that originally defined it, it required, to hold it together, a voice rather than a class ethic and idealized ethos, for in the place of the sophisticated and graceful voice of poets such as Chrétien, we begin to sense a more earnest and anxious narrative stance, less confident, though not without irony, humor, and self-awareness. The development of such a voice is not without importance for the poetry of the next century, especially that of Chaucer. . . .

*Notes*

[1] The classic distinction is W. P. Ker, *Epic and Romance: Essays on Medieval Literature* (2nd ed., 1908; rpt. New York: Dover, 1957). See too Auerbach, *Mimesis*, pp. 123-142; Vinaver, *The Rise of Romance*, pp. 1-14; Bloomfield, "Episodic Motivation and Marvels in Epic and Romance," pp. 97-128; D. M. Hill, "Romance as Epic," *English Studies* 44 (1963): 95-107. For a judicious survey of scholarship, see Lillian Herlands Hornstein, "Middle English Romances," *Recent Middle English Scholarship and Criticism: Survey and Desiderata*, ed. J. Burke Severs (Pittsburgh: Duquesne Univ. Press, 1971), pp. 55-95. Recent studies such as Robert W. Hanning, *The Individual in Twelfth-Century Romance* (New Haven, Conn.: Yale Univ. Press, 1977), suggest interesting distinctions within "romance" itself along the lines of the present chapter. A similar distinction between thirteenth- and twelfth-century romance in France is made in an important article by Per Nykrog, "Two Creators of Narrative Form in Twelfth-Century France: Gautier D'Arras—Chrétien de Troyes," *Speculum* 48 (1973): 258-276, though his distinction seems to be based primarily on aesthetic differences. An important attempt to categorize the romances by length is Dieter Mehl, *The Middle English Romances of the Thirteenth and Fourteenth Centuries* (London: Routledge, 1968).

[2] W. P. Ker "Metrical Romances, 1200-1500, I," *The Cambridge History of English Literature*, ed. A. W. Ward and A. R. Waller (Cambridge: Cambridge Univ. Press, 1907-1908), p. 277.

[3] On the social context of medieval lyrics, see Stephen G. Nichols, Jr., "The Medieval Lyric and Its Public," *Medievalia et Humanistica*, NS 3 (1972): 133-153.

[4] Among the most important of recent researches is the attempt by Paul Strohm to deduce medieval generic definitions from terms in the texts themselves. See his "*Passioun, Lyf, Miracle, Legende*: Some Generic Terms in Middle English Hagiographical Narrative, I and II," *Chaucer Review* 10 (1975): 62-75, 154-171; "*Storie, Spelle, Geste, Romaunce, Tragedie*: Generic Distinctions in the Middle English Troy Narratives," *Specu-*

*lum* 46 (1971): 348-359; and "Some Generic Distinctions in the *Canterbury Tales,*" *Modern Philology* 68 (1971): 321-328. A summary of definitions is available in Mehl, *Middle English Romances*, pp. 13-22.

[5] For the purpose of convenience, all line numbers from the romances in this chapter are to the edition by Walter H. French and Charles B. Hale, *Middle English Metrical Romances*, 2 vols. (1930; rpt. New York: Russell and Russell, 1964). Archaic letters have been modernized both here and in other Middle English extracts.

[6] Auerbach, *Mimesis*, pp. 143-173.

[7] Unfortunately for our analysis, the road back to Denmark is contained in a missing leaf. In addition, a copyist's error seems to have omitted the journey back to England.

[8] On the relation of chronicle to romance, see the important comments by M. Dominica Legge, *Anglo-Norman Literature and its Background* (Oxford: Clarendon, 1963), pp. 139-175. My comments on the "ground of being" of medieval history draw upon Brandt, *The Shape of Medieval History*.

[9] Perhaps such evasion is characteristic of medieval political theory in general. See John Peter, *Complaint and Satire in Early English Literature* (Oxford: Clarendon, 1956); and Arthur B. Ferguson, *The Articulate Citizen and the English Renaissance* (Durham, N.C.: Duke Univ. Press, 1965), pp. 1-131.

[10] Ernst Kantorowicz, *The King's Two Bodies: A Study in Medieval Political Theology* (Princeton, N.J.: Princeton Univ. Press, 1958), prints a number of illustrations. His discussion informs this scene. On the political theme in *Havelok*, see Mehl, *Middle English Romances*, pp. 161-172; and David Staines, "*Havelok the Dane:* A Thirteenth-Century Handbook for Princes," *Speculum* 51 (1976): 602-623.

[11] Auerbach, *Mimesis*, pp. 110-111.

[12] For an interesting reading of *Havelok* in social terms and for a comparison with a French analogue, see John Halverson, "*Havelok the Dane* and Society," *Chaucer Review* 6 (1971): 142-151.

[13] Mehl, *Middle English Romances*, p. 172.

[14] See Robert W. Hanning, "*Havelok the Dane:* Structure, Symbols, Meaning," *Studies in Philology* 64 (1967): 586-605; and Judith Weiss, "Structure and Characterization in *Havelok the Dane*," *Speculum* 44 (1969): 247-257.

[15] See G. R. Owst, *Literature and Pulpit in Medieval England* (Cambridge: Cambridge Univ. Press, 1933). . . .

**W. R. J. Barron (essay date 1987)**

SOURCE: "*King Horn* and *Havelok the Dane*," in *English Medieval Romance*, Longman, 1987, pp. 65-74.

[*In the following excerpt, Barron considers the relative popularity of* King Horn *and* Havelok the Dane *and contends that while the realism of* Havelok *has more appeal for today's readers, that was not necessarily true in the case of its original audience.*]

. . . In the earliest of the English romances, *King Horn* (c. 1225), history is so throughly absorbed into folklore that, though the period of the Viking raids provides the violent social context of the action, specific historical events and characters cannot be identified. The Anglo-Norman version, which predates it by half a century, seems independently derived from a common original, perhaps a folk-tale told by people of Norwegian descent in the west of England.[3] As a boy, Horn is set adrift with his companions by Saracen pirates (late substitutes for Viking originals?) who have killed his father, the King of Sudene; he lands in Westernesse where Rymenild, the King's daughter, falls in love with him. When his false companion Fikenild betrays them to King Aylmer, Horn is banished, sails to Ireland, and serves King Thurston, killing the Saracen giant who had killed his own father but refusing the King's daughter in marriage. Hearing that Rymenild is being forced into marriage with King Mody, he returns in disguise to Westernesse, kills the bridegroom, denounces Fikenild's treachery, and sets out with his faithful companion Athulf to regain his father's kingdom. Meanwhile Fikenild tries to force Rymenild into marrying him, but Horn again returns in disguise, kills him, rewards the faithful with kingdoms and brides, and reigns in his own land with Rymenild.

*Horn* is immediately recognizable as a folk-tale of the exile-and-return type involving the familiar motifs of revenge, recovery of the patrimony, and the winning of a bride. Its form is that of the multimove story which several times repeats the same basic pattern of incidents: the victim hero suffers a misfortune or experiences a lack of something essential to him, leaves home, is tested by adventures involving a villain, emerges victorious to return home in disguise and be recognized by some token or test, only to recommence the pattern of events as the result of some new misfortune, villany, or continuing lack. The repeated pattern stands out clearly in *Horn*, though it involves the usual improbabilities and irrationalities of folk-tale. Horn conceals his royal birth in both the courts he visits for no apparent reason; by pretending to be a thrall he makes himself an unsuitable suitor for Rymenild, yet her father seems to feel his kingdom threatened by this humble stranger; the readiness with which the King lets Fikenild cow him into giving Rymenild to him is equally unexplained. The logic of folk-tale, however, is not that of reason but of feeling; it is a fantasy on which the rational mind has imposed sufficient order to allow the working out of the conflict between the hero's wishes and inhibitions.

Like someone engaged in a ritual, Horn goes through six moves, crossing water between each of them and in each enacting variations on the same theme. In Sudene he is a prince deprived of the protection and freed from the restraint of a father by circumstances for which he has no responsibility. In Westernesse he is a thrall whose love for Rymenild would threaten the kingdom; when she dreams that a fish has broken her net, Horn predicts that an ill-wisher will destroy their happiness, as if willing his own banishment. In Ireland, under the name Godmod (Goodmind), he avenges his father by killing the Saracen giant who slew him and, though he refuses the Princess offered him, serves her father for seven years. Back in Westernesse, he throws off his beggar's disguise to declare his true identity, joking with Rymenild about a net which has been set for seven years, shows no awe of her father the King, and kills the rival suitor, King Mody. Crossing to Sudene with his true friend Athulf, he claims his own throne. Returning to Westernesse, Horn overthrows Fikenild, his rival for Rymenild who once suggested that his love for her threatened her father's kingdom, and finally overcomes, now that he is king in his own right, his persistent feeling that to marry a princess and become a king is a disloyal act against a reigning monarch. The underlying theme is clearly that of the maturation of an individual: the various kings are representatives of the father-figure from whose control he struggles to free himself; the good and bad companions are aspects of his personality which further or inhibit his half-realized desire to rival his father and grow to full adult power and independence.[4]

It is impossible to tell how far the original audience, with its greater familiarity with folk-tale, would be consciously aware of this level of meaning where the modern reader sees only the shadowy outline of a male-Cinderella story. But just as today a fairy-tale can be the medium of pantomime or of political allegory, so in *Horn* a familiar folk-tale pattern contributes its underlying meaning to an exemplary poem on the making of a good king. The plethora of kings in the poem are not just the gilt gingerbread figures of fairy-tale; they exemplify, positively or negatively, the condition to which Horn was born and for which circumstances require him to demonstrate his fitness, reflecting, perhaps, the original shaping of the folk-tale in the Viking age when royal birth could not secure the succession without outstanding personal qualities. From the beginning, Horn's beauty (a useful adjunct to royal charisma) is stressed; he has courtly talents of manner, speech, skill in harping which earn him golden opinions at Aylmer's court; these qualities win him the love of a princess, which discretion and loyalty to her father as his overlord will not allow him to accept until he has achieved knighthood and proved his valour in battle; though it was Rymenild who made all the advances, he limits his claim on her fidelity to seven years, remains faithful to her through seven years of exile, but still refuses to demand her in marriage until he has regained his patrimony and can claim her as an equal.

The folk-tale pattern of repetition with variation serves this theme also. Of the three fights against pagans in which Horn proves his fitness for his father's role of defender of faith and nation, details of the first echo the King's last battle when Fortune overwhelms him with unfair odds only to favour his son when he is similarly overmatched; the second, a David and Goliath encounter in which he kills the giant who slew his father, shows him as the champion of a Christian society whose own leaders have failed to stem the pagan influx; the third, when he reconquers his own kingdom, demonstrates the fruits of valour in the rescue of his mother, the founding of churches, and revitalization of a Christian society. His valour is rooted in faith but also in love: the ring which Rymenild gave him serves as a talisman strengthening him in battle. His initial seduction by her makes him seem a puppet without will, but the inversion of that incident when he refuses a princess freely offered by her father shows him making a free choice in deference to prior obligations of duty to his deserted people and fidelity to Rymenild. Horn's changing status in the love relationship is indicated by the symbolism of Rymenild's dream, when he still fails to ask for her hand after being knighted, that a fish has escaped her net; when he returns in disguise to rescue her from King Mody, he identifies himself as a fisher come to fish! Horn in turn dreams of the drowning Rymenild thrust under by Fikenild and returns again to kill the false friend whose earlier treachery had found him still naïve and vulnerable. The fatherless castaway, with the aid of Fortune and his own physical and spiritual powers, has assumed the authority of a Christian king, scourge of pagans and protector of other kingdoms.[5]

The English version of *Horn* in some 1550 three-stress couplets, about a quarter of the French counterpart, has the spare and sinewy directness of saga. An omniscient narrator outlines action, introduces actors, switches locations but, apart from the occasional ominous phrase warning of dangers ahead, gives no insights into character or motivation. The terse couplets carry the action forward with the absolute minimum of detail needed to establish situation and imply motive:

> A morewe tho the day gan springe,     *when*
> The King him rod an huntinge.
> At hom lefte Fikenhild,

That was the wurste moder child.
Horn ferde into bure       *went*
To sen aventure.

(ll. 649-54)[6]

The individual scenes, each a moment of intense dramatic action, follow one another without explicit connection, their frequently ironic relationship being implicit in the pattern of repetition and inversion. Each is self-contained, carrying forward Horn's feud against the Saracens and his winning of Rymenild alternately but largely independently, the episodes achieving their internal climax and resolution without affecting each other except at the causal level, separate phases in the development of the public and the private man. The public sphere provides the greatest variety of adventure and the long time-span which tests the constancy of the lovers, but their relationship remains the central focus kept continually in mind by Horn's desire to make himself worthy of Rymenild, by her ring which inspires his valour, by the dreams which betray their concern for each other even when apart, and by Horn's various disguises which stress the continuing threat to their union. The narrative procedure is formulaic, moving from episode to episode in a dozen words, scarcely varied, which sketch the repeated sea voyages:

The whyght him gan stonde       *breeze*
                                      *arose*
And drof till Irelonde.
To lond he him sette       *disembarked*
And fot on stirop sette.

(ll. 761-64)

They function like blackouts between the scenes of some experimental drama whose coherence depends upon the emotional interplay between episodes and the ability of the audience to interpret the conventions of parallelism and contrast in situations, themes, and characters.[7]

It is a production without décor; the schematic procedure has no place for description and even the repeated references to the hero's good looks have narrative function, moving his Saracen captors to spare the boy's life and causing Rymenild to distinguish him from his companions. Only Horn has any degree of individuality; the other characters are the formulaic stereotypes of folk-tale—father, faithful and unfaithful friend, foreign king, his marriageable daughter—and even Rymenild is presented only in terms of her passionate love for Horn and the passionate anger she turns on those who come between them. He responds with an undemonstrative fidelity, acting to remove the barriers between them with a simple, manly directness so devoid of courtly address that one might think him motivated more by need to avenge his father and advance his own career than deserve her love. When he expresses emotion, throwing off one of his many disguises, it is with the same directness with which he acts:

He wiped that blake of his swere       *dirt,*
                                          *neck*

And sede, 'Quen so swete and dere,
Ich am Horn thin owe.       *own*
Ne canstu me noght knowe?
Ich am Horn of Westernesse.
In armes thu me kusse!'

(ll. 1213-18)

The highly dramatized action constantly breaks into speech, statements rather than dialogue, in which the characters declare their feelings and intentions where their French counterparts explain theirs. With characteristic economy, they convey the import of past action or prepare for events to come, the unemotional content made vivid by the sparse context, like speeches in a ballad.[8]

Failure to appreciate how the structural pattern of folk-tale serves the epic theme of a good king's survival as champion of Christian values in the face of paganism without and treachery within has, until recently, caused *Horn* to be undervalued in relation to **Havelok** where the popular appeal of a folk hero dominates the social theme.[9] His tale of exile and return, vaguely coloured by memories of the union of England and Denmark under Canute, was given undeserved authenticity by inclusion in Gaimar's *Estoire des Engleis* from which, about 1200, it was adapted as a brief Anglo-Norman poem in imitation of Marie's *lais*. Towards the end of the century, an English poet working, most probably, in Lincolnshire, made a much fuller adaptation from a related Anglo-Norman source.[10] It tells how, on the deaths of their parents, Goldborough, heiress to the throne of England, is entrusted as ward to Earl Godrich and Havelok, Prince of Denmark, to Earl Godard who usurps his throne and hands him over to the fisherman Grim to be killed. Recognizing his royal birth by a miraculous light shining from Havelok's mouth, Grim flees with him to England and founds Grimsby; the boy becomes a scullion in Godrich's castle at Lincoln, attracts attention by his great strength, and is married to Goldborough whom the Earl had promised her father to give to the strongest man in the kingdom. Havelok dreams that he will become a great king, returns to Denmark where his king-light wins him knighthood, defeats Godard, returns to England, defeats Godrich, and, after doing exemplary justice on the two traitors, rules in both kingdoms.

The similarity of the basic folk-tale pattern of the deprived boy winning back his heritage to that in *Horn* is evident. But this male Cinderella accepts the ashes as his element: growing up in Grim's cottage, his hearty appetite makes him ashamed to eat without working and he sells fish for him until, in a time of famine, he costs more to feed than he can earn, when his foster-father sends him to seek his fortune in Lincoln, barefoot and dressed in an old sail. He wins his first job carrying supplies for the Earl's cook by shoving the other porters into the mud and he labours in the castle kitchen, breaking firewood and carrying water like a beast of burden but 'Als he was strong, so was he softe' (l. 991):

| | |
|---|---|
| It ne was non so litel knave, | *child* |
| For to leiken ne forto plawe, | *sport* |
| That he ne wolde with him pleye; | |
| The children that yeden in the weye | |
| | *ran* |
| Of him, he deden all here wille, | |
| And with him leikeden here fille. | |
| Him loveden alle, still and bolde, | *shy* |
| Knightes, children, yunge and olde. | |

(ll. 949-56)[11]

In the new clothes with which the cook provides him, he is the handsomest man in England, a novice yet champion stone-putter—but only because he is too 'sore adrad' to disobey the cook's order to compete. When, still a virgin, he is forced to marry Goldborough, to prevent her being shamed at court he takes her away to Grimsby where Grim's children, whose father is now dead, serve them as lord and lady. Only when his wife, alerted by the king-light which an angel explains to her in a dream, interprets his own prophetic dream of possessing Denmark and England does Havelok remember his childhood· and pray for divine aid against Godard. On landing in Denmark with Grim's three sons to reconquer his heritage, his ignorance of arms is demonstrated by an incident in which he does great slaughter among the thieves who attack his lodging by flailing them with the bar of the door, impressing Earl Ubbe so that, recognizing him as Denmark's heir, he knights him and has him crowned king. Thereafter the blood royal begins to show as Havelok knights Grim's sons, captures and condemns Godard, invades England, defeats Godrich in single combat, makes the English do fealty to their true queen, and rewards all the friends of his youth, giving noble husbands to Grim's daughters and Godrich's earldom to his former cook, while his own union with Goldborough provides rulers for many kingdoms:

| | |
|---|---|
| He geten children hem bitwene | *begot* |
| Sones and doughtres right fivetene, | |
| Wharof the sones were kinges alle, | |
| So wolde God it sholde bifalle, | |
| And the doughtres alle quenes: | |
| Him stondes well that good child strenes. | |
| | *begets* |

(ll. 2978-83)

The fairy-tale ending and the proverbial truism represent the dominant tone of *Havelok* with its naïve hero

become a leader of men by force of circumstances, motivated by good sense rather than any awareness of natural superiority, its acknowledgement of harsh necessity in the famine which causes Grim to send his foster-son away to the city, and practical piety in Havelok's foundation of a priory in Grim's memory. But instead of the generalized never-never-land of fairy-tale it is set in a polity which mirrors contemporary concepts of good and bad government. The England of King Athelwold in which it begins is an idealized medieval state in which equity and good order are maintained by a stern but just monarch who enforces his laws with impartial rigour, earning the respect and love of all classes. England under the usurper Godrich and Denmark under Godard suffer all the ill effects of tyrannical rule: both demand oaths of loyalty from all subjects but allow them no part in the government; Godrich creates an oppressive bureaucracy to enforce his personal will and coerces his barons to support him in fighting Havelok by threatening to reduce them to thralls, a flagrant violation of law; the inherent weakness of Godard's tyranny is demonstrated by the attack on Havelok's lodging and the rapidity with which his barons desert the Earl to join their rightful prince. The view of kingship which emerges reflects contemporary English theory: the absolute power of a king ruling by divine right needs to be modified by the willing consent of the governed if it is not to degenerate into tyranny.

Against the record of contemporary failure in practice, Havelok's career reads like the idealized biography of an Athelwold: pious, selfless, just and generous. It is not the king-mark but his personal characteristics of courage, loyalty, strength, good sense, and amiability which distinguish him as he rises from the lowest social class to be doubly conqueror and king. In each he displays the virtues appropriate to his social position: slaving uncomplainingly as a porter, and as king rewarding loyal adherents however humble and punishing his opponents, after due legal process, with drastic penalties—Godard is flayed alive and Godrich burnt—which satisfy both the rigorous justice of folk-tale and contemporary precedent.[12] His development from the gentle giant who goes in fear of his master the cook to an imperious monarch may not be psychologically convincing, but it expresses the ideal of the virtues of the good king as rooted in the best qualities of the ordinary man which is at the heart of the poem. The English poet has fused the individual and social·roles of his hero much more successfully than the author of the Anglo-Norman *lai* who, in putting a courtly gloss on the folk-tale, sets it in the age of Arthur, makes Grim a baron unaccountably given to fishing, and Havelok a rather passive figure carried along by events rather than one who, initially ignorant of his royal birth, earns the right to rule by his own efforts.[13]

The English redactor has not only taken much greater space, some three thousand four-stress lines, than either French version, but has structured the narrative to underline his dual theme of personal and regal virtues. Though Goldborough is inevitably passive, her role as victim parallels that of Havelok, allowing reduplication of the situation in which a land initially well ruled falls into the power of a man who breaks his feudal troth, usurps the right of the legitimate heir, and rules with the viciousness to be expected from one who lacks divine ordination. Their forced union, intended by Godrich as a degradation of the Princess, has the opposite effect, uniting her with 'the best man' physically and morally and preparing the eventual triumph of right over wrong. Havelok's actions when he comes to power parallel those of Athelwold in a way which promises that under him England will be as well ruled as in the past. There, as in Denmark, the people admit their fault in submitting to usurpers, acknowledging that they have a part to play in government, just as the fidelity of Grim and his sons is contrasted with the treachery of their betters. The two countries, repeatedly evoked as 'al Denemark' and 'al Engelond', are made active participants, most vividly in the prophetic dream which the English redactor transferred from Goldborough to Havelok who sees himself embracing his future kingdoms in his arms.[14]

The emotional as well as the thematic significance of the action is heightened by the recapitulation of key episodes: repeated recollection of the scene in which Havelok saw his sisters killed on Godard's orders keeps the usurper's crimes in mind until retribution overtakes him; periodic appearances of his king-mark declare the hero's royal birth throughout his humble youth; frequent comparison of the two usurpers with Judas and the devil and references to the oaths of loyalty they have broken maintain animosity against them during their long absences from the action. Frequent interventions by the narrator, displaying his personal bias, direct the audience's reactions: he repeatedly curses the two traitors, calls down maledictions upon them or prays for a blessing or divine aid for hero and heroine; he draws attention to changes of scene and the progress of the action, allowing the minstrel who assumed his voice in performance to make direct contact with the listeners. The minstrel would also have been able to make effective use of the many passages of direct speech, not only dramatic dialogue but the monologues of Godard and Godrich meditating the fate of their wards, the dying speeches of their royal fathers, the speech of Ubbe exhorting the Danes to rally to their true prince, recapitulating his wrongs just when they are about to be revenged. The patterned structure and pointed narration achieve a clarity of outline which allows the poet to indulge in incidental detail, developing the minor characters, in particular Grim, beyond the folk-tale stereotypes on which they are based.[15] His delight in description gives the often brief scenes,

particularly those of humble life, a vividness which has, perhaps, unduly influenced opinions on the popular character of the poem. But whoever designed the dual theme subtly interrelated, the clear-cut narrative, the economic style in which the swift-running couplets carry a mass of detail without falling back on line-filling formulae, rising to rhetorical tirades or crystallizing into popular proverbs which underscore meaning, he was more probably a trained cleric than a wayside entertainer.[16]

Both *Horn* and **Havelok** are manifestly in the romance mode, fantasies of wish-fulfilment which express a dual idealism of personal maturation and social stability while acknowledging the realities of life for a fatherless boy and the limitations of good government in a troubled age. Both show the structural pattern of repetition and variation familiar from the *Chanson de Roland* and the works of Chrétien, perhaps a legacy of their common folklore inheritance, but none the less with full appreciation of the value of such narrative procedures for thematic emphasis. In other respects their relationship to the romance genre is more various: *Horn*, with its stress on personal qualities of leadership employed in defence of faith and fatherland, inspired by a love which is served rather than indulged and whose goal is marriage for dynastic ends, shares the social values of the epic, the limited scale of the *lai* and the dramatic narrative elisions of the ballad; **Havelok** fills out a similar structure with a wealth of naturalistic detail and vividness of narration reminiscent of the popular tale rather than the distanced, atmospheric romance. Modern critics, attracted by **Havelok**'s realism, assume that their preference reflects that of a popular English audience to whom the style and conventions of *roman courtois* would have been alien but whose pious and sentimental tastes approved the moral rectitude of the hard-working hero, a model apprentice-boy, and the idealized picture of monarchic rule. But Havelok is essentially a Perceval-figure whose inherent qualities display themselves in a disparate context; the contrast between royal birth and humble circumstances can be appreciated from above as well as below and **Havelok** may not so much reflect what the lower classes thought of their rulers as what the ruling classes liked to think humbler people thought of them.[17] The effect of the human detail, the touches of comedy, the vivid style is to modify the dangers of piety, bathos, and exaggeration arising from the attempt to span social and moral spheres so widely separated. The same dangers exist in *Horn* but are avoided there by a strictly schematic presentation of all spheres, both humble and regal, in terms of familiar plot situations, a self-consistent version of reality which does not challenge comparison with the real world.[18]

However attractive to us, contemporary audiences do not seem to have found the realism of **Havelok** a more satisfactory solution. Though his association with Grimsby kept the hero's reputation alive in folk tradition and won him mention in later chronicles, the Anglo-Norman *lai* fathered no Continental adaptations and the English version did not live on in the chapbooks. The Anglo-Norman Horn story, on the other hand, was transformed into a pedagogic French prose romance which, though it smothered the primitive power of the original in using it to exemplify proper gentlemanly behaviour, found its way into English, German, Dutch, and Icelandic versions by the end of the sixteenth century. The English story reappears in *Horn Child* (c. 1320) stylistically distorted by a particularly inept tail-rhyme stanza, while its true nature was recognized by the ballad-makers of whose work nine examples stretching back to the fourteenth century remained current until the nineteenth. The fact that none of the surviving versions seems to derive directly from another, and that the three texts of *King Horn* vary so much in verbal detail that scarcely a line is exactly the same in all three implies a lively, widely dispersed tradition acceptable at many social levels.[19] The occurrence of *Horn* and **Havelok** in the Bodleian MS Laud Misc. 108 in association with one of many texts of the *South English Legendary*, a vastly popular compilation of saints' lives, folklore, natural science, and recent history, has suggested that they too would appeal to an audience of limited sophistication anxious for instruction and moral edification. Such a context may indicate one aspect of their appeal, but all that can be certainly known of the audiences for which they were *originally* written is that they were not French-speaking; the quality of the Anglo-Norman versions does not suggest that the interests, tastes, and literary discrimination of those for whom the English texts were composed were in any way inferior. . . .

## Notes

. . .[3] See H. G. Leach, *Angevin Britain and Scandinavia* (Cambridge, Massachusetts, 1921), pp. 328-31, and M. D. Legge, *Anglo-Norman Literature and its Background* (Oxford, 1963), pp. 96-104.

[4] See Anne Wilson, *Traditional Romance and Tale* (Ipswich, 1976), pp. 59-62, and Derek Brewer, *Symbolic Stories* (Cambridge, 1980), pp. 64-65.

[5] See Georgianna Ziegler, 'Structural Repetition in *King Horn*', *Neuphilologische Mitteilungen*, 81 (1980), 403-08.

[6] Text from Cambridge University MS Gg. 4.27 (II), normalized and modernized by D. B. Sands, *Middle English Verse Romances* (New York, 1966), pp. 15-54.

[7] See Mary Hynes-Berry, 'Cohesion in *King Horn* and *Sir Orfeo*', *Speculum*, 50 (1975), 652-70.

[8] H. L. Creek, 'Character in the Matter of England Romances', *Journal of English and Germanic Philology*, 10 (1911), 429-52, 585-609.

[9] See, for example, George Kane, *Middle English Literature* (London, 1951), pp. 48-49: 'This story is loosely episodic, distorted by gratuitous duplication, inartistically expressed . . . '; 'absurdities . . . arise in it out of disregard for narrative structure and out of inadequate motivation. . . . '

[10] On the historical background see Leach, pp. 324-28. Characteristic of *Havelok*'s vague Norse associations are various attributes of Grim which connect him with Odin, notably the name of one of his sons, Hugh Raven, reminiscent of Huginn, one of the two ravens who are the god's familiars, suggesting that the story may have originated as a hero-myth in which the protagonist was aided by Odin in one of his many disguises (see Edmond Reiss, '*Havelok the Dane* and Norse Mythology', *Modern Language Quarterly*, 27 (1966), 115-24).

[11] Text from Bodleian Library MS Laud Misc. 108, normalized and modernized by Sands, pp. 55-129.

[12] See W. R. J. Barron, 'The Penalties for Treason in Medieval Life and Literature', *Journal of Medieval History*, 7 (1981), 187-202.

[13] See Sheila Delany and V. Ishkanian, 'Theocratic and Contractual Kingship in *Havelok the Dane*', *Zeitschrift für Anglistick und Amerikanistik*, 22 (1974), 290-302; John Halverson, '*Havelok the Dane* and Society', *Chaucer Review*, 6 (1971), 142-51; David Staines, '*Havelok the Dane*: A Thirteenth-century Handbook for Princes', *Speculum*, 51 (1976), 602-23.

[14] See Judith Weiss, 'Structure and Characterisation in *Havelok the Dane*', *Speculum*, 44 (1969), 247-57.

[15] Comparison with cognate versions of the Helpful Fisherman story suggests that the English poet deliberately retained that part of the tradition which showed Grim as initially cruel and venial, providing narrative tension and a dramatic change in behaviour after he has seen the kingmark which are lacking in the more consistent characterization of the French version (see Maldwyn Mills, 'Havelok and the Brutal Fisherman', *Medium Aevum*, 36 (1967), 219-30).

[16] The stylistic aspects of *Havelok* are particularly well treated in Dieter Mehl, *The Middle English Romances of the Thirteenth and Fourteenth Centuries* (London, 1968), pp. 161-72.

[17] See J. C. Hirsh, '*Havelok* 2933: A Problem in Medieval Literary History', *Neuphilologische Mitteilungen*, 78 (1977), 339-47 (p. 343).

[18] See J. M. Ganim, 'History and Consciousness in Middle English Romance', *The Literary Review*, 23 (1980), 481-96 (pp. 484-87).

[19] See J. R. Hurt, 'The Texts of *King Horn*', *Journal of the Folklore Institut*, 7 (1970), 47-59 (p. 49). . . .

**Sheila Delany (essay date 1990)**

SOURCE: "The Romance of Kingship: *Havelok the Dane*," in *Medieval Literary Politics*, Manchester University Press, 1990, pp. 61-73.

[*In the following essay, Delany sketches the historical background of* Havelok the Dane, *summarizes its plot, and asserts its importance in describing the beginnings of social mobility and change in thirteenth-century England.*]

In claiming romance for the 'mythos of summer', Northrop Frye associates the genre with 'wish-fulfillment dream'. At the same time, Frye introduces an important qualification to the utopian or fantastic dimension of romance: the quest-romance 'is the search of the libido or desiring self for a fulfillment that will deliver it from the anxieties of reality but will still contain that reality' (p. 193). The Middle English verse romance **Havelok the Dane** exemplifies this double perspective in the two dimensions in which it explores the nature of kingship—a topic of the first importance in English public life of the thirteenth century, when **Havelok** was composed. The poem operates simultaneously on mythic and political levels, defining kingship in the same terms as were used in contemporary discussions of kingship: a compromise between the royal prerogative conferred by divine ordination, and the practical limitations imposed on royal power by social structure. That compromise is incarnated in the person of Havelok, who rules in two registers: as theologically ordained monarch and figural hero, saviour of the kingdom; and as socially responsible leader of a multi-class nation united under law.

A brief resumé of the historical background must precede my reading of the poem.

By the late thirteenth century, the Norman and Angevin effort to centralise government had produced in England a strong sense of national unity. It had also engendered significant baronial resistance to royal power. And, especially with the thirteenth-century boom in the wool trade, a powerful bourgeoisie was clamouring—or, more accurately, manoeuvring—for extended influence in local governments and in Parliament.[1] The net result of these social forces was neither an outright rejection of absolute monarchy, nor thorough repression of dissidence and ambition.

Instead, a balance was eventually achieved between royal power and the rights of subjects of various classes, which some scholars have called a 'partnership' of the interested parties: king, barons, wealthy merchants and burgesses (Tout, p. 135; Wilkinson). From a modern point of view this balance remains a conservative one, in which theocratic notions were not fully replaced but were rather tempered by the exigencies of English class structure.

Such an adjustment appears, for example, in the Great Charter of 1215. John, 'by the grace of God king of England', acting 'by the will of God, . . . to the honour of God and for the exalting of the holy church and the bettering of our realm', is forced nonetheless to limit the power of the Crown, to specify the rights of barons and other classes, and, in article 61, to reassert the legal right of resistance.[2]

But Magna Carta is a programmatic and not a theoretical document. A more fully developed statement of limited monarchy appears in the work of the jurist Henry Bracton (d. 1268), *De Legibus et Consuetudinibus Angliae*. So finely balanced is Bracton's treatise that it was quoted during the seventeenth century by royalists and parliamentarians alike. Bracton conceives the king both above and below the law, divinely appointed but, just because of this, obliged to govern properly:

> The king himself must be, not under Man, but under God and the Law, because the Law makes the king. . . . For there is no king where arbitrary will dominates, and not the Law. And that he should be under the law because he is God's vicar, becomes evident through the similitude with Jesus Christ in whose stead he governs on earth. For He, God's true Mercy, though having at His disposal many means to recuperate ineffably the human race, chose before all other expedients the one which applied for the destruction of the devil's work; that is, not the strength of power, but the maxim of Justice, and therefore he wished to be under the Law in order to redeem those under the Law. For he did not wish to apply force, but reason and judgment.[3]

The success of Bracton's book (it became the basis of legal literature in the reign of Edward I) reflected the attempts being made in historical practice to redefine the nature, rights and obligations of kingship. Those attempts were evident throughout the century in several ways: the constant claims of barons and burgesses to participate in government, the baronial crisis of 1298 and the subsequent Confirmation of Charters, the development of Parliament as a legislative organ.

The concern with the nature of kingship that dominated English public life in the thirteenth century was given literary expression in **Havelok the Dane**. In its Middle English version, **Havelok** was probably composed during the reign of Edward I (1272-1307), though the precise date is uncertain.[4] The stylistic simplicity of *Havelok*, its humor and energy, and its attention to physical detail have caused many critics to call it 'bourgeois romance'. Yet since the medieval bourgeoisie included a very wide range of wealth and social status, from great banking families and mercantile magnates down to the local brewer and baker, the adjective 'bourgeois' does little to pinpoint the actual politics of a given work. My view of *Havelok* is that the main purpose of the poem is to define the nature of kingship in the person of its eponymous hero. What emerges is the characteristically English resolution, familiar from thirteenth-century theory and practice: Havelok reigns by divine right and also by consensus; he is born to rule, but, unaware of this, he earns the right to rule. In this chapter, therefore, I want first to show that Havelok is established as theocratic king, and then to indicate how that status is qualified and limited by contractual notions.

The single extant copy of *Havelok* is found in a collection of saints' lives (MS. Laud Misc. 108, Bodleian), and its imposing title seems more appropriate to a religious story than to romance: *Incipit Vita Havelok Quondam Rex Angliae et Danemarchie*. This placement need not be coincidental, for the romance presents Havelok as a worker of miracles. As rightful king, moreover—king by heredity and divine right—he is not only protected by God but becomes the instrument of divine justice. In this sense, Havelok is a figural hero: not a Christ-figure, but one whose literal or historical role in the narrative duplicates the archetypal victory of good over evil.

After an invocation to Christ (15-22), the story opens with a description of the idyllic reign of Athelwold, the English king whose daughter Havelok will marry and whose ideal government he will duplicate. The description is a conventional one, with many antecedents and analogues in medieval literature and historiography.[5] Yet the convention serves a special literary purpose here, and is tailored to show particular virtues. Athelwold's piety takes the form of justice, as it ought to do when the king is God's representative on earth; in Bracton's phrase, *'Dum facit justiciam, vicarius est Regis Eterni, minister autem diaboli dum declinat ad iniuriam'* (f. 107b). As we will see, the story includes both types. Athelwold, however, administers the strait retributive justice expected of *'vicarius Regis Eterni'*.

> He lovede God with all his might,
> And holy kirke and soth and right.
> Right-wise men he lovede alle,
> And overall made hem forto calle.
> Wreyeres and wrobbers made he falle
> And hated hem so man doth galle; . . .
>
> (35-40)

Friend to fatherless, protector of widows and maidens (71-97), Athelwold practises the primary Christian virtue of *caritas*, feeding the poor and winning Christ's reward in duplicating Christ's goodness (98-105). Loved by all, Athelwold is mourned by all in his fatal illness. He entrusts his small daughter Goldeboru to the wardship of Earl Godrich of Cornwall. It is a sacred trust, and the ceremony is a religious one which includes

> the messebook,
> The caliz, and the pateyn ok,
> The corporaus, the messe-gere . . .
>
> (186-8)

Thereupon the king takes to his deathbed; his preparation is that of a saint and includes prayer, confession and self-flagellation. Then Athelwold distributes all his goods and money (218-25), an act which reminds us that 'it is easier for a camel to go through the eye of the needle than for a rich man to enter the kingdom of God' (Mark 10:25). Athelwold dies calling on Christ and repeating Christ's dying words (from Luke 23:46; lines 228-31).

After the sorrow of the populace is somewhat abated, bells are rung and masses sung,

> That God self shulde his soule leden
> Into hevene biforn his Sone
> And ther withuten ende wone.
>
> (245-7)

The extended portrait of Athelwold and his reign has thus set a standard for godly rule which will not be easily met.

The idyllic condition of England ends abruptly, less by Athelwold's death than by the treachery of the evil Earl Godrich. Despite his holy vow to guard both Goldeboru and England, Godrich establishes a strict and oppressive bureaucracy (248-79), and when Goldeboru comes of age withholds the kingdom from her. As Athelwold was linked with Christ and the saints, Godrich is compared with Judas and Satan (319, 1100-1, 1133-4). Like Judas, Godrich betrays God and his leader for material gain: he has broken a religious vow and usurped the throne from its divinely ordained occupant. The author calls for miraculous intervention to restore Goldeboru (and, by implication, England), like Lazarus, to her former condition (331-3).

Godrich's usurpation figurally re-enacts the archetypal Christian conflict of good and evil; plainly the hero who can perform the prayed-for feat of liberation must be Christ's agent.

The narrative turns now to Denmark, where the preceding story of betrayal is repeated (though it is told less amply). Birkabein, the good and holy king, entrusts his heirs to Earl Godard. Godard kills the two girls in a particularly bloody way (465-75), and arranges to have Havelok killed by his serf, Grim. Go-dard's momentary pity on the boy is called 'miracle fair and good' (500), and Godard, like his English counterpart, is compared to Judas and to Satan (422-5, 482, 496, 506, 1409, 1411, 2229, 2512). Christ's curses are heaped on him (426-46), and another miracle is prayed for so that Havelok may avenge himself (542-4). In fact a sequence of 'miracles' has already begun, as noted above. The first of them (not explicitly la-belled as such) was that which caused 'the dumb to speak': the seven-year-old Havelok's extraordinary access of rhetoric which had prompted Godard's pity. Another providential miracle occurs immediately after the prayer: in the dimness of their cottage, Grim and his wife see a light shining from Havelok's mouth 'als it were a sunnebem'; they also notice the 'kine-merk' on his shoulder (later we discover that it is a golden cross: 1262-3, 2139-40). These signs of divine appoint-ment cause Grim to commit himself to Havelok rather than to the diabolical Godard. He does so in a prayer-like passage which deliberately exploits the ambiguity of the words 'lord' and 'freedom':

> 'Loverd, have mercy
> Of me and Leve, that is me by!
> Loverd, we aren bothe thine,
> Thine cherles, thine hine . . .
> Thoru other man, loverd, than thoru thee
> Shal I nevere freeman be.
> Thou shalt me, loverd, free maken.
> For I shall yemen thee and waken;
> Thoru thee wile I freedom have.'
>
> (617-31)

The theological dimension of this speech is intensified by the resemblance of Grim's repentance to that of Peter after he denies Christ; as Peter 'broke down and wept' (Mark 14:72) so Grim 'sore gret' (615). We may add that Grim, like Peter, is a fisherman; that he is Havelok's first subject, as Peter was the first apostle; and that his role as founder of the town of Grimsby parallels Peter's as founder of the Church (Matthew 16:18). Again the symbolism is a deft and unobtrusive reminder of Havelok's theocratic role.

With his family and Havelok, Grim sails to England, settles at Grimsby, and becomes a prosperous fisher-man and merchant. Havelok finds work in nearby Lin-coln, where his good qualities endear him to all (945-88). So well-known is Havelok that Godrich, attending Parliament in Lincoln, decides to use him in order to rid himself of Goldeboru. Having promised to wed Goldeboru to the 'hexte' (highest) man in the land, Godrich thinks he will observe only the literal mean-ing of that promise (the tallest man), unaware that in so doing he providentially fulfills its moral and social meanings as well (the best man, the most exalted) and prepares his own downfall. The forced marriage is performed by the Archbishop of York, who 'cam to the parlement / Als God him havede thider sent' (1179-80). Thus the marriage is consecrated by the highest ecclesiastical authority.

Havelok now returns with his royal bride to Grimsby, where the holy marks of kingship are revealed for the second time. Goldeboru does not understand their full significance until an angel's voice interprets them and reveals Havelok's destiny. With this heavenly commu-nication Goldeboru is able to interpret Havelok's pro-phetic dream and to help him plan a strategy for win-ning the throne of Denmark. Havelok consecrates his project at church, and sets sail for Denmark.

In Denmark Havelok does battle with a group of thieves who, as 'Caimes kin and Eves' (2045) par-ticipate in the nature of archetypal Biblical sinners. After this victory the holy king-marks are again re-vealed, this time to the royal justice Ubbe. Re-cognised at last as rightful ruler heir in his own land, Havelok is able to bring Godard to the hideous death he deserves. Returning to England, Havelok engages in climactic single combat with Godrich. He shows his mercy by offering to forgive if Godrich will re-nounce all claim to the throne. When mercy is re-jected, justice must be done, and Godrich meets as painful a death as Godard had done. Havelok is made king, rewards are distributed, fealty is taken 'on the bok'. A new golden age begins for England under a divinely appointed king who equals Athelwold in strength, virtue and piety.

To read ***Havelok*** from a religious point of view reveals a king who is virtually a saviour-figure: he defeats diabolical opponents, avenges those who have been wronged, and brings a new reign of harmony, love and peace. But the poem also develops another aspect of Havelok's rule, simultaneously with the theocratic. That is the political or contractual side of his rule, to which I now turn.

Reviewing the beginning of ***Havelok***, we find that England's golden age under Athelwold is defined in political as well as in religious terms. The king is dis-tinguished by his ability to make and enforce good laws (27-9), and his reign by a remarkable consensus among all social classes:

> Him lovede yung, him lovede olde,
> Erl and barun, dreng and thain,
> Knight, bondeman, and swain,
> Widwes, maidnes, prestes and clerkes,
> And alle for hise gode werkes.
>
> (30-4)

The theme of consensus is constant in the story, and it is as important a key to judgment as the religious sym-bols discussed above. Again and again the author emphasises that the good ruler governs on behalf of and with the approval of his population, at least the middle and upper classes. Thus when Athelwold falls ill,

> He sende writes sone anon
> After his erles evereich on:
> And after hise baruns, riche and povre,
> Fro Rokesburw all into Dovere . . .
>
> (136-9)

This council of earls and barons chooses Godrich as ward of Athelwold's daughter, just as Godard is chosen ward of Birkabein's children by a similar council of Danish barons and knights (364-82).

Havelok's influence when he works as a cook's helper in Lincoln transcends class lines (955-8), a trait which anticipates the contractual character of his rule. When Goldeboru interprets Havelok's prophetic dream, she is careful to include among his future loyal subjects 'Erl and baroun, dreng and thain, / Knightes and burgeys and swain' (1327-8). When Ubbe discovers Havelok's holy light, he summons his entire retinue of 'knightes and sergaunz'. The formulaic list is repeated when Ubbe promises that Havelok shall take fealty of the entire population (2138-85), when he summons them (2194-5) and when the oath is sworn (2258-65). When the ceremony is done, Ubbe sends out an even more general writ throughout the entire country to castles, boroughs and towns, knights, constables and sheriffs (2274-89). When Godard is caught, his sentence is decided by a popular assembly which includes knights and burgesses (2465-73). Godrich is judged by a more limited but still representative jury of his peers (761-5).

In contrast to Athelwold and Havelok, the usurpers Godrich and Godard govern autocratically. Godard makes decisions solely on the basis of personal will (249-59). He demands a loyalty oath from all subjects without admitting any to partnership in government (260-2), and Godard does the same in Denmark (437-42). Godrich rules by fear alone, creating an oppressive bureaucracy in order to enforce his ambitious schemes (266-79). When Godrich rallies his barons for battle with Havelok, not only does he fail to seek their advice, but he coerces by threatening to reduce them to thralls (2564-5)—a flagrant and unheard-of violation of custom and law.[6]

Although consensus is an important feature of kingship in *Havelok*, the poem puts forth nothing like what we would now call a 'democratic' social ideal—nor did political and legal theory of the time. The 'partnership' mentioned earlier included barons, smaller landholders (knights) and the upper bourgeoisie. Peasants and labourers were not considered to have legitimate class interests other than what was defined for them by their lords or employers: this was to remain generally true in England well into the seventeenth century, and even through the Civil War (MacPherson, Part 3). The interests represented in *Havelok* are those of the newly powerful propertied classes: they hoped to share the privilege of government, but had no intention of extending that privilege beyond themselves.

Among Athelwold's virtues is his prompt attention to crimes against property. Thieves are the particular object of his hatred (39-43), and his zeal against them makes England a safe place for wealthy people and travelling merchants (45-58).[7] Indeed the prosperity accruing from commercial activity seems to constitute a large part of England's 'ease' in praise of which the author concludes this passage (59-61).

Acquisition of wealth and property appears in the poem as an honourable pursuit and one requiring virtuous character. Grim's loyalty to Havelok, as well as his industry, is rewarded by prosperity, which, by the time he dies, amounts to a large family fortune in money, goods and livestock (1221-8). Even as Godard's thrall, Grim had not been badly off; he owned substantial livestock (699-702) and a well-equipped ship sturdy enough to sail to England (706-13). Still, Grim is not free, and he acknowledges that only Havelok can make him free (618-31). This would seem at first to infringe contemporary feudal law, for a serf could be directly manumitted only by his overlord (in this case Godard), not by the king. The only way in which the king could be said to confer freedom was through the law of year and day. This privilege, included in many borough charters, provided that any person who lived peacefully in the borough in his own house for the stipulated period, would automatically become free.[8] What Grim seems to anticipate, the, is that his path to freedom lies through the borough privileges which were the essence of the alliance between king and upper bourgeoisie.

As a youth, Havelok heartily adopts the middle-class work ethic; he helps Grim to sell fish, for

> It is no shame forto swinken;
> The man that may well eten and drinken
> That nought he have but on swin long;
> To liggen at hom it is full strong.
>
> (799-802)

But a shortage ('dere') of grain forces Havelok to seek full-time work in Lincoln instead. The situation there is grim. Havelok remains unemployed and hungry for two days, until

> The thridde day herde he calle;
> 'Bermen, bermen, hider forth alle!'
> Povre that on fote yede
> Sprongen forth so sparke of glede,
> Havelok shof dune nine or ten
> Right amidewarde the fen,

And stirte forth to the cook,
Ther the erles mete he took
That he boughte at the bridge;
The bermen let he alle lidge,
And bar the mete to the castel,
And gat him there a ferthing wastel.

(867-78)

Noteworthy in this passage are, first, the large number of unemployed who, at the cook's call, 'spring forth like sparks from a coal'; and, second, Havelok's brutal fervour in shoving his hungry competitors into the mud. The incident is repeated the next day. So impressed is the earl's cook with this eagerness that he offers Havelok a steady job. Havelok accepts, stipulating no other wages than enough to eat (901-20). Havelok is as conscientious a worker as we might expect from his behaviour so far: he does everything (931-42) and afterward does more:

Wolde he nevere haven rest
More than he were a best.
Of alle men was he mest meke,
Lauhwinde ay and blithe of speke;
Ever he was glad and blithe;
His sorwe he couthe full well mithe.

(943-8)

In short, Havelok is presented as an ideal worker. Yet we must acknowledge that he is an ideal worker only from the point of view of an employer. He is extremely competitive with other workers, works for nothing, gladly works to the point of exhaustion, and never complains but always smiles. None of this behaviour could be considered either realistic or admirable by an audience of ordinary workers, though it would suit the taste of their urban employers or manorial supervisors.

With Havelok's experience in Lincoln we see that his movement through the story, after Godard's usurpation, is to be a progression from lowest to highest social class. He begins as the foster-child of a serf, at Grimsby becomes a free fisherman's assistant, and at Lincoln an employee in the earl's household. That progression continues when, after marrying Goldeboru, Havelok returns to Denmark as a merchant, is knighted by Ubbe in token of his victory over the thieves, and finally achieves the throne. Presumably Havelok's experience of all classes will enlarge his political sympathies when he is king, and teach him the needs of his entire population. At the same time Havelok's social ascent permits him to display, in each condition, the noblest side of his nature and the one most appropriate to the particular class, whether cheerful acquiescence or valiant self-defense.

Nearly two hundred lines are lost from that portion of the poem which narrates the crossing to Denmark, a project supported and financed by Grim's (now wealthy) sons. When the text resumes we find Havelok conversing with Ubbe. It is Ubbe's function, as justice, to grant foreign merchants permission to sell their goods, and to receive for that privilege a toll or hanse: in this case a very valuable gold ring (1632-4). Ubbe invites Havelok and Goldeboru to dine with him, guaranteeing, with an elegant play on her name the safety of Havelok's most valuable property':

'And have thou of hire no drede;
Shall hire no man shame bede.
By the fey I owe to thee,
Thereof shall I myself boru be.'

(1664-7)

Despite this assurance, Havelok worries lest someone abduct his wife (1668-73), and Ubbe himself, acknowledging the possibility, sends a special guard to Havelok's lodging. When the attack occurs, its motive is unclear. Huwe Raven is sure that *raptus* is the aim of the sixty armed invaders (868-70), but Havelok's wealthy host Bernard Brun thinks it is robbery (1955-9). Though the local burgesses agree with Bernard, rejoicing that he has lost no property ('tinte no catel', 2023). Ubbe continues to emphasise the protection of Goldeboru.

Beside letting the poet display some of his most vigorous verse, and Havelok his formidable courage and strength, the battle episode underscores the need for a strong just king and a centralised administration. Again this point of view coincides with the interests of the upper bourgeoisie, whose property and fortunes could be protected, whose liberties and privileges could be granted and maintained, only by a strong centralised government. When we recall that under Athelwold no merchant travelling in England would have encountered the least trouble (45-8), the entire episode shows Godard's abysmal failure to sustain the moral tone of Denmark and to make it safe for the middle classes. Since Godrich has been unable to establish a judicial system or a public police force, Ubbe, fearing retaliation from friends of the slaughtered thieves, removes Havelok to his own well-protected house—where of course the recognition scene occurs.

A curious feature of Havelok's accession to kingship is its complete secularity. In Denmark, Ubbe summons the population, who confer the kingdom upon Havelok (2316-19). Of the English accession we hear only that the feast lasted more than forty days (2948-50). The Danish accession emphasises the ancient electoral principle, and conspicuously absent from both accounts is any mention of a traditional coronation ceremony. There is no reference to a crown; no bishops or other ecclesiastical figures are present; Havelok is neither consecrated nor anointed with holy oil; he wears no coronation robes, so closely resembling sacerdotal vestments; nor does he take anything resembling the traditional English coronation oath with its promise to safeguard the Church.

My argument is admittedly *ex silentio*: nonetheless the omission of a coronation ceremony, with its heavy ecclesiastical overtones, is significant. First, such a ceremony could have provided the author with an ideal opportunity for ceremonial description, an opportunity most medieval authors welcomed in such events as weddings, dubbings, battles, and so on. Indeed we have already seen that our author enjoys and excels at physical description and detail: the death of Athelwold, the battle at Bernard's, and other *loci* prove that. Second, even more surprising than the poet's bypassing a splendid literary opportunity is his ignoring an event which in his own time was an extremely important one in English public life, and which had been important for generations.[9] Both literary and social tradition, then, suggest that a coronation scene would be an obvious climax in the poem. Its omission, however, is neither accidental nor inconsistent.

In part the secularity of Havelok's accession may reflect the nationalistic sentiment that infused thirteenth-century English public life, for that sentiment was largely a product of England's assertion of sovereignty against papal intervention to emphasise the rights of *regnum* over those of *sacerdotium*. It stresses the inviolable unity of the nation.

But beyond this, the secular coronation rounds out the new definition of kingship offered in **Havelok**, and here a historical analogue cannot be ignored. Like Havelok, Edward I became king in an unusual manner. Since he was abroad when his father died in 1272, Edward's succession was proclaimed immediately by hereditary right and will of the magnates. This was confirmed by oath of fealty from knights and burgesses, and Edward began to reign from the date of his election. It was the first time that full legal recognition had been extended to an heir before coronation, for Edward was formally crowned—that is, he received ecclesiastical approval—only two years later, on his return to England. Thus Edward's accession itself showed that the English notion of kingship had already moved well away from the theocratic extreme, and that the will of those governed had become as significant a factor as the will of God. 'The double note, of conservatism and experiment, which was to sound throughout his reign, seemed already struck before he began it' (Johnstone, p. 393). It is the same double note that *Havelok* strikes.

At the end of the romance, the theme of social mobility emerges again. The rise of Grim and Havelok has already validated social mobility, while the villainy of Earls Godard and Godrich indicates that rank cannot guarantee character. Havelok himself underlines the importance of moral, rather than social, superiority when

he refers to Godard as a 'thrall' (1408); later the author calls Godrich a 'mixed [filthy] cherl' (2533), rhyming 'cherl' with 'erl' to intensify the paradox.[10] Now, social mobility is extended to Havelok's supporters. Grim's three sons are elevated to knights and barons (2346-53), and Grim's daughters are raised even higher. One of them is given in marriage to the Earl of Chester, the other to Havelok's former employer, the cook, who is now by Havelok's grant Earl of Cornwall. These rewards, especially the last, may seem extravagant, and Halvorsen has called this scene 'a peasant fantasy'.[11] But the scene is neither fantastic, nor expressive of peasant aspirations; it represents the social reality and realistic ambitions of the upper bourgeoisie and knighthood.

I would point out, first, that a post in a noble household was often a prestigious sinecure. The Earl's 'cook' may have been himself a wealthy tenant-knight with merely supervisory duties. Though the exact duty of a nobleman's 'cook' is not known, it is known that William the Conqueror gave his 'cook' half a hide of land, and that the Count of Boulogne conferred on his 'cook' the estate of Wilmiton (Pollock and Maitland, pp. 262-71). Moreover, the period was one of rapid and often dramatic social change. Serfs left the manor to become free labourers or artisans; artisans might amass sufficient capital and property to become burgesses; recently wealthy merchants and financiers bought estates and titles, intermarried with nobility, adopted an aristocratic life-style, and aspired to participate in government. In 1307, perhaps only a few years after **Havelok** was composed, the young Edward II created Piers Gavaston, a knight's son, Earl of Cornwall—a title whose two previous holders had been king's sons. Joan, daughter of Edward I and widow of the Earl of Gloucester, in 1295 married a knight, to whom Edward eventually entrusted the Gloucester inheritance. However it was not only in Edward's private life that he confirmed social mobility, but also in his deliberate expansion of 'the community of the realm' to include the upper middle classes, as in the 'Model Parliament' of 1295. For Edward recognised that the upper bourgeoisie was both a valuable financial resource, and a reliable ally against the barons. Thus the reward scene in **Havelok** represents little that had not been, or would not soon be, accomplished in reality.

The idea of theocratic monarchy in England would long outlive the thirteenth century, though the history of Richard II shows that Tudor and Stuart monarchs could assert with impunity what their predecessors could not. Still, the origins of its demise in the Civil War of 1642 lay precisely, and paradoxically, in the 'partnership'— the gradual institutional adjustments—by which monarchy survived in the thirteenth century. To the beginning of that fruitful change **Havelok the Dane** bears witness.

*Notes*

[1] See Power and, for a convenient summary of scholarship on medieval English government and social structure, Wickson.

[2] Text in McKechnie. Article 61, McKechnie notes, was 'nothing more nor less than legalised rebellion' (p. 153); and though it was scarcely a feasible concession, it is nonetheless a significant one.

[3] Bracton, *De Leg.*, f. 5b, in the edition of Woodbine, vol. 2, p. 33; quoted in Kantorowiz, p. 156. See also Schulz, Pollock, and Maitland, vol. I; and McIlwain, Chapter 4.

[4] The later limit is generally taken to be 1303, the date of composition of Robert Mannyng's *Handlyng Synne*, which seems to imitate parts of *Havelok*. Skeat's discussion of final -e suggests that the poem was originally written before 1300, and other internal evidence points to a date after 1296. See 'Introduction' (revised by K. Sisam) to W. Skeat's edition (Oxford, 2nd ed. 1915). All quotations in my text are from the edition of Sands. The two earlier versions of the Havelok story are Geoffrey Gaimer's Anglo-Norman *Estorie des engles*, and the Old French *Lai d'Havelok*, both twelfith century.

[5] Thus Bede's *History* (2:16) praises the great peace in Britain under King Edwin, commenting on the king's special care for travellers. The *Anglo-Saxon Chronicle* for 1087 commends the righteousness and piety of William the Conqueror, his mildness to good men and severity to bad; his reign is described as a time when 'a man might go over the kingdom unhurt, with his bosom full of gold'. The Peterborough continuation of the *Chronicle* claims that under Henry I a man could carry treasure anywhere without being molested. For some details in my account of the religious theme, I am indebted to a paper by V. Ishkanian, my graduate student at Simon Fraser University.

[6] The reduction of free men to servile status was not in itself unheard of in the later thirteenth century, for it was a widely debated legal question whether performance of base services over several generations could make free stock servile (Pollock and Maitland, p. 410). Opinion generally ran that it could not. As applied to magnates the threat can have had no real social analogue, and is meant to show the hyperbolic viciousness of Godrich's nature, as well as his contempt for the law of the land.

[7] This may allude to Edward's special campaign against robbery, embodied in the Statute of Winchester (1285). The Statute specifies the duties oftowns and hundreds, lords, sheriffs and bailiffs in expanding roads, cutting forests, guarding estates, and general surveillance against

strangers: see *Records of the Borough of Northampton* (Northampton, 1889) vol. I, pp. 416-19. This was only one of Edward's many attempts to investigate and correct the bureaucratic abuses of the previous regime and his own; the results of his official inquiries appear in the Hundred Rolls and in various county assize rolls.

[8] Pollock and Maitland add that the same law applied to serfs who escaped to the king's domain. As a borough privilege, the law of year and day helped to create a pool of free labour required by the bourgeoisie. Encouraged partly by this law, serfs and villeins deserted the manors in considerable numbers; see Dobb, Chapter 2.

[9] See Richardson. A convenient guide to scholarship on the coronation ceremonies and oaths is the bibliography in Hoyt. Schramm provides a full study of the ceremony and its tradition.

[10] The relation of rank and character is a familiar theme in the literature of the twelfth through fourteenth centuries. It is debated in *De Arte Honesti Amandi* of Andreas Capellanus (Dialogues two and three). In Jean de Meun's continuation of the *Roman de la Rose*, Reason shows that the nobleman who seeks only pleasure becomes Satan's serf (4396-8). Chaucer, following Jean, would take up the question of true 'gentilesse' in his *Wife of Bath's Tale*, and it would be illustrated (through from a different angle) by Langland in the person of Piers Plowman.

[11] While I admire Halvorsen's wish to place *Havelok* in its social context, his concept of class is vague and inaccurate. He suggests, for instance, that 'middle class' is preferable to 'bourgeois' as a designation for this type of literature, because the former term is more inclusive, ranging from 'the villager and peasant at one end [of the social spectrum] and powerful burgher and even petty nobility at the other'. But it is just this inclusiveness that produces imprecision: witness Halvoren's inclusion of peasants in the middle class with no specification as to rich or poor peasant, servile or free, etc. My argument is that *Havelok* is by no means as diffuse in its ideology as Halvorsen implies: its range of social consciousness does not include that of villagers and peasants but is limited to that of burgesses and barons. One would be surprised to find a work of literature so false to social reality that it could claim identity of values among classes so divergent in their interests.

Such, however, appears to be the vision of David Staines, whose discussion of *Havelok* is hopelessly confused as far as class and class ideology are concerned. For Staines, the poem expresses social ideas suitable to royalty and 'the lower classes' alike. This would be quite a juggling act, even if Staines had enlightened us as to the referent of 'lower classes' and explained what they are lower than: lower than the king? lower than the bourgeoisie? lower than the artisanate? The article beautifully illustrates the need for precision in class terminology.

Susan Crane rightly rejects the peasant view, arguing that *Havelok* 'attends to some interests that the barony shared with the emerging professional and mercantile class' (p. 44); she characterises the poem as 'a utopian vision of harmony and happiness' (p. 44), 'a romance of the law' (p. 48).

## Thorlac Turville-Petre (essay date 1994)

SOURCE: "*Havelok* and the History of the Nation," in *Readings in Medieval English Romance*, edited by Carol M. Meale, D.S. Brewer, 1994, pp. 121-34.

[*In the following essay, Turville-Petre argues that* Havelok the Dane *is better considered as history than romance and that this was the way it was viewed by contemporary readers of the chronicles.*]

The establishment and exploration of a sense of national identity is a major preoccupation of English writers of the late thirteenth and early fourteenth centuries: who are the English; where do they come from; what constitutes the English nation? The English chronicles of the period, Robert of Gloucester's *Chronicle* of c.1300, the *Anonymous Short English Metrical Chronicle* of *post* 1307, and Robert Manning's *Chronicle* written in 1338,[1] have a central role to play in answering such questions, as they relate 'all þe story of Inglande' in order to give 'þe lewed' an understanding of 'þe state of þe land' (Manning I, 3-12), thus shaping a sense of national identity based on the history of England. Other kinds of work are also important in this shaping, particularly the 'romances' with their portrayal of English heroes of the past.

Though we are accustomed to classing *Havelok*[2] as a romance, it would be closer to the medieval view of the work to call it a history.[3] We rarely have much evidence on the way in which contemporary readers classified a medieval work, but it is clear that *Havelok* was unhesitatingly accepted as a history in the early fourteenth century. In 1310 Rauf de Boun incorporated into his Anglo-Norman chronicle *Le Petit Bruit*,[4] written for the Earl of Lincoln, a synopsis of the English poem which he referred to as 'l'estorie de Grimesby' (p. 15, 1. 13), and Robert Manning from Bourne in south Lincolnshire attempted to fit the poem's account into his *Chronicle*, but found difficulties with its chronology, and was assailed by doubts on all sides: 'Right story can me not ken þe certeynte what spellis' (II, p. 25).[5] These chroniclers took *Havelok* to be a historical work, and tried (in Manning's case unsuccessfully) to transform it into another *kind* of history.

Hayden White, discussing the 'fantasy that real events are properly represented when they can be shown to display the formal coherency of a story', analyses the three traditional kinds of historical representation.[6] The first two, annal and chronicle, are non-narrative. Annals present a vertical set of events where chronology is the principle of organisation, with 'no suggestion', he says, 'of any necessary connection between one event and another'. The second form, the chronicle, he writes, 'aspires to narrativity, but . . . usually is marked by a failure to achieve narrative closure', in that it breaks off 'in *media res*, in the chronicler's own present'. The third type is narrative history proper, where events are patterned as though they possessed coherence and an order of meaning, quite uncharacteristic of events as they actually occur. The annal presents itself as the most artless form of historical writing, the narrative history as the most crafted. *Havelok* is clearly an example of the latter, with its balanced structure of parallel events—Goldeborw, heiress of the king of England deprived of her inheritance by earl Godrich, as Havelok is deprived of the Danish throne by earl Go-dard; with its pattern of stability, conflict and return to stability, as Havelok and Goldeborw restore the peace and just rule that Godrich and Godard have upset; and with the final claim by the author that he has stayed awake many nights over the crafting of 'þe rym'.[7] The historical setting is established at once as *are dawes*, 'former times' (27), and the king of England named as Athelwold (106), pointing clearly to Anglo-Saxon England.[8] The poet himself is probably responsible for supplying this and many other names not in the analogues, such as Godrich, earl of Cornwall, and William Wendut, son of Grim, names which lend a historical and factual air. Above all, the poet lays great emphasis on legal practices and social institutions: the formal oath of regency taken by Godrich (185-209), his appointment of local justices, sheriffs, beadles, greaves and 'grith-sergeans' (263-67), the act of homage, *manrede*, named no fewer than eleven times, the writ of summons of the feudal levy (2549-66), and the formal pronouncement of sentence of execution on Godrich (2819-38).[9] The effect of all this is to suggest that the poem deals with serious matters of constitutional importance, and this effect is in no way undercut by the poet's opening address to a listening audience[10] and his appeal to 'fil me a cuppe of ful god ale' (14); not an invitation to drunkeness and *ribaudie*, but rather marking the presence of the poet-narrator as shaper and interpreter of historical events.

It is as chronicle history that the story of Havelok makes its first appearance. In Gaimar's *L'Estoire des Engleis* of about 1135, the events are set in the time of King Constantine, nephew of Arthur. The Dane Adelbriht rules East Anglia, and the Briton Edelsi rules in Lin-colnshire. Adelbriht's daughter Argentille is deprived of her inheritance by Edelsi, but Havelok, son of King Gunter of Denmark, wins it back for her, and Havelok and Argentille together rule East Anglia for 20 years.

The story reappears in the late thirteenth century in the *Anglo-Norman Brut* chronicle. The later Middle English translation of this begins:

> After Kyng Constantynus deth þere were ij kynges
> in Britaigne: þat on me callede Adelbright, þat was
> a Danoys, þat helde þe contre of Northfolc and
> Southfolc; þat oþere hit Edelf, and was a Britoun,
> þat helde Nichole, Lyndeseye, and al þe lande vnto
> Hunber.
>
> (91.23-26)[11]

The English poem differs from the Anglo-Norman versions in two fundamental respects: that the setting is England, not ancient Britain, and that Athelwold is king of the county as a whole, not just of East Anglia. This causes problems for the chroniclers who depend on the English poem, since there is no obvious place for Athelwold in the sequence of English kings. Rauf de Boun boldly makes room for him as the son of Edmund Ironside, taking the entirely logical step of tying the story in to a period of actual Danish rule in England, with Havelok father of king Canute, so that his marriage to Athelwold's daughter Goldeborw results in a succession of Anglo-Danish kings. Manning, a much more serious historian, is entirely stumped by the problem of accommodating this interloper. His source, Peter of Langtoft, lands him in trouble by mentioning Havelok in connection with Alfred's wars with the Danes, but none of the established historical authorities offer further guidance:

> Noiþer Gildas, no Bede, no Henry of
> Huntynton,
> No William of Malmesbiri, ne Pers of
> Bridlynton,
> Writes not in þer bokes of no kyng
> Athelwold,
> Ne Goldeburgh his douhtere, ne Hauelok not
> of told.
>
> (II, p. 25)

The elegant solution that Manning or his reviser eventually adopted at this point in the revision of the *Chronicle* in the Lambeth manuscript was to rewrite the passage, dropping the reference to the English poem, and summarising instead the Anglo-Norman version with its setting on the local and not the national stage.

The tension in Manning's first puzzled account of Havelok resides in the conflict between the apparently authenticating evidence on the ground and the silence of reputable historians:

> Men sais in Lyncoln castelle ligges ȝit
> a stone
> Þat Hauelok kast wele forbi euerilkone;
> And ȝit þe chapelle standes þer
> he weddid his wife.
>
> (II, p. 26)

Just so, today, believers in Robin Hood point to the sad remains of his tree, Major Oak. The chroniclers frequently draw attention to the present witnesses of past events, the ancient castles, abbeys and tombs that authenticate or commemorate the historical record, and to towns whose names perpetuate the story of their foundation, such as Thongcastle (modern Caistor in Lincolnshire), so named, as Manning reports, after Hengist acquired the site by encircling it with a bull's hide cut into thongs.[12] For a Lincolnshire audience, this is the effect, or at least a part of it, of the detailed descriptions in *Havelok* of local scenes at Lincoln and Grimsby. The name Grimsby is a living reminder of its foundation by Grim:

> And for þat Grim þat place aute
> Þe stede of Grim þe name laute,
> So þat Grimesbi it calle
> Þat þer-offe speken alle;
> And so shulen men callen it ay
> Bituene þis and Domesday.
>
> (744-49)

Though the action takes place at a *time* long past, the *place* is here, Lincoln, that fish-market on High Bridge, from where Havelok climbs up the path to our ancient castle (in fact founded only two years after the Conquest). Godrich is led to execution 'Bi-souþe þe borw unto a grene/Þat þare is yet' (2829-30). Havelok's Lincoln still stands.[13]

But such physical manifestations are more than authenticating evidence. They are the demonstration that past actions have their consequences in present conditions; Grimsby as it is today is the product of a train of historical events beginning with Grim's landing on the Humber shore. The very point of recalling events of the past is that they have relevance to the present: 'gude it is, for many thynges,/For to here þe dedis of kynges' (Manning I, 15-16). The vernacular writers of this period make this point more obvious by bringing their histories up to recent times, unlike Wace. . . , who had ended in the distant past. Robert of Gloucester and Manning can in this way explore the working-out of historical processes that have led to contemporary conditions, whether it be the origins of the Scottish wars or the social divisions of society since the Conquest.

The local descriptions in *Havelok* are particularly memorable, but the English poem differs from Gaimer and the related Anglo-Norman accounts in setting the local scenes within a national framework. Nothing could demonstrate this more directly than the summons to a parliament at Lincoln; the nation literally comes to the locality:

> In þat time al Hengelond
> Þ'erl Godrich hauede in his hond,
> And he gart komen into þe tun
> Mani erl and mani barun,
> And alle þat liues were
> In England þanne wer þere,
> Þat þey haueden after sent
> To ben þer at þe parlement.
>
> (1000-07)

Nor was this an unbelievable event, since parliament did indeed meet at Lincoln in 1301, an event recorded by Manning in some detail (II, p. 312). Since the poem opens not with the local scenes but with a description of England, we are in a position to envisage the region within the nation. The concerns of the poem centre on the relationship between the region and the nation, a topic which is foreshadowed at the accession of the wicked Godrich as regent of England by his appointment of local officials throughout the land, so that 'al Engelond' could be controlled as the beast is by the goad (266-79).

The national setting is very quickly and effectively established. There was a king of olden days who was loved by all his people:

> Erl and barun, dreng and þayn,
> Knict, bondeman and swain,
> Wydues, maydnes, prestes and clerkes,
> And al for hise gode werkes.
>
> (31-34)

So effective was his justice that:

> Þanne micthe chapmen fare
> Þuruth Englond wit here ware,
> And baldelike beye and sellen
> Oueral þer he wilen dwellen;
> In gode burwes and þer-fram
> Ne funden he non þat dede hem sham.
>
> (51-56)

These opening fifty-six lines have named the kingdom, England, and have given a sense of the diversity of its population and an idea of the extent of its territory in the towns through which chapmen travel in perfect safety. Through an implicit contrast with present conditions, the poet suggests that the nation *then* both is and yet isn't the nation *now:*

> Þanne was Engelond at hayse;
> Michel was svich a king to preyse
> Þat held so Englond in grith!

> Krist of heuene was him with;
> He was Engelondes blome.
>
> (59-63)

In these few lines the poet constructs the framework for his portrayal of the nation, the details of which he fills in later. So its geographical extent is made more specific by twice marking the limits as bounded by Dover and Roxburgh. From the whole nation within these bounds Athelwold summons his barons to attend his deathbed at Winchester (138-39, 158), and Godrich dispatches justices 'Al Engelond to faren þorw,/Fro Douere into Rokesborw' (264-65) in order to establish his control as national leader. At the same time, the unity of the nation is repeatedly stressed by the phrase 'al Engelond' (250, 277, 278 etc.).[14]

There has been some discussion about the reference to Roxburgh, in the belief that it provides evidence to date the poem after 1295 when Roxburgh was surrendered to Edward I.[15] But there is no reason to assume that Roxburgh was (or had recently been) in English hands at the time of writing. The poet is indeed saying that it was a part of the England of *are dawes*, and therefore perhaps implying that it should still be. This is certainly the view of chroniclers; Manning, following his source Langtoft, reports that Edward I had called on the testimony of chronicles to demonstrate that his lordship of Scotland was sanctioned by history (II, p. 190), and furthermore he quotes Merlin's prophecy that the three parts of the island Brutus conquered would one day be reunited, in ironic recognition that this had not yet happened (II, p. 282).

It has similarly been proposed that Godrich's title of earl of Cornwall is a sly reference to Henry II's brother Richard, earl of Cornwall between 1227 and 1272; that the introduction of Reyner, earl of Chester as Godard's ally refers to the alliance between Richard of Corwall and Ranulf of Chester in 1227; and that the officiation of the Archbishop of York at Havelok's wedding in Lincoln reflects the summons of this archbishop to the Lincoln parliament in 1301.[16] These suggestions rest on a basic misunderstanding of the poet's treatment of history. The main point of all these titles is that they are familiar in English history and reasonably ancient; just as there'll always be an England, so there'll always be an Archbishop of York. A more particular point about the two earls is that their presence in Lincoln underlines that *national* issues are at stake, since both Cornwall and Chester are a very long way from Lincolnshire. It might also be added that neither earldom was in the hands of a long-established family to which the poet's references might unfortunately point;[17] indeed Cornwall was actually vacant from 1300 until Edward II invested his favourite Piers Gaveston with the title in 1307, and Chester was also vacant until the future Edward II himself took the title in 1301.

These titles, then, help to build up an impression of an England of geographical range and familiar institutions. What we are hearing about is not contemporary England, and yet it bears a relationship with the nation as it now is. The present grows out of the past; but it *is* the past, not a confused medley of past and present.

Exploring the relationship between the nation past and the nation present is a theme fundamental to the chronicles. 'It is wisdom for to wytten/Þe state of þe land' (I, 11-12) declares Manning at the outset of his chronicle. The nation is to be defined through the story of its origins and development, with the focus upon the history of the *people* of the nation. We should not be surprised that the concept of nation is fundamentally a racist one; after all, the Latin word *natio* means 'breed' or 'stock',[18] so that the associations of race or *kynde* are built into the word in its early vernacular use. Furthermore, the pattern on which the English chronicles are constructed gives additional emphasis to the ethnic basis of nationalism. 'After þe Bretons þe Inglis camen', says Manning (I, 35), and from that point on the chronicle becomes a history of *us*, of the people 'whereof is comen oure Inglis kynde' (I, 48). Manning goes on directly to discuss his use of the English language (I, 71-128), which is the living demonstration of his kinship with Hengist and Horsa.

The Saxons stand at the heart of the English nation. Everyone else is 'the other', and in this construction that includes the Normans, who defeated us at the battle of Hastings, so that 'our fredom þat day for euer toke þe leve' (II, p. 71), and they have oppressed us ever since with serfdom and taxation.[19] Ancient hostilities are perpetuated in modern social structures, and the English nation is ruled by 'þat folc of Normandie/Þat among vs wonieþзvt' as Robert of Gloucester writes in his late-thirteenth-century *Chronicle* (54-55). Not surprisingly, the *Anglo-Norman Brut* offers a different notion of the structure of society, but even so it is based on an ethnic concept of 'nation'. England is torn apart by the diverse origins of its peoples, so that such discord 'entre gent de une nacioun' had never been seen before the civil war of 1322. In the words of the later Middle English translation:

> Hit was no wonder, for þe grete lordes of Engeland were nouзt alle of o nacioun, but were mellede wiþ oþere nacions, þat is forto seyn, somme Britons, somme Saxones, somme Danois, somme Peghtes, somme Frenchemen, somme Normans, somme Spaignardes, somme Romayns, somme Henaudes, some Flemyngus, and of oþere diuerse naciouns, þe whiche nacions acorded nouзt to þe kynde bloode of Engeland.
>
> (*Brut,* p. 220, ll. 17-23)

Ethnic nationalism, defining the nation in these terms of the 'native blood of England', has no place for the Danes and those descended from them. It is not a question of people *becoming* English by long and diligent service to the nation; they just *aren't* English and, when it comes to the crunch, blood will out. This is the idea, I suppose, behind Robert of Gloucester's curious comment in his preliminary historical survey, that England has often been attacked by 'þe folc of Denemarch, þat ne beþ noзt зvt isome' (52)— 'who are not yet at one/not yet integrated'; a remark quite at odds with his source.[20]

When it comes to giving a full account of the Viking attacks, Robert of Gloucester gives the slant that is universal among medieval historians, whether they write in English, French or Latin. The Vikings attack and seize by force; they murder, loot and burn:

> Þat luþer folc of Denemarch robbede and
>    slowe uaste,
> Chirchen and abbeys barnde and adoun caste;
> Men leye vnbured to-drawe, þat reuþe it was
>    ynou;
> Þat feble folc to wildernesse and to wodes
>    faste drou.
>
> (6086-89)

East Anglia in particular is terrorised by their depredations:

> to Estangle aзen
>    hii come;
> Þere hii barnde and robbede and þat folc to
>    grounde slowe
> And, as wolves among ssep, reuliche hom to-
>    drowe.
>
> (5297-99)

It is as an example of a major theme in his chronicle, the 'gyle/Of folc of þe sulue lond' (4-5), 'the treachery of the country's own people', that Robert relates the events leading up to the election of a Danish king to the throne of England, for Cnut could never have won the crown 'зif false traytors nadde ybe here of Engelonde' (6145). The noble Edmund, nicknamed Ironside for his strength, yet 'debonere and milde' to all who were honourable, is chosen king by those lords who were not 'fals ne luþer' (6134), and struggles to defeat Cnut. Duke Edric treacherously pretends that Edmund has been killed in battle, and cries out 'Englissemen, Englissemen, fleþ anon, ich rede' (6195), so that the English forces lose the opportunity to defeat the Danes. After more inconclusive battles, Edmund comes to a reconciliation with Cnut, but is murdered at the instigation of 'þe luþer duc Edric' (6330) shortly afterwards, stabbed in the privy. Cnut calls a parliament which complaisantly agrees to deprive Edmund's sons of their rightful heritage, 'Alas, alas þe tricherie' (6427), so that Cnut 'huld him þo al clene king of al Engelonde/Of Norþwey and of Denemarch' (6432-33).

As it turns out, Cnut mends his ways and becomes a thoroughly good king; he is generous to the church (6507-21), makes the best laws that could be (6606-07), 'and louede Englissemen and Engelond þerto' (6506). But this does not alter the fact that he and his two sons were not the rightful heirs:

> Kinges of Denemarch in þis manere were
> Kinges here of þis lond, kinges ech after oþer,
> Þe sone verst after þe fader, þe broþer after þe
>     broþer;
> And Engelond was out of kunde six and tuenti
>     зer.
>
>                  (6673-76)

With the accession of Edward the Confessor, England returns at last to the 'riзt eir of kunde' (6680), and the *Anglo-Norman Brut* reports that the English barons decreed that 'neuermore after þat tyme no man þat was a Danois, þouз he were ner so grete a man amonges ham, he shulde neuer bene Kyng of Engeland' (p. 126, ll. 3-5), because the Danes had behaved so offensively to the native English:

> If þe Englisshemen hade nouзt bowede adoun here heuedes to done reuerence vnto þe Danois, þai shulde haue bene bete and defoulede; and soche maner despites and vilonyes deden þe Danois to our Englisshemen.
>
>                  (p. 126, ll. 10-13)

The story of England as offered by all the chronicles presents the Vikings as invaders, Cnut and his sons as foreign kings ruling as a consequence of English treachery, and the Danes as arrogant aliens imposing themselves on a resentful native population. With this script it is impossible to be a loyal Englishman and at the same time to have pride in one's Danish ancestry. This is a most unsatisfactory plot for the people of north Lincolnshire, who preserved a memory of their Danish heritage which is expressed most clearly by *Havelok* itself, but is also indicated by their continued (though rapidly dwindling) use of Scandinavian personal names throughout the thirteenth century,[21] and other bits and pieces of evidence, such as the dedication of the Augustinian abbey of Wellow in Grimsby to St Olaf as well as St Augustine.[22]

The fact is that the chronicle-accounts give only part, and that a small part, of the story of the Vikings in England. In recent years, place-name scholars and archaeologists have brought forward conclusive evidence to show that Viking settlement must have been on a massive scale in some parts of the country, and nowhere more so than in north Lincolnshire. Kenneth Cameron admits that 'literary sources tell us no details concerning the extent and the density of Viking settlements in eastern England',[23] but he uses the distribution-patterns of Scandinavian, English and hybrid place-names and field-names in the east Midlands to show that occupation by members of the *micel here*, the 'great army' that invaded in the year 865, was followed by waves of secondary settlement by farmers from Scandinavia on a very considerable scale, extending over a long period up to the eleventh century. The settlers moved onto sites that had been deserted by the English, reclaiming marginal land, subdividing some of the more prosperous estates, and gradually intermarrying with the native inhabitants. The field-names of north Lincolnshire are a particularly rich source of Danish words, including many agricultural terms such as *eng*, 'meadow', *garðr*, 'enclosure', *hafri,* 'oats' and *haugr*, 'mound',[24] all pointing to the interests of the new settlers. Excavations have shown that parts of Lincoln itself were laid out in Viking times, to an extent previously unsuspected.[25] Cameron illustrates another aspect of settlement with one particularly telling detail. The name of one north Lincolnshire *wapentake*—itself a Scandinavian term for a district from which members of the local assembly were drawn—is *Lawress*, 'the coppice of Law-Wulf', evidently preserving the honorific title of the head-man famous for his knowledge of the law. Cameron comments:

> A single name makes the political and human situation clear. Groups of Vikings settled in the district which they themselves formed, or took over, under their own lawman, and they settled in sufficient numbers to have dominated it and to have been able to impose features of their own social structure on it.
>
>                  (p. 133)

The poet of *Havelok* addresses the Anglo-Danish descendants of this population. The chronicles tell only of pagan bands raping and pillaging; *Havelok* presents a revisionist view of the Vikings, bringing justice, peace and social integration. It is a rewrite, indeed, of the story of Edric's treachery towards his king Edmund Ironside and the wrongful accession of the Danish Cnut, as we have heard it told by Robert of Gloucester. Thus the golden age of Anglo-Saxon England under Edmund (now appearing as Athelwold) is destroyed by the traitor within, Edric (now Godrich). The Danes under Cnut (now recast as Havelok) establish peace and justice once again, not by conquest or treachery, but by just succession. *Havelok* indeed proffers the standard image of the Viking pillagers, but does so in a context that demands that it be rejected, as the traitor Godrich calls on his English troops to resist the Danish invaders:

> 'Lokes hware here at Grimesbi
> His uten-laddes here comen,
>          [*soldiers from abroad*]
> And haues nu þe priorie numen.
> Al þat euere mithen he finde,

He brenne kirkes and prestes binde;
He strangleth monkes and nunnes baþe.'

(2580-85)

This accusation is patently untrue, and indeed comes immediately after we have been told that Havelok founded a priory at Grimsby in honour of Grim.

The crucial difference between Cnut and Havelok is that Havelok succeeds to the throne of England by lawful right, through the inheritance of his wife. The author repeats no fewer than six times that Goldeborw is the *eir*, the *rihte eir*,[26] and this is fully and elaborately acknowledged by the English after Havelok's victory:

Þan þe Englishe men þat sawe,
Þat þei wisten, heye and lawe,
Þat Goldeboru þat was so fayr
Was of Engeland rith eyr,
And þat þe king hire hauede wedded,
And haueden ben samen bedded,
He comen alle to crie 'merci'
Vnto þe king at one cri,
And beden him sone manrede and oth
Þat he ne sholden, for lef ne loth,
Neueremore ageyn him go
Ne ride, for wel ne for wo.

(2767-78)

Following this, six earls go to fetch Godrich, the English fall to their knees before Goldeborw and admit 'Englond auhte for to ben/Youres, and we youre men' (2801-2), and then, after judgement has been duly pronounced on Godrich by his peers, the English offer homage:

Hauelok anon manrede tok
Of alle Englishe on þe bok,
And dide hem grete oþes swere
Þat he sholden him god feyth bere.

(2851-54)

Havelok's lawful right to the crown through his wife is an especially prominent feature on the contemporary Grimsby seal, in which Havelok holds up to Goldeborw a large ring, above which is a crown.[27] But the symbolic importance of marriage in the poem is much more than that. *Havelok* ends with the weddings of Grim's daughters: the earl of Chester who had fought on Godrich's side is married to Gunnild, and they settle in Chester and have five fine sons; Godrich's cook Bertram is given the earldom of Cornwall, now vacant, and marries Leuiue, and they settle on his estates and produce many children. Havelok and Goldeborw themselves have fifteen children; the sons all become kings and the daughters queens. In each case there is intermarriage between Danes and English, and Anglo-Danish offspring, and in this way the Danes become part

of the English national stock, of the *nation*, in an image of integration and of peaceful settlement, represented too by Havelok's distribution of land to his followers, 'His Denshe men to feste wel/Wit riche landes and catel' (2939-40). Though granted land in England, many of Havelok's retinue choose to return to Denmark (2952-62), and this must in fact have been a common arrangement in the early days of settlement.

More than any other so-called 'romance', *Havelok* communicates a sense of a society, a diversity of people together involved in the actions of just kings and faithless lords. One mark of this is the expression of social inclusiveness used first of the followers of Athelwold and then repeated five times throughout the poem:

Erl and barun, dreng and þayn,
Knict, bondeman and swain,
Wydues, maydnes, prestes and clerkes.

(31-33)

But even more significantly, these inter-knit ranks of society play a central part in the action through the career and the person of Havelok himself, as he moves through the social hierarchy from poverty to power, from 'cherles sone' (1093) to king, carrying fish, swilling dishes, and inheriting two thrones.[28] The poem ends with a vision of harmony throughout society, as people not only of different ranks but also of different ethnic origins witness the coronation in London, 'Henglische and Denshe, heye and lowe' (2946). With this formula, Danish and English, rich and poor, are finally integrated into one nation of England.

*Notes*

[1] *The Metrical Chronicle of Robert of Gloucester*, 2 vols, ed. by William Aldis Wright, Rolls Series (London, 1887). *An Anonymous Short English Metrical Chronicle*, ed. by Ewald Zettl, EETS [Early English Text Society] 196 (1935). The two parts of Manning's *Chronicle* are edited separately: part I (to Cadwalader) as *The Story of England by Robert Manning of Brunne, A.D. 1338*, ed. by Frederick J. Furnivall, 2 vols, Rolls Series (London, 1887); Part II as *Peter Langtoft's Chronicle*, ed. by Thomas Hearne, 2 vols (Oxford, 1725; reprinted London, 1810). References to part I are by line, part II by page.

[2] Ed. by G.V. Smithers (Oxford: Clarendon Press, 1987).

[3] See Rosalind Field, 'Romance as History, History as Romance', in *Romance in Medieval England*, ed. by Maldwyn Mills, Jennifer Fellows and Carol M. Meale (Cambridge: Brewer, 1991), pp. 163-73.

[4] Ed. by Diana B. Tyson, ANTS Plain Texts Series, 4 (London, 1987).

[5] Havelok is also mentioned in some versions of the *Short Metrical Chronicle*; see Zettl's discussion, p. lxxvi n. 2, and p. lxxxv.

[6] Hayden White, 'The Value of Narrativity in the Representation of Reality', in *The Content of the Form* (Baltimore, Maryland: Johns Hopkins University Press, 1987), pp. 1-25; quotations on pp. 4, 6, 5.

[7] A characterisation of the poem that Manning also uses (II, p. 26).

[8] Bede mentions two local Anglo-Saxon kings of that name, and St Ethelwold was well known in the east Midlands through his association with Thorney and Peterborough.

[9] See *Havelok*, ed. by Smithers, pp. lix, lxiii.

[10] The opening address of *Havelok*, 'Herknet to me, gode men' (1), is actually paralleled by the first line of the *Short Metrical Chronicle*, 'Herkeneþ hiderward ȝe lordlynges'.

[11] *The Brut, or the Chronicles of England*, part 1, ed. by F.W.D. Brie, EETS 131 (1906). The Anglo-Norman text is not edited, but Smithers prints from MS Rawlinson D.329 its account of Havelok (*Havelok*, pp. xxv-xxvi).

[12] Manning I, 7505-22. The source is Geoffrey of Monmouth vi.11, and ultimately the story of Dido at Carthage. For forms of Caistor/Thongcastle, see Kenneth Cameron, *The Place-Names of Lincolnshire*, 2, English Place-Name Society, vol. 64-5 (Nottingham, 1991), pp. 87-8.

[13] For much background information see J.W.F. Hill, *Medieval Lincoln* (Cambridge: Cambridge University Press, 1948), who says (p. 231 n. 1, p. 345) that the gallows stood on Canwick Hill to the south of the city. Hill also quotes an Anglo-Norman poem describing how St Hugh of Lincoln's murderer was dragged by horses to a gibbet outside the city.

[14] Noted by Judith Weiss, 'Structure and Characterisation in *Havelok the Dane*', *Speculum*, 44 (1969), 247-57.

[15] See especially G.V. Smithers, 'Four notes on *Hauelok*', in *So Meny People, Longages and Tonges*, ed. by Michael Benskin and M.L. Samuels (Edinburgh: Benskin and Samuels, 1981), pp. 191-209.

[16] See *Havelok*, ed. by Smithers, notes to ll. 178, 2608, 1179-80.

[17] Such association was a possibility. At any rate, more glorious figures of romance might be eagerly taken up by noble families in search of worthy forebears, as with the Beauchamp family's appropriation of the story of Guy of Warwick; on which see Emma Mason, 'Legends of the Beauchamps' Ancestors', *Journal of Medieval History*, 10 (1984), 25-40.

[18] See Hans-Dietrich Kahl, 'Einige Beobachtungen zum Sprachgebrauch von *natio* im mittelalterlichen Latein mit Ausblicken auf das neuhochdeutsche Fremdwort "Nation"', *Nationes*, 1 (1978), 63-108.

[19] For discussion of the theme of the Norman Yoke, see Thorlac Turville-Petre, 'Politics and Poetry in the Early Fourteenth Century: the Case of Robert Manning's *Chronicle*', *Review of English Studies*, 39 (1988), 1-28.

[20] Henry of Huntingdon, his source at this point, on the contrary says that the Danes occupied the land but afterwards died out: 'sed postea deperierunt' (*Historia Anglorum*, ed. by Thomas Arnold, Rolls Series London, 1879, p. 8). Robert of Gloucester immediately follows his comment with the remark that the Normans are still living among us.

[21] See Gillian Fellows Jensen, *Scandinavian Personal Names in Lincolnshire and Yorkshire* (Copenhagen: Akademisk Forlag, 1968), esp. p. xvii.

[22] See Edward Gillett, *A History of Grimsby* (London: Oxford University Press, 1970), p. 8; *Victoria History of the County of Lincoln*, ed. by William Page (London: James Street, 1906), ii, 161; Bruce Dickins, 'The Cult of S. Olave in the British Isles', *Saga Book of the Viking Society*, 13 (1937-45), 53-80.

[23] 'Viking Settlement in the East Midlands. The Place-Name Evidence', *Beiträge zur Namenforschung*, Neue Folge 23 (1985), 129-53; quotation on p. 131.

[24] Kenneth Cameron, private communication.

[25] See Christina Colyer and M.J. Jones, 'Excavations at Lincoln. Second Interim Report', *Antiquaries Journal*, 59 (1979), 50-91; cited in Cameron, 'Viking Settlement', p. 151.

[26] See the discussion by Smithers, *Havelok*, p. lvii.

[27] Illustrated in Smithers, *Havelok*, fig. 1; discussed pp. 160-7.

[28] On social stratification and mobility in the poem, see Susan Crane, *Insular Romance: Politics, Faith, and Culture in Anglo-Norman and Middle English Literature* (Berkeley, Los Angeles and London: University of California Press, 1986), pp. 40-52; and Sheila Delany, 'The Romance of Kingship: *Havelok the Dane*', in *Medieval Literary Politics* (Manchester: Manchester University Press, 1990), pp. 61-73.

## FURTHER READING

Reiss, Edmund. "*Havelok the Dane* and Norse Mythology." *Modern Language Quarterly* XXVII, No. 2 (June 1966): 115-24.

   Focuses on the character Grim, particularly concerning parallels, connections, and relationships to Odin in Norse mythology.

Smithers, G. V. Introduction to *Havelok*, translated by G. V. Smithers, pp. xi-xciii. Oxford: Clarendon Press, 1987.
   Extensive treatment that includes a survey of various manuscripts, alternate versions, sources, subject, date of composition, account of the language used, and bibliography.

# Petronius

## c. 20-66

(Full name Gaius Petronius Arbiter.) Roman novelist and poet.

### INTRODUCTION

Viewed by many critics as the first novelist, Petronius is the author of the *Satyricon* (circa 63-66), an episodic, satiric portrait of first-century Roman society. The *Satyricon,* only portions of which are extant, displays many different literary styles and its prose is interspersed with poetry, in some cases of considerable length. Its present fragmented state reflects its discontinuous plot, with one episode followed by another, and a host of appearing and disappearing characters. Scholars of the *Satyricon* have also noted that its realism and attention to detail make it an excellent source of information about its historical period. Because the *Satyricon* contains arguably pornographic content, critics have debated whether or not Petronius was a moralist: was he simply commenting without judgment on the scenes he depicts, or was he conveying his disapproval? Regardless of the answer, he is critically acclaimed for originality, characterizations, and mastery of comedy rich in parody, wit, and wordplay.

### Biographical Information

The famous historian Tacitus writes of Petronius in his *Annals,* and his account is almost all that is known of Petronius. Petronius's days were passed in sleep, Tacitus writes, his nights in business and pleasure. He was regarded as a man of luxury. But Petronius also demonstrated energy and ability as proconsul and later consul elect of Bithynia, and he was chosen by the Roman Emperor Nero to be one of his intimate associates. It is believed that Petronius began writing the *Satyricon* around the time he was befriended by Nero. By 63 he was the leading cultural figure at Nero's palace and was officially declared *elegantiae arbiter,* or arbiter of good taste. Nero, according to Tacitus, thought nothing charming or elegant without first consulting Petronius for his approval. This led to jealousy on the part of the ruthless Tigellinus, head of Nero's guards and a rival confidant. Tigellinus aroused Nero's suspicions concerning an assassination plot involving a friend of Petronius's, Flavius Scaevinus. Tigellinus bribed a slave to become an informer and threw into prison many of Petronius's domestics who could have supported his innocence. On his way to Nero, who was heading to Campania, to try to persuade him of his innocence, Petronius was arrested and detained at Cumae. According to the legend, Petronius opened his veins, but bound them up again, prolonging his death, only to reopen them while conversing with friends on light topics. On some of his slaves he lavished gifts; others he ordered whipped. He dined and then slept a little so that his suicide might seem more natural. In his will, Petronius fully described Nero's perversions, naming both male and female partners who joined him in his acts, and sent the report under seal to Nero. Then Petronius broke his signet-ring so that it could not be abused after his death.

### Major Works

The *Satyricon* is the only known work by Petronius. It appears to have been written to be read aloud, quite possibly as a court entertainment. The title likely refers to both satyr and satire. Although it is impossible to know for certain the length of the entire work, some scholars have estimated that ninety percent of it has been lost. Surviving are portions of eight major episodes comprising 141 short chapters, of which chapters 26 to 78 concern themselves with the "Cena Trimalchionis," or "Trimalchio's Dinner," which is the only complete episode. In addition, there are some thirty fragments extant. All portions appear to be from books fourteen, fifteen, and sixteen, but it is not known how many books were in the original; some scholars surmise that there may have been twenty, or even twenty-four, while others believe such a massive book very unlikely. The *Satyricon*'s setting shifts through southern Italy and the story is narrated by Encolpius, a Greek freedman who is the hero (some say anti-hero) of the story. Scholars have debated to what extent Encolpius's voice is Petronius's own. Because of the nature of the plot—an "amazing medley of riotous and indecent adventures," according to G. M. A. Grube—the *Satyricon* is difficult to summarize. It details the wandering adventures and misadventures of three intelligent rogues with no morals: Encolpius, his friend Ascyltos, and Giton, a boy. The centerpiece of the surviving *Satyricon,* the "Cena," depicts a banquet of the newly-rich, hosted by the multi-millionaire Trimalchio, who ostentatiously displays his wealth. For all their pretensions and airs, host and guests are revealed through their conversations and actions as ignorant vulgarians, wasteful and consumed with greed.

### Critical Reception

Critics have lavished praise on Petronius for his skill at

characterization. They have pointed out his modernity in revealing the essence of the characters through dialogue and action rather than by declarations of the author. The *Satyricon* has also been singled out for its variety: characters are rapidly introduced and as rapidly disappear, and the scenes and situations also change quickly. The work has also especially been extolled for its realism. Two areas of special interest to scholars are categorizing the *Satyricon* by genre and determining the purpose Petronius's purpose in writing it. The *Satyricon* defies traditional categorization: though many scholars view it as clearly a satire, others have insisted that it is not. It has been called the first novel, but others have asserted that it is not a novel at all. It has been viewed as mime, epic, picaresque novel, comedy, parody, Menippean satire, Milesian tale, erotic elegy, prose fiction, realistic novel, and various combinations of the above. Gareth Schmeling has contended that Petronius wrote each episode of the *Satyricon* in a recognizable format, thus one episode is picaresque, the next mime, another novel. Froma I. Zeitlin has pointed out that the *Satyricon* violates the notion that genres should be pure and contended that Petronius deliberately confounded readers' expectations. She has termed the style of the *Satyricon* a "synthesis of incongruous juxtapositions of styles and varying planes of literary suggestiveness which yield to and crowd in upon each other with a general effect of confusion." Scholars have much debated Petronius's stance in his novel, and the views that he is moral or immoral have each been vociferously defended.

## PRINCIPAL WORK

*Satyricon* (novel) c. 63-66

## PRINCIPAL ENGLISH TRANSLATIONS

*Petronius: Cena Trimalchionus* [edited by Martin S. Smith] 1983

*The Satyricon* [translated by William Arrowsmith] 1983

*Petronius* [translated by Michael Heseltine; revised by E. H. Warmington] 1987

*The Satyricon* [translated by P. G. Walsh] 1997

## CRITICISM

### Edwin W. Bowen (essay date 1903)

SOURCE: "An Ancient Roman Novel," *The South At-

*lantic Quarterly*, Vol. II, January to October, 1903, pp. 125-36.

[*In the following essay, Bowen summarizes the* Satyricon, *with particular emphasis on the section called "Trimalchio's Dinner."*]

Fiction is the all-prevailing form of literature today. There is hardly a civilized nation whose literature is not now dominated by the novel. In France, Germany, Italy, and Russia this form of literature is conceded to be supreme; and in England and America the tyranny of the novel is acknowledged without question. How long fiction will continue to reign supreme is a problem to which the future alone can give a definite and correct answer. There are some among us, however, who assume the role of the prophet and jauntily inform us that the novel is already doomed. An eminent French *littérateur* recently announced with all the gravity and authority of an oracle that within the next half century the novel will have become a thing of the past. The modern newspaper, it is surmised, is destined to supplant entirely the novel, whose territory it is already beginning to invade. It is an easy enough matter to venture such off-hand predictions and oracular vaticinations, but the world usually discounts them and takes them with many grains of salt. Such inspired predictions, like those of Cassandra, fail to create confidence and do not carry conviction to many minds.

The present tyranny of the novel has not been of very long duration. We do not have to go very far back in our literary history before we arrive at a period when the novel, far from being supreme, was almost entirely neglected. Yet the novel as a form of literary expression is of a hoary antiquity. We are all aware that fiction was known among the ancient Greeks and Romans. But the fiction of these nations took the form of poetry, for the most part, and very rarely appeared as prose. Yet a few Greek and Roman writers of fiction adopted prose as the medium of expression; and some fragments of their works of fiction have actually come down to us. All students of Greek literature are tolerably well acquainted with the so-called Milesian Tales. These tales are the earliest forms of prose fiction found in the literature of the Hellenes. This species of literary expression was cultivated by Aristides and others about the third or fourth century, B.C. As to the specific form of these prose stories comparatively little is definitely known, except that they were brief, witty, and more or less indecent. Now, whether the last named quality was an essential characteristic or a mere accident in the constitution of those novelettes which have survived the tooth of time, is a question we are not here concerned with. For I do not propose in the present paper to treat of the Milesian Tales in general, but simply and briefly to draw attention to a novel by a Roman author who wrote in imitation of these tales. It is interesting to note in passing that the Milesian

Tales were the prototypes of the romances which were so popular during the Middle Ages and are so widely disseminated among all the European literatures.

The Milesian Tales found their way to Rome through the teaching of Parthenius of Nicæa, a native Greek who taught at Rome during the first century, B.C. It will be recalled that this Greek scholar was a tutor of the poet Vergil and that his influence upon the Mantuan bard was so strong that the poet translated and published several of his teacher's poems, as, for example, the poem *Moretum,* which is frequently attributed to Vergil as its original author. Parthenius had a flourishing school among the cultured classes of Rome. He so impressed himself upon the family of the Cæsars that Tiberius, some years after Parthenius's death, had a bust of him set up in the imperial library. Young men aspiring to become men of letters affected to write in imitation of the style of Parthenius. One of the most conspicuous of his imitators was Petronius, the *maitre de plaisirs* of Nero's reign.

Of Petronius, or Gaius Petronius, to give his full name, very little is known. Indeed, the little information which we have is unsatisfactory and downright tantalizing. For we are not absolutely sure that the Gaius Petronius, mentioned in history as the *arbiter elegantiarum* under Nero, is the author of the novel in question which has come down to us. Gaius Petronius is the Petronius whom the skilful novelist Henryk Sienkiewicz has portrayed with masterly touch in his engaging "Quo Vadis;" and it is worth while to remark in passing that the sketch of Petronius given by the Polish novelist is, in all essential points, true to history. There is a brief but graphic description of Petronius found in the Annals of the Roman historian Tacitus. According to Tacitus, in the year 66 A.D. Petronius fell a victim to the dire jealousy of Tigellinus, the infamous court favorite of Nero, and in consequence thereof forfeited his life. In the strong summary of Petronius's life given in his Annals the philosophic Roman historian says: "His days were passed in sleep, his nights in the duties or pleasures of life; where others toiled for fame he lounged into it, and he had the reputation not, like most members of that profligate society, of a dissolute wanton, but of a trained master of luxury. A sort of careless ease, an entire absence of self-consciousness added a peculiar charm and grace to whatever he did. Yet while proconsul in Bithynia, he showed himself vigorous and capable. Then surrendering himself to vice, or simulating it, he became the boon companion—the arbiter of elegance—of Nero; and such was his influence and such his authority in all matters of taste that the emperor regarded nothing delicate or charming except what Petronius had first put the stamp of his approval upon. Thus the jealousy of Tigellinus was aroused against Petronius as the purveyor of pleasure and the rival of himself."

Tigellinus, whose influence with the dissolute Nero was unbounded, accused Petronius of being an intimate and confederate of the traitor Scaevinus; and he cut off all Petronius's means of self-defence by speedily arresting his slaves and throwing them into prison, so that they could not testify in behalf of their master's innocence. He then directed his attack upon Petronius himself, and he persuaded the suspicious and wicked Nero to have him arrested while he was accompanying the emperor on a journey to Cumae. Here at Cumae Petronius was placed under arrest at the command of Nero; and here anticipating the dire consequences of the displeasure which he had incurred, he deliberately had his own veins opened and thus took his own life. Some relate that, realizing that his life was forfeited, Petronius gave a grand banquet to his friends and at the conclusion himself arose and, in the presence of his guests, had his veins opened, meantime chatting with those around him as if nothing unusual were happening. Others say that he employed the interval between his arrest and his death in writing a satire upon the vices and debauchery of Nero and his profligate court, and sealed it and sent it to the emperor. Tacitus tells us that he made his will and that, contrary to the practice of those condemned to death during those times, he did not flatter the emperor or any of his corrupt court favorites, but satirized their vices, giving a description of each new kind of debauchery.

Such, in brief, is the portrait of Gaius Petronius, the Beau Brummell of Nero's reign, which the Roman historian has handed down to us. It is generally assumed by modern scholarship that this Petronius is the author of the interesting and entertaining Roman novel which has been preserved in Latin literature. This novel was published under the title of **"Satira"** and extended through sixteen books. Only fragments of it have been preserved to our time, and these are hardly sufficient to enable us to determine definitely whether the novel was strictly a novel with a plot or not. The **"Satira"** is more in the nature of a romance than a satire. It is a narrative in a brilliant style, a series of episodes strung together with no natural sequence or logical connection. The fragment preserved to us contains two very engaging episodes. The one is the famous story of the Matron of Ephesus, which is one of the most important of the Milesian Tales. The other is Trimalchio's dinner party, which is a masterpiece of comic literature.

Some scholars have contended that in the **"Satiria"** we have the scurrilous and drastic satire of Nero and his court which Petronius composed immediately before his death and sent to the emperor with his compliments. But this Neronian hypothesis rests upon a flimsy basis and has been almost entirely abandoned by scholars of the present day. For it is altogether improbable that Petronius could have written so voluminous a diatribe (the **"Satira"** originally contained at least sixteen books) against the emperor during the short interim between his arrest and his death; and even granted that Petronius could have done so, it is not to be supposed that Nero would have permitted such a book to exist without making an effort to suppress it. Moreover, there is much in the book which cannot, except by a strained and far-fetched theory, be interpeted as referring to Nero. We may, therefore, safely reject the Neronian hypothesis as untenable. But we are unable to determine the date of the composition of the **"Satira,"** except that it must have been written prior to the year 66 A.D.

The **"Satira"** seems to have lent itself readily to quotation during the period in the Dark Ages when Latin was little read and studied. For we find excerpts from it and allusions to it, comparatively frequently, in the works of the grammarians and scholars of those times, such as Macrobius, Servius, Lydus, Jerome, Fulgentius and Priscian. Moreover, there are known to be extant at least twenty-one manuscripts of the work, distributed throughout the libraries of Europe. This argues a tolerably wide acquaintance with the book on the part of mediaeval scholars. The language of the **"Satira"** is remarkable as being the *sermo plebeius*, i.e. the everyday speech of the Roman common people. Solecisms abound and there is much of what by convention is called slang. Yet the language is not uniformly vulgar or provincial. Sometimes it rises to the dignity and rank of classic Latin. But more frequently it is a mere vulgar *patois*, such as was heard only in plebeian circles of society and among the lowest classes of the imperial city. It was perhaps the unclassical character of the Latinity that induced a certain French scholar during the seventeenth century to produce a forgery and to attempt to foist the fraudulent manuscript upon the public. The language naturally offered a tempting bait to unscrupulous scholars to fill out the gap and make spurious additions to the fragmentary work.

Trimalchio's dinner party, which forms the greater part of the **"Satira,"** gives what we may presume to be a faithful picture of the typical life of the Roman *bourgeoisie*. It is a bit of character-sketching almost worthy of the pen of Dickens, and the humor is sustained throughout. It is a matter for regret that parts of it are coarse—perhaps indecent is the word that ought to be used—but we must bear in mind that the book is the product of an immoral age, when men's tastes, by overstimulation, had become jaded, and unusual and unnatural methods were employed to produce desired effects. The narrative reads like a twentieth century dime novel, or like what the English call a "shilling shocker."

Trimalchio is a grotesque specimen of the *nouveaux riches*. He is a man of obscure origin who was once a slave, but on obtaining his freedom he got a start in life and amassed a vast fortune beyond the dreams of avarice. He is a bald, red-faced, unlettered fellow, inordinately fond of ostentation and vulgar display, proud of his accumulated fortune, conceited and a gourmand withal. Yet he desires above all things to appear a man of literary attainments and takes the deepest pleasure in airing his scant erudition. But almost invariably, while masquerading in the attire of a scholar, he would show the cloven foot which betrayed him. His wife is Fortunata, a sharp, shrewd, lemonfaced little woman to whose frugality and thrift Trimalchio frankly confesses his indebtedness for a large share of his success. She is not so inordinately vain as her husband, and therefore she does not make such ludicrous blunders in displaying her knowledge. There are two companions of Trimalchio—Encolpius and Ascyltus—both of whom are invited, along with others, to the dinner party. The narrative of their experience is set forth by Petronius in a comic vein, remarkable alike for its racy humor and flashing wit. The details of the dinner are given in full—a dinner rendered conspicuous by its lavish profusion as well as its shocking lack of taste.

The guests meet at the magnificently furnished house of Trimalchio at the appointed hour, and the dinner begins. But the host, for some reason or other, does not appear at the sumptuous table when the guests all take their seats. He waits till the dinner is begun and well under way, before he enters the room and takes the seat of honor, which has been reserved for him. He thereupon informs his guests, presumably to compose them, what inconvenience he was put to, to keep his engagement to dine with them. After this speech he becomes utterly listless, and with a nonchalant air he falls to picking his teeth with a pin and then, by way of diversion, begins a game of checkers with a friend sitting next to him. According to the Roman fashion, a course of eggs is first served. But the guests are startled at the manner in which the eggs are served. For the eggs are placed under a wooden hen with outstretched wings sitting upon a tray; and, on breaking the shells, which are simply pastry, each guest draws out a plump reed-bird surrounded by yolk of egg, well seasoned with salt and pepper. At this juncture Trimalchio abandons his game of checkers and begins his dinner. Wine now commences literally to flow like water and is poured over the hands of each guest. Then wine-jars are brought in, containing "Falernian Opimian, one hundred years old" and are placed one at each plate. This elicits from the host the polite remark, addressed to the guests, "I did not put nearly such good liquor on my table yesterday, and yet the people who dined with me then were socially very much superior to you."

The next course served is one of all sorts of rich viands—capons, hare, sow's paunch, fish, kidneys, roast beef, meat pie, lobster, and goose. The guests, now warmed up by the copious draughts of the genuine old Opimian, begin to talk freely; and one of them for the enlightenment of Encolpius, undertakes a brief description, in an undertone, of the different personages at the table and intersperses his description with racy side-remarks about the hostess Fortunata. Trimalchio, too, lets his tongue wag and airs his learning amid the profuse display of his wealth. "Tell me," says he to one of those sitting near him, "do you remember the Twelve Labors of Hercules, or the story of Ulysses, and how the Cyclops twisted his thumb after he had been turned into a pig? When I was a boy I used to read these things in Homer; and with my own eyes I once saw the Sibyl at Cumae hanging in a great jar, and when the young men asked her, 'Sibyl, what do you want?', she said, 'I want to die!'," [I quote here and elsewhere from Professor Peck's admirable translation of **"Trimalchio's Dinner."**]

A slave serving grapes recites some of Trimalchio's verses to the company, and as a reward receives his freedom. Trimalchio suddenly rises from the table to go to the next room for something, and while he is away, the conversation becomes quite general. One comments on the trite topic of the weather and the shortness of the day; another deplores the practice of daily baths, which consume so much time. They fall to cracking jokes and telling anecdotes of friends who have lately died. One laments the degeneracy of the times and, *laudator temporis acti* that he is, revels in the reminiscences of the good old times when he was a boy, just come from Asia. One of the freedmen ventures to give his views on education, which I quote in part as showing the style of the novel.

"Well, Agememnon," says he, "you look as though you were saying, 'Why is this bore babbling?' Why, simply because you, who know how to talk book talk, won't speak at all. You don't belong to our set, and so you make fun of every thing a poor man says. I know you are cracked on account of your learning, but what good is it all to you? Some day I'll persuade you to come out to my country place and look at my humble dwelling. We'll find something there to chew on,—chickens and eggs—and it will be rather nice there even though the drought this year has burnt everything brown. Still, we'll find something to fill our bellies with. My little shaver is growing up to be a pupil of yours. Already he can say his table of four times; and if he lives, you'll find him a very faithful pupil, for when he has any time to himself, he never takes his head out of a book. He's clever and has good stuff in him, though he's crazy after pet birds. I've already killed three goldfinches of his and told him that the weasel ate them up; but he took up some other non-sense, and just now he's very fond of painting. He's just given Greek the go-by, and he's begun to take hold of Latin very well, even though his teacher is too easy-going and doesn't stick to one thing, but just comes and sets him a lesson to learn, and never wants to take any pains himself. I've also another tutor for him who doesn't know very much, to be sure, but who's very diligent and teaches more than he understands himself.

On the quarter-days he comes to the house and is perfectly satisfied with whatever you pay him. I've just bought the boy some law books, because I want to have him get a little snack of law for home use, for this is a practical bread-and-butter subject. The boy has really pottered over literature long enough, and if he doesn't care about it in the end, I've decided to teach him a trade,—either the barber's, or the auctioneer's, or else the lawyer's,—and then nothing but death can take it from him. That's why I say to him every day, 'My dear boy, believe me, whatever you learn you learn for your own good. Just look at Phileros, the lawyer. If he hadn't learned law, he wouldn't be able today to keep the wolf from the door. Why, not very long ago he was carrying around goods for sale, on his back, whereas now, he matches himself against Norbanus.' Yes, learning is a treasure; but still a trade never dies."

Trimalchio then returns from the next room whither he has gone, and the conversation wanes. But the dinner proceeds as before. A huge roasted pig is served, whole and apparently undrawn. The guests are amazed and sit with bated breath. But they are soon reassured when a carver comes in, and slashing right and left, opens the roasted pig and out come the well-seasoned sausages, tumbling over the dish. The astonishment of those at the table breaks forth into a burst of applause, and the host rewards the cleverness of his *chef* with the present of a silver crown and a cup handed him on a salver of Corinthian bronze. Trimalchio uses this occasion to deliver a lecture on Corinthian bronze and bric-a-brac in general, explaining to his entire satisfaction how Corinthian bronze was first made by Hannibal from the melting down of the metal taken at the capture of Troy. In his conversation Trimalchio gets his mythology wofully mixed, as when in reference to the relief work upon his cups he explains a figure of Daedalus shutting up Niobe in the Trojan horse, or the figure of Cassandra killing her sons. He next has a slave enter the dining hall and read the official report of what has happened on his estates the preceding day, in imitation of the Roman *acti diurna*. Then musicians and actors are introduced to contribute to the entertainment of the company.

During one of the performances Trimalchio is accidently struck on the neck by one of the acrobats. This furnishes him the inspiration for an epigram which he composes upon the spot and reads to his admiring audience. He also composes some verses which he recites and then proceeds to deliver off-hand a lecture on poetry. The guests now begin to feel the effects of their liberal potations, and two of them fall to quarrelling and pour forth a flood of choice Billingsgate, which Trimalchio as peacemaker at length succeeds in checking. A troop of declaimers in costume enter and recite from Homer. The host then tells the story of the Trojan war, according to its own version, which, I need hardly add, is a long departure from the accepted account. "Do you know what play they are acting?" says Trimalchio to one of the guests seated near him, referring to the troop of declaimers. "Diomede and Ganymede were two brothers. Their sister was Helen. Agamemnon carried her off and put a deer in her place for Diana, and so now Homer explains how the Trojans and Parentines are waging war. Agamemnon, you must know, came off victor and gave his daughter Iphigenia to be the wife of Achilles. Thereupon Ajax went mad, and presently now will show us the *dènouement*."

After further feasting the sumptuous and elaborate dinner is finally concluded, and the viands being removed, the guests fall to telling stories. Niceros relates as his story the interesting and realistic tale of the werewolf, and Trimalchio follows with a hair-raising witch story which he vows is actual fact. Though the werewolf story is somewhat long, I make bold to quote it because it illustrates Petronius's method and art as a story-teller and is itself one of the most notably realistic stories in all Latin literature.

"When I was still a slave," says Niceros, beginning his tale, "I used to live in a little street where Gavilla lives now. At that time, as the gods would have it, I fell in love with the wife of Terentius, the inn-keeper. You must have known her; her name was Melissa, native of Tarentum, and a very kissable girl, too. Yet there wasn't anything wrong in my love for her, but I just liked her because she had such nice ways. . . . As it happened, her husband died at his place in the country, so I tried by hook and by crook to get to her, for you know a friend in need is a friend indeed. As chance would have it, my master had gone to Capua to look after some wares; and so, seizing the opportunity, I asked the man who was staying with us to go with me as far as the fifth milestone. He was a soldier, as bold as hell. We set off about cock-crow, while the moon was still shining as bright as mid-day. At last we came to a cemetery, and my companion went off among the tombstones, while I took a rest, humming a tune and counting the monuments. Presently, when I looked at my companion, he had undressed and put all his clothes by the roadside. My heart was in my mouth, and I sat there like a dead man; but he walked around his clothes and all of a sudden was turned into a wolf. Now, don't imagine that I am fooling you, for I wouldn't tell any lies for the world. But, as I was going on to say just now, he was turned into a wolf, and began to howl and then ran off into the woods. At first I did not know where I was, but when I went up to his clothes to pick them up, lo and behold, they had all been turned into stone! Well, I was about ready to die of fright, but I drew my sword and all along the road I cut and thrust at every shadow until I reached my friend's house. When I entered as pale as a ghost, I almost fainted. The sweat was running down my crotch, my eyes were

fixed, and it was with the greatest difficulty that I was brought to. Melissa wondered at me to think that I was out so late, and she said, 'If you'd only come sooner, you might have been of some help to me; for a wolf has just entered the grounds and attacked our flocks and made them bleed like a butcher. He didn't get off unhurt, however, for one of my slaves struck him in the neck with a spear.' After I heard this I couldn't close my eyes; but as soon as it was bright daylight, I hurried home like a plundered pedlar; and when I came to the place where the clothes had been turned into a stone, I found nothing there but a pool of blood. But when I reached home, there lay my friend the soldier, in his bed like a stuck pig, with the doctor putting a plaster on his neck. Then I knew that he was a werewolf, and from that day on I couldn't have eaten a mouthful of bread with him even if you had killed me. I leave it to others to say what they think of this; but if I have lied to you, I hope your honors will have nothing more to do with me."

Toward the end a friend of Trimalchio's with his wife enters the dining-room and both sit down at the table. Trimalchio, moved by maudlin sentimentality, orders a slave to bring him his will, which he reads, and after giving the arrangements for his funeral, he begins to weep bitterly. At length he rises from the table and the guests follow him to the baths where they take a hot bath. The bath finished, they all proceed to another dining-hall where a second elaborate dinner is served. During this meal Trimalchio, by way of amusement, trumps up a quarrel with Fortunata, and throwing first a cup at her head, afterwards fires a volley of invectives and select vituperation, after which peace is again restored. The wine-jars are again filled. Trimalchio stretches himself out, full length, as if dead, and lying there invites the company to consider him as if lying in state and begs each one to say pleasant thigs about him as though he were actually dead. The hornblowers now play a funeral march over his body and so the dinner at last ends.

I have thus given a somewhat detailed account of **"Trimalchio's Dinner."** It is the longest and most important fragment of Petronius's lost novel, and illustrates the author's dramatic power and art better than any other fragment. It serves also to show us the breadth and compass of the Milesian Tale, as it grew and flourished after being transplanted from the genial soil of Hellas to sunny Italy. It shows us, further, the nearest approach, among the Greeks and Romans, to our own novel. After reading **"Trimalchio's Dinner"**—a mere fragment of Petronius's **"Satira"**—we are convinced that its loss forms no inconsiderable gap in the literary remains of the Romans, and we can but deplore the untoward accident, if accident it was, that deprived us of the missing parts of the novel. For the book is unique; and in point of vividness and dramatic power there is nothing comparable to it in the entire range of Latin literature. It is conceived along the line of the broadest humor. It abounds in wit and fun and is intensely human. We feel that it would almost do credit to the art of our own Fielding, the creator of Tom Jones and Amelia.

## Frank Frost Abbott (essay date 1907)

SOURCE: "The Use of Language as a Means of Characterization in Petronius," _Classical Philology_, Vol. II, No. 1, January, 1907, pp. 43-50.

[_In the following essay, Abbott explains how Petronius expresses both the individuality and culture level of his characters through their vocabulary, colloquialisms, pronunciation, word-formation, and inflectional forms._]

The character and culture of a man are revealed by his dress, his conduct, his attitude toward the world, by the subjects in which he shows an interest, and by his manner of speech, and upon the use which writers of fiction have made of these indications of character depends the clearness with which we conceive the essential qualities of the people whom they depict. Among the Latin writers no one has equaled Petronius, it seems to me, in the portrayal of character, and the purpose of this paper is to call attention to one method which he has used with great success in attaining his end. His book, especially the main extant episode, while not lacking in external incidents of lively interest, is essentially a character study. In holding the attention of the reader he relies less, for instance, than the other great ancient novelist, Apuleius, upon description. When Petronius gives us an account of the house or the dress of Trimalchio, the appearance of Habinnas, and the jewels of Fortunata, it is incidental to his main purpose. In Apuleius descriptions are freely given for their own sake, as the writer naïvely remarks on one or two occasions. The subjects about which people in the _Goden Ass_ and in Latin comedy talk, and the attitude which they take toward the world in their remarks, throw some light upon their character. This is true, for instance, of the miser and Thelyphron in Apuleius and of Pseudolus in Plautus, but the situation usually determines the subject of conversation and gives it its color. The tricky slave, for example, is bent upon thwarting the procurer, and his whole mind is centred upon this subject. But in Plautus, in Terence, and in Apuleius there is perhaps nothing quite comparable with the unrestrained flow of conversation at Trimalchio's table, where each speaker, with the cockles of his heart warmed by the hundred-year-old Opimian, talks about the things which make up the real interests of life for him and frankly states his optimistic or pessimistic view of gods and men. The gloomy philosophy of Seleucus, the rough-and-ready standards of Phileros, the querulous senility of Ganymedes, or the prosy optimism of

Echion comes out with marvelous clearness in the choice which each makes of a subject and in the sentiments which he expresses about it. But it is in the careful distinction which he draws between the speech of the cultivated and that of the illiterate that the pre-eminence of Petronius as an artist comes out most clearly. The people who figure in the _Satirae_ fall into two well-marked classes. In the first group are men like the poet Eumolpus, the rhetorician Agamemnon, the anti-hero Encolpius, and his attendant Giton. They all live by their wits and are unscrupulous and vicious, but they are all men of some education and taste, who are fairly versed in the practices of good society. Eumolpus was of course a professional man of letters; Encolpius is characterized as a _scholasticus_ (10), and remarks to Ascyltus _et tu litteras scis et ego_ (10), so that the writer represents them as men whose training would enable them to speak good Latin. Trimalchio and his freedman friends make up the other group. They are quite illiterate, as every one knows, and their conversation smacks of the junk shop and the stonecutter's yard. It is not easy in a brief space to bring out in its full significance the differences which Petronius makes between the language and style of the one set of men and those of the other, but a comparison of passages of similar length in which men of the two respective groups are talking will illustrate the point with sufficient clearness. I have chosen for examination the conversation running from p. 27, l. 37, to p. 31, l. 12, in Bücheler's fourth edition, and for comparison with it the two conversations which extend from p. 68, l. 9, to p. 71, l. 12, and from p. 73, l. 16, to p. 74, l. 16. The freedmen Dama, Seleucus, Phileros, Ganymedes, and Echion are talking in the first passage; Eumolpus, Encolpius, and Giton are the speakers in the other sections.

From these chosen pages I shall set down with very slight comment the words and phrases which belong to the people's speech and are at variance with formal usage. My sole purpose is to show one point in the technique of Petronius, to bring out the way in which he makes men of different degrees of culture reveal themselves in their language.

Taking up the passage from p. 27 to p. 31, and discussing, first, vocabulary, pronunciation, word-formation, and inflectional forms, we find that it contains the following colloquial elements:

a) Of words belonging exclusively to the plebeian vocabulary there occur _bucca_ (44), [The references are to sections.] _burdubasta_ (45), _caldicerebrius_ (45), _cicaro_ (46), _filix_ (45), _linguosus_ (43), _miscix_ (45), _merus_ (45) and _pullarius_ (43) with transferred meaning, _staminatus_ (41), _sestertiarius_ (45), _tertiarius_ (45), and _frunisci_ (44).

b) _baliscus_ (42), _balneus_ (41), _caelus_ (45), _fatus_ (42), and _vinus_ (41) appear as masculine nouns; _schema_ and *stigma* as feminines of the 1. declension, and *nervia* (45), and *librum* (46) as neuters. The occurrence of these nouns in *-us* and the assignment of Greek nouns in *-a* to the first declension, in the speech of the illiterate in Petronius, furnish one of the earliest indications we have of the elimination of the neuter gender in vulgar Latin (cf. Appel *De genere neutro intereunte in lingua latina*; W. Meyer *Die Schicksale des lat. Neutrums im romanischen*; Suchier "Der Untergang der geschlechtlosen Substantivform," *Archiv f. lat. Lex.* III, p. 161). The analogical nominatives *librum* (cf. *cultrum* for *culter*) and *nervia* (pl.) are like many similar vulgar forms against which the author of the *Appendix Probi* warns his readers.

*c*) The syncopated colloquial forms *bublum* (44), *caldicerebrius* (45), *calfacio* (41), and *cardeles* (46) need no comment. In the same field of colloquial pronunciation are *oricularios* (43), *percolopabant* (44), *plodo* (45), and *plovebat* (44). The forms *oricularios* and *plodo* attest a well-known vulgar pronunciation of *au. plovebat,* which from Festus (330. 29 Th. de Ponor) we infer is an archaic form, is one of the interesting cases in which popular Latin has retained a form which has dropped out of the literary speech. As for *percolopabant*, one may well ask if Petronius is not nodding here. We should not be at all surprised at hearing the unaspirated pronunciation from an illiterate Italian in Rome or northern Italy, but in Cumae, in the mouth of the Greek Ganymedes, like *tisicus* in 64, it seems to be a slip on the part of the author.

*d*) The favorite popular endings *-arius, -atus* (Stolz *Hist. Gram.*, pp. 424 f.), which are used eleven times in the *Cena* alone, *-ax, -osus, -im*, and the diminutive ending, are well represented by *pullarius* (43), *sestertiarius* (45 *bis*), *tertiarius* (45), *staminatus* (41), *abstinax* (42), *salax* (43), *linguosus* (43), *urceatim* (44), *bellus* (42), *servulus* (46), and *amasiunculus* (45).

*e*) *arguto* (46) and *verso* (41) perhaps show the colloquial fondness for iteratives, and *arguto* and *delector* (45), with an active meaning, illustrate the freedom with which deponent verbs admit an active form or vice versa in colloquial speech. *vinciturum* (45) is perhaps a clever plebeian attempt, like similar cases in Plautus, to distinguish the corresponding tense forms of *vinco* and *vivo*, while *diibus* (44) finds parallels in the plebeian inscriptions.

*f*) There are several interesting deviations from formal usage in the matter of syntax, and they are all indications of the breaking-down of the synthetic system which had reached such a high point of development in formal Latin. Of the prepositions those which take both the accusative and the ablative are most liable to confusion, and *fui in funus* (42) does not surprise us, since it is a short-hand phrase for the full expression "I went to, and was present at the funeral." The same careless brevity is responsible for the use of *foras* in the sentence *nunc populus est domi leones, foras vulpes* (44). *unus de nobis* (44), while not very unusual, is a precursor of the analytical form of the partitive expression. In twenty-five or thirty other cases in the *Satirae* the partitive idea is expressed by *de* or *ex* with the ablative. *prae literas* (46) illustrates a more general confusion of the accusative and ablative than *fui in funus* does (cf. Suchier *Archiv* III, p. 165). Analogy explains sufficiently *te persuadeam* (46), *meos fruniscar* (44) and *quod frunitus est* (43). The popular mind grasps the broad truth, with slight regard for the subtle limitations which the grammarian puts on it in practice, that the accusative is the case of the direct object, and this general principle it is likely to extend to any transitive verb in the language, and in this category fall *persuadere* and *frunisci*, although perhaps in the case of *frunisci* one may say that of the two constructions allowable in early times after *frui* and its derivatives popular speech retained the accusative, because this construction conformed to the general case usage after transitive verbs. In a similar way *aediles male eveniat* (44) is probably to be explained, although Bücheler regards the use of the accusative here as a Grecism. *male evenire* conveys an idea sufficiently transitive to justify to the popular mind the case commonly used after transitive verbs. *belle erit* (46) illustrates a colloquial usage common enough from the time of Plautus on. The indicative in the indirect question, *nemo curat, quid annona mordet* (44), and *quod* with the indicative for the accusative and infinitive in *subolfacio quod. . . . daturus est* (45), and *dixi quod mustella comedit* (46) are early instances of a deviation, common enough later, from formal modal usage.

From this brief examination of the favorite forms, words, and syntactical usages of Dama and his friends we come now to a discussion of their style:

*g*) They are rather fond of long words like *frunisci* (43) and *argutare* (46).

*h*) They are very free in the use of such epithets as *aediles trium cauniarum* (44), *sestertiarius homo* (45 *bis*), *burdubasta* (45), *loripes* (45), *discordia non homo* (43), *stips* (43), *terrae filius* (43), *servi oricularii* (43), *pullarius* (43), and *linguosus* (43). Of a complimentary character are *cicaro meus* (46), *fortunae filius* (43), *omnis minervae homo* (43), and *piper, non homo* (44).

*i*) Their favorite oath is *mehercules* (43 *bis*, 44, 45) which Cicero condemns (*Or.* 157) as an undesirable form.

*j*) *modo, modo me appellavit* (42), and the double negative in *neminem nihil boni facere oportet* (42), as I have tried to show in the *University of Chicago Studies in Classical Philology* III, pp. 72 f., are both instances of the colloquial use of duplication for emphasis. Perhaps *olim oliorum* (43) belongs to the same category.

*k*) A far more striking colloquial characteristic of the passage which we are considering than any of those thus far mentioned is the extraordinarily liberal use made of popular and proverbial expressions like *amicus amico* (44), *udi mures* (44), *pro luto esse* (44), *micare in tenebris* (44), *urceatim plovebat* (44) *serva me, servabo te* (44), *animam ebulliit* (42), and *habet unde* (45). In these four pages there are no less than seventy-five such phrases.

*l*) Equally noteworthy is the use by the speakers of asyndeton and of short, co-ordinate sentences and paratactical expressions. Some of these characteristics may be illustrated by a few lines from the remarks of Phileros (43): *plane Fortunae filius, in manu illius plumbum aureum fiebat. facile est autem, ubi omnia quadrata currunt. et quot putas illum annos secum tulisse? septuaginta et supra. sed corneolus fuit, aetatem bene ferebat, niger tamquam corvus*. The frequent employment of *nam* and of *et* merely as narrative particles to introduce a new statement, of which one case occurs in this passage (*et quot putas*, etc.), is characteristic of all the speakers of this group.

At pp. 68-71 and 73-74 it will be remembered that Eumolpus, Encolpius, and Giton are talking together. Using the rubrics adopted above, we notice the following colloquialisms: (*a*) *excanduit* (100) in a figurative sense; (*d*) *tremebundus* (100) with a favorite colloquial ending; (*e*) the colloquial phrases *quid ergo* (102) and *quis nobiscum Hannibal navigat* (101), although these expressions would not surprise one in formal Latin, and (*i*) the expletive *per fidem* (100). No other deviations from formal usage seem to occur anywhere in the four pages. The contrast, therefore, between the Latin which Dama and his friends use in conversation and that which Petronius puts into the mouths of his more cultivated characters is very striking.

To make sure that this difference in language is characteristic of the whole ***Satirae***, let us take another passage, this time of about two pages, in the Bücheler edition, including 26-30. The speaker is the narrator Encolpius. Of colloquialisms we find: (*a*) *unus* (26), perhaps used as the indefinite article; (*c*) the form *hoc* (26) for *huc*; (*e*) the favorite colloquial periphrasis with *coepi* in *errare coepimus* (27), *interrogare coepi* (29), *rogare coepit* (30), and perhaps *conaremur intrare* (30) should be mentioned in this connection, and finally (*h*) *deliciae* (28) may be noted, although the word is not uncommon in formal Latin. The few words quoted from Trimalchio in 26, and the brief remarks of slaves in 26, 30 and 31 have, of course, been left out of consideration.

If Petronius has not exaggerated the peculiarities of his freedmen, there is no piece of Latin literature which shows in so interesting a fashion the difference between the *sermo urbanus* and the *sermo plebeius*, and, what is more to our purpose, no writer has so clearly indicated the standing or the culture of his different characters in their speech as Petronius has done.

He seems, too, to give individuality to his characters by showing their fondness for certain words or phrases. Friedländer, in his edition of the ***Satirae***, p. 218, has already noted that *ad summam, recte,* and *curabo* with the subjunctive are favorites with the freedman Hermeros. In our first passage Seleucus, within a half page, uses *quid si non* twice, and both the cases of duplication noted above occur in his remarks. Seven of the eleven plebeian words are used by the rag-dealer Echion, while two of the four instances of *mehercules* are found in what Phileros says. Of the other two speakers Dama says too little to reveal his peculiarities, and perhaps the most marked quality of Ganymedes is his staccato style.

Finally it seems possible to detect certain differences between the styles of Trimalchio drunk and Trimalchio sober. Plautus has brought out some of the comic aspects of drunkenness in his plays. The sentimental, helpless attitude of Callidamates in the *Mostellaria*, and his thick-tongued utterance furnish one type of the drunken man; the sternly moral tone and the fluent discourse of Stasimus in the *Trinummus* illustrate the effect of stimulants upon a different temperament, but no Latin writer has made so interesting and accurate a psychological study of the effects of intoxication as Petronius has in the case of Trimalchio. Under the mellowing influence of the wine the host forgets his dignity as land-holder and *sevir Augustalis*. With the gradual change in his conduct and manner, which Petronius skilfully depicts, we are not concerned here. But his language, as well as his manner, undergoes a subtle change and loses the few suggestions of the polite world which it shows in the early part of the dinner. The admission of the cook and of the other slaves to share in the festivities (76) is typical of the frank relapse of Trimalchio's demeanor and speech to those of his former servile condition in life, and the gradual change in them is very cleverly indicated by Petronius; but it is a change whose subtlety can be appreciated only from one's own reading and not through an analysis made by another.

### Frank Frost Abbott (essay date 1909)

SOURCE: "Petronius: A Study in Ancient Realism," in *Society and Politics in Ancient Rome: Essays and Sketches*, Charles Scribner's Sons, 1909, pp. 115-30.

[*In the following essay, Abbott provides background on Petronius's time, credits him with being the creator*

*of the novel, and praises him for the modernity of his
realism, particularly with regard to characterization.*]

The Latin novelist, Petronius, of the first century of
our era, has been strangely neglected, as it seems to
me. In our latest, and in other respects our best, history
of the early novel even his name is not mentioned. It
is a perilous thing to discuss the work of an author
whose life and writings are so little known to the general public; and when even the professional student of
literary history ignores his existence, it is like flying in
the face of Providence. But the important position which
Petronius holds as the creator of a new *genre* of literature may properly justify the imprudence. Furthermore
the small circle of his admirers is likely to be enlarged
in the near future, since two good translations into
English of a portion of his work have lately appeared,
and he may at last be rescued from the obscurity in
which he languishes.

Perhaps it is not quite correct to say that the facts in
the life of Petronius are not widely known to-day.
Whoever has read the "Quo Vadis," of Sienkiewicz,
his great Polish follower in the field of prose fiction,
will know what manner of man Petronius was, and
many of us who remember the incident where the hero
of Quo Vadis purchases at the book shop of Avirnus
a copy of his **Satyricon** for a friend, Vinicius, bidding
him keep the author's name a secret, may wonder
whether the book has survived the wreck of the Roman
Empire, and, if it has, what its character and value are.
A part of it has come down to us, perhaps a fourth or
fifth of the entire work. In subject and in treatment it
is exactly such a production as one would expect from
the pen of a man like Petronius. The reader will remember in the novel of Sienkiewicz the closing hours
of the life of Petronius. The description is founded
upon fact, for it is based upon the pages of the historian Tacitus. After holding securely for a long time the
unique position of director-in-chief of the imperial
pleasures under the capricious voluptuary, Nero,
Petronius at last saw another supplant him in the
emperor's favor. Knowing that his days were numbered,
he decided not to wait for the inevitable sentence of
death, but, inviting his friends to dinner, he opened
one or more of his veins and passed away in the enjoyment of those pleasures to which he had given so many
years of his life; and it was characteristic of the man
that he bound up the wounds when the conversation
took a turn which interested him, and that, as Tacitus
tells us, he did not pass these last hours in discoursing
on the immortality of the soul and the teachings of the
sages, but in listening to the recital of gay and trifling
verses. This is the only information of present interest
which the ancients have left us concerning the great
Roman realist. Perhaps it would help us to a more
intelligent understanding of his work, to sketch in somewhat fully, as a background to this impressionist view
of Petronius, which Tacitus gives us, a picture of the

times in which he lived; but a few words must suffice
upon this point.

In the period of one hundred years which intervened
between the middle of the first century B.C. and the
middle of the first century A.D. Roman life and character had undergone tremendous changes of a social,
political, and religious nature. The beginning of this
period is distinguished by the completion of Pompey's
conquests in the East, and the consequent influx into
Italy of thousands of Greeks and Orientals, who
brought with them, to undermine the comparatively
simple life of the Roman, the standards of luxury of
the ancient and effete civilizations. Many of the newcomers were slaves, and the cheapness of their labor
soon drove the peasant proprietors from the country
districts of Italy to Rome, to swell the number of idle
men already in the metropolis. The Romans were quick
also to appreciate the opportunities which the Orient
offered them for making fortunes, and the Eastern
provinces were soon filled with Roman tax-gatherers,
traders, and bankers, who came back ultimately to
spend their money in Italy with all the prodigality
which the exaggerated Oriental ideas of luxury could
develop in parvenus. Political changes at home and
abroad in this period were almost as marked as economic changes. The brain and brawn of every citizen had been needed in the early struggles of Rome
for existence, and in her later contests for supremacy
with rivals like Carthage. But at the beginning of
our era Rome's enemies abroad were not to be
feared, and the men who protected her far-away
frontiers were no longer the citizens who left the
field and the bench, to return to them later with the
addition of those forceful qualities which come from
military discipline, but professional soldiers who
passed their lives in the provinces. In civil life the
emperor had gained so complete a mastery that there
was no longer any outlet for the political ambition
of the man of genius, nor any opportunity for the
average citizen to gratify his natural desire for a
part in the control of affairs. A religion with a strong
spiritual or moral tendency like Judaism might have
stemmed the tide setting toward selfishness and
materialism, but, as a writer upon morals has remarked, "the Roman religion, though in its best
days an admirable system of moral discipline, was
never an independent source of moral enthusiasm."
In the period which we are considering the Roman
had outgrown his religion.

The extension of his horizon, and an acquaintance with
more highly developed religious and philosophical
systems had shown him the narrowness and puerility
of his own faith, and as yet nothing had come to take
its place. As a result of the social conditions which
developed out of these changes men's thoughts were
turned in upon themselves, and their lives were given
over to the gratification of their personal tastes. The

# T. PETRONI ARBITRI
# SATYRICON,

Super profligatis Neronianæ tempestatis
moribus:

## COMMENTARIIS, SIVE EX-
## CVRSIBVS MEDICO-PHILOSOPHICIS:

Itemque NOTIS VNIVERSALIBVS & PER-
PETVIS recens adornatum.

IN QVIBVS DIFFICILIMA QVÆQVE LOCA, ATQVE

*à variis Interpretibus partim studio prætermissa, partim nequaquam
tentata, adamussim explicantur, illustranturque:*
EDITIO NOVA ET LOCVPLETISSIMA;

TAM MEDICIS, POETIS, QVAM PHILOSOPHIS, HISTO-
ricis, Oratoribus, Antiquariis, Philologis, Criticis ac Politicis vti-
lis ac necessaria.

ACCESSIT AD MANTISSAM SYLLOGE CLARISS. ALIQVOT INTERPRETVM,
*quorum in* PETRONIVM *Castigationes hûc-usque nondum editæ.*
NOVITER RECENSENTE

## JO. PETRO LOTICHIO, MED. D.

eiusdemque in Academia Rintelana P. P.

FRANCOFVRTI AD MOENVM,

Typis exscribebat Wolfgangus Hofmannus, Sumptibus LVCÆ JENNISI.
ANNO M. DC. XXIX.

*Title page of the 1629 edition of* Satyricon.

literature of the period reflected the temper of the times, as a literature always does. The age of heroic achievement which could furnish an inspiration to lofty flights of the Muse was past. The labored efforts of Lucan in writing an epic on the civil war, and the artificial tragedies of Seneca, illustrate this fact for the generation of Petronius, if any illustration is needed. It was a period of introspection, when each man's thoughts were limited to himself and those about him, when he had no share and no interest in the greater concerns of politics or religion or philosophy. The realistic romance dealing with the affairs of everyday life is the natural product of such a state of society, and it was in such circumstances that the great realistic novel of Petronius, which is also, I think, the earliest-known romance of any sort, saw the light of day. It is a significant fact that prose fiction made its appearance after every other independent form of literature in prose and verse had come into existence and lived its life, so to speak. The same statement may be made of the development of romance among the Greeks and in modern times. Prose fiction always seems to spring up in an imitative rather than in a creative literary period. As I have already said, only a portion of the work of Petronius is extant, but even the part left us forms an invaluable contribution to the literature of prose fiction, and furnishes a striking proof of the genius of its author.

The action of the story in its complete form, as the contemporaries of Petronius had it, took place in certain Italian and provincial towns. Three principal episodes of considerable length have come down to us, and in them the scene is laid in two Italian towns. Some one has said that our own novelist Howells was the first writer to reproduce accurately the local color of different towns within the borders of the same country. I am afraid that Howells's supporters must yield to Petronius his claim to this distinction. When one follows the hero in the novel of Petronius from the shores of the Bay of Naples, where the scene is at first laid, to Croton, in Southern Italy, he comes into an entirely different atmosphere. He passes out of the circle of Rome's influence. The provincial aristocracy of the little Campanian village, making its crude attempts to imitate the manners of the metropolis, gives place to the elegant depravity of a town which was essentially Greek in its mode of life; and the differences which existed between the two types of society are presented in so subtle a fashion that even a close student, like Zola, of the characteristics which society of the same grade shows in different modern cities might admire the result. The hero of the romance is a Greek freedman who lives by his wits. Gathered about him in the story is a picturesque group of adventurers, parvenus, tradesmen, professional poets, fortune hunters, and petty provincial magistrates. It is an interesting fact that in this novel of Petronius women for the first time, in so far as I know, play an important part in literature. The narrative literature of the earlier period deals mainly

with the doings of men and their relations to one another, and it is primarily addressed to men. A late writer has acutely surmised that the romance of chivalry was written for women, and that we owe to them the beginnings of the modern novel. What has just been noted of the *Satiræ* of Petronius would indicate the same origin for the ancient novel with equal probability.

In Greek and Roman epic and tragic poetry a primary motive was regularly employed which is not regarded as essential in modern literature; I mean the wrath of an offended deity or the unpitying action of fate. It is true that heredity in the prose dramas of Ibsen and society in many of the so-called problem novels of to-day serve the same dramatic purpose, but that element is not an *essential* one with us, and a modern author in composing a piece of imaginative literature would not feel bound to introduce it. We are likely, therefore, to forget that it *was* an essential factor with the Romans. Although he was creating a new form of literature, Petronius observes literary conventions in introducing this factor. The mishaps of his rascally hero are due to the anger of Priapus, who was as much an object of ridicule as of reverence among the Romans. The introduction of this motive and the choice of this god as the offended deity give a unity to the story, and make it a delightful satire upon the epic. The hero, Encolpius, driven by his rascalities from one town to another, becomes a realistic Odysseus. The book satisfies our modern conception of a novel, then, in having a well-defined plot, and it may also truly be said of it, I think, that each incident is a natural result of the action of two forces, the character of the hero and his environment. It must be confessed, however, that the development of the plot is not followed out as continuously in this ancient novel as it is in a modern one. Long episodes are introduced which do not help along the action, and the movement is frequently interrupted by literary disquisitions or by poems.

In one important particular the novel of Petronius stands apart from all ancient imaginative literature and takes its place by the side of our latest modern fiction: I mean in its realism. This is true of its individual incidents, of its portrayal of contemporaneous society, and of the way in which the various characters are presented. I have already mentioned the skill of Petronius in reproducing local color. But since the treatment is intensely realistic, while we have a true picture of a certain class, the romance of Petronius gives us a one-sided view of contemporaneous society, just as realistic novels of the same type do to-day. The realistic treatment which Petronius has adopted in his novel puts it in marked contrast to the early Greek romances, which appeared somewhat later. The Marvellous Things Beyond Thule is a fair specimen of these productions. The hero and the heroine in this story, Dinias and Dercyllis by name, after surviving perils at the hands of robbers, assassins, and magicians; after witnessing murders, suicides, and resurrections; having exhausted the possibilities of adventure from Hades to the North Pole—are finally transported to the moon to round off their experiences.

I am not aware that any one has called attention to the fact that the modern realistic novel made its first appearance in circumstances very similar to those in which the romance of Petronius was written. It is equally remarkable that in both cases the same phase of society is represented. The state of society in Spain in the sixteenth century, when the picaresque novel appeared, was the same as that of Italy in the first century of our era. In both countries the old aristocracy had disappeared, and a plutocracy had taken its place. The importation of slave labor had driven the peasant proprietors out of the country districts of Italy, while in Spain a similar result was produced by the heavy taxes which made agriculture unprofitable. The Inquisition in Spain, like the *delatio* in Italy, developed a spirit of suspicion and selfishness, and broke the ties which ordinarily bind men to one another. The ancient and the modern realistic novel grew in similar soils. The resemblance which the Spanish novel bears to its Latin predecessor is still more striking. Both are rogue stories; both are autobiographical; both are based on a careful study of society. Magic, the supernatural, and the element of perilous adventure are carefully excluded. The Spaniard as well as the Italian has made free use of the folk tale. His work, like that of Petronius, has a marked element of satire in it; and it bears the same relation to the romance of chivalry that the Latin novel bears to the epic. Such a marked resemblance in treatment would on *a priori* grounds lead one to think that Mendoza and Aleman found their inspiration in the Satiræ of Petronius, but there seems to be no reason for supposing that either of them was familiar with the work of the Roman. The Italian and the Spanish realistic novel were spontaneous products of a similar situation.

One of the fundamental principles of modern realism, as enunciated, for instance, by Zola and Howells and Garland, is that the characters of the persons concerned shall be revealed to the reader by their words and actions, without comment or explanation on the part of the author. This principle has been scrupulously observed by Petronius, and there is not a single instance in his novel where the artist destroys the illusion by obtruding his own personality into the scene he is painting. As for his characters, they stand out with marvellous distinctness—the roué Encolpius, the poetaster Eumolpus, the parvenu Trimalchio, and the shrewd housewife Fortunata. Even the minor characters are portrayed with as much clearness and individuality as the figures in one of Meissonier's pictures. Let me try to convey a feeble impression from Petronius's own book of his cleverness in portraying minor characters and of the humor and sprightliness of his dialogue. The scene is a dinner party given by a parvenu.

The guests are all or almost all freedmen, a rag merchant, a retired dealer in tombstones, an after-dinner poet, and men of that type. Conversation has become general under the mellowing influence of the Falernian, and the tedious, tactless Seleucus, who has just come from a funeral, discourses in a maudlin fashion on the insignificance of man in the economy of nature, and proceeds to describe in detail the last sickness of his friend and the scenes at his funeral, until the plain speaker Phileros cuts short his lugubrious tale by remarking that the dear departed would pull a copper out of the mud with his teeth, if he got a chance, and that, having lived seventy years and left a round hundred thousand, he ought to have been satisfied. Ganymedes, the pessimist of the company, has been waiting impatiently for Phileros to bring his remarks to an end, and with that delightful inconsequence which characterizes the conversation of men of his type begins a long lament for the good old times, when the worthy Safinius flourished, whose oratorical power depended not on the new-fangled arts of logic and composition, but on the strength of his voice. With the men of that time you could play *mora* in the dark, but as for our days—well, the less said the better, and in view of the prevalent dishonesty and irreligion it's no wonder that times are bad and that the gods are rheumatic when we ask them to come to our relief. But the rag dealer, Echion, has no such gloomy views of the Fatherland. It's all in the way you look at things. In fact, if you lived somewhere else, you would be saying that pigs walked the streets here already roasted. In reality the future is very bright, for Titus is going to give a show at the amphitheatre, and there's every prospect of a fight to the finish, and it won't be anything like the show which Glyce gave with his hamstrung gladiators, who were ready to drop if you blew at them. And so the dinner goes merrily on, until the host, whose vanity grows more evident, calls for his will to be read. The reading of the will draws forth such loud wails and cries of lamentation from the slaves, who have an eye single to their own advancement, that the local fire company supposes the host's house to be on fire and comes rushing in with axes and ladders. The dinner is brought to an inglorious end. All of this—and the whole story, in fact—is told with delightful cynicism, a sparkling wit, and with charming simplicity and lucidity of style.

Quintilian, the great Roman literary critic, confessed by implication that satire was the only new form of literature which his countrymen had produced, and critics of subsequent times have in the main accepted his *dictum*. It seems to me, however, that the Romans may successfully lay claim to the creation of prose fiction also. There is no earlier extant novel than that of Petronius, nor is there any reference in ancient literature to an earlier work of that sort, so far as I know, so that Petronius is at the same time the creator of a new *genre* of literature and the author of one of the world's greatest pieces of realistic fiction.

## Frank Frost Abbott (essay date 1911)

SOURCE: "The Origin of the Realistic Romance among the Romans," *Classical Philology*, Vol. VI, No. 3, July, 1911, pp. 257-70.

[*In the following excerpt, Abbott searches in other genres—including the epic, the serious heroic romance, the mime, and the prologue of comedy—for elements that could have influenced Petronius's composition of the first known realistic romance.*]

One of the most fascinating and tantalizing problems of literary history concerns the origin of prose fiction among the Romans. We can trace the growth of the epic from its infancy in the third century before Christ as it develops in strength in the poems of Naevius, Ennius, and Cicero until it reaches its full stature in the *Aeneid*, and then we can see the decline of its vigor in the *Pharsalia*, the *Punica*, the *Thebais*, and *Achilleis*, until it practically dies a natural death in the mythological and historical poems of Claudian. The way also in which tragedy, comedy, lyric poetry, history, biography, and the other types of literature in prose and verse came into existence and developed among the Romans can be followed with reasonable success. But the origin and early history of the novel is involved in obscurity. The great realistic romance of Petronius of the first century of our era is without a legally recognized ancestor, and has no direct descendant. The situation is the more surprising when we recall its probable size in its original form. Of course only a part of it has come down to us, some one hundred and ten pages in all. Its great size probably proved fatal to its preservation in its complete form, or at least contributed to that end, for it has been estimated that it ran from six hundred to nine hundred pages, being longer therefore than the average novel of Dickens and Scott. Consequently we are not dealing with a bit of ephemeral literature, but with an elaborate composition of a high degree of excellence, behind which we should expect to find a long line of development. We are puzzled not so much by the utter absence of anything in the way of prose fiction before the time of Petronius as by the difficulty of establishing any satisfactory logical connection between earlier forms of literature and the romance of Petronius. We are bewildered, in fact, by the various possibilities which the situation presents. The work shows points of similarity with several antecedent forms of composition, but the gaps which lie in any assumed line of descent are so great as to make us question its correctness.

If we call to mind the present condition of this romance and those characteristic features of it which are pertinent to the question at issue, the nature of the problem and its difficulty also will be apparent at once. Out of the original work, in a rather fragmentary form, only four or five main episodes are extant, one of which is the brilliant story of the Dinner of Trimalchio. The action takes place for the most part in southern Italy, and the principal characters are freedmen who have made their fortunes and degenerate freemen who are picking up a precarious living by their wits. The freemen, who are the central figures in the novel, are involved in a great variety of experiences, most of them of a disgraceful sort, and the story is a story of low life. Women play an important rôle in the narrative, more important perhaps than they do in any other kind of ancient literature—at least their individuality is more marked. The efficient motif is erotic. I say the efficient, because the conventional motif which seems to account for all the misadventures of the anti-hero Encolpius is the wrath of an offended deity. A great part of the book has an atmosphere of satire about it which piques our curiosity and baffles us at the same time, because it is hard to say how much of this element is inherent in the subject itself and how much of it lies in the intention of the author. It is the characteristic of parvenu society to imitate smart society to the best of its ability, and its social functions are a parody of the like events in the upper set. The story of a dinner party, for instance, given by such a *nouveau riche* as Trimalchio would constantly remind us by its likeness and its unlikeness, by its sins of omission and commission, of a similar event in correct society. In other words it would be a parody on a proper dinner, even if the man who described the event knew nothing about the usages of good society, and with no ulterior motive in mind set down accurately the doings of his upstart characters. For instance, when Trimalchio's chef has three white pigs driven into the dining-room for the ostensible purpose of allowing the guests to pick one out for the next course, with the memory of our own monkey breakfasts and horseback dinners in mind, we may feel that this is a not improbable attempt on the part of a Roman parvenu to imitate his betters in giving a dinner somewhat out of the ordinary. Members of the smart set at Rome try to impress their guests by the value and weight of their silver plate. Why shouldn't the host of our story adopt the more direct and effective way of accomplishing the same object by having the weight of silver engraved on each article? He does so. It is a very natural thing for him to do. In good society they talk of literature and art. Why isn't it natural for Trimalchio to turn the conversation into the same channels, even if he does make Hannibal take Troy and does confuse the epic heroes and some late champions of the gladiatorial ring? In other words, much of that which is satirical in the *Satirae* of Petronius is so only because we are setting up in our minds a comparison between the doings of these rich freedmen and the requirements of good taste and moderation. But it seems possible to detect a satirical or a cynical purpose on the part of the author carried father than is involved in the choice of his subject and the realistic presentation of his characters. Petronius seems to delight in putting his most admirable sentiments in the mouths of contemptible characters. Some of the best literary criticism we have of the period he presents through the medium of the parasite rhetorician Agamemnon. That happy phrase characterizing Horace's style, "curiosa felicitas," which has perhaps never been equaled in its brevity and appositeness, is coined by the incorrigible poetaster Eumolpus. It is he too who composes and recites the two rather brilliant epic poems incorporated into the *Satirae*, one of which is received with a shower of stones by the bystanders. The impassioned eulogy of the careers of Democritus, Chrysippus, Lysippus, and Myron, who had endured hunger, pain, and weariness of body and mind for the sake of science, art, and the good of their fellow-men, and the diatribe against the pursuit of material comforts and pleasure which characterized the people of his own time are put in the mouth of the same *roué* Eumolpus. These situations have the true Horatian humor about them. The most serious and systematic discourse which Horace has given us, in his *Satires*, on the art of living comes from the crack-brained Damasippus, who has made a failure of his own life. In another of his poems, after having set forth at great length the weaknesses of his fellow-mortals, Horace himself is convicted of being inconsistent, a slave to his passions, and a victim of hot temper by his own slave Davus. We are reminded again of the literary method of Horace in his *Satires* when we read the dramatic description of the shipwreck in Petronius. The blackness of night descends upon the water; the little bark which contains the hero and his friends is at the mercy of the sea; Lichas, the master of the vessel, is swept from the deck by a wave; Encolpius and his comrade Giton prepare to die in each other's embrace, but the tragic scene ends with a ridiculous picturè of Eumolpus bellowing out above the roar of the storm a new poem which he is setting down upon a huge piece of parchment. Evidently Petronius has the same dread of being taken too seriously which Horace shows so often in his *Satires*. The cynical, or at least unmoral, attitude of Petronius is brought out in a still more marked way at the close of this same passage. Of those upon the ill-fated ship the degenerates Encolpius, Giton, and Eumolpus, who have wronged Lichas irreparably, escape, while the pious Lichas meets a horrible death. All this seems to make it clear that not only does the subject which Petronius has treated inevitably involve a satire upon contemporary society, but that the author takes a satirical or cynical attitude toward life.

Another characteristic of the story is its realism. There are no marvelous adventures, and in fact no improbable incidents in it. The author never obtrudes his own personality upon us, as his successor Apuleius sometimes does, or as Thackeray has done. We know what the people in the story are like, not from the author's description of them, but from their actions, from the subjects about which they talk, and from the way in which they talk. Agamemnon converses as a rhetori-

cian might talk, Habinnas like a millionaire stone-cutter, and Echion like a rag-dealer, and their language and style is what we should expect from men of their standing in society and of their occupations. The conversations of Trimalchio and his freedmen guests are not witty, and their jests are not clever. This adherence to the true principles of realism is the more noteworthy in the case of so brilliant a writer as Petronius, and those of us who recall some of the preternaturally clever conversations in the pages of Henry James and other contemporary novelists may feel that in this respect he is a truer artist than they are.

One other characteristic of the novel of Petronius must be noted in this connection. It is cast in the prose-poetic form, that is, passages in verse are inserted here and there in the narrative. In a few cases they are quoted, but for the most part they are the original compositions of the novelist. They range in length from couplets to poems of three hundred lines. Sometimes they form an integral part of the narrative, or again they illustrate a point, elaborate an idea in poetry, or are exercises in verse.

We have tried to bring out the characteristic features of this romance in order that we may see what the essential elements are of the problem which faces one in attempting to explain the origin of the type of literature represented by the work of Petronius. What was there in antecedent literature which will help us to understand the appearance on Italian soil in the first century of our era of a long erotic story of adventure, dealing in a realistic way with everyday life, marked by a satirical tone, and with a leaning toward the form of the *prosimetrum*? This is the question raised by the analysis of the characteristics of the story which we have made above. We have no ambitious hope of solving it, yet the mere statement of a puzzling but interesting problem is stimulating to the imagination and the intellect, and I am tempted to take up the subject because the discovery of certain papyri in Egypt within recent years has led to the formulation of a new theory of the origin of the romance of perilous adventure, and may, therefore, throw some light on the source of our realistic novel of everyday life. My purpose, then, is to speak briefly of the different genres of literature of the earlier period with which the story of Petronius may stand in some direct relation, or from which the suggestion may have come to Petronius for his work. Several of these lines of possible descent have been skilfully traced by others. In their views here and there I have made some modifications, and I have called attention to one or two types of literature, belonging to the earlier period and heretofore unnoticed in this connection, which may help us to understand the appearance of the realistic novel.

It seems a far cry from this story of sordid motives and vulgar action to the heroic episodes of epic poetry, and yet the **Satirae** contain not a few more or less direct suggestions of epic situations and characters. The conventional *motif* of the story of Petronius is the wrath of an offended deity. The narrative in the *Odyssey* and the *Aeneid* rests on the same basis. The ship of their enemy Lichas on which Encolpius and his companions are cooped up reminds them of the cave of the Cyclops; Giton hiding from the town crier under a mattress is compared to Ulysses underneath the sheep and clinging to its wool to escape the eye of the Cyclops, while the woman whose charms engage the attention of Encolpius at Croton bears the name of Circe. It seems to be clear from these reminiscences that Petronius had the epic in mind when he wrote his story, and his novel may well be a direct or an indirect parody of an epic narrative. Rohde in his analysis of the serious Greek romance of the centuries subsequent to Petronius has postulated the following development for that form of story: Travelers returning from remote parts of the world told remarkable stories of their experiences. Some of these stories took a literary form in the *Odyssey* and the *Tales of the Argonauts*. They appeared in prose too in narratives like the story of *Sinbad the Sailor* of a much later date. A more definite plot and a greater dramatic intensity were given to these tales of adventure by the addition of an erotic element which often took the form of two separated lovers. Some use is made of this element, for instance, in the relations of Odysseus and Penelope, perhaps in the episode of Aeneas and Dido, and in the story of Jason and Medea. The intrusion of the love *motif* into the stories told of demi-gods and heroes, so that the whole narrative turns upon it, is illustrated by such tales in the *Metamorphoses* of Ovid as those of Pyramus and Thisbe, Pluto and Proserpina, or Meleager and Atalanta. The love element, which may have been developed in this way out of its slight use in the epic, and the element of adventure form the basis of the serious Greek romances of Antonius Diogenes, Achilles Tatius, and the other writers of the centuries which follow Petronius.

Before trying to connect the **Satirae** with a serious romance of the type just mentioned, let us follow another line of descent which leads us to the same objective point, viz., the appearance of the serious story in prose. We have been led to consider the possible connection of this kind of prose fiction with the epic by the presence in both of them of the love element and that of adventure. But the Greek novel has another rather marked feature. It is rhetorical, and this quality has suggested that it may have come, not from the epic, but from the rhetorical exercise. Support has been given to this theory within recent years by the discovery in Egypt of two fragments of the Ninos romance. The first of these fragments reveals Ninos, the hero, pleading with his aunt Derkeia, the mother of his sweetheart, for permission to marry his cousin. All the arguments in support of his plea and against it are put

forward and balanced one against the other in a very systematic way. He wins over Derkeia. Later in the same fragment the girl pleads in a somewhat similar fashion with Thambe, the mother of Ninos. The second fragment is mainly concerned with the campaigns of Ninos. Here we have the two lovers, probably separated by the departure of Ninos for the wars, while the hero, at least, is exposed to the dangers of the campaign. It was pointed out after the discovery of this find that the large part taken in the story by the carefully balanced arguments indicated that the story grew out of exercises in argumentation in the rhetorical schools.[1] The elder Seneca has preserved for us in his *Controversiae* specimens of the themes which were set for students in these schools. The student was asked to imagine himself in a supposed dilemma and then to discuss the considerations which would lead him to adopt the one or the other line of conduct. Some of these situations suggest excellent dramatic possibilities, conditions of life, for instance, where suicide seemed justifiable, misadventures with pirates, or a turn of affairs which threatened a woman's virtue. Before the student reached the point of arguing the case, the story must be told, and out of these narratives of adventure, told at the outset to develop the dilemma, may have grown the romance of adventure, written for its own sake. The story of Ninos has a peculiar interest in connection with this theory, because it was probably very short, and consequently may give us the connecting link between the rhetorical exercise and the long novel of the later period, and because it is the earliest known serious romance. On the back of the papyrus which contains it are some farm accounts of the year 101 A.D. Evidently by that time the roll had become waste paper, and the story itself may have been composed a century or even two centuries earlier. So far as this second theory is concerned we may raise the question in passing whether we have any other instance of a genre of literature growing out of a schoolboy exercise. Usually the teacher adapts to his purpose some form of creative literature already in existence.

Leaving this objection out of account for the moment, the romance of love and perilous adventure may possibly be then a lineal descendant either of the epic or of the rhetorical exercise. Whichever of these two views is the correct one, the discovery of the Ninos romance fills in a gap in one theory of the origin of the realistic romance of Petronius, and with that we are here concerned. Before the story of Ninos was found, no serious romance and no title of such a romance anterior to the time of Petronius was known. This story, as we have seen, may well go back to the first century before Christ, or at least to the beginning of our era. It is conceivable that stories like it, but now lost, existed even at an earlier date. Now in the century, more or less, which elapsed between the assumed date of the appearance of these Greek narratives and the time of Petronius, the extraordinary commercial development of Rome had created a new aristocracy—the aristocracy of wealth. In harmony with this social change the military chieftain and the political leader who had been the heroes of the old fiction gave way to the substantial man of affairs of the new, just as Thaddeus of Warsaw has yielded his place in our present day novels to Silas Lapham, and the bourgeois erotic story of adventure resulted, as we find it in the extant Greek novels of the second and third centuries of our era. If we can assume that this stage of development was reached before the time of Petronius we can think of his novel as a parody of such a romance. If, however, the bourgeois romance had not appeared before 50 A.D., then, if we regard his story as a parody of a prose narrative, it must be a parody of such a heroic romance as that of Ninos, or a parody of the longer heroic romances which developed out of the rhetorical narrative. If excavations in Egypt or at Herculaneum should bring to light a serious bourgeois story of adventure, they would furnish us the missing link. Until, or unless, such a discovery is made the chain of evidence is incomplete.

The two theories of the realistic romance which we have been discussing assume that it is a parody of some anterior form of literature, and that this fact accounts for the appearance of the satirical or cynical element in it. Other students of literary history, however, think that this characteristic was brought over directly from the Milesian tale[2] or the Menippean satire.[3] To how many different kinds of stories the term "Milesian tale" was applied by the ancients is a matter of dispute, but the existence of the short story before the time of Petronius is beyond question. Indeed we find specimens of it. In its commonest form it presented a single episode of everyday life. It brought out some human weakness or foible. Very often it was a story of illicit love. Its philosophy of life was: No man's honesty and no woman's virtue are unassailable. In all these respects save in the fact that it presents one episode only, it resembles the **Satirae** of Petronius. At least two stories of this type are to be found in the extant fragments of the novel of Petronius. One of them is related as a well-known tale by the poet Eumolpus, and the other is told by him as a personal experience. More than a dozen of them are inbedded in the novel of Apuleius, the *Metamorphoses*, and modern specimens of them are to be seen in Boccaccio and in Chaucer. In fact they are popular from the twelfth century down to the eighteenth. Long before the time of Petronius they occur sporadically in literature. A good specimen, for instance, is found in a letter commonly attributed to Aeschines in the fourth century B.C. As early as the first century before Christ collections of them had been made and translated into Latin. This development suggests an interesting possible origin of the realistic romance. In such a collection as those just mentioned of the first century B.C., the central figures were different in the different stories, as is

the case, for instance, in the *Canterbury Tales*. So original a writer as Petronius may well have thought of connecting these different episodes together by making them the experiences of a single individual. The Encolpius of Petronius would in that case be in a way an ancient Don Juan. If we compare the *Arabian Nights* with one of the groups of stories found in the Romances of the Round Table we can see what this step forward would mean. The tales which bear the title of the *Arabian Nights* all have the same general setting and the same general treatment, and they are put in the mouth of the same story-teller. The Lancelot group of Round Table stories, however, shows a nearer approach to unity since the stories in it concern the same person and have a common ultimate purpose, even if it is vague. When this point had been reached the realistic romance would have made its appearance. We have been thinking of the realistic novel as being made up of a series of Milesian tales. We may conceive of it, however, as an expanded Milesian tale, just as scholars are coming to think of the epic as growing out of a single hero-song rather than as resulting from the union of several such songs.

To pass to another possibility, it is very tempting to see a connection between the **Satirae** of Petronius and the prologue of comedy. Plautus thought it necessary to prefix to many of his plays an account of the incidents which preceded the action of the play. In some cases he went so far as to outline in the prologue the action of the play itself in order that the spectators might follow it intelligently. This introductory narrative runs up to seventy-six lines in the *Menaechmi*, to eighty-two in the *Rudens*, and to one hundred and fifty-two in the *Amphitruo*. In this way it becomes a short realistic story of everyday people involving frequently a love intrigue and told in the iambic senarius, the simplest form of verse. Following it is the more extended narrative of the comedy itself with its incidents and dialogue. This combination of the condensed narrative in the story form, presented usually as a monologue in simple verse, and the expanded narrative in the dramatic form, with its conversational element, may well have suggested the writing of a realistic novel in prose. A slight, though not a fatal, objection to this theory lies in the fact that the prologues to comedy subsequent to Plautus changed in their character, and contain little narrative. This is not a serious objection, for the plays of Plautus were still known to the cultivated in the later period.

The mine gives us still more numerous points of contact with the work of Petronius than comedy does.[4] It is unfortunate both for our understanding of Roman life and for our solution of the question before us that only fragments of this form of dramatic composition have come down to us. Even from them, however, it is clear that the mime dealt with everyday life in a very frank, realistic way. The new comedy has its conventions in the matter of situations and language. The matron, for instance, must not be presented in a questionable light, and the language is the conversational speech of the better classes. The mime recognizes no such restrictions in its portrayal of life. The married woman, her stupid husband, and her lover are common figures in this form of the drama, and if we may draw an inference from the lately discovered fragments of Greek mimes, the speech was that of the common people. Again, the new comedy has its limited list of stock characters—the old man, the tricky slave, the parasite, and the others which we know so well in Plautus and Terence, but as for the mime, any figure to be seen on the street may find a place in it—the rhetorician, the soldier, the legacy hunter, the innkeeper, or the town crier. The doings of kings and heroes were parodied. We are even told that a comic Hector and Achilles were put on the stage, and the gods did not come off unscathed. All of these characteristic features of the mine remind us in a striking way of the novel of Petronius. His work, like the mime, is a realistic picture of low life which presents a great variety of characters, and shows no regard for conventional morals. It is especially interesting to notice the element of parody, which we have already observed in Petronius, in both kinds of literary productions. The theory that Petronius may have had the composition of his *Satirae* suggested to him by plays of this type is greatly strengthened by the fact that the mime reached its highest point of popularity at the court in the time of Nero, in whose reign Petronius lived. In point of fact Petronius refers to the mime frequently. One of these passages is of peculiar significance in this connection. Encolpius and his comrades are entering the town of Croton and are considering what device they shall adopt so as to live without working. At last a happy idea occurs to Eumolpus and he says "why don't we construct a mime?" and the mime is played, with Eumolpus as a fabulously rich man at the point of death, and the others as his attendants. The role makes a great hit, and all the vagabonds in the company play their assumed parts in their daily life at Croton with such skill that the legacy hunters of the place load them with attentions and shower them with presents. This whole episode in fact may be thought of as a mime cast in the narrative form, and the same conception may be applied with great plausibility to the entire story of Encolpius.

We have thus far been attacking the question with which we are concerned from the side of the subject-matter and tone of the story of Petronius. Another method of approach is suggested by the Menippean Satire,[5] the best specimens of which have come down to us in the fragments of Varro, one of Cicero's contemporaries. These satires are an olla podrida, dealing with all sorts of subjects in a satirical manner, sometimes put in the dialogue form, and cast in a *mélange* of prose and verse. It is this last characteristic which is of special interest to us in this connection, because in the prose of Petronius verses are freely used. Occasionally the verses in the *Satirae* are quoted from another source, but usually they are the compositions of Petronius himself. If it were not aside from our immediate purpose it would be interesting to follow the history of this prose-poetical form from the time of Petronius on. After him it does not seem to have been used very much until the third and fourth centuries of our era. However, Martial in the first century prefixed a prose prologue to five books of his *Epigrams*, and one of these prologues ends with a poem of four lines. The several books of the *Silvae* of Statius are also preceded by prose letters of dedication. That strange imitation of the *Aulularia* of Plautus of the fourth century, the *Querolus*, is in a form half prose and half verse. A sentence begins in prose and runs off into verse, as some of the epitaphs also do. The *Epistles* of Ausonius of the same century are compounded of prose and a great variety of verse. By the fifth and sixth centuries a *mélange* of verse or a combination of prose and verse is very common, as one can see in the writings of Martianus Capella, Sidonius Apollinaris, Ennodius, and Boethius. It recurs again in modern times, for instance, in Dante's *La Vita Nuova*, in Boccaccio, *Aucassin et Nicollette*, the *Heptameron*, the *Celtic Ballads*, the *Arabian Nights*, and in *Alice in Wonderland*. A little thought suggests that it is not an unnatural medium of expression. A change from prose to verse or from one form of verse to another suggests a change in the emotional condition of a speaker or writer. We see that clearly enough illustrated in tragedy or comedy. In the thrilling scene in the *Captives* of Plautus, for example, where Tyndarus is in mortal terror lest the trick which he has played on his master, Hegio, may be discovered and he be consigned to work in chains in the quarries, the verse is the trochaic septenarius. As soon as the suspense is over it drops to the iambic senarius. If we should arrange the commoner Latin verses in a sequence according to the emotional effects which they produced, at the bottom of the series would stand the iambic senarius. Above that would come trochaic verse, and we should rise to higher planes of exaltation as we read the anapaestic, or cretic, or bacchiac. The greater part of life is commonplace. Consequently the common medium for conversation or for the narrative in a composition like comedy made up entirely of verse is the senarius. Now this form of verse in its simple, almost natural, quantitative arrangement is very close to prose, and it would be a short step to substitute prose for it as the basis of the story, interspersing verse here and there to secure variety, or when the emotions were called into play, just as lyric verses are interpolated in the iambic narrative. In this way the combination of different kinds of verse in the drama, and the prosimetrum of the Menippean Satire and of Petronius may be explained, and we see a possible line of descent from comedy and this form of satire to the *Satirae*.

These various theories of the origin of the romance of Petronius—that it may be related to the epic, to the serious heroic romance, to the bourgeois story of adventure developed out of the rhetorical exercise, to the Milesian tale, to the prologue of comedy, to the verse-*mélange* of comedy or the mime, or to the prose-poetical Menippean satire—are not, of necessity, it seems to me, mutually exclusive. His novel may well be thought of as a parody of the serious romance, with frequent reminiscences of the epic, a parody suggested to him by comedy and its prologue, by the mime, or by the short cynical Milesian tale, and cast in the form of the Menippean satire, or, so far as subject-matter and realistic treatment are concerned, the suggestion may have come directly from the mime, and if we can accept the theory of some scholars, who have lately studied the mime, that it sometimes contained both prose and verse, we may be inclined to regard that type of literature as the immediate progenitor of the novel even in the matter of external form, and leave the Menippean satire out of the line of descent. Whether the one or the other of these explanations of its origin recommends itself to us as probable or not, it is interesting to note, as we leave the subject, that, so far as our present information goes, the realistic romance seems to have been the invention of Petronius.

### Notes

[1] Cf. Schmid, "Der griechische Roman," *Neue Jahrb.*, Bd. XIII (1904), 465-85; Wilcken, in *Hermes* XXVIII, 161 ff., and in *Archiv f. Papyrusforschung* I, 255 ff.; Grenfell-Hunt *Fayûm Towns and Their Papyri* (1900) 75 ff. and *Rivista di Filologia* XXIII, 1 ff.

[2] Some of the important late discussions of the Milesian tale are by Bürger *Hermes* (1892) 351 ff.; Norden *Die antike Kunstprosa* II, 602, 604 n.; Rohde *Kleine Schriften* II, 25 ff.; Bürger *Studien zur Geschichte d. griech. Romans* I (*Programm von Blankenburg a. H.* 1902); W. Schmid *Neue Jahrb. f. d. klass. Alt.* (1904) 474 ff.; Lucas, "Zu den Milesiaca des Aristides," *Philologus* 61 (1907), 16 ff.

[3] On the origin of the *prosimetrum* cf. Hirzel *Der Dialog* 381 ff.; Norden *Die Antike Kunstprosa* 755.

[4] Cf. Rosenblüth *Beiträge zur Quellenkunde von Petrons Satiren* (Berlin, 1909).

[5] This theory in the main is suggested by Rohde *Der griechische Roman*[2] 267 (Leipzig, 1900) and by Ribbeck *Geschichte d. röm. Dichtung*[2] III, 150.

### Keith Preston (essay date 1915)

SOURCE: "Some Sources of Comic Effect in Petronius," *Classical Philology*, Vol. X, No. 3, July, 1915, pp. 257-70.

*[In the following essay, Preston examines some of the techniques and devices used by Petronius for comic effect, including surprise, buffoonery, intoxication, and the continual introduction of new characters.]*

The relation of Petronius to comedy is a subject which has already engaged the attention of scholars. In his very valuable studies on the literary sources of Petronius, Collignon[1] devotes considerable space to this topic. Starting with a collection of all explicit references to drama, in the *Satiricon*, the more significant of which have to do with the mime, he proceeds to examine the literary material of his author for points of resemblance to the mime and the new comedy. His comparison shows, quite conclusively, that Petronius was very greatly influenced by the former; as for the new comedy, at least in so far as it is represented by Plautus and Terence, Collignon finds but few parallels.

The influence of the mime on Petronius can, in truth, hardly be exaggerated. Reich,[2] in his somewhat sweeping manner, asserts the intimate connection between mime and the *Satiricon*. Thomas[3] has some excellent remarks on the same subject, and Rosenblüth in his work on the sources of Petronius[4] rehearses and considerably augments the material collected by Collignon. As regards such matters as explicit reference to mime and comedy, resemblances in language and style to such fragments as we have of mime, typical characters, and episodes, and the element of parody which is common to Petronius and the mime, the studies referred to above, particularly those of Collignon and Rosenblüth, are fairly complete. I wish, then, in the present paper, to accept their conclusions in regard to mime and Petronius, and discuss mainly some matters of technique in the handling of comic episodes which will bear further emphasis.

There is apparent, at the outset, a certain regularity about Petronius' treatment of comic episodes, and a repetition of several recognized devices for farcical effect. The thesis that Petronius was writing mainly for comic effect needs no defense; in fact, through one of his characters, he voices the feeling that tragic episodes, except for purposes of parody, are quite against the proprieties in this comedy of low life. Cf. Petr. 80. 3 where Giton, interposing himself as peacemaker between his jealous admirers, who are on the point of engaging in a sword fight, "petebatque suppliciter ne Thebanum par humilis taberna spectaret."[5] It is not detracting from Petronius, who has shown his powers of restrained and subtle humor in many places, to say that he conceived of himself primarily as a [*gelotopoidos*], and that there is a decided element of the theatrical in his constant insistence upon laughter and applause. The humor of an incident is not left to make its own appeal to the reader; we are told that it provoked "gales of laughter," or "bursts" of applause. Thus *risus* and *plausus* are combined: 11. 2, risu plausuque; 18. 7, complosis manibus in tantum repente risum effusa; 20. 6, ancilla risu meo prodita complosit manus; 36. 4, damus plausum. . . . et res. . . . ridentes aggredimur; cf. for plausus only, 50. 1, 68. 6. As for *risus*, we find such strong expressions as: 24. 5, Giton et risu dissolvebat ilia sua; 57. 1, usque ad lacrimas rideret; 20. 7, non indecenti risu latera commovit; 58. 1, risum iam diu compressum etiam indecenter effudit; 140. 10, ingenti risu; 10. 3, diffusi in risum. The number of times which *risus, rideo,* etc., recur in Petronius is striking; cf. Segebade and Lommatzsch, *Lexicon Petronianum, s.v.* Nowhere else in Latin literature is such a premium put upon laughter; indeed, the conventional Roman attitude with reference to hearty laughter as related to *gravitas* may be seen from Quint. vi. 3. 8: risus res levis et quae ab scurris et mimis moveatur. I believe that Thomas[6] makes a very acute observation when he says that the keynote of the **Satiricon** is struck in Petronius 19. 1: omnia mimico risu exsonuerant.

More significant still, for comparison with farce, is the manner in which the author accelerates action toward the close of an episode, if several characters are on the scene, engaging everyone in a free-for-all, or ending the incident abruptly by the rapid exit of one of the principals, accompanied often by a slamming of doors. These swift disappearances are particularly characteristic; in fact, Encolpius and his associates seem always to be leaving the stage on the dead run; cf. 6. 2: subduxi me et cursim Ascylton persequi coepi; 15.8: praecipites abimus praeclusisque foribus ridere. . . . operuit 90. 1: et ille. . . . operuit caput extraque templum profugit; 91. 3: extraho Gitona raptimque in hospitium meum pervolo. Praeclusis deinde foribus; 94. 7; continuo limen egressus adduxit repente ostium cellae et ad Gitona investigandum cucurrit; 138. 3: aniculae. . . . per aliquot vices secutae fugientem "prende furem" clamant, evasi tamen omnibus digitis inter praecipitem decursam cruentatis. That type of farcical climax in which every character is engaged in frenzied activity is seen to great advantage in the mimic marriage, Petr. 26, in itself a theme that had probably been treated on the stage.[7] It is hardly possible to dwell on the details of this picture, but the desired effects are skilfully produced. The same may be said of the even more objectionable passage, Petr. 140 f. To make possible description of events in progress on either side of a closed door, Petronius has them watched through a keyhole or chink; cf. 26. 4, 96. 1, 140. 11. This was a favorite stage device.[8]

Out-and-out buffoonery of a mild and a more drastic order is, of course, inseparable from this sort of farce. Blows (*verbera*) are not uncommon; cf. 11. 4: lorum de pera solvit et me coepit non perfunctorie verberare; 79. 11: verberibus excitavi; cf. also 15. 1: misit in faciem Ascylti tunicam; 95. 5: urceolum fictilem in

Eumolpi caput iaculatus est, solvitque clamantis frontem et de cella se proripuit. The grand mêlée or fracas in which everybody engages is another example of the kind of climax noted above; cf. Eumolpus' encounter with the insularii, Petr. 95. 7-9, and the combat on shipboard, 108. 7-13. The breaking of dishes is more than once employed for comic effect; cf. 22. 3, 64. 10, 70. 5. At 53. 11 of the Cena the fall of a mountebank from his ladder is disastrous to Trimalchio, and in 136. 1-3, Oenothea's tumble from a rickety stool is described with an evident straining after comic effect: fracta est putris sella, quae staturae altitudinem adiecerat, anumque pondere suo deiectum super foculum mittit. frangitur ergo cervix cucumelae ignemque modo convalescentem restinguit. vexat cubitum ipsa stipiti ardenti faciemque totam excitato cinere perfundit. consurrexi equidem turbatus anumque non sine risu erexi. For similar mischances cf. the enforced bath of Ascyltos and Encolpius, 72. 7-8, and the humiliation of Fortunata, 67. 12.

In the series of detached and more or less independent episodes that make up what remains to us of the *Satiricon*, the most extended, the most interesting, and the most complete in itself is the *Cena Trimalchionis*. The *Cena* is, to all intents and purposes, a literary mime, yet it preserves the same dramatic qualities that we have noted in other parts of the **Satiricon**. As a literary mime, it may be compared with Theocritus 15, where we have, as in the *Cena*, a change of scene within the mime, and, to a less degree than in Petronius, the introduction of new characters. The *Cena* compares also with Herondas and Theocritus, and other authors of the literary mime, in many points of language and style which have been adequately discussed elsewhere.[9] For present purposes, the thing to be observed is the way in which Petronius gives life, movement, and a dramatic climax to what might naturally have been a more or less stationary picture.

The element of surprise is of course important, and, in this connection, the culinary conceits of Trimalchio and his cooks have a special value. We are not to suppose that banquets, even parvenu banquets, were featured by such extravagances, nor can we assume that these bizarre devices are lugged in by Petronius merely for satirical effect. The attitude of the reader must be that of Encolpius, exasperated appreciation; these things are cheaply sensational, it is true, but they are successful sensations, and the animated menu is not the least feature in the interest of the *Cena*. Quite in line with such devices is the continual introduction of new entertainers, new slaves, new guests (Habinnas and Scintilla), and new demonstrations from the musical *familia* of Trimalchio, which Encolpius compares to the chorus of a pantomime: Petr. 31. 7: pantomimi chorum, non patris familiae triclinium crederes. One of the stock subjects of imitation in mime was intoxication,[10] a source of humor which was not neglected also in the new comedy, as in Plaut. *Most.* 315ff.; *Pseud.* 1285 ff.; and elsewhere. This kind of comic effect is handled with particular skill in the *Cena*; the vinous exaltation of Trimalchio and his guests, increasing by slow but clearly indicated stages, gradually speeds up the action of the piece and culminates in the turbulent finale, where Trimalchio invites the celebration of his own funeral—"consonuere cornicines funebri strepitu— unus praecipue servus libitinarii illius qui inter hos honestissimus erat tam valde intonuit ut totam concitaret viciniam. itaque vigiles qui custodiebant vicinam regionem, rati ardere Trimalchionis domum, effregerunt ianuam subito et cum aqua securibusque tumultuari suo iure coeperunt. nos occasionem opportunissimam nacti Agamemnoni verba dedimus raptimque tam plane quam ex incendio fugimus." Cf. Cicero *Pro Caelio* 65: mimi ergo est exitus, non fabulae, in quo cum clausula non invenitur, fugit aliquis e manibus, deinde scabillae concrepant, aulaeum tollitur.

A more drastic form of buffoonery is that phallic element, which is so pronounced in the **Satiricon** (cf. particularly 129. 1, 92. 9-11, 108. 10, 132, 140), and which seems almost certainly traceable, in part at least, to the mime.[11] The scene of the **Satiricon** is laid in Southern Italy. It is a probable inference that some part of the action, at least, was placed at Tarentum, to which city the ship of Lichas, himself a Tarentine (100. 7), was conveying the principal characters at the time of the shipwreck (cf. 101. 1). Other references to Tarentum, 38. 2, 61. 6, 48. 2, seem to indicates a predilection for that city on the part of Petronius, or at least a special familiarity with it. In view of this, we must allow a considerable importance to the fact that the type of mime that flourished most in this locale is known to have been distinctly phallic in character.[12] It is extremely unlikely that Petronius, in a work so evidently designed to win popular favor, went very far beyond the standards to which·his intended public was accustomed; if he was writing for a public that had been educated down to such frank buffoonery by long familiarity with a coarsened stage, the phallic element in Petronius may be easily explained. For comparison with mime, it is worth noting that the interest, in most of these scenes, is not sensual, but comic, and the comic effects, as in other episodes, are very largely those of surprise, misadventure, and personal humiliation.

The fact that one set of characters is carried through the loose adventures of the **Satiricon**, the continued attachment between Encolpius and Giton, and the part that jealousy plays in this attachment, have been made grounds for the hypothesis that the work of Petronius was modeled upon a lost genre of Greek satirical romances, which were a parody of the serious romances of love. This theory, proposed and defended with considerable ingenuity by Heinze, is subscribed to by Thomas.[13] Aside from the inherent improbability that all trace of such Greek originals should have been lost,

the **Satiricon** fails to reveal any consistent scheme of parody on the serious Greek romances as we know them. The mere fact that "l'amour Grec" is the central theme in the **Satiricon** would hardly have impressed the reading public of Petronius' time as a delicious parody of the Greek romance, for the same theme inspired countless poems in Greek and roman literature where no one would suspect parody, and, for all we know, may also have been the subject of serious romances. I fail to see a refinement of parody in the fact that, in contrast to the persistently faithful lovers of Longus, Achilles Tatius, and their school, we have a pair who are persistently and consistently unfaithful. The spasmodic jealousy of Encolpius is humorous only where it results, as it frequently does, in his personal discomfiture; in this he corresponds to what we know of the zelotypus as a recognized type in mime and comedy; cf. Juv. 8. 197, Zelotypus Thymeles, stupidi collega Corinthi. As for the wrath of Priapus, this is undoubtedly parody, but it is parody of a sort that was familiar to the mime and intimately connected with the phallic element therein.[14] In general, it is clear that the sex interest in the main narrative of Petronius is incidental to a sort of rough phallic comedy. A close analysis of episodes is unnecessary, but their tone may be amply explained by assuming that in writing them the author was conforming to the conventions of an impure type of farce.[15]

For the literary relationship between Petronius and the mime, such points of technique, though less tangible than some other considerations, are perhaps safer and more certain in the end. Insistence upon "the laugh," swift and sudden action, with a pronounced fondness for the mêlée, surprises of all kinds, horseplay, violence, and drastic buffoonery, were certainly common to mime and to Petronius. Resemblances in style and subject-matter between the rather meager remains of the dramatic mime and the **Satiricon** lose something of their significance when we note that most of these elements are found also in the new comedy. For example, the use of proverbs and the moralizing tendency[16] are common throughout comedy. Epic parody, like the Ulysses references in the **Satiricon** of which Klebs has made so much, is found, among other places, in Plaut. *Bacch.* 925 f., where the siege of Troy is played upon in an elaborate comparison. The gods are burlesqued occasionally in comedy, as well as in mime and in Petronius, particularly in the *Amphitruo* of Plautus, which has itself been compared to the *Fabulae Rhinthonicae*. Ruses and strategies, important, as we know, in mime and in Petronius, are too common in comedy to need specific mention, and disguises, like that of Giton and Encolpius on the ship of Lichas, are employed by Plautus, not only in the *Casina*, which Rosenblüth mentions, but also in the *Miles* iv. 6 and 7, where Pleusicles masquerades as a sailor, in *Trinummus* iv. 2, *Pseudolus* iv 1. 2, *Persa* iv. 4, and elsewhere. The episode in Petronius in which Giton is hid beneath the bed, and, later, betrayed by a sneeze, is compared by Rosenblüth[17] to those scenes in mime where the adulterer, upon the approach of the lawful husband, concealed himself in some improvised shelter, for instance a chest (*cista*); cf. Juv. vi. 42 and scholion: qui totiens superveniente marito sub cista celatus est ut in mimo. That the comic use of such hiding-places was a familiar [*topos*] in Attic comedy may be inferred from Xenarchus 4K: 9-11. . . .

Forecasting the action by means of dreams, as in Petronius 17. 20, and 104. 2-3, is characteristic not only of mime but of comedy; cf. Plaut. *Merc.* ii. 1, and *Rudens* iii. 1. The combat, Petr. 95. 6, in which spits, meat-forks, and other improvised weapons are employed, is paralleled in Terence *Eun.* 771 ff., though, with the reserve that is characteristic of comedy, in the *Eunuchus* the soldier and his followers stop short of blows. Threats of violence are common in comedy, actual blows are rare. The *Amphitruo*, distinctive also in some other respects, is a notable exception to this rule; cf. i. 1. In mentioning (*op. cit.*, p. 151) the peculiar relations existing between master and slaves, as, for example, in Petr. 126. 5, 64. 11-12, 45. 7, 69. 3, 75. 11, Rosenblüth might well have noted that this theme, which, as he shows, was common in mime, appears also very frequently in comedy; cf. *Casina* 460: illuc est, illuc, quod hic hunc fecit vilicum, etc.; *Persa* 191. 2; *Asin.* 799 f. (cf. Petr. 64. 11-12).

In comic characters, what is left to us of the **Satiricon** does not offer a large number of the familiar types, but we find quite as much evident contact with comedy in this respect as exists with mime. The physician,[18] as he is alluded to in Petr. 42. 5, 47. 2, 56. 2, may be compared with the comic medicus in *Menaechmi*, act v. Schoolmasters are only just barely mentioned in the **Satiricon**, but if it is worth while considering the type,[19] Lydus, the paedagogus in the *Bacchides*, is a fine representative. Another type that is worth something more than a casual glance is the cook; the versatile and aggressive cook of Trimalchio (cf. Petr. 49, 74. 5, 70. 12) has a strong family resemblance to the braggart cook in comedy as represented in Plaut. *Pseud.* iii. 2, in the *Aululari*, and in numberless other plays of the new comedy, as we can infer from the comic fragments. The captator theme, as developed in Petr. 116 ff., is not, to be sure, very extensively handled in existing remains of comedy, but Periplectomenus, *Miles* 705-15, describes the advantages that accrue to a wealthy bachelor from legacy-hunting friends and relatives in a way that reminds the reader of the joyous experiences of Eumolpus and his suite during their sojourn at Crotona.

Perhaps the most perfectly conventional comic type in the **Satiricon** is Chrysis, the go-between or intermediary in the Circe-Polyaenos episode, Petr. 126 ff. Chrysis, like Milphidippe in the *Miles*, is the bearer of proposals from her mistress, in this case a noble lady of Crotona, to a gallant who has been seen and admired from afar. The slave employed on such a mission is variously styled in comedy conciliatrix: *Miles* 1400, itaque ancilla conciliatrix quae erat internuntia; *Miles* 986, haec celox illius quae egreditur internuntia; or interpres, *Miles* 952. Like Pyrgopolinices in the *Miles*, Encolpius fatuously affects to believe that the ancilla is herself enamored of him; cf. Petr. 126. 8; itaque oratione blandissima plenus "rogo" inquam "numquid illa quae me amat, tu es?" Cf. *Miles* 1038, Py.: "di tibi dent quaecumque optes." Mil.: "tecum aetatem exigere ut liceat." Py. "nimium optas." Mil.: "non me dico, sed eram meam quae te demoritur." The fact that this identical twist is given the conversation in Petronius and in the *Miles* tempts one to translate the phrase that follows, frigidum schema, not, "a clumsy turn of speech," but a "stale gambit." At any rate, a cordial understanding is established between Encolpius and Chrysis, and a bantering conversation follows in 8-11; and cf. 12: procedentibus deinde longius iocis. Such intimate chaff between amator and ancilla is characteristic of comedy; cf. the long jesting conversation between Astaphium and Diniarchus, *Truc.* 115 ff.

It would be possible to strengthen an argument for the debt of Petronius to comedy by a number of details which hardly belong under the title of this study. For example, the use of erotic epistles (cf. Petr. 129, 130) is a device that may well have been common in comedy (cf. Plaut. *Pseud.* 64 f.), but this might easily be over-emphasized. Much more significant is the passage 81. 3, where Encolpius reviews the past action of the story in a mournful soliloquy. In tone and purpose this tirade belongs clearly with the so-called morologia of comic lovers.[20] Both these points would lead naturally to a consideration of the sermo amatorius in Petronius, which, particularly in the Circe and Polyaenos episode, and in the Milesian tales, shows many reminiscences of comic diction; this, however, would require an extended study in itself. Such reference as I have made to comedy has been designed to show that, on the side of typical characters and comic material, Petronius may be somewhat more indebted to the new comedy than has been acknowledged by Collignon and Rosenblüth. His attitude toward this material, and his technique in the handling of comic episodes, seem to me to support their conclusions in regard to the very considerable influence of mime on Petronius.

*Notes*

[1] A. Collignon, Étude sur Pétrone, Paris, 1892.

[2] H. Reich, *Der Mimus*, Berlin, 1903, p. 35.

[3] Emile Thomas, *Pétrone*, Paris, 1902, p. 172.

[4] M. Rosenblüth, *Beitrage zur Quellenkunde von Petrons Satiren*, Berlin, 1909, pp. 36-55.

[5] One is tempted, though this is, perhaps, over-subtle, to see, in these words, a direct contrast between classic tragedy and comedy, as specialized in the tabernariae. The reference to tragedy is clear, for in Thebanum par we have an obvious allusion to the tragic case of Eteocles and Polinices; cf. also the high-flown language that follows "neve sanguine mutuo pollueremus familiaritatis clarissimae sacra." In view of this it may be significant that Giton here refers to the lodging, elsewhere called cella, deversorium, in the words humilis taberna.

[6] *Op. cit.*, p. 213.

[7] Cf. Rosenblüth, *op. cit.*, p. 53, referring to the *Nuptiae* of Laberius.

[8] Rosenblüth, *op. cit.*, p. 50.

[9] Rosenblüth, *op. cit.*, pp. 37 f.

[10] Athen. 621 C: [(*magodos*) *panta poiei ta exo kosmou hypokrinomenos pote men gyneika kai moikhous mastropoos pote d'andra methoonta*].

[11] Rosenblüth, *op. cit.*, p. 52.

[12] The use of the phallus was carried into comedy probably from the Bacchic celebrations; cf. Führ, *De Mimis Graecorum*, p. 24. Phallic comedy, so popular in the Dorian states, came to Tarentum and Southern Italy by way of Sparta, as it did to Syracuse by way of Corinth (cf. Nairn, *Mimes of Herondas*, Introduction, p. xxiii). Vase paintings from Southern Italy show the phallus as part of the costume of actors in the mimes that were popular there (cf. O. Jahn, *Beschreibung der Vasensammlung Konig Ludwigs in d. Pinak. in München 1854*, 8 S. CCXXVII f.), and the same symbol appears to have figured in Roman mime (cf. Grysar, "Der Romische Mimus," *Sitzungsberichte der Wiener Akademie der Wissenschaften philosophisch-historische Klasse*, 1854, XXII, 270, who cites Schol. ad Juvenal vi. 68; penem ut habent in mimo). In general cf. also Reich, *op. cit.*, I, 17.

[13] M. R. Heinze, "Petr. und der griechische Roman," *Hermes*, XXXIV (1899), 494-519; Thomas, *op. cit.*, p. 207 f.

[14] Cf. Collignon, *op. cit.*, p. 281, quoting Augustine *Civ. dei* vi. 75; Rosenblüth, *op. cit.*, p. 52.

[15] Rosenblüth, *op. cit.*, p. 52, n. 1, notes that in mime and in Petronius the same frankness is used in regard to all bodily functions; he compares Petr. 47, 2, 117. 12, with Pomp. 4 Rib.[3], and the [*Porde*] of the Oxyrhynchos mime. In his second example from Petronius, 117. 12, the scurrility of Corax and Giton is provoked by the fact that they are acting as porters, and are laden beyond their strength. Note the similar situation of Xanthias in Aristophanes *Ranae* i. 1, where Dionysus deprecates the same form of jest (line 8), and cf. von Leeuwen *ad locum* for the prevalence in comedy of this form of humor.

[16] Rosenblüth, *op. cit.*, p. 45.

[17] *Op. cit.*, p. 50 and p. 78, n. 3.

[18] Rosenblüth, *op. cit.*, p. 54.

[19] Rosenblüth, *op. cit.*, p. 54.

[20] Cf. *Merc.* i. 4-5: vi amoris facere. qui aut dii aut soli aut lunae miserias narrant suas; *Persa* 49: amoris vitio, non meo nunc tibi morologus fio. Cf. also Leo *Plaut, Forsch.*,[2] p. 151, n. 1.

## C. W. Mendell (essay date 1917)

SOURCE: "Petronius and the Greek Romance," *Classical Philology*, Vol. XII, No. 2, April, 1917, pp. 158-72.

[*In the following essay, Mendell argues that the* Satyricon *is not a realistic but rather a romantic novel, and that it is neither a parody nor a satire, although it contains elements of both.*]

Some years ago Professor Abbott published in *Classical Philology*[1] a stimulating article entitled "The Origin of the Realistic Romance among the Romans." In that article he indicated many possible sources from which Petronius may have drawn something of his tone or matter. As Abbott himself suggests, all of these are sources for various specific characteristics of Petronius rather than ancestors from which the literary type proceeded. He concludes with the statement that "so far as our present information goes, Petronius seems to have been the inventor of the realistic romance."

Among the possible sources of Petronius, Abbott mentions the love romances of the Greeks which, if we could be sure that they were written in their developed form as early as the time of Petronius, would furnish a type of source different from the rest. Heinze[2] assumed for the romances an early date and developed the theory that Petronius wrote a parody of them. He finds in this way a forerunner of the type rather than of particular characteristics. I believe that this is the right direction in which to look for the literary ancestor of Petronius and that there are more indications of this relation than Heinze makes use of; furthermore, that Abbott's enumeration of characteristics reinforces rather than controverts this view, but that Heinze's theory of the parody nature of the novel is not the correct one.

I am skeptical of the propriety of calling Petronius' work a *realistic* romance, if that implies, as it seems to, an attempt on the part of the author to present human life essentially as it is.[3] The term "realistic" was presumably first applied to the book because it dealt with everyday folk, not with superhuman or heroic characters. But so did the love romances. That the hero and heroine were superlatively beautiful and in most ways extremely noble did not of necessity remove them from the sphere of possibility. Frankly accepted impossibilities were excluded from these romances, indicating a conscious effort at realism. But they still without apology introduced improbabilities of an extreme sort, and a succession of unusual experiences which in their total are quite incredible even though no particular one is by itself impossible. And this is just what Petronius does. He never asks us to believe in marvels, but he sends his characters through a series of adventures which the most credulous mind could not find probable. And even so we have but a small portion of them.

A parallel from another literary field may make more clear the actual position of Petronius in the scale of realism. Greek tragedy dealt with exalted characters of the heroic past; gods and goddesses and personages purely mythological. Aeschylus did not scruple to deal with impossibilities; there was good ground for Aristophanes' thrusts at his horse-cocks and goat-stags; his gods and his sea-nymphs and his winged Erinyes all trod the earth among his characters. Euripides made the drama much more realistic, and although mythical kings and princes and the dwellers on Olympus still make up the personnel, they show the emotions and actions of real people. The New Comedy took the next step. The logical successor of Euripides' tragedy, it reduced every detail to the plane of the common-place. Ordinary people with ordinary emotions are its material, and it is called, in contrast to tragedy, "the mirror of life." But it is a *speculum vitae* only by comparison. It depicts only one side of life and that too distorted by exaggeration, with experiences treading on the heels of one another in such rapid succession and with such a persistently comic phase that they can hardly be termed, with any strictness of expression, realistic.

What is true of the New Comedy in this respect is roughly true of Petronius' work. It does not show the marvels of the early tales of adventurous travel. It confines itself to what might conceivably happen, but not to any truthfully realistic depiction of life. The romance of adventure, pure and simple, presented the frankly impossible with the utmost confidence. The romance of love confined itself to the realms of possibility so far as incidents go and, like Euripides, presented persons of an exalted rank, in a serious fashion,

acting in a natural and human manner. Petronius reduced the characters to middle and low society and dwelt on a very different phase of their experiences. Just what that phase was and the resultant tone of the treatment will appear later.

The acceptance of some such evolution of the prose romance does not imply that with the beginning of one type the preceding ceased to be written, but merely that in a general way this was the order of their first appearance and development of type.[4] This Heinze doubts. He thinks that there is no such relation between the romance of adventure and the erotic romance. They are, he holds, two totally different and unrelated types, alike only in the one point that their plots are not stationary. He seems, however, to be influenced by the fact that he places the only writer of the romance of adventure that we know, Antonius Diogenes, too late to influence Petronius, while at the same time he posits erotic romances before the time of the Roman novelist. This is too cavalier. Even without the evidence of Lucian in the introduction to his *True History*, it would be clear that the romance of adventure was a very slight variation from the professedly historic work of such logographers as Ctesias and Iamboulos. Without positive proof it is almost impossible to give up the generally accepted theory of development which recognizes a logical sequence from the novel of adventure to the erotic romance.

The dating of Greek romances is at best a hazardous undertaking. But there is certainly no ground for putting Antonius Diogenes later than Petronius. It has been assumed that his bilingual name disproves the statement of Photius that he lived shortly after the time of Alexander.[5] But Livius Andronicus came to Rome in 275 B.C.; Rome had come much into contact with Greek cities in such a way as to acquire Greek slaves long before that; Naples and Cumae were Roman before 300; and before Alexander began his conquests Rome had conquered many a Greek in Campania. Furthermore, regardless of exact dating, his nearness to Ctesias and the other logographers makes it more than likely that he wrote before formal rhetoric had begun its sway.

The erotic romances, too, must be given much earlier dates than they used to receive. Jebb stated without hesitation that Chariton was a writer of the fifth century,[6] but a papyrus of 100 A.D. with a considerable fragment of his novel deducts from this date more than two hundred years at a blow.[7] The Ninos fragment cannot have been written later than 50 A.D., and in all probability was distinctly earlier.[8] These two romances have one thing in common which seems to me significant. Chariton's novel has much more deliberate rhetoric than the others that we possess, and the Ninos fragments indicate that that romance was similar to Chariton's in this respect. In psychological analysis, in balanced arguments, in brilliant descriptions, and in dramatic scenes, Chariton is far ahead of Xenophon, for example, or Achilles Tatius. It seems therefore not improbable that, although Rohde was wrong in his *actual* date for Chariton, he was right in his *relative* dating, and that the two romances of whose dates we have some slight indication are among the latest.[9] If Chariton is two hundred years and more older than he was generally believed to be, there is no reason to think that the rest may not be too, and internal evidence strongly suggests that they mark an earlier stage of development.

In consideration of the possibility of an early date for the romances, it seems not unlikely that too little weight has been given to a passage from Plautus.[10] In *Men.* 247, Messenio says to his master: "Quin nos hinc domum | redimus nisi si historiam scripturi sumus?" He has already complained of the traveling as follows: "Histros Hispanos Massilienses Hiluros | mare superum omne Graeciamque exoticam | orasque Italicas omnis, qua adgreditur mare | sumus circumvecti." This sounds more like material for a romance than for a history, and his conclusion indicates the further ground of similarity which led him to associate their wanderings with those of the romantic hero: "Hominem inter vivos quaeritamus mortuom; | nam invenissemus iam diu, sei viveret." There is nothing to contradict this interpretation in the other instances of the use of *historia* in Plautus.[11]

It is obvious since the discovery of the Ninos fragments that the rhetoric which could have influenced the romance was the rhetoric taught by such men as Seneca and his predecessors, not the rhetoric of the new sophistic. The balancing of arguments and the descriptive chapters are exactly the sort of thing which the regular rhetorical training would have cultivated. It by no means follows that the romances were expanded rhetorical exercises. The condensed plots which Seneca and the other rhetoricians collected were much more probably summaries of longer stories which the teacher presented in the form of an abstract for the pupil to practice on. The fact that many of them deal with actual historical incidents bears out this supposition and the modern case system of studying law furnishes a fair parallel. That the school teacher invented and the novelist borrowed is certainly a harder theory than the reverse. Parthenius, some thirty years before Christ, culling plots for Gallus to use, is a good example of the sort of thing that Seneca probably did to obtain for his classroom the material that has survived him. The interesting point for the present study is that he evidently had romances from which to draw.

Another parallel from the drama may serve to clarify the understanding of this development of type. Even in the time of Aeschylus the desire for the romantic element was strong. Colonization had no doubt fostered it. In Aeschylus it is satisfied by the marvelous, the supernatural, and the strange. Such long stories as Io's of her wanderings have little reason for existing except as they cater to a public craving for romance. In the later dramatists, who catered to less naïve audiences, the strange and weird drop out and the love element enters to make good the romantic loss. Euripides incurs the charge of degrading the stage by introducing women in love among his characters. Finally, in the New Comedy, the love element is more regularly the central theme, but is reduced to a lower plane and treated with much less of dignity and seriousness.

So the romantic element in prose story-telling proceeds from the original travel motif with its marvels of imagination, the sort of thing that Lucian reproduces as an extravaganza in his *True History*, to the love story with adventure as a contributory element. And when it has run its course on the high and arid plane of pure romance, it is revived by an infusion of Roman salt by Petronius. Even in the part that rhetoric plays in these two very different fields the parallel holds roughly. The rhetoric of the Greek romance is the rhetoric of Euripides; the naturalness of Petronius is the naturalness of the New Comedy.

If we could be absolutely sure what the *Milesian Tales* were and just what Aristides wrote, one step in the development of the romance might be cleared up. But entire agreement on this point seems impossible; I merely venture a suggestion. Ovid's phrase (*Tristia* ii. 413), "Iunxit Aristides Milesia crimina [or carmina] secum, Pulsus Aristides nec tamen urbe sua est," is pretty generally taken to indicate that Aristides formed some kind of a whole out of the Milesian stories which he found or invented. The tone of the Milesian tale was presumably erotic and piquant.[12] Now it seems to me that the second reference of Ovid to Aristides (*Tristia* ii. 443) implies that his book was in reality a consecutive story: "Vertit Aristidem Sisenna nec obfuit illi Historiae turpis inseruisse iocos." *Fabula* and not *historia* is the regular word for short incidental stories. Many references to Petronius and Apuleius confirm the results of a study of Ovid's usage on this point.[13] *Historia* indicates something sustained,[14] and such a meaning is demanded by the passage in order to make possible the insertion of the *ioci* which, as elsewhere in Ovid, are evidently erotic anecdotes. Sisenna then inserted short anecdotes into his translation of the book of Aristides. (Possibly Ovid was misled into thinking that the original book of Aristides was a compilation, by the title of it which was very likely *Milesiaca* after the analogy of the *Babylonica* of Iamblichus and the *Indica* and the like of his predecessors.) The resultant book was the novel that caused scandal when found in the luggage of one of Crassus' officers after the battle of Carrhae, and it was probably in its Latin version that it was known to the Romans who refer to it. So it is not strange that the scandalous insertions came to be looked on by them as the essential part of the romance and that the name of the Greek romance that gave them a setting was misconstrued into a title for them.

In view of some such possibility, Apuleius' statement about his own work in his introduction is significant: "At ego tibi sermone isto Milesio varias fabulas conseram," etc. He means that in addition to merely Latinizing the *Onos* of Lucius of Patrae he will insert stories of erotic flavor and it is in these that much of his originality lies. He speaks of the inserts as *fabulae*, with the exception noted above, as does Petronius in introducing the story of the Matron of Ephesus (110, 113).

If this supposition about the *Milesian Tales* be true, then it is in the Latin romances only, in Sisenna, Petronius, and Apuleius, that there are short inserted anecdotes. The Greek romances have numberless episodic digressions which seem to take the reader far afield, but *fabulae* deliberately introduced as short stories they do not have. It looks very much as though the introduction of these were a Roman contribution to the romance. But before considering this point further it will be convenient to consider the characteristics of Petronius as presented by Abbott and to see how they bear on the suggested relation between the Greek and the Roman romance.

Professor Abbott, in outlining the characteristics of Petronius' novel that must be considered in looking for a predecessor, notes, first, the place, Southern Italy; second, the generally low class of characters; third, the prominence of women; fourth, the efficient motif, erotic in spite of the framework furnished by an offended deity; fifth, the baffling tone of satire; sixth, the realism; seventh, the character-drawing, and, finally, the prose-poetic form. These must be compared one by one with the characteristics of the romance.

The scenes of the Greek novels range pretty freely over the known world, although one point is worth noting which I think has not been brought out. The range of scene is confined to the old Greek world, not to the expanded Roman world. Persia, Asia Minor, Egypt, Southern Italy, Sicily form the stage on which the characters of romance move. If the novels were a late invention, if they did not, as I believe they do, go back to Hellenistic times, this would be difficult to explain, but it is perfectly natural in the case of a type of literature firmly fixed before Rome had widened the bounds of the world. The early romance of adventure had treated in splendidly cavalier style Scythia and Thule, the lower world and the moon, until the tendency toward realism led the romancer to limit himself to the world his readers knew. But to return to the point, the scenes cover always a considerable range. Southern Italy and Sicily figure in Xenophon of Ephesus and also in Chariton, who is the representative of the romance who comes nearest to Petronius. The scene of

the Roman novel in the fragment we possess is Southern Italy; there is indication that Massilia, too, figured in the story, and the haphazard wandering of the characters leaves little room for doubt that the scenes were even more varied.

The characters of the romances are mixed. From the great king of Persia to a humble herdsman, all stages of society are represented. The hero and heroine, ordinarily half-way between these extremes, are, in the greatest variety of ways, brought into contact with prince and pauper, pirate and pander. In Petronius there are no real potentates. But, granted the criteria by which his middle-class folk gauge position, the range is like that of the Greek. From Habinnas and Trimalchio to the fisherman who picks up the heroes after the wreck, we have the counterparts of the romantic satrap and vassal. The general type of character must be noted (it is distinctly low by comparison), but the range of character is just as important, and in that Chariton and Petronius are alike.

In the matter of the prominence of women, I can find no reason to draw any distinction between Petronius and the romance. In Chariton, Callirhoe, Plangon, and Stateira are very prominent and sharply differentiated, and every romance furnishes its quota of well-drawn women. Manto, the Potiphar's wife of Xenophon, his ugly Kuno, Melite, the scheming widow of Achilles Tatius, the splendid farmer's daughter of Iamblichus—these can hardly be said to play a less important part than men.

In motif again there is little distinction beyond that of tone. The efficient motif of the romances is erotic just as much as is that of Petronius. In the romance it is circumstance that drives on the lovers through a mad succession of experiences even though these circumstances are sometimes motivated by the anger of a god offended by the obstinacy or arrogance of the lovers. Petronius, too, gives realism by making the force of circumstances govern the plot, but behind circumstances, he reminds us several times, is the anger of the offended Priapus. Like the low caste of his characters this choice of offended deity must be remembered as significant.

The baffling tone of satire is peculiar to Petronius. The romances are beyond all else ingenuous. The realism I have already discussed. The trend away from marvels had gone as far in Chariton as in Petronius. The only difference lies in the class of people treated: in keeping with his middle-class people, Petronius' adventures and melodramatic situations are middle class. I am inclined also to detect less difference than is usually found in the matter of character-drawing. What difference there is seems to me to be a result of the individual skill of a particular artist, not a question of type. As psychological analysis began to enter into the romance, characterization began to be more prominent. It is one of the chief results of strong rhetorical influences. And Chariton in particular depicts individualities: the faithful Polycharmus, a second Pylades, the gentleman Dionysius, the oriental queen Stateira, the big-hearted countrywoman Plangon; they are all real characters though not done with the genius of Petronius. Few of the romancers seem to have been men of high genius. Finally, the prose-poetic form is peculiar to Petronius.

It is clear, I think, that in most of its characteristics Petronius' book is not far removed from the Greek romance. Further points of similarity might be noted. Heinze has dwelt on the framework and motivation, on the union and separation of Giton and Encolpius, on the steady chain of misfortunes, on the constant erotic temptations of the heroes. I would add the insistence on hair-breadth escapes which are the mainstay of both the Roman and the Greek novelist in holding attention, and the prevailing willingness of the characters to give up and die when crises arise. Details, too, bear out the parallel which framework and general characteristics make so clear. To name a few: the cloak motif or recognition by means of a garment (Petr. 12ff.) is almost identical in the use made of it with the incident of Iamblichus in which Sinonis tries to sell a cloak and is arrested for robbing a tomb. Encolpius before the pictures (Petr. 83) recalls the opening of Achilles Tatius. The argument over punishment (Petr. 107) may be paralled in any romance, perhaps best by the arguments of the pirates and the trial scene in Chariton. The shipwreck (Petr. 114, 115) might be taken bodily from Achilles Tatius or Xenophon of Ephesus. The comparison of Circe's beauty to that of a goddess (Petr. 126) suggests the familiar conceit that the Greek heroine would be taken for Aphrodite on the street. The magic potions of Greek romance are perhaps paralleled by the disgusting magic of Petronius (Petr. 134 ff.).

With all these points of similarity which cannot be mere coincidences, there remain the essential differences noted in passing: the class of characters treated, the baffling tone of satire, the prosepoetic form, and I would add the insertion of anecdotes unrelated to the plot.

It is time to consider the name under which the novel of Petronius has come down to us. Buecheler's ***Petronii Satirae*** is the accepted designation, but this title does not describe the book correctly if it implies conformity with one of the two types of satire distinguished by Quintilian, the Horatian and the Varronian. The hexameter form of the first is an unsurmountable obstacle, and Varro like Horace wrote short satires collected into books, not one long and continuous composition divided into chapters. It is not surprising, therefore, to find that there is practically no manuscript authority

for designating Petronius' book as a satire. On the other hand, it will not be difficult to see how the designation crept in during later years.

The majority of the best manuscripts read *saturicon*, either in superscription or in colophon (so BDEFG[15]). B, the oldest, has **"Petronii Arbitri Saturicon."** In the eleventh-century Paris manuscript alone appears any form of the word *satura*: "Petronii arbitri satirarum l. incipit," and this is corrected in the margin by the same or a contemporary hand to "Petronii arbitri affranii Satirici lib. incip." This has the appearance of being an attempt to remedy the strange-looking form *satiricon*, further changed to **Satyri** in the Trau manuscript (A), and modern editors have been equally prone to change it to suit their purposes. Savaron in his notes on Sidonius Apollinaris[16] says: "Petronii libellus mera est satura Varroniana, ut suo loco dicitur, ipse tamen Saturicum sive Satiricum maluit inscribere: quo modo commentarium dicitur pro commentario libro: Apologeticus pro apologetico libro." Casaubon says[17] that it is not worth while discussing why Petronius preferred **Satiricum** to **Satyra**. As a matter of fact there is no reason to think that he did. **Saturicon** is in all probability the Latinization of the Greek genitive plural, and the *satirarum* of P, which has been largely responsible for the classification of Petronius' novel as a satire, was an attempt by the copyist to correct this. The longer fragment of the Trau manuscript (A) shows that there were at least sixteen books in the novel so that [*biblia*] was probably the word understood in the Greek title which Petronius wished to suggest. His title . . . gives fair warning of the kind of romance that is coming, at the same time indicating clearly that here is no satire proper.

The characterization of Petronius' book which made appropriate his designation of it and which also led to its later classification as satire is twofold: first, characteristics of content, second, those of form. In content the two branches of satire did not differ widely. Aulus Gellius (ii. 18. 6) indicates the nature of Varro's subject-matter to some extent, explaining that he was called Menippean because he modeled his work on that of the Cynic Menippus. The writings of Menippus were partly philosophical but rarely in a wholly serious tone.[18] Varro's subjects have a range as wide as Horace's: literary, philosophical, mythological, satires on the miser, on wills, on the education of children, on food and dinners, and on Priapus. The field of satire seems not to have varied much from Lucilius' day to Juvenal's, and from this field Petronius chose many an object for satiric attack. Oratory and poetry, education, the influence of money, the wealthy upstart, the *recitationes*, Priapus, the *captatores*, the women's devotion to a gladiator, magic, all are touched on by Petronius as well as by Varro and Horace and Juvenal. And so they are by Martial. The difference is that in the novelist and in the epigrammatist they are incidental, in the satirists they are the chief themes of the satires, treated for their own sake. In Petronius they are quite subordinate to the story. They indicate the satiric spirit of the author but do not prove him a satirist.

This point is well illustrated by the enumeration of characteristics in the thesis of Rosenblüth. After outlining the peculiarities common to Petronius and to satire, he proceeds to list those common to Petronius and to the mime, and practically every point which he brings up is applicable to satire as well, while the one thing that would be significant in Petronius, the dramatic form, is, of course, wanting. He cites, for example, the mixture of real names and appropriate nicknames, the use of colloquialisms, types of character, enchantments, mimic episodes, and so on. No doubt the mime, like the epic, like the prologues of comedy, had its influence in the formation of the romantic type. And so, in a greater degree, satire, the literary type truly congenial to the Roman, encroaching as it did on the epigram, on the lyric, on drama, and even on history, encroached also on the romance, and is responsible for incidental subjects in Petronius and for much of the tone throughout. But the novel of Petronius is neither mime nor satire. The essentials of its literary type are those of the romance.

In form it is the Varronian satire only with which Hirzel and Schmid, Rohde and Ribbeck would allign Petronius.[19] Whatever theory we may hold of its origin or precise nature, there can be no doubt of the existence as far back as the time of Cicero of this prosimetric form of essay, probably not precisely defined as satire. And from the point of view of form there is a real and essential resemblance between Varro and Petronius and a difference between Petronius and the Greek romance. But in this respect too I think that an incidental resemblance is mistaken for identity of type. The metrical portions of the novel do not, with two or three short exceptions, further the narrative, while in the Varronian satire, so far as can be judged by the remains, the discourse was carried on indiscriminately by the metrical parts and by the prose. Seneca's farce on the death of Claudius furnishes a striking example of the actual mixing of prose and verse and shows the difference between such metrical passages and the insertions in Petronius which, except for form, are much like the ethnographical lore inserted in the romances. The Menippean satire made it seem natural to the Roman to introduce metrical inserts into his continuous discourse, just as the influence of satire in general led him to introduce satiric attacks on various familiar abuses.

In so far as the characters treated by Petronius are of a different class from those of the Greek romance I believe that this too is due to the spirit of satire. It is to a satirist like Juvenal ·that we must look for a parallel, to a man of nearly the same period who saw practically the same conditions. If he chose a bourgeois society to assail, it is only natural that Petronius should attack the same class, a class coming into great prominence during the early empire without too much credit in the eyes of the aristocracy. But I have already indicated that I do not feel the difference in this respect between the Roman and the Greek to be very great. It should be borne in mind that the part of the novel which we possess deals with a provincial town where Habinnas the *sevir* would be a man of no inconsiderable position.

Finally, like Sisenna and like Apuleius, Petronius inserts into his narrative anecdotes which are in no wise relevant or necessary to the progress of his novel, stories introduced for their own sake and not merely digressions in which even a Chariton might indulge. Such anecdotes are foreign to the atmosphere of feverish haste which marks most of the Greek romances, but absolutely in keeping with the rambling and casual tone of satire. Horace is full of them and rarely feels the need of his apology, *non longa est fabula*, which, however, is significant when taken in connection with the use of *fabula* by Ovid, Petronius, and Apuleius.

This scrutiny of the characteristics of Petronius as outlined by Abbott shows that the baffling tone of satire, the prose-poetic form, the class of characters treated, and, in addition to these, the insertion of anecdotes not strictly a part of the plot, are presumably the result of the influence of satire, while the remaining characteristics supplement the evidence which serves to define the literary type of the work as erotic romance.

Now, although Heinze maintains the similarity between Petronius and the erotic romance, he finds the tone of the former to be one of parody and makes this the determining factor in explaining the relation between the two. He cites the general tone of epic parody, the tragic pose of killing one's self at every crisis, always given up on a very slight pretext, and, finally, the exaggerated attitude toward dangers of every sort.

These are all parody in detail: of themselves they do not justify a characterization of the whole work. And when we stop to notice how such detailed parody appears in other branches of Latin literature, not remote from the romance, their significance seems even less probably that which Heinze would make it. For example, so far as the tone of epic parody is concerned,· Horace and Juvenal offer much more obvious instances of the same, yet no one would feel that the satire of Horace and Juvenal was adequately defined as parody. The Roman comedy has passages which very obviously parody the tragedy, such as the recognition scene in the *Menaechmi*, but such details do not make the comedy as a whole a parody. The comedy furnishes also numerous instances of characters who express a fixed determination to die, usually a slave or a weak-willed lover, and this determination presently vanishes. Dangers in the comedy are magnified enormously. But these facts do not prove that comedy belongs to the parody type of literature. It is true, to be sure, that the tone of the novel as a whole is largely a matter of feeling or impression and therefore dangerous ground for argument, but, so far as the consensus of feeling goes, the tone would seem to be nearer to one of realism than to one of parody, and I therefore feel more confident of my own impression that the tone of parody is confined to details.

To show that the romance as a whole was a parody it would be necessary, I think, to show that in its entirety, especially in so far as its main lines are concerned, the parody was obvious and sustained. Lucian, in the preface to his *True History*, gives fair warning that he is writing a parody and the reader is never given an opportunity to doubt the sincerity of the warning. The *Will of the Little Pig* is sustained parody. But if Petronius were the same, we should expect something more in the way of burlesque setting and fewer men with a normally developed sense of humor would have swallowed the romance as realistic and satiric.

Finally, the long incident of Trimalchio's dinner, forming as it does so considerable a portion of even the entire work, would be out of place in a parody of the erotic romance. Parody, as Heinze himself says in another connection, implies something parodied, and such an incident would be so totally foreign to the spirit and purpose of romance as to be utterly out of place in the parody. The dinner of the *nouveau riche* was an accepted subject of satire thoroughly congenial to the highly original writer of a romance penned in the satiric vein.

My conclusions are these. The novel of Petronius is not, strictly speaking, a realistic novel. It is an erotic romance and belongs to the developed, not to the early, type of romance. Its essential type characteristics are those of the romance. It is not a parody although it contains parody. It is not a satire although strongly influenced by the satiric spirit. It is a real romance written by a truly Roman artist; his national characteristics appear in the satiric bent, in the setting, and in much of the tone; his personal impress is felt in the excellent characterization, in the genial humor, and in the wealth of invention.

### Notes

[1] VI (1911), 257 ff.

[2] R. Heinze, "Petron und der griechische Roman," *Hermes*, XXXIV (1899), 494 ff.

[3] This is the position maintained by Martin Rosenblüth in a Kiel dissertation: *Beiträge zur Quellenkunde von Petrons Satiren* (Berlin, 1909). Bürger also calls Petronius' work *ein echt realistischen Sittenroman*; see "Der antike Roman vor Petronius," *Hermes*, XXVII (1892), 345 ff.

[4] This distinction is clearly drawn by Otmar Schissel von Fleschenberg in *Entwickelungsgeschichte des griechischen Romanes im Alterthum* (Halle, 1913).

[5] This is the position of J. S. Phillimore in his article on the romances in *English Literature and the Classics* (Oxford, 1912).

[6] See *A Companion to Greek Studies*, Cambridge, 1906, p. 161.

[7] Grenfell, Hunt, and Hogarth, *Fayum Towns and Their Papyri*, p. 74.

[8] See U. Wilcken, "Ein neuer griechischer Roman," *Hermes*, XXVIII (1893), 161 ff.

[9] Rohde, *Der griechische Roman und seine Vorläufer*, 2d ed., p. 521: "Nur so viel scheint eine genauere Betrachtung seines Romanes zu lehren, dass er die Romane des Iamblichus, Heliodorus und nicht am wenigsten den des Xenophon vor Augen hatte und nachbildete." A fragment of Achilles Tatius of a date not later than 300 puts another of the romances much earlier than Rohde's dating. See *Oxyrhyncus Popyri*, X, 135, No. 1250.

[10] Professor Henry W. Prescott has kindly called to my attention the fact that this point is brought out by Bousset, *Zeitschr. f. d. Neutestamentl. Wiss.*, 1904, pp. 18 ff.

[11] *Bacchides* i. 2. 50; *Trinummus* ii. 2. 100. R. Reitzenstein, *Das Märchen von Amor und Psyche bei Apuleius*, pp. 32 ff. and 62 ff., interprets *historia* and *fabula* differently, but to take *historiae inseruisse* as "wrote at intervals while engaged on a serious work" is very hard, and the whole argument is based on the unfounded claim that Apuleius found his entire matter in Sisenna.

[12] The best summaries of the evidence are Hans Lucas, "Zu den *Milesiaca* des Aristides," *Philologus*, LXVI (1907), 16 ff., and Otmar Schissel von Fleschenberg, *Die griechische Novelle* (Halle, 1913).

[13] Cf. Petr. 39, 61, 92, 110, etc.; Apul. i. 20, 26; ii. 15, 20, etc.; Ovid *Met.* iv. 53; *Ex ponto* iii. 2. 97; *Tristia* iv. 10. 68, etc.

[14] Cf. Quint. *Inst. Orat.* ii. 4. 2; in Apul. viii. 1, *historia* is used instead of the usual *fabula* and the insertion turns out to be a miniature romance.

[15] See Buecheler's edition of 1862.

[16] *Epistulae* viii. 11. Cited by Burmann, edition of Petronius (1709), p. 2.

[17] *De Satyra* ii. 4. Cited by Burmann, edition of Petronius (1709), p. 2.

[18] Cf. Riese edition of Varro, Introd., p. 9.

[19] Hirzel, *Der Dialog* (Leipzig, 1895), II, 37; Schmid, "Der griechische Roman," *Neue Jahrbücher*, 1904, I, 476; Rohde, *Der griechische Roman*, 2d ed. (Leipzig, 1900), p. 267; Ribbeck, *Geschichte der römischen Dichtung*, III, 150.

## B. E. Perry (essay date 1925)

SOURCE: "Petronius and the Comic Romance," *Classical Philology*," Vol. XX, No. 1, January, 1925, pp. 31-49.

[*In the following essay, Perry rejects several proposed literary forerunners of the* Satyricon, *contending that its more likely model was the straightforward comic narrative.*]

In the present state of our knowledge, and owing to the nature of the problem itself, any attempt to account for the origin and peculiarities of Petronius' *Satyricon* must involve, at one point or another, the assumption of something that cannot be definitely proved. The following study is subject, of course, to these limitations. It is undertaken, however, in the belief that certain facts of ancient literary history have not hitherto received their proper evaluation in this connection, and that some advance may yet be made toward a more probable and comprehensive solution of this important problem.[1]

The *Satyricon*, or rather what remains of it, relates, in autobiographical form, the low-life adventures of a degenerate rhetorician, Encolpius—a fellow of negative character who lives, though not very successfully, by his wits and by the arts of the parasite. Accompanied by a young favorite named Giton, whose loyalty constantly wavers, this anti-hero, Encolpius, wanders aimlessly about, constantly involved in ludicrous intrigues with low, though sometimes educated, companions and everywhere pursued, it would seem, by the wrath of an offended Priapus.[2] Into this general framework are introduced . . . such elaborate side shows as Trimalchio's dinner, the brilliant harangues on the decay of liberal arts, the long poem on the Civil War, or the story of the matron of Ephesus. The realistic portrayals of men and manners throughout combine to give us a gay, but often grotesque panorama of society unmasked and unrobed; and, to borrow a phrase from Petronius himself, "everything resounds with mimic laughter."[3]

Such, in brief, is the *Satyricon*. When we ask ourselves how such a story came to be written, and what known type, or types, of literature may have served as its chief model or forerunner, we are confronted with several interesting possibilities.[4] The Menippean satire, the mime, the epic, the Greek erotic romance, and the Milesian tales have each apparently contributed something to the tone, or the subject-matter, or the structure of Petronius' work. It is an easy matter, in fact, to discover sources for various specific characteristics of the *Satyricon*; and it is likewise easy to see that Petronius must be credited with a considerable amount of originality in the handling of his basic literary model, whatever that may have been. In attempting to decide what this model most probably was, we ought to look for a form of literature which bears the most fundamental similarity to the *Satyricon*, not in the details of subject-matter, or even plot, so much as in the main tendency of the story and its more radical type characteristics. The fact, for instance, that the *Satyricon* contains a long description of a banquet is surely less significant in the question of its origin than the fact that it is, by and large, a narrative of adventure. And, when we have chosen that form of literature which appears to make the nearest approach to the *Satyricon*, we shall want to define as far as possible the originality of Petronius, and to account for the gap existing between his work and its assumed literary ancestor. The narrower the gap, and the more readily it may be explained in terms of literary growth and practice, so much the more probable will be our choice of the original model or logical forerunner. The chief difficulty with many of the suggested lines of descent lies in the fact that they postulate such wide gaps between the *Satyricon* and its supposed antecedents, and such radical innovation or reconstruction on the part of Petronius, as can scarcely be paralleled in literary history. This, I think, should be avoided if at all possible. We should keep to the historical and evolutionary method, even if it becomes necessary to assume a missing link.

For the sake of a little orientation, let me review briefly a few of the more important theories heretofore advocated.

The view that the *Satyricon* is a Menippean satire expanded into a romance (whatever that means) has been held by such a formidable array of scholars as Rohde,[5] Ribbeck,[6] W. Schmid,[7] Hirzel,[8] and more recently by J. Geffcken.[9] None of these men, however, has had much to say on the subject beyond a few *obiter dicta*. They note the title of the work, *Satyricon* or *Satirae*, the mixture of prose and poetry as in Varro, and the recurrence of numerous themes common to satire. But it is hard to see how any of these similarities can be regarded as fundamental.

The title as given in the manuscripts ranges from **Satirarum libri** and **Saturicon**, or its intended equivalent **Satyrici libri**, through various obvious corruptions of these words. The best manuscripts have **Saturicon**;[10] and it is surely much more probable that an original Greek genitive **Satyricon** has been misunderstood and corrupted into the familiar Latin **Satirae** than, conversely, that **Satirae** has evolved into the less familiar but correct form **Satyricon** (*sc. libri*). The propriety of such a title is not hard to understand; it falls in line with the usual title of a Greek romance, such as (Suidas, *s.v.* Iamblichus), (Heliodorus), etc.,[11] and probably meant simply a romance dealing with things of a *satyr-like* character. That is, in fact, exactly what we have in Petronius' work; for Priapus plays an important part in the plot, and the activities of Encolpius, Giton, and Ascyltus are pre-eminently *satyrica* in this sense, that is, *phallic*. The genitive ending in -*on* shows clearly enough that Petronius regarded his title as Greek, i.e., not derived from Latin *satira*; and this Greek word . . . regularly had the meaning satyr-like or pertaining to satyrs, whether applied to the drama or to anything else, from the earliest times to the latest.[12] The elder Pliny uses the word in this sense when he speaks of *saturica signa*, i.e., statues of Priapus (xix. 50) or *saturicos motus* (of certain birds, x. 138); and Plutarch applies it to men who resemble satyrs, either in outward appearance (*Cato* 7) or in conduct (*Galba* 16; *Pericles* 13). The title **Satyricon** (*sc. libri*) is therefore thoroughly appropriate to an obscene novel; whereas, **Satirae,** which regularly means a number of separate satirical essays, seems much less appropriate and more difficult to explain.

As for the recurrence in the **Satyricon** of numerous themes common to satire (a very loosely defined type), it should be remembered that many of these are also common to other forms of literature, and that even in their aggregate they are probably not much more numerous than the themes belonging to the mime,[13] for instance, or to the Milesian tale (i.e., realistic novella). As Professor Mendell observes, it is natural that satire should have influenced the novel of Petronius as it did other forms of Roman literature, epigram, lyric, mime, history, and even epic (see Petronius' *Bellum Civile*); but the fact of this influence, which is also reflected in the prose-poetic form, does not go far toward convincing us that the **Satyricon** is essentially or primarily a satire, or that it owes its origin to satire. In the main narrative, which is what we have to explain, Petronius differs from Varro and the satirists in that he shows no evidence of moral seriousness. Everything is presented from a purely objective point of view, to all appearances merely for fun, and without any traces of the author's approval or disapproval. If Petronius had any ulterior philosophical purpose in describing the bur-lesque adventures of Encolpius, then he has concealed that purpose very effectively; for the tone is nearly everywhere gay and always unmoral.[14] On the other hand, the brilliant harangues on literature and art, and the clever, often beautiful, poems that have been inserted into the main story undoubtedly represent the author's own serious thought and his best artistic effort. That these are formally subordinated to the burlesque narrative, and that they are put into the mouths of rascals, or even ridiculed at times, may be explained as due to Petronius' dislike of posing as serious or didactic. To do so, even in the guarded manner of Horace, would not only be distasteful to him as a sophisticated courtier, but, in the realm of poetry at least, even dangerous. Petronius must have known Nero well enough to beware of his jealousy. If he was to give expression to that poetic genius which he possessed in a greater degree than anyone of his age, he must not, like the ill-fated Lucan, profess to be a poet, but only a trifler. Accordingly, the **Satyricon** consists mainly in a purely burlesque and unmoral novel (a form apparently despised by ancient critics), while the artistic expression of the author is made to appear incidental and playful. Which of the two elements took precedence in the author's mind and was responsible for the writing of the book, we have, of course, no means of determining; but the composition of a long, burlesque novel, though it served a definite purpose and gave the author many an opportunity for self-expression, was probably no mere means to an end but likewise an end in itself. Such a performance rings true to the character of the cynical *arbiter elegantiae* as described by Tacitus—the man who regarded nothing more worth while than idle amusement and who, at the hour of death, "listened to no discourses on the immortality of the soul or teachings of the philosophers, but only to trivial songs and light verses."

Since the story part of the **Satyricon** has every appearance of being written primarily to amuse, we may conclude that it is not a satire, expanded and incidentally taking on the form of a romance, but rather a romance which has been influenced to some extent by satire. It is possible, of course, that this romance was the first of its kind, and that it was created on the basis of no better prototype than a Menippean satire; but the transition here seems too abrupt, and there are other forms of ancient literature which make a nearer approach.

The attempt to establish some sort of connection between the work of Petronius and the Greek erotic romances, though always inviting, was long delayed by the prevailing belief that the latter species did not come into being before the second century A.D. But this date for the origin of the Greek romance is now known to be wrong. The discovery of the Ninus romance on a papyrus which had become waste paper in 101 A.D. has shown very clearly that the erotic romance, as a type, must have been in existence at least by the middle of the first century A.D., probably much earlier.[15] It is possible, therefore, that Petronius took his pattern for the *Satyricon* from the Greek romances. This hypothesis would explain in some measure the provenience of the general type, a story of adventure featuring two lovers whose experiences sometimes bear a close *outward* resemblance to those of the Greek hero and heroine. But, even so, we have still to account for the vast difference in nature between the two species of romance: the Greek is idealized and serious, while Petronius is realistic and burlesque.

Richard Heinze has attempted to explain this difference on the theory that the *Satyricon* was written as a deliberate parody upon the Greek romance.[16] Most critics will admit that the *Satyricon* does contain parody on romantic love, but that this parody was the dominating motif and *raison d'être* of the entire romance is by no means clear. The parody is too poorly sustained. It appears to be merely incidental. In such a work as Heinze assumes the *Satyricon* to be, the long episode of Trimalchio's dinner would be quite out of place. Then, too, we find parody on the epic as well as on the romance. Encolpius more than once compares himself to Ulysses and, like the Homeric hero, he, too, is pursued over land and sea by the wrath of a deity, in this case Priapus. But the authors of genuine parodies, such as Lucian's *True History,* or the *Battle of the Frogs and Mice,* never leave us in doubt about the thing parodied. From beginning to end, the tendency is everywhere obvious and the parallelism in technique and motivation carefully sustained. Of course it is difficult to say just what constitutes parody. It is easy to agree with Heinze in general when he says that the *Satyricon* stands in about the same relation to the serious Greek romance that comedy or satyr-drama does to tragedy. In both cases we observe a sort of reaction. But it is hard to believe that the parallelism between the two romances was so close as between the two kinds of drama, or that in either case the origin of the comic type is to be explained as due to intentional parody. The *Satyricon* is to the Greek romance no more than what *Gil Blas* or *Lazarillo de Tormes* are to the romance of chivalry.

The most recent writer on this subject is Professor C. W. Mendell (*loc. cit.*). Mendell rejects the theory of a deliberate parody and, regarding the machinery of the plot in the *Satyricon* as its most essential element, maintains that Petronius' work represents merely an advanced stage in the development of the serious erotic novel. He thus fails to account for the burlesque and unmoral tendency except in so far as it may be due to the influence of satire and the sophisticated age and surroundings in which the Roman writer lived. To this it may be objected that, besides the inherent improbability of any literary type radically changing its primary tone and tendency except by parody, there is no

evidence that such a transition took place, unless it was due entirely to the wilful invention of Petronius. The latest of the Greek erotic romances written long after Petronius are quite as idealized and as serious as the earliest. They show no tendency whatever to replace heroes with anti-heroes, as Petronius has done, nor to change the serious tone to the comic. As ancient comedy appears to have sprung from a different type of origin from that of tragedy, and as both types remained distinct throughout antiquity and characterized by a different tone and tendency, so, I believe, the comic unmoral novel, though formally influenced by the conventions of the serious romance, must have been comic or at least realistic at the start.

The history of the novel in later times would suggest this. The humorous, realistic, and somewhat unmoral history of the roguish Gil Blas, though less exaggerated, is fundamentally the same kind of story as the *Satyricon*. Yet its origins are not to be sought in the serious romance of chivalry but directly in the rogue stories of Spain, such as that of *Lazarillo de Tormes*. And these rogue stories themselves, if they did not, as seems most probable,[17] result from the grouping about one character of numerous stock tricks and *facetiae*, at least did not grow out of the serious romances.

But to return to Petronius. The question as to whether or not the *Satyricon* was preceded by other romances of a burlesque or realistic or picaresque nature has generally taken the form of a dispute as to whether the lost *Milesiaka* of one Aristides, translated by Sisenna, was a collection of stories or a continuous romance like that of Petronius.[18] The question is at least an open one; but since the ancient *testimonia* are quite ambiguous on this point, we shall do better, I think, to leave Aristides out of the reckoning altogether and to admit that, so far as explicit testimony goes, we cannot be absolutely sure of the existence of any comic romance prior to the time of Petronius. But lack of *testimonia* in the field of ancient fiction means very little; and it would not be at all surprising if many comic romances, of which we now have no knowledge, were in circulation in the days of Petronius.[19] When I say "comic romance" I do not mean a romance resembling the *Satyricon* in all its wealth of realistic tableaux and numerous side shows, but rather a straightforward story of manifold adventure related chiefly for the sake of the fun and in the spirit of burlesque. That such a romance existed in Greek before the time of Petronius appears to me to be extremely probable, and it is only when we make this assumption that the origin and peculiarities of the *Satyricon* can be explained satisfactorily and in accord with the facts and tendencies of ancient literary history.

We know that a comic romance did actually evolve in Greek literature. The [*Loukios e Onos*] of Lucian, familiarly known through Apuleius' interpolated version as the story of the *Golden Ass*, is just such a romance as I have in mind. The foundation on which it was built was a short folk-tale which related the transformation of a young man into an ass as a punishment for some folly or for some offense against the witches.[20] The author of the [*Onos*], or rather of its original,[21] has taken this simple situation and made it into a "romance" by giving it an introduction and a conclusion and by adding to the number of the experiences which the young man undergoes. The added experiences in this case were suggested partly by Aesopic fables and proverbs relating to the ass; but there is also, as in Petronius, obvious borrowing from the epic, the comedy, the erotic romance, and the mime.[22] Now the basic story of the *Satyricon* is closely analogous, both in formation and tendency to the [*Onos*]. It consists mainly in a series of comic episodes suggested by or taken bodily from various convenient sources, especially the mime, and related smoothly and, no doubt, as in the [*Onos*], with much originality and invention, as the experiences of one man.[23] Without reaching a climax such a story might be prolonged indefinitely. The only logical end would be the death of the protagonist or want of comic experiences to assign to him. The adventures of Encolpius were probably represented as the result of his having offended Priapus, while those of Lucius resulted from his own fatal curiosity about magic. In both cases the cause of the adventures serves as a loose framework on which the episodes are hung, and which gives them the only thread of unity they possess, apart from the biographical form. Other romances of the same type may have had a different framework. This framework merely supplies the want of a plot; and the fact that it differs in the two romances is no more significant than the fact that Plautus' *Menaechmi* turns on a different plot from that of his *Trinummus*.

Nor do I believe that the erotic element is any more essential. The pairing of Encolpius and Giton as lovers with Ascyltus as a foil appears to be merely a device for creating comic situations. Their mock love affair involves no sustained dramatic suspense as in the erotic romances properly so called, nor is the interest here, as there, at all psychological. Unlike the picturesque characters of serious romance, Encolpius and Lucius, as human souls, attract neither our interest nor our sympathy. They are far from being even clever rogues. They are merely the vehicles of burlesque. The primary and ever present purpose of both the *Satyricon* and the [*Onos*] is simply to amuse the reader by the objective presentation of consecutive comic scenes. And herein the type is defined. So long as the episodes are presented for the sake of the fun, and not for love's sake or for the sake of realism, they may be either erotic or non-erotic, real or imaginary. Erotic scenes lend themselves very readily to burlesque, and it is for that reason no doubt that they figure so prominently; but their value is purely comic,

and their importance no greater than that of numerous other burlesque scenes of a different nature.

Likewise, the presence or absence of realism in the primary situation seems unimportant. The difference between the [*Onos*] and the *Satyricon* in this respect is merely a difference in the particular devices employed toward the same end, namely, to create a potentially comic situation or framework. Such matters of plot-technique, or choice of theme, are variable within the limits of universally recognized and well-defined literary genres. Aristophanes' *Peace* and his *Acharnians* are both comedies, and written for the same political purpose, though the former deals with a frankly impossible situation, and the latter with a situation within the range of possibility; so, too, with the *Amphitryo* of Plautus as compared with the other plays; and so with Horace's *Satires*. Without differing in what we call type, they may deal with either possibilities or impossibilities. The supernatural incidents in the [*Onos*] are not told as such for their own sake, but in a spirit of burlesque, and they are strictly subordinate to the author's main purpose—comedy and amusement. As soon as Lucius becomes an ass his experiences are as realistic as those of Encolpius. Burlesque naturally adheres to the commonplace; but any device may be employed to support it.

Apart from the formation and purpose of the two stories of adventure, we note many other points of similarity. One of the most peculiar features of the [*Onos*], as of the *Satyricon*, consists in the absence of any moral personality in the leading characters. Outside the popular novella with which the [*Onos*] is closely associated in origin, one looks in vain for this strange quality in almost any other form of ancient literature. The conventional rogue, or even the parasite, usually acts with some spiritual energy, and has some kind of self-respect; but the peculiar thing about Lucius and Encolpius is that they relate the most extravagant and ironical farces all at their own expense. Provided it be comic, there is no act or predicament, however absurd or humiliating even to a rogue, to which they will not readily confess. The things that Lucius tells about himself, though humiliating, are generally less debasing than the experiences of the Roman Encolpius; but the tendency and the odd effect are exactly the same. In most narrative literature the episodes are adapted in some measure to suit the character, typical or individual, of the protagonists; but in the [*Onos*] and in the *Satyricon* the episodes exist for their own sakes, and the persons who are made to enact them tend thereby to become mere puppets. Accordingly, Lucius and Encolpius are fictitious persons representative of contemporary society, as is usual in comedy; whereas, in the erotic romance the characters generally belong to history or local legend and their experiences, except in the latest of the romances, that of Achilles Tatius, are represented as taking place in a far-off past. It is probably mere coincidence that both Lucius and Encolpius are educated Romans, the former an author, the latter a rhetorician; but in the erotic novel, the characters are never either Roman or literary. The [*Onos*] and the **Satyricon** are also alike in that they are both independent of the conventional geographical background of the erotic novels, for the latter rarely or never take us so far west as the home of Trimalchio, nor so far north on the mainland of Greece as the setting of the [*Onos*]. Like the **Satyricon**, the [*Onos*] has the autobiographical form, contains many comic reminiscences of the epic and the erotic romance, and also many similarities in the motives and situations. To enumerate these here would take too long, but I think I have made it clear that the basic story of the **Satyricon** is identical in type essentials with the story of Lucius.[24]

The question now arises, Was this type originated by Petronius and imitated, as scarcely any other Roman type was, by the Greeks, or did both representatives spring up independently? Neither of these suppositions seems at all plausible. In nearly every department of literature the Romans were inspired by Greek models Why not here too? Is it not more likely that the first specimen of a comic romance was simple and straightforward like the [*Onos*], rather than a story like that of Petronius, which is imbedded, and almost lost, in a maze of digressions and embellishments of every sort? Petronius' work in sixteen books or more has every appearance of being a developed rather than a primitive (i.e., the first) specimen of the comic romance; and it is therefore very probable that the **Satyricon** was preceded by other comic romances of the more simple type, presumably in Greek.[25]

This sort of novel may have originated in the same way as the [*Onos*], that is, from the expansion of popular tales that were either ironical or humorous at the start or *potentially* so by virtue of their subject-matter. A fairy tale of real intrinsic beauty is likely to retain its ideal character perennially; but a realistic tale, or a naïvely superstitious one, however serious it may be at the start, owing to its essentially homely character, is apt to become ironical or burlesque as society becomes more sophisticated. One may see this process at work in Apuleius' tale of Socrates and Aristomenes (*Met.* i. 5-20). It is true that not many of these popular tales were likely to become expanded into "romances," because the single incident with which they usually dealt often offorded no good framework for further episodes. But when fancy has once changed a man into an ass, nothing is more natural than that his recorded experiences in that form should be augmented, not indeed by popular repetition—for in a novella of this sort where the protagonist is variable and of no personal importance or identity there can be no popular biographical interest—but by the conscious literary effort of a writer already familiar with the *Odyssey* and with the serious prose romances. Besides the ass-story we may imagine

others equally capable of expansion. The clever thief who stole from the treasure-house of Rhamsinitus (*Hdt.* ii. 121) is waging a war of wits with the king until such time as the latter pardons him. The situation here provides a natural framework into which any number of episodes might be worked without any organic readjustment. The difference between a story of this kind and the [*Onos*] is purely quantitative and artistic. We call the former a novella instead of a romance because it is popular rather than literary and because it contains fewer episodes; but the two types are structurally identical and spiritually very closely akin. Since the gap between them is very slight, it may well have been bridged by writers who lived before the time of Petronius. Such a development is more to be expected in an age that witnessed the elaboration of the mime, the new comedy, and the serious bourgeoise romance, and in which the realistic novella emerged from oral tradition into literature, than in the later and much less creative period of the second century A.D. (date of the [*Onos*]). After a few novels had been written on the basis of folklore plots, it would be very easy for any writer to create a plot of his own on the same simple principles, and this is probably what Petronius has done, possibly others before him. . . .

But there is more to account for in Petronius than the basic story. What shall we say of the poetry, the declamations, the inserted *fabulae*, and the vivid and detailed representations of scenes from real life? I believe most of this is to be strictly Roman and to have originated with Petronius. The practice of dressing up Greek models with various embellishments and digressions and of departing more or less from their conventional standards in form and range of content was apparently not uncommon among Roman writers. They wanted to contribute something original. Their attitude is somewhat typified by that of Phaedrus as expressed in the Prologue of his second book (l. 8): *Equidem omni cura morem servabo senis (Aesopi)| sed si libuerit aliquid interponere, | dictorum sensus ut delectet varietas, | bonas in partes, lector, accipias velim;* and at the beginning of the third book (l. 38): *ego porro illius semita feci viam | et cogitavi plura quam reliquerat*; and his fifth book professes to be entirely original. Likewise, Ovid's *Metamorphoses*, though based in large part on Greek collections of myths, is undoubtedly original in respect to its *Rahmenerzählung*, which cannot be paralleled in Greek, and to its mixture of epic, lyric, historical, and philosophical passages. These combinations and the arts by which the various myths are formally strung together may be accredited to the invention of the Roman artist himself. If we bear in mind the great amount of heterogeneous matter that Apuleius in his *Metamorphoses* has crowded into the framework of the straightforward Greek story of Lucius, we shall have no need to wonder at the discursiveness of Petronius nor at his apparent aberrations from the norm of his Greek predecessors. The two Roman writers have treated their Greek models in almost exactly the same manner. Let us consider the various features separately.

Petronius differs from the "[*Onos*] and from Greek writers generally in the degree of realism he employs. By "realism" I mean the concrete, detailed, and vivid representation of scenes from ordinary or low life, often described for their own artistic value. We meet with some of this realism in the Greek comedy, in Greek mimes, and elsewhere; but on the whole it is less vivid and more incidental. Greek writers are likely to make less of it than the Romans.[26] At any rate, this is the case in the story of Lucius; for the Latin version of Apuleius contains many a graphic sketch of persons and things which, in the Greek version, were alluded to in more general terms or briefly dismissed.[27] It is probable, therefore, that the extreme realism of Petronius is Roman; and that just as the Romans never, so far as we know, developed an idealized romance, so probably the Greeks never had a truly realistic one, that is, realistic in the same degree as Petronius. The realism in the "[*Onos*], which I assume to be more or less typical of that of the lost novels of the same type, is purely incidental to the narrative; whereas in Apuleius and in Petronius it is often paraded for its independent value; cf. *Met.* ix. 12-13; and the description of Trimalchio's dinner.

That which has been said of the difference in point of realism between the Roman and Greek novels applies also to character-drawing; for the characters in Apuleius, as well as in Petronius, are described far more vividly and realistically than they are in the "[*Onos*] or in any other Greek romance. Since Apuleius has made a great advance in this respect over his Greek original, it is easy to believe that Petronius has done likewise.

Along with concreteness we observe greater obscenity, and more of it in Petronius than in the "[*Onos*], or, in fact, in any known Greek work. The Greek tends to keep it subordinate, the Roman to give it greater prominence, and often to make it coarser by representing it more concretely. This again could be amply illustrated from Apuleius, to say nothing of Catullus and Martial in contrast with the Greek *Anthology* (quantitatively and qualitatively).

Another feature worth mentioning is the insertion of short stories more or less independent of the plot. Such stories are those about the werwolf, the matron of Ephesus, and that of Eumolpus in chapters 85-87. Apuleius has inserted seventeen or more such independent stories into his translation of the Greek Luciad, and Ovid tells us that Sisenna added *ioci* to his translation of Aristides. These *ioci*, as Professor Mendell observes, may have been short stories; but in any case it is important to note that Sisenna did add some em-

bellishments of his own, and that it is only in the Roman novels, never in the Greek, that independent stories are inserted.

The long poems on the fall of Troy and on the Civil War, respectively, and the lengthy discussions of literature and art, interrupt the progress of the main narrative and are introduced chiefly for their intrinsic interest. At first thought, it would seem difficult to parallel this sort of procedure elsewhere, but here again a comparison with Apuleius proves instructive. Apuleius does not indeed introduce long poems, doubtless because he was less interested in poetry than Petronius; but he does introduce philosophical digressions and ornate descriptions, and these, like the digressions of Petronius, stand apart as artistic units, treated for their own sake and retarding the narrative. The difference in nature or length between the separate artistic entertainments of Petronius and those of Apuleius are due only to individual taste. Petronius as *arbiter elegantiae* at Nero's court was interested in literary criticism and matters of taste. It is not surprising, therefore, that he felt the challenge of Lucan's *Pharsalia* and was tempted to imitate or rival or parody that poem in his *Civil War*. Apuleius, on the other hand, being more interested in his prose style, exercises his talent in describing the house of Byrrhena, or the robber's cave, or in writing an essay on the beauty of human hair, or describing in ornate prose the ceremonies in the worship of Isis and Osiris, all of which he has added of his own accord to the Greek original, and which are unessential to the story. Likewise, the shorter poems in the **Satyricon** rarely advance the action, but, like the others, seem to be introduced for their independent interest. Sometimes, of course, they illustrate a point in the text, or a situation, quite effectively and humorously, but they seem to be added for the sake of embellishment rather than as a matter of form. Many of them are of surprising beauty and stand in the same odd contrast to their coarse surroundings as do the artistic effusions of Apuleius.

When Apuleius puts the beautiful story of Cupid and Psyche into the mouth of a villainous old hag, he is doing the same sort of thing that Petronius does when he puts elegant criticism into the mouth of Eumolpus. As a mystic, Apuleius is induced to leave out the original burlesque ending of the ass-story, and to substitute therefor a twenty-five-page chapter describing in a solemn, religious tone the majesty of Isis and Osiris. As a platonic philosopher and a Carthaginian senator, he puts into the mouth of Lucius a page of denunciation against corrupt judges and an eloquent eulogy of Socrates, but at the end he remarks: "Behold, shall we suffer an ass to philosophize? I return whence I left off, to the main story" (*Met.* x. 33). In the same way, Petronius has allowed his degenerates to philosophize on literature and art, or in fact on any of the numerous subjects in which he is interested, and which may add to the reader's entertainment.

These embellishments probably do not belong to the comic, unmoral novel as a Greek type but are added in accordance with the fancy of the individual Roman writer; and this in turn will be qualified by the age in which the author lives and its cultural and literary background. Much of the subject-matter of Petronius, as well as the discursive nature of his writing and his love of variety, shows the influence of Roman satirè; but it is not as a moralist that the *arbiter elegantiae* is interested in society but as an entertainer.

To sum up, I believe that the basic story of the **Satyricon** was patterned after, or at any rate preceded by, some straightforward comic narrative like the "[*Onos*]; and that the criticism of art and literature, the poetry, the character-drawing, and the realistic tableaux are due to the originality of Petronius.

### Notes

[1] Read at the meeting of the Ohio Classical Conference at Delaware, October, 1923, under the title, "Petronius and his Greek Sources."

[2] Cf. chap. 139:

[3] Chap. 19, *omnia mimico risu exsonuerant*. I agree with Preston (*Class. Phil.*, X, 261) and Thomas (*Pétrone*, p. 213) that the keynote of the *Satyricon* is struck in this passage. Preston observes very justly that Petronius "conceived of himself primarily as a [*gelotopoios*]" and that "nowhere else in Latin literature is such a premium put on laughter."

[4] These are discussed in an interesting article by Professor F. F. Abbott, *Class. Phil.*, VI, 257 ff.

[5] *Der Griechische Roman*,[3] p. 267.

[6] *Röm. Dichtung*[2], III, 150.

[7] *Neue Jahrb. f. d. kl. Alt.*, XIII (1904), 476.

[8] *Der Dialog*, II, 37.

[9] *Neue Jahrb. f. d. kl. Alt.*, XXVII (1911), 485.

[10] That is, BDEFG*pt*. See Bücheler's Preface in the edition of 1862, pp. xiv, xxv-xxvi, and 2. *Petronii arbitri satirarum 1*. is the reading of P; but P seems to be the only MS in which any form of the noun *satira* occurs.

[11] Cf. C. W. Mendell in *Class. Phil.*, XII (1917), 168; and Suidas. . . . These titles are cited in the nominative, of course, but they probably appeared on the title-page in the genitive followed by [*logoi*] or [*biblia*] plus a numeral, or with the numeral alone. Strictly, the work of Petronius should be cited not as *Satyricon,* but as *Satyrica*.

[12] The meaning "satirical," or "belonging to satire," appears to be late and to have originated with grammarians who associated Roman satire with the Greek satyr-drama; so Lydus, *De Mag.* 41. After a prolonged search through the lexicons and *indices verborum*, I am unable to find any instance earlier than Lactantius or the *scholia* on Juvenal i. 168, in which the word *satyricus* has reference to satire, either in Greek or in Latin. That it may have been so used by grammarians in the time of Petronius is not improbable; but the other meaning was certainly common, and of much longer standing.

[13] See the parallels listed by M. Rosenblüth, *Beiträge zur Quellenkunde von Petrons Satiren*, pp. 36-55.

[14] Professor Abbott observes with a great deal of truth that much of what appears to be satirical in Petronius is so only because we are setting up in our own minds a comparison between the abuses described (perhaps merely for fun) and the requirements of good taste. The subject-matter of the *Satyricon*, like that of the realistic novella, by its very nature may be regarded as constituting a satire on society; but this does not mean that the author is a satirist, if by "satirist" we mean one whose chief purpose, like that of Varro, Horace, or Juvenal, is to criticize society from an ethical point of view. For this implies either an attempt to correct, or moral indignation or reaction to things as they are. But the only inference, if any, that Petronius by his tone would encourage us to draw seems to be that society is incorrigible and not worth worrying about; and that it is the part of wisdom not, like the satirists, to carp at conditions which are sadly inevitable, but to look only for amusement in the comedy of human life. Petronius is a cynic; but his cynicism is not that of the school, or of Menippus, who would scale heaven for philosophical truth. It is deeper and more somber; it springs evidently from a profound though latent pessimism, from the cosmic disillusionment of the man of the world.

[15] See the scholarly monograph of B. Lavagnini, *Le Origini del Romanzo Greco*, Pisa, 1921. Lavagnini shows in a very convincing way that the romance evolved from the elaboration, popular and historiographical, of local legends in Hellenistic times; cf. *AJP*, XLIV, 371 ff., and, for the early date, Mendell, *op. cit.*, pp. 161-62, 165; and W. Schmid in Rohde's *Gr. Roman*,[3] p. 610.

[16] *Hermes*, XXXIV (1899), 494-519.

[17] See Chandler, *Romances of Roguery*, pp. 6 ff.

[18] For the views of the leading disputants on this subject see the summary of Rosenblüth, *op. cit.*, pp. 87-90. The most important ancient testimony is to be found in the following passages: Ovid, *Trist.* ii. 413-14; *ibid.* 443-44; Ps. Lucian, *Amores* 1; Plutarch, *Crassus* 32. From these passages, and from a few very meager fragments, the most that can be inferred with certainty about the [*Milesiaka*] is that they were obscene and partly at least in prose. That they *may* have been partly in verse also has been inferred by Norden (*Antike Kunstprosa*, II, 756) from the words *nocte vagatrix* quoted by the grammarian Charisius from Sisenna's translation. The plural title may mean no more than it does in Lucian's [*Alethe diegemata*], or in the [*Aithiopika*] of Heliodorus.

[19] The ancient literary critics evidently regarded this kind of writing as trivial and beneath their serious consideration. Hence they tend to ignore it. That it was popular, there can be no doubt (cf. Jerome in Bücheler's *Petronius*, p. 243); but it must have circulated rather among laymen than among men of literary profession. The novels of Petronius and Apuleius are mentioned occasionally by ancient writers, but generally in a tone of disparagement. Outside of Photius and Suidas, references to Greek romances are extremely rare and meager; and even in these encyclopedias you will look in vain for mention of Longus or Chariton, whose novels would be quite unheard of were it not for the survival of their manuscripts. Likewise, the two erotio novels mentioned by Suidas under the name of Xenophon (cf. *supra*) are apparently mentioned by no other ancient writer. Moreover, some of the ethnographical titles that have come down to us and are generally believed to refer to historical works, may in reality have been the titles of romances. Thus, if Suidas had not added that [*estide ton panu aiskhron*] we would assume that the [*Rodiaka*] of Philip of Amphipolis was history; but the descriptive remarks of our lexicographer, and a casual reference in Theodorus Priscian (*Res Medicae*, 11), make it clear that the book was erotic fiction; and who knows but that it antedated Petronius? Along with Aristides, Ovid (*Trist.* ii. 415 ff.) mentions two other naughty books whose authors were not exiled:

> *Nec qui descripsit corrumpi semina matrum*
> *Eubius, impurae conditor historiae*
> *Nec qui composuit nuper Sybaritica fugil.*

Either one of these books may have been a continuous romance like that of Petronius, and the term *historia* strongly suggests this; for the usage cf. Mendell, *op. cit.*, pp. 163-64; Propertius, ii. 1, 13-16; see also Bürger in *Hermes*, XXVII (1892), 354-55. That they were written in a humorous vein seems probable from the analogy of the stories of adultery in Apuleius, Petronius, and elsewhere.

Robert, *Hermes*, XXXVI (1901), 364 ff., believes that certain wall paintings found in the *casa Farnesina* at Rome represent scenes from a picaresque romance prior to Petronius. But in this, too, there is no certainty.

[20] K. Weinhold (*Sitzungsb. d. königl. Preuss. Acad. d. Wissen.* [1892], pp. 475 ff.) points out eight analogues to this story in the folklore of Europe and India. He summarizes as follows: *Das Urgeschichtchen mag so gelautet haben: ein junger Mann kommt mit Frauen in zu vertraute Beziehung, und wird zur Busse in einen Esel verwandelt, dem gewisse seiner Anlagen entsprechen. Nur sein Äusseres, nicht seine innere Natur wird von der Verwandlung betroffen. Er hat ein mühsames Leben zu führen, bis es ihm gelingt, die Kräuter zu geniessen, welche bestimmt sind, ihn zu entzaubern.* For other legends, less typical, to be sure, than those discussed by Weinhold, but dealing with the same theme, see the story of Peter the Huntsman, in Grimm's *Fairy Tales* and that of the rogue Ali of Cairo in the *Arabian Nights* (Burton's translation, VII, 197-99). Cf. also my dissertation, pp. 43 ff.

[21] The [*Onos*] is an epitome of a longer work of the same nature entitled [*Metamorphoseis*] and ascribed by Photius (*Bibl.* 129) to one Lucius of Patrae (the ass in the story). The real author of this lost original, however, was probably Lucian; cf. Perry, *op. cit.*, pp. 59 ff.

[22] For Aesopic motifs in the [*Onos*] see Crusius in *Philologus,* XLVII (1888), 448. Epic parody and reminiscences are listed, though not exhaustively, by Neukamm, *De Luciano Asini Auctore* (Leipzig, 1914), pp. 92-93, who also points out the influence of comedy (pp. 94, 87-88). Several matters in the [*Onos*], such as the adventure with the robbers, their cave, their plans for torturing (chap. 25; cf. Xenophon of Ephesus iv. 6), the [*daimon baskanos*] (19), the resolve of Lucius to commit suicide rather than become a eunuch (33), the setting up of [*anathemata*] at the end (cf. Longus and Xenophon, *ad. fin.*), as well as occasional stylistic features (e.g., the soliloquies of Lucius in 5, 15, and 23; cf. Chariton vi. 6; Xenophon ii. 10, iii. 5; Heliodorus ii. 4; Achilles Tatius iii. 10) remind us of the erotic romance. For the mimic motifs in the [*Onos*] compare chap. 51 with the statement of Suetonius in *Nero* 12 and Martial in *Liber Spect.* 5. See also Rosenblüth, *op. cit.,* p. 65 (top). In commenting on the boisterous theatrical element in Petronius, Preston (*loc. cit.*) observes that the humor of an incident is seldom left to make its own appeal to the reader, but "we are told that it provoked 'gales of laughter' or 'bursts' of applause." . . .

[23] By this I do not mean to imply that there was ever any progress of development from collections of separate stories or *Schwänke* to novels like that of Petronius. This is the view of K. Bürger (*Studien zur Geschichte des griechischen Romans* [Erster Teil, 1902], pp. 20 ff.) and of Schissel von Fleschenberg (*Entwicklungsgeschichte des griechischen Romans*

[Halle, 1913], pp. 3 ff.), who assume that Aristides' *Milesiaka* was some kind of a collection—*Rahmenerzählung*, according to Schissel—and that there was a tendency among writers of such collections to weld together the separate stories more closely so as to give them some inner unity, and that finally they came to be told smoothly as the experiences of one man. To me, this theory of development seems very improbable; cf. the remarks of W. Schmid in Rohde's *Gr. Roman*[3], pp. 607 f.

[24] This fact is recognized, though somewhat vaguely, by Bürger (*op. cit.*) and by Collignon (*Étude sur Pétrone*, p. 49), neither of whom has made an adequate and discriminating comparison.

[25] Cf. the remarks of Leo, *Die Kultur der Gegenwart*, Teil I, Abt. 8 (Leipzig, 1912), p. 459: *Die Form des Schelmenromans, die das Buch hatte, war gewiss in den Unterschichten der griechischen Litteratur vorhanden; was solche Produktion wert ist das hängt ganz von der Persönlichkeit ab, die das Ihrige in die Form hineinlegt.* Wilamowitz (*op. cit.*, p. 190) is of the same opinion.

[26] Cf. the interesting remarks of F. A. Wright, *AJP*, XLII, 169: "The habit which the Roman poets have of working up a long passage from a few lines in some Greek original by the addition of a mass of realistic details deserves more study than it has yet received." He cites several examples from the works of Vergil, Ovid, and Horace.

[27] A fuller discussion of the various phases of Apuleius' originality in the *Metamorphoses* will be found in an article of mine which appears in *TAPA*, LIV. 196 ff.

## Philip Schuyler Allen (essay date 1928)

SOURCE: "The Approach to Romanesque Poetry," in *The Romanesque Lyric: Studies in Its Background and Development from Petronius to the Cambridge Songs 50-1050*, University of North Carolina Press, 1928, pp. 66-83.

[*In the following excerpt, Allen examines some of Petronius's poetry, explaining how it breaks with Roman tradition and why some critics have scorned it.*]

In my preceding narrative I have several times used the phrase Romanesque poetry to describe a certain manner of early European metrical writing.

As so applied, my choice of the word Romanesque is determined by the current application of the same attributive term to transitional types in the history of the fine and decorative arts. When thus employed Romanesque of course specifies "belonging to or desig-

nating the early medieval style of art and ornament derived from those of the Roman empire." As hitherto used in the domain of art Romanesque describes mainly that modification of the classical Roman form which was introduced between the reigns of Constantine and Justinian and which was an avowed attempt to adapt classical forms to Christian purposes.

Now I want to have a single word with which to refer to whatever poetry in western Europe since the Augustan Age derives its main elements of plan and construction, its purpose, theme, and imagery from Roman verse. I need one term like Romanesque to specify a distinct departure from Roman writing and yet a sideline descendant of it—a term, in short, which will run like a stout golden thread through the Silver Age, through the revival of letters under Hadrian, the African schools of Fronto and Tertullian, the fourth-century renaissance, and those two centuries after the troubadour Fortunatus, which seem so sterile of creative literary production but are so fruitful and significant with regard to polyphonic music. It is the lack of animating ideation of six centuries of Latin writing, caused by the failure to achieve one all-embracing phrase for their activity, which has led critics to speak of decay, debasement, preciosity, and final extinction when characterizing the natural and ordered stages that poetry had to undergo on its long pilgrimage from Rome to Canterbury. Whatever else may be said of such a phrase as Romanesque poetry, it will be agreed that its use may help to explain every historical departure of Latin writing from the classic idealism or formalism of Augustan Rome. No phrase is so satisfactory, so little vague as Romanesque poetry to indicate that the matter of verse has come to predominate over its form. Romanesque presumes in art the quality of the personal, ephemeral, emotional, or sensual, as opposed to that of the ideal or ethos. It notes that less attention is paid to objective methods of composition than to the expression of subjective feeling—hence it always suggests *romantic* as opposed to *classical*.

It will still be rashly contended by some people that Romanesque poetry is but a corrupted imitation of Roman writing, and yet this is never true, for it is a new thing in the world, the slowly matured product of a long period and of many influences. Let me say most emphatically that even where Romanesque poetry is but a short remove from debased Roman art, if it is yet definitely removed and contains at least one new element or unit which is entirely absent from Roman—no matter how slight that element (as of personal appeal or pathos or fancy) may seem to be—then the style of art and ornament in poetry is no longer Roman, it is Romanesque; whether in whole or in part, it is an entity as separate from Roman as a Romance language is separate from the Latin tongue.

There are two well worn paths between which the

modern student of Romanesque poetry ordinarily chooses when he approaches the merging of Latin tradition with Gothic and Frankish culture in the Gaul of the fifth and sixth centuries. Because I propose to follow neither of these clearly marked trails, I feel it incumbent upon me to state promptly the reasons for my nonconformance to custom in this regard.

The first of these hallowed routist routes from decadent classical poetry to that which we term Romanesque *starts* with Horace and Catullus and with such moments of Vergil as carry the idyllic manner to a higher tension. A beginning is made with this trio because most modern critics not unreasonably consider them to be the finest exemplars of Latin lyric verse. This first path *ends* with Martianus Capella, Cassiodorus, Boethius, Colum Cille, Columban, Gregory of Tours, and Venantius Fortunatus, and—except for a vivid revival in the rococo measures of fourth-century lyric art—is felt to run all the way downhill to the tawdry Romanesque rhetoric that marks its inglorious close. The critic who pads the hoof along this route and approaches the study of Romanesque poetry from this direction finds, laudably enough, that the successors of the Augustan Age are less and less able to sustain the splendor of Horatian diction, and to him poor sixth-century poets inevitably assume the rôle of mendicants at the end of a trail that swoops sharply down from the summits to the sunset.

Now I gain neither healing nor help in my poetic pilgrimage by proceeding from the assumption that Romanesque poetry is only a barbarous corruption of classical molds. Such an assumption feeds me indeed with Rome but robs me of Whitechapel and Strawberry Hill. It causes my historic sense to atrophy, for it fosters a biased scholastic connoisseurship at the expense of all power fully to enjoy poetry written during the parlous centuries of Gothic Night. Such preconception as to the nature of Romanesque verse takes no account of that changed character of people in western Europe and of that consequent shifting in expression to embody new social conditions to which I have devoted much space in my opening chapters. Such prejudgment demands of me æsthetic snobbery, in that I am supposed to prefer meticulous copyings of poetic masterpieces to the confusing experiments and innovations of rebellious racy art. It blinds me to all values that lie outside the pale of conventional classic complacency. Such a recapture of the romantic spirit in verse as mirrors, no matter if dully, new efforts put forth by men in the first century of Christ, finds no sympathetic response in him who willfully ascribes each deviation from Augustan norm to a perversion of taste. This amateur of decadent Græco-Roman verse extols the ancient priests of poetry but decries its newer prophets. He is so content to exalt the stagnant art of the pagan past that he belittles the advance in poetic endeavor during six centuries—their incessant, restless

experiment; their tireless speculation about æsthetics; their unwearying effort to apply them to the actual production of poetry and to exert the conscious human will upon art as it had not been exerted before.

So much, then, in the way of reaction against the first of the paths by which the modern student of Romanesque is unfortunately wont to approach the merging of Roman pagan tradition with Gothic and Frankish ideals of taste. Let us now turn to the second path, the one that starts with the world of medieval poetry, of which, by consensus of opinion, the ecclesiastical and vagabond Latin verse of the twelfth and thirteenth centuries furnishes him with many noblest examples. From this point of audition the modernist critic harks back to thin earliest notes of Latin Romanesque as these loose themselves waveringly from the full-stopped diapason of classical sound. Such a critic's ears still tingle reminiscently with the mad catachresis of canonical Latin poured forth by Gerbert and Fulbert and Wipo, by Serlo and Gerald and Baudri, by Alan and Adam and Hildebert and Nigel, Bernard and Walter, and Philip le Breton, by him of Salisbury and Vinesauf and Vendôme and Rennes and Morlaix and Grevia, by Peter of Blois and Reginald of Canterbury and Henry of Huntingdon and Hildebert of Lavardin and Hugo of Orleans and Godefrid of Rheims, by Hilary and Abelard and Odo of Orleans, Golias, Archipoeta, Mapes and Primas, and all who belong to the graceless Order of Goliards, whose names do not linger in the knowledge of men but who wrote imperishable MSS of modern song, like Cambridge and St. Omer and Queen Christine and Benedictbeurn. And to the ears of such a critic the Latin poems of fourth and sixth-century Gaul—Gothic, baroque, and rococo—give out a satisfying tone; their singers no longer seem to seek our alms but rather stand prophetic and erect at the beginning of that polyphonic path which strikes sharply upward from a dawn-filled horizon to the table-land of medieval Latin lyric utterance.

I cannot truthfully say that I treasure the result gained from following this second pathway chosen by the modernist more highly than the attitude gained through following the first one, the way invariably affected by the classicist. For neither classicist nor modernist regards his journeying in Romanesque poetry as an end in itself. To either critic the road offers no place of sojourn, but only a causeway between two points. It has to them no high reason for individual existence in and of itself—both types of critic see it only in direct relation to what has preceded it or to what follows after. They do not apply their historical sense to the study of Romanesque poetry. They do not apply to it certain psychological tests that are now familiar to every modern man of culture, in an attempt to discover if Romanesque verse (like sculpture, architecture, mosaic, carving) is a characteristic art, or, on the other hand, if it expresses the racial and social temper of the time which produces it. Critics seek no real values in Romanesque poetry as such, and, therefore, find none. Critics censure the rebellious quality in Romanesque, forgetful that it is just the mark of high artistry so to exercise its individual will as to die fighting a world that will not change. Better far is such rebellion than the harmony of dull and complacent monotones that ruled the Græco-Roman decadence; particularly after new ages and novel societies had come to the front of the western stage.

In our critical analysis of poetry, any judgment at which we may arrive depends upon the viewpoint from which the subject is approached. It is maintained by some that an atom has energy when studied in *vacuo animæ*, irrespective of the mood of the scientific observer. But certainly a Romanesque poem—or sculpture or cathedral or carving or mosaic—has neither charm nor meaning unless it be in the mind of its beholder. "Reared as I had been among people who despised Gothic architecture," said Goethe, "I fed fat my distaste for those overloaded and complex ornaments which by their grotesquerie appeared to preach the gospel of gloom. And then all at once I saw the new revelation—the very thing that had seemed to me so contemptible now engaged my spirit, and conversely. A sudden perception of beauty in all its forms thereupon flooded my soul."

It is as hard for us to realize there was a time when Goethe turned his back upon the Strasbourg minster, as it was for his contemporaries to learn he could regard this edifice with a favoring eye. But that is not the point. The point is that Gothic notions such as dwell in a church wall, the doggerel of folk-song, the broadsides of Lutheran prose, the art of Shakespeare and even of Pindar were not conceptually or conceivably beautiful to Goethe until the moment when through Herder's teaching he felt them so to be. And thereafter they had for him necessitous, inherent beauty.

When with a mind single to the beauty of classical Roman poetry the student pursues a path which leads from Horace to the provinces, he finds the long flourishing of Romanesque a dreary time indeed. And in a Gallo-Roman society subservient to its military element, where barbarian slaves who gained ascendancy over a brutal soldiery might spawn on the throne of the Cæsars, he cannot hope to see the profession of poetry in a flourishing condition. Then it seems to him inevitable that the cult represented by Horace and the elegiac poets should become esoteric, and its enjoyment be confined to a rapidly diminishing class, whose sole source of inspiration and whose only audience is of the academy. Then he sighs at the divorce of tradition from contemporary thought, at the very moment when the opposite is true. He grieves over the increasing divergence of written and spoken Latin, and makes an ill face as an *elocutio novella*, the idiom of common life,

rises ever more sensibly to the surface. And finally, when a poet's meaning can no longer be deciphered by reference to the pages of Forcellini's *totius latinitatis lexicon*—what wicked irony sparkles in this title!—when a poet's contemporaries exalt him if he but spell correctly and his phrases parse, then does the amateur of Augustan poetry exclaim with unction, Rome is dead! And he refuses to sanction the Hisperic speech of a sixth century which has basely denied its birthright.

But when with a mind full of the beauty of resurgent thirteenth-century Latin lyric verse the modern student impatiently seeks the first indications of breaking in the stiff, implacable ritual of classical meters, then there is a freshness as of dawn in the new style that makes itself felt in the latter years of the principate of Augustus: the straining after romantic effect, the love of startling color and gorgeous imagery, the surfeit of brilliant epigram, the sense of masquerade and elaborate felicity of expression. Such a student holds high the Silver Age for the unexpected service it was to render that period of the Middle Ages when Greek was a hidden mystery to the western world—it was then that Lucan and Statius, Juvenal and Persius, and even the humble author of the *Ilias Latina* did their part in keeping the lamp alive and illumining the darkness before the budding morrow of the Renaissance. He finds vastly engaging many a half-forgotten line of Ausonius, Sidonius, and Venantius. For he sees a new nation coming into existence among the ruins of classical civilization in Gaul, and knows that a new idiom with firefly gleams of *lai* and *chanson* is being evolved. And his spirit chafes for the bright morning that is to come when Rome shall at last give up her reluctant ghost—a suicide, like Werther's, too long delayed! And the moment this modern student's eye surely catches the first gray foreshadowings of Carolingian renaissance, he longs to cry out, Rome is not dead but risen! And for him there exists meaning in every poetic excrescence of this old life that is real, not alone in the happier births of literary genius, but in the lucubrations of Vergil the Grammarian, and in the *Hisperica famina*, the *Lorica*, the *Rubisca*, the *Adelphus adelpha*, the *Vita Columbani*, and the *Antiphonary of Bangor*.

Perhaps I shall make myself clearest in distinguishing the attitude of classicist and modernist (romanticist) towards Romanesque poetry by taking refuge in concrete illustration.

A classicist who would derive his criteria for judging all Romanesque poetry by Horace's standard of performance finds little to admire in the verses of Petronius. For Horace, in the words of Garrod, is not profound, not ecstatic. He has discovered what we might have thought did not exist: the poetry of good sense. It is in virtue of this that he appeals to nearly all the moods of the average man and satisfies most needs, save the very highest. Horace is wise without pedantry, noble

without cant, at all points humane and genuine. He has
a hard, cool mind. For him life streams by like the
passage of some peaceful Saturnalia. The scene has its
dark patches, but Horace moves serenely amid its shifting phases; solidly content with life, the kindly uncle
of the whole human race. By habit he speaks in lofty
tones to Time and the world; his sonorous verse is
pitched to the greatness of the empire it reflects; he
has a high, moral seriousness and a supreme instinct
for measure and proportion.

Whereas, if he speak of them at all, the classicist refers
to the epigrams of lyric Petronius with bare tolerance,
citing them for want of better as stock examples of a
Latin that has already become Silver, on its foredoomed
way to being of baser metal yet: bronze, iron, pewter,
lead, tin, and scrap. For by the day of Petronius the
great movement of the Latin-speaking provinces had
begun. While still in a sense subordinate to Italy, these
provinces had grown to be organic parts of the empire
instead of subject countries. The municipal institutions
and civic energy of Rome were multiplied in a thousand centers of local life in Italy and Gaul, Spain and
Africa. Like the empire itself, Latin poetry had taken
a broader basis. The exquisite austerity of the old verse
was gone, and its diction, formed by a purer taste amid
a grave and exclusive public, was eclipsed by new and
striking styles. As the political extinction of Rome
proper approached and the one overwhelming interest
of the City ceased to absorb individual passion and
emotion, the tension on poetry and art became relaxed.
Feeling grew more humane and personal, social and
family life reassumed their real importance; and gradually there grew up a thing new to literature, the Romanesque, the romantic spirit. With its passionate sense
of beauty in nature, idyllic poetry reacted on the sense
of beauty in simple human life; the elegy and the epigram are full of a new freshness of feeling, and the
personal lyric is born, with its premonitions of a simple
pathos which is as alien to the older Roman spirit as
it is close to the feeling of medieval romance.

Now no one has brought the phantom of freshness into
the Latin poetry of love and nature more definitely
than Petronius. In fact, if we except a very few of the
best poems of Propertius, Latin elegiacs have nothing
to show that combines such perfection of form with
such sensuous charm. Therefore, your modernist finds
(with a start of surprise) in the lyric Petronius the words
and the tone of today:

### ENCOURAGEMENT TO EXILE

Leave thine own home, O youth, seek distant
    shores!
For thee a larger order somewhere shines—
Fear not thy fate! For thee through unknown
    pines
Under the cold north-wind the Danube pours;

For thee in Egypt the untroubled lands
Wait, and strange men behold the setting sun
Fall down and rise. Greatly be thou as one
Who disembarks, fearless, on alien sands. (1)

### THE MALADY OF LOVE IS NERVES

Night's first sweet silence fell, and on my bed
Scarcely I closed defeated eyes in sleep
When fierce Love seized me by the hair, and
    said,
(Night's bitter vigil he had bade me keep),
"Thou slave," he said, "a thousand amorous
    girls
Hast thou not loved? And canst thou lie
    alone?
O hard of heart!" I leaped, and he was gone,
And with my garment in disordered swirls,
And with bare feet I sought his path where
    none
There was by which to go. And now I run,
Being weary, and to move brings me no
    peace;
And turning back is bitter, and to stay
Most shames me in the midmost of my way—
And all men's voices slowly sink and cease;
The singing birds, my dogs that, faithful, keep
My house, the roaring streets, to me are still.
Alone of men, I dread my couch, my sleep—
I follow after Love, lord of my will. (2)

### NOBLESSE OBLIGE

Pride of birth or degree proves no man to be
    upright—
Noble alone is he whose hands have never
    known fear. (3)

### ILLUSION

Our eyes deceive us, and our sense
Weighs down our reason with pretense,
And in false ways goes wandering:
The tower that stands wellnigh four-square
Loses sharp corners in blue air
And softens to a rounded thing;
The liquor of Hyblæan bees,
My hunger sated, fails to please;
I hate the smell of cinnamon!
For this thing or for that, why weep
Or smile, except our senses keep
A doubtful battle never won. (4)

### WE ARE SUCH STUFF AS DREAMS . . .

Dreams that delude with flying shade men's
    minds
No airy phantoms are, nor sent by gods
From any shrine of theirs, but each man only

Weaves for himself his dream. And when in
  sleep,
Conquered, his limbs repose, and quiet comes,
Then the imponderable mind pursues
In darkness the slow circuit of the day.—
If towns have shook before him and sad cities
Under the weight of flames have been down-
  razed,
Javelins and fleeing armies he beholds,
The funerals of kings and plains wide-watered
With rivers of shed blood. If he's an orator,
Statutes and courts appear before his eyes;
He looks with terror on tribunals thronged
With multitudes. The miser hides his riches
And digs up buried treasure, and the huntsman
Drives through the shaken woods his yelling
  dogs.
The sailor dreams of shipwreck; from the
  waves,
Gasping, he takes his vessel, or in death
Seizes on it and sinks. And the adultress
Dreams, and so yields herself. The woman
  writes
In dreams unto her lover: why, the dog,
Sleeping, believes he follows on the hare!—
So all night long endured, the wounds of day
Doubly are sorrow to the miserable. (5)

NEALCE

Nealce, forever
  That night shall be dear
Asleep in my bosom
  That first saw you here;
And dear be the spirit,
  The lamp and the bed
When softly you came to
  A joy that is fled.
And now we are older
  We still must endure

The pitiful trouble
  Of age that is sure;
And since the brief years
  We shall lose with delay,
Let us kiss as of old,
  Let us love as we may.
Ours once was a passion
  Too sudden to spend—
Ah, now let us guard it
  Lest quickly it end! (6)

REMEMBERED SHORES

O sweeter to me than life may be is the sea and the
sand where I May come once more, a remembered
shore that I love changelessly; And day is fair in
that region where I swam as the naiad swims, The
cold sea-maid with whom I played a wager of hands

and limbs. And the fountain's pool all day is cool,
and the seaweed washes in, And O the sand, and
the quiet land where love knows never a sin! I have
lived my life. And not the strife of fortune can take
from me What time has given—a quiet haven, the
past, and the shore, and the sea. (7)

Now Petronius, as my reader will recall, lived in the
days of Nero and would be famous as a lyric poet but
for two things: first, his verse is overshadowed by his
most remarkable novel, the **Satyricon**; second, classicist critics are prone to abuse him, in common with his
great contemporaries Seneca, Martial, Juvenal, Lucan,
Phædrus, and Statius, because he did not follow in all
things linguistic and literary the mold of an age long
dead—as if the future should abuse our poets for doing
aught but ape Dryden and Pope. Be that as it may,
there is but one first-century lyric with which we may
reasonably compare the above-given odes of Petronius,
and that one is Statius's well-known *Apostrophe to
Sleep*. From the classicist point of view, it is a far more
deserving ode than any of Petronius (because it adheres more tightly in form and manner to traditional
verse). But I doubt if the modernist will agree with this
verdict, although the translation has been designedly
cast into a form best suited to display to English readers the virtues of its original: a verse-scheme after Sir
Philip Sidney's hexameter sonnet.

APOSTROPHE TO SLEEP

What have I done, O Sleep, gentlest of
  heaven's sons,
    That, miserable, I only forfeit the boons you
    spill?
    The flocks are silent each one, and beast
    and bird are still,
The truculent streams lie quiet, the sea-wave
  no more runs,
Curved tree-tops droop in slumber like men
  (and weary ones)—
    The seventh moon my staring eyeballs now
    doth fill,
    And morning and evening stars, seven
    dawns with dewy chill
Have sprinkled me in pitsy. Where shall I
  speak my orisons?

Sleep, is there any, lying in a fair girl's arms
  all night
    Who sighs and sends you from him? Hither
    let him send!
    Shed not your wing-feathers upon my
    sleepless eyes—
    Let happier souls pray so. Mine be the
    lesser prize:
    Go by with airy stride, touching with your
    wand's end—
No more than that—my face, even though the
  touch be light. (8)

But, however classicist and modernist may feel as to the difference between the art of Petronius and Statius, one important fact is manifest. A crack of division has occurred—call it a flaw, if you insist—which marks off two sorts of lyric verse in the first century. One sort is the Statius ode which clings to traditional Roman ideas and forms, as ivy clings to an old oak; it represents the past. The other sort is the Petronius epigram which varies, if slightly, yet always definitely, from Roman ideas and forms of the past. It foreshadows the end of ancient poetry; it contains germinally the inner spirit of romantic revolt; the amateur of modern verse turns to it without shock of sudden transition. It is not Roman except in the modeling of its verses. It is Romanesque.

For the first time in Latin verse we have in the epigrams of Petronius the most genuine and pathetic expression of a man's weariness. The best of them speak of quiet country and seaside, of love deeper than desire and founded on the durable grace of mind as well as the loveliness of the flesh,[1] of simplicity and escape from court. They speak of these things in a new way and with unmatched sincerity—they give us a poetic naturalism as unexpected as it is real. Therefore, as I am more concerned to describe the actualities of poetry than to characterize it according to the passing notions of any one day, I conceive it my duty not to give Petronius a bad name and then proceed to depreciate him—nor a good name and then rush forward in his praise—but rather to assign him his presumptive place in the scheme of things.

There is no more convenient place to which to assign the beginning of the history of the Romanesque lyric than the considerable number of epigrams, attributed with more or less certainty to Petronius,[2] which are preserved in the fragments of the *Latin Anthology*, seven of which have been quoted in translation above. It is with these epigrams of the age of Nero that the crack of division appears in Latin poetry which never thereafter heals, no matter how powerfully one abortive attempt after another is put forth during the following centuries to bridge the widening gap between western European verse and its pagan predecessors.

We must pause here to be quite sure of our ground. First, we must acknowledge readily that long before Petronius there veined Latin poetry elements that are curiously not Greek and not Roman, that breathe somehow of modernity of mood; of a tenderness and a sensibility that belong to romantic rather than to classic worlds. No one, it seems to me, not even Mackail, has written so well of this elusive Italian quality in Roman poetry as has H. W. Garrod, this quality that robs it of the danger of passing at its best for rhetoric, and at its worst for prose. This *ingenium molle*, we are told, whether in passion as with Propertius[3] or as with Vergil in reflection, is that deep and tender sensibility which

is the least Roman thing in the world and which in its subtlest manifestations is perhaps the peculiar possession of the Celt.[4] The unelaborate magic of Catullus is that of the Celtic temperament—the fourth *Æneid* is the triumph of an unconscious Celticism over the whole moral plan of Vergil's epic. Even before the Augustan Age Latin poetry is *facetus*—it glows and dances; has *lepor*—is clean and sprightly; has *venustas*—is possessed of a melting charm. Often enough, too, in the poetry of personal invective—in the *Epodes* and some of the *Odes* of Horace, in Catullus, and in the Vergilian *Catalepton*—we have that *Italum acetum,* that vinegar of coarse and biting wit from the countryside which has its origin in the casual ribaldry of the *vindemiatores*, in the rudely improvised dramatic contests of the harvest-home; pert and ready and unscrupulous in assigning its object inalienably to the pit. And the quickened force of this wit is like to seem to a modern man as up-to-date and recent as any songs irrepressible Heine borrowed from a similar source: the south-German reaping-couplets, *schnaderhüpfeln.*

If these things be true, then why not begin our history of the Romanesque lyric with Catullus, say, whose poetry is much less actually classic than that of Vergil and Horace, wherein are exhibited in a greater degree the qualities of grandeur, harmony, and stability? The passion of the senses so lifts more than one elegy of Catullus into regions where the moral judgment stands abashed, that nothing in the world seems significant save the personal trouble of a soul on fire. Why not begin with him?

Because, as Garrod is prompt to explain, although the quickening force in the best Augustan poetry is the Italian blood, yet not without reason do we speak of this poetry as Roman. For it was made by Italians who were already Romanized; the Italian spirit worked always under the spell of Rome and not under any merely external compulsion. And the spell of Rome was still over the whole of Roman poetry. The Italians were only a nation through Rome—it had behind it a great life and expressed a great people, their conscious deeds and their national ideals. Until the Christian Era has begun and we possess in the date of the birth of Christ a greatest symbolic indication of the ending of an ancient world of Roman life and poetry, it is vastly convenient for us to regard that world as a classical entity and to disregard the patent fact that side by side with it—ever since the influx into Italian art of Alexandrian models, at least—there had been a new world of poetry growing up which had with that classical entity so little in common that it is only confusing to take the former into account. In the way of literary analysis it is worth while to hunt out even in Ennius (B.C. 239-169) an Italian vividness and a colored phraseology that is neither Greek nor Roman—a swiftness, wild agitated tones, and a prophetic fury wrought by fire that are mayhap half Calabrian, half Celtic. But we must not forget that the Italian and the Roman elements of Latin poetry are never really so separate and disparate as in literary analysis they would seem to be. And thus for many reasons it is best to treat as of one composite but integrating mold the poetry written in Latin to the closing days of the Augustan Age—for the sound of it all is the sound of a great nation.[5]

That there is more than the convenience of criticism in such a position is evident when we recall with Mackail that it is only in the growth and life of the new (Christian) world that the decay and death of the old can be viewed with equanimity, or in a certain sense can be historically justified. For it is the law of poetry that life comes only by death—she replenishes one thing out of another and does not suffer anything to be forgotten before she has been recruited by the death of something else: *materies opus est ut crescant postera saecla.* Poetry works out Roman classical forms towards a definite goal of perfection: the expression of one great national life and spirit. For such forms we have one name that fits like a tight cap: Roman. When great new forces begin to destroy the beauty of Roman forms of verse, forces that are strangers to them, and flaw them beyond their ability to recover, then poetry with passionless action breaks up perishable Roman materials and begins anew. Here, late in the afternoon of the Augustan Age, comes this new melting down of the primitive matter of Roman forms, to prepare it for alien civilizations. This moment in the gradual evolution of the purpose of history begins the period of Romanesque.

Other lyric poets of early Romanesque besides Petronius are but names to us: Gætulicus, consul in 26 A.D., whose mistress, Cæsennia, was herself a poetess; Cæsius Bassus, Vagellius, Sosianus, Montanus, Lucilius junior, Sulpicia, and some of Pliny's poet friends. Luckily, however, there has survived to us from these days the pastoral writing of an unknown author, from the first twenty-four lines of whose *Lydia* the following brace of sonnets have been most honestly derived:

LYDIA

I

Fair fields and meadows, how I envy you
    That are more fair since in you, silent-
wise,
    Love's fairest damsel plays or stands and
sighs.
You have my Lydia's voice, you have her
    view,
Her eyes to smile before. Doth she pursue
    Some song of mine her voice hath
learned to prize?
    She sings—my ears have heard her in
that guise.
Teach her to love. Ye fields, I envy you.

O there is no place made so fortunate,
    And there's no earth knows such
beatitude
        As that wherein she sets her snowy
feet;
Or where with rosy hand the vine-branch rude
    She plucks somewhile before the grape
is sweet
        And ripens to its Dionysian state.

II

Among the many colors of the flowers
    She'll lay her limbs that breathe the
breath of spring,
    And to the sweet crushed grasses
whispering,
Shyly retell the story of love's hours.
Then shall rejoice the fields and forest-bowers,
    The water-brooks shall then run loitering,
    The fountains freeze, and bright birds
cease to sing
What time my dear makes lament for love's
    powers.

I envy you, ye fields. You have my joy,
    And she is yours my bliss is fashioned
of.
        My dying members waste away with
sorrow,
My heat of life the cold of death doth
    borrow—
        She is not here, my lady and my love!
        I envy you, ye fields. You have my
joy. (9)

The appearance so early in the history of Romanesque idyl of the Petrarchistic manner is of vital interest. Judged by Vergil's standard of performance, the *Lydia* is deemed not only too slight and ineffectual to be included with his works but too negligible even to be the famous poem of like name written by Valerius Cato.[6] Says Frank, our verse abounds with conceits that a neurotic and sentimental pupil of Propertius—not too well practiced in verse writing—would be likely to cull from his master. We have here the situation of Goethe and the Strasbourg minster over again, in the case of Frank and *Lydia*; but of Goethe before the moment of conversion to that "grotesquerie" which is a glory of the Elizabethan lyrics.

This grotesquerie is the final triumph of the romantic over the classical attitude. Whether more implicitly real, as in our pieces from Petronius, or definitely mannered, as in the *Lydia*, we have come with it from an age of reason to an age of feeling.

Romanticism is a literature dominated by the lyrical element. Lyricism is individualism; it expresses ideas and emotions that are ours. Emotions, in turn, are of two sorts: sentiments of love and hate, hope and despair, enthusiasm and melancholy. Some of these emotions are concerned with the universe, the materials with which we construct the image of the exterior world—sensations. Others of these emotions are muscular—odors and taste. This second set romanticists leave to the realists; their own lyricism is sentimental and picturesque.

Under romanticism the emotions of others interest us only as they are men like us; hence the poet becomes the representative of humanity. Lyricism transports us into the realm of the universal—the sadness and desire of the individual become the problem of life and death, emotionally considered. Ours not to seek the reason behind the *moi* that is sad or desirous; ours to lay aside the exercise of intelligence and reflection, to leave behind psychology, science, exact method, steps in logic, the art of thinking and rationalizing. Lyric poetry, picturesque literature, living history—these are the things that count in an age of Romanesque. Against the rules are the definition of genres, the interior laws of each form, all precepts of taste.

To the modern reader who—whether consciously or not—studies classical Roman poetry with a bias that favors the personal element in art, the most serious defect of Augustan writing lies in the weakness of its lyrical impulse. In the words of Sikes, whether we understand lyric in its original sense as a poem sung by a single voice or a chorus, to the lyre, or extend the definition to any short poem which gives perfect expression to a mood of the highest imaginative intensity, we must admit that Roman poetry does not often satisfy the definition.[7] Quintilian's remark that "Horace is about the only lyric poet of Rome" indicates that the Romans themselves realized this weakness and knew their poets rarely *sing*.[8] They speak, says Sikes, they recite or even chant; but they do not commonly break out into that ecstasy of emotion which seems to demand music as its medium. Though he never lacks the perfect expression, Horace seldom rises to imaginative intensity: no burning moments, no absorbing passion, no thrill of rapture for gratified desire, no spasm of torture in frustrate hope; his equal muse is strange alike to the highest joys and the deepest despair.

The most that we may expect from such a situation is the social lyric suited exactly to the whims and tastes of a leisured caste. In so far as Catullus in the intimate lyric and Vergil in the more personal type of idyl had anticipated Romanesque elements of poetry, they were destined to be without discoverable posterity. The individual lyric of Catullus had been made of no account by Horace.

## Notes

[1] See Mackail, *Select Epigrams from the Greek An-*thology*, p. 32: The literary treatment of the passion of love is one of the matters in which the ancient world stands farthest apart from the modern world. Perhaps the action of love on human lives differs but little from one age to another, but the form in which it is expressed was altered in western Europe in the Middle Ages, and ever since we have spoken a different language. Strangely enough in this regard, the *Nealce* of Petronius finds its closest parallels in the lyrics of the Elizabethan Age.

[2] Immediately following the epigrams assigned to Seneca, Codex Vossianus, Q. 86, gives sixteen epigrams, each headed by the word *item*. Of these, two are quoted by Fulgentius as the work of Petronius. Especially in view of the fact that they all bear a marked family resemblance to one another, there is, therefore, a strong presumption that they are all by the author of the *Satyricon*. Further, there are eleven epigrams published by Binet in his edition of Petronius (Poitiers, 1579) from a MS originally in the cathedral library of Beauvais, but now lost. The first of the series is quoted by Fulgentius as being by Petronius, and there is no reason for doubting the accuracy of Binet or his MS as to the rest. These poems are followed by eight other epigrams, the first two of which Binet ascribes to Petronius on stylistic grounds, but without MS authority. Lastly, four epigrams are preserved by Codex Vossianus F., iii, under the title Petronii; of these, the first two are found in the extant portions of the *Satyricon*. The evidence for the Petronian authorship of these thirty-seven poems is not conclusive, but the evidence against such authorship is of the slightest. See Bæhrens, *Poetæ Latini Minores*, IV, 74-89, 90-100, 101-108, 120, 121; Haseltine's edition of Petronius (Loeb Library), and especially H. E. Butler, *Post-Augustan Poetry from Seneca to Juvenal* (Oxford, 1909), pp. 134 f.

[3] Propertius, in whose Umbrian blood there was possibly some admixture of the Celtic, speaks of himself as *mollis in omnes*. H. W. Garrod, *The Oxford Book of Latin Verse* (Oxford, 1921), p. xviii. Of the makers of Roman poetry very few indeed are Roman. Livius and Ennius were half-Greeks from Calabria. Nævius and Lucilius were natives of Campania. Accius and Plautus—and later Propertius—were Umbrian. Cæcilius was an Insubrian Gaul. Catullus, Bibaculus, Ticidas, Cinna, Vergil, were Transpadanes. Asinius Gallus came from Gallia Narbonensis, Horace from Apulia. Of the considerable poets of the empire, Lucan, Seneca, Martial, are of Spanish birth. A Spanish origin has been conjectured for Silius. Claudian is an Alexandrian, Ausonius a Gual, Statius and Juvenal are Campanians, Persius an Etrurian. Rome's rôle in the world is the absorption of outlying genius. See Garrod, *op. cit.*, pp. xv f.

[4] The subtle and moving effects in the *Eclogues* of this *molle ingenium* are well characterized by Mackail when

he speaks of the note of brooding pity which pierces the immature and tremulous cadences of Vergil's earliest period. We are passed out of classicism into what we call romanticism. The Celtic spirit—for that is what it is—is overmastering. It constantly girds a poet and carries him whither he would not. See Garrod, *op. cit.*, p. xix.

[5] The argument all through here is Garrod's.

[6] *Lydia*, poem, verses 104 to 183 (end) of *Diræ*. Despite its attribution to Valerius Cato by Ellis (*Amer. Jour. Philol.*, 1882, pp. 271-284; *ibid.*, 1890, pp. 1-15), its publication in 1907 in the Oxford text of *Appendix Vergiliana*, and the opinion of Lindsay (*Class. Rev.*, 1918, p. 62), most Latinists today join with Tyrrell in considering it the work of an unknown poet contemporary with Petronius. See Tenney Frank, *Vergil* (New York, 1922), p. 131.

[7] E. E. Sikes, *Roman Poetry* (New York, 1923), p. 9. The reader will, of course, recognize my restatement of Lanson's famous passage in the preceding paragraph on romanticism.

[8] Somehow I cannot feel with Sikes that Quintilian's failure to say a word in this connection of Catullus is primarily due to his ranking the latter as a writer of lampoon and epigram, and therefore technically outside the lyrical canon. It would seem more reasonable to presume that Quintilian and other critics of the early Empire found Catullus too prone to be guided by his emotions, too apt to be unreticent and self-revelatory, too preoccupied with his sex and his soul, too slow to subordinate reason to feeling, too little restrained by the rules governing an artistic if corrupt generation, to be considered in the first flight of aspirants for lyric fame. But see Sikes, *op. cit.*, pp. 9 ff.

Nepos in "Atticus," lists Lucretius and Catullus as the leading poets of the late Republic, and Velleius Paterculus some sixty years later (circa 30 A.D.) lists Lucretius, Catullus, and Varro in the same connection. This may or may not be significant of critical insight. Sikes himself declares that an urban life, highly artificial and conventional, dominated by "good taste," shrinking from any form of eccentricity, could not foster the intensity of personal emotion which overflows in lyrical utterance. Sikes grants that the statement that the Augustans were intent on repressing "enthusiasm" may seem in flat opposition to the subjective poetry of the elegiac writers who are chiefly occupied with their own loves or (as in Ovid's *Tristia*) their own misfortunes. But he contends rightly that Propertius and Ovid were not minded to be *lyrical*; they made no song of either their passion or their woe; they may have felt deeply and truly, but their feeling was restrained by the code of refinement and good breeding. The elegy must conform to the character of a Roman gentleman, who may be a profligate but must never forget to be an artist. Since Roman art was typical rather than personal, the lover must not emphasize the individuality of his mistress or himself. Celia or Delia or Corinna, says Sikes, is any mistress for any lover.

## Moses Hadas (essay date 1929)

SOURCE: "Oriental Elements in Petronius," *The American Journal of Philology*, Vol. L, No. 4, October-November, 1929, pp. 378-85.

[*In the following essay, Hadas gives specific examples of Oriental elements in the speech of particular characters in the* Satyricon.]

The art of Petronius in suiting language to character has often been noticed.[1] It has been pointed out, for example, that the Greeks in the Cena are recognizable by peculiarities in their speech.[2] On the other hand, Professor Tenney Frank's calculations have demonstrated the preponderance of the Oriental element in the Rome and Italy of the early Empire.[3] Trimalchio himself proclaims his Asiatic origin,[4] and we should certainly expect that some of his guests were similarly derived. If Petronius is as skilful a realist in suiting his speeches to his characters as his critics have shown him to be, we might logically expect to find certain Oriental elements in the speech of the guests at the Cena.

The process of assimilation whereby the Easterners took on the habits and speech of Rome went on constantly,[5] yet traces of Eastern origin must have persisted for two or more generations, in idiom if not in pronunciation, and in habits of thought if not in outward behaviour. Organization of foreign groups according to ethnic origins[6] would tend to perpetuate racial peculiarities. Conversation among peoples of foreign extraction in New York is apt to betray foreign traces, and the same condition must have prevailed in Rome. I submit for consideration the following examples from the **Satyricon**:[7]

26. 9 Trimalchio. Friedlaender[8] cites the opinion of Bücheler that the name is Semitic. There can be little doubt that *-malchio* represents the root . . . which is frequently used like its equivalent *rex* for a very wealthy or elegant person; the *tri-* is an intensive prefix as in *trifur, trismegistus*.

31. 2 Vinum dominicum ministratoris gratia est. Friedlaender puts the emphasis on *dominicum*: "Die gratia ministratoris besteht darin, dass er vinum dominicum, nicht einen geringeren vorsetzt." But in Babylonian Talmud, Baba Kama 92b, an Aramaic proverb occurs: "The wine is the master's, the thanks the

butler's." Our passage seems to be simply a parallel of this proverb.

34. 8 Potantibus . . . larvam argenteam attulit servus. Though the famous Bosco Reale cup shows the skeleton used as an ornamental design, with probably the same purpose of serving as a *memento mori*, the origin of the custom is almost certainly Eastern. Herodotus II 78 says that wealthy Egyptians had skeletons brought in at their banquets, and Plutarch, whose testimony may be independent, also refers to this practise.[10] The *memento mori* motive in connection with the enjoyment of food and drink is frequent in Scriptures: Isaiah 22. 13, 56. 12; Eccles. 2. 24; Luke 12. 19; I Cor. 15. 32.

35. On this chapter Sage[11] remarks that Trimalchio's "exactness in astrology is amazing when we think of his capacity for blundering in history, geography, and mythology." It is of course what we should expect of an Oriental.

37. 8 nummorum nummos; cf. 43. 8 olim oliorum. This usage is often explained as a Hebraism (e. g. by Friedlaender) on the analogy of *Song of Songs*, *Vanity of vanities*, *Heaven of heavens*, etc. Suess says categorically:[12] "Nil exstat in his sermonibus, quod merito possit ad auctoritatem patrii sermonis syriaci aut hebraici revocari." He adduces parallels to the present usage from Vergil, Catalepton 5. 6, and Varro, L. L. VII 27, neither of which seems convincing.

37. 10 Babaecalis. No satisfactory explanation of this word has been offered. Mr. Sedgwick reports:[13] "Mr. Ulric Gantillon suggests that the word may be a pretentious and derogatory inflation of the Persian *beg* (Turkish *bey*)." However that may be I feel sure that this word as well as *burdubasta* (45. 11; see below) and perhaps *tangomenas* (34. 7 and 73. 6) are transliterated Oriental words. I would call attention to the late Professor W. R. Newbold's article, *Five Transliterated Aramaic Inscriptions*,[14] and especially to his interpretation of C. I. L. IV 760,[15] where he makes the unintelligible letters TCLOfTORGC into Aramaic words quite in keeping with the obscenity of the Latin part of the inscription, and quite worthy of one of Trimalchio's guests.

37. 10 In rutae folium. Martial XI 13. 5 makes it clear that this expression is a proverbial one for small size. "A leaf of myrtle" is frequently used in a similar sense in rabbinic writings.[16] The leaves of rue and myrtle are not dissimilar.

38. 13 Sociorum olla male fervet. An exact parallel to this proverb in Erubin 3a and Baba Batra 24b has been pointed out by W. Bacher:[17] "A pot which is the common property of a number of partners is neither cold nor hot." Friedlaender corrects the note of his first edition on the basis of this suggestion.

41. 3 Servus tuus. The use of this phrase by a free person for the sake of politeness seems unparalleled in Latin. It is the regular Hebrew usage. . . . Examples are cited from Genesis 18. 3, I Sam. 20. 7, 8, II Kings 8. 13, etc.

41. 12 Matus. The usual explanation of this word is that of e. g. Sedgwick:[19] "vulg. for *madidus*, itself slang." . . . Is not this the sort of expression that might continue, in a Latinized form, in the speech of Trimalchio and his associates?

42. 2 Cor nostrum cotidie liquescit. This seems to be a Semitic conceit. Cf. Joshua 7. 5: "Wherefore the hearts of the people melted and became as water." Psalms 22. 14: "I am poured out like water: my heart also in the midst of my body is even like melting wax."

42. 2 Nec sane lavare potui; fui enim hodie in funus. Roman usage did not forbid a mourner to wash, and the present passage seems to indicate some sort of ritual prohibition rather than simply preoccupation. Such a prohibition does occur in the Talmud, Moed Katan 15b: "A mourner may not wash". Furthermore prohibition of bathing, as well as of certain other physical comforts, was always understood as being involved in any fast.

44. 3 Serva me, servabo te. Similar expressions may be found in all languages, as for example our "Scratch my back and I'll scratch yours"; but Baba Mezia 80a has a literal version of the present passage.

44. 14 Nunc populus est domi leones, foras vulpes. This antithesis occurs frequently in Greek, being found as far back as Aristophanes, Pax 1189. It may be worth mentioning, however, that the proverbial expression seems implied in a passage in the Talmud, Baba Kama 117b: "The lion you spoke of [when he was at a great distance] has turned into a fox [now that he is here]." The rabbis frequently use "lion" to denote a distinguished or worthy person,[23] and *leones* in 44. 4 is a parallel to this usage: "o si haberemus illos leones, quos ego hic inveni, cum primum ex Asia veni."

44. 17 Nemo ieiunium servat. Fasting was rare among the Romans and the *ieiunium Cereris* appears to be the only fast that was kept annually, so that Friedlaender can say, "Vielleicht stand im Original: Nemo Cereris jejunium servat." To Eastern peoples fasting was very familiar. The Pharisees fasted on Mondays and Thursdays and on numerous special occasions. An entire treatise of the Talmud, Taanit,[24] is devoted to the regulation of fast days, especially those proclaimed for seasons of drouth.

44.18 Iovem aquam exorabant: itaque statim urceatim plovebat. The following story from Taanit was widely known, and may conceivably have been in the mind of the speaker: "Honi the Circle-drawer was therefore asked to pray that rain should fall. . . . He then drew a circle and placed himself in its center, and said . . . 'I swear by Thy great Name that I will not move from here until Thou showest mercy to Thy children'. . . . The rain then came down with vehemence, each drop as big as the opening of a barrel."[25]

45.8 Sed qui asinum non potest stratum caedit. The identical proverb is found in the Midrash, Tanhuma P'kude 4.

45.11 Burdubasta. The exact phonetic transliteration of this word into Aramaic gives the meaning "pit of shamefulness". This explanation of this word seems to me more plausible than any heretofore suggested.

46.8 Primigeni. This not uncommon slave name is perhaps a reflection of the special privileges accorded to the firstborn son among Semitic peoples.[28] Here it may not be a proper name, but used as in the address of Jacob to Reuben, Genesis 49.3: "Reuben, thou art my firstborn, my might, and the beginning of my strength."

46.8 Quidquid discis tibi discis. Cf. Proverbs 9.12: "If thou be wise, thou shalt be wise for thyself."

47.1 Unguento manus lavit. Burmann comments:[29] "non succurrat similis luxuriae exemplum." The Mischa mentions the custom of scenting the hands at meals by means of incense passed on a brazier.[30] Lavish use of perfumery is characteristic of Eastern countries; scriptural references illustrating such use (though not for the washing of hands) are: Canticles 3.6; Proverbs 7.17; Psalms 45.9; Luke 7.46.

52.3 Petraitis. Sedgwick notes:[31] "Cognomen of Lycian god *Men*, Lebas-W 668, 676—CIA 3.73. But here no doubt for Tetraites who occurs as gladiator five times in inscriptions coupled with Prudens." Perhaps the confusion of names is in itself significant.

57.8 In alio peduclum vides, in te ricinum non vides. Cf. Matthew 7.5: "Thou hypocrite, first cast out the beam out of thine own eye; and then shalt thou see clearly to cast out the mote out of thy brother's eye." Also, Luke 6.41.[32]

65.5 Habinnas. The name in this form does not occur in C. I. L., but Abinnerici (gen.) does occur (IV 2585, 2599, 2600, 2601), and its recurrence in Josephus, Ant. Jud. XX 22 (Niese) . . . establishes its Syrian or Jewish origin. Several Talmudic sages were called Abina or Abin.[33] Furthermore the name Abban . . . occurs in the apocryphal Acts of Thomas, which is proven to be of Syriac origin. Professor F. C. Burkitt declared the name to be Semitic,[34] and subsequently proves his guess.[35]

68.8 Recutitus est. Perhaps a conscious disparagement by one who considered himself advanced beyond a barbaric practise. The practise is always associated with Jews; cf. 102. 14 circumcide nos ut iudaei videamur, and Frag. 37 (Bücheler).[36]

69.9 De *fimo* facta sunt. "A favorite oriental trick according to Sir R. Burton," Sedgwick.[37]

72.10 Nemo unquam convivarum per eandem ianuam emisus est, alia intrant alia exeunt. Cf. Ezekiel 46.9: "But when the people of the land shall come before the Lord in the solemn feasts, he that entereth in by way of the north gate to worship shall go out by way of the south gate; and he that entereth by the way of the south gate shall go forth by the way of the north gate: he shall not return by the way of the gate whereby he came in, but shall go forth over against it."[38] Apparently Trimalchio's notion of elegance in this regard is ultimately derived from the Temple arrangement or something cognate.

74.12 Urceolum frigidum ad malam eius admovit. Yoma 78a: "Raba used to cool himself on Atonement Day with the outside of a vessel of water."

77.4 Cusuc. Mr. Sedgwick remarks:[39] "It is no doubt Eastern. Mr. Gantillon sends me the following note: 'Cusuc is the Persian *kushk,* a light Summer palace, pavilion, portico. In Turkish it became *kosk,* pronounced *kyosk,* whence the French *kiosque.* Trimalchio says: "Cusuc *erat,* nunc *templum est.*" The word must have brought with it into the slang of his day both the sense of flimsiness and of the promise of a more pretentious building, temple or palace.'"

80.1 Age, inquit, nunc et puerum dividamus: iocari putabam discedentem: at ille gladium paricidali manu strinxit. H. Lucas[40] recognizes in this a version of the Judgment of Solomon, but says that it is derived through a Greek source. R. Engelmann[41] enumerates no less than five examples of the representation of the Judgment of Solomon in Roman art, and I do not see why the story cannot have migrated directly without Greek intervention.

94.1 O felicem, inquit, matrem tuam, quae te talem peperit. Cf. Luke 11.27: "Blessed is the womb that bare thee and the paps which thou hast sucked."

105.4 Placuit quadragenas utrique plagas imponi. Forty stripes is regularly the maximum corporal punishment in all rabbinic legal writings, on the basis of Deuteronomy 25.3: "Forty stripes he may give him, and not exceed."

111. The possibility that the origin of the story of the Widow of Ephesus is ultimately Oriental has been widely recognized. I would add that three versions of

the story, in details apparently independent of each other and of our text, are extant in medieval Hebrew literature, ranging in date from the ninth to the thirteenth centuries.[42] Perhaps this may indicate a persistent independent tradition, from which Petronius may have drawn directly.

*Notes*

[1] F. F. Abbott, The Use of Language as a Means of Characterization in Petronius, *Classical Philology* II (1907), 43-50.

[2] Abbott, *loc. cit.*; A. H. Salonius, Die Griechen und das Griechische in Petrons Cena Trimalchionis, Helsingfors and Leipzig 1927 (known to me only through the review of G. Meyer in Gnomon V (1929), 144-150).

[3] Race Mixture in the Roman Empire, *American Historical Review* XXI (1915-1916), 689-708; and Economic History of Rome, ch. X.

[4] Satyricon 29. 3, 75. 10.

[5] For instances of assimilation through Romanization of names, see Mary L. Gordon, The Nationality of Slaves under the Early Roman Empire, *Journal of Roman Studies* XIV (1924), 93-111.

[6] See especially George LaPiana, Foreign Groups in Rome During the First Centuries of the Empire, *Harvard Theological Review* XX (1927), 183-403.

[7] I am not here considering oriental affinities of the romance as a whole, such as are suggested by Karl Kerenyi, Die Griechisch-Orientalische Romanliteratur, Tübingen, 1927; of this work see Indices IV and VI.

[8] L. Friedlaender, Petronii Cena Trimalchionis etc.,[2] Leipzig 1906. . . .

[10] Sept. Sap. Conviv. 148 A, quoted in the Petronius edition of P. Burmann (Amsterdam 1743), p. 194.

[11] Evan T. Sage, Petronius, *The Satiricon*, New York and London 1929.

[12] Guilelmus Suess, Petronii imitatio sermonis plebei qua necessitate coniungatur cum grammatica illius aetatis doctrina, Dorpat 1927, p. 8.

[13] W. B. Sedgwick, *Classical Review* XXXIX (1925), p. 117.

[14] In *American Journal of Archaeology* XXX (1926), pp. 288-329.

[15] *Ibid.*, p. 295.

[16] . . . bHullin 47b, and elsewhere.

[17] In *Jewish Quarterly Review* IV (1892), pp. 168-170. . . .

[19] W. B. Sedgwick, The Cena Trimalchionis of Petronius, Oxford 1925. . . .

[23] M. Jastrow, A Dictionary of the Targumim, the Talmud, etc., I p. 118.

[24] This treatise is excellently edited and translated in the Schiff Library of Jewish Classics, by H. Malter, Philadelphia 1928.

[25] The translation is that of Malter, *op. cit.*, pp. 167 f. . . .

[28] S. A. Cook in Encyc. Biblica, s. v. Firstborn (II 1525). The word constituted an honorable title among the Semites; see W. Robertson Smith, The Religion of the Semites[2], pp. 458 ff.

[29] *Op. cit.*, p. 314.

[30] Berakhot VI 6; cf. Jastrow, *op. cit.*, II, p. 738.

[31] W. B. Sedgwick, *Classical Review* XXXIX (1925), p. 118.

[32] Many rabbinic parallels are cited in Strack und Billerbeck, Kommentar zum Neuen Testament aus Talmud und Midrasch, München 1922, I, p. 446.

[33] Jewish Encyc. I, pp. 63-64.

[34] *Journal of Theological Studies* I (1900), p. 288.

[35] *Ibid.* II (1901), p. 429: "In a Latin papyrus dated 166 A.D. and published among the Palaeographical Society's Facsimiles (Series II, plate 190), we learn that C. Fabullius Macer, a lieutenant in the Imperial Fleet of triremes on the Tigris, bought a seven-year-old slave who came from the country beyond the river and answered to the name of Abban or Eutyches (Puerum natione transfluminianum nomine Abban quem Eutychen sive quo alio nomine vocatur [sic]). The name of the slave is obviously identical with that of the merchant who bought the Apostle Thomas to be a carpenter."

[36] See Theodore Reinach, Textes d'auteurs grecs et romains relatifs au Judaisme, Paris 1895, Index s. v. *circoncision*.

[37] W. B. Sedgwick, *Classical Review* XXXIX (1925), p. 118.

[38] The Code of Maimonides, under *Hilkhoth Tefila*,

prescribes that all synagogues have two entrances.

[39] *Loc. cit.*

[40] Festschrift zu Otto Hirschfelds 60. jährigem Geburtstag, p. 269.

[41] Ein neues Urtheil Salomonis und die Friesbilder der Casa Tiberina, Hermes XXXIX (1904), pp. 146-154.

[42] Cf. í. Davidson's edition of Joseph Zabara, Sepher Shaashuim, New York 1914, pp. lii ff.

## F. A. Todd (essay date 1940)

SOURCE: "The *Satiricon* of Petronius," in *Some Ancient Novels: 'Leucieppe'; 'Daphnis and Chloe'; 'The Satiricon'; 'The Golden Ass,'* Books for Libraries Press, 1968, pp. 65-101.

[*In the following essay, first published in 1940, Todd provides an overview of the* Satyricon, *including a consideration of its possible models, and a detailed synopsis of the Trimalchio's Dinner section.*]

From Achilles Tatius and Longus we pass to Petronius and Apuleius, and find that in the novel, if in little else, the Romans not only equalled but even excelled the Greeks. In discussing the *Leucippe and Clitophon* and the *Daphnis and Chloe* it was necessary, at times, to exchange the part of expositor and critic for that of apologist; but the **Satiricon** and the *Golden Ass*, considered as works of art, need no defence.

In the *Daphnis and Chloe* we encountered the sole example, in antiquity, of a union of the romance with the pastoral; in the work of Petronius we shall find the romance in combination with satire. In this respect, as in many others, the **Satiricon** is both unique, in the ancient literatures, and characteristically Roman. Everybody is familiar with Quintilian's boast *Satira quidem tota nostra est*. Satire, Quintilian claimed, unlike other forms of literature, was not of Greek origin but an independent creation of Rome. The earliest *satura* was a medley, as the name itself denotes: a medley either of different kinds of verse or else of intermingled verse and prose. Lucilius, in the latter half of the second century before Christ, after experimenting with a variety of metres, finally chose a single metre, the dactylic hexameter, as the appropriate vehicle. He further used *satura*[1] for the purposes of polemic, and so made the name *satura*, for the first time, connote 'satire' in the sense that the word has borne ever since, namely, a censorious description and criticism of human affairs. His example was followed more or less closely by Horace and Persius and Juvenal. But the medley did not die out altogether. Varro, a contemporary of Cicero in the first century before Christ, wrote,

in vast bulk, what he called 'Menippean Satires', a work partly in prose and partly in verse, of which some hundreds of short fragments are still extant. The name 'Menippean' indicated his indebtedness to the Cynic philosopher Menippus who, in the third century before Christ, had written humorously on philosophical themes. In the time of Nero, beyond which we need not go, there appeared two works in the same tradition. Seneca wrote the *Apocolocyntosis*, which is satire pure and simple; and Petronius wrote the **Satiricon** (some think that it should be called **Satirae**), which is not true satire but a satirical novel cast in the Menippean mould. That is the work to which we now turn our attention.

There is no sound reason for doubting that the author of this remarkable work was that Gaius[2] Petronius whose death under Nero, in the year 66 after Christ, is recorded by the historian Tacitus in the sixteenth book of the *Annals*. In the seventeenth chapter of that book Tacitus mentions the death of four eminent Romans, of whom one was Petronius. Then in the eighteenth chapter he writes:

> 'In telling of C. Petronius I must recall briefly his earlier career. His day would be passed in sleep, his night in the duties and pleasures of life. As industry advances others to fame, so had indolence advanced him; and he was regarded not as a debauchee and prodigal, like most of those who waste their substance, but as a man of tutored voluptuousness. And the more unrestrained were his words and deeds, the more suggestive of a certain recklessness of self, with the greater approval were they interpreted as evidence of simplicity. Yet as governor of Bithynia, and soon afterwards as consul, he showed himself vigorous and an able man of affairs. Then, slipping back into vice, or in simulation of vice, he was received into the select company of Nero's intimates as *elegantiae arbiter*, "arbiter of taste", determining which of the pleasures of superabundance should be approved by the Emperor. He thus incurred the jealousy of Tigellinus, who regarded him as a rival, his superior in the science of pleasure. Tigellinus therefore applied himself to the Emperor's cruelty, his ruling passion, charging Petronius with having been the friend of Scaevinus. He bribed a slave to give information, made defence impossible, and imprisoned the greater part of his household.

> 'It chanced that just then Caesar was visiting Campania, and Petronius, having travelled as far as Cumae, was being detained there. He endured no longer the postponement of fear or hope. Yet he did not banish life in haste. Having cut his veins, he would bind them up and open them again as he pleased. Meanwhile he would speak to his friends, but not on serious topics nor to make a parade of fortitude; and he would listen to them regaling him, not with disquisitions on immortality nor with the doctrines of philosophers, but with light poems and ribald verses. On some of his slaves he bestowed

his bounty, on others a flogging. He dined and he slept, so that his death, though forced, should seem to be natural. Even in his will he did not, as did many of those who perished, flatter Nero or Tigellinus or any other of the powerful. But he wrote a full account of the Emperor's deeds of shame, adding the names of his male and female accomplices and specifying severally their novel forms of debauchery; and this he sent under seal to Nero. Then he broke his signet-ring, so that it might not presently serve to endanger others.'

There was grim humour in his presentation to the Emperor. Many victims of Imperial tyranny made rich presents to the tyrant or his minister, so that their kinsfolk or friends might be allowed to inherit the rest.[3] One imagines Nero expectantly opening the parcel—and extracting from it a catalogue of the abominations he had committed. Petronius was a man of bad life, a man infected with that cynical contempt for morality which was characteristic of Nero's court, and yet was not incapable of the lesser kinds of heroism. Galsworthy might well have taken from him a hint for his 'Old English', that unrepentant but gallant old sinner who goes down with colours flying. One might say of Petronius what Talthybius the herald says of Polyxena in Euripides' play:[4] . . . 'much thought he took to fall becomingly': . . . 'like a gentleman'. He was a fit subject for the pencil of Tacitus, the greatest artist in portraiture among all the ancient historians.

A theory that the account of Nero's excesses to which Tacitus refers was no other than the *Satiricon* has found enough support to require mention, but need not delay us long. To write such a work in a few days, at most, and in the circumstances described by Tacitus, would surely have been beyond human powers; and if it had nevertheless been written and sent to Nero as a recognizable lampoon on himself and his court, Nero would certainly have caused it to be destroyed. But in fact there is not in all the novel a character who, viewed as a whole, bears the slightest resemblance to Nero, whereas there are many the delineation of whom bears witness to close observation and study of actual types which could have had no place at an Imperial court. There is no need, however, to labour the argument. It is conceivable, no doubt, that Petronius wrote the *Satiricon* for Nero; but if he did so, he wrote it not for Nero's discomfiture but for his delectation.

I have been calling the novel *Satiricon*, but there is no certainty about the name. Bücheler, the distinguished German editor of Petronius, called it *Satirae*, 'Satires'; improbably, since so obvious a title was not likely to be corrupted into the other recorded names. The name which has gained widest currency in English is *Satyricon*, with a *y*, objectionable because it implies a non-existent connexion with satyrs, and to be regarded as a corrupt spelling of *Satiricon*, the form given (though not on that account necessarily correct) in the

oldest manuscript. If *Satiricon* is right, it is a facetiously coined hybrid genitive plural, Latin with a Greek termination, equivalent to *Satiricon libri*, 'books of satirical matters,' i.e. 'Satires'.[5]

Of the text of Petronius' novel we now possess only fragments, presumably detached from the complete work by anthologists. In their sum, they amount, in Bücheler's minor edition, to about a hundred and twenty printed octavo pages. Many of these were known and edited in the fifteenth and sixteenth centuries; but by far the longest and best of them exists in a single manuscript, the famous *Codex Traguriensis*, discovered at Trau in Dalmatia about 1650. It constitutes about a third of what is extant, and contains the episode of the *Cena Trimalchionis*, 'Trimalchio's Dinner', on which the fame of Petronius is most securely based. If some other fragments survive only as witnesses to the depravity of the excerptor, 'Trimalchio's Dinner', at least, owes its preservation to intrinsic merit. With the omission of a·very few vulgarities it is fit for the reading of the most modest of youths and maidens. The Trau manuscript[6] states that our excerpts from the *Satiricon* are from the fifteenth and sixteenth books. The statement rests on its sole authority, and is scarcely credible. Even if we assumed that the sixteenth book was also the last, though that is not asserted; further, that the extant fragments represent nearly the whole of Books XV and XVI, though that is neither asserted nor probable; we should still be committed to a work of fiction of a length quite unexampled in antiquity, a work longer than all the sixteen books of Tacitus' *Annals*, longer even than the *Pickwick Papers*.

The standard edition of the Latin text of Petronius is that by Bücheler, and there is a convenient edition of the Latin, with an English translation by Heseltine, in the Loeb Classical Library. I mention also the serviceable edition, with French translation, critical apparatus, and a few explanatory notes, by Ernout in the Budé collection. The episode of Trimalchio's Dinner may be read in a number of separate editions, of which I name only that by W. D. Lowe, with English version and useful commentary. There are also many translations of the whole work, in various languages, without Latin text. Perhaps the most useful of these, for the English reader, is that by J. M. Mitchell in the *Broadway Translations*, though like others it is marred by too free a use of modern colloquialisms where the Latin affords no warrant for them.

It is not possible to reconstruct the whole story, nor even, though attempts have been made, to divine, with any near approach to certainty, its central idea. There is much in the surviving fragments that is not narrative at all. For instance, there is much poetry, including an *epyllion*, a miniature epic, of nearly three hundred lines on the Civil War, and a poem of sixty-five lines on the Sack of Troy; there are also verses which neither are, nor are intended to be, poetry; there is much literary criticism: for instance, the famous characterization of Horace's poetry, *Horatii curiosa felicitas*, 'Horace's elaborate felicity', is thrown off casually by one of Petronius' characters; and so forth. But let me give a summary.

The action begins in an unnamed town, perhaps Cumae, not far from Naples, and shifts from time to time to other parts of southern Italy. The period is the principate of Nero. The narrator is Encolpius, who is also the central figure of the story.

In the earlier part of the narrative the principal characters are two young men named Encolpius and Ascyltos, and a lad named Giton who is their retainer. They are precious rogues, all three of them: a set of well-educated but needy adventurers, always willing to play the sponger, not averse from a little casual crime. Their morals are deplorable, and they have no redeeming virtues. In fact, it would be hard to imagine a more disreputable gang.

The story, as we now have it, opens abruptly. We find the two young men engaged in a discussion with a rhetorician named Agamemnon; or rather, Encolpius and Agamemnon do the talking while Ascyltos, finding them tedious, manages to slip away undetected. Encolpius laments the decay of oratory, and criticizes sarcastically, though justly, the training given by the schools of rhetoric. Agamemnon admits that his strictures are reasonable, but throws the blame on the pupils and their parents: in order to earn a living, the teacher of rhetoric must provide the sort of instruction that the pupil likes and that the parent at least countenances; among lunatics, he too must rave. He concludes his reply by setting out his ideas in some impromptu verses after the manner of Lucilius. Meanwhile Ascyltos has disappeared. After some alarming and unsavoury adventures in the back streets of the town, the two associates manage to find their lodgings, but presently have a violent quarrel which nevertheless ends in reconciliation. Here there is a gap in the narrative.

We next encounter the rogues involved in a little matter of stolen property. They had purloined some gold pieces and sewn them into a ragged tunic, which they had then had the ill luck to lose, leaving themselves with no more than a couple of pence. But they had also stolen a fine cloak. Coming into a market-place, they chance upon the rustic owners of the cloak who have found the lost tunic and are trying to sell it. Ascyltos makes an opportunity of assuring himself that the gold pieces are still in it. The friends think of suing for recovery in the courts, but wisely decide that this would not be safe. On the other hand, the owners of the splendid cloak recognize their property. Now ensues a pretty piece of wrangling, in the course of which the bystand-ers propose to impound both garments until a judge can settle the dispute: there is some reason to suspect, as they justly observe, that both articles have been stolen. Ascyltos, however, contrives to procure an exchange, which is apparently to the advantage of the rustics, and the adventurers go off to their inn with the booty.

The next episode is an adventure in which the three are made to suffer for an act of sacrilege. Soon after this, we find them again in the company of the rhetorician Agamemnon, who conducts them to a dinner-party given by the freedman Trimalchio, the description of which, as I have said, takes up about a third of the extant portion of the novel. Of this I postpone consideration.

After the dinner-party there is another quarrel between Encolpius and Ascyltos, and Ascyltos goes off with Giton. Encolpius later recovers Giton, and Ascyltos, having come back in search of the boy, retires discomfited and disappears from the story. In the meantime Encolpius, in depression of spirits, visits a picture-gallery, where he admires works by the old Greek masters. While he thus seeks distraction in the gallery, he meets an old man named Eumolpus, who in the rest of the narrative fills the place left vacant by the withdrawal of Ascyltos.

Eumolpus thus introduces himself: 'I am a poet', he says, 'and a poet, as I hope, not of the meanest inspiration, if only one may put trust in chaplets: though partiality bestows these on the undeserving too. "Why then", you ask, "are your clothes so shabby?" Just for that reason: love of genius never made a man rich.' The two men fall into conversation, and Eumolpus, on this first acquaintance, does not scruple to relate the discreditable particulars of an amorous exploit. Turning to more serious topics, they discuss the decay of art, and Eumolpus, prompted by a picture, composes on the spot, and recites, a poem on the *Sack of Troy*. (In title, but in nothing else, this recalls the poem that Nero is said to have sung, to his own accompaniment, while Rome was burning.)[7] Eumolpus' poem proves that he is indeed a poet of parts, but disapproving hearers throw stones at him till he runs away. Encolpius, though complaining that Eumolpus, during an acquaintance of less than two hours, has spoken more often like a poet than like a human being, takes him to dinner on condition that he indulge his mania no more that day.

Hereafter Encolpius and Eumolpus join forces, and we presently find them, with Giton, on board ship. As happened so often, luck was out. The vessel proves to be the property of a certain Lichas, of Tarentum, who has on board, as passenger, a woman named Tryphaena. These were the very people whom Encolpius and Giton most wished to avoid, since they had been the victims of an earlier escapade. At their wits' end, the rascals try to disguise themselves by shaving their heads and eyebrows, but only make matters worse, because, according to the ancient superstition, to cut the hair on a sea-voyage was to invite disaster. The culprits were thrashed for bringing misfortune on the ship. Worse still, they were recognized, and for a time things threatened to go hardly with them until at last a truce was arrived at. There ensued a terrible storm, in which the ship was wrecked and Lichas was drowned. Tryphaena escaped in a boat, and Encolpius and Giton, having been rescued by fishermen, discover Eumolpus in the skipper's cabin spouting poetry with a roar as of a caged beast, and, even in the face of death, filling a huge parchment with his verses. Him, too, they save.

The three friends, safe ashore, find that they are near Crotona, a city notorious for the addiction of its inhabitants to legacy-hunting, one of the popular vices of the time. This happy circumstance suggests to Eumolpus the idea of passing himself off for a wealthy, childless, ailing old man, and thus enriching himself and his two accomplices at the expense of the Crotoniates, who will pay court to him and make gifts. This 'confidence trick' is duly put into execution, and for a time is very profitable. The tricksters live well, if not virtuously, save only that Encolpius is disappointed in a love-affair. But the generosity of the Crotoniates at last begins to flag, and it becomes clear that danger is at hand. Eumolpus therefore announces that his testament will provide only for those, other than his freedmen, who will consent to eat his dead body in public. 'Shut your eyes', he says, 'and imagine that you are eating, not human flesh, but a hundred thousand pounds. And anyhow we'll find some seasonings to change the taste.' And he proceeds to cite allegedly historical precedents for his proposal. The rest of the story is lost.

Observe how very different is all this from the Greek novels. In the *Satiricon* we have no lovely and virtuous heroine, no enamoured and much-enduring hero, no pirates, no rhetorical prinking or posturing or acrobatics, nothing in fact of the stock-in-trade of your Tatiuses and Longuses and the rest of them. I grant the shipwreck, but how differently Petronius manages it, and with what dramatic effect! Nor can the *Satiricon* be rightly regarded as a parody of Greek Romance. Parody by its very nature implies a measure of similarity; but the *Satiricon* differs widely from the Greek novels in the essentials both of pattern and of substance. Those who have maintained[8] that Petronius based his novel, by way either of imitation or of parody, on Greek original or originals, may be fairly asked, but will be asked vainly, for trace or record of a possible original. Where there is demonstrable parody or imitation it is of Latin, even of contemporary Latin, as in Eumolpus' poem, after Lucan, on the Civil War. One may doubt whether these critics have any firmer basis for their theories than the assumption, too widely current, that whatever is good in Latin literature must necessarily have been derived from Greek sources. The *Satiricon* stands alone, without exemplar and without peer; no one but a Roman could have written it, and no Roman but Petronius.

But if I thus claim for Petronius that his work is unique, I must not be thought to maintain that he owes nothing to any predecessor. It was the brain of a a god that gave birth to Pallas, unbegotten and unconceived. The finite genius of man can do no more than cultivate the seed that forebears have sown, or engraft new scions on a stock whose roots are set deep in a past incalculably remote. To recur to an example of which I have already made some mention, Quintilian affirms that Satire is entirely Roman; and if he means that the Romans invented and developed Satire as a separate, well-defined literary species, he speaks truth. And yet Roman satire, before it reached its full development, drew much from the Greeks, without losing its title to essential originality: from drama in the Old Attic Comedy of Aristophanes and the other masters; from the lampoon in Archilochus; from philosophy in the writings of Menippus the Cynic and Bion the Cyrenaic; and so forth: and who shall trace all of these back to their ultimate sources? And so it is with all forms in all literatures. Forgive me for repeating doctrine so well worn as to be trite: Literature is an organism; and though its members are multitudinous and their variety untold, all draw life from a parent stem.

The form of Petronius' novel, a mixture of prose and verse, in which prose greatly predominates, proves his indebtedness to Roman satire of the kind called Menippean, such satire as Varro had written. Perhaps there was a revival of interest in this form in Petronius' day, for to the same period, the Neronian Age, belongs Seneca's Menippean satire the *Apocolocyntosis*, the '*Pumpkinification*' (not Deification) of the Emperor Claudius: a poor thing, in the worst of taste, quite unworthy of its distinguished author. Although it is Menippean in form, Petronius' satire approximates more closely in spirit to that of Horace, taking nothing too seriously, 'telling the truth with a laugh', preferring urbane humour both to ridicule and to moral indignation—for which, indeed, Petronius would have found small warrant in his own character and tastes.

In some details the *Satiricon* is obviously indebted, for manner or matter, or for both, to what were known as the Milesian Tales, although, no less obviously, these cannot have served as model for the whole work. Of the Milesian Tales I have already made passing mention, as one of the factors that contributed to the making of the Greek Romance. They came to be associated with the name of Aristides of Miletus, who collected, and committed to writing, many *novelle* of diverse ages and origins. Some of these were derived from literature, but most, as seems probable, from oral tradition;

ordinarily they were both humorous and licentious. You will find many examples of the type in the *Arabian Nights* and the *Decameron*; and there are many more, not recorded in literature, that are still current among people whose taste in fiction is not over-delicate. Aristides' collection of Milesian Tales was translated into Latin in the first half of the first century before Christ by Sisenna—the historian Sisenna, of whom Cicero[9] unkindly said that his pre-eminence among Roman historians merely showed how poor were the achievements of the Romans in this field. Sisenna's version enjoyed great popularity. Plutarch, in his *Life of Crasus*, narrates that when the Romans had been defeated by the Parthians at Carrhae, a copy of Aristides' book (presumably in Sisenna's translation) was found in the pack of a Roman soldier; whereupon the Parthian general spoke contemptuously of Romans as men who even in war could not abstain from obscenities.

The most notable specimen of the Milesian Tale in Petronius is the famous story of the Matron of Ephesus told by the poet Eumolpus on board ship.[10] It is the story of a matron so famed for her wifely virtue that women came from far and near to look upon her. So devoted was she to her husband that on his death she joined him in his underground tomb, determined to end her life there by starvation. Her parents came, her kinsfolk, and even the magistrates, but all failed to wean her from her resolve. Her sole attendant was a faithful handmaiden, who kept the lamp burning in the tomb. And there the widow sat, weeping and foodless, for five days. Then some robbers were crucified, and a soldier was posted to watch the bodies. Seeing a light in the tomb, and hearing sounds of lamentation, he went to investigate. Moved by the woman's grief and beauty, he tried to comfort her, and offered her his own food and wine. She refused them, redoubling her manifestations of grief; but the maid, seduced by the appetizing odours, made a hearty meal, and at last, reinforcing her arguments with an apposite quotation, or rather misquotation, from Virgil,[11]

> Think'st thou that ash or shades of buried
>     dead
> Give heed to this?

persuaded her mistress to do likewise. Thus refreshed, the widow recovered something of her interest in life, and presently noticed, for the first time, that the soldier was a good-looking and well-spoken young fellow. The soldier, helped by another of the maid's quotations from Virgil,[12]

> And wilt thou fight against a love approved?

ventured to pay court to her; but while the courtship proceeded and the soldier was neglecting his duty, the parents of one of the robbers removed his body from the cross and carried it away. The soldier feared for his life, and therefore, paradoxically, resolved to end it; but the good woman, 'no less pitiful than virtuous', could not bear the loss of a second dear one, and gave him the body of her husband to fix on the cross.

Petronius, then, owed something to the Satire, and something to the Milesian Tale. But there, so far as can be discerned, his specific indebtedness ends. There can be few examples, in any literature, of a work so nearly perfect in its kind that owes so little to predecessors: nothing, in fact, but framework and a few incidentals. Let us consider the *Satiricon* again in relation to the Greek novels. New discoveries, while they afford evidence that there were other kinds of novel, chiefly of quasi-historical content, nevertheless confirm the traditional view, based on the extant examples, that the typical Greek novel was a love-story. In the *Ninus* we have love in combination with what purports to be history. But the *Satiricon*, in any relevant sense, is neither amatory nor historical. In the Greek novels one is accustomed to find, because of their very nature, a heroine as well as a hero, whereas in the *Satiricon* the female characters are subsidiary and incidental. Unless professedly historical, the Greek novels are timeless. Chariton, it is true, makes his heroine the daughter of Hermocrates the Syracusan, a notable historical personage in the fifth century before Christ, and Heliodorus makes his Egypt a Persian satrapy; but these indications of date have no significance for the story, and the other novelists, in this main class, do not even hint, consciously, at a date. The *Satiricon*, on the other hand, while quite certainly not to be classed as an historical novel, is plainly dated by Petronius in the Neronian Age, and is therefore a novel of contemporary life and manners. In the Greek novels that we know, there is always a contrast and conflict of virtue and villainy, whereas in the *Satiricon*, while there is some villainy and plenty of vice, there is no virtue of positive kinds at all. The chief characters of the Greek novels are persons of wealth and consideration, those of the *Satiricon* are totally undistinguished. The Greek novels exhibit characters who, with few exceptions, are not individuals but types: in Petronius, every character is clear-cut and lifelike. This realism in the invention and delineation of characters is matched by an equal realism in the scenes. The Greek novelists usually lack the skill, even if they have the desire, to give the reader a clear impression of a scene: one may imagine, but does not see, 'what it was like to be there'. But Petronius, with a few deft touches, gives you the whole scene with an almost photographic sharpness and particularity: the narrow winding streets, the footpaths, the market-places, the inns, the stews with their inscriptions, the baths, the houses of rich and poor, the fresco-paintings, and all the rest. All are made vivid and convincing, with effortless art; and how true they are to reality the remains of Pompeii and Herculaneum bear witness.

All the Greek novelists whose work is extant were professional rhetoricians—'sophist-rhetoricians'—and their novels are products of their art. This accounts, as we have seen, for many of their most striking characteristics: their unrealities and absurdities, their irrelevancies drawn from the common-place book, their artificiality, their passion for display. Rhetoric, they are convinced, can never come amiss, however improbable or inappropriate the circumstances. Chaereas about to commit suicide;[13] Clitophon contemplating his sweetheart's severed neck;[14] Daphnis watching Chloe asleep;[15] even Habrocomes and Anthea in the bridal chamber;[16] all make speeches that smell, even if they do not positively reek, of the rhetorician's lamp. Hardly less rhetorical is the mould in which the narrative passages are cast. But what of Petronius? Petronius in this matter of rhetoric is a portent. He lived in an age when rhetoric formed the staple of the Roman higher education; a rhetoric, moreover, which, concurrently with the suppression of liberty in public life and in the courts, had become more and more widely divorced from reality. Its marks are almost everywhere on Latin literature of the Silver Age, though the greatest writers avoid its extravagances. In Petronius we encounter the phenomenon of an Imperial writer entirely free from the taint of rhetoric, though himself, no doubt, trained in the customary schools. The schools, on the principle of 'safety first', prescribed to their pupils for declamation or debate themes that had little or no relation to real life. Hear what Petronius, through the mouth of Encolpius, says about them at the opening of the *Satiricon*:

> 'Isn't it the same kind of Fury that plagues our declaimers? They cry: "For the freedom of the people was I wounded thus!"; "I sacrificed this eye for you!"; "Give me a guide to guide me to my children, for my hamstrings have been cut and cannot support me!". Even this sort of thing would be endurable, if it paved the way to eloquence. But the only issue of this bombast and of this meaningless burble of phrase-making is that the learners, when they come to the bar, think themselves translated into another world. In my opinion, youngsters become absolute numskulls in the schools because they neither hear of nor see anything of our everyday experience: nothing but pirates, with chains, standing on the shore; or tyrants composing edicts that sons shall cut off their fathers' heads; or oracles, given to stop a pestilence, that three or more virgins shall be sacrificed; honey-balls of rhetoric, every word and deed sprinkled with poppy and sesame. Those who are brought up amongst this sort of thing can no more be sound of taste than those who live in a kitchen can be pleasant of smell. With all respect, you rhetoricians have been the first of all to ruin eloquence.'

So Petronius eschews rhetoric, and in this respect also is sharply distinguished from the authors of the Greek romances. In the narrative passages, and the speech of

his educated persons, his latinity is as pure and as free from artificialities as you will find in any prose writer after Cicero. But of this more presently.

The *Satiricon* is thoroughly Roman both in matter and spirit, and I ask forbearance if, in emphasizing this, I draw attention again to some points on which I have touched already. We have seen how the generalizing Greek genius tends to exhibit the type rather than the individual, in literature as well as in other forms of art; and in so far as Rome is under the influence of Greece, the same tendency persists, as may be observed notably in Latin Comedy. But the Roman is by nature a realist, interested in the particular rather than in the general. It was not by accident that in sculpture, for instance, the Romans achieved their best work in historical sculptures and in portraits, as is proved by countless surviving examples. In the *Satiricon* there are many types: the millionaire freedman, the teacher of rhetoric, the poet-adventurer, the patchwork-blanket maker, the monumental mason, the quarrelsome wife, and so forth; but each of these is strongly individualized and each is drawn with a vivid realism that has not been surpassed even in the modern novel: in the ancient literatures there is nothing to approach it. Miraculous skill in the delineation of character is among the greatest of Petronius' virtues as a novelist: no matter how insignificant the character may be, however small a part he may play, there he stands before us, individual and complete and·alive. What mere marionettes, in comparison, are most of the characters of the Greek novels!

The characters of Petronius are all of types familiar in the Rome and Italy of his day, accurately observed and sketched with a humour which gives to him a very high place among the humorists of the world. How thoroughly he enjoyed writing his book! Latin literature as a whole, like the Peers in *Iolanthe*, is 'dignified and stately'. It is written for men of station, and is apt to shut out from its august consideration men of lowlier degree—the slave, the freedman, the tradesman, the artisan. From literature we learn little about the common folk of Rome and Italy. But all Petronius' characters are taken from the humbler walks of life. They include the rich with the poor, the educated with the ignorant; but one and all are, as I have said, altogether undistinguished. This indolent courtier, this able and energetic statesman—for he was both—this cultured voluptuary, took a most comprehensive interest in humanity; and it amused him to record the lives and idiosyncrasies and conversation of men and women whom the average Roman noble would regard either not at all or with indulgent contempt. That most of his characters bear Greek names is due not to derivation from some Greek source, but primarily, one may suppose, to the fact that the scenes of the story are laid in southern Italy,[17] a land thickly studden with towns of Greek origin, the towns of what was once called 'Great

Greece'. This at any rate makes the use of Greek names appropriate. But it is also possible, I think, that Petronius preferred the thin disguise of foreign names when indicating, as he often does, by his choice of name some characteristic or occupation of the bearer. Of this device, of course, though it is now out of fashion, even modern literature has furnished many examples, and Petronius makes free, though not invariable, use of it.[18] Thus Encolpius suggests 'Cuddle'; Ascyltos 'Thickskin'; Giton 'Neighbour'; Eumolpus 'Sweetsong'. The chief rhetorician is called Agamemnon, 'King of men', and his second-in-command is therefore named Menelaus. Tryphaena is voluptuous, as her name denotes; Circe is as amorous as Homer's enchantress; Pannychis is 'Miss Nightrevel'. Trimalchio, the fabulously wealthy freedman, has a hybrid name, half Greek and half Semitic, which has been interpreted 'Thrice Blessed'.

Petronius is no less complete a realist in language than in character-drawing. Latin falls into three main divisions, all of which are abundantly represented in Petronius. In narrative passages he uses literary Latin which, though less formal than the Latin of the more dignified masters, is of such excellence that because of it the Council of Trent refrained from putting the **Satiricon** on the Index. His educated characters, such as Encolpius and Eumolpus, speak what was known as *sermo urbanus* or *sermo cotidianus*, the everyday Latin of educated Romans, the Latin best exemplified in the correspondence of Cicero and his friends. But the humbler, uneducated persons, such as Trimalchio and his associates, speak the *sermo plebeius*, for which indeed Petronius is one of our chief authorities. This was the speech of the common people, 'Vulgar Latin' as it is sometimes called, the sort of Latin from which the Romance languages—Italian, French, Spanish, and the rest—are in the main descended. In Petronius we find a Campanian variety of Vulgar Latin, in which there is a considerable admixture of Greek words; just the sort of Latin, except that in Petronius there are few vagaries of spelling to indicate popular pronunciations, that is to be read in the multitude of inscriptions scribbled, in the same era, on walls in the Campanian towns of Pompeii and Herculaneum, and now recorded in volume IV of the great Corpus of Latin Inscriptions. In vocabulary and accidence and syntax it differs very greatly even from the everyday colloquial speech of the educated, and still more from literary Latin; it abounds in hybrids and slang and irregular formations that would horrify a purist, and exhibits a delightful uncertainty in the use of genders and declensions and conjugations; but withal it is vigorous, forthright, and racy, admirably adapted to the expression of simple ideas, and, in Petronius' use of it, contributes, hardly less than the thoughts of which it is the vehicle, to our comprehension and realization of character. Petronius' astonishing skill in adapting speech to character will become apparent,

I hope, when I come, as I shall do now, to the episode of Trimalchio's Dinner.

Trimalchio's Dinner is a study of a vulgar multimillionaire and his friends, a good-humoured satire on the freedmen *nouveaux riches* of whom there were so many in Imperial Rome. Agamemnon, the professor of rhetoric, has himself been bidden to the dinner-party, and has obtained invitations for Encolpius, Ascyltos, and Giton. These three forget all their troubles, put on their best clothes, and go off to the baths. At the baths, says Encolpius, 'all at once we see a bald-headed old man dressed in a red tunic and playing ball among long-haired pages. It was not so much the pages that had made us look, though they were worth looking at, as his lordship himself, who was wearing dress-shoes and taking exercise with a green ball. He wouldn't pick up a ball that had touched the ground, but a slave had a bag full of them, from which he kept supplying the players.' This was Trimalchio, their host. After exercise and the bath, he donned a scarlet wrap, entered his palanquin, and moved off homeward preceded by four liveried footmen and a go-cart containing his bleareyed wizened favourite, 'uglier than Trimalchio himself'.

Following their host, the friends presently reach the house. Here again they encounter the ostentation of gay colours, costly as well as abnormal, and therefore a favourite extravagance of Trimalchio and his household. At the door there was a janitor dressed in green with a cherry-coloured girdle, shelling peas in a silver dish; and above, in a golden cage, a magpie was squawking a how-do-you-do to the guests as they came in. This was only a foretaste of the splendours of the house. They pass through a long colonnade decorated, in fresco-painting, with scenes from the life of Trimalchio, and enter a vast hall, the *atrium* of the mansion, in which the pictures are of scenes from the *Iliad* and the *Odyssey* and a recent gladiatorial show. And so they reach the dining-hall. Here everything was done to music: if a slave rendered a service, he sang; if he was asked for something, he sang; and the singing was very bad. In fact, it was more like a vaudeville show than a gentleman's dining-room.

With excellent dramatic effect, Petronius delays Trimalchio's entrance till after the *hors-d'œuvres*. At last Trimalchio, his shaven head protruding from a voluminous scarlet cloak, a fringed and purple-bordered table-napkin about his neck, a silver toothpick in action, is carried in to the music of a band and set down on the couch in the midst of a pile of tiny cushions. 'My friends', he says, with exquisite courtesy, 'I didn't want to come to dinner yet, but rather than keep you waiting by my absence I have quite forgone my own pleasure. Still, you'll let me finish my game of chess first.' And this he does, swearing the while 'like a millhand'.

Trimalchio does his guests extremely well, in wine as well as food. 'Wine', he says, 'is life. This is real Opimian. What I served yesterday wasn't as good, and my guests were much finer gentlemen.' But he must not only be lavish, he must also be original; and his idea of originality is to serve a series of 'freak' dishes such as we used to be told would be provided on great occasions by the baser sort of modern American millionaire. It is all very ingenious, all very costly, and all most marvellously vulgar. A wooden hen, brooding on peahen's eggs in a basket of straw, is brought in to the accompaniment of music. The eggs are handed round, and Trimalchio expresses the fear that they are addled; but they prove to contain dainty figpeckers in a paste of flour and devilled yolk-of-egg. There was a great circular tray on which were represented the signs of the Zodiac, and on each sign was an appropriate dish: beef on the Bull, mullet on the Fish, kidneys on the Twins, and so on. A wild boar, the most highly prized of all ancient game, was carried in: a gigantic bearded slave, garbed as a huntsman, ripped it up with a hunting-knife, and out flew, not 'four-and-twenty blackbirds', but a flock of thrushes, one of which was given to each guest.

All the dinner is of a piece with that. And the servants are in keeping. We meet a cook who can make anything out of anything: goose and fish and game-fowl out of plain pig, fish out of a sow's matrix, pigeon out of fat bacon, squab out of ham; Trimalchio, with pretty wit, as he says, has dubbed him Daedalus. There is the carver happily named Carpus, whence one of Trimalchio's standing jokes: when a dish is brought in, Trimalchio cries 'Carpe, carpe!' that is 'Carver, carve 'er!' And there is the well-meaning young slave who insults the master by picking up a silver dish that he has dropped, instead of letting it be swept out with the debris of the meal.

The company does not spend all the time in eating and drinking. There is plenty of talk, and plenty of entertainment. Trimalchio, who is no dull-witted ignoramus—a man needs education these days, even at dinner; and his patron, bless him, saw to it that he was made a man among men—Trimalchio bids a guest tell of the twelve labours of Hercules, and how the Cyclops screwed Ulysses' thumb out, tales that he used to read in Homer when a boy. And he knows how Hannibal invented Corinthian bronze at the sack of Troy, how Ajax went mad because Iphigenia married Achilles, how Niobe was shut up in the Trojan Horse by Daedalus. It is excellent fooling. A guest tells a gruesome tale of a werewolf, the first werewolf story in literature, which Trimalchio caps with a still more horrifying tale of witches. A secretary reads out his report, 'as though it were the City Gazette':[19]

*July 26th*: On the estate at Cumae, property of Trimalchio, born 30 boys, 40 girls; transferred from threshing-floor to granary, 500,000 pecks of grain; oxen broken in, 500.

*Same date*: The slave Mithridates was crucified for cursing our master Gaius; put away in the safe, because it could not be invested, £100,000.

*Same date*: A fire, originating in the overseer Nasta's house, occurred in the gardens at Pompeii.[20]

On hearing this last entry recited, Trimalchio exclaims 'What's that? When were the gardens at Pompeii bought for me?' 'Last year,' replies the secretary, 'and so they haven't come on the books yet.' Trimalchio flared up and said, 'If properties are bought for me and I don't know within six months, I won't 'ave them entered on my books.'

Trimalchio grows maudlin and causes his will to be read, so that he may be loved as much in life as in death. All the beneficiaries are touched by his generosity. He then reduces himself and the company to tears by giving directions for his funeral. Here are some of them, addressed to his friend the monumental mason Habinnas, who will have the contract for making the tomb.[21]

Turning to Habinnas, he said: 'What about it, dear old friend? Are you building my monument as I told you to? I'm mighty anxious to have you paint by the feet of my statue a pup, and wreaths of flowers, and perfumes, and all Petraites's[22] fights, so that thanks to you I may enjoy life when I'm dead. Make the frontage a hundred feet, the depth two-hundred: I want all sorts of fruit about my ashes, and lots of vines. It's plain wrong to have a man's houses nice when he's alive and not to bother about those where we have to be longer. And that is why above all I want put on it "This monument is not to descend to the heir".

'Yes, and I'll see to it that I provide in my will for not being insulted when I am dead. I am going to put one of my freedmen in charge of my tomb to guard it, so that folk mayn't make a dash to my monument to do their business. And please do ships[23] under full sail (on the wall) of my monument, and me sitting on a platform in official robes with five gold rings and pouring out cash to a crowd out of a bag; for you know, I gave a banquet at two shillings a head. I'd like the dinin'-'all to be did too. And you'll do the whole people doing themselves well. On my right you'll put a statue of my dear Fortunata[24] with a dove in her hand: and have her with her pup on a lead tied to her belt; and put my kid[25], and some large jars sealed so as not to let the wine spill. And you may carve a broken urn and a boy crying over it. A sundial in the middle, so that whoever looks at the time reads my name willy nilly. And the inscription—think carefully—how will this do? "C. Pompeius Trimalchio Maecenatianus[26] rests here. He was appointed an

Augustal[27] in his absence. He could have been on every civil service panel at Rome, but refused. Dutiful, brave, and loyal, he grew from small beginnings and left thirty millions of sesterces. And he never went to a lecture. Farewell: and thou also.'"

After this lugubrious performance all are dissolved in tears, even Encolpius the narrator. At the suggestion of Trimalchio, they all troop out and take a hot bath, during which Encolpius and his friends try to escape. Unsuccessful in their attempt, they return with the rest to renew the festivity. At last Trimalchio ordered hornblowers to be fetched into the dining-room and to 'play something pretty' while he pretended to be dead. The band struck up a dirge. One of the bandsmen, the son of an undertaker, outblew the others and produced such a thunderous din that the whole neighbourhood was aroused, and the fire brigade, thinking that the house was afire, smashed in the door and set to work with water and axes. In the confusion the friends at last made their escape.

Here is Fortunata, the appropriately named wife of Trimalchio, as described to Encolpius, in chapter 37, by his neighbour at table:

> 'That's Trimalchio's wife: Fortunata is her name; she measures her cash by the peck. And only the other day, what was she? You'll excuse me, sir, you wouldn't have taken bread from her hand. Now, without why or wherefore, she's God almighty and Trimalchio's factotus. In fact, if it's mid midday and she tells him it's dark, he'll believe her. He doesn't know what he has: he's fairly rolling in it; but this bitch[28] sees to everything, and where you wouldn't expect it. She's a steady, sensible body, full of good ideas: why, look at all this gold! But she has a nasty tongue, and clacks and clacks in bed. If she likes you she likes you, if she doesn't she doesn't.'

And having introduced her, Petronius leaves her to reveal herself, for the rest, by word and action.

I have tried in this translation, and elsewhere, to give you something of the flavour of the Latin, a task not easy to accomplish. So much turns, in the speech of Petronius' humbler characters, on the use of a vulgar word or inflexion or turn of phrase for which it is hard to find a satisfactory analogue in English. One can only do one's best, avoiding the excesses of colloquialism and vulgarism, not justified by the Latin, that mar some of the current versions. Some of these humble folk at Trimalchio's party know very well that their speech is vulgar and ungrammatical, and are sensitive about it. Here again Petronius' psychology is exactly right. Thus Echion the blanket-maker,[29] after a long discourse, notices that the rhetorician Agamemnon is smiling at his blunders, and forthwith, in his indignation, blunders worse: 'I can see you're saying, Agamemnon, "Why is that nuisance babbling?" Because you, who *can* gab, won't gab. You're not one of our bunch, and so make fun of the way us *poor* coves talk. We know *you* are silly with edication.'

Here is Seleucus,[30] fresh from a funeral, speaking after another guest has mentioned baths and wine. The type is not yet extinct:

> 'I don't take a bath every day. A bath is like the laundryman:[31] the water has teeth. Every day, and our innards melt. But when I've got inside a mug of mead,[32] to hell with the cold. Anyhow I couldn't have had a bath, for I was to a funeral to-day. Chrysanthus—a nice, decent chap he was—has snuffed out. It was only the other day he spoke to me. It seems as if I was talking with him now. Dear, oh dear! We are just blown bags on legs. We're of less account than flies. Flies have *some* good in them, anyhow; but we are of no more account than bubbles. And suppose he hadn't starved himself. For five days he didn't chuck water into his mouth, and not a speck of bread. And yet he's joined the majority.[33] 'Twas the doctors did for him, or rather his bad 'oroscope; for a doctor is nothing but a comfort to the mind. Still, he had a lovely funeral, with a proper bier and a lovely pall. The mourning was very fine (he set some of his people free), even if his wife was stingy with her tears. Suppose he hadn't treated her well. But your woman who *is* a woman is a regular kite. Nobody oughtn't to do none of them a kindness: it's just like chucking it into a well. But an old love sticks like a crab.'

And next let us listen to Ganymedes the pessimist:[34]

> 'What he's telling us is neither here nor there. But nobody minds how prices is pinching. Good God! I haven't been able to find a mouthful of bread today. And how the drought lasts! We've been starving for a year now. Blast the Flour Board.[35] They're up to their games with the millers: "you scratch my back, I'll scratch yours". And so the small man is in trouble; for with those big bugs it's always Christmas. Oh, if only we had those stout fellers I found here when I first came from Asia! A man could live then. . . . The way they used to wallop those stiffs and put the fear of God into them! Yes, and I remember Safinius. He lived up by the old arch in those days, when I was a lad. A perfect peppercorn: hot!—wherever he went he singed the ground. But he was straight, he was sure, a friend to a friend, a man you wouldn't mind playing odd-and-even with in the dark. . . . A penny loaf was more than enough for two; but now I've seen a bull's eye bun bigger. Dear, oh dear! it's getting worse every day. This colony is growing backwards like a calf's tail.'

In the speech of all the uneducated persons there is a vulgar element, but this element varies in amount and kind with the individual. Petronius is too close an observer and too true an artist to make all speak alike, and he differentiates one character from another not only in what is said but also in the manner of saying it. To illustrate satisfactorily, in translations, this aspect of Petronius' realism would be extremely difficult if not actually impossible, and I venture only on a single example. Niceros, who tells the story of the werewolf,[36] makes a specialty of the 'bulls' that we call Irish. Admonished by Trimalchio not to be so glum, he says he is afraid that those scholar fellows will laugh at him; but plucking up courage he adds: 'Well, that's their business. I'll tell it all the same. Let them laugh: it doesn't hurt me. It's better to be laughed at than made ridiculous.' And so he begins his tale:

'When I was still in service, we were living in Narrow Street: Gavilla has the house now.' (Note how these details give an air of reality to the narrative as when we are told that Safinius 'used to live by the old arch'.) 'There, as the gods willed, I fell in love with the wife of Terence who used to keep the pub; you knew her: Melissa from Tarentum, the prettiest peach of a woman. But so help me, it was not for her looks or for what I could get that I went with her, but because she was a good honest lass. If I asked her for anything, she never said no. If she made a penny, I had a ha'penny; (all that I had) I gave her to mind, and I was never took down. Her man breathed his last out at the homestead. And so, by tooth and toe-nail, I made and managed a way to come to her. You know, it's trouble that shows the friend.

It happened that the master was out to Capua to fix up some odds and ends. Taking my chance, I persuaded of a guest of ours to come with me as far as the fifth milestone. A soldier he was, strong as the devil. We vamoose about cockcrow; the moon was as bright as at midday. We come among the tombs: my man goes to do his job by the pillars, and I sit there singing and counting the pillars. Then, when I looked back for my mate, he undressed himself and put all his clothes by the roadside. My heart was in my mouth, and I stood like I was dead. But he made a ring of water round his clothes, and suddenly turned into a wolf. Don't think I am joking: I wouldn't tell a lie, not for anybody's fortune. But as I was going to say, when he turned into a wolf he began to howl and ran off into the wood. At first I didn't know where I was; then I went to pick up his clothes, but they were turned into stone. Didn't I just die of fear! Still, I drew my sword, and whackity-whack!,[37] I cut at the shadows until I came to the homestead of my lady friend. I came in like a corpse; I nearly snuffed out; the sweat fairly flew between my legs; my eyes went dead; I hardly came to at all. My lass Melissa wondered why I was out walking so late, and says she: "If you had come sooner, you would at least have helped us. A wolf came into the homestead; and all the cattle, he let 'em blood like a butcher. But he didn't have the laugh of us, even if he did get away: one of our people ran him through with a spear." When I heard this, I could not sleep another wink; but when it was broad day I ran for my master Gaius' house

like a robbed publican, and when I came to the place where the clothes had been turned into stone I found nothing but blood. And when I got home, my soldier was lying in bed like a bullick and the doctor was seeing to his neck. I knew then that he was a change-skin, and after that I couldn't have taken a bite of bread with him, not if you had killed me first.'

But in observing the guests, perhaps we have been too neglectful of the host. Before we leave the dinner, let us hear what Trimalchio has to say for himself. By this time all the company are a little the worse for liquor, and Trimalchio so far forgets himself as to kiss a pretty servant. His wife Fortunata is furious; she swears at him and calls him 'riff-raff' and 'disgrace' and, finally, 'dog'. Trimalchio throws a cup at her and hits her on the cheek. There are tears on the one side and vilification on the other: Trimalchio won't have her statue on his tomb, for even then she would give him no peace. He won't even let her kiss him when he's dead. Habinnas, who is to make the tomb, and his wife Scintilla both beg him to relent, until Trimalchio, bursting into tears, speaks as follows:[38]

'Habinnas, sure as I 'ope you may enjoy your pile, if I did wrong, spit in my face. I kissed a thoroughly good girl, not because she's pretty but because she's good. She knows her ten-times, she can read a book at sight, she has made herself a fancy-dress out of her allowance and bought a chair and two ladles out of her own money. Doesn't she deserve to have me take notice of her? But Fortunata says no. You would, would you, Madame high-heels? Take my advice: don't let your luck give you the stomach-ache, you kite; don't make me show my teeth, sweetie, or you'll feel my dander. You know me: when I once make up my mind there's no budging. me. But let us remember the living. Please enjoy yourselves, friends. You know, I was once just like you: it was merit that brought me to this. It's the little brain that makes men, everything else is plain rubbidge. "I buy well, I sell well"; though others will tell you differently. I am bursting with success. What, snuffler? Still crying? I'll soon make you cry, for what's coming to you. Well, as I was going to say, it was levelheadedness that brought me to this fortune. When I came from Asia, I was just so high as this candelabrus is. In fact, every day I used to measure myself by it. And so as to get a moustache under my beak quicker, I used to rub oil from the lamps on my lips. For fourteen years I was the boss's favourite: there's nothing wrong in what the boss tells you to do. And I pleased the missus too. You know what I mean. I say nothing: I'm not one to boast.

Well, by the grace of God, I ran the house and, look you, took the boss's fancy. In short, he made me co-heir with the Emperor, and I got a nobleman's fortune. But nobody's never satisfied. I must needs try trading. To cut it short, I built five ships, I loaded wine—it was just gold in those days—, I sent them to Rome. You'd think I'd ordered it: all the ships were wrecked. It's not a story, it's the truth. In one day Neptune swallowed three hundred thousand pounds. Think I lost heart? No! Why, I thought this loss nobbut a mouthful, practically nothing. I built a second lot, bigger and better and luckier, so that everybody was saying I was a stout fellow. You know, a great ship is a stout ship. I loaded up again, with wine and fat bacon and beans and scent and slaves. This time Fortunata did the decent thing: she sold all her gold and all her clothes and put a hundred sovereigns into my hand. That was the yeast that made my pile rise. Things go so fast when the gods will. On a single trip I cleared a round hundred thousand pounds. At once I bought back all the properties that had belonged to my patron. I build a house, I buy up slaves and cattle; everything I touched grew like a honeycomb. When I found that I had more than all my home-town together, 'twas "hand from the board!".[39] I got clear of trading and began financing freedmen. But when I wanted to retire from my business, an astrologer wouldn't 'ave it. This was a Greek bloke, name of Serapa, who had happened to come to our colony:[40] he was in the know with the gods. He even told me what I had forgotten, explained everything to me from A to Z. He knew me inside out: could almost tell me what I had had for dinner yesterday. You'd have thought he had always lived with me. I ask you, Habinnas—you were there, I think—: "That's how you came by your missus"; "You are not very lucky in your friends"; "No one ever makes you a fair return"; "You have great estates"; "You are nursing a viper in your bosom"; and—I touch wood[41]—that I still have left to live thirty years and four months and two days. And besides, I'm soon to receive a legacy. This my 'oroscope tells me. If I manage to join my estates up with Apulia,[42] I'll have come far enough in life. In the meantime, under Mercury's eye, I have built this house. As you know, it was a bit of a shanty: now it's a palace. It has four dining-rooms, twenty private rooms, two marble colonnades; upstairs, a lot of small rooms, my own bedroom, this viper's lair, a first-rate crib for the janitor. There's plenty of room for guests. In fact, when Scaurus came here, there was nowhere he preferred to stay, and he has friends of his father to stay with at the seaside. And there is plenty else that I'll show you presently. Believe me, have a penny, and you're worth a penny; have something, and you'll be thought something. So your friend, who was once a frog, is now a king.'

Trimalchio then orders in his funeral robes for the inspection of his guests; the bandsmen are brought in to play a dirge; the fire-brigade arrives; and so the party breaks up in confusion.

What direct influence, if any, the **Satiricon** has had on modern literature I shall not attempt to estimate. It is the first picaresque novel, and on that account, if on no other, would demand attention. All of it is heartless, and the grossness of parts is extreme. But in humour, and in brilliance of conception and execution, it is a masterpiece; and the loss of the Trimalchio episode, so narrowly averted, would have caused a lamentable impoverishment of the world's literature.

*Notes*

[1] Later, the spelling *satira* becomes current.

[2] Tacitus calls him Gaius, the Elder Pliny and Plutarch call him Titus. Even a contemporary can err in such matters, as Wilamowitz, for instance, in an appreciation of Jebb called him Sir Robert Jebb, a slip perpetuated in the reprint of his *Kleine Schriften*, i, p. 461.

[3] Annaeus Mela, who met his death at the same time as Petronius, is a case in point: cp. Tacitus, *Ann.* xvi. 17.

[4] *Hecuba,* 569.

[5] For this view, see Ernout in the Budé edition of Petronius, p. xxxviii, n. 2.

[6] It is now in Paris.

[7] Suetonius, *Nero,* 38.

[8] e.g. R. Heinze, 'Petron und der griechische Roman', in *Hermes*, xxxiv (1899), pp. 494-519.

[9] *Brutus,* 228.

[10] III f.

[11] *Aeneid*, iv. 34 *id cinerem aut manes credis curare sepultos?* but the maid substitutes *sentire* for the received text *curare*.

[12] From the same speech of Anna to Dido: *Aen.* iv. 38.

[13] Chariton, i. 5.

[14] Achilles Tatius, v. 7.

[15] Longus, i. 25.

[16] Xenophon of Ephesus, i. 9.

[17] A couple of fragments, preserved by other writers, point to the possibility, though not the certainty, that the scene of a lost part of the novel was Massilia (the modern Marseilles), an ancient Greek foundation in which Greek names would be equally appropriate.

[18] It is perhaps relevant to observe that in Latin fiction a Greek name does not necessarily imply Greek nationality or derivation or even habits. In Martial's Epigrams, for instance, there is nothing un-Roman about a Chaerestratus who for lack of a few pounds loses his

right to a place on the Knights' benches in the theatre (Mart. Epigr. v. 25).

[19] 53, 1 ff. The *Urbis acta* were the *acta diurna* ('Daily News'), the official daily gazette of Rome.

[20] This, I have no doubt, is the meaning of *in hortis Pompeianis*, not, as Ernout (Indices, p. 210) strangely takes it, 'in the gardens belonging to Pompeius', i.e. to (Pompeius) Trimalchio. A local name is needed, as in *praedio Cumano*, just above; and Trimalchio's estates extend not only to Pompeii but far beyond.

[21] Chapter 71.

[22] An eminent gladiator. Trimalchio (ch. 52) already has a number of cups decorated with his exploits in the arena.

[23] These are to symbolize Trimalchio's trading ventures by sea.

[24] His wife, with whom we shall find him quarrelling violently.

[25] *Cicaronem meum*: presumably the favourite, mentioned above.

[26] This imposing array of names, assumed by Trimalchio on receiving his freedom, does no more than suggest the eminence, wealth, and munificence of Trimalchio's former masters. Chronology, propriety, and the context alike forbid us to suppose that Petronius represents his Trimalchio as a quasi-historical character, formerly the slave of Maecenas and, after him, of a Pompeius.

[27] The *Augustales*, six in number, held a sort of honorary magistracy. In the towns of southern Italy they were always freedmen.

[28] This, it seems, is the meaning of *lupatria*. If I understand it aright, the name is not a reflection on Fortunata's morals, which, in the context, are not impugned. On vulgar lips a coarse word may merely express some strong emotion, as, in this instance, of admiration. Similarly in English one may hear a word which, if taken literally, would be a foul insult, used as an expression of affection and sympathy by those who lack both refinement and an adequate vocabulary.

[29] Ch. 46. Echion is a *centonarius*, a maker of the rag blankets which, soaked in water, were used for putting out fires.

[30] Ch. 42.

[31] Literally 'fuller'. The *fullo* was the bleacher and laundryman and 'cleaner' of the Roman world, here the butt of the ancient jest that we now direct at the laundryman.

[32] Mead is an excellent substitute for a cloak. Cp. *Gammer Gurton's Needle*: 'No frost nor snow, no wind, I trow, | Can hurt me if it wold: | I am so wrapped within and lapped | Of jolly good ale and old.'

[33] Seleucus does use this *cliché, abiit ad plures*, much as Niceros (below) says *supremum diem obiit* 'breathed his last'.

[34] Ch. 44.

[35] The *aediles,* whose duties included superintendence of markets and food supplies.

[36] Chapters 61 and 62.

[37] The manuscript gives *matauitatau*, which has been variously emended. May it not be, after all, as one of the seventeenth century editors suggested, an onomatopoeic coinage? I should put stresses on the second and last syllables. Note that the incongruity of a sword noisily *whacking* unsubstantial shadows is quite in the manner of the speaker.

[38] Chapters 75 to 77. I make one small change *pudoris causa*.

[39] i.e. 'the game is over'.

[40] The 'colony', of course, is a town with 'colonial' status.

[41] Literally, 'why shouldn't I tell you?' Like his fellows, Trimalchio is superstitious; but he decides, being emboldened with wine, to take the risk.

[42] A modest hope. Trimalchio will be content, say, with no more than a third of Italy.

### Gilbert Bagnani (essay date 1954)

SOURCE: "The Date and Authorship of the 'Satyricon'," in *The Phoenix*, Vol. II, 1954, pp. 3-26.

[*In the following essay, Bagnani explains the difficulties and contradictions that must be overcome in determining the authorship and date of composition of the* Satyricon; *rejects arguments of other scholars that involve circular reasoning; and concludes that it was written by the Petronius described in Tacitus's* Annals *around the year 60.*]

*Notes upon books outdo the books themselves.*

J. BRAMSTON

The present state of the "Petronius Question" can only be described as unsatisfactory. Though "the accepted date and authorship are likely to remain in favour," we are constantly being reminded that these assumptions "are only presumptive, not proved."[1] It is characteristic of the unsatisfactory state of the question that the very same passage has been used to prove that the *Satiricon* was written after Commodus, and to prove that it was written under Nero. In Chapter 57, Hermeros, reaching the bellicose state of intoxication rather sooner than the others, looks round to find someone with whom to quarrel and, lighting on Ascyltos, lets out a torrent of Billingsgate. Amongst other endearments he says: *eques Romanus es, et ego regis filius.* E. V. Marmorale[2] assumes that Ascyltos is wearing the equestrian gold ring (*cf.* 58. 10), and that Hermeros consequently believes him to be really a knight. Since this is obviously impossible, Marmorale argues that Ascyltos must have received the *ius anuli aurei* by imperial decree as a concession of *ingenuitas*, a practice that becomes general only after Commodus. On the other hand, A. Momigliano[3], reviving a suggestion of N. Heinsius,[4] sees in *et ego regis filius* an oblique reference to Pallas who, *regibus Arcadiae ortus, veterrimam nobilitatem usui publico postponeret, seque inter ministros principis haberi sineret.*[5] He considers this an argument "which alone is sufficient to date Petronius in the Neronian time" and adds: "the allusion could not be understood—and would no longer be interesting—after Nero."

The difficulties and contradictions implicit in Marmorale's theory have been effectively examined by numerous scholars, including Maiuri[6] and R. Browning,[7] but even the last-mentioned assumes that Hermeros believes Ascyltos to be a knight. Now it is quite obvious, as Sedgwick rightly pointed out,[8] that the whole passage cannot be taken seriously. Hermeros is not deceived by the *anuli buxei*, and, as "a self-made man and proud of it," an inverted snob, he is the last person on earth to advance spurious claims to gentility. He advances a preposterous and obviously false claim to royal blood to beat Ascyltos' even more preposterous and obviously false claim to equestrian rank. "If you're a Roman knight, well then, I'm a King's son!" It is just a part of that ritual of abuse used in only slightly different forms *semper, ubique et ab omnibus.* There is a story that a certain gentleman, strolling with the late Lord Curzon, stopped to talk to an old family retainer, the widow of a sergeant-major in the Indian Army. Life in India having been mentioned, Curzon chipped in with: "That must have been when I was Viceroy." Whereupon the old lady countered with "Ye was, was ye? Well, me 'usband, 'e was Commander-in-Chief, 'e was!"

An allusion to Pallas is possible only if the *Satiricon* was written in the time of Nero; otherwise it might just as well be an allusion to Maecenas or, indeed, to anyone else. Throughout the whole course of the Empire there must have arrived in Rome every year a host of "aliens" who could claim—frequently with perfect truth—that their "birth, beyond all questions, springs From great and noble, though forgotten, kings."[9] The different interpretations of this one short passage illustrate the exceptional importance of the problem of the date and authorship for the full understanding of the work itself. It is obviously full of allusions, but their interpretation depends entirely on the precise dating of the work; they cannot be used to date it. If we can prove that the *Satiricon* was written for the amusement of Nero's court, then the *ego regis filius* may have been intended as an allusion to Pallas, or, more probably, may have been taken by some contemporary readers as an allusion to Pallas, but it is perfectly comprehensible without any such allusion. The sentence with which Trimalchio ends his epitaph (71. 12), *nec umquam philosophum audivit*, is a perfectly good *boutade* and need not be anything more. But if the *Satiricon* was written for the entertainment of Nero at a time when Seneca was falling from favour, we can easily suppose that the author hoped that the Emperor, on reading the passage, might exclaim, "Lucky fellow! I wish I could say as much!"

Nothing is more subjective than the interpretation of an author's allusions. When Lord Chesterfield's *Letters to his Son* were published in 1774 the description of the "respectable Hottentot"[10] was almost universally understood as a reference to Johnson, and it undoubtedly fits Johnson better than any allusions in the *Satiricon* fit their alleged prototypes. But everyone is now agreed that the allusion is to Lyttelton, and Birkbeck Hill points out that, had the letter been published when it was written and not twenty-three years later, an allusion to Johnson would never have been suspected.[11] The explanation of the allusions in the *Satiricon* depends entirely on the date; to use them as an element of dating is to argue in a circle. The most that can be said is that no historical or literary allusion has been found that is hopelessly inconsistent with an early date, and the same can be said of the proper names; but this can hardly be used as a conclusive proof that the work was written during the first century, and still less that it was written in the time of Nero.[12]

The precise dating of the work itself is also the only way by which we can identify the author. There is no direct evidence whatsoever to connect the author with the Petronius of Tacitus. The facts are clear and not in dispute. The late authors and MSS that mention our author call him indifferently Petronius, Arbiter, or Petronius Arbiter, and obviously consider Arbiter to be his regular *cognomen*. From the account of Tacitus[13] it is equally obvious that *Arbiter Elegantiarum* was an appellation or nickname given by Society or by Tacitus himself to Nero's favourite, and was not a formal *cognomen*. Tacitus implies that Petronius had no *cogno-*

*men*. Two explanations of these facts are equally possible, indeed equally plausible: that later authors turned the nickname into a *cognomen*, or that the descendants of Petronius adopted the nickname as the regular *cognomen* of their branch of the *gens Petronia*. In the present state of our knowledge what must be avoided is the usual circular argument: that since it was written by the Petronius of Tacitus the **Satiricon** was written in the time of Nero, and that since it was written in the time of Nero it must have been written by the Petronius of Tacitus.

If it can be proved by conclusive internal evidence, without any reference to the name of the author, that the work must have been written between A.D. 55 and 65 there can be no reasonable doubt that it was written by the Petronius of Tacitus. And thus we return once more to the essential question: the precise dating of the work itself by internal evidence alone.

. . . . .

An absolute *terminus ante quem* and *post quem* are easily fixed. Maiuri has rightly pointed out that *malui civis Romanus esse quam tributarius* (57. 4) would be meaningless after the Constitutio Antoniniana of A.D. 212,[14] which is therefore an absolute terminus. The first author to quote the "Arbiter" is Terentianus Maurus,[15] whose date, however, is only slightly less uncertain than that of Petronius himself, though most scholars are now agreed in placing his activity towards the end of the second century.[16] His statement that people in his own day were in the habit of singing the songs of Petronius has been used as an argument that Terentianus and Petronius were contemporaries.[17] It can, of course, be interpreted this way, but let us remember that Addison heard Venetian gondoliers sing the songs of Tasso, and that we ourselves *solemus cantare*—or whistle—both the latest musical and the songs of Shakespeare and Jonson.[18]

An equally definite *terminus a quo* is given by the simple consideration that, though the *cognomen* Arbiter could be borne by any descendant of the Petronius of Tacitus, it could not possibly be borne by anyone earlier. And therefore the work itself, though it may be later than the time of Nero, cannot possibly be earlier. This terminus is confirmed and rendered more precise by the close relationship between Petronius and the younger Seneca and Lucan,[19] a relationship that is quite undeniable, but that may be explained in various ways. Petronius may be consciously and deliberately imitating, criticizing, and parodying Seneca; on the other hand he may be a contemporary, moving in the same or a similar circle, influenced by the same ideas and ideals, and drawing his material from the same common stock. For example: ·the parallel between Trimalchio and the Calvisius Sabinus, described by Seneca in *Ep. ad Luc.* 27, is extremely close and can

hardly be fortuitous,[20] but it is equally explicable on the supposition that Petronius developed and expanded Seneca's charactersketch, or on the supposition that he too was acquainted with Calvisius and drew from life, without any knowledge of Seneca's letter. We cannot therefore maintain that the **Satiricon** must necessarily have been written after the publication of the *Letters to Lucilius*.

The same considerations apply to the undoubtedly close relationship with Lucan.[21] It is quite possible to argue that Petronius' *de Bello Civili* is a satire on or a parody of Lucan's poem. On the other hand it is equally arguable that Eumolpus is genuinely expounding the theories of Petronius on how an epic poem should be written. In this case it is unnecessary to suppose that Petronius knew the whole of Lucan's poem, or even the first book. It would be enough for him to know that Lucan was planning an epic poem on the Civil War— and the Senecan coterie will have put out a good deal of advance publicity—and to have sufficient knowledge of "the wonderful boy's" style to form a pretty shrewd idea of what the public was likely to get. A certain connexion has been pointed out between the first lines of the two poems.[22] This does not necessarily prove that the **Satiricon** was written after A.D. 60 when Lucan published his first book.[23] Parts of Lucan's poem may have been read in Seneca's salon before publication; it is not inconceivable that Lucan may have admired the *sidus* conceit and borrowed it from Petronius and not vice versa; and finally both poets may have independently made use of a fashionable conceit. The only positive statement we can make is that the **Satiricon** must have been written after Lucan was known to be engaged on an epic poem on the Civil War, i.e., not earlier than *ca.* A.D. 58.

To resume: Petronius is contemporary with, or later than, Seneca and Lucan, and contemporary with, or earlier than, Terentianus Maurus, and the **Satiricon** cannot have been written before A.D. 58 or after A.D. 212. Is it possible to reduce these limits still further?

. . . . .

We have already seen that up till now all attempts to fix ·a definite date by explaining the allusions have been subjective and based only too frequently on circular reasoning. The same can be said of the endless discussions of Petronius' alleged literary theories, especially of the interpretation of the opening dialogue between Encolpius and Agamemnon (1-5).[24] A. D. Nock has rightly pointed out the danger of taking the passage as a serious contribution to the question.[25] Petronius' main object may well be to poke fun at the stock controversies between the different schools of rhetoric and to parody the stock arguments that were now centuries old. In this case the famous *nuper*[26] of 2. 7—*nuper ventosa istaec et enormis loquacitas*

*Athenas ex Asia commigravit*—may represent the translation of an early Hellenistic or even fourth-century original when the statement was literally true.

The investigation of the Latinity of Petronius,[27] a happy hunting ground for philologists, lexicographers, and candidates for the Ph.D., leads to a dead end as far as dating the work is concerned. We know too little to be able to date "vulgar" Latin. It is only through an accident that the closest parallels with the language of Petronius are furnished by the *Ludus de morte Claudii* and the Pompeian graffiti, that is to say by documents dating between A.D. 55 and 79. And even if our material were far more extensive than it is, it is an open question whether we could date it with any degree of approximation. A spoken language or dialect usually changes much more slowly than the literary dialect, which is immediately affected by literary fashions or by the example of an influential author. The difference between the literary Italian of Boccaccio—or, for that matter, even of Manzoni—and the modern literary Italian of, say, Malaparte or Moravia, is enormous: but when Boccaccio reproduces the spoken Tuscan of his own time in the mouths of comic characters such as Calandrino and Buffalmacco it is not very different, wit included, from the language spoken today by Tuscan peasants. The most cursory glance at Hofmann's *Umgangssprache* shows that Petronius shares many peculiarities with Plautus, many others with the author of the *Peregrinatio Aetheriae*, and many with both. Even if all Marmorale's philological arguments in favour of a late dating were sound, they would prove only that the **Satiricon** *might* have been written at the end of the second century, not that it *was*.

What renders the question so peculiarly difficult is that we cannot be quite certain that Petronius is ever wholly serious. The first line of the *schedium Lucilianae humilitatis* (5. 1) is given by practically all the MSS as

*artis severae si quis amat effectus*

and practically all modern editors, except Sage, emend the *amat* to *ambit*. Marmorale maintains the reading of the MSS and sees in the false quantity a proof that Petronius was writing at a time when the feeling for quantity was lost.[28] Now, the merit of Petronius as a poet may be a matter of opinion, but that he is a competent versifier is not; and to find a time when even a schoolboy poetaster did not know, or might forget, the quantity of the first syllable of *amare*, the most overworked verb in the whole of a poet's vocabulary, we should have to go to the darkest of the Dark Ages. If the text is sound the false quantity is intentional, and what both Marmorale and the editors forget is that the *schedium* is a parody of Lucilius. It is also incredibly bad: nowhere else is Petronius guilty of such really appalling doggerel. The conclusion is obvious: Petronius has a low opinion of Lucilius as a poet.

Horace's remark that the verses of Lucilius were *duri* (*S.* 1. 4. 8), and that they ran *incomposito pede* (*S.* 1. 10. 1), is merely a polite way of saying that they frequently did not scan.[29] And we know from the eight verses prefixed to this tenth Satire—which, if not Horatian, are probably ancient—that old editors of Lucilius, like modern editors of Petronius, were given to emendation. Petronius, wishing to parody Lucilius, deliberately introduces a false quantity, and, to make the point perfectly obvious to the meanest intelligence, makes the blunder in the very first line with the most familiar of all verbs.

If the *horti Pompeiani* of 53.5 are to be understood as "the farms at Pompeii," the **Satiricon** could be dated with certainty before the eruption of A.D. 79, for Maiuri's argument[30] that the area round Vesuvius cannot have been cultivated for over a century after the eruption is quite unanswerable. Unfortunately one cannot exclude the interpretation "the farms of Pompeius," on the analogy of *Horti Sallustiani*, etc. To ask who then can this Pompeius be, is quite beside the point; agreed that it cannot be Trimalchio's patron, but Pompeius is a common *nomen* throughout the Empire, and there is no reason whatever to suppose that any particular Pompeius is meant.

The hypothesis of a late second-century date can be excluded with certainty, not by considering this or that detail, but by observing the entire and perfectly consistent picture given in the **Satiricon** of contemporary life and manners, and of social and economic conditions. The perusal of any Handbook of Private Antiquities—Marquardt, Blümner, Friedländer, Carcopino—is enough to convince an unbiased reader that the **Satiricon** reflects the manners and customs of the first century. Marmorale has sought to meet this objection by quoting parallels from the *Historia Augusta*.[31] Now it is quite obvious that, whatever view we take of the value of the *Historia Augusta* as a record of historical events, it is entirely valueless as evidence for the *mores* of the second or early third century—though it may possibly have considerable value as evidence for those of the late fourth or early fifth.

To prove that the **Satiricon** reflects the social and economic conditions of the first century of the Empire would involve writing still another book on Roman life.[32] But, besides the arguments advanced by so many others, I should like to stress a few that seem to me quite decisive. In the *Graeca urbs* the municipal magistracies are flourishing and the leading men of the town are straining every nerve, and spending a great deal of money, in order to get elected.[33] By A.D. 180 they would have been working even harder to avoid by every means in their power election to municipal office. Nor is there any trace in the **Satiricon** of those great corporations and collegia that from the middle of the second century on are so important a part of the economic life of the Empire, and this in a city which, whether it be Puteoli or not,[34] is certainly intended to represent an important commercial city of Campania.

The complete absence of any religious feeling in Petronius has often been pointed out, and is indeed one of his most obvious characteristics. He pokes more or less good-humoured fun at astrology and divination,[35] omens and prodigies,[36] ghosts and were-wolves. He obviously considers mysticism and mystery religions an outlet for wealthy nymphomaniacs. Philosophy does not come off much better; certainly Trimalchio's Epicureanism is hardly a recommendation for the school. Nor is Petronius merely disapproving of religious innovations or aberrations; the old Roman religion is laughed at with equal impartiality.[37] The picture of the good old days when "our great ladies went up the hill to the Temple of Jupiter in their best clothes, their feet bare, their hair loose, their thoughts pure, to pray for rain. And of course down it came at once in buckets—if that didn't do it, what would?—and everyone went home like drowned rats,"[38] is one of the best things in the whole book, but its creator can hardly be considered an enthusiastic supporter of the Augustan religious programme. Personally I find it most unfortunate that this passage invariably comes to my mind when looking at the Ara Pacis.

Such indifference to religion is hardly conceivable at any period after the accession of Hadrian, when even scepticism, as in Lucian, becomes militant and doctrinaire. The author who most resembles Petronius is certainly Apuleius, but the close formal resemblance between the two works[39]—both picaresque novels with a considerable amount of obscenity—must not blind us to their essential, their fundamental difference. Apuleius' novel is a profoundly moral work, a kind of Divine Comedy, the regeneration of sinful man through Isis and her mysteries. Petronius' "heroes" are quite definitely unregenerate and their creator quite obviously wants to keep them that way. If one of the main threads of the novel is the loss and recovery by Encolpius of his virility,[40] it is a metamorphosis very different from Lucius's. When Apuleius digresses we get the masterpiece of Cupid and Psyche: when Petronius digresses we get the Pergamene Boy and the Matron of Ephesus, also masterpieces, but of a very different kind. Fulgentius himself would find it hard to interpret the *Satiricon* allegorically, and, if Petronius is a "Moralist,"[41] he is a moralist of a very peculiar type, certainly not the Johnsonian.

Even though we can unhesitatingly affirm that the *Satiricon* reflects the *mores* of the first century, it does not follow that it reflects those of the time of Nero, still less that the problems of the date and authorship are solved, as most commentators directly or indirectly imply. Manners and customs change with every de-

cade. Johnson once rightly "observed, that all works which describe manners, require notes in sixty or seventy years, or less";[42] and if manners had changed so greatly in sixty years as to render much of *The Spectator* unintelligible in 1773, we can assume that there must have been an at least equal change of manners between the time of Claudius and that of Nerva. Unfortunately we know too little about the details of Roman life to do more than date by centuries, and though the *Satiricon* reflects the manners of the first century, we cannot say whether it reflects the early, the middle, or the final decades. Admittedly the general impression would seem to favour a Julio-Claudian rather than a Flavian date, but this is a merely subjective impression. The luxury of Trimalchio would appear to be pre-Flavian, but Tacitus' claim that the Flavian was an age of almost "Victorian" respectability after the excesses of the Julio-Claudians,[43] is hardly borne out by Juvenal and Martial, who, more than any other authors, are a commentator's seconds in his duel with the text of the *Satiricon*. It is true that Encolpius seems to take it for granted that, in a case of disputed possession, the interdictal procedure will be followed,[44] and Frontinus has been cited as proving that, by the Flavian period, this cumbersome procedure was avoided as much as possible.[45] But our text of Frontinus is in a most unsatisfactory state—it may well have been interpolated—and in any case Frontinus is referring to immovables and not to *utrubi*, the only one of the possessory interdicts applicable to the case of the cloak.

It would be easy to advance a theory that the *Satiricon* was written in the first decade of the second century by some descendant of the original Arbiter in order to satirize Domitianic society.[46] Such a theory would explain the close relationship between Petronius on the one hand and Juvenal, Martial, Quintilian, Statius, and Tacitus on the other, without postulating any conscious borrowing one from another. In such a case Tacitus would have presumably based his detailed account of the death of the Arbiter—with an oblique explanation of the origin of the *cognomen*—on a couple of letters written to him by, say, a grand-nephew, one of his literary friends. The amphitheatre at Puteoli is the new Flavian one, and Ganymedes' lament on the decay of the city (44) genuinely reflects the decay of Campania under the Flavians, and is not the typical grouse of a typical *laudator temporis acti*.

To resume: we can now say that the *Satiricon* cannot have been written before A.D. 58 at the earliest, nor after about A.D. 118 at the latest. Can these limits be reduced still further? Can proof be found that will conclusively assign the work to one of these six decades? The road leading to this goal is strewn with the warning bones of my predecessors, but *audaces fortuna iuvat*: let's try again!

. . . . .

Echion, the rag-and-bone man, in enumerating the attractions of the coming games, mentions specifically (45. 7-8) *dispensatorem Glyconis, qui deprehensus est cum dominam suam delectaretur, videbis populi rixam inter zelotypos et amasiunculos. Glyco autem, sestertiarius homo, dispensatorem ad bestias dedit.* It is clear from this that Glyco used his absolute power of life and death over his slaves to be revenged on his steward, and that he was legally entitled to do so, even though a considerable section of public opinion was against him. This absolute power of a master over his slaves was restricted by a Lex Petronia cited by Modestinus (*D* 48. 8. 11. 1-2): *servo sine iudice ad bestias dato, non solum qui vendidit poena, verum et qui comparavit tenebitur, post legem Petroniam et senatus consulta ad eam legem pertinentia dominis potestas ablata est ad bestias depugnandas suo arbitrio servos tradere: oblato tamen iudici servo, si iusta sit domini querella, sic poenae tradetur.*[47]

It is quite clear that Glyco acted *suo arbitrio*;[48] had he obtained the condemnation of his steward from a jurisdictional magistrate Echion would have used the technical expression *dispensatorem damnandum dandumque ad bestias curavit.* Moreover, had the Lex Petronia been in force, no magistrate would have been disposed to condemn the steward and admit that Glyco's was a *iusta querella*. Indeed, this was just the sort of case for which the law was drafted: a master's punishing his slave for a crime for which the master himself was directly or indirectly responsible. And if a steward had the opportunity *delectari dominam*, the *dominus* was, to put it as mildly as possible, negligent. The point is made by Echion himself: *quid servus peccavit, qui coactus est facere?* a direct echo of the phrase attributed by the elder Seneca[49] to the orator Haterius, *impudicitia in ingenuo crimen est, in servo necessitas.* Even on the very unlikely hypothesis that the magistrate had been "fixed" or was a *zelotypus*[50] and willing to condemn the steward, the facts would have necessarily been brought out in court. In this case Glyco, under the Lex Iulia, would have had to proceed against his wife and divorce her: otherwise he would lay himself open to the savage penalties that the law comminated against complaisant husbands and to the great danger of prosecution by any *delator*. Echion's thumb-nail sketch of the unattractive Glyco proves not only that the wife was not punished for her peccadillo, but also that a divorce was the last thing the good-for-nothing Glyco would want. He had obviously married the daughter of Hermogenes, a prominent if not a highly respected citizen, for her money and for her family influence and connexions, and he would lose all by a divorce. Of course the facts were well known—*hoc est se ipsum traducere*—but only through gossip, and no *delator*, without concrete evidence, would dare launch a prosecution under the Lex Iulia. This was the fundamental weakness of that law as of all statutes rendering adultery a criminal offence: the natural repugnance of husbands to prosecute, and the utter impossibility of compelling them to do so. The wisest man may not avoid getting cuckolded, but only a congenital idiot sticks antlers over his front door. Sensible people behaved like Trimalchio's own master; a too attractive slave was sent off to some distant country estate.[51]

Since Glyco certainly condemned his steward to the amphitheatre *suo arbitrio*, the only possible conclusion is that the Lex Petronia was not yet in force; and it consequently follows that the **Satiricon** was written before the passage of the Lex Petronia. Even if Petronius did not place the action of the novel in his own day, this is not the kind of accuracy an ancient author would be inclined to bother about, and, indeed, the whole point of the story would be missed if its readers were used to the conditions created by that statute. Unfortunately the date of the Lex Petronia *de servis* is uncertain: some civilians date it in A.D. 19,[52] others in A.D. 61.[53] It would be easy to say that, since the **Satiricon** cannot be earlier than A.D. 58, the latter are right and Petronius furnishes the proof; but to date the Lex Petronia by the **Satiricon** and then date the **Satiricon** by the Lex Petronia is too much like that circular reasoning we have already condemned. We must try to establish the date of the Lex Petronia without reference to the **Satiricon**.

. . . . .

Four *leges publicae populi Romani* are designated as Petroniae and, since they have occasionally been confused, it may be well to examine them all, keeping in mind the following considerations. The *gens Petronia*, of Umbro-Etruscan origin, is not known in Rome till about the middle of the second century B.C.[54] and did not become prominent till the Civil Wars.[55] On the other hand, legislation by *lex rogata* submitted to the comitia fell gradually into disuse during the early Empire and ceased with Nerva, being replaced either by Senatusconsulta or imperial constitutions and rescripts. Moreover, during this period, the right to submit legislation to the comitia was, in practice, limited to the consuls, ordinary or suffect.

1. The Lex Petronia *de praefectis municipiorum*: known only through epigraphic evidence.[56] It is earlier than A.D. 79 since it is mentioned on an inscription at Pompeii.[57] If it is really referred to in the Fasti Venusini, it would be earlier than 32 B.C. and might in that case be tribunician,[58] but the interpretation of the reference in the Fasti is dubious.[59] The lex belongs probably to late republican or early imperial times, but its date, and even its purpose, are quite uncertain. It is mentioned here only because it has been confused with the Lex Petronia *de servis*.[60]

2. Lex Petronia *de adulterii iudicio*:[61] mentioned in a rescript of Valerian and Gallienus of 256, *C* 9. 9. 16. 2: *. . . quia et decreto patrum et lege Petronia ei, qui iure viri delatum adulterium non peregit, numquam postea id crimen deferre permittitur.* The rescript distinguishes quite clearly the lex from a *decretum patrum*, i.e., a Senatusconsultum, that preceded it. Given the subject-matter of the lex there can be little doubt that this Senatusconsultum is the famous SC Turpilianum *de abolitionibus D* 48. 16 and *C* 9. 45; indeed the lex is merely a particular application of the general principle. It follows therefore that both the SC and the lex were proposed by the same person, P. Petronius Turpilianus, consul ordinarius in A.D. 61. He probably proposed the Senatusconsultum a few years earlier when praetor.

3. Lex Iunia Petronia *de liberalibus causis*.[62] Known from *D* 40. 1. 24. *pr.* (*Hermogenianus, libro primo iuris epitomarum*): *lege Iunia Petronia, si dissonantes pares iudicum existant sententiae, pro libertate pronuntiari iussum.* This is an extremely puzzling statute: it obviously deals with suits *de libertate* before the centumviral court. Its range was later extended by a constitution of Antoninus Pius (Paul, *D* 42. 1. 38. *pr.*), probably to the courts of the provincial governors. Its date can hardly be disputed; it was passed in the second half of A.D. 19 by the consul ordinarius M. Iunius Silanus and the consul suffectus P. Petronius P. f. who succeeded the other ordinarius L. Norbanus Balbus. There is no reason whatever to connect this law in any way with the lex Petronia *de servis*;[63] indeed the two laws deal with entirely different fields of law. The Iunia Petronia belongs to the Law of Civil Procedure, the Petronia *de servis* to the Law of Property, and no Roman jurist would confuse the two. To think of a Roman Law of Slavery is entirely modern; for a Roman slavery was merely a special section of the general law of property, or, in certain cases, of persons. The real difficulty is the relation between this law and the Lex Iunia (Norbana) that gave birth to that horrible abortion, Junian Latinity. If the latter was passed at the beginning of A.D. 19—and this is the more widely held opinion—it seems very strange that legislation should have to be introduced only a few months later to deal with a point of procedure that had been overlooked by the drafters of the original statute, especially as there is no doubt whatever that Roman legal draughtsmanship was of a very high order. The Iunia Petronia seems rather to be *ad hoc* legislation, designed to meet a practical difficulty that had arisen in the courts, i.e., the centumviral court in a particular case tried a short time previously had divided fifty-fifty. The institution of Junian Latinity must have enormously increased both the number and the complexity of the *causae liberales*, and therefore the Iunia Petronia would logically appear to have been passed after disputes on *status* had been before the courts for some time. Since the date of the Iunia Petronia is far more certain than that of the

Iunia Norbana, this would seem to be a strong argument in support of those who date Junian Latinity to the earlier part of the reign of Augustus.[64]

4. We now come to the Lex Petronia *de servis*.[65] We have seen that there is absolutely no reason to connect it in any way with the Iunia Petronia of A.D. 19, and thus the only possibility of dating it is by considering its position in the development of the Roman concept of slavery. In this connexion the revolutionary nature of the Lex Petronia does not seem to have been fully appreciated. From the point of view of Roman Law slaves are merely a particular type of property, and it is a basic principle of law that an owner can do what he pleases with property to which he has a clear title. That in practice this absolute right was limited—and not only in the case of slaves—by custom, public opinion, self-interest, and other extra-legal but important considerations, does not affect the strictly legal position in the slightest.[66] Now the Lex Petronia explicitly prohibits an owner from disposing of certain property *suo arbitrio*, explicitly recognizes that this right existed, and explicitly abolishes it; *potestas ablata est.* So revolutionary an innovation seems to me incredible under the principates of either Augustus or Tiberius, in such matters rather rigidly conservative, admirers of *ius, fas, mos maiorum*, and other equally repulsive Roman ideals.[67] The Iunia Petronia, as I have pointed out, merely establishes a *presumptio iuris* in procedure, but does not touch in any way the, so to speak, "common law" rights of ownership.

The Lex Petronia would appear to be the legal expression of that growing feeling of humanity towards slaves that is so marked in both Seneca and the *Satiricon*. This feeling was expressed also in the legislation by Claudius which is the first attempt, and a rather half-hearted one, to limit the unfettered rights of slave owners. If Suetonius[68] is to be trusted, the Claudian law consisted of two parts. The first part, the main one, laid down that, if a master exposed a sick slave to avoid the trouble or expense of curing him and the slave recovered, the slave was free and his former master could not claim him. In itself this would hardly be a restriction of property rights, but rather an enactment that, under certain circumstances, if an owner abandoned certain property, he lost his title to it.[69] The real object of the law was to oblige owners to look after sick slaves, but it was obvious to the legal draughtsmen that this object could be easily defeated and the law circumvented by an owner who, finding he could no longer expose his slave and being still unwilling to look after him, simply put him to death. It was therefore further enacted that in such a case—and in such a case alone—the killing of the slave would be held as equivalent to murder.

There was left, however, a further loophole. If a slave, sick, old, or unproductive, could not be in practice either exposed or killed, he could still be used to provide entertainment at the games, and the person who gave the *munus* would probably pay the owner something for him. The Lex Petronia effectively plugged this loophole and, under the influence of the humanitarian ideas of the time, enacted the first general limitation of the rights of slave owners. The Lex Petronia is therefore later than Claudius.

To this conclusion there is one objection that must be examined. Aulus Gellius (5. 14. 27), in telling the famous story of Androcles and the Lion, places the following words in Androcles' mouth: (*dominus*) *me statim rei capitalis damnandum dandumque ad bestias curavit*. The phrase expresses in technical legal language the procedure followed after the Lex Petronia. Since the incident almost certainly took place under Gaius,[70] the Lex Petronia would appear to have been in force at this time. But we must remember that Gellius is writing in the second half of the second century after Christ, and is, moreover, translating from the Hellenistic Greek of Apion, a native Egyptian. It is highly improbable that the latter made use of such technical legal language. Aelian also tells the story (*de Nat. An.* 7. 48) and, though he summarizes and turns direct into indirect speech, he is probably verbally closer to the original. . . . This is nothing like as specific a statement as that of Gellius, indeed it is a masterpiece of ambiguity. We can only conclude therefore that Gellius, who, though not a jurist, was familiar with and fond of using legal Latin, finding in Apion a vague expression such as "my master held an inquiry on what I had done wrong, and I was condemned to the beasts,"[71] translated it by the technical phrase that would be used by his own contemporaries, forgetting, or more probably not knowing, that the procedure before a magistrate was not yet in force in the time of Apion.

Having thus proved, I hope, that the Lex Petronia *de servis* is a post-Claudian *lex rogata* strongly influenced by the general humanitarianism of the time, seen in both Seneca and Petronius, we must try to establish its precise date. There is no indication that comitial legislation was continued under the Flavians, whose policy indeed was directed at decreasing the authority of the consuls, and the only consul of the *gens Petronia* that we know of in this period is M. Petronius Umbrinus, suffect in A.D. 81.[72] The revival of comitial legislation under Nerva is itself open to a good deal of doubt,[73] and in any case we know of no Petronius who held a consulship in those years. It therefore follows that the probabilities in favour of a Neronian date are overwhelming. Since the lex must have been sponsored by a consul, ordinary or suffect, we have four possibilities during this period:[74] A. Petronius Lurco, suffect during the latter part of A.D. 58; P. Petronius Turpilianus, ordinary consul in 61; T. Petronius Niger, suffect in some year between 63 and 70; and the Arbiter himself, suffect in some year of Nero's reign before A.D. 66.

Unfortunately our only complete lists of consuls for the reign are those for the years 56-59 and 62.

Until we can complete these consular lists it is impossible to choose between the various possibilities with any degree of confidence; in the present state of our knowledge the most we can do is to examine and weigh certain probabilities. That the author of this legislation was A. Petronius Lurco seems to me improbable in the extreme. This conjecture would oblige us to assign the **Satiricon** to the first part of A.D. 58, a date which, though not actually impossible, is highly unlikely, given the relationship not only with Lucan's poem but also with Nero's own *Troiae Halosis*. Most writers on the subject of the Lex Petronia have attributed it to Petronius Turpilianus during his consulship in the first part of A.D. 61, and on the whole, in the present state of our knowledge, this is perhaps the most probable hypothesis, for he was the author of the SC Turpilianum and of another *lex rogata*, the Lex Petronia *de adulterii iudicio*. The comitia must have met only rarely in this period, and presumably as much legislation as possible would have been presented to them. On the other hand we do not know whether Petronius Turpilianus was influenced by the humanitarian movement of the time— we know of him only as a reliable man in an emergency and a good administrator of unquestioned loyalty—and the two leges Petroniae have nothing in common except their name.

There is, moreover, a general consideration which, while not being real evidence and still less proof, deserves to be kept in mind. Legislation so revolutionary as our Lex Petronia is usually passed after some particular case has drawn the attention of both lawyers and public to the unsatisfactory state of the law. Such an event occurred in A.D. 61 when the city prefect, Pedianus Secundus, was murdered by one of his slaves. From the account of Tacitus[75] it would appear that the crime took place in the second half of the year, after Turpilianus had left for Britain. In such cases the law prescribed that the whole *familia*—in this case over four hundred people—should be executed, and the Senate refused to modify the law, notwithstanding the entreaties of the populace, covertly supported by the Emperor himself. Any humanitarian proposal would be popular in such circumstances, and, given the temper of the people and the attitude of the Senate, it would be more likely to be submitted to the comitia as a *lex rogata*, rather than enacted by Senatusconsultum or imperial constitution. If this reasoning is correct, the author of our legislation was either the Arbiter or T. Petronius Niger.

The possibility that Petronius "Arbiter" may have been the author of this legislation cannot be excluded. Tacitus states that, as consul, he was surprisingly and unexpectedly active, and it is not easy to see what activity, except legislative, was possible for a suffect consul under the later Julio-Claudians. The Lex Petronia is also the kind of legislation we might expect both from the person described by Tacitus and from the author of the **Satiricon**. Since he was a favourite of Nero's, we can reasonably conjecture that the Arbiter reached the consulship when he was at the height of his influence, that is to say after Seneca's had begun to decline and before Tigellinus' had become overwhelming. We should therefore expect his consulship to fall in one of the two years A.D. 60 and 61.[76] In favour of the year 60 is the consideration that Nero might want a close personal friend, his own *arbiter elegantiarum*, to be consul for the celebration of the Neroneia; and this, of course, might be the chief activity to which Tacitus referred. On the other hand, it is quite possible that two members of the same *gens*, close relations and favourites of the Emperor, might hold the consulship in the same year as a particular mark of imperial favour.[77] Finally, the candidature of our only recently resurrected T. Petronius Niger cannot be absolutely dismissed. In its favour is the confusion made by Pliny and Plutarch about the *praenomen* of the Arbiter, which they both give as T(itus).[78] It is not outside the range of possibility that they confused the author of a well-known lex with the author of a notorious novel. In this case the Lex Petronia might be of any date between 61 and 70.

To resume: I hope I have proved, without reference to the **Satiricon**, that the Lex Petronia *de servis* was enacted under Nero, probably by Petronius Turpilianus in A.D. 61, possibly by Petronius Arbiter or by T. Petronius Niger between A.D. 60 and the end of the reign.

. . . . .

I have already said that the question of the authorship depends on that of the date. If the **Satiricon** is of the time of Nero it follows inevitably that it was written by the Petronius of Tacitus. Having proved that the **Satiricon** was written between A.D. 58 and 65 I submit that it was written by Petronius "Arbiter." That an anonymous work written at this time should have been fathered on him is so intrinsically improbable and so devoid of any semblance of proof as to require no contradiction. The main arguments of those who consider the "Petronian" authorship of the **Satiricon** a question that cannot be answered are best put by Émile Thomas:

> Pour la question de l'identité de personne entre le Pétrone de Tacite et l'auteur du roman, l'obstacle principal est toujours celui-ci. . . . Dans le portrait si vivant que Tacite a tracé du consulaire et de sa fin, il n'est pas question de son talent d'écrivain; en fait d'ouvrage de Pétrone, Tacite ne cite que le pamphlet envoyé à Néron: comment expliquer ce silence, si ce même consulaire avait écrit un roman très lu, très répandu et qui lui a survécu? D'autre part, nous ne connaissons pas la vie de l'auteur du *Satiricon*: mais nous constatons que, dans tant de pages, il n'y a pas une allusion, pas un mot qui se rapporte à la vie publique: comment comprendre qu'un homme, mêlé de si près à la politique de son temps, ait pu écrire un long ouvrage où rien ne rappelle ce qu'il a fait, ce qu'il a vu, ni même, avec pleine clarté et en toute précision l'histoire de son temps?[79]

M. Thomas' book is as full of good things as a plum pudding, but in this particular case his observations are not arguments, they are impertinences. M. Thomas who, like nearly all Frenchmen, is an admirable writer, is here quite calmly telling two of the very greatest artists in prose, Tacitus and Petronius, how to write history, and how to write novels. He joins those critics, ancient and modern, who blame Jane Austen for not depicting English sentiment during the Napoleonic Wars, Charles Dickens for dealing with "low" life, and Rudyard Kipling for ignoring the struggles of Indian nationalism. Any great artist has the right to make his own rules of relevance. It is obvious that all ancient historians, Polybius not excluded, had very different ideas from modern historians on what was relevant. No doubt a modern historian, with his academic career in mind, would, in the text and in the footnotes, have given us a complete biography of Petronius, the exact date of his birth, his full *cursus honorum* and list of works, with dates, places of publication, and variant editions. It would all be extremely useful and valuable; but how dull!

The space that Tacitus devotes to Petronius is actually a confirmation of the importance of Petronius as an author. Tacitus gives him two full chapters, twice as much as he gives Lucan, whose epic poem also is not referred to. Petronius was not one of the more important political figures of the time; the interest that Tacitus so clearly shows must be due to some other reason, and that reason can only be literary. The author of the *Dialogus de oratoribus* had read and studied the **Satiricon**; and a master of prose, such as Tacitus, could hardly fail to admire another great artist, however different. To a specialist in antithesis, the contrast between the *flâneur*, the dandy, the writer of salacious novels, and the capable administrator, the acute critic, the artist in living and writing, must have been fascinating. It is the same contrast, the same antithesis that we ourselves find so fascinating in Pepys, the hedonist, and Pepys, the saviour of the Navy; in Boswell, the friend of Johnson, and in Boswell, the friend of Wilkes. Of course we can hardly expect that Tacitus, that high-minded and serious Stoic, that Olympian dispenser of eternal praise or infamy, and, not to put too fine a point on it, that superlative prig, should openly avow his fascination and admiration. But he devotes to Petronius an amount of space which, given the general economy of the *Annals*, is not otherwise explicable. And I cannot help feeling that, in his description of the death of Petronius, the Stoic Tacitus was uncomfortably aware that the way this dandy met his death was far more dignified than the Stoic posturings of Seneca or Thrasea.

The authorship and, within very narrow limits, the date of composition being thus established, the purpose and the occasion of the publication follow with a high degree of probability. The *Satiricon* was written for the amusement of Nero and his *pauci familiares* on the occasion of the Neroneia of A.D. 60. The general assumption in the *Satiricon* that the simplest way of getting a fortune is to find hidden treasure would seem to refer to the early Neronian legislation on treasure-trove and echo the passage of Calpurnius (*Ecl.* 4. 117 ff.).[80] By this time the influence of Seneca was declining and the sly digs at philosophers in general and Seneca in particular would be appreciated. The *Troiae Halosis* and the *de Bello Civili*, in this case, are neither parodies nor criticisms, but merely exercises on themes that were popular in the small coterie for which Petronius was writing. Momigliano's remark: "he described the big themes of the literary life of his days (the Imperial poetry on Troy included) as subjects not for emperors and lofty people but for dubious, amusing, and vulgar members of a low society"[81] is true and penetrating. A highly sophisticated society would enjoy the joke: that the joke was also a very subtle indictment of that society itself would scarcely be apparent, and may not have been deliberately intended by the author. It would therefore appear more probable that Lucan, in revising his poem for publication, took some hints from Petronius, than that Petronius was attacking Lucan's poem.

The subsequent consulship of Petronius proves that Nero appreciated the work. But, as an author, Petronius had overreached himself. In writing a highly topical skit for the amusement of a very restricted group he forfeited his popularity with a wider public and with the professional critics and literary historians. The *Satiricon* is, and must always have been, a most disconcerting work. Like Peacock's novels, which in certain ways it rather resembles, it obstinately refuses to be fitted into any literary genre. After the passing of the society for which he wrote, and the growing emphasis in the following generations on "high seriousness" and formal education, Petronius was naturally neglected. No one could really expect Quintilian, or any "educationist" ancient or modern, to recommend the *Satiricon* as a model to his pupils. Tacitus had read him and reluctantly admired him, but we can hardly blame him for not publicly declaring his admiration. The best thing schoolmasters, rhetoricians, and literary historians can do is to ignore so original an author. The *Satiricon* is relegated to the category "curious" and to grammarians on the look-out for strange expressions and usages. It is not surprising that so much of Petronius has been lost:

what is really surprising is that so much has been preserved.

The *Satiricon* will continue to remain a puzzling and fascinating work. It is true enough that Petronius' avowed purpose was to amuse Nero's court and that he apparently succeeded in accomplishing this purpose, but is this all? Can anyone be as completely detached as Petronius seems to be? What does he really think of the society he is describing or the society for which he is writing? Is he really a satirist? a moralist? The Sphinx smiles and remains inscrutable.

*Notes*

[1] J. Whatmough, *CP* 44 (1949) 274, reviewing Marmorale, *Questione*: cf. W. Suess, *Gnomon* 23 (1951) 312-317, and A. Ernout, *RevPhil* 24 (1950) 120.

[2] Marmorale, *Questione* 317-323.

[3] Momigliano, 100.

[4] Burman, *Satyricon*[2] (Amsterdam 1745) 1. 372.

[5] Tacitus, *Ann.* 12. 53.

[6] *Petroniana* 101-128.

[7] *CR* 63 (1949) 12.

[8] W. B. Sedgwick, *The Cena Trimalchionis*[2] (Oxford 1950) 115. A salutary warning that one must not take any statement of Petronius too seriously had been issued by A. D. Nock, *CR* 46 (1932) 173.

[9] Though Charles Churchill's *Prophecy of Famine* was published early in 1763, these lines (273-274) are directed against the Scots in general, not against Lord Bute in particular, and still less against Boswell, even though the latter arrived in London that very year, and on one occasion characteristically informed George III that he was the Pretender's cousin in the seventh degree (*Malahide Papers* 16. 101). The early Empire seems to have attributed as much importance to quarterings as a minor German court. Besides the claim that Maecenas and Pallas were *atavis editi regibus,* a royal pedigree was also provided for Nero's concubine Acte (Suet., *Nero* 28. 1), while the Vitellii were given a descent from Faunus, King of the Aborigines (Suet., *Vitell.* 1. 2).

[10] Letter to his son of 28 February O.S. 1751 (*Letters,* ed. Bonamy Dobrée, 4. 1685).

[11] Boswell, *Life of Johnson*, ed. Hill-Powell, 1. 267, n. 2.

[12] Most of the alleged allusions have been effectively

examined and criticized by Marmorale, *Questione* 63-104. He convincingly refutes, 99, L. Hermann's attempt in *AntCl* 11 (1942) 87-89 to place the *Cena* in A.D. 34: there is not the slightest reason to suppose that Scaurus, Pompeius, and others mentioned are historical or even real persons. Recent attempts at allusion-hunting, equally ingenious and unconvincing, are those of P. Grimal, *RevPhil* 16 (1942) 161-168, and of Richard H. Crum, *CW* 45 (1952) 161-170. Trimalchio's second cognomen Maecenatianus does not *necessarily* indicate that he had been a slave of Maecenas; H. W. Haley, *HSCP* 2 (1891) 13.

[13] *Ann* 16. 17: *inter paucos familiarium Neroni adsumptus est, elegantiae arbiter . . .* (and *cf. infra* 49, n. 13).

[14] Maiuri, *Petroniana* 127. In dealing with this point Marmorale, *Questione* 324-325, is more than usually unconvincing. I shall forbear discussing the long controversy started by U. E. Paoli, "L'Età del Satyricon," *StItal* 14 (1937) 3-46. Since there is no reason whatever to see in *Sat.* 70. 10 a case of *manumissio per mensam* (it is clearly contradicted by the fact that Trimalchio intends to manumit all his slaves *testamento*, 71. 1), *cadit quaestio: cf.* R. Henrion, *RBPh* 22 (1943) 198.

[15] *De Metris* 2489 (*GLK* 6. 399) "Arbiter"; and 2852 (*ibid.* 6. 409) "Petronius."

[16] Schanz-Hosius, *Gesch. d. Röm. Lit.* 3³ (Munich 1922) 27.

[17] Marmorale, *Questione* 290-291: *cf.* Schanz-Hosius, *loc. cit.*

[18] The attempt to prove that Terentianus considers Petronius one of the *poetae novelli* (E. Castorina in *Giorn. it. di Filologia* 1. 213) is wholly unconvincing.

[19] Collignon, 149-165 and 291-311; Maiuri, *Cena* 17-24; Marmorale, *Questione* 224-235.

[20] Maiuri, *Cena* 19.

[21] Collignon, 149-226; H. Stubbe, "Die Verseinlagen im Petron" *Philologus*, Suppl. 25, 2 (1933) 67-151; a summary of the various theories in Sage, 207.

[22] R. J. Getty, *CP* 46 (1951) 29.

[23] Though, as Momigliano, 97, points out, Miss Toynbee's interpretation, 87, of the passage in Suetonius is open to doubt, the fact is not.

[24] Collignon, 63-108; Marmorale, *Questione* 275-286; Sage, 207; E. Paratore, *Il Satyricon* (Florence 1933) 2. 1-24; L. Alfonsi, *RFIC*, N.S., 26 (1948) 46-53.

[25] *CR* 46 (1932) 173, pointing out the close connexion between this passage of Petronius and Philo, *de Plantatione* 157-159.

[26] Collignon, 83; Marmorale, *Questione* 284-286. Sage, 146, rightly suspected that "Petronius was following some Greek source and failed to remove the evidence." If, however, the whole passage is a deliberate parody of stock arguments, the failure is intentional.

[27] There is a summary of the question and a fairly complete bibliography in Marmorale, *Questione* 124-223; but *cf.* Excursus I.

[28] Marmorale, *Questione* 292.

[29] Or that Horace and his contemporaries were unable to scan them, even as the English Augustans were unable to scan Chaucer or Donne. Lucilius might have answered in the words of Alfieri, *son duri, duri, disaccentati? . . . non son cantati!* G. Suess, "Petronii imitatio sermonis plebei," *Acta et Comment. Univ. Tartuensis*, B13, 1 (Dorpat 1927) rightly points out the close dependence of Petronius on Lucilius, but this does not mean that Petronius necessarily admired him.

[30] *Cena* 186; *Petroniana* 110-112.

[31] *Questione* 297-313; for a discussion of the problem of the *Historia Augusta* see S. Mazzarino, *Aspetti Sociali del Quarto Secolo* (Roma 1941) 345-370.

[32] The close connexion between manners and customs as depicted in the *Cena* and the life of Pompeii and Herculaneum has been admirably brought out in Maiuri, *Cena*. If 53. 3, *Mithridates servus in crucem actus est, quia Gai nostri genio male dixerat*, could be taken seriously, the date of the work would be earlier than Hadrian, who seems to have forbidden masters to put slaves to death *arbitrio* (Mommsen, *Strafrecht* 617; W. W. Buckland, *Law of Slavery* [Cambridge 1908] 37; F. Schulz, *Principles of Roman Law* [Oxford 1936] 220—though we should like to have better evidence of the fact than the *Historia Augusta*). It would be dangerous, however, to stress this point since the whole episode of the recitation of the *Acta* is farcical in the extreme.

[33] *Sat.* 45. 10 (Echion): *subolfacio quia nobis epulum daturus est Mammaea, binos denarios mihi et meis.*

[34] The case for Puteoli has been excellently put by Maiuri, *Cena* 5-14 and *Petroniana* 106-108; *contra*, Marmorale, *Questione* 117-133, Paratore, *Il Satyricon* 1. 179-211 and *Paideia* 3 (1948) 265. I do not believe with Paratore that the *Graeca urbs* is imaginary nor with Maiuri that the name was deliberately concealed. If the *Satiricon* was written in the time of Nero, the identification with Puteoli is highly probable since it is

still the most important town of Campania, but it is impossible to identify the city with such certainty as to date the work itself. Moreover Cumae is excluded only on the basis of Trimalchio's reference to it in 48. 8, and it seems to me extremely difficult to take this as a reference to the Italian Cumae. Either he is referring to the Aeolic Cumae (so Marmorale, *Cena* 78), or, more probably, the text is corrupt.

[35] J. G. W. M. De Vreese, *Petron 39 und die Astrologie* (Amsterdam 1927), has greatly elucidated these passages, but has made the fundamental mistake of taking them seriously, *cf. infra* 58, n. 52.

[36] It is enough to compare the point of view of Petronius in such matters with that of Dio Cassius, a highly educated Senator, to exclude the possibility of their being contemporaries. *Cf.* M. A. Levi, *Nerone e i suoi tempi* (Milan 1949) 219.

[37] Contempt for the official religion is even more marked in the *Ludus de morte Claudii*; Collignon, 28.

[38] *Sat.* 44. 18: *antea stolatae ibant nudis pedibus in clivum, passis capillis, mentibus puris, et Iovem aquam exorabant. itaque statim urceatim plovebat—aut tunc, aut nunquam—et omnes redibant udi tanquam mures* (*redibant udi*, Jacobs, Bücheler, Maiuri; *ridebant udi*, Sage, Ernout, Terzaghi; *ridebant uvidi*, Marmorale; *ridebant ut dii*, H).

[39] Collignon, 40-46; Marmorale, *Questione* 247-262.

[40] C. Marchesi, *Petronio* (Milan 1940) 41-42. The same considerations apply to the generally accepted theory that the plot of the novel is the Wrath of Priapus. Far too little is left of the work to allow us to consider the various attempts at reconstructing the plot as anything more than exercises in ingenuity. From fr. 4 it seems probable—though not certain—that part of the action took place in Massilia, but the *Memphitides puellae* of fr. 19 are no kind of proof that anything took place in Egypt.

[41] G. Highet, "Petronius the Moralist," *TAPA* 72 (1941) 176-194.

[42] Boswell, *Life*, 3 April 1773 (ed. Hill-Powell, 2. 212).

[43] *Ann.* 3. 55.

[44] *Sat.* 13. 4: *iure civili dimicandum, ut si nollent alienam rem domino reddere, ad interdictum venirent.*

[45] F. Schulz, *Classical Roman Law* (Oxford 1951) 62, quoting an alleged statement of Frontinus: *magna alea est ad interdictum deducere, cuius est executio perplexissima.* But this sentence is to be found not in Frontinus, but in Agennius Urbicus (*Corpus*

*Agrimensorum Romanorum*, ed. C. Thulin [Leipzig 1913] 1. 1. 34, lines 2-3) and, though his source is undoubtedly Frontinus, his verbal accuracy is by no means certain. The phrase with which Frontinus, in the certain fragments of his work (*Corpus*, 1. 1. 6, lines 13-14), refers to the interdict, *de possessione controversia est, de qua ad interdictum, hoc est iure ordinario, litigatur*, hardly supports Schulz, and is almost an echo of Petronius.

[46] A Flavian date was suggested by G. H. Kraffert, *Neue Beiträge* (Verden 1888) 8.

[47] The text seems sound and uninterpolated, except that the term *iudex* has been substituted for that of the original jurisdictional magistrate, praetor, or prefect: *cf. Index interpolationum* 3. 536.

[48] Marmorale's note on this passage, *Cena* 64, "la *Lex Petronia* riconosceva al padrone *ad bestias depugnandas suo arbitrio servos suos tradere*," is simply not true. L. Friedländer, *Cena Trimalchionis*² (Leipzig 1906) 265, supposed that Glyco had obtained a judgement fom the urban prefect. I deal with this supposition in the text.

[49] Seneca Rh., *Controv.* 4, *Praef.* 10; and *cf.* Trimalchio's own remark (75. 11): *nec turpe est quod dominus iubet.* L. Debray, *NRHD* 43 (1919) 42, n. 6, interprets *peccare* in the technical sense "to commit a delict."

[50] That *zelotypus* could also mean "cuckold" would seem to be indicated by its survival in this sense well into the Middle Ages; *cf.* J. Gessler, *AntCl* 11 (1942) 85.

[51] *Sat.* 69. 3.

[52] Girard, *Manuel élémentaire du droit romain*⁸ (Paris 1929) 109; Leonhard-Weiss in *RE* 12. 2. 2401.

[53] A. Bouché-Leclerq, *Manuel des institutions romaines* (Paris 1886) 410: Rotondi, *Leges publicae populi romani* (1912) 468 followed by P. de Francisci, *Storia del Diritto Romano* (Milan 1938) 2. 1. 434 and H. H. Scullard in *Oxford Classical Dictionary* 501.

[54] F. Münzer in *RE* 19. 1. 1193: *in Wirklichkeit sind Petronier in Rom vor der Mitte des 2 Fhdts. v. Chr. nicht bekannt, und es sind in der republikanischen Zeit immer nur wenige und unbedeutende gewesen;* and *cf. infra* 51 and n. 30.

[55] The first Petronius to have been politically important would appear to have been the one proscribed for some unspecified participation in the murder of Caesar; *RE* 19. 1. 1231 and *infra* 52.

[56] Rotondi, *Leges publicae* 439.

[57] *CIL* 10. 858 = *ILS* 6359.

[58] So G. Niccolini, *Fasti dei Tribuni della Plebe* (Milan 1934) 444, followed by T. R. S. Broughton, *Magistrates of the Roman Republic* 2 (New York 1952) 474.

[59] *Cf.* A. Degrassi, *Fasti Consulares* (II 13. 1 [Rome 1947]) 1. 256 with bibliography: *cf. infra* 52, n. 36.

[60] It is frequently asserted that the L. P. *de servis* is mentioned in an inscription at Pompeii; Buckland, *Law of Slavery* 36, n. 7, and G. A. Petropoulos, *Historia tou Romaïkou Dikaiou* (Athens 1944) 385, n. 5. The inscription *CIL* 10. 858 (see above, n. 57) refers to the L. P. *de praefectis*.

[61] Rotondi, *Leges publicae* 468.

[62] *Ibid.* 464.

[63] As does Karlowa, *Röm. Rechtsgeschichte* 1. 620, followed by R. Hanslik in *RE* 19. 1. 1999 and all those who date the L. P. *de servis* to A.D. 19.

[64] *Cf.* H. Last in *CAH* 10. 888-890.

[65] Rotondi, *Leges publicae* 468.

[66] The statement of F. Schulz, *Classical Roman Law* 335, that "classical ownership did not imply an unlimited right over a thing" is true enough for the classical period, but the fact that it had to be restricted by law and imperial constitutions proves that it was originally as free as possible. Of course a slave though a "res" was always a "persona"; *cf.* Buckland, *Law of Slavery* 3-4.

[67] N. A. Mashkin, *Principat Augusta* (Moscow 1949) as reviewed by Ch. Wirszubski *FRS* 42 (1952) 117, advances the thesis that the whole of the policy of Augustus was dictated by slave owners and directed to increase their power and rights. This is, of course, fantastic, but undoubtedly the Lex Aelia Sentia and above all the SC Silanianum of A.D. 10 (*D* 29. 5; *C* 6. 35; Buckland, *Law of Slavery* 95-97) aggravated the position of slaves and might be considered reactionary legislation. The Lex Iunia Petronia may well be an attempt by Tiberius to modify the stringency of his predecessor's statutes, in much the same way as he dealt with the Papia Poppaea: it would be characteristic of Tiberius to adopt so indirect an approach to a problem.

[68] Suet., *Claud.* 25. 2: *cum quidam aegra et adfecta mancipia in insulam Aesculapi taedio medendi exponerent, omnes qui exponerentur liberos esse sanxit, nec redire in dicionem domini, si convaluissent; quod si quis necare quem mallet quam exponere, caedis crimine teneri*, confirmed by Dio Cassius 60. 29. 7 and Modestinus in *D* 48. 8. 2. From the phraseology it would appear that Suetonius is copying from the actual law or from some law book.

[69] It would be an exception to the general rule that ownership in *res mancipi* is not lost by *derelictio; cf.* Schulz, *Classical Roman Law* 362. If *C* 7. 6. 1. 3 (Justinian) is to be trusted, it would appear that Claudius also determined that slaves who gained their freedom in this way should have Latin status. On this legislation of Claudius see G. May, *RHD* 15 (1936) 215.

[70] The text of Gellius does not preserve the name of the Emperor in whose reign the incident is supposed to have occurred: in 5. 14. 15 some editions print *a C(aio) Cesare,* but the *praenomen* is a conjecture of L. Müller's. Apion, however, taught in Rome under Tiberius and Claudius, and was a member of the Alexandrine embassy to Gaius; *cf. FHG* 3. 506.

[71] . . . We have already pointed out that this whole passage is farcical in the extreme (*supra* 11, n. 32) and here Petronius is possibly satirizing the trials *inter cubiculum principis*; but the joke would be pointless if such informal trials had not been a common practice.

[72] *Cf. infra* 53 my reconstruction of the stemma of the Petronii, and *RE* 19. 1. 1230, n. 80.

[73] *Cf.* V. Arangio-Ruiz, *Storia del Diritto Romano*[3] (Napoli 1942) 231.

[74] *Vide infra* the stemma of the Petronii on p. 53 and notes.

[75] *Ann.* 14. 42-45.

[76] Some as yet unpublished tablets from Herculaneum have completed the consular lists for A.D. 62 (see the *Aggiunte* in Degrassi's *Fasti Consolari*). Of course Petronius might have been consul in 63, 64, or 65, but his influence during these years would have been on the wane. Moreover, had he been consul at the time of the great fire or the year before his death, we should expect Tacitus to have made some reference to the fact. The way the historian speaks of his consulship would indicate that it had taken place some time before his death.

[77] For example, the case of the two Vitellii quoted *infra* 47, n. 4.

[78] *Vide infra* 50 and note 21: it is quite impossible to identify this Petronius with the Arbiter, even admitting that the latter's *praenomen* was Titus. In the name of the former, Niger is no nickname but the official *cognomen* since it appears in an official act. He therefore

had the *tria nomina*. The "Arbiter," like the prefect of Egypt and the consul of A.D. 19, had only *praenomen* and *nomen*. Had he had a *cognomen* Tacitus would certainly have given it.

[79] É. Thomas, *Pétrone—l'envers de la société romaine*[3] (Paris 1912) 50, n. 1.

[80] On the legislation concerning treasure-trove *cf.* Momigliano, 98.

[81] Momigliano, 100. Petronius would have heartily subscribed to Chesterfield's dictum (of 10 May O.S. 1748; *Letters* ed. Dobrée 3. 1146): "Whatever poets may write, or fools believe, of rural innocence and truth, and of the perfidy of Courts, this is most undoubtedly true—that shepherds and ministers are both men; their nature and passions the same, the modes of them only different."

## LIST OF ABBREVIATIONS

*AJP*: American Journal of Philology

*AntCl*: L'Antiquité Classique

*BPW*: Berliner Philologische Wochenschrift

*C*: Codex Iustinianus

*CAH*: Cambridge Ancient History

*CIL*: Corpus Inscriptionum Latinarum

Collignon: A. Collignon, *Étude sur Pétrone* (Paris 1892)

*CP*: Classical Philology

*CQ*: Classical Quarterly

*CR*: Classical Review

*CW*: Classical Weekly

*D*: Digesta Iustiniani

*FHG*: Fragmenta Historicorum Graecorum (Müller)

*GLK*: Grammatici Latini, ed. Keil

*H*: Codex Traguriensis, Parisinus 7989

*HSCP*: Harvard Studies in Classical Philology

*II*: Inscriptiones Italiae

*ILS*: Inscriptiones Latinae Selectae (Dessau)

*JRS*: Journal of Roman Studies

*Lud.*: *Ludus de morte Claudii*, quoted from the edition by Carlo F. Russo, *L. Annaei Senecae Divi Claudii* '[*Apokolokyntosis*], Biblioteca di Studi Superiori, Filologia Latina III (Florence 1948)

Maiuri, *Cena*: A. Maiuri, *La Cena di Trimalchione* (Naples 1945)

Maiuri, *Petroniana*: A. Maiuri, *Petroniana, PP* 3 (1948) 101-128

Marmorale, *Cena*: E. V. Marmorale, *Petronii Arbitri Cena Trimalchionis,* Biblioteca di Studi Superiori, Filologia Latina I (Florence 1947)

Marmorale, *Questione*: E. V. Marmorale, *La Questione Petroniana* (Bari 1948)

Momigliano: A. Momigliano, "Literary Chronology of the Neronian Age," *CQ* 38 (1944) 96-100

*NJbb*: Neue Jahrbücher für das klassische Altertum

*NRHD*: Nouvelle Revue historique de droit français et étranger

*PIR*: Prosopographia Imperii Romani

*PP*: La Parola del Passato

*RBPh*: Revue belge de philologie et d'histoire

*RE*: Pauly-Wissowa, Real-Encyclopädie der classischen Altertumswissenschaft

*RendLinc*: Rendiconti della R. Accademia dei Lincei

*RevPhil*: Revue de Philologie

*RFIC*: Rivista di Filologia e d'Istruzione Classica

*RHD*: Revue historique de droit français et étranger

*RhM*: Rheinisches Museum

Russo: C. F. Russo's introduction and notes to *Lud.*

Sage: Petronius, *The Satiricon*, edited with introduction and notes by Evan T. Sage (New York 1929)

*Sat.*: *Petronii Satiricon*; if not otherwise stated references are to the text edited by A. Ernout (3rd ed., Paris, Budé, 1950)

*StItal*: Studi Italiani di Filologia Classica

*TAPA*: Transactions of the American Philological Association

Toynbee: J. M. C. Toynbee, "Nero Artifex: The *Apocolocyntosis* Reconsidered," *CQ* 36 (1942) 83-93

*WS*: Wiener Studien

*ZSS*: Zeitschrift der Savigny-Stiftung, Romanistische Abteilung

## J. Allen Cabaniss (essay date 1960)

SOURCE: "The *Satyricon* and the Christian Oral Tradition," *Greek, Roman & Byzantine Studies*, Vol. 3, 1960, pp. 36-9.

[*In the following essay, Cabaniss contends that Petronius was familiar with the pre-literary Christian gospel and presents several passages from the* Satyricon *that he believes allude to it.*]

Several years ago I offered a tentative suggestion that some "minor, but nonetheless tantalizing, resemblances between the famous Milesian tale of the matron of Ephesus" in the *Satiricon* and the Biblical account of Christ's burial were the result of cynical and garbled use by Petronius of an oral version of the new Christian gospel which he may have heard, perhaps in Bithynia.[2] So modest was my proposal that I supposed there were no other resemblances. I now believe, however, that at several other points the oral version of the Christian tradition impinges upon Petronius's picaresque romance.

There are a few details of his life[3] to which I wish first to direct attention, since they apparently lend credence to the possibility and even probability of this influence. In A.D. 39, when Petronius was only nineteen or twenty years old, he accompanied his uncle, Publius, when that kinsman became governor of the province of Syria. For a while he may have enjoyed the life of Antioch-on-the-Orontes as well as a visit to Egypt.

It is well then to remember that he was in Palestine at the very time when the new religious movement was creating its initial stir in legal trials and persecutions. It was indeed in Antioch about this very time that "Christians" first received that appellation (Acts 11:26). And St. Paul had visited there about 38.[4] The governor, Publius Petronius, was indeed indirectly involved in these affairs. It was he whom Caligula ordered to install the imperial image in the Temple at Jerusalem and it was in the summer of 40 that he advanced to obey the order. This particular effort caused such dismay among both Jews and Christians that its effect can still be read in the pages of the New Testament (cf. Mark 13:14). Because Publius Petronius realized its folly he delayed and tried to dissuade the emperor. The latter, infuriated at such an attitude, decreed the governor's suicide, but the execution was not accom-

plished, for Caligula himself was assassinated on 24 January 41.[5]

If within the years 40-42 the young Petronius traveled anywhere in the eastern Mediterranean area he would have inevitably seen and heard about the new movement. And when he did become governor of Bithynia in 55-56, he was in an area where the Christian mission was unusually successful.[6] It was probably while he was in Bithynia, about 56, that St. Paul was enduring his Caesarean imprisonment under the governor Felix. What is of interest is the apparent association of Felix's wife Drusilla in the government (Acts 24:24). Her name would have a familiar ring to Petronius because it was the same as that of Emperor Caligula's sister, whose deification-proceedings he had attended and ridiculed somewhat earlier.[7] All in all there is every reason to surmise that Petronius did in fact have ample opportunity to gain some knowledge of the Christian gospel while it was in its pre-literary stage. It is a fact that his name of that of a member of his family (his uncle Publius? another?) was remembered by Christians and entered the Christian tradition. For according to the apocryphal Gospel of Peter (about 150) 8.31,[8] the centurion guarding Christ's sepulcher bears the name of Petronius.

I shall not again treat the story of the matron of Ephesus, nor the mention by both St. Paul and Petronius of a woman named Tryphaena,[9] but, contrary to my former statement, I now assert that the remark in *Satiricon* 74, "haec dicente eo gallus gallinaceus cantavit," is significant in view of the identical sentiment and a number of similar words in Luke 22:60. . . .

There are six other places where Biblical allusions spring immediately to mind, First, there is the statement near the end of *Satiricon* 63, that witches (mulieres plussciae . . . nocturnae) exist who "turn downward what is upward" (quod sursum est, deorsum faciunt). Similarly at Thessalonica the early Christians (who were also people of the nighttime[10]) were said (Acts 17:6), about 49 or 50, to be those who "upset the world." . . .

Secondly, near the beginning of *Satiricon* 75, Habinnas reminds Trimalchio that "we are men, not gods" (homines sumus, non dei). So about 46-49 St. Paul at Lystra had to defend himself against divine worship as an apparition of Hermes by crying out (Acts 14:15), "We are indeed men like you." . . .

Third, toward the beginning of *Satiricon* 78 occurs the remark by Trimalchio of his graveclothes, "See to it, Stichus, that neither mice nor moths touch them" (Vide tu . . . , Stiche, ne ista mures tangant aut tineae). Surely this is an echo of the original which lies beneath Matt. 6:20, "but lay up treasures for yourselves in heaven where neither moth nor rust destroys." . . .

Fourth, in the middle of **Satiricon** 105, it was decided that to appease the guardian-deity of the ship "forty stripes be inflicted on each one" (placuit quadragenas utrique plagas imponi). Perhaps of no great significance, but nonetheless, the Apostle records (II Cor. 11:24) that five times he received from the Jews stripes to the number of "forty less one." . . .

Fifth, the first line of a metrical passage in **Satiricon** 109 states: "Fallen are the hairs—that which alone is the glory of the body" (Quod solum formae decus est, cecidere capilli). In like manner St. Paul believes (I Cor. 11:15) that for a woman her hair "is her glory." There is here also a faint reminiscence of the Lord's declaration (Matt. 10:30), "Even the hairs of your head are all numbered." . . .

Sixth, midway through **Satiricon** 131 an old woman performs a spell thus: "she soon took up on her middle finger dust mixed with spittle and signed the forehead" (mox turbatum sputo pulverem medio sustulit digito frontemque . . . signavit) of a man who protested all the while. So when Christ healed the blind man at the pool of Siloam (John 9:6), "He spat upon the ground and made clay out of the spittle, and put the clay upon his eyes." . . . This, of course, is a folk-pattern that can be frequently discovered.

In addition to these six points we may also add a certain cynical commendation of celibacy (qui vero nec uxores unquam duxerunt . . . ad summos honores perveniunt, id est soli militares, soli fortissimi atque etiam innocentes habentur [**Sat.** 116, ad fin.], which agrees in part with some tendencies in primitive Christianity. And we should perhaps also add the account of the shipwreck (**Sat.** 113-115) which in many ways parallels the account of St. Paul's adventures in Acts 27.

Let us admit that each of these points singly is not very impressive, but the cumulative effect is quite strong. To me it seems quite apparent that Petronius had heard some oral accounts of the Christian message and mission and that he employed many words, phrases, and situations from it to give a certain piquant flavor to his romance.

*Notes*

This paper was presented at the Third International Congress on Patristic Studies Christ Church, Oxford, 21-25 September 1959.

² Allen Cabaniss, "A Footnote to the 'Petronian Question'," *CP* 49 (1954) 98-102.

³ Gilbert Bagnani, *Arbiter of Elegance: A Study of the Life & Works of C. Petronius* (The Phoenix, Suppl. vol. II [Toronto 1954]). Despite his intemperate language, I believe that Bagnani has made his case that the *Satiricon* was written by Petronius between A.D. 58 and 65. Referring to my remarks in *CP* (*supra* n. 2), Bagnani states ambiguously (op.cit. 64, n. 71): "If these similarities are anything more than coincidences—which seems to me doubtful—Petronius may possibly have heard some vague accounts of the Crucifixion while in Bithynia." Bagnani's sentence does not lend itself to precise grammatical analysis and I cannot decide whether he agrees with me or not.

⁴ Philip Carrington, *The Early Christian Church,* 1: *The First Christian Century* (Cambridge 1957) 67.

⁵ *ibid.* 72.

⁶ *ibid.* 130, 439f.

⁷ Bagnani, *op.cit.* 48.

⁸ M. R. James, *The Apocryphal New Testament* (Oxford 1950) 90.

⁹ Cabaniss, *op.cit.*

¹⁰ Cabaniss, "Early Christian Nighttime Worship," *Journal of Bible and Religion* 25 (1957) 30-33.

## J. P. Sullivan (essay date 1961)

SOURCE: "The *Satyricon* of Petronius: Some Psycho-Analytical Considerations," *The American Imago*, Vol. 18, No. 4, Winter, 1961, pp. 353-69.

[*In the following essay, Sullivan contends that the psychosexual interests—particularly exhibitionism—of the characters in the* Satyricon *reflect Petronius's own, and are thus valid evidence in a psychoanalysis of the author.*]

1. Psycho-analytical studies like those of Freud on Dostoevsky and Jones on *Hamlet*, have thrown much light on modern works of literature, but except for mythological investigations like those of Otto Rank and Theodor Reik there has been no equivalent work undertaken for classical literature. Even the interest in the *Oedipus* cycle is predominantly a mythological interest. Yet ancient authors, just as much as modern, were governed in their art by their individual aims, wishes, stresses and unconscious pre-occupations and are therefore amenable to similar investigation; they have also the added attraction of belonging to societies radically different from the society with which psycho-analysis is mainly concerned. The autonomy of art compared with the directed nature of other activities offers the widest scope for the psychology of the individual to show itself, for its manifestations are directed only by internal and, to a lesser extent, literary and

cultural forces. Psychoanalytical methods applied even to ancient literary works may provide a key for understanding the societies which produced them, and because of their very remoteness we cannot afford to neglect any means we have to realize the common humanity underlying them. Abraham's analysis in 1912 of Amenhotep IV demonstrated that psycho-analysis could elucidate purely historical problems; it is not impossible that literary problems may be similarly elucidated with the aid of psycho-analytical methods. One such problem is the concern of this paper.

The *Satiricon* of Petronius, as we have it, is a mere fragment of the original, consisting of 141 short chapters, full of gaps but presenting eight major episodes in addition to a number of detachable poems and discussions which are only loosely connected with the apparently picaresque plot. Its date and authorship are disputed, although scholarly opinion on literary, linguistic and historical grounds is inclined to attribute it to the first century A.D. The real debate is whether it was the work of Gaius (or Titus) Petronius, the courtier of Nero, whose life and death are described by Tacitus (Annals XVI, 16-20). The traditional attribution rests on the coincidence that the name *Petronius* in our MSS is also the name of the historical figure and the possibility that his reputation as *arbiter elegantiae* in Nero's Court may have added the element *Arbiter* to his name in MSS and citations. Counterbalancing this is a natural reluctance to attribute the work to the man because it seems too good to be true—just as Baconians deny Shakespearian authorship as too surprising to be true. Those willing to accept the attribution have based their acceptance partly on the similarity between the character of the courtier and the character of the novel. J. W. Duff, for example, says (*Literary History of Rome in the Silver Age*, pp. 172-3):

It may be affirmed that the Tacitean portrait of Petronius wears the very features to be expected in the author of a novel depicting low and vicious life in tones which argue intimacy of knowledge and at the same time the almost cynically detached spirit of the spectator.

This is highly subjective and there seems some critical confusion in making a novel the mirror of its author. The difference between the character of an author and the character of his work may be immense. If psychological criteria are to be used, they should not be as vague and impressionistic as this.

The character of the *Satiricon* will become evident as the episodes are examined in detail. The novel is partly *realistic* in its intentions; it is a highly self-conscious work of art based upon certain critical theories, which may be established from literary discussions in the work itself. Petronius was reacting in language, themes and treatment against the artificiality and remoteness from life of Silver Age literature. Suetonius' anecdotes (*Nero*, 26) of the Emperor leaving his palace to wander round the lower quarters of home is a parallel worth mentioning. Petronius too seems to have adopted the naive realist's heresy that the sordid side of life is alone really life as it is lived.

There is a revealing paragraph in a short story by a modern author, Miss Mary McCarthy. A young man in hospital hears what he thinks are the screams of a cancer patient.

He knew immediately that he was not meant to hear; these shrieks were being wrung from a being against its will; yet in this fact, precisely, lay their power to electrify the attention. "A dying woman screaming in the night", the young man repeated musingly, as the cries stopped, at their very summit, as abruptly as they had started, leaving a pounding stillness, "this is the actual; the actual, in fact, is *that which should not be witnessed*. The actual," he defined, pronouncing the syllables slowly and distinctly in a pedagogical style, "under which may be subsumed the street accident, the plane crash, the atrocity, is pornography.[1]

In Petronius what is of interest for our purposes is the type of situation chosen for realistic treatment. The first episode which calls for attention is chs. 16-26, where the narrator Encolpius and his two friends, fall into the hands of Quartilla, a priestess of Priapus. This god plays a significant role in the work; he is the author of various misfortunes which happen to Encolpius, who in some way has offended him. The main event of this first episode is the defloration of the seven year old Pannychis by Giton, Encolpius' young catamite, and the conditions under which this takes place.

Itaque cum inclusi iacerent, consedimus ante limen thalami, et in primis Quartilla per rimam improbe diductam adplicuerat oculum curiosum lusumque puerilem libidinosa speculabatur diligentia. me quoque ad idem spectaculum lenta manu traxit, et quia considerantium cohaeserant vultus, quidquid a spectaeulo vacabat, commovebat obiter labra et me tamquam furtivis subinde oculus verberabat . . . (26)[2]

This is the first patent example of scopophilia in the work. Although Quartilla is sexually aroused, Encolpius indicates he does not enjoy her attentions. His description of her kisses as furtive is significant—*me tamquam furtivis subinde osculis verberabat.*

There is a similar incident in the last section of the story where Encolpius is with his friend Eumolpus in Croton. Eumolpus, posing as a rich childless and ailing old man, is entrusted with the care of two children by an unscrupulous woman who hopes for a legacy.

Eumolpus, qui tam frugi erat ut illi etiam ego puer viderer, non distulit puellam invitare ad pygesiaca sacra. sed et podagricum se esse lumborumque solutorum omnibus dixerat, et si non servasset integram simulationem periclitabatur totam paene tragoediam. itaque ut constaret mendacio fides, puellam quidem exoravit ut sederet supra commendatam bonitatem, Coraci autem imperavit ut lectum in quo ipse iacebat subiret positisque in pavimento manibus dominum lumbis suis commoveret. ille lente parebat imperio puellaeque artificium pari motu remunerabat. cum ergo res ad effectum spectaret, clara Eumolpus voce exhortabatur Coraca ut spissaret officium. sic inter mercennarium amicamque positus senex veluti oscillatione ludebat. hoc semel iterumque ingenti risu, etiam suo, Eumolpus fecerat. itaque ego quoque, ne desidia consuetudinem perderem, dum frater sororis suae automata per clostellum miratur, accessi tentaturus an pateretur iniuriam. nec se reiciebat a blanditiis doctissimus puer, sed me numen inimicum ibi quoque invenit. (140)[3]

Here there are two cases of *scopomixia* and in each the scenes witnessed are of a perverse nature. But this is not all. Voyeurism and exhibitionism are psycho-analytical polarities and the latter is also exemplified in Petronius. Immediately before the child-marriage occurs the following incident:

Stabat inter haec Giton et risu dissolvebat ilia sua. itaque conspicata eum Quartilla, cuius esset puer, diligentissima sciscitatione quaesivit. eum ego fratrem meum esse dixissem, 'quare ergo' inquit 'me non basiavit?' vocatumque ad se in osculum adplicuit. mox manum etiam demisit in sinum et pertractato vasculo tam rudi 'haec' inquit 'belle cras in promulside libidinis nostrae militabit; hodie enim post asellum diaria non sumo.' (24)[4]

Despite differences—handling rather than looking at a forbidden object—this is surely a sort of exhibitionism. Not that Giton is depicted as an exhibitionist but rather that the author here is subjecting Giton to these experiences.

After the second instance of voyeurism there is an even more patent example of exhibitionism. Although after watching Eumolpus through the key-hole Encolpius was frustrated by his impotence, yet after a hiatus in the MSS we find him talking to Eumolpus:

'dii maiores sunt, qui me restituerunt in integrum . . .' haec locutus sustuli tunicam Eumolpoque me totum approbavi. at ille primo exhorruit, deinde ut plurimum crederet, utraque manu deorum beneficia tractat. (140)[5]

In this exhibitionism there is also the motif of *handling* the genitals, which seems to argue conclusively that the scene between Quartilla and Giton was exhibitionist too in its significance, just as voyeurism is

psychologically compatible with the desire to touch what is seen. And another example might be cited from ch. 105 where the narrator is recognised despite his disguise by his enemy Lichas, who "ran up and looked at neither my hands nor my face, but straightway dropped his eyes and ran his officious hand to my genitals."

Apart from these uncomplicated examples there is also a less obvious case. Early in the work Encolpius quarrels with his friend Ascyltos over the affections of Giton. Ascyltos leaves in a rage.

. . . osculisque tandem bona fide exactis alligo artissimis complexibus puerum fruorque votis usque ad invidiam felicibus. nec adhuc quidem omnia erant facta, cum Ascyltos furtim se foribus admovit discussisque fortissime claustris invenit me cum fratre ludentem. risu itaque plausuque cellulam implevit, opertum me amiculo evolvit et 'quid agebas' inquit 'frater sanctissime?' (11)[6]

In the light of earlier instances the scopophilic aspects of this are patent. From the narrator's view-point it is exhibitionism (in fiction it is the author's psychology we are concerned with and the question of the voluntary or involuntary nature of the incident may be disregarded). On Ascyltos' side it is voyeurism. If the latter is stressed, the usual parallel is not far to seek. Later in the work Encolpius and Ascyltos part and Giton elects to go with Ascyltos. He is recovered by Encolpius through a chance meeting at the public baths and they give Ascyltos the slip. It turns out that Giton was in charge of Ascyltos' clothes which were stolen when he left. Eumolpus describes the subsequent scene:

' . . . circumire omnes angulos coepi et clara voce Encolpion clamitare. ex altera parte invenis nudus, qui vestimenta perdiderat, non minore clamoris indignatione Gitona flagitabat. et me quidem pueri tanquam insanum imitatione petulantissima deriserunt, illum autem frequentia ingens circumvenit cum plausu et admiratione timidissima. habebat enim inguinum pondus tam grande ut ipsum hominem laciniam fascini crederes. o iuvenem laboriosum: puto illum pridie incipere, postero die flnire.' (92)[7]

From the author's standpoint, the exhibitionism here is not one or two enjoying the sight but an admiring crowd. A crowd standing around someone in the Roman public baths, where almost everyone was naked, is rather unexpected in a Latin author and seems to spring from phantasy rather than any probable incident in real life.

Here then in a short fragmentary work are two, possibly three, cases of mixoscopy and three (if the extension from sight to touch is admitted) of exhibitionism. It would be temerarious to pronounce on the prevalence of such perversion in Roman life, but it can be stated with certainty that it is not a traditional literary topic in extant classical literature in the way the incest-motif is. Petronius has not gone to earlier authors for his sexual material as he clearly has for his satirical subjects. There is of course the retelling in classical authors of certain myths involving scopophilia and exhibitionism (the story of Actaeon e.g. who was torn to pieces by dogs for witnessing Diana bathing and Baubo's piece of exhibitionism to amuse Demeter), but in general examples of scopophilia or exhibitionism in literature are notoriously few. The classic story of Candaules, who hid Gyges behind his bedroom door to enable him to see his wife naked (Herodotus I, 8-12) is not relevant: neither Candaules' wife nor Gyges were willing participants. We find that outside Petronius the only non-mythical examples of scopophilia are some possible references in the Greek Anthology and Martial.[8] Exhibitionism is almost as rare for literary purposes.[9] Although we cannot say for certain what we would find in the bulk of Latin literature which is unfortunately lost to us, the evidence indicates that in these instances Petronius is not adapting traditional sexual motifs or borrowing such themes from earlier authors, although he does this elsewhere.[10] These subjects in Petronius' novel must therefore be a genuine reflection of his own psychosexual interests whether they were grounded in his sexual behaviour or in his phantasy life. Petronius is the only ancient author who makes extensive use of these themes, although the subjects are much more common in modern literature, Marcel Proust being the most obvious example.

2. To understand how pervasive a theme scopophilia is in the *Satiricon*, it is necessary to examine disguised aspects of this instinct by reference to Freud's scheme for it. . . .[11]

It is irrelevant whether the characters expose themselves of their own accord or through circumstances, for the author is autonomous here, but so far incidents in the *Satiricon* of active scopophilia have been paralleled by overt or covert exhibitionism. . . . In c. 140 (quoted above) Encolpius found himself impotent, a disability he blamed on Priapus. He is first aware of this when he is impotent with a Crotonian lady named Circe. After his unsuccessful attempt with Circe, Encolpius goes to bed alone

> conditusque lectulo totum ignem furoris in eam
> converti, quae mihi omnium malorum causa fuerat:
>
> ter corripui terribilem manu bipennum,
> ter languidior coliculi repente thyrso
> ferrum timui, quod trepido male debat usum.
> nec iam poteram, quo modo conficere libebat;
> namque illa metu frigidior rigente bruma
> confugerat in viscera mille operta rugis.
> ita non potuit supplicio caput aperire,

> sed furciferae mortifero timore lusus
> ad verba, magis quae poterant nocere, fugi.
>
> (132)[12]

Encolpius (despite certain feelings of shame) goes on to abuse his genitals for failing him. This incident plainly falls into Freud's . . . category: even the dual nature of that category is realised, as Encolpius and his penis are treated as separate subjects occupying our attention in turn. The very ambivalence of Encolpius in this castration attempt (is his penis part of himself or not?) suggests the auto-erotism underlying scopophilia. Petronius thus illustrates all the Freudian classifications, not aetiologically or in their psychoanalytical priority as Freud does, but as unconnected aspects of the same preoccupation.

In the light of the above certain elements in the work arguably relate to the less obvious transformations of scopophilia. Some of them are significant only when viewed in connection with the more obvious scopophilic themes, but some also display their scopophilic nature to the most cursory examination.

Freud pointed out (*in Der Witz und seine Beziehung zum Unbewussten*) that obscene humour and wit represent exposure in a psychological sense. The *Satiricon* traditionally belongs to the class of *curiosa*. It is not pornographic in the worst sense, but it does make use of conventionally obscene subjects; their treatment is humorous and there are frequent examples of obscene wit in the conversations (e.g. ch. 92—"Tanto magis expedit *inguina* quam *ingenia* fricare"). The two Milesian tales, the well-known *Widow of Ephesus* and the other describing the seduction of a pupil by Eumolpus, may be adduced as similar evidence. It is true that obscene poems and writings were produced by highly respectable Roman figures such as the younger Pliny (cf. *Epistles* VI 14, 4) and it was then conventionally less disreputable to have written such things than it is now, but it was not so common as to make the question of psychological predilections unimportant.

Scopophilia particularly shows itself in the desire to see what is forbidden, whether by law, social custom or, ultimately, incest taboos. Abraham says of a neurotic patient:

> "In this as in other cases the prohibition of looking at his mother originated in the more particular prohibition of seeing her naked, and in especial of seeing her genitals."[13]

Along with the mixoscopy of the *Satiricon* there is a concentration on more general *secrets*: the word *secretum* (as well as synonyms like *obscurus* etc.) occurs frequently. At times it describes out of the way places and these instances may well be dictated by the exigencies of a picaresque plot. The same may be argued of the impersonations and disguises of the last two episodes, and the fact that more than half the scenes take place at dusk or at night or in an atmosphere of darkness and failing light, guttering lamps and burning torches. But the use of *secrets* in the plot itself may be susceptible of deeper interpretation.

Encolpius' offence which made him fall foul of Quartilla (16-26) was the witnessing and consequent profanation of some rites of Priapus, an unforgivable sacrilege (*inexpiabile scelus*). Quartilla stresses the secret nature of these rites (*tot annorum secreta*) and the danger of their becoming common knowledge. There were various secret cults in the Roman world but the ceremonies in honour of Priapus are self-avowedly sexual. Expiation for the offence requires a licentious all-night vigil in the god's honour, and it is during this that the first scopophilic incident occurs. Throughout this episode there are allusions to secrets (e.g. *"Both of us swore in the most solemn terms that so horrible a secret would perish between us"* c. 21.) Again, when Encolpius is apparently the victim of a sexual assault (the text is fragmentary here), Ascyltos "had covered his head with his cloak; he had been warned it was dangerous to be involved in other people's secrets" (21). It might be added that among the verse fragments attributed to Petronius there is a retelling of the story of Midas and his asses' ears and how the secret leaked out—the moral being that men cannot keep secrets (*Nam citius flammas mortales ore tenebunt / quam secreta tegant*—fr. 28).

The significance of these features of the work is brought out by Abraham's remark on a neurotic patient—

> . . . the early forcing away of his seopophilie instinct from its real objects and aims led not only to a typical brooding but also to a morbid propensity towards secret and mystical things . . . I need hardly refer to the countless similar phenomena that are to be found in folk-psychology—on the one hand, secret cults, mysteries, oeeultist movements, etc, and on the other, religious prohibitions against inquiring into the most secret things.
>
> (*op. cit.,* p. 219)

Even the two ghost stories in Petronius gain significance from Abraham's further remarks on the same patient:

> Concerning the significance of ghosts . . . when later the prohibition against looking and knowing had obtained a hold over him, his repressed wish for a repetition of the pleasurable impressions of childhood was displaced on to 'ghosts'. He longed all the time to see ghosts.
>
> (*ibid.,* p. 220)

Abraham also explains the significance of the Cyclops story in relation to scopophilia and castration anxiety. Allusions to the Cyclops theme in the **Satiricon** are found in 48, 97, 98 and 101—patently it attracted Petronius. The motif of blinding is not specifically used, the story being generally offered as a comparison with some situation in which the characters find themselves. One instance comes near this however and is psycho-analytically important. In c. 48, Trimalchio, displaying his inaccurate knowledge of mythology, asks Agamemnon if he knows "the story of Ulysses, how the Cyclops tore his thumb out with pincers". Here the underlying notion of castrating the father has been replaced by the more basic anxiety that the father will castrate oneself. Trimalchio's mistake is of considerable interest for the author's psychology.

The whole motif of castration in the **Satiricon** must be brought into relation with the scopophilic elements. The castration anxiety evinced may be taken as the fear of punishment for forbidden looking. The reversal by Trimalchio of the traditional Cyclops' story is paralleled by the lack of active castration (directed as it was against the father) in the work. The two castration scenes are both concerned with self-castration. The first is Giton's move to castrate himself with a blunted razor because his sexual attractions have caused so much trouble and jealousy among his friends. He had earlier attempted to cut his throat with the same razor (94). These attempts at self-mutilation or suicide, although not serious on Giton's part, always lead to Encolpius' trying to cut his throat too. These incidents are to be compared with Encolpius' frustrated self-castration in c. 132 (cited earlier in another connection). This last takes place after Encolpius' sexual failure with Circe, and thus is connected with the theme of sexual inadequacy and sexual envy.

Abraham mentions a patient who had once seen his father naked when he was nine years old and

> . . . had inspected his genitals with great interest. His phantasies . . . often reverted to that scene. And yet the thoughts associated with it were by no means purely pleasurable; on the contrary, he was continually worried by the question whether his genitals would attain the size of his father's . . . he fell prey to the tormenting belief . . . that his penis was too small.
>
> (*ibid.,* p. 186)

There are two situations in the **Satiricon** reminiscent of this: the jealous reference to the size of Asclytos' genitals in c. 92 (Ascyltos, it will be remembered, being a rival for Giton's affections), and the final return to normal of Encolpius' own genitals in c. 139, when he exhibits them to his other rival, Eumolpus, a fatherly figure with strong sexual inclinations. Feelings of sexual inferiority is often a motive for certain types of scopophilia, particularly for male interest in male genitals, just as any natural physical disability often prompts curiosity about the hidden part of normal people's lives. All of these sexual incidents fit a scopophilic pattern and it is to be noticed that Encolpius, the narrator and the hero (or anti-hero) of the work, is the one who generally exemplifies the pattern.[14] It is he who displays the sexual inadequacy, the sexual envy, the castration anxiety, the scopophilic and exhibitionist traits to the full, and seems therefore the main vehicle of the author's phantasy in these respects, just as Eumolpus is the main vehicle of the author's views on poetry. Encolpius is not made out a sympathetic character, he is more of an unfortunate scape-goat. Although, like Proust's narrator, Encolpius does not seem aware of the perverseness of these scopophilic situations, Petronius takes care to *place* Encolpius in a way Proust does not in comparable situations. This is as indicative of Petronius' artistic sensibility as the incidents chosen are of his psychological preoccupations.

3. I have attempted in this paper to show how Petronius with his explicit intention of writing a work of a realist nature has chosen as the main element of his realism various sexual motifs and has concentrated on such perversions of the sexual instinct as are related to scopophilia and its polarity, exhibitionism. In this I suggest that he was directed by his own phantasies and sexual interests; the frank nature of the work, its very originality allowed his preoccupations much greater rein, as they were less fettered by literary models, conventions or stock themes. Consequently more is deducible about his psychology than is usual with many ancient or modern authors. Not that these are the only interests exemplified; I have not tried to discuss the sexual orientation of the work as a whole. For instance, most of the male characters are accepted as sexually ambivalent. This was a natural convention in the ancient world with its greater tolerance of homosexuality. The assumption of ambivalence also gives the work a greater variety of sexual topics; Petronius is adopting an accepted Roman belief (cp. Suetonius on Julius Caesar, 54). In view of this convention deductions about Petronius' own sexual orientation are not easy to make, but the evidence presented above reveals a preoccupation with scopophilic themes, and the rarity of this does allow psychoanalytical deductions to be made.

This has one practical application. There are literary and historical reasons for attributing the *Satiricon* to the courtier described by Tacitus and mentioned by the Elder Pliny and Plutarch. But the material in this paper may perhaps offer another possible argument for the attribution. The account of Petronius given in Tacitus' *Annals* XVI, 16-20 may be summarized as follows:

> He was a man who spent his days sleeping and his nights working or enjoying himself. Industry is the usual foundation of success, but with him it was idleness . . . Yet as proconsul in Bithynia and later as consul he showed himself a vigor and capable administrator. His subsequent return to his old habits . . . led to his admission to the small circle of Nero's intimates, where he became the Arbiter of Elegance . . .

Accused of complicity in a plot against the Emperor, Petronius decided to commit suicide and ended his life in the way he had lived.

> Even in the codicils to his will, he refused to put down any of the usual death-bed flatteries for Nero . . . Instead he wrote out a full description of the Emperor's vicious activities, prefaced with the names of his male and female partners, and specifying the novel forms his lust had taken. This document he sent under seal to Nero . . . Nero's puzzlement as to how his nocturnal ingenuities were known was resolved by blaming Silia. This was not an insignificant person, but a senator's wife in fact, who had been a chosen partner in all the Emperor's vices and also a close friend of Petronius. She was exiled for her lack of discretion about what she had seen and experienced.

The most interesting features of this account, which may be related to the features of the *Satiricon* I have been discussing, are Petronius' nocturnal habits and the great interest shown in the Emperor's sexual life.

To examine them in order: Petronius did not simply use the nights for pleasure, which might be dependent upon general conventions, which were not so different at least in the early Empire from what they are now. He used them also for work—this may point to a deliberate avoidance of daytime as a time for any activity at all. It is important however that Tacitus specially refers to this habit and thus implies it was a fairly unusual or at least significant characteristic deserving the historian's comment. In the work itself perhaps half of the episodes take place in darkness, the characters are frequently lost in the dark, lamps and lighting are often mentioned. In all cases, as obviously in some, this might be demanded by the situation and it would be unwise to deduce much from it. But one of the characteristics of scopophilia is the fear of light and the avoidance of it. Abraham is again the most convenient text (cf. *op. cit.* section III, pp. 201-206) where he says that darkness has both a positive and a negative significance for the scopophilic. Obviously Abraham is drawing on case-histories of neurotic patients and it is unlikely that Petronius has any really neurotic intolerance of daylight. This would be hardly feasible in view of his record as a capable administrator. But he did have a preference for night which Tacitus took pains to point out and this may well indicate a scopophilic disposition.

But the most important feature of the courtier is surely the great interest he took in the details of the sexual life of the Emperor. This was a dangerous interest, and Silia suffered on suspicion of pandering to it. It was also a strong interest, which must have involved close questioning of Silia (if it really was she who was his source) about Nero's associates and the practices in which she took part. This interest must strike us as morbid to some degree and reflects the scopophilic instinct in its vicarious aspect. The connection of graphic and verbal obscenity with scopophilia is well-known. Prompted by revenge, Petronius chose to write down a careful account of all he knew about the Emperor's sexual proclivities, based on careful study, it would seem, for the blow struck home to Nero, and produced a violent reaction. This connects the courtier with our author and it is on this fact in particular that the psycho-analytical argument for the attribution of the **Satiricon** to the Petronius described by Tacitus may be based. It has at least slightly more definition than the traditional psychological argument which has held the field for so long.

### Notes

[1] 'The Old Men' in *Cast a Cold Eye,* p. 147.

[2] When they were shut in and lying down, we sat round the doorway. Quartilla was one of the first to put an inquisitive eye to a treacherous little crack and begin spying on their childish play with prurient curiosity. Her insistent hand dragged me down to have a look too. Our faces were pressed together as we watched and whenever she could spare a moment from the sight, she'd move her lips close to mine in passing and furtively pester me with kisses."

[3] Eumolpus, who was so unfastidious that even I seemed a boy to him, did not hesitate a moment to invite the girl to some ritual buttock-thumping. However, he had told everyone that he had gout and a weakness in the loins and if he did not keep up his pretence, he would bei in danger of ruining the whole plot. So to ensure that the lie was not discredited, he actually persuaded the girl to sit on top of the upright nature to which she had been entrusted, but ordered Corax to get under the bed he was lying on, and with his hands on the floor to move his master up and down with his thighs. Corax carried out his orders gently and the expertness of the girl responded with similar movements. Then when things were looking forward to the desired result, Eumolpus loudly urged Corax to increase the speed. Placed like this between his servant and his girl friend the old man lookd as if he was on a swing. Eumolpus repeated this performance amid roars of laughter, including his own. Not unnaturally I for my part, not to get out of the habit through lack of practice, approached the brother, who was admiring his sister's tricks through the keyhole, and tried to see if he would accept my advances. The shrewd lad did not reject my overtures but the unfriendly god dogged me in this situation too."

[4] Giton was standing there while all this went on and was splitting his sides laughing. Catching sight of him, Quartilla with great interest asked whose the boy was. I replied he wasy my little friend. 'Indeed!' said Quartilla, 'Why hasn't he given me a kiss?' And calling him to her, she pressed her lips to his. Then she slipped her hand into his clothes and felt his immature little tool.

'This,' she said 'will do nicely tomorrow as an *hors d'oeuvre* to our love feast. For the moment, I don't want ordinary stuffing after a nice piece of meat'.

[5] 'There are mightier gods who have restored me to full health . . . ' With this I lifted my tunic and showed off all I had to Eumolpus. At first he was stunned, then to convince himself to the full, he ran both hands over the gifts of the gods.

[6] At last our kisses were without restraint. I hugged the boy close to me. I had what I wanted and anyone would have envied my luck. But we were still in the middle of this when Ascyltos came quietly to the door, absolutely shattered the bolts and found me having a gay time with Giton. He filled the little room with laughter and applause. He rolled me out of the cloak I was lying in and said:

'What were you up to, my pious old friend?'

[7] 'I began going round every nook and cranny and calling out *Encolpius!* in a loud voice. And somewhere else a naked young man, who had lost his clothes, was yelling for someone called Giton with equally indignant shouts. And while the boys just ridiculed me as a lunatie with the most impudent imitations, a huge crowd surrounded him with applause and the most awe-struck admiration. You see, he had such enormous sexual organs that you'd think the man was just an attachment to his penis. What a man for the job! I think he starts yesterday and finishes tomorrow.'

[8] e.g. *Anth. Pal.* V, 225 and XII, 40 and 27. Cf. also Martial XI, 70.

[9] The gross man in Theophrastus (*Characters,* XI) lifts his tunic up in front of ladies. The *cordax*, a frankly exhibitionistic dance, might also be mentioned, as Trimalchio in the *Satiricon* is anxious for his wife to perform it for the amusement of his guests (52, 8).

[10] One of the female characters in the work, Circe, is a type of woman often satirized in Roman literature, the woman who likes inferior lovers. Although Freud remarks that this desire is less common in women that in men (*Collected Papers*, Vol. IV (English Edition), p. 211), she is a recognizable literary type even in modern times (compare Madame Philibert in Thomas Mann's *Felix Krull*).

[11] *Instincts and their Vicissitudes* (1915) *Collected Papers* Vol. IV (English Edition), p. 73.

[12] And hidden in bed I turn the whole blaze of my anger against the one who had been the cause of all my troubles. Three times I seized the terrible two-edged blade in my hand, three times, suddenly softer than a length of stalk, I shuddered before the steel, which badly served my trembling hand. Now I could not do what a moment ago I was eager to achieve. For she was colder than the frost of winter through fear and took refuge inside my vitals, covered with a thousand wrinkles. So I could not uncover her head for punishment, but tricked by the mortal fear of the rascally thing, I took refuge in insults which could hurt even more.

[13] 'Restriction and Transformations of Scopophilia in Psycho-neurotics', *Selected Papers* (English Edition, 1949), p. 177.

[14] Not of course invariably. Scopophilic behaviour is found in many of the other characters. Moreover certain characteristics of the famous vulgarian Trimalchio serve also as a vehicle for the less obvious transformations of the instinct that dominates the work. Urolagnia and coprolagnia are part of the complex of voyeurism: Trimalchio (like the Emperor Claudius cf. Suetonius 32) is greatly interested in the excretory functions and gives a long and vulgar description of his own internal economy (47); references to chamber-pots and similar subjects are frequent in this part of the work (cf. cc. 27, 41 *et al.*).

## Herbert Musurillo (essay date 1961)

SOURCE: "Life a Dream: The Poetry of Petronius," in *Symbol and Myth in Ancient Poetry*, Fordham University Press, 1961, pp. 159-64.

[*In the following essay, Musurillo examines Petronius's use of dream symbolism in his poetry and describes how it works on more than one level.*]

Petronius Arbiter is chiefly known as the author of that curious and sometimes scatological novel, the **Satyricon**. That he is to be identified with the Master of the Revels of Nero's court who enjoyed a rather theatrical suicide in A.D. 66 is most likely, there being very little serious evidence to challenge the traditional point of view.[1] But he has also left us a very striking collection of lyrics and short elegies which will repay serious study, since they are quite modern in their poetic technique.

We get a brief glimpse of Petronius' talent for symbolic composition in the brief and unfortunately corrupt fragment 84 which begins *O litus vita mihi dulcius*.

Following the most commonly accepted text, we may translate:

> O shore sweeter than life! Ah sea!
> How happy I am that I can come straightway
> To the land I love.
> Ah, lovely day!
> This is the country spot where once I used
> To rouse the water-nymphs with swimming-stroke.
> Here is the spring's pool. There the weeds that the sea
> Washed up. Here the sure haven of my silent hopes.
> I have lived. And no meaner fate can ever destroy for us
> The blessings of time past.

The setting is somewhat ambiguous, but it would seem to be as follows. An old man returns—at least in reverie—to the scenes of his childhood, to the country lake of Italy where he used to swim as a boy. As he thinks of the joys he had, the quiet pool suddenly becomes a kind of symbol of the peace and security he has finally achieved in old age. He is happy in the remembrance of Time Past. Almost as in *The Lake* of Lamartine, the spring and its cool basin stand as a permanent token of happiness that cannot be destroyed. Despite the obscurities of the poem, it is masterly in its brevity.

But perhaps Petronius' greatest power may be seen in his use of dream-symbolism. In that beautiful elegiac poem, *Lecto compositus* (frag. 99 Baehrens), a young man in his first sleep is awakened by Amor tugging him by the hair. "How can you, my servant," says Cupid, "lie alone?" He leaps up and dashes out into the night with bare feet and tunic ungirt; then, bewildered by the various streets, he stands stock still like a wandering madman; he can move neither forward nor backward. Suddenly he is aware that

> Silent are men's voices and all street sounds;
> Silent the song of the birds and the noise of faithful watchdogs.
>
> I of all men stand alone,
> And I am afraid of sleep.
> Great lord of Desire, I am at your service
> (11-14).

It is like an anxiety dream or a dream of wish-fulfilment. But all at once in the silence of the night, passion yields to a philosophic awareness of man's fundamental loneliness. The conclusion is ambiguous: *sequor imperium, magne Cupido, tuum* (14); but the stark picture of the pathetic, bewildered sleepwalker is unforgettable.

Petronius' most interesting dream poem is frag. 30 (Buecheler; frag. 121 Baehrens), *Somnia quae mentes ludunt*. It is easy to hazard the guess that it occurred in one of the lost sections of the **Satyricon**; a similar poem, in fact, may be found in 128. The ostensible theme of fragment 30 is that dreams are merely a continuation of the day's activities—in Freudian terminology, the "day's residues." In translation:

> Dreams that trick the mind with flitting shadows,
> Come not from the shrines of the gods or powers of heaven.
> Each man makes his own. For when sleep presses
> On the body crushed with weariness, then the mind
> Can play without burden, pursuing at night whatever
> Occurred by day. The man who makes towns tremble
> In war, and destroys unhappy cities by fire,
> Sees spears and routed hosts and dying kings
> And plains flowing with shed blood. Lawyers
> See statutes and law-courts, and gaze in terror
> On a judge's bench that is merely within the heart.
> The miser buries his wealth, discovers treasure.
> The hunter shakes the woodland with his pack.
> The sailor saves his ship or, drowning, grips it.
> The courtesan writes her lover; the adulteress yields.
> The drowsing dog barks at the spoor of the hare.
> The wounds of the unhappy perdure through the hours of night.

On a superficial reading of the poem, the theme seems almost a commonplace of the sort found frequently in literature with an Epicurean tinge. For the Epicureans attempted to combat the view held by the superstitious masses and encouraged by the Stoics, that dreams could be communications from the gods. Indeed, the second century dream writer, Artemidorus of Daldis, incorporating what seems to have been Stoic material, taught that in addition to dreams prompted by bodily needs there was a true class of prognostic dreams due to divine influence: the "theorematic" or vision-dreams, which embodied a clear indication of the future, and the allegorical or obscure dreams, which required expert interpretation.[3] Stoic dream theory, as reflected particularly by Posidonius, seems to have had an important influence on Christian allegorism chiefly through the writings of Philo Judaeus. For Philo utilized Stoic theory in his attempt to explain the three types of dreams which occurred in the Old Testament, the divine, the angelic and the non-divine.[4]

It is logical to suppose, then, that our poet is attempting to refute this prophetic theory of dreams, and, for this reason, he takes only such examples which would readily fit his case. The instances are obviously tailored to picture continuations, or possible continuations, of the day's activity. He does not treat, as do other theoreticians, the body-need dream, the fantastic allegorical dream or the theophany type of dream, which poets like Sappho, Tibullus and Propertius could describe so well. But, it is precisely this selectivity, among other things, which arouses suspicion that the poem may have a level of meaning which is not completely on the surface, though not irrelevant to the Epicurean view of life.

As we begin reading the first line, it is not immediately clear that the *somnia* which trick the mind are *night* dreams in the literal sense. Before the meaning becomes specified the associations of "vague fancies" and "pretenses," which can be attached to the word *somnia*, seem very present. Again, they deceive the mind "at the time of hovering shadows," or "by means of flickering shadows," perhaps like the "images of things," *rerum simulacra*, that flutter through the air in Lucretius 4. 32. Further, can the "shadows," *umbrae*, mean "ghosts"? Indeed, it is not completely clear what it is that each man makes for himself until we come to the "sleep" and "weariness" of the succeeding lines, and then it becomes obvious that the poet is dealing with the prophetic theory of dreams and, perhaps, the practice of incubation.

Thereafter, the sequence of the various dream narratives is clear: the soldier, the orator, the miser (at least as a type from the mime), the hunter, the sailor, the women of ill repute. The dreams are of the sort that one would today call wish-fulfillment dreams and, at least in the case of the terrified orator and drowning sailor, anxiety dreams. A modern Freudian analyst might perhaps tend to see more, especially in the sacking of cities, the plain flowing with blood, the hunter and his hounds, the sinking sailor and the unfaithful women. But these images are familiar enough from ancient accounts of dreams, as we find them, for example, in the Hellenistic papyri and especially in the *Dream Book* of Artemidorus. The pathetic little line on the barking dog—in Lucretius, incidentally, the dog wakes itself up—should not, I feel, be deleted, nor should *latrat* ("barks") be changed to *lustrat* ("follows" the tracks of). The detail would seem to have been a regular Epicurean topic, to show the affinity between animals and men, and is similarly developed by Lucretius.[5]

But it is the ambiguity of the final line, *In noctis spatium*, ("The wounds of the unhappy," etc.) that suggests an entirely different reading of the poem. What is meant by the "wounds" and who are the unhappy? One possibility that occurs is that the lines refer to those who are in sorrow, or otherwise ill. Or, again, because of the previous reference to lovers and their ladies, we may legitimately think of the "wounds of love"; the image is frequent enough in the elegiac poets. Hence physical pain, moral affliction, the pangs of love—all seem possible. But still we are not sure whether the line is intended to refer to a type of dreamer not previously mentioned, or is meant to be a summary of all the types of dreams that have gone before. After the mention of the dog, we should have expected the list to be complete. It is this final possibility, that the last line sums up the entire poem, which presents an entirely new dimension in imagery. For all of the dreamers that the poem describes are all in search of happiness in one form or another, aptly symbolized by the hunter and the courtesan; and thus all might be described as "unhappy" and suffering from "wounds." In this way, the final line of the poem, "The wounds of the unhappy perdure through the hours of night," would resume the meaning of the entire fragment. Dreams merely continue the unhappy quest of our conscious lives; in the Epicurean view, they are symbolic of man's pursuit of happiness without benefit of providence. Like hounds we too merely bark at the hare's scent.

Thus a further nuance suggests itself. If dreams are merely a prolongation of what we do by day—and, indeed, the poet speaks of the dream activity almost as though he were describing men's daily lives—Petronius may be hinting, though not expressly stating, that all these absorbing interests are, in a sense, mere dreams, *somnia*. This would bring us back to the ambiguity we noted in the first line, where *somnia*, "dreams," could have the suggestion of "idle fancies." Hence what the sailor, the courtesan, the warrior do in their dreams is hardly less substantial than what they do in the light. If this suggestion is correct, the poem would have two levels of meaning. On the first level, it would represent a fairly straightforward case against the prophetic theory of dreams as supported by the Stoic school. This would confirm the impression we get from the poem quoted in Ch. 128 of the **Satyricon** as well as the slighting reference in Ch. 10 to "dream-interpretations," *somniorum interpretamenta*. But I cannot escape the impression that on a second and more poetic level the fragment would seem to be saying something about the dream quality of life: that the most absorbing interests of men, their passions and ambitions, are little more than dreams.

### Notes

1 See the discussion in G. Bagnani, *Arbiter of Elegance: A Study of the Life and Works of C. Petronius* (The *Phoenix*, suppl. vol. 2, Toronto, 1954) 3 ff., with the bibliography cited.

2 For the text I have departed somewhat from A. Riese, *Anth. lat.*, pars prior, fasc. 2 (Leipzig 1870)651, in order to reflect the MS tradition more closely. See also F. Buecheler, *Petronii Saturae et liber Priapeorum*[6] (cur. W. Heraeus, Berlin 1922) frag. 30, 121.

3 For the literature in general, see H. Kenner, *Pauly-Wissowa* 18 (1939) 448-459, *s.v.* 'Oneiros.' For the Epicurean view, see Lucretius 4.962-1036, with the commentary of C. Bailey (Oxford 1947)3.1295ff. On Artemidorus of Daldis, who flourished about A.D. 170, see Nilsson, *Gesch. griech. Rel.* 1 (Munich 1950)499. Cf. also R. Pack, "Lexical and Textual Notes on Artemidorus," *Trans. of the Amer. Philol. Assoc.* 90 (1959) 180-84, with bibliography. It is interesting to note that Sigmund Freud in his *Traumdeutung*, ch. ii, pointed out that his own theory ultimately went back to the principles of Artemidorus, based on the association of ideas. If one may be allowed to oversimplify, however, the difference in Freudian dream-analysis primarily consists in the fact that (a) the analyst is to draw the associations from the dreamer himself, and (b) Freudian dream-symbolism is almost wholly sexual.

4 For a discussion of the influence of Stoic dream theory on Philo, see H. A. Wolfson, *Philo* (Cambridge, 1948) 2.55ff.

5 See Lucr. 4.987ff., with Bailey's commentary *ad loc.*, 1297ff.

### G. M. A. Grube (essay date 1965)

SOURCE: "Petronius," in *The Greek and Roman Critics*, University of Toronto Press, 1965, pp. 262-8.

[*In the following excerpt, Grube outlines Petronius's thoughts on poetry, particularly his attack on declamations and his assessment that the arts had reached a degenerated state in Rome.*]

. . . [Petronius] is always superbly alive.[1] In that amazing medley of riotous and indecent adventures which make up the **Satyricon** we find several passages bearing on literature. The book as we have it begins with a violent tirade against the practice of declamations which Encolpius addresses to a teacher of rhetoric called Agamemnon. It may be quoted here as a typical denunciation, making, in a more lively manner, most of the criticisms which recur throughout the century:

> Are declaimers pursued by another kind of Furies when they shout: 'These wounds were received on behalf of our public freedom', 'this eye was lost for your sake', 'give me a guide to lead me to my children for these hamstrung knees cannot support my body'? Even these things could be endured if they opened the way for future orators. As it is, these inflated subjects and empty-sounding phrases

advance them so little that when they get to court they think themselves transported to another world. I think our adolescents become so very stupid at school because they don't hear or see anything related to actual life, but pirates standing ready with chains[2] on the shore, despots issuing edicts ordering sons to cut off their fathers' heads, oracular responses in times of pestilence demanding the sacrifice of three or more virgins, honeyed word-dumplings; every word and deed dipped in syrup and oil. Young people brought up on such a diet no more acquire wisdom than kitchen servants acquire a pleasant perfume. If you'll allow me to say so, you teachers have been the first to destroy eloquence. The stimulation of smooth, empty, ridiculous sound effects has enfeebled and destroyed the body of your speeches. Young men were not confined to declamations when Sophocles and Euripides discovered the words of proper speech, when Pindar and the nine lyrists scrupled to use lines from Homer. Not to go to the poets as my witnesses, certainly neither Plato nor Demosthenes indulged in this sort of exercise. Great and, if I may so put it, modest speech is neither mottled nor turgid, but rises in natural beauty. This windy and enormous verbosity recently invaded Athens from Asia and it blew upon young minds as they rose to great things like an effluvium from a pestilential constellation, while eloquence, its rules corrupted, stood by in silence. Who, since Thucydides and Hypereides, has equalled their fame? Even poetry did not shine with a healthy hue, but all the arts of speech were fed on the same diet and produced nothing capable of lasting to old age. Painting too has come to the same end after the audacity of the Egyptians discovered a short cut to so great an art.

Agamemnon makes no real reply; in fact he agrees in principle. He blames it all on the parents. If you teach the young properly you will be left without pupils, for parents will send them where they get quicker results. It's no good teaching them the right things; they no longer have the patience. The result is that nowadays the young just waste their time at school and learn nothing worthwhile.

Later (83) Encolpius visits a gallery of paintings which contains works of Apelles and other classical painters. He there meets a shabby old man, a poet (which explains his shabbiness, for 'the love of talent never made a man rich') and they discuss the degeneration of taste, all due to the love of money, which has corrupted all the arts, and philosophy as well. It should be added that the poet, before discoursing upon the corruption of the age, tells a story of his relation to a boy-pupil which is certainly not to his credit!

Petronius' work is a *satura*, he passes from prose to verse with the greatest of ease, and it is hard to be sure where he is serious, especially in his poetry. Probably nowhere entirely. No passage is more puzzling, however, than where he has been understood to criticize Lucan, especially for doing away with the divine apparatus in his epic of the civil war. It begins, in prose, as follows (118):

> Poetry has led many astray. For as soon as one has constructed feet into verses and clothed a rather tender meaning in a periodic structure of words, he thinks at once that he has scaled Helicon. Thus those who are trained in the service of the courts have often taken refuge in the quiet pursuit of poetry as in a happier haven; they think that it is easier to construct a poem than a *controversia* embroidered with sparkling little maxims (*sententiolis vibrantibus pictam*). But a more genuine spirit has no liking for such uninspired work[3]; it cannot conceive anything or bring it to birth unless it is steeped in a vast stream of literature. One must avoid, so to speak, all slovenly diction, use expressions far removed from the common people, with the result (as expressed by Horace)[4] 'I hate the vulgar crowd and I avoid it.' Besides this, one should be careful that one's pithy phrases (*sententiae*) do not stand out from the body of one's discourse, but shine as a colouring worked into the cloth itself. Homer is a proof of this, so are the lyric poets, our Roman Virgil and Horace's diligent felicity (*curiosa felicitas*). The others have either not seen the path which leads to poetry, or, if they saw it, have been afraid to take it. Anyone who undertakes a great work on the Civil War will collapse under the burden, unless he is full of literature. It is not a question of describing events in verse, historians do this much better; but the spirit must freely range over byways, interventions by the gods, and swoop over mythical content, so that the poem appears to be the prophesying of a frenzied mind rather than a scrupulously reliable statement of facts before witnesses—as in the following effusion, if it please you, though it still needs final polishing: . . .

The 'effusion' which follows is a poem of two hundred and ninety-six hexameters, which read like the beginning of an epic on Caesar's invasion of Italy. That there is meant to be a reference to Lucan when Petronius refers to epics on the civil wars seems obvious, especially as Lucan was the only Roman epic poet *not* to make use of the usual divine apparatus. There are also many echoes of the *Pharsalia* in the poem. But what else refers to him, and what is the purpose of the poem itself?[5]

The general discussion of poetry in the first part of the passage, quoted above, is not particularly original: too many people write poetry; anyone who can put a few verses together thinks himself a poet; poetry is not merely a pleasant relaxation for tired orators; it requires inspiration and a deep knowledge of great literature; poetic diction is very different from ordinary speech. Most of these ideas can be paralleled in Horace, Cicero and elsewhere.[6] One imagines that the sophisticated courtier of Nero shared Horace's contempt for the mob, even though he could make individual members of it come wonderfully to life in his own work and speak their own language. Brilliant phrases that stand out from the body of a work are certainly a weakness of Lucan's, but so they were of all contemporary work, whether in verse or prose, not excluding Petronius himself, or the poem which follows, and one doubts that he would here have Lucan specifically in mind.[7] We have already seen that Petronius was an adherent of the 'classical' school and are not surprised that he chooses Homer and the Greek lyrists as models, but it is interesting to find Virgil and Horace now recognized as the Roman classics, and the phrase which he coins to describe the poetry of Horace—*curiosa felicitas*, where the adjective implies care or diligence while the noun implies luck or a gift from the gods, i.e. natural talent, is a deservedly famous critical phrase, frequently quoted.

It is with the mention of epics on the civil war that Lucan inevitably comes to our minds. He must have been in Petronius' mind also, for the *Pharsalia* was, as far as we know, the only contemporary poem of the kind.[8] But when he repeats his general requirement, namely that such a poet must be steeped in great literature, he need not imply that Lucan was not so steeped, which he obviously was. Petronius goes on to make three further points, and they are made in one sentence, i.e. they go together. The epic poet should not be primarily concerned to give the facts, which is the historian's job, but he must be prepared to range over by-ways[9] which are no part of a historical account, he must bring in the gods, and he must be inspired. All this, Petronius repeats, is where he differs from the historian. A poem is a poem, not a history. This is probably intended as a not unfriendly criticism of Lucan but even here, except for the gods, Petronius need not be thinking of him exclusively.

What he seems to imply is that to write an epic on recent or contemporary history is a very difficult task indeed, perhaps that the subject is more suitable for a historian. He does not say that without the usual divine apparatus it will fail, but he expresses the opinion that one should stick to the laws of the genre, including the gods. That, and the other characteristics, the inclusion of *ambages*, for example—i.e. the less direct pressing on with the story but amplification of episodes (one thinks of Dido and the visit to Hades in the *Aeneid*)— and the poetic frenzy generally, remain essential to any epic, whatever its subject.

As for Petronius' poem as a whole, its intention cannot be judged in isolation. Poems of varying length are scattered throughout the work; they are usually short, often echo other poets, and are frequently humorous in intent, just as he often uses a dignified and epic diction at the most undignified moments. Sometimes the poems seem to have no other purpose than the author's own amusement, and there does not seem ever to be any intended parody or serious criticism of the authors from whom phrases are borrowed. The nearest parallel to the *Bellum Civile* is a poem of sixty-five *senarii* on the fall of Troy which the same Eumolpus improvises as Encolpius is intently looking at a picture on the subject in a picture gallery (89). This bears much the same relation to the second book of the *Aeneid* as the poem on the civil war bears to the *Pharsalia*. There, certainly, no criticism of Virgil is intended. At the end of it, passers-by throw stones at Eumolpus but he is used to that sort of reception. Yet the poem is not deliberately bad; indeed it is not without merit considered in itself as an exercise in rhetorical poetry, and it seems to have no other purpose.

The *Bellum Civile* itself is much longer. It consists of five panels.[10] The first depicts the Romans, having conquered the world, exploiting all its resources to feed their luxury and corruption—a powerful indictment (1-60). Then we have a scene where Pluto rises from the nether world and addresses Fortuna; they contemplate the Roman world and decide to stir up civil war; dread omens follow (67-140). We then see Caesar high up in the Alps addressing his troops and marching forward, overcoming all difficulties (141-208). Then the scene shifts to Rome where all is fear and confusion, and even the great Pompey, in spite of his past glories, takes to flight (209-44). Peace, Faith, Justice and Concord leave the earth while evil spirits, Fury, Treason, Madness among them, rise up from the world below. The gods take sides. Discord rises and calls the peoples and the Roman nobles to war (245-95). There the poem abruptly ends.

Clearly, it conforms to the requirements just enunciated by Petronius himself. No specific historical event is mentioned except that Caesar crossed the Alps. There are plenty of digressions or byways (*ambages*) such as the whole first panel on the luxury of Rome, and the scenes where the gods intervene. In fact little that is found here would find a place in a reliable historical account. The gods fill more than a third of the poem. Moreover, the many echoes, not only of Lucan, but of Virgil, Livy and others,[11] show that the author is 'full of literature'. We may not think that such echoes and reworking of others' phrases and ideas is the best way of showing one's acquaintance with literature, but it was certainly the fashion of the day and a practice taught in the schools where our author was trained, however much he may have disliked them. The diction is poetic, and though there are powerful lines and *sententiae*, they do not quite stand out as they do in other writers of the time, including Lucan. As for poetic genius, it is a competent, in places a striking poem, and Petronius does not claim to be a great poet.

The implied criticism of Lucan remains on this general level. Attempts to find parody, or criticism in detail have not been successful; the whole poem is no more a parody of Lucan than the other poem on the fall of Troy is a parody of Virgil. One imagines Petronius saying: 'My dear Lucan, to write an epic on recent history is almost impossible, and you are not succeeding any better by breaking the rules of the genre. You should keep the divine apparatus and worry a great deal less about what actually happened. Now if I were to attempt so difficult a task, this is how I'd do it. . . .' As far as it goes, the poem is serious; it is also highly competent; but Petronius cannot be serious for very long, and after less than three hundred lines he gives up. No other hidden meanings, abstruse criticisms or parodies are probably intended. It is just a rather lengthy illustration of what he has just said, no more and no less.

The passages we have discussed are, unfortunately, the only relevant passages on poetry and literature to be found in Petronius as we have him: the attack on declamations, the degenerate state of all the arts, and the reflections on poetry in general which we have just discussed. One wishes there were more, for the author of the **Satyricon** obviously was fully qualified to give us more, had he chosen; indeed he may have done so, since we only have fragments of his fifteenth and sixteenth books. If so, the loss is much to be regretted, for he had a far more mature mind than Persius and a far deeper appreciation of poetry and literature generally than the younger Seneca ever had.

*Notes*

[1] I am taking for granted that the Petronius mentioned by Tacitus in *Annals* XVI, 18-19 is the author of the *Satyricon*. This is now generally accepted. See Gilbert Bagnani, *Arbiter of Elegance*, Toronto, 1957, and references there.

[2] *cum catenis*: 'Pirates on the shore waving handcuffs', i.e. waiting for the shipwrecked, as G. Bagnani translates it in *Studies in honour of B. L. Ullman* p. 230, instead of the usual translation 'pirates in chains'. Professor Bagnani also draws my attention to the curiously archaic nature of the passage: not only are all the examples of the good old days Greek classical writers, but the Asiatic style is said to have *recently* (*nuper*) invaded Athens! Since we are dealing with Petronius, this is obviously deliberate, but the intent is obscure. He is probably satirizing the Graccomania of contemporary professors of rhetoric.

[3] Reading, with most MSS., *sanitatem* instead of *vanitatem*. The word is here used in contrast to the inspiration of the true poet, it is the [*Sophrosyne*] of Plato in the *Phaedrus* (above, p. 57).

[4] *Odes* III, I, 1.

[5] For a full discussion of all the problems raised by this famous passage of Petronius see A. Collignon, *Etude*

*Sur Pétrone* 101-226. See also Florence Th. Baldwin, *The Bellum Civile.*

[6] See Collignon 101-5.

[7] Excessive use of striking and epigrammatic *sententiae* is a vice which developed with the abuse of declamations, and it is not, as such, dealt with by Horace or Cicero, though one thinks of Horace's advice that no part should be elaborated at the expense of the whole (*A.P.* 32-37). Collignon (p. 102) quotes Cicero, *De Orat.* III, 25 (96) that a definite tone should pervade the whole speech, but the following sentence goes on to say that certain ornaments—*quasi verborum et sententiarum flores*—should *not* be scattered throughout the speech. Cicero is of course not referring to *sententiae* in the later technical sense; he means ideas or content as opposed to *verba*, i.e. figures of thought and figures of speech. Parallels for *sententiae* that stand out too much are rarer with later authors. Collignon (p. 105) cites Tacitus, *Dialogus* 21, and one might add Quintilian 8, 5, 25-34.

[8] Under Augustus L. Varius Rufus, Cornelius Severus, and Rabirius wrote epics on contemporary history, and we know that the emperor wanted Horace to do so, but we do not know of any epic on recent or contemporary history between their day and Lucan's.

[9] *Ambages* means a detour or digression, and here seems to mean such digressions or side issues as would have no place in a historical account.

[10] Such a division covers the whole poem, except five lines (61-65) immediately after the first section. These tell how Fortune had raised three generals—Crassus killed in Parthia, Pompey killed by the shores of Egypt and Caesar in Rome—as if the burden of their ashes were too great and the earth had widely separated their deaths. This is no doubt intended as an introductory reference to the triumvirate, but the rhetorical exaggeration is one of the least successful in the whole poem.

[11] All these are carefully studied by Collingnon pp. 150-62 and 165-76.

*Abbreviations used in the Notes and Bibliography*

*AJP* American Journal of Philology

*CP* Classical Philology

*CQ* Classical Quarterly

*CR* Classical Review

*HSCP* Harvard Studies in Classical Philology

*JRS* Journal of Roman Studies

*LSJ* Liddell and Scott, Greek-English Lexicon, revised by Stuart Jones and Roderick Mackenzie

*RE* Pauly-Wissowa, *Realenzyklopädie der klassischen Altertumswissenschaft*

*REG* Revue des études grecques

*REL* Revue des études latines

*Rh.M.* Rheiniches Museum

*TAPA* Transactions and Proceedings of the American Philological Association

### John Sullivan (essay date 1968)

SOURCE: "The Humour of Petronius," in *The Satyricon of Petronius: A Literary Study*, Faber and Faber Limited, 1968, pp. 214-31.

[*In the following essay, Sullivan discusses Petronius's wide range of humor, including the humor of incongruity, literary humor, farce, mime situations, verbal wit, and satiric dialogue.*]

i. *Some General Considerations*

Nothing is more boring than writing about what is comic, and so one approaches the subject of Petronius' humour with a heavy heart, though it is almost the first characteristic of the **Satyricon** that the reader notices. L. Dugas' sound remarks come to mind:

> Il n'est pas de fait plus étudié que le rire; il n'en est pas qui ait eu le don d'exciter davantage la curiosité du vulgaire et celle des philosophes; il n'en est pas sur lequel on ait recueilli plus d'observations et bâti plus de théories, et avec cela il n'en est pas qui demeure plus inexpliqué. On serait tenté de dire avec les sceptiques qu'il faut être content de rire et de ne pas chercher à savoir pourquoi on rit, d'autant que peut-être la réflexion tue le rire, et qu'il serait alors contradictoire qu'elle en découvrît les causes . . . [1]

Nevertheless it would be cowardly, in a work aiming at some sort of comprehensiveness, to shirk the subject, even though the remarks that follow offer merely one possible pattern of analysis, and do not purport to cover all the possible aspects of Petronius' humour. Some of these have been discussed earlier under different heads, the comic satire, for instance, and the extensive stretches of literary parody. Indeed it is difficult to disentangle the pure humour from the finer play of wit in the style and conception of the work, which offers subtler, but not necessarily inferior, amusement.

The staple of most humour and comedy is the incongruous, the linking together in unexpected ways of diverse concepts, language, situations, persons, or modes of experience and behaviour. Petronius' humour is no exception. Unfortunately, even this sort of humour tends to be topical and dependent on fashion, and frequently fades within a century. The reason is often linguistic or social change whereby jokes are lost and absurdity diminished. We are not very much amused nowadays by the references to 'horns' in Elizabethan literature. With the **Satyricon**, therefore, a great imaginative effort is often needed to see just what the purely topical incongruities are, although, luckily, some of the humour flows from perennial springs. The basic humour of the **Satyricon** consists in the application of a refined, literary, and stylistically sophisticated narrative medium to the disreputable low-life adventures and sexual escapades of a number of unprincipled and generally worthless characters. The *nostalgie de la boue* that perhaps dictated this choice of subject, which contrasts so strongly with some of the literary digressions, has already been examined, and here we need merely inspect the techniques and mechanisms used. Particularly noticeable is the contrast between the short, polished, and rhythmic sentences, with their constant literary allusions, and the high degree of excitement, despair, astonishment, shame, suffering, laughing, crying, and ecstasy they describe. The narrative is full of references to the narrator's being thunderstruck, frightened to death, delirious with happiness and so on, yet the prose itself, economically and smoothly, records these horrors and raptures without any ornate or effusive reinforcements of the feelings described, except where deliberate parody is intended.[2] The effect is an ironic distancing of the writer's material, which enhances the amusing quality of the work: something of the sort may be seen in the early novels of Evelyn Waugh and Anthony Powell.

Sometimes the incongruity that is fundamental to the humour is between the high moral sentiments, the sensible, sometimes serious, literary criticism, and the persons that voice them, whether the narrator Encolpius, a timorous and suspicious criminal of (to us) strange origins and unknown destination, or the immoral, opportunistic poetaster, Eumolpus. Sometimes the incongruity is between the style of the prose or verse and the lowliness or absurdity of the incidents, or, alternatively, between the highflown declamatory style of some of the characters, Giton, for instance, or even Chrysis, and the actual station or attainments in life. The tragic style is frequently invoked and parodied, as the references to *tragoedia* (108.11) and tragic subjects (*Thebanum par* 80.3; cf. 132.13) might lead us to expect. The use of epic style and references, especially of Vergilian or Homeric epic, for the most unlikely or obscene subjects is even more noticeable. Not only is the Wrath of Priapus a parody of the

Wrath of Poseidon in the *Odyssey*, but Homer is drawn on for such incidents as Lichas' lewd recognition of Encolpius (105.9), which burlesques Eurycleia's identification of Odysseus.

The use of elevated, lyrical, or rhetorical language for unseemly subjects is frequent enough in English literature and may be found in Rochester, Dorset, and in such minor productions as the anonymous *Panegyric on Cundums*, just as the use of elegant and high-flown prose for erotic matters is familiar to us from such novels as John Cleland's *Memoirs of a Lady of Pleasure*. Petronius has a highly differentiated style, or set of styles, but this is certainly one use to which he puts his abilities for comic effect. As Samuel Johnson remarks in his *Life of Cowley*:

> Language is the dress of thought: and as the noblest mien or most graceful action would be degraded and obscured by a garb appropriated to the gross employments of rustics or mechanics, so most heroic sentiments will lose their efficacy, and the most splendid ideas lose their magnificence, if they are conveyed by vulgar mouths and contaminated by inelegant applications.

The best example of this literary erotic humour is the episode with Circe (126 ff.). The narrative contains a number of reminiscences of Ovid's amatory works, particularly in the description of Circe and her powers;[3] the climax of the story (or should one say anticlimax?), Encolpius' impotence, which is followed by Circe's beratings of him, and his own soliloquy over the offending member, whose failure has deprived him of such joy, draws heavily on Ovid's well-known elegy on *his* impotence (*Am.* 3.7). The theme is a popular one, being found in the roughly contemporary *Priapea* (83, attributed to Tibullus), and it was to enjoy a long history. Maximianus in the fourth century elaborated on the Ovidian description with some originality (*Elegy* V), and the Earl of Rochester's poems, *The Imperfect Enjoyment*, *On Leaving his Mistress*, and *The Disappointment*, all turn on the topic.

Petronius elaborates on Ovid in a number of ways. He splits up the basic action into several dramatic scenes: Chrysis is brought back as a witness; Giton, rather than another woman, is given the blame; Ovid's simple self-reproaches become in the hero's soliloquy an opportunity for reflections on obscenity (132.15); and the usual Petronian motif of castration is invoked.

Apart from heightening the action in this way, Petronius keeps up the play of literary humour. Ovid is kept continually in mind in this whole section. Even at 135, when Encolpius is seeking a cure for his impotence, we have the parodic allusions to the Baucis and Philemon story, treated by Callimachus in the *Hecale* and rehandled by Ovid in the *Metamorphoses*. Even Encolpius' slaughter of the goose at 136.4 ff. seems to recall the more hospitable slaughter of the goose for Theseus in the Alexandrian epyllion which Ovid inserted into his work (*Met.* 8.620-724). At this point in the *Satyricon*, not content with Ovidian allusions, Petronius adds a parody of Vergil cast in the more suggestive sotadic metre:

> ter corripui terribilem manu bipennem,
> ter languidior coliculi repente thyrso
> ferrum timui, quod trepido male dabat usum.
> nec iam poteram, quod modo conficere
>     libebat;
> namque illa metu frigidior rigente bruma
> confugerat in viscera mille operta rugis.
> ita non potui supplicio caput aperire,
> sed furciferae mortifero timore lusus
> ad verba, magis quam poterant nocere, fugi.
>
> (132.8)

> Three times I took the murd'rous axe in hand,
> Three times I wavered like a wilting stalk
> And curtsied from the blade, poor instrument
> In trembling hands—I could not what I would.
> From terror colder than the wintry frost,
> It took asylum far within my crotch,
> A thousand wrinkles deep.
> How could I lift its head to punishment?
> Cozened by its whoreson, mortal fright,
> I fled for aid to words that deeper bite.

Not satisfied with the echoes of Vergil in this poem, Petronius adds a cento of Vergilian lines to describe the appearance of Encolpius' penis:

> illa solo fixos oculos aversa tenebat,
> nec magis incepto vultum sermone movetur
> quam lentae salices lassove papavera collo.[4]
>
> (132.11)

> She held her eyes averted and down-cast
> Nor altered aught her face at this address
> Than supple willow or drooping poppyhead.

The piquancy of the wit is irreverently enhanced by the fact that the first two lines were used by Vergil to describe the pathetic meeting of Dido and Aeneas in the underworld, and half of the last line comes from the description of the death of Euryalus.

The parody is not confined to the frankly sexual situations. Legal language, diplomatic language, and the tones of erotic elegy also, are employed in more innocent contexts, such as the scene where Eumolpus negotiates a truce between the adventurers and their pursuers (109.2), or the episode where he plots against the legacy hunters (117.5); and Ovid is largely drawn on for Encolpius' initially romantic encounters with Circe. Similar use is made of philosophical doctrines or commonplaces, Stoic and Epicurean. As we have seen, Trimalchio's enlightened speech on the common humanity of slave and free: *'et servi homines sunt et aeque unum lactem biberunt, etiam si illos malus fatus oppresserit'* (71.1-'Slaves are human too and they drank one and the same milk as us, even if an unlucky fate has put them down'), is meant as the keynote of what, to Petronius, would be his absurd and tasteless treatment of his household, in which undue familiarity and harsh treatment (cf. 28.7, 52.5, 53.3 etc) irrationally alternate. The purpose is, in a way, satiric, and the savagely ironic glance at such sentiments in Seneca's *Epistulae Morales* adds the literary element to the humour.[5]

The attraction of the humour of incongruity and surprise for Petronius may be seen further in the two stories which Eumolpus retells at different points in the narrative, the stories of the Boy of Pergamum and the Widow of Ephesus (85 ff., 111 ff.). In each case, the point of the story lies in the reversal of roles: the young body becomes the would-be seducer, and Eumolpus is reduced to stern measures to avoid what he formerly desired so eagerly; the Widow, that paragon of chastity, is willing to sacrifice anything, even the husband she doted on enough to die for, to save the new lover she has acquired.[6] The pellucid style of the narrative contrasts vividly with the unseemliness of the themes, and here, as elsewhere, Petronius avoids any vulgar or obscene language of the sort we find in Catullus or Martial. Eumolpus, for all his wicked ways, is as chaste in his prose as in his poetry.

ii. *Mime and Comedy Situations*

*A priori*, it is perhaps a surprise that the great sophistication of style and literary allusion is at the service not simply of picaresque adventures and sexual descriptions, but also of individual scenes which seem to be drawn from mime and comedy. The picaresque and sexual elements are explicable by Petronius' artistic assumptions, even where we might criticize them, and something of the sort must be invoked to explain his free use of mime, for its influence is unmistakable.[7] The question is, what was the particular attraction of mime and comedy for Petronius, and to what use does he put this inspiration in the *Satyricon*?

Despite the literary tradition of Sophron, Herodas, and Theocritus, and the perhaps better than average efforts of such Roman writers as Laberius and Publilius Syrus, who, besides being a favourite writer of Trimalchio's (55.5), is quoted by Seneca about nine times in the *Epistulae Morales*, the mime in Rome in our period was hardly a respectable literary or artistic form. With the pantomime, it seemed to provide what the twentieth century gets from soap opera, farce, melodrama, strip-tease, ballet, interpretative dancing in the style of Isadora Duncan, or the miming of Marcel Marceau.

But however trite, obscene, or even cruel it may have been, its general popularity is well-documented for the first century.[8] Martial writes with complete unconcern about a realistic performance of the Pasiphae story in the amphitheatre and the actual crucifixion of a criminal in a production of the famous *Laureolus* mime;[9] the notoriety that made such actors as Latinus and Bathyllus stock butts for the satirists is as indicative of their standing as are the fierce, if prejudiced, protests of Christian writers such as Tertullian.[10] An analogous addiction to gladiatorial games was present in quite well-educated people, the emperor Claudius being an obvious example (Suet. *Claud.* 21), and Seneca would at least drop in on them, if only to be shocked (*Ep.* 7.3). On the other hand we are familiar with professors of philosophy who like detective fiction or soccer; eminent papyrologists and literary critics share a fondness for P. G. Wodehouse or thrillers. Petronius' perhaps condescending interest in mime may have been analogous; and the *nostalgie de la boue*, which has been postulated as a dominating impulse in him, might find equal satisfaction in making use of this sort of 'art', particularly if he could fit its themes, with the resulting incongruity, into his highly literary framework.

It is perhaps an exaggeration to say that the key to the whole *Satyricon* is in the words: *omnia mimico risu exsonuerant*,[11] but words, incidents, even titles from mime, occur in the narrative. Before we examine the end to which this art-form is put by Petronius, it might be well to summarize such relevant characteristics of the mime in the early principate as might appeal to him.

There is, first of all, the theory of the mime which would commend itself as consonant with Petronius' own literary principles. Its origin was popularly thought to be *mimetic*, imitative of real life,[12] hence the naturalism of even such Alexandrian mime writers as Herodas and Theocritus. By an obvious progression due to the principles of realism, we have the concentration on the lower aspects of life, and the careful, if stereotyped, observation of everyday affairs and language, particularly of the lower classes. The obscenity of the mime, Martial's *mimica licentia*, is not unconnected with this.[13] To Petronius' mind this art-form would have an aim similar to his own intentions in the *Satyricon*: to narrate frankly the behaviour of ordinary, i.e. inferior, people (*quodque facit populus, candida lingua refert,* 132.15) and the pleasures of sex (*concubitis, Veneris gaudia,* ibid.).

Other characteristics of the mime, literary and non-literary, that must have appealed to Petronius would be the colloquial speech, such stock figures as the procurer or go-between (like Chrysis), the *cinaedus*, the excluded lover (cf. Encolpius *inclusus*, 94.7 ff.), and so on. In particular one of the features of mime was imposture and deception, and this alone would relate the whole world of the **Satyricon** to the mime.

Specifically, however, the first direct reference we find is in the Quartilla scene. Quartilla and her maids have arrived; the promises of Encolpius are accepted, and the priestess' threat of possible force has been made. Suddenly the three women burst out laughing, to the surprise and consternation of the trio, and at this point the phrase, if we can trust the variant reading for *nimio, omnia mimico risu exsonuerant* (19.1) occurs. From the context it appears that some sort of deception is being practised on the three; from what follows, it is presumably that the apparently harmless and weak women are backed by forces greater than the trio can hope to match. The laughter is described as *mimicus* because it is the sort of laughter which the stage deception excites, hearty and cruel. Even the mock marriage of Giton and Pannychis (25.1 ff.) has the features of mime, and may have been suggested by Laberius' *Nuptiae.*[14]

The same impression is left by Petronius' use of the word at 117.4, where Eumolpus, having thought of a deception which he can practise on the Crotonian legacy hunters (*mendacium*, 117.2, 5), wishes he had a large stage setting (*scaena*), and better dress and equipment, but asks why they are delaying the production of the mime (*quid ergo cessamus mimum componere?* 117.4), the mime being of course that of the poor old man, who pretends to be rich and ill, and so profitably deceives the legacy hunters.

The motif of the mime is particularly pervasive in the *Cena.*[15] Not only does Trimalchio like real mimes, as the song (35.6) from the *Laserpiciarius mimus* or *The Asafoetida Man*, and the imitation of Publilius Syrus (55.6) indicate, but many of the scenes put on for the entertainment of the guests involve some sort of humorous trick, deception, or joke, and are reminiscent of mimes. There can be little doubt that these entertainments, like some of the others put on by Trimalchio, are yet another indication of his low taste. Encolpius' sour remarks make this clear: *pantomimi chorum, non patris familiae triclinium crederes* (31.7). The sneer is directed not so much against mime itself, as against Trimalchio's bad taste in spoiling the dinner and the conversation by his unremitting attempts to impress and amuse his guests. His taste for such things as mime, Atellan farce, and acrobats is genuine (cf. 53.12-13), whereas Petronius' own interest would be self-conscious and critical. As with Herodas and Theocritus, it is the elevation of a popular art form into a higher literary genre or a more sophisticated context.

There are however one or two incidents of a farcical nature in the **Satyricon** which perhaps surprise the non-Anglo-Saxon reader more than anything else, unless of course this type of anal humour appeals to him. Trimal-

chio's ill-mannered emphasis on excretory functions (41.9, 47.2-6) may be excused as satiric, a fact underlined by the guests' laughter (47.7), but the farting scene with Eumolpus' servant Corax would be more puzzling were it not consistent with the frequently low nature of the incidents in the **Satyricon**. It must also be remembered that this type of humour exercises a certain hearty, or morbid, appeal to some writers. Such Rabelaisian interests may be seen in Ben Jonson, whose *Famous Voyage* also makes use of the mock-heroic style, Jonathan Swift, Mark Twain, at least in his *1601*, and, most importantly for our purposes, Aristophanes, who, in the opening scene of the *Frogs*, has Dionysus' slave Xanthus behave in much the same way as Corax for the same reasons.

In sum, it may be said that mime subjects and situations provide part of the grist for Petronius' sophisticated and literary mill. They provide the melodrama, the movement, and incident, for the picaresque plot and some of its farcical humour. There are swift disappearances, violence, quarrels, concealments, enforced baths, impostures, and dramatic *bouleversements.*[16] Not all should be attributed to the direct influence of mime—satire and comedy have similar features—but the insistence in certain episodes on laughter and applause, ideas so opposed to the upper class Roman notion of *gravitas,*[17] again indicates perhaps that one source of humour that Petronius was drawing upon was, as I have suggested, the fusing of typical incidents from the plots of mime with a highly literary language and treatment—once more the humour of incongruity.

Naturally the modern reader does not always appreciate the references to so unrestorably topical a form. The dead conventions are alien to him, as the conventions of *Gammer Gurton's Needle* and the humour of many Shakespearean comedies are alien also. He will notice of course the contrast between the refined style and literary discussions, and the buffoonery of much of the action, but he will not be able to perceive easily the *deliberateness* of the contrast between the action and the language. One would have to turn to modern analogies to realize the effect that Petronius seems to be aiming at. Several come to mind. A simple analogy may be seen in the novels of P. G. Wodehouse, whose relation to stage comedy with its embarrassing social situations, elaborate plots, and unmaskings, is approximately the same as Petronius' to mime. The analogy is strengthened when one considers Wodehouse's ironic use of English colloquialisms and literary allusions—the inversion of *milieux* corresponds to the difference between a democratic and an aristocratic society's tastes. After all, farcical situations, with some exceptions, are culturally determined. Lovers in chests, or laundry baskets, predicaments so dear to the Romans and the Elizabethans, are out of place in the efficient housing of today. Adulterous lovers who run into family friends at airports fit our different patterns of behaviour, although the situations may be just as comical.

It is important not to claim too much now for the humour of incident in Petronius, although we can realize that his comedy was probably a good deal funnier for his audience than we can properly appreciate, just as his literary allusions, imitations, and parodies must have excited a more immediate response, and thus a greater pleasure, from the instant recognition of incongruity than we can hope to achieve by our laborious restoration of the original contexts. Here again, perhaps, the limited analogy of Wodehouse, with Bertie Wooster's mangled Shakespeare, might be borne in mind.

### iii. *Verbal Wit*

At the opposite extreme to the farcical incidents employed by Petronius for the action proper, there is the almost equally large element of verbal wit, which more readily satisfies our expectations of such a literate and polished writer. The most obvious form in which this verbal wit shows itself is the pun. Humour of the punning sort was more popular with the Romans than with us, as the extant examples of Cicero's witticisms prove. Even such oddities as a fondness for rebuses, a liking shared by Trimalchio and the Emperor Augustus,[18] exemplify this taste.

Puns may be tendentious, sexual, for example, or simply plays upon words; again they may rely on a simple change of a letter or syllable, or involve the *double entendre* proper. Petronius uses most of these varieties. As an example of the first may be instanced Eumolpus' wry but neat comment on Ascyltos' success in being picked up at the baths: *'tanto magis expedit inguina quam ingenia fricare'* (92.11), which may be translated loosely by 'A polished wick is more profitable than a polished wit'. There are a number of *double-entendres* proper, both in the narrative and the dialogue. Quartilla's little joke on examining Giton's miniature sexual equipment (24.7) provides a convenient example:

> 'haec' inquit 'belle cras in promulside libidinis nostrae militabit; hodie enim post asellum diaria non sumo.'

Loosely,

> 'Tomorrow,' she said, 'this will serve nicely as hors d'oeuvre to tempt my appetite. For the present I don't want a common shrimp after such a nice cod-piece.'

The actual joke depends on a double meaning of *asellus,* which can be both a fish and that great Ro-

man symbol of lust and sexual potency, the ass. Similar sexual puns and double meanings may be found at 11.4 (*dividere cum fratre*); 17.7 ff. (*medicina*); 24.1-4 (*embasicoetas*); 126.10 (*in equestribus sedeo*); 131.7 (the Ovidian *leporem excitavi*); 140.2,7 (*bonitas*); and 140.13 (*deorum beneficia*).

Puns and double meanings, of course, are funnier when they rely on the powerful reinforcement of a sexual reference. And it must be said that most of the puns in Encolpius' narrative and the dialogue outside the *Cena* are of this sort. Trimalchio, however, although he is given his fair share of sexual allusion (e.g. 69.3), is limited in his verbal humour to puns which are either childishly naïve or ponderously artificial; these are not meant in themselves to be funny, but are intended by their very weakness to satirize Trimalchio's deficiencies in wit. Examples of these are: *hoc est ius cenae* (35.7), which plays upon the double meaning of *ius* (*law* and *sauce*); *'Carpe, carpe'* (36.7), which would come over into English as 'Carver, carve 'er!'; and *secundae mensae* (68.1-2), which relies on the literal meaning 'second tables' and the idiomatic meaning of 'dessert'. The joke about *Corinthea vasa* and *Corinthus* (50.2-4) is too weak even to bear explication, as Encolpius' sardonic *ille melius* underlines.

As is clear, these 'jokes' sometimes rely on staging and props to be made at all, and Trimalchio's most elaborate joke is practically a tableau (41.6 ff.). Here a slave named Dionysus plays the different avatars, as it were, of the God of Wine. Trimalchio orders him to play the Italian god of wine, Liber, and the boy interprets this adjectivally as *liber* (free), and puts on a freedman's cap. Trimalchio compounds the joke by adding that the guests cannot deny *me . . . habere liberum patrem*, which plays upon the two possible meanings, *Father Liber* and *a free father*.[19] The fondness for this elaborate situational pun, as we may describe it, may be seen also in the Zodiac dish served by Trimalchio (35.2 ff., 39.4 ff.); here the various foods placed over the signs of the Zodiac generally show some sort of conceptual relationship to their sign, which is explicated at tiresome length by Trimalchio.[20] It would be equally tiresome to examine the rebus-tickets which are distributed among the guests, and which elicit odd presents for them to take home (56.8 ff.). The only bearable example is perhaps *'muraena et littera'* (*lamprey and a letter*), which receives a mouse with a frog attached instead of the expected lamprey (*murem cum rana alligata / muraena*), and a stick of beet (*beta* meaning both 'beet' and the Greek letter *beta*).

All this, of course, in so far as it is funny at all, is purely second-order humour, and is at the service of the satiric portrait. The real humour of the *Cena*—fortunately—consists in something much more comic and human. Verbal wit is exhibited also in Petronius' choice of names for his characters, although it must be admitted that he lacks the fantasy and richness of a Peacock or a Dickens. Almost all of the names are Greek, a fact that may be explained by Petronius' choice of low characters who, to the Roman mind, would be ex-slaves or *Graeculi*, and by the fact that Greek names have more expressive possibilities than standard Latin names. Quartilla is one of the few exceptions: her name is a diminutive of the Latin *quarta* (*fourth*)—such numerical names being not uncommon for slaves. There might possibly be an allusion in the diminutive to her early sexual proclivities, which she describes at 25.4 ff.: *'Iunonem meam iratam habeam, si umquam me meminerim virginem fuisse'* ('Juno's curse on me, if I remember ever being a virgin'). But usually the names are appropriately Greek, with the further exception of Proculus in Trimalchio's circle of freedmen. The importunate poet is ironically named Eumolpus ('the sweet singer'); Ascyltos' name (something like 'Mr. Takeit') fits Eumolpus' envious description of him: *'o iuvenem laboriosum: puto illum pridie incipere, postero die finire'*—'What a man for the job! I think he starts yesterday and finishes tomorrow' (92.9-10). Some of the names are less vividly descriptive. Tryphaena means, roughly, 'luxurious' and so is appropriate for a *demimondaine* who travels around solely in the pursuit of pleasure (101.5). Similarly 'Oenothea' ('Wine-goddess') aptly describes the bibulous priestess of Priapus (134.8 and ff.), as well as being perhaps a humorous allusion to the Homeric Eidothea. Some of the names of the minor characters are simply slave names (e.g. Corax and Psyche). The mythological names on the other hand do usually have point. Circe and 'Polyaenus', Agamemnon and Menelaus, provide mildly joking allusions to Homeric characters, and Lichas, the licentious sea-captain, derives his name from the Hercules myth with a possible overtone of perverse sexual practices.[21]

### iv. *Characterization*

Petronius' principal genius is for humorous characterization, which is deployed largely through the medium of dialogue, and this perhaps is the side of the *Satyricon* which appeals most to the reader, familiar as he is with the developed techniques of the novel. Encolpius is usually the victim, as the plot requires, and his characterization for various reasons differs from the others (see above, pp. 116 ff.). He is very emotional and suggestible, but his infrequent moments of ecstasy (78.8 and 126.13 ff.), or bravery (82.1 ff.), are more than balanced by his almost immediate return to despair, frustration, or cowardice. He is generally depicted as pessimistic, timorous, and self-pitying. He is rarely allowed to shine, if we except the opening scene and the *apologia* for the work (132.15), where he is presumably voicing the author's own views, and tends more to be the foil, if not a butt, for the other characters. He is the target of Quartilla's practical jokes (24.2 etc); of Ascyltos' sardonic cracks (10.1; 11.4); of Giton's infidelity (80.6; 113.4); of Eumolpus' disdain-

ful unkindness (94.1 ff., 109.8); of Circe's sarcastic irony (128.1; 130.4-6) and brutality (132.2). One has to remember of course that Petronius is not interested in exploring the consistencies or inconsistencies of Encolpius' character as a modern novelist might be, but rather in using him as the excuse for the different episodes or the foil for the other characters.

The characterization of the other figures in the *Satyricon* is predominantly satiric in the conventional sense of the term, even though there is no impression given of moral indignation. With the crew of libidinous women that stalk the pages of the *Satyricon*, the problem for the author is simply one of differentiation, as we have seen (pp. 119 ff.). Not all the techniques employed are humorous, although an exception might be made of the delightfully ironic tone of Circe's letter to Encolpius (129.4-9). The transcendence of Petronius' initial satiric aims by a stronger comic and novelistic impulse in the creation of Trimalchio has been also examined earlier (pp. 151-57 above).

Eumolpus is perhaps the most suitable figure with which to illustrate Petronius' techniques of character depiction in detail. We are first presented with a physical description:

> ecce autem . . . intravit pinacothecam senex canus, exercitati vultus et qui videbatur nescio quid magnum promittere, sed cultu non proinde speciosus, ut facile appareret eum < ex > hac nota litteratorum esse quos odisse divites solent.
>
> (83.7-8)

> All of a sudden, however . . . a white-haired old man entered the picture-gallery. His face was lined and seemed to have in it a promise of something impressive. But his appearance was shabby, and this made it clear that he belonged to the class of intellectuals so hated generally by the rich.

As with Quartilla and Circe, his first address is conciliatory and righteous:

> 'ego' inquit 'poeta sum et ut spero non humillimi spiritus, si modo coronis aliquid credendum est, quas etiam ad imperitos deferre gratia solet. 'quare ergo' inquis 'tam male vestitus es?' propter hoc ipsum. amor ingenii neminem umquam divitem fecit . . . non dubie ita est: si quis vitiorum omnium inimicus rectum iter vitae coepit insistere, primum propter morum differentiam odium habet; quis enim potest probare diversa? deinde qui solas extruere divitias curant, nihil volunt inter homines melius credi quam quod ipsi tenent. insectantur itaque, quacumque ratione possunt, litterarum amatores, ut videantur illi quoque infra pecuniam positi.'
>
> (83.8-84.3)

'I am a poet,' he said, 'and a poet of no mean ability, I like to think, at least if bardic crowns are to be trusted when favouritism confers them even on mediocrity. 'Why,' you ask, 'are you so badly dressed then?' For this one reason—concern for the arts never made anyone rich . . . No doubt about it. If a man sets his face against every temptation and starts off on the straight and narrow, he's immediately hated because of his different ways. No one can approve of conduct different from his own. And secondly, those who are interested in piling up money don't want anything else in life regarded as better than what they have themselves. So they persecute lovers of literature in any way possible to show that they too are inferior to wealth.'

As we have observed, Petronius is particularly fond of the humour of contrast and incongruity, and this lofty tone of dedication and disdain for lower pleasures is quickly deflated for the reader by the anecdote of Eumolpus' adventure in Pergamum where he manages by a clever deception to seduce his host's young son. The tale is clearly a familiar *conte*, but at the same time its narration by Eumolpus shows him to be a lecherous and hypocritical old fraud: Circe's initial demureness and the brutality and libidinousness of her true nature provide an analogous contrast. Eumolpus in fact completely inverts the poetic *topos* that we find in Catullus, Ovid, Martial, and others.[22] Whatever we think of his poetry, it is rarely playful (as at 109.9-10), and never obscene (whereas his life is anything but chaste). Eumolpus becomes then a suitable new rival for Giton's affections, and a natural leader in the imposture practised on the legacy hunters at Croton. The highly sexual episode involving Philomela's little daughter (140) is a perfect example of the combination in him of lechery and deceit. His relations with Encolpius and Giton are a similar blend, and his trickery is evident also in his attempts to deceive Lichas and Tryphaena on board ship (104.3 ff.).

It may be noted, however, that Eumolpus has many virtues; he is resourceful and courageous, as well as lecherous and cunning (cf. 95, 108, 117). Analogously, we do not have to take the literary criticism of the **Satyricon** and the moral criticism as vitiated simply by the speaker. The moralizing speeches (88, 140.14 etc), apart from their parodic intentions, provide a deliberate counterpoint to the immoral actions of Eumolpus and the others. What validity they might have is undercut by their dramatic function, and provide no evidence, positive or negative, by consistency or contrast, of the author's own views. It is unlikely, for instance, that his Epicureanism would be offended by Eumolpus' philosophy of *carpe diem* (cf. 99.1, 132.15, particularly lines 5-8), but its presentation is above all governed by Petronius' sceptical and opportunistic humour. The literary criticism, on the other hand, contrasts with nothing. It is not undercut by issuing from Eumolpus; it is merely appropriate, even when valid, for Eumolpus'

important trait is that he is mad about poetry. Inopportune reciters and poets are of course frequent subjects of satire in Latin literature,[23] and the satiric intent here is made quite obvious by the crowd's hostile reception of Eumolpus' poem on the Fall of Troy (90.1), and by Encolpius' own chidings (90.1, 90.3, 93.3). But there is no need to be sceptical about Eumolpus' function as a vehicle of the author's literary criticism (are we to assume that Petronius did *not* think that Horace displayed *curiosa felicitas*?) or to feel that its insights are necessarily out of character when coming from Eumolpus.

I have not tried here to do more than outline the broader strokes used in the delineation of character in the **Satyricon**. Much of the differentiation of character, as was noted earlier, is achieved by a careful attention to the style of each speaker's dialogue, and, where relevant, monologue.[24] This aspect of Petronius' character drawing, however, concerns his parodic intentions, and not, strictly speaking, his comic characterization.

*Notes*

[1] *La psychologie du rire* (Paris, 1902), p. 1.

[2] For a more complete analysis, see J. K. Schoenberger, *Glotta* 31 (1951), 22 ff., and P. A. George, *Arion* 5 (1966), 336 ff.

[3] Cf. Collignon, pp. 260 ff.

[4] *Aen.* 6. 469-70; *Ecl.* 5.16; *Aen.* 9.436.

[5] See above, pp. 193 ff.

[6] The story was a very popular one, see E. Grisebach, *Die Wanderung der Novelle von der treulosen Witwe durch die Weltliteratur* (Berlin, 1886) and P. Ure, 'The Widow of Ephesus: Some Reflections on an International Comic Theme', *Durham Univ. Journal* 18 (1956), 1 ff.

[7] See M. Rosenblüth, *Beiträge zur Quellenkunde von Petronius' Satiren* (Kiel, 1909); F. Möring, *De Petronio mimorum imitatore* (Münster, 1915), a more moderate statement; K. Preston, 'Some Sources of the Comic Effect in Petronius', *CP* 10 (1915), 260 ff.; and R. Cahen, *Le Satiricon et ses origines* (Paris, 1925), pp. 38 ff., 70 ff.

[8] For its general characteristics, see H. Reich, *Der Mimus* (Berlin, 1903), vol. I, pp. 35 ff.

[9] *Lib. Spectac.* 5.7.

[10] Cf. e.g. Juv. 1.36, 6.63; Tert. *Spect.* 17.1-5. For ancient judgments on the mime and Christian criticisms, see Reich, *op. cit.,* pp. 50 ff., 109 ff.

[11] E. Thomas, *Pétrone* (Paris, 1912), p. 213.

[12] Diomedes' description (*GLK* I, p. 491), which depends on Theophrastus, reads: *mimus est sermonis cuius libet < et > motus sine reverentia, vel factorum et turpium cum lascivia imitatio.* . . . Cf. W. Ridgeway, *The Drama and Dramatic Dances of Non-European Peoples* (Cambridge, 1915), p. 10: 'Amongst primitive people all dances are mimetic and pantomimic'.

[13] Mart. 8 *praef.*; cf. Val. Max. 2.10.8.

[14] Rosenblüth, *op. cit.*, p. 37.

[15] Given the various literary influences that make themselves felt in the *Cena*, Rosenblüth's comparison (*op. cit.*, p. 53) of the whole episode to the mimes of Herodas and Theocritus must not be taken too seriously.

[16] See Preston (*art. cit.* above) for an exhaustive—and exhausting—survey of the possibilities.

[17] Cf. Quint. *Inst.* 6.3.8: *risus res levis et quae a scurris et mimis moveatur.*

[18] Compare 56.8-10 with Suet. *Aug.* 75.

[19] See A. E. Housman, *CR* 32 (1918), 162.

[20] Where the text is nonsensical, I would suggest: *super scorpionem locustam* (following Gaselee), *super sagittarium oculatam, super capricornum caprum et cornutam.*

[21] See further the explanations in the index of names to Ernout's edition.

[22] See p. 104, n. 2.

[23] Cf. e.g. Juv. 1.2 ff., 3.9; Mart. 3.44, 45.

[24] See pp. 119 ff., and P. A. George, *Arion* 5 (1966), 336 ff.

### Bibliography

This is not a complete bibliography of Petronius, as there is little here on the text or the manuscript tradition, on the details of the language and style, or on the various philological and historical problems. It does however include the main editions, and some of the general, or critical, works on Petronius, as well as the more important articles and books on the work and its background which are cited in the notes. A reasonably complete bibliography may be compiled with the aid of S. Gaselee, 'The Bibliography of Petronius', *Trans. of the Bibliographical Society* 10 (1909) 141-233; M. Stirling, *Addenda et Corrigenda to 'The Bibliography of Petronius' by Stephen Gaselee*, Pts. I and II, 1931

(MS in the Cambridge University Library); *L'Année Philologique;* E. Lommatzsch, *Bursians Jahresberichte für das klassische Altertum* 175 (1919) 98 ff.; 204 (1925) 215 ff.; 235 (1932) 142 ff.; 260 (1938) 94 ff.; R. Helm, *ibid.* 282 (1945) 5 ff.; R. Muth, *Anzeiger für die Altertumswissenschaft* 9 (1956) 1-22; H. C. Schnur, *CW* 50 (1957) 133-6, 141-3; and A. Rini, *Petronius in Italy* (New York, 1937).

Abbott, F. F., 'The Use of Language as a Means of Characterisation in Petronius', *CP* 2 (1907) 43 ff.

————, 'The Origin of the Realistic Romance among the Romans', *CP* 6 (1911) 257 ff.

Altamura, D., 'Quibus ex Graeca lingua translatis verbis in Cena Trimalchionis enarranda Petronius usus sit', *Latinitas* 6 (1958) 194 ff.

Arrowsmith, W., *The Satyricon of Petronius.* Translated and with an Introduction. Ann Arbor 1959.

————, 'Luxury and Death in the *Satyricon*', *Arion* 5 (1966) 304 ff.

Auerbach, E., *Mimesis, the Representation of Reality in Western Literature* (trans.) (New York 1957).

Bacon, H. H., 'The Sibyl in the Bottle', *Virginia Quarterly Review* 34 (1958) 262 ff.

Bagnani, G., 'And Passing Rich', *Phoenix Supplt.* 1 (Toronto 1952) 218 ff.

————, *Arbiter of Elegance, Phoenix Supplt.* 2 (Toronto 1954).

————, 'Encolpius: Gladiator Obscenus', *CP* 51 (1956) 24 ff.

————, 'The House of Trimalchio', *AJP* 75 (1954) 16 ff.

————, 'Trimalchio', *Phoenix* 8 (1954) 77 ff.

Bailey, C., *Epicurus*, Oxford 1926.

Baldwin, F. T., *The Bellum Civile of Petronius*, New York 1911.

Balsdon, J. P. V. D., *Roman Women*, London 1963.

Barnes, J. W. B., 'Egypt and the Greek Romance', *Mitteil. aus. d. Papyrussamml. d. Öst.-Nat. Bibl.* n.s. 5 (1956) 29 ff.

Beck, C., *The Age of Petronius*, Cambridge, Mass. 1856.

Bendz, G. 'Sprachliche Bemerkungen zu Petron', *Eranos* 39 (1941) 27 ff.

Bickel, E., 'Petrons Simplicitas bei Tacitus', *RhM* 90 (1941) 269 ff.

Birt, T., 'Zu Petron', *PhW* 45 (1925) 95.

Bogner, H., 'Petronius bei Tacitus', *H* 76 (1941) 223 f.

Boissier, G., *Étude sur la vie et les ouvrages de M. T. Varron*, Paris 1861.

————, *L'Opposition sous les Césars*, Paris 1875.

Bonner, S. F., *Roman Declamation under the Empire*, Liverpool 1948.

Borszák, K., 'Die *Simplicitas* und römische Puritanismus', *EPhK* 70 (1947) 1 ff.

Browning, R., 'The Date of Petronius', *CR* 63 (1949) 12-14.

————, 'The Date of Petronius', *CR* 63 (1949) 28-9.

Bücheler, F. *Petronii Arbitri Satirarum Reliquiae*, Berlin 1862.

Bürger, K., 'Der antike Roman vor Petronius', *H* 27 (1892) 345 ff.

Burman, *Titi Petronii Arbitri Satyricôn quae supersunt*. Curante Petro Burmanno. Editio altera. Amsterdam, 1743.

Cahen, R., *Le Satiricon et ses origines*, Paris 1925.

Carratelli, G. Pugliese, 'Tabulae ceratae Herculanenses', *PP* 3 (1946) 381.

Ciaffii, V., *La Struttura del Satyricon*, Turin 1955.

————, *Petronio e Apuleio*, Turin 1960.

Cichorius, C., 'Petronius und Massilia', *Römische Studien*, Leipzig 1922, pp. 438 ff.

Cizek, E., 'Autour de la date du Satyricon de Pétrone', *Stud. Clas.* 7 (1965) 197 ff.

Collignon, A., *Étude sur Pétrone. La Critique littéraire, l'imitation et la parodie dans le Satiricon*, Paris 1892.

Cordier, A., *L'allitération latine. Le procédé dans l'"Enéide" de Virgile*, Paris 1939.

Courtney, E., 'Parody and Literary Allusion in Menippean Satire', *Philologus* 106 (1962) 86 ff.

Crum, R. H., 'Petronius and the Emperors', *CW* 45 (1951) 161 ff., 197 ff.

de Guerle, J. N. M., *Recherches Sceptiques sur Pétrone*, Paris 1797.

de Vreese, J. G. W. M. *Petron 39 und die Astrologie*, Amsterdam 1927.

Desmouliez, A., 'Sur la polémique entre Cicéron et les Atticistes', *REL* 30 (1952) 168 ff.

Downer, J. W., *Metaphors and Wordplays in Petronius*, Waco, Texas 1913.

Duff, A. M., *Freedmen in the Early Roman Empire*, Cambridge 1958.

Dugas, L., *La psychologie du rire*, Paris 1902.

Enia, M., *Il Satiricon e il suo autore Petronio Arbitro*, Palermo 1899.

Ernout, A., *Le Satiricon de Pétrone*. Texte et Traduction. 4th edn. Paris 1958.

Faider, P., *Études sur Sénèque*, Ghent 1921.

Feix, J., *Wortstellung und Satzbau in Petrons Roman*, Breslau 1934.

Ficari, Q., *La figura di Trimalchione nel'Satiricon' di Petronio Arbitro*, Lucera 1910.

Freud, S., *Jokes and their Relation to the Unconscious*, London 1960.

Friedländer, L., *Petronii Cena Trimalchionis*, 2nd edn. Leipzig 1906.

Garrido, I. M., 'A Note on Petronius' *Satyricon* 135', *CR* 44 (1930) 10 f.

Gaselee, S., *Some Unpublished Materials for an Edition of Petronius*, (1909). Unpubld. Diss. Camb. Univ. Lib.

George, P. A., 'Style and character in the *Satyricon*', *Arion* 5 (1966) 336 ff.

Gottschlich, J., 'De parodiis Senecae apud Petronium', *Miscellaneorum Philologicorum libellus zu Friderici Haase Jubiläum* (Breslau 1863).

Gresseth, G. K., 'The Quarrel between Lucan and Nero', *CP* 52 (1957) 24 ff.

Griffin, M. T., 'De Brevitate Vitae', *JRS* 52 (1962) 104-13.

Grimal, P., 'Sur quelques noms propres de la *Cena Trimalchionis*', *RPh* 16 (1942) 161 ff.

Griesbach, E., *Die Wanderung der Novelle von der treulosen Wittwe durch die Weltliteratur*, Berlin 1886.

Grube, G. M. A., *The Greek and Roman Critics*, London 1965.

von Guericke, A., *De linguae vulgaris reliquiis apud Petronium et in inscriptionibus parietariis Pompeianis*, Gumbinnen 1875.

Haley, H. W., 'Quaestiones Petronianae', *HSCP* 2 (1891) 1 ff.

Haskins, C. E., *M. Annaei Lucani Pharsalia* (ed.). With an Introduction by W. E. Heitland. Cambridge 1887.

Hausrath, A., 'Die ionische Novellistik', *NJA* 33 (1914) 441 ff.

Headlam, W., *Herodas*, Cambridge 1922.

Heinz, K., *Das Bild Kaiser Neros*, Bern 1948.

Heinze, R., 'Petron und der griechische Roman', *H* 34 (1889) 494 ff.

Heitland, W. E., see Haskins.

Helm, R., *Der antike Roman*, 2nd. edn. Göttingen 1956.

Heraeus, W., *Die Sprache des Petronius und die Glossen*, Leipzig 1899.

Herter, H., *De Priapo*, Giessen 1932.

Hertling, C., *Quaestiones mimicae*, Strasburg 1899.

Highet, G., 'Petronius the Moralist', *TAPA* 72 (1941) 176 ff.

———, *Juvenal the Satirist*, Oxford 1956.

Hirzel, R., *Der Dialog*, Leipzig 1895.

Housman, A. E., 'Jests of Cicero, Plautus and Trimalchio', *CR* 32 (1918) 162.

Iannelli, C., 'Dissertatio tertia qua Petronii Arbitri aetas constituitur', *In Perottinum codicem . . . Dissertationes Tres* (Naples 1811) pp. 117-316.

Jensen, C., *Philodemus über die Gedichte, fünftes Buch*, Berlin 1923.

Kent, R. G., see Sturtevant.

Kempe, P., *De clausulis Petronianis*, Greifswald 1922.

Kindt, B., 'Petron und Lucan', *Philologus* 51 (1892) 355 ff.

Klebs, E., 'Zur Komposition von Petronius' Satirae', *Philologus* 47 (1889) 623 ff.

———, 'Petroniana', *Philologus Suppltbd.* 6 (1893) 659 ff.

Lavagnini, B., *Eroticorum Graecorum fragmenta papyracea*, Leipzig 1922.

Le Coultre, J., 'Notes sur Pétrone', *Mélanges Boissier* (Paris 1903) pp. 326 ff.

Levi, M. A., *Nerone e i suoi tempi*, Milan 1949.

Lommatzsch, E. (with J. Segebade), *Lexicon Petronianum*, Leipzig 1898.

Ludwig, E., *De Petronii sermone plebeio*, Marburg 1869.

McCague, E. S., *Clausulae in Petronius* (1930). Unpubld. Thesis. Univ. of Pittsburgh.

MacKendrick, P. L., '*The Great Gatsby* and Trimalchio', *CJ* 45 (1950) 307 ff.

Maiuri, A., *La Cena di Trimalchione di Petronio Arbitro*, Naples 1945.

———, 'Petroniana', *PP* 3 (1948) 103 ff.

Marbach, A., *Wortbildung, Wortwahl und Wortbedeutung als Mittel der Characterzeichnung bei Petron*, Giessen 1931.

Marchesi, C., *Petronio*, Rome 1921.

Marmorale, E. V., '*Cena Trimalchionis*' *testo critico e commento*, Florence 1947.

———, *La questione Petroniana*, Bari 1948.

Martin, J., *Symposion, die Geschichte einer literarischen Form*, Paderborn 1931.

Martins, F., 'A crise do meravilhoso na epopeia Latina', *Humanitas* 1 (1947) 25 ff.

Mason, H. A., 'Is Juvenal a Classic?': *Critical Essays in Roman Literature: Satire*, London 1963, pp. 93 ff.

Mendell, C. W., 'Petronius and the Greek Romance', *CP* 12 (1917) 158 ff.

Michenaud, G., 'Les sons du vers Virgilien', *LEC* 21 (1953) 343 ff.

Momigliano, A., 'Literary Chronology of the Neronian Age', *CQ* 38 (1944) 96 ff.

Möring, F., *De Petronio mimorum imitatore*, Münster 1915.

Mössler, J. G., *Commentatio de Petronii poemate 'De Bello civili'*, Breslau 1842.

———, *Quaestionum Petroniarum specimen quo poema 'De bello civili' cum 'Pharsalia' Lucani comparatur*, Hirschberg 1857.

Müller, K., *Petronii Arbitri Satyricon*, Munich 1961.

———, (with W. Ehlers), *Petronius Satyrica: Schelmengeschichte*, Munich 1965.

Münscher, K., *Senecas Werke, Untersuchungen zur Abfassungszeit und Echtheit, Philologus Suppltbd.* 16 (Leipzig 1922).

Nelson, H. L. W., *Ein Unterrichtsprogramm aus neronischer Zeit, dargestellt auf Grund von Petrons Satiricon, c. 5*, Amsterdam 1956.

Norden, E., *Die antike Kunstprosa*, Leipzig 1909.

Pack, R., 'The Criminal Dossier of Encolpius', *CP* 55 (1960) 31 ff.

Paratore, E., *Il Satyricon di Petronio I-Introduzione, II-Commento*, Florence 1933.

Pepe, L., *Studi Petroniani*, Naples 1957.

———, 'Sul monumento sepolcrale di Trimalchione', *GIF* 10 (1957) 293 ff.

Perrochat, P., *Commentaire exégétique et critique du Festin de Trimalchion*, 2nd edn. Paris 1952.

Perry, B. E., 'Petronius and the Comic Romance', *CP* 20 (1925) 31 ff.

Pétrequin, J. E., *Nouvelles recherches historiques et critiques sur Pétrone*, Paris, 1869.

Preston, K., 'Some sources of the comic effect in Petronius', *CP* 10 (1915) 260 ff.

Raith, O., *Petronius ein Epikureer*, Nuremberg 1963.

Rattenbury, R. M., 'Romance: The Greek Novel', *New Chapters in Greek Literature. Third Series*, Oxford 1933, pp. 211 ff.

Reich, H., *Der Mimus*, Berlin 1903.

Révay, J., 'Horaz und Petron', *CP* 17 (1922) 202 ff.

Ribezzo, F., 'I frammenti di libro XIV di Petronio', *RIGI* 15 (1931) 41 ff.

Rohde, E., *Der griechische Roman und seine Vorläufer*, 3rd edn. Leipzig 1914.

Rose, K. F. C., *The Date and Author of the Satyricon* (1962). Unpubld. Thesis. Bodleian Library, Oxford.

———, 'The Author of the *Satyricon*', *Latomus* 20 (1961) 821 ff.

———, 'The Date of the *Satyricon*', *CQ* 12 (1962) 166 ff.

———, 'Time and Place in the *Satyricon*', *TAPA* 93 (1962) 402 ff.

———, 'The Petronian Inquisition: An Auto-da-Fé', *Arion* 5 (1966) 275 ff.

Rosenblüth, M., *Beiträge zur Quellenkunde von Petronius' Satiren*, Berlin 1909.

Rostagni, A., 'Filodemo control l'estetica classica', *Scritti Minori* I (Turin 1955) pp. 349 ff.

Rowell, H. T., 'The Gladiator Petraites and the Date of the *Satyricon*' *TAPA* 89 (1958) 12 ff.

Rudd, W. J. N., *The Satires of Horace*, Cambridge 1966.

Sage, E. T., 'Atticism in Petronius', *TAPA* 46 (1915) 47 ff.

Salonius, A. H., *Die Griechen und das Griechische in Petrons Cena Trimalchions*, Helsingförs-Leipzig 1927.

Schissel von Fleschenberg, O., 'Die künstlerische Absicht in Petrons "Saturae" ', *WS* 33 (1911) 264 ff.

Schmid, D., *Der Erbschleicher in der antiken Satire*, Tübingen 1951.

Schnur, H. C., *The Age of Petronius Arbiter* (1957). Unpubld. Diss. New York Univ.

———, 'The Economic Background of the *Satyricon*', *Latomus* 18 (1959) 790 ff.

Schoenberger, J. K., 'Zum Stil des Petronius', *Glotta* 31 (1951) 22 ff.

Schraidt, N. E., 'Literary and Philosophical Remains in the *Satyricon* of Petronius Arbiter', *CJ* 35 (1939) 154 ff.

Segebade, J., see Lommatzsch.

Sgobbo, I., 'Frammenti dello libro XIV delle "Saturae" di Petronio', *RAL* 6.6. (1930) 355 ff.

Shero, L. R., 'The *Cena* in Roman Satire', *CP* 18 (1923) 126 ff.

Sinko, T., 'De famis et libidinis in fabula Petroniana momento', *Eos* 36 (1935) 385 ff.

―――, 'De reconstructione fabulae Menippeae Petronii', *Meander* 12 (1957) 79 ff.

Sochatoff, A. F., 'The Purpose of Petronius' *Bellum civile*: A Re-examination', *TAPA* 93 (1962) 449 ff.

Sparrow, J., *Half-Lines and Repetitions in Virgil*, Oxford 1931.

Steele, R. B., 'Literary Adaptations and References in Petronius', *CJ* 15 (1920) 283 ff.

Strilciw, N., 'De arte rhetorica in Petronii saturis conspicua', *Eos* 30 (1927) 367 ff.

Stubbe, H., *Die Verseinlagen im Petron*, *Philologus Suppltbd.* 25 (Leipzig 1933).

Studer, G., 'Über das Zeitalter des Petronius Arbiter', *RhM* 2 (1843) 50 ff., 202 ff.

Sturtevant, E. H. (with R. G. Kent), 'Elision and Hiatus in Latin Prose and Verse', *TAPA* 46 (1915) 148 ff.

Sullivan, J. P., 'Realism and Satire in Petronius': *Critical Essays on Latin Literature: Satire*, (London 1963) pp. 73 ff.

―――, *Petronius: The Satyricon and the Fragments. Translated and with an Introduction.* (Penguin Classics) Harmondsworth 1965.

Süss, W., *De eo quem dicunt inesse Trimalchionis cenae sermoni vulgari*, Dorpat 1926.

―――, *Petronii imitatio sermonis plebei qua necessitate coniungatur cum grammatica illius aetatis doctrina*, *Acta et Comm. Univ. Tartuensis* 13 (1927) 103 ff., Dorpat 1926.

―――, 'Zu Lucilius' ( II) *H* 62 (1927) 349 ff.

Thomas, E., *Pétrone*, 3rd edn. Paris 1912.

―――, 'Pétrone et le roman grec', *RIPB* 45 (1900) 157 ff.

Thomas, P., *L'âge et l'auteur du Satyricon*, Ghent 1905.

Trampe, E., *De Lucani arte metrica*, Berlin 1884.

Tremoli, P., *Le iscrizioni di Trimalchione*, Trieste 1960.

Trenkner, S., *The Greek Novella in the Classical Period*, Cambridge 1958.

Ure, P., 'The Widow of Ephesus. Some Reflections on an International Comic Theme', *Durham Univ. Journ.* 18 (1956) 1 ff.

Usener, H., *Epicurea*, Leipzig 1887.

Veyne, P., 'Vie de Trimalchion', *Annales Économies Sociétés Civilisations* 16 (1961) 213 ff.

―――, 'Trimalchio Maecenatianus', *Hommages à Albert Grenier* (Brussels 1962) pp. 1617 ff.

Veyne, P., *'Arbiter Elegantiae'*, *RPh* 37 (1963) 258 f.

―――, 'Le "je" dans le *Satiricon*', *REL* 42 (1964) 301 ff.

Westerburg, M., 'Petron und Lucan', *RhM* 38 (1883) 92 ff.

Wilamowitz-Moellendorf, U. von, 'Asianismus und Atticismus', *H* 35 (1900) 1 ff.

Wilcken, U. 'Ein neuer griechischer Roman', *H* 28 (1893) 92 ff.

―――, 'Eine neue Roman-Handschrift', *Archiv f. Papyrusforschung* 1 (1901) 255 ff.

Wilkinson, L. P., 'Philodemus and Poetry', *G & R* 2 (1933) 144 ff.

*List of Abbreviations*

Abbreviations for standard classical periodicals, where not obvious, usually conform to the conventions of *L'Année Philologique*; for ancient authors cited in the notes, to the lists in Lewis and Short and Liddell-Scott-Jones. *RE* is one of the standard abbreviations for *Pauly-Wissowa-Kroll-Mittelhaus, Real-Encyklopädie der classischen Altertumswissenschaft*. The following list of abbreviations is peculiar to this book:

*BC Carmen de bello civili*, chapters 119-124.1 of the *Satyricon*.

Bücheler *Petronii Saturae* recensuit Franciscus Buecheler. Berlin, 1862.

Burman *Titi Petronii Arbitri Satyricōn quae supersunt.* Curante Petro Burmanno. Editio altera. Amsterdam, 1743.

Ciaffi Ciaffi, V., *La Struttura del Satyricon*. Turin, 1955.

Collignon Collignon, A., *Étude sur Pétrone*. Paris. 1892.

Gaselee Gaselee, S., *Materials for an Edition of Petronius* (1907-1908). Unpublished Thesis. Cambridge University Library.

Müller *Petronii Arbitri Satyricon cum Apparatu Critico* edidit Konrad Müller. Munich, 1961.

Müller[2] *Petronius Satyrica.* Lateinisch-Deutsch von Konrad Müller und Wilhelm Ehlers. Munich, 1965.

Maiuri Maiuri, A. *La Cena di Trimalchione di Petronio Arbitro.* Naples, 1945.

Paratore Paratore, E., *Il Satyricon di Petronio.* Vols. I and II. Florence, 1933.

Rose Rose, K. F. C., *The Date and Author of the Satyricon* (1962). Unpubld. Thesis. Bodleian Library, Oxford.

## Gareth Schmeling (essay date 1969)

SOURCE: "Petronius: Satirist, Moralist, Epicurean, Artist," *The Classical Bulletin*, Vol. 45, No. 4, February, 1969, pp. 49-50, 64.

[*In the following essay, Schmeling considers Petronius's intent in the* Satyricon, *concluding that the author sought to entertain, and that the moral aspects of the satire are present only as a part of the means to the end of producing art.*]

In 1941 Gilbert Highet noted that Petronius, writing as a satirist, ought also to be considered a moralist.[1] This was novel and perhaps even a bit shocking. In 1963 Oskar Raith proposed that Petronius be regarded as an Epicurean, but one without a moral stance.[2] William Nethercut[3] proposed (perhaps on the analogy of Highet's satirist-equals-moralist theory) that just as surely as Petronius had adopted the position of an Epicurean, so he had assumed "the posture of one who relates observation from an ethical standpoint to a clearly defined situation, [and thus] can be fairly grouped among the moralists."[4] Although not necessarily agreeing that Petronius was an Epicurean, many scholars would second Nethercut's motion to accept Petronius as a moralist.[5] Then in 1967 John Sullivan set forth evidence for his view that Petronius was not a satirist, moralist, or Epicurean, but an artist.[6] All these studies have pointed up a "new Petronian question."

What was Petronius' intent in writing the **Satyricon**? It is my concern here to try to determine the intent of the author, perhaps at more than one level. The tone of the

**Satyricon**, that is, the attitude of Petronius toward the characters and their actions, is very much disputed but surely has some bearing on the intent. While the sense, the literal meaning of the **Satyricon**, is usually intelligible where the manuscripts are good, the tone of the author and his relationship to the narrator is not always clear.[7] The feeling of the reader (his experience and imagination as related to the **Satyricon**) works to interpret the sense. My concern is not to discuss the literary merits of the **Satyricon** in view of the intent of the author or to judge the **Satyricon** by the feelings of the reader, but rather to try to discuss the author's intent itself. Although I am concerned with intent here, it is perhaps irrelevant to the value of the work as a piece of literature.

Before Highet's essay in 1941 the prevailing view of Petronius and his **Satyricon** was, at best, that they were unfit for mixed company and, at worst (in the words of P. Massen), that *liberque in eodem cum suo auctore rogo flagrare debuit, non alia luce dignior.* Highet develops his argument in this direction: Petronius used the form of a Menippean satire, and to the ancient writer genre was rigidly defined and by itself disclosed the intent of the author. The intent of a satirist is, by definition, moral. Because no audience could approve of murder, theft, and outlawry, Highet reasons that Petronius must have described the false taste of his characters with an eye to correcting them: "To show their repulsiveness, to describe their constant danger and guilt . . . is to be a moralist and a satirist."[8] Highet later took this same approach to Juvenal.[9]

Oskar Raith's monograph on Petronius as Epicurean has received less than enthusiastic reviews. Nevertheless, Nethercut has accepted it and has built his Petronius-the-moralist theory on it: an Epicurean must have an ethical standpoint and consequently must be some kind of moralist.

The last in the line of theories dealing with the "new Petronian question" is that Petronius is an artist.[10] Sullivan believes that Petronius was driven to write the **Satyricon** not by the motives of a satirist but rather by those of an artist. Petronius uses his material to entertain, not to correct, censure, or chastise. If the tone does approach the satirical it is because Petronius means to use satire as a form of entertainment. The "abnormal" sexual adventures, far from being a guide book of how-not-to (Highet's view), can be judged psychoanalytically to reveal Freudian symptoms of scopophilia in the dramatic characters and perhaps in Petronius himself: "The regular choice of such incidents for insertion into the narrative may reflect an unconscious pattern of attention."[11]

It seems to me that Petronius is determined to entertain his listeners with stories of thefts, sexual adventures and misadventures. Even in the *Cena Trimalchionis* we learn of past sexual escapes and witness new ones. If it were Petronius' intent to present a coherent moral program, the atmosphere of the novel would suggest that he had failed. From beginning to end Petronius portrays the seamy side of first century provincial life. After such total immersion in what appear to be immoral stories, it would be unnatural to conclude the *Satyricon* with a moral message. Even a scene in which a character seems to condemn aberrant morals is probably not to be taken seriously. Agamemnon, who represents the worst in rhetoricians, condemns Asian rhetoric; Encolpius condemns the infidelity of his lover, only to be found more unfaithful; Eumolpus, who had just alluded to Horace's advice about *limae labor,* reels off a 295 line epyllion from the top of his head, while he is walking along the road to Croton, *versus dictabat stans pede in uno.*

An artistic approach to one episode may help illustrate Petronius' intent in the *Satyricon*. The Quartilla story (*Sat.* 16-26), though of considerable length, has seldom been considered. The scene which opens with Quartilla crashing through the outer door, closes with Quartilla peeping through the chink in the inner door at the deflowering ceremony of Pannychis. The eye of the audience follows Quartilla as she enters the room, but remains in the doorway, so to speak, and views the action from there. The whole Quartilla episode shows a constant effort to direct the spectator-reader in a special way. The scene (perhaps with dominant overtones from the mime) begins with Petronius inviting the audience to view his small portrait through the opened front door. The direction is set. After experiments on several levels of *amor* the story closes with the youth Giton consummating a marriage with seven-year-old Pannychis. Petronius presents the scene in such a way as to make sure the audience notes the direction. Along with Quartilla, who is the first to put her eye to the chink to see the consummation, the audience is also invited to view the scene. Petronius has developed a telescope effect whereby the audience (spectator-reader) first takes in the scene broadly through the outside door, then more narrowly through the inside door, and finally all attention is focused through the chink in the inside door.

Whether we can appreciate such scenes, or whether such scenes have any merit whatever, is not our concern here. We are not considering whether it is art or pornography, but rather what Petronius' intent was in writing it. He does not seem to have written it because he was a satirist-moralist or an Epicurean-moralist. Satirists and moralists do not immerse their audience in lengthy, well wrought scenes of "immorality," and then expect it to reject their work of art. Satirists and moralists work within a defined moral system, which can be recognized. But where is Petronius' system? Material is chosen by Petronius not because it fits his moral outlook, but rather because of its richness and

adaptability to his wit, humor, or satire. This is the difference between a satirist and an artist (Sullivan). Furthermore, we cannot assume out of hand with Highet that all the world disapproves of theft, murder, and outlawry.[12] At the same time it is not necessary for Petronius to approve or disapprove of the actions of his characters, who are, after all, instruments of his form of art and not mirrors of his own character. His intent was to produce an art-form, and thus he must be considered an artist. Our feelings toward his creation of art are irrelevant. We may consider it bawdy, risqué, or even pornographic. Petronius' intent was to entertain, and he decided that the best way to do it was through a novel form using wit, parody, satire, yes, even "immoral" scenes.[13]

*Notes*

[1] G. Highet, "Petronius the Moralist," *TAPA* 72 (1941) 176-194.

[2] O. Raith, *Petronius ein Epikureer* (*Erlanger Beiträge zur Sprach und Kunstwissenschaft* [Nuremberg 1963]). H. Musurillo, "Dream Symbolism in Petronius Frag. 30," *CP* 53 (1958) 108-110, had earlier hinted at this.

[3] W. Nethercut, "Petronius, Epicurean and Moralist," *CB* 43 (1967) 53-55. Nethercut does not take into account the work of E. Courtney, "Parody and Literary Allusion in Menippean Satire," *Philologus* 106 (1962) 86-100, which absolutely destroys Highet's tenet that Petronius wrote as a moralist, or the work of G. Gellie, "A Comment on Petronius," *AUMLA* 10 (1959) 89-100, who reads the *Satyricon* as a form of entertainment very closely tied to the mime.

[4] Although Nethercut (supra, n. 3) accepts the findings of Raith that Petronius was an Epicurean, most reviewers of Raith's monograph do not agree with him. Eight disagree with Raith: R. Browning, *CR* 15 (1965) 67-69; J. Delz, *Gnomon* 38 (1966) 213-215; C. de Meo, *Latinitas* 14 (1966) 305-306; G. Franco, *Maia* 18 (1966) 303-306; J. Kaimowitz, *AJP* 87 (1966) 478-481; J. Preaux, *RBPh* 43 (1965) 601-602; K. Rose, *Latomus* 22 (1964) 109-110; R. Verdière, *AC* 33 (1964) 502. Three agree with Raith: V. Tandoi, *A&R* 10 (1965) 177-178; P. Veyne, *REA* 66 (1964) 446-450; W. Krenkel, *DLZ* 87 (1966) 692-694; one abstains: E. des Places, *RSR* 52 (1964) 475-476.

[5] A partial list would include: W. Arrowsmith, *Arion* 5 (1966) 304-331; H. Bacon, *Virginia Quarterly Review* 34 (1958) 262-276; P. MacKendrick, *CJ* 45 (1950) 307-314; A. Sochatoff, *TAPA* 93 (1962) 449-458.

[6] J. P. Sullivan, *Arion* 6 (1967) 71-88; this was followed in 1968 by what must be the best treatment of Petronius in many years, *The Satyricon of Petronius: A Literary Study* (London 1968).

[7] See also E. Auerbach, *Mimesis,* tr. W. Trask (Garden City 1957) 20-43; P. George, "Style and Character in the Satyricon," *Arion* 5 (1966) 336-358; P. Veyne, "Le 'je' dans le Satiricon," *REL* 42 (1964) 301-324.

[8] Highet (supra, n. 1) p. 183.

[9] 'G. Highet, *Juvendal the Satirist. A Study* (New York 1954). H. A. Mason, "Is Juvenal a Classic," *Critical Essays in Latin Literature: Satire,* ed. J. P. Sullivan (London 1963) 93-176, is highly critical of Highet's methods and results in *Juvenal the Satirist.* Mason views Juvenal above all else as a wit and artist; this would run directly counter to Highet's conclusions.

[10] Sullivan, supra n. 6.

[11] Sullivan, *The Satyricon of Petronius,* 250.

[12] Highet, supra, n. 1, p. 193.

[13] O. Kiefer, *Sexual Life in Ancient Rome,* tr. G. & H. Highet (New York 1952) comments: "It may be said that the *Satyricon* is tolerable enough on the hypothesis that it is a classical book; but that its frank descriptions would nowadays be felt to indicate, not art, but pornography." Kiefer apparently does not understand the problem. Some credit should be given here to G. Boissier, *L' Opposition sous les Césars* (Paris 1900) 258, who apparently was the first to hint that Petronius wrote the *Satyricon* to entertain.

## H. D. Rankin (essay date 1971)

SOURCE: "Some Comments on Petronius's Portrayal of Character," in *Petronius the Artist: Essays on the Satyricon and its Author,* Martinus Nijhoff, 1971, pp. 11-31.

[*In the following essay, Rankin studies some of the major characters in the* Satyricon *as well as the discontented society in which they lived.*]

Within the broken economy of the *Satyricon*'s remains, Petronius' characters move convincingly. There are few characters in the work that are not drawn with their own special life. The Roman satiric tradition,[1] and the works of the Greek characterologists who were possibly in some rapport with the Athenian New Comedy,[2] provided a copious history and abundant material and models for his character-drawing. Nor must we omit to mention the influence upon him of older classical authors.[3] Part of the standard rhetorical education was concerned with the bundles of qualities that represented recurrent personality types.[4] Petronius took this material, which he thought was inadequate in itself and rather jaded,[5] and added to it his own digested observations of life, forming a blend of unprecedented origi-

nality in Roman letters. Life as well as literature produced his characterisation, and it is probably its contact with life which gives it its greatest measure of vigour.[6]

This aspect of Petronius' genius has produced some of the most fascinating human material in Roman literature. It is a pity that some of the ablest Petronian criticism of recent decades has emphasised so much the limitations placed upon his character-drawing power by the literary forms of his age.[7] I hope to suggest that many of the reservations expressed in such criticisms, are unnecessarily restrictive. Apart from the most prominent personae, characters in general in the *Satyricon* appear and disappear rapidly, almost as if they were flashed on to a screen.[8] They are presented with what seems to be great economy, though the cinematic impression is enhanced by the broken nature of our text. Little enough is said in narrative: they are allowed, for a considerable part, to reveal themselves by means of their own words,[9] which need not be plentiful, but are usually pregnant. Even minor characters have a sufficient depth of dimension to suggest that they have lives to lead outside the boundaries of the text.[10] In the case of the principal characters, of whom we have more particular information, we are aware that only a portion is visible above the surface. Conscious or unconscious motives are adumbrated, which may provide a basis for psychoanalytical interpretation.[11] However, the more apparently self-revealing are the words uttered by these characters, the more difficult it is to fathom their natures. They share this measure of opacity with their creator, Petronius.[12] It will be recalled also how difficult it is to estimate the personality and motives of Ovid, who, even when he is at his most apparently self-revealing, seems to keep back the essence of his personality.

Just as Petronius could penetrate other people's characters, we may infer from Tacitus' biography of him that he could analyse his own personality.[13] His insight is clearly revealed even in those minor characters who have their brief say at Trimalchio's dinner-party.[14] They are self-deceptive and yet strangely innocent boasters in their pretence that they are not merely parasites of one of their own kind who has had astonishing success. Their aggressiveness reveals a latent sense of their own lowly position,[15] which is indicated also by the crudeness of their speech and style.[16] This aggressiveness is an imitation of Trimalchio's superb arrogance which itself is a metamorph of his original lowness. Later in the work (112), Lichas, the shipowner, shows anger at the widow of Ephesus, whose story is told,[17] because he compares her defections with those of his own wife—a snap identification that occurs in his irritated and irrational mind. These are examples of the angles from which Petronius chooses to view his participants in the human tragi-farce. Certain female figures, such as Quartilla, Tryphaena, and the widow of

Croton, are sinister and sexually menacing, as well as being ridiculous. Oenothea and Proselenus are lower counterparts of Quartilla.[18] The principal three characters, Encolpius, Ascyltos and Giton, are markedly unstable, and are, like the characters of mime,[19] essentially "on the run,"[20] pursued by the intractability of the world and the inevitability of debasing misfortunes: they have no policy and in no respect are they in control of their actions. Trimalchio and his friends, however, are a circle of people who exhibit a credible, vivid, but also farcical social pattern consisting of satellites around a rich man who wishes to assume that everybody and everything orbits about him.

None of these are merely "types," though it would be possible to refer them in a general way to the human typology of the Satire, Mime, New Comedy, which was influenced by the "characterology" of Fourth Century philosophers such as Plato,[21] Aristotle,[22] Theophrastus.[23] Typology in a sense goes back to the sophists;[24] Plato produced his own array of human types in the *Republic*, which probably was influenced by Sicilian mime.[25] Aristotle's presentation of character is incidental to his philosophy, but Theophrastus presented specimens of the human personality with the meticulous care of an artist. Characterology thus stood with one foot in the philosopher's lecture hall, and the other in the kitchen of the Menippean satire. Its rhetorical and philosophical associations rigidified in the typical Greek novel, where characters are allowed to possess very few idiosyncrasies,[26] and move along almost entirely predictable lines. This sterility is probably parodied by Petronius, along with that of other literary genres; he stigmatises especially the contemporary rhetorical education, as rigid and inane. The base from which he mounts his attack is an appreciation and knowledge of the older classical authors. The epic in particular influences his approach to decadent contemporary practices. His satirical mimesis is directed against such writers as Publilius Syrus and Lucan.[27] Knowledge of the older classics provides Petronius with the necessary field of reference outside his own time and place, and he has in this antiquity a measure, mainly literary, but not exclusive of ethical implication,[28] which he can place against the debauchery and slackness, both moral and literary, of those with whom he has to live. He is not a *laudator temporis acti* of the same bitter stamp as Aristophanes, or even of the same kind as his own minor characters, one of whom (44) bemoans (a human touch) at once the decay of religion and the high price of bread.[29] He has sympathy, and he is more tolerant of the foibles of his contemporaries than he appears to be at first glance. Quite simply, he seems to have a range of awareness of literature that is very wide, surpassing all but a few of the intellectuals of his time.[30] This extends far beyond the common limits of an age of stale rhetoric and inferior popular song. As Menippus,[31] and as Petronius' own predecessors in Roman satire[32] attempted to improve and criticise

standards of social custom, so Petronius attempted in the cultural sphere to suggest standards of taste, which were not merely classical, or archaic, but were intended to be reasonable.[33]

Before we come to discuss the individual characters, we may consider an important submerged entity in the work. It is not the author's own personality; though this is of importance in the *Satyricon*, and is inevitably revealed in it and by it. It is the society itself of the First Century B.C. which is the most striking implicit "character" in the *Satyricon*. This age was the mother of Petronius and all his characters, and also of Nero and Seneca and Tigellinus. It was an age of great economic growth in the shadow of a principate which had struck root, and it produced patches of prosperity[34] from which a number of individuals benefited to a vast degree. Secure communications, the absence of serious civil war, a centralised administration composed of new men, *equites*, or freedmen—all were factors which contributed towards the increase in prosperity. Archaeological evidence from the remains of trading cities such as Ostia, is itself sufficient testimony to the movement of these times.[35] They wanted cultural anchorage, and to be admired as great patrons. They lacked judgment, but they were eager. Education was spread thinner to meet the new demand.[36] The arts adopted self-conscious and extreme forms in order to meet this demand which always sought to purchase something new and original.[37] Many of the restraints of ancient *religio* were dissolved, but the new men were more superstitious than the Republican oligarchy.[38] Philosophy was represented on as many levels of respectability as the worship of the gods. The so-called "Stoic Opposition" of those who opposed the principate in eager retrospect for the Republic's *libertas* were strongly influenced by philosophical ideas.[39] On lower levels of social and political endeavour, the philosophical basis for life was supplied by Cynic streetcorner preachers.[40]

The advent of the new rich had broken the continuity with the past almost as effectively as the civil conflict had decimated the senatorial aristocracy, and ended the hope of the old Republic's restoration. Society held the possibility of an exciting and rewarding career even for the humblest person, though not for many of such. In this society, a poor boy, even if he were an ex-slave from an Eastern province of the empire, could possibly end as a millionaire and enjoy not only the power conferred by his wealth, but a new status.[41] It was easy for Greek or Hellenised intellectuals to make a living from the nascent cultural tastes of such men.[42] A society of wandering philosophers ranged the country like goliardic singers, or like Jack Kerouac's characters in *On the Road*. Society easily tolerated the light burden which they represented. But at the same time this was an age which was heartbreaking to its more refined spirits.[43] The intellectuals' attitude to such a soceity of the rich was often *odi et amo*, and in the case of some of the less fortunate, this was speedily reduced to *odi*. The attitudes that emanated from affluence and the decreasingly less critical attitudes to materialist values depressed the intellectuals of First Century A.D. Italy, just as Plato was depressed by Syracuse.[44] The **Satyricon** reveals the dilemma of the intellectual who is torn between his desire to participate in an exciting prosperity, and his awareness of the thinness of the cultural superficies upon which his patrons oblige him to perform. Petronius expresses his difficulties in one mode; later on, Tacitus, who had clearly some sympathy for Petronius' predicament,[45] expresses his hatred of the frustrating times in another. Tacitus had the advantage of surviving to write in a period when the empire had its opportunity to draw breath after its first prolonged attack of horrors.[46] Tacitus was a man of archaic strictness and integrity.[47] Even more frustrated was Juvenal, expressing his common-sense Roman animus against a society which profited intellectual frauds and let men of worth subsist on pittances.[48]

But Petronius had the deepest comprehension of the discontents of Imperial society. He could empathise the experiences of the depressed and disaffiliated. He was less stiffened by *gravitas* than Tacitus, and not so thwarted as Juvenal. He floated with the stream for a long time, though he was at last immersed. He was jocular rather than jaundiced in his writing, and the statement which his work in general enunciates, is a calm one, no matter how irrational or hysterical are some of its components.[49] Notwithstanding this, he is doomed, and he knows it. His characters from time to time express hysterical despair, and then are switched away from it. Is this his own despair? Did he cultivate a volatility which could turn it aside for a period? If we hypothesise a literary receptacle for such despair, perhaps we might suggest that Encolpius, who narrates the novel as we have it, plays the author's part. Possibly this Encolpius is Petronius, as Petronius might have been if he had been unsuccessful. The onus of proof, however, still lies with those who would go so far as Conrad Cichorius who suggests that there are indications of a connection between Petronius and the city of Massilia from which Encolpius may have fled as scapegoat.[50] Massiliote connections, even if they are established in the case both of the author and his creation, are not conclusive evidence for the author's life-history, but the fact that the story (at least in the surviving portion) is in Encolpius' hands, counts for something. He is the mouthpiece for the intellectual discontents of the age, and his sexual impotence itself might be taken as a symbol of the age's intellectual futility. The symbolism may or may not be there, but if it is, it may even have been unconsciously implanted by this most self-conscious author. The theme of impotence is appropriate. The intellectual, in spite of Seneca and others, was powerless. The First Century A.D. was not the age of Petronius, or even of Gaius and Nero; it was in an important sense, the age of Trimalchio.

Where, within the bounds of antiquity or modernity, could one find a time more appropriate to a disillusioned wanderer like Encolpius than the age of which he is a product? Encolpius is a displaced and anomic man. He is an Odysseus for whom there is no known destination, and no homecoming of which we are aware.[51] Encolpius is carried off helpless by the tide of First Century society; he is certainly less able than Petronius to keep his footing against it. Nevertheless, Encolpius can, to some extent, discriminate the experience that flows over him. He has a high intelligence which has been sharpened by a good education. But he does not discriminate to any purpose. He allows his emotions to bear him off, and surrenders to their power in no romantic sense, but because he sees no sufficient reason to do anything else. He moves rapidly from the pole of hysterical misery and near suicide to that of extreme hilarity and unfounded optimism.[52] He has rejected conventional civilisation apart from the margin that gives him subsistence, and even this he does not positively accept.[53] He is a casual predator and occasional parasite. Even in his suicidal moments,[54] he must live, and so he must remain in some relation with his environment. Somewhere or somehow, perhaps even from the beginning, he lost the centripetal forces of conscience or reflection, and he gives the impression of a personality which has no persistent inner core, but is composed of waves of anxiety.[55] He has moved back from the "guilt culture" to the "shame culture," and he is swiftly leaving the ambience of the "shame culture" also in his retrogressive journey.[56] His personality has something of the shape of that of a Homeric hero[57] debased and chronologically displaced. He is mutable, unreflectingly egoistic, and seems to be capable of unlimited variability of attitudes which are not linked by any common element other than his capacity to react swiftly towards immediate or short term pleasure stimuli.[58]

Encolpius' "interior monologue" does not entail a Socratic observation of self so much as the egotistic objectivity of a Homeric hero describing what is happening within him, but with almost indulgent objectivity refraining from moral judgment on himself. Such a personality freely admits discreditable motives and calmly discusses their ineluctable influence upon his attitude and action. Homeric man is thought to be concerned with the circumstances of outward honour, and is not shameless. But no mark or public ridicule diverts Encolpius from his ways for more than a short time: Encolpius does not care.

To pursue the Homeric analogy a little further, we might argue that the difference between the Homeric and Petronian casts of personality was essentially this: the Homeric characters, if we follow (though at some distance) the Dodds/Snell view of their problem, were preconscientious, whereas the people we encounter in Petronius' narrative are postconscientious. The former belong to a time when conscientious self-control was not generally a condition of remaining a member of human society: the latter to a time when changing views about society and art allowed the long outmoded fluid, primitivistic shape of personality to be a possible object of artistic attention once more. This analogy is hardly affected, whether we regard "Homer" as more concerned with depicting a primitive age, or as treating a decadent one in a romantically primitivising style. On the other hand, Homeric influence in Petronius has been sufficiently striking to cause Klebs and many others to see a Homeric parody in his work. The Greek novel had Homeric associations, particularly with the *Odyssey*,[59] and Klebs' position was that Encolpius is a species of dishonourable Odysseus, pursued by the wrath of Priapus, as his illustrious predecessor was by the relentless anger of Poseidon.[60] There is a long tradition of parody connected with the Odyssey and the view that a novel which contains some specific Homeric parodies is itself a Homeric parody, remains attractive.[61] If we equate Encolpius with Odysseus, however approximately, we are faced with a pathetic and absurd "Odysseus" which perhaps is reminiscent of that in the Cynic tradition.[62] He is a wanderer with no home to go to, and no Penelope, faithful or otherwise, awaits his return.[63] How he ended in the full text of the novel, it is impossible to say. Perhaps, after all, a home was found for the wanderer—as happens to Lucius in the *Metamorphoses* of Apuleius, but considering the nature of the *Satyricon*, it is hard to imagine a serious ending, unless perhaps, as itself a final joke on the part of the author. The Odyssean homecoming is, however, paralleled by the reunion of parted lovers in the Hellenistic novel's tradition, and it is possible that Petronius ended his work with some brutal jest along these lines, involving Giton and Encolpius. His brand of realism would hardly allow any end to the wanderings that was free either from tragedy or farce. We cannot exclude the Odyssean analogy, whether we think it comes direct or by means of the Hellenistic romances. Though the text of the *Satyricon* is much broken, the cause and effect of divine wrath is easily enough seen. The origin of his bad luck may occur in the part of the novel that is lost. We are not informed what his transgression was, but clearly it was grossly offensive to Priapus.[64] In fact, Encolpius consistently commits acts which offend the gods. He manages (somewhat unnecessarily) to slaughter a sacred goose of Priapus,[65] which depresses his credit even further with the deity - and this incident reminds us of Odysseus' men killing the oxen of the Sun. A striking effect of his sin is that he is plagued by impotence.[66] His would-be mistress, Chrysis, expresses the opinion that Encolpius' fixation on Giton is the cause of his impotence, but this naturalistic explanation need not detract from the general probability of the divine curse upon him.[67] At all events, until almost the end, incidents of apparent good fortune in sexual matters turn out badly for him.[68]

Encolpius' name itself suggests sensuality and Hellenic origins.[69] Others also in the *Satyricon* have Greek names: Ascyltos for example and Giton, Encolpius' two principal companions, also Eumolpus. Agamemnon and Menelaus are minor characters, rhetoricians whose too Homeric names in themselves represent a satire upon their profession. These Greeks or Hellenised Italiotes, are probably of good education, but this is not necessarily true of Giton whose name is a a typical slave name and need not, Greek though it is, suggest an Hellenic origin. He is somewhat more vulgar than his two associates, certainly more than Encolpius, and of these two, Ascyltos seems to be rather more coarse and insensitive than Encolpius. Ascyltos' name in itself suggests something of a bravo.[70] His sexual prowess is as notable as his selfishness, and he has great physical strength. Encolpius is hardly his inferior in respect of selfishness, but he lacks the unthinking aggressiveness of his friend. Ascyltos' potency is in sharp contrast with the inhibitions that torment Encolpius. He is more violent than Encolpius, and has about him something of the aura of a gladiatorial tough and criminal bar-fly.[71] His attitude to Encolpius alternates between predatory friendship and cool treachery. The bone of contention between them is again and again the boy Giton and his sexual attractions. In some respects Ascyltos can be seen as a coarser, hostile shadow of Encolpius. We get the impression, however, that Encolpius would wish to be as aggressive himself, if he had the courage and the opportunity.[72] There is no real friendship, no *amicitia* between these two. Indeed, the tenor of the novel implies an attack upon the concept of friendship. In ch. 80 there is a bitter little poem about the fallibility and unreliability of friends, which is almost as pessimistic as any Shakespearean locus on the subject.[73]

The boy Giton is the catalyst of trouble between these two characters, and he is the third point of the persistent triangle of relationships. He is a species of "femme fatale" and he sees himself as a source of quarrelling who separates the two friends and reunites them (for more trouble) according to his whim or convenience.[74] He applies moral blackmail, by threatening to kill himself or offering himself to be killed, when rows which he has engineered flare up more fiercely than is suitable to his purpose of playing off one of the friends against the other.[75] Like other suicide threats[76] and attempts in the *Satyricon*, Giton's promises of self-destruction are not to be taken seriously. This suggests as much as anything else, a general sense of the devaluation of life. These wanderers do not care for life sufficiently to succeed in killing themselves, or even to be serious in intending to do so. It requires a Stoic or Cynic conviction to do that. They are simply the victims of outbursts of anomic despair which soon pass, so that they can revert to their old habits once more. The physically weaker members of this triad, Encolpius and Giton, are more hysterical than the more elementary Ascyltos.[77] Later in the **Satyricon**, when Ascyltos has been replaced by Eumolpus, Giton's manoeuvres in playing off Eumolpus against Encolpius are conducted with much greater finesse, and with less violent results. Even though he is a fraud in everything but his bad habits and love of dubious poetry, Eumolpus is not a violent personality. Like any other professional rhetorician or poet in the context of the **Satyricon**, he lives off his capacity to dupe the public and is perfectly contented with his way of life. He cannot be prevented, in fact, from exhibiting his art.[78] This is true also of Agamemnon and his satellite Menelaus. However, to return to Giton: there is no doubt that he possesses a cynical self-centredness and bland insolence which might ensure his survival and perhaps even make his fortune. This was an age in which ex-slaves could become rich and powerful. Giton, it turns out, is a slave; though he is a runaway, he pretends, for purposes of social convenience, to be the slave of Encolpius[79] and Ascyltos. It is just possible that Giton might develop into a magnate of similar type to Trimalchio, but it may be that Giton does not show the same shrewdness as Trimalchio in the choice of those to whom he prostitutes himself,[80] and this, together with his irrationality, may prescribe limits to his future success. Nevertheless, if he should fall into the right hands, he could be imagined as prosperous and powerful.

Trimalchio is an excellently realised character: not simply because we have so much more continuous text about him than about other individuals. It is a question of character itself. Trimalchio and his friends have a more positive view of the world, are concerned in action, and lacking any kind of introspection, develop some amazing foibles which remind the reader quite strongly of Dickens' characters. Trimalchio is a contrast to Encolpius and Ascyltos, who are buffeted about by circumstances which they make no consistent attempt to resist. Trimalchio's thoughtless dynamism and pomposity are thrown into relief by the "beatnik" passivity of these two, and of the other intellectuals, such as Agamemnon. Some of the minor figures surrounding Trimalchio, in that they are obviously hangers-on and parasites, approach the irregularity of life of Encolpius and his friends, but Trimalchio himself sets a standard of a successful career that outshines anything else of the kind that there is in the book as we have it. Credit is surely due to a person who was a slave in his youth, was a foreigner in Italy,[81] and suffered the serious reverses of his early business career. Against his ignorance and vulgarity, faults, by the way, which have been somewhat overstressed by critics,[82] there is set his immense energy and psychological resilience. It was no small achievement, having been sold into slavery in a foreign country, to gain freedom and a fortune.[83] Like other young slaves, Trimalchio was used as a sexual object by his master and later by his mistress.[84] So far from being broken in spirit by this

(or rendered touchy and unbalanced like Giton), Trimalchio set to work to maximise the advantages that could come to him from this situation. Eventually, he ceases to be the utensil, and becomes the user, for he so prevails upon the affections of his master that he obtains manumission and inherits money from him. This change from the slave situation is probably a more frequent version and a more plausible one of the Stoic paradox that only a slave is really a king.[85] Trimalchio went into a trading venture with his inheritance and when the ships laden with his merchandise came to grief, he found himself in a very difficult position. However, he liquified whatever property he had, and his wife sold her jewellery, so that he could remain solvent and try once more. This time the voyage in which he invested turned out to be a prosperous one, and he began to be rich. He then took to the more profitable and secure occupation of financing freedmen like himself.[86] No doubt the freedmen who are present at his dinner-party are in his debt.

The gloomy prognostications about the economic state of Italy that are uttered by some of the minor characters at the *Cena* may be true, for ancient prosperity was patchy, but they also indicate their own relative lack of success in the game which Trimalchio has played with genius(44). The period was a prosperous one, and social advances and social mobility were remarkable in it. Trimalchio's rise in status was phenomenal even for this time. In Ostia, a prosperous seaport that attracted people from all parts of the empire, there was a notable increase in people of freedman stock who were in high places in the community, though (unlike Trimalchio) their families only became established as a local ruling class after three generations.[87] On the other hand we know that *principes* ruled through freedmen,[88] who held high offices on the principial staff.

Much has been made of the view that Petronius despised and disliked people of Trimalchio's type. There is little evidence to support this. Petronius does not seem to have marked or consistent sympathy with any of his characters[89]—even the Encolpius who is possibly identified with himself. He shows comprehension of many aspects of human behaviour, and it is fairer to say that he understood Trimalchio rather than that he despised him. The portrait is a satirical one, and thus it has in it an element of attack, but there is little to suggest active dislike. On the other hand, Trimalchio, like the society which produced him, and like the literature which speciously (in Petronius' opinion) malnourished that society, is a fair target for mockery. There is a certain directness in Trimalchio's personality that Petronius surely did not despise. Trimalchio was ignorant but not decadent, intolerable company but not without humanity, indecent but generous, and by the standards of his time, not cruel. Trimalchio had his own form of *simplicitas*,[90] and though we have no reason to believe that Petronius would necessarily have approved entirely of anybody's *simplicitas*, (including his own),[91] he was surely, on the evidence of his literary skill as presented by the **Satyricon**, capable of making a connection between the ripe outspokenness of Trimalchio, and his own sophisticated outspokenness. Trimalchio is the reverse of Petronius' own coin—according to Tacitus' description of Petronius' character. Trimalchio is a person of heroic dimensions, whose only enemy is the inevitable death which he has tried to buy off with the splendid funeral that his wealth could procure, and to which he looks forward with a thoughtless enthusiasm as if it were a day of personal triumph. Like a heroic character of epos, he is volatile and rude,[92] but his bark is worse than his bite. He threatens dire punishments to his slaves at various points in the **Satyricon**, but always allows the offenders to go free. His mercy earns him the appearance of magnanimity, and the occasions for its exercise may be supposed to have been contrived to that end, but nevertheless, his abstention from harsh punishment is real. Whether it is sincere or not makes little difference. The number of tricks and deceptions which he has arranged to startle the guests may suggest that the offences which he forgives are concocted. We have an example of the rigged offence in the case of the pig which the cook has apparently forgotten to gut, but which in fact is stuffed with sausages which look like entrails. The cook is on the verge of punishment, but is let off.[93] This is a very clear example of the theme of pretence that runs through the work. At all events, Trimalchio remembers the slave condition which he once endured. "Slaves are human beings," he says, and invites them to the table, where they succeed in crowding the guests off the couches.[94] It is characteristic of the usual attitude that the household slaves have the benefits of his forgiveness, but not the rustic ones. When the minutes of his estate administration are read out, we find that the country slaves are not so well treated as those who are in personal contract with their master in the house. (53) This agrees not only with the customary attitude of ancient slave-owners, but also with the rather limited scope of human sympathy that is observable in Trimalchio. Perhaps even more than other characters, his sympathy is engaged by what is before his eyes, or happens to be an immediate object of apprehension. This is illustrated by Trimalchio's flirtation with his boyfriend, Croesus, in the presence of Fortunata. (64) He is insensitive to everything but the matter that is before his attention. This type of personality could concentrate intensely upon individual transactions of business from which his prosperity grew. This is combined, as it easily can be, with the enduring love of property which has however, little in it of the narrow obsession of the miser. Trimalchio wishes to be like a prince, who can spend lavishly and not count the cost. He realises his desire for self-assertion by conspicuous expenditure from apparently inexhaustible wealth, rather than by the oppression of fellow creatures.[95] He admits slaves to the human family but he does not question the fact of slavery as an institution. His perceptions are short-term, immediately concentrated, and exclude peripheral distractions; his bursts of bad temper are connected with this trait; so also is his rudeness and his inability to appreciate the finality of death—though his attitude on this last point was common enough in all kinds of temperaments. For him, death means nothing but the glories of his funeral and monument, and he does not conceive of his ego being absent, or even attenuated at the occasion of his final public appearance. It is not final. There will always be Trimalchio. His rudeness is of a piece with the shortness of grain in his perceptive personality. The immediate is all-important, and the game of draughts must be finished before the guests are attended to. (33) So too, he says, the wine served is better tonight than it was when, a couple of nights back, he had much more important people to dinner. (34) Last century, and some part of this one, periods not distinguished for good manners, have shown remarkable sensitivity to Trimalchio's rudeness. A number of authors have criticised him for it. But his rudeness is simply shortness of grain and inability to comprehend more than one thing concentratedly at a time. There is also the rudeness of pure energy: we may be reminded of the rudeness of manner in the Elizabethan age, when people of high social standing freely behaved in the rough fashion of Mr. Walter Releigh towards his father: "Box about t'will come to my father anon"—without any great harm being intended by it.[96] Certainly Trimalchio is not nearly so complex or vulnerable a personality as F. Scott Fitzgerald's Gatsby, with whom he has been compared.[97]

Fortunata and Scintilla are the only female characters in Petronius who are not presented as menacing. They are pathetic and absurd (but not unsympathetic) ex-slaves or freedwomen whose husbands have become wealthy and powerful, and who are consequently a little insecure. Fortunata, Trimalchio's wife, is not necessarily (as has been supposed) of native Roman stock.[98] This suggestion, which was based upon her name, is not convincing, for her name ("Lucky") is precisely the kind of name that might be given to a slave girl. She has been a dancer, and is reproached by her husband in a quarrel, with this fact: *"fulcipedia,"* he calls her—"hoofer." Their quarrels are violent and bitter, but the marriage (in spite of Trimalchio's male concubines) seems to be a real one. In early years, we are told, Fortunata helped the common financial cause by selling off her jewels so that Trimalchio could use the money to make one more attempt to retrieve his imperiled fortunes—"at this point Fortunata did the decent thing,"[99] says her gracious spouse. In spite of her dubious past, or because of the perpetual insecurity[100] and social contempt which it represented, she has become the model of the careful housewife. Her personality is tenuous and without colour, and her tears and impotent rage do nothing but exasperate Trimalchio in their quarrels. He is also said to be sometimes rather in fear of her. (52, 11) Scintilla, Habinnas' wife, is more or less a duplicate of Fortunata. Her name is also of the kind of pet name, "Spark," that would be quite appropriate for a slave girl. She is dominated by her husband, but the relationship, as it is depicted in our text, does not give evidence of such extremes as that of Trimalchio and Fortunata. There is a certain comradeship between the two women in their situation of gilded adversity. They admire each other's jewels; they comfort each other against the drunken horseplay and infidelity of their husbands with their respective slaves.[101]

These respectable housewives are quite distinct from the other female characters in the book. The others are menacing and sexually dominating. They provide occasions for Encolpius to prove himself impotent; those who attempt to cure him with rituals, do so in a shameful and terrifying fashion. These women represent the opposite pole of femininity to the embourgeoised Fortunata and Scintilla. Quartilla, the priestess of Priapus, treats Encolpius and his friends with similar impropriety and sexual menace. She is contemptuous of their manhood, informed as she is by the inspiration of a fertility deity whose power transcends mere individual potency, and whose worship jestingly makes light of it. The element of menace is also to be seen in Tryphaena, Circe, and Chrysis. In a more intensified and absurd form the qualities of Quartilla appear in Oenothea and Proselenos, whose ritual for curing Encolpius of his impotence amounts to a painful, obscene assault, almost more terrifying to him than Quartilla's minatory amorousness.[102]

The element of ritual and the influence of the malign god Priapus, to some extent explain the aggressiveness of the women who are so closely associated with his worship. But other women such as Tryphaena, Circe, Chrysis, and Philomela, are no less aggressive—not to speak of the treachery and unreliability of feminine nature which is implied by the folk-tale of the "Widow of Ephesus".[103] Encolpius, while consistently falling foul of female anger, is none the less attracted to women and wishes to be successful in his love affairs with them, but he meets nothing but humiliation. Also, he is impotent in his homosexual relationships (140) except in the case of Giton.

Something about Encolpius puts him in a position of impotence and contempt vis-à-vis the female characters—this something is whatever has made him impotent. The aggressiveness of the women is stimulated by Encolpius—it is not an inevitable or usual characteristic of womankind in the work's *Weltanschauung*. Others fare much better. We might say that Lichas fared marginally better than Encolpius if we had more information about him, but we gather that he has been badly worsted in a transaction involving his wife called Hedyle.[104] His attitude to Tryphaena is far from being even positive, much less dominating. He is thwarted and frantic, but after the fashion of an ordinary man and not one who is cursed with a notable disability like Encolpius. A more successful man in this sphere is Eumolpus. He presents a contrast to his fellow intellectuals. Encolpius is young, but Eumolpus is elderly; Encolpius does not create anything, but Eumolpus utters long tracts of rather boring verse, and even under threat of stoning, cannot be brought to desist.[105] Eumolpus is a wanderer, like the others; he is somewhat mad, but unlike them, his craziness seems to have some purpose,—even though the purpose itself lacks sanity, let alone honesty. He is buoyant, hopeful, full of schemes, where they are lassitudinous, and it is he who conceives the notion of passing himself off in Croton as a rich old man with no children who might well be a good quarry for legacy-hunters. He enjoys himself in a positive sense at the public's expense. He lives the life of an active and colourful rascal. His activity with Philomela's daughter, and with the boy whom he seduced while he was his tutor, testify to his potency.[106] He is not so much the victim of his own desires (as are Encolpius, Giton and Ascyltos) as the cunning manipulator of them to gain his own special ends. He resembles more than the others, a "popularizing" Epicurean type who regards the world as a place in which he must live, as comfortably as possible.[107] His only passion is for the recitation of his own bad poetry.

The power of Petronius' character portrayal, and the way in which it is wedded to the styles of speech which the characters respectively use, which is individual while it still remains Petronian, makes it the more regrettable that large tracts of the book are lost. There are, as it is, many minor characters who create their own atmospheres, such as the haughty steward who magnanimously forgives his fellow slave a whipping,[108] the greasy kitchen slave who impertinently challenges Trimalchio to a bet (they are supporters of rival racing teams).[109] The fact that they all speak the same language which is Petronius' own distinctive language, without any abatement in the individuality which they possess, may remind us of (say) Dickens, but would I think, remind Petronius' contemporaries of Homer. A writer of powerful communicative genius leaves his reader with a sense of the inevitability of his mode of presentation and context. His characters are all imbued with his peculiar thought and emit the special flavour of his own philosophy of life. This, I would suggest, is true of Petronius' portrayals of character.

### Notes

[1] J. P. Sullivan takes the view that the *Satyricon* rather than being a *Kreuzung der Gattungen* is a natural development within the boundaries of Menippean satire:

*The Satyricon of Petronius* London 1968, 115, *cf.* 89; C. A. Van Rooy, *Studies in Classical Satire and Related Literary Theory*, Leiden 1965, 154-5. But *cf.* W. Kroll, *Studien zum Verständnis der Römischen Literatur*, Darmstadt 1959, 223-4 "Die Kreuzung der Gattungen."

[2] Ariston of Ceos, Aratos, and Philodemos the Epicurean philosopher of the First Century B.C. wrote characterologies: see Schmid-Stählin, *Geschichte der Griechischen Literatur* II, 1. 64. The view that Menander had been a pupil of Theophrastus is best treated with caution: A. Lesky, *History of Greek Literature* (transl. Willis, De Heer) London 1966, 644-5. . . .

[3] Sullivan 165, 167.

[4] S. F. Bonner, *Roman Declamation in the Late Republic and Early Empire*, California 1949, 160-1.

[5] *Satyricon* 1. 1-3.

[6] Which Sullivan does not regard as naturalistic in the modern sense: 97; E. Auerbach, *Mimesis*, transl. Trask, Princeton 1953, 28-33.

[7] Sullivan, 97, 101, 104: "the work is not so much a depiction of the real, for our moral instruction, as a denigration of the real." See also refs at note 6 above.

[8] *Cf.* E. Dujardin, *Le Monologue Intérieur*, Paris 1931, 47-8.

[9] Sullivan 59, 69, 82; R. Hirzel, *Der Dialog*, Lips 1895, II 37.

[10] 30, 6-11; 70, 13.

[11] Sullivan, ch. VII 232-253; which is a modification of his paper "The *Satyricon* of Petronius, some Psychoanalytical Considerations," *American Imago* Vol. 18, 1961, 325-369: he argues that Petronius had scopophilic tendencies.

[12] See Tacitus' account of his personality: *Annales* XVI, 17-20.

[13] The expressions in Tacitus' biography: *ac dicta factaque eius quanto solutiora et quandam sui neglegentiam praeferentia, tanto gratius in speciem simplicitatis accipiebantur.* (*Annales* XVI, 18,2) and: *neque tamen praeceps vitam expulit, sed incisas venas, ut libitum, obligatas aperire rursum et adloqui amicos, non per seria aut quibus gloriam constantiae peteret. audiebatque referentis nihil de immortalitate animae et sapientium placitis, sed levia carmina et facilis versus.* (19, 2) suggest a certain capacity for self-examination.

[14] 41,9; 46; Frank Frost Abbott, "The Use of language as a means of Characterisation in Petronius," *Classical Philology* 2, 43-50. On the style of the more sophisticated characters: Peter George's article "Style and Character in the Satyricon," *Arion* Vol. V, 3, 336-358 analyses the literary elements in their talk.

[15] Perhaps they were agents of his: H. C. Schnur, "The Economic Background of the *Satyricon*," *Latomus*, 18, 1959, 790-9, 792.

[16] Abbott, 43-4.

[17] For Lichas' reaction to the story: 113, 2-4: *at non Lichas risit, sed iratum commovens caput "si iustus" inquit "imperator fuisset, debuit patris familiae corpus in monumentum referre, mulierem affigere cruci". non dubie redierat in animum Hedyle expilatumque libidinosa migratione navigium. sed nec foederis verba permittebant meminisse, nec hilaritas, quae occupaverat mentes, dabat iracundiae locum*: Assuming that Hedyle is his wife.

[18] Also the un-named girl accompanying the peasants: 14, 5 *mulier operto capite, quae cum rustico steterat*, who, if 16, 3 (*illa scilicet quae paulo ante cum rustico steterat*) is accepted as genuine, may be the maid of Quartilla. On this question, Sullivan 46-7, Nisbet's review of Konrad Müller's text *Journal of Roman Studies* 1962, 227-8.

[19] *The Mimes of Herodas* by W. Headlam, A. D. Knox, Cambridge 1966, Introduction esp. *xxii-xxiii*.

[20] For this comical "chase" associated wlth the mime: Cicero *Pro Caelio* 65: *Mimi ergo iam exitus, non fabulae; in quo cum clausula non invenitur, fugit aliquis e manibus, dein scabilla concrepant, aulaeum tollitur*: see R. G. Austin's comment *ad. loc. M. Tulli Ciceronis, Pro Marco Caelio Oratio*, Oxford 1952.

[21] *Rep.* 548 d. *Gorg.* 493 d: R. G. Ussher's comments, *The Characters of Theophrastus* Intro. 27; For Plato's description of the "timocratic" man: *Rep.* 549 d ff; the "democratic" man: 559 d ff., the "tyrannical" man: 571 a ff. H. Reich, *Der Mimus*, Berlin 1903 Bd. II, 355, 360, 363.

[22] On resemblances between Theophrastus' [*Kharakteres*] and Aristotle, Ussher, 8-11, who is careful to stress the difference in style and time of Theophrastus' work from those of his master (at *Rhet.* 9, 26; III, 7. 6, for example). Also E. Schwartz, *Ethik der Griechen* edit. Richter, Stuttgart 1951, 16 f.

[23] Characterology as such first emerges in its full form with Theophrastus' [*Kharakteres*] Schmid-Stählin, II, 1. 64. Ussher does not agree with the view that this work has a direct ethical purpose, and suggests that it

might have been intended to serve for a *Poetic*.

[24] If we accept that Thucydides' descriptions of the character of peoples (as in Thuc. I, 70) or individuals (Pericles: Thuc. II, 65) or the so-called Melian Dialogue (Thuc. V, 84-114) are (a) sufficiently in the manner of [*ethopoia*] (b) are sophistic and dialogue: R. Hirzel, *Der Dialog* I, 45, 53; Protagoras was said to be the inventor of the "Socratic" dialogue Diog. 9, 53 (Hirzel 56).

[25] Reich, *op. cit.*

[26] F. A. Todd, *Some Ancient Novels*, Oxford 1940, 80.

[27] Sullivan 67, 168-9, 191-2; H. Stubbe, "Die Verseinlagen im Petron," *Philologus Supplement* bd. XXV Hefte, 1933 (esp. 103) argues that stylistically, the *Bellum Civile* poem is Vergilian rather than imitative of Lucan's style, and an implied criticism of L. on stylistic as well as other grounds. *cf.* K. F. C. Rose, "Problems of Chronology in Lucan's career," *T. A. P. A.* Vol. XCVII, 1966, 379-396.

[28] Sullivan, 259: "If there is a 'quasi-moral' principle at work, it is the principle, invoked sometimes by Horace also, of taste, be it taste in literature or behaviour; but taste itself dictates that even this be not taken too seriously" *surtout pas de zèle*: *cf.* J. F. Killeen on Petronius, "James Joyce's Roman Prototype," *Comparative Literature* IX, 3, 1957, 193-203, rejects alike (201) the tendency to see ethically significant implications and intentions in the *Satyricon* (Burman, Klebs and others) and in *Ulysses*.

[29] 44. 2, 3, 17, 18; Schnur, *op. cit.*; P. A. Brunt, "The Roman Mob," *Past and Present*, 35, 1966, 3-27.

[30] A. Rini, *Petronius in Italy*, N. Y. 1957. 159. E. Courtney, "Parody and Literary allusion in Menippean Satire," *Philologus* 102, 1/2, 1962, 86-100.

[31] E. Zeller, *Philosophie der Griechen* II i. (ed. 5 Darmstadt 1963) 286-7; E. Rohde, *Der Griechische Roman*, Hildesheim 1960, 267.

[32] Note above 28; Varros' work sometimes had a distinct political purpose, . . . Hirzel I, 455.

[33] Sullivan, 89; G. M. A. Grube, *The Greek and Roman Critics*, London 1965, 196-8; L. P. Wilkinson, "Philodemus and Poetry", *Greece and Rome* 2. 1933, 144 ff.

[34] On the relative smallness of Trimalchio's fortune, Sullivan, 150.

[35] Schnur, 791; Russell Meiggs, *Roman Ostia*, Oxford 1960, 70.

[36] Meiggs, 222-3.

[37] Petronius ridicules artistic extremes in his parodies, but it may be recalled that in fact, at a celebration of games given by Nero, *inter pyrricharum argumenta taurus Pasiphaaen ligneo invencae simulacro abditam iniit, ut multi spectantium crediderunt* (Suet, *Nero* 12) *cf.* 21: *inter cetera cantavit Canacen parturientem Oresten matricidam etc.*

[38] *cf.* the story of the *versipellis*, 62, also its echo 63, and the resultant superstitious dread on the part of Trimalchio's guests in 64. The Roman senatorial "establishment" at least endeavoured to control the introduction of new magico-religious ideas into the city: A. Toynbee, *Hannibal's Legacy*, Oxford 1965, Vol. II, 400 f, 912 f; Augustus caused a large number of the Sibylline oracles to be destroyed in 12 B.C. on the grounds that: *nullis vel parum idoneis auctoribus ferebatur*, whereas he preserved the genuine ones (Suet. *Aug* 31. 1.). On this question see G. W. Clarke "The Burning of Books and Catullus 36", *Latomus* XXVII, 515 ff. The attitude of the Republican ruling class to magic and the like was essentially social—they feared that it might subvert society, indeed the attitude that underlay the S. C. *de Bacchanalibus*, 186 B.C. is strikingly persistent in Tacitus' stigmatisation of Christianity as an *exitiabilis superstitio* (*Annales* XV, 44, 4). Though the magic dreads of Trimalchio and his friends may be native Italian in origin and thus not eligible for suppression and severe reprobation, few respectable persons of the Republic would have admitted them, and in Imperial times, adherents of the Republican style like Tacitus, would have despised them. Servilia gave money to *magi* to see if her father Soranus would be spared, which is made a charge against her in her trial together with her father (Tac. *Annales* XVI, 30, 2; 31, 1).

[39] Stoics could hardly be expected to feel much sympathy with the pretensions of a princeps who allowed himself to be worshipped as a god, as emerges in the reign of Gaius, E. V. Arnold, *Roman Stoicism*, London 1911, 393, and on the "Old Roman"—Stoic opposition to Nero, 394-9; B. W. Henderson, *The Life and Principate of the Emperor Nero*, London 1903, 294-302, also ch. XI *passim*.

[40] There was some of this plain outspokenness even in such respectable figures as Demetrius the Cynic, the friend of Thrasea: Dio Cassius 66, 11, 13; Suet Vesp. 13. See also H. Musurillo, *Acts of the Pagan Martyrs*, Oxford 1954.

[41] 75, 10 - 77, 7.

[42] A. H. Salonius: "Die Griechen und das Griechische in Petrons Cena Trimalchionis", *Societas Scientiarum Fennica, Commentationes Humanarum Litterarum*,

Helsingfors 1927, II i, 15.

[43] Even under an earlier and more humane dispensation, Horace had been able to withdraw from too close an association with the *princeps*, Suet. *Vita Horati* 25, C. L. Roth.

[44] Plato *Ep.* VII 326 b, c.

[45] This is indicated by the amount of interest shown by Tacitus in the life history of P. *cf.* H. D. Rankin, "On Tacitus' Biography of Petronius," *Classica et Mediaevalia* XXVI. 1-2 1965, 233-45; (see below, 106-108).

[46] Tacitus, *Histories* I, 1.

[47] R. Syme, *Tacitus*, Oxford 1958, 553.

[48] Juvenal III 147-53, VII 66 ff. G. Highet, *Juvenal the Satirist*, Oxford 1959, 7-19.

[49] A statement of what B. E. Perry, *The Ancient Romances, A Literary-Historical Account of their Origins*, California 1967, calls his "profound but latent pessimism." This coolness is characteristic of Epicurean literary doctrine: Sullivan 57; Grube, 195-6; Wilkinson 146, 149-50; Philodemus *Über Die Gedichte*, C. Jensen, Berlin 1923, II, 21 - III 5 (ff. 11,13).

[50] C. Cichorius, "Petronius und Massilia," *Römische Studien* Berlin 1922, 138-9.

[51] Such as the final reconciliation with life in Apuleius' *Metamorphoses*.

[52] For examples of his instability, 16-25; 80, 7; 82, 4.

[53] As in the case of the "beats" so it might be said of P's character that: "the pursuit of long-range goods is abandoned for the pleasures and the anguish of the moment." Elwin H. Powell in Arnold H. Rose, *Human Behavior and Social Process, An Interactionist Approach*, London 1962, 361.

[54] 80, 7.

[55] *Cf.* J. P. Donleavy's "Sebastian Dangerfield" in *The Ginger Man*, or (a most extreme example of antiheroism) Keith Waterhouse's *Jubb*.

[56] E. R. Dodds, *The Greeks and the Irrational*, California 1951, 17 ff.

[57] Dodds, *op. cit.* in his chapter "Agamemnon's Apology" *passim*.

[58] *Cf.* G. S. Kirk, *Homer and the Epic*, Cambridge 1965, 101-2, on the "monumental" aspect of Homer's

work exemplified in his use of pre-existing material.

[59] A theme drawn into Hellenistic literature and into the novel via the later tragedy: E. Rohde, *Der Griechische Roman und seine Vorläufer*, Hildesheim 1960, 110, 111.

[60] E. Klebs, "Zur Composition von Petronius' Satirae," *Philologus* 47, 1889, 623-635.

[61] Courtney, *op. cit.*

[62] R. Hoïstad, *Cynic Hero and Cynic King*, Uppsala 1948: and (without prejudice to the question whether or not Antisthenes is classifiable as a proto-cynic), Mullach, Frag. Antist. 25, 26, 27, ([*homerika*] of Antisthenes) deal with Odysseus.

[63] A conjecture which (I suggest) is not unreasonable in itself but the probability of which is inevitably subject to the incomplete nature of the text which we possess.

[64] Klebs, *op. cit.*; Cichorius, *op. cit.*; Sullivan, 40 ff.

[65] 136, 5-6.

[66] 128, 2, 8-9; 129, 5-7; 133, 3; 134; 139, 4 (probably); 140, 11.

[67] 128, 8-9.

[68] R. Heinze, "Petron und der Griechische Roman," *Hermes* XXXIV 1899, 494-519, esp. 498.

[69] Salonius, 6: "auf dem Schoss Sitzenden." The name does occur in inscriptions etc. H. Stephanus, *Thesaurus L. Gr.* s.v.; Pape, *Griechische Eigennamen*.

[70] Salonius 6: it means "undisturbed, untouched." . . .

[71] Notice his extreme aggressiveness and brutalised physique and mentality, 80; 92, 2: there is something "gladiatoral" perhaps about Encolpius' past: see 9, 9; 81, 3; 130, 20. In 80 we have the distinct impression of an inexpert gladiatorial combat between E. and A. See Burmann's comments *ad loc*, and the note of Gonsalius de Salas (in the Burmann edition).

[72] 82, 1-3: *haec locutus gladio latus cingor, et ne infirmitas militiam perderet, largioribus cibis excito vires. mox in publicum prosilio furentisque more omnes circumeo porticus. sed dum attonito vultu efferatoque (animo) nihil aliud quam caedem et sanguinem cogito frequentiusque manum ad capulum, quem devoveram, refero, notavit me miles, sive ille planus fuit sive nocturnus grassator, et "quid tu" inquit "commilito ex qua legione es aut cuius centuria?"*

[73] 80, 9:

> nomen amicitiae sic, quatenus expedit, haeret;
> calculus in tabula mobile ducit opus.
> cum fortuna manet, vultum servatis, amici;
> cum cecidit, turpi vertitis ora fuga.

[74] He comes between them when they are about to fight, announces that he is the cause of dissension, offers himself to be killed, 80, 4: he quite unexpectedly (from Encolpius' point of view) elects to go off with Ascyltos. Later (91, 8) he admits: *cum duos armatos viderem, ad fortiorem confugi.*

[75] 80, 4; 94, 15; 101, 7; 108, 11.

[76] 30, 7; 94, 8; 97, 9; 101, 2; 108, 10-11; 132.

[77] 92, 7-11.

[78] Even at the risk of a stoning, 90, 1 or a beating, 92, 6.

[79] The reference to him as a *gladiator* 9, 9, might suggest slave status: Tryphaena's remark, 105, 11: *meruisse quidem contumeliam aliquam fugitivos, quibus in odium bona sua venissent*, might also suggest this; it is possible that the plurals simply refer to Giton.

[80] 75, 11.

[81] Trimalchio is not Roman: *tam magnus ex Asia veni quam hic candelabrus est*: 75, 10: on the question of the Semitic name: *Trimalchio* see L. Friedländer's note on 26, *Petronii Cena Trimalchionis*, Amsterdam 1960, 209; W. D. Lowe, *Petronii Cena Trimalchionis*, Cambridge 1905, 3. Salonius, 6; Meiggs, 224: "Malchio, Malchus" etc.

[82] For instance: Dill, *Roman Society from Nero to Marcus Aurelius*; Salonius 20: J. W. Duff, *Roman Satire*, Cambridge 1937, 101-5; J. W. Duff, *Freedmen in the Early Empire*, repr. Cambridge 1958, 126: we may recall the traditional anti-intellectualism of the Romans: C. Marius was completely ignorant of Greek culture: Sallust *Jug.* 85. No doubt Petronius used Trimalchio as a figure for his satire: Sullivan 150-7 gives a balanced estimate of the whole question.

[83] 75, 10 suggests this: so also do the references to *ipsimus* and *ipsima* (75, 11) *cf.* the voluntary entry into servitude of one of T's friends 57, 4.

[84] Notes: 81, 83 above: also Herodas *Mime*, V.

[85] We may note that an absurd version of this familiar paradox is attributed to Bion: Hoïstad: 178. B. was reputed to be the author of a book . . . from which apophthegms on the subject may be derived: Mullach

fg. 1.

[86] 76, 9-10 *postquam coepi plus habere quam tota patria mea habet, manum de tabula: sustuli me de negotiatione et coepi (per) libertos faenerare.*

[87] Meiggs, 70.

[88] Duff, *Freedmen* etc. ch. VIII.

[89] Sullivan, 265-7.

[90] The question of Petronius' *simplicitas* as suggested by the phrase of Tacitus *in speciem simplicitatis* which describes how people regarded P's more outrageous actions and sayings (Tac. *Annales* XVI, 18, 2) has been subject to many different interpretations: see Stubbe, "Die Verseinlagen in Petronius," *Philologus* suppl. 25 Hft. 2. 150-1; H. Bogner, *Hermes* 1941, 223-4; E. Bickel, *RhM* 1941, 269-72. Quite probably archaic "simplicity" is intended (Bickel) in some form or other. One of the best descriptions of *species simplicitatis* in modern literature is to be found in F. Scott Fitzgerald's *Tender is the Night*, Bodley Head edit. Vol. II, London 1959, 91: the outrageous, apparently innocent joke about the bathing-dress.

[91] Tacitus probably liked P's *apparent* simplicity as reflecting old Roman character (quite irrespective of what lay behind the appearance). For Tacitus' conservative tastes: Syme, *Tacitus*, 553.

[92] *Cf.* note 58 above: Petronius has this "rudeness" under perfect artistic control: Abbott points out (49-50) how the language and manner of Trimalchio undergo a change as he becomes more affected by drink in the course of the dinner.

[93] 49, 8-9.

[94] 71, 1: *diffusus hac contentione Trimalchio "amici" inquit "et servi homines sunt et aeque unum lactem biberunt, etiam si illos malus fatus oppresserit."*

[95] Note 34 above; Schnur *op. cit.*: even if Trimalchio's fortune is in fact only of moderate size, he acts on the assumption that it is enormous, which is presumably part of the satire upon him and his kind.

[96] Especially the rough play at the dinner party in which Sir W. cuffed his son, who in turn hit his neighbour saying, "Box about t'will come to my father anon." John Aubrey, Life of Sir Walter Raleigh: *Aubrey's Brief Lives* edit. O. Lawson Dick, London 1949, 319.

[97] Paul Mackendrick, "The Great Gatsby and Trimalchio," *Classical Journal* 45, 7, 1950, 304-14.

[98] Salonius, 7.

[99] 76, 7: *hoc loco Fortunata rem piam fecit*: tribute is paid to her business acumen earlier in the text (37).

[100] Fortunata's low early status is attested not only by her husband's drunken abuse of her as *milva, fulcipedia* 75, 6, but also in 37, 3: *ignoscet mihi genius tuus, noluisses de manu illius panem accipere.*

[101] 67, 6-10: They examine each other's jewellery in a comradely fashion; 47, 12: Scintilla comforts Fortunata in her quarrel with Trimalchio. Both have trouble with husbands who have favourite boy slaves: 69, 1-2; 74, 8.

[102] 134-138: description of a ritual which combines tedium, fear and pain in a fashion that parallels the Quartilla episode (16-25), save that the later episode is more fragmentary: the original text must have been a very minutely detailed account of an obscene ceremony.

[103] 111-113.

[104] 113, 3-4 *non dubie redierat in animum Hedyle expilatumque libidinosa migratione navigium. sed nec foederis verba permittebant meminisse, nec hilaritas, quae occupaverat mentes. dabat iracundiae locum.*

[105] Sullivan 194-5: some of Eumolpus' discourse is possibly a parody of Seneca.

[106] 85-87; 140.

[107] See: Sullivan 110, 212-13.

[108] Notes 10, 93 above.

[109] Note 10 above.

## Bibliography

Note: Abbreviations: Apart from the usual abbreviations of the titles of well-known works and periodicals (*e.g. R-E* for *Real-Encyclopaedie, PLM* for *Poetae Latini Minores, etc.*) I have sometimes used abbreviations in the notes which are not familiar but which I hope are easily understandable from the context, *e.g.* "*R.R.*" near "Syme" will stand for "Roman Rsevolution", or *D.P.* in the context with "H. Herter" will be "De Priapo".

TEXTS, COMMENTARIES, AND TRANSLATIONS

*Petronius, The Satyricon,* translated by William Arrowsmith, New York, 1960.

*Petronii Satirae et Liber Priapeorum,* ed. F. Buecheler, Berlin, 1871.

*Titi Petronii Arbitri Satyricôn quae supersunt cum integris notis Doctorum Virorum Commentariis; et Notes Nicolai Heinsii et Guilielmi Goesii nunc primum editis, accedunt Jani Dousae Praecidanea, D. Jos Ant Gonsali de Salas Commenta, variae Dissertationes et Praefationes,* etc., curante Petro Burmanno, Trajecti ad Rhenum, 1709.

*Petronii Saturae recensuit* Franciscus Buecheler *exemplar ex editione anni MDCCCLXII anastatice iteratum; adiectae sunt Varronis et Senecae Saturae similesque reliquiae ex editione sexta anni MDCCCCXII a* Guilielmo Heraeo *curata repetita et supplementa,* Berlin, 1958.

*Pétrone, Le Satyricon,* Texte établi et traduit par A. Ernout, Paris, 1967.

*Petronii Cena Trimalchionis,* mit Deutscher übersetzung und erklärenden Anmerkungen, von Ludwig Friedländer, Leipzig, 1891.

*Titi Petronii Arbitri Equitis Romani Satyricon, cum Fragmento nuper Tragurii reperto; Accedunt diversorum Poetarum Lusus in Priapum, Pervigilium Veneris, Ausonii cento nuptialis, Cupido crucifixus, Epistolae de Cleopatra et alia nonnulla, omnia commentariis et notis Doctorum Virorum illustrata,* concinnante Michaele Hadrianide, Amstelodami, 1669.

*Petronius,* with an English Translation by Michael Heseltine; *Seneca, Apocolocyntosis,* with an English Translation by W. H. D. Rouse, (Loeb Classical Series) London, 1916.

*Petronii Cena Trimalchionis,* edited with critical and explanatory notes and translated into English Prose, W. D. Lowe, Cambridge, 1905.

*Petronius, The Satyricon, translated by* J. M. Mitchell, with an Introduction and notes, London, 1923.

*Petronii Arbitri Satyricon* cum apparatu critico edidit Konrad Müller, München, 1961.

*Petronii Cena Trimalchionis,* herausgegeben von Helmut Schmeck, vierte, neubearbeitete und verbesserte Auflage (Sammlung Vulgärlateinische Texte) Heidelberg, 1954.

*Petronii Arbitri Satiricon cum uberioribus commentarii instar, notis,* Johannes A. Woweren, Amsterodami, 1626.

*Priapeia sive Diversorum Poetarum in Priapum Lusus; illustrati Commentariis Gasperis Schoppi, Franci; L. Apulii Madavrensis, Anexomenos ab eodem illustratus etc. etc.* Patavii, 1664.

*Petronius, The Satyricon and the Fragments* translated

with an introduction by John Sullivan, London, 1965.

OTHER WORKS

Abbott, Frank Frost, "The Use of Language as a means of characterisation in Petronius", C.P. 2, 1907, 43-50

Arnold, E. V., *Roman Stoicism,* London, 1911.

Bagnani, G., "Arbiter of Elegance", *Phoenix* Suppl. 2, Toronto, 1954.

Bickel, E., "Petrons Simplicitas bei Tacitus" *Rheinisches Museum* 90, 1941, 269ff.

Barré, see Roux.

Bogner, H, "Petronius bei Tacitus" *Hermes* 76, 1941, 223f.

Bucheit, V., "Studien zum Corpus *Priapeorum*", *Zetemata* Hft. 22, München, 1962.

Bürger, K., "Der Antike Roman vor Petronius", *Hermes,* 27, 1892, 345 ff.

Cichorius, C., *Römische Studien,* Berlin, 1922.

Clarke, G. W., "The Burning of Books and Catullus 36", *Latomus* XXVII, 1968, 575ff.

Courtney, E., "Parody and Literary Allusion in Menippean Satire", *Philologus* 102, 1/2 1962, 86-100.

Dudley, D. R., *A History of Cynicism,* London, 1937.

Durkheim, E., *Suicide,* (trans. Spaulding, Simpson), Glencoe, Illinois, 1951.

Duff, J. W., *Freedmen in the Early Roman Empire,* Cambridge, repr. 1958.

Duff, J. W., *Roman Satire,* Cambridge, 1937.

Elliott, R. C., *The Power of Satire,* Princeton, 1960.

Fowler, Ward W., *The Religious Experience of the Roman People,* London, 1911.

Geiger, K. A., *Der Selbstmord im Klassischen Altertum,* Augsburg, 1888.

George, P., "Style and Character in the *Satyricon*", Arion V, 1966, 336-358.

Heinze, R., "Petron und der Griechischen Roman", *Hermes* XXXIV 1899, 494-519.

Henderson, B. W., *The Life and Principate of the Emperor Nero,* London, 1903.

Herter, H., *De Priapo,* Giessen, 1932.

Highet, G., "Petronius the Moralist", *T.A.P.A.* 1941, 179-194.

Hirzel, R., *Der Dialog* (repr.), Hildesheim, 1963.

Hirzel, R., *Der Selbstmord (Archiv für Religionswissenschaft* 1906), repr. Darmstadt, 1967.

Hoïstad, R., *Cynic Hero and Cynic King,* Uppsala, 1948.

Kerenyi, K., *Die Griechisch-Orientalische Romanliteratur in Religionsgeschichtlicher Beleuchtung,* Tübingen, 1927.

Killeen, J. F., "James Joyce's Roman Prototype", *Comparative Literature* IX·3, 1957, 193-203.

Klebs, E., "Zur Composition von Petronius' Satirae", *Philologus* 47, 1889, 623-635.

Kroll, W., *Studien zum Verständnis der Römischen Literatur,* Darmstadt (repr.), 1959.

Latte, K., *Römische Religionsgeschichte* (Handbuch der Altertumswissenschaft), München, 1960.

Luck, G., *Latin Love Elegy,* London, 1959.

MacKendrick, Paul, "The Great Gatsby and Trimalchio", *Classical Journal* 45, 7, 1950, 304-314.

Marx, F. A., "Tacitus und die Literatur der exitus illustrium virorum", *Philologus* XLVI, 1937, 83-103.

Perry, B. E., *The Ancient Romances, A Literary-Historical Account of their Origins,* (Sather Classical Lectures) California, 1967.

Raith, O., *Petronius Ein Epikureer,* Erlangen, 1963.

Reich, H., *Der Mimus,* Berlin, 1903.

Rini, A., *Petronius in Italy,* N.Y., 1937.

Rohde, E., *Der Griechische Roman,* Hildesheim, 1960.

Rose, K. F. C., "The Author of the Satyricon", *Latomus* XX, 1961, 811-825; "The Date of the Satyricon", *C.Q.* NS XIII, 1, 1962, 166-168; "Problems of Chronology in Lucan's Career", *T.A.P.A.* XCVII 1966, 379-396; "Time and Place in the Satyricon", *T.A.P.A.* XCIII 1962, 402-9; "The Petronian Inquisition, an Auto-da-Fé", *Arion* 1966, 275-301.

Roux, H., Barré, M.L., *Herculaneum et Pompeii, Recueil Général des Peintures, Bronzes, etc.*, Paris, 1872.

Solonius, A. H., "Die Griechen und das Griechische in Petrons Cena Trimalchionis". *Societas Scientiarum Fennica Commentationes Humanarum Literarum* II, 1, 15. Helsingfors, 1927.

Sayre, F., *Diogenes of Sinope, A Study of Greek Cynicism.* Baltimore, 1938.

Schnur, H. C., "The Economic Background of the Satyricon", *Latomus* 18. 1959, 790 ff.

Stanford, W. B., "Ulyssean Qualities in Leopold Bloom", *Comparative Literature* 5, 1953, 125-136; *The Ulysses Theme,* Oxford, 1954.

Stengel, E., *Suicide and Attempted Suicide,* London, 1964.

Sullivan, J. P., *The Satyricon of Petronius, A Literary Study,* London, 1968.

Stubbe, H., "Die Verseinlagen im Petron", *Philologus* Suppltbd. 25, Leipzig, 1925.

Syme, R., *Sallust,* California 1964; *Tacitus,* Oxford 1958; *The Roman Revolution,* Oxford, 1939.

Todd, F. A., *Some Ancient Novels,* Oxford, 1940.

Toynbee, A., *Hannibal's Legacy,* Oxford, 1965.

Wagenwoort, H., *Roman Dynamism,* Oxford, 1947.

Wilkinson, L. P., "Philodemus and Poetry", $\bar{G}$. & R. 2, 1933, 144ff.

Wissowa, G., *Religion und Kultus der Römer,* München, 1912.

Zeller, E., *Philosophie der Griechen,* ed. 5., Darmstadt, 1963.

**Froma I. Zeitlin (essay date 1971)**

SOURCE: "Petronius as Paradox: Anarchy and Artistic Integrity," *Transactions and Proceedings of the American Philological Association*, Vol. 102, 1971, pp. 631-84.

[*In the following essay, Zeitlin contends that the inconsistencies, ambiguities, and incongruities of the* Satyricon *are deliberate and that they reflect Petronius's worldview, which embraced irrationality, chaos, and disintegration.*]

The recent renewal of interest in the **Satyricon** has produced many new and valuable insights into this strange work.[1] But enigmatic it still remains—both in respect of its form or genre and of the purpose or stance of the author—while contradictory theories continue to be vigorously propounded, attacked, and defended.[2]

Perhaps this enigmatic quality of the **Satyricon,** aggravated by the fragmentary condition of the text, will inevitably defeat the possibility of any consensus among its readers, but the present lack of consensus may also be a clear indication that a new approach to the **Satyricon** is needed. It might be argued that any ambiguous work of literature which fundamentally defies the ready classifications and explications that are offered by conventional criticism ought to be reexamined in unconventional terms. For its resistance to definition by rigorous classical canons may well be a clue to its purpose, and the uneasiness its ambiguity may create in the reader by baffling his expectations may well be a key to its meaning.[3]

There are some criteria even in the controversial field of aesthetic theory by which we try to evaluate literature.[4] The first posits in a work of art an organic connection between form and content, where artistic form imposes itself upon and disciplines its "formless" subject matter to create a "symbolic integrity of a work of art."[5] The second requires that fusion of form and content should result in some significant statement, implicit or explicit, about the human condition as perceived by the artist, who may legitimately select his material from the entire range of human experience. But we often ask more than this by adding a third criterion—an expectation that art achieve a formal intelligible ordering of experience to satisfy a deeply felt human need of apprehending an intelligible world order. Aesthetics, in this sense, can independently play the same role as religion or political ideology by guaranteeing a viable concept of a world-order rather than just a world-view.

As soon as the third expectation is applied to Petronius, the reader is apt to shake his head in disbelief, for Petronius seems not to order experience but to disorder it, by irony and ambiguity of tone, by disorganized plot, by shifting characterizations, and by bewildering incongruities, to name only a few of his more prominent "failings." But when it is examined in terms of the first two criteria, we should expect to find in the **Satyricon** an inner coherence and an interrelation of form, style, literary devices, plot, mode of characterization, themes, images, and symbols which create a world-view that is intelligible when seen within the framework of its own inner logic. If Petronius sees the world as irrational, confused, and illusory, this *Weltanschauung* should be accepted as his legitimate right. Although it need not be adopted or even admired by the reader, the *existence* of this view can be acknowledged and understood.

The purpose of this paper, then, is to take an approach to the *Satyricon* that accepts its paradoxes, its inconsistencies, its ambiguities, its absurdities, and its incongruities as integral emblems of a world-view that expresses a consistent vision of disintegration through the inter-relatiionship of form and content. What has been called "literary opportunism"[6] will then prove to be conscious artistic choice.

This approach first asks for a genuine acceptance of the radical originality of the *Satyricon,* so that it may be judged in terms of its own premises, although assistance can and should be sought in comparisons with literary works of later ages which display similar characteristics. Although the special originality of the *Satyricon* has been acknowledged by many, the deeper implications of this recognition have not been explored.[7]

Secondly, this approach requires a relinquishing of the canons of classical or neo-classical aesthetic theory as our standard for judging Petronius, while, at the same time, allowing Petronius his own close acquaintance with those canons. For, as I hope to prove, the *Satyricon* is a radically anti-classical work, which, by its subversion and rejection of classical aesthetic theory with its attendant expectations, sets out to project a radically anti-classical world-view.

### I. *Genre and Classical Genre Theory*

The classical theory of genres, which reigned supreme in antiquity and still continues to exercise a strong influence today, especially on critics of classical literature, must judge Petronius a hopeless misfit. This theory, as has been observed, is "the . . . doctrine of purity of genre. . . . Though it was never worked out with sharp consistency, there was a real aesthetic principle . . . involved: it was the appeal to a rigid unity of tone, a stylized purity and 'simplicity,' a concentration on a single emotion . . . as on a single plot or theme. There was an appeal also to specialization and pluralism: each kind of art has its own capacities and its own pleasure. . . . Classical theory had too its social differentiation of genres. . . . And that sharp distinction in the *dramatis personae* proper to each kind has its concomitants in the doctrine of 'decorum' (class 'mores') and the separation of styles and dictions into high, middle, low. It had, too, its hierarchy of kinds, in which not merely the rank of the characters and the style counted as elements but also the length or size (the capacity for sustaining power) and the seriousness of tone."[8]

But the *Satyricon* violates many of these prescriptions. For instance, it exhibits no rigid unity of tone, no stylistic purity and simplicity, no concentration on a single emotion, and probably not on a single plot or theme (certainly if the Aristotelian doctrine of the causal plot is taken as the only acceptable norm).

In descriptive terms, the *Satyricon* belongs to no traditional classical genre; it contains elements from many and varied genres in prose and poetry. It has affinities with epic, with the *Reiseroman,* with romance, with formal satire (both Lucilian and Menippean), with the Milesian tale, and with the mime, among others.[9] It may use or abuse elements from all these genres, but it has metamorphosed this blend of genres into something singular, a "unique hybrid," as it has been called.[10] The absence of any one traditional category into which the *Satyricon* can comfortably fit might then be taken, paradoxically, as a salient descriptive quality of the work. Its guiding principle seems to be an incongruous, unexpected juxtaposition or fusion of genres, undertaken with the deliberate intention of defeating the expectations of an audience accustomed, far more than we, to an organizing literary form.

The theory of genres not only implies the principle of order in defining the nature of the form and content with a given genre, but its procedure of classification and differentiation of separate genres is also a principle of ordering aesthetic experience. Therefore, Petronius, both by his rejection of a single form and by his mixture of established forms, introduces a fundamental disorder into his work.

There are further implications involved in Petronius' rejection of traditional genre theory. Although genres may be universal categories, which transcend time and place, each culture, each tradition "will have disqualified certain forms and means of expressions as invalid and impossible; by the same process, it will suggest others as now possible and valid."[11] Although, in one sense, as we shall see, the *Satyricon* is a product consonant with its time, in another sense, Petronius, on his own initiative, overturns this principle too. For in addition to the mixture of genres, he raises to the literary level sub-literary prose fiction and the still more substandard mime, thus enlarging the range and focus of subject matter and its treatment which are permissible for literature. On the other hand, in contrast to the upgrading of some genres, a reverse process is going on at the same time—the debasement of legitimate genres, especially epic, by parodistic and ironic techniques. In his treatment of the different genres within the work, he often reverses the doctrine of decorum in reference both to style and to *dramatis personae,* which creates still another kind of disorder.[12]

For viable literature, however, there must be a tension between the inherent limitations imposed by the form and all it represents and the necessary freedom allowed to the individual artist to exercise creative invention within these limits (leading often, in the case of the great artist, even to the expansion of a given form) to affect the audience with a sense of both recognition and novelty. "The genre represents, so to speak, a sum of aesthetic devices at hand, available to the artist and already intelligible to the reader. . . . The totally familiar and repetitive pattern is boring; the totally novel form will be unintelligible . . .".[13]

The separation of form from creative invention signals the exhaustion of form; the literature of each successive age must revitalize the current forms, expanding them by cross-fertilization from other forms, drawn both from literary and non-literary sources. It should be free also to develop forms appropriate to the ethos of the age. But the classical theory of genres, by its "regulatory and prescriptive" rules established for existing forms and by its unwillingness to tolerate other aesthetic systems,[14] became a still more rigid and confining system in the hands of the Romans. For they did not address themselves, for the most part, to the creation and development of their own organic forms but adapted (often successfully) to their own special needs the organic forms of another and, in many ways, alien culture. But once those special needs had been defined, they did not encourage the free development of new or changing standards. On the contrary, they canonized existing standards with eventually stultifying effects. Even satire (the one genre which the Romans claimed for their own, and which, according to one derivation, signified "medley" or "potpourri"), a form that inherently should have been able to tolerate a wider range of experimentation, rapidly standardized satirical material and treatment into recognizable *topoi.*

It is well-known that Nero's literary tastes encouraged experimentation and discussion of styles and practices. Silver Latin literature did mark an attempt to revitalize old forms, although it was hampered in its task by a lack of political freedom.[15] But it should be noted that, with the exception of Petronius, the experimentation was confined to work within the existing genres such as satire, epic, and tragedy, and here rhetoric played far too great a role. But rhetoric, which has been accused as the cause of the decline in Roman literature, was, at least, one of the ways in which the traditional forms might be given a new and different touch. Yet since rhetoric puts the emphasis on stylistic brilliance and superficial effects, it is ultimately an empty substitute for the aesthetic freedom denied to literature by current political conditions and by too early and too rigid definitions of genres.

The choice, however, by a specific culture of its acceptable genres is dictated to a large extent by the needs of the society which range beyond the limits of pure aesthetic enjoyment, based on inherited tradition and values and yet capable of alteration and expansion to suit the demands of the living age. In this sense, the literary form can be viewed as an "institution of society—as church, university or state is an institution."[16] An acceptance of the traditional literary norms is, in some sense, a conformity, perhaps even a commitment, to the larger social norms.

This is an especially valid observation for Roman society, which was highly institutionalized in many ways, which required for its psychic needs a high degree of organization, and which, in general, clung tenaciously to tradition. Literature, too, had been institutionalized to some extent; Roman prose and poetry, particularly in the preceding Augustan age, had often been closely allied to the programs of the state, and its practice had been encouraged and subsidized by the formal system of literary patronage offered to the artists by the upper classes and later by the court.

The theory of genres, viewed as an institution of society, upholds the orderly status quo through its formal ordered structure. By its contents, it also lends support to the ideals of that society. It may then be legitimate to regard Petronius' rejection of its tenets as an implicit rejection of other larger institutions and their ideologies. This suggestion seems to be verified by the content of the *Satyricon,* which, as we shall see, hits out in varied oblique ways at the other institutions of Roman society.

In one sense, Petronius' rejection of the theory of genres can be seen as a genuine aesthetic experiment in the revitalization of literature and also as a rejection of the traditional values of his society and its institutions. In another sense, his technique of mixing generes can be viewed as a device used to create an impression of disorder, which he felt to be an appropriate representation of reality for his particular age.

Such a theory, based on observation of the text, is complicated, however, by the tenets of traditional literary criticism offered by Agamemnon, Encolpius, and Eumolpus in the *Satyricon,* which have often been taken as expressions of the "real" opinions of Petronius and have been extracted from the text for insertion into histories of literary criticism. Petronius, thereby, has been marked as a literary conservative, who looks back to the classical norms of the past for his models.[17]

But, taken in context, the formal expositions of clichés in praise of the past in the arts and sciences (88), in the rules set down for formal educational training based on immersion in the classics of the past (5), and in the prescriptions for writing poetry in the epic genre, also based on the models of the past (118), are undercut in a complex way by those who make the formal expositions. For example, Agamemnon does not follow his own regimen for educational training. Eumolpus, in his *Bellum Civile,* is not consistent in the principles he propounds on the technique of writing epic poetry, which makes his role as an arbiter of literary standards appear incongruous.[18] The resulting epic effort, a pastiche of Lucan and Vergil, faithful to neither and yet not a creative new fusion, seems to me to question the very notion that epic poetry or any other literary genre can be reduced to a single set formula which will guarantee its success. I would go still further and see, by extension, an oblique attack on a society which lives by a faith in such established technical rules and rejects freer experimentation in favor of conscious archaization and legislation of norms. Vergil and Horace were, after all, standards of achievement for *their* age, and no amount of wishful thinking can assimilate the product of a *cupientis exire beluae gemitus* (115.1) to that of a *furentis animi vaticinatio* (118.6).

Eumolpus is always ready with a set piece to match a specific occasion. Shorn tresses on shipboard suggest a vapid *elegidarion* on hair (109.9-10); a corpse washed up on the beach evokes a verse epitaph (115.20); a painting in an art gallery calls for an *ekphrasis* (89), and Eumolpus' poem on the capture of Troy is no more successful as poetry than his *Bellum Civile*.

Most significant of all, of course, is the undermining of the value of rigid classical prescriptions by Petronius' own violations of the tradition in the *Satyricon*. For while Eumolpus' mixture of Seneca and Vergil in the *Troiae Halosis* (the crossing of genres) and of Lucan and Vergil in the *Bellum Civile* (the crossing of generations) may be viewed as further evidence of Petronius' technique of deliberate confusion, nevertheless, the woeful sterility of Eumolpus' derivative creations, containing the lesser of both the new and the old, provides a strong contrast to Petronius' own fertile and imaginative use of a similar technique in the body of the text.

Moreover, the moralizing statements, representative of an even more traditional Roman attitude, characterized by a nostalgia for the idealized past, have generally been recognized as undercut and partially invalidated by the behavior of those who voice them. If the objects of satire become the satirists themselves, as do the moralist philosophers, by the same reasoning the practitioners of literary criticism are equally subject to satire, especially since the teachers of both types of dogma are the same men. Especially too since art and morals are joined together in the traditional Roman unity (88).

This is not to say that the moralizing statements aimed at the excesses of the present are not objectively true, given the evidence of Seneca and of the **Satyricon** itself, or that the statements on art, which castigate the literary vices of the present and recognize the great achievements of the past, have no external validity. One ambiguity lies in the relationship established between the external validity of the complaints and their *traditional* presentation (which includes the *traditional* prescription for their amelioration by a return to the

conditions of the past). The personal characters of the individual speakers create a second ambiguity. The behavior of those who theorize, but who do not, and probably cannot, put their theories into practice, demonstrates the insufficiency of the theories as a valid guide to life or to art. The suspicion thus grows that the traditional rules for the diagnosis and cure of the present ills, which were formulated in the past and maintained in a closed and stagnant system, may be, after all, pure cant.

Satire often takes as its theme the "setting of ideas and generalizations and theories and dogmas over against the life they are supposed to explain," . . . so that "satire may often represent the collision between a selection of standards from experience and the feeling that experience is bigger than any set of beliefs about it."[19] This skeptical attitude towards dogmatic pronouncements seems to me, in fact, precisely what Petronius aims to project in these scenes. He surely satirizes Stoicism and he even satirizes Epicureanism, too.[20] His statements on art seem not so much to advocate a fixed position in the literary controversies of his day, but to demonstrate the futility of explaining art by intellectual theories.[21] Thus, his mixture of genres can be seen also as another expression of his rejection of fixed theoretical criteria for aesthetic theory.

*Mode and Form*

To project his sense of the unintelligibility of the world, Petronius had to make his view intelligible to the audience. There is a balance necessary between the recognition of a given literary form by the audience and the expectation of novelty, a requirement which normally leads to a slow development within or even outside a genre form. Petronius cannot deny the expectations of the audience altogether. To do so would be to produce a totally private and uncommunicable work.

The comic mode is traditionally the mode most open to free invention of plot, to fantasy, to absurdities, to reversals of roles and to other confusions.[22] It is therefore an effective literary means for obtaining from the audience an acceptance of novelty in plot, and perhaps, to a lesser degree, in form. It is also, to some extent, a protective device, for it can legitimately allow the members of the "outer" audience to respond to a comic work on the level of amiable nonsense. Yet the comic mode, too, preserves the underlying, shifting relationship between humor and gravity which is essential in great comedy and to which the members of the "inner," more perceptive audience can respond, if they wish.

In addition, intrinsic to the use of a fictional narrative or novelistic form are the paucity of rigid conventions and a concomitant need for wide invention so as to create an impression of the complex sprawl of life.[23] In truth, this basic "formlessness" is an indigenous and legitimate trait of the novel, the art form which Henry James called "that loose and baggy monster."[24] This fact has not always been recognized in its full implications, for adherents of neo-classical theory have applied to the European novel the classical Aristotelian standard of the causal plot and hence made the standard of the genre the "realistic" novel.[25] But if we grant that the *Satyricon,* despite its mixture of classical genres, nevertheless belongs to a species of narrative fiction and is entitled to be called a novel, then we can judge Petronius according to the norms of fiction.

By the criteria of modern theory, we need not judge Petronius against the classical standard of the causal plot, to his detriment; nor need we judge him by the neo-classical norm of the "realistic" novel. We can also understand that the use of satire in a novel is different from satire encompassed within the limits of its own more slender form.[26] Moreover, we are free to compare his fictional mode with other types of fiction that have appeared since his time—notably, the picaresque novel of Renaissance Spain (which his work seems to anticipate) and some of our modern novels.[27] It is significant that the evaluations of both have suffered when the "realistic" novel is held to be the norm.

Yet, at the same time, in our approach to Petronius, first, we can recognize his own unconventional use of the novel form as an acceptable literary form along with its implications. Secondly, we can refer back to the stylized prose romance in antiquity and to the epic, that other long fictional form, both of which Petronius recalls in his work for his own particular purposes. Thirdly, we can keep in mind the Aristotelian requirement of causality for all fictional plots, which he rejects, as he did the formal theory of genres.

In other words, we have a distinct advantage in that we can estimate the shock value of the *Satyricon* for an audience of Petronius' time, but we are not limited by the constrictions of classical theory in our own assessment of the meaning and value of Petronius' work.

Modern theory asks only that "this world or *kosmos* of a novelist—this pattern or structure or organism, which includes plot, characters, setting, world-view, 'tone'— is what we must scrutinize when we attempt to compare a novel with life or to judge ethically or socially a novelist's work."[28] The word "kosmos" here may seem ironical, if kosmos is felt to bear its root meaning, since the salient feature of the world of Petronius is its lack of kosmos or order. But when kosmos is interpreted as "world," then Petronius should be judged in terms of his own "creative and humorous presentation of an imaginatively realized world."[29]

If a novel is, as Stendhal says, "a mirror carried along the road,"[30] then who is to say that that mirror may not be crazed and even cracked and so produce its own highly individual refractions? But to understand the particular nature of these refractions in Petronius, we must first examine his style and then the plot and other components of his world-view.

## II. *Style*

Sullivan remarks with some justice that Petronius exhibits "several distinguishable styles" in the *Satyricon;* the first, an "elaborate style . . . used for literary criticism, parody, and various rhetorical purposes;" the second, a "plain but careful rhythmical style which is the chief narrative medium, a kind of artistic *sermo urbanus,*" differentiated for "leisurely elaboration . . . and rapid descriptions of action;" and the third, a "vulgar style (*sermo plebeius*)" used primarily in the *Cena* to imitate proletarian daily speech. The conclusion drawn is that "in each case, Petronius would see a particular style as suitable to a particular subject matter and this would be part of his and the Roman idea of literary decorum."[31]

This analysis of the several styles of the *Satyricon,* valid as it may be, does not, however, convey a sense of the style of the book, taken as a whole. That style might be described as eclectic, varied, or even multitudinous. The *sermo urbanus,* often taken as the preferred style of Petronius himself, is one voice in a dissonant chorus of voices, albeit an important stabilizer in the continuity of the first-person narrative. One could better describe the style of the *Satyricon* as a synthesis of incongruous juxtapositions of styles and varying planes of literary suggestiveness which yield to and crowd in upon each other with a general effect of confusion. The high level of verbal wit also contributes to the stylistic complexity.

In addition, there is the shift between poetry and prose that makes an irregular alternation between two fundamentally different modes of discourse. But the general principle of variation applies to both modes, for the styles of poetry in the text are also varied in tone, genre, and length. The distinction might be better subsumed under the general rubric of rapid stylistic variety. This trait has been attributed to a brilliant "literary opportunism" which capriciously moves from style to style as a display of technical virtuosity and wit.[32] I would attribute it rather to another fundamental statement made by the work—namely, that the insistence on a fluidity and plasticity and changeability of styles in a rapid series of incongruities is an intentional device designed to represent stylistically those same qualities of confusion in the world. In other words, stylistic disorder mirrors world disorder.

Moreover, the frequent use of puns, verbal wit, literary allusions, and, above all, parody, appeals to the reader's education and intellectual skills as well as to his sense of humor. Thus an inherent antithesis is created between the flow of the plot and the demands of recognition in these verbal techniques which slow down and usually break the narrative of action and episode. There is a "rhythm created . . . by interplay between the narrative . . . and the verbal surface. The verbal play constantly interrupts our attention to the narrative—we are constantly torn from the story to consider, ponder, and admire the intense activity of the verbal level. Our attention is constantly alternating between style and action in a way that gives birth to an instantaneous and irregular rhythm in reading the book." And this "jagged reading rhythm suggests a correspondence with the jagged episodic plot, the rush of events, and the internal chaos of the characters"[33] which I will explore in a later section. In addition, the rhythm of the narrative is also broken by other formal devices such as the digressions on literature, art, philosophy, and morals, and even, to some extent, by the inserted Milesian tales.

The stylistic incongruities have been observed and well analyzed by Sullivan, but these matters are treated under the heading of "Humor," an appropriate rubric but one that effectively removes from consideration an approach to these incongruities that might see them as expressive of more than a comic versatility.

On the one hand, he describes Petronius' distribution of styles as consonant with the Roman doctrine of decorum. For example, when Encolpius speaks of literature or of art, he employs a polished rhetorical style. But, on the other hand, Sullivan sees the "basic humor" of the work as "an application of a refined literary and stylistically sophisticated narrative medium to disreputable low-life adventures and sexual escapades of a number of unprincipled . . . characters."[34] This technique is clearly a violation of the doctrine of decorum where the relationship between form and content is disrupted, and that relationship is thereby held up to scrutiny.

Morcover, Sullivan continues by nothing that there is "sometimes an incongruity . . . between the high moral sentiments, the sensible, sometimes serious literary criticism and the persons that voice them . . . sometimes an incongruity . . . between the style of the prose or verse and the lowliness or absurdity of the inci.dents, or alternatively, between the high-flown declamatory style of some of the characters and the actual station or attainments in life."[35] But this last incongruity, while again a violation of the doctrine of decorum, is, in another sense, the fulfillment of a second stylistic dictum, namely, consonance of style with character—*qualis vir, talis oratio.*[36]

The freedmen in the *Cena,* regardless of their accomplishments, speak with a style that betrays their origins. But Eumolpus, who shifts his style to suit the appropriate subject, although all his styles are appropriate to an educated man, expresses his shifting and opportunistic nature through the instability of his style.[37] Encolpius, another even more unstable character, is a better case in point. In the digressions he responds to the rhetorical nature of the subjects with rhetorical prose. Events he generally narrates in the *sermo urbanus,* but as soon as he is confronted with positive action on his own, or more precisely, when his emotions are directly involved, he generally lapses into a mock-heroic or sentimental romantic style. This lapse reveals his bookish pretensions and his corresponding naiveté about real life. This stylistic habit also reflects the disparity between the actual events and his own inflated view of them. He must constantly draw his emotional responses, not from inner conviction, but from stock responses to stock situations. This perverse habit ironically calls into question the theory behind the doctrine of decorum. It calls into question the "handbook" approach to life, much as Eumolpus' poetry calls into question the "handbook" approach to literature. Thus Petronius uses stylistic incongruities also for genuine characterizations of his incongruous personages,[38] who, by their instability and unreality, reflect the culture which produced them.

The dense literary texture, which I noted earlier in connection with the jagged and disorderly reading rhythm, serves another even more important function. The **Satyricon,** both in style and in the themes of some episodes, is permeated with reminiscences of other genres and other styles, ranging, in effect, through the whole of the classical tradition. The enumeration of the categories of oratory, historiography, legal and diplomatic formulae, epic, epistolography, erotic elegy, philosophical essay, satire, romance, tragedy, and comedy probably does not exhaust the list.[39] In the process, the text also touches on most of the major figures in Latin literature, with a special preference for the Augustans of the preceding age.[40] But the chief mode of literary allusion is parody in all of its different forms, a technique which distorts the primary references.

Parodistic technique has generally been considered a secondary literary activity, effective on the level of humor or of literary criticism. For in the mimetic theory put forth by Aristotle, art should imitate life, while parody "does not imitate an action in nature; it imitates another work of art."[41] But recently it has been shown to possess an important aesthetic of its own by its imitation of art. Parody expresses what is often inexpressible in other ways when it is practiced on its highest level by those of marked artistic merit. Cervantes, Shakespeare, Proust, Joyce, and Mann, for instance, use parody in important and primary ways.[42]

Parody works backwards; it dislocates the union of form and content and thus raises the larger question of the gap between "art and life, between artifact and nature, between real and irreal," which art has tried to solve.[43] It lays open to examination the validity of the marriage between certain art forms and certain modes of thought and action which have become legitimate for them. In the process, parodistic technique will seek to push art beyond the restrictions laid upon it by formal requirements. But parody, especially where art is closely bound up with social and cultural ideas as it was in Rome, asks too for a scrutiny of the ideas and actions inherent in the forms. Eumolpus, as the poet, is determined to play the classical role of poet as ethical teacher. By the failure of his academic poetry, and by the gap exposed between his preachings and practice, he is the most persuasive argument for the impotence of the old forms to validate existence in a new and different age.

In Petronius the secondary form of parody is embedded in the primary form of the novel, and can make no claim to stand on its own; it must serve to make some contribution to the whole. To some critics its only contribution may be that of humor or of limited literary criticism of individuals, but it is important to note that it is "generally at the end of a tradition when established forms are exhausted, that this kind of original [use of] parody will appear."[44] Otherwise, when the canonical forms are still felt to be viable, then "parody is in fact the province of poets of lesser range", used more as "forms of homage."[45] What parody does in this later stage is to "dramatize the pathos of dissonance" between form and content. "It revokes in effect those relationships which would usually occur in art during periods of relative cultural health when primary forms supply the mode of expression. . . . In a culture where usurpation of function and confusion of polarities are the rule, the very instability of parody becomes the means of stabilizing the subject matter which is itself unstable and fluid, and parody becomes a major mode of expression for civilization in a state of transition and flux."[46]

For Petronius parody seems less of a stabilizer and more of a continuing statement about the cultural and spiritual crisis of his time. The past is invoked through literary allusions only to be distorted and made comic, while the literary and moral digressions, which lay claim to a "serious" consideration, cast doubt on the validity of their traditional precepts by their cliché-ridden presentations. In effect, parody in Petronius, by embracing an entire literary tradition, expresses the incongruity and absurdity of an entire culture.

The individual incongruities of Petronius' style evoke laughter from the audience. Collectively, they seem to evoke a certain sense of loss for what was once taken for granted in a more secure and ordered world where form and content attained a stable fusion. As one critic has remarked, "what most distinguishes the *Satyricon* is its extraordinary style, a style that is a conglomeration of every Greek and Roman style reduced to mock-

ery and held together by that special quality" which "is a melancholy like no other in literature . . . As a living body is sustained and nourished by its bloodstream, the style of Petronius is suffused by a sense of indefinable sorrow which haunts and corrupts all possible achievement. The nostalgia of the gutter and the melancholy of grandeur flow together and wash away the very idea of accomplishment."[47]

Behind the anti-hero stands always the hero who once existed. Petronius' technique exposes the basic incongruity between the sordidness of reality and the literary texture which recalls a reality that no longer exists, while his disorderly conglomeration of styles reflects the confusions of the present reality as expressed in the clearest fashion by the plot and its characters.

### III. *Content: Plot and Character*

"Picaresque novel," a term often used to describe the *Satyricon,* is a reference to a genre of fiction "created" during the Renaissance in Spain and later taken up by other European writers.[48] The genre is distinguished by an episodic plot using a first-person narrative in which an itinerant rogue or picaro undergoes a series of sensational low-life adventures. Strong social satire and a cynical realism are also important elements of this form, but critics, when they apply the epithet "picaresque" to the *Satyricon,* rarely seem to consider these corollaries, nor have they investigated the larger implications of the genre.

But this is not surprising, since, in general, studies of the novel have tended to denigrate the worth of the picaresque type on the premise that, in a neo-classical evaluation based on Aristotelian doctrine, the episodic plot is not as satisfying as the causal plot of the "realistic" novel. Recently, however, critics have adopted new attitudes towards the picaresque in which the techniques of that form are seen as expressive of a worldview which is different from that posed in the "realistic" novel, but one that is not inferior.[49] The picaresque need not be deemed a primitive type of fiction which preceded a more mature development of prose fiction. This point is borne out by the renewal of the picaresque mode in modern fiction.[50] Picaresque form, then, like that of the *Satyricon,* represents conscious artistic choice rather than technical failure.

Although many of the observations I shall make on the *Satyricon* proceeded originally from my study of the text itself, the recent work on the picaresque novel parallels my own conclusions closely enough to warrant application of the special features belonging to the later picaresque form to the *Satyricon.* Viewing Petronius within the picaresque frame has the advantage of identifying his work as a recurrent literary phenomenon which arises in response to similar social conditions in history, which gives us a wider perspective. But, at the same time, it allows us to assess the originality of the work when placed in its own Roman context and within the frame of the ancient classical tradition. Moreover, the use of the picaresque as a point of reference will enable us to see the significant variations from the type in the *Satyricon* and to gauge their import.

## Plot

Picaresque form and its devices aim at projecting a view of a chaotic and disordered world. The picaresque novel sees experience as fragmented, disjointed, and unstable. It is unlike the "realistic" novel, which, by its causal plot, projects an underlying rational principle which guides the world in which cause and effect assert a basic cosmic order in human events. It is unlike comedy in which the world is first turned topsy-turvy and made chaotic, but order is reaffirmed at the end in the re-establishment of social norms. It is unlike romance which seems to set forth a chaotic unpatterned world like that of the picaresque, for "in romance cause and effect do operate," although "the probability of their operation is more remote than in the realistic novel. There is an ordering of events, but it is not a probable ordering: the wonderful romance plot unravels a complicated pattern of chance and coincidence that works mysteriously towards some end."[51] That end is the perfect union of love which has overcome the random blows of Fortune and triumphs at the last.

The picaresque, by contrast, never really resolves the chaotic appearance of the world. Although our text of the *Satyricon* is fragmentary, ancient testimonia which presumably refer to the work as a whole, do not give the impression that a radically un-picaresque ending made any restoration of harmony or an assertion of classical values. Scurrilous and scabrous it probably remained until the end.[52]

The picaresque plot asserts that experience is ultimately devoid of order and intelligibility. Episode follows upon episode without true causal connection. The result is a kind of jagged fragmentation. Anything can and does happen, including "the fantastic, the improbable, and the weird."[53]

The *Satyricon* displays these same features in its variety of episodes. Think, for example, of the *Cena* which ranges back and forth between the realistic and the grotesque, of the bizarre scenes on board the ship, and of the surrealistic quality of the Croton adventure. As in the picaresque, "nothing strictly *happens*. The . . . plot merely records fragmented happening after fragmented happening."[54] This impression of fragmentation in the *Satyricon* is magnified by the mutilated state of the text, but transitions, when they occur (as after the Cena [79]), only reinforce the impression of haphazard adventure.[55]

Generally, characters appear and disappear in the *Satyricon,* as in the picaresque, with no lasting effects. Once the trio has given Agamemnon the slip at the end of the Cena (78.8), we hear no further allusion to him. Quartilla fades from view just as effortlessly. When characters make a brief reappearance, they do so purely by coincidence, and there is no guarantee of an orderly pattern to the hero's experience which might give it some coherence. What emerges instead is a "dance pattern" which teases us with the possibility of a meaningful pattern but which is then denied.[56] The unwelcome reunion with Lichas and Tryphaena is an example of this device. After the furor and the commotion die down, the corpse of Lichas is washed up on the shore to provide a starting point for mock philosophical remarks on the human condition (115.7-20), but then it is cremated and forgotten. The characters assume new roles and turn resolutely towards the new adventure in Croton.

In the *Satyricon* a variation of the "dance pattern" occurs among the main characters themselves which lends a frenetic pace to the proceedings. Encolpius and his companions rapidly come and go, now finding each other, now losing each other. They shift alliances and sexual liaisons. Ascyltos steals away from Encolpius at the rhetorical discussion (6.1) and meets him again coincidentally at the brothel (7.4). The two quarrel over Giton and plan to break up the threesome. This solution is postponed (10.4-7), but later Giton goes with Ascyltos leaving the astounded Encolpius alone (80.5-8). Giton then returns to Encolpius at the inn (91.1-7); soon Ascyltos comes to look for Giton (97.1-3). Giton and Encolpius make their escape with Eumolpus, the new third man and the new rival for Giton (99.4-6). Ascyltos now disappears never to reappear in the extant text. Many other more temporary combinations are possible too—in the orgy scene with Quartilla, on board the ship, and in Croton. Circe is exchanged for Chrysis, and so on. This type of complicated but ultimately meaningless "dance pattern" points to the inability of the hero and his companions to form lasting emotional ties and will be examined further in a later discussion of character.

Not only is the plot disjointed and episodic; it is frequently punctuated by digressions of varying sorts, which, as I mentioned in the analysis of style, contributes to a jagged reading rhythm and which makes the action appear still more episodic.

Another device often used to enhance the chaos of the episodic plot is the rapid pace of action. Events pile upon events within a given episode and have "the effect of dazzling both reader and picaro with the accumulated chaos of life's action."[57] This happens frequently in the *Satyricon.* For example, in the Quartilla episode (16-26.6) Quartilla enters unexpectedly with a maid and a small serving girl and tricks the three male characters into an orgy. Catamites enter and add to the confusion. More attendants enter, a banquet begins, and after further sexual antics, they all fall asleep—but only for a short while. Two thieves burst in, wreak havoc, and wake everyone up, but they avoid detection by another trick. Festivities are renewed; more entertainers come in, another catamite follows, and Giton is finally paired off with the young serving girl, while Quartilla continues her amatory games. The scene breaks off here and further chaos probably followed to put an end to the episode.

The element of slapstick in the orgy is tempered by the rapid succession of unpleasant tricks and the unwelcome assaults upon the characters.[58] Tricks and random violence are commonplace events of the picaresque world. The world is shown to be chaotic and illusory, and the hero can and must adapt to it by playing his own tricks. The scene at the inn after the pinacotheca episode shows an elaborate pattern of tricks and countertricks (92-99). Characters are locked in and out, a mock suicide is enacted, violence erupts. The confusion grows apace as more and more characters become involved, until finally, after a temporary reconciliation, escape is made to a new chaotic experience on board the ship, which itself follows a variation of the same pattern.

Episodes are not resolved; they disintegrate. Often events get out of hand, and the hasty exit of the hero and his confrères concludes the scene. Something like this must have happened in the brothel scene (8.4). It happens at the end of the *Cena* (78.5-8), and in the pinacotheca (90.1). The sea storm, that universal image of turbulence, puts an end to the entanglements on board the ship (114-115.5). It happens again at the end of the Oenothea scene (138.3-4).

Typically, unpredictable and often unpleasant accidents occur which further emphasize the chaotic and even malevolent aspect of reality. Violence, assault, or punishment far out of proportion to the so-called "crime" is a familiar pattern in the picaresque as in the *Satyricon.* For instance, Oenothea, the witch, tumbles off a rotten stool and crashes down on the hearth. The neck of the pot breaks and puts out the fire. Oenothea is singed by a burning coal and rushes off to get some live embers for the fire. Meanwhile, Encolpius is attacked by some angry geese and he batters the leader of the flock to death, unaware that it is a sacred bird (136.1-5).

Violence inflicted upon the hero most often takes place within the sexual milieu. These sexual scenes are usually regarded as pornographic, but the patterning of unpredictable sexual tricks or accidents assault the hero rather than arouse him. The whole sadistic tenor of the Quartilla scene is an obvious example (especially 21.1, 26.7). Encolpius' brief rendezvous with Giton is inter-

rupted by Ascyltos who suddenly bursts into the room and threatens Encolpius with a lashing (11). Encolpius' impotence earns him a flogging ordered by Circe (132.2-4), and the treatments prescribed for his ailment by both Proselenos and Oenothea involve unpleasant violence (131.4-6; 134.3-6; 138.1-2).[59] Verbal assaults are common too throughout (9.6-9; 57.1-3; 58; 81.4-5).

A particular device used in the *Satyricon* to heighten the senseless drift of experience might be seen in the recurrent pattern of Encolpius losing his way. The first time he ends up in a brothel (6.3-7.4), the second time in a fishpond (72.7-73.2). The third time he is rescued by Giton's forethought in marking out the way with chalk, but not until he and his companions have dragged their bleeding feet for nearly a whole hour over the flints and broken pots which lie out in the road (79.1-5).

The last pattern which contributes to the general impression of chaos in the world is the rapid change in the hero's own fortunes. Events constantly assault the hero, but he cannot ultimately claim control over them. "His fortune goes up or down as it pleases. His fate is in the lap of the gods, but the gods are continually dropping it" which leads to a "senseless and unstoppable whirling."[60]

Fortuna is often invoked in the *Satyricon. O lusum Fortunae mirabilem,* exclaims Encolpius at the discovery of the long-lost tunic (13.1). After the loss of Giton, he observes: *non multum oportet consilio credere, quia suam habet Fortuna rationem* (82.6). He reacts in a similar way to the recognition of Lichas' voice (100.3; 101.1). When the storm begins, he laments that Fortune will not even allow Giton and himself to die in a lovers' embrace (114.8). His speech over the corpse of Lichas rhetorically elevates the theme of the mutability of men's fortunes (115.8-17). But his genuine awareness of his precarious position is revealed in the skeptical attitude he takes towards his present good fortune in Croton (125):

> Eumolpus, drunk with his success, had so far forgotten the past that he began to boast to his intimates that no one in Croton dared to cross him and that, for any crimes we might commit, he could easily get us off through the influence of his new friends. For my part, thanks to the excellent food and the other gifts which Fortune showered on us in prodigious profusion, I had begun to put on weight again and had almost convinced myself that luck was no longer my enemy. Still, I couldn't help reflecting now and then on our present life and how it had come about. "What would happen," I used to wonder, "if one of these legacy-chasers had the wit to send off to Africa for information and then exposed us? Or suppose Eumolpus' hired servant got bored with his present luck and dropped a hint to his friends, or gave the whole show away out of

spite? No mistake about it: we'd have to run for it, right back to our old life of poverty. Why, we'd have to start begging again. And, gods in heaven, an outlaw's life is a miserable business. Always waiting to be punished. . . . " (tr. Arrowsmith).

This concept of a cruel and random fortune contradicts the view that the **Satyricon** is patterned on a comic wrath of Priapus which would make some sense of Encolpius' adventures.[61] But if one takes the wrath of Priapus as a single motif, rather than as a controlling frame,[62] an incongruous analogy to the *Odyssey* rather than an accepted fact, the Fortuna theme retains its primary force as an expression of the perilous chaos of the world.

The objective devices of a picaresque plot—the rush of events, the jagged reading rhythm, the accidents and sudden violence, and references to a malevolent Fortuna—all interact to project a chaotic sense of reality. Furthermore, the picaresque world is illusory and unreal. It is a world of appearances, tricks, deceptions, and counter-deceptions. Nothing and no one turns out to be what it or he seems. Hence arises the prominent element of satire in the picaresque genre which strips off the mask and reveals the hypocrisy of society and its members. All the conventional values and conventions of respectability are exposed. The insistent theme in the picaresque and in the **Satyricon** is that the world is roguish.

The respectable *matrona* tricks Encolpius and brings him to a brothel (6.4-7.2). An equally unassuming *paterfamilias* deceives Ascyltos in the same way (8.2-3). Philomela, another *matrona,* acts as procuress for her daughter, after age has withered her charms (140.1-4). The Widow of Ephesus deceives her neighbors and relatives, thereby proving the inconstancy of womankind (111-112). The earnest tutor wins the family's confidence only to corrupt the Pergamene boy by his tricks (85-87). The idealized goddess-figure Circe has a taste for vulgarity (126.1-7). The innocence of youth too is unmasked in the person of the Pergamene boy who proves an apt pupil, while Giton's modest demeanor and coy naiveté hide his unscrupulous manipulations.

Institutions are similarly treated both in the picaresque and in the **Satyricon.** Justice guaranteed by due process of law is rightly suspected by Ascyltos and the others (14.1-2; cf. 15.2-5). Religion is exposed as a fraud by its lecherous priestess Quartilla. She bemoans sacrilege but prescribes an orgy as mock expiation and as remedy for her ague (16.2-18.5). Oenothea's wrath at the killing of the goose is immediately assuaged by the offer of money (137.5-9). Philosophical dogmas are held up to ridicule as are the philosophers, and moralists receive the same unmasking. Traditional education is attacked, and the rhetorician is shown un-

equal to his preaching. Likewise, the traditional theories of art, as I have pointed out earlier, are shown to be clusters of clichés and the poet who follows those precepts turns out jejune verses. Eumolpus is no ethical guide of men; he is a corrupt teacher.[63] In addition to the exposure of the favorite Roman traditions of prescriptive ethical and aesthetic theory, Roman political ideology, centering about the fall of Troy and the Civil War, is slyly emptied of its meaning and subverted.[64]

In its revelation of social and intellectual hypocrisy, the **Satyricon** serves to "break up the lumber of stereotypes, fossilized beliefs, superstitious terrors, crank theories, pedantic dogmatism [and] oppressive fashions,"[65] thus performing an important function of satire and irony. But when the **Satyricon,** by its accidents, tricks, and chaotic events, shows the world in general to be a chaos of appearances, it takes up the function of a still more radical irony. The "technique of disintegration" is used to cast doubt "even on ordinary common sense as the standard. For common sense too has certain implied dogmas, notably that the data of sense experience are reliable and consistent, and that our customary associations with things form a solid basis for interpreting the present and predicting the future. . . . "[66] "In the riotous chaos of . . . Petronius [and others]," Frye finds that "satire plunges through to its final victory over common sense. When we have finished with their weirdly logical fantasies of debauch, dream, and delirium we wake up wondering if Paracelsus' suggestion is right that the things seen in delirium are really there, like stars in the daytime and invisible for the same reasons."[67] Petronius, by his various picaresque devices, uses satire and irony in his novel to show that "heroism and effective action are absent, disorganized or foredoomed to defeat, and that confusion and anarchy reign over the world."[68]

### The Cena as Microcosm

The *Cena* has often been treated separately from the rest of the work both because it is a digression in the adventures of Encolpius and because of its realistic language and portraiture. But I have deliberately deferred consideration of the *Cena* until the picaresque world-view in the **Satyricon** was outlined. For the *Cena* provides a microcosm of the larger world confronting Encolpius, and it does so on several different ironic levels. Seen as a whole, the *Cena* represents a shifting, unreliable, and unpredictable reality.

The host, Trimalchio, is himself a shifting character, unstable and arbitrary, who now blows hot, now cold. He is capricious, for instance, in his treatment of his wife. He is even more capricious in his treatment of his slaves, playing now the tyrant, now the benefactor.[69] But even his harsh actions towards his slaves are suspect, since the anger is more than often feigned or, at least, assuaged with ease. He vacillates between vulgarity and attempts at erudition. Above all, he alternates between pretensions to greater status than he actually has and his pride in his humble beginnings.

Trimalchio is a master impresario of tricks, deceits, and disguises. The *trompe l'oeil* painting of the dog which terrifies Encolpius (29.1) is an emblem of this theme of deception and illusion which continues throughout the *Cena*. The dishes are never what they seem; they invariably conceal something else within. As has been pointed out, the archetypal artist Daedalus is reduced to the cook who metamorphoses pork into a myriad of other forms.[70] Moreover, the presentation of the dishes and of the other events at the *Cena* is usually carefully staged, but designed to simulate spontaneity, which reinforces the resemblance to real life.

Deceit and disguise are expressed on still another level in the digressive stories of the werewolf and the changeling boy (61.6-62; 63.3-10). No one is what he seems; human forms are unstable, and beneath the humorous veneer lies the uneasy sensation that the world is not rational or coherent.[71] When Trimalchio philosophizes that, after literature, the hardest professions are those of the doctor and of the moneychanger, because the doctor must know the insides of men and a moneychanger must see the copper beneath the silver (56.1-3), he is only reacting to a world whose reality proves to be illusory and counterfeit, and, therefore, ultimately unintelligible.

This chaotic reality is mirrored in the *Cena* by the constant series of planned and occasionally unplanned surprises. Ceilings yawn to discharge their contents; acrobats and other entertainers perform their tricks; riddles and puns are visually enacted. Dogs burst in; thrushes fly out. The steward of the estate intrudes unexpectedly into the banquet milieu with his reading of the daily gazette (53.1-10). Each new presentation promises a new derangement of sensibilities.

Accidents, too, both planned and unplanned, add to the chaotic atmosphere. Violence and assault are often feigned but sometimes real. Proposed punishments are too extravagant for offenses both real and imaginary, or the slave is punished ultimately for a different and more trivial offense. A cook is threatened with a flogging for his stupidity in having forgotten to gut the pig, when, in truth, he has substituted sausages and blood puddings for entrails (49-50.1). But dishes are dropped (34.2-3; 52.3-4), and a clumsy acrobat injures Trimalchio (54.1-2). Dogs first enter on cue in a hunting tableau to introduce a dish of game (40.1-4). But later, Scylax, Trimalchio's huge dog, is brought in. A real dog-fight ensues, which ends in the upsetting of a lamp and the breaking of glassware, while some of the guests are unpleasantly spattered with oil (64.6-10). Two boys simulate a quarrel and smash each other's

water pots only to release a cascade of oysters and cockles for the guests (70.4-6). But later Trimalchio quarrels with Fortunata in earnest and hurls a cup in her face (74.8-11). This type of real violence is concentrated towards the end of the *Cena* as the outside world begins to intrude more and more, and Trimalchio, the stage director, begins to lose control over the proceedings.

The rhythm of the picaresque world is maintained in the hectic "rush of events." Slaves move with lightning speed; dishes are whisked in and out; foods are prepared and cooked in an instant. Conversations interrupt the flow of events at irregular intervals, and the whole episodic effect is one of frenetic assault on the guests. One event of staged chaos follows on the heels of another until the fire brigade, deceived as to the meaning of the trumpet blast, rushes in and hacks down the doors, making a grand finale of unstaged chaos (78.5-8). The real world finally destroys the artificial world staged at the banquet, but, on closer inspection, the two are found to be the same. Thus artifice and nature both support and reinforce each other, while each casts doubt on the reality of the other with an ironic ambiguity. The *Cena* shows life to be a *theatrum mundi*, a theme that runs through the **Satyricon** in the frequent references to the mime and the stage.[72]

Another aspect of the **Satyricon's** world-view is also stressed in the *Cena*. Incongruities and confusions appear on many levels. Like the *trompe l'oeil* painting of the dog which is paradigmatic of the theme of illusion, the motif of incongruity is signalled at the very beginning of the episode by the paintings of the *Iliad* and the *Odyssey* grouped with one that depicts the gladiatorial games (29.9). Colors are juxtaposed in jarring combinations. Slaves recline with guests at the table.

The verbal level is often confused. Here too vulgarity alternates with feigned refinement. Greek and Latin are intermixed. The freedmen ramble on at will on a variety of topics. The long speech of Echion, for instance, has an effect that is close to a stream-of-consciousness (45-46). Jokes and poor puns proliferate, confusing the primary meaning of words. Trimalchio leaps from subject to subject as the fancy strikes him. Aetiologies are distorted; chronologies and characters of myth and history are confounded. The colloquial speech in the *Cena* has been praised for its faithful reproduction of vulgar diction, but this trait too supports the confused and disorganized impression of the outside world which invades the formal literary symposium.

Moreover, there is a confusion of modalities. The basic one involves a confusion between life and death which frames the *Cena* and which is thematically developed throughout, and this confusion reaches its climax in the great scene at the end of the banquet in which the feast turns into a mock funeral for Trimalchio (77.7-78.1-7).[73]

Encolpius reacts to the staged microcosm of chaos and illusion with amazement, terror, consternation, anxiety, apprehension, bewilderment, disgust, and only rarely with laughter, not unlike his reactions to events in the outside world.[74] It is only the enlarged scale and the concentrated focus of the *Cena* that make it different from the other episodes in this respect.

But there is still another level on which the *Cena* operates which makes the microcosmic analogy even more cogent. Encolpius is an outsider to the milieu of the freedmen at the banquet. Even if his role of *scholasticus* is an assumed one, his educational training and his outlook put him into a different category. The picaro's position is inevitably that of a misfit in society who wanders through life freed from the normal restraints and obligations imposed on respectable people. It is this position as a marginal man which allows the picaro his delicious satiric view of a hierarchical system. Encolpius, in this role, can observe the antics at the banquet and can present a detached view of the proceedings.

But the particular society into which Encolpius is thrust in the *Cena,* while a discernible and defined stratum of the social heap, is itself a marginal and precarious one, which can thus mirror, to some extent, the position of the picaro. Freedmen are torn between two worlds— that of slavery and that of freedom and respectability. The guests at the *Cena* constantly reveal their anxiety at their ambiguous status. The frequent definitions of what a man really is, the insistence on the theme of *libertas* in jest and in earnest,[75] and the proud statement of one freedman that he was a slave for forty years, but no one could tell whether he was a slave or a free man (57.9) are expressions of this deep preoccupation.

The key to status, in their eyes, is the acquisition of wealth, but wealth itself is a shifting and variable commodity, subject finally to the whims of Fortune. Capricious Fortuna, here more than elsewhere in the extant text, is felt to be the determining factor in man's fate. A man may be a millionaire one day and a pauper the next. Speculation may succeed, but failure is possible too. The memory of poverty and slavery haunts them. One can try to stave off the effects of Fortuna by learning a trade, by asserting the value of initiative and hard work, but luck is always needed.

Auerbach has commented upon this concept of changing fortunes, no longer viewed against the classical stable social order, but now seen as historical change against a background of social disorder. "For him [the freedman], the world is in ceaseless motion, nothing is certain, and wealth and social position are highly unstable."[76] He further notes that prior to Petronius "in the mimetic literary art of antiquity, the instability of fortune almost always appears as a fate which strikes from without and affects only a limited area [and a few special individuals], not as a fate which results from the inner processes of the real, historical world."[77] In the narrative which Auerbach cites (37-38.1-12) "four persons are mentioned who are all in the same boat, all engaged in the same turbulent pursuit of unstable Fortune. Though each of them individually has his private destiny, their destinies are all similar; their lot, for all its turbulence, is the common lot, common and vulgar. And behind the four persons who are described, we see the entire company, every member of which, we surmise, has a similar destiny which can be described in similar terms. Behind them again, we see in imagination a whole world of similar lives, and finally find ourselves contemplating an extremely animated historico-economic picture of the perpetual ups and downs of a mob of fortune-hunters scrambling after wealth and stupid pleasures. . . . Such a society most clearly reflects the ups and downs of existence, because there is nothing to hold the balance for it; its members have neither inward tradition nor outer stability; they are nothing without money."[78]

Thus, the *Cena,* as microcosm of an unstable and illusory reality, moves up to still another plane—that of a reflection of the general society itself in which Encolpius, another reflection of that society, moves. The values of the freedmen are not very different from those of the *ingenui* or those of the society as a whole. Money is everywhere the standard by which men are judged in the **Satyricon.** Even the gods are not immune (88.10). All dream of hidden treasure (38.8; 88.8; 128.6), and the imposture of Eumolpus in that grotesque world of legacy hunters, where all pretense to any other interest in life is abandoned (116.3-9), only confirms the social norm. The freedmen aim for status and respectability, and while their distortions of elegance and taste demonstrate the gulf that yawns between them and the stable upper classes, their preoccupations are the same, and, at least, admitted with greater honesty. The satire of the *Cena* can move in the other direction to expose the foibles of the dominant group. For if the freedmen must ape the mores of established society, generally, in their values and aspirations, and specifically, in the staging of a banquet extravagant in its excesses and ostentation, the society itself, which they are so desperate to join, becomes the primary target of the satiric barb.

Encolpius, as picaro, is freed from the rat race for wealth and status. He is well aware of the degradations and dangers of poverty, but he never seeks to acquire wealth for its own sake. He travels light, as picaros do, but he has his own non-picaresque illusions and pretensions which weigh him down with invisible baggage and prevent him from forming any realistic view of the inconstant world.

In the *Cena*, the pretensions to literature and to philosophy satirize the gaucherie of the freedmen, but the inadequacy of these standards as a sign of aristocracy and *humanitas* is also mocked. There are important flashes of this ironic insight in the *Cena*, when *rhetores* and *obsonatores* end up under the same zodiacal sign (39.12; cf. 39.5), where practical education is praised, with some truth, over aspirations to higher culture (46.3-8; 58.7-14), and above all, when the freedmen, in turn, expose the hollow pretensions of the *scholastici* guests (48.4-6; 57.8-11).

Thus, the *Cena*, on several levels, serves as a microcosm of the world of the **Satyricon.** The external techniques of Petronius—the mixture of styles and genres,[79] the episodic, irregular "rush of events," and the succession of tricks, deceits, and illusions—convey a sense of disordered chaos. The *Cena* reveals the world of the freedmen and the world of society at large as a chaos of appearances. But it also exposes the picaresque hero as another chaos of appearances. To assess the importance of his unmasking, we must now turn to an examination of the character of the picaresque hero.

### Character

An examination of the characterization of Encolpius and his friends might best be conducted by viewing their personalities against the typical traits of the picaresque hero. Then it can be shown how, in many instances, Encolpius never learns to be a true picaro, and therein lies the special quality of the **Satyricon,** and perhaps the meaning of its message.

The picaro, as mentioned earlier, is inherently an outsider to his society—an outsider who lives on its fringes, exploits its hierarchical structure, but is not enslaved by it. He "is an inveterate displaced person. He has no home, no calling, no sure set of values."[80] He is mobile, burdened with few material possessions (10.4), and is always ready to move on with the episodic flow of life. He has no fixed destination or purpose which would give coherence to his trials and adventures.

In order to survive in the disordered and chaotic world, the protagonist must be able to divine the roguishness of the world and to guarantee his own existence by joining it as a rogue. The world provides his education as a picaro, and this "pattern of education by the world reflects on the world more than on the picaro. . . . In affirming the world's outer chaos by becoming a picaro, the hero gives up hope of personality and order. Having become a manipulator of appearances, the picaresque character settles into the non-reality of becoming an appearance itself."[81]

The picaro or rogue is a scoundrel, a delinquent, but not a criminal who does harm for its own sake.[82] The pressure of outward events often engenders the roguish pattern. Hunger, for instance, is an effective goad in the picaresque novel,[83] and Encolpius, in his prayer to Priapus, pleads straitened circumstances as justification for his transgressions (133.vv. 6-9).[84]

The world is full of illusions in which the picaro is assailed by tricks of all kinds, as Encolpius is tricked by the old lady at the beginning, by Quartilla, by the events in the *Cena,* by Ascyltos, by Giton, and later by Eumolpus. In retaliation, the picaro learns to play tricks too. Encolpius, however, shows only a limited aptitude for trickery, and one that is also not initiatory but collaborative. In the marketplace (12-15), in the plans for disguise on board the ship (101.6-103.5), and in the preparations for the mime at Croton (117.1-10), he follows along with the schemes of others. In this respect, he never completes his picaresque education, but retains a fundamental naiveté. He is an intermittent rogue, who never masters the art of gratuitous trickery, and yet neither does he remain virtuous and incorruptible.

In order to meet the shifting picaresque world, the picaro must and does assume "protean forms." He should be adept at role-playing and disguise. "Typically, he can turn his hand to anything, assume the disguise of every profession and vocation."[85] The picaro often takes on the slave or servant role under a succession of masters. For "the servant's position offers him the opportunity both to observe and to take advantage of society without being concerned with many of the demands that society makes on the individuals belonging to it. Servitude implies, among other things, irresponsibility. The picaro takes what he can from others because he never collects the various kinds of baggage of his 'own' which would encumber him. Servitude allows him in this way to be his own master, in fact, though not in form, as he could not be were he to take a 'respectable' place in society. . . . By voluntarily becoming a serving man he retires from the general scramble for status and respect and puts himself in a position to survey that scramble with great clarity."[86]

Encolpius is only a partial picaro, for, at least, in the extant portions of the text, he poses mainly as a *scholasticus* and only twice briefly as a slave. Here his intellectual pretensions preclude him from assuming a lowly role for long or in earnest. The picaro is most often a member of the lower classes, generally a young man with too high a degree of intelligence or education for his station.[87] Encolpius and his friends, on the other hand, can be characterized as "bohemians—the unemployable, overeducated, miseducated members of the *lumpen* intelligentsia."[88] Thus when Encolpius adopts the role of slave, he does so not so much as a change in form, but as the playing of a trick. On board the ship Encolpius and Giton pose temporarily as branded fugitive slaves to avoid detection. Ironically, the disguise closely approximates reality, for, in the eyes of Lichas and Tryphaena, they are fugitives from justice, but their disgrace is short-lived. In the second instance, Encolpius' role as a slave in Croton is part of a more commodious trick in which the master is also fictitious. This type of role playing seems to be more of a comic adjustment to society without a real sacrifice of integrity of personality.[89] Encolpius remains a figure who looks at society *de haut en bas,* although it will be shown that it is this view which is ultimately illusionary.

The true picaro becomes radically "other-directed," and as "the infinitely adaptable man . . . he sits on the pole furthest from integrity. He speaks of the thousand daily compromises we make with reality, of our lack of true inner stability, our lack of self, our lack of heroism."[90] In later literature, the hero, no longer a true picaresque figure, may vacillate between "protean disguiser or adjuster to circumstances, and the adamant inner directed romance hero" as is the case, for instance, with Smollett's *Roderick Random*.[91] But Roderick Random finds himself in a true romance situation with his beloved Narcissa, while Encolpius' romantic view of his sordid and unromantic liaisons is only an illusion on his part. Giton, Ascyltos, and Circe may speak in the same terms as Encolpius, but they are not fundamentally deceived by their illusions. Consequently, their behavior approaches role-playing of romantic parodies, while Encolpius genuinely suffers.[92] This is the single most radical difference between Encolpius and the picaro. Picaros harbor no illusions, and are willing "to deal with the world on its own corrupt terms."[93] But Encolpius, when events touch him personally, relinquishes the picaresque view in favor of self delusion. Yet the chaotic reality of his circumstances divined beneath his romantic outlook remains recognizably picaresque. In the *Satyricon* it is only the picaro who does not acquiesce in the full acceptance of this world, but, at the same time, he does not possess the internal stability with which to resist the circumstances of that world.

One of the prominent traits of the picaro is his loneliness and fundamental lack of real love. Real attachment to others provides a meaningful haven of security in the chaotic rush of life. For a picaro, the lack of attachment is "a practical reaction to the disorder [in the world]. If things are chaotic outside, one cannot practically attach oneself to any person or thing; Fortune will blast all attachments, or other men will be revealed as unable to reciprocate love. . . . The unanchored self (or non-self) is the only possible self in such a world."[94] Feeling for others exists, even compassion, or "a gesture in the direction of human solidarity, but it is scarcely

an emotional attachment that organizes the picaro's psyche or behavior in any deeper or lasting way."[95]

Encolpius forms no lasting relationships despite his illusions, nor do any of his friends. The "dance pattern" of these shifting alliances, as I have pointed out earlier, is symptomatic of this instability of personality. Giton plays off Ascyltos and later Eumolpus against Encolpius. Ascyltos steals Giton away but is later seen in the baths going home with the highest bidder for his prodigious equipment (92.7-10). Encolpius, who might have us believe otherwise, was involved in some relationship with Tryphaena, Lichas, and Lichas' wife, and later with Ascyltos before taking up the liaison in earnest with Giton.[96] In Croton he shifts back and forth between Giton and Circe. In fact, his ambivalence as a bisexual is indicative of his basic instability. Although, by his reactions and by his language, he distinguishes between the random sexual escapades (which we have seen as further evidence of a chaotic world), and those attachments in which he is emotionally involved, he cannot remain for long with those passions which he persists in viewing as genuine romantic loves. Thus the loneliness that he experiences after the loss of Giton (81.1-3), in one sense, is another reflection of a romantic reaction to the separation from his beloved, but, on the other hand, is an externally valid expression of the true loneliness that falls to the lot of the picaro.

The organizing principle of the world of romance is one of true love which withstands all vicissitudes and provides stability in an unstable world. The romance hero, after his suffering and after his loneliness, eventually finds a final and permanent union with his beloved. The constancy of his love enables him to persevere. Encolpius fluctuates, changes his resolves, and changes his partners. His reunion with Giton proves to be a shallow and absurd echo of the romance world, for the constancy of chastity gives way to random promiscuity.

In short, Encolpius displays a strange kind of internal instability of character. On the one hand, he possesses traits that are typical of the picaro. He is willing to assume different roles, willing to participate in roguish trickery. He shows inconstancy in his resolutions; he alternately flees and rejoins the world, alternately threatens suicide and embraces life. The picaro is unlike those "characters in whose inner stability, whether throughout the work (comic, romance) or at the end (tragic), we feel joy and exaltation . . . The picaro is neither a round nor a flat character. A flat character is defined by one trait [the miser, the cuckold], a round character, by the organic interrelation or organization of his traits. The picaro differs from the flat in having many traits, from the round in having shifting traits that present no order, that seem random in their appearances and disappearances and connections. While most literary characters speak for the ordered side of our personalities, he speaks for the disordered side."[97] Sullivan's description of Encolpius' character as "disorganized and fragmentary," . . . as "alternately romantic and cynical, brave and timorous, malevolent and cringing, jealous and rational, sophisticated and naive"[98] might seem to label Encolpius as a pure picaro. But the instability of the picaro is supported by the picaro's clear view of the roguish world to which he belongs.

However, when Encolpius tries to organize his emotional life in terms of the diametrically opposed world of romance, he only succeeds in disorganizing his personality still further, this time in a non-picaresque way. Because of these romantic and heroic illusions, he is rarely able to maintain even a temporary mastery over events or to preserve his own picaresque independence. More often than the true picaro, he becomes a victim.

The successful picaro alternates between mastery of and subjection to life's chaotic events, and these alternations of fortune, although not organized in any coherent way, reflect his attunement to the chaotic world. Encolpius never fully joins that world, although the world in the *Satyricon* is shown to be truly picaresque. Thus he obtains few of the benefits of his position.

The theme of freedom has been proposed as an important theme of the picaresque form, supplying a counterbalance to the uneasiness aroused by the external chaos. The picaro is seen as a genuine affirmation of the individual man, and of his "longing for a free natural existence . . . unhampered by conventions of a complex social order."[99] The picaro, "by remaining apart from the stability of the fixed social order, takes upon himself both more freedom and more vulnerability than the ordinary, socially 'adjusted' man. Rugged individualist that he must be, the picaro has to assume direct and personal responsibility for shaping the course of his existence, and in this regard he is freer than other men. . . . The picaro as master of his fate is the jack-of-all-trades, skilled manipulator, adept deceiver, artist of disguises, adaptable to all situations and all men. The picaro as the butt of fortune is the man of many adversities, continually tossed on the breakers of a sea of vicissitudes, never allowed rest or security."[100] Encolpius more frequently falls into the second category.

If one searches the *Satyricon* for a character who plays this picaresque role more fully, Eumolpus emerges as the most likely candidate, although his pretensions to art, providing that he seriously believes them, may somewhat disqualify him. Life has its ups and downs for him; he is stoned in the gallery (90.1); he receives similar treatment in the bath and has difficulty in retrieving his clothes, unlike the more fortunate Ascyltos (92.6-11). The mutilated end of our extant text sug-

gests that time is running out on his imposture in Croton (141.1). In the story of the Pergamene boy he first shows his roguish abilities and then is tricked in turn by his apt pupil (85-87). He displays a real flair for gratuitous trickery; he masterminds the disguise on board the ship, while the others flounder in more impractical plans. He dreams up the scheme in Croton. He can play many roles; he appears now as a serious poet and teacher, now as a bawdy raconteur, now as a practiced diplomat, now as a wealthy old man who is grief stricken over the loss of his only son. He adapts to situations with ease, and when fisticuffs are called for in the inn, he is equal to the occasion and accepts his injuries with equanimity (95.4-9; 98.7). Relationships for him are sexually oriented. He has no other interest in Giton than his physical beauty, and when Philomela offers him her daughter, he works out a plan whereby he can maintain the illusion of his impotence and enjoy the girl at the same time (140.1-11).

For Eumolpus impotence is part of his disguise of debility. For Encolpius it becomes an unpleasant fact of his existence. Picaros are lusty, healthy fellows with a strong appeal to women. Encolpius' appetites may be broader, but he most often falls short of fulfillment. The theme of impotence which is associated with the recurrent motif of death is unusual for a well-adjusted picaro, but it is an excellent image for the picaro manqué.

Encolpius' physical impotence parallels his inability to meet the modern world on its own terms. When it is objected that the *Satyricon* presents no "unified point of view," the burden of this "failure" falls on the narrator who should be able to supply that "missing" outlook.[101] To strip off the mask from others he ought to have some sense of honesty, if only a uniform cynicism. Encolpius does not, for while he prepares a face to meet the faces that he meets, he is unable to peer behind his own mask with any consistency. A narrator who can see the pack on another's back but not on his own provides shifting planes of irony and ambiguity which are often difficult to fathom. His failure to present a stable ordered personality, *qua* picaro, is due to the conditions a picaresque world imposes on him. But his impotence, emotional illusions, and false rhetoric are due to the defects of his formal traditional education which do not allow him to complete the picaresque education which the world demands of him. Encolpius, the anti-hero in a world in which heroism is dead, persists in the fantasy of viewing his life in heroic terms and gauging his responses accordingly. He is an outsider, like all picaros, because of his loss of place in the social hierarchy. But he is even more a psychic outsider, who by persisting in living in a vanished mode, can never come to terms with the world.

He is an odd combination of the picaresque and quixotic types. To a roguish world he often responds with the appropriate roguishness. But, as a quixotic type, he projects himself as a kind of noble simpleton who sees the world through the lens of myth, epic, and romance. Yet nobility is precisely the trait he is lacking, for he has not the virtue and the strength that lies behind the idealistic faith of Cervantes' hero. Don Quixote "rejects society as it is—and brings himself to see the world as it is not . . . because he has culled from literature an ideal image of what the society should be. . . . The picaro's imagination is pragmatic, the Don's idealistic. . . . The picaro improvises his manner of acting as he goes; he preserves a strong sense of spontaneity in the way he lives. Don Quixote, on the other hand, tries to follow a pattern that he has learned from the printed page: life for him amounts to the fulfillment of a duty—both to himself and to the world. In sum, the picaro lives by ear; Don Quixote lives by the book."[102] Encolpius, too, lives by the book, although in a shallow and hedonistic way, for he feels no sense of duty either to himself or to the world. What is even more important, he does not continually live in this fashion, a situation which deranges his character still further. A violent clash results between the picaresque mold and the quixotic mutant which renders Encolpius even more unstable than the world around him, and produces another level of chaos that approaches the schizophrenic.

But by this technique, the nature of the chaos in Petronius' world is more closely defined. For the present world which is revealed as chaotic and illusionary is held up against a background of the established literary tradition. This tradition, in turn, points to a heroic and romantically idealized view of the Roman world which was perpetuated through literature but was finally trivialized through the emptiness of rhetoric. Rhetoric is a symptom of this vacuum that exists between the facts of the present and the values of the past. It is also a cause of the disparity. Hence the images of death and of impotence and of losing one's way are important metaphors of the failure of culture. The *vitrea fracta,* the phrase which describes the *sententiae* of rhetoric (10.1), are also strewn over the ground outside Trimalchio's house on whose fragments the characters, unable to find their way, cut and bloody their feet (79.1-3). The broken glass fragments of rhetoric supply a mirror of life that is inevitably distorted, deranged, and ultimately fragmentary.[103] Serious intellectual activities are also ironically refracted, for no character is capable of speaking about them without resort to rhetoric. The ideas and their rhetorical presentation are indissolubly bound up with each other.

Encolpius, in two instances, makes his plight clear to the reader. In the opening attack against the traditional education of his day, he exposes its irrelevancies and unrealities (1-2); it fails to prepare students to cope actively with life; it is intoxicated with the sheer flow of empty verbiage; it constricts free development of the intellect by the use of the set speech. In short, its effect is one of enervation and paralysis. In his diagnosis, Encolpius unwittingly exposes the reasons for his own vulnerability to circumstances and his own failure to adapt successfully to the outside world. When he accuses the rhetoricians of fostering absurdities of language, *ut corpus orationis enervaretur* (2.2), his later impotence takes on an added meaning.[104] But Encolpius, nevertheless, commits the same faults he castigates. He "is naive enough and suggestible enough to parrot his teacher, hypocrisy and all."[105] His speech against declamation is revealed as still another declamation, and this is the term that Agamemnon uses to cut off the verbal flood (3.1).[106] His language and his presentation betray his lack of real understanding of the stultifying limitations of Roman education. In addition, the remedies of a return to the literature of the past which he and Agamemnon propose, will, if carried out, perhaps sharpen his literary tastes but will not help him solve his real-life problems. He will only increase his bookish pretensions without any palpable growth in emotional maturity.

In the second instance, Encolpius has another important inkling of the gap that lies between his private reality of epic and romance and the objective reality of life. The placement of these remarks is significant, for Encolpius, distraught by his physical impotence, determines to lop off his offending member, a plan, which, in his typical inconstancy, he fails to carry out. He grasps the need for language and behavior which are both honest and realistic, but this insight can be no permanent truth for him. He lapses immediately into parodistic verse which recalls literary approaches to the same problem, and thus his statement is given the same air of unreality (132.6-15).

It is, in my opinion, an egregious error to isolate this passage as the personal view of Petronius who is said to be advocating a return to an earlier classical tradition of simplicity.[107] The very terms of Encolpius' presentation deny this, and, moreover, he has not had difficulty before in speaking of these matters in a refined way. Frankness is surely one of the refreshing attributes he has exhibited on occasion, but only when he plays the role of picaro. Perhaps Encolpius here is trying to bridge the gap between the picaresque vision he occasionally shares and the romantic vision he too often entertains, but the mode of his observation shows that he fails to grasp its essential import. The burden of the past becomes too great and overwhelms him; he has only composed another *declamatio,* as he himself calls it, and words are again substituted for action (133.1). When Encolpius scolds Eumolpus for his "disease" of spouting literature, he remarks that he has spent two hours with him, *et saepius poetice quam humane locutus es* (90.3). Unfortunately, Encolpius suffers from a variation of the same malady, but he cannot make that diagnosis; hence the irony of his situation.

## IV. *World-View*

It is therefore idle to look in the **Satyricon** for a conventional moralist who takes up the terms of a moribund set of dogmas offered in fossilized form. Petronius surely is no neo-Epicurean, no neo-satirist in the old tradition, no neo-classicist who looks back to established time-hallowed forms for a revitalization of the present.

All his techniques point instead to a radically anti-classical stance. He thumbs his nose at the doctrine of the purity of genres, at stylistic uniformity, and at the doctrine of decorum. Literature of the past is reduced to parody and absurdity. Traditional philosophical and moralistic views are undermined and even annulled. What is more, his entire tale is anti-classical in viewpoint.

One has only to compare the *Odyssey* or its later definition in the *Aeneid* to gauge the difference. Odysseus is a rogue, it is true—the archetypal rogue of Western literature—but he never becomes a true picaro. He exults in gratuitous trickery, but he has an integrated ordered personality and the fixed destination of a stable ordered society about which he organizes his existence. He normally maintains his mastery over circumstances. The external chaos of the world resides permanently in the fabulous and mysterious regions of the remote world. Chaos at home in the social frame gives way to the order which is reestablished by Odysseus himself and validated by the gods' assurance of justice.

The *Aeneid* has its own set of referents for creating a coherent world in which the framework of history embraces the past, the present, and the future of Rome. In plot, in the patterning and interrelationship of books, in its poetic exposition of themes, the Roman epic represents a point at which the *furor* of passion and irrationality yields, at least for a time, to the stable order achieved by the application of high ideals and reason and sanctioned by Fate.

The **Satyricon** sees only a disorderly world unsupported by the rational guidance of the gods or their substitutes. The balance, the symmetry, the perfection of pure form that resides in the classical mode finds a radical antithesis in the hectic rush of irrational episodes narrated in a mixture of styles and genres. "The **Satyricon** is all uproar, guffaws, rumpus, commotion, but behind its noise there is always present a long recurrent note—the ebb and flow of human irrelevance."[108] This is a world where "things fall apart; the center cannot hold;/ Mere anarchy is loosed upon the world."[109] Where the center is lost, purpose and direction are also lost.

Classicism feels secure in the proven models of the past which have demonstrated their validity as artistic representations of human existence, while the **Satyricon** rejects the forms of the past and confounds the organizing principles of classical theory. Yet there is also a poignant regret for what is past and gone, and the ghosts of the past which hover over the **Satyricon** only increase the uneasiness engendered by the new picaresque world. But there is no turning back to the old models in these changed circumstances. Petronius is a revolutionary who articulates in art his sense of a transitional society in the throes of a cultural and social crisis.

There is one other example of a classical author who approaches Petronius in his concept of the world, and he does so by techniques that are also meant to express the turbulence of another cultural crisis. That author is Euripides writing in the declining days of the Athenian democracy, "haunted by the disappearance of the old integrated culture and the heroic image of man that had incarnated that culture."[110] Allowing for the fundamental difference in mode between tragedy and comedy, in form between drama and novel, in temperament between Greek and Roman, Euripides and Petronius show many startling similarities.

Like Petronius, the drama of Euripides assumes "a universe devoid of rational order or of an order incomprehensible to men . . .", a feeling which he "reports with great clarity and honesty . . . [as] the widening gulf between reality and tradition; between the operative and professed values of his culture; between fact and myth; . . . between life and art."[111]

Euripides mixes genres and tones so that tragedy slides towards comedy, romance, and melodrama. A late play, like the *Helen,* defies satisfactory classical genre description. The *Helen* is an excellent example since its philosophical premise rests on the confusion between reality and illusion.[112] "At any point in a tragedy, the comic, or more accurately, the pathetic or ludicrous, can erupt with poignant effect, intensifying the tragic or toughening it with parody."[113] Aeschylus, for instance, is held before the audience in a parodistic way, notably in the recognition scene in the *Electra* and in the outburst of the Phrygian slave in the *Orestes,* which is an absurd imitation of the mad scene of Cassandra in the *Agamemnon.*

Euripides, like Petronius, is an antitraditional artist who experiments with various forms, with innovations in language and music, with new plots and with old ones given new complications in a sharp contrast to the austere economy of the traditional drama (e.g., *Ion*). His plays are crowded with characters and with rapid series of actions, rendering a more complex view of life. Coincidences and improbabilities abound.

Realism is another feature of Euripidean theater, which creates a dissonance in the drama. Incongruities are everywhere. Myth conflicts with the more sordid reality of experience, and the harshness of their juxtaposition is not softened (e.g., *Heracles*). The heroic figure is domesticated, debased, and deheroized, like Jason or Orestes. In Euripides, realism invades the mythological sphere with disquieting effects;[114] in Petronius, the situation is reversed.

In Euripides, characters assume elaborate disguises and plot intricate deceptions (e.g., *Helen, Iphigenia in Tauris, Electra*). The passions and irrationalities of human behavior are thrust into prominence. Derangement and abnormality of personality are explored (e.g., *Orestes, Electra*). Emphasis is laid on the plight of the individual who is adrift and isolated in a chaotic world, whether in actual exile (*Iphigenia in Tauris, Helen*) or in a state of psychological alienation (*Electra, Orestes*).[115] Heroes are often weak and inconstant. They waver in resolution and change their minds, reflecting the epistemological problem of the world's coherence (*Hippolytus, Iphigenia in Aulis*).[116] *Tyche,* blind and senseless Fortune, gains in importance, and the restoration of the order demanded by the myth is often effected artificially by the *deus ex machina,* sometimes a mechanical contrivance in the fuller sense of the word (*Orestes, Electra*). "His theater everywhere insists upon a scrupulous and detailed recreation of the complexity of reality and the difficulty of moral judgment."[117] In his chaotic contemporary world, Euripides, like Petronius, responded to the loss of the coherent social system and its attendant values with revolutionary ideas and techniques.

But Euripides is not as nihilistic or ironic as Petronius. He questions old values in the search for new ones. In vaunting the individual and his solitary experience as the ultimate touchstone of action, he sees redemption in the loyalty of personal relationships, in the assumption of inner moral convictions, in the power of the young, the old, the weak, and the innocent to redeem their society and to recreate its values.[118]

Petronius is more difficult to read. He has not suggested any unambiguous solutions to the problem of establishing a new order or even of effecting a means for revitalization. Parody is ultimately an unstable and temporary mode of expression appropriate to the experience of an unstable world. The colloquial speech of the freedmen may reflect an aesthetic experiment, a "rebarbarization" of literature,[119] but the contents of their conversations, while they are to be commended for their more realistic view of the world, also display an enslavement to the general values of the society which the freedmen yearn to enter. Nor can the old

tradition that once validated social norms serve to re-establish order, for Petronius has diagnosed one important symptom of the cultural failure in Encolpius' enslavement to the past.

He has not offered an aesthetic and ideological alternative in his world, but he has used new form, new technique, and new content to diagram the predicament of his age. The ironic approach he adopts, like that of the picaresque, "need not have any positive moral purpose; it is critical without necessarily assuming a clear standard of desired behavior. Ultimately, picaresque irony is an individualist, asocial exercise of the intellect, and as such it reflects the condition of rootlessness which is the heart of the picaresque situation."[120] It is an "irony of disintegration," but it is not a bitter denunciation. Instead there is laughter, exuberance, and vitality.

The one important positive aspect of his vision is finally that exuberance, that vitality, that rich sense of the comic tempered with compassion and with understanding.[121] This sense of the comic sees the absurdity of man, his society, and his world, but it makes that vision endurable through the medium of wit and irony which expresses not hatred and disgust but a sense of partnership in and commitment to the human condition. Habinnas sums up this insight that informs the ***Satyricon:*** *Nemo nostrum . . . non peccat. Homines sumus, non dei* (75.1). It is an insight that renounces the classical hero, both comic and tragic, and his aspirations to moments of superhuman achievement, but one that is consonant with the changed condition of the world.

*Historical Perspective*

The ***Satyricon,*** in its ambiguities, ironies, parodies, and incongruities, is essentially related to those forms of literature which unsettle the reader by their anarchic view of life, and which generally appear in times of cultural and social stress of varying kinds. The picaresque novel, for instance, arises in Spain in the wake of the breakup of the feudal order and in Germany during the chaos of the Thirty Years' War.[122] Uncertainty, dislocation, and anxiety are the impulses which produce a cynical realism, a satire of society, and a distrust of dogma and tradition.

In the Rome of Petronius' time several sets of conditions encourage the genesis of a work like the ***Satyricon.*** First, there are the special conditions at the court of Nero. A literary salon existed dedicated to experimentation, and the courtiers were imbued by their emperor with sophisticated tastes, a strong iconoclastic sense, a contempt for the conventions of Roman aristocratic life, and a *nostalgie de la boue*.[123] The ***Satyricon*** could easily find acceptance and even inspiration from such an audience.

On another level, however, the shifting and capricious temper of a deranged ruler must also be taken into consideration. Nero, who may have encouraged an unconventional and frank acknowledgement of men's secret desires and vices (Suet. 29), invited hypocrisy and flattery too by destroying those who asserted or seemed to assert any independence of thought or action. His paranoid fears, which often prompted arbitrary and irrational behavior, would tend to create an atmosphere in which the world of the courtiers must have appeared chaotic and illusionary. The echoes of court practices in the *Cena* and the reminiscences of the traits of Nero and other emperors in the figure of Trimalchio support this assumption still further.[124]

Secondly, the political climate of the Neronian age, owing to the repressive imperial policies, had demoralized the senatorial class, whose major function and source of prestige had been active public service; it also demoralized the lower classes who felt still less of a share in controlling their own destinies. This group, energized by spectacles which channelled off their aggressive instincts and de-energized or pacified by the hydrotherapeutic influences of the baths, had, to a large degree, also lost any real sense of national purpose. The intellectuals perhaps suffered a larger degree of alienation. Augustan ideals of the lofty goals of Roman destiny became for many of them another rigid convention, like the moral conventions, openly subscribed to and privately denied. The sense of communal values was thereby seriously diminished.

The third factor, the larger socio-economic situation, is still more important. This was "an age of great economic growth in the shadow of a principate which had struck root, and it produced patches of prosperity from which a number of individuals benefited to a vast degree."[125] It was the beginning of a time of physical and social mobility. The *Cena,* in its presentation of the freedmen's milieu, reflects the disruption of that hierarchical society in which each man knew his place and his prospects. The urban sprawl of a polyglot, cosmopolitan population in a technologically complex society leads always, even as in our own time, to a dehumanization of man. The individual loses a sense of participation in a coherent group, and turns inward to personal and private means of the validation of life. This movement towards individual standards is evident already in Euripides' response to the more limited social crisis of his age. It is still more evident in the social developments of the Hellenistic age which gave rise to the prose romance.[126] It also becomes a factor in Roman literature of the late Republic; the writers of that period responded to the complexities of urban life with an emphasis on the worth of personal experience.[127]

That Petronius should create a character who is a delinquent, an outsider, a marginal man, who belongs in no social milieu, who has no past or future, no destination or purpose beyond passing pleasures and the will to survive, whose personality is unstable, whose relationships are insecure, and who should have learned by experience that the world is roguish, unpredictable, and ultimately without any coherent design, marks the first step taken in literature towards the vision of our modern desacralized world and the image of the radically alienated man who is familiar to us from the pages of modern fiction.

But, in another more positive sense, the *Satyricon,* like the picaresque form but on a diminished scale, "affirms the primacy of individual experience—to begin with, the most basic aspects of individual experience—in a kind of existence where any larger order must be very much in question. It is a literary form characteristic of a period of disintegration, both social disintegration and disintegration of belief. Like Descartes, the picaresque writer finds any existing systems to be of the shakiest kind, and he too, tries to effect a basic reconstruction by beginning again with the one self-evident fact of the experiencing 'I'."[128]

This condition accounts for the fact that in cultural history the novel itself receives late acceptance as a serious and important literary genre. "The novel is the form of literature which most fully reflects this individualist and innovating reorientation. Previous literary forms had reflected the general tendency of their culture to make conformity to traditional practice the major test of truth; the plots of classical and Renaissance epic, for example, are based on past history or fable, and the merits of the author's treatment are judged largely according to a view of literary models in the genre. This literary traditionalism is first and most fully challenged by the novel, whose primary criterion was truth to individual experience—the individual experience which is always unique and therefore new."[129]

Here, in this perspective, lies the basis for an evaluation of Petronius and the radical originality of his work seen within its classical context. The use of a long fictional narrative as his form becomes a significant and important choice. Within the loose confines of that form, Petronius has succeeded in creating an inner coherence and logic which is proper to its purpose of commentary upon and elucidation of the human condition. Form, style, and content are all integrated into a unitary world-view, which may dismay us by its vision of anarchy, but which we may admire paradoxically for the integrity of its presentation in Petronius' art.

## Notes

[1] This paper came into being largely as a result of an undergraduate seminar on Petronius given at Rutgers University in the spring of 1971. Special acknowledgement is made to Myron Jaworsky, Ronald Kopnicki, and Kathleen Miller for their contributions.

I am indebted to Professors Gilbert Highet and S. Palmer Bovie and to Craig Knobles who offered many valuable suggestions.

[2] Textual references to the Satyricon will be cited from the Budé edition, ed. A. Ernout (Paris 1923; repr. 1967).

The following bibliographical references are used: Alter = Robert Alter, *Rogue's Progress: Studies in the Picaresque Novel* (Cambridge, Mass. 1964); Arrowsmith I = William Arrowsmith, "Luxury and Death in the *Satyricon,*" *Arion* 5 (1966) 304-31; Arrowsmith II = William Arrowsmith, "Euripides' Theater of Ideas" in *Euripides: A Collection of Critical Essays,* ed. E. Segal (Englewood Cliffs, New Jersey 1968) 13-33; Booth = Wayne C. Booth, *The Rhetoric of Fiction* (Chicago 1961); Cameron = Averil M. Cameron, "Myth and Meaning in Petronius: Some Modern Comparisons," *Latomus* 29 (1970) 397-425; Courtney = E. Courtney, "Parody and Literary Allusion in Menippean Satire," *Philologus* 106 (1962) 86-100; Frye = Northrop Frye, *Anatomy of Criticism* (1957; repr. New York 1968); George = Peter George, "Style and Character in the *Satyricon,*" *Arion* 5 (1966) 336-58; Kiremidjian = G. D. Kiremidjian, "The Aesthetics of Parody," *Journal of Aesthetics and Art Criticism* 28 (1970) 231-42; Miller = Stuart Miller, *The Picaresque Novel* (Cleveland 1967); Perry = Ben E. Perry, *The Ancient Romances* (Berkeley and Los Angeles 1967); Rankin = H. D. Rankin, "Some Comments on Petronius' Portrayal of Character," *Eranos* 68 (1970) 123-47; Rexroth = Kenneth Rexroth, "Petronius, the *Satyricon,*" in *Classics Revisited* (New York 1969) 99-103; Sullivan = J. P Sullivan, *The Satyricon of Petronius: A Literary Study* (Bloomington, Ind. and London 1968); Veyne = P. Veyne, "Le 'je' dans le *Satiricon,*" *REL* 42 (1964) 301-24; Walsh = P. G. Walsh, *The Roman Novel* (Cambridge 1970); Wellek and Warren = René Wellek and Austin Warren, *Theory of Literature*[3] (New York 1956); Zeitlin = Froma I. Zeitlin, "Romanus Petronius: A Study of the *Troiae Halosis* and the *Bellum Civile,*" *Latomus* 30 (1971) 56-82.

[3] Such is the case, for example, with Laurence Sterne's *Tristam Shandy.* "Is it simply a scrambled comic novel . . . ? Is it a collection of playful speculative essays like Montaigne's, but with a more fictional sugar coating than Montaigne felt necessary? Or is it a satire in the tradition of Swift's *A Tale of the Tub,* taking in, as Sterne himself put it, 'everything which I find laugh-at-able in my way'?" Booth 222. See further Booth's analysis of the work—the problem of formal coherence and the unity of *Tristam Shandy,* 221-40.

[4] If the following exposition of some basic principles of literary theory seems too rudimentary to be mentioned, I ask the reader's indulgence. Such an exposition, oversimplified as it is, seems to me to be neces-

sary in view of much of the recent evaluations of Petronius which tend to ignore these principles.

[5] Kiremidjian 236. By form I mean "the aesthetic structure of a literary work—that which makes it literature." By content (or materials) I mean "human behavior experience . . . and human ideas and attitudes." Wellek and Warren 241. See their entire chapter, "Evaluation," 238-51 and the bibliography cited therein.

[6] Sullivan 266-67.

[7] Sullivan 81-83 calls the *Satyricon* "a highly original work unparalleled in ancient literature," but lays his emphasis on the debts Petronius owes to tradition (especially to Menippean satire) which, in his opinion, predetermined Petronius' choice of material. Courtney 100, too, concludes that Petronius' "exuberant genius . . . embarked on a 'Kreuzung der Gattungen' which for breadth and audacity has no parallel in ancient literature and which completely overrides the extremely formal canons of ancient literary theory," but he too relates this feature mainly to the tradition of Menippean satire. Walsh 7 asserts that "nothing remotely comparable to its plot survives in Greek literature, and the Roman atmosphere of many of its episodes encourages the belief that he has brought to birth a new type of fiction," but in his analysis he too stresses the importance of the formative genres. Perry 186-90, 202-10 offers the most illuminating discussion of the originality of the *Satyricon.* But, while he rejects the usual emphasis on *Quellenforschungen,* he attributes the adoption of this radically unusual form to Petronius' desire for "a safe place in which to experiment artistically with various types of poetry, rhetorical declamation, and criticism" 209. Cameron comes closer to an appreciation of the wider implications of Petronius' originality as expressed through the interrelationship of form and content. See especially 423-24 and cf. Arrowsmith I, 304-25.

[8] Wellek and Warren 234. See J. F. D'Alton, *Roman Literary Theory and Criticism* (New York 1931; repr. 1962) 398-482 for a full discussion of the classical theory of kinds and for enumeration of the ancient sources. See also Perry 18-27.

[9] For a discussion of the various influences on the *Satyricon* with relevant bibliography, see especially Perry 186-89, Walsh 7-31, Sullivan 89-98, 115-57, and Veyne 310-12.

[10] Cameron 404. See also W. Kroll, "Die Kreuzung der Gattungen" in *Studien zum Verständnis der römischen Literatur* (1924; repr. Darmstadt 1969) 223-24. "Petronius makes use of various types of subject matter that were topical or prominent in . . . antecedent literary forms . . . ; but these for him were simply building materials. Like so many bricks, they tell us

nothing about the architectural scheme of the *Satyricon* as a whole and the purpose that guided the author in the construction of it." Perry 206.

Courtney 90 and Sullivan 81-114 insist that Menippean satire is to be classified in this category. But I concur in Cameron's judgment that "there is no sign that there existed in the shadowy satires of Varro anything of the rich invention of the *Satyricon*." 404. See also G. Schmeling, "The *Satyricon:* Forms in Search of a Genre," *CB* 47 (1971) 49-50. Despite the presence in Menippean satire of genre mixture, literary allusions, parody, and prosimetric form, the scale of the *Satyricon* (even in its mutilated state), its characterizations, its complicated plot, and its whole conception militate against such a narrow viewpoint.

[11] Kiremidjian 236.

[12] "Parody, in effect, violates the doctrine of decorum, by making a relationship between a genre and its style which is not proper or decorous at all," but, in fact, is "a reverse relationship." George Watson, *The Study of Literature* (New York 1969) 94. This technique of sundering the union of form and content was, of course, an accepted technique in antiquity. See P. Lelièvre, "The Basis of Ancient Parody," *G&R* NS 1 (1954) 66-81, J. Cèbes, *La caricature et la parodie dans le monde romain antique* (Paris 1966), and Courtney 86-100. Yet nowhere else in antiquity is parody used so pervasively and with such a wide range of targets. The effect of Petronius' extravagant engagement with parodistic expression deserves an examination of the deeper implications which parody may bear over and beyond its humorous appeal and its value as a mode of literary criticism. But since parody in Petronius extends beyond the main genre categories to general stylistic considerations, this examination will be deferred for the moment.

[13] Wellek and Warren 235.

[14] Wellek and Warren 233-34.

[15] On the literary interests of the Neronian court, see Sullivan 81-86 and J. P. Sullivan, "Petronius Seneca and Lucan: A Neronian Literary Feud?", *TAPA* 99 (1968) 454-55.

[16] Wellek and Warren 226 and see their chapter, "Literature and Society," 94-109. See also Harry Levin, "Literature as an Institution," *Accent* 6 (1946) 159-68 (repr. in *Criticism,* eds. Schorer, Miles, McKenzie [New York 1948] 546-53).

[17] See E. Sage, "Atticism in Petronius," *TAPA* 46 (1915) 47-57, and Sullivan 158-70 who sees the two characteristics of Petronius' criticism as "propriety and classicism." 165.

[18] I am in agreement here with Walsh 49-50, who remarks that "in keeping with the characterization of the conservative theorist of mediocre talent, the poem handles the theme of the civil war in a traditionalist manner, but in style [often] echoes the stridency and monotonous versification of the poet whom Eumolpus is condemning. The irony is characteristic of Petronius." Although Vergil's influence on the versification is also apparent (see George E. Duckworth, "Five Centuries of Latin Hexameter Poetry: Silver Age and Late Empire," *TAPA* 98 [1967] 106-7, n. 83), mannerisms of Lucan are also prominent. For the theory that this poem is a serious critique of Lucan, see Sullivan 165-86 and for the ideological implications of the poem beyond the confines of literary method, see Zeitlin 67-82.

[19] Frye 229, 230.

[20] On the satirical treatment of Stocism and Seneca, its leading exponent, see Sullivan 193-211 and Sullivan (above, note 15) 461-62. Although it has been claimed recently that Petronius espouses a popular brand of Epicureanism (see O. Raith, *Petronius ein Epikureer* [Nuremberg 1963], Walsh 50, 82, 109-10, and, to some extent, Sullivan 33, 88, 108, 212 and Sullivan [above, note 15] 465), the text does not seem to support any consistent adherence to a single philosophy. In fact, on shipboard, Epicurus earns a satirical reference of his own. Eumolpus cites Epicurus' disdain for the vatic properties of dreams in order to dissuade Lichas and Tryphena from investigating the meaning of their dreams (104.3), but these dreams, in fact, turn out to convey accurate information.

[21] See the exposition of this theory in Sullivan 85-89 and its sequel in Sullivan (above, note 15) 453-67, where the evidence and the arguments seem to me to be less convincing. In any case, Sullivan 268 recognizes that "it must be confessed that Petronius' literary theories and artistic practice finally impress the reader, despite their successes, as not quite fully thought out. His complaints about the unreality of contemporary rhetoric are not consonant with his traditionalist's admiration of Vergilian epic; his defence of the realism of the *Satyricon* . . . conflicts with the differently conceived fantasy of much of the Crotonian episode, as well as with many of the irrelevant insertions, prose and verse, which serve merely to display his stylistic invention and skills." Frye's remarks on the use of satire and irony provide a useful explanation of this apparent "gap" between theory and practice. "The romantic fixation which revolves around the beauty of perfect form, in art or elsewhere, is also a logical target for satire. The word satire is said to come from *satura,* or hash, and a kind of parody of form seems to run all through its tradition, from the mixture of prose and verse in early satire to the jerky cinematic changes of scene in Rabelais. . . . *Tristam Shandy* and *Don Juan* illustrate very clearly the constant tendency to

self-parody in satiric rhetoric which prevents even the process of writing itself from becoming an over-simplified convention or ideal. . . . An extraordinary number of great satires are fragmentary, unfinished, or anonymous. In ironic fiction a good many devices turning on the difficulty of communication . . . serve the same purpose" 233-34.

[22] On the recurrent features of the comic mode, see Frye 163-86. On the freedom of invention allowed to comedy, see Perry 89, although I cannot agree with his notion that no rules whatsoever apply to the writing of comedy. Perry's definition of a comic novel is also useful to this discussion—"anything that one would call burlesque, picaresque, satirical, realistic, disillusioning, unmoral or unideal" 87. Satire should be subsumed under the larger rubric of the comic mode insofar as it exhibits "wit or humor founded on fantasy or a sense of the grotesque or absurd," Frye 224, but it should be remembered that satire is not the only source of the comic in the *Satyricon*. The mime, as well as comic drama, exercise an important influence.

[23] See Ian Watt, *The Rise of the Novel* (London 1957) 13.

[24] Henry James, Preface to the revised version of *The Tragic Muse,* in *The Art of the Novel: Critical Prefaces* (New York 1934) 84.

[25] See Miller 9-10; see also Booth 23-60. On the *Satyricon*'s failure as a "realistic" novel, see Sullivan 96-98.

[26] "Whereas the novelist aims at understanding the complexities of life, satire aims at simplification, at a pretence of misunderstanding, and at denunciation. The sheer size of the open-ended form of the novel has also much to do with the difficulty that satirists have in using it: Satire seems to require a light and closed form which helps to make a simple point effectively— the form is itself a component of wit without which satire is unbearable. It follows that no full-length novel is likely to be satirical throughout, and indeed not one example among the classics comes to mind." Matthew Hodgart, *Satire* (New York and Toronto 1969) 214. See his entire chapter, "Satire in the Novel," 214-40.

[27] Walsh 224-43 has pointed out the relationship of Petronius (and Apuleius) with the picaresque novel, but he has confined himself to speculations as to the influence of the Roman writers on later literature. (See further below, note 48.) There have been several studies on similarities between Petronius and more modern writers—Cameron on Petronius and Joyce, Pound, and Eliot, H. D. Rankin, "Notes on the Comparison of Petronius with Three Moderns," *AAntHung* 18 (1970) 197-213 [Proust, Joyce, and Fitzgerald], P. MacKendrick, "The Great Gatsby and Trimalchio," *CJ*

45 (1950) 307-14, and William Arrowsmith, Introduction to his translation of the *Satyricon* (New York 1960) viii, who suggests a comparison with Vladimir Nabokov's *Lolita*.

[28] Wellek and Warren 214.

[29] Sullivan 264 but he never makes clear what he means by this phrase.

[30] "Un roman: c'est un miroir qu'on promène le long d'un chemin." Stendhal (Henri Beyle), *Le rouge et le noir: Chronique du XIX͡e siècle,* ed. Henri Martineau (Paris 1953) 76.

[31] Sullivan 164.

[32] Sullivan 267 is the leading proponent of this view.

[33] Miller 112. This statement describes the style of Francisco de Quevedo's *El Buscón,* a picaresque novel of the Spanish Renaissance (1616), but it is even more applicable to the *Satyricon*.

[34] Sullivan 215.

[35] Sullivan 215-16.

[36] See George 337 and 357, n. 2.

[37] See George on Eumolpus, 347-48.

[38] For a discussion of Petronius' subtle discrimination in the speaking styles of his personages to reveal character, see George 336-58.

[39] For an exhaustive and sometimes overzealous list of literary allusions in the *Satyricon,* see A. Collignon, *Étude sur Pétrone* (Paris 1892). See too Courtney 86-99 and Walsh 32-52.

[40] See Walsh 35-36. For a more detailed study of Petronius' use of Vergil and Ovid, see Zeitlin 58-82.

[41] Kiremidjian 233.

[42] See Kiremidjian's discussion 232, 234-35. On the modern writers, see, for example, Hugh Kenner, *Dublin's Joyce* (Bloomington, Ind. 1956) 7-18, and Erich Heller, *Thomas Mann; The Ironic German* (Boston 1958; rev. ed. New York 1961) 253-90.

[43] Kiremidjian 237.

[44] Kiremidjian 240.

[45] Kiremidjian 241.

[46] Kiremidjian 242.

[47] Rexroth 101.

[48] The earliest example of the picaresque novel (but considered by some critics to be proto-picaresque or a precursor of the picaresque) is the anonymous *Lazarillo de Tormes* (1554). Other notable Spanish representatives include Mateo Alemán, *Guzmán de Alfarache* (Part I publ. 1599, Part II, 1604), and Francisco de Quevedo, *El Buscón* (1616). A lone Elizabethan entry is Thomas Nashe, *The Unfortunate Traveller* (1594). Alain René Lesage heralds the French tradition with *Gil Blas* (1715/1724/1735), although most recent criticism detects many important deviations from the norm. The main German contender is Hans Jacob Christoffels von Grimmelshausen, *Der abenteuerliche Simplicissimus* (1668) which uses the historical background of the Thirty Years' War as the setting for the hero's picaresque adventures. The English tradition includes, again with reservations, Tobias Smollett, *Roderick Random* (1748) and Daniel Defoe, *Moll Flanders* (1722). Henry Fielding, *Tom Jones* (1749), which owes much to the genre, is not in fact a picaresque novel.

On the history of the picaresque novel and for a more complete list of representatives of the form, see Alberto del Monte, *Itinerario del romanzo picaresco spagnuolo* (Firenze 1957) and Alexander Parker, *Literature and the Delinquent: The Picaresque Novel in Spain and Europe 1599-1753* (Edinburgh 1967). For other more detailed studies of the characteristics of the genre, see especially Alter and Miller.

[49] Miller 9, 132. This contention informs his entire study of the picaresque genre in which he takes a structural and not a historical approach.

[50] More modern "revivals" of the picaresque might include Stendhal, *Le rouge et le noir* (1830), Mark Twain, *Huckleberry Finn* (1884), Saul Bellow, *The Adventures of Augie March* (1953), Thomas Mann, *The Confessions of Felix Krull* (1955), Joyce Cary, *The Horse's Mouth* (1944), and Ralph Ellison, *Invisible Man* (1947). One or more of the novels of Céline, Henry Miller, Thomas Pynchon, William Burroughs, Jean Genet, and Günther Grass have also been mentioned as possible contenders. But there is no general consensus on any of these later works.

[51] Miller 10.

[52] See Sullivan 77, and see his collection of ancient testimonia, 111-14.

[53] Miller 10.

[54] Miller 12.

[55] Perhaps this is why the frequent lacunae in the text do not, for the most part, seriously diminish the reader's enjoyment or even comprehension.

[56] On the "dance pattern," see Miller 13-20.

[57] Miller 21, and see his discussion of the rhythm in picaresque novels, 21-27.

[58] See especially *Sat.* 20, 21.1-3, 26.7. On the prevalence of physical violence in the picaresque novel as a reflection of social disorder, see Alter 66.

[59] Sullivan's treatment of the pornographic elements of the *Satyricon* isolates voyeurism and exhibitionism as the chief perversions, which he interprets as peculiarities of Petronius himself, 238-53. Since he stands virtually alone among Petronian scholars in his willingness to discuss this hitherto taboo subject, other critics have accepted his conclusions without any further qualifications (e.g., Walsh and Cameron). His theory can be questioned on several grounds. First of all, voyeurism and exhibitionism are only minor motifs in the range of pornographic situations which Petronius sets before us. Second of all, these two acts are integral ingredients of any pornographic work which typically includes orgies and other scenes of group sex. (See Drs. Eberhard and Phyllis Kronhausen, *Pornography and the Law; The Psychology of Erotic Realism and Hard Core Pornography*[2] (New York 1964) 228-84, 314-15). The extant portions of the *Satyricon* present rather the multiplicity and variety of sexual possibilities with the attendant breaking of taboos which are the major distinguishing marks of pornographic literature in any age. Homosexual and heterosexual encounters, brothels, composite sexual scenes, incest motifs (Philomela's offspring), seduction of children (the defloration of Pannychis, the Pergamene Boy), the permissive mother figure (Philomela), sadism, flagellation, inversion of religious ritual, even mild necrophilia (The Widow of Ephesus) and so on are all found in Petronius in addition to the incidents of voyeurism and exhibitionism. The most striking characteristics of almost all these encounters in Petronius, however, are the high level of sadism involved and the generally low level of satisfaction obtained. The pornographic imagination projects fantasies of super-sexual prowess (size and performance), not random assault and impotence. It also projects its characters as willing or at least acquiescent participants in almost every type of sexual activity. The two Milesian tales with their successful consummations which both partners eventually enjoy are representative of the usual pornographic scheme. The Circe episode, on the other hand, is an excellent example of Petronian adaptation (or perhaps parody?) of pornographic material. What should be a typical pornographic experience turns instead into failure, humiliation, and rejection. Most often, sex in the *Satyricon* is either a source of frustration or an assault upon an unwilling victim. See below in the discussion

of character for further implications of Encolpius' impotence.

[60] Miller 28.

[61] This is the theory first proposed by E. Klebs. "Zur Komposition von Petronius' Satirae," *Philologus* 47 (1889) 623-55.

[62] See Sullivan 93.

[63] On the roguishness of society and its institutions in the picaresque vision, see Alter 94-95.

[64] For this thesis, see Zeitlin 56-82.

[65] Frye 233. In his scheme, this type of activity is termed "second-phase irony."

[66] Frye 234. This technique of disintegration characterizes "third-phase irony."

[67] Frye 235. The Croton episode fits into his category of "sixth-phase irony"—demonic epiphany with its image of the "femme fatale" and its setting of "the city of dreadful night in the desert" 238-39.

[68] Frye 192. He sees this as the archetypal theme of satire and irony.

[69] *Interdiu severa, nunc hilaria* (64.13). See Walsh's analysis of Trimalchio, 129-30 and see Rankin 135-36.

[70] Cameron 406-7 on *Sat.* 70.1-2.

[71] On the theme of metamorphosis, see especially Arrowsmith I, 311-12 and 315. See also Zeitlin 63.

In Ovid, metamorphosis is a change to a permanent new state of being. In Petronius, change is only temporary and hence unreliable. (I am indebted to Ronald Kopnicki for this observation.) Cf. too the metamorphosis of Lucius at the end of Apuleius' novel. On the general meaning of metamorphosis in antiquity, see H. Rüdiger, "Nachwort" zur Übersetzung der *Eselromans von Apuleius* von A. Rode (Zurich 1960) 517-59.

[72] See Walsh 24-25 and *Sat.* 19.1, 80.9, 94.15, 106.1, 117.4.

[73] See Arrowsmith I, 306-12, for a fuller exposition of this point.

[74] Veyne 301-6 contends that Encolpius' reactions to the *Cena* as narrator display a false naiveté in contrast to his behavior in the rest of the text. See Sullivan 215 for a more accurate description.

[75] See especially 40.3-41.4, 41.6-8, and 71.1-2.

[76] Erich Auerbach, *Mimesis,* tr. Willard Trask (Princeton 1953) 28.

[77] *Ibid.* 29.

[78] *Ibid.* 29-30.

[79] This is seen in the new use of the symposium form, the variety of intellectual topics covered by Trimalchio and his guests, and by the different kinds of verse insertions.

[80] Alter 123.

[81] Miller 56-57.

[82] See Parker (above, note 48) 3-6.

[83] Hunger is a dominant element in the Spanish picaresque novels. On this theme in *Lazarillo de Tormes,* see Alter 1-10. Cf. too *El Buscón,* especially chapters 3 and 4.

[84] See Sullivan 40-42 on speculations as to Encolpius' earlier role at Massilia as ritual scapegoat. The victim is fed at public expense for a year before being driven from the city.

[85] Miller 70.

[86] Alter 16-17.

[87] See Miller on the origins of the typical picaresque hero, 47-55. Unless Encolpius were a thoroughgoing imposter (and the organization of his personality seems to preclude this), his educational training and his outlook would seem to indicate at least an upper middle-class background.

[88] Rexroth 101, who remarks that Encolpius and his friends are the first of their kind in literature, but they are not, as he states, to become "the common characters of all picaresque romances."

[89] Miller 75 on the character of Gil Blas. Encolpius is never called upon to perform the duties required of a slave, or to remain for long in a servile imposture. He plays only a temporary game. On the other hand, Lucius in *The Golden Ass,* by his transformation into an ass, a beast of burden, is compelled to endure the real hardships engendered by his situation.

[90] Miller 72. "The picaresque character is not merely a rogue, and his chaos of personality is greater than any purely moral chaos. It reflects a total lack of structure in the world, not merely a lack of ethical or social structure." Miller 131.

[91] See Miller's analysis of the shift in Roderick

Random's character, 93-94, and Alter 77-79.

[92] Giton expresses himself in the same type of literary language that Encolpius uses (George 338-42) but he does so as an adaptation to his situation, not as an indication of his outlook on life. He has rather a "cynical self-centeredness and a bland insolence which might ensure his survival and perhaps even make his fortune." Rankin 133. Love for him is a pose, an attitude by which he ingratiates himself with others and gratifies his own narcissistic desires. Encolpius, on the other hand, despite the extravagant hollowness of his language, is genuinely infatuated with the boy, and his jealousy is not feigned.

[93] Alter 110.

[94] Miller 78.

[95] Miller 79, and see Alter 10.

[96] *Sat.* 105.9, 106.2, 108.11, 113.3 and see Sullivan 43-44.

[97] Miller 45-46 and on the distinction between the round and flat character, see further in W.K. Wimsatt, *The Verbal Icon: Studies in the Meaning of Poetry* (Lexington, Ky. 1949) 77-79.

[98] Sullivan 119. In his view, however, Encolpius' character is "disorganized and fragmentary, not because he is at odds with himself or suffering from a spiritual instability . . . but because he is the structural and narrative link for the different themes that Petronius has chosen as well as the victim of certain comic and satiric situations." See also Veyne 308, n. 1, who holds similar views, but cf. Rankin's evaluation of Encolpius' instability, 128-30, which he interprets as a reflection of the conditions of the age rather than as an expedient for the author's different purposes.

[99] Parker (above, note 48) 16, 17.

[100] Alter 71-72.

[101] See Sullivan 267 for this widely held view, but on the host of complex problems raised by the techniques of the unreliable narrator and of impersonal narration, see Booth's brilliant discussion, 149-65, 271-391.

[102] Alter, 108-9.

[103] I owe this observation to Myron Jaworsky.

[104] On the theme of impotence and its relationship to language, see Arrowsmith I, 309, 318-20.

[105] George 351.

[106] George 351; Walsh 84-85.

[107] This is Sullivan's contention 33, 109-110, 259.

[108] Rexroth 101-2.

[109] W. B. Yeats, "The Second Coming" in *Collected Poems* (New York 1959) 184-85.

[110] Arrowsmith II, 15.

[111] Arrowsmith II, 16, 18.

[112] See Ann Pippin [Burnett], "Euripides' *Helen:* A Comedy of Ideas," *CP* 55 (1960) 151-63.

[113] Arrowsmith II, 22.

[114] Arrowsmith II, 17-20.

[115] See Christian Wolff, *Aspects of the Later Plays of Euripides* (unpubl. diss. Harvard 1963).

[116] See B. M. W. Knox, "Second Thoughts in Greek Tragedy," *GRBS* 7 (1966) 213-32, on the indecisiveness of Euripidean characters.

[117] Arrowsmith II, 24.

[118] See Wolff (above, note 119) and H. Förs, *Dionysos und die Stärke der Schwachen im Werk des Euripides,* Diss. Tübingen (Munich 1964).

[119] "Rebarbarization" is used in the sense of a return or resort to subliterary modes of expression (such as those found in folk or oral literature [e.g., ballad, mime] and to subliterary interests such as a "preoccupation with the physical sexual experience.") The effect of this "rebarbarization" can be a renewal of cultural vigor. See the valuable article, "Literature" by Max Lerner and Edwin Mums, Jr., *Encyclopedia of the Social Sciences* 9 (1933), especially 526-27. See also the discussion of this concept in Wellek and Warren 235-36.

[120] Alter 102. By contrast to this type of irony, one might point to Fielding's use of responsible social irony. "His [Fielding's] irony, far from being radically disturbing like that of Swift, is, in intention, corrective and orthodox; it undermines deviations from a healthy, sensible, social morality; it prunes society of perversions. Unlike the irony of Gibbon or Samuel Butler II, it does not unsettle traditional ethics and Christian orthodoxy—it is the irony of integration rather than disintegration." A.R. Humphreys, "Fielding's Irony: Its Methods and Effects," *Review of English Studies,* 18 (1942) 183. See also Alter 102-3.

[121] See Arrowsmith I, 326.

[122] See Alter *passim,* del Monte (above, note 48), and O. Borgers, "Le roman picaresque. Réalisme et fiction," *Lettres Romanes* 14 (1960) 295-305; 15 (1961) 23-38, 135-48.

[123] On the theory that the *Satyricon* was composed for an audience of Nero's courtiers, see K. F. C. Rose, "The Petronian Inquisition: An Auto-da-Fé," *Arion* 5 (1966) 292-95.

[124] See Walsh 137-39 and R. H. Crum, "Petronius and the Emperors," *CW* 45 (1952) 161-67; 197-201.

[125] Rankin 126.

[126] See Perry 44-95.

[127] On this subjective element in Latin literature, see Brooks Otis, "The Uniqueness of Latin Literature," *Arion* 6 (1967) 185-206.

[128] Alter 84.

[129] Watt (above, note 23) 13.

## Christopher Gill (essay date 1973)

SOURCE: "The Sexual Episodes in the *Satyricon,*" *Classical Philology*, Vol. LXVIII, No. 2, April, 1973, pp. 172-85.

[*In the following essay, Gill takes issue with J. P. Sullivan's (see excerpt dated 1961) psychoanalytic reading of the sexual scenes in the* Satyricon, *advocating instead a literary approach which views them in terms of their function of stressing the bizarre and the shocking.*]

Scenes in the *Satyricon* which include a strongly sexual element compose a not inconsiderable amount of the extant text. The actions of the main protagonists outside the *Cena,* Encolpius and Giton, and of the characters they encounter, involve incidents and adventures in which the erotic drive plays an important part and which are sometimes overtly sexual. The two "Milesian" tales recounted within the main story, the Woman of Ephesus and the Boy of Pergamum, are narratives of sexual seduction. These parts of the *Satyricon* are written with no less invention and verbal skill than the remainder of the work. Until quite recently, however, they have received little scholarly attention, for obvious reasons. The one modern critic who has considered them closely, J. P. Sullivan, is primarily concerned to use these episodes as psychoanalytic data to reconstruct the sexuality of the author, although his analysis has been subsequently transposed into literary discussions of the *Satyricon.*[1] It seems worthwhile then to appraise the distinctively literary qualities of these

scenes, within the context of the style of the whole work; and that is the aim of this article.

First, however, Sullivan's analysis is worth criticizing in detail. His argument contains logical weaknesses, but more significant is the way in which certain elements in a scene are singled out and given an interpretation which seems unnatural to a reader who is attending to the fictional whole. This trait is perhaps characteristic of studies of literature by followers of Freud,[2] but it is the more irritating in a critic who, when he is not being psychoanalytic, can be sensitive to the overall tone of the work, and with whose understanding of that tone I largely agree. Furthermore, I share Sullivan's view that there is a kind of "voyeurism" in the *Satyricon,* though this trait, I shall argue, lies not in the psychosexual, but in the literary, character of the work.

In his analysis of the sexual episodes, Sullivan's main point is that the *Satyricon* contains an unusually large number of scenes which include examples of two related psychosexual themes, scopophilia and exhibitionism, and "disguised aspects" of these themes, such as castration and sadism (pp. 238 ff.). Since Petronius, in his depiction of actions of the scopophilic-exhibitionist type "is not following any obvious literary tradition, or borrowing the themes from earlier authors," it is argued that his "large use of them is the more striking, and . . . must therefore be a genuine reflection of his own psychosexual interests, whether these were grounded in his sexual behaviour or in his fantasy life" (pp. 244-45). The scopophilic tendencies of the author of the *Satyricon,* Sullivan argues, are consistent with the character of Petronius as Tacitus describes him (*Ann.* 16. 17-20). The historian comments on Petronius' "nocturnal habits and the great interest he showed in the Emperor's sexual life" (p. 251). Since "one of the characteristics of scopophilia is the fear of light," the penchant for nocturnal life shown by Petronius, combined with his voyeuristic curiosity about Nero's erotic activities, add up to a "psychoanalytic argument for the attribution of the *Satyricon* to the Petronius described by Tacitus" (p. 253).

The exposition of this thesis is open to criticism, most obviously on the grounds that the evidence for the psychosexual themes is slighter than Sullivan admits, and that the argument he bases on that evidence is logically flawed. A recent *Dictionary of Psychoanalysis* defines scopophilia as a "sexual perversion in which the subject's preferred form of sexual activity is looking at the sexual parts or activities of others."[3] In none of the instances Sullivan selects is the act of looking the "preferred form" of sexual activity.[4] In only one case is stress laid on the pleasure obtained by a character from the act of looking (*Sat.* 26. 5, Quartilla's observation of the sexual union of Giton and Pannychis), and in that case, as in *Sat.* 140. 11, the looking is in fact a stimulus to a more overt form of sexual activity which the character apparently "prefers."[5] The same degree of misrepresentation occurs in the examples of exhibitionism. The exhibitionist finds his preferred form of sexual activity, and his erotic gratification, in deliberately exposing his genitals to someone else (*Dictionary*, p. 47, cf. p. 116). Of the four examples of exhibitionism given by Sullivan,[6] only one shows a character deliberately exposing his genitals to someone else (*Sat.* 140. 12-13), and in this case his aim is not sexual gratification, but the wish to demonstrate that he is no longer impotent.[7] In the course of maintaining that all four scenes are genuine instances of exhibitionism, Sullivan's reasoning becomes strained. Describing a scene in which a woman touches a boy's penis (*Sat.* 24. 7), Sullivan comments, "Despite differences—handling rather than looking at a forbidden object—this is surely *a sort of* exhibitionism" (p. 241, italics mine). In order to strengthen this point Sullivan cites the scene in which a man does expose his genitals (*Sat.* 140. 12-13) and notes that in this scene it also happens that another person handles the penis. He concludes: "In this exhibitionism there is also the motif of handling the genitals, which *seems to argue conclusively* that the scene between Quartilla was exhibitionist too in its significance" (p. 241, italics mine). Sullivan is asserting that, since, in a scene of exposure (which he terms "exhibitionism") there was, incidental to the exposure, handling of the penis by another, it follows that handling of the penis (without any self-exposure) constitutes an act of exhibitionism. The flaw in this argument is surely apparent.

In the development of the argument, Sullivan's discussion of one passage is illustrative of the whole style of his application of psychoanalytic method to the literary text. The argument moves from the "uncomplicated examples" of the sexual themes to a "less obvious case" in which Ascyltus finds Encolpius making love to Giton (*Sat.* 11, p. 242). Ascyltus "rolled me [Encolpius] out of the cloak I was lying in and said, 'What were you up to, you most reverend brother?'" The comment is made: "In the light of earlier instances the scopophilic aspects of this are patent. From the narrator's viewpoint it is exhibitionism . . . On Ascyltus' side it is voyeurism" (p. 242). This statement raises doubts in the mind of someone who considers the fictional situation as it is presented. Is there in fact any "voyeurism" in Ascyltus' action, any indication that this is his "preferred form of sexual activity"? The situation is that a man finds his sexual rival in bed with someone he is attracted to. Not surprisingly, he wants to find out, and to stop, what is going on. He "rolls" Encolpius "out of the cloak" to do this. Then, with sardonic amusement, combined perhaps with pleasure at having interrupted the consummation of the act, he asks his "most reverend brother" i.e., his friend or (former) sexual partner, what he was up to. One may genuinely wonder if there is any "voyeurism" on Ascyltus' part

or "exhibitionism" on Encolpius' part; for the actions seem to be otherwise motivated. But Sullivan, apparently anticipating this objection, attempts to answer it by saying that "the question of the voluntary or involuntary nature of the incident from the character's point of view may be disregarded" (p. 242). To this can be compared a later statement that in fiction, "It is irrelevant whether the characters expose themselves of their own accord, or through force of circumstances" (p. 245). This flexibility in the definition of what counts as voyeurism or exhibitionism enables Sullivan to include in his examples of exhibitionism a scene in which the display of genitals is not deliberate, let alone a "preferred form of sexual activity," namely the scene in which Ascyltus is naked because he is at the baths (*Sat.* 92. 7-9).[8] But in all these cases a point is being ignored. If we do not take into account "the voluntary or involuntary nature of the incident from the character's point of view," what possible criterion do we have for deciding whether the artistic depiction of a given act is, or is not, an instance of scopophilia or exhibitionism? If we allow the wide limits that Sullivan recommends, what sexual act is there which could *not* be interpreted as scopophilic or exhibitionist? For in any sexual act, or in the foreplay to a sexual act, if it is described in any detail, there is likely to be some point at which one character touches or sees another's genitals. It is thus hard to see how pointing out these features in the *Satyricon* helps to define the distinctive psychosexuality which underlies the work.

Furthermore, there seems to be a certain lack of consistency in the way in which characters are used as indexes of the author's predilections. On the one hand, as in the instance just discussed, what is important is not the intention explicitly put in the mind of the character by the author, but the sexual by-product (which a critic may detect) of a particular scene. But on the other hand, one of the characters at least, Encolpius, is described as being, in his actions and feelings in the story, virtually identical with the author in his psychosexuality, "the main vehicle of the author's fantasy" (p. 249). If one is to make a psychological analysis of a work, does not a choice have to be made between seeing characters as the direct expression of the writer's impulses, and seeing them as units in the construction of a fictional scene which, incidentally, displays the predilections of the author? Apart from attempting this consistency of method in discussing the author's employment of characters, should not the analyst pay some attention to another feature of the literary work, namely tone? Is no account to be taken of the difference between the brisk flippancy of Petronius' depiction of sexual actions (including those which involve Encolpius, the alleged psychosexual *alter ego* of the author) and, say, the passionate seriousness of Plato's description of the struggle of the mind with physical lust given in Socrates' "palinode" (*Phaedrus* 251 ff.)? It may be that flippancy of tone is regarded by Freudian critics as a cover, or disguise, for the perhaps un-conscious impulses of the author's *libido:* but if that is the critic's opinion, it should be clearly stated. More generally, it may be doubted whether it is enough for the psychoanalyst to single out only the overtly sexual elements in a work, particularly when they are closely connected with the rest of the book in terms of the plot and the tone of the narrative, and consider them as data on their own. It is quite possible that only a con-sideration of the story as a whole, or of the stylistic character present throughout the work, can provide the analyst with the material he needs. Freud's analyses of Da Vinci and Dostoevsky attempt a more thoroughgo-ing analysis of the men and their works, and within that total examination many of the more illuminating details he fastens on, in dreams or artistic works, are not explicitly sexual at all.[9] But what served as a cor-rective to undirected speculation in the case of Da Vinci and Dostoevsky, namely biographical evidence about the men in question, is almost wholly lacking in the case of a fragmentary text, whose attribution to the Neronian courtier, while customary, is essentially con-jectural. For this reason, a psychoanalysis of the **Satyricon** of any certainty may very well be impos-sible.

At all events, such an analysis is not the aim of the present discussion. The view to be stated here is that the sexual elements, and the manner of their presenta-tion, are best explained, not by attempted reconstruc-tion of the author's psychosexuality, but by reference to the literary character of the surviving work and (as far as can be discovered) the intentions of the author in this work. The sexual episodes have not so far been studied in this way. Before examining the specifically erotic scenes, some observations will be made about the general character of the work. The interpretation of the **Satyricon** given here is largely in agreement with those of P. G. Walsh (who does not give special con-sideration to the sexual episodes) and of Sullivan him-self, in the non-Freudian parts of his book. Not all points of resemblance between their views on this subject and what is stated here will be noted.[10]

A reader of the **Satyricon** today, especially one com-ing to the book in translation, may feel it to be a pe-culiarly "modern" work in a number of ways: in the realistic reproduction of ordinary people and their speech in the *Cena,* in the striking and bizarre quality of the surface action, as well as the almost surrealistic lack of sequence in the plot, and in the amorality and sexual ambivalence of the characters. The last three of these aspects were the ones particularly emphasized by Federico Fellini in his film version of the book. A closer inspection of the Latin text discloses a more complex impression. The effect of discontinuity in the action is fostered by the incompleteness of our text, and, in particular, it seems, by the vagaries of the excerptors who originated the manuscript traditions on

which the reconstruction of the work outside the *Cena* depends.[11] Nevertheless, even when the whole of a passage has been handed down more or less intact (as the *Cena* has), piling of incident on incident within a single context is more common than sequential devel-opment and deepening of the human situation. The impression of a deliberately striking surface action is a real one; but the actions, however peculiar, are played out on the more familar terrain of a complex literary background. Pastiche, parody, and juxtaposition of divergent styles compose a continuous literary texture, sometimes closely fitted to the action described and the theme discussed, sometimes ironically at variance with it. The literary works generally seen as underly-ing the text include the *Odyssey,* the Greek romance, the Milesian tale, the poems of Virgil and Ovid, Horace's *Satires,* Lucan's *Pharsalia,* the Roman mime, Seneca's tragedies and moral epistles. In the relation-ship of the **Satyricon** to this literary context, it is es-pecially hard to distinguish pastiche (straightforward imitation of a certain style) from parody (pointed ex-aggeration of that style), as, for instance, the continued controversy about the level of seriousness of the *Bellum civile* and *Halosis Troiae* demonstrates.[12] The sustained allusiveness, so characteristic of Roman literature, is dominant here, but often, it seems, without the purpo-siveness that would place the allusions within an artis-tically independent whole. The *Cena,* with its nonliter-ary Latin, imitating what we take to have been the speech of ordinary men, is something of an exception. But in this case the mixture of parody and pastiche is derived not from literature but from life, and the same problem, of distinguishing genuine *mimesis* of a man-ner of speech (and of a human character) from parody of it, applies with equal force, particularly in the case of Trimalchio.

The **Satyricon,** in short, is not the type of work com-mended by theorists such as Horace, in which the author, with a sincerity of artistic purpose, creates out of the parts of his work a unity in which the style is appropriate both to the subject matter and to the cho-sen genre.[13] Rather this work, as it proceeds, deliber-ately juxtaposes examples of different styles, and the aim of the juxtaposition seems not to be to create a unity by accumulation but to exploit the possibilities of each individual demonstration. In its prosimetrical combination of the styles of more cohesive genres, the work resembles the "Menippean" satires of Varro and the *Apocolocyntosis* of Seneca. But the **Satyricon** lacks the sustained moral intention we can infer from our remains of Varro's satires (whether these are spoken in the first person or couched in narrative and dramatic form). And in the range and scale of its differing forms of fictional and poetic display, it surpasses both the Varronian works and the (equally allusive) *Apocolocyntosis.* The second book of Horace's *Satires* might be thought to stand close to the *Cena* in provid-ing a series of personal vignettes without explicit comment by the author; but, apart from the stylistic differences, implicit comment and criticism is much closer to the surface in Horace. The "voice" of the *Satyricon,* the authentic voice of the author, is not expressed in the various formal displays of the work, but lies behind those words; and even when some implicit comment or intention is sensed by a reader, the point is often less than completely clear. Sometimes the author can be heard in the brisk, rhythmically compact, and dispassionate Latin of the narrative, so often ironically at variance with the violence of the characters' actions and passions which that narrative is used to relate.[14] If one had to imagine a historical context for this kind of work, one could hardly imagine a more plausible setting than oral presentation by an educated and observant consular to a group of like-minded associates in or around the Neronian court. The "voice" of the work can thus be seen as precisely that of its discriminating author, periodically trying out on his audience successive experiments in literary and "real-life" styles, each episode combining the temporary impact of the striking or surprising with the intellectual pleasure of a recognizable stylistic context.

The distinctively sexual episodes are not divergent, in their style, from the work as a whole; indeed, the qualities of language and construction in these scenes may be seen as symptomatic, and illuminative, of the literary character of the *Satyricon.* The element of the striking and bizarre in the action is amply present in the sheer choice of sexual combinations: a eunuch attempting sexual assault on a man (23-24),[15] an attempted seduction of a young man by a girl ending in impotence (126 ff.), a love triangle involving male homosexuals (9-11 and elsewhere), a courtesan sampling a young boy, and then arranging a union between the boy and a pre-pubertal girl (24-26), and so on. Underneath the strangeness of the surface activity lies a more complex literary context than at first appears. Contrary to what one might suppose (in the face of the rich variety of sexual practice described), the language of these episodes contains comparatively few of the words which recur in the "obscene insult poems" of Catullus, the *Priapea,* and Martial.[16] The literary background drawn on is of a more elaborate kind. Walsh shows how a strident love quarrel between Encolpius and Ascyltus breaks down, under analysis, into pairs of opposing statements, with almost metrical composition, antithesis, and isocolon, drawn directly from the language of the rhetorical schools (p. 87, *Sat.* 9. 8). In the romantic crises among the three males in the earlier fragments (9 ff., cf. 79 ff.), and especially in the consultations on board ship which precede the "treaty" governing sexual relationships (100 ff.), whole speeches read like *declamationes,* whether they are couched in the mode of accusation or defense, general reflection, or *supplicatio.*[17] The love poems placed periodically in the narrative, and the love letters exchanged in the Circe episodes, evoke existing erotic literature, par-

ticularly the poetry of Ovid.[18] Within the sexual combinations of the story, names of greater figures from literature are employed, like Circe and Polyaenus, Tarquin and Lucretia,[19] and by allusions to epic poetry we are reminded of romantic and emotional encounters between Zeus and Hera as well as Dido and Aeneas.

This allusiveness, like pastiche, is in part simply characteristic of the practice throughout the work. Thus the tales of the Woman of Ephesus and the Boy of Pergamum represent, we must assume (lacking as we do Sisenna's translation of Aristides' collection of *Milesiaka*), a Petronian exercise in the type of the Milesian tale, just as the inserted stories in the *Metamorphoses* represent Apuleius' offerings in the same genre.[20] But in addition the very elaborateness of the literary imitations and references lends a certain unreality to the erotic encounters, particularly when it is juxtaposed to the slightness or sordidness of the human protagonists. The verses recalling the environment of the love-making between Zeus and Hera in the *Iliad* precede the ignominious impotence of a very un-Odyssean Polyaenus.[21] The response, or lack of response, of the man's inadequate organ to his urgent harangue is described in the same words as Dido's rejection of Aeneas' belated overtures in Hades.[22] When characters like Giton speak in a pastiche of rhetorical prose, the effect is not to increase the stature of the figures, but to make the scenes in which the speeches occur commensurately more theatrical.[23]

This ironic disparity between style and content has been noted in the contrast between the "short, polished, and rhythmic sentences" of the narrative "and the high degree of excitement, despair, and astonishment" which the words attribute to the characters, including the narrator himself (Sullivan, p. 158). There is often a similar disparity in the description of sexual acts. The more physical and intimate the actions are, the more obliquely they are expressed. Encolpius' desire for privacy is attributed to his wish "ut veterem cum Gitone meo rationem reducerem" (10). Eumolpus tells how an *eques,* discovering the well-endowed Ascyltus in the baths, led him away, "ut tam magna fortuna solus uteretur" (92). Philomela's daughter, ripe for corruption, is invited to take her seat on the "commendatam bonitatem" of Eumolpus (140). When Encolpius' virility is restored, Eumolpus confirms the restoration by running both hands over the "deorum beneficia" (140). In Quartilla's orgy, Encolpius, battered by the attentions of a eunuch, complains that his friend Ascyltus "solus ferias agit," at which the assailant promptly "equum mutavit" (24). Of the same eunuch, whose perspiration at his sexual labors has removed part of his make-up powder, it is said (in a simile of Lucretian rather than epic character) "ut putares [*sc.* eum] detectum parietem nimbo laborare" (23. 5). This urbane ornamentation, or periphrasis, in descrbing the physical or the sexual lends an irony, and a degree of unreality, to the event presented, and gives a tone of prurient indirectness to the narrative.

There is also a secondary effect, in some cases, of implicit parody of the literary works whose phrases, or style, are thus incongruously taken out of context. This applies to the allusions to the epic poems as well as to the antitheses and *sententiae* borrowed from the rhetorical schools. On the level of plot, the homosexual *renversement* of the heterosexual themes and situations of the Greek romance incidentally satirizes the originals which are adapted.[24] Similarly, the rhetorical heightening of the speeches made by the lovers at moments of stress renders the moments themselves more theatrical and burlesques *en passant* the lamentations of the heroes of romance.[25] In cases where the pastiche is of works which are themselves mannered, or which depend on the satiric reversal of existing literary models, the **Satyricon** reinforces the effect of the original. Thus the allusions to Ovid's poetry heighten the verbal artificiality already present in the model. And the narration of the Milesian tales most probably emphasizes a salient feature of the Milesian tradition, the cynical reversal of accepted moral and literary norms (such as that of *pudicitia* in wives, maidens, and boys) which were already enshrined in the idealized tradition of historiography and romance.[26]

The rich artificiality of the language used to describe sexual events, and the disparity between verbal style and physical content (or sometimes between different styles in the same episode), do not reinforce the fictional reality of the action presented. Rather they tend to make each scene a temporary performance or display, the directness of the sexual impact undercut by the self-conscious style of the presentation. This quality of the language of the work is supplemented by the way in which characters are used, in the construction of particular situations, to make scenes into theatrical spectacles. What is characteristic of the **Satyricon** is the self-conscious presentation by the author (through his characters) of a series of exhibitions of verbal or fictional virtuosity, designed for an audience capable of relishing the contrived grotesquerie of the display. In a number of sexual incidents the same structure of actors-performance-audience is created, with the characters in the story acting as surrogates for author and audience. While some of the characters enact a parody of a normal sexual act—and themselves relish the comic and aesthetic aspects of what they are doing—others serve as the appreciative audience of those parodies. Of this kind is the climax of Quartilla's orgy, the "marriage" of the adolescent Giton and the seven-year-old Pannychis (**Sat.** 25-26). Quartilla originates this scene, and stage-manages it, using an enthusiastic chorus ("iam embasicoetas praeferebat facem, iam ebriae mulieres longum agmen plaudentes fecerant") and a compliant hero and heroine ("non repugnaverat puer, ac ne puella quidem tristis expaverat nuptiarum nomen") to com-

pose a *spectaculum* of which she is the most excited spectator. Of this kind, too, is the copulation engineered by Eumolpus, his slave, and Philomela's the verbal expression itself an object of urbane amusement. The whole scene is essentially a game, played by the fictional characters with their bodies, and by the author with his language. The one, relatively minor, element in this scene which Sullivan singles out, the boy's observation of the sexual act, can now be seen as only one of the units out of which Petronius forms his elaborately perverse construction.

In creating individual spectacles through the agency of the characters, Petronius makes sexual episodes like this one consonant with other sections of the **Satyricon.** In particular, the *Cena*, insofar as it is engineered by Trimalchio, consists of a series of incidents of a superficially bizarre or shocking character (slaves threatened with terrible punishments for culinary mistakes, 49; acrobats falling from ceilings, 54; a roof collapsing only to disclose gifts suspended by a pulley, 60), which turn out to have been organized in advance by the host and are enacted by his slaves. The sheer excess of the food, together with the relentless pursuit of novelty by means of elaborate disguises (the work of "Daedalus" the chef), corresponds to the sexual plethora, enlivened by peculiar unions and reversals of ordinary mating roles, in such events as Quartilla's orgy. Above all, in the culmination of the *Cena*, the scene in which Trimalchio anticipates his end and the others respond with lamentation (71-72), a scene which is virtually a staged "death" of Trimalchio, the way in which characters use their words and reactions to create a travesty of an organic event is analogous to the way characters employ their bodies and responses to construct a grotesque machine for sexual intercourse in Eumolpus' bedroom at Croton. The intermittent, usually sarcastic, comments of the narrator reinforce our disposition to take a detached and aesthetic view of the sights which Trimalchio provides.[30]

Whether the displays of the *Cena* and the sexual *spectacula* mimic the home life of an emperor whose love of personal and artistic exhibition is well attested,[31] and whose erotic experiments apparently received a similar presentation,[32] is not certainly verifiable. What can be said is that this proffering of self-enclosed exhibitions, in which the internal roles adopted by the characters mirror the artistic practice of the author, is consistent with the over-all composition of the **Satyricon.** The author of this work is consistently the stage manager of the successive episodes of his verbal *Cena*, in which what is important is the temporary impact of a particular scene rather than any internal thread of connection running throughout the whole. This literary "Daedalus" is more concerned with a series of transformations of the existing diet of Roman literature and language than with the achievement of a new and autonomous work or genre. His work lacks the kind of aesthetic unity which comes from matching of subject matter, genre, and verbal style, a unity whose function is to give to the reader the pleasure and benefit appropriate to the type of mimetic work produced.[33] The "proper pleasure" the **Satyricon** affords is a detached enjoyment of the skill with which the author manipulates the styles of ordinary speech and literary forms and juxtaposes different styles, both to each other and to an often deliberately inappropriate subject matter. The ironic detachment invited from a reader (resembling in kind, if not in degree of enthusiasm, the critical position of the narrator of the *Cena*) corresponds to a similar detachment on the part of the writer, who does not fuse his personality with the work he creates. And yet, while the author is ironically separable from his characters and situations, he does not use them in the service of a detectable satiric intention, as Horace and Juvenal do. Instead of making us hear his voice, either as creative artist or satirist, he retains a detachment from his work which we might (repeating the Freudian term in a different context) call "voyeuristic." This attitude to his literary work, once diagnosed, may be susceptible of psychological interpretation, on Freudian or perhaps Eriksonian lines, as being the attitude of a man who has not moved from the satirical mimicry of the emotional adolescent to the mature self-responsibility of the independent artist. That is more than I can say.

## A Note on the "Realism" of the *Satyricon*

The **Satyricon** is sometimes seen as remarkable primarily for its realism, whether that realism is seen in faithfulness to ordinary language, or in depiction of the actualities of sexual life, or in techniques of fictional presentation.[34] So far as I can tell from reading Sullivan's discussion of this question (pp. 98 ff.), he sees Petronius as a realist in some sense, and in his argument he cites, as others do, the eightline verse at 132. 15 ff. There Petronius, apparently speaking *in propria persona,* seems to defend the inclusion of sexual elements in his work, in part by claiming that his work represents the whole of human reality. This is not the place to consider the whole question of realism in the **Satyricon;** but the lines in 132, which fall within the context of a sexual episode, can be appropriately considered here, particularly as they may affect our understanding of the objectives of the sexual scenes. The verse itself is as follows:

> quid me constricta spectatis fronte Catones
>    damnatisque novae simplicitatis opus?s
> sermonis puri non tristis gratia ridet,
>    quodque facit populus, candida lingua refert.
> nam quis concubitus, Veneris quis gaudia
>    nescit?
>    quis vetat in tepido membra calere toro?
> ipse pater veri doctos Epicurus amare
>    iussit, et hoc vitam dixit habere [*telos*].

Why do you Catos look at me with furrowed brow and condemn my work with its novel simplicity? My pure narrative smiles with a cheerful attractiveness; whatever people do, my frank tongue reports. Who is ignorant of love-making and the joys of Venus? Who forbids that our limbs should glow in the warmth of the bed? Why, Epicurus himself, the father of truth, ordered men of understanding to love, and said that this was the "prime goal" of life.

Part of the claim here is that sex is part of *quodque facit populus,* and that a work which aims to present a straightforward depiction of human life must include it. This claim resembles statements in other writers of the Silver Age who lay stress on the inclusiveness of their writing (Iuv. 1. 85-86), or who defend their decision to depict what really happens in human life rather than repeat the formulas of literary tradition (Iuv. 1. 19 ff., Mart. 10. 4. 11-12). Petronius' statement is made with particular clarity, and, if it is to be taken with absolute seriousness, it must end all debate about the literary objectives of the sexual episodes.[35]

But it is not at all certain that in these lines Petronius has stepped out of the current of his work and given a complete and ingenuous statement of his intentions. Is not our reading of his claim influenced by the context in which it is placed? The sequence of events immediately before the statement is this. Encolpius lies on his bed and harangues (in nine lines of quasi-Virgilian verse) his limp penis. In three lines, composed of actual lines from Virgil,[36] the organ's failure to respond is described. Encolpius pulls himself up short at the ridiculousness of what he is doing. But then he changes his mind and decides that, if in Homer and tragedy characters can curse their eyes, heart, etc., and in real life sick men can curse their diseased feet, hands, etc., then he, Encolpius, can legitimately harangue his inadequate organ. Then, without a break in the received text, comes the literary credo. At first one might suppose that the speech is part of the story, and represents Encolpius' defending his address to his private parts; but the allusions to an *opus,* the phrase *sermonis puri,* and so on, indicate that here Petronius is defending his presentation of Encolpius' address. But how curious a peg on which to hang a credo of literary realism! The credo justifies Encolpius' impotent harangue—hardly the glowing pleasures of sex the claim speaks of, *concubitus, Veneris gaudia, in tepido membra calere toro, amare.* The juxtaposition of such a scene, so curious an example of the sexual, and so ironically composed in mock-epic style, to a claim of an all-embracing depiction of humanity's passion, is incongruous. Indeed, the incongruity is such that it has the effect of undercutting the claim, of making the claim itself seem a piece of rhetoric or pastiche, a version of the literary "statement of intentions,"[37] rather than the author's final and unqualified statement on his work. The context invites us to read the claim in an ironic tone of voice, dwelling, perhaps with particular relish, on phrases like *novae simplicitatis, sermonis puri, non tristis, candida lingua,* phrases employed in the literary statements of other writers, here rendered disingenuous by the situation.[38] Furthermore, just as the claim inappropriately mimics more serious literary statements, the allusion to Epicurus gives a deliberately simplified version of that thinker's views of the erotic and of pleasure as the goal of life.[39] Even if the claim were not undercut in these ways, it would be undercut, or at least belied, by the practice of sexual depiction within the work. Petronius' *candida lingua* does not report the whole range of human sexual experience; his selection is slanted towards acts which have a surprising effect, the perverse, bizarre, or amusing in erotic combination. Nor are these *Veneris gaudia* presented with the kind of "cheerful attractiveness" which would make a reader respond warmly to the "Epicurean" objective of a life rich in sexual activity. Whether one thinks of the different kinds of *Angst* that the erotic protagonist, Encolpius, suffers, or of the contrived performances of more effective voluptuaries, the impact of the sexual description is different from the purpose avowed in the credo. It is ironic detachment from the characters (perhaps combined with an aesthetic appreciation of the scenes they compose) that the *erotica* of this work invite, and not a spontaneous responsiveness to their experiences. Thus the claim of realism, at least in connection with the presentation of the sexual, must be seen as simply another piece of Petronian pastiche, a literary pose momentarily adopted by the author, rather than an attempt to break out of his work and speak directly and sincerely to his audience.[40]

### Notes

[1] The first statement of these views was given in "The *Satyricon* of Petronius—Some Psycho-analytic Considerations," *The American Imago,* XVIII (1961), 353-69. This psychoanalytic argument was subsequently transposed into two literary discussions: "Realism and Satire in Petronius," *Critical Essays on Latin Literature: Satire* (London, 1963), pp. 73 ff., esp. "A Digression on the Genesis of the Sexual Episodes," pp. 78-82; and "The Sexual Themes of the *Satyricon,*" ch. vii of *The Satyricon of Petronius* (London, 1969), pp. 232-53. It is to the most recent statement of these views that the page references in this article refer.

[2] See, for instance, the well-known analysis of Hamlet by Ernest Jones, of which the final version was published as *Hamlet and Oedipus* (London, 1949). More recently one may compare the subtle, but still (for many readers) implausible interpretation of certain scenes in *Oliver Twist* by Steves Marcus, "Who is Fagin?" in an appendix to *Dickens: From Pickwick to Dombey* (London, 1965), pp. 358-78, esp. 370 ff.

[3] *A Critical Dictionary of Psychoanalysis,* ed. Charles Rycroft (London, 1968). The entry under "scopophilia" refers the reader to "voyeurism," p. 175, from which the words quoted are taken.

[4] Sullivan's examples of scopophilia (pp. 238-43) are: 26. 4-5 (Encolpius and Quartilla watching the love-making of Gilton and Pannychis), 140 (Encolpius and Philomela's son watching the love-making of Eumolpus and Philomela's daughter), and 11 (Ascyltus interrupting the love-making of Encolpius and Giton), which is also put forward as an example of exhibitionism.

[5] *Sat.* 26. 4-5: "itaque cum inclusi iacerent, consedimus ante limen thalami, et in primis Quartilla per rimam improbe diductam adplicuerat oculum curiosum lusumque puerilem libidinosa speculabatur diligentia. me quoque ad idem spectaculum lenta manu traxit, et quia considerantium haeserant vultus, quicquid a spectaculo vacabat, commovebat obiter labra et me tamquam furtivis subinde oculis verberabat." *Sat.* 140. 11: "itaque ego quoque, ne desidia consuetudinem perderem, dum frater sororis suae automata per clostellum miratur, accessi temptaturus an pateretur iniuriam. nec se reiciebat a blanditils doctissimus puer, sed me numen inimicum ibi quoque invenit." All quotations are from the edition of K. Müller (Munich, 1961).

[6] The examples of exhibitionism are: 24. 6-7 (Quartilla playing with Giton's penis), 92. 7-9 (Ascyltus, naked at the baths, admired by those present for the size of his penis), 140. 12-13 (Encolpius showing his restored virility to Eumolpus), and 11 (in which Encolpius is considered the exhibitionist), cf. n. 4. Sullivan, pp. 240-43.

[7] "'dii maiores sunt qui me restituerunt in integrum . . .' haec locutus sustuli tunicam Eumolpoque me totum approbavi. at ille primo exhorruit, deinde ut plurimum crederet, utraque manu deorum beneficia tractat."

[8] " . . . ex altera parte iuvenis nudus, qui vestimenta perdiderat, non minore clamoris indignatione Gitona flagitabat . . . illum autem frequentia ingens circumvenit, cum plausu et admiratione timidissima. habebat enim inguinum pondus tam grande ut ipsum hominem laciniam fascini crederes. o iuvenem laboriosum: puto illum pridie incipere, postero die finire."

[9] *Five Lectures on Psycho-Analysis: Leonardo da Vinci and Other Works* (London, 1957), in *The Standard Edition of the Complete Psychological Works of Sigmund Freud,* ed. James Strachey. "Dostoevsky and Parricide," tr. D. F. Tait, in *Dostoevsky: Stavrogin's Confession, etc.* (London, 1947).

[10] P. G. Walsh, *The Roman Novel* (Cambridge, 1970), hereafter simply "Walsh."

[11] The traditions L and O; see Müller's *Praefatio,* pp. xxxvii ff. Sullivan notes that the habits of the original excerptor of L can be detected by comparison with H in the *Cena* (pp. 37-38). After giving quite full extracts at the beginning, he limits himself to verse and generalities. Similarly in other episodes he may have preserved the opening incidents fully, before losing interest and retaining only verse, generalities, and, perhaps, strikingly dramatic or sexual passages.

[12] Walsh, "Eumolpus, the *Halosis Troiae,* and *De Bello Civili,*" *CP,* LXIII (1968), 208 ff., gives a recent discussion of the issues.

[13] This, broadly speaking, is Horace's advice in the *Ars poetica.* He advocates sincerity of artistic purpose, in that he calls for a fusion of the writer's creative gifts (*ingenium*) with an artistic correlative to those gifts, a work suited to the writer's talents (38-40, cf. 366 ff.), which fulfils his intentions (73 ff.), and is given verbal shape through determined *ars* (295 ff., 408 ff.). What is commended is integration of the poet's mind with his work, not ironic detachment from it and exploitation of the incongruous possibilities of all available styles. The notion of a quasi-moral seriousness, as part of a writer's duty, is present in the assertion that "scribendi recte sapere est et principium et fons" (309, cf. 310), and in the statement that "omne tulit punctum qui miscuit utile dulci, slectorem delectando pariterque monendo" (343-44).

[14] Cf. Sullivan, p. 158.

[15] The assault, apparently, is of a passive kind, *clunibus baslisque,* 24. 4.

[16] Inspection shows several uses of *inguina, scortum, clunes, coitus;* also *anus, cinaedus, spatalocinaedus, spintria,* and the obscure *pigiciaca* (see n. 29 below). It is not a large vocabulary relative to the amount of sexual action.

[17] Cf. Walsh, pp. 100 ff.

[18] Cf. Walsh, pp. 42 and 106; Sullivan, pp. 189-90, 217-18, 236.

[19] Circe and Polyaenus, 127 ff., Tarquin and Lucretia, 9.5.

[20] Cf. Walsh, pp. 10 ff.

[21] 127. 9; cf. *Il.* 14. 347 ff.

[22] 132. 11, lines 1-2; cf. *Aen.* 6. 469 ff.

[23] Cf. P. George, "Style and Character in the *Satyricon,*" *Arion,* V (1966), 336-58, esp. 338-52 on Giton.

[24] E. Courtney, "Parody and Allusion in Menippean Satire," *Philologus,* CVI (1962), 86 ff., notes ironic reversals of the romance plot. For instance, in the romance, in exceptional cases, the hero attracts men; in the *Satyricon,* correspondingly, the hero Encolpius, occasionally becomes involved with women (p. 93). On the relative chronology of the romance and the *Satyricon,* see Walsh, pp. 8-9, 78 ff. B. Perry, *The Ancient Romances* (Berkeley, 1967), dates the *Ninus ca.* 100 B.C., and the works of Chariton, together with a postulated prototype for the *Recognitiones* of ps.-Clement, in the first century after Christ (p. 350).

[25] Courtney, p. 94.

[26] For the relation between idealized historiography and romance, see Perry, ch. iv, "Birth of the Ideal Greek Romance," pp. 149-80.

[30] 47. 8, 65. 1, 69. 7, 54. 3-4.

[31] Tac. *Ann.* 14. 14, 15. 33, 16. 4; Suet. *Nero* 20 ff.

[32] Tac. *Ann.* 15. 37; Suet. *Nero* 18-19; Iuv. 10. 333 ff.,

[33] The terminology used in this sentence is that of ancient literary critics, notably Horace and Aristotle (cf. n. 13 above).

[34] E.g., E. Auerbach, *Mimesis* (Princeton, 1953), ch. ii.

[35] E.g., A. Collignon, *Étude sur Petrone* (Paris, 1892), pp. 53-55, takes these lines as a serious personal statement by the author, justifying the depiction of love-making on Epicurean grounds.

[36] For the first two lines see *Aen.* 6.-469 ff. (cf. 1. 482). For the third line see *Ecl.* 3. 83, 5. 16; *Aen.* 9. 436.

[37] For such statements of intentions, comments by the author indicating the nature of the work he is offering, see, e.g., Hor. *Epist.* 1. 1. 1 ff.; Ov. *Am.* 1. 1, *Rem. Am.* 357-96; Mart. 1. *Epist. ad lect.* Such statements may be in themselves amusingly or artfully presented, as is the case with Ovid *Am.* 1. 1 and Mart. 1. *Epist. ad lect.,* but they are not normally placed in a context which renders them incongruous.

[38] On the employment of these phrases in Latin literature, see H. Stubbe, "Die Verseinlagen im Petron," *Philologus,* Supp. XXV (1933), 150-54. *Simplicitas* (cf. Sullivan, p. 99, n. 1) and *sermo purus* (cf. E. T. Sage, "Atticism in Petronius," *TAPA,* XLVI [1915], 54) connote the unadorned simplicity of the "Attic" style of prose. (In fact, Atticist slogans, if partly appropriate to the narrative style of the *Satyricon,* are inadequate to cover the range of styles self-consciously employed within the whole work.) Also *simplicitas,* as well as *candidus* and *purus,* denotes frankness and directness,

an abandonment of guile or restraint (just as *non tristis*—equivalent in literary terms to *iocosus,* Hor. *Ser.* 1. 10. 11—implies a "carnival" freedom from *severitia* or *tristitia,* which is a severe attitude expressed in a weighty style, Cic. *Brut.* 30. 113, cf. Mart. 1. *Epist. ad lect.*). This *apologia* undercuts its own claims to *simplicitas*—already contradicted by the sophistication of the *opus* Petronius presents—by its slick employment of artistic slogans. (Cf. the disingenuousness with which Martial cites the *Romana simplicitas* of Augustus' obscene verses as a justification for his own oblique and contrived compositions.)

[39] For Epicurus pleasure is the *telos* of life. He includes the sexual pleasures with other sensations under the heading of the pleasurable and the good (Diog. Laert. 10. 6); but in his more detailed scheme of pleasures it would seem that sexual pleasures come in the category of those which are physical but not necessary (*Ep. ad Men.* 127). Furthermore, he makes disparaging remarks about the possible ill-effects of love (Diog. Laert. 10. 118) and the disturbing frenzy of erotic desire (Hermias *In Phaedr.,* p. 76), a theme developed by Lucretius at 4. 1058.

[40] I should like to acknowledge the valuable comments and criticisms made on earlier drafts of this article by Professor P. G. Walsh of Edinburgh University, Professor G. S. Kirk of Bristol University, and Dr. R. Phillips of Yale University.

### Roger Beck (essay date 1973)

SOURCE: "Some Observations on the Narrative Technique of Petronius," *The Phoenix,* Vol. XXVII, No. 1, Spring, 1973, pp. 42-61.

[*In the following essay, Beck attempts to reconcile discrepancies in the character of Encolpius by considering him as two separate persons: the narrator and the subject of the narration.*]

One of the most problematic questions in the *Satyricon* is the character of the hero and narrator of the story, Encolpius himself. Critics rightly point out the fluctuations and seeming inconsistencies in Petronius' portrayal of him, as the following pen sketches from two recent studies show: "alternatively romantic and cynical, brave and timorous, malevolent and cringing, jealous and rational, sophisticated and naive" (J. P. Sullivan[1]); "simple soul and man of the world, sadist and soft-hearted sentimentalist, parasitic flatterer and ingenuous guest" (P. G. Walsh[2]). Explanations of these seeming inconsistencies, however, differ widely. Some find the self-contradictory character convincing in itself, in an Aristotelian sense consistently inconsistent. H. D. Rankin sees him in a rather modern light as a decayed intelligence, registering and aware of the experiences that flow over him but unable to confront and master them, a victim of random emotions and anxieties.[3] For Walsh the inconsistencies are primarily a matter of Encolpius' position as narrator: "He is the chameleon of the I-narrator who sees the complexities within himself but only the consistent traits in others."[4] Others explain the discrepancies in terms of the economy of the *Satyricon* as a whole. Sullivan insists that "Encolpius' character is disorganized and fragmentary, not because he is at odds with himself and suffering from a spiritual instability that the author is interested in exploring, but because he is the structural and narrative link for the different themes that Petronius has chosen, as well as the victim of certain comic and satiric situations. The character of Encolpius . . . is composed *of those traits, even if contradictory, which are appropriate responses to the demands of the particular episode*" (*loc. cit.* [n. 1]; Sullivan's italics). On a somewhat different tack, P. George accounts for the discrepancy between the quality and sophistication of the narrative and the naivety, stupidity, and poor taste of the narrator in terms of the author's wish to retain the vividness and the comic and satiric possibilities of first person narrative without stunting himself with the limitations of a style appropriate to the narrator.[5]

It will be noted that both of the last two explanations (George and Sullivan) imply a certain failure on Petronius' part, despite the brilliance of individual episodes (or, perhaps, because of it), to sustain an overall plausibility and consistency in the writing of narrative fiction; or at least they suggest a willingness to sacrifice plausibility and consistency of narration for other effects. This, to some extent, is typical of the mainstream of Petronian criticism which tends to treat the *Satyricon* primarily in terms of parody, satire, and a medley of literary entertainment (the heaviest arguments being concerned with the genres that go to make the mixture and with Petronius' attitude towards them), and only secondarily as an extended novel.[6] In the study that follows I propose to take an opposite approach and to suggest a means of reconciling the discrepancies in Encolpius' character that at the same time sees in the *Satyricon* a well-wrought, sophisticated, and self-consistent work of narrative fiction.

The key to the solution is, I believe, a realization that in dealing with Encolpius one is concerned not with a single person but with two: Encolpius the narrator and Encolpius the subject of the narration. Not only are they two distinct persons separated by what is presumably a considerable span of time (the narrator is looking back on his own *past* adventures) but they are also two very *different* characters. The narrator, as we shall see, is sophisticated and competent, while his former self is chaotic and naïve. Strictly speaking, one should say only that *that version* of his former self *which the narrator chooses to present* is chaotic and naïve. For we should be aware that the Encolpius who is the protagonist in the adventures related is as much the creation of the Encolpius who tells the story as are the other characters who make their appearance in the novel. And as we shall also see, there is excellent reason to suppose that the very last thing that interests Encolpius the narrator is an accurate, factual reconstruction of his own past life and character. In the **Satyricon** we have in fact two levels of creation: the author creates the narrator and the narrator creates the narrative together with the various characters (himself included), using as a basis—but as no more than that— his own past experiences. In a sense, of course, the author creates the totality of the work, but to be aware of this alone is to rest on a generality which ignores the particular approach here taken by Petronius. The genius of the **Satyricon,** considered as a work of narrative fiction, lies in the subtlety with which Petronius has delineated a highly sophisticated and complex narrator who defines himself brilliantly and consistently in the telling of his story.

That there is a real difference between the narrator and his former self and that an awareness of this difference might help in appreciating the structure and economy of the **Satyricon** is a consideration that has so far played virtually no part in the criticism of the work.[7] This unfortunate state of affairs is due to a number of factors. First, the mutilation of the text has deprived us of the beginning and end of the novel, points at which we might reasonably expect that the author would have shown us the narrator introducing and concluding his narration. At the most elementary level, then, we are never made aware of the narrator as an individual existing in his own right outside the context of the narrative, as we are, for example, by Clitophon's meeting with the author in Achilles Tatius' *Leucippe and Clitophon* or by Apuleius' introduction of himself to his audience in the *Metamorphoses.* Secondly, Petronius' narrator does not draw attention to himself by frequent use of a first person clearly referring to his present rather than his former self (a rare example occurs in 65.1 where the narrator comments on the *matteae* served at the banquet: *quarum etiam recordatio me, si qua est dicenti fides, offendit*). Thirdly, as we shall see, the narrator takes considerable pains to avoid the sort of aloof, superior, and judicious tone that would reveal beyond question his separate identity as a distinct person distanced from the action and looking back at past events from the vantage point of hindsight and experience. Finally, though, the main reason why the distinction between the narrator and his former self is generally ignored may well be a matter of the marginal status of prose fiction as a genre in ancient literature. Classical antiquity simply does not possess a large corpus of sophisticated prose fiction, and as a result the necessary critical approaches, such as "point of view" analysis, evolved in the study of other literatures are not by and large known to classicists or applied to such novels as fall within their sphere. Fortunately,

with T. Hägg's recently published *Narrative Technique in Ancient Greek Romances* an excellent start has been made at remedying this deficiency.[8]

The starting point for an assessment of Encolpius as narrator must surely be Encolpius' own attitude towards the telling of his tale, since it is that which determines the whole character of the narration and thus of the novel itself. Why does he tell his story, what purpose is the narrative intended to serve? Lacking any explicit statement of aims, one must work backwards from the evidence of the structure and tone of the narrative itself. The answer is not difficult to find. It is abundantly clear that Encolpius' main—one is even tempted to say exclusive—aim in recounting his adventures is to *entertain*. One receives throughout the novel the consistent impression of a narrator *shaping* the adventures and encounters of his past life into episodes which will delight and amuse. The clearest proof of this is the narrator's use of realism. Where realism serves the end of effective story-telling realism is maintained. Thus, in the *cena,* where the main thrust of the narration is to build up a picture of a freedman magnate and his circle, realism dominates both the narrative and the reported speeches, since realism will clearly produce the effect desired. Yet even here unrealistic elements intrude when they contribute to the building of the narrator's portrait of Trimalchio and his world, for example the fantastic exaggerations of the bulletin read out by the *actuarius* (53.2): on a single day on a single estate 30 boys and 40 girls born, 500,000 *modii* of grain processed, 500 oxen broken in! When, however, different effects are aimed at in the story-telling, realism is sometimes jettisoned entirely. Take, for example, the introduction to the adventures with the legacy hunters at Croton. Here the narrator intends to entertain us with satire of sorts, and to set the scene he has the adventurers meet a certain *vilicus* who obligingly gives them a thumb-nail sketch of the predators and their prey (116.6-9):

> *In hac . . . urbe non litterarum studia celebrantur, non eloquentia locum habet, non frugalitas sanctique mores laudibus ad fructum perveniunt, sed quoscumque homines videritis, scitote in duas partes esse divisos. nam aut captantur aut captant. in hac urbe nemo liberos tollit, quia quisquis suos heredes habet, non ad cenas, non ad spectacula admittitur, sed omnibus prohibetur commodis, inter ignominiosos latitat. qui vero nec uxorem umquam duxerunt nec proximas necessitudines habent, ad summos honores perveniunt, soli fortissimi atque etiam innocentes habentur. adibitis . . . oppidum tamquam in pestilentia campos, in quibus nihil aliud est nisi cadavera quae lacerantur aut corvi qui lacerant.*
>
> [Müller's text]

In that town literature and the arts go utterly unhonored; eloquence there has no prestige; and those who lead the good and simple life find no admirers. Any man you meet in that town you may be certain belongs to one of two classes: the makers of wills and those who pursue the makers of wills. You will find no fathers there, for those with natural heirs of their own are regarded as pariahs. A father is someone who is never invited to dinner, never entertained, who, in short, is compelled to spend his life, outcast and excluded, among the poor and obscure. Those, however, who remain bachelors in perpetuity and have no close relatives are held in the highest honor and esteem: they and they alone are men of honor and courage, brave as lions, paragons without spot or flaw. In short, sirs, you are going to a place which is like a countryside ravaged by the plague, a place in which you will see only two things: the bodies of those who are eaten, and the carrion crows who eat them.

[Arrowsmith's translation]

Now the point here is not that such a tirade is unrealistic in content; people frequently castigate cities in an exaggerated way as moral cesspools where only rogues thrive. Rather, the point is that such a speech with its neat summary of the state of affairs, its brisk style and clever antitheses is utterly implausible in the mouth of a farm bailiff encountered by chance by a party that has lost its way on a country road. Since the narrator, as we know from the *cena,* is more than capable of reporting realistically the talk of the uneducated, we must assume that he has other motives for presenting the conversation with the *vilicus* as he does. Here, as in other situations, the principle at work appears to be the effective presentation of the episode as an entertaining tale shaped to a certain pattern. The pattern here is a satiric farce in which legacy hunters prey on the rich, the rich on legacy hunters, and Eumolpus and company on all comers. The speech of the *vilicus* provides with considerable neatness, but also with total lack of plausibility if verisimilitude is taken into account, an alluring introduction to the episode.

The narrator gives us, then, not a precise and factual account of his past life and adventures but a version of them shaped imaginatively for the entertainment of an audience. In effect, he offers implicitly what Apuleius offers explicitly (*varias fabulas conseram auresque tuas benivolas lepido susurro permulceam,* 1.1), and he offers it perhaps more whole-heartedly, since in Apuleius' case a good part of the author-narrator's purpose—though unstated—is the glorification of Isis and the redeemed life. In the **Satyricon** there is no such ulterior motive at work. Petronius portrays a narrator spinning tales to amuse an audience, tales which we may suppose to be *based* on the narrator's experiences, but not an accurate *reconstruction* of them. Realism can at any point be sacrificed for effect, and we can never know just how close we come to the "facts" of the narrator's past life, though we can be quite sure that most of the time there is a high propor-

tion of fantasy, imagination, and artistic editing to the mixture. Continuity and consistency in the **Satyricon** lie not in the *content* of the narration but in the *persona* of the narrator as an artist shaping a highly selective and fanciful autobiography.

It is the *persona* of the narrator that above all justifies the frequent appearance of verse in his story-telling. The verse is an organic part of the narrative because the narrator himself is firmly characterized throughout as a self-conscious practitioner of the art of words, as one who moulds the experiences of life into literary forms, and as a fascinated student of the poetic imagination—and its delusions. Moreover, the subjects of his narrative are often themselves the devotees—and victims—of rhetoric, of poetry, and of literary culture in general. They include not only such obvious figures as Eumolpus and Agamemnon, but also the hero's sexual associates (Giton and Ascyltus), and above all his own past self. The difference between the narrator's approach to literary culture and that of the subjects of his narration is a topic I hope to explore more fully on a later occasion. At present the point I wish to emphasize is simply that it is the ubiquitous literary concerns of the narrator and his subjects that permit the frequent resort to verse without any loss of the novel's unity. This, indeed, is one of Petronius' subtlest achievements: the transformation of his chosen genre, the mixed prose and verse medium of Menippean satire, into coherent narrative fiction. The means that won him this triumph is the creation of his cultured and imaginative narrator. To realize the nature of Petronius' achievement one has only to compare the near contemporary *Apocolocyntosis* in which the movement from prose to verse is inexplicable in terms of any logic of narrative or character, and which therefore remains more or less at the level of a satiric medley.

The verse in the **Satyricon** may be divided into two categories: that which the narrator attributes to characters other than himself and that which he either attributes to his own past self or else presents in his own person as narrator. The first category is obviously the more straightforward, in that in each instance the verse must be presented as the spoken words of the character to whom it is attributed. More often than not the verse in this category is realistic enough, in the sense that it fits the character and the occasion. The best example of this sort is perhaps Eumolpus' "little elegy on hair" (*capillorum elegidarion*) and the hendecasyllables that follow (109.9-10). What could be more natural than that in the merry-making following the reconciliation on Lichas' ship the irrepressible old aesthete should deliver himself of a humorous medley of prose and verse, taking as an obvious starting point the ludicrously shorn and painted appearance of Giton and Encolpius?

> . . . *cum Eumolpus et ipse vino solutus dicta voluit*
> *in calvos stigmososque iaculari, donec consumpta*

*frigidissima urbanitate rediit ad carmina sua coepitque capillorum elegidarion dicere.*

[109.8]

. . . when Eumolpus, being well in his cups, got the idea of throwing out some quips about bald heads and brandmarks, until exhausting his weak witticisms he went back to his poetry and began reciting a little elegy on hair.

[Sullivan's translation]

Just as realistic (if we grant the convention of the narrator's total recall of lengthy poetry) is Eumolpus' *Sack of Troy* (89) with its genesis in the conversation between the two newly met *littérateurs* and the picture that confronts them in the gallery; even his *Civil War* (119 ff.), despite its huge length, is reasonable enough, given his addiction to verse-making and recitation and the established tastes and interests of the narrator which lead him to report it. Other examples of verse that fits both character and situation without any violation of realism are the lines of Agamemnon on training for the arts (5) and the execrable pieces of Trimalchio on mortality (34.10 and 55.3). Of verse that is unrealistic in this sense the best example is probably Tryphaena's appeal to the combatants on board Lichas' ship (108.14). In "real" life such murderous conflicts springing from the passions of desperate men (*rabies libidine perditorum collecta*, 108.8) are seldom settled by the measured rhetoric of Vergilian hexameters. But realism is, of course, the last thing that interests the narrator in his description of the fight. Rather, his aim is to turn the fracas into an entertaining farce. Hence Giton's histrionics with the dummy razor (108.10-11), and hence too the narrator's ironic elevation of the brawl into "no commonplace war" (*non tralaticium bellum*, 108.12) which can only be settled by due ritual (*data . . . acceptaque ex more patrio fide*, 108.13) and the formulas of solemn treaty (109.2-3). Into this presentation Tryphaena's verse with its pretentious allusions to the sea flights of Paris and Medea fits admirably. The heroic and tragic overtones render the actual mêlée by contrast only the more ludicrous.

A further example of verse which is unrealistic and implausible in its given context is the poem of Oenothea on her powers as a witch (134.12). The poem merits some close attention since it leads us directly to certain highly significant features of the narrator's over-all design. The content of the poem is commonplace enough. Oenothea simply attributes to herself the standard accomplishments of witchcraft that one meets throughout ancient literature:[9] control of crop growth, the raising and stilling of tempests, power over animals, and—the supreme accomplishment—the ability to change the motions of the heavenly bodies. If one accepts lines 11-16 (see Müller *ad loc.*), Oenothea then cites the great mythical practitioners of her art: Medea, Circe, Proteus. In both language and content the poem

is utterly trite. What gives it point is nothing in the poem itself but rather the contrast between, on the one side, the claims that it makes and the images that it conjures up, and on the other, the reality of Oenothea's person and abilities. For as the narrative proceeds, it becomes abundantly clear that Oenothea is a drunken, incompetent, libidinous, and venal hag whose "magic" cannot fool even the credulous Encolpius. This counterpicture the narrator paints in vivid detail: the dilapidated state of her cottage with its loose pegs (135.4) and rotten stool collapsing under her weight and scattering the fire needed for the ritual (136.1-2), the snack of decaying pig's head (135.4 and 136.1) and the spitting out of the bean shells *veluti muscarum imagines* (135.6), the quick change of attitude over the slaughtered goose once payment is offered (137.7-8), the pretense of divination by the nuts which even Encolpius realizes sink or swim in the wine depending on whether or not their kernels are properly formed (137.10), and finally the drunken and lecherous pursuit as Encolpius makes his escape (138.3). So glaring, then, is the contrast between the pretensions of the verse and the sordidness of the actual situation that one is lead to suppose that it is an intended element in the narrator's design. The verse is included not for its own sake (and certainly not for its artistic merits), but deliberately to set up this contrast between illusion and reality—though here, of course, one must bear in mind the fact that the "real" world is as much the narrator's creation as is the never-never land of poetic delusion (the farcical element built into the world of the everyday should keep us aware that this side of things is also shaped artistically, not merely recorded). What, though, is the purpose of this contrast? To suppose that it is intended to make a point about Oenothea herself, that her performances do not measure up to her pretensions, is to run into an immediate difficulty. For the narrator draws the contrast in so extreme a manner that it becomes scarcely credible that so squalid and uncultured a person could possibly entertain and express in correct—though hackneyed—form the literate and imaginative sentiments attributed to her in the verse. In other words, if we suppose that the contrast is purely a matter of opposite traits in Oenothea *alone*, we must also admit that the narrator's over-all portrait of her fails to achieve either unity or plausibility. There is, however, another possibility. Might we not suppose that the verse represents not the narrator's reconstruction of Oenothea's own pretensions to magical powers, but rather the reconstruction of what he himself in the past, with the fervid literary imagination that he carried into all his adventures, would *expect* a witch to claim on first encounter? The verse, on this supposition, would not really be Oenothea's at all, but rather the imaginings of Encolpius himself *projected* on to Oenothea in his later re-shaping of his adventures for narration. The interpretation is admittedly a complicated one. It depends for its plausibility on the realization that this would merely be a variation on a game which the narrator is constantly playing in his story-telling: the drawing of contrasts between the delusions engendered on his own past thinking by literary stereotypes and the often squalid truth about the people whom he met and the adventures which befell him. Most often this contrast is effected by means of the verse which the narrator either presents in his own person or attributes specifically to his own past self. It is to the verse of this type that we must now turn.

The verse of Encolpius falls naturally into two groups. The first, which is much the smaller, consists of those poems which are presented as the words and thoughts of the protagonist *in situ*. Encolpius' supplication of Priapus (133.3) is one such poem; it is set out unambiguously as his spoken words on the particular occasion: *positoque in limine genu* sic deprecatus sum *numen aversum* (133.2). Another is the poem in which he attributes his misfortunes to the wrath of Priapus and assimilates his sufferings to the pattern of the divine persecution of the great heroes (139.2). The present tenses (*persequitur, sequitur*) guarantee it as his own words, or at least his thoughts (the absence of its prose framework from the text prevents us from knowing which), *in situ*. The same is true of the flamboyant challenge to Jupiter to sample Circe's charms (126.18). Again, the text is mutilated in its surroundings, but we could well construe it as a conceit spoken aloud to compliment and impress Circe herself (such an interpretation would fit well with the sentence that appears next in the text: *delectata illa risit . . .* , 127.1). Finally, I would also classify as Encolpius' words *in situ* the verse deprecating the censoriousness of would-be *Catones* (132.15), which I shall argue is actually a continuation of his soliloquy in defense of the rhetorical onslaught which he has just delivered against his recalcitrant member.

I am well aware that such a reading of the verse at 132.15 runs counter to the generally accepted interpretation. Most critics have understood the piece not as the words of Encolpius at all, but as a direct appeal by Petronius himself justifying, in his own person, the approach and subject matter of the **Satyricon.** Such, for example, was Collignon's opinion: "Il semble même qu'à un moment donné, Pétrone s'applique ouvertement à mettre son récit sous le patronage d'Épicure. Au chapitre 132 se lit une pièce de quatre distiques, où l'on croit entendre *l'auteur lui-même s'adressant à ses lecteurs et non plus cette fois par la bouche d'un de ses personnages*" (my italics).[10] The same view is adopted, as an unargued assumption, by both Arrowsmith ("a rare aside, that defends [Petronius'] work from the attacks of prudery")[11] and Sullivan ("an aside of the author to his audience, explaining part of his intentions and principles in a defense of the subjects of the **Satyricon** and his literary treatment of them").[12]

The view is a difficult one to refute. For it depends not on any evidence in the text that can be challenged as a matter of fact, but on an unexamined and fixed determination to discover at all costs the presence— and opinions, whether aesthetic or moral—of the author himself in his work. It is this preconception of the nature of the **Satyricon** as necessarily a vehicle for the tastes and opinions of its author (if only we could agree what they are!) that leads critics to seize on the verse at 132.15 as Petronius' direct address to us in his own proper person. But, in fact, we are not dealing with an author such as Fielding, part of whose technique—and a highly successful part—consists in regularly and explicitly entering his own work to explain, to justify and to point the moral. The verse to the *Catones* would be the *only* such intrusion to be found in the very substantial portions of the **Satyricon** that have survived. We would have to assume, then, that for the sake of a meagre few lines of personal apologetics the author has chosen to sabotage his whole carefully contrived effect of a story communicated throughout not by himself but by a narrator with his own distinct and subtly drawn *persona* recreating his own adventures.

But, in fact, the generally accepted view of the poem, with its disastrous implications for Petronius' narrative technique, is quite unnecessary. The poem may be read—and read more naturally—as a continuation, without any break, of the rhetorical soliloquy that immediately precedes it. Shortly beforehand Encolpius had delivered his tirade. He had then, however, experienced feelings of shame at having "bandied words with that part of the body which men of the stricter sort (*severioris notae homines*) usually do not admit even to their thoughts" (132.12). But his mood now veers again, and he reflects that his imprecations are only natural. His words are given in direct speech (132.13-14):

> *Quid autem ego . . . mali feci, si dolorem meum naturali convicio exoneravi? aut quid est quod in corpore humano ventri male dicere solemus aut gulae capitique etiam, cum saepius dolet? quid? non et Ulixes cum corde litigat suo, et quidam tragici oculos suos tamquam audientes castigant? podagrici pedibus suis male dicunt, chiragrici manibus, lippi oculis, et qui offenderunt saepe digitos, quicquid doloris habent in pedes deferunt.*

What's so unnatural or wrong about working off one's feelings with a little plainspoken abuse? Don't we curse our guts, our teeth, our heads, when they give us trouble? Didn't Ulysses himself have a parley with his heart? Why, the way those heroes in the tragic plays strut around cursing their eyes, you'd think their eyes had ears. Gouty people damn their toes; arthritics curse their joints; the crud-eyed blast their eyes and even toe-stubbers take out their feelings on their feet.

[Arrowsmith's translation]

It is at this point that the poem is introduced. The first four lines are as follows:

> *Quid me constricta spectatis fronte Catones*
>   *damnatisque novae simplicitatis opus?*
> *Sermonis pur; non tristis gratia ridet*
>   *quodque facit populus, candida lingua*
>   *refert.*

Why do you censors stare at me with frowning brow and condemn a work of novel simplicity? The lively charm of pure language laughs through it, and what the people do my candid tongue reports.[13]

The continuity of this first part of the verse with the preceding prose passage is seamless. The *Catones,* surely, are the *severioris notae homines* whom we met above. Encolpius is now addressing them directly as if they were present (he is, in fact, solioquizing) and debating with him on standards of propriety in speech. The development of the rhetoric is typical of Encolpius, as the narrator (who is, of course, his later self) reveals him to us. In his soliloquy Encolpius moves from the reality of his own impotence to a debate with imaginary adversaries on the propriety of making a declamation out of it. In precisely the same way the earlier oration over the drowned Lichas (115.8-19) had drifted away from the here and now of the individual corpse on the sea shore to the generalities of a classroom exercize complete with imagined objectors to the line of argument:

> *At enim fluctibus obruto non contingit sepultura.*
> *tamquam intersit, periturum corpus quae ratio*
> *consumat, ignis an fluctus an mora. quicquid feceris,*
> *omnia haec eodem ventura sunt. ferae tamen corpus*
> *lacerabunt. tamquam melius ignis accipiat; immo*
> *hanc poenam gravissimam credimus, ubi servis*
> *irascimur.*

[115.17-18]

But I hear someone object: those who drown at sea die unburied. Lord, lord, as though it mattered how this deathbound flesh should die! Fire or water or the wear and tear of time, what does it matter? Death or death: the end is always the same. But objectors again: wild beasts may mutilate the body. And so? Is the fire that someday cremates your corpse more friendly? Gentle fire, the cruelest death to which an angry master can sentence his slave?

[Arrowsmith's translation]

Surely, then, the *novae simplicitatis opus* of the poem's second line need be understood as no more than the

tirade against the offending member. To accept this interpretation, it is not necessary to believe that the tirade *really is* "a work of novel simplicity" or that it has in fact all the qualities ascribed to it (purity and candour of language, liveliness and charm). We need only admit that Encolpius himself might well make such a claim. Given his talent for grandiose fantasies (cf. the sacrifice and festival promised to Priapus in 133.3), the supposition is perfectly plausible. If the term *opus* seems out of all proportion to the few sentences actually recorded, it can be accounted for by Encolpius' exaggerated sense of literary self-importance. Even when first introduced, the tirade is called an *oratio* (the choice of term reflecting, I take it, Encolpius' own estimation at the time): *erectus igitur in cubitum* hac fere oratione *contumacem vexavi* (132.9).

On this reading, the expression *quod facit populus* need be taken to refer to no more than what Encolpius has just been saying that people as a matter of fact habitually do, which is to curse those parts of their bodies which give them trouble. The fourth line of the poem, then, is merely a recapitulation in verse of what has already been argued in detail in prose. Encolpius claims that his tirade has the merit of "candour" (*candida lingua*) because it reflects the idiom of ordinary people (*quod facit populus*). As he had said earlier (132.13), he has only relieved his feelings with "natural invective" (*naturali convicio*).

But, in fact, the expression *quod facit populus* is usually construed in a very different sense. Its meaning is generally understood not from what precedes it, but from what follows. For the poem continues (lines 5-8):

> *nam quis concubitus, Veneris quis gaudia*
>   *nescit?*
>     *quis vetat in tepido membra calere toro?*
> *ipse pater veri doctos Epicurus amare*
>   *iussit et hoc vitam dixit habere [telos].*

All men born know of mating and the joys of love; all men are free to let their limbs glow in a warm bed. Epicurus himself, the true father of truth, bade wise men be lovers, and said that herein lay the goal of life.

[Heseltine's Loeb translation]

Reading back from line 5 to 4, it is natural enough to suppose that "what the people do" is to be understood in the present context as love-making. The inference seems guaranteed by the conjunction *nam:*

>   *quodque facit populus candida lingua*
>     *refert.*
> nam *quis concubitus, Veneris quis gaudia*
>   *nescit?*

Now if this equation of *quod facit populus* with *concubitus* and the *gaudia Veneris* is accepted, it follows that the subject matter of the *novae simplicitatis opus* is also *concubitus* and the *gaudia Veneris*. In that case the *novae simplicitatis opus* must be construed as something other than Encolpius' tirade, the subject of which was rather different and much more specific, namely his own impotent member. Since there is no other internal candidate for the *novae simplicitatis opus,* it is tempting to equate it with the **Satyricon** itself and to suppose that the author is here thrusting himself forward to justify his own subject matter.

And yet, as I have argued, this interpretation involves the supposition that here and here only in the entire preserved text does the author choose to violate his otherwise carefully maintained pretense that the **Satyricon** is the continuous autobiography of a narrator with a distinct and definite *persona* of his own. It also involves the supposition of a considerable lacuna immediately prior to the verse to allow first for the change of speakers from Encolpius *in situ* to the author in his own person, and secondly for the shift of subject matter from the propriety of speaking about certain parts of the body to the propriety of treating of sexual matters in general. It is the first of these changes that is the really awkward one. Surely, it is quite inconceivable that at one moment Encolpius the protagonist—not even Encolpius the narrator—should be speaking, and at the next, and without any transition, Petronius in his own voice.[14] And yet it is well-nigh impossible to imagine what form a transitional sentence or passage, alerting us to the fact that the verse will be the author's own apology, could conceivably take. An easy transition to and from authorial comment is precisely what Petronius has denied himself by the very skill and consistency with which he presents the **Satyricon** exclusively as a story told by his narrator Encolpius.

I suggest, then, that we return to an interpretation of the poem as a continuation of Encolpius' soliloquy, understanding the *novae simplicitatis opus* as his recent tirade and *quod facit populus* as the everyday practice, which he has just been discussing, of cursing mis-functioning parts of the body. With this reading we must, of course, postulate a lacuna between lines 4 and 5, since there will now be a *non sequitur* between Encolpius' claim that his speech only reflects the common habit of damning one's faulty members and the rhetorical question "who is ignorant of lovemaking?" We may suppose that in the missing section Encolpius developed his argument to the point of demanding from his imaginary opponents the right to speak of sexual matters at large, on the grounds of their universality and their prime importance in human life. This intervening prose passage dropped out, and the two verse passages were conflated, with the conjunction *nam* suggesting a sort of spurious continuity. Such a

conflation of two pieces of verse can be exactly paralleled in 80.9, where two separate pairs of couplets have likewise coalesced into a single verse passage, though in that instance the lack of real continuity between the two is more readily apparent.

A significant feature of the verse at 132.15 (if my interpretation is correct) is the way in which the original tirade is built up in Encolpius' imagination into a full-scale literary *opus*. This quality of exaggeration is also present in the other pieces of verse which are presented as the words or thoughts of the protagonist in action. Significantly, the exaggeration often takes the form of a flight of fancy into the world of literature and myth along much the same lines as the poem on Oenothea's powers (134.12), which I suggested above should properly be read as the hero's own fantasy projected into the witch's mouth. Thus, in his prayer to Priapus (133.3) Encolpius commits himself not only to the sacrifice of a goat and a litter of piglets (lines 13-15) but also to an entire festival complete with chorus of suitably inebriated and dancing youths (line 16 f.):

> *Spumabit pateris hornus liquor, et ter ovantem*
> *circa delubrum gressum feret ebria pubes.*

> New wine will foam in bowls, and thrice around
> thy shrine the tipsy youth will tread its joyous dance.

The image is that of a rustic revel of the type that features regularly in idealizing poetry about the simple, pious life of the countryside.[15] But it is utterly inappropriate to Encolpius with his radically different *milieu* and style of life. For, in sober fact, how on earth is this city boy of presumably slender means going to assemble all those dancing yokels to redeem his vow for him? But, clearly, the faithful fulfilment of his promises is not the consideration uppermost in Encolpius' mind.[16] He is indulging in a literary fantasy in which he enters a pastoral world to act as master of ceremonies in a festival modelled on the best poetic stereotypes. Much the same "trip" into the world of literature is also evident in the verse at 139.2, though there the realm entered is that of epic and heroic myth. With magnificent hyperbole the impotent Encolpius classes himself, as the victim of Priapus' wrath, with the archetypal victims of divine jealousy, Hercules, Laomedon, Pelias, Telephus, and Ulysses:

> *me quoque per terras, per cani Nereos aequor*
> *Hellespontiaci sequitur gravis ira Priapi.*

> [line 7 f.]

> Me too over land and grey Nereus' sea the harsh
> anger of Hellespontine Priapus pursues.

In view of the wide-spread belief that the wrath of Priapus is a major theme in the composition of the

*Satyricon* as a whole,[17] it is, I believe, most important to bear in mind that we have only the word of Encolpius the protagonist, not of Encolpius the narrator, as assurance that his sufferings stem from the individual attentions of an outraged god. The hypothesis of divine persecution may well be no more than a fantasy spun by the hero partly to salvage his dignity in the humiliating circumstances of sexual impotence and partly because, in any case, he is by nature a compulsive spinner of such fantasies.

So far we have been discussing only those pieces of verse which are presented directly as the words or thoughts of Encolpius *in situ*. A much larger group consists of pieces which Encolpius offers in his role of narrator. These pieces are contemporaneous with the prose narrative; they look back on the past adventures from the same later standpoint in time. Most of them are characterized by past tenses: e.g., *qualis nox* fuit *illa* (79.8), *nobilis aestivas platanus* diffuderat *umbras* (131.8), *ter* corripui *terribilem manu bipennem* (132.8), *non Indum* fulgebat *ebur* (135.8). When present tenses are used, they tend to be the timeless presents of general propositions: e.g., *nomen amicitiae sic, quatenus* expedit, haeret (80.9), *quisquis* habet *nummos, secura* navigat *aura* (137.9).

Now of all these pieces only a single one actually functions as narrative in advancing the telling of the story. That piece is the verse at 132.8, which describes Encolpius' attempt at self-mutilation and its failure: *ter corripui terribilem manu bipennem*. The rest are a medley of background description (e.g., on the beauties of nature as the setting for the meeting with Circe, 131.8), moralizing (e.g., on the limits of friendship, 80.9.1-4), commentary on the action (e.g., the extended simile comparing the sexual failure with Circe to the loss of a hoard of gold that a dreamer experiences on awaking, 128.6), and literary and mythical allusions (e.g., the comparison between the victory over the geese and the routing of the Stymphalian birds by Hercules and of the Harpies by the Argonauts, 136.6). Do we conclude, then, that these pieces represent the studied evaluations and literary reflections of the narrator looking back on his past life and adventures? The answer, unfortunately, cannot be a simple yes. For to suppose such would be to ignore a persistent and significant feature of many of these pieces. In perhaps the majority of instances the verse, *taken in context*, is somehow inappropriate, ludicrous, or downright false. Furthermore, the error or absurdity belongs not to Encolpius the narrator, whose concern is to draw attention to it in an oblique and subtle way, but rather to Encolpius the protagonist in action.

Let us take as an example the verse description of Oenothea's cottage (135.8). The place is characterized as a model of rustic simplicity. The appearance and furnishings are described in terms which are favourable

or at least neutral (with the exception, perhaps, of the wine-stained pottery at line 7 and the rather careless application of daub to wattle at line 8 f.). It is the sort of place, indeed, that prompts thoughts of Hecale, the old woman immortalized by Callimachus as an archetype of peasant hospitality. Now the most striking thing about this verse description is that it is clean contrary to the facts as given in the prose narrative. Oenothea's cottage, as we have seen already, is a ramshackle and filthy hovel and its owner a slovenly hag (no Hecale she!). The contrast between prose and verse can be seen at its clearest in the edible provisions that each makes mention of. The prose speaks of dirty beans (*grana sordidissimis putaminibus vestita,* 135.5) and a decaying pig's head, the veteran of countless snacks (*sincipitis vetustissima particula mille plagis dolata,* 135.4; *coaequale natalium suorum sinciput,* 136.1), while the verse describes only fruit and sweet smelling herbs (*mitia sorba/et thymbrae veteres et passis uva racemis/inter odoratas pendebant texta coronas,* lines 12-14). Now the contrast between the sordid reality of the prose and the idealizing fantasies of the verse is too marked, too vivid, and too entertaining to be a matter of chance discrepancy or of careless composition. We must assume, then, that it is an effect intentionally engineered by Encolpius the narrator. It follows, therefore, that the illusions of the verse are not *his* illusions; *he* does not see Oenothea and her shack in the idealizing light of the verse. Whose illusions are they, then? Surely they must represent the poetic fantasies in which, as we have seen already, the narrator's *former* self, Encolpius the protagonist, used constantly to indulge. Though the language of the verse with its past tenses seems to emanate from the narrator looking back in time, the sentiments are very much those of the hero in the thick of his adventures. Like the flight of fancy in the prayer to Priapus (133.3), the reflections on Oenothea's cottage are clearly the imaginings of the Encolpius who lives half his life in a never-never land of myth and literature and whose imagination is easily triggered into fantastic poetic responses, however inappropriate or even ludicrous. Thus, the mere fact of the *paupertas* of Oenothea's dwelling place (135.7) is enough to prompt the hero's musings on the commonplace theme of the simple life free from the burden of riches (lines 1-3 of the poem), and by a sort of literary osmosis the shack, despite its all too obvious squalour, is transformed into the rustic and fragrant haunt of a Hecale. The beginnings of this drift into fantasy are caught precisely in the prose sentence that introduces the verse: *mirabar equidem paupertatis ingenium singularumque rerum quasdam artes.* Though presented in the format of a narrator's description, the verse that follows is clearly a reconstruction of the hero's intrigued reflections (*mirabar equidem*) at the time.

Let us look at some of the other passages in which the narrator's verse, by reason of some obviously deliberate contrast with a sordid or ludicrous prose reality, seems to be a reconstruction of Encolpius' fantasies at the time. One such piece is the verse comparing the victory over the geese to the routing of the Stymphalian birds or the Harpies (136.6). The verb *reor* (line 2 of the verse) should be the narrator's present: "In just such a way I think the Stymphalian birds . . . fled" (*tales . . . Stymphalidas . . . fugisse reor*). But it reflects, I believe, more the pretensions to mythic grandeur of the hero himself in action. For once again the narrative makes it abundantly clear that the actual fray is a very different matter from its imagined counterparts, and since the narrator is controlling this contrast between reality and illusion it cannot be he who is the spinner of illusion, except in the sense of *re-creating* his own past fantasies. The passage is a particularly interesting one in that the hero's fantasies are allowed to spill over into the preceding prose (136.4-5), where we find, often in the same sentence, a subtle mixture of heroic posturing and absurd or very ordinary reality. In the protagonist's imagination his foes are viciously formidable (*impetum in me faciunt foedoque ac veluti rabioso stridore circumsistunt trepidantem*) and their leader a sort of Mezentius: *dux et magister saevitiae.* But probably they are only looking for their midday meal (*qui, ut puto, medio die solebant ab anu diaria exigere*), and part of the injuries which they inflict on Encolpius, the tearing of his tunic and the breaking of his sandal straps, are scarcely compatible with heroic dignity. Again, Encolpius defends himself *armata manu,* but his weapon is actually a table leg, and a diminutive table leg (*pedem mensulae*) at that! Finally, the battering to death of the *dux* which had been rash enough to bite Encolpius' leg is spoken of as an act of epic vengeance: *morte me anseris vindicavi.*

Yet another piece of verse in which there is a jarring contrast between the poetry and its prose context is the implied comparison of the lovemaking with Circe to the [*hieros gamos*] of Jupiter and Juno (127.9). The hero's musings (*Idaeo quales fudit de vertice flores / terra parens*) are triggered by the varied plant cover on to which Circe lowers him (127.8): *implicitumque me bracchiis . . . deduxit in terram vario gramine indutam.* But the love-making itself is a bathetic anticlimax, trailing off into Circe's shrill and vulgar questioning (128.1): *numquid te osculum meum offendit? numquid spiritus ieiunio marcens? numquid alarum sum negligens?* What could be more extreme than this contrast between the fantasy of the [*hieros gamos*], that most fructiferous of all unions, and the actual impotence of Encolpius' performance, or between the imagined floral idyll and Circe's real anxieties about her personal hygiene? Again, the contrast is clearly an effect produced by the narrator, and the comparison with the [*hieros gamos*], so false to the realities of the situation, can only be the fantasy of the hero in the moments

before disappointment strikes. The same, surely, is true of the ecstatic poem on the mutual joys of that night which in fact ends so crushingly with Giton's choice of Ascyltus as his "brother" (79.8): *qualis nox fuit illa, di deaeque.* The verse implies a union of souls in the high passion that unites the two bodies: *et transfudimus hinc et hinc labellis/errantes animas* (line 3 f.). But as events immediately show, such a union is an illusion: Giton will jilt Encolpius for another man, seemingly at whim. Indeed, in this particular passage the narrator, in what I take to be one of his rare uses of a first person referring to his present rather than his past self, himself alludes to this very discrepancy between the illusions and the realities of his earlier life. For at the end of the verse the prose resumes with the sentence, *sine causa gratulor mihi* ("but I flatter myself without good cause," 79.9). The narrator is here saying that the picture which he has just painted of a highly romantic and, by implication, exclusive passion is unfounded in reality; for Ascyltus, he continues, made off with the boy. The single present (*gratulor*), followed by an immediate switch to past tenses (*nam cum . . . remisissem . . . manus, Ascyltos . . . subduxit mihi . . . puerum et in lectum transtulit suum*), suggests that this is certainly the narrator's comment at the time of narration and not the protagonist's at the time of the original action.[18]

Naturally, not all of the narrator's verse demonstrates the sort of ludicrous contrast with its prose context that would make it unequivocally a reconstruction of the protagonist's musings *in situ.* Some of the pieces are sound and unexceptionable comments on the situations as they really were. For example, the verse on the power of money (137.9) is an appropriate enough general response to Oenothea's sudden change of attitude over the slaughter of the goose when payment is offered. It would not be inconsistent, then, to imagine that here the verse is the narrator's own commentary, since such a supposition would not contradict what we know of his sophisticated clearsightedness. But we can, of course, equally well imagine it to be Encolpius' own reflection at the time, a reflection which for once squarely hits the mark and which is then echoed and endorsed by his later self in the process of narration. The same two options are also open for the verse in which the hero's reaction to the fiasco with Circe is compared to the sense of loss experienced on awaking from a dream of hoarded gold (128.6). We could take the verse, which is forceful and to the point, either as exclusively the narrator's own composition at the time of narration or else as his reconstruction of a comparison which he made at the time of the original experience. It is impossible to decide for certain, though since we are told that the hero was in fact musing at the time (*ego contra damnatus et quasi quodam visu in horrorem perductus interrogare animum meum coepi, an vera voluptate fraudatus essem,* 128.5), it is perhaps best to interpret the verse as echoing, in part, the contents of those reflections.[19]

By and large, however, the dominant impression that emerges from the narrator's verse, as from that which is directly attributed to the protagonist *in situ,* is one of a hero who constantly—perhaps even compulsively—indulges in flights of fancy, mainly into a world of literary stereotypes, in contexts which render his fantasies both ludicrous and perversely inappropriate to the prose realities of his life, character, *milieu,* and adventures. The contrast between the hero's fantasies and the real situations in which he lives and moves is established by the narrator through the subtle and humorous juxtaposing of verse and prose. The narrator allows his audience to draw its conclusions about the hero—and about himself—from the contrasts alone. Nowhere does he intrude into his narrative to say in so many words that his protagonist, his own former self, lived much of his life surrounded by an aura of self-induced illusion and literary fantasy. Yet that is the conclusion that inescapably emerges. It is a conclusion, moreover, that helps us answer the problem with which this study started: the apparent character conflict between Encolpius as the cool and rational sophisticate and Encolpius as the deluded simpleton. The cool and rational sophisticate is the Encolpius who delicately and amusingly shapes his narrative in such a manner as to point up, without specific comment, the fantasies of his subject; the deluded simpleton is the earlier Encolpius who himself dreamt up and experienced the fantasies.

In dealing with the contrast between narrator and protagonist as seen in certain of the verse passages and their prose contexts, one has not, of course, covered (even by implication) the whole topic of the relationship between the two. Much remains to be examined in the prose alone. Much, moreover, remains to be said about the way in which the narrator presents characters other than his own past self. But these topics must wait for separate treatment. For the present I hope that I have established enough to suggest first that a distinction can and should be drawn between Encolpius as narrator and Encolpius as protagonist, and secondly that what Petronius offers us in the **Satyricon** is a portrait of Encolpius the narrator shaping an amusing and sophisticated version of his past life and adventures which includes, as a theme of major interest, a detailed treatment of his own chaotic and fantasy-ridden former self.

To conclude, I should emphasize the fact that both the hero's fantasies and the contrasted "realities" of his life and adventures as presented in the narrative are constructions of the narrator which may in fact correspond only loosely to the hero's "actual" fantasies and "actual" experiences. As I suggested earlier, the narrator's primary concern seems to be to shape his life and adventures into well-organized and entertaining episodes, even on occasions at the expense of realism and verisimilitude. Thus, not only the verse fantasies but also the prose "realities" may well contain certain deliberate inventions of the narrator designed simply to make the contrast more dramatic. For his aim is not to present an accurate case study of his earlier fantasies but to shape them for our entertainment. What his own feelings towards them actually are, it is difficult to tell (perhaps, in any case, it is the wrong question to ask of such a narrator). But a possible hint is offered by a strange phenomenon which we have already noted: the presentation of most of the protagonist's fantasies in the form of the narrator's own verse compositions looking back from a later standpoint in time. It is as if the narrator were fondly reliving the follies and fantasies of the past by giving expression to them as his own compositions of the present. It is a subtle device. For by identifying with his own past self in this way, the narrator avoids the sort of aloof and heartless ridicule of his subject which would render both himself and his narrative far less attractive than they are. Indeed, I believe that this identification of the narrator with his protagonist contributes in large measure to that atmosphere of good humour and moral sanity which the **Satyricon** somewhat paradoxically maintains. In place of unfeeling condemnation, callous contempt, and unpitying laughter, we are invited to feel sympathy with the young Encolpius as absurdly but gamely he confronts his unedifying experiences with the grand fantasies of myth and literature. To a great extent we feel this sympathy because the older Encolpius who is telling the story retains it himself.

*Notes*

[1] *The Satyricon of Petronius* (Bloomington and London 1968) 119.

[2] *The Roman Novel* (Cambridge 1970) 81.

[3] "Some Comments on Petronius' Portrayal of Character," *Petronius the Artist: Essays on the* Satyricon *and its Author* (The Hague 1971) 11-31, 19.

[4] *Loc cit.* (n. 2). Walsh adds that the contradictions are also "explicable in part by the comic pose of the anti-hero as simpleton" (*ibid.*); cf. P. Veyne, "Le 'je' dans le Satiricon," *REL* 42 (1964) 301-324, who sees a consistent pose of *fausse naïveté* in Encolpius' conduct at the *cena.*

[5] "Style and Character in the *Satyricon,*" *Arion* 5 (1966) 336-358, esp. 349 ff.

[6] This observation is perhaps somewhat unfair to George who, in the earlier part of his article (above, n. 5), demonstrates brilliantly the care which Petronius takes to make the rhetoric of different persons (in particular

Giton) match and define their characters in the context of the narrative.

[7] The possibility of a distinction is intimated by Veyne (*op. cit.* [n. 4]) but is not further explored: "L'auto-ironie du *Satiricon* se justifait-elle par la conversion finale d'un Encolpe parvenu, après tous ses voyages, au port de la sagesse?" (307).

[8] Stockholm 1971. See in particular (*i*) Hägg's chapter on "Points of View" (112-137) and especially the section on Achilles Tatius (124 ff.) whose novel, like Petronius', takes the form of a first person narration, and (*ii*) his bibliography with its coverage of writers, especially American, on the novel in general.

[9] Cf. Ap. Rhod. 3.531-533, Virg. *Ecl.* 8.69-71, 95-99, *Aen.* 4.487-491, Tib. 1.2.43-52, Ovid *Am.* 2.1.23-28.

[10] *Étude sur Petrone* (Paris 1892) 53.

[11] In the introduction to his translation (Ann Arbor 1959), xvi.

[12] *Op. cit.* (n. 1) 98.

[13] My translation here is intentionally as literal as possible. In general, the versions of the published translations are coloured by their common conviction that the poem is Petronius' *apologia* for the *Satyricon* (see esp. Arrowsmith's version).

[14] Strangely enough, just such an unsignalled and abrupt switch from Encolpius to the author is implied by both Sullivan and Arrowsmith. Both critics believe that the poem is Petronius' own apology, but in their translations neither of them marks a lacuna in front of the verse. Collignon (*loc. cit.*[n. 10]) was more aware of the difficulties involved in reading the poem as authorial comment: "Ces quatre distiques ne se lient pas étroitement avec ce qui précède. On peut, avec M. Buecheler, supposer une lacune. Ou bien il y a eu transposition de ce morceau primitivement placé ailleurs à l'endroit qu'il occupe aujourd'hui."

[15] Cf. Virg. *Georg.* 1.338-347, 2.527-531, Hor. *Odes* 3.18.

[16] A fair indication of Encolpius' break with reality as his poetic fancy runs away with him is his claim *non sanguine tristi/perfusus venio, non templis impius hostis/admovi dextram* (lines 6-8). But the crimes of homicide and temple desecration are precisely those that he has recently confessed in his letter to Circe (130.2): *hominem occidi, templum violavi*. In the poem, however, Encolpius is deluding himself into the role of the guiltless suppliant. Therefore, *by definition of the role assumed,* he *cannot* have committed the crimes which in other circumstances he will openly—even somewhat boastfully—admit.

[17] See, for example, the following observations of Sullivan (*op. cit.* [n. 1] 42) and Walsh (*op. cit.* [n. 2] 76): " . . . the wrath of the god . . . provides one of the mainsprings of the plot." "The pervasive motif . . . is of a hero beset by the anger of Priapus." This view was first put forward by E. Klebs, "Zur Komposition von Petronius Satirae," *Philologus* 47 (1889) 623 ff. Strictly speaking, all that we are entitled to claim is, I believe, (*a*) that Encolpius the protagonist, a character whom we know to be hopelessly prone to fantasy and melodrama, *imagines himself on certain occasions* to be the victim of the anger of Priapus, and (*b*) that these imaginings are understandable in view of (*i*) the nature of his ailment at Croton (i.e., impotence) and (*ii*) his occasional entanglements with people such as Quartilla who are genuinely connected with the cult of Priapus.

[18] Such, though, is not the usual reading implied by the translations. Cf., for example, Arrowsmith ("Alas, I boasted of my happiness too soon") and Sullivan ("I congratulated myself too soon").

[19] The prose tells us that the theme of Encolpius' self-questioning was *an vera voluptate fraudatus essem*. If the verse is also taken as re-creating Encolpius' reflections at the time, then the prose summary of his line of inquiry must be understood to mean "whether it was real (as opposed to illusory or dream-like) pleasure that I had been deprived of." Encolpius, in other words, is left wondering after Circe's departure whether the whole experience might not have been a dream—or nightmare. I stress this point because the translators for the most part imply that the pleasure was accepted as real enough and that the only question that engages Encolpius' thoughts is whether or not he had lost it: " . . . wondering if I were now cut off forever from my only hope of joy" (Arrowsmith), " . . . whether I had been robbed of the chance of true pleasure" (Sullivan). This, I believe, misses the point. The emphatic word in the indirect question is *vera*, which should be understood predicatively.

**T. Wade Richardson (essay date 1984)**

SOURCE: "Homosexuality in the *Satyricon*," *Classica et Mediaevalia*, Vol. XXXV, No. 1984, pp. 105-27.

[*In the following excerpt, Richardson states that "the* Satyricon *provides one of the most comprehensive accounts of homosexual activity in Roman times,"* stressing that Petronius used homosexual elements in his writing for their comic possibilities and that he did not view homosexuality as perverse.*]

Classical homosexuality has its bibliography, but the subject has lacked the methodical analysis that one expects of scholarship. This is particularly true of the *Satyricon,* whose homosexual incident has not received, to my knowledge, a separate consideration. The scattered references to the topic in wider studies either neutralize it by treating it as a part of the ancient sexual smorgasbord, or else find in Petronius satirical and even moralizing tendencies consistent with a stance of disapproval and suspiciously modern. Neither position is capable of doing justice to the sexual ambience of the work.[1]

One may quickly ponder the possible reasons for this deficiency. Perhaps most scholars have not found the subject absorbing or germane, or perhaps they have distrusted their ability to deal with it impartially. For when homosexuality has been broached there has been a failure to recognize distinctions and typologies that are a common feature in present sociological research;[2] consequently inferences have been too general. At fault I believe is a two-thousand-year Christian tradition which has united with the Western legal system to obliterate the distinction between homosexual desire, homosexual acts, and the condition of homosexuality. Christianity in extreme form teaches that a sinful thought is the same as a sinful act, and the law in its application has not (until recently, at any rate) encouraged society to differentiate homosexual behaviour.

The literary implications of vagueness on the topic of homosexuality in the *Satyricon* are not inconsiderable. Since it is unlikely that Petronius designed the work to be a "possession for all time" his treatment of homosexual incident will reflect the norms and incorporate the attitudes and assumptions of first-century Roman society, as identifiable by that segment of society which makes up the writer's public. The writer's personal views are harder to recover, and I am not going to attempt to do so with any precision. Yet because there is a convenant between author and audience it is safe to assume that Petronius is seeking the comprehension and reaction of his public, and it will in turn respond in the only ways available to it—in the case of the *Satyricon* chiefly with laughter. It is a measure of the work's cleverness that it has been found fresh and entertaining throughout the centuries down to our own, but the modern response can be misleading, for Petronius' timeless humour tempts one into assuming that he holds up views on sexuality similar to the spectrum of our own. In the case of homosexuality, given the differences in conditioning, this seems unlikely, and the inability of scholars to agree on the ultimate thrust of the work is one of the results.

There are severe shortcomings in extracting information on homosexuality from the *Satyricon* and using it as a sort of sociological document. Views on homosexuality in Greek and Roman literature are rarely explicit but are almost always implied in the most unself-conscious manner. Moreover, the quality of the

evidence is likely to vary according to the reliability of the particular literary genre as an expression of realism.[3] Nothing like raw data is available. Yet it is probably a fair statement that the *Satyricon* provides one of the most comprehensive accounts of homosexual activity in Roman times. For if one subtracts it from Roman literature our information on the subject will certainly be far sparser. Thus a commitment to evaluating the homosexual material exists, and it would be submitting unduly to scholarly pessimism or fastidiousness to avoid discerning possible social attitudes behind treatment of homosexuality and pointing to literary conclusions that may or may not follow.

There is little doubt that in homosexuality in the modern era, contrary to classical times, one is faced with a phenomenon that has gone underground. Proof of this lies in the vocabulary of discrimination. It is surely significant that the Greeks would have found the concept of 'a homosexual' (for which they had no word) hard to comprehend. For them homosexual desire coexisted peacefully with heterosexual, and such is also true of the activity which the desire generated[4] (although it was more appropriate at some stages in life than in others, as shall be seen). There is, according to Dover, no evidence in the Greek sources that such desire itself was morally bad or 'contrary to nature', and the acts themselves met with that designation rarely and in a narrower sense than that used today.[5] The average Greek could develop homosexual interests but maintain a heterosexual orientation and was thus not today's 'homosexual'—who is defined in the careful language of sociology as "a person whose erotic concerns are quite persistently and predominantly directed towards members of [his] own sex".[6] Unusually intense or protracted homosexual enthusiasm may have been a matter of comment, but was not greatly disapproved.[7]

It has been assumed that in the *Satyricon* Encolpius, Ascyltus, Giton, Eumolpus and others practise their homosexuality within a Greek mould.[8] We should test this proposition and its implications for interpretation of the work. If in fact it appears to be true, is the author depicting unRoman phenomena to go with the *Graeca urbs* of the setting, or is there no essential difference between Greek and Roman perceptions in the practical application of homosexuality?

For purposes of comparison one may recapitulate Dover's findings on Greek homosexuality: it operated under numerous rules and constraints, and seems far more likely to have been indulged in by the wealthy, leisured class, for erotic dalliance and emotional involvement with desirable young citizen males involved an investment of time for hanging about gymnasia and money for courting gifts.[9] Typically, it concerned a relationship between a senior partner who might be a youth or an older man, and a junior who might be a boy or youth before the beard was grown. The older partner or erastes occupied the role of pursuer, and the younger or eromenos that of pursued.[10] Rigid convention within the homosexual ethos prescribed modes of behaviour for every aspect of this relationship from the spiritual to the carnal, with reward for conformity being the continued support of an important segment of public opinion.[11] Erastes initiated the relationship, in which admiration and love for the younger male could express itself in forms of sexual release. The eromenos, who stood to gain from his own and society's contemplation of the devotion of his older friend, conceived his role as a granter of favours (if the relationship was to continue), and could never in the convention initiate sexual contact or show sexual enjoyment. On the sexual plane the relationship was ostensibly entirely selfish, and eromenos had to suppress genital tension and channel it into the concept of service.[12] One is entitled to some disbelief in the practical maintenance of this code, but the literary evidence takes one no further.[13] It seems that the best way to perpetuate this relationship was not to hold up to society the contradiction inherent in the approval of homosexual pursuit and ridicule of homosexual submission.[14]

The reasons for development and maintenance of this type of homosexuality among the Greeks are still a matter for speculation.[15] The outward manifestations of it, as described, in the classical and postclassical periods, when it was already perhaps two hundred years old,[16] have led researchers to seek its origins in mutually reinforcing psychological and sociological causations: the apparently inadequate performance of the Greek father in counselling his son,[17] and the idealization of adolescence and desire to perpetuate it.[18] The Greek father preferred to counsel another man's son and developed an erotic interest in him, while the boy modelled himself on this surrogate father/erastes. As for adolescence, Devereux perceives the Greeks as exploiting the undifferentiated sexuality of males in pubescence, and channelling it in all its representations, from fantasy to physical well-being, into homosexual modes.[19] The evidence from art and literature reveals in relationships between eromenos and erastes a strongly phallic-centered interest, suggesting that homosexual behaviour of the Greeks was rooted in sexual immaturity.[20] It was not therefore a psychiatric perversion or pathology but a psychological and affective state satisfying a cultural demand for such behaviour, artificially prolonged into adulthood. The Greek attitude to women is perhaps germane: Dover suggests that a general devaluation of their intellectual and emotional qualities in a society that depended more on male attributes for survival tended to foster male grouping and damage relations between husband and wife or (unexpectedly) father and son.[21]

These interpretations are not without difficulties. The view, something of a commonplace and based on good

evidence, that homosexual activity declined or ceased after marriage, is hard to reconcile with the theory of displaced fathering. If "pursuit of eromenoi was characteristic of the years before marriage"[22] fathers would not routinely be part of it, and one cannot see how relations between husband and wife would be affected. Further, the quality of the evidence raises a chronic difficulty in that it is fullest (while not being prolix) several hundred years after the inception of homosexual practice. Nevertheless, Devereux's main point that Greek homosexual behaviour reflected actually a pseudo-homosexual condition and that consequently the Greeks were not a nation of borderline psychotics should stand, and is directly applicable to our concern in the *Satyricon*.[23]

Schmeling, perhaps reflecting a generally-held impression, makes the provocative remark that Encolpius, Ascyltus and Giton were brought up in the Greek tradition of sexuality, but, contrary to "the pre-Platonic homosexuals of ancient Greece who regularly developed into heterosexuals", are "psychiatrically perverts" (a term borrowed from Devereux).[24] This view, not elaborated but presumably based on perceptions of the behaviour and attitudes expressed by the *Satyricon* protagonists, invites an inspection of the evidence and a testing against the criteria for psychiatrical perversion adduced by Devereux. In view of the above description of the Greek tradition and Devereux's explanation of it, one wonders if there may be a contradiction in being so brought up but perverted. One wonders, further, if this is purely a modern judgment, or whether the author has his characters exhibiting abnormal patterns with conscious intent.

The ability to reflect a Greek tradition in the *Satyricon* implies awareness of the unchanged nature of a homosexual ethos through half a millennium of Greek culture and an intact transference into a more-or-less Roman landscape. A good case for uniformity may be made. On the Greek side Dover finds a promising illustration of the prospects of continuity of homosexual culture in the enduring incidence of graffiti, especially *kalos*-graffiti, reflecting unchanging sentiment of artist, customer or general public.[25] Although there is evidence in Hellenistic poetry to suggest a shift in taste in eromenoi over a couple of centuries from the muscular athlete of the fifth-century palaestra towards a more effeminate style,[26] the ethos appears unaffected and survives to be treated with obvious comprehension by Plutarch in Roman times. As part of the nostalgic, antiquarian movement Plutarch actually provides better evidence for the homosexual ethos of the Greek classical and postclassical periods, but his great interest in the affairs of historical erastai and eromenoi, together with a remark about a contemporary attitude of utter contempt for men who enjoy playing the passive role,[27] which is identical with the classical view,[28] suggest a cultural continuum despite a greatly changed world and presumably a modification of the sociological conditions that brought the homosexual ethos into being.

Further, the celebrated borrowings by the Romans of Greek literature and art from the third century B.C. on that make it possible to treat the classical world as a "Greco-Roman cultural amalgam"[29] appear to have brought knowledge of sexual styles also—a knowledge which seems to have fused solid with Roman hegemony of the classical world. The most remarkable product of this apparent fusion that distinguishes the classical world from our own is the admissibility of homosexual desire. In Greece erotic response in a male to another's physical beauty was, as I have mentioned, normal and natural, for it is the inescapable assumption lying behind many types of literary evidence, from the discussions on love in Plato and Xenophon to the argumentation of Aeschines, from the crude humour of Aristophanes to the equally crude gusto of Theocritus. The acceptance of the bisexual character of desire must of course have given an important degree of sanction to its practical expression in homosexual acts, as at the very least a method of releasing sexual tension akin to sexual relations with women without procreation as the object. Sexual acts of either sort could and did meet with disapproval and constraint on moral grounds, but chiefly insofar as the practitioner exhibited a lack of self-control that made him a bad risk in other areas.[30]

As for what 'a homosexual' is, and for what produced this condition in the male and when, which is the arena for modern debate on the subject in the clinical literature and popular press, it was something of a non-issue. This was, I think, firstly because clinical psychiatry was an uninvented science and Greek public opinion was incapable of recognizing a genetically determined basis for homosexuality; and secondly because Greek law seems to have taken almost no account of circumstances outside the individual's control.[31] Aristotle goes a little of the way when distinguishing between the roles of nature and habituation in making passive homosexuality pleasurable—a rare attempt at exonerating those subject to the first influence if not the second even if it be produced by outrage in boyhood![32]

In Rome the proof of fusion of sexual attitudes may be found in the Latin poets, particularly those with links to satire. Lucil. 8.325 in describing a womanly ideal, *quod gracila est, pernix, quod pectore puro, quod puero similis,* demonstrates a clear parallel in Roman taste for fondness for the human form in its state of non-differentiation. One compares Lucr. 4.1053-4 *sive puer membris muliebribus hunc iaculatur,/ seu mulier toto iactans e corpore amorem* with the often-observed Greek tendency to lump together young males indiscriminately with women as sexual prizes (For the implied response of the two classes, the boy passive, the woman loving and passionate, cf. above, n.21.). A final example from a near-contemporary of Petronius establishes a well-marked pattern of the bisexuality of desire in males of first-century Rome.[33] Mart. 2.28 is a poem which for the poet's purposes covers all fields of sexual endeavour—apparently five: the three things that may be presumed to have the respect of the poet or his *persona* (in descending order?) are what Sextillus is *not.* He is not a *pedico,* nor a *fututor,* nor an *irrumator.* The two things that remain are passed over in mock-silence and rumour may take its pick: Sextillus is either a *fellator* or a *cinaedus.* The poem clearly implies the acceptability of the boy as a sex-object on a level with women, and the social disapproval of male roles considered demeaning as non-masculine. These attitudes differ in no important respect from those of classical Greece, as established by Aristophanes. For despite differences in genre and audience the two embody the sexual prejudices of their day.

As for any debate in Rome between heredity, conditioning or mere licentiousness governing the adoption of homosexual life styles, Aristotle's extenuating attitude based on the dictates of nature has its Roman reflexion from a surprising quarter: Juv. 2.15-17 *verius ergo/ et magis ingenue Peribomius; hunc ego fatis/ inputo, qui vultu morbum incessuque fatetur.* On the distinction between desire and practice I think it would be safe to say that Rome on the whole must have found homosexual attachment harder to approve on cultural grounds. There is a comparative dearth of literature with homosexual themes. The social conditions in the Roman family appear to have been different, and women of citizen-status are argued to have occupied a higher position.[34] The educational benefits of these relationships in Greece which seem to have fanned homosexual sentiment were rather attenuated in a Roman ethos developing under different political influences. Finally, the austere bent of Roman society from its outset affected the availability of the leisure time and luxury disposables that were so much a part of the Greek homosexual scene.

One concludes, then, that the Romans lacked a home-grown homosexual ethos, but probably under Greek influence were capable of acknowledging the validity of bisexual desire—the only necessary precondition for the admission of homosexual acts. Yet the general tenor of public opinion, if we find its at least partial and consistent echo in Cicero, Livy, Juvenal, Pliny and Suetonius, was not favourable.[35] The homosexual attachment was harder to justify in this Roman milieu, but it could be contemplated, as I shall argue that the **Satyricon** proves; and the Romans who dared pursued their homosexual pleasures with a typically practical bent. Expanding opportunities for sensual gratification with either sex were the perquisites of growing luxury and world conquest. Master-slave relationships proliferated and must have set squarely in the Roman consciousness a manifest destiny, expressed so nobly by Vergil, governing rights of conquered over subject, exploiter over exploited.[36] Yet insofar as this was expressed sexually, the difference in Roman society saw to it that only pederasty had anything of a following, and other types of homosexual expression met with the incomprehension that they do nowadays, though not necessarily for the same reasons. The argument that they were contrary to natural or divine or moral law was not so fully developed.[37] Homosexuality as viewed in Rome appears from the external evidence to fulfill a number of Greek requirements. We may now turn to the *Satyricon* for possible confirmation of these modes.

*Encolpius, Ascyltus and Giton.* The plot of the novel concerns the adventures of three young friends. The principal character, Encolpius, a sexually-mature youth (*adulescens,* 3.1), has had an *amicitia* with Ascyltus, a contemporary. The early history of the relationship is compromised by the state of the text, but it is clear from the type of bickering that erupts in c.9 that sexual togetherness was a feature of it, and that this had made the pals, in the current idiom, *fratres.* In the quarrel Encolpius accuses Ascyltus of attempting to rape his later-acquired *frater,* Giton, a somewhat younger youth. The pair had enjoyed a *vetustissima consuetudo* (80.6), now threatened by the robust courtship of the more powerful (*fortiorem,* 91.8) Ascyltus. In the triangle that is formed the two older youths become rivals— Encolpius self-pityingly and Ascyltus arrogantly—for the affections of Giton, and appear to lose the sexual interest in each other that had commenced with the 'seduction' of Ascyltus "in the park" (9.10) before our *Satyricon* commences. A truce is declared so as not to threaten an invitation to dinner—after which, Ascyltus declares, he will move out and seek another *frater* (10.6). Encolpius cheats on the terms by sneaking in to have a cuddle with his love, and receives a thrashing for not sharing. Other adventures take the trio's minds off sexual jealousies for a time: the recovery of their cloak, the ordeal at Quartilla's, and the long intermezzo of dinner with Trimalchio. Immediately after, Ascyltus gets into Giton's bed. This treachery and dissension, it is decided, cannot go on: Giton is to be allowed to choose his preferred 'mate'. He chooses Ascyltus, and the new couple leave Encolpius to a suicidal despair. Some time later Encolpius spots Giton in a bath-house, apparently down in the dumps. He hurries him off and resumes his old standing. Ascyltus comes round to reclaim his prize, but a search fails to turn him up and he departs, never to be heard from again.

Within this framework it is possible to discern two types of homosexual grouping. The attachment of the twentyish coevals Encolpius and Ascyltus, and their separate attachment to a youth a few years their junior and still in the late stages of boyhood. Both types of relationship conform, therefore, to two central variet-

ies of Greek homosexual coupling for which the vase paintings cited by Dover provide such extraordinarily clear visual evidence in their respective depiction of sexual acts between youthful coevals, and different ones between an older and a younger male.[38] Dover notes, however, that in the Greek evidence the reciprocal desire of partners belonging to the same age category is virtually unknown.[39] If this be accepted one must interpret the obviously reciprocal sexual acts between contemporaries as expressions of an attachment that existed outside the erastes/eromenos relationship—an attachment largely if not totally of a sexual kind that found it convenient to seek sexual release in homosexual ways and with a degree of mutuality denied to the more formal affair. With Encolpius and Ascyltus the division between erastes and eromenos is equally obscure, and their *amicitia* meets practical needs more than sentimental and emotional ones.[40] Their sexual needs are fulfilled in other ways also, for it is clear from a taunt of Ascyltus that relationships of a heterosexual nature were not excluded—surely an important consideration in a review of the sexuality of the pair: *'ne tum quidem, cum fortiter faceres, cum pura muliere pugnasti'* (9.9). The slur holds two implications: firstly, that Encolpius performed better with disreputable women (the wife of Lichas? 106.2), and his later failures with a "decent" woman, Circe, support this; secondly, his present impotence is known to Ascyltus—a matter of interest because for all Encolpius' effeteness he was the sexual initiator in their own relationship (9.10).

In addition both friends have sexual encounters with other males. That Lichas' liaison was sexual is clear by his method of destroying Encolpius' disguise: *continuo ad inguina mea admovit officiosam manum et 'salve' inquit 'Encolpi'* (105.9). Later he tries to put the relationship back on its old footing (109.8). However, there is some evidence that Encolpius is moving out of the sexual object or eromenos stage:[41] *tam frugi erat [Eumolpus] ut illi etiam ego puer viderer* (140.5). It took an inveterate sexual opportunist like Eumolpus to think of Encolpius as a boy, and he confirms personally "with both hands" the young man's recovery (140.13). Ascyltus too is in demand in brothel and baths, among allegedly respectable old gentlemen, for the size of his genitals. The roles these two young cocksmen played is not clear, but one assumes they were not choosy in trading their bodies for the tangibles of life.[42]

The second grouping in the plot is that of Encolpius and Giton. Dover's visual evidence[43] establishes that physically these two fulfill the Greek requirements for the typical erastes/eromenos relationship, described above. The senior partner is a youth, beardless or lightly-bearded, and the junior is a boy, immature and about a head shorter. Giton is "about sixteen" (97.2) and *mollis,* that is, possessing undifferentiated secondary sexual characteristics.[44] Lest anyone think that a Mediterranean boy of his age should have reached full sexual growth, Petronius signals his status conclusively to his audience in the Quartilla scene: he has a "novice tool" (*vasculo tam rudi*, 24.7) that will do for an hors d'oeuvre and a *lusum puerilem* (26.4). He is thus entering the years of the growing spurt of such erotic appeal to the ancient male for its combining of physical appeal with mental receptivity.

As for mental attributes, what kept the homosexual relationship functioning was the ability of the older male to exploit adolescent fantasies of service, loyalty and hero-worship, and develop the liaison into a fully-fledged emotional affair. The couple were, in different ways, "in love" and enjoyed a sentimental and sexual relationship that had its own justification and did not suggest or mimic heterosexual practice. The Encolpius/Giton affair is loaded with resemblances to such a multifaceted Greek homosexual relationship, and it is this relationship which is reproduced by Petronius with all the physical and emotional paraphernalia—ironically, as we shall see.[45]

Giton's physical beauty is such that it captivates Encolpius, moves Ascyltus to lust, and attracts all other males (Eumolpus, the sailors on Lichas' ship) and females (Quartilla, Tryphaena). This is fully in keeping with the eromenoi of Greek literature who are similarly appealing.[46] Yet alongside these physical requirements Petronius portrays him as possessing (or, more accurately, portrays Encolpius as perceiving him to possess, for the portrait is not free from irony) a character in its main lines appropriate and desirable in a sex-object. The old-fashioned ideal in classical Greece abhorred flirtatiousness in a beautiful boy and encouraged passivity.[47] Giton apparently reflects this ideal, for Encolpius perceives him to be demure (*verecundissimus,* 25.3), tender-hearted (thus receptive to a lover—*mitissimus,* 93.4) and tactful (in a quarrel with Eumolpus he leaves the room so that Encolpius' anger may cool, 94.4). He has spirit (he lets out a giggle here and there) but is not overtly provocative and, rather, uses his innate shrewdness (*pectus sapientiae plenum,* 91.9) to exploit the typical opportunities presented to an eromenos to torment his erastes with doubt and jealousy. Eumolpus too is smitten with this special erotic combination (*raram . . . mixturam cum sapientia forma,* 94.1) which matches Encolpius' perception (*moderationis verecundiaeque verba, quae formam eius egregie decebant,* 93.4).[48] He is the perfect minion, in contrast to the rivals whom Encolpius fends off, who are all the opposite—*libidinosi* (Ascyltus, 10.7; Quartilla, 24.7; Tryphaena, 113.3; Eumolpus, 94.5).[49]

The sexual aspects of the relationship are treated in the veiled Greek manner to which Dover alerts us. Certainly there is no overt expectation by Encolpius of reciprocated sexual desire in the scenes of physical union. The Greek eromenos got the satisfaction of being desired and admired, and this evidently seems enough for Giton: *postquam se amari sensit, supercilium altius sustulit* (91.7). For consummation of Encolpius' desire Petronius employs language romantic and vague but nonetheless suggestive of approaching (intercrural) orgasm: *alligo artissimis complexibus puerum fruorque votis usque ad invidiam felicibus. nec adhuc omnia erant facta, cum . . .* (11.1-2). This tallies with the Greek evidence, which shrinks from portraying or hinting at anal copulation in cross-age affairs.[50] The intercrural method is possibly confirmed when Socrates compares Kritias' desire for Euthydemos as no better than a pig's wanting to scratch himself against a stone.[51] It seems fair to conclude that in relations between senior and junior partner, where fear of exploitation was present, anal copulation with a male could symbolize respective positions of dominance and submissiveness that might damage the emotional balance of the relationship.[52]

Giton's passivity is a byword. He apparently froze so well when Ascyltus got into bed with him that his acquiescence could be mistaken for sleep (79.9) In his sexual role he certainly could not initiate, but two other options remained: he could be *repugnans* or *non repugnans*. No small element of Petronius' humour derives from the lover's bedevilment over which of the two he is on a given occasion. He is led off unprotesting by the *virguncula* (20.8), and is fondled unresisting by Tryphaena. He displays alarming sympathies for Eumolpus, and leaves with Ascyltus right after spinning a yarn of rejection. Later, he swears ambiguously that *nullam vim factam* (133.2).

Where romantic passion exists, intrigue, jealousy and violence are present, whether the context be heterosexual or homosexual, and the latter has its own tradition in Greek history of lurid goings-on. That homosexual lovers' quarrels were a cliché is perceived from X. *Smp.* 8.4, where Socrates mimics an eromenos, "I beg you Antisthenes, please don't beat me up!" In my view it is this very tradition that Petronius exploits for humorous effect with Ascyltus' violent progress and intimidating behaviour (drawing his sword, 9.4-5; whipping, 11.4; suggesting cutting Giton in half, 79.9f.).

The finishing touch to this melodrama, this *fabula inter amantes,* is supplied by an attempted suicide. Encolpius decides to end it all by hanging himself. Giton bursts in, savours the scene and resolves as a gesture of his love to die first: *'erras' inquit 'Encolpi, si putas contingere posse ut ante moriaris'* (94.10). He grabs a razor, slashes at his throat and falls to the ground. Encolpius picks up the instrument and prepares to die alongside him, when he notes that it is a blunt one for practising: it was a *mimica mors.*

Dover refers to suicide's "conspicuous role" in the numerous homosexual love stories recounted by Plutarch.[53] Moreover, everyone in Petronius' audience would be familiar with the cliché of the readiness of erastes and eromenos to endure pain and death to prove their devotion, the most inspirational example being the conduct of The Sacred Band at Chaeronea.[54] Yet despite the immediacy of these examples and their appropriateness to the context of the present affair scholars have perceived the roots of the **Satyricon** in essentially heterosexual genres of epic (as travesty of it) and Greek Romance (parody of it), with admixtures of the Milesian tale, mime, Menippean and Lucilian satire, and farce.[55] It seems that an important ingredient has been left out of the stew, for the mockery inherent in the blanket substitution of a homosexual plot for the heterosexual ones appears to hold up to criticism homosexuality per se, whereas the use of themes perceived as homosexual achieves a more subtle humour that invites the audience to laugh at the indignities imposed on the young of intemperate love of any sort. I think this may answer the question of why it is so difficult to see unambiguous disapproval of homosexual conduct in the **Satyricon.**

This is not to say, however, that people have not tried.[56] Smith believes that Petronius is making a special parodic or even moral point at the expense of Encolpius and Trimalchio merely when they admire the physical qualities of boys;[57] and Coffey, in his acceptance (though with reservations) of the **Satyricon** as a parody of Greek romance ("there is a homosexual couple, Encolpius a cowardly braggart, a thief and a trickster, and Giton, effeminate sharing most of the traits of a Greek heroine,") implies the recognition of homosexuals as a class and an invitation to contemplate the ridiculousness of homosexuality itself.[58] None of these views would be tenable in a first-century world familiar with the Greco-Roman bisexual ethos and free from the guilt attached to homosexual eros because there was no need to repress it. Petronius' careful depiction, *con amore,* of a familiar homosexual style in the Roman world must have provoked appreciation, laughter, and perhaps even nostalgia in his own audience.

The sustained parody (if that is not too strong a word) in the Encolpius/Giton affair is that of a homosexual and not of a heterosexual relationship gone awry. That is to say, Petronius' knowledgeable audience sees in Giton not the attributes of a Greek heroine but those of a passive little eromenos in the Greek mould played to the hilt and undercut by the Roman boy's special brand of slyness. Encolpius for his part behaves like a mooning erastes only more so, trying to juggle a homosexual emotionalism with a hearty appetite for all sexual diversions, and his activity has come to a standstill on all fronts: *neque puero neque puellae bona sua vendere potest* (134.8). His plight was, I suspect, a familiar one. For psychological reasons sexually mature women would always present more of a challenge in that satisfaction will be sought in return, and pressure to perform would be far greater than with an immature boy who could not permit himself to have sexual demands.[59] Such are the normal problems of classical youth. Petronius' special achievement is in investing the affair with sympathetic humour. A past genius of comedy, Aristophanes, could only raise a laugh by reducing the homosexual ethos to its crudest physical aspects.[60] The author of the **Satyricon** adopts a more subtle method.

*Eumolpus.* Eumolpus the seedy poet is not a lad or a youth, but represents the third class of man: the mature male. Indeed, he is rather old, a *senex canus* (83.7). Yet apparently despite his advanced years he is sexually active and has a particular enthusiasm for boys at what one could call the ideal eromenos stage. Encolpius finds this out as soon as the two meet, for Eumolpus launches into an account of a sexual bout in Pergamum with the young son of a local dignitary—a lad as capable as Giton of playing the erastes/eromenos game.[61] For the moment Encolpius is cheered, but typically fails to see the danger signals, and when Giton returns contritely the old man takes a prompt fancy to the boy. Furthermore, he makes it plain what he has in mind: *laudo Ganymedem* (92.3). Things go from bad to worse when Giton displays a sympathy for him in contrast to Encolpius' contempt for his poetry, and the compliments flow (94.1).

The scene is now set for another round of elaborate sexual humour. Sexuality, even homosexuality, I have argued was condoned by Roman society in the young man, Petronius' point being the comicality not of the acts themselves but of an exaggerated emotionalism under its influence. But the same acts in the unemotional elderly receive no such acceptance and may be viewed as a fit subject for some friendly 'ribbing'. As an older man Eumolpus cannot claim merely to be in love and having his head turned. He must stalk his prey with cunning and cynicism for more immediate and practical ends, and the writer has him play the strongest suit available to his years: he must pass for that old Greek cliché the personal guide and educator responsible for the young boy's morals. Thus while accepting hospitality at Pergamum, whenever the subject of pederasty (*usus formosorum*, 85.3) comes up he rails convincingly and looks grim, with the result that he is soon made teacher and chaperone of the host's comely son. Later, with Giton he makes the same but rather less convincing offer of *paedagogus et custos* (94.2).[62] The trick is as familiar to Encolpius (*'tu libidinosus'*) as to Petronius' audience: the wolf offers to guard the sheep.

The subterfuges to which Eumolpus must resort to achieve his ends reflect society's attitude to his pastime, and our knowing author gives him a hypocritical stance to (pretend to) salve a guilty conscience: *si quis vitiorum omnium inimicus rectum iter viae coepit insistere, primum propter morum differentiam odium habet; quis enim potest probare diversa?* (84.1).[63] True enough, but the delicious irony of Petronius' point is that here society may be justified in that Eumolpus differs by being more 'immoral' than most. Yet by his recognition of the old man's plight the author does not let go of sympathy for him. Eumolpus and the other elderly gentlemen are consigned to pursuing their homosexual habits with extreme caution, approximating the situation in classical Greece where a mature man was expected to put aside such eros. Naturally the ambivalence of sexual desire continued, but the acts were not countenanced. This is a standard which Petronius may have thought too rigid, for I see the essence of his comedy in making the audience laugh at the rigidities of the structures of man. There is a veiled plea for more flexibility.

Eumolpus as an older man, and an intelligent one, needed not only to exercise discretion but also to be able to justify (or to make a show of justifying) his presence around boys. Petronius, in what I believe to be one of his most masterly comic touches, has him do so by appealing to the *homosexual* ideals of ancient Greece and setting a familiarity with the eternally ambiguous nature of love constantly to his own advantage. Plato's *Symposium* and *Phaedrus* and Xenophon's *Symposium* are the *loci classici* for discussion (in homosexual metaphor) in which participants explore the benefits mutual to eromenos and erastes in a 'love' relationship, taking into proper account that sexual activity in such a relationship can be stimulated either by eros, the complex and laudable longing of the soul to partake of beauty, or else by mere bodily craving. Nobly expressed, this "compound of an educational with a genital relationship"[64] allowed the senior partner to train the eromenos by his good example, and the junior granted the erastes his body as reward and encouragement.[65] Paraphrased in blunt language the ethos provided that the "acceptance of the teacher's thrusting penis between [the boy's] thighs or in his anus is the fee which the pupil pays for good teaching, or alternatively, a gift from a younger person to an older person whom he has come to love and admire."[66] It is this ethos that Eumolpus seeks to exploit, and with a hypocrisy, irony and cynicism that must have appeared to the audience as highly amusing. As we have seen, he poses as educator for the Pergamene Boy and Giton, and is able to provide for the children of Philomela an actual *bonitas* (140.2) corresponding to the Greek *agathos*. I would even go further, and suggest that behind Petronius' pun of Eumolpus' "upright nature" there lurks a familiarity with the apparent ancient Greek notion that the communication of semen from penis to anus is an act of symbolic educational transference.[67] Although the *pigiciaca sacra* in the scene is problematic,[68] it appears from the activity which follows that

Eumolpus has chosen the girl's anus—for its greater accessibility over her brother's—while Encolpius is allowed to try his luck with yet another *doctissimus puer* (140.11). In Eumolpus, therefore, we have more corroboration that Petronius holds up a product, no less than the young trio, of the Greek and Roman cultural amalgam. In the old sexual adventurer the author's target shifts, but his antecedents are similar and his comic aim is just as sure.

*Other Characters.* The equally elderly Trimalchio, rather under the weather as the evening progresses, kisses a pretty boy too soundly (74.8), and his wife appeals for fair treatment. An ugly scene ensues. Trimalchio becomes defensive, making the stock excuse that he was rewarding the boy's ways and not his looks, but the viciousness of his counter-attack reveals that Fortunata has struck home: as an old man and in mixed company he could not give such evidence of homosexual desire.[69] He had been indiscreet. Society constrained him as it did the *patresfamiliae* and Lichas. The double standard which cursed elderly males by permitting bisexual desire while curbing behaviour provokes enjoyment in the audience of the discomfort it produces. One might compare the potential for gossip nowadays in any extramarital sexual habits of respectable mature figures.[70]

The *cinaedi* are a case apart, and would appear to be fair game for a laugh of a different sort for their ridiculous, campy appearance and unabashed sexual antics which their physical circumstances seem to have given them leave to pursue with special vigour. It is clear from the language which Encolpius uses what *he* thinks of this class who are capable of arousal and orgasm (as modern medicine confirms) although confined by surgery to active pursuit of passive postures: *immundissimo me basio conspuit* (23.4). Encolpius may have been crippled emotionally, but he was a cut above them. As usual it is unclear what Petronius thinks, and we cannot be sure of any invitation to the reader. The novelist of all ages is permitted this ambiguity. Certainly Encolpius' violent reaction does not necessarily do him credit. Yet one can be sure that his utter disgust delineates the humour in the situation without criticizing the activity itself. Is the reader invited to convict Encolpius of hypocrisy? I think not, for this circus side-show is too separate from Encolpius' own affair, and the audience could not accept the assault of the *cinaedi* as a dose of his own medicine as easily perhaps as we can today.

Finally we may consider the view expressed by Schmeling (n. 24) that Encolpius, Ascyltus and Giton are "psychiatrically perverts". From the setting of the remark it appears intended as a modern judgment on the basis of modern clinical knowledge, and not something of which the writer himself is aware. The basis for it, one recalls, is that the trio appear to have no hope of shedding their homosexuality and developing exclusively heterosexual habits in maturity. The first response to this is that there is no way of telling, since the protagonists are still youths at the end of the story. Actually, there appears, to me at any rate, to be no evidence of their preoccupation's future permanence. It is not, one remembers, viewed by Petronius as a 'perversion'. If their homosexuality conforms to the Greek type, as Schmeling seems to suggest, and as I hope to have demonstrated, there is on the contrary strong *prima facie* support for arguing that the youths' present frenetic sexual adventurism in general and homosexual habits in particular will cease when they get older. Petronius' compositional method may be said to foreshadow this, for Encolpius the narrator of his own youthful misadventures is already capable of viewing them with an ironic detachment as he draws the audience into having a laugh at his own expense. Further, it is possible to follow him in a kind of progression from neurotic impotence, through attempts to prove himself sexually with a mature and 'decent' woman, to the triumph of his 'restoration' at the end: *dii maiores sunt qui me restituerunt in integrum* (140.12). I think a good deal of the comic point is lost for Petronius' own audience if it is being asked to accept the present homosexual habits of the trio as permanent.

Petronius is thus unaware of their 'perversion'. Insofar as this may be a modern reading we may apply the criteria of Devereux.[71] For perversion in a psychiatric sense to be present three conditions are suggested: it must be stable (permanent), compulsive (uncontrollable) and anti-hedonistic. Devereux acquits routine Greek homosexuality of the first count on the basis that it was a culturally-standardized stage of evolution towards heterosexuality (particularly, one adds, in certain phases of youth). Encolpius goes free, as seen, on the same grounds. The role of compulsion is very much diminished because homosexuality was not denied to Encolpius and did not produce guilt. Thus the anxiety or panic accompanying denial could not be present. Furthermore, as seen, Encolpius sought balancing remedies that controlled his urge with Giton. Denial of satisfaction for Encolpius came not from society but from impotence, producing anxiety of a different sort. The data we possess, however, shows that he has functioned heterosexually in the past and hopes to do so again. For homosexuality to follow the third condition, anti-hedonism, it must be accompanied by fear of loss of control, and must be channelled into non-sexual, aggressive drives. Functioning as a 'normal' successful homosexual erastes Encolpius would exhibit no externalized hostility as the product of self-hatred or anti-hedonism. One concludes, then, that he and his friends were no more genuine perverts than the average Greek.

The Roman attitude to this homosexuality, if not precisely that of the Greeks, was far closer to the Greek ethos than to our own. The author is thus not, in my view, applying an artificial Greek standard to go with the *Graeca urbs,* but is employing a wider type of realism in his novel. The audience is capable of recognizing and identifying with the conditions under which the characters function, and is amused and titillated by the responsive chord which they strike. Our own literary understanding and appreciation of the **Satyricon** should be based on Petronius' relatively limited and contemporary vision of his subject—which is not to disparage him but to recognize the full literary and cultural mainsprings of his humour. We may credit the author by not adopting analyses supposing attitudes to homosexuality more in keeping with the orthodoxies of the present day.

*Notes*

An earlier version of this paper was given at the annual conference of the Classical Association of Canada, Saskatoon, June 1979.

[1] On the Greek side K. J. Dover has greatly improved the situation with two studies, *Greek Popular Morality in the Time of Plato and Aristotle* (Oxford 1974) and *Greek Homosexuality* (Cambridge, Mass. 1978), cited hereinafter as *GPM* and *GH*. The bibliography in the latter is, despite a disclaimer, a good guide to literature on homosexuality ancient and modern. See particularly G. Devereux, *Greek Pseudo-Homosexuality and the 'Greek Miracle',* SO 42 (1967) 69-92. For the *Satyricon* see J. P. Sullivan, *The 'Satyricon' of Petronius: a Literary Study* (London 1968), esp. 234-236, M. Smith (ed.), *Petronius: Cena Trimalchionis* (Oxford 1975) *ad loc.,* M. Coffey, *Roman Satire* (London 1976) 178-203, P. G. Walsh, *The Roman Novel* (Cambridge 1970), esp. 82-83, J. Fisher, *Métaphore et interdit dans le discours érotique de Pétrone, CEA* 5 (1976) 5-15, G. Schmeling, *The 'Exclusus Amator' Motif in Petronius,* in *Fons Perennis: Saggi critici in onore del Vittorio d'Agostino* (Turin 1971) 333-357.

[2] For example see A. Bell and M. Weinberg, *Homosexualities: A Study of Diversity Among Men and Women* (New York 1978).

[3] On the quality of evidence from different types of literature see Dover *GPM* 8-22 and *GH* 11-14.

[4] See Dover *GH* 1, 12, 23, 61-62, 65, 201.

[5] See Dover *GH* 165-170.

[6] D. J. West, *Homosexuality Re-Examined* (Minneapolis 1977) 1.

[7] See Dover *GH* 23, 73.

[8] See Schmeling (above, n. 1) 346.

⁹ See Dover *GH* 54-55, 92, 150.

¹⁰ See Dover *GH* 85, 164.

¹¹ See Dover *GH* 107.

¹² See Dover *GH* 44, 91, 163.

¹³ See Dover *GH* 103.

¹⁴ On the 'complicated' attitude of Greek society see Dover *GH* 185, 190-191. Comedy expresses a greater hostility than philosophy to boys who play the role of eromenoi (Dover *GH* 146). Approval of the relationship required the muting of the tendency to see sexual acts between males in terms of dominant and subordinate roles (see Dover *GH* 101-106, 140).

¹⁵ Here Dover is cautious and brief. See his remarks in *GPM* 213-216 and *GH* 201-203. Devereux, *art. cit.* (n. 1) is the major source for theories on psychological and sociological origins of Greek homosexuality.

¹⁶ On the difficulty of the earliest literary evidence for the Greek homosexual ethic see Dover *GH* 194-201.

¹⁷ Devereux 78.

¹⁸ Devereux 80. Cf. Dover *GH* 135 on "youthening" in art.

¹⁹ Cf. Devereux 75-76.

²⁰ For "phallos-centeredness" see Devereux 74. For representations of the penis in art and their significance see Dover *GH* 124-135. For emotions inspired by the sight of a boy's penis see Dover *GH* 124, 137, 156. n.6.

²¹ Dover *GH* 202. The low opinion among Greek males of the intellect and self-control of women (Dover *GH* 12, 67, 201) is perhaps connected with the well-known Greek view of their hypersexuality (Dover *GH* 36 n. 18, 96, 102, 170). In other words, giving in to sexual desire and enjoyment was the result of emotional weakness inherent in women. The belief in greater feminine pleasure out of sex goes back at least to Hes. *Fr.* 275: Teiresias, who has been both male and female, says women get nine-tenths of it (see Dover *GPM* 101). I should like to associate the possibly true reason for this apparent observation with a suggestion by Devereux in another context that "the Greek woman was psychosexually mature at an earlier age than the Greek man" (Devereux 74). The homosexual ethos postponed the boy's sense of sexual identity and discouraged overt enjoyment, while the girl's was completed earlier. Greater maturity produced heightened sexual intensity with no fear of loss of control. See also Devereux 72.

²² Dover *GH* 171; cf. *GPM* 213.

²³ Devereux 80.

²⁴ Schmeling, *art. cit.* (n.1) 346 n.18.

²⁵ Dover *GH* 112-115.

²⁶ Dover *GH* 79.

²⁷ Plu. *Mor.* 768a. See Dover *GH* 4, 103 n.87.

²⁸ In Greek comedy all homosexual submission is contemptible (Dover *GH* 142-148). In Theoc. 5.116-119 the slur is that Lakon *enjoyed* playing the woman's role. Dover *GH* 104. For contempt for *cinaedi* see Mart. 2.53, 71, 73, etc.

²⁹ Dover *GH* 4.

³⁰ Dover *GH* 30. Homosexuality appears not to have been singled out for special criticism until Pl. *Lg.* 838e-839g, where the Athenian advocates abstaining from males in order to follow nature and avoid erotic fury and insanity (Dover *GH* 166). For eros as a 'sickness' and a 'madness' see Dover *GPM* 210-211.

³¹ See Dover *GH* 108-109.

³² Arist. *EN* 1148g15-9a20. Quoted by Dover *GH* 168.

³³ For other examples see Sullivan (*op. cit.*, n. 1) 235 n.1.

³⁴ See on this S. Pomeroy, *Goddesses, Whores, Wives and Slaves* (New York 1975) 149f.

³⁵ E.g. Cic. *Catil.* 2.23, Plin. *Epist.* 9.17, Juv. 2, Suet. *Cal.* 36.

³⁶ M. Cary and H. H. Scullard, *A History of Rome* (London 1975³) 173 and 606 n. 10 quotes Cic. *Verr.* 2.3.12 for the rationale of provincial taxes as a war indemnity levied upon conquered people, or alternatively, because provinces and revenues are the property, as it were, of the Roman people (*Verr.* 2.2.7).

³⁷ But see Juv. 2.132f. on homosexual marriage.

³⁸ For homosexual acts between coevals see R200, R223 (anal), R243 (anal), R954; between a senior and a junior partner: B114, B250, B486, R502, R573 (none anal).

³⁹ Dover *GH* 16.

⁴⁰ Encolpius is, however, sentimental enough to have viewed Ascyltus as *carissimum sibi commilitonem fortunaeque etiam similitudine* (80.8). Ascyltus is the unemotional type, yet acknowledges a mutual commit-

ment: *'sic dividere cum fratre nolito'* (11.4).

[41] In the Greek ethos this passage is well marked. See Dover *GH* 58, 68 for "female characteristics" of boys; 86: "once the beard was grown, a young male was supposed to be passing out of the eromenos stage"; 171.

[42] In the brothel, 8.3; at the baths, 92.10, with an *eques Romanus ut aiebant infamis*. In better days Encolpius was a veritable sexual Achilles (129.1).

[43] Dover *GH* R27, R59, R196, R547, R637, R651, R851.

[44] The Greek literary evidence behaves sometimes as if the terms for the junior partner, *pais* and *neaniskos*, are interchangeable, sometimes as if they represent two distinct phases (see Dover *GH* 85-6); there is a similar ambivalence in the *Satyricon* with *puer* and *ephebus*. In the Greek ethos accosting a boy too young to judge one's character was illegal (Dover *GH* 48-49). At what age this should be, and in whose opinion, are questions asked by Dover but not answered.

[45] Perhaps at variance with this view is Walsh, *op. cit.* (n.1) 83: "The whole relationship between Encolpius and Giton is a comedy of manners without satirical intent". My belief is that there is so much irony that parodic point is inescapable.

[46] See Dover *GH* 172 for citations: the *paidika* of Jason of Pherai; the soft beauty of Dionysus in Eur. *Bacchae*.

[47] See Dover *GH* 28, 84-85.

[48] For this sentiment cf. Verg. *Aen.* 5.344 *gratior pulchro veniens in corpore virtus* (of the comely Euryalus).

[49] Encolpius in his black despair after the departure of Ascyltus with Giton recants and even accuses Giton of *libido,* of behaving like a kept woman *(mulier secutuleia)* and of performing *opus muliebre* in jail (80.3-6). If this be true we must recall that Giton was a slave and not a citizen and did not practise vice, like Encolpius, *despite* being free *(stupro liber, stupro ingenuus)*. At this low point in his life Encolpius' perception of himself and Giton in the idealized erastes/eromenos love-affair is severely shaken.

[50] See above, n. 38.

[51] See Dover *GH* 123 n. 38, 159. For Roman observation of this habit cf. Lucil. 9.356 *scaberat ut porcus contritis arbore costis.*

[52] Anal copulation with women is depicted not infrequently. See Dover *GH* B51, B634, R543, R545, R577. One should avoid, with Dover, seeing 'political' significance in this. E. Segal, in a review of Dover and using his evidence, *New York Times Book Review* April 8, 1979, 36: "this rare sexual proclivity only emphasized the male attitude toward the female: she must be dominated and debased", makes an inference which Dover is not prepared to do. Contempt for the anally-penetrated male does not prove contempt for the anally-penetrated female, as Segal argues. Another possible reason for this practice is less invidious: "hetairai may commonly have insisted on anal intercourse as a simple contraceptive measure" (Dover *GH* 101). There are dangers in interpreting mute visual evidence sociologically, for we have no way of telling at whose instigation the acts proceeded, and why.

[53] Dover *GH* 51-52.

[54] See Dover *GH* 192.

[55] E.g. M. Smith, *op. cit* (n. 1) xv-xviii.

[56] E.g. J. Fisher, *art. cit.* (n. 1) 14: " . . . l'homosexuel est, dans tout le roman, exception faite des relations Encolpe-Giton-Ascylte, constamment décrié."

[57] Smith 55, 97.

[58] M. Coffey, *op. cit.* (n. 1) 184.

[59] See above, n. 21.

[60] See Dover *GH* 148.

[61] I differ with R. Beck, *Eumolpus poeta, Eumolpus fabulator: A Study of Characterization in the "Satyricon", Phoenix* 33,3 (1979) 249, in that I do not believe that Petronius presents the view of the boy's "insatiable sexuality" (to contrast with the model of innocence seduced). The boy's desires are meretricious and not sexual, and he is more conniving and mock-affectionate (86.7 *cervicem meam iunxit amplexu*) than passionate. This venal *ephebus plenae maturitatis* has boasted to his friends of the wealth of his lover (87.4), and he will lose face if Eumolpus does not "pay up" in a manner befitting the boy's beauty. He allows *(male repugnans)* the affair to be renewed for this reason, and not *voluptatis causa* (although Eumolpus flatters himself with thinking *'ille non indelectata nequitia mea'*). The tables are turned: the exploiter is exploited. For the Greek view, that "the attentions of the erastes, assuring a boy that he is not ugly, are welcome to him for that reason alone", see Dover *GH* 89, quoting the famous scene in Pl. *Smp.* 219g when Socrates did not try to seduce Alcibiades.

[62] Giton plays right along with him: *'pater carissime*

(ironically), *in tua sumus custodia'* (99.8). He is well aware of how to inflame the old lecher.

[63] For a similar sentiment cf. Ov. *Am.* 3.4.17 *nitimur in vetitum semper cupimusque negata.*

[64] Dover *GH* 202.

[65] See Dover *GH* 91, quoting Pl. *Smp.* 184c (points made by Pausanias): the erastes subordinates himself in any way to an eromenos who has granted him favours, and the eromenos performs any service for one who makes him [*sophos*] and [*agathos*]. Such is the proper setting for "favours". Cf. Dover *GH* 190.

[66] Dover *GH* 91.

[67] On this see E. Bethe, *Die dorische Knabenliebe, RhM* N.F. 62 (1907) 465-474; T. Vanggaard, *Phallos* (New York 1972) 32-33; Devereux, *art. cit.* (n. 1) 80; Dover *GH* 202-203. For knowledge as the 'fruit' of this union see Dover *GH* 164. For other instances of the sexual signification of *bona* cf. (of Encolpius) *neque puero neque puellae bona sua vendere potest* (134.8); (of Tryphaena) *in odium bona sua venissent* (104.11). For *bonae artes* as sexual seduction see Ov. *Ars.* 1.459. See on this N. P. Gross, *CJ* 74,4 (1979) 305.

[68] For a restatement of the possibilities see B. Baldwin, *"Pigiciaca Sacra". A Fundamental Problem in Petronius?, Maia* 29 (1977) 119-121. For possible parody of a religious rite see Schmeling *art. cit.* (n. 1) 24-25. Add a Spartan custom, according to Hagnon of Tarsus *ap.* Ath. 602d, "before marriage it is customary for the Spartans to associate with virgin girls as with paidika," (tr. Dover *GH* 188). For anal copulation with women see above, n.52.

[69] The freedmen are on the whole rather asexual. They gossip about one of their number who was *pullarius* and *adhuc salax* at over seventy (43.7f.). They appear to have little interest in the young men at dinner, and even when provoked do not seem conscious of the relationship of Giton and Encolpius. The worst thing Giton is called is a *cepa cirrata* (58.2). Smith *op.cit.* (n. 1) 68 believes that certain details depict Trimalchio as effeminate. This may be so, but I doubt if it should be linked with any inference of passive homosexuality—despite the symbolism of his slave-boy Croesus riding on his back!

[70] See L. Humphreys, *Tearoom Trade. Impersonal Sex in Public Places* (Chicago 1970) for modern homosexual analogues.

[71] Devereux, *art. cit.* (n.1) 72-73.

## Niall W. Slater (essay date 1990)

SOURCE: "Character Voices," in *Reading Petronius,* The Johns Hopkins University Press, 1990, pp. 137-54.

[*In the following essay, Slater contends that it is the content and occasion of language more than its form that results in the sense of individual characterizations in the* Satyricon.]

Our initial linear experience (in the previous chapters) of Petronius's novel is over. This experience itself has been a fiction: I who write and, most likely, you who read are not first-time readers of the **Satyricon.** We began by attempting to forget our previous experiences of reading Petronius and strove to construct a new "first reading." While our construct will not correspond in every particular to everyone's or anyone's first reading of the **Satyricon,** this is a useful exercise nonetheless, for it helps us to remember and revitalize aspects of the reading experience we regularly choose to forget.

We have thus used the axis of time to unify our experience of reading. If nothing else, the first-person voice of the narrator has also raised in our minds as readers an expectation of unity. Yet we have encountered and recorded in detail in our first reading the tendency of the actual experience of reading the **Satyricon** to fragment—stylistically, generically, and socially as well as physically. That very fragmentation of experience now invites, even more demands, that we become re-readers of the **Satyricon**—but what kind of re-readings are licit? What approaches can supplement but not violate our initial framework? What detective games can we play without abolishing the temporality of the text?

One strategy of re-reading, which does attempt to respect this temporality, confronts and seeks to abolish the physical fragmentation of the text by playing ever more intensely the game of reconstructing the missing bits. In our first reading we have done some minimal reconstruction work, though an attempt has been made to avoid digressions from the existing text. There is a challenge to reading an only partially surviving work. Experienced readers of classical texts are familiar with this challenge; we are used to lost books of Livy and missing acts of Menander. That very familiarity is, however, a danger. It conditions us to read in certain ways, and especially encourages us to play the game of filling in the gaps in these texts in time-honored fashion, promising honor (what Stanley Fish has so candidly called "the profession's highest rewards")[1] to those who offer the most compelling reconstruction of the missing bits. Clues within the text become tools for filling in gaps in narrative. ("What is Encolpius doing in Marseilles? What is the chronology of the Quartilla episode?") The problem with this approach pursued alone is that we further disorder an already damaged text without necessarily haveing understood its original order. We may thus gather together all the scattered references to Lichas, Tryphaena, and Lichas's wife in order to reconstruct the missing prehistory of Encolpius's relations to these three, but we have by no means thereby "explained" the episode on Lichas's ship as we now have it.

This problem seems particularly acute for the *Satyricon,* where the evidence suggests that we have at least thirteen books to reconstruct before our fragments even begin. Doubts about what might have been in the lost books might have paralyzed interpretation, had not trained readers of ancient texts a method of reading at their disposal to assist in the reconstruction of the lost parts of the work, even in the absence of explicit references to those missing portions in the surviving text. That method is generic criticism.

This is indeed a legitimate way of re-reading certain classical texts. We know enough about Menandrian comedy and the conditions of its creation, performance, and reception to allow the construction of a generic archetype. Surviving plays show enough structural features in common that we can say with some certainty what the end of the fourth act of a Menander play is likely to be or who of a given cast of characters is likely to be introduced in the first act. The hope of constructing such an archetype for the *Satyricon* explains many generic approaches to the work.

But is this a legitimate way of re-reading the *Satyricon*? It is one of only two surviving Roman novels, and the other, the *Golden Ass,* does not offer us a model for reconstructing Petronius. The problem of parody enormously complicates the generic approach. Which generic model shall we look to? Were there, for example, other explicit *Odyssey* references, parallel to Encolpius playing Polyaenus with Circe, which would "prove" that the *Satyricon* was a parody of epic? Were there other banquet scenes and parodies of Roman social customs which would conclusively make the work satire?

I shall not answer these questions; instead, I intend to examine the premises behind them. The assumption seems to be that the genre of a work is determined by the proportion from a certain language system in the full conglomeration. If more than 50 percent of the language is that of epic, then the genre is epic, or at least parody of epic. This assumes that the fundamentally mixed nature of the existing text of the *Satyricon* can be tamed or disciplined by the recovery of a more unitary body of missing language. I deny this assumption.

Part of the reason for insisting on the linear experience of our first reading has been precisely to recover the sense of literary mixture in the *Satyricon.* A typical generic approach begins by radically disordering the text along the axis of time. It may, for example, take the references to Priapus from the end of the *Satyricon* and read backwards, looking only for bits of epic parody in the text which can be said to lead up to the "theme" of the wrath of Priapus. This approach demands that the reader become an archaeologist of, or, perhaps better, a detective within, the text.

The model of the reader as detective is already a familiar one, but nonetheless useful. Many fictions seem to invite the reader to operate as a detective, or more precisely to operate as the fictional archetypes in detective stories do. John Winkler has discussed this analogy in illuminating detail for the later Roman novel of Apuleius,[2] and we may yet discover that Petronius is playing a kindred game. The unspoken assumption is that a text of literary quality is "difficult"; it possesses a meaning that must be wrested from it by the power of the reader/detective over the text. Some approaches assume that the text is composed according to the "fair-play" rules of detective fiction.[3] All of the facts are there. It is up to the reader/detective to discard irrelevancies and red herrings, rearrange the chronology of presentation into a chronology of action (as with alibis based on time), and produce (for the reader's pleasure) the truth, the hidden reality behind the rhetoric of seeming. Other, more deconstructionist, approaches assume we can insert a lever and pry loose the meaning the text wishes at all costs to conceal.

The reader/detective thus creates a hierarchy within the text as he reads. A generic approach based on the epic model, at its extreme, "reveals" to us a hidden text, made up only of epic and Priapic references, which we presume Petronius has intentionally buried under all his other material. The remaining poems, folktales, situations from mime, or other parodies become filler or, even worse, a collection of red herrings designed as a test, devices to divert us from the supposed buried treasure the author has created for the reader/detective to ferret out, the "real meaning."

No doubt some texts, especially those based on parody of, or allusion to, a single other work of literature, are composed on such principles. Even there, an analysis that simply extracts the allusions does justice to neither the author's rhetoric of presentation nor the reader's reception of the text. In such texts, however, once the hidden armature of the text parodied or alluded to is revealed, its existence is usually indisputable. The fact that so many texts or genres are parodied or alluded to in the *Satyricon* suggests there is no such hidden armature, or at the very least no hierarchy in which one parody is central and all others peripheral.

We must rather confront the mixture of languages, subjects, and style in the *Satyricon* as we have it. Nor is it enough to label the mixture *prosimetrum* or

Menippean satire and declare that we have solved the generic question; the labels simply beg the question. What is the effect of this continual shifting among kinds of language as a reading experience?

A recognition of this mixture of language systems, which he terms *heteroglossia,* is the foundation of M. Bakhtin's approach to the novel. In his view the novel itself is opposed to genre; it has no genre itself but coopts into itself the other literary genres (notably epic, but also satire, lyric, etc.). Bakhtin then subdivides the novel into two "lines." In the first, the novel takes the subjects and concerns of the other genres, but reworks them in a new, spuriously "unified," literary language. As he says: "Novels of the First Line, as we have seen, incorporate a multitude of different semiliterary genres drawn from everyday life, and proceed to eliminate their brute heteroglossia, replacing it everywhere with a single-imaged, 'ennobled' language."[4] One might say that the novel absorbs a class of signifieds from the various genres while using and creating a new and apparently unified set of signifiers to discuss these matters. For example, the epistolary novel brings into literary prose a range of subjects and narrative patterns new to high literature, but they are absorbed into, and represented by, the exiting literary language. In the Second Line, the newly incorporated genres bring with them their distinctive signifiers as well. In Bakhtin's terms, a genuine sense of dialect becomes apparent; texts speak in two or more distinctive voices, and the linguistic texture of the novel becomes dialogized.

Our two surviving Roman novels fall linguistically into these two lines: it is apparent that there is a characteristically Apuleian style, whereas there is no single Petronian style. The rich and variegated language of the *Golden Ass* is nonetheless shared by characters of widely different social and generic backgrounds: the maid Fotis speaks a language as richly literate as that of Lucius himself. In the *Satyricon,* however, language is a good indicator of social status, and a character such as Circe's maid, Chrysis, who speaks in a literate vein despite her status, is quite unusual.[5] In Petronius the various language systems are not submerged and absorbed into a unified literary style. Encolpius on the decline of rhetoric sounds nothing like Echion (45) on the decline of gladiatorial fights. Put another way, the freedmen's solecisms are grammatical, our heroes' those of taste.

On a crude level this is one explanation for the "modernity" so many readers have experienced in the *Satyricon.* Bakhtin's distinction between First and Second Line novels is not strictly a chronological one, but First line novels, as represented by romance and chivalric fiction, are generally prior to linguistically and socially heteroglot fictions. The matter of the genres mixes before their media do. The *Satyricon* is thus a novel very much before its time.

Auerbach's brilliant essay on the *Satyricon* in *Mimesis* sees this change from the unified language of epic to the heteroglot language of Petronius as a key advance in realism: "Petronius' literary ambition, like that of the realists of modern times, is to imitate a random, everyday, contemporary milieu with its sociological background, and to have his characters speak their jargon without recourse to any form of stylization. Thus he reached the ultimate limit of the advance of realism in antiquity."[6] The *Satyricon* has thus taken the same step beyond the unified literary language of the Greek romance that the later novel (the preeminent example being *Don Quixote*) takes beyond chivalric and sentimental romance.[7]

The *Satyricon* in turn makes this unified language of romance one of the objects of its own representation, a development key to Bakhtin's Second Line novel:

> As a counterweight to "literariness," novels of the Second Line foreground a critique of literary discourse as such, and primarily novelistic discourse. This *auto-criticism of discourse* [italics Bakhtin's] is one of the primary distinguishing features of the novel as a genre. Discourse is criticized in its relationship to reality; its attempt to faithfully reflect [*sic*] reality, to manage reality and to transpose it . . . And in its further development, the novel of the Second Line remains in large measure a novel that tests literary discourse.[8]

This objectification of the prior novel form serves not only the purposes of realism (as we shall see), though that is an important aspect of it: there *are* literary people in the world who can only be represented in this way. The process also has metafictional implications for other literary forms represented within the *Satyricon* and for the characters who introduce this "literariness" into their own discourse.

I propose to begin re-reading the *Satyricon* by examining in turn the various language systems that have gone into its construction. Here I may seem to violate the axis of time so important to our first reading by gathering examples of language from the whole work by social stratum or generic affinity. This violation is more apparent than real. Unlike the approaches I have criticized, in theory all the language of the *Satyricon* can be reexamined in this way; no preliminary hierarchization takes place such as occurs when we re-read with a single generic model in mind. Moreover, a language system in Bakhtin's terms is a synchronic entity. In examining the range of expression from a given language system actually used in the *Satyricon,* we are therefore simultaneously exploring the repertoire of the reader implicated in this text. The repertoire does *not* come into being along the time axis of the reading process, but in theory exists in the mind of the reader from the beginning. An example is in order here. At 29.1, Encolpius is frightened by the painted dog into a pratfall. At 72.7, a real watchdog frightens Ascyltus and Encolpius as they are trying to escape from Trimalchio's house, and both end up in the fish-pond. These two incidents are part of a ring structure. Note, however, that the second event simply does not *exist* when the reader encounters the first. Whatever the first encounter with a dog means, its meaning is not "explained" by the second encounter. That is only a meaning *added to* the meaning of the original encounter in its original context. On the other hand when a word such as *versipellis* occurs in Niceros's story of the werewolf in sections 61-62, we can presume this concept to be part of the linguistic universe of the reader of the *Satyricon* from the beginning. The language system of ghost and horror stories from which this comes is therefore potentially present throughout the novel.

How do we establish the occurrence of various language systems in the *Satyricon?* Individual instances are established by *difference*. The formal markers of change are often obvious: for instance, from Eumolpus reciting hexameter poetry to Encolpius describing events on the road to Croton, or from Agamemnon summarizing a *controversia* for Trimalchio's amusement to Niceros's quite different entertainment in the form of the werewolf story. Yet this leaves us with a welter of instances and no general principle as yet for dealing with them.

Only by gathering together instances of a given language system from the whole of the *Satyricon* are we enabled in turn to judge the impact of a language system in its context and to relate the instances of a given language system to its use in Roman culture at large in Petronius's time. Each instance of a language system has at least three valences, three horizons to read against. The first is its immediate context, the alien language system it is placed next to in the narrative of the *Satyricon.* Our first reading has given particular attention to this valence. The second is to other, non-contiguous, examples of that language system in Petronius. The third is to the language system as a whole and its place in the discourse of Roman culture outside the given text. As we fragment the text of the *Satyricon* into its constituent language systems in the course of our re-reading, we shall focus particularly on these last two valences.

Yet considerable problems remain in defining individual language systems. Shall we group system by speaker, by linguistic form, or by function in the narrative? Our first reading has addressed the marked shifts of language within the narrative. For our re-reading to enrich, rather than simply suppress, the experiences of our first reading, we must look at as many potential language systems as possible. Two somewhat different approaches to the heteroglossia of Petronian narrative are implicit in the brief excerpts quoted above from Auerbach and Bakhtin himself. Auerbach sees the heteroglossia of Petronian narrative in social terms: the speech of slaves and freedmen versus that of free citizens, the uneducated versus the educated. Bakhtin sees this already filtered through literary forms. Auerbach describes Petronius's language as "jargon without recourse to any form of stylization"; Bakhtin suggests that a stylization has already occurred in such minor literary forms as mime or epistolography. We must beware simply collapsing these categories. The "semi-literary" of Bakhtin's hierarchy need not be identical with the "unstylized jargon" of the freedmen and slaves. Bakhtin's classification in a sense is nearer to what literary history and our close reading of the *Satyricon* have already suggested: the speech of the freedmen, for example, is not simply a transcription from nature, but shows considerable influence from such popular forms as mime. Yet Bakhtin himself refers to the passage cited above to "brute heteroglossia" which is "drawn from everyday life." The effect certainly is to conceal, not reveal, any literary (in our sense of the word) origin for certain language systems in Petronius.

Insofar as social and literary classifications of the *Satyricon*'s heteroglossia are in competition, we need not adjudicate their claims beforehand. Both ways of reading will help us hear the polyphonic nature of this remarkable text more clearly. I propose to begin by examining the social and character differences encoded in its language and shall turn in the next chapter to the literary voices of the text.

In beginning our re-reading of the *Satyricon* with a search for social difference in language, we must beware a certain danger. Petronius's characters, especially the freedmen at Trimalchio's table, are so different from the rest of Latin literature and so individually memorable that it is tempting to proclaim each an island unto himself and assume beforehand that their character differences are expressed in the form as well as the content of their language. My goal at the moment, however, is not to offer a full study of characterization in Petronius; character is the sum of many language systems, not just the social. We must begin more simply, with the way the characters speak.

Social difference in language in the *Satyricon* paradoxically is at once both obvious and elusive. At first glance it is clear that the Latin of the freedmen at Trimalchio's table is neither that of Vergil and Cicero nor that of the work's more educated characters. Early philological interest quickly focused on the evidence the text provided for the distinction between *sermo urbanus* and *sermo plebeius* (roughly, literary and colloquial language). Vocabulary and idiom, the variations from standard genders or inflectional endings, sentence structure and rhythm of speech were all investigated carefully—and, supplemented by comedy, inscriptions, and other scattered sources, yielded a good bit of information.[9]

Yet it is difficult to refine this distinction of *sermo plebeius* and *sermo urbanus* any further—and indeed we may in fact wonder how representative the freedmen in the *Cena* are of a Roman *sermo plebeius*. A glance at their names suggests the problem: Trimalchio, Habinnas, Niceros, Hermeros. These are not native Latin speakers. On the other hand, neither are Lichas and Tryphaena, yet their Latin seems of a piece with the *sermo urbanus* of Encolpius and Eumolpus. Indeed, the social class of characters other than the freedmen in the **Satyricon** is hard to judge. One scholar dubbed Encolpius and Ascyltus the *Lumpenintelligentsia,* which seems at once wonderfully apt and yet still insufficient to fix them on the social scale.

The first-person form of narration also imposes restrictions on our investigation of socially based language systems. We tend to forget how little we have that is not Encolpius—though certainly his own language, both in direct discourse and in narration, is compounded of many systems. We may begin by looking briefly at the language of the freedmen as a single system; thereafter the analysis will turn to the language of individual characters, where distinctions are more those of style than of vocabulary and syntax.

Many features of the freedmen's speech are peculiarities of single words, where it is often difficult to distinguish the errors of the non-native speaker from the uneducated native. Trimalchio (39.5-6) and Echion, for example, both use the form *caelus* instead of *caelum.* Seleucus (42.5) and Trimalchio (71.1, 77.2) also speak of "fate" as *fatus* rather than *fatum*. While these might in isolation seem errors of one who has learned Latin as a second language, there is ample evidence (including some changes to feminine forms) for the tendency of the neuter to disappear in colloquial Latin.[10] All the instances of changes of gender in the **Satyricon** occur in the *Cena*.[11]

Other peculiarities seem specific to lower-class language. The freedmen are fond of coining adjectives with grand-sounding endings, such as *-ax* and *-osus:* for example, *abstinax* (42.5), *nugax* (52.4), *salax* (43.8), *dignitosus* (57.10), and *sucosus* (38.6).[12] A contrary tendency, real or specious modesty, appears in the extensive use of diminutives, a common feature of informal speech at many social levels. The tone often verges on sarcasm. When Hermeros attacks Ascyltus for laughing at himself and his fellow freedmen, there is considerable pride in this statement that

> glebulas emi, lamellulas paravi . . .
>
> (57.6)

I bought a little land, I got together a little silver . . .

and when he challenges Giton to a little bet (*sponsiunculam,* 58.8), the diminutive suggests his contempt for his opponent. Certainly diminutives are not unique to the speech of the freedmen, but they are more common here than elsewhere.

Pecularities of syntax worth noting include the tendency to use the accusative even when another oblique case would be expected (as at 44.16, *meos fruniscar*) and the use of *quod* and *quia* clauses where one would still expect the infinitive plus accusative construction in indirect speech.[13] These, too, are tendencies that triumph in later Latin.

Turning from vocabulary and grammar, we also find features of style shared broadly among the freedmen. Their speech is notably telegraphic, even for after-dinner conversation. These men speak in short sentences and to the point. Here is Ganymedes complaining about the decay of religion:

> nemo enim caelum caelum putat, nemo jejunium servat, nemo Jovem pili facit, sed omnes opertis oculis bona sua computant. antea stolatae ibant nudis pedibus in clivum, passis capillis, mentibus puris, et Jovem aquam exorabant. itaque statim urceatim plovebat; aut tunc aut numquam: et omnes redibant udi tamquam mures.
>
> (44.17-18)

No one thinks heaven is heaven, no one keeps a fast, no one cares a straw for Jupiter, but they all shut their eyes [to everything else] and count their money. Once upon a time matrons used to climb the hill with bare feet, hair down, minds pure, and pray to Jupiter for rain. And it immediately poured down in buckets—either then or never—and they all came back drowned like mice.

Partly the effect arises from the parataxis: strings of phrases tied together with *nam* and *et* or no connectives at all.[14] Partly also it is a result of the liberal use of proverbial expressions and cliché phrases (such as *udi tamquam mures* and *urceatim plovebat*).

Such proverbs and clichés are virtually a language system of their own. A phrase such as *serva me, servabo te* (44.3: "You scratch my back, I'll scratch yours") is at once part of everyone's language and no one's in particular. Formal speech and writing avoid such phrases precisely because they are not original or distinctive; they are the values of the culture thinking out loud. When Echion says *colubra restem non parit* (45.9; literally, "A snake doesn't give birth to a rope"), he is expressing not so much a thought in proverbial form as a demand for his audience's affirmation of his previous statements. At times these demands and stock phrases threaten to crowd out any real ideas at all.[15] Here is Phileros on the late Chrysanthus:

> puto mehercules illum reliquisse solida centum, et omnia in nummis habuit. de re tamen ego verum dicam, qui linguam caninam comedi: durae buccae fuit, linguosus, discordia, non homo. frater ejus fortis fuit, amicus amico, manu plena, uncta mensa. et inter initia malam parram pilavit, sed recorrexit costas illius prima vindemia: vendidit enim vinum, quantum ipse voluit.

> (43.2-4)

> By Hercules I think he left a hundred thousand minimum, and all of it in cash. And I'm telling the truth about this: I've eaten the dog's tongue:[16] mean-mouthed, talkative, an argument, not a man. His brother was a real man, a friend to a friend, free with his money and a good host. And when he was starting out he had some bad luck, but his first vintage patched him up: he sold his wine at whatever price he wanted.

Between Phileros's insistence on his own truthfulness and his rhythmic, but stereotypical, paean to Chrysanthus and his brother, there is hardly room for any real narrative or description, which boils down to this: Chrysanthus, a hard man in contrast to his brother, had reverses and successes. One imagines that Phileros describes anyone he approves of as an *amicus amico,* for example.

Some differences among the individual freedmen make themselves felt, of course, but these are expressed more often through the content and occasion than the form of their language. The first speakers after their host's temporary departure in 41.9 are, like Trimalchio, also haunted by the theme of time. Dama complains that the day goes by so fast that "you turn around, and it's night" (*dum versas te, nox fit,* 41.10). Seleucus tells of the funeral he has just attended, and Ganymedes (a wonderfully ironic name for the man who sounds the oldest of all of them in his outlook) goes on about the days when men were men and women were devout and chaste. This group of freedmen seems in general older and less directly dependent on Trimalchio himself. Later we meet Niceros, whom Trimalchio can call on for a rendition of the werewolf story (61-62), and Plocamus, who gives an unintelligible performance in Greek. These, like Hermeros, who leaps to Trimalchio's defense when he thinks Ascyltos and Giton are laughing at him (57-58),[17] seem more directly dependent on Trimalchio. There are, then, differences of status within the group of freedmen, but these are not marked by form of speech.

The effect is of a language system independent of the individual speaker, encoding the freedmen's basic val-ues (individualism coupled with strong class loyalty). Consequently it is difficult to distinguish between individual freedmen on the basis of language: their much-praised realism consists more in their deviations from the *sermo urbanus* than in distinctions among themselves.[18]

Our task of listening for individual voices is not simplified as we turn from the freedmen to the other characters of the novel. In a deservedly well-known article of 1966, Peter George undertook an analysis of the style of the non-freedmen as an expression of their character. It is no disparagement of his work, however, to note that he showed more clearly what these characters' style was not: their own. George begins with a discussion of Giton's style and concludes, quite rightly, that it is the style of the declamation exercise, all epi-grams and dramatic poses. Moreover it is *bad* rhetoric, an expression of Giton's immature and undisciplined character.[19] Paradoxically though, Giton's style is defined by its lack of personality: it is his insofar as it is not his. Where the freedmen lose themselves in the clichés of everyday life, Giton loses himself in the conceits of rhetoric. So, too, George's discussion of the maid Chrysis's style merely compounds a negative definition: in one passage she speaks in the language of the slave-and-freedmen social stratum to which she belongs, while in another she apes the rhetorical man-nerisms of the social-climbing set of Encolpius, Ascyltus, and Giton.[20] Neither style is her own in any real sense. Although the rhetorical style is clearly adopted, the more colloquial style is not marked by any personal idiosyncrasy and so blends with the rest of the *sermo plebeius* in Petronius.

Eumolpus would seem the most promising candidate for an analysis of his personal voice, in that he speaks more of the **Satyricon** than anyone other than Encolpius. While the bulk of this is in the form of his two poems, the *Bellum civile* and the *Trojae halosis,* which present their own stylistic problems, there is still ample material from prose contexts to consider. Yet a distinctive voice for Eumolpus remains elusive. There is no stylistic overlap between his poetry and prose; in fact, George notes that "his prose is less colored by poeticisms than that of any of the other literati."[21] George admires Eumolpus's style and discusses how his character is the appropriate narrator for the Milesian tales in the **Satyricon,** but then he goes on to say that Eumolpus's style is "notable for just that blend of literary vigor" that characterizes the best prose in Petronius.[22] That means *Encolpius's* style.[23] In other words, Eumolpus's style is just the same as Encolpius's style, absent the vices sporadically "characteristic" of the latter. Thus Eumolpus emerges just as stylistically schizophrenic as Chrysis, though where she divides between the *sermo plebeius* and an attempt at *sermo urbanus,* Eumolpus divides between a polished *sermo urbanus,* which he shares with the other educated characters (even though he may excel in it) and a poetic style which we have ample reason to believe is not his own (and shall return to below).

When confronted with the challenge of identifying a characteristic voice and language for Encolpius, the immediate response is to throw up our hands. It is not merely that, since he is the first-person narrator, technically every word of the **Satyricon** is in "his" voice. Our situation is not materially improved if we limit our consideration to the language Encolpius speaks out loud in the course of the novel. As George notes:

> Encolpius's style of speech shows no slavish adherence to one particular model or set of models: if it did, the sheer quantity of what he says would make for monotony. But this does not mean that Encolpius is less imitative than Giton; on the contrary. Many of the variations in his style are *ad hoc* imitations of the style of the person to whom he is speaking at the time.[24]

Thus Encolpius, somewhat more successfully than Giton, speaks the languages of others; it is an intensely literary style.

This brief survey has suggested that there is less than meets the eye to the social and character differences of language systems in this novel. The broad distinction of *sermo plebeius* and *sermo urbanus* suffices to generate the heteroglossia of sociological background that Auerbach praises, but it is much more difficult to trace finer social distinctions of speech. Variations within the language of the more educated characters are more a function of the literary models they use or misuse than characteristic expressions of individual psyches. Our next step must therefore be an exploration of the literary language system of the **Satyricon.**

*Notes*

[1] Fish 1981, 371.

[2] Winkler 1985, esp. 60-69. My discussion of reading and detective fiction owes a great deal to his. See also Guetti 1982.

[3] S. S. Van Dine's list of twenty rules is the classic, first published in the *American Magazine,* September 1928 (conveniently reprinted in Haycraft 1946, 189-96, which also contains Ronald Knox's "Decalogue," 194-96).

[4] Bakhtin 1981, 410.

[5] Many words appear nowhere in Latin literature between Plautus in the second century B.C. and Apuleius in the second century A.D. In his excellent analysis of Apuleius's style, Tatum 1979, 147, notes the Plautine

exuberance in Fotis's style. He further notes: "Although stylistic variation abounds in Apuleius' work, his novel never attains the variety of characterizations so distinctive in Petronius' *Satyricon.* The qualities of Petronius' characters are reflected in their speech . . . Such verisimilitude never appears in Apuleius" (149). On Chrysis's style, see George 1966, 342-46.

[6] Auerbach 1953, 30. He does regard the *Satyricon* as not fully realistic in the modern sense because of its failure to anchor this mixture of languages in a concept of historical forces that produced them (31-33).

[7] It is, in point of fact, earlier than the surviving examples of the Greek romance. New discoveries could easily revise our picture of the history of ancient prose fiction. At the moment, though, the essentially unified language of Longus or Heliodorus seems typical of the Greek romance.

[8] Bakhtin 1981, 412.

[9] The discussion of the *sermo urbanus* and the *sermo vulgaris* or *sermo plebeius* begins with Buechler in his edition of 1867. One of the most important works here is Abbot 1907. Smith 1975, xxix-xxx, provides an excellent short bibliography on linguistic questions and a very useful outline of the linguistic idiosyncracies of the freedmen in his appendix 2 (220-24). What follows is deeply indebted to Abbott and Smith. The title of Petersmann 1985 promises a great deal more in this area than it delivers. Petersman 1986 offers much the same material, but the sections on *sermo urbanus* and *sermo vulgaris* (401-7) are useful. A copy of Heraeus 1899 came to hand too late to be incorporated in this analysis but contains important parallel materials.

[10] Smith 1975, 221.

[11] Swanson 1963, 253.

[12] Smith 1975, 222-23. Abbot 1907, 46, also notes the use of the popular endings *-arius* and *-atus.*

[13] E.g., *dixi quia mustella comedit,* 46.4.

[14] Abbott 1907, 48.

[15] Abbot 1907, 48, counts seventy-five such examples in the space of four pages of text.

[16] Meaning obscure. Suggestions range from a medicinal plant (Heseltine) to a reference to Cynic philosophers (Sage and Gilleland, ad loc.).

[17] Hermeros in this passage is given one touch that is emphatically not freedman's speech. He imagines Ascyltos asking him a question with the word *servivisti* in it: "Why are you a slave?" The normal form of the

verb was contracted (*servisti*). This is the only uncontracted *-vis-* perfect in Petronius. Vine 1988, who points this out, suggests Hermeros is mocking the hypercorrect speech of intellectuals and characterizing Ascyltos as such. That is too subtle a touch for Hermeros's character; Petronius happily sacrifices consistency of character here for a good joke.

[18] Abbott 1907, 49, argues for some individuality: seven of eleven "plebeian" words in his sample are spoken by Echion; Phileros is fond of the oath *mehercules*. Smith 1975, 223, notes the prevalence of Graecisms in Hermeros's speech.

[19] George 1966, 338-42.

[20] Ibid., 342-46. The colloquial passage cited is 126.8-10, where she rejects Encolpius's advances; the more rhetorical is 126.2.

[21] George 1966, 348. Cf. Gagliardi 1981, 364: "Tra Eumolpo poeta ed Eumolpo personaggio, in somma, si ricompone qui una frattura altrove sempre operante."

[22] George 1966, 347.

[23] George indeed believes that one can distinguish Petronius's style from Encolpius's style, despite the first-person form of narration. This procedure seems to me merely to divide the prose one admires ("Petronius's style") from everything else ("Encolpius's style") on no principal other than taste. Roger Beck 1975 has attempted a functionally similar, but unpersuasive, division of Encolpius into younger and older selves. The recent attempt of Jones 1987 to refine Beck's approach in fact demonstrates its unworkability. See above ch. III n. 26 and ch. VI n. 33.

[24] George 1966, 350.

### Works Cited

Abbot, Frank Frost. 1907. "The Use of Language as a Means of Characterization in Petronius." *Classical Philology* 2: 43-50. . . .

Auerbach, Erich. 1953. *Mimesis*. Translated by W.R. Trask. Princeton. . . .

Bakhtin, M. M. 1981. *The Dialogic Imagination: Four Essays*. Edited by M. Holquist. Translated by C. Emerson and M. Holquist. Austin. . . .

Beck, Roger. 1975. "Encolpius at the *Cena*." *Phoenix* 29: 271-83. . . .

Fish, Stanley. 1972. *Self-Consuming Artifacts*. Berkeley and Los Angeles.

———. 1980. *Is There a Text in This Class? The Authority of Interpretive Communities*. Cambridge, Mass.

———. 1983. "Profession Despise Thyself: Fear and Self-Loathing in Literary Studies." *Critical Inquiry* 10: 349-64.

———. 1984. "Fear of Fish: A Reply to Walter Davis." *Critical Inquiry* 10: 695-705.

———. 1985a. "Anti-Professionalism." *New Literary History* 17: 89-108.

———. 1985b. "Resistance and Independence: A Reply to Gerald Graff." *New Literary History* 17: 119-27.

———. 1987. "Change." *South Atlantic Quarterly* 86.4: 423-44. . . .

George, Peter. 1966. "Style and Character in the *Satyricon*." *Arion* 5: 336-58. . . .

Guetti, James. 1982. "Detective Fiction." *Raritan* 2.1: 133-54.

Haycraft, H. 1946. *The Art of the Mystery Story*. Reprinted New York, 1975. . . .

Heraeus, Wilhelm. 1899. *Die Sprache des Petronius und die Glossen*. Leipzig. . . .

Heseltine, M. 1969. *Petronius*. Revised by E. H. Warmington. Cambridge, Mass. . . .

Jones, F. 1987. "The Narrator and the Narrative of the *Satyricon*." *Latomus* 46: 810-19. . . .

Petersmann, H. 1985. "Umwelt, Sprachsituation und Stilschichten in Petrons 'Satyrica.'" *ANRW* II. 32.3: 1687-1705.

———. 1986. "Petrons 'Satyrica.'" In *Die römische Satire*, edited by J. Adamietz, 383ff. Darmstadt. . . .

Sage, E. T. 1969. *Petronius: The Satyricon*. Revised and expanded by B. Gilleland. New York. . . .

Smith, Martin S., ed. 1975. *Petronii Arbitri Cena Trimalchionis*. Oxford. . . .

Tatum, James. 1979. *Apuleius and the Golden Ass*. Ithaca, N.Y. . . .

Vine, Brent. 1988. "A Note on *servivisti* (Petr. 57.4)." *AJP* 109: 543-46. . . .

## FURTHER READING

Arrowsmith, William."Luxury and Death in the *Satyricon*." *Arion* V, No. 3 (Autumn 1966): 304-31.

Explores the theme he finds in the *Cena* segment of the *Satyricon*--an excess of luxury that, when uncontrolled, can bring death.

Beck, Roger. "Eumolpus *Poeta*, Eumolpus *Fabulator:* A Study of Characterization in the *Satyricon*." *Phoenix* XXXIII, No. 3 (Autumn 1979): 239-53.

Contends that the many-sided characterization of the poet Eumolpus in the *Satyricon* demonstrates Petronius's sophistication.

Best, Edward E., Jr. "Attitudes toward Literacy Reflected in Petronius." *Classical Journal* 61 (November 1965): 72-76.

Argues that many passages in the *Satyricon* suggest a widespread literacy among the common Roman people.

Boyce, Bret. *The Language of the Freedmen in Petronius'* Cena Trimalchionis. Leiden, The Netherlands: E. J. Brill, 1991, 113 p.

Comprehensive study of the characteristics of the language of the freedmen in the *Cena* and how Petronius uses language to portray character.

Cameron, Averil. "Petronius and Plato." *The Classical Quarterly* XIX, No. 2 (November 1969): 367-70.

Discusses how Petronius's character Habinnas is modeled after Alcibiades from Plato's *Symposium*.

_____. "Myth and Meaning in Petronius: Some Modern Comparisons." *Latomus* XXIX, No. 2 (April-June 1970): 397-425.

Examines how Petronius uses epic—specifically the *Odyssey*—to demonstrate the emptiness of modern life.

Connors, Catherine. *Petronius the Poet: Verse and Literary Tradition in the "Satyricon."* Cambridge: Cambridge University Press, 1998, 166 p.

Examines the poems of the *Satyricon,* their implications, and their relation to mime, Menippean satire, and prosimetric Greek fiction.

Courtney, E. "Parody and Literary Allusion in Menippean Satire." *Philologus* 106 (1962): 86-100.

Contends that the *Satyricon* is a parody of the novel.

Currie, H. MacL. "Petronius and Ovid." *Studies in Latin Literature and Roman History* V (1989): 317-35.

Discusses Ovid's influence on Petronius.

de la Mare, Albinia Catherine. "The Return of Petronius to Italy." In *Medieval Learning and Literature: Essays Presented to Richard William Hunt,* edited by J. J. G.

Alexander and M. T. Gibson, pp. 220-54. Oxford: Clarendon Press, 1976.

Describes various fifteenth-century manuscripts of the *Satyricon* and their derivations.

Dietrich, B. C. "Petronius: Satyr of Satirist." *Movimento Europeo per la Difesa del Latino* XVII, No. 1 (January-June 1970): 17-43.

Discusses the *Satyricon*'s sharp literary criticism and its concern with the human condition; also summarizes its plots and characters.

George, Peter. "Style and Character in the *Satyricon*." *Arion* V, No. 3 (Autumn 1966): 336-58.

Presents a character and content study of the *Satyricon* based on a critical analysis of its style.

Heseltine, Michael. Introduction to *Petronius.* Translated by Michael Heseltine, revised by E. H. Warmington, pp. ix-xlvi. Cambridge: Harvard University Press, 1987.

Introduction that includes discussion of assorted manuscripts and editions.

Jones, Frederick M. "Realism in Petronius." *Groningen Colloquia on the Novel* IV (1991): 105-20.

Contends that the contemporary audience of the *Satyricon* would have considered what modern critics call realism as verisimilitude, but with a radical subjective element.

Lees, Francis Noel. "Mr. Eliot's Sunday Morning *Satura:* Petronius and *The Waste Land*." In *T. S. Eliot: The Man and His Work,* edited by Allen Tate, pp. 345-54. London: Chatto & Windus, 1967.

Examines the influence of the *Satyricon* on Eliot's *The Waste Land.*

Panayotakis, Costas. *Theatrum Arbitri: Theatrical Elements in the* Satyrica *of Petronius.* Leiden, The Netherlands: E. J. Brill, 1995, 225 p.

Examines possible influences of Roman comic drama on the *Satyricon.*

Ramage, Edwin S., David L. Sigsbee, and Sigmund C. Fredericks. "Seneca and Petronius: Menippean Satire under Nero." In their *Roman Satirists and Their Satire: The Fine Art of Criticism in Ancient Rome,* pp. 89-113. Park Ridge, N.J.: Noyes Press, 1974.

Discusses difficulties in categorizing the *Satyricon* before explaining why it is best viewed as a sophisticated Menippean satire.

Rankin, H. D. "Saturnalian Wordplay and Apophoreta in *Satyricon* 56." *Classica et Mediaevalia* XXIII, No. 1-2 (1962): 134-42.

Presents many examples of word-play and puns found in the *Satyricon.*

_____. "Some Themes of Concealment and Pretence in

Petronius' *Satyricon*." *Latomus* XXVIII, No. 1 (January-March 1969): 99-119.

Explains how the elements of concealment, secrecy, and social pretense that occur in the *Satyricon* mirror characteristics Petronius saw in his own society.

Reeve, M. D. "Petronius." In *Texts and Transmission: A Survey of the Latin Classics,* edited by L. D. Reynolds, pp. 295-300. Oxford: Clarendon Press, 1983.

Discusses various early manuscripts of the *Satyricon* and how they were used by other writers.

Richardson, Wade. *Reading and Variant in Petronius: Studies in the French Humanists and Their Manuscript Sources.* Toronto: University of Toronto Press, 1993, 187 p.

Studies the textual tradition of the *Satyricon* and evaluates different versions of the text.

Sandy, Gerald. "Satire in the *Satyricon*." *American Journal of Philology* XC, No. 3 (July 1969): 293-303.

Explains that the *Satyricon* is both amoral and satirical.

_____. "Petronius and the Tradition of the Interpolated Narrative." *Transactions and Proceedings of the American Philological Association* 101 (1970): 463-76.

Discusses how and why Petronius introduces his framed narratives.

Schmeling, Gareth. "The *Satyricon*: Poems in Search of a Genre." *The Classical Bulletin* 47, No. 4 (February, 1971): 49-53.

Rejects the designation of either satire or parody for the *Satyricon*, instead concluding that it should be identified (with some qualifications)as a novel or romance.

———. "The *Satyricon:* The Sense of an Ending." *Rheinisches Museum für Philologie* 134, Nos. 3-4 (1991): 352-77.

Concentrates on the "outrageous" and always unpredictable endings and projected endings of episodes of the *Satyricon.*

Shey, H. James. "Petronius and Plato's *Gorgias*." *The Classical Bulletin,* 47, No. 6 (April, 1971): 81-4.

Offers evidence that many motifs dramatized by Petronius were borrowed from Plato's *Gorgias.*

Slater, Niall W. "'Against Interpretation': Petronius and Art Criticism." *Ramus* 16, Nos. 1-2 (1987): 165-76.

Contends that Petronius parodies the ideal of *mimesis* in the visual arts.

Sochatoff, A. Fred. "Imagery in the Poems of the *Satyricon*." *Classical Journal* 65 (May 1970): 340-44.

Examines how Petronius reveals his characters through use of imagery in their poetry.

Tacitus. "Testamonia." *Arion* V, No.3 (Autumn 1966): 273-74.

Provides a vivid sketch of how the jealousy of a rival confidant of Nero's led to Petronius's death. Tacitus's *Annals,* where this excerpt first appeared, was written in the second century.

Walsh, P. G. "The Satyricon." In his *The Roman Novel: The "Satyricon" of Petronius and the "Metamorphoses" of Apuleius,* pp. 67-110. Cambridge: Cambridge University Press, 1970.

Overview of the *Satyricon* that discusses its origin, purpose, action, tone, and humor.

# CLASSICAL AND MEDIEVAL LITERATURE CRITICISM

## INDEXES

Literary Criticism Series
Cumulative Author Index

Literary Criticism Series
Cumulative Topic Index

*CMLC* Cumulative Nationality Index

*CMLC* Cumulative Title Index

*CMLC* Cumulative Critic Index

# How to Use This Index

### The main references

> Calvino, Italo
> 1923–1985 ....... **CLC 5, 8, 11, 22, 33, 39,**
> **73; SSC 3**

list all author entries in the following Gale Literary Criticism series:

**BLC** = *Black Literature Criticism*
**CLC** = *Contemporary Literary Criticism*
**CLR** = *Children's Literature Review*
**CMLC** = *Classical and Medieval Literature Criticism*
**DA** = *DISCovering Authors*
**DAB** = *DISCovering Authors: British*
**DAC** = *DISCovering Authors: Canadian*
**DAM** = *DISCovering Authors: Modules*
　　　*DRAM*: *Dramatists Module*; **MST**: *Most-Studied Authors Module*;
　　　**MULT**: *Multicultural Authors Module*; **NOV**: *Novelists Module*;
　　　**POET**: *Poets Module*; **POP**: *Popular Fiction and Genre Authors Module*
**DC** = *Drama Criticism*
**HLC** = *Hispanic Literature Criticism*
**LC** = *Literature Criticism from 1400 to 1800*
**NCLC** = *Nineteenth-Century Literature Criticism*
**PC** = *Poetry Criticism*
**SSC** = *Short Story Criticism*
**TCLC** = *Twentieth-Century Literary Criticism*
**WLC** = *World Literature Criticism, 1500 to the Present*

### The cross-references

> See also CANR 23; CA 85-88;
> obituary CA116

list all author entries in the following Gale biographical and literary sources:

**AAYA** = *Authors & Artists for Young Adults*
**AITN** = *Authors in the News*
**BEST** = *Bestsellers*
**BW** = *Black Writers*
**CA** = *Contemporary Authors*
**CAAS** = *Contemporary Authors Autobiography Series*
**CABS** = *Contemporary Authors Bibliographical Series*
**CANR** = *Contemporary Authors New Revision Series*
**CAP** = *Contemporary Authors Permanent Series*
**CDALB** = *Concise Dictionary of American Literary Biography*
**CDBLB** = *Concise Dictionary of British Literary Biography*
**DLB** = *Dictionary of Literary Biography*
**DLBD** = *Dictionary of Literary Biography Documentary Series*
**DLBY** = *Dictionary of Literary Biography Yearbook*
**HW** = *Hispanic Writers*
**JRDA** = *Junior DISCovering Authors*
**MAICYA** = *Major Authors and Illustrators for Children and Young Adults*
**MTCW** = *Major 20th-Century Writers*
**NNAL** = *Native North American Literature*
**SAAS** = *Something about the Author Autobiography Series*
**SATA** = *Something about the Author*
**YABC** = *Yesterday's Authors of Books for Children*

See also CA 65-68; CANR 11, 43, 78

**Aston, James**
See White, T(erence) H(anbury)

**Asturias, Miguel Angel** 1899-1974 **CLC 3, 8, 13; DAM MULT, NOV; HLC**
See also CA 25-28; 49-52; CANR 32; CAP 2; DLB 113; HW 1; MTCW 1, 2

**Atares, Carlos Saura**
See Saura (Atares), Carlos

**Atheling, William**
See Pound, Ezra (Weston Loomis)

**Atheling, William, Jr.**
See Blish, James (Benjamin)

**Atherton, Gertrude (Franklin Horn)** 1857-1948 **TCLC 2**
See also CA 104; 155; DLB 9, 78, 186

**Atherton, Lucius**
See Masters, Edgar Lee

**Atkins, Jack**
See Harris, Mark

**Atkinson, Kate** **CLC 99**
See also CA 166

**Attaway, William (Alexander)** 1911-1986 **CLC 92; BLC 1; DAM MULT**
See also BW 2, 3; CA 143; DLB 76

**Atticus**
See Fleming, Ian (Lancaster); Wilson, (Thomas) Woodrow

**Atwood, Margaret (Eleanor)** 1939- **CLC 2, 3, 4, 8, 13, 15, 25, 44, 84; DA; DAB; DAC; DAM MST, NOV, POET; PC 8; SSC 2; WLC**
See also AAYA 12; BEST 89:2; CA 49-52; CANR 3, 24, 33, 59; DLB 53; INT CANR-24; MTCW 1, 2; SATA 50

**Aubigny, Pierre d'**
See Mencken, H(enry) L(ouis)

**Aubin, Penelope** 1685-1731(?) **LC 9**
See also DLB 39

**Auchincloss, Louis (Stanton)** 1917- **CLC 4, 6, 9, 18, 45; DAM NOV; SSC 22**
See also CA 1-4R; CANR 6, 29, 55; DLB 2; DLBY 80; INT CANR-29; MTCW 1

**Auden, W(ystan) H(ugh)** 1907-1973 **CLC 1, 2, 3, 4, 6, 9, 11, 14, 43; DA; DAB; DAC; DAM DRAM, MST, POET; PC 1; WLC**
See also AAYA 18; CA 9-12R; 45-48; CANR 5, 61; CDBLB 1914-1945; DLB 10, 20; MTCW 1, 2

**Audiberti, Jacques** 1900-1965 **CLC 38; DAM DRAM**
See also CA 25-28R

**Audubon, John James** 1785-1851 **NCLC 47**

**Auel, Jean M(arie)** 1936- **CLC 31, 107; DAM POP**
See also AAYA 7; BEST 90:4; CA 103; CANR 21, 64; INT CANR-21; SATA 91

**Auerbach, Erich** 1892-1957 **TCLC 43**
See also CA 118; 155

**Augier, Emile** 1820-1889 **NCLC 31**
See also DLB 192

**August, John**
See De Voto, Bernard (Augustine)

**Augustine** 354-430 **CMLC 6; DA; DAB; DAC; DAM MST; WLCS**
See also DLB 115

**Aurelius**
See Bourne, Randolph S(illiman)

**Aurobindo, Sri**
See Ghose, Aurabinda

**Austen, Jane** 1775-1817 **NCLC 1, 13, 19, 33, 51; DA; DAB; DAC; DAM MST, NOV; WLC**

See also AAYA 19; CDBLB 1789-1832; DLB 116

**Auster, Paul** 1947- **CLC 47**
See also CA 69-72; CANR 23, 52, 75; MTCW 1

**Austin, Frank**
See Faust, Frederick (Schiller)

**Austin, Mary (Hunter)** 1868-1934 **TCLC 25**
See also CA 109; DLB 9, 78, 206

**Autran Dourado, Waldomiro**
See Dourado, (Waldomiro Freitas) Autran

**Averroes** 1126-1198 **CMLC 7**
See also DLB 115

**Avicenna** 980-1037 **CMLC 16**
See also DLB 115

**Avison, Margaret** 1918- **CLC 2, 4, 97; DAC; DAM POET**
See also CA 17-20R; DLB 53; MTCW 1

**Axton, David**
See Koontz, Dean R(ay)

**Ayckbourn, Alan** 1939- **CLC 5, 8, 18, 33, 74; DAB; DAM DRAM**
See also CA 21-24R; CANR 31, 59; DLB 13; MTCW 1, 2

**Aydy, Catherine**
See Tennant, Emma (Christina)

**Ayme, Marcel (Andre)** 1902-1967 **CLC 11**
See also CA 89-92; CANR 67; CLR 25; DLB 72; SATA 91

**Ayrton, Michael** 192]-1975 **CLC 7**
See also CA 5-8R; 61-64; CANR 9, 21

**Azorin** **CLC 11**
See also Martinez Ruiz, Jose

**Azuela, Mariano** 1873-1952 **TCLC 3; DAM MULT; HLC**
See also CA 104; 131; HW 1, 2; MTCW 1, 2

**Baastad, Babbis Friis**
See Friis-Baastad, Babbis Ellinor

**Bab**
See Gilbert, W(illiam) S(chwenck)

**Babbis, Eleanor**
See Friis-Baastad, Babbis Ellinor

**Babel, Isaac**
See Babel, Isaak (Emmanuilovich)

**Babel, Isaak (Emmanuilovich)** 1894-1941(?) **TCLC 2, 13; SSC 16**
See also CA 104; 155; MTCW 1

**Babits, Mihaly** 1883-1941 **TCLC 14**
See also CA 114

**Babur** 1483-1530 **LC 18**

**Bacchelli, Riccardo** 1891-1985 **CLC 19**
See also CA 29-32R; 117

**Bach, Richard (David)** 1936- **CLC 14; DAM NOV, POP**
See also AITN 1; BEST 89:2; CA 9-12R; CANR 18; MTCW 1; SATA 13

**Bachman, Richard**
See King, Stephen (Edwin)

**Bachmann, Ingeborg** 1926-1973 **CLC 69**
See also CA 93-96; 45-48; CANR 69; DLB 85

**Bacon, Francis** 1561-1626 **LC 18, 32**
See also CDBLB Before 1660; DLB 151

**Bacon, Roger** 1214(?)-1292 **CMLC 14**
See also DLB 115

**Bacovia, George** **TCLC 24**
See also Vasiliu, Gheorghe

**Badanes, Jerome** 1937- **CLC 59**

**Bagehot, Walter** 1826-1877 **NCLC 10**
See also DLB 55

**Bagnold, Enid** 1889-1981 **CLC 25; DAM DRAM**
See also CA 5-8R; 103; CANR 5, 40; DLB 13,

160, 191; MAICYA; SATA 1, 25

**Bagritsky, Eduard** 1895-1934 **TCLC 60**

**Bagrjana, Elisaveta**
See Belcheva, Elisaveta

**Bagryana, Elisaveta** **CLC 10**
See also Belcheva, Elisaveta
See also DLB 147

**Bailey, Paul** 1937- **CLC 45**
See also CA 21-24R; CANR 16, 62; DLB 14

**Baillie, Joanna** 1762-1851 **NCLC 71**
See also DLB 93

**Bainbridge, Beryl (Margaret)** 1933- **CLC 4, 5, 8, 10, 14, 18, 22, 62; DAM NOV**
See also CA 21-24R; CANR 24, 55, 75; DLB 14; MTCW 1, 2

**Baker, Elliott** 1922- **CLC 8**
See also CA 45-48; CANR 2, 63

**Baker, Jean H.** **TCLC 3, 10**
See also Russell, George William

**Baker, Nicholson** 1957- **CLC 61; DAM POP**
See also CA 135; CANR 63

**Baker, Ray Stannard** 1870-1946 **TCLC 47**
See also CA 118

**Baker, Russell (Wayne)** 1925- **CLC 31**
See also BEST 89:4; CA 57-60; CANR 11, 41, 59; MTCW 1, 2

**Bakhtin, M.**
See Bakhtin, Mikhail Mikhailovich

**Bakhtin, M. M.**
See Bakhtin, Mikhail Mikhailovich

**Bakhtin, Mikhail**
See Bakhtin, Mikhail Mikhailovich

**Bakhtin, Mikhail Mikhailovich** 1895-1975 **CLC 83**
See also CA 128; 113

**Bakshi, Ralph** 1938(?)- **CLC 26**
See also CA 112; 138

**Bakunin, Mikhail (Alexandrovich)** 1814-1876 **NCLC 25, 58**

**Baldwin, James (Arthur)** 1924-1987 **CLC 1, 2, 3, 4, 5, 8, 13, 15, 17, 42, 50, 67, 90; BLC 1; DA; DAB; DAC; DAM MST, MULT, NOV, POP; DC 1; SSC 10, 33; WLC**
See also AAYA 4; BW 1; CA 1-4R; 124; CABS 1; CANR 3, 24; CDALB 1941-1968; DLB 2, 7, 33; DLBY 87; MTCW 1, 2; SATA 9; SATA-Obit 54

**Ballard, J(ames) G(raham)** 1930- **CLC 3, 6, 14, 36; DAM NOV, POP; SSC 1**
See also AAYA 3; CA 5-8R; CANR 15, 39, 65; DLB 14, 207; MTCW 1, 2; SATA 93

**Balmont, Konstantin (Dmitriyevich)** 1867-1943 **TCLC 11**
See also CA 109; 155

**Baltausis, Vincas**
See Mikszath, Kalman

**Balzac, Honore de** 1799-1850 **NCLC 5, 35, 53; DA; DAB; DAC; DAM MST, NOV; SSC 5; WLC**
See also DLB 119

**Bambara, Toni Cade** 1939-1995 **CLC 19, 88; BLC 1; DA; DAC; DAM MST, MULT; WLCS**
See also AAYA 5; BW 2, 3; CA 29-32R; 150; CANR 24, 49; CDALBS; DLB 38; MTCW 1, 2

**Bamdad, A.**
See Shamlu, Ahmad

**Banat, D. R.**
See Bradbury, Ray (Douglas)

**Bancroft, Laura**
See Baum, L(yman) Frank

**Banim, John** 1798-1842 **NCLC 13**

See also DLB 116, 158, 159

**Banim, Michael** 1796-1874     **NCLC 13**
    See also DLB 158, 159

**Banjo, The**
    See Paterson, A(ndrew) B(arton)

**Banks, Iain**
    See Banks, Iain M(enzies)

**Banks, Iain M(enzies)** 1954-     **CLC 34**
    See also CA 123; 128; CANR 61; DLB 194;
    INT 128

**Banks, Lynne Reid**     **CLC 23**
    See also Reid Banks, Lynne
    See also AAYA 6

**Banks, Russell** 1940-     **CLC 37, 72**
    See also.CA 65-68; CAAS 15; CANR 19, 52,
    73; DLB 130

**Banville, John** 1945-     **CLC 46, 118**
    See also CA 117; 128; DLB 14; INT 128

**Banville, Theodore (Faullain) de** 1832-1891
    **NCLC 9**

**Baraka, Amiri** 1934-**CLC 1, 2, 3, 5, 10, 14, 33,**
    **115; BLC 1; DA; DAC; DAM MST, MULT,**
    **POET, POP; DC 6; PC 4; WLCS**
    See also Jones, LeRoi
    See also BW 2, 3; CA 21-24R; CABS 3; CANR
    27, 38, 61; CDALB 1941-1968; DLB 5, 7,
    16, 38; DLBD 8; MTCW 1, 2

**Barbauld, Anna Laetitia** 1743-1825**NCLC 50**
    See also DLB 107, 109, 142, 158

**Barbellion, W. N. P.**     **TCLC 24**
    See also Cummings, Bruce F(rederick)

**Barbera, Jack (Vincent)** 1945-     **CLC 44**
    See also CA 110; CANR 45

**Barbey d'Aurevilly, Jules Amedee** 1808-1889
    **NCLC 1; SSC 17**
    See also DLB 119

**Barbour, John** c. 1316-1395     **CMLC 33**
    See also DLB 146

**Barbusse, Henri** 1873-1935     **TCLC 5**
    See also CA 105; 154; DLB 65

**Barclay, Bill**
    See Moorcock, Michael (John)

**Barclay, William Ewert**
    See Moorcock, Michael (John)

**Barea, Arturo** 1897-1957     **TCLC 14**
    See also CA 111

**Barfoot, Joan** 1946-     **CLC 18**
    See also CA 105

**Barham, Richard Harris** 1788-1845**NCLC 77**
    See also DLB 159

**Baring, Maurice** 1874-1945     **TCLC 8**
    See also CA 105; 168; DLB 34

**Baring-Gould, Sabine** 1834-1924     **TCLC 88**
    See also DLB 156, 190

**Barker, Clive** 1952-     **CLC 52; DAM POP**
    See also AAYA 10; BEST 90:3; CA 121; 129;
    CANR 71; INT 129; MTCW 1, 2

**Barker, George Granville** 1913-1991 **CLC 8,**
    **48; DAM POET**
    See also CA 9-12R; 135; CANR 7, 38; DLB
    20; MTCW 1

**Barker, Harley Granville**
    See Granville-Barker, Harley
    See also DLB 10

**Barker, Howard** 1946-     **CLC 37**
    See also CA 102; DLB 13

**Barker, Jane** 1652-1732     **LC 42**

**Barker, Pat(ricia)** 1943-     **CLC 32, 94**
    See also CA 117; 122; CANR 50; INT 122

**Barlach, Ernst** 1870-1938     **TCLC 84**
    See also DLB 56, 118

**Barlow, Joel** 1754-1812     **NCLC 23**
    See also DLB 37

**Barnard, Mary (Ethel)** 1909-     **CLC 48**
    See also CA 21-22; CAP 2

**Barnes, Djuna** 1892-1982**CLC 3, 4, 8, 11, 29;**
    **SSC 3**
    See also CA 9-12R; 107; CANR 16, 55; DLB
    4, 9, 45; MTCW 1, 2

**Barnes, Julian (Patrick)** 1946- **CLC 42; DAB**
    See also CA 102; CANR 19, 54; DLB 194;
    DLBY 93; MTCW 1

**Barnes, Peter** 1931-     **CLC 5, 56**
    See also CA 65-68; CAAS 12; CANR 33, 34,
    64; DLB 13; MTCW 1

**Barnes, William** 1801-1886     **NCLC 75**
    See also DLB 32

**Baroja (y Nessi), Pio** 1872-1956**TCLC 8; HLC**
    See also CA 104

**Baron, David**
    See Pinter, Harold

**Baron Corvo**
    See Rolfe, Frederick (William Serafino Austin
    Lewis Mary)

**Barondess, Sue K(aufman)** 1926-1977 **CLC 8**
    See also Kaufman, Sue
    See also CA 1-4R; 69-72; CANR 1

**Baron de Teive**
    See Pessoa, Fernando (Antonio Nogueira)

**Baroness Von S.**
    See Zangwill, Israel

**Barres, (Auguste-) Maurice** 1862-1923**TCLC**
    **47**
    See also CA 164; DLB 123

**Barreto, Afonso Henrique de Lima**
    See Lima Barreto, Afonso Henrique de

**Barrett, (Roger) Syd** 1946-     **CLC 35**

**Barrett, William (Christopher)** 1913-1992
    **CLC 27**
    See also CA 13-16R; 139; CANR 11, 67; INT
    CANR-11

**Barrie, J(ames) M(atthew)** 1860-1937 **TCLC**
    **2; DAB; DAM DRAM**
    See also CA 104; 136; CANR 77; CDBLB
    1890-1914; CLR 16; DLB 10, 141, 156;
    MAICYA; MTCW 1; SATA 100; YABC 1

**Barrington, Michael**
    See Moorcock, Michael (John)

**Barrol, Grady**
    See Bograd, Larry

**Barry, Mike**
    See Malzberg, Barry N(athaniel)

**Barry, Philip** 1896-1949     **TCLC 11**
    See also CA 109; DLB 7

**Bart, Andre Schwarz**
    See Schwarz-Bart, Andre

**Barth, John (Simmons)** 1930-**CLC 1, 2, 3, 5, 7,**
    **9, 10, 14, 27, 51, 89; DAM NOV; SSC 10**
    See also AITN 1, 2; CA 1-4R; CABS 1; CANR
    5, 23, 49, 64; DLB 2; MTCW 1

**Barthelme, Donald** 1931-1989**CLC 1, 2, 3, 5, 6,**
    **8, 13, 23, 46, 59, 115; DAM NOV; SSC 2**
    See also CA 21-24R; 129; CANR 20, 58; DLB
    2; DLBY 80, 89; MTCW 1, 2; SATA 7;
    SATA-Obit 62

**Barthelme, Frederick** 1943-     **CLC 36, 117**
    See also CA 114; 122; CANR 77; DLBY 85;
    INT 122

**Barthes, Roland (Gerard)** 1915-1980**CLC 24,**
    **83**
    See also CA 130; 97-100; CANR 66; MTCW
    1, 2

**Barzun, Jacques (Martin)** 1907-     **CLC 51**
    See also CA 61-64; CANR 22

**Bashevis, Isaac**
    See Singer, Isaac Bashevis

**Bashkirtseff, Marie** 1859-1884     **NCLC 27**

**Basho**
    See Matsuo Basho

**Bass, Kingsley B., Jr.**
    See Bullins, Ed

**Bass, Rick** 1958-     **CLC 79**
    See also CA 126; CANR 53; DLB 212

**Bassani, Giorgio** 1916-     **CLC 9**
    See also CA 65-68; CANR 33; DLB 128, 177;
    MTCW 1

**Bastos, Augusto (Antonio) Roa**
    See Roa Bastos, Augusto (Antonio)

**Bataille, Georges** 1897-1962     **CLC 29**
    See also CA 101; 89-92

**Bates, H(erbert) E(rnest)** 1905-1974**CLC 46;**
    **DAB; DAM POP; SSC 10**
    See also CA 93-96; 45-48; CANR 34; DLB 162,
    191; MTCW 1, 2

**Bauchart**
    See Camus, Albert

**Baudelaire, Charles** 1821-1867 **NCLC 6, 29,**
    **55; DA; DAB; DAC; DAM MST, POET;**
    **PC 1; SSC 18; WLC**

**Baudrillard, Jean** 1929-     **CLC 60**

**Baum, L(yman) Frank** 1856-1919     **TCLC 7**
    See also CA 108; 133; CLR 15; DLB 22; JRDA;
    MAICYA; MTCW 1, 2; SATA 18, 100

**Baum, Louis F.**
    See Baum, L(yman) Frank

**Baumbach, Jonathan** 1933-     **CLC 6, 23**
    See also CA 13-16R; CAAS 5; CANR 12, 66;
    DLBY 80; INT CANR-12; MTCW 1

**Bausch, Richard (Carl)** 1945-     **CLC 51**
    See also CA 101; CAAS 14; CANR 43, 61; DLB
    130

**Baxter, Charles (Morley)** 1947- **CLC 45, 78;**
    **DAM POP**
    See also CA 57-60; CANR 40, 64; DLB 130;
    MTCW 2

**Baxter, George Owen**
    See Faust, Frederick (Schiller)

**Baxter, James K(eir)** 1926-1972     **CLC 14**
    See also CA 77-80

**Baxter, John**
    See Hunt, E(verette) Howard, (Jr.)

**Bayer, Sylvia**
    See Glassco, John

**Baynton, Barbara** 1857-1929     **TCLC 57**

**Beagle, Peter S(oyer)** 1939-     **CLC 7, 104**
    See also CA 9-12R; CANR 4, 51, 73; DLBY
    80; INT CANR-4; MTCW 1; SATA 60

**Bean, Normal**
    See Burroughs, Edgar Rice

**Beard, Charles A(ustin)** 1874-1948 **TCLC 15**
    See also CA 115; DLB 17; SATA 18

**Beardsley, Aubrey** 1872-1898     **NCLC 6**

**Beattie, Ann** 1947-**CLC 8, 13, 18, 40, 63; DAM**
    **NOV, POP; SSC 11**
    See also BEST 90:2; CA 81-84; CANR 53, 73;
    DLBY 82; MTCW 1, 2

**Beattie, James** 1735-1803     **NCLC 25**
    See also DLB 109

**Beauchamp, Kathleen Mansfield** 1888-1923
    See Mansfield, Katherine
    See also CA 104; 134; DA; DAC; DAM MST;
    MTCW 2

**Beaumarchais, Pierre-Augustin Caron de** 1732-
    1799     **DC 4**
    See also DAM DRAM

**Beaumont, Francis** 1584(?)-1616**LC 33; DC 6**
    See also CDBLB Before 1660; DLB 58, 121

**Beauvoir, Simone (Lucie Ernestine Marie**
    **Bertrand) de** 1908-1986**CLC 1, 2, 4, 8, 14,**

**31, 44, 50, 71; DA; DAB; DAC; DAM MST, NOV; WLC**
See also CA 9-12R; 118; CANR 28, 61; DLB 72; DLBY 86; MTCW 1, 2

**Becker, Carl (Lotus)** 1873-1945 **TCLC 63**
See also CA 157; DLB 17

**Becker, Jurek** 1937-1997 **CLC 7, 19**
See also CA 85-88; 157; CANR 60; DLB 75

**Becker, Walter** 1950- **CLC 26**

**Beckett, Samuel (Barclay)** 1906-1989 **CLC 1, 2, 3, 4, 6, 9, 10, 11, 14, 18, 29, 57, 59, 83; DA; DAB; DAC; DAM DRAM, MST, NOV; SSC 16; WLC**
See also CA 5-8R; 130; CANR 33, 61; CDBLB 1945-1960; DLB 13, 15; DLBY 90; MTCW 1, 2

**Beckford, William** 1760-1844 **NCLC 16**
See also DLB 39

**Beckman, Gunnel** 1910- **CLC 26**
See also CA 33-36R; CANR 15; CLR 25; MAICYA; SAAS 9; SATA 6

**Becque, Henri** 1837-1899 **NCLC 3**
See also DLB 192

**Beddoes, Thomas Lovell** 1803-1849 **NCLC 3**
See also DLB 96

**Bede** c. 673-735 **CMLC 20**
See also DLB 146

**Bedford, Donald F.**
See Fearing, Kenneth (Flexner)

**Beecher, Catharine Esther** 1800-1878 **NCLC 30**
See also DLB 1

**Beecher, John** 1904-1980 **CLC 6**
See also AITN 1; CA 5-8R; 105; CANR 8

**Beer, Johann** 1655-1700 **LC 5**
See also DLB 168

**Beer, Patricia** 1924- **CLC 58**
See also CA 61-64; CANR 13, 46; DLB 40

**Beerbohm, Max**
See Beerbohm, (Henry) Max(imilian)

**Beerbohm, (Henry) Max(imilian)** 1872-1956 **TCLC 1, 24**
See also CA 104; 154; CANR 79; DLB 34, 100

**Beer-Hofmann, Richard** 1866-1945 **TCLC 60**
See also CA 160; DLB 81

**Begiebing, Robert J(ohn)** 1946- **CLC 70**
See also CA 122; CANR 40

**Behan, Brendan** 1923-1964 **CLC 1, 8, 11, 15, 79; DAM DRAM**
See also CA 73-76; CANR 33; CDBLB 1945-1960; DLB 13; MTCW 1, 2

**Behn, Aphra** 1640(?)-1689 **LC 1, 30, 42; DA; DAB; DAC; DAM DRAM, MST, NOV, POET; DC 4; PC 13; WLC**
See also DLB 39, 80, 131

**Behrman, S(amuel) N(athaniel)** 1893-1973 **CLC 40**
See also CA 13-16; 45-48; CAP 1; DLB 7, 44

**Belasco, David** 1853-1931 **TCLC 3**
See also CA 104; 168; DLB 7

**Belcheva, Elisaveta** 1893- **CLC 10**
See also Bagryana, Elisaveta

**Beldone, Phil "Cheech"**
See Ellison, Harlan (Jay)

**Beleno**
See Azuela, Mariano

**Belinski, Vissarion Grigoryevich** 1811-1848 **NCLC 5**
See also DLB 198

**Belitt, Ben** 1911- **CLC 22**
See also CA 13-16R; CAAS 4; CANR 7, 77; DLB 5

**Bell, Gertrude (Margaret Lowthian)** 1868-1926

**TCLC 67**
See also CA 167; DLB 174

**Bell, J. Freeman**
See Zangwill, Israel

**Bell, James Madison** 1826-1902 **TCLC 43; BLC 1; DAM MULT**
See also BW 1; CA 122; 124; DLB 50

**Bell, Madison Smartt** 1957- **CLC 41, 102**
See also CA 111; CANR 28, 54, 73; MTCW 1

**Bell, Marvin (Hartley)** 1937- **CLC 8, 31; DAM POET**
See also CA 21-24R; CAAS 14; CANR 59; DLB 5; MTCW 1

**Bell, W. L. D.**
See Mencken, H(enry) L(ouis)

**Bellamy, Atwood C.**
See Mencken, H(enry) L(ouis)

**Bellamy, Edward** 1850-1898 **NCLC 4**
See also DLB 12

**Bellin, Edward J.**
See Kuttner, Henry

**Belloc, (Joseph) Hilaire (Pierre Sebastien Rene Swanton)** 1870-1953 **TCLC 7, 18; DAM POET; PC 24**
See also CA 106; 152; DLB 19, 100, 141, 174; MTCW 1; YABC 1

**Belloc, Joseph Peter Rene Hilaire**
See Belloc, (Joseph) Hilaire (Pierre Sebastien Rene Swanton)

**Belloc, Joseph Pierre Hilaire**
See Belloc, (Joseph) Hilaire (Pierre Sebastien Rene Swanton)

**Belloc, M. A.**
See Lowndes, Marie Adelaide (Belloc)

**Bellow, Saul** 1915- **CLC 1, 2, 3, 6, 8, 10, 13, 25, 33, 34, 63, 79; DA; DAB; DAC; DAM MST, NOV, POP; SSC 14; WLC**
See also AITN 2; BEST 89:3; CA 5-8R; CABS 1; CANR 29, 53; CDALB 1941-1968; DLB 2, 28; DLBD 3; DLBY 82; MTCW 1, 2

**Belser, Reimond Karel Maria de** 1929-
See Ruyslinck, Ward
See also CA 152

**Bely, Andrey** **TCLC 7; PC 11**
See also Bugayev, Boris Nikolayevich
See also MTCW 1

**Belyi, Andrei**
See Bugayev, Boris Nikolayevich

**Benary, Margot**
See Benary-Isbert, Margot

**Benary-Isbert, Margot** 1889-1979 **CLC 12**
See also CA 5-8R; 89-92; CANR 4, 72; CLR 12; MAICYA; SATA 2; SATA-Obit 21

**Benavente (y Martinez), Jacinto** 1866-1954 **TCLC 3; DAM DRAM, MULT; HLCS 1**
See also CA 106; 131; HW 1, 2; MTCW 1, 2

**Benchley, Peter (Bradford)** 1940- **CLC 4, 8; DAM NOV, POP**
See also AAYA 14; AITN 2; CA 17-20R; CANR 12, 35, 66; MTCW 1, 2; SATA 3, 89

**Benchley, Robert (Charles)** 1889-1945 **TCLC 1, 55**
See also CA 105; 153; DLB 11

**Benda, Julien** 1867-1956 **TCLC 60**
See also CA 120; 154

**Benedict, Ruth (Fulton)** 1887-1948 **TCLC 60**
See also CA 158

**Benedict, Saint** c. 480-c. 547 **CMLC 29**

**Benedikt, Michael** 1935- **CLC 4, 14**
See also CA 13-16R; CANR 7; DLB 5

**Benet, Juan** 1927- **CLC 28**
See also CA 143

**Benet, Stephen Vincent** 1898-1943 **TCLC 7;**

**DAM POET; SSC 10**
See also CA 104; 152; DLB 4, 48, 102; DLBY 97; MTCW 1; YABC 1

**Benet, William Rose** 1886-1950 **TCLC 28; DAM POET**
See also CA 118; 152; DLB 45

**Benford, Gregory (Albert)** 1941- **CLC 52**
See also CA 69-72, 175; CAAE 175; CAAS 27; CANR 12, 24, 49; DLBY 82

**Bengtsson, Frans (Gunnar)** 1894-1954 **TCLC 48**
See also CA 170

**Benjamin, David**
See Slavitt, David R(ytman)

**Benjamin, Lois**
See Gould, Lois

**Benjamin, Walter** 1892-1940 **TCLC 39**
See also CA 164

**Benn, Gottfried** 1886-1956 **TCLC 3**
See also CA 106; 153; DLB 56

**Bennett, Alan** 1934- **CLC 45, 77; DAB; DAM MST**
See also CA 103; CANR 35, 55; MTCW 1, 2

**Bennett, (Enoch) Arnold** 1867-1931 **TCLC 5, 20**
See also CA 106; 155; CDBLB 1890-1914; DLB 10, 34, 98, 135; MTCW 2

**Bennett, Elizabeth**
See Mitchell, Margaret (Munnerlyn)

**Bennett, George Harold** 1930-
See Bennett, Hal
See also BW 1; CA 97-100

**Bennett, Hal** **CLC 5**
See also Bennett, George Harold
See also DLB 33

**Bennett, Jay** 1912- **CLC 35**
See also AAYA 10; CA 69-72; CANR 11, 42, 79; JRDA; SAAS 4; SATA 41, 87; SATA-Brief 27

**Bennett, Louise (Simone)** 1919- **CLC 28; BLC 1; DAM MULT**
See also BW 2, 3; CA 151; DLB 117

**Benson, E(dward) F(rederic)** 1867-1940 **TCLC 27**
See also CA 114; 157; DLB 135, 153

**Benson, Jackson J.** 1930- **CLC 34**
See also CA 25-28R; DLB 111

**Benson, Sally** 1900-1972 **CLC 17**
See also CA 19-20; 37-40R; CAP 1; SATA 1, 35; SATA-Obit 27

**Benson, Stella** 1892-1933 **TCLC 17**
See also CA 117; 155; DLB 36, 162

**Bentham, Jeremy** 1748-1832 **NCLC 38**
See also DLB 107, 158

**Bentley, E(dmund) C(lerihew)** 1875-1956 **TCLC 12**
See also CA 108; DLB 70

**Bentley, Eric (Russell)** 1916- **CLC 24**
See also CA 5-8R; CANR 6, 67; INT CANR-6

**Beranger, Pierre Jean de** 1780-1857 **NCLC 34**

**Berdyaev, Nicolas**
See Berdyaev, Nikolai (Aleksandrovich)

**Berdyaev, Nikolai (Aleksandrovich)** 1874-1948 **TCLC 67**
See also CA 120; 157

**Berdyayev, Nikolai (Aleksandrovich)**
See Berdyaev, Nikolai (Aleksandrovich)

**Berendt, John (Lawrence)** 1939- **CLC 86**
See also CA 146; CANR 75; MTCW 1

**Beresford, J(ohn) D(avys)** 1873-1947 **TCLC 81**
See also CA 112; 155; DLB 162, 178, 197

**Bergelson, David** 1884-1952 **TCLC 81**

**Berger, Colonel**
See Malraux, (Georges-)Andre
**Berger, John (Peter)** 1926- **CLC 2, 19**
See also CA 81-84; CANR 51, 78; DLB 14, 207
**Berger, Melvin H.** 1927- **CLC 12**
See also CA 5-8R; CANR 4; CLR 32; SAAS 2;
SATA 5, 88
**Berger, Thomas (Louis)** 1924-**CLC 3, 5, 8, 11, 18, 38; DAM NOV**
See also CA 1-4R; CANR 5, 28, 51; DLB 2;
DLBY 80; INT CANR-28; MTCW 1, 2
**Bergman, (Ernst) Ingmar** 1918- **CLC 16, 72**
See also CA 81-84; CANR 33, 70; MTCW 2
**Bergson, Henri(-Louis)** 1859-1941 **TCLC 32**
See also CA 164
**Bergstein, Eleanor** 1938- **CLC 4**
See also CA 53-56; CANR 5
**Berkoff, Steven** 1937- **CLC 56**
See also CA 104; CANR 72
**Bermant, Chaim (Icyk)** 1929- **CLC 40**
See also CA 57-60; CANR 6, 31, 57
**Bern, Victoria**
See Fisher, M(ary) F(rances) K(ennedy)
**Bernanos, (Paul Louis) Georges** 1888-1948 **TCLC 3**
See also CA 104; 130; DLB 72
**Bernard, April** 1956- **CLC 59**
See also CA 131
**Berne, Victoria**
See Fisher, M(ary) F(rances) K(ennedy)
**Bernhard, Thomas** 1931-1989 **CLC 3, 32, 61**
See also CA 85-88; 127; CANR 32, 57; DLB 85, 124; MTCW 1
**Bernhardt, Sarah (Henriette Rosine)** 1844-1923 **TCLC 75**
See also CA 157
**Berriault, Gina** 1926- **CLC 54, 109; SSC 30**
See also CA 116; 129; CANR 66; DLB 130
**Berrigan, Daniel** 1921- **CLC 4**
See also CA 33-36R; CAAS 1; CANR 11, 43, 78; DLB 5
**Berrigan, Edmund Joseph Michael, Jr.** 1934-1983
See Berrigan, Ted
See also CA 61-64; 110; CANR 14
**Berrigan, Ted** **CLC 37**
See also Berrigan, Edmund Joseph Michael, Jr.
See also DLB 5, 169
**Berry, Charles Edward Anderson** 1931-
See Berry, Chuck
See also CA 115
**Berry, Chuck** **CLC 17**
See also Berry, Charles Edward Anderson
**Berry, Jonas**
See Ashbery, John (Lawrence)
**Berry, Wendell (Erdman)** 1934- **CLC 4, 6, 8, 27, 46; DAM POET**
See also AITN 1; CA 73-76; CANR 50, 73; DLB 5, 6; MTCW 1
**Berryman, John** 1914-1972**CLC 1, 2, 3, 4, 6, 8, 10, 13, 25, 62; DAM POET**
See also CA 13-16; 33-36R; CABS 2; CANR 35; CAP 1; CDALB 1941-1968; DLB 48; MTCW 1, 2
**Bertolucci, Bernardo** 1940- **CLC 16**
See also CA 106
**Berton, Pierre (Francis Demarigny)** 1920- **CLC 104**
See also CA 1-4R; CANR 2, 56; DLB 68; SATA 99
**Bertrand, Aloysius** 1807-1841 **NCLC 31**
**Bertran de Born** c. 1140-1215 **CMLC 5**
**Besant, Annie (Wood)** 1847-1933 **TCLC 9**

See also CA 105
**Bessie, Alvah** 1904-1985 **CLC 23**
See also CA 5-8R; 116; CANR 2, 80; DLB 26
**Bethlen, T. D.**
See Silverberg, Robert
**Beti, Mongo** **CLC 27; BLC 1; DAM MULT**
See also Biyidi, Alexandre
See also CANR 79
**Betjeman, John** 1906-1984 **CLC 2, 6, 10, 34, 43; DAB; DAM MST, POET**
See also CA 9-12R; 112; CANR 33, 56; CDBLB 1945-1960; DLB 20; DLBY 84; MTCW 1, 2
**Bettelheim, Bruno** 1903-1990 **CLC 79**
See also CA 81-84; 131; CANR 23, 61; MTCW 1, 2
**Betti, Ugo** 1892-1953 **TCLC 5**
See also CA 104; 155
**Betts, Doris (Waugh)** 1932- **CLC 3, 6, 28**
See also CA 13-16R; CANR 9, 66, 77; DLBY 82; INT CANR-9
**Bevan, Alistair**
See Roberts, Keith (John Kingston)
**Bey, Pilaff**
See Douglas, (George) Norman
**Bialik, Chaim Nachman** 1873-1934 **TCLC 25**
See also CA 170
**Bickerstaff, Isaac**
See Swift, Jonathan
**Bidart, Frank** 1939- **CLC 33**
See also CA 140
**Bienek, Horst** 1930- **CLC 7, 11**
See also CA 73-76; DLB 75
**Bierce, Ambrose (Gwinett)** 1842-1914(?) **TCLC 1, 7, 44; DA; DAC; DAM MST; SSC 9; WLC**
See also CA 104; 139; CANR 78; CDALB 1865-1917; DLB 11, 12, 23, 71, 74, 186
**Biggers, Earl Derr** 1884-1933 **TCLC 65**
See also CA 108; 153
**Billings, Josh**
See Shaw, Henry Wheeler
**Billington, (Lady) Rachel (Mary)** 1942- **CLC 43**
See also AITN 2; CA 33-36R; CANR 44
**Binyon, T(imothy) J(ohn)** 1936- **CLC 34**
See also CA 111; CANR 28
**Bioy Casares, Adolfo** 1914-1999**CLC 4, 8, 13, 88; DAM MULT; HLC; SSC 17**
See also CA 29-32R; CANR 19, 43, 66; DLB 113; HW 1, 2; MTCW 1, 2
**Bird, Cordwainer**
See Ellison, Harlan (Jay)
**Bird, Robert Montgomery** 1806-1854**NCLC 1**
See also DLB 202
**Birkerts, Sven** 1951- **CLC 116**
See also CA 128; 133; CAAS 29; INT 133
**Birney, (Alfred) Earle** 1904-1995**CLC 1, 4, 6, 11; DAC; DAM MST, POET**
See also CA 1-4R; CANR 5, 20; DLB 88; MTCW 1
**Biruni, al** 973-1048(?) **CMLC 28**
**Bishop, Elizabeth** 1911-1979 **CLC 1, 4, 9, 13, 15, 32; DA; DAC; DAM MST, POET; PC 3**
See also CA 5-8R; 89-92; CABS 2; CANR 26, 61; CDALB 1968-1988; DLB 5, 169; MTCW 1, 2; SATA-Obit 24
**Bishop, John** 1935- **CLC 10**
See also CA 105
**Bissett, Bill** 1939- **CLC 18; PC 14**
See also CA 69-72; CAAS 19; CANR 15; DLB 53; MTCW 1

**Bissoondath, Neil (Devindra)** 1955-**CLC 120; DAC**
See also CA 136
**Bitov, Andrei (Georgievich)** 1937- **CLC 57**
See also CA 142
**Biyidi, Alexandre** 1932-
See Beti, Mongo
See also BW 1, 3; CA 114; 124; MTCW 1, 2
**Bjarme, Brynjolf**
See Ibsen, Henrik (Johan)
**Bjoernson, Bjoernstjerne (Martinius)** 1832-1910 **TCLC 7, 37**
See also CA 104
**Black, Robert**
See Holdstock, Robert P.
**Blackburn, Paul** 1926-1971 **CLC 9, 43**
See also CA 81-84; 33-36R; CANR 34; DLB 16; DLBY 81
**Black Elk** 1863-1950 **TCLC 33; DAM MULT**
See also CA 144; MTCW 1; NNAL
**Black Hobart**
See Sanders, (James) Ed(ward)
**Blacklin, Malcolm**
See Chambers, Aidan
**Blackmore, R(ichard) D(oddridge)** 1825-1900 **TCLC 27**
See also CA 120; DLB 18
**Blackmur, R(ichard) P(almer)** 1904-1965 **CLC 2, 24**
See also CA 11-12; 25-28R; CANR 71; CAP 1; DLB 63
**Black Tarantula**
See Acker, Kathy
**Blackwood, Algernon (Henry)** 1869-1951 **TCLC 5**
See also CA 105; 150; DLB 153, 156, 178
**Blackwood, Caroline** 1931-1996**CLC 6, 9, 100**
See also CA 85-88; 151; CANR 32, 61, 65; DLB 14, 207; MTCW 1
**Blade, Alexander**
See Hamilton, Edmond; Silverberg, Robert
**Blaga, Lucian** 1895-1961 **CLC 75**
See also CA 157
**Blair, Eric (Arthur)** 1903-1950
See Orwell, George
See also CA 104; 132; DA; DAB; DAC; DAM MST, NOV; MTCW 1, 2; SATA 29
**Blair, Hugh** 1718-1800 **NCLC 75**
**Blais, Marie-Claire** 1939-**CLC 2, 4, 6, 13, 22; DAC; DAM MST**
See also CA 21-24R; CAAS 4; CANR 38, 75; DLB 53; MTCW 1, 2
**Blaise, Clark** 1940- **CLC 29**
See also AITN 2; CA 53-56; CAAS 3; CANR 5, 66; DLB 53
**Blake, Fairley**
See De Voto, Bernard (Augustine)
**Blake, Nicholas**
See Day Lewis, C(ecil)
See also DLB 77
**Blake, William** 1757-1827 **NCLC 13, 37, 57; DA; DAB; DAC; DAM MST, POET; PC 12; WLC**
See also CDBLB 1789-1832; CLR 52; DLB 93, 163; MAICYA; SATA 30
**Blasco Ibanez, Vicente** 1867-1928 **TCLC 12; DAM NOV**
See also CA 110; 131; HW 1, 2; MTCW 1
**Blatty, William Peter** 1928-**CLC 2; DAM POP**
See also CA 5-8R; CANR 9
**Bleeck, Oliver**
See Thomas, Ross (Elmore)
**Blessing, Lee** 1949- **CLC 54**

NOV, POP; SSC 29; WLC
See also AAYA 15; AITN 1, 2; CA 1-4R; CANR
2, 30, 75; CDALB 1968-1988; DLB 2, 8;
MTCW 1, 2; SATA 11, 64

Bradford, Gamaliel 1863-1932        TCLC 36
See also CA 160; DLB 17

Bradley, David (Henry), Jr. 1950-    CLC 23,
118; BLC 1; DAM MULT
See also BW 1, 3; CA 104; CANR 26; DLB 33

Bradley, John Ed(mund, Jr.) 1958-    CLC 55
See also CA 139

Bradley, Marion Zimmer 1930-CLC 30; DAM
POP
See also AAYA 9; CA 57-60; CAAS 10; CANR
7, 31, 51, 75; DLB 8; MTCW 1, 2; SATA 90

Bradstreet, Anne 1612(?)-1672LC 4, 30; DA;
DAC; DAM MST, POET; PC 10
See also CDALB 1640-1865; DLB 24

Brady, Joan 1939-                        CLC 86
See also CA 141

Bragg, Melvyn 1939-                      CLC 10
See also BEST 89:3; CA 57-60; CANR 10, 48;
DLB 14

Brahe, Tycho 1546-1601                   LC 45

Braine, John (Gerard) 1922-1986CLC 1, 3, 41
See also CA 1-4R; 120; CANR 1, 33; CDBLB
1945-1960; DLB 15; DLBY 86; MTCW 1

Bramah, Ernest 1868-1942                TCLC 72
See also CA 156; DLB 70

Brammer, William 1930(?)-1978          CLC 31
See also CA 77-80

Brancati, Vitaliano 1907-1954           TCLC 12
See also CA 109

Brancato, Robin F(idler) 1936-          CLC 35
See also AAYA 9; CA 69-72; CANR 11, 45;
CLR 32; JRDA; SAAS 9; SATA 97

Brand, Max
See Faust, Frederick (Schiller)

Brand, Millen 1906-1980                  CLC 7
See also CA 21-24R; 97-100; CANR 72

Branden, Barbara                         CLC 44
See also CA 148

Brandes, Georg (Morris Cohen) 1842-1927
TCLC 10
See also CA 105

Brandys, Kazimierz 1916-                 CLC 62

Branley, Franklyn M(ansfield) 1915-CLC 21
See also CA 33-36R; CANR 14, 39; CLR 13;
MAICYA; SAAS 16; SATA 4, 68

Brathwaite, Edward (Kamau) 1930-CLC 11;
BLCS; DAM POET
See also BW 2, 3; CA 25-28R; CANR 11, 26,
47; DLB 125

Brautigan, Richard (Gary) 1935-1984CLC 1,
3, 5, 9, 12, 34, 42; DAM NOV
See also CA 53-56; 113; CANR 34; DLB 2, 5,
206; DLBY 80, 84; MTCW 1; SATA 56

Brave Bird, Mary 1953-
See Crow Dog, Mary (Ellen)
See also NNAL

Braverman, Kate 1950-                    CLC 67
See also CA 89-92

Brecht, (Eugen) Bertolt (Friedrich) 1898-1956
TCLC 1, 6, 13, 35; DA; DAB; DAC; DAM
DRAM, MST; DC 3; WLC
See also CA 104; 133; CANR 62; DLB 56, 124;
MTCW 1, 2

Brecht, Eugen Berthold Friedrich
See Brecht, (Eugen) Bertolt (Friedrich)

Bremer, Fredrika 1801-1865              NCLC 11

Brennan, Christopher John 1870-1932TCLC
17
See also CA 117

Brennan, Maeve 1917-1993                 CLC 5
See also CA 81-84; CANR 72

Brent, Linda
See Jacobs, Harriet A(nn)

Brentano, Clemens (Maria) 1778-1842NCLC
1
See also DLB 90

Brent of Bin Bin
See Franklin, (Stella Maria Sarah) Miles
(Lampe)

Brenton, Howard 1942-                    CLC 31
See also CA 69-72; CANR 33, 67; DLB 13;
MTCW 1

Breslin, James 1930-1996
See Breslin, Jimmy
See also CA 73-76; CANR 31, 75; DAM NOV;
MTCW 1, 2

Breslin, Jimmy                           CLC 4, 43
See also Breslin, James
See also AITN 1; DLB 185; MTCW 2

Bresson, Robert 1901-                    CLC 16
See also CA 110; CANR 49

Breton, Andre 1896-1966CLC 2, 9, 15, 54; PC
15
See also CA 19-20; 25-28R; CANR 40, 60; CAP
2; DLB 65; MTCW 1, 2

Breytenbach, Breyten 1939(?)-   CLC 23, 37;
DAM POET
See also CA 113; 129; CANR 61

Bridgers, Sue Ellen 1942-                CLC 26
See also AAYA 8; CA 65-68; CANR 11, 36;
CLR 18; DLB 52; JRDA; MAICYA; SAAS
1; SATA 22, 90

Bridges, Robert (Seymour) 1844-1930 TCLC
1; DAM POET
See also CA 104; 152; CDBLB 1890-1914;
DLB 19, 98

Bridie, James                            TCLC 3
See also Mavor, Osborne Henry
See also DLB 10

Brin, David 1950-                        CLC 34
See also AAYA 21; CA 102; CANR 24, 70; INT
CANR-24; SATA 65

Brink, Andre (Philippus) 1935-   CLC 18, 36,
106
See also CA 104; CANR 39, 62; INT 103;
MTCW 1, 2

Brinsmead, H(esba) F(ay) 1922-           CLC 21
See also CA 21-24R; CANR 10; CLR 47;
MAICYA; SAAS 5; SATA 18, 78

Brittain, Vera (Mary) 1893(?)-1970 CLC 23
See also CA 13-16; 25-28R; CANR 58; CAP 1;
DLB 191; MTCW 1, 2

Broch, Hermann 1886-1951                TCLC 20
See also CA 117; DLB 85, 124

Brock, Rose
See Hansen, Joseph

Brodkey, Harold (Roy) 1930-1996         CLC 56
See also CA 111; 151; CANR 71; DLB 130

Brodskii, Iosif
See Brodsky, Joseph

Brodsky, Iosif Alexandrovich 1940-1996
See Brodsky, Joseph
See also AITN 1; CA 41-44R; 151; CANR 37;
DAM POET; MTCW 1, 2

Brodsky, Joseph 1940-1996 CLC 4, 6, 13, 36,
100; PC 9
See also Brodskii, Iosif; Brodsky, Iosif
Alexandrovich
See also MTCW 1

Brodsky, Michael (Mark) 1948-           CLC 19
See also CA 102; CANR 18, 41, 58

Bromell, Henry 1947-                     CLC 5

See also CA 53-56; CANR 9

Bromfield, Louis (Brucker) 1896-1956TCLC
11
See also CA 107; 155; DLB 4, 9, 86

Broner, E(sther) M(asserman) 1930- CLC 19
See also CA 17-20R; CANR 8, 25, 72; DLB 28

Bronk, William (M.) 1918-1999           CLC 10
See also CA 89-92; CANR 23; DLB 165

Bronstein, Lev Davidovich
See Trotsky, Leon

Bronte, Anne 1820-1849                  NCLC 71
See also DLB 21, 199

Bronte, Charlotte 1816-1855 NCLC 3, 8, 33,
58; DA; DAB; DAC; DAM MST, NOV;
WLC
See also AAYA 17; CDBLB 1832-1890; DLB
21, 159, 199

Bronte, Emily (Jane) 1818-1848NCLC 16, 35;
DA; DAB; DAC; DAM MST, NOV, POET;
PC 8; WLC
See also AAYA 17; CDBLB 1832-1890; DLB
21, 32, 199

Brooke, Frances 1724-1789               LC 6, 48
See also DLB 39, 99

Brooke, Henry 1703(?)-1783              LC 1
See also DLB 39

Brooke, Rupert (Chawner) 1887-1915 TCLC
2, 7; DA; DAB; DAC; DAM MST, POET;
PC 24; WLC
See also CA 104; 132; CANR 61; CDBLB
1914-1945; DLB 19; MTCW 1, 2

Brooke-Haven, P.
See Wodehouse, P(elham) G(renville)

Brooke-Rose, Christine 1926(?)-         CLC 40
See also CA 13-16R; CANR 58; DLB 14

Brookner, Anita 1928- CLC 32, 34, 51; DAB;
DAM POP
See also CA 114; 120; CANR 37, 56; DLB 194;
DLBY 87; MTCW 1, 2

Brooks, Cleanth 1906-1994 CLC 24, 86, 110
See also CA 17-20R; 145; CANR 33, 35; DLB
63; DLBY 94; INT CANR-35; MTCW 1, 2

Brooks, George
See Baum, L(yman) Frank

Brooks, Gwendolyn 1917- CLC 1, 2, 4, 5, 15,
49; BLC 1; DA; DAC; DAM MST, MULT,
POET; PC 7; WLC
See also AAYA 20; AITN 1; BW 2, 3; CA 1-
4R; CANR 1, 27, 52, 75; CDALB 1941-
1968; CLR 27; DLB 5, 76, 165; MTCW 1,
2; SATA 6

Brooks, Mel                              CLC 12
See also Kaminsky, Melvin
See also AAYA 13; DLB 26

Brooks, Peter 1938-                      CLC 34
See also CA 45-48; CANR 1

Brooks, Van Wyck 1886-1963              CLC 29
See also CA 1-4R; CANR 6; DLB 45, 63, 103

Brophy, Brigid (Antonia) 1929-1995 CLC 6,
11, 29, 105
See also CA 5-8R; 149; CAAS 4; CANR 25,
53; DLB 14; MTCW 1, 2

Brosman, Catharine Savage 1934-         CLC 9
See also CA 61-64; CANR 21, 46

Brossard, Nicole 1943-                   CLC 115
See also CA 122; CAAS 16; DLB 53

Brother Antoninus
See Everson, William (Oliver)

The Brothers Quay
See Quay, Stephen; Quay, Timothy

Broughton, T(homas) Alan 1936-          CLC 19
See also CA 45-48; CANR 2, 23, 48

Broumas, Olga 1949-                      CLC 10, 73

See also CA 85-88; CANR 20, 69

**Brown, Alan** 1950- **CLC 99**
See also CA 156

**Brown, Charles Brockden** 1771-1810 **N C L C 22, 74**
See also CDALB 1640-1865; DLB 37, 59, 73

**Brown, Christy** 1932-1981 **CLC 63**
See also CA 105; 104; CANR 72; DLB 14

**Brown, Claude** 1937- **CLC 30; BLC 1; DAM MULT**
See also AAYA 7; BW 1, 3; CA 73-76

**Brown, Dee (Alexander)** 1908- **CLC 18, 47; DAM POP**
See also AAYA 30; CA 13-16R; CAAS 6; CANR 11, 45, 60; DLBY 80; MTCW 1, 2; SATA 5

**Brown, George**
See Wertmueller, Lina

**Brown, George Douglas** 1869-1902 **TCLC 28**
See also CA 162

**Brown, George Mackay** 1921-1996 **CLC 5, 48, 100**
See also CA 21-24R; 151; CAAS 6; CANR 12, 37, 67; DLB 14, 27, 139; MTCW 1; SATA 35

**Brown, (William) Larry** 1951- **CLC 73**
See also CA 130; 134; INT 133

**Brown, Moses**
See Barrett, William (Christopher)

**Brown, Rita Mae** 1944- **CLC 18, 43, 79; DAM NOV, POP**
See also CA 45-48; CANR 2, 11, 35, 62; INT CANR-11; MTCW 1, 2

**Brown, Roderick (Langmere) Haig-**
See Haig-Brown, Roderick (Langmere)

**Brown, Rosellen** 1939- **CLC 32**
See also CA 77-80; CAAS 10; CANR 14, 44

**Brown, Sterling Allen** 1901-1989 **CLC 1, 23, 59; BLC 1; DAM MULT, POET**
See also BW 1, 3; CA 85-88; 127; CANR 26; DLB 48, 51, 63; MTCW 1, 2

**Brown, Will**
See Ainsworth, William Harrison

**Brown, William Wells** 1813-1884 **NCLC 2; BLC 1; DAM MULT; DC 1**
See also DLB 3, 50

**Browne, (Clyde) Jackson** 1948(?)- **CLC 21**
See also CA 120

**Browning, Elizabeth Barrett** 1806-1861 **NCLC 1, 16, 61, 66; DA; DAB; DAC; DAM MST, POET; PC 6; WLC**
See also CDBLB 1832-1890; DLB 32, 199

**Browning, Robert** 1812-1889 **NCLC 19; DA; DAB; DAC; DAM MST, POET; PC 2; WLCS**
See also CDBLB 1832-1890; DLB 32, 163; YABC 1

**Browning, Tod** 1882-1962 **CLC 16**
See also CA 141; 117

**Brownson, Orestes Augustus** 1803-1876 **NCLC 50**
See also DLB 1, 59, 73

**Bruccoli, Matthew J(oseph)** 1931- **CLC 34**
See also CA 9-12R; CANR 7; DLB 103

**Bruce, Lenny** **CLC 21**
See also Schneider, Leonard Alfred

**Bruin, John**
See Brutus, Dennis

**Brulard, Henri**
See Stendhal

**Brulls, Christian**
See Simenon, Georges (Jacques Christian)

**Brunner, John (Kilian Houston)** 1934-1995

**CLC 8, 10; DAM POP**
See also CA 1-4R; 149; CAAS 8; CANR 2, 37; MTCW 1, 2

**Bruno, Giordano** 1548-1600 **LC 27**

**Brutus, Dennis** 1924- **CLC 43; BLC 1; DAM MULT, POET; PC 24**
See also BW 2, 3; CA 49-52; CAAS 14; CANR 2, 27, 42; DLB 117

**Bryan, C(ourtlandt) D(ixon) B(arnes)** 1936- **CLC 29**
See also CA 73-76; CANR 13, 68; DLB 185; INT CANR-13

**Bryan, Michael**
See Moore, Brian

**Bryant, William Cullen** 1794-1878 **NCLC 6, 46; DA; DAB; DAC; DAM MST, POET; PC 20**
See also CDALB 1640-1865; DLB 3, 43, 59, 189

**Bryusov, Valery Yakovlevich** 1873-1924 **TCLC 10**
See also CA 107; 155

**Buchan, John** 1875-1940 **TCLC 41; DAB; DAM POP**
See also CA 108; 145; DLB 34, 70, 156; MTCW 1; YABC 2

**Buchanan, George** 1506-1582 **LC 4**
See also DLB 152

**Buchheim, Lothar-Guenther** 1918- **CLC 6**
See also CA 85-88

**Buchner, (Karl) Georg** 1813-1837 **NCLC 26**

**Buchwald, Art(hur)** 1925- **CLC 33**
See also AITN 1; CA 5-8R; CANR 21, 67; MTCW 1, 2; SATA 10

**Buck, Pearl S(ydenstricker)** 1892-1973 **CLC 7, 11, 18; DA; DAB; DAC; DAM MST, NOV**
See also AITN 1; CA 1-4R; 41-44R; CANR 1, 34; CDALBS; DLB 9, 102; MTCW 1, 2; SATA 1, 25

**Buckler, Ernest** 1908-1984 **CLC 13; DAC; DAM MST**
See also CA 11-12; 114; CAP 1; DLB 68; SATA 47

**Buckley, Vincent (Thomas)** 1925-1988 **CLC 57**
See also CA 101

**Buckley, William F(rank), Jr.** 1925- **CLC 7, 18, 37; DAM POP**
See also AITN 1; CA 1-4R; CANR 1, 24, 53; DLB 137; DLBY 80; INT CANR-24; MTCW 1, 2

**Buechner, (Carl) Frederick** 1926- **CLC 2, 4, 6, 9; DAM NOV**
See also CA 13-16R; CANR 11, 39, 64; DLBY 80; INT CANR-11; MTCW 1, 2

**Buell, John (Edward)** 1927- **CLC 10**
See also CA 1-4R; CANR 71; DLB 53

**Buero Vallejo, Antonio** 1916- **CLC 15, 46**
See also CA 106; CANR 24, 49, 75; HW 1; MTCW 1, 2

**Bufalino, Gesualdo** 1920(?)- **CLC 74**
See also DLB 196

**Bugayev, Boris Nikolayevich** 1880-1934 **TCLC 7; PC 11**
See also Bely, Andrey
See also CA 104; 165; MTCW 1

**Bukowski, Charles** 1920-1994 **CLC 2, 5, 9, 41, 82, 108; DAM NOV, POET; PC 18**
See also CA 17-20R; 144; CANR 40, 62; DLB 5, 130, 169; MTCW 1, 2

**Bulgakov, Mikhail (Afanas'evich)** 1891-1940 **TCLC 2, 16; DAM DRAM, NOV; SSC 18**
See also CA 105; 152

**Bulgya, Alexander Alexandrovich** 1901-1956

**TCLC 53**
See also Fadeyev, Alexander
See also CA 117

**Bullins, Ed** 1935- **CLC 1, 5, 7; BLC 1; DAM DRAM, MULT; DC 6**
See also BW 2, 3; CA 49-52; CAAS 16; CANR 24, 46, 73; DLB 7, 38; MTCW 1, 2

**Bulwer-Lytton, Edward (George Earle Lytton)** 1803-1873 **NCLC 1, 45**
See also DLB 21

**Bunin, Ivan Alexeyevich** 1870-1953 **TCLC 6; SSC 5**
See also CA 104

**Bunting, Basil** 1900-1985 **CLC 10, 39, 47; DAM POET**
See also CA 53-56; 115; CANR 7; DLB 20

**Bunuel, Luis** 1900-1983 **CLC 16, 80; DAM MULT; HLC**
See also CA 101; 110; CANR 32, 77; HW 1

**Bunyan, John** 1628-1688 **LC 4; DA; DAB; DAC; DAM MST; WLC**
See also CDBLB 1660-1789; DLB 39

**Burckhardt, Jacob (Christoph)** 1818-1897 **NCLC 49**

**Burford, Eleanor**
See Hibbert, Eleanor Alice Burford

**Burgess, Anthony** **CLC 1, 2, 4, 5, 8, 10, 13, 15, 22, 40, 62, 81, 94; DAB**
See also Wilson, John (Anthony) Burgess
See also AAYA 25; CDBLB 1960 to Present; DLB 14, 194; DLBY 98; MTCW 1

**Burke, Edmund** 1729(?)-1797 **LC 7, 36; DA; DAB; DAC; DAM MST; WLC**
See also DLB 104

**Burke, Kenneth (Duva)** 1897-1993 **CLC 2, 24**
See also CA 5-8R; 143; CANR 39, 74; DLB 45, 63; MTCW 1, 2

**Burke, Leda**
See Garnett, David

**Burke, Ralph**
See Silverberg, Robert

**Burke, Thomas** 1886-1945 **TCLC 63**
See also CA 113; 155; DLB 197

**Burney, Fanny** 1752-1840 **NCLC 12, 54**
See also DLB 39

**Burns, Robert** 1759-1796 **LC 3, 29, 40; DA; DAB; DAC; DAM MST, POET; PC 6; WLC**
See also CDBLB 1789-1832; DLB 109

**Burns, Tex**
See L'Amour, Louis (Dearborn)

**Burnshaw, Stanley** 1906- **CLC 3, 13, 44**
See also CA 9-12R; DLB 48; DLBY 97

**<Burr, Anne** 1937- **CLC 6**
See also CA 25-28R

**Burroughs, Edgar Rice** 1875-1950 **TCLC 2, 32; DAM NOV**
See also AAYA 11; CA 104; 132; DLB 8; MTCW 1, 2; SATA 41

**Burroughs, William S(eward)** 1914-1997 **CLC 1, 2, 5, 15, 22, 42, 75, 109; DA; DAB; DAC; DAM MST, NOV, POP; WLC**
See also AITN 2; CA 9-12R; 160; CANR 20, 52; DLB 2, 8, 16, 152; DLBY 81, 97; MTCW 1, 2

**Burton, Sir Richard F(rancis)** 1821-1890 **NCLC 42**
See also DLB 55, 166, 184

**Busch, Frederick** 1941- **CLC 7, 10, 18, 47**
See also CA 33-36R; CAAS 1; CANR 45, 73; DLB 6

**Bush, Ronald** 1946- **CLC 34**
See also CA 136

See Holdstock, Robert P.

**Carlson, Ron(ald F.)** 1947-          **CLC 54**
See also CA 105; CANR 27

**Carlyle, Thomas** 1795-1881    **NCLC 70; DA;**
   **DAB; DAC; DAM MST**
See also CDBLB 1789-1832; DLB 55; 144

**Carman, (William) Bliss** 1861-1929 **TCLC 7;**
   **DAC**
See also CA 104; 152; DLB 92

**Carnegie, Dale** 1888-1955          **TCLC 53**

**Carossa, Hans** 1878-1956           **TCLC 48**
See also CA 170; DLB 66

**Carpenter, Don(ald Richard)** 1931-1995**C L C**
   **41**
See also CA 45-48; 149; CANR 1, 71

**Carpenter, Edward** 1844-1929        **TCLC 88**
See also CA 163

**Carpentier (y Valmont), Alejo** 1904-1980**CLC**
   **8, 11, 38, 110; DAM MULT; HLC**
See also CA 65-68; 97-100; CANR 11, 70; DLB
   113; HW 1, 2

**Carr, Caleb** 1955(?)-              **CLC 86**
See also CA 147; CANR 73

**Carr, Emily** 1871-1945             **TCLC 32**
See also CA 159; DLB 68

**Carr, John Dickson** 1906-1977       **CLC 3**
See also Fairbairn, Roger
See also CA 49-52; 69-72; CANR 3, 33, 60;
   MTCW 1, 2

**Carr, Philippa**
See Hibbert, Eleanor Alice Burford

**Carr, Virginia Spencer** 1929-       **CLC 34**
See also CA 61-64; DLB 111

**Carrere, Emmanuel** 1957-            **CLC 89**

**Carrier, Roch** 1937-**CLC 13, 78; DAC; DAM**
   **MST**
See also CA 130; CANR 61; DLB 53; SATA
   105

**Carroll, James P.** 1943(?)-         **CLC 38**
See also CA 81-84; CANR 73; MTCW 1

**Carroll, Jim** 1951-                **CLC 35**
See also AAYA 17; CA 45-48; CANR 42

**Carroll, Lewis**    **NCLC 2, 53; PC 18; WLC**
See also Dodgson, Charles Lutwidge
See also CDBLB 1832-1890; CLR 2, 18; DLB
   18, 163, 178; DLBY 98; JRDA

**Carroll, Paul Vincent** 1900-1968    **CLC 10**
See also CA 9-12R; 25-28R; DLB 10

**Carruth, Hayden** 1921- **CLC 4, 7, 10, 18, 84;**
   **PC 10**
See also CA 9-12R; CANR 4, 38, 59; DLB 5,
   165; INT CANR-4; MTCW 1, 2; SATA 47

**Carson, Rachel Louise** 1907-1964    **CLC 71;**
   **DAM POP**
See also CA 77-80; CANR 35; MTCW 1, 2;
   SATA 23

**Carter, Angela (Olive)** 1940-1992 **CLC 5, 41,**
   **76; SSC 13**
See also CA 53-56; 136; CANR 12, 36, 61; DLB
   14, 207; MTCW 1, 2; SATA 66; SATA-Obit
   70

**Carter, Nick**
See Smith, Martin Cruz

**Carver, Raymond** 1938-1988 **CLC 22, 36, 53,**
   **55; DAM NOV; SSC 8**
See also CA 33-36R; 126; CANR 17, 34, 61;
   DLB 130; DLBY 84, 88; MTCW 1, 2

**Cary, Elizabeth, Lady Falkland** 1585-1639
   **LC 30**

**Cary, (Arthur) Joyce (Lunel)** 1888-1957
   **TCLC 1, 29**
See also CA 104; 164; CDBLB 1914-1945;
   DLB 15, 100; MTCW 2

**Casanova de Seingalt, Giovanni Jacopo** 1725-
   1798                              **LC 13**

**Casares, Adolfo Bioy**
See Bioy Casares, Adolfo

**Casely-Hayford, J(oseph) E(phraim)** 1866-1930
   **TCLC 24; BLC 1; DAM MULT**
See also BW 2; CA 123; 152

**Casey, John (Dudley)** 1939-         **CLC 59**
See also BEST 90:2; CA 69-72; CANR 23

**Casey, Michael** 1947-               **CLC 2**
See also CA 65-68; DLB 5

**Casey, Patrick**
See Thurman, Wallace (Henry)

**Casey, Warren (Peter)** 1935-1988     **CLC 12**
See also CA 101; 127; INT 101

**Casona, Alejandro**                  **CLC 49**
See also Alvarez, Alejandro Rodriguez

**Cassavetes, John** 1929-1989         **CLC 20**
See also CA 85-88; 127

**Cassian, Nina** 1924-                **PC 17**

**Cassill, R(onald) V(erlin)** 1919-    **CLC 4, 23**
See also CA 9-12R; CAAS 1; CANR 7, 45; DLB
   6

**Cassirer, Ernst** 1874-1945          **TCLC 61**
See also CA 157

**Cassity, (Allen) Turner** 1929-       **CLC 6, 42**
See also CA 17-20R; CAAS 8; CANR 11; DLB
   105

**Castaneda, Carlos (Cesar Aranha)** 1931(?)-
   1998                          **CLC 12, 119**
See also CA 25-28R; CANR 32, 66; HW 1;
   MTCW 1

**Castedo, Elena** 1937-               **CLC 65**
See also CA 132

**Castedo-Ellerman, Elena**
See Castedo, Elena

**Castellanos, Rosario** 1925-1974**CLC 66; DAM**
   **MULT; HLC**
See also CA 131; 53-56; CANR 58; DLB 113;
   HW 1; MTCW 1

**Castelvetro, Lodovico** 1505-1571     **LC 12**

**Castiglione, Baldassare** 1478-1529    **LC 12**

**Castle, Robert**
See Hamilton, Edmond

**Castro, Guillen de** 1569-1631        **LC 19**

**Castro, Rosalia de** 1837-1885 **NCLC 3; DAM**
   **MULT**

**Cather, Willa**
See Cather, Willa Sibert

**Cather, Willa Sibert** 1873-1947    **TCLC 1, 11,**
   **31; DA; DAB; DAC; DAM MST, NOV;**
   **SSC 2; WLC**
See also AAYA 24; CA 104; 128; CDALB 1865-
   1917; DLB 9, 54, 78; DLBD 1; MTCW 1, 2;
   SATA 30

**Catherine, Saint** 1347-1380         **CMLC 27**

**Cato, Marcus Porcius** 234B.C.-149B.C.
   **CMLC 21**
See also DLB 211

**Catton, (Charles) Bruce** 1899-1978   **CLC 35**
See also AITN 1; CA 5-8R; 81-84; CANR 7,
   74; DLB 17; SATA 2; SATA-Obit 24

**Catullus** c. 84B.C.-c. 54B.C.       **CMLC 18**
See also DLB 211

**Cauldwell, Frank**
See King, Francis (Henry)

**Caunitz, William J.** 1933-1996       **CLC 34**
See also BEST 89:3; CA 125; 130; 152; CANR
   73; INT 130

**Causley, Charles (Stanley)** 1917-     **CLC 7**
See also CA 9-12R; CANR 5, 35; CLR 30; DLB
   27; MTCW 1; SATA 3, 66

**Caute, (John) David** 1936-     **CLC 29; DAM**

**NOV**
See also CA 1-4R; CAAS 4; CANR 1, 33, 64;
   DLB 14

**Cavafy, C(onstantine) P(eter)** 1863-1933
   **TCLC 2, 7; DAM POET**
See also Kavafis, Konstantinos Petrou
See also CA 148; MTCW 1

**Cavallo, Evelyn**
See Spark, Muriel (Sarah)

**Cavanna, Betty**                     **CLC 12**
See also Harrison, Elizabeth Cavanna
See also JRDA; MAICYA; SAAS 4; SATA 1,
   30

**Cavendish, Margaret Lucas** 1623-1673**LC 30**
See also DLB 131

**Caxton, William** 1421(?)-1491(?)     **LC 17**
See also DLB 170

**Cayer, D. M.**
See Duffy, Maureen

**Cayrol, Jean** 1911-                 **CLC 11**
See also CA 89-92; DLB 83

**Cela, Camilo Jose** 1916-**CLC 4, 13, 59; DAM**
   **MULT; HLC**
See also BEST 90:2; CA 21-24R; CAAS 10;
   CANR 21, 32, 76; DLBY 89; HW 1; MTCW
   1, 2

**Celan, Paul**     **CLC 10, 19, 53, 82; PC 10**
See also Antschel, Paul
See also DLB 69

**Celine, Louis-Ferdinand CLC 1, 3, 4, 7, 9, 15,**
   **47**
See also Destouches, Louis-Ferdinand
See also DLB 72

**Cellini, Benvenuto** 1500-1571        **LC 7**

**Cendrars, Blaise** 1887-1961      **CLC 18, 106**
See also Sauser-Hall, Frederic

**Cernuda (y Bidon), Luis** 1902-1963  **CLC 54;**
   **DAM POET**
See also CA 131; 89-92; DLB 134; HW 1

**Cervantes (Saavedra), Miguel de** 1547-1616
   **LC 6, 23; DA; DAB; DAC; DAM MST,**
   **NOV; SSC 12; WLC**

**Cesaire, Aime (Fernand)** 1913-   **CLC 19, 32,**
   **112; BLC 1; DAM MULT, POET; PC 25**
See also BW 2, 3; CA 65-68; CANR 24, 43;
   MTCW 1, 2

**Chabon, Michael** 1963-              **CLC 55**
See also CA 139; CANR 57

**Chabrol, Claude** 1930-              **CLC 16**
See also CA 110

**Challans, Mary** 1905-1983
See Renault, Mary
See also CA 81-84; 111; CANR 74; MTCW 2;
   SATA 23; SATA-Obit 36

**Challis, George**
See Faust, Frederick (Schiller)

**Chambers, Aidan** 1934-              **CLC 35**
See also AAYA 27; CA 25-28R; CANR 12, 31,
   58; JRDA; MAICYA; SAAS 12; SATA 1, 69

**Chambers, James** 1948-
See Cliff, Jimmy
See also CA 124

**Chambers, Jessie**
See Lawrence, D(avid) H(erbert Richards)

**Chambers, Robert W(illiam)** 1865-1933
   **TCLC 41**
See also CA 165; DLB 202; SATA 107

**Chandler, Raymond (Thornton)** 1888-1959
   **TCLC 1, 7; SSC 23**
See also AAYA 25; CA 104; 129; CANR 60;
   CDALB 1929-1941; DLBD 6; MTCW 1, 2

**Chang, Eileen** 1920-1995            **SSC 28**
See also CA 166

See also CA 89-92; 139; CANR 20, 46; DLBY 80; MTCW 1

**Comfort, Alex(ander)** 1920-**CLC 7; DAM POP**
See also CA 1-4R; CANR 1, 45; MTCW 1

**Comfort, Montgomery**
See Campbell, (John) Ramsey

**Compton-Burnett, I(vy)** 1884(?)-1969 **CLC 1, 3, 10, 15, 34; DAM NOV**
See also CA 1-4R; 25-28R; CANR 4; DLB 36; MTCW 1

**Comstock, Anthony** 1844-1915 **TCLC 13**
See also CA 110; 169

**Comte, Auguste** 1798-1857 **NCLC 54**

**Conan Doyle, Arthur**
See Doyle, Arthur Conan

**Conde, Maryse** 1937- **CLC 52, 92; BLCS; DAM MULT**
See also Boucolon, Maryse
See also BW 2; MTCW 1

**Condillac, Etienne Bonnot de** 1714-1780 **L C 26**

**Condon, Richard (Thomas)** 1915-1996 **CLC 4, 6, 8, 10, 45, 100; DAM NOV**
See also BEST 90:3; CA 1-4R; 151; CAAS 1; CANR 2, 23; INT CANR-23; MTCW 1, 2

**Confucius** 551B.C.-479B.C. **CMLC 19; DA; DAB; DAC; DAM MST; WLCS**

**Congreve, William** 1670-1729 **LC 5, 21; DA; DAB; DAC; DAM DRAM, MST, POET; DC 2; WLC**
See also CDBLB 1660-1789; DLB 39, 84

**Connell, Evan S(helby), Jr.** 1924- **CLC 4, 6, 45; DAM NOV**
See also AAYA 7; CA 1-4R; CAAS 2; CANR 2, 39, 76; DLB 2; DLBY 81; MTCW 1, 2

**Connelly, Marc(us Cook)** 1890-1980 **CLC 7**
See also CA 85-88; 102; CANR 30; DLB 7; DLBY 80; SATA-Obit 25

**Connor, Ralph** **TCLC 31**
See also Gordon, Charles William
See also DLB 92

**Conrad, Joseph** 1857-1924 **TCLC 1, 6, 13, 25, 43, 57; DA; DAB; DAC; DAM MST, NOV; SSC 9; WLC**
See also AAYA 26; CA 104; 131; CANR 60; CDBLB 1890-1914; DLB 10, 34, 98, 156; MTCW 1, 2; SATA 27

**Conrad, Robert Arnold**
See Hart, Moss

**Conroy, Pat**
See Conroy, (Donald) Pat(rick)
See also MTCW 2

**Conroy, (Donald) Pat(rick)** 1945- **CLC 30, 74; DAM NOV, POP**
See also Conroy, Pat
See also AAYA 8; AITN 1; CA 85-88; CANR 24, 53; DLB 6; MTCW 1

**Constant (de Rebecque), (Henri) Benjamin** 1767-1830 **NCLC 6**
See also DLB 119

**Conybeare, Charles Augustus**
See Eliot, T(homas) S(tearns)

**Cook, Michael** 1933- **CLC 58**
See also CA 93-96; CANR 68; DLB 53

**Cook, Robin** 1940- **CLC 14; DAM POP**
See also BEST 90:2; CA 108; 111; CANR 41; INT 111

**Cook, Roy**
See Silverberg, Robert

**Cooke, Elizabeth** 1948- **CLC 55**
See also CA 129

**Cooke, John Esten** 1830-1886 **NCLC 5**
See also DLB 3

**Cooke, John Estes**
See Baum, L(yman) Frank

**Cooke, M. E.**
See Creasey, John

**Cooke, Margaret**
See Creasey, John

**Cook-Lynn, Elizabeth** 1930- **CLC 93; DAM MULT**
See also CA 133; DLB 175; NNAL

**Cooney, Ray** **CLC 62**

**Cooper, Douglas** 1960- **CLC 86**

**Cooper, Henry St. John**
See Creasey, John

**Cooper, J(oan) California** (?)- **CLC 56; DAM MULT**
See also AAYA 12; BW 1; CA 125; CANR 55; DLB 212

**Cooper, James Fenimore** 1789-1851 **NCLC 1, 27, 54**
See also AAYA 22; CDALB 1640-1865; DLB 3; SATA 19

**Coover, Robert (Lowell)** 1932- **CLC 3, 7, 15, 32, 46, 87; DAM NOV; SSC 15**
See also CA 45-48; CANR 3, 37, 58; DLB 2; DLBY 81; MTCW 1, 2

**Copeland, Stewart (Armstrong)** 1952- **CLC 26**

**Copernicus, Nicolaus** 1473-1543 **LC 45**

**Coppard, A(lfred) E(dgar)** 1878-1957 **TCLC 5; SSC 21**
See also CA 114; 167; DLB 162; YABC 1

**Coppee, Francois** 1842-1908 **TCLC 25**
See also CA 170

**Coppola, Francis Ford** 1939- **CLC 16**
See also CA 77-80; CANR 40, 78; DLB 44

**Corbiere, Tristan** 1845-1875 **NCLC 43**

**Corcoran, Barbara** 1911- **CLC 17**
See also AAYA 14; CA 21-24R; CAAS 2; CANR 11, 28, 48; CLR 50; DLB 52; JRDA; SAAS 20; SATA 3, 77

**Cordelier, Maurice**
See Giraudoux, (Hippolyte) Jean

**Corelli, Marie** 1855-1924 **TCLC 51**
See also Mackay, Mary
See also DLB 34, 156

**Corman, Cid** 1924- **CLC 9**
See also Corman, Sidney
See also CAAS 2; DLB 5, 193

**Corman, Sidney** 1924-
See Corman, Cid
See also CA 85-88; CANR 44; DAM POET

**Cormier, Robert (Edmund)** 1925- **CLC 12, 30; DA; DAB; DAC; DAM MST, NOV**
See also AAYA 3, 19; CA 1-4R; CANR 5, 23, 76; CDALB 1968-1988; CLR 12, 55; DLB 52; INT CANR-23; JRDA; MAICYA; MTCW 1, 2; SATA 10, 45, 83

**Corn, Alfred (DeWitt III)** 1943- **CLC 33**
See also CA 104; CAAS 25; CANR 44; DLB 120; DLBY 80

**Corneille, Pierre** 1606-1684 **LC 28; DAB; DAM MST**

**Cornwell, David (John Moore)** 1931- **CLC 9, 15; DAM POP**
See also le Carre, John
See also CA 5-8R; CANR 13, 33, 59; MTCW 1, 2

**Corso, (Nunzio) Gregory** 1930- **CLC 1, 11**
See also CA 5-8R; CANR 41, 76; DLB 5, 16; MTCW 1, 2

**Cortazar, Julio** 1914-1984 **CLC 2, 3, 5, 10, 13, 15, 33, 34, 92; DAM MULT, NOV; HLC; SSC 7**
See also CA 21-24R; CANR 12, 32; DLB 113;

HW 1, 2; MTCW 1, 2

**CORTES, HERNAN** 1484-1547 **LC 31**

**Corvinus, Jakob**
See Raabe, Wilhelm (Karl)

**Corwin, Cecil**
See Kornbluth, C(yril) M.

**Cosic, Dobrica** 1921- **CLC 14**
See also CA 122; 138; DLB 181

**Costain, Thomas B(ertram)** 1885-1965 **C L C 30**
See also CA 5-8R; 25-28R; DLB 9

**Costantini, Humberto** 1924(?)-1987 **CLC 49**
See also CA 131; 122; HW 1

**Costello, Elvis** 1955- **CLC 21**

**Costenoble, Philostene**
See Ghelderode, Michel de

**Cotes, Cecil V.**
See Duncan, Sara Jeannette

**Cotter, Joseph Seamon Sr.** 1861-1949 **TCLC 28; BLC 1; DAM MULT**
See also BW 1; CA 124; DLB 50

**Couch, Arthur Thomas Quiller**
See Quiller-Couch, SirArthur (Thomas)

**Coulton, James**
See Hansen, Joseph

**Couperus, Louis (Marie Anne)** 1863-1923 **TCLC 15**
See also CA 115

**Coupland, Douglas** 1961- **CLC 85; DAC; DAM POP**
See also CA 142; CANR 57

**Court, Wesli**
See Turco, Lewis (Putnam)

**Courtenay, Bryce** 1933- **CLC 59**
See also CA 138

**Courtney, Robert**
See Ellison, Harlan (Jay)

**Cousteau, Jacques-Yves** 1910-1997 **CLC 30**
See also CA 65-68; 159; CANR 15, 67; MTCW 1; SATA 38, 98

**Coventry, Francis** 1725-1754 **LC 46**

**Cowan, Peter (Walkinshaw)** 1914- **SSC 28**
See also CA 21-24R; CANR 9, 25, 50

**Coward, Noel (Peirce)** 1899-1973 **CLC 1, 9, 29, 51; DAM DRAM**
See also AITN 1; CA 17-18; 41-44R; CANR 35; CAP 2; CDBLB 1914-1945; DLB 10; MTCW 1, 2

**Cowley, Abraham** 1618-1667 **LC 43**
See also DLB 131, 151

**Cowley, Malcolm** 1898-1989 **CLC 39**
See also CA 5-8R; 128; CANR 3, 55; DLB 4, 48; DLBY 81, 89; MTCW 1, 2

**Cowper, William** 1731-1800 **NCLC 8; DAM POET**
See also DLB 104, 109

**Cox, William Trevor** 1928- **CLC 9, 14, 71; DAM NOV**
See also Trevor, William
See also CA 9-12R; CANR 4, 37, 55, 76; DLB 14; INT CANR-37; MTCW 1, 2

**Coyne, P. J.**
See Masters, Hilary

**Cozzens, James Gould** 1903-1978 **CLC 1, 4, 11, 92**
See also CA 9-12R; 81-84; CANR 19; CDALB 1941-1968; DLB 9; DLBD 2; DLBY 84, 97; MTCW 1, 2

**Crabbe, George** 1754-1832 **NCLC 26**
See also DLB 93

**Craddock, Charles Egbert**
See Murfree, Mary Noailles

**Craig, A. A.**

SATA-Brief 30

**Da Ponte, Lorenzo** 1749-1838    **NCLC 50**

**Dario, Ruben** 1867-1916    **TCLC 4; DAM MULT; HLC; PC 15**
See also CA 131; HW 1, 2; MTCW 1, 2

**Darley, George** 1795-1846    **NCLC 2**
See also DLB 96

**Darrow, Clarence (Seward)** 1857-1938 **TCLC 81**
See also CA 164

**Darwin, Charles** 1809-1882    **NCLC 57**
See also DLB 57, 166

**Daryush, Elizabeth** 1887-1977    **CLC 6, 19**
See also CA 49-52; CANR 3; DLB 20

**Dasgupta, Surendranath** 1887-1952 **TCLC 81**
See also CA 157

**Dashwood, Edmee Elizabeth Monica de la Pasture** 1890-1943
See Delafield, E. M.
See also CA 119; 154

**Daudet, (Louis Marie) Alphonse** 1840-1897 **NCLC 1**
See also DLB 123

**Daumal, Rene** 1908-1944    **TCLC 14**
See also CA 114

**Davenant, William** 1606-1668    **LC 13**
See also DLB 58, 126

**Davenport, Guy (Mattison, Jr.)** 1927- **CLC 6, 14, 38; SSC 16**
See also CA 33-36R; CANR 23, 73; DLB 130

**Davidson, Avram (James)** 1923-1993
See Queen, Ellery
See also CA 101; 171; CANR 26; DLB 8

**Davidson, Donald (Grady)** 1893-1968 **CLC 2, 13, 19**
See also CA 5-8R; 25-28R; CANR 4; DLB 45

**Davidson, Hugh**
See Hamilton, Edmond

**Davidson, John** 1857-1909    **TCLC 24**
See also CA 118; DLB 19

**Davidson, Sara** 1943-    **CLC 9**
See also CA 81-84; CANR 44, 68; DLB 185

**Davie, Donald (Alfred)** 1922-1995 **CLC 5, 8, 10, 31**
See also CA 1-4R; 149; CAAS 3; CANR 1, 44; DLB 27; MTCW 1

**Davies, Ray(mond Douglas)** 1944-    **CLC 21**
See also CA 116; 146

**Davies, Rhys** 1901-1978    **CLC 23**
See also CA 9-12R; 81-84; CANR 4; DLB 139, 191

**Davies, (William) Robertson** 1913-1995 **C L C 2, 7, 13, 25, 42, 75, 91; DA; DAB; DAC; DAM MST, NOV, POP; WLC**
See also BEST 89:2; CA 33-36R; 150; CANR 17, 42; DLB 68; INT CANR-17; MTCW 1, 2

**Davies, W(illiam) H(enry)** 1871-1940 **TCLC 5**
See also CA 104; DLB 19, 174

**Davies, Walter C.**
See Kornbluth, C(yril) M.

**Davis, Angela (Yvonne)** 1944- **CLC 77; DAM MULT**
See also BW 2, 3; CA 57-60; CANR 10

**Davis, B. Lynch**
See Bioy Casares, Adolfo; Borges, Jorge Luis

**Davis, Harold Lenoir** 1894-1960    **CLC 49**
See also CA 89-92; DLB 9, 206

**Davis, Rebecca (Blaine) Harding** 1831-1910 **TCLC 6**
See also CA 104; DLB 74

**Davis, Richard Harding** 1864-1916 **TCLC 24**
See also CA 114; DLB 12, 23, 78, 79, 189;

DLBD 13

**Davison, Frank Dalby** 1893-1970    **CLC 15**
See also CA 116

**Davison, Lawrence H.**
See Lawrence, D(avid) H(erbert Richards)

**Davison, Peter (Hubert)** 1928-    **CLC 28**
See also CA 9-12R; CAAS 4; CANR 3, 43; DLB 5

**Davys, Mary** 1674-1732    **LC 1, 46**
See also DLB 39

**Dawson, Fielding** 1930-    **CLC 6**
See also CA 85-88; DLB 130

**Dawson, Peter**
See Faust, Frederick (Schiller)

**Day, Clarence (Shepard, Jr.)** 1874-1935 **TCLC 25**
See also CA 108; DLB 11

**Day, Thomas** 1748-1789    **LC 1**
See also DLB 39; YABC 1

**Day Lewis, C(ecil)** 1904-1972    **CLC 1, 6, 10; DAM POET; PC 11**
See also Blake, Nicholas
See also CA 13-16; 33-36R; CANR 34; CAP 1; DLB 15, 20; MTCW 1, 2

**Dazai Osamu** 1909-1948    **TCLC 11**
See also Tsushima, Shuji
See also CA 164; DLB 182

**de Andrade, Carlos Drummond** 1892-1945
See Drummond de Andrade, Carlos

**Deane, Norman**
See Creasey, John

**de Beauvoir, Simone (Lucie Ernestine Marie Bertrand)**
See Beauvoir, Simone (Lucie Ernestine Marie Bertrand) de

**de Beer, P.**
See Bosman, Herman Charles

**de Brissac, Malcolm**
See Dickinson, Peter (Malcolm)

**de Chardin, Pierre Teilhard**
See Teilhard de Chardin, (Marie Joseph) Pierre

**Dee, John** 1527-1608    **LC 20**

**Deer, Sandra** 1940-    **CLC 45**

**De Ferrari, Gabriella** 1941-    **CLC 65**
See also CA 146

**Defoe, Daniel** 1660(?)-1731    **LC 1, 42; DA; DAB; DAC; DAM MST, NOV; WLC**
See also AAYA 27; CDBLB 1660-1789; DLB 39, 95, 101; JRDA; MAICYA; SATA 22

**de Gourmont, Remy(-Marie-Charles)**
See Gourmont, Remy (-Marie-Charles) de

**de Hartog, Jan** 1914-    **CLC 19**
See also CA 1-4R; CANR 1

**de Hostos, E. M.**
See Hostos (y Bonilla), Eugenio Maria de

**de Hostos, Eugenio M.**
See Hostos (y Bonilla), Eugenio Maria de

**Deighton, Len**    **CLC 4, 7, 22, 46**
See also Deighton, Leonard Cyril
See also AAYA 6; BEST 89:2; CDBLB 1960 to Present; DLB 87

**Deighton, Leonard Cyril** 1929-
See Deighton, Len
See also CA 9-12R; CANR 19, 33, 68; DAM NOV, POP; MTCW 1, 2

**Dekker, Thomas** 1572(?)-1632    **LC 22; DAM DRAM**
See also CDBLB Before 1660; DLB 62, 172

**Delafield, E. M.** 1890-1943    **TCLC 61**
See also Dashwood, Edmee Elizabeth Monica de la Pasture
See also DLB 34

**de la Mare, Walter (John)** 1873-1956 **TCLC 4,**

53; **DAB; DAC; DAM MST, POET; SSC 14; WLC**
See also CA 163; CDBLB 1914-1945; CLR 23; DLB 162; MTCW 1; SATA 16

**Delaney, Franey**
See O'Hara, John (Henry)

**Delaney, Shelagh** 1939- **CLC 29; DAM DRAM**
See also CA 17-20R; CANR 30, 67; CDBLB 1960 to Present; DLB 13; MTCW 1

**Delany, Mary (Granville Pendarves)** 1700-1788 **LC 12**

**Delany, Samuel R(ay, Jr.)** 1942- **CLC 8, 14, 38; BLC 1; DAM MULT**
See also AAYA 24; BW 2, 3; CA 81-84; CANR 27, 43; DLB 8, 33; MTCW 1, 2

**De La Ramee, (Marie) Louise** 1839-1908
See Ouida
See also SATA 20

**de la Roche, Mazo** 1879-1961    **CLC 14**
See also CA 85-88; CANR 30; DLB 68; SATA 64

**De La Salle, Innocent**
See Hartmann, Sadakichi

**Delbanco, Nicholas (Franklin)** 1942- **CLC 6, 13**
See also CA 17-20R; CAAS 2; CANR 29, 55; DLB 6

**del Castillo, Michel** 1933-    **CLC 38**
See also CA 109; CANR 77

**Deledda, Grazia (Cosima)** 1875(?)-1936 **TCLC 23**
See also CA 123

**Delibes, Miguel**    **CLC 8, 18**
See also Delibes Setien, Miguel

**Delibes Setien, Miguel** 1920-
See Delibes, Miguel
See also CA 45-48; CANR 1, 32; HW 1; MTCW 1

**DeLillo, Don** 1936- **CLC 8, 10, 13, 27, 39, 54, 76; DAM NOV, POP**
See also BEST 89:1; CA 81-84; CANR 21, 76; DLB 6, 173; MTCW 1, 2

**de Lisser, H. G.**
See De Lisser, H(erbert) G(eorge)
See also DLB 117

**De Lisser, H(erbert) G(eorge)** 1878-1944 **TCLC 12**
See also de Lisser, H. G.
See also BW 2; CA 109; 152

**Deloney, Thomas** 1560(?)-1600    **LC 41**
See also DLB 167

**Deloria, Vine (Victor), Jr.** 1933- **CLC 21; DAM MULT**
See also CA 53-56; CANR 5, 20, 48; DLB 175; MTCW 1; NNAL; SATA 21

**Del Vecchio, John M(ichael)** 1947- **CLC 29**
See also CA 110; DLBD 9

**de Man, Paul (Adolph Michel)** 1919-1983 **CLC 55**
See also CA 128; 111; CANR 61; DLB 67; MTCW 1, 2

**De Marinis, Rick** 1934-    **CLC 54**
See also CA 57-60; CAAS 24; CANR 9, 25, 50

**Dembry, R. Emmet**
See Murfree, Mary Noailles

**Demby, William** 1922- **CLC 53; BLC 1; DAM MULT**
See also BW 1, 3; CA 81-84; DLB 33

**de Menton, Francisco**
See Chin, Frank (Chew, Jr.)

**Demijohn, Thom**
See Disch, Thomas M(ichael)

**de Montherlant, Henry (Milon)**

See Montherlant, Henry (Milon) de
**Demosthenes** 384B.C.-322B.C.    **CMLC 13**
See also DLB 176
**de Natale, Francine**
See Malzberg, Barry N(athaniel)
**Denby, Edwin (Orr)** 1903-1983    **CLC 48**
See also CA 138; 110
**Denis, Julio**
See Cortazar, Julio
**Denmark, Harrison**
See Zelazny, Roger (Joseph)
**Dennis, John** 1658-1734    **LC 11**
See also DLB 101
**Dennis, Nigel (Forbes)** 1912-1989    **CLC 8**
See also CA 25-28R; 129; DLB 13, 15; MTCW
1
**Dent, Lester** 1904(?)-1959    **TCLC 72**
See also CA 112; 161
**De Palma, Brian (Russell)** 1940-    **CLC 20**
See also CA 109
**De Quincey, Thomas** 1785-1859    **NCLC 4**
See also CDBLB 1789-1832; DLB 110; 144
**Deren, Eleanora** 1908(?)-1961
See Deren, Maya
See also CA 111
**Deren, Maya** 1917-1961    **CLC 16, 102**
See also Deren, Eleanora
**Derleth, August (William)** 1909-1971**CLC 31**
See also CA 1-4R; 29-32R; CANR 4; DLB 9;
DLBD 17; SATA 5
**Der Nister** 1884-1950    **TCLC 56**
**de Routisie, Albert**
See Aragon, Louis
**Derrida, Jacques** 1930-    **CLC 24, 87**
See also CA 124; 127; CANR 76; MTCW 1
**Derry Down Derry**
See Lear, Edward
**Dersonnes, Jacques**
See Simenon, Georges (Jacques Christian)
**Desai, Anita** 1937-**CLC 19, 37, 97; DAB; DAM
NOV**
See also CA 81-84; CANR 33, 53; MTCW 1,
2; SATA 63
**Desai, Kiran** 1971-    **CLC 119**
See also CA 171
**de Saint-Luc, Jean**
See Glassco, John
**de Saint Roman, Arnaud**
See Aragon, Louis
**Descartes, Rene** 1596-1650    **LC 20, 35**
**De Sica, Vittorio** 1901(?)-1974    **CLC 20**
See also CA 117
**Desnos, Robert** 1900-1945    **TCLC 22**
See also CA 121; 151
**Destouches, Louis-Ferdinand** 1894-1961**C L C
9, 15**
See also Celine, Louis-Ferdinand
See also CA 85-88; CANR 28; MTCW 1
**de Tolignac, Gaston**
See Griffith, D(avid Lewelyn) W(ark)
**Deutsch, Babette** 1895-1982    **CLC 18**
See also CA 1-4R; 108; CANR 4, 79; DLB 45;
SATA 1; SATA-Obit 33
**Devenant, William** 1606-1649    **LC 13**
**Devkota, Laxmiprasad** 1909-1959 **TCLC 23**
See also CA 123
**De Voto, Bernard (Augustine)** 1897-1955
**TCLC 29**
See also CA 113; 160; DLB 9
**De Vries, Peter** 1910-1993 **CLC 1, 2, 3, 7, 10,
28, 46; DAM NOV**
See also CA 17-20R; 142; CANR 41; DLB 6;
DLBY 82; MTCW 1, 2

**Dexter, John**
See Bradley, Marion Zimmer
**Dexter, Martin**
See Faust, Frederick (Schiller)
**Dexter, Pete** 1943-    **CLC 34, 55; DAM POP**
See also BEST 89:2; CA 127; 131; INT 131;
MTCW 1
**Diamano, Silmang**
See Senghor, Leopold Sedar
**Diamond, Neil** 1941-    **CLC 30**
See also CA 108
**Diaz del Castillo, Bernal** 1496-1584    **LC 31;
HLCS 1**
**di Bassetto, Corno**
See Shaw, George Bernard
**Dick, Philip K(indred)** 1928-1982**CLC 10, 30,
72; DAM NOV, POP**
See also AAYA 24; CA 49-52; 106; CANR 2,
16; DLB 8; MTCW 1, 2
**Dickens, Charles (John Huffam)** 1812-1870
**NCLC 3, 8, 18, 26, 37, 50; DA; DAB; DAC;
DAM MST, NOV; SSC 17; WLC**
See also AAYA 23; CDBLB 1832-1890; DLB
21, 55, 70, 159, 166; JRDA; MAICYA; SATA
15
**Dickey, James (Lafayette)** 1923-1997 **CLC 1,
2, 4, 7, 10, 15, 47, 109; DAM NOV, POET,
POP**
See also AITN 1, 2; CA 9-12R; 156; CABS 2;
CANR 10, 48, 61; CDALB 1968-1988; DLB
5, 193; DLBD 7; DLBY 82, 93, 96, 97, 98;
INT CANR-10; MTCW 1, 2
**Dickey, William** 1928-1994    **CLC 3, 28**
See also CA 9-12R; 145; CANR 24, 79; DLB 5
**Dickinson, Charles** 1951-    **CLC 49**
See also CA 128
**Dickinson, Emily (Elizabeth)** 1830-1886
**NCLC 21, 77; DA; DAB; DAC; DAM
MST, POET; PC 1; WLC**
See also AAYA 22; CDALB 1865-1917; DLB
1; SATA 29
**Dickinson, Peter (Malcolm)** 1927-**CLC 12, 35**
See also AAYA 9; CA 41-44R; CANR 31, 58;
CLR 29; DLB 87, 161; JRDA; MAICYA;
SATA 5, 62, 95
**Dickson, Carr**
See Carr, John Dickson
**Dickson, Carter**
See Carr, John Dickson
**Diderot, Denis** 1713-1784    **LC 26**
**Didion, Joan** 1934- **CLC 1, 3, 8, 14, 32; DAM
NOV**
See also AITN 1; CA 5-8R; CANR 14, 52, 76;
CDALB 1968-1988; DLB 2, 173, 185;
DLBY 81, 86; MTCW 1, 2
**Dietrich, Robert**
See Hunt, E(verette) Howard, (Jr.)
**Difusa, Pati**
See Almodovar, Pedro
**Dillard, Annie** 1945-    **CLC 9, 60, 115; DAM
NOV**
See also AAYA 6; CA 49-52; CANR 3, 43, 62;
DLBY 80; MTCW 1, 2; SATA 10
**Dillard, R(ichard) H(enry) W(ilde)** 1937-
**CLC 5**
See also CA 21-24R; CAAS 7; CANR 10; DLB
5
**Dillon, Eilis** 1920-1994    **CLC 17**
See also CA 9-12R; 147; CAAS 3; CANR 4,
38, 78; CLR 26; MAICYA; SATA 2, 74;
SATA-Essay 105; SATA-Obit 83
**Dimont, Penelope**
See Mortimer, Penelope (Ruth)

**Dinesen, Isak**    **CLC 10, 29, 95; SSC 7**
See also Blixen, Karen (Christentze Dinesen)
See also MTCW 1
**Ding Ling**    **CLC 68**
See also Chiang, Pin-chin
**Diphusa, Patty**
See Almodovar, Pedro
**Disch, Thomas M(ichael)** 1940-    **CLC 7, 36**
See also AAYA 17; CA 21-24R; CAAS 4;
CANR 17, 36, 54; CLR 18; DLB 8;
MAICYA; MTCW 1, 2; SAAS 15; SATA 92
**Disch, Tom**
See Disch, Thomas M(ichael)
**d'Isly, Georges**
See Simenon, Georges (Jacques Christian)
**Disraeli, Benjamin** 1804-1881    **NCLC 2, 39**
See also DLB 21, 55
**Ditcum, Steve**
See Crumb, R(obert)
**Dixon, Paige**
See Corcoran, Barbara
**Dixon, Stephen** 1936-    **CLC 52; SSC 16**
See also CA 89-92; CANR 17, 40, 54; DLB 130
**Doak, Annie**
See Dillard, Annie
**Dobell, Sydney Thompson** 1824-1874 **N C L C
43**
See also DLB 32
**Doblin, Alfred**    **TCLC 13**
See also Doeblin, Alfred
**Dobrolyubov, Nikolai Alexandrovich** 1836-1861
**NCLC 5**
**Dobson, Austin** 1840-1921    **TCLC 79**
See also DLB 35; 144
**Dobyns, Stephen** 1941-    **CLC 37**
See also CA 45-48; CANR 2, 18
**Doctorow, E(dgar) L(aurence)** 1931- **CLC 6,
11, 15, 18, 37, 44, 65, 113; DAM NOV, POP**
See also AAYA 22; AITN 2; BEST 89:3; CA
45-48; CANR 2, 33, 51, 76; CDALB 1968-
1988; DLB 2, 28, 173; DLBY 80; MTCW 1,
2
**Dodgson, Charles Lutwidge** 1832-1898
See Carroll, Lewis
See also CLR 2; DA; DAB; DAC; DAM MST,
NOV, POET; MAICYA; SATA 100; YABC 2
**Dodson, Owen (Vincent)** 1914-1983 **CLC 79;
BLC 1; DAM MULT**
See also BW 1; CA 65-68; 110; CANR 24; DLB
76
**Doeblin, Alfred** 1878-1957    **TCLC 13**
See also Doblin, Alfred
See also CA 110; 141; DLB 66
**Doerr, Harriet** 1910-    **CLC 34**
See also CA 117; 122; CANR 47; INT 122
**Domecq, H(onorio) Bustos**
See Bioy Casares, Adolfo; Borges, Jorge Luis
**Domini, Rey**
See Lorde, Audre (Geraldine)
**Dominique**
See Proust, (Valentin-Louis-George-Eugene-)
Marcel
**Don, A**
See Stephen, SirLeslie
**Donaldson, Stephen R.** 1947- **CLC 46; DAM
POP**
See also CA 89-92; CANR 13, 55; INT CANR-
13
**Donleavy, J(ames) P(atrick)** 1926-**CLC 1, 4, 6,
10, 45**
See also AITN 2; CA 9-12R; CANR 24, 49, 62,
80; DLB 6, 173; INT CANR-24; MTCW 1,
2

**Donne, John** 1572-1631LC 10, 24; DA; DAB; DAC; DAM MST, POET; PC 1; WLC
See also CDBLB Before 1660; DLB 121, 151

**Donnell, David** 1939(?)- **CLC 34**

**Donoghue, P. S.**
See Hunt, E(verette) Howard, (Jr.)

**Donoso (Yanez), Jose** 1924-1996CLC 4, 8, 11, 32, 99; DAM MULT; HLC; SSC 34
See also CA 81-84; 155; CANR 32, 73; DLB 113; HW 1, 2; MTCW 1, 2

**Donovan, John** 1928-1992 **CLC 35**
See also AAYA 20; CA 97-100; 137; CLR 3; MAICYA; SATA 72; SATA-Brief 29

**Don Roberto**
See Cunninghame Graham, R(obert) B(ontine)

**Doolittle, Hilda** 1886-1961CLC 3, 8, 14, 31, 34, 73; DA; DAC; DAM MST, POET; PC 5; WLC
See also H. D.
See also CA 97-100; CANR 35; DLB 4, 45; MTCW 1, 2

**Dorfman, Ariel** 1942- **CLC 48, 77; DAM MULT; HLC**
See also CA 124; 130; CANR 67, 70; HW 1, 2; INT 130

**Dorn, Edward (Merton)** 1929- **CLC 10, 18**
See also CA 93-96; CANR 42, 79; DLB 5; INT 93-96

**Dorris, Michael (Anthony)** 1945-1997 **C L C 109; DAM MULT, NOV**
See also AAYA 20; BEST 90:1; CA 102; 157; CANR 19, 46, 75; DLB 175; MTCW 2; NNAL; SATA 75; SATA-Obit 94

**Dorris, Michael A.**
See Dorris, Michael (Anthony)

**Dorsan, Luc**
See Simenon, Georges (Jacques Christian)

**Dorsange, Jean**
See Simenon, Georges (Jacques Christian)

**Dos Passos, John (Roderigo)** 1896-1970 C L C 1, 4, 8, 11, 15, 25, 34, 82; DA; DAB; DAC; DAM MST, NOV; WLC
See also CA 1-4R; 29-32R; CANR 3; CDALB 1929-1941; DLB 4, 9; DLBD 1, 15; DLBY 96; MTCW 1, 2

**Dossage, Jean**
See Simenon, Georges (Jacques Christian)

**Dostoevsky, Fedor Mikhailovich** 1821-1881 NCLC 2, 7, 21, 33, 43; DA; DAB; DAC; DAM MST, NOV; SSC 2, 33; WLC

**Doughty, Charles M(ontagu)** 1843-1926 TCLC 27
See also CA 115; DLB 19, 57, 174

**Douglas, Ellen** **CLC 73**
See also Haxton, Josephine Ayres; Williamson, Ellen Douglas

**Douglas, Gavin** 1475(?)-1522 **LC 20**
See also DLB 132

**Douglas, George**
See Brown, George Douglas

**Douglas, Keith (Castellain)** 1920-1944 T C L C 40
See also CA 160; DLB 27

**Douglas, Leonard**
See Bradbury, Ray (Douglas)

**Douglas, Michael**
See Crichton, (John) Michael

**Douglas, (George) Norman** 1868-1952 T C L C 68
See also CA 119; 157; DLB 34, 195

**Douglas, William**
See Brown, George Douglas

**Douglass, Frederick** 1817(?)-1895NCLC 7, 55; BLC 1; DA; DAC; DAM MST, MULT; WLC
See also CDALB 1640-1865; DLB 1, 43, 50, 79; SATA 29

**Dourado, (Waldomiro Freitas) Autran** 1926- CLC 23, 60
See also CA 25-28R; CANR 34; DLB 145; HW 2

**Dourado, Waldomiro Autran**
See Dourado, (Waldomiro Freitas) Autran

**Dove, Rita (Frances)** 1952-CLC 50, 81; BLCS; DAM MULT, POET; PC 6
See also BW 2; CA 109; CAAS 19; CANR 27, 42, 68, 76; CDALBS; DLB 120; MTCW 1

**Doveglion**
See Villa, Jose Garcia

**Dowell, Coleman** 1925-1985 **CLC 60**
See also CA 25-28R; 117; CANR 10; DLB 130

**Dowson, Ernest (Christopher)** 1867-1900 TCLC 4
See also CA 105; 150; DLB 19, 135

**Doyle, A. Conan**
See Doyle, Arthur Conan

**Doyle, Arthur Conan** 1859-1930TCLC 7; DA; DAB; DAC; DAM MST, NOV; SSC 12; WLC
See also AAYA 14; CA 104; 122; CDBLB 1890-1914; DLB 18, 70, 156, 178; MTCW 1, 2; SATA 24

**Doyle, Conan**
See Doyle, Arthur Conan

**Doyle, John**
See Graves, Robert (von Ranke)

**Doyle, Roddy** 1958(?)- **CLC 81**
See also AAYA 14; CA 143; CANR 73; DLB 194

**Doyle, Sir A. Conan**
See Doyle, Arthur Conan

**Doyle, Sir Arthur Conan**
See Doyle, Arthur Conan

**Dr. A**
See Asimov, Isaac; Silverstein, Alvin

**Drabble, Margaret** 1939-CLC 2, 3, 5, 8, 10, 22, 53; DAB; DAC; DAM MST, NOV, POP
See also CA 13-16R; CANR 18, 35, 63; CDBLB 1960 to Present; DLB 14, 155; MTCW 1, 2; SATA 48

**Drapier, M. B.**
See Swift, Jonathan

**Drayham, James**
See Mencken, H(enry) L(ouis)

**Drayton, Michael** 1563-1631 **LC 8; DAM POET**
See also DLB 121

**Dreadstone, Carl**
See Campbell, (John) Ramsey

**Dreiser, Theodore (Herman Albert)** 1871-1945 TCLC 10, 18, 35, 83; DA; DAC; DAM MST, NOV; SSC 30; WLC
See also CA 106; 132; CDALB 1865-1917; DLB 9, 12, 102, 137; DLBD 1; MTCW 1, 2

**Drexler, Rosalyn** 1926- **CLC 2, 6**
See also CA 81-84; CANR 68

**Dreyer, Carl Theodor** 1889-1968 **CLC 16**
See also CA 116

**Drieu la Rochelle, Pierre(-Eugene)** 1893-1945 TCLC 21
See also CA 117; DLB 72

**Drinkwater, John** 1882-1937 **TCLC 57**
See also CA 109; 149; DLB 10, 19, 149

**Drop Shot**
See Cable, George Washington

**Droste-Hulshoff, Annette Freiin von** 1797-1848 NCLC 3
See also DLB 133

**Drummond, Walter**
See Silverberg, Robert

**Drummond, William Henry** 1854-1907T C L C 25
See also CA 160; DLB 92

**Drummond de Andrade, Carlos** 1902-1987 CLC 18
See also Andrade, Carlos Drummond de
See also CA 132; 123

**Drury, Allen (Stuart)** 1918-1998 **CLC 37**
See also CA 57-60; 170; CANR 18, 52; INT CANR-18

**Dryden, John** 1631-1700LC 3, 21; DA; DAB; DAC; DAM DRAM, MST, POET; DC 3; PC 25; WLC
See also CDBLB 1660-1789; DLB 80, 101, 131

**Duberman, Martin (Bauml)** 1930- **CLC 8**
See also CA 1-4R; CANR 2, 63

**Dubie, Norman (Evans)** 1945- **CLC 36**
See also CA 69-72; CANR 12; DLB 120

**Du Bois, W(illiam) E(dward) B(urghardt)** 1868-1963 CLC 1, 2, 13, 64, 96; BLC 1; DA; DAC; DAM MST, MULT, NOV; WLC
See also BW 1, 3; CA 85-88; CANR 34; CDALB 1865-1917; DLB 47, 50, 91; MTCW 1, 2; SATA 42

**Dubus, Andre** 1936- CLC 13, 36, 97; SSC 15
See also CA 21-24R; CANR 17; DLB 130; INT CANR-17

**Duca Minimo**
See D'Annunzio, Gabriele

**Ducharme, Rejean** 1941- **CLC 74**
See also CA 165; DLB 60

**Duclos, Charles Pinot** 1704-1772 **LC 1**

**Dudek, Louis** 1918- **CLC 11, 19**
See also CA 45-48; CAAS 14; CANR 1; DLB 88

**Duerrenmatt, Friedrich** 1921-1990 CLC 1, 4, 8, 11, 15, 43, 102; DAM DRAM
See also CA 17-20R; CANR 33; DLB 69, 124; MTCW 1, 2

**Duffy, Bruce** 1953(?)- **CLC 50**
See also CA 172

**Duffy, Maureen** 1933- **CLC 37**
See also CA 25-28R; CANR 33, 68; DLB 14; MTCW 1

**Dugan, Alan** 1923- **CLC 2, 6**
See also CA 81-84; DLB 5

**du Gard, Roger Martin**
See Martin du Gard, Roger

**Duhamel, Georges** 1884-1966 **CLC 8**
See also CA 81-84; 25-28R; CANR 35; DLB 65; MTCW 1

**Dujardin, Edouard (Emile Louis)** 1861-1949 TCLC 13
See also CA 109; DLB 123

**Dulles, John Foster** 1888-1959 **TCLC 72**
See also CA 115; 149

**Dumas, Alexandre (pere)**
See Dumas, Alexandre (Davy de la Pailleterie)

**Dumas, Alexandre (Davy de la Pailleterie)** 1802-1870 NCLC 11; DA; DAB; DAC; DAM MST, NOV; WLC
See also DLB 119, 192; SATA 18

**Dumas, Alexandre (fils)** 1824-1895NCLC 71; DC 1
See also AAYA 22; DLB 192

**Dumas, Claudine**
See Malzberg, Barry N(athaniel)

**Dumas, Henry L.** 1934-1968 **CLC 6, 62**
See also BW 1; CA 85-88; DLB 41

**du Maurier, Daphne** 1907-1989**CLC 6, 11, 59;
DAB; DAC; DAM MST, POP; SSC 18**
See also CA 5-8R; 128; CANR 6, 55; DLB 191;
MTCW 1, 2; SATA 27; SATA-Obit 60

**Dunbar, Paul Laurence** 1872-1906 **TCLC 2,
12; BLC 1; DA; DAC; DAM MST, MULT,
POET; PC 5; SSC 8; WLC**
See also BW 1, 3; CA 104; 124; CANR 79;
CDALB 1865-1917; DLB 50, 54, 78; SATA
34

**Dunbar, William** 1460(?)-1530(?) **LC 20**
See also DLB 132, 146

**Duncan, Dora Angela**
See Duncan, Isadora

**Duncan, Isadora** 1877(?)-1927 **TCLC 68**
See also CA 118; 149

**Duncan, Lois** 1934- **CLC 26**
See also AAYA 4; CA 1-4R; CANR 2, 23, 36;
CLR 29; JRDA; MAICYA; SAAS 2; SATA
1, 36, 75

**Duncan, Robert (Edward)** 1919-1988 **CLC 1,
2, 4, 7, 15, 41, 55; DAM POET; PC 2**
See also CA 9-12R; 124; CANR 28, 62; DLB
5, 16, 193; MTCW 1, 2

**Duncan, Sara Jeannette** 1861-1922 **TCLC 60**
See also CA 157; DLB 92

**Dunlap, William** 1766-1839 **NCLC 2**
See also DLB 30, 37, 59

**Dunn, Douglas (Eaglesham)** 1942- **CLC 6, 40**
See also CA 45-48; CANR 2, 33; DLB 40;
MTCW 1

**Dunn, Katherine (Karen)** 1945- **CLC 71**
See also CA 33-36R; CANR 72; MTCW 1

**Dunn, Stephen** 1939- **CLC 36**
See also CA 33-36R; CANR 12, 48, 53; DLB
105

**Dunne, Finley Peter** 1867-1936 **TCLC 28**
See also CA 108; DLB 11, 23

**Dunne, John Gregory** 1932- **CLC 28**
See also CA 25-28R; CANR 14, 50; DLBY 80

**Dunsany, Edward John Moreton Drax Plunkett**
1878-1957
See Dunsany, Lord
See also CA 104; 148; DLB 10; MTCW 1

**Dunsany, Lord** **TCLC 2, 59**
See also Dunsany, Edward John Moreton Drax
Plunkett
See also DLB 77, 153, 156

**du Perry, Jean**
See Simenon, Georges (Jacques Christian)

**Durang, Christopher (Ferdinand)** 1949-**C L C
27, 38**
See also CA 105; CANR 50, 76; MTCW 1

**Duras, Marguerite** 1914-1996**CLC 3, 6, 11, 20,
34, 40, 68, 100**
See also CA 25-28R; 151; CANR 50; DLB 83;
MTCW 1, 2

**Durban, (Rosa) Pam** 1947- **CLC 39**
See also CA 123

**Durcan, Paul** 1944-**CLC 43, 70; DAM POET**
See also CA 134

**Durkheim, Emile** 1858-1917 **TCLC 55**

**Durrell, Lawrence (George)** 1912-1990 **C L C
1, 4, 6, 8, 13, 27, 41; DAM NOV**
See also CA 9-12R; 132; CANR 40, 77; CDBLB
1945-1960; DLB 15, 27, 204; DLBY 90;
MTCW 1, 2

**Durrenmatt, Friedrich**
See Duerrenmatt, Friedrich

**Dutt, Toru** 1856-1877 **NCLC 29**

**Dwight, Timothy** 1752-1817 **NCLC 13**
See also DLB 37

**Dworkin, Andrea** 1946- **CLC 43**

See also CA 77-80; CAAS 21; CANR 16, 39,
76; INT CANR-16; MTCW 1, 2

**Dwyer, Deanna**
See Koontz, Dean R(ay)

**Dwyer, K. R.**
See Koontz, Dean R(ay)

**Dwyer, Thomas A.** 1923- **CLC 114**
See also CA 115

**Dye, Richard**
See De Voto, Bernard (Augustine)

**Dylan, Bob** 1941- **CLC 3, 4, 6, 12, 77**
See also CA 41-44R; DLB 16

**Eagleton, Terence (Francis)** 1943-
See Eagleton, Terry
See also CA 57-60; CANR 7, 23, 68; MTCW 1,
2

**Eagleton, Terry** **CLC 63**
See also Eagleton, Terence (Francis)
See also MTCW 1

**Early, Jack**
See Scoppettone, Sandra

**East, Michael**
See West, Morris L(anglo)

**Eastaway, Edward**
See Thomas, (Philip) Edward

**Eastlake, William (Derry)** 1917-1997 **CLC 8**
See also CA 5-8R; 158; CAAS 1; CANR 5, 63;
DLB 6, 206; INT CANR-5

**Eastman, Charles A(lexander)** 1858-1939
**TCLC 55; DAM MULT**
See also DLB 175; NNAL; YABC 1

**Eberhart, Richard (Ghormley)** 1904- **CLC 3,
11, 19, 56; DAM POET**
See also CA 1-4R; CANR 2; CDALB 1941-
1968; DLB 48; MTCW 1

**Eberstadt, Fernanda** 1960- **CLC 39**
See also CA 136; CANR 69

**Echegaray (y Eizaguirre), Jose (Maria Waldo)**
1832-1916 **TCLC 4; HLCS 1**
See also CA 104; CANR 32; HW 1; MTCW 1

**Echeverria, (Jose) Esteban (Antonino)** 1805-
1851 **NCLC 18**

**Echo**
See Proust, (Valentin-Louis-George-Eugene-)
Marcel

**Eckert, Allan W.** 1931- **CLC 17**
See also AAYA 18; CA 13-16R; CANR 14, 45;
INT CANR-14; SAAS 21; SATA 29, 91;
SATA-Brief 27

**Eckhart, Meister** 1260(?)-1328(?) **CMLC 9**
See also DLB 115

**Eckmar, F. R.**
See de Hartog, Jan

**Eco, Umberto** 1932- **CLC 28, 60; DAM NOV,
POP**
See also BEST 90:1; CA 77-80; CANR 12, 33,
55; DLB 196; MTCW 1, 2

**Eddison, E(ric) R(ucker)** 1882-1945**TCLC 15**
See also CA 109; 156

**Eddy, Mary (Ann Morse) Baker** 1821-1910
**TCLC 71**
See also CA 113; 174

**Edel, (Joseph) Leon** 1907-1997 **CLC 29, 34**
See also CA 1-4R; 161; CANR 1, 22; DLB 103;
INT CANR-22

**Eden, Emily** 1797-1869 **NCLC 10**

**Edgar, David** 1948- **CLC 42; DAM DRAM**
See also CA 57-60; CANR 12, 61; DLB 13;
MTCW 1

**Edgerton, Clyde (Carlyle)** 1944- **CLC 39**
See also AAYA 17; CA 118; 134; CANR 64;
INT 134

**Edgeworth, Maria** 1768-1849 **NCLC 1, 51**

See also DLB 116, 159, 163; SATA 21

**Edmonds, Paul**
See Kuttner, Henry

**Edmonds, Walter D(umaux)** 1903-1998 **C L C
35**
See also CA 5-8R; CANR 2; DLB 9; MAICYA;
SAAS 4; SATA 1, 27; SATA-Obit 99

**Edmondson, Wallace**
See Ellison, Harlan (Jay)

**Edson, Russell** **CLC 13**
See also CA 33-36R

**Edwards, Bronwen Elizabeth**
See Rose, Wendy

**Edwards, G(erald) B(asil)** 1899-1976**CLC 25**
See also CA 110

**Edwards, Gus** 1939- **CLC 43**
See also CA 108; INT 108

**Edwards, Jonathan** 1703-1758 **LC 7; DA;
DAC; DAM MST**
See also DLB 24

**Efron, Marina Ivanovna Tsvetaeva**
See Tsvetaeva (Efron), Marina (Ivanovna)

**Ehle, John (Marsden, Jr.)** 1925- **CLC 27**
See also CA 9-12R

**Ehrenbourg, Ilya (Grigoryevich)**
See Ehrenburg, Ilya (Grigoryevich)

**Ehrenburg, Ilya (Grigoryevich)** 1891-1967
**CLC 18, 34, 62**
See also CA 102; 25-28R

**Ehrenburg, Ilyo (Grigoryevich)**
See Ehrenburg, Ilya (Grigoryevich)

**Ehrenreich, Barbara** 1941- **CLC 110**
See also BEST 90:4; CA 73-76; CANR 16, 37,
62; MTCW 1, 2

**Eich, Guenter** 1907-1972 **CLC 15**
See also CA 111; 93-96; DLB 69, 124

**Eichendorff, Joseph Freiherr von** 1788-1857
**NCLC 8**
See also DLB 90

**Eigner, Larry** **CLC 9**
See also Eigner, Laurence (Joel)
See also CAAS 23; DLB 5

**Eigner, Laurence (Joel)** 1927-1996
See Eigner, Larry
See also CA 9-12R; 151; CANR 6; DLB 193

**Einstein, Albert** 1879-1955 **TCLC 65**
See also CA 121; 133; MTCW 1, 2

**Eiseley, Loren Corey** 1907-1977 **CLC 7**
See also AAYA 5; CA 1-4R; 73-76; CANR 6;
DLBD 17

**Eisenstadt, Jill** 1963- **CLC 50**
See also CA 140

**Eisenstein, Sergei (Mikhailovich)** 1898-1948
**TCLC 57**
See also CA 114; 149

**Eisner, Simon**
See Kornbluth, C(yril) M.

**Ekeloef, (Bengt) Gunnar** 1907-1968 **CLC 27;
DAM POET; PC 23**
See also CA 123; 25-28R

**Ekelof, (Bengt) Gunnar**
See Ekeloef, (Bengt) Gunnar

**Ekelund, Vilhelm** 1880-1949 **TCLC 75**

**Ekwensi, C. O. D.**
See Ekwensi, Cyprian (Odiatu Duaka)

**Ekwensi, Cyprian (Odiatu Duaka)** 1921-**CLC
4; BLC 1; DAM MULT**
See also BW 2, 3; CA 29-32R; CANR 18, 42,
74; DLB 117; MTCW 1, 2; SATA 66

**Elaine** **TCLC 18**
See also Leverson, Ada

**El Crummo**
See Crumb, R(obert)

**Fisher, Dorothy (Frances) Canfield** 1879-1958
TCLC **87**
See also CA 114; 136; CANR 80; DLB 9, 102;
MAICYA; YABC 1
**Fisher, M(ary) F(rances) K(ennedy)** 1908-1992
CLC **76, 87**
See also CA 77-80; 138; CANR 44; MTCW 1
**Fisher, Roy** 1930- CLC **25**
See also CA 81-84; CAAS 10; CANR 16; DLB
40
**Fisher, Rudolph** 1897-1934TCLC **11; BLC 2;
DAM MULT; SSC 25**
See also BW 1, 3; CA 107; 124; CANR 80; DLB
51, 102
**Fisher, Vardis (Alvero)** 1895-1968 CLC **7**
See also CA 5-8R; 25-28R; CANR 68; DLB 9,
206
**Fiske, Tarleton**
See Bloch, Robert (Albert)
**Fitch, Clarke**
See Sinclair, Upton (Beall)
**Fitch, John IV**
See Cormier, Robert (Edmund)
**Fitzgerald, Captain Hugh**
See Baum, L(yman) Frank
**FitzGerald, Edward** 1809-1883 NCLC **9**
See also DLB 32
**Fitzgerald, F(rancis) Scott (Key)** 1896-1940
TCLC **1, 6, 14, 28, 55; DA; DAB; DAC;
DAM MST, NOV; SSC 6, 31; WLC**
See also AAYA 24; AITN 1; CA 110; 123;
CDALB 1917-1929; DLB 4, 9, 86; DLBD 1,
15, 16; DLBY 81, 96; MTCW 1, 2
**Fitzgerald, Penelope** 1916- CLC **19, 51, 61**
See also CA 85-88; CAAS 10; CANR 56; DLB
14, 194; MTCW 2
**Fitzgerald, Robert (Stuart)** 1910-1985CLC **39**
See also CA 1-4R; 114; CANR 1; DLBY 80
**FitzGerald, Robert D(avid)** 1902-1987CLC **19**
See also CA 17-20R
**Fitzgerald, Zelda (Sayre)** 1900-1948TCLC **52**
See also CA 117; 126; DLBY 84
**Flanagan, Thomas (James Bonner)** 1923-
CLC **25, 52**
See also CA 108; CANR 55; DLBY 80; INT
108; MTCW 1
**Flaubert, Gustave** 1821-1880NCLC **2, 10, 19,
62, 66; DA; DAB; DAC; DAM MST, NOV;
SSC 11; WLC**
See also DLB 119
**Flecker, Herman Elroy**
See Flecker, (Herman) James Elroy
**Flecker, (Herman) James Elroy** 1884-1915
TCLC **43**
See also CA 109; 150; DLB 10, 19
**Fleming, Ian (Lancaster)** 1908-1964 CLC **3,
30; DAM POP**
See also AAYA 26; CA 5-8R; CANR 59;
CDBLB 1945-1960; DLB 87, 201; MTCW
1, 2; SATA 9
**Fleming, Thomas (James)** 1927- CLC **37**
See also CA 5-8R; CANR 10; INT CANR-10;
SATA 8
**Fletcher, John** 1579-1625 LC **33; DC 6**
See also CDBLB Before 1660; DLB 58
**Fletcher, John Gould** 1886-1950 TCLC **35**
See also CA 107; 167; DLB 4, 45
**Fleur, Paul**
See Pohl, Frederik
**Flooglebuckle, Al**
See Spiegelman, Art
**Flying Officer X**
See Bates, H(erbert) E(rnest)

**Fo, Dario** 1926- CLC **32, 109; DAM DRAM;
DC 10**
See also CA 116; 128; CANR 68; DLBY 97;
MTCW 1, 2
**Fogarty, Jonathan Titulescu Esq.**
See Farrell, James T(homas)
**Folke, Will**
See Bloch, Robert (Albert)
**Follett, Ken(neth Martin)** 1949- CLC **18;
DAM NOV, POP**
See also AAYA 6; BEST 89:4; CA 81-84; CANR
13, 33, 54; DLB 87; DLBY 81; INT CANR-
33; MTCW 1
**Fontane, Theodor** 1819-1898 NCLC **26**
See also DLB 129
**Foote, Horton** 1916-CLC **51, 91; DAM DRAM**
See also CA 73-76; CANR 34, 51; DLB 26; INT
CANR-34
**Foote, Shelby** 1916-CLC **75; DAM NOV, POP**
See also CA 5-8R; CANR 3, 45, 74; DLB 2,
17; MTCW 2
**Forbes, Esther** 1891-1967 CLC **12**
See also AAYA 17; CA 13-14; 25-28R; CAP 1;
CLR 27; DLB 22; JRDA; MAICYA; SATA
2, 100
**Forche, Carolyn (Louise)** 1950- CLC **25, 83,
86; DAM POET; PC 10**
See also CA 109; 117; CANR 50, 74; DLB 5,
193; INT 117; MTCW 1
**Ford, Elbur**
See Hibbert, Eleanor Alice Burford
**Ford, Ford Madox** 1873-1939TCLC **1, 15, 39,
57; DAM NOV**
See also CA 104; 132; CANR 74; CDBLB
1914-1945; DLB 162; MTCW 1, 2
**Ford, Henry** 1863-1947 TCLC **73**
See also CA 115; 148
**Ford, John** 1586-(?) DC **8**
See also CDBLB Before 1660; DAM DRAM;
DLB 58
**Ford, John** 1895-1973 CLC **16**
See also CA 45-48
**Ford, Richard** 1944- CLC **46, 99**
See also CA 69-72; CANR 11, 47; MTCW 1
**Ford, Webster**
See Masters, Edgar Lee
**Foreman, Richard** 1937- CLC **50**
See also CA 65-68; CANR 32, 63
**Forester, C(ecil) S(cott)** 1899-1966 CLC **35**
See also CA 73-76; 25-28R; DLB 191; SATA
13
**Forez**
See Mauriac, Francois (Charles)
**Forman, James Douglas** 1932- CLC **21**
See also AAYA 17; CA 9-12R; CANR 4, 19,
42; JRDA; MAICYA; SATA 8, 70
**Fornes, Maria Irene** 1930-CLC **39, 61; DC 10;
HLCS 1**
See also CA 25-28R; CANR 28; DLB 7; HW 1,
2; INT CANR-28; MTCW 1
**Forrest, Leon (Richard)** 1937-1997 CLC **4;
BLCS**
See also BW 2; CA 89-92; 162; CAAS 7; CANR
25, 52; DLB 33
**Forster, E(dward) M(organ)** 1879-1970 C L C
**1, 2, 3, 4, 9, 10, 13, 15, 22, 45, 77; DA; DAB;
DAC; DAM MST, NOV; SSC 27; WLC**
See also AAYA 2; CA 13-14; 25-28R; CANR
45; CAP 1; CDBLB 1914-1945; DLB 34, 98,
162, 178, 195; DLBD 10; MTCW 1, 2; SATA
57
**Forster, John** 1812-1876 NCLC **11**
See also DLB 144, 184

**Forsyth, Frederick** 1938-CLC **2, 5, 36; DAM
NOV, POP**
See also BEST 89:4; CA 85-88; CANR 38, 62:
DLB 87; MTCW 1, 2
**Forten, Charlotte L.** TCLC **16; BLC 2**
See also Grimke, Charlotte L(ottie) Forten
See also DLB 50
**Foscolo, Ugo** 1778-1827 NCLC **8**
**Fosse, Bob** CLC **20**
See also Fosse, Robert Louis
**Fosse, Robert Louis** 1927-1987
See Fosse, Bob
See also CA 110; 123
**Foster, Stephen Collins** 1826-1864 NCLC **26**
**Foucault, Michel** 1926-1984 CLC **31, 34, 69**
See also CA 105; 113; CANR 34; MTCW 1, 2
**Fouque, Friedrich (Heinrich Karl) de la Motte**
1777-1843 NCLC **2**
See also DLB 90
**Fourier, Charles** 1772-1837 NCLC **51**
**Fournier, Henri Alban** 1886-1914
See Alain-Fournier
See also CA 104
**Fournier, Pierre** 1916- CLC **11**
See also Gascar, Pierre
See also CA 89-92; CANR 16, 40
**Fowles, John (Philip)** 1926-CLC **1, 2, 3, 4, 6,
9, 10, 15, 33, 87; DAB; DAC; DAM MST;
SSC 33**
See also CA 5-8R; CANR 25, 71; CDBLB 1960
to Present; DLB 14, 139, 207; MTCW 1, 2;
SATA 22
**Fox, Paula** 1923- CLC **2, 8**
See also AAYA 3; CA 73-76; CANR 20, 36,
62; CLR 1, 44; DLB 52; JRDA; MAICYA;
MTCW 1; SATA 17, 60
**Fox, William Price (Jr.)** 1926- CLC **22**
See also CA 17-20R; CAAS 19; CANR 11; DLB
2; DLBY 81
**Foxe, John** 1516(?)-1587 LC **14**
See also DLB 132
**Frame, Janet** 1924-CLC **2, 3, 6, 22, 66, 96; SSC
29**
See also Clutha, Janet Paterson Frame
**France, Anatole** TCLC **9**
See also Thibault, Jacques Anatole Francois
See also DLB 123; MTCW 1
**Francis, Claude** 19(?)- CLC **50**
**Francis, Dick** 1920-CLC **2, 22, 42, 102; DAM
POP**
See also AAYA 5, 21; BEST 89:3; CA 5-8R;
CANR 9, 42, 68; CDBLB 1960 to Present;
DLB 87; INT CANR-9; MTCW 1, 2
**Francis, Robert (Churchill)** 1901-1987 C L C
**15**
See also CA 1-4R; 123; CANR 1
**Frank, Anne(lies Marie)** 1929-1945TCLC **17;
DA; DAB; DAC; DAM MST; WLC**
See also AAYA 12; CA 113; 133; CANR 68;
MTCW 1, 2; SATA 87; SATA-Brief 42
**Frank, Bruno** 1887-1945 TCLC **81**
See also DLB 118
**Frank, Elizabeth** 1945- CLC **39**
See also CA 121; 126; CANR 78; INT 126
**Frankl, Viktor E(mil)** 1905-1997 CLC **93**
See also CA 65-68; 161
**Franklin, Benjamin**
See Hasek, Jaroslav (Matej Frantisek)
**Franklin, Benjamin** 1706-1790 LC **25; DA;
DAB; DAC; DAM MST; WLCS**
See also CDALB 1640-1865; DLB 24, 43, 73
**Franklin, (Stella Maria Sarah) Miles (Lampe)**
1879-1954 TCLC **7**

See also CA 104; 164

**Fraser, (Lady) Antonia (Pakenham)** 1932-
CLC 32, 107
See also CA 85-88; CANR 44, 65; MTCW 1,
2; SATA-Brief 32

**Fraser, George MacDonald** 1925-        **CLC 7**
See also CA 45-48; CANR 2, 48, 74; MTCW 1

**Fraser, Sylvia** 1935-                        **CLC 64**
See also CA 45-48; CANR 1, 16, 60

**Frayn, Michael** 1933-CLC 3, 7, 31, 47; DAM
DRAM, NOV
See also CA 5-8R; CANR 30, 69; DLB 13, 14,
194; MTCW 1, 2

**Fraze, Candida (Merrill)** 1945-        **CLC 50**
See also CA 126

**Frazer, J(ames) G(eorge)** 1854-1941TCLC 32
See also CA 118

**Frazer, Robert Caine**
See Creasey, John

**Frazer, Sir James George**
See Frazer, J(ames) G(eorge)

**Frazier, Charles** 1950-                **CLC 109**
See also CA 161

**Frazier, Ian** 1951-                        **CLC 46**
See also CA 130; CANR 54

**Frederic, Harold** 1856-1898            **NCLC 10**
See also DLB 12, 23; DLBD 13

**Frederick, John**
See Faust, Frederick (Schiller)

**Frederick the Great** 1712-1786            **LC 14**

**Fredro, Aleksander** 1793-1876            **NCLC 8**

**Freeling, Nicolas** 1927-                **CLC 38**
See also CA 49-52; CAAS 12; CANR 1, 17,
50; DLB 87

**Freeman, Douglas Southall** 1886-1953 **T C L C
11**
See also CA 109; DLB 17; DLBD 17

**Freeman, Judith** 1946-                **CLC 55**
See also CA 148

**Freeman, Mary Eleanor Wilkins** 1852-1930
**TCLC 9; SSC 1**
See also CA 106; DLB 12, 78

**Freeman, R(ichard) Austin** 1862-1943 **T C L C
21**
See also CA 113; DLB 70

**French, Albert** 1943-                    **CLC 86**
See also BW 3; CA 167

**French, Marilyn** 1929-CLC 10, 18, 60; DAM
DRAM, NOV, POP
See also CA 69-72; CANR 3, 31; INT CANR-
31; MTCW 1, 2

**French, Paul**
See Asimov, Isaac

**Freneau, Philip Morin** 1752-1832        **NCLC 1**
See also DLB 37, 43

**Freud, Sigmund** 1856-1939                **TCLC 52**
See also CA 115; 133; CANR 69; MTCW 1, 2

**Friedan, Betty (Naomi)** 1921-            **CLC 74**
See also CA 65-68; CANR 18, 45, 74; MTCW
1, 2

**Friedlander, Saul** 1932-                **CLC 90**
See also CA 117; 130; CANR 72

**Friedman, B(ernard) H(arper)** 1926- CLC 7
See also CA 1-4R; CANR 3, 48

**Friedman, Bruce Jay** 1930-            **CLC 3, 5, 56**
See also CA 9-12R; CANR 25, 52; DLB 2, 28;
INT CANR-25

**Friel, Brian** 1929-    **CLC 5, 42, 59, 115; DC 8**
See also CA 21-24R; CANR 33, 69; DLB 13;
MTCW 1

**Friis-Baastad, Babbis Ellinor** 1921-1970 C L C
12
See also CA 17-20R; 134; SATA 7

**Frisch, Max (Rudolf)** 1911-1991CLC 3, 9, 14,
18, 32, 44; DAM DRAM, NOV
See also CA 85-88; 134; CANR 32, 74; DLB
69, 124; MTCW 1, 2

**Fromentin, Eugene (Samuel Auguste)** 1820-
1876                                    **NCLC 10**
See also DLB 123

**Frost, Frederick**
See Faust, Frederick (Schiller)

**Frost, Robert (Lee)** 1874-1963CLC 1, 3, 4, 9,
10, 13, 15, 26, 34, 44; DA; DAB; DAC;
DAM MST, POET; PC 1; WLC
See also AAYA 21; CA 89-92; CANR 33;
CDALB 1917-1929; DLB 54; DLBD 7;
MTCW 1, 2; SATA 14

**Froude, James Anthony** 1818-1894 NCLC 43
See also DLB 18, 57, 144

**Froy, Herald**
See Waterhouse, Keith (Spencer)

**Fry, Christopher** 1907- CLC 2, 10, 14; DAM
DRAM
See also CA 17-20R; CAAS 23; CANR 9, 30,
74; DLB 13; MTCW 1, 2; SATA 66

**Frye, (Herman) Northrop** 1912-1991CLC 24,
70
See also CA 5-8R; 133; CANR 8, 37; DLB 67,
68; MTCW 1, 2

**Fuchs, Daniel** 1909-1993                **CLC 8, 22**
See also CA 81-84; 142; CAAS 5; CANR 40;
DLB 9, 26, 28; DLBY 93

**Fuchs, Daniel** 1934-                    **CLC 34**
See also CA 37-40R; CANR 14, 48

**Fuentes, Carlos** 1928-CLC 3, 8, 10, 13, 22, 41,
60, 113; DA; DAB; DAC; DAM MST,
MULT, NOV; HLC; SSC 24; WLC
See also AAYA 4; AITN 2; CA 69-72; CANR
10, 32, 68; DLB 113; HW 1, 2; MTCW 1, 2

**Fuentes, Gregorio Lopez y**
See Lopez y Fuentes, Gregorio

**Fugard, (Harold) Athol** 1932-CLC 5, 9, 14, 25,
40, 80; DAM DRAM; DC 3
See also AAYA 17; CA 85-88; CANR 32, 54;
MTCW 1

**Fugard, Sheila** 1932-                    **CLC 48**
See also CA 125

**Fuller, Charles (H., Jr.)** 1939-CLC 25; BLC 2;
DAM DRAM, MULT; DC 1
See also BW 2; CA 108; 112; DLB 38; INT 112;
MTCW 1

**Fuller, John (Leopold)** 1937-            **CLC 62**
See also CA 21-24R; CANR 9, 44; DLB 40

**Fuller, Margaret**                        **NCLC 5, 50**
See also Ossoli, Sarah Margaret (Fuller
marchesa d')

**Fuller, Roy (Broadbent)** 1912-1991CLC 4, 28
See also CA 5-8R; 135; CAAS 10; CANR 53;
DLB 15, 20; SATA 87

**Fulton, Alice** 1952-                    **CLC 52**
See also CA 116; CANR 57; DLB 193

**Furphy, Joseph** 1843-1912                **TCLC 25**
See also CA 163

**Fussell, Paul** 1924-                    **CLC 74**
See also BEST 90:1; CA 17-20R; CANR 8, 21,
35, 69; INT CANR-21; MTCW 1, 2

**Futabatei, Shimei** 1864-1909            **TCLC 44**
See also CA 162; DLB 180

**Futrelle, Jacques** 1875-1912            **TCLC 19**
See also CA 113; 155

**Gaboriau, Emile** 1835-1873              **NCLC 14**

**Gadda, Carlo Emilio** 1893-1973        **CLC 11**
See also CA 89-92; DLB 177

**Gaddis, William** 1922-1998CLC 1, 3, 6, 8, 10,
19, 43, 86

See also CA 17-20R; 172; CANR 21, 48; DLB
2; MTCW 1, 2

**Gage, Walter**
See Inge, William (Motter)

**Gaines, Ernest J(ames)** 1933- CLC 3, 11, 18,
86; BLC 2; DAM MULT
See also AAYA 18; AITN 1; BW 2, 3; CA 9-
12R; CANR 6, 24, 42, 75; CDALB 1968-
1988; DLB 2, 33, 152; DLBY 80; MTCW 1,
2; SATA 86

**Gaitskill, Mary** 1954-                    **CLC 69**
See also CA 128; CANR 61

**Galdos, Benito Perez**
See Perez Galdos, Benito

**Gale, Zona** 1874-1938TCLC 7; DAM DRAM
See also CA 105; 153; DLB 9, 78

**Galeano, Eduardo (Hughes)** 1940- CLC 72;
HLCS 1
See also CA 29-32R; CANR 13, 32; HW 1

**Galiano, Juan Valera y Alcala**
See Valera y Alcala-Galiano, Juan

**Galilei, Galileo** 1546-1642                **LC 45**

**Gallagher, Tess** 1943-    **CLC 18, 63; DAM
POET; PC 9**
See also CA 106; DLB 212

**Gallant, Mavis** 1922-    CLC 7, 18, 38; DAC;
DAM MST; SSC 5
See also CA 69-72; CANR 29, 69; DLB 53;
MTCW 1, 2

**Gallant, Roy A(rthur)** 1924-            **CLC 17**
See also CA 5-8R; CANR 4, 29, 54; CLR 30;
MAICYA; SATA 4, 68

**Gallico, Paul (William)** 1897-1976        **CLC 2**
See also AITN 1; CA 5-8R; 69-72; CANR 23;
DLB 9, 171; MAICYA; SATA 13

**Gallo, Max Louis** 1932-                    **CLC 95**
See also CA 85-88

**Gallois, Lucien**
See Desnos, Robert

**Gallup, Ralph**
See Whitemore, Hugh (John)

**Galsworthy, John** 1867-1933TCLC 1, 45; DA;
DAB; DAC; DAM DRAM, MST, NOV;
SSC 22; WLC
See also CA 104; 141; CANR 75; CDBLB
1890-1914; DLB 10, 34, 98, 162; DLBD 16;
MTCW 1

**Galt, John** 1779-1839                        **NCLC 1**
See also DLB 99, 116, 159

**Galvin, James** 1951-                        **CLC 38**
See also CA 108; CANR 26

**Gamboa, Federico** 1864-1939            **TCLC 36**
See also CA 167; HW 2

**Gandhi, M. K.**
See Gandhi, Mohandas Karamchand

**Gandhi, Mahatma**
See Gandhi, Mohandas Karamchand

**Gandhi, Mohandas Karamchand** 1869-1948
**TCLC 59; DAM MULT**
See also CA 121; 132; MTCW 1, 2

**Gann, Ernest Kellogg** 1910-1991        **CLC 23**
See also AITN 1; CA 1-4R; 136; CANR 1

**Garcia, Cristina** 1958-                    **CLC 76**
See also CA 141; CANR 73; HW 2

**Garcia Lorca, Federico** 1898-1936TCLC 1, 7,
49; DA; DAB; DAC; DAM DRAM, MST,
MULT, POET; DC 2; HLC; PC 3; WLC
See also CA 104; 131; DLB 108; HW 1, 2;
MTCW 1, 2

**Garcia Marquez, Gabriel (Jose)** 1928-CLC 2,
3, 8, 10, 15, 27, 47, 55, 68; DA; DAB; DAC;
DAM MST, MULT, NOV, POP; HLC; SSC
8; WLC

See also AAYA 3; BEST 89:1, 90:4; CA 33-36R; CANR 10, 28, 50, 75; DLB 113; HW 1, 2; MTCW 1, 2

**Gard, Janice**
See Latham, Jean Lee

**Gard, Roger Martin du**
See Martin du Gard, Roger

**Gardam, Jane** 1928-                        **CLC 43**
See also CA 49-52; CANR 2, 18, 33, 54; CLR 12; DLB 14, 161; MAICYA; MTCW 1; SAAS 9; SATA 39, 76; SATA-Brief 28

**Gardner, Herb(ert)** 1934-                **CLC 44**
See also CA 149

**Gardner, John (Champlin), Jr.** 1933-1982
**CLC 2, 3, 5, 7, 8, 10, 18, 28, 34; DAM NOV, POP; SSC 7**
See also AITN 1; CA 65-68; 107; CANR 33, 73; CDALBS; DLB 2; DLBY 82; MTCW 1; SATA 40; SATA-Obit 31

**Gardner, John (Edmund)** 1926-**CLC 30; DAM POP**
See also CA 103; CANR 15, 69; MTCW 1

**Gardner, Miriam**
See Bradley, Marion Zimmer

**Gardner, Noel**
See Kuttner, Henry

**Gardons, S. S.**
See Snodgrass, W(illiam) D(e Witt)

**Garfield, Leon** 1921-1996                **CLC 12**
See also AAYA 8; CA 17-20R; 152; CANR 38, 41, 78; CLR 21; DLB 161; JRDA; MAICYA; SATA 1, 32, 76; SATA-Obit 90

**Garland, (Hannibal) Hamlin** 1860-1940
**TCLC 3; SSC 18**
See also CA 104; DLB 12, 71, 78, 186

**Garneau, (Hector de) Saint-Denys** 1912-1943
**TCLC 13**
See also CA 111; DLB 88

**Garner, Alan** 1934-**CLC 17; DAB; DAM POP**
See also AAYA 18; CA 73-76; CANR 15, 64; CLR 20; DLB 161; MAICYA; MTCW 1, 2; SATA 18, 69

**Garner, Hugh** 1913-1979                  **CLC 13**
See also CA 69-72; CANR 31; DLB 68

**Garnett, David** 1892-1981                **CLC 3**
See also CA 5-8R; 103; CANR 17, 79; DLB 34; MTCW 2

**Garos, Stephanie**
See Katz, Steve

**Garrett, George (Palmer)** ·1929-**CLC 3, 11, 51; SSC 30**
See also CA 1-4R; CAAS 5; CANR 1, 42, 67; DLB 2, 5, 130, 152; DLBY 83

**Garrick, David** 1717-1779        **LC 15; DAM DRAM**
See also DLB 84

**Garrigue, Jean** 1914-1972                **CLC 2, 8**
See also CA 5-8R; 37-40R; CANR 20

**Garrison, Frederick**
See Sinclair, Upton (Beall)

**Garth, Will**
See Hamilton, Edmond; Kuttner, Henry

**Garvey, Marcus (Moziah, Jr.)** 1887-1940
**TCLC 41; BLC 2; DAM MULT**
See also BW 1; CA 120; 124; CANR 79

**Gary, Romain**                            **CLC 25**
See also Kacew, Romain
See also DLB 83

**Gascar, Pierre**                          **CLC 11**
See also Fournier, Pierre

**Gascoyne, David (Emery)** 1916-          **CLC 45**
See also CA 65-68; CANR 10, 28, 54; DLB 20; MTCW 1

**Gaskell, Elizabeth Cleghorn** 1810-1865**NCLC 70; DAB; DAM MST; SSC 25**
See also CDBLB 1832-1890; DLB 21, 144, 159

**Gass, William H(oward)** 1924-**CLC 1, 2, 8, 11, 15, 39; SSC 12**
See also CA 17-20R; CANR 30, 71; DLB 2; MTCW 1, 2

**Gasset, Jose Ortega y**
See Ortega y Gasset, Jose

**Gates, Henry Louis, Jr.** 1950-**CLC 65; BLCS; DAM MULT**
See also BW 2, 3; CA 109; CANR 25, 53, 75; DLB 67; MTCW 1

**Gautier, Theophile** 1811-1872    **NCLC 1, 59; DAM POET; PC 18; SSC 20**
See also DLB 119

**Gawsworth, John**
See Bates, H(erbert) E(rnest)

**Gay, John** 1685-1732        **LC 49; DAM DRAM**
See also DLB 84, 95

**Gay, Oliver**
See Gogarty, Oliver St. John

**Gaye, Marvin (Penze)** 1939-1984          **CLC 26**
See also CA 112

**Gebler, Carlo (Ernest)** 1954-           **CLC 39**
See also CA 119; 133

**Gee, Maggie (Mary)** 1948-               **CLC 57**
See also CA 130; DLB 207

**Gee, Maurice (Gough)** 1931-             **CLC 29**
See also CA 97-100; CANR 67; CLR 56; SATA 46, 101

**Gelbart, Larry (Simon)** 1923-           **CLC 21, 61**
See also CA 73-76; CANR 45

**Gelber, Jack** 1932-              **CLC 1, 6, 14, 79**
See also CA 1-4R; CANR 2; DLB 7

**Gellhorn, Martha (Ellis)** 1908-1998 **CLC 14, 60**
See also CA 77-80; 164; CANR 44; DLBY 82, 98

**Genet, Jean** 1910-1986**CLC 1, 2, 5, 10, 14, 44, 46; DAM DRAM**
See also CA 13-16R; CANR 18; DLB 72; DLBY 86; MTCW 1, 2

**Gent, Peter** 1942-                       **CLC 29**
See also AITN 1; CA 89-92; DLBY 82

**Gentlewoman in New England, A**
See Bradstreet, Anne

**Gentlewoman in Those Parts, A**
See Bradstreet, Anne

**George, Jean Craighead** 1919-           **CLC 35**
See also AAYA 8; CA 5-8R; CANR 25; CLR 1; DLB 52; JRDA; MAICYA; SATA 2, 68

**George, Stefan (Anton)** 1868-1933**TCLC 2, 14**
See also CA 104

**Georges, Georges Martin**
See Simenon, Georges (Jacques Christian)

**Gerhardi, William Alexander**
See Gerhardie, William Alexander

**Gerhardie, William Alexander** 1895-1977
**CLC 5**
See also CA 25-28R; 73-76; CANR 18; DLB 36

**Gerstler, Amy** 1956-                     **CLC 70**
See also CA 146

**Gertler, T.**                             **CLC 34**
See also CA 116; 121; INT 121

**Ghalib**                                  **NCLC 39**
See also Ghalib, Hsadullah Khan

**Ghalib, Hsadullah Khan** 1797-1869
See Ghalib
See also DAM POET

**Ghelderode, Michel de** 1898-1962**CLC 6, 11; DAM DRAM**

See also CA 85-88; CANR 40, 77

**Ghiselin, Brewster** 1903-                **CLC 23**
See also CA 13-16R; CAAS 10; CANR 13

**Ghose, Aurabinda** 1872-1950             **TCLC 63**
See also CA 163

**Ghose, Zulfikar** 1935-                   **CLC 42**
See also CA 65-68; CANR 67

**Ghosh, Amitav** 1956-                     **CLC 44**
See also CA 147; CANR 80

**Giacosa, Giuseppe** 1847-1906            **TCLC 7**
See also CA 104

**Gibb, Lee**
See Waterhouse, Keith (Spencer)

**Gibbon, Lewis Grassic**                   **TCLC 4**
See also Mitchell, James Leslie

**Gibbons, Kaye** 1960-**CLC 50, 88; DAM POP**
See also CA 151; CANR 75; MTCW 1

**Gibran, Kahlil** 1883-1931 **TCLC 1, 9; DAM POET, POP; PC 9**
See also CA 104; 150; MTCW 2

**Gibran, Khalil**
See Gibran, Kahlil

**Gibson, William** 1914- **CLC 23; DA; DAB; DAC; DAM DRAM, MST**
See also CA 9-12R; CANR 9, 42, 75; DLB 7; MTCW 1; SATA 66

**Gibson, William (Ford)** 1948-   **CLC 39, 63; DAM POP**
See also AAYA 12; CA 126; 133; CANR 52; MTCW 1

**Gide, Andre (Paul Guillaume)** 1869-1951
**TCLC 5, 12, 36; DA; DAB; DAC; DAM MST, NOV; SSC 13; WLC**
See also CA 104; 124; DLB 65; MTCW 1, 2

**Gifford, Barry (Colby)** 1946-            **CLC 34**
See also CA 65-68; CANR 9, 30, 40

**Gilbert, Frank**
See De Voto, Bernard (Augustine)

**Gilbert, W(illiam) S(chwenck)** 1836-1911
**TCLC 3; DAM DRAM, POET**
See also CA 104; 173; SATA 36

**Gilbreth, Frank B., Jr.** 1911-           **CLC 17**
See also CA 9-12R; SATA 2

**Gilchrist, Ellen** 1935-**CLC 34, 48; DAM POP; SSC 14**
See also CA 113; 116; CANR 41, 61; DLB 130; MTCW 1, 2

**Giles, Molly** 1942-                       **CLC 39**
See also CA 126

**Gill, Eric** 1882-1940                     **TCLC 85**

**Gill, Patrick**
See Creasey, John

**Gilliam, Terry (Vance)** 1940-            **CLC 21**
See also Monty Python
See also AAYA 19; CA 108; 113; CANR 35; INT 113

**Gillian, Jerry**
See Gilliam, Terry (Vance)

**Gilliatt, Penelope (Ann Douglass)** 1932-1993
**CLC 2, 10, 13, 53**
See also AITN 2; CA 13-16R; 141; CANR 49; DLB 14

**Gilman, Charlotte (Anna) Perkins (Stetson)**
1860-1935          **TCLC 9, 37; SSC 13**
See also CA 106; 150; MTCW 1

**Gilmour, David** 1949-                     **CLC 35**
See also CA 138, 147

**Gilpin, William** 1724-1804               **NCLC 30**

**Gilray, J. D.**
See Mencken, H(enry) L(ouis)

**Gilroy, Frank D(aniel)** 1925-            **CLC 2**
See also CA 81-84; CANR 32, 64; DLB 7

**Gilstrap, John** 1957(?)-                 **CLC 99**

MULT; HLC
See also CA 85-88; CANR 32, 61; HW 1, 2; MTCW 1, 2

**Gozzano, Guido** 1883-1916 **PC 10**
See also CA 154; DLB 114

**Gozzi, (Conte) Carlo** 1720-1806 **NCLC 23**

**Grabbe, Christian Dietrich** 1801-1836**NCLC 2**
See also DLB 133

**Grace, Patricia** 1937- **CLC 56**

**Gracian y Morales, Baltasar** 1601-1658**LC 15**

**Gracq, Julien** **CLC 11, 48**
See also Poirier, Louis
See also DLB 83

**Grade, Chaim** 1910-1982 **CLC 10**
See also CA 93-96; 107

**Graduate of Oxford, A**
See Ruskin, John

**Grafton, Garth**
See Duncan, Sara Jeannette

**Graham, John**
See Phillips, David Graham

**Graham, Jorie** 1951- **CLC 48, 118**
See also CA 111; CANR 63; DLB 120

**Graham, R(obert) B(ontine) Cunninghame**
See Cunninghame Graham, R(obert) B(ontine)
See also DLB 98, 135, 174

**Graham, Robert**
See Haldeman, Joe (William)

**Graham, Tom**
See Lewis, (Harry) Sinclair

**Graham, W(illiam) S(ydney)** 1918-1986 **C L C 29**
See also CA 73-76; 118; DLB 20

**Graham, Winston (Mawdsley)** 1910- **CLC 23**
See also CA 49-52; CANR 2, 22, 45, 66; DLB 77

**Grahame, Kenneth** 1859-1932**TCLC 64; DAB**
See also CA 108; 136; CANR 80; CLR 5; DLB 34, 141, 178; MAICYA; MTCW 2; SATA 100; YABC 1

**Granovsky, Timofei Nikolaevich** 1813-1855 **NCLC 75**
See also DLB 198

**Grant, Skeeter**
See Spiegelman, Art

**Granville-Barker, Harley** 1877-1946**TCLC 2; DAM DRAM**
See also Barker, Harley Granville
See also CA 104

**Grass, Guenter (Wilhelm)** 1927-**CLC 1, 2, 4, 6, 11, 15, 22, 32, 49, 88; DA; DAB; DAC; DAM MST, NOV; WLC**
See also CA 13-16R; CANR 20, 75; DLB 75, 124; MTCW 1, 2

**Gratton, Thomas**
See Hulme, T(homas) E(rnest)

**Grau, Shirley Ann** 1929- **CLC 4, 9; SSC 15**
See also CA 89-92; CANR 22, 69; DLB 2; INT CANR-22; MTCW 1

**Gravel, Fern**
See Hall, James Norman

**Graver, Elizabeth** 1964- **CLC 70**
See also CA 135; CANR 71

**Graves, Richard Perceval** 1945- **CLC 44**
See also CA 65-68; CANR 9, 26, 51

**Graves, Robert (von Ranke)** 1895-1985 **C L C 1, 2, 6, 11, 39, 44, 45; DAB; DAC; DAM MST, POET; PC 6**
See also CA 5-8R; 117; CANR 5, 36; CDBLB 1914-1945; DLB 20, 100, 191; DLBD 18; DLBY 85; MTCW 1, 2; SATA 45

**Graves, Valerie**

See Bradley, Marion Zimmer

**Gray, Alasdair (James)** 1934- **CLC 41**
See also CA 126; CANR 47, 69; DLB 194; INT 126; MTCW 1, 2

**Gray, Amlin** 1946- **CLC 29**
See also CA 138

**Gray, Francine du Plessix** 1930- **CLC 22; DAM NOV**
See also BEST 90:3; CA 61-64; CAAS 2; CANR 11, 33, 75; INT CANR-11; MTCW 1, 2

**Gray, John (Henry)** 1866-1934 **TCLC 19**
See also CA 119; 162

**Gray, Simon (James Holliday)** 1936- **CLC 9, 14, 36**
See also AITN 1; CA 21-24R; CAAS 3; CANR 32, 69; DLB 13; MTCW 1

**Gray, Spalding** 1941-**CLC 49, 112; DAM POP; DC 7**
See also CA 128; CANR 74; MTCW 2

**Gray, Thomas** 1716-1771**LC 4, 40; DA; DAB; DAC; DAM MST; PC 2; WLC**
See also CDBLB 1660-1789; DLB 109

**Grayson, David**
See Baker, Ray Stannard

**Grayson, Richard (A.)** 1951- **CLC 38**
See also CA 85-88; CANR 14, 31, 57

**Greeley, Andrew M(oran)** 1928- **CLC 28; DAM POP**
See also CA 5-8R; CAAS 7; CANR 7, 43, 69; MTCW 1, 2

**Green, Anna Katharine** 1846-1935 **TCLC 63**
See also CA 112; 159; DLB 202

**Green, Brian**
See Card, Orson Scott

**Green, Hannah**
See Greenberg, Joanne (Goldenberg)

**Green, Hannah** 1927(?)-1996 **CLC 3**
See also CA 73-76; CANR 59

**Green, Henry** 1905-1973 **CLC 2, 13, 97**
See also Yorke, Henry Vincent
See also CA 175; DLB 15

**Green, Julian (Hartridge)** 1900-1998
See Green, Julien
See also CA 21-24R; 169; CANR 33; DLB 4, 72; MTCW 1

**Green, Julien** **CLC 3, 11, 77**
See also Green, Julian (Hartridge)
See also MTCW 2

**Green, Paul (Eliot)** 1894-1981**CLC 25; DAM DRAM**
See also AITN 1; CA 5-8R; 103; CANR 3; DLB 7, 9; DLBY 81

**Greenberg, Ivan** 1908-1973
See Rahv, Philip
See also CA 85-88

**Greenberg, Joanne (Goldenberg)** 1932- **C L C 7, 30**
See also AAYA 12; CA 5-8R; CANR 14, 32, 69; SATA 25

**Greenberg, Richard** 1959(?)- **CLC 57**
See also CA 138

**Greene, Bette** 1934- **CLC 30**
See also AAYA 7; CA 53-56; CANR 4; CLR 2; JRDA; MAICYA; SAAS 16; SATA 8, 102

**Greene, Gael** **CLC 8**
See also CA 13-16R; CANR 10

**Greene, Graham (Henry)** 1904-1991**CLC 1, 3, 6, 9, 14, 18, 27, 37, 70, 72; DA; DAB; DAC; DAM MST, NOV; SSC 29; WLC**
See also AITN 2; CA 13-16R; 133; CANR 35, 61; CDBLB 1945-1960; DLB 13, 15, 77, 100, 162, 201, 204; DLBY 91; MTCW 1, 2;

SATA 20

**Greene, Robert** 1558-1592 **LC 41**
See also DLB 62, 167

**Greer, Richard**
See Silverberg, Robert

**Gregor, Arthur** 1923- **CLC 9**
See also CA 25-28R; CAAS 10; CANR 11; SATA 36

**Gregor, Lee**
See Pohl, Frederik

**Gregory, Isabella Augusta (Persse)** 1852-1932 **TCLC 1**
See also CA 104; DLB 10

**Gregory, J. Dennis**
See Williams, John A(lfred)

**Grendon, Stephen**
See Derleth, August (William)

**Grenville, Kate** 1950- **CLC 61**
See also CA 118; CANR 53

**Grenville, Pelham**
See Wodehouse, P(elham) G(renville)

**Greve, Felix Paul (Berthold Friedrich)** 1879-1948
See Grove, Frederick Philip
See also CA 104; 141; 175; CANR 79; DAC; DAM MST

**Grey, Zane** 1872-1939 **TCLC 6; DAM POP**
See also CA 104; 132; DLB 212; MTCW 1, 2

**Grieg, (Johan) Nordahl (Brun)** 1902-1943 **TCLC 10**
See also CA 107

**Grieve, C(hristopher) M(urray)** 1892-1978 **CLC 11, 19; DAM POET**
See also MacDiarmid, Hugh; Pteleon
See also CA 5-8R; 85-88; CANR 33; MTCW 1

**Griffin, Gerald** 1803-1840 **NCLC 7**
See also DLB 159

**Griffin, John Howard** 1920-1980 **CLC 68**
See also AITN 1; CA 1-4R; 101; CANR 2

**Griffin, Peter** 1942- **CLC 39**
See also CA 136

**Griffith, D(avid Lewelyn) W(ark)** 1875(?)-1948 **TCLC 68**
See also CA 119; 150; CANR 80

**Griffith, Lawrence**
See Griffith, D(avid Lewelyn) W(ark)

**Griffiths, Trevor** 1935- **CLC 13, 52**
See also CA 97-100; CANR 45; DLB 13

**Griggs, Sutton Elbert** 1872-1930(?)**TCLC 77**
See also CA 123; DLB 50

**Grigson, Geoffrey (Edward Harvey)** 1905-1985 **CLC 7, 39**
See also CA 25-28R; 118; CANR 20, 33; DLB 27; MTCW 1, 2

**Grillparzer, Franz** 1791-1872 **NCLC 1**
See also DLB 133

**Grimble, Reverend Charles James**
See Eliot, T(homas) S(tearns)

**Grimke, Charlotte L(ottie) Forten** 1837(?)-1914
See Forten, Charlotte L.
See also BW 1; CA 117; 124; DAM MULT, POET

**Grimm, Jacob Ludwig Karl** 1785-1863**NCLC 3, 77**
See also DLB 90; MAICYA; SATA 22

**Grimm, Wilhelm Karl** 1786-1859**NCLC 3, 77**
See also DLB 90; MAICYA; SATA 22

**Grimmelshausen, Johann Jakob Christoffel von** 1621-1676 **LC 6**
See also DLB 168

**Grindel, Eugene** 1895-1952
See Eluard, Paul
See also CA 104

Grisham, John 1955-  **CLC 84; DAM POP**
See also AAYA 14; CA 138; CANR 47, 69;
MTCW 2
Grossman, David 1954-  **CLC 67**
See also CA 138
Grossman, Vasily (Semenovich) 1905-1964
**CLC 41**
See also CA 124; 130; MTCW 1
Grove, Frederick Philip  **TCLC 4**
See also Greve, Felix Paul (Berthold Friedrich)
See also DLB 92
Grubb
See Crumb, R(obert)
Grumbach, Doris (Isaac) 1918-**CLC 13, 22, 64**
See also CA 5-8R; CAAS 2; CANR 9, 42, 70;
INT CANR-9; MTCW 2
Grundtvig, Nicolai Frederik Severin 1783-1872
**NCLC 1**
Grunge
See Crumb, R(obert)
Grunwald, Lisa 1959-  **CLC 44**
See also CA 120
Guare, John 1938-  **CLC 8, 14, 29, 67; DAM**
**DRAM**
See also CA 73-76; CANR 21, 69; DLB 7;
MTCW 1, 2
Gudjonsson, Halldor Kiljan 1902-1998
See Laxness, Halldor
See also CA 103; 164
Guenter, Erich
See Eich, Guenter
Guest, Barbara 1920-  **CLC 34**
See also CA 25-28R; CANR 11, 44; DLB 5,
193
Guest, Judith (Ann) 1936-  **CLC 8, 30; DAM**
**NOV, POP**
See also AAYA 7; CA 77-80; CANR 15, 75;
INT CANR-15; MTCW 1, 2
Guevara, Che  **CLC 87; HLC**
See also Guevara (Serna), Ernesto
Guevara (Serna), Ernesto 1928-1967
See Guevara, Che
See also CA 127; 111; CANR 56; DAM MULT;
HW 1
Guicciardini, Francesco 1483-1540  **LC 49**
Guild, Nicholas M. 1944-  **CLC 33**
See also CA 93-96
Guillemin, Jacques
See Sartre, Jean-Paul
Guillen, Jorge 1893-1984  **CLC 11; DAM**
**MULT, POET; HLCS 1**
See also CA 89-92; 112; DLB 108; HW 1
Guillen, Nicolas (Cristobal) 1902-1989  **C L C**
**48, 79; BLC 2; DAM MST, MULT, POET;**
**HLC; PC 23**
See also BW 2; CA 116; 125; 129; HW 1
Guillevic, (Eugene) 1907-  **CLC 33**
See also CA 93-96
Guillois
See Desnos, Robert
Guillois, Valentin
See Desnos, Robert
Guiney, Louise Imogen 1861-1920  **TCLC 41**
See also CA 160; DLB 54
Guiraldes, Ricardo (Guillermo) 1886-1927
**TCLC 39**
See also CA 131; HW 1; MTCW 1
Gumilev, Nikolai (Stepanovich) 1886-1921
**TCLC 60**
See also CA 165
Gunesekera, Romesh 1954-  **CLC 91**
See also CA 159
Gunn, Bill  **CLC 5**

See also Gunn, William Harrison
See also DLB 38
Gunn, Thom(son William) 1929-**CLC 3, 6, 18,**
**32, 81; DAM POET; PC 26**
See also CA 17-20R; CANR 9, 33; CDBLB
1960 to Present; DLB 27; INT CANR-33;
MTCW 1
Gunn, William Harrison 1934(?)-1989
See Gunn, Bill
See also AITN 1; BW 1, 3; CA 13-16R; 128;
CANR 12, 25, 76
Gunnars, Kristjana 1948-  **CLC 69**
See also CA 113; DLB 60
Gurdjieff, G(eorgei) I(vanovich) 1877(?)-1949
**TCLC 71**
See also CA 157
Gurganus, Allan 1947-  **CLC 70; DAM POP**
See also BEST 90:1; CA 135
Gurney, A(lbert) R(amsdell), Jr. 1930-  **C L C**
**32, 50, 54; DAM DRAM**
See also CA 77-80; CANR 32, 64
Gurney, Ivor (Bertie) 1890-1937  **TCLC 33**
See also CA 167
Gurney, Peter
See Gurney, A(lbert) R(amsdell), Jr.
Guro, Elena 1877-1913  **TCLC 56**
Gustafson, James M(oody) 1925-  **CLC 100**
See also CA 25-28R; CANR 37
Gustafson, Ralph (Barker) 1909-  **CLC 36**
See also CA 21-24R; CANR 8, 45; DLB 88
Gut, Gom
See Simenon, Georges (Jacques Christian)
Guterson, David 1956-  **CLC 91**
See also CA 132; CANR 73; MTCW 2
Guthrie, A(lfred) B(ertram), Jr. 1901-1991
**CLC 23**
See also CA 57-60; 134; CANR 24; DLB 212;
SATA 62; SATA-Obit 67
Guthrie, Isobel
See Grieve, C(hristopher) M(urray)
Guthrie, Woodrow Wilson 1912-1967
See Guthrie, Woody
See also CA 113; 93-96
Guthrie, Woody  **CLC 35**
See also Guthrie, Woodrow Wilson
Guy, Rosa (Cuthbert) 1928-  **CLC 26**
See also AAYA 4; BW 2; CA 17-20R; CANR
14, 34; CLR 13; DLB 33; JRDA; MAICYA;
SATA 14, 62
Gwendolyn
See Bennett, (Enoch) Arnold
**H. D.**  **CLC 3, 8, 14, 31, 34, 73; PC 5**
See also Doolittle, Hilda
H. de V.
See Buchan, John
Haavikko, Paavo Juhani 1931-  **CLC 18, 34**
See also CA 106
Habbema, Koos
See Heijermans, Herman
Habermas, Juergen 1929-  **CLC 104**
See also CA 109
Habermas, Jurgen
See Habermas, Juergen
Hacker, Marilyn 1942-  **CLC 5, 9, 23, 72, 91;**
**DAM POET**
See also CA 77-80; CANR 68; DLB 120
Haeckel, Ernst Heinrich (Philipp August) 1834-
1919  **TCLC 83**
See also CA 157
Hafiz c. 1326-1389  **CMLC 34**
Hafiz c. 1326-1389(?)  **CMLC 34**
Haggard, H(enry) Rider 1856-1925 **TCLC 11**
See also CA 108; 148; DLB 70, 156, 174, 178;

MTCW 2; SATA 16
Hagiosy, L.
See Larbaud, Valery (Nicolas)
Hagiwara Sakutaro 1886-1942 **TCLC 60; PC**
**18**
Haig, Fenil
See Ford, Ford Madox
Haig-Brown, Roderick (Langmere) 1908-1976
**CLC 21**
See also CA 5-8R; 69-72; CANR 4, 38; CLR
31; DLB 88; MAICYA; SATA 12
Hailey, Arthur 1920-**CLC 5; DAM NOV, POP**
See also AITN 2; BEST 90:3; CA 1-4R; CANR
2, 36, 75; DLB 88; DLBY 82; MTCW 1, 2
Hailey, Elizabeth Forsythe 1938-  **CLC 40**
See also CA 93-96; CAAS 1; CANR 15, 48;
INT CANR-15
Haines, John (Meade) 1924-  **CLC 58**
See also CA 17-20R; CANR 13, 34; DLB 212
Hakluyt, Richard 1552-1616  **LC 31**
Haldeman, Joe (William) 1943-  **CLC 61**
See also CA 53-56; CAAS 25; CANR 6, 70,
72; DLB 8; INT CANR-6
Hale, Sarah Josepha (Buell) 1788-1879**NCLC**
**75**
See also DLB 1, 42, 73
Haley, Alex(ander Murray Palmer) 1921-1992
**CLC 8, 12, 76; BLC 2; DA; DAB; DAC;**
**DAM MST, MULT, POP**
See also AAYA 26; BW 2, 3; CA 77-80; 136;
CANR 61; CDALBS; DLB 38; MTCW 1, 2
Haliburton, Thomas Chandler 1796-1865
**NCLC 15**
See also DLB 11, 99
Hall, Donald (Andrew, Jr.) 1928- **CLC 1, 13,**
**37, 59; DAM POET**
See also CA 5-8R; CAAS 7; CANR 2, 44, 64;
DLB 5; MTCW 1; SATA 23, 97
Hall, Frederic Sauser
See Sauser-Hall, Frederic
Hall, James
See Kuttner, Henry
Hall, James Norman 1887-1951  **TCLC 23**
See also CA 123; 173; SATA 21
Hall, Radclyffe
See Hall, (Marguerite) Radclyffe
See also MTCW 2
Hall, (Marguerite) Radclyffe 1886-1943
**TCLC 12**
See also CA 110; 150; DLB 191
Hall, Rodney 1935-  **CLC 51**
See also CA 109; CANR 69
Halleck, Fitz-Greene 1790-1867  **NCLC 47**
See also DLB 3
Halliday, Michael
See Creasey, John
Halpern, Daniel 1945-  **CLC 14**
See also CA 33-36R
Hamburger, Michael (Peter Leopold) 1924-
**CLC 5, 14**
See also CA 5-8R; CAAS 4; CANR 2, 47; DLB
27
Hamill, Pete 1935-  **CLC 10**
See also CA 25-28R; CANR 18, 71
Hamilton, Alexander 1755(?)-1804 **NCLC 49**
See also DLB 37
Hamilton, Clive
See Lewis, C(live) S(taples)
Hamilton, Edmond 1904-1977  **CLC 1**
See also CA 1-4R; CANR 3; DLB 8
Hamilton, Eugene (Jacob) Lee
See Lee-Hamilton, Eugene (Jacob)
Hamilton, Franklin

See Silverberg, Robert

**Hamilton, Gail**
See Corcoran, Barbara

**Hamilton, Mollie**
See Kaye, M(ary) M(argaret)

**Hamilton, (Anthony Walter) Patrick** 1904-1962 **CLC 51**
See also CA 113; DLB 191

**Hamilton, Virginia** 1936- **CLC 26; DAM MULT**
See also AAYA 2, 21; BW 2, 3; CA 25-28R; CANR 20, 37, 73; CLR 1, 11, 40; DLB 33, 52; INT CANR-20; JRDA; MAICYA; MTCW 1, 2; SATA 4, 56, 79

**Hammett, (Samuel) Dashiell** 1894-1961 **C L C 3, 5, 10, 19, 47; SSC 17**
See also AITN 1; CA 81-84; CANR 42; CDALB 1929-1941; DLBD 6; DLBY 96; MTCW 1, 2

**Hammon, Jupiter** 1711(?)-1800(?) **NCLC 5; BLC 2; DAM MULT, POET; PC 16**
See also DLB 31, 50

**Hammond, Keith**
See Kuttner, Henry

**Hamner, Earl (Henry), Jr.** 1923- **CLC 12**
See also AITN 2; CA 73-76; DLB 6

**Hampton, Christopher (James)** 1946- **CLC 4**
See also CA 25-28R; DLB 13; MTCW 1

**Hamsun, Knut** **TCLC 2, 14, 49**
See also Pedersen, Knut

**Handke, Peter** 1942- **CLC 5, 8, 10, 15, 38; DAM DRAM, NOV**
See also CA 77-80; CANR 33, 75; DLB 85, 124; MTCW 1, 2

**Hanley, James** 1901-1985 **CLC 3, 5, 8, 13**
See also CA 73-76; 117; CANR 36; DLB 191; MTCW 1

**Hannah, Barry** 1942- **CLC 23, 38, 90**
See also CA 108; 110; CANR 43, 68; DLB 6; INT 110; MTCW 1

**Hannon, Ezra**
See Hunter, Evan

**Hansberry, Lorraine (Vivian)** 1930-1965 **CLC 17, 62; BLC 2; DA; DAB; DAC; DAM DRAM, MST, MULT; DC 2**
See also AAYA 25; BW 1, 3; CA 109; 25-28R; CABS 3; CANR 58; CDALB 1941-1968; DLB 7, 38; MTCW 1, 2

**Hansen, Joseph** 1923- **CLC 38**
See also CA 29-32R; CAAS 17; CANR 16, 44, 66; INT CANR-16

**Hansen, Martin A(lfred)** 1909-1955 **TCLC 32**
See also CA 167

**Hanson, Kenneth O(stlin)** 1922- **CLC 13**
See also CA 53-56; CANR 7

**Hardwick, Elizabeth (Bruce)** 1916- **CLC 13; DAM NOV**
See also CA 5-8R; CANR 3, 32, 70; DLB 6; MTCW 1, 2

**Hardy, Thomas** 1840-1928 **TCLC 4, 10, 18, 32, 48, 53, 72; DA; DAB; DAC; DAM MST, NOV, POET; PC 8; SSC 2; WLC**
See also CA 104; 123; CDBLB 1890-1914; DLB 18, 19, 135; MTCW 1, 2

**Hare, David** 1947- **CLC 29, 58**
See also CA 97-100; CANR 39; DLB 13; MTCW 1

**Harewood, John**
See Van Druten, John (William)

**Harford, Henry**
See Hudson, W(illiam) H(enry)

**Hargrave, Leonie**
See Disch, Thomas M(ichael)

**Harjo, Joy** 1951- **CLC 83; DAM MULT**
See also CA 114; CANR 35, 67; DLB 120, 175; MTCW 2; NNAL

**Harlan, Louis R(udolph)** 1922- **CLC 34**
See also CA 21-24R; CANR 25, 55, 80

**Harling, Robert** 1951(?)- **CLC 53**
See also CA 147

**Harmon, William (Ruth)** 1938- **CLC 38**
See also CA 33-36R; CANR 14, 32, 35; SATA 65

**Harper, F. E. W.**
See Harper, Frances Ellen Watkins

**Harper, Frances E. W.**
See Harper, Frances Ellen Watkins

**Harper, Frances E. Watkins**
See Harper, Frances Ellen Watkins

**Harper, Frances Ellen**
See Harper, Frances Ellen Watkins

**Harper, Frances Ellen Watkins** 1825-1911 **TCLC 14; BLC 2; DAM MULT, POET; PC 21**
See also BW 1, 3; CA 111; 125; CANR 79; DLB 50

**Harper, Michael S(teven)** 1938- **CLC 7, 22**
See also BW 1; CA 33-36R; CANR 24; DLB 41

**Harper, Mrs. F. E. W.**
See Harper, Frances Ellen Watkins

**Harris, Christie (Lucy) Irwin** 1907- **CLC 12**
See also CA 5-8R; CANR 6; CLR 47; DLB 88; JRDA; MAICYA; SAAS 10; SATA 6, 74

**Harris, Frank** 1856-1931 **TCLC 24**
See also CA 109; 150; CANR 80; DLB 156, 197

**Harris, George Washington** 1814-1869 **NCLC 23**
See also DLB 3, 11

**Harris, Joel Chandler** 1848-1908 **TCLC 2; SSC 19**
See also CA 104; 137; CANR 80; CLR 49; DLB 11, 23, 42, 78, 91; MAICYA; SATA 100; YABC 1

**Harris, John (Wyndham Parkes Lucas) Beynon** 1903-1969
See Wyndham, John
See also CA 102; 89-92

**Harris, MacDonald** **CLC 9**
See also Heiney, Donald (William)

**Harris, Mark** 1922- **CLC 19**
See also CA 5-8R; CAAS 3; CANR 2, 55; DLB 2; DLBY 80

**Harris, (Theodore) Wilson** 1921- **CLC 25**
See also BW 2, 3; CA 65-68; CAAS 16; CANR 11, 27, 69; DLB 117; MTCW 1

**Harrison, Elizabeth Cavanna** 1909-
See Cavanna, Betty
See also CA 9-12R; CANR 6, 27

**Harrison, Harry (Max)** 1925- **CLC 42**
See also CA 1-4R; CANR 5, 21; DLB 8; SATA 4

**Harrison, James (Thomas)** 1937- **CLC 6, 14, 33, 66; SSC 19**
See also CA 13-16R; CANR 8, 51, 79; DLBY 82; INT CANR-8

**Harrison, Jim**
See Harrison, James (Thomas)

**Harrison, Kathryn** 1961- **CLC 70**
See also CA 144; CANR 68

**Harrison, Tony** 1937- **CLC 43**
See also CA 65-68; CANR 44; DLB 40; MTCW 1

**Harriss, Will(ard Irvin)** 1922- **CLC 34**
See also CA 111

**Harson, Sley**
See Ellison, Harlan (Jay)

**Hart, Ellis**
See Ellison, Harlan (Jay)

**Hart, Josephine** 1942(?)- **CLC 70; DAM POP**
See also CA 138; CANR 70

**Hart, Moss** 1904-1961 **CLC 66; DAM DRAM**
See also CA 109; 89-92; DLB 7

**Harte, (Francis) Bret(t)** 1836(?)-1902 **TCLC 1, 25; DA; DAC; DAM MST; SSC 8; WLC**
See also CA 104; 140; CANR 80; CDALB 1865-1917; DLB 12, 64, 74, 79, 186; SATA 26

**Hartley, L(eslie) P(oles)** 1895-1972 **CLC 2, 22**
See also CA 45-48; 37-40R; CANR 33; DLB 15, 139; MTCW 1, 2

**Hartman, Geoffrey H.** 1929- **CLC 27**
See also CA 117; 125; CANR 79; DLB 67

**Hartmann, Sadakichi** 1867-1944 **TCLC 73**
See also CA 157; DLB 54

**Hartmann von Aue** c. 1160-c. 1205 **CMLC 15**
See also DLB 138

**Hartmann von Aue** 1170-1210 **CMLC 15**

**Haruf, Kent** 1943- **CLC 34**
See also CA 149

**Harwood, Ronald** 1934- **CLC 32; DAM DRAM, MST**
See also CA 1-4R; CANR 4, 55; DLB 13

**Hasegawa Tatsunosuke**
See Futabatei, Shimei

**Hasek, Jaroslav (Matej Frantisek)** 1883-1923 **TCLC 4**
See also CA 104; 129; MTCW 1, 2

**Hass, Robert** 1941- **CLC 18, 39, 99; PC 16**
See also CA 111; CANR 30, 50, 71; DLB 105, 206; SATA 94

**Hastings, Hudson**
See Kuttner, Henry

**Hastings, Selina** **CLC 44**

**Hathorne, John** 1641-1717 **LC 38**

**Hatteras, Amelia**
See Mencken, H(enry) L(ouis)

**Hatteras, Owen** **TCLC 18**
See also Mencken, H(enry) L(ouis); Nathan, George Jean

**Hauptmann, Gerhart (Johann Robert)** 1862-1946 **TCLC 4; DAM DRAM**
See also CA 104; 153; DLB 66, 118

**Havel, Vaclav** 1936- **CLC 25, 58, 65; DAM DRAM; DC 6**
See also CA 104; CANR 36, 63; MTCW 1, 2

**Haviaras, Stratis** **CLC 33**
See also Chaviaras, Strates

**Hawes, Stephen** 1475(?)-1523(?) **LC 17**
See also DLB 132

**Hawkes, John (Clendennin Burne, Jr.)** 1925-1998 **CLC 1, 2, 3, 4, 7, 9, 14, 15, 27, 49**
See also CA 1-4R; 167; CANR 2, 47, 64; DLB 2, 7; DLBY 80, 98; MTCW 1, 2

**Hawking, S. W.**
See Hawking, Stephen W(illiam)

**Hawking, Stephen W(illiam)** 1942- **CLC 63, 105**
See also AAYA 13; BEST 89:1; CA 126; 129; CANR 48; MTCW 2

**Hawkins, Anthony Hope**
See Hope, Anthony

**Hawthorne, Julian** 1846-1934 **TCLC 25**
See also CA 165

**Hawthorne, Nathaniel** 1804-1864 **NCLC 39; DA; DAB; DAC; DAM MST, NOV; SSC 3, 29; WLC**
See also AAYA 18; CDALB 1640-1865; DLB

1, 74; YABC 2

**Haxton, Josephine Ayres** 1921-
See Douglas, Ellen
See also CA 115; CANR 41

**Hayaseca y Eizaguirre, Jorge**
See Echegaray (y Eizaguirre), Jose (Maria Waldo)

**Hayashi, Fumiko** 1904-1951    **TCLC 27**
See also CA 161; DLB 180

**Haycraft, Anna**
See Ellis, Alice Thomas
See also CA 122; MTCW 2

**Hayden, Robert E(arl)** 1913-1980 **CLC 5, 9, 14, 37; BLC 2; DA; DAC; DAM MST, MULT, POET; PC 6**
See also BW 1, 3; CA 69-72; 97-100; CABS 2; CANR 24, 75; CDALB 1941-1968; DLB 5, 76; MTCW 1, 2; SATA 19; SATA-Obit 26

**Hayford, J(oseph) E(phraim) Casely**
See Casely-Hayford, J(oseph) E(phraim)

**Hayman, Ronald** 1932-    **CLC 44**
See also CA 25-28R; CANR 18, 50; DLB 155

**Haywood, Eliza (Fowler)** 1693(?)-1756 **LC 1, 44**
See also DLB 39

**Hazlitt, William** 1778-1830    **NCLC 29**
See also DLB 110, 158

**Hazzard, Shirley** 1931-    **CLC 18**
See also CA 9-12R; CANR 4, 70; DLBY 82; MTCW 1

**Head, Bessie** 1937-1986 **CLC 25, 67; BLC 2; DAM MULT**
See also BW 2, 3; CA 29-32R; 119; CANR 25; DLB 117; MTCW 1, 2

**Headon, (Nicky) Topper** 1956(?)-    **CLC 30**

**Heaney, Seamus (Justin)** 1939- **CLC 5, 7, 14, 25, 37, 74, 91; DAB; DAM POET; PC 18; WLCS**
See also CA 85-88; CANR 25, 48, 75; CDBLB 1960 to Present; DLB 40; DLBY 95; MTCW 1, 2

**Hearn, (Patricio) Lafcadio (Tessima Carlos)** 1850-1904    **TCLC 9**
See also CA 105; 166; DLB 12, 78, 189

**Hearne, Vicki** 1946-    **CLC 56**
See also CA 139

**Hearon, Shelby** 1931-    **CLC 63**
See also AITN 2; CA 25-28R; CANR 18, 48

**Heat-Moon, William Least**    **CLC 29**
See also Trogdon, William (Lewis)
See also AAYA 9

**Hebbel, Friedrich** 1813-1863 **NCLC 43; DAM DRAM**
See also DLB 129

**Hebert, Anne** 1916- **CLC 4, 13, 29; DAC; DAM MST, POET**
See also CA 85-88; CANR 69; DLB 68; MTCW 1, 2

**Hecht, Anthony (Evan)** 1923- **CLC 8, 13, 19; DAM POET**
See also CA 9-12R; CANR 6; DLB 5, 169

**Hecht, Ben** 1894-1964    **CLC 8**
See also CA 85-88; DLB 7, 9, 25, 26, 28, 86

**Hedayat, Sadeq** 1903-1951    **TCLC 21**
See also CA 120

**Hegel, Georg Wilhelm Friedrich** 1770-1831 **NCLC 46**
See also DLB 90

**Heidegger, Martin** 1889-1976    **CLC 24**
See also CA 81-84; 65-68; CANR 34; MTCW 1, 2

**Heidenstam, (Carl Gustaf) Verner von** 1859-1940    **TCLC 5**

See also CA 104

**Heifner, Jack** 1946-    **CLC 11**
See also CA 105; CANR 47

**Heijermans, Herman** 1864-1924    **TCLC 24**
See also CA 123

**Heilbrun, Carolyn G(old)** 1926-    **CLC 25**
See also CA 45-48; CANR 1, 28, 58

**Heine, Heinrich** 1797-1856 **NCLC 4, 54; PC 25**
See also DLB 90

**Heinemann, Larry (Curtiss)** 1944-    **CLC 50**
See also CA 110; CAAS 21; CANR 31; DLBD 9; INT CANR-31

**Heiney, Donald (William)** 1921-1993
See Harris, MacDonald
See also CA 1-4R; 142; CANR 3, 58

**Heinlein, Robert A(nson)** 1907-1988 **CLC 1, 3, 8, 14, 26, 55; DAM POP**
See also AAYA 17; CA 1-4R; 125; CANR 1, 20, 53; DLB 8; JRDA; MAICYA; MTCW 1, 2; SATA 9, 69; SATA-Obit 56

**Helforth, John**
See Doolittle, Hilda

**Hellenhofferu, Vojtech Kapristian z**
See Hasek, Jaroslav (Matej Frantisek)

**Heller, Joseph** 1923- **CLC 1, 3, 5, 8, 11, 36, 63; DA; DAB; DAC; DAM MST, NOV, POP; WLC**
See also AAYA 24; AITN 1; CA 5-8R; CABS 1; CANR 8, 42, 66; DLB 2, 28; DLBY 80; INT CANR-8; MTCW 1, 2

**Hellman, Lillian (Florence)** 1906-1984 **CLC 2, 4, 8, 14, 18, 34, 44, 52; DAM DRAM; DC 1**
See also AITN 1, 2; CA 13-16R; 112; CANR 33; DLB 7; DLBY 84; MTCW 1, 2

**Helprin, Mark** 1947- **CLC 7, 10, 22, 32; DAM NOV, POP**
See also CA 81-84; CANR 47, 64; CDALBS; DLBY 85; MTCW 1, 2

**Helvetius, Claude-Adrien** 1715-1771    **LC 26**

**Helyar, Jane Penelope Josephine** 1933-
See Poole, Josephine
See also CA 21-24R; CANR 10, 26; SATA 82

**Hemans, Felicia** 1793-1835    **NCLC 71**
See also DLB 96

**Hemingway, Ernest (Miller)** 1899-1961 **CLC 1, 3, 6, 8, 10, 13, 19, 30, 34, 39, 41, 44, 50, 61, 80; DA; DAB; DAC; DAM MST, NOV; SSC 1, 25; WLC**
See also AAYA 19; CA 77-80; CANR 34; CDALB 1917-1929; DLB 4, 9, 102, 210; DLBD 1, 15, 16; DLBY 81, 87, 96, 98; MTCW 1, 2

**Hempel, Amy** 1951-    **CLC 39**
See also CA 118; 137; CANR 70; MTCW 2

**Henderson, F. C.**
See Mencken, H(enry) L(ouis)

**Henderson, Sylvia**
See Ashton-Warner, Sylvia (Constance)

**Henderson, Zenna (Chlarson)** 1917-1983 **SSC 29**
See also CA 1-4R; 133; CANR 1; DLB 8; SATA 5

**Henkin, Joshua**    **CLC 119**
See also CA 161

**Henley, Beth**    **CLC 23; DC 6**
See also Henley, Elizabeth Becker
See also CABS 3; DLBY 86

**Henley, Elizabeth Becker** 1952-
See Henley, Beth
See also CA 107; CANR 32, 73; DAM DRAM, MST; MTCW 1, 2

**Henley, William Ernest** 1849-1903    **TCLC 8**
See also CA 105; DLB 19

**Hennissart, Martha**
See Lathen, Emma
See also CA 85-88; CANR 64

**Henry, O.**    **TCLC 1, 19; SSC 5; WLC**
See also Porter, William Sydney

**Henry, Patrick** 1736-1799    **LC 25**

**Henryson, Robert** 1430(?)-1506(?)    **LC 20**
See also DLB 146

**Henry VIII** 1491-1547    **LC 10**
See also DLB 132

**Henschke, Alfred**
See Klabund

**Hentoff, Nat(han Irving)** 1925-    **CLC 26**
See also AAYA 4; CA 1-4R; CAAS 6; CANR 5, 25, 77; CLR 1, 52; INT CANR-25; JRDA; MAICYA; SATA 42, 69; SATA-Brief 27

**Heppenstall, (John) Rayner** 1911-1981    **CLC 10**
See also CA 1-4R; 103; CANR 29

**Heraclitus** c. 540B.C.-c. 450B.C.    **CMLC 22**
See also DLB 176

**Herbert, Frank (Patrick)** 1920-1986 **CLC 12, 23, 35, 44, 85; DAM POP**
See also AAYA 21; CA 53-56; 118; CANR 5, 43; CDALBS; DLB 8; INT CANR-5; MTCW 1, 2; SATA 9, 37; SATA-Obit 47

**Herbert, George** 1593-1633    **LC 24; DAB; DAM POET; PC 4**
See also CDBLB Before 1660; DLB 126

**Herbert, Zbigniew** 1924-1998 **CLC 9, 43; DAM POET**
See also CA 89-92; 169; CANR 36, 74; MTCW 1

**Herbst, Josephine (Frey)** 1897-1969 **CLC 34**
See also CA 5-8R; 25-28R; DLB 9

**Hergesheimer, Joseph** 1880-1954    **TCLC 11**
See also CA 109; DLB 102, 9

**Herlihy, James Leo** 1927-1993    **CLC 6**
See also CA 1-4R; 143; CANR 2

**Hermogenes** fl. c. 175-    **CMLC 6**

**Hernandez, Jose** 1834-1886    **NCLC 17**

**Herodotus** c. 484B.C.-429B.C.    **CMLC 17**
See also DLB 176

**Herrick, Robert** 1591-1674 **LC 13; DA; DAB; DAC; DAM MST, POP; PC 9**
See also DLB 126

**Herring, Guilles**
See Somerville, Edith

**Herriot, James** 1916-1995 **CLC 12; DAM POP**
See also Wight, James Alfred
See also AAYA 1; CA 148; CANR 40; MTCW 2; SATA 86

**Herrmann, Dorothy** 1941-    **CLC 44**
See also CA 107

**Herrmann, Taffy**
See Herrmann, Dorothy

**Hersey, John (Richard)** 1914-1993 **CLC 1, 2, 7, 9, 40, 81, 97; DAM POP**
See also AAYA 29; CA 17-20R; 140; CANR 33; CDALBS; DLB 6, 185; MTCW 1, 2; SATA 25; SATA-Obit 76

**Herzen, Aleksandr Ivanovich** 1812-1870 **NCLC 10, 61**

**Herzl, Theodor** 1860-1904    **TCLC 36**
See also CA 168

**Herzog, Werner** 1942-    **CLC 16**
See also CA 89-92

**Hesiod** c. 8th cent. B.C.-    **CMLC 5**
See also DLB 176

**Hesse, Hermann** 1877-1962 **CLC 1, 2, 3, 6, 11, 17, 25, 69; DA; DAB; DAC; DAM MST, NOV; SSC 9; WLC**
See also CA 17-18; CAP 2; DLB 66; MTCW 1,

2; SATA 50

**Hewes, Cady**
See De Voto, Bernard (Augustine)

**Heyen, William** 1940-			**CLC 13, 18**
See also CA 33-36R; CAAS 9; DLB 5

**Heyerdahl, Thor** 1914-			**CLC 26**
See also CA 5-8R; CANR 5, 22, 66, 73; MTCW
1, 2; SATA 2, 52

**Heym, Georg (Theodor Franz Arthur)** 1887-
1912					**TCLC 9**
See also CA 106

**Heym, Stefan** 1913-			**CLC 41**
See also CA 9-12R; CANR 4; DLB 69

**Heyse, Paul (Johann Ludwig von)** 1830-1914
**TCLC 8**
See also CA 104; DLB 129

**Heyward, (Edwin) DuBose** 1885-1940 **T C L C
59**
See also CA 108; 157; DLB 7, 9, 45; SATA 21

**Hibbert, Eleanor Alice Burford** 1906-1993
**CLC 7; DAM POP**
See also BEST 90:4; CA 17-20R; 140; CANR
9, 28, 59; MTCW 2; SATA 2; SATA-Obit 74

**Hichens, Robert (Smythe)** 1864-1950 **T C L C
64**
See also CA 162; DLB 153

**Higgins, George V(incent)** 1939-**CLC 4, 7, 10,
18**
See also CA 77-80; CAAS 5; CANR 17, 51;
DLB 2; DLBY 81, 98; INT CANR-17;
MTCW 1

**Higginson, Thomas Wentworth** 1823-1911
**TCLC 36**
See also CA 162; DLB 1, 64

**Highet, Helen**
See MacInnes, Helen (Clark)

**Highsmith, (Mary) Patricia** 1921-1995**CLC 2,
4, 14, 42, 102; DAM NOV, POP**
See also CA 1-4R; 147; CANR 1, 20, 48, 62;
MTCW 1, 2

**Highwater, Jamake (Mamake)** 1942(?)- **C L C
12**
See also AAYA 7; CA 65-68; CAAS 7; CANR
10, 34; CLR 17; DLB 52; DLBY 85; JRDA;
MAICYA; SATA 32, 69; SATA-Brief 30

**Highway, Tomson** 1951-**CLC 92; DAC; DAM
MULT**
See also CA 151; CANR 75; MTCW 2; NNAL

**Higuchi, Ichiyo** 1872-1896			**NCLC 49**

**Hijuelos, Oscar** 1951- **CLC 65; DAM MULT,
POP; HLC**
See also AAYA 25; BEST 90:1; CA 123; CANR
50, 75; DLB 145; HW 1, 2; MTCW 2

**Hikmet, Nazim** 1902(?)-1963		**CLC 40**
See also CA 141; 93-96

**Hildegard von Bingen** 1098-1179	**CMLC 20**
See also DLB 148

**Hildesheimer, Wolfgang** 1916-1991	**CLC 49**
See also CA 101; 135; DLB 69, 124

**Hill, Geoffrey (William)** 1932- **CLC 5, 8, 18,
45; DAM POET**
See also CA 81-84; CANR 21; CDBLB 1960
to Present; DLB 40; MTCW 1

**Hill, George Roy** 1921-			**CLC 26**
See also CA 110; 122

**Hill, John**
See Koontz, Dean R(ay)

**Hill, Susan (Elizabeth)** 1942-	**CLC 4, 113;
DAB; DAM MST, NOV**
See also CA 33-36R; CANR 29, 69; DLB 14,
139; MTCW 1

**Hillerman, Tony** 1925- **CLC 62; DAM POP**
See also AAYA 6; BEST 89:1; CA 29-32R;

CANR 21, 42, 65; DLB 206; SATA 6

**Hillesum, Etty** 1914-1943			**TCLC 49**
See also CA 137

**Hilliard, Noel (Harvey)** 1929-		**CLC 15**
See also CA 9-12R; CANR 7, 69

**Hillis, Rick** 1956-				**CLC 66**
See also CA 134

**Hilton, James** 1900-1954			**TCLC 21**
See also CA 108; 169; DLB 34, 77; SATA 34

**Himes, Chester (Bomar)** 1909-1984**CLC 2, 4,
7, 18, 58, 108; BLC 2; DAM MULT**
See also BW 2; CA 25-28R; 114; CANR 22;
DLB 2, 76, 143; MTCW 1, 2

**Hinde, Thomas**				**CLC 6, 11**
See also Chitty, Thomas Willes

**Hindin, Nathan**
See Bloch, Robert (Albert)

**Hine, (William) Daryl** 1936-		**CLC 15**
See also CA 1-4R; CAAS 15; CANR 1, 20; DLB
60

**Hinkson, Katharine Tynan**
See Tynan, Katharine

**Hinton, S(usan) E(loise)** 1950- **CLC 30, 111;
DA; DAB; DAC; DAM MST, NOV**
See also AAYA 2; CA 81-84; CANR 32, 62;
CDALBS; CLR 3, 23; JRDA; MAICYA;
MTCW 1, 2; SATA 19, 58

**Hippius, Zinaida**				**TCLC 9**
See also Gippius, Zinaida (Nikolayevna)

**Hiraoka, Kimitake** 1925-1970
See Mishima, Yukio
See also CA 97-100; 29-32R; DAM DRAM;
MTCW 1, 2

**Hirsch, E(ric) D(onald), Jr.** 1928-		**CLC 79**
See also CA 25-28R; CANR 27, 51; DLB 67;
INT CANR-27; MTCW 1

**Hirsch, Edward** 1950-			**CLC 31, 50**
See also CA 104; CANR 20, 42; DLB 120

**Hitchcock, Alfred (Joseph)** 1899-1980**CLC 16**
See also AAYA 22; CA 159; 97-100; SATA 27;
SATA-Obit 24

**Hitler, Adolf** 1889-1945			**TCLC 53**
See also CA 117; 147

**Hoagland, Edward** 1932-			**CLC 28**
See also CA 1-4R; CANR 2, 31, 57; DLB 6;
SATA 51

**Hoban, Russell (Conwell)** 1925- **CLC 7, 25;
DAM NOV**
See also CA 5-8R; CANR 23, 37, 66; CLR 3;
DLB 52; MAICYA; MTCW 1, 2; SATA 1,
40, 78

**Hobbes, Thomas** 1588-1679			**LC 36**
See also DLB 151

**Hobbs, Perry**
See Blackmur, R(ichard) P(almer)

**Hobson, Laura Z(ametkin)** 1900-1986**CLC 7,
25**
See also CA 17-20R; 118; CANR 55; DLB 28;
SATA 52

**Hochhuth, Rolf** 1931- **CLC 4, 11, 18; DAM
DRAM**
See also CA 5-8R; CANR 33, 75; DLB 124;
MTCW 1, 2

**Hochman, Sandra** 1936-			**CLC 3, 8**
See also CA 5-8R; DLB 5

**Hochwaelder, Fritz** 1911-1986**CLC 36; DAM
DRAM**
See also CA 29-32R; 120; CANR 42; MTCW 1

**Hochwalder, Fritz**
See Hochwaelder, Fritz

**Hocking, Mary (Eunice)** 1921-		**CLC 13**
See also CA 101; CANR 18, 40

**Hodgins, Jack** 1938-			**CLC 23**

See also CA 93-96; DLB 60

**Hodgson, William Hope** 1877(?)-1918 **T C L C
13**
See also CA 111; 164; DLB 70, 153, 156, 178;
MTCW 2

**Hoeg, Peter** 1957-				**CLC 95**
See also CA 151; CANR 75; MTCW 2

**Hoffman, Alice** 1952- **CLC 51; DAM NOV**
See also CA 77-80; CANR 34, 66; MTCW 1, 2

**Hoffman, Daniel (Gerard)** 1923-**CLC 6, 13, 23**
See also CA 1-4R; CANR 4; DLB 5

**Hoffman, Stanley** 1944-			**CLC 5**
See also CA 77-80

**Hoffman, William M(oses)** 1939-		**CLC 40**
See also CA 57-60; CANR 11, 71

**Hoffmann, E(rnst) T(heodor) A(madeus)** 1776-
1822				**NCLC 2; SSC 13**
See also DLB 90; SATA 27

**Hofmann, Gert** 1931-			**CLC 54**
See also CA 128

**Hofmannsthal, Hugo von** 1874-1929**TCLC 11;
DAM DRAM; DC 4**
See also CA 106; 153; DLB 81, 118

**Hogan, Linda** 1947- **CLC 73; DAM MULT**
See also CA 120; CANR 45, 73; DLB 175;
NNAL

**Hogarth, Charles**
See Creasey, John

**Hogarth, Emmett**
See Polonsky, Abraham (Lincoln)

**Hogg, James** 1770-1835			**NCLC 4**
See also DLB 93, 116, 159

**Holbach, Paul Henri Thiry Baron** 1723-1789
**LC 14**

**Holberg, Ludvig** 1684-1754			**LC 6**

**Holden, Ursula** 1921-			**CLC 18**
See also CA 101; CAAS 8; CANR 22

**Holderlin, (Johann Christian) Friedrich** 1770-
1843				**NCLC 16; PC 4**

**Holdstock, Robert**
See Holdstock, Robert P.

**Holdstock, Robert P.** 1948-			**CLC 39**
See also CA 131

**Holland, Isabelle** 1920-			**CLC 21**
See also AAYA 11; CA 21-24R; CANR 10, 25,
47; CLR 57; JRDA; MAICYA; SATA 8, 70;
SATA-Essay 103

**Holland, Marcus**
See Caldwell, (Janet Miriam) Taylor (Holland)

**Hollander, John** 1929-		**CLC 2, 5, 8, 14**
See also CA 1-4R; CANR 1, 52; DLB 5; SATA
13

**Hollander, Paul**
See Silverberg, Robert

**Holleran, Andrew** 1943(?)-			**CLC 38**
See also CA 144

**Hollinghurst, Alan** 1954-			**CLC 55, 91**
See also CA 114; DLB 207

**Hollis, Jim**
See Summers, Hollis (Spurgeon, Jr.)

**Holly, Buddy** 1936-1959			**TCLC 65**

**Holmes, Gordon**
See Shiel, M(atthew) P(hipps)

**Holmes, John**
See Souster, (Holmes) Raymond

**Holmes, John Clellon** 1926-1988		**CLC 56**
See also CA 9-12R; 125; CANR 4; DLB 16

**Holmes, Oliver Wendell, Jr.** 1841-1935**TCLC
77**
See also CA 114

**Holmes, Oliver Wendell** 1809-1894 **NCLC 14**
See also CDALB 1640-1865; DLB 1, 189;
SATA 34

Holmes, Raymond
See Souster, (Holmes) Raymond
Holt, Victoria
See Hibbert, Eleanor Alice Burford
Holub, Miroslav 1923-1998 **CLC 4**
See also CA 21-24R; 169; CANR 10
Homer c. 8th cent. B.C.- **CMLC 1, 16; DA;**
**DAB; DAC; DAM MST, POET; PC 23;**
**WLCS**
See also DLB 176
Hongo, Garrett Kaoru 1951- **PC 23**
See also CA 133; CAAS 22; DLB 120
Honig, Edwin 1919- **CLC 33**
See also CA 5-8R; CAAS 8; CANR 4, 45; DLB
5
Hood, Hugh (John Blagdon) 1928-**CLC 15, 28**
See also CA 49-52; CAAS 17; CANR 1, 33;
DLB 53
Hood, Thomas 1799-1845 **NCLC 16**
See also DLB 96
Hooker, (Peter) Jeremy 1941- **CLC 43**
See also CA 77-80; CANR 22; DLB 40
hooks, bell **CLC 94; BLCS**
See also Watkins, Gloria
See also MTCW 2
Hope, A(lec) D(erwent) 1907- **CLC 3, 51**
See also CA 21-24R; CANR 33, 74; MTCW 1,
2
Hope, Anthony 1863-1933 **TCLC 83**
See also CA 157; DLB 153, 156
Hope, Brian
See Creasey, John
Hope, Christopher (David Tully) 1944- **CLC**
**52**
See also CA 106; CANR 47; SATA 62
Hopkins, Gerard Manley 1844-1889 **NCLC**
**17; DA; DAB; DAC; DAM MST, POET;**
**PC 15; WLC**
See also CDBLB 1890-1914; DLB 35, 57
Hopkins, John (Richard) 1931-1998 **CLC 4**
See also CA 85-88; 169
Hopkins, Pauline Elizabeth 1859-1930**TCLC**
**28; BLC 2; DAM MULT**
See also BW 2, 3; CA 141; DLB 50
Hopkinson, Francis 1737-1791 **LC 25**
See also DLB 31
Hopley-Woolrich, Cornell George 1903-1968
See Woolrich, Cornell
See also CA 13-14; CANR 58; CAP 1; MTCW
2
Horatio
See Proust, (Valentin-Louis-George-Eugene-)
Marcel
Horgan, Paul (George Vincent O'Shaughnessy)
1903-1995 **CLC 9, 53; DAM NOV**
See also CA 13-16R; 147; CANR 9, 35; DLB
212; DLBY 85; INT CANR-9; MTCW 1, 2;
SATA 13; SATA-Obit 84
Horn, Peter
See Kuttner, Henry
Hornem, Horace Esq.
See Byron, George Gordon (Noel)
Horney, Karen (Clementine Theodore
Danielsen) 1885-1952 **TCLC 71**
See also CA 114; 165
Hornung, E(rnest) W(illiam) 1866-1921
**TCLC 59**
See also CA 108; 160; DLB 70
Horovitz, Israel (Arthur) 1939-**CLC 56; DAM**
**DRAM**
See also CA 33-36R; CANR 46, 59; DLB 7
Horvath, Odon von
See Horvath, Oedoen von

See also DLB 85, 124
Horvath, Oedoen von 1901-1938 **TCLC 45**
See also Horvath, Odon von
See also CA 118
Horwitz, Julius 1920-1986 **CLC 14**
See also CA 9-12R; 119; CANR 12
Hospital, Janette Turner 1942- **CLC 42**
See also CA 108; CANR 48
Hostos, E. M. de
See Hostos (y Bonilla), Eugenio Maria de
Hostos, Eugenio M. de
See Hostos (y Bonilla), Eugenio Maria de
Hostos, Eugenio Maria
See Hostos (y Bonilla), Eugenio Maria de
Hostos (y Bonilla), Eugenio Maria de 1839-1903
**TCLC 24**
See also CA 123; 131; HW 1
Houdini
See Lovecraft, H(oward) P(hillips)
Hougan, Carolyn 1943- **CLC 34**
See also CA 139
Household, Geoffrey (Edward West) 1900-1988
**CLC 11**
See also CA 77-80; 126; CANR 58; DLB 87;
SATA 14; SATA-Obit 59
Housman, A(lfred) E(dward) 1859-1936
**TCLC 1, 10; DA; DAB; DAC; DAM MST,**
**POET; PC 2; WLCS**
See also CA 104; 125; DLB 19; MTCW 1, 2
Housman, Laurence 1865-1959 **TCLC 7**
See also CA 106; 155; DLB 10; SATA 25
Howard, Elizabeth Jane 1923- **CLC 7, 29**
See also CA 5-8R; CANR 8, 62
Howard, Maureen 1930- **CLC 5, 14, 46**
See also CA 53-56; CANR 31, 75; DLBY 83;
INT CANR-31; MTCW 1, 2
Howard, Richard 1929- **CLC 7, 10, 47**
See also AITN 1; CA 85-88; CANR 25, 80; DLB
5; INT CANR-25
Howard, Robert E(rvin) 1906-1936 **TCLC 8**
See also CA 105; 157
Howard, Warren F.
See Pohl, Frederik
Howe, Fanny (Quincy) 1940- **CLC 47**
See also CA 117; CAAS 27; CANR 70; SATA-
Brief 52
Howe, Irving 1920-1993 **CLC 85**
See also CA 9-12R; 141; CANR 21, 50; DLB
67; MTCW 1, 2
Howe, Julia Ward 1819-1910 **TCLC 21**
See also CA 117; DLB 1, 189
Howe, Susan 1937- **CLC 72**
See also CA 160; DLB 120
Howe, Tina 1937- **CLC 48**
See also CA 109
Howell, James 1594(?)-1666 **LC 13**
See also DLB 151
Howells, W. D.
See Howells, William Dean
Howells, William D.
See Howells, William Dean
Howells, William Dean 1837-1920**TCLC 7, 17,**
**41**
See also CA 104; 134; CDALB 1865-1917;
DLB 12, 64, 74, 79, 189; MTCW 2
Howes, Barbara 1914-1996 **CLC 15**
See also CA 9-12R; 151; CAAS 3; CANR 53;
SATA 5
Hrabal, Bohumil 1914-1997 **CLC 13, 67**
See also CA 106; 156; CAAS 12; CANR 57
Hroswitha of Gandersheim c. 935-c. 1002
**CMLC 29**
See also DLB 148

Hsun, Lu
See Lu Hsun
Hubbard, L(afayette) Ron(ald) 1911-1986
**CLC 43; DAM POP**
See also CA 77-80; 118; CANR 52; MTCW 2
Huch, Ricarda (Octavia) 1864-1947**TCLC 13**
See also CA 111; DLB 66
Huddle, David 1942- **CLC 49**
See also CA 57-60; CAAS 20; DLB 130
Hudson, Jeffrey
See Crichton, (John) Michael
Hudson, W(illiam) H(enry) 1841-1922 **TCLC**
**29**
See also CA 115; DLB 98, 153, 174; SATA 35
Hueffer, Ford Madox
See Ford, Ford Madox
Hughart, Barry 1934- **CLC 39**
See also CA 137
Hughes, Colin
See Creasey, John
Hughes, David (John) 1930- **CLC 48**
See also CA 116; 129; DLB 14
Hughes, Edward James
See Hughes, Ted
See also DAM MST, POET
Hughes, (James) Langston 1902-1967**CLC 1,**
**5, 10, 15, 35, 44, 108; BLC 2; DA; DAB;**
**DAC; DAM DRAM, MST, MULT, POET;**
**DC 3; PC 1; SSC 6; WLC**
See also AAYA 12; BW 1, 3; CA 1-4R; 25-28R;
CANR 1, 34; CDALB 1929-1941; CLR 17;
DLB 4, 7, 48, 51, 86; JRDA; MAICYA;
MTCW 1, 2; SATA 4, 33
Hughes, Richard (Arthur Warren) 1900-1976
**CLC 1, 11; DAM NOV**
See also CA 5-8R; 65-68; CANR 4; DLB 15,
161; MTCW 1; SATA 8; SATA-Obit 25
Hughes, Ted 1930-1998 **CLC 2, 4, 9, 14, 37,**
**119; DAB; DAC; PC 7**
See also Hughes, Edward James
See also CA 1-4R; 171; CANR 1, 33, 66; CLR
3; DLB 40, 161; MAICYA; MTCW 1, 2;
SATA 49; SATA-Brief 27; SATA-Obit 107
Hugo, Richard F(ranklin) 1923-1982 **CLC 6,**
**18, 32; DAM POET**
See also CA 49-52; 108; CANR 3; DLB 5, 206
Hugo, Victor (Marie) 1802-1885**NCLC 3, 10,**
**21; DA; DAB; DAC; DAM DRAM, MST,**
**NOV, POET; PC 17; WLC**
See also AAYA 28; DLB 119, 192; SATA 47
Huidobro, Vicente
See Huidobro Fernandez, Vicente Garcia
Huidobro Fernandez, Vicente Garcia 1893-
1948 **TCLC 31**
See also CA 131; HW 1
Hulme, Keri 1947- **CLC 39**
See also CA 125; CANR 69; INT 125
Hulme, T(homas) E(rnest) 1883-1917 **TCLC**
**21**
See also CA 117; DLB 19
Hume, David 1711-1776 **LC 7**
See also DLB 104
Humphrey, William 1924-1997 **CLC 45**
See also CA 77-80; 160; CANR 68; DLB 212
Humphreys, Emyr Owen 1919- **CLC 47**
See also CA 5-8R; CANR 3, 24; DLB 15
Humphreys, Josephine 1945- **CLC 34, 57**
See also CA 121; 127; INT 127
Huneker, James Gibbons 1857-1921**TCLC 65**
See also DLB 71
Hungerford, Pixie
See Brinsmead, H(esba) F(ay)
Hunt, E(verette) Howard, (Jr.) 1918- **CLC 3**

See also AITN 1; CA 45-48; CANR 2, 47
**Hunt, Kyle**
  See Creasey, John
**Hunt, (James Henry) Leigh** 1784-1859**N C L C**
  **1, 70; DAM POET**
    See also DLB 96, 110, 144
**Hunt, Marsha** 1946-                    **CLC 70**
  See also BW 2, 3; CA 143; CANR 79
**Hunt, Violet** 1866(?)-1942        **TCLC 53**
  See also DLB 162, 197
**Hunter, E. Waldo**
  See Sturgeon, Theodore (Hamilton)
**Hunter, Evan** 1926-  **CLC 11, 31; DAM POP**
  See also CA 5-8R; CANR 5, 38, 62; DLBY 82;
    INT CANR-5; MTCW 1; SATA 25
**Hunter, Kristin (Eggleston)** 1931-    **CLC 35**
  See also AITN 1; BW 1; CA 13-16R; CANR
    13; CLR 3; DLB 33; INT CANR-13;
    MAICYA; SAAS 10; SATA 12
**Hunter, Mollie** 1922-                  **CLC 21**
  See also McIlwraith, Maureen Mollie Hunter
  See also AAYA 13; CANR 37, 78; CLR 25; DLB
    161; JRDA; MAICYA; SAAS 7; SATA 54,
    106
**Hunter, Robert** (?)-1734              **LC 7**
**Hurston, Zora Neale** 1903-1960**CLC 7, 30, 61;**
  **BLC 2; DA; DAC; DAM MST, MULT,**
  **NOV; SSC 4; WLCS**
    See also AAYA 15; BW 1, 3; CA 85-88; CANR
    61; CDALBS; DLB 51, 86; MTCW 1, 2
**Huston, John (Marcellus)** 1906-1987 **CLC 20**
  See also CA 73-76; 123; CANR 34; DLB 26
**Hustvedt, Siri** 1955-                  **CLC 76**
  See also CA 137
**Hutten, Ulrich von** 1488-1523         **LC 16**
  See also DLB 179
**Huxley, Aldous (Leonard)** 1894-1963 **CLC 1,**
  **3, 4, 5, 8, 11, 18, 35, 79; DA; DAB; DAC;**
  **DAM MST, NOV; WLC**
    See also AAYA 11; CA 85-88; CANR 44;
    CDBLB 1914-1945; DLB 36, 100, 162, 195;
    MTCW 1, 2; SATA 63
**Huxley, T(homas) H(enry)** 1825-1895 **N C L C**
  **67**
    See also DLB 57
**Huysmans, Joris-Karl** 1848-1907**TCLC 7, 69**
  See also CA 104; 165; DLB 123
**Hwang, David Henry** 1957-  **CLC 55; DAM**
  **DRAM; DC 4**
    See also CA 127; 132; CANR 76; DLB 212;
    INT 132; MTCW 2
**Hyde, Anthony** 1946-                   **CLC 42**
  See also CA 136
**Hyde, Margaret O(ldroyd)** 1917-       **CLC 21**
  See also CA 1-4R; CANR 1, 36; CLR 23; JRDA;
    MAICYA; SAAS 8; SATA 1, 42, 76
**Hynes, James** 1956(?)-                 **CLC 65**
  See also CA 164
**Ian, Janis** 1951-                      **CLC 21**
  See also CA 105
**Ibanez, Vicente Blasco**
  See Blasco Ibanez, Vicente
**Ibarguengoitia, Jorge** 1928-1983      **CLC 37**
  See also CA 124; 113; HW 1
**Ibsen, Henrik (Johan)** 1828-1906 **TCLC 2, 8,**
  **16, 37, 52; DA; DAB; DAC; DAM DRAM,**
  **MST; DC 2; WLC**
    See also CA 104; 141
**Ibuse, Masuji** 1898-1993               **CLC 22**
  See also CA 127; 141; DLB 180
**Ichikawa, Kon** 1915-                   **CLC 20**
  See also CA 121
**Idle, Eric** 1943-                      **CLC 21**

See also Monty Python
  See also CA 116; CANR 35
**Ignatow, David** 1914-1997   **CLC 4, 7, 14, 40**
  See also CA 9-12R; 162; CAAS 3; CANR 31,
    57; DLB 5
**Ihimaera, Witi** 1944-                  **CLC 46**
  See also CA 77-80
**Ilf, Ilya**                            **TCLC 21**
  See also Fainzilberg, Ilya Arnoldovich
**Illyes, Gyula** 1902-1983              **PC 16**
  See also CA 114; 109
**Immermann, Karl (Lebrecht)** 1796-1840
  **NCLC 4, 49**
    See also DLB 133
**Ince, Thomas H.** 1882-1924           **TCLC 89**
**Inchbald, Elizabeth** 1753-1821       **NCLC 62**
  See also DLB 39, 89
**Inclan, Ramon (Maria) del Valle**
  See Valle-Inclan, Ramon (Maria) del
**Infante, G(uillermo) Cabrera**
  See Cabrera Infante, G(uillermo)
**Ingalls, Rachel (Holmes)** 1940-      **CLC 42**
  See also CA 123; 127
**Ingamells, Reginald Charles**
  See Ingamells, Rex
**Ingamells, Rex** 1913-1955            **TCLC 35**
  See also CA 167
**Inge, William (Motter)** 1913-1973  **CLC 1, 8,**
  **19; DAM DRAM**
    See also CA 9-12R; CDALB 1941-1968; DLB
    7; MTCW 1, 2
**Ingelow, Jean** 1820-1897             **NCLC 39**
  See also DLB 35, 163; SATA 33
**Ingram, Willis J.**
  See Harris, Mark
**Innaurato, Albert (F.)** 1948(?)-     **CLC 21, 60**
  See also CA 115; 122; CANR 78; INT 122
**Innes, Michael**
  See Stewart, J(ohn) I(nnes) M(ackintosh)
**Innis, Harold Adams** 1894-1952       **TCLC 77**
  See also DLB 88
**Ionesco, Eugene** 1909-1994**CLC 1, 4, 6, 9, 11,**
  **15, 41, 86; DA; DAB; DAC; DAM DRAM,**
  **MST; WLC**
    See also CA 9-12R; 144; CANR 55; MTCW 1,
    2; SATA 7; SATA-Obit 79
**Iqbal, Muhammad** 1873-1938           **TCLC 28**
**Ireland, Patrick**
  See O'Doherty, Brian
**Iron, Ralph**
  See Schreiner, Olive (Emilie Albertina)
**Irving, John (Winslow)** 1942-**CLC 13, 23, 38,**
  **112; DAM NOV, POP**
    See also AAYA 8; BEST 89:3; CA 25-28R;
    CANR 28, 73; DLB 6; DLBY 82; MTCW 1,
    2
**Irving, Washington** 1783-1859 **NCLC 2, 19;**
  **DA; DAB; DAC; DAM MST; SSC 2; WLC**
    See also CDALB 1640-1865; DLB 3, 11, 30,
    59, 73, 74, 186; YABC 2
**Irwin, P. K.**
  See Page, P(atricia) K(athleen)
**Isaacs, Jorge Ricardo** 1837-1895     **NCLC 70**
**Isaacs, Susan** 1943-       **CLC 32; DAM POP**
  See also BEST 89:1; CA 89-92; CANR 20, 41,
    65; INT CANR-20; MTCW 1, 2
**Isherwood, Christopher (William Bradshaw)**
  1904-1986     **CLC 1, 9, 11, 14, 44; DAM**
  **DRAM, NOV**
    See also CA 13-16R; 117; CANR 35; DLB 15,
    195; DLBY 86; MTCW 1, 2
**Ishiguro, Kazuo** 1954-  **CLC 27, 56, 59, 110;**
  **DAM NOV**

See also BEST 90:2; CA 120; CANR 49; DLB
    194; MTCW 1, 2
**Ishikawa, Hakuhin**
  See Ishikawa, Takuboku
**Ishikawa, Takuboku** 1886(?)-1912 **TCLC 15;**
  **DAM POET; PC 10**
    See also CA 113; 153
**Iskander, Fazil** 1929-                **CLC 47**
  See also CA 102
**Isler, Alan (David)** 1934-            **CLC 91**
  See also CA 156
**Ivan IV** 1530-1584                    **LC 17**
**Ivanov, Vyacheslav Ivanovich** 1866-1949
  **TCLC 33**
    See also CA 122
**Ivask, Ivar Vidrik** 1927-1992         **CLC 14**
  See also CA 37-40R; 139; CANR 24
**Ives, Morgan**
  See Bradley, Marion Zimmer
**Izumi Shikibu** c. 973-c. 1034        **CMLC 33**
**J. R. S.**
  See Gogarty, Oliver St. John
**Jabran, Kahlil**
  See Gibran, Kahlil
**Jabran, Khalil**
  See Gibran, Kahlil
**Jackson, Daniel**
  See Wingrove, David (John)
**Jackson, Jesse** 1908-1983             **CLC 12**
  See also BW 1; CA 25-28R; 109; CANR 27;
    CLR 28; MAICYA; SATA 2, 29; SATA-Obit
    48
**Jackson, Laura (Riding)** 1901-1991
  See Riding, Laura
  See also CA 65-68; 135; CANR 28; DLB 48
**Jackson, Sam**
  See Trumbo, Dalton
**Jackson, Sara**
  See Wingrove, David (John)
**Jackson, Shirley** 1919-1965   **CLC 11, 60, 87;**
  **DA; DAC; DAM MST; SSC 9; WLC**
    See also AAYA 9; CA 1-4R; 25-28R; CANR 4,
    52; CDALB 1941-1968; DLB 6; MTCW 2;
    SATA 2
**Jacob, (Cyprien-)Max** 1876-1944       **TCLC 6**
  See also CA 104
**Jacobs, Harriet A(nn)** 1813(?)-1897**NCLC 67**
**Jacobs, Jim** 1942-                    **CLC 12**
  See also CA 97-100; INT 97-100
**Jacobs, W(illiam) W(ymark)** 1863-1943
  **TCLC 22**
    See also CA 121; 167; DLB 135
**Jacobsen, Jens Peter** 1847-1885      **NCLC 34**
**Jacobsen, Josephine** 1908-          **CLC 48, 102**
  See also CA 33-36R; CAAS 18; CANR 23, 48
**Jacobson, Dan** 1929-                 **CLC 4, 14**
  See also CA 1-4R; CANR 2, 25, 66; DLB 14,
    207; MTCW 1
**Jacqueline**
  See Carpentier (y Valmont), Alejo
**Jagger, Mick** 1944-                   **CLC 17**
**Jahiz, al-** c. 780-c. 869            **CMLC 25**
**Jakes, John (William)** 1932-  **CLC 29; DAM**
  **NOV, POP**
    See also BEST 89:4; CA 57-60; CANR 10, 43,
    66; DLBY 83; INT CANR-10; MTCW 1, 2;
    SATA 62
**James, Andrew**
  See Kirkup, James
**James, C(yril) L(ionel) R(obert)** 1901-1989
  **CLC 33; BLCS**
    See also BW 2; CA 117; 125; 128; CANR 62;
    DLB 125; MTCW 1

**James, Daniel (Lewis)** 1911-1988
　See Santiago, Danny
　See also CA 174; 125
**James, Dynely**
　See Mayne, William (James Carter)
**James, Henry Sr.** 1811-1882　　**NCLC 53**
**James, Henry** 1843-1916 **TCLC 2, 11, 24, 40,
　47, 64; DA; DAB; DAC; DAM MST, NOV;
　SSC 8, 32; WLC**
　See also CA 104; 132; CDALB 1865-1917;
　DLB 12, 71, 74, 189; DLBD 13; MTCW 1,
　2
**James, M. R.**
　See James, Montague (Rhodes)
　See also DLB 156
**James, Montague (Rhodes)** 1862-1936 **T C L C
　6; SSC 16**
　See also CA 104; DLB 201
**James, P. D.** 1920-　　　　　　**CLC 18, 46**
　See also White, Phyllis Dorothy James
　See also BEST 90:2; CDBLB 1960 to Present;
　DLB 87; DLBD 17
**James, Philip**
　See Moorcock, Michael (John)
**James, William** 1842-1910　　**TCLC 15, 32**
　See also CA 109
**James I** 1394-1437　　　　　　　　**LC 20**
**Jameson, Anna** 1794-1860　　　　**NCLC 43**
　See also DLB 99, 166
**Jami, Nur al-Din 'Abd al-Rahman** 1414-1492
　**LC 9**
**Jammes, Francis** 1868-1938　　　　**TCLC 75**
**Jandl, Ernst** 1925-　　　　　　　　**CLC 34**
**Janowitz, Tama** 1957-　　**CLC 43; DAM POP**
　See also CA 106; CANR 52
**Japrisot, Sebastien** 1931-　　　　　**CLC 90**
**Jarrell, Randall** 1914-1965**CLC 1, 2, 6, 9, 13,
　49; DAM POET**
　See also CA 5-8R; 25-28R; CABS 2; CANR 6,
　34; CDALB 1941-1968; CLR 6; DLB 48, 52;
　MAICYA; MTCW 1, 2; SATA 7
**Jarry, Alfred** 1873-1907　**TCLC 2, 14; DAM
　DRAM; SSC 20**
　See also CA 104; 153; DLB 192
**Jarvis, E. K.**
　See Bloch, Robert (Albert); Ellison, Harlan
　(Jay); Silverberg, Robert
**Jeake, Samuel, Jr.**
　See Aiken, Conrad (Potter)
**Jean Paul** 1763-1825　　　　　　　　**NCLC 7**
**Jefferies, (John) Richard** 1848-1887**NCLC 47**
　See also DLB 98, 141; SATA 16
**Jeffers, (John) Robinson** 1887-1962**CLC 2, 3,
　11, 15, 54; DA; DAC; DAM MST, POET;
　PC 17; WLC**
　See also CA 85-88; CANR 35; CDALB 1917-
　1929; DLB 45, 212; MTCW 1, 2
**Jefferson, Janet**
　See Mencken, H(enry) L(ouis)
**Jefferson, Thomas** 1743-1826　　　**NCLC 11**
　See also CDALB 1640-1865; DLB 31
**Jeffrey, Francis** 1773-1850　　　　**NCLC 33**
　See also DLB 107
**Jelakowitch, Ivan**
　See Heijermans, Herman
**Jellicoe, (Patricia) Ann** 1927-　　**CLC 27**
　See also CA 85-88; DLB 13
**Jen, Gish**　　　　　　　　　　　　**CLC 70**
　See also Jen, Lillian
**Jen, Lillian** 1956(?)-
　See Jen, Gish
　See also CA 135
**Jenkins, (John) Robin** 1912-　　　　**CLC 52**

See also CA 1-4R; CANR 1; DLB 14
**Jennings, Elizabeth (Joan)** 1926-　**CLC 5, 14**
　See also CA 61-64; CAAS 5; CANR 8, 39, 66;
　DLB 27; MTCW 1; SATA 66
**Jennings, Waylon** 1937-　　　　　　**CLC 21**
**Jensen, Johannes V.** 1873-1950　　**TCLC 41**
　See also CA 170
**Jensen, Laura (Linnea)** 1948-　　　**CLC 37**
　See also CA 103
**Jerome, Jerome K(lapka)** 1859-1927**TCLC 23**
　See also CA 119; DLB 10, 34, 135
**Jerrold, Douglas William** 1803-1857**NCLC 2**
　See also DLB 158, 159
**Jewett, (Theodora) Sarah Orne** 1849-1909
　**TCLC 1, 22; SSC 6**
　See also CA 108; 127; CANR 71; DLB 12, 74;
　SATA 15
**Jewsbury, Geraldine (Endsor)** 1812-1880
　**NCLC 22**
　See also DLB 21
**Jhabvala, Ruth Prawer** 1927-**CLC 4, 8, 29, 94;
　DAB; DAM NOV**
　See also CA 1-4R; CANR 2, 29, 51, 74; DLB
　139, 194; INT CANR-29; MTCW 1, 2
**Jibran, Kahlil**
　See Gibran, Kahlil
**Jibran, Khalil**
　See Gibran, Kahlil
**Jiles, Paulette** 1943-　　　　　　　**CLC 13, 58**
　See also CA 101; CANR 70
**Jimenez (Mantecon), Juan Ramon** 1881-1958
　**TCLC 4; DAM MULT, POET; HLC; PC
　7**
　See also CA 104; 131; CANR 74; DLB 134;
　HW 1; MTCW 1, 2
**Jimenez, Ramon**
　See Jimenez (Mantecon), Juan Ramon
**Jimenez Mantecon, Juan**
　See Jimenez (Mantecon), Juan Ramon
**Jin, Ha** 1956-　　　　　　　　　　**CLC 109**
　See also CA 152
**Joel, Billy**　　　　　　　　　　　**CLC 26**
　See also Joel, William Martin
**Joel, William Martin** 1949-
　See Joel, Billy
　See also CA 108
**John, Saint** 7th cent. -　　　　　　**CMLC 27**
**John of the Cross, St.** 1542-1591　　　**LC 18**
**Johnson, B(ryan) S(tanley William)** 1933-1973
　**CLC 6, 9**
　See also CA 9-12R; 53-56; CANR 9; DLB 14,
　40
**Johnson, Benj. F. of Boo**
　See Riley, James Whitcomb
**Johnson, Benjamin F. of Boo**
　See Riley, James Whitcomb
**Johnson, Charles (Richard)** 1948-**CLC 7, 51,
　65; BLC 2; DAM MULT**
　See also BW 2, 3; CA 116; CAAS 18; CANR
　42, 66; DLB 33; MTCW 2
**Johnson, Denis** 1949-　　　　　　　**CLC 52**
　See also CA 117; 121; CANR 71; DLB 120
**Johnson, Diane** 1934-　　　　　**CLC 5, 13, 48**
　See also CA 41-44R; CANR 17, 40, 62; DLBY
　80; INT CANR-17; MTCW 1
**Johnson, Eyvind (Olof Verner)** 1900-1976
　**CLC 14**
　See also CA 73-76; 69-72; CANR 34
**Johnson, J. R.**
　See James, C(yril) L(ionel) R(obert)
**Johnson, James Weldon** 1871-1938 **TCLC 3,
　19; BLC 2; DAM MULT, POET; PC 24**
　See also BW 1, 3; CA 104; 125; CDALB 1917-

1929; CLR 32; DLB 51; MTCW 1, 2; SATA
31
**Johnson, Joyce** 1935-　　　　　　　**CLC 58**
　See also CA 125; 129
**Johnson, Judith (Emlyn)** 1936-　　**CLC 7, 15**
　See also CA 25-28R; 153; CANR 34
**Johnson, Lionel (Pigot)** 1867-1902 **TCLC 19**
　See also CA 117; DLB 19
**Johnson, Marguerite (Annie)**
　See Angelou, Maya
**Johnson, Mel**
　See Malzberg, Barry N(athaniel)
**Johnson, Pamela Hansford** 1912-1981**CLC 1,
　7, 27**
　See also CA 1-4R; 104; CANR 2, 28; DLB 15;
　MTCW 1, 2
**Johnson, Robert** 1911(?)-1938　　　**TCLC 69**
　See also BW 3; CA 174
**Johnson, Samuel** 1709-1784**LC 15; DA; DAB;
　DAC; DAM MST; WLC**
　See also CDBLB 1660-1789; DLB 39, 95, 104,
　142
**Johnson, Uwe** 1934-1984　　**CLC 5, 10, 15, 40**
　See also CA 1-4R; 112; CANR 1, 39; DLB 75;
　MTCW 1
**Johnston, George (Benson)** 1913-　　**CLC 51**
　See also CA 1-4R; CANR 5, 20; DLB 88
**Johnston, Jennifer** 1930-　　　　　　**CLC 7**
　See also CA 85-88; DLB 14
**Jolley, (Monica) Elizabeth** 1923-**CLC 46; SSC
　19**
　See also CA 127; CAAS 13; CANR 59
**Jones, Arthur Llewellyn** 1863-1947
　See Machen, Arthur
　See also CA 104
**Jones, D(ouglas) G(ordon)** 1929-　　**CLC 10**
　See also CA 29-32R; CANR 13; DLB 53
**Jones, David (Michael)** 1895-1974**CLC 2, 4, 7,
　13, 42**
　See also CA 9-12R; 53-56; CANR 28; CDBLB
　1945-1960; DLB 20, 100; MTCW 1
**Jones, David Robert** 1947-
　See Bowie, David
　See also CA 103
**Jones, Diana Wynne** 1934-　　　　　**CLC 26**
　See also AAYA 12; CA 49-52; CANR 4, 26,
　56; CLR 23; DLB 161; JRDA; MAICYA;
　SAAS 7; SATA 9, 70
**Jones, Edward P.** 1950-　　　　　　**CLC 76**
　See also BW 2, 3; CA 142; CANR 79
**Jones, Gayl** 1949-　　**CLC 6, 9; BLC 2; DAM
　MULT**
　See also BW 2, 3; CA 77-80; CANR 27, 66;
　DLB 33; MTCW 1, 2
**Jones, James** 1921-1977　　**CLC 1, 3, 10, 39**
　See also AITN 1, 2; CA 1-4R; 69-72; CANR 6;
　DLB 2, 143; DLBD 17; DLBY 98; MTCW 1
**Jones, John J.**
　See Lovecraft, H(oward) P(hillips)
**Jones, LeRoi**　　　　　　**CLC 1, 2, 3, 5, 10, 14**
　See also Baraka, Amiri
　See also MTCW 2
**Jones, Louis B.** 1953-　　　　　　　**CLC 65**
　See also CA 141; CANR 73
**Jones, Madison (Percy, Jr.)** 1925-　　**CLC 4**
　See also CA 13-16R; CAAS 11; CANR 7, 54;
　DLB 152
**Jones, Mervyn** 1922-　　　　　　　**CLC 10, 52**
　See also CA 45-48; CAAS 5; CANR 1; MTCW
　1
**Jones, Mick** 1956(?)-　　　　　　　**CLC 30**
**Jones, Nettie (Pearl)** 1941-　　　　　**CLC 34**
　See also BW 2; CA 137; CAAS 20

Jones, Preston 1936-1979 **CLC 10**
See also CA 73-76; 89-92; DLB 7
Jones, Robert F(rancis) 1934- **CLC 7**
See also CA 49-52; CANR 2, 61
Jones, Rod 1953- **CLC 50**
See also CA 128
Jones, Terence Graham Parry 1942- CLC 21
See also Jones, Terry; Monty Python
See also CA 112; 116; CANR 35; INT 116
Jones, Terry
See Jones, Terence Graham Parry
See also SATA 67; SATA-Brief 51
Jones, Thom 1945(?)- **CLC 81**
See also CA 157
Jong, Erica 1942- CLC 4, 6, 8, 18, 83; DAM
**NOV, POP**
See also AITN 1; BEST 90:2; CA 73-76; CANR
26, 52, 75; DLB 2, 5, 28, 152; INT CANR-
26; MTCW 1, 2
Jonson, Ben(jamin) 1572(?)-1637 **LC 6, 33;**
**DA; DAB; DAC; DAM DRAM, MST,**
**POET; DC 4; PC 17; WLC**
See also CDBLB Before 1660; DLB 62, 121
Jordan, June 1936-CLC 5, 11, 23, 114; BLCS;
**DAM MULT, POET**
See also AAYA 2; BW 2, 3; CA 33-36R; CANR
25, 70; CLR 10; DLB 38; MAICYA; MTCW
1; SATA 4
Jordan, Neil (Patrick) 1950- **CLC 110**
See also CA 124; 130; CANR 54; INT 130
Jordan, Pat(rick M.) 1941- **CLC 37**
See also CA 33-36R
Jorgensen, Ivar
See Ellison, Harlan (Jay)
Jorgenson, Ivar
See Silverberg, Robert
Josephus, Flavius c. 37-100 **CMLC 13**
Josipovici, Gabriel 1940- **CLC 6, 43**
See also CA 37-40R; CAAS 8; CANR 47; DLB
14
Joubert, Joseph 1754-1824 **NCLC 9**
Jouve, Pierre Jean 1887-1976 **CLC 47**
See also CA 65-68
Jovine, Francesco 1902-1950 **TCLC 79**
Joyce, James (Augustine Aloysius) 1882-1941
**TCLC 3, 8, 16, 35, 52; DA; DAB; DAC;**
**DAM MST, NOV, POET; PC 22; SSC 3,**
**26; WLC**
See also CA 104; 126; CDBLB 1914-1945;
DLB 10, 19, 36, 162; MTCW 1, 2
Jozsef, Attila 1905-1937 **TCLC 22**
See also CA 116
Juana Ines de la Cruz 1651(?)-1695 **LC 5;**
**HLCS 1; PC 24**
Judd, Cyril
See Kornbluth, C(yril) M.; Pohl, Frederik
Julian of Norwich 1342(?)-1416(?) **LC 6**
See also DLB 146
Junger, Sebastian 1962- **CLC 109**
See also AAYA 28; CA 165
Juniper, Alex
See Hospital, Janette Turner
Junius
See Luxemburg, Rosa
Just, Ward (Swift) 1935- **CLC 4, 27**
See also CA 25-28R; CANR 32; INT CANR-
32
Justice, Donald (Rodney) 1925- CLC 6, 19,
**102; DAM POET**
See also CA 5-8R; CANR 26, 54, 74; DLBY
83; INT CANR-26; MTCW 2
Juvenal c. 60-c. 13 **CMLC 8**
See also Juvenalis, Decimus Junius

See also DLB 211
Juvenalis, Decimus Junius 55(?)-c. 127(?)
See Juvenal
Juvenis
See Bourne, Randolph S(illiman)
Kacew, Romain 1914-1980
See Gary, Romain
See also CA 108; 102
Kadare, Ismail 1936- **CLC 52**
See also CA 161
Kadohata, Cynthia **CLC 59**
See also CA 140
Kafka, Franz 1883-1924TCLC 2, 6, 13, 29, 47,
53; DA; DAB; DAC; DAM MST, NOV;
SSC 5, 29; WLC
See also CA 105; 126; DLB 81; MTCW 1, 2
Kahanovitsch, Pinkhes
See Der Nister
Kahn, Roger 1927- **CLC 30**
See also CA 25-28R; CANR 44, 69; DLB 171;
SATA 37
Kain, Saul
See Sassoon, Siegfried (Lorraine)
Kaiser, Georg 1878-1945 **TCLC 9**
See also CA 106; DLB 124
Kaletski, Alexander 1946- **CLC 39**
See also CA 118; 143
Kalidasa fl. c. 400- **CMLC 9; PC 22**
Kallman, Chester (Simon) 1921-1975 **CLC 2**
See also CA 45-48; 53-56; CANR 3
Kaminsky, Melvin 1926-
See Brooks, Mel
See also CA 65-68; CANR 16
Kaminsky, Stuart M(elvin) 1934- **CLC 59**
See also CA 73-76; CANR 29, 53
Kandinsky, Wassily 1866-1944 **TCLC 92**
See also CA 118; 155
Kane, Francis
See Robbins, Harold
Kane, Paul
See Simon, Paul (Frederick)
Kane, Wilson
See Bloch, Robert (Albert)
Kanin, Garson 1912- **CLC 22**
See also AITN 1; CA 5-8R; CANR 7, 78; DLB
7
Kaniuk, Yoram 1930- **CLC 19**
See also CA 134
Kant, Immanuel 1724-1804 **NCLC 27, 67**
See also DLB 94
Kantor, MacKinlay 1904-1977 **CLC 7**
See also CA 61-64; 73-76; CANR 60, 63; DLB
9, 102; MTCW 2
Kaplan, David Michael 1946- **CLC 50**
Kaplan, James 1951- **CLC 59**
See also CA 135
Karageorge, Michael
See Anderson, Poul (William)
Karamzin, Nikolai Mikhailovich 1766-1826
**NCLC 3**
See also DLB 150
Karapanou, Margarita 1946- **CLC 13**
See also CA 101
Karinthy, Frigyes 1887-1938 **TCLC 47**
See also CA 170
Karl, Frederick R(obert) 1927- **CLC 34**
See also CA 5-8R; CANR 3, 44
Kastel, Warren
See Silverberg, Robert
Kataev, Evgeny Petrovich 1903-1942
See Petrov, Evgeny
See also CA 120
Kataphusin

See Ruskin, John
Katz, Steve 1935- **CLC 47**
See also CA 25-28R; CAAS 14, 64; CANR 12;
DLBY 83
Kauffman, Janet 1945- **CLC 42**
See also CA 117; CANR 43; DLBY 86
Kaufman, Bob (Garnell) 1925-1986 **CLC 49**
See also BW 1; CA 41-44R; 118; CANR 22;
DLB 16, 41
Kaufman, George S. 1889-1961CLC 38; DAM
**DRAM**
See also CA 108; 93-96; DLB 7; INT 108;
MTCW 2
Kaufman, Sue **CLC 3, 8**
See also Barondess, Sue K(aufman)
Kavafis, Konstantinos Petrou 1863-1933
See Cavafy, C(onstantine) P(eter)
See also CA 104
Kavan, Anna 1901-1968 **CLC 5, 13, 82**
See also CA 5-8R; CANR 6, 57; MTCW 1
Kavanagh, Dan
See Barnes, Julian (Patrick)
Kavanagh, Julie 1952- **CLC 119**
See also CA 163
Kavanagh, Patrick (Joseph) 1904-1967 **C L C**
**22**
See also CA 123; 25-28R; DLB 15, 20; MTCW
1
Kawabata, Yasunari 1899-1972 **CLC 2, 5, 9,**
**18, 107; DAM MULT; SSC 17**
See also CA 93-96; 33-36R; DLB 180; MTCW
2
Kaye, M(ary) M(argaret) 1909- **CLC 28**
See also CA 89-92; CANR 24, 60; MTCW 1,
2; SATA 62
Kaye, Mollie
See Kaye, M(ary) M(argaret)
Kaye-Smith, Sheila 1887-1956 **TCLC 20**
See also CA 118; DLB 36
Kaymor, Patrice Maguilene
See Senghor, Leopold Sedar
Kazan, Elia 1909- **CLC 6, 16, 63**
See also CA 21-24R; CANR 32, 78
Kazantzakis, Nikos 1883(?)-1957 **TCLC 2, 5,**
**33**
See also CA 105; 132; MTCW 1, 2
Kazin, Alfred 1915-1998 **CLC 34, 38, 119**
See also CA 1-4R; CAAS 7; CANR 1, 45, 79;
DLB 67
Keane, Mary Nesta (Skrine) 1904-1996
See Keane, Molly
See also CA 108; 114; 151
Keane, Molly **CLC 31**
See also Keane, Mary Nesta (Skrine)
See also INT 114
Keates, Jonathan 1946(?)- **CLC 34**
See also CA 163
Keaton, Buster 1895-1966 **CLC 20**
Keats, John 1795-1821NCLC 8, 73; DA; DAB;
**DAC; DAM MST, POET; PC 1; WLC**
See also CDBLB 1789-1832; DLB 96, 110
Keene, Donald 1922- **CLC 34**
See also CA 1-4R; CANR 5
Keillor, Garrison **CLC 40, 115**
See also Keillor, Gary (Edward)
See also AAYA 2; BEST 89:3; DLBY 87; SATA
58
Keillor, Gary (Edward) 1942-
See Keillor, Garrison
See also CA 111; 117; CANR 36, 59; DAM
POP; MTCW 1, 2
Keith, Michael
See Hubbard, L(afayette) Ron(ald)

**Keller, Gottfried** 1819-1890 **NCLC 2; SSC 26**
See also DLB 129
**Keller, Nora Okja** **CLC 109**
**Kellerman, Jonathan** 1949- **CLC 44; DAM POP**
See also BEST 90:1; CA 106; CANR 29, 51; INT CANR-29
**Kelley, William Melvin** 1937- **CLC 22**
See also BW 1; CA 77-80; CANR 27; DLB 33
**Kellogg, Marjorie** 1922- **CLC 2**
See also CA 81-84
**Kellow, Kathleen**
See Hibbert, Eleanor Alice Burford
**Kelly, M(ilton) T(erry)** 1947- **CLC 55**
See also CA 97-100; CAAS 22; CANR 19, 43
**Kelman, James** 1946- **CLC 58, 86**
See also CA 148; DLB 194
**Kemal, Yashar** 1923- **CLC 14, 29**
See also CA 89-92; CANR 44
**Kemble, Fanny** 1809-1893 **NCLC 18**
See also DLB 32
**Kemelman, Harry** 1908-1996 **CLC 2**
See also AITN 1; CA 9-12R; 155; CANR 6, 71; DLB 28
**Kempe, Margery** 1373(?)-1440(?) **LC 6**
See also DLB 146
**Kempis, Thomas a** 1380-1471 **LC 11**
**Kendall, Henry** 1839-1882 **NCLC 12**
**Keneally, Thomas (Michael)** 1935- **CLC 5, 8, 10, 14, 19, 27, 43, 117; DAM NOV**
See also CA 85-88; CANR 10, 50, 74; MTCW 1, 2
**Kennedy, Adrienne (Lita)** 1931- **CLC 66; BLC 2; DAM MULT; DC 5**
See also BW 2, 3; CA 103; CAAS 20; CABS 3; CANR 26, 53; DLB 38
**Kennedy, John Pendleton** 1795-1870 **NCLC 2**
See also DLB 3
**Kennedy, Joseph Charles** 1929-
See Kennedy, X. J.
See also CA 1-4R; CANR 4, 30, 40; SATA 14, 86
**Kennedy, William** 1928- **CLC 6, 28, 34, 53; DAM NOV**
See also AAYA 1; CA 85-88; CANR 14, 31, 76; DLB 143; DLBY 85; INT CANR-31; MTCW 1, 2; SATA 57
**Kennedy, X. J.** **CLC 8, 42**
<indeSee also Kennedy, Joseph Charles
See also CAAS 9; CLR 27; DLB 5; SAAS 22
**Kenny, Maurice (Francis)** 1929- **CLC 87; DAM MULT**
See also CA 144; CAAS 22; DLB 175; NNAL
**Kent, Kelvin**
See Kuttner, Henry
**Kenton, Maxwell**
See Southern, Terry
**Kenyon, Robert O.**
See Kuttner, Henry
**Kepler, Johannes** 1571-1630 **LC 45**
**Kerouac, Jack** **CLC 1, 2, 3, 5, 14, 29, 61**
See also Kerouac, Jean-Louis Lebris de
See also AAYA 25; CDALB 1941-1968; DLB 2, 16; DLBD 3; DLBY 95; MTCW 2
**Kerouac, Jean-Louis Lebris de** 1922-1969
See Kerouac, Jack
See also AITN 1; CA 5-8R; 25-28R; CANR 26, 54; DA; DAB; DAC; DAM MST, NOV, POET, POP; MTCW 1, 2; WLC
**Kerr, Jean** 1923- **CLC 22**
See also CA 5-8R; CANR 7; INT CANR-7
**Kerr, M. E.** **CLC 12, 35**
See also Meaker, Marijane (Agnes)

See also AAYA 2, 23; CLR 29; SAAS 1
**Kerr, Robert** **CLC 55**
**Kerrigan, (Thomas) Anthony** 1918- **CLC 4, 6**
See also CA 49-52; CAAS 11; CANR 4
**Kerry, Lois**
See Duncan, Lois
**Kesey, Ken (Elton)** 1935- **CLC 1, 3, 6, 11, 46, 64; DA; DAB; DAC; DAM MST, NOV, POP; WLC**
See also AAYA 25; CA 1-4R; CANR 22, 38, 66; CDALB 1968-1988; DLB 2, 16, 206; MTCW 1, 2; SATA 66
**Kesselring, Joseph (Otto)** 1902-1967 **CLC 45; DAM DRAM, MST**
See also CA 150
<indexb**Kessler, Jascha (Frederick)** 1929- **CLC 4**
See also CA 17-20R; CANR 8, 48
**Kettelkamp, Larry (Dale)** 1933- **CLC 12**
See also CA 29-32R; CANR 16; SAAS 3; SATA 2
**Key, Ellen** 1849-1926 **TCLC 65**
**Keyber, Conny**
See Fielding, Henry
**Keyes, Daniel** 1927- **CLC 80; DA; DAC; DAM MST, NOV**
See also AAYA 23; CA 17-20R; CANR 10, 26, 54, 74; MTCW 2; SATA 37
**Keynes, John Maynard** 1883-1946 **TCLC 64**
See also CA 114; 162, 163; DLBD 10; MTCW 2
**Khanshendel, Chiron**
See Rose, Wendy
**Khayyam, Omar** 1048-1131 **CMLC 11; DAM POET; PC 8**
**Kherdian, David** 1931- **CLC 6, 9**
See also CA 21-24R; CAAS 2; CANR 39, 78; CLR 24; JRDA; MAICYA; SATA 16, 74
**Khlebnikov, Velimir** **TCLC 20**
See also Khlebnikov, Viktor Vladimirovich
**Khlebnikov, Viktor Vladimirovich** 1885-1922
See Khlebnikov, Velimir
See also CA 117
**Khodasevich, Vladislav (Felitsianovich)** 1886-1939 **TCLC 15**
See also CA 115
**Kielland, Alexander Lange** 1849-1906 **TCLC 5**
See also CA 104
**Kiely, Benedict** 1919- **CLC 23, 43**
See also CA 1-4R; CANR 2; DLB 15
**Kienzle, William X(avier)** 1928- **CLC 25; DAM POP**
See also CA 93-96; CAAS 1; CANR 9, 31, 59; INT CANR-31; MTCW 1, 2
**Kierkegaard, Soren** 1813-1855 **NCLC 34**
**Kieslowski, Krzysztof** 1941-1996 **CLC 120**
See also CA 147; 151
**Killens, John Oliver** 1916-1987 **CLC 10**
See also BW 2; CA 77-80; 123; CAAS 2; CANR 26; DLB 33
**Killigrew, Anne** 1660-1685 **LC 4**
See also DLB 131
**Kim**
See Simenon, Georges (Jacques Christian)
**Kincaid, Jamaica** 1949- **CLC 43, 68; BLC 2; DAM MULT, NOV**
See also AAYA 13; BW 2, 3; CA 125; CANR 47, 59; CDALBS; DLB 157; MTCW 2
**King, Francis (Henry)** 1923- **CLC 8, 53; DAM NOV**
See also CA 1-4R; CANR 1, 33; DLB 15, 139; MTCW 1

**King, Kennedy**
See Brown, George Douglas
<indexbo**King, Martin Luther, Jr.** 1929-1968 **CLC 83; BLC 2; DA; DAB; DAC; DAM MST, MULT; WLCS**
See also BW 2, 3; CA 25-28; CANR 27, 44; CAP 2; MTCW 1, 2; SATA 14
**King, Stephen (Edwin)** 1947- **CLC 12, 26, 37, 61, 113; DAM NOV, POP; SSC 17**
See also AAYA 1, 17; BEST 90:1; CA 61-64; CANR 1, 30, 52, 76; DLB 143; DLBY 80; JRDA; MTCW 1, 2; SATA 9, 55
**King, Steve**
See King, Stephen (Edwin)
**King, Thomas** 1943- **CLC 89; DAC; DAM MULT**
See also CA 144; DLB 175; NNAL; SATA 96
**Kingman, Lee** **CLC 17**
See also Natti, (Mary) Lee
See also SAAS 3; SATA 1, 67
**Kingsley, Charles** 1819-1875 **NCLC 35**
See also DLB 21, 32, 163, 190; YABC 2
**Kingsley, Sidney** 1906-1995 **CLC 44**
See also CA 85-88; 147; DLB 7
**Kingsolver, Barbara** 1955- **CLC 55, 81; DAM POP**
See also AAYA 15; CA 129; 134; CANR 60; CDALBS; DLB 206; INT 134; MTCW 2
**Kingston, Maxine (Ting Ting) Hong** 1940- **CLC 12, 19, 58; DAM MULT, NOV; WLCS**
See also AAYA 8; CA 69-72; CANR 13, 38, 74; CDALBS; DLB 173, 212; DLBY 80; INT CANR-13; MTCW 1, 2; SATA 53
**Kinnell, Galway** 1927- **CLC 1, 2, 3, 5, 13, 29; PC 26**
See also CA 9-12R; CANR 10, 34, 66; DLB 5; DLBY 87; INT CANR-34; MTCW 1, 2
**Kinsella, Thomas** 1928- **CLC 4, 19**
See also CA 17-20R; CANR 15; DLB 27; MTCW 1, 2
**Kinsella, W(illiam) P(atrick)** 1935- **CLC 27, 43; DAM NOV, POP**
See also AAYA 7; CA 97-100; CAAS 7; CANR 21, 35, 66, 75; INT CANR-21; MTCW 1, 2
**Kinsey, Alfred C(harles)** 1894-1956 **TCLC 91**
See also CA 115; 170; MTCW 2
**Kipling, (Joseph) Rudyard** 1865-1936 **TCLC 8, 17; DA; DAB; DAC; DAM MST, POET; PC 3; SSC 5; WLC**
See also CA 105; 120; CANR 33; CDBLB 1890-1914; CLR 39; DLB 19, 34, 141, 156; MAICYA; MTCW 1, 2; SATA 100; YABC 2
**Kirkup, James** 1918- **CLC 1**
See also CA 1-4R; CAAS 4; CANR 2; DLB 27; SATA 12
**Kirkwood, James** 1930(?)-1989 **CLC 9**
See also AITN 2; CA 1-4R; 128; CANR 6, 40
**Kirshner, Sidney**
See Kingsley, Sidney
**Kis, Danilo** 1935-1989 **CLC 57**
See also CA 109; 118; 129; CANR 61; DLB 181; MTCW 1
**Kivi, Aleksis** 1834-1872 **NCLC 30**
**Kizer, Carolyn (Ashley)** 1925- **CLC 15, 39, 80; DAM POET**
See also CA 65-68; CAAS 5; CANR 24, 70; DLB 5, 169; MTCW 2
**Klabund** 1890-1928 **TCLC 44**
See also CA 162; DLB 66
**Klappert, Peter** 1942- **CLC 57**
See also CA 33-36R; DLB 5
**Klein, A(braham) M(oses)** 1909-1972 **CLC 19;**

DAB; DAC; DAM MST
See also CA 101; 37-40R; DLB 68

**Klein, Norma** 1938-1989 **CLC 30**
See also AAYA 2; CA 41-44R; 128; CANR 15, 37; CLR 2, 19; INT CANR-15; JRDA; MAICYA; SAAS 1; SATA 7, 57

**Klein, T(heodore) E(ibon) D(onald)** 1947- **CLC 34**
See also CA 119; CANR 44, 75

**Kleist, Heinrich von** 1777-1811 **NCLC 2, 37; DAM DRAM; SSC 22**
See also DLB 90

**Klima, Ivan** 1931- **CLC 56; DAM NOV**
See also CA 25-28R; CANR 17, 50

**Klimentov, Andrei Platonovich** 1899-1951
See Platonov, Andrei
See also CA 108

**Klinger, Friedrich Maximilian von** 1752-1831 **NCLC 1**
See also DLB 94

**Klingsor the Magician**
See Hartmann, Sadakichi

**Klopstock, Friedrich Gottlieb** 1724-1803 **NCLC 11**
See also DLB 97

**Knapp, Caroline** 1959- **CLC 99**
See also CA 154

**Knebel, Fletcher** 1911-1993 **CLC 14**
<indexSee also AITN 1; CA 1-4R; 140; CAAS 3; CANR 1, 36; SATA 36; SATA-Obit 75

**Knickerbocker, Diedrich**
See Irving, Washington

**Knight, Etheridge** 1931-1991 **CLC 40; BLC 2; DAM POET; PC 14**
See also BW 1, 3; CA 21-24R; 133; CANR 23; DLB 41; MTCW 2

**Knight, Sarah Kemble** 1666-1727 **LC 7**
See also DLB 24, 200

**Knister, Raymond** 1899-1932 **TCLC 56**
See also DLB 68

**Knowles, John** 1926- **CLC 1, 4, 10, 26; DA; DAC; DAM MST, NOV**
See also AAYA 10; CA 17-20R; CANR 40, 74, 76; CDALB 1968-1988; DLB 6; MTCW 1, 2; SATA 8, 89

**Knox, Calvin M.**
See Silverberg, Robert

**Knox, John** c. 1505-1572 **LC 37**
See also DLB 132

<Knye, Cassandra
See Disch, Thomas M(ichael)

**Koch, C(hristopher) J(ohn)** 1932- **CLC 42**
See also CA 127

**Koch, Christopher**
See Koch, C(hristopher) J(ohn)

**Koch, Kenneth** 1925- **CLC 5, 8, 44; DAM POET**
See also CA 1-4R; CANR 6, 36, 57; DLB 5; INT CANR-36; MTCW 2; SATA 65

**Kochanowski, Jan** 1530-1584 **LC 10**

**Kock, Charles Paul de** 1794-1871 **NCLC 16**

**Koda Shigeyuki** 1867-1947
See Rohan, Koda
See also CA 121

**Koestler, Arthur** 1905-1983 **CLC 1, 3, 6, 8, 15, 33**
See also CA 1-4R; 109; CANR 1, 33; CDBLB 1945-1960; DLBY 83; MTCW 1, 2

**Kogawa, Joy Nozomi** 1935- **CLC 78; DAC; DAM MST, MULT**
See also CA 101; CANR 19, 62; MTCW 2; SATA 99

**Kohout, Pavel** 1928- **CLC 13**

See also CA 45-48; CANR 3

**Koizumi, Yakumo**
See Hearn, (Patricio) Lafcadio (Tessima Carlos)

**Kolmar, Gertrud** 1894-1943 **TCLC 40**
See also CA 167

**Komunyakaa, Yusef** 1947- **CLC 86, 94; BLCS**
See also CA 147; DLB 120

**Konrad, George**
See Konrad, Gyoergy

**Konrad, Gyoergy** 1933- **CLC 4, 10, 73**
See also CA 85-88

**Konwicki, Tadeusz** 1926- **CLC 8, 28, 54, 117**
See also CA 101; CAAS 9; CANR 39, 59; MTCW 1

**Koontz, Dean R(ay)** 1945- **CLC 78; DAM NOV, POP**
See also AAYA 9; BEST 89:3, 90:2; CA 108; CANR 19, 36, 52; MTCW 1; SATA 92

**Kopernik, Mikolaj**
See Copernicus, Nicolaus

**Kopit, Arthur (Lee)** 1937- **CLC 1, 18, 33; DAM DRAM**
See also AITN 1; CA 81-84; CABS 3; DLB 7; MTCW 1

**Kops, Bernard** 1926- **CLC 4**
See also CA 5-8R; DLB 13

**Kornbluth, C(yril) M.** 1923-1958 **TCLC 8**
See also CA 105; 160; DLB 8

**Korolenko, V. G.**
See Korolenko, Vladimir Galaktionovich

**Korolenko, Vladimir**
See Korolenko, Vladimir Galaktionovich

**Korolenko, Vladimir G.**
See Korolenko, Vladimir Galaktionovich

**Korolenko, Vladimir Galaktionovich** 1853-1921 **TCLC 22**
See also CA 121

**Korzybski, Alfred (Habdank Skarbek)** 1879-1950 **TCLC 61**
See also CA 123; 160

**Kosinski, Jerzy (Nikodem)** 1933-1991 **CLC 1, 2, 3, 6, 10, 15, 53, 70; DAM NOV**
See also CA 17-20R; 134; CANR 9, 46; DLB 2; DLBY 82; MTCW 1, 2

**Kostelanetz, Richard (Cory)** 1940- **CLC 28**
See also CA 13-16R; CAAS 8; CANR 38, 77

**Kostrowitzki, Wilhelm Apollinaris de** 1880-1918
See Apollinaire, Guillaume
See also CA 104

**Kotlowitz, Robert** 1924- **CLC 4**
See also CA 33-36R; CANR 36

**Kotzebue, August (Friedrich Ferdinand) von** 1761-1819 **NCLC 25**
See also DLB 94

<inKotzwinkle, William 1938- **CLC 5, 14, 35**
See also CA 45-48; CANR 3, 44; CLR 6; DLB 173; MAICYA; SATA 24, 70

**Kowna, Stancy**
See Szymborska, Wislawa

**Kozol, Jonathan** 1936- **CLC 17**
See also CA 61-64; CANR 16, 45

**Kozoll, Michael** 1940(?)- **CLC 35**

**Kramer, Kathryn** 19(?)- **CLC 34**

**Kramer, Larry** 1935- **CLC 42; DAM POP; DC 8**
See also CA 124; 126; CANR 60

**Krasicki, Ignacy** 1735-1801 **NCLC 8**

**Krasinski, Zygmunt** 1812-1859 **NCLC 4**

**Kraus, Karl** 1874-1936 **TCLC 5**
See also CA 104; DLB 118

**Kreve (Mickevicius), Vincas** 1882-1954 **TCLC 27**

See also CA 170

**Kristeva, Julia** 1941- **CLC 77**
See also CA 154

**Kristofferson, Kris** 1936- **CLC 26**
See also CA 104

**Krizanc, John** 1956- **CLC 57**

**Krleza, Miroslav** 1893-1981 **CLC 8, 114**
See also CA 97-100; 105; CANR 50; DLB 147

**Kroetsch, Robert** 1927- **CLC 5, 23, 57; DAC; DAM POET**
See also CA 17-20R; CANR 8, 38; DLB 53; MTCW 1

**Kroetz, Franz**
See Kroetz, Franz Xaver

**Kroetz, Franz Xaver** 1946- **CLC 41**
See also CA 130

**Kroker, Arthur (W.)** 1945- **CLC 77**
<See also CA 161

**Kropotkin, Peter (Aleksieevich)** 1842-1921 **TCLC 36**
See also CA 119

**Krotkov, Yuri** 1917- **CLC 19**
See also CA 102

**Krumb**
See Crumb, R(obert)

**Krumgold, Joseph (Quincy)** 1908-1980 **CLC 12**
See also CA 9-12R; 101; CANR 7; MAICYA; SATA 1, 48; SATA-Obit 23

**Krumwitz**
See Crumb, R(obert)

**Krutch, Joseph Wood** 1893-1970 **CLC 24**
See also CA 1-4R; 25-28R; CANR 4; DLB 63, 206

**Krutzch, Gus**
See Eliot, T(homas) S(tearns)

**Krylov, Ivan Andreevich** 1768(?)-1844 **NCLC 1**
See also DLB 150

**Kubin, Alfred (Leopold Isidor)** 1877-1959 **TCLC 23**
See also CA 112; 149; DLB 81

**Kubrick, Stanley** 1928- **CLC 16**
See also AAYA 30; CA 81-84; CANR 33; DLB 26

**Kumin, Maxine (Winokur)** 1925- **CLC 5, 13, 28; DAM POET; PC 15**
See also AITN 2; CA 1-4R; CAAS 8; CANR 1, 21, 69; DLB 5; MTCW 1, 2; SATA 12

**Kundera, Milan** 1929- **CLC 4, 9, 19, 32, 68, 115; DAM NOV; SSC 24**
See also AAYA 2; CA 85-88; CANR 19, 52, 74; MTCW 1, 2

**Kunene, Mazisi (Raymond)** 1930- **CLC 85**
See also BW 1, 3; CA 125; DLB 117

**Kunitz, Stanley (Jasspon)** 1905- **CLC 6, 11, 14; PC 19**
See also CA 41-44R; CANR 26, 57; DLB 48; INT CANR-26; MTCW 1, 2

**Kunze, Reiner** 1933- **CLC 10**
See also CA 93-96; DLB 75

**Kuprin, Aleksandr Ivanovich** 1870-1938 **TCLC 5**
See also CA 104

**Kureishi, Hanif** 1954(?)- **CLC 64**
See also CA 139; DLB 194

**Kurosawa, Akira** 1910-1998 **CLC 16, 119; DAM MULT**
See also AAYA 11; CA 101; 170; CANR 46

**Kushner, Tony** 1957(?)- **CLC 81; DAM DRAM; DC 10**
See also CA 144; CANR 74; MTCW 2

**Kuttner, Henry** 1915-1958 **TCLC 10**

See also CA 108; 136; CANR 69; SATA 65

Lesage, Alain-Rene 1668-1747    LC 2, 28

Leskov, Nikolai (Semyonovich) 1831-1895
   NCLC 25; SSC 34

Lessing, Doris (May) 1919-CLC 1, 2, 3, 6, 10,
   15, 22, 40, 94; DA; DAB; DAC; DAM MST,
   NOV; SSC 6; WLCS
   See also CA 9-12R; CAAS 14; CANR 33, 54,
   76; CDBLB 1960 to Present; DLB 15, 139;
   DLBY 85; MTCW 1, 2

Lessing, Gotthold Ephraim 1729-1781   LC 8
   See also DLB 97

Lester, Richard 1932-      CLC 20

Lever, Charles (James) 1806-1872   NCLC 23
   See also DLB 21

Leverson, Ada 1865(?)-1936(?)     TCLC 18
   See also Elaine
   See also CA 117; DLB 153

Levertov, Denise 1923-1997 CLC 1, 2, 3, 5, 8,
   15, 28, 66; DAM POET; PC 11
   See also CA 1-4R; 163; CAAS 19; CANR 3,
   29, 50; CDALBS; DLB 5, 165; INT CANR-
   29; MTCW 1, 2

Levi, Jonathan      CLC 76

Levi, Peter (Chad Tigar) 1931-    CLC 41
   See also CA 5-8R; CANR 34, 80; DLB 40

Levi, Primo 1919-1987   CLC 37, 50; SSC 12
   See also CA 13-16R; 122; CANR 12, 33, 61,
   70; DLB 177; MTCW 1, 2

Levin, Ira 1929-      CLC 3, 6; DAM POP
   See also CA 21-24R; CANR 17, 44, 74; MTCW
   1, 2; SATA 66

Levin, Meyer 1905-1981   CLC 7; DAM POP
   See also AITN 1; CA 9-12R; 104; CANR 15;
   DLB 9, 28; DLBY 81; SATA 21; SATA-Obit
   27

Levine, Norman 1924-      CLC 54
   See also CA 73-76; CAAS 23; CANR 14, 70;
   DLB 88

Levine, Philip 1928-CLC 2, 4, 5, 9, 14, 33, 118;
   DAM POET; PC 22
   See also CA 9-12R; CANR 9, 37, 52; DLB 5

Levinson, Deirdre 1931-      CLC 49
   See also CA 73-76; CANR 70

Levi-Strauss, Claude 1908-      CLC 38
   See also CA 1-4R; CANR 6, 32, 57; MTCW 1,
   2

Levitin, Sonia (Wolff) 1934-      CLC 17
   See also AAYA 13; CA 29-32R; CANR 14, 32,
   79; CLR 53; JRDA; MAICYA; SAAS 2;
   SATA 4, 68

Levon, O. U.
   See Kesey, Ken (Elton)

Levy, Amy 1861-1889      NCLC 59
   See also DLB 156

Lewes, George Henry 1817-1878   NCLC 25
   See also DLB 55, 144

Lewis, Alun 1915-1944      TCLC 3
   See also CA 104; DLB 20, 162

Lewis, C. Day
   See Day Lewis, C(ecil)

Lewis, C(live) S(taples) 1898-1963CLC 1, 3, 6,
   14, 27; DA; DAB; DAC; DAM MST, NOV,
   POP; WLC
   See also AAYA 3; CA 81-84; CANR 33, 71;
   CDBLB 1945-1960; CLR 3, 27; DLB 15,
   100, 160; JRDA; MAICYA; MTCW 1, 2;
   SATA 13, 100

Lewis, Janet 1899-1998      CLC 41
   See also Winters, Janet Lewis
   See also CA 9-12R; 172; CANR 29, 63; CAP
   1; DLBY 87

Lewis, Matthew Gregory 1775-1818NCLC 11,

62
   See also DLB 39, 158, 178

Lewis, (Harry) Sinclair 1885-1951 TCLC 4,
   13, 23, 39; DA; DAB; DAC; DAM MST,
   NOV; WLC
   See also CA 104; 133; CDALB 1917-1929;
   DLB 9, 102; DLBD 1; MTCW 1, 2

Lewis, (Percy) Wyndham 1882(?)-1957T C L C
   2, 9; SSC 34
   See also CA 104; 157; DLB 15; MTCW 2

Lewisohn, Ludwig 1883-1955      TCLC 19
   See also CA 107; DLB 4, 9, 28, 102

Lewton, Val 1904-1951      TCLC 76

Leyner, Mark 1956-      CLC 92
   See also CA 110; CANR 28, 53; MTCW 2

Lezama Lima, Jose 1910-1976CLC 4, 10, 101;
   DAM MULT; HLCS 1
   See also CA 77-80; CANR 71; DLB 113; HW
   1, 2

L'Heureux, John (Clarke) 1934-      CLC 52
   See also CA 13-16R; CANR 23, 45

Liddell, C. H.
   See Kuttner, Henry

Lie, Jonas (Lauritz Idemil) 1833-1908(?)
   TCLC 5
   See also CA 115

Lieber, Joel 1937-1971      CLC 6
   See also CA 73-76; 29-32R

Lieber, Stanley Martin
   See Lee, Stan

Lieberman, Laurence (James) 1935- CLC 4,
   36
   See also CA 17-20R; CANR 8, 36

Lieh Tzu fl. 7th cent. B.C.-5th cent. B.C.
   CMLC 27

Lieksman, Anders
   See Haavikko, Paavo Juhani

Li Fei-kan 1904-
   See Pa Chin
   See also CA 105

Lifton, Robert Jay 1926-      CLC 67
   See also CA 17-20R; CANR 27, 78; INT
   CANR-27; SATA 66

Lightfoot, Gordon 1938-      CLC 26
   See also CA 109

Lightman, Alan P(aige) 1948-      CLC 81
   See also CA 141; CANR 63

Ligotti, Thomas (Robert) 1953-CLC 44; SSC
   16
   See also CA 123; CANR 49

Li Ho 791-817      PC 13

Liliencron, (Friedrich Adolf Axel) Detlev von
   1844-1909      TCLC 18
   See also CA 117

Lilly, William 1602-1681      LC 27

Lima, Jose Lezama
   See Lezama Lima, Jose

Lima Barreto, Afonso Henrique de 1881-1922
   TCLC 23
   See also CA 117

Limonov, Edward 1944-      CLC 67
   See also CA 137

Lin, Frank
   See Atherton, Gertrude (Franklin Horn)

Lincoln, Abraham 1809-1865      NCLC 18

Lind, Jakov      CLC 1, 2, 4, 27, 82
   See also Landwirth, Heinz
   See also CAAS 4

Lindbergh, Anne (Spencer) Morrow 1906-
   CLC 82; DAM NOV
   See also CA 17-20R; CANR 16, 73; MTCW 1,
   2; SATA 33

Lindsay, David 1878-1945      TCLC 15

See also CA 113

Lindsay, (Nicholas) Vachel 1879-1931 T C L C
   17; DA; DAC; DAM MST, POET; PC 23;
   WLC
   See also CA 114; 135; CANR 79; CDALB
   1865-1917; DLB 54; SATA 40

Linke-Poot
   See Doeblin, Alfred

Linney, Romulus 1930-      CLC 51
   See also CA 1-4R; CANR 40, 44, 79

Linton, Eliza Lynn 1822-1898      NCLC 41
   See also DLB 18

Li Po 701-763      CMLC 2

Lipsius, Justus 1547-1606      LC 16

Lipsyte, Robert (Michael) 1938-CLC 21; DA;
   DAC; DAM MST, NOV
   See also AAYA 7; CA 17-20R; CANR 8, 57;
   CLR 23; JRDA; MAICYA; SATA 5, 68

Lish, Gordon (Jay) 1934-    CLC 45; SSC 18
   See also CA 113; 117; CANR 79; DLB 130;
   INT 117

Lispector, Clarice 1925(?)-1977    CLC 43;
   HLCS 1; SSC 34
   See also CA 139; 116; CANR 71; DLB 113;
   HW 2

Littell, Robert 1935(?)-      CLC 42
   See also CA 109; 112; CANR 64

Little, Malcolm 1925-1965
   See Malcolm X
   See also BW 1, 3; CA 125; 111; DA; DAB;
   DAC; DAM MST, MULT; MTCW 1, 2

Littlewit, Humphrey Gent.
   See Lovecraft, H(oward) P(hillips)

Litwos
   See Sienkiewicz, Henryk (Adam Alexander
   Pius)

Liu, E 1857-1909      TCLC 15
   See also CA 115

Lively, Penelope (Margaret) 1933- CLC 32,
   50; DAM NOV
   See also CA 41-44R; CANR 29, 67, 79; CLR
   7; DLB 14, 161, 207; JRDA; MAICYA;
   MTCW 1, 2; SATA 7, 60, 101

Livesay, Dorothy (Kathleen) 1909-CLC 4, 15,
   79; DAC; DAM MST, POET
   See also AITN 2; CA 25-28R; CAAS 8; CANR
   36, 67; DLB 68; MTCW 1

Livy c. 59B.C.-c. 17      CMLC 11
   See also DLB 211

Lizardi, Jose Joaquin Fernandez de 1776-1827
   NCLC 30

Llewellyn, Richard
   See Llewellyn Lloyd, Richard Dafydd Vivian
   See also DLB 15

Llewellyn Lloyd, Richard Dafydd Vivian 1906-
   1983      CLC 7, 80
   See also Llewellyn, Richard
   See also CA 53-56; 111; CANR 7, 71; SATA
   11; SATA-Obit 37

Llosa, (Jorge) Mario (Pedro) Vargas
   See Vargas Llosa, (Jorge) Mario (Pedro)

Lloyd, Manda
   See Mander, (Mary) Jane

Lloyd Webber, Andrew 1948-
   See Webber, Andrew Lloyd
   See also AAYA 1; CA 116; 149; DAM DRAM;
   SATA 56

Llull, Ramon c. 1235-c. 1316      CMLC 12

Lobb, Ebenezer
   See Upward, Allen

Locke, Alain (Le Roy) 1886-1954 TCLC 43;
   BLCS
   See also BW 1, 3; CA 106; 124; CANR 79; DLB

51
**Locke, John** 1632-1704     **LC 7, 35**
See also DLB 101
**Locke-Elliott, Sumner**
See Elliott, Sumner Locke
**Lockhart, John Gibson** 1794-1854   **NCLC 6**
See also DLB 110, 116, 144
**Lodge, David (John)** 1935-**CLC 36; DAM POP**
See also BEST 90:1; CA 17-20R; CANR 19,
53; DLB 14, 194; INT CANR-19; MTCW 1,
2
**Lodge, Thomas** 1558-1625     **LC 41**
**Lodge, Thomas** 1558-1625     **LC 41**
See also DLB 172
**Loennbohm, Armas Eino Leopold** 1878-1926
See Leino, Eino
See also CA 123
**Loewinsohn, Ron(ald William)** 1937-**CLC 52**
See also CA 25-28R; CANR 71
**Logan, Jake**
See Smith, Martin Cruz
**Logan, John (Burton)** 1923-1987    **CLC 5**
See also CA 77-80; 124; CANR 45; DLB 5
**Lo Kuan-chung** 1330(?)-1400(?)    **LC 12**
**Lombard, Nap**
See Johnson, Pamela Hansford
**London, Jack**   **TCLC 9, 15, 39; SSC 4; WLC**
See also London, John Griffith
See also AAYA 13; AITN 2; CDALB 1865-
1917; DLB 8, 12, 78, 212; SATA 18
**London, John Griffith** 1876-1916
See London, Jack
See also CA 110; 119; CANR 73; DA; DAB;
DAC; DAM MST, NOV; JRDA; MAICYA;
MTCW 1, 2
**Long, Emmett**
See Leonard, Elmore (John, Jr.)
**Longbaugh, Harry**
See Goldman, William (W.)
**Longfellow, Henry Wadsworth** 1807-1882
   **NCLC 2, 45; DA; DAB; DAC; DAM MST,
POET; WLCS**
See also CDALB 1640-1865; DLB 1, 59; SATA
19
**Longinus** c. 1st cent. -     **CMLC 27**
See also DLB 176
**Longley, Michael** 1939-     **CLC 29**
See also CA 102; DLB 40
**Longus** fl. c. 2nd cent. -     **CMLC 7**
**Longway, A. Hugh**
See Lang, Andrew
**Lonnrot, Elias** 1802-1884     **NCLC 53**
**Lopate, Phillip** 1943-     **CLC 29**
See also CA 97-100; DLBY 80; INT 97-100
**Lopez Portillo (y Pacheco), Jose** 1920-**CLC 46**
See also CA 129; HW 1
**Lopez y Fuentes, Gregorio** 1897(?)-1966**CLC
32**
See also CA 131; HW 1
**Lorca, Federico Garcia**
<See Garcia Lorca, Federico
**Lord, Bette Bao** 1938-     **CLC 23**
See also BEST 90:3; CA 107; CANR 41, 79;
INT 107; SATA 58
**Lord Auch**
See Bataille, Georges
**Lord Byron**
See Byron, George Gordon (Noel)
**Lorde, Audre (Geraldine)** 1934-1992**CLC 18,
71; BLC 2; DAM MULT, POET; PC 12**
See also BW 1, 3; CA 25-28R; 142; CANR 16,
26, 46; DLB 41; MTCW 1, 2
**Lord Houghton**

See Milnes, Richard Monckton
**Lord Jeffrey**
See Jeffrey, Francis
**Lorenzini, Carlo** 1826-1890
See Collodi, Carlo
See also MAICYA; SATA 29, 100
**Lorenzo, Heberto Padilla**
See Padilla (Lorenzo), Heberto
**Loris**
See Hofmannsthal, Hugo von
**Loti, Pierre**     **TCLC 11**
See also Viaud, (Louis Marie) Julien
See also DLB 123
**Louie, David Wong** 1954-     **CLC 70**
See also CA 139
**Louis, Father M.**
See Merton, Thomas
**Lovecraft, H(oward) P(hillips)** 1890-1937
   **TCLC 4, 22; DAM POP; SSC 3**
See also AAYA 14; CA 104; 133; MTCW 1, 2
**Lovelace, Earl** 1935-     **CLC 51**
See also BW 2; CA 77-80; CANR 41, 72; DLB
125; MTCW 1
**Lovelace, Richard** 1618-1657    **LC 24**
See also DLB 131
**Lowell, Amy** 1874-1925   **TCLC 1, 8; DAM
POET; PC 13**
See also CA 104; 151; DLB 54, 140; MTCW 2
**Lowell, James Russell** 1819-1891   **NCLC 2**
See also CDALB 1640-1865; DLB 1, 11, 64,
79, 189
**Lowell, Robert (Traill Spence, Jr.)** 1917-1977
  **CLC 1, 2, 3, 4, 5, 8, 9, 11, 15, 37; DA; DAB;
DAC; DAM MST, NOV; PC 3; WLC**
See also CA 9-12R; 73-76; CABS 2; CANR 26,
60; CDALBS; DLB 5, 169; MTCW 1, 2
**Lowenthal, Michael (Francis)** 1969-**CLC 119**
See also CA 150
**Lowndes, Marie Adelaide (Belloc)** 1868-1947
   **TCLC 12**
See also CA 107; DLB 70
**Lowry, (Clarence) Malcolm** 1909-1957**TCLC
6, 40; SSC 31**
See also CA 105; 131; CANR 62; CDBLB
1945-1960; DLB 15; MTCW 1, 2
**Lowry, Mina Gertrude** 1882-1966
See Loy, Mina
See also CA 113
**Loxsmith, John**
See Brunner, John (Kilian Houston)
**Loy, Mina**     **CLC 28; DAM POET; PC 16**
See also Lowry, Mina Gertrude
See also DLB 4, 54
**Loyson-Bridet**
See Schwob, Marcel (Mayer Andre)
**Lucan** 39-65     **CMLC 33**
See also DLB 211
**Lucas, Craig** 1951-     **CLC 64**
See also CA 137; CANR 71
**Lucas, E(dward) V(errall)** 1868-1938   **TCLC
73**
See also DLB 98, 149, 153; SATA 20
**Lucas, George** 1944-     **CLC 16**
See also AAYA 1, 23; CA 77-80; CANR 30;
SATA 56
**Lucas, Hans**
See Godard, Jean-Luc
**Lucas, Victoria**
See Plath, Sylvia
**Lucian** c. 120-c. 180     **CMLC 32**
See also DLB 176
**Ludlam, Charles** 1943-1987    **CLC 46, 50**
See also CA 85-88; 122; CANR 72

**Ludlum, Robert** 1927-**CLC 22, 43; DAM NOV,
POP**
See also AAYA 10; BEST 89:1, 90:3; CA 33-
36R; CANR 25, 41, 68; DLBY 82; MTCW
1, 2
**Ludwig, Ken**     **CLC 60**
**Ludwig, Otto** 1813-1865    **NCLC 4**
See also DLB 129
**Lugones, Leopoldo** 1874-1938   **TCLC 15;
HLCS 1**
See also CA 116; 131; HW 1
**Lu Hsun** 1881-1936   **TCLC 3; SSC 20**
See also Shu-Jen, Chou
**Lukacs, George**     **CLC 24**
See also Lukacs, Gyorgy (Szegeny von)
**Lukacs, Gyorgy (Szegeny von)** 1885-1971
See Lukacs, George
See also CA 101; 29-32R; CANR 62; MTCW 2
**Luke, Peter (Ambrose Cyprian)** 1919-1995
   **CLC 38**
See also CA 81-84; 147; CANR 72; DLB 13
**Lunar, Dennis**
See Mungo, Raymond
**Lurie, Alison** 1926-    **CLC 4, 5, 18, 39**
See also CA 1-4R; CANR 2, 17, 50; DLB 2;
MTCW 1; SATA 46
**Lustig, Arnost** 1926-     **CLC 56**
See also AAYA 3; CA 69-72; CANR 47; SATA
56
**Luther, Martin** 1483-1546    **LC 9, 37**
See also DLB 179
**Luxemburg, Rosa** 1870(?)-1919   **TCLC 63**
See also CA 118
**Luzi, Mario** 1914-     **CLC 13**
See also CA 61-64; CANR 9, 70; DLB 128
**Lyly, John** 1554(?)-1606**LC 41; DAM DRAM;
DC 7**
See also DLB 62, 167
**L'Ymagier**
See Gourmont, Remy (-Marie-Charles) de
**Lynch, B. Suarez**
See Bioy Casares, Adolfo; Borges, Jorge Luis
**Lynch, David (K.)** 1946-     **CLC 66**
See also CA 124; 129
**Lynch, James**
See Andreyev, Leonid (Nikolaevich)
**Lynch Davis, B.**
See Bioy Casares, Adolfo; Borges, Jorge Luis
**Lyndsay, Sir David** 1490-1555    **LC 20**
**Lynn, Kenneth S(chuyler)** 1923-   **CLC 50**
See also CA 1-4R; CANR 3, 27, 65
**Lynx**
See West, Rebecca
**Lyons, Marcus**
See Blish, James (Benjamin)
**Lyre, Pinchbeck**
See Sassoon, Siegfried (Lorraine)
**Lytle, Andrew (Nelson)** 1902-1995   **CLC 22**
See also CA 9-12R; 150; CANR 70; DLB 6;
DLBY 95
**Lyttelton, George** 1709-1773    **LC 10**
**Maas, Peter** 1929-     **CLC 29**
See also CA 93-96; INT 93-96; MTCW 2
**Macaulay, Rose** 1881-1958   **TCLC 7, 44**
See also CA 104; DLB 36
**Macaulay, Thomas Babington** 1800-1859
   **NCLC 42**
See also CDBLB 1832-1890; DLB 32, 55
**MacBeth, George (Mann)** 1932-1992**CLC 2, 5,
9**
See also CA 25-28R; 136; CANR 61, 66; DLB
40; MTCW 1; SATA 4; SATA-Obit 70
**MacCaig, Norman (Alexander)** 1910-**CLC 36;**

DAB; DAM POET
See also CA 9-12R; CANR 3, 34; DLB 27

**MacCarthy, Sir(Charles Otto) Desmond** 1877-1952                                    **TCLC 36**
See also CA 167

**MacDiarmid, Hugh CLC 2, 4, 11, 19, 63; PC 9**
See Grieve, C(hristopher) M(urray)
See also CDBLB 1945-1960; DLB 20

**MacDonald, Anson**
See Heinlein, Robert A(nson)

**Macdonald, Cynthia** 1928-          **CLC 13, 19**
See also CA 49-52; CANR 4, 44; DLB 105

**MacDonald, George** 1824-1905          **TCLC 9**
See also CA 106; 137; CANR 80; DLB 18, 163, 178; MAICYA; SATA 33, 100

**Macdonald, John**
See Millar, Kenneth

**MacDonald, John D(ann)** 1916-1986 **CLC 3, 27, 44; DAM NOV, POP**
See also CA 1-4R; 121; CANR 1, 19, 60; DLB 8; DLBY 86; MTCW 1, 2

**Macdonald, John Ross**
See Millar, Kenneth

**Macdonald, Ross**          **CLC 1, 2, 3, 14, 34, 41**
See also Millar, Kenneth
See also DLBD 6

**MacDougal, John**
See Blish, James (Benjamin)

**MacEwen, Gwendolyn (Margaret)** 1941-1987 **CLC 13, 55**
See also CA 9-12R; 124; CANR 7, 22; DLB 53; SATA 50; SATA-Obit 55

**Macha, Karel Hynek** 1810-1846          **NCLC 46**

**Machado (y Ruiz), Antonio** 1875-1939 **TCLC 3**
See also CA 104; 174; DLB 108; HW 2

**Machado de Assis, Joaquim Maria** 1839-1908 **TCLC 10; BLC 2; HLCS 1; SSC 24**
See also CA 107; 153

**Machen, Arthur**          **TCLC 4; SSC 20**
See also Jones, Arthur Llewellyn
See also DLB 36, 156, 178

**Machiavelli, Niccolo** 1469-1527 **LC 8, 36; DA; DAB; DAC; DAM MST; WLCS**

**MacInnes, Colin** 1914-1976          **CLC 4, 23**
See also CA 69-72; 65-68; CANR 21; DLB 14; MTCW 1, 2

**MacInnes, Helen (Clark)** 1907-1985 **CLC 27, 39; DAM POP**
See also CA 1-4R; 117; CANR 1, 28, 58; DLB 87; MTCW 1, 2; SATA 22; SATA-Obit 44

**Mackay, Mary** 1855-1924
See Corelli, Marie
See also CA 118

**Mackenzie, Compton (Edward Montague)** 1883-1972          **CLC 18**
See also CA 21-22; 37-40R; CAP 2; DLB 34, 100

**Mackenzie, Henry** 1745-1831          **NCLC 41**
See also DLB 39

**Mackintosh, Elizabeth** 1896(?)-1952
See Tey, Josephine
See also CA 110

**MacLaren, James**
See Grieve, C(hristopher) M(urray)

**Mac Laverty, Bernard** 1942-          **CLC 31**
See also CA 116; 118; CANR 43; INT 118

**MacLean, Alistair (Stuart)** 1922(?)-1987 **CLC 3, 13, 50, 63; DAM POP**
See also CA 57-60; 121; CANR 28, 61; MTCW 1; SATA 23; SATA-Obit 50

**Maclean, Norman (Fitzroy)** 1902-1990 **CLC 78; DAM POP; SSC 13**

See also CA 102; 132; CANR 49; DLB 206

**MacLeish, Archibald** 1892-1982 **CLC 3, 8, 14, 68; DAM POET**
See also CA 9-12R; 106; CANR 33, 63; CDALBS; DLB 4, 7, 45; DLBY 82; MTCW 1, 2

**MacLennan, (John) Hugh** 1907-1990 **CLC 2, 14, 92; DAC; DAM MST**
See also CA 5-8R; 142; CANR 33; DLB 68; MTCW 1, 2

**MacLeod, Alistair** 1936- **CLC 56; DAC; DAM MST**
See also CA 123; DLB 60; MTCW 2

**Macleod, Fiona**
See Sharp, William

**MacNeice, (Frederick) Louis** 1907-1963 **CLC 1, 4, 10, 53; DAB; DAM POET**
See also CA 85-88; CANR 61; DLB 10, 20; MTCW 1, 2

**MacNeill, Dand**
See Fraser, George MacDonald

**Macpherson, James** 1736-1796          **LC 29**
See also Ossian
See also DLB 109

**Macpherson, (Jean) Jay** 1931-          **CLC 14**
See also CA 5-8R; DLB 53

**MacShane, Frank** 1927-          **CLC 39**
See also CA 9-12R; CANR 3, 33; DLB 111

**Macumber, Mari**
See Sandoz, Mari(e Susette)

**Madach, Imre** 1823-1864          **NCLC 19**

**Madden, (Jerry) David** 1933-          **CLC 5, 15**
See also CA 1-4R; CAAS 3; CANR 4, 45; DLB 6; MTCW 1

**Maddern, Al(an)**
See Ellison, Harlan (Jay)

**Madhubuti, Haki R.** 1942- **CLC 6, 73; BLC 2; DAM MULT, POET; PC 5**
See also Lee, Don L.
See also BW 2, 3; CA 73-76; CANR 24, 51, 73; DLB 5, 41; DLBD 8; MTCW 2

**Maepenn, Hugh**
See Kuttner, Henry

**Maepenn, K. H.**
See Kuttner, Henry

**Maeterlinck, Maurice** 1862-1949          **TCLC 3; DAM DRAM**
See also CA 104; 136; CANR 80; DLB 192; SATA 66

**Maginn, William** 1794-1842          **NCLC 8**
See also DLB 110, 159

**Mahapatra, Jayanta** 1928-          **CLC 33; DAM MULT**
See also CA 73-76; CAAS 9; CANR 15, 33, 66

**Mahfouz, Naguib (Abdel Aziz Al-Sabilgi)** 1911(?)-
See Mahfuz, Najib
See also BEST 89:2; CA 128; CANR 55; DAM NOV; MTCW 1, 2

**Mahfuz, Najib**          **CLC 52, 55**
See also Mahfouz, Naguib (Abdel Aziz Al-Sabilgi)
See also DLBY 88

**Mahon, Derek** 1941-          **CLC 27**
See also CA 113; 128; DLB 40

**Mailer, Norman** 1923- **CLC 1, 2, 3, 4, 5, 8, 11, 14, 28, 39, 74, 111; DA; DAB; DAC; DAM MST, NOV, POP**
See also AITN 2; CA 9-12R; CABS 1; CANR 28, 74, 77; CDALB 1968-1988; DLB 2, 16, 28, 185; DLBD 3; DLBY 80, 83; MTCW 1, 2

**Maillet, Antonine** 1929-          **CLC 54, 118; DAC**

See also CA 115; 120; CANR 46, 74, 77; DLB 60; INT 120; MTCW 2

**Mais, Roger** 1905-1955          **TCLC 8**
See also BW 1, 3; CA 105; 124; DLB 125; MTCW 1

**Maistre, Joseph de** 1753-1821          **NCLC 37**

**Maitland, Frederic** 1850-1906          **TCLC 65**

**Maitland, Sara (Louise)** 1950-          **CLC 49**
See also CA 69-72; CANR 13, 59

**Major, Clarence** 1936- **CLC 3, 19, 48; BLC 2; DAM MULT**
See also BW 2, 3; CA 21-24R; CAAS 6; CANR 13, 25, 53; DLB 33

**Major, Kevin (Gerald)** 1949-          **CLC 26; DAC**
See also AAYA 16; CA 97-100; CANR 21, 38; CLR 11; DLB 60; INT CANR-21; JRDA; MAICYA; SATA 32, 82

**Maki, James**
See Ozu, Yasujiro

**Malabaila, Damiano**
See Levi, Primo

**Malamud, Bernard** 1914-1986 **CLC 1, 2, 3, 5, 8, 9, 11, 18, 27, 44, 78, 85; DA; DAB; DAC; DAM MST, NOV, POP; SSC 15; WLC**
See also AAYA 16; CA 5-8R; 118; CABS 1; CANR 28, 62; CDALB 1941-1968; DLB 2, 28, 152; DLBY 80, 86; MTCW 1, 2

**Malan, Herman**
See Bosman, Herman Charles; Bosman, Herman Charles

**Malaparte, Curzio** 1898-1957          **TCLC 52**

**Malcolm, Dan**
See Silverberg, Robert

**Malcolm X**          **CLC 82, 117; BLC 2; WLCS**
See also Little, Malcolm

**Malherbe, Francois de** 1555-1628          **LC 5**

**Mallarme, Stephane** 1842-1898 **NCLC 4, 41; DAM POET; PC 4**

**Mallet-Joris, Francoise** 1930-          **CLC 11**
See also CA 65-68; CANR 17; DLB 83

**Malley, Ern**
See McAuley, James Phillip

**Mallowan, Agatha Christie**
See Christie, Agatha (Mary Clarissa)

**Maloff, Saul** 1922-          **CLC 5**
See also CA 33-36R

**Malone, Louis**
See MacNeice, (Frederick) Louis

**Malone, Michael (Christopher)** 1942- **CLC 43**
See also CA 77-80; CANR 14, 32, 57

**Malory, (Sir) Thomas** 1410(?)-1471(?) **LC 11; DA; DAB; DAC; DAM MST; WLCS**
See also CDBLB Before 1660; DLB 146; SATA 59; SATA-Brief 33

**Malouf, (George Joseph) David** 1934- **CLC 28, 86**
See also CA 124; CANR 50, 76; MTCW 2

**Malraux, (Georges-)Andre** 1901-1976 **CLC 1, 4, 9, 13, 15, 57; DAM NOV**
See also CA 21-22; 69-72; CANR 34, 58; CAP 2; DLB 72; MTCW 1, 2

**Malzberg, Barry N(athaniel)** 1939-          **CLC 7**
See also CA 61-64; CAAS 4; CANR 16; DLB 8

**Mamet, David (Alan)** 1947- **CLC 9, 15, 34, 46, 91; DAM DRAM; DC 4**
See also AAYA 3; CA 81-84; CABS 3; CANR 15, 41, 67, 72; DLB 7; MTCW 1, 2

**Mamoulian, Rouben (Zachary)** 1897-1987          **CLC 16**
See also CA 25-28R; 124

**Mandelstam, Osip (Emilievich)** 1891(?)-1938(?) **TCLC 2, 6; PC 14**
See also CA 104; 150; MTCW 2

See also DLB 4, 45, 51, 117

**McKay, Festus Claudius** 1889-1948
See McKay, Claude
See also BW 1, 3; CA 104; 124; CANR 73; DA; DAC; DAM MST, MULT, NOV, POET; MTCW 1, 2; WLC

**McKuen, Rod** 1933-                                    **CLC 1, 3**
See also AITN 1; CA 41-44R; CANR 40

**McLoughlin, R. B.**
See Mencken, H(enry) L(ouis)

**McLuhan, (Herbert) Marshall** 1911-1980
**CLC 37, 83**
See also CA 9-12R; 102; CANR 12, 34, 61; DLB 88; INT CANR-12; MTCW 1, 2

**McMillan, Terry (L.)** 1951- **CLC 50, 61, 112; BLCS; DAM MULT, NOV, POP**
See also AAYA 21; BW 2, 3; CA 140; CANR 60; MTCW 2

**McMurtry, Larry (Jeff)** 1936-**CLC 2, 3, 7, 11, 27, 44; DAM NOV, POP**
See also AAYA 15; AITN 2; BEST 89:2; CA 5-8R; CANR 19, 43, 64; CDALB 1968-1988; DLB 2, 143; DLBY 80, 87; MTCW 1, 2

**McNally, T. M.** 1961-                                  **CLC 82**
**McNally, Terrence** 1939-     **CLC 4, 7, 41, 91; DAM DRAM**
See also CA 45-48; CANR 2, 56; DLB 7; MTCW 2

**McNamer, Deirdre** 1950-                            **CLC 70**
**McNeal, Tom**                                          **CLC 119**
**McNeile, Herman Cyril** 1888-1937
See Sapper
See also DLB 77

**McNickle, (William) D'Arcy** 1904-1977 **C L C 89; DAM MULT**
See also CA 9-12R; 85-88; CANR 5, 45; DLB 175, 212; NNAL; SATA-Obit 22

**McPhee, John (Angus)** 1931-                        **CLC 36**
See also BEST 90:1; CA 65-68; CANR 20, 46, 64, 69; DLB 185; MTCW 1, 2

**McPherson, James Alan** 1943-     **CLC 19, 77; BLCS**
See also BW 1, 3; CA 25-28R; CAAS 17; CANR 24, 74; DLB 38; MTCW 1, 2

**McPherson, William (Alexander)** 1933- **C L C 34**
See also CA 69-72; CANR 28; INT CANR-28

**Mead, George Herbert** 1873-1958       **TCLC 89**
**Mead, Margaret** 1901-1978                         **CLC 37**
See also AITN 1; CA 1-4R; 81-84; CANR 4; MTCW 1, 2; SATA-Obit 20

**Meaker, Marijane (Agnes)** 1927-
See Kerr, M. E.
See also CA 107; CANR 37, 63; INT 107; JRDA; MAICYA; MTCW 1; SATA 20, 61, 99

**Medoff, Mark (Howard)** 1940-            **CLC 6, 23; DAM DRAM**
See also AITN 1; CA 53-56; CANR 5; DLB 7; INT CANR-5

**Medvedev, P. N.**
See Bakhtin, Mikhail Mikhailovich

**Meged, Aharon**
See Megged, Aharon

**Meged, Aron**
See Megged, Aharon

**Megged, Aharon** 1920-                               **CLC 9**
See also CA 49-52; CAAS 13; CANR 1

**Mehta, Ved (Parkash)** 1934-                       **CLC 37**
See also CA 1-4R; CANR 2, 23, 69; MTCW 1

**Melanter**
See Blackmore, R(ichard) D(oddridge)

**Melies, Georges** 1861-1938                        **TCLC 81**

**Melikow, Loris**
See Hofmannsthal, Hugo von

**Melmoth, Sebastian**
See Wilde, Oscar

**Meltzer, Milton** 1915-                               **CLC 26**
See also AAYA 8; CA 13-16R; CANR 38; CLR 13; DLB 61; JRDA; MAICYA; SAAS 1; SATA 1, 50, 80

**Melville, Herman** 1819-1891 **NCLC 3, 12, 29, 45, 49; DA; DAB; DAC; DAM MST, NOV; SSC 1, 17; WLC**
See also AAYA 25; CDALB 1640-1865; DLB 3, 74; SATA 59

**Menander** c. 342B.C.-c. 292B.C.        **CMLC 9; DAM DRAM; DC 3**
See also DLB 176

**Mencken, H(enry) L(ouis)** 1880-1956 **T C L C 13**
See also CA 105; 125; CDALB 1917-1929; DLB 11, 29, 63, 137; MTCW 1, 2

**Mendelsohn, Jane** 1965(?)-                       **CLC 99**
See also CA 154

**Mercer, David** 1928-1980**CLC 5; DAM DRAM**
See also CA 9-12R; 102; CANR 23; DLB 13; MTCW 1

**Merchant, Paul**
See Ellison, Harlan (Jay)

**Meredith, George** 1828-1909      **TCLC 17, 43; DAM POET**
See also CA 117; 153; CANR 80; CDBLB 1832-1890; DLB 18, 35, 57, 159

**Meredith, William (Morris)** 1919-**CLC 4, 13, 22, 55; DAM POET**
See also CA 9-12R; CAAS 14; CANR 6, 40; DLB 5

**Merezhkovsky, Dmitry Sergeyevich** 1865-1941 **TCLC 29**
See also CA 169

**Merimee, Prosper** 1803-1870**NCLC 6, 65; SSC 7**
See also DLB 119, 192

**Merkin, Daphne** 1954-                               **CLC 44**
See also CA 123

**Merlin, Arthur**
See Blish, James (Benjamin)

**Merrill, James (Ingram)** 1926-1995**CLC 2, 3, 6, 8, 13, 18, 34, 91; DAM POET**
See also CA 13-16R; 147; CANR 10, 49, 63; DLB 5, 165; DLBY 85; INT CANR-10; MTCW 1, 2

**Merriman, Alex**
See Silverberg, Robert

**Merriman, Brian** 1747-1805                       **NCLC 70**

**Merritt, E. B.**
See Waddington, Miriam

**Merton, Thomas** 1915-1968 **CLC 1, 3, 11, 34, 83; PC 10**
See also CA 5-8R; 25-28R; CANR 22, 53; DLB 48; DLBY 81; MTCW 1, 2

**Merwin, W(illiam) S(tanley)** 1927- **CLC 1, 2, 3, 5, 8, 13, 18, 45, 88; DAM POET**
See also CA 13-16R; CANR 15, 51; DLB 5, 169; INT CANR-15; MTCW 1, 2

**Metcalf, John** 1938-                                 **CLC 37**
See also CA 113; DLB 60

**Metcalf, Suzanne**
See Baum, L(yman) Frank

**Mew, Charlotte (Mary)** 1870-1928         **TCLC 8**
See also CA 105; DLB 19, 135

**Mewshaw, Michael** 1943-                          **CLC 9**
See also CA 53-56; CANR 7, 47; DLBY 80

**Meyer, June**
See Jordan, June

**Meyer, Lynn**
See Slavitt, David R(ytman)

**Meyer-Meyrink, Gustav** 1868-1932
See Meyrink, Gustav
See also CA 117

**Meyers, Jeffrey** 1939-                               **CLC 39**
See also CA 73-76; CANR 54; DLB 111

**Meynell, Alice (Christina Gertrude Thompson)** 1847-1922                                          **TCLC 6**
See also CA 104; DLB 19, 98

**Meyrink, Gustav**                                      **TCLC 21**
See also Meyer-Meyrink, Gustav
See also DLB 81

**Michaels, Leonard** 1933- **CLC 6, 25; SSC 16**
See also CA 61-64; CANR 21, 62; DLB 130; MTCW 1

**Michaux, Henri** 1899-1984                 **CLC 8, 19**
See also CA 85-88; 114

**Micheaux, Oscar (Devereaux)** 1884-1951
**TCLC 76**
See also BW 3; CA 174; DLB 50

**Michelangelo** 1475-1564                           **LC 12**
**Michelet, Jules** 1798-1874                       **NCLC 31**
**Michels, Robert** 1876-1936                     **TCLC 88**
**Michener, James A(lbert)** 1907(?)-1997 **C L C 1, 5, 11, 29, 60, 109; DAM NOV, POP**
See also AAYA 27; AITN 1; BEST 90:1; CA 5-8R; 161; CANR 21, 45, 68; DLB 6; MTCW 1, 2

**Mickiewicz, Adam** 1798-1855                    **NCLC 3**
**Middleton, Christopher** 1926-                   **CLC 13**
See also CA 13-16R; CANR 29, 54; DLB 40

**Middleton, Richard (Barham)** 1882-1911
**TCLC 56**
See also DLB 156

**Middleton, Stanley** 1919-                    **CLC 7, 38**
See also CA 25-28R; CAAS 23; CANR 21, 46; DLB 14

**Middleton, Thomas** 1580-1627 **LC 33; DAM DRAM, MST; DC 5**
See also DLB 58

**Migueis, Jose Rodrigues** 1901-                 **CLC 10**
**Mikszath, Kalman** 1847-1910               **TCLC 31**
See also CA 170

**Miles, Jack**                                          **CLC 100**
**Miles, Josephine (Louise)** 1911-1985**CLC 1, 2, 14, 34, 39; DAM POET**
See also CA 1-4R; 116; CANR 2, 55; DLB 48

**Militant**
See Sandburg, Carl (August)

**Mill, John Stuart** 1806-1873                **NCLC 11, 58**
See also CDBLB 1832-1890; DLB 55, 190

**Millar, Kenneth** 1915-1983    **CLC 14; DAM POP**
See also Macdonald, Ross
See also CA 9-12R; 110; CANR 16, 63; DLB 2; DLBD 6; DLBY 83; MTCW 1, 2

**Millay, E. Vincent**
See Millay, Edna St. Vincent

**Millay, Edna St. Vincent** 1892-1950 **TCLC 4, 49; DA; DAB; DAC; DAM MST, POET; PC 6; WLCS**
See also CA 104; 130; CDALB 1917-1929; DLB 45; MTCW 1, 2

**Miller, Arthur** 1915-**CLC 1, 2, 6, 10, 15, 26, 47, 78; DA; DAB; DAC; DAM DRAM, MST; DC 1; WLC**
See also AAYA 15; AITN 1; CA 1-4R; CABS 3; CANR 2, 30, 54, 76; CDALB 1941-1968; DLB 7; MTCW 1, 2

**Miller, Henry (Valentine)** 1891-1980**CLC 1, 2, 4, 9, 14, 43, 84; DA; DAB; DAC; DAM MST, NOV; WLC**

MTCW 1, 2

**Moravia, Alberto** 1907-1990 **CLC 2, 7, 11, 27, 46; SSC 26**
See also Pincherle, Alberto
See also DLB 177; MTCW 2

**More, Hannah** 1745-1833      **NCLC 27**
See also DLB 107, 109, 116, 158

**More, Henry** 1614-1687      **LC 9**
See also DLB 126

**More, Sir Thomas** 1478-1535      **LC 10, 32**

**Moreas, Jean**      **TCLC 18**
See also Papadiamantopoulos, Johannes

**Morgan, Berry** 1919-      **CLC 6**
See also CA 49-52; DLB 6

**Morgan, Claire**
See Highsmith, (Mary) Patricia

**Morgan, Edwin (George)** 1920-      **CLC 31**
See also CA 5-8R; CANR 3, 43; DLB 27

**Morgan, (George) Frederick** 1922-      **CLC 23**
See also CA 17-20R; CANR 21

**Morgan, Harriet**
See Mencken, H(enry) L(ouis)

**Morgan, Jane**
See Cooper, James Fenimore

**Morgan, Janet** 1945-      **CLC 39**
See also CA 65-68

**Morgan, Lady** 1776(?)-1859      **NCLC 29**
See also DLB 116, 158

**Morgan, Robin (Evonne)** 1941-      **CLC 2**
See also CA 69-72; CANR 29, 68; MTCW 1;
SATA 80

**Morgan, Scott**
See Kuttner, Henry

**Morgan, Seth** 1949(?)-1990      **CLC 65**
See also CA 132

**Morgenstern, Christian** 1871-1914      **TCLC 8**
See also CA 105

**Morgenstern, S.**
See Goldman, William (W.)

**Moricz, Zsigmond** 1879-1942      **TCLC 33**
See also CA 165

**Morike, Eduard (Friedrich)** 1804-1875 **NCLC 10**
See also DLB 133

**Moritz, Karl Philipp** 1756-1793      **LC 2**
See also DLB 94

**Morland, Peter Henry**
See Faust, Frederick (Schiller)

**Morley, Christopher (Darlington)** 1890-1957 **TCLC 87**
See also CA 112; DLB 9

**Morren, Theophil**
See Hofmannsthal, Hugo von

**Morris, Bill** 1952-      **CLC 76**

**Morris, Julian**
See West, Morris L(anglo)

**Morris, Steveland Judkins** 1950(?)-
See Wonder, Stevie
See also CA 111

**Morris, William** 1834-1896      **NCLC 4**
See also CDBLB 1832-1890; DLB 18, 35, 57, 156, 178, 184

**Morris, Wright** 1910-1998 **CLC 1, 3, 7, 18, 37**
See also CA 9-12R; 167; CANR 21; DLB 2, 206; DLBY 81; MTCW 1, 2

**Morrison, Arthur** 1863-1945      **TCLC 72**
See also CA 120; 157; DLB 70, 135, 197

**Morrison, Chloe Anthony Wofford**
See Morrison, Toni

**Morrison, James Douglas** 1943-1971
See Morrison, Jim
See also CA 73-76; CANR 40

**Morrison, Jim**      **CLC 17**

See also Morrison, James Douglas

**Morrison, Toni** 1931- **CLC 4, 10, 22, 55, 81, 87; BLC 3; DA; DAB; DAC; DAM MST, MULT, NOV, POP**
See also AAYA 1, 22; BW 2, 3; CA 29-32R; CANR 27, 42, 67; CDALB 1968-1988; DLB 6, 33, 143; DLBY 81; MTCW 1, 2; SATA 57

**Morrison, Van** 1945-      **CLC 21**
See also CA 116; 168

**Morrissy, Mary** 1958-      **CLC 99**

**Mortimer, John (Clifford)** 1923- **CLC 28, 43; DAM DRAM, POP**
See also CA 13-16R; CANR 21, 69; CDBLB 1960 to Present; DLB 13; INT CANR-21; MTCW 1, 2

**Mortimer, Penelope (Ruth)** 1918-      **CLC 5**
See also CA 57-60; CANR 45

**Morton, Anthony**
See Creasey, John

**Mosca, Gaetano** 1858-1941      **TCLC 75**

**Mosher, Howard Frank** 1943-      **CLC 62**
See also CA 139; CANR 65

**Mosley, Nicholas** 1923-      **CLC 43, 70**
See also CA 69-72; CANR 41, 60; DLB 14, 207

**Mosley, Walter** 1952- **CLC 97; BLCS; DAM MULT, POP**
See also AAYA 17; BW 2; CA 142; CANR 57; MTCW 2

**Moss, Howard** 1922-1987 **CLC 7, 14, 45, 50; DAM POET**
See also CA 1-4R; 123; CANR 1, 44; DLB 5

**Mossgiel, Rab**
See Burns, Robert

**Motion, Andrew (Peter)** 1952-      **CLC 47**
See also CA 146; DLB 40

**Motley, Willard (Francis)** 1909-1965 **CLC 18**
See also BW 1; CA 117; 106; DLB 76, 143

**Motoori, Norinaga** 1730-1801      **NCLC 45**

**Mott, Michael (Charles Alston)** 1930- **CLC 15, 34**
See also CA 5-8R; CAAS 7; CANR 7, 29

**Mountain Wolf Woman** 1884-1960      **CLC 92**
See also CA 144; NNAL

**Moure, Erin** 1955-      **CLC 88**
See also CA 113; DLB 60

**Mowat, Farley (McGill)** 1921- **CLC 26; DAC; DAM MST**
See also AAYA 1; CA 1-4R; CANR 4, 24, 42, 68; CLR 20; DLB 68; INT CANR-24; JRDA; MAICYA; MTCW 1, 2; SATA 3, 55

**Mowatt, Anna Cora** 1819-1870      **NCLC 74**

**Moyers, Bill** 1934-      **CLC 74**
See also AITN 2; CA 61-64; CANR 31, 52

**Mphahlele, Es'kia**
See Mphahlele, Ezekiel
See also DLB 125

**Mphahlele, Ezekiel** 1919-1983 **CLC 25; BLC 3; DAM MULT**
See also Mphahlele, Es'kia
See also BW 2, 3; CA 81-84; CANR 26, 76; MTCW 2

**Mqhayi, S(amuel) E(dward) K(rune Loliwe)** 1875-1945 **TCLC 25; BLC 3; DAM MULT**
See also CA 153

**Mrozek, Slawomir** 1930-      **CLC 3, 13**
See also CA 13-16R; CAAS 10; CANR 29; MTCW 1

**Mrs. Belloc-Lowndes**
See Lowndes, Marie Adelaide (Belloc)

**Mtwa, Percy** (?)-      **CLC 47**

**Mueller, Lisel** 1924-      **CLC 13, 51**
See also CA 93-96; DLB 105

**Muir, Edwin** 1887-1959      **TCLC 2, 87**

See also CA 104; DLB 20, 100, 191

**Muir, John** 1838-1914      **TCLC 28**
See also CA 165; DLB 186

**Mujica Lainez, Manuel** 1910-1984      **CLC 31**
See also Lainez, Manuel Mujica
See also CA 81-84; 112; CANR 32; HW 1

**Mukherjee, Bharati** 1940- **CLC 53, 115; DAM NOV**
See also BEST 89:2; CA 107; CANR 45, 72; DLB 60; MTCW 1, 2

**Muldoon, Paul** 1951- **CLC 32, 72; DAM POET**
See also CA 113; 129; CANR 52; DLB 40; INT 129

**Mulisch, Harry** 1927-      **CLC 42**
See also CA 9-12R; CANR 6, 26, 56

**Mull, Martin** 1943-      **CLC 17**
See also CA 105

**Muller, Wilhelm**      **NCLC 73**

**Mulock, Dinah Maria**
See Craik, Dinah Maria (Mulock)

**Munford, Robert** 1737(?)-1783      **LC 5**
See also DLB 31

**Mungo, Raymond** 1946-      **CLC 72**
See also CA 49-52; CANR 2

**Munro, Alice** 1931- **CLC 6, 10, 19, 50, 95; DAC; DAM MST, NOV; SSC 3; WLCS**
See also AITN 2; CA 33-36R; CANR 33, 53, 75; DLB 53; MTCW 1, 2; SATA 29

**Munro, H(ector) H(ugh)** 1870-1916
See Saki
See also CA 104; 130; CDBLB 1890-1914; DA; DAB; DAC; DAM MST, NOV; DLB 34, 162; MTCW 1, 2; WLC

**Murdoch, (Jean) Iris** 1919- **CLC 1, 2, 3, 4, 6, 8, 11, 15, 22, 31, 51; DAB; DAC; DAM MST, NOV**
See also CA 13-16R; CANR 8, 43, 68; CDBLB 1960 to Present; DLB 14, 194; INT CANR-8; MTCW 1, 2

**Murfree, Mary Noailles** 1850-1922      **SSC 22**
See also CA 122; DLB 12, 74

**Murnau, Friedrich Wilhelm**
See Plumpe, Friedrich Wilhelm

**Murphy, Richard** 1927-      **CLC 41**
See also CA 29-32R; DLB 40

**Murphy, Sylvia** 1937-      **CLC 34**
See also CA 121

**Murphy, Thomas (Bernard)** 1935-      **CLC 51**
See also CA 101

**Murray, Albert L.** 1916-      **CLC 73**
See also BW 2; CA 49-52; CANR 26, 52, 78; DLB 38

**Murray, Judith Sargent** 1751-1820 **NCLC 63**
See also DLB 37, 200

**Murray, Les(lie) A(llan)** 1938- **CLC 40; DAM POET**
See also CA 21-24R; CANR 11, 27, 56

**Murry, J. Middleton**
See Murry, John Middleton

**Murry, John Middleton** 1889-1957 **TCLC 16**
See also CA 118; DLB 149

**Musgrave, Susan** 1951-      **CLC 13, 54**
See also CA 69-72; CANR 45

**Musil, Robert (Edler von)** 1880-1942 **TCLC 12, 68; SSC 18**
See also CA 109; CANR 55; DLB 81, 124; MTCW 2

**Muske, Carol** 1945-      **CLC 90**
See also Muske-Dukes, Carol (Anne)

**Muske-Dukes, Carol (Anne)** 1945-
See Muske, Carol
See also CA 65-68; CANR 32, 70

**Musset, (Louis Charles) Alfred de** 1810-1857

See also Norris, (Benjamin) Frank(lin, Jr.)
See also CDALB 1865-1917; DLB 12, 71, 186
**Norris, (Benjamin) Frank(lin, Jr.)** 1870-1902
**TCLC 24**
See also Norris, Frank
See also CA 110; 160
**Norris, Leslie** 1921- **CLC 14**
See also CA 11-12; CANR 14; CAP 1; DLB 27
**North, Andrew**
See Norton, Andre
**North, Anthony**
See Koontz, Dean R(ay)
**North, Captain George**
See Stevenson, Robert Louis (Balfour)
**North, Milou**
See Erdrich, Louise
**Northrup, B. A.**
See Hubbard, L(afayette) Ron(ald)
**North Staffs**
See Hulme, T(homas) E(rnest)
**Norton, Alice Mary**
See Norton, Andre
See also MAICYA; SATA 1, 43
**Norton, Andre** 1912- **CLC 12**
See also Norton, Alice Mary
See also AAYA 14; CA 1-4R; CANR 68; CLR
50; DLB 8, 52; JRDA; MTCW 1; SATA 91
**Norton, Caroline** 1808-1877 **NCLC 47**
See also DLB 21, 159, 199
**Norway, Nevil Shute** 1899-1960
See Shute, Nevil
See also CA 102; 93-96; MTCW 2
**Norwid, Cyprian Kamil** 1821-1883 **NCLC 17**
**Nosille, Nabrah**
See Ellison, Harlan (Jay)
**Nossack, Hans Erich** 1901-1978 **CLC 6**
See also CA 93-96; 85-88; DLB 69
**Nostradamus** 1503-1566 **LC 27**
**Nosu, Chuji**
See Ozu, Yasujiro
**Notenburg, Eleanora (Genrikhovna) von**
See Guro, Elena
**Nova, Craig** 1945- **CLC 7, 31**
See also CA 45-48; CANR 2, 53
**Novak, Joseph**
See Kosinski, Jerzy (Nikodem)
**Novalis** 1772-1801 **NCLC 13**
See also DLB 90
**Novis, Emile**
See Weil, Simone (Adolphine)
**Nowlan, Alden (Albert)** 1933-1983 **CLC 15;
DAC; DAM MST**
See also CA 9-12R; CANR 5; DLB 53
**Noyes, Alfred** 1880-1958 **TCLC 7**
See also CA 104; DLB 20
**Nunn, Kem** **CLC 34**
See also CA 159
**Nye, Robert** 1939- **CLC 13, 42; DAM NOV**
See also CA 33-36R; CANR 29, 67; DLB 14;
MTCW 1; SATA 6
**Nyro, Laura** 1947- **CLC 17**
**Oates, Joyce Carol** 1938-**CLC 1, 2, 3, 6, 9, 11,
15, 19, 33, 52, 108; DA; DAB; DAC; DAM
MST, NOV, POP; SSC 6; WLC**
See also AAYA 15; AITN 1; BEST 89:2; CA 5-
8R; CANR 25, 45, 74; CDALB 1968-1988;
DLB 2, 5, 130; DLBY 81; INT CANR-25;
MTCW 1, 2
**O'Brien, Darcy** 1939-1998 **CLC 11**
See also CA 21-24R; 167; CANR 8, 59
**O'Brien, E. G.**
See Clarke, Arthur C(harles)
**O'Brien, Edna** 1936- **CLC 3, 5, 8, 13, 36, 65,**

116; DAM NOV; SSC 10
See also CA 1-4R; CANR 6, 41, 65; CDBLB
1960 to Present; DLB 14; MTCW 1, 2
**O'Brien, Fitz-James** 1828-1862 **NCLC 21**
See also DLB 74
**O'Brien, Flann** **CLC 1, 4, 5, 7, 10, 47**
See also O Nuallain, Brian
**O'Brien, Richard** 1942- **CLC 17**
See also CA 124
**O'Brien, (William) Tim(othy)** 1946- **CLC 7,
19, 40, 103; DAM POP**
See also AAYA 16; CA 85-88; CANR 40, 58;
CDALBS; DLB 152; DLBD 9; DLBY 80;
MTCW 2
**Obstfelder, Sigbjoern** 1866-1900 **TCLC 23**
See also CA 123
**O'Casey, Sean** 1880-1964 **CLC 1, 5, 9, 11, 15,
88; DAB; DAC; DAM DRAM, MST;
WLCS**
See also CA 89-92; CANR 62; CDBLB 1914-
1945; DLB 10; MTCW 1, 2
**O'Cathasaigh, Sean**
See O'Casey, Sean
**Ochs, Phil** 1940-1976 **CLC 17**
See also CA 65-68
**O'Connor, Edwin (Greene)** 1918-1968**CLC 14**
See also CA 93-96; 25-28R
**O'Connor, (Mary) Flannery** 1925-1964 **C L C
1, 2, 3, 6, 10, 13, 15, 21, 66, 104; DA; DAB;
DAC; DAM MST, NOV; SSC 1, 23; WLC**
See also AAYA 7; CA 1-4R; CANR 3, 41;
CDALB 1941-1968; DLB 2, 152; DLBD 12;
DLBY 80; MTCW 1, 2
**O'Connor, Frank** **CLC 23; SSC 5**
See also O'Donovan, Michael John
See also DLB 162
**O'Dell, Scott** 1898-1989 **CLC 30**
See also AAYA 3; CA 61-64; 129; CANR 12,
30; CLR 1, 16; DLB 52; JRDA; MAICYA;
SATA 12, 60
**Odets, Clifford** 1906-1963**CLC 2, 28, 98; DAM
DRAM; DC 6**
See also CA 85-88; CANR 62; DLB 7, 26;
MTCW 1, 2
**O'Doherty, Brian** 1934- **CLC 76**
See also CA 105
**O'Donnell, K. M.**
See Malzberg, Barry N(athaniel)
**O'Donnell, Lawrence**
See Kuttner, Henry
**O'Donovan, Michael John** 1903-1966**CLC 14**
See also O'Connor, Frank
See also CA 93-96
**Oe, Kenzaburo** 1935- **CLC 10, 36, 86; DAM
NOV; SSC 20**
See also CA 97-100; CANR 36, 50, 74; DLB
182; DLBY 94; MTCW 1, 2
**O'Faolain, Julia** 1932- **CLC 6, 19, 47, 108**
See also CA 81-84; CAAS 2; CANR 12, 61;
DLB 14; MTCW 1
**O'Faolain, Sean** 1900-1991 **CLC 1, 7, 14, 32,
70; SSC 13**
See also CA 61-64; 134; CANR 12, 66; DLB
15, 162; MTCW 1, 2
**O'Flaherty, Liam** 1896-1984**CLC 5, 34; SSC 6**
See also CA 101; 113; CANR 35; DLB 36, 162;
DLBY 84; MTCW 1, 2
**Ogilvy, Gavin**
See Barrie, J(ames) M(atthew)
**O'Grady, Standish (James)** 1846-1928 **T C L C
5**
See also CA 104; 157
**O'Grady, Timothy** 1951- **CLC 59**

See also CA 138
**O'Hara, Frank** 1926-1966 **CLC 2, 5, 13, 78;
DAM POET**
See also CA 9-12R; 25-28R; CANR 33; DLB
5, 16, 193; MTCW 1, 2
**O'Hara, John (Henry)** 1905-1970**CLC 1, 2, 3,
6, 11, 42; DAM NOV; SSC 15**
See also CA 5-8R; 25-28R; CANR 31, 60;
CDALB 1929-1941; DLB 9, 86; DLBD 2;
MTCW 1, 2
**O Hehir, Diana** 1922- **CLC 41**
See also CA 93-96
**Okigbo, Christopher (Ifenayichukwu)** 1932-
1967 **CLC 25, 84; BLC 3; DAM MULT,
POET; PC 7**
See also BW 1, 3; CA 77-80; CANR 74; DLB
125; MTCW 1, 2
**Okri, Ben** 1959- **CLC 87**
See also BW 2, 3; CA 130; 138; CANR 65; DLB
157; INT 138; MTCW 2
**Olds, Sharon** 1942- **CLC 32, 39, 85; DAM
POET; PC 22**
See also CA 101; CANR 18, 41, 66; DLB 120;
MTCW 2
**Oldstyle, Jonathan**
See Irving, Washington
**Olesha, Yuri (Karlovich)** 1899-1960 **CLC 8**
See also CA 85-88
**Oliphant, Laurence** 1829(?)-1888 **NCLC 47**
See also DLB 18, 166
**Oliphant, Margaret (Oliphant Wilson)** 1828-
1897 **NCLC 11, 61; SSC 25**
See also DLB 18, 159, 190
**Oliver, Mary** 1935- **CLC 19, 34, 98**
See also CA 21-24R; CANR 9, 43; DLB 5, 193
**Olivier, Laurence (Kerr)** 1907-1989 **CLC 20**
See also CA 111; 150; 129
**Olsen, Tillie** 1912-**CLC 4, 13, 114; DA; DAB;
DAC; DAM MST; SSC 11**
See also CA 1-4R; CANR 1, 43, 74; CDALBS;
DLB 28, 206; DLBY 80; MTCW 1, 2
**Olson, Charles (John)** 1910-1970**CLC 1, 2, 5,
6, 9, 11, 29; DAM POET; PC 19**
See also CA 13-16; 25-28R; CABS 2; CANR
35, 61; CAP 1; DLB 5, 16, 193; MTCW 1, 2
**Olson, Toby** 1937- **CLC 28**
See also CA 65-68; CANR 9, 31
**Olyesha, Yuri**
See Olesha, Yuri (Karlovich)
**Ondaatje, (Philip) Michael** 1943-**CLC 14, 29,
51, 76; DAB; DAC; DAM MST**
See also CA 77-80; CANR 42, 74; DLB 60;
MTCW 2
**Oneal, Elizabeth** 1934-
See Oneal, Zibby
See also CA 106; CANR 28; MAICYA; SATA
30, 82
**Oneal, Zibby** **CLC 30**
See also Oneal, Elizabeth
See also AAYA 5; CLR 13; JRDA
**O'Neill, Eugene (Gladstone)** 1888-1953**TCLC
1, 6, 27, 49; DA; DAB; DAC; DAM DRAM,
MST; WLC**
See also AITN 1; CA 110; 132; CDALB 1929-
1941; DLB 7; MTCW 1, 2
**Onetti, Juan Carlos** 1909-1994 **CLC 7, 10;
DAM MULT, NOV; HLCS 1; SSC 23**
See also CA 85-88; 145; CANR 32, 63; DLB
113; HW 1, 2; MTCW 1, 2
**O Nuallain, Brian** 1911-1966
See O'Brien, Flann
See also CA 21-22; 25-28R; CAP 2
**Ophuls, Max** 1902-1957 **TCLC 79**

**Pasternak, Boris (Leonidovich)** 1890-1960
**CLC 7, 10, 18, 63; DA; DAB; DAC; DAM
MST, NOV, POET; PC 6; SSC 31; WLC**
See also CA 127; 116; MTCW 1, 2

**Patchen, Kenneth** 1911-1972    **CLC 1, 2, 18;
DAM POET**
See also CA 1-4R; 33-36R; CANR 3, 35; DLB
16, 48; MTCW 1

**Pater, Walter (Horatio)** 1839-1894    **NCLC 7**
See also CDBLB 1832-1890; DLB 57, 156

**Paterson, A(ndrew) B(arton)** 1864-1941
**TCLC 32**
See also CA 155; SATA 97

**Paterson, Katherine (Womeldorf)** 1932-**C L C
12, 30**
See also AAYA 1; CA 21-24R; CANR 28, 59;
CLR 7, 50; DLB 52; JRDA; MAICYA;
MTCW 1; SATA 13, 53, 92

**Patmore, Coventry Kersey Dighton** 1823-1896
**NCLC 9**
See also DLB 35, 98

**Paton, Alan (Stewart)** 1903-1988 **CLC 4, 10,
25, 55, 106; DA; DAB; DAC; DAM MST,
NOV; WLC**
See also AAYA 26; CA 13-16; 125; CANR 22;
CAP 1; DLBD 17; MTCW 1, 2; SATA 11;
SATA-Obit 56

**Paton Walsh, Gillian** 1937-
See Walsh, Jill Paton
See also CANR 38; JRDA; MAICYA; SAAS 3;
SATA 4, 72

**Patton, George S.** 1885-1945        **TCLC 79**

**Paulding, James Kirke** 1778-1860    **NCLC 2**
See also DLB 3, 59, 74

**Paulin, Thomas Neilson** 1949-
See Paulin, Tom
See also CA 123; 128

**Paulin, Tom**                **CLC 37**
See also Paulin, Thomas Neilson
See also DLB 40

**Paustovsky, Konstantin (Georgievich)** 1892-
1968                    **CLC 40**
See also CA 93-96; 25-28R

**Pavese, Cesare** 1908-1950    **TCLC 3; PC 13;
SSC 19**
See also CA 104; 169; DLB 128, 177

**Pavic, Milorad** 1929-                **CLC 60**
See also CA 136; DLB 181

**Pavlov, Ivan Petrovich** 1849-1936    **TCLC 91**
See also CA 118

**Payne, Alan**
See Jakes, John (William)

**Paz, Gil**
See Lugones, Leopoldo

**Paz, Octavio** 1914-1998**CLC 3, 4, 6, 10, 19, 51,
65, 119; DA; DAB; DAC; DAM MST,
MULT, POET; HLC; PC 1; WLC**
See also CA 73-76; 165; CANR 32, 65; DLBY
90, 98; HW 1, 2; MTCW 1, 2

**p'Bitek, Okot** 1931-1982        **CLC 96; BLC 3;
DAM MULT**
See also BW 2, 3; CA 124; 107; DLB 125;
MTCW 1, 2

**Peacock, Molly** 1947-                **CLC 60**
See also CA 103; CAAS 21; CANR 52; DLB
120

**Peacock, Thomas Love** 1785-1866 **NCLC 22**
See also DLB 96, 116

**Peake, Mervyn** 1911-1968        **CLC 7, 54**
See also CA 5-8R; 25-28R; CANR 3; DLB 15,
160; MTCW 1; SATA 23

**Pearce, Philippa**                **CLC 21**
See also Christie, (Ann) Philippa

See also CLR 9; DLB 161; MAICYA; SATA 1,
67

**Pearl, Eric**
See Elman, Richard (Martin)

**Pearson, T(homas) R(eid)** 1956-        **CLC 39**
See also CA 120; 130; INT 130

**Peck, Dale** 1967-                **CLC 81**
See also CA 146; CANR 72

**Peck, John** 1941-                **CLC 3**
See also CA 49-52; CANR 3

**Peck, Richard (Wayne)** 1934-        **CLC 21**
See also AAYA 1, 24; CA 85-88; CANR 19,
38; CLR 15; INT CANR-19; JRDA;
MAICYA; SAAS 2; SATA 18, 55, 97

**Peck, Robert Newton** 1928-        **CLC 17; DA;
DAC; DAM MST**
See also AAYA 3; CA 81-84; CANR 31, 63;
CLR 45; JRDA; MAICYA; SAAS 1; SATA
21, 62

**Peckinpah, (David) Sam(uel)** 1925-1984 **C L C
20**
See also CA 109; 114

**Pedersen, Knut** 1859-1952
See Hamsun, Knut
See also CA 104; 119; CANR 63; MTCW 1, 2

**Peeslake, Gaffer**
See Durrell, Lawrence (George)

**Peguy, Charles Pierre** 1873-1914    **TCLC 10**
See also CA 107

**Peirce, Charles Sanders** 1839-1914 **TCLC 81**

**Pena, Ramon del Valle y**
See Valle-Inclan, Ramon (Maria) del

**Pendennis, Arthur Esquir**
See Thackeray, William Makepeace

**Penn, William** 1644-1718            **LC 25**
See also DLB 24

**PEPECE**
See Prado (Calvo), Pedro

**Pepys, Samuel** 1633-1703    **LC 11; DA; DAB;
DAC; DAM MST; WLC**
See also CDBLB 1660-1789; DLB 101

**Percy, Walker** 1916-1990**CLC 2, 3, 6, 8, 14, 18,
47, 65; DAM NOV, POP**
See also CA 1-4R; 131; CANR 1, 23, 64; DLB
2; DLBY 80, 90; MTCW 1, 2

**Percy, William Alexander** 1885-1942**TCLC 84**
See also CA 163; MTCW 2

**Perec, Georges** 1936-1982        **CLC 56, 116**
See also CA 141; DLB 83

**Pereda (y Sanchez de Porrua), Jose Maria de**
1833-1906                    **TCLC 16**
See also CA 117

**Pereda y Porrua, Jose Maria de**
See Pereda (y Sanchez de Porrua), Jose Maria
de

**Peregoy, George Weems**
See Mencken, H(enry) L(ouis)

**Perelman, S(idney) J(oseph)** 1904-1979 **C L C
3, 5, 9, 15, 23, 44, 49; DAM DRAM; SSC
32**
See also AITN 1, 2; CA 73-76; 89-92; CANR
18; DLB 11, 44; MTCW 1, 2

**Peret, Benjamin** 1899-1959        **TCLC 20**
See also CA 117

**Peretz, Isaac Loeb** 1851(?)-1915    **TCLC 16;
SSC 26**
See also CA 109

**Peretz, Yitzkhok Leibush**
See Peretz, Isaac Loeb

**Perez Galdos, Benito** 1843-1920    **TCLC 27;
HLCS 1**
See also CA 125; 153; HW 1

**Perrault, Charles** 1628-1703        **LC 2**

See also MAICYA; SATA 25

**Perry, Brighton**
See Sherwood, Robert E(mmet)

**Perse, St.-John**
See Leger, (Marie-Rene Auguste) Alexis Saint-
Leger

**Perutz, Leo(pold)** 1882-1957        **TCLC 60**
See also CA 147; DLB 81

**Peseenz, Tulio F.**
See Lopez y Fuentes, Gregorio

**Pesetsky, Bette** 1932-                **CLC 28**
See also CA 133; DLB 130

**Peshkov, Alexei Maximovich** 1868-1936
See Gorky, Maxim
See also CA 105; 141; DA; DAC; DAM DRAM,
MST, NOV; MTCW 2

**Pessoa, Fernando (Antonio Nogueira)** 1888-
1935**TCLC 27; DAM MULT; HLC; PC 20**
See also CA 125

**Peterkin, Julia Mood** 1880-1961        **CLC 31**
See also CA 102; DLB 9

**Peters, Joan K(aren)** 1945-            **CLC 39**
See also CA 158

**Peters, Robert L(ouis)** 1924-            **CLC 7**
See also CA 13-16R; CAAS 8; DLB 105

**Petofi, Sandor** 1823-1849            **NCLC 21**

**Petrakis, Harry Mark** 1923-            **CLC 3**
See also CA 9-12R; CANR 4, 30

**Petrarch** 1304-1374 **CMLC 20; DAM POET;
PC 8**

**Petrov, Evgeny**                **TCLC 21**
See also Kataev, Evgeny Petrovich

**Petry, Ann (Lane)** 1908-1997    **CLC 1, 7, 18**
See also BW 1, 3; CA 5-8R; 157; CAAS 6;
CANR 4, 46; CLR 12; DLB 76; JRDA;
MAICYA; MTCW 1; SATA 5; SATA-Obit 94

**Petursson, Halligrimur** 1614-1674        **LC 8**

**Peychinovich**
See Vazov, Ivan (Minchov)

**Phaedrus** c. 18B.C.-c. 50            **CMLC 25**
See also DLB 211

**Philips, Katherine** 1632-1664        **LC 30**
See also DLB 131

<indexboPhilipson, Morris H.** 1926-**CLC 53**
See also CA 1-4R; CANR 4

**Phillips, Caryl** 1958-    **CLC 96; BLCS; DAM
MULT**
See also BW 2; CA 141; CANR 63; DLB 157;
MTCW 2

**Phillips, David Graham** 1867-1911 **TCLC 44**
See also CA 108; DLB 9, 12

**Phillips, Jack**
See Sandburg, Carl (August)

**Phillips, Jayne Anne** 1952-**CLC 15, 33; SSC 16**
See also CA 101; CANR 24, 50; DLBY 80; INT
CANR-24; MTCW 1, 2

**Phillips, Richard**
See Dick, Philip K(indred)

**Phillips, Robert (Schaeffer)** 1938-    **CLC 28**
See also CA 17-20R; CAAS 13; CANR 8; DLB
105

**Phillips, Ward**
See Lovecraft, H(oward) P(hillips)

**Piccolo, Lucio** 1901-1969            **CLC 13**
See also CA 97-100; DLB 114

**Pickthall, Marjorie L(owry) C(hristie)** 1883-
1922                    **TCLC 21**
See also CA 107; DLB 92

**Pico della Mirandola, Giovanni** 1463-1494**LC
15**

**Piercy, Marge** 1936- **CLC 3, 6, 14, 18, 27, 62**
See also CA 21-24R; CAAS 1; CANR 13, 43,
66; DLB 120; MTCW 1, 2

See also CA 126; CANR 63

**Power, Susan** 1961-                                    **CLC 91**

**Powers, J(ames) F(arl)** 1917-**CLC 1, 4, 8, 57;**
**SSC 4**
See also CA 1-4R; CANR 2, 61; DLB 130;
MTCW 1

**Powers, John J(ames)** 1945-
See Powers, John R.
See also CA 69-72

**Powers, John R.**                                      **CLC 66**
See also Powers, John J(ames)

**Powers, Richard (S.)** 1957-              **CLC 93**
See also CA 148; CANR 80

**Pownall, David** 1938-                      **CLC 10**
See also CA 89-92; CAAS 18; CANR 49; DLB
14

**Powys, John Cowper** 1872-1963**CLC 7, 9, 15,**
**46**
See also CA 85-88; DLB 15; MTCW 1, 2

**Powys, T(heodore) F(rancis)** 1875-1953
**TCLC 9**
See also CA 106; DLB 36, 162

**Prado (Calvo), Pedro** 1886-1952      **TCLC 75**
See also CA 131; HW 1

**Prager, Emily** 1952-                        **CLC 56**

**Pratt, E(dwin) J(ohn)** 1883(?)-1964 **CLC 19;**
**DAC; DAM POET**
See also CA 141; 93-96; CANR 77; DLB 92

**Premchand**                                        **TCLC 21**
See also Srivastava, Dhanpat Rai

**Preussler, Otfried** 1923-                    **CLC 17**
See also CA 77-80; SATA 24

**Prevert, Jacques (Henri Marie)** 1900-1977
**CLC 15**
See also CA 77-80; 69-72; CANR 29, 61;
MTCW 1; SATA-Obit 30

**Prevost, Abbe (Antoine Francois)** 1697-1763
**LC 1**

**Price, (Edward) Reynolds** 1933-**CLC 3, 6, 13,**
**43, 50, 63; DAM NOV; SSC 22**
See also CA 1-4R; CANR 1, 37, 57; DLB 2;
INT CANR-37

**Price, Richard** 1949-                      **CLC 6, 12**
See also CA 49-52; CANR 3; DLBY 81

**Prichard, Katharine Susannah** 1883-1969
**CLC 46**
See also CA 11-12; CANR 33; CAP 1; MTCW
1; SATA 66

**Priestley, J(ohn) B(oynton)** 1894-1984**CLC 2,**
**5, 9, 34; DAM DRAM, NOV**
See also CA 9-12R; 113; CANR 33; CDBLB
1914-1945; DLB 10, 34, 77, 100, 139; DLBY
84; MTCW 1, 2

**Prince** 1958(?)-                              **CLC 35**

**Prince, F(rank) T(empleton)** 1912-    **CLC 22**
See also CA 101; CANR 43, 79; DLB 20

**Prince Kropotkin**
See Kropotkin, Peter (Aleksieevich)

**Prior, Matthew** 1664-1721                    **LC 4**
See also DLB 95

**Prishvin, Mikhail** 1873-1954              **TCLC 75**

**Pritchard, William H(arrison)** 1932- **CLC 34**
See also CA 65-68; CANR 23; DLB 111

**Pritchett, V(ictor) S(awdon)** 1900-1997 **C L C**
**5, 13, 15, 41; DAM NOV; SSC 14**
See also CA 61-64; 157; CANR 31, 63; DLB
15, 139; MTCW 1, 2

**Private 19022**
See Manning, Frederic

**Probst, Mark** 1925-                          **CLC 59**
See also CA 130

**Prokosch, Frederic** 1908-1989          **CLC 4, 48**
See also CA 73-76; 128; DLB 48; MTCW 2

**Propertius, Sextus** c. 50B.C.-c. 16B.C. **C M L C**
**32**
See also DLB 211

**Prophet, The**
See Dreiser, Theodore (Herman Albert)

**Prose, Francine** 1947-                        **CLC 45**
See also CA 109; 112; CANR 46; SATA 101

**Proudhon**
See Cunha, Euclides (Rodrigues Pimenta) da

**Proulx, Annie**
See Proulx, E(dna) Annie

**Proulx, E(dna) Annie** 1935-  **CLC 81; DAM**
**POP**
See also CA 145; CANR 65; MTCW 2

**Proust, (Valentin-Louis-George-Eugene-)**
**Marcel** 1871-1922 **TCLC 7, 13, 33; DA;**
**DAB; DAC; DAM MST, NOV; WLC**
See also CA 104; 120; DLB 65; MTCW 1, 2

**Prowler, Harley**
See Masters, Edgar Lee

**Prus, Boleslaw** 1845-1912                    **TCLC 48**

**Pryor, Richard (Franklin Lenox Thomas)** 1940-
**CLC 26**
See also CA 122; 152

**Przybyszewski, Stanislaw** 1868-1927**TCLC 36**
See also CA 160; DLB 66

**Pteleon**
See Grieve, C(hristopher) M(urray)
See also DAM POET

**Puckett, Lute**
See Masters, Edgar Lee

**Puig, Manuel** 1932-1990**CLC 3, 5, 10, 28, 65;**
**DAM MULT; HLC**
See also CA 45-48; CANR 2, 32, 63; DLB 113;
HW 1, 2; MTCW 1, 2

**Pulitzer, Joseph** 1847-1911                **TCLC 76**
See also CA 114; DLB 23

**Purdy, A(lfred) W(ellington)** 1918- **CLC 3, 6,**
**14, 50; DAC; DAM MST, POET**
See also CA 81-84; CAAS 17; CANR 42, 66;
DLB 88

**Purdy, James (Amos)** 1923- **CLC 2, 4, 10, 28,**
**52**
See also CA 33-36R; CAAS 1; CANR 19, 51;
DLB 2; INT CANR-19; MTCW 1

**Pure, Simon**
See Swinnerton, Frank Arthur

**Pushkin, Alexander (Sergeyevich)** 1799-1837
**NCLC 3, 27; DA; DAB; DAC; DAM**
**DRAM, MST, POET; PC 10; SSC 27;**
**WLC**
See also DLB 205; SATA 61

**P'u Sung-ling** 1640-1715          **LC 49; SSC 31**

**Putnam, Arthur Lee**
See Alger, Horatio, Jr.

**Puzo, Mario** 1920-1999 **CLC 1, 2, 6, 36, 107;**
**DAM NOV, POP**
See also CA 65-68; CANR 4, 42, 65; DLB 6;
MTCW 1, 2

**Pygge, Edward**
See Barnes, Julian (Patrick)

**Pyle, Ernest Taylor** 1900-1945
See Pyle, Ernie
See also CA 115; 160

**Pyle, Ernie** 1900-1945                        **TCLC 75**
See also Pyle, Ernest Taylor
See also DLB 29; MTCW 2

**Pyle, Howard** 1853-1911                      **TCLC 81**
See also CA 109; 137; CLR 22; DLB 42, 188;
DLBD 13; MAICYA; SATA 16, 100

**Pym, Barbara (Mary Crampton)** 1913-1980
**CLC 13, 19, 37, 111**
See also CA 13-14; 97-100; CANR 13, 34; CAP

1; DLB 14, 207; DLBY 87; MTCW 1, 2

**Pynchon, Thomas (Ruggles, Jr.)** 1937-**CLC 2,**
**3, 6, 9, 11, 18, 33, 62, 72; DA; DAB; DAC;**
**DAM MST, NOV, POP; SSC 14; WLC**
See also BEST 90:2; CA 17-20R; CANR 22,
46, 73; DLB 2, 173; MTCW 1, 2

**Pythagoras** c. 570B.C.-c. 500B.C.    **CMLC 22**
See also DLB 176

**Q**
See Quiller-Couch, SirArthur (Thomas)

**Qian Zhongshu**
See Ch'ien Chung-shu

**Qroll**
See Dagerman, Stig (Halvard)

**Quarrington, Paul (Lewis)** 1953-        **CLC 65**
See also CA 129; CANR 62

**Quasimodo, Salvatore** 1901-1968        **CLC 10**
See also CA 13-16; 25-28R; CAP 1; DLB 114;
MTCW 1

**Quay, Stephen** 1947-                          **CLC 95**

**Quay, Timothy** 1947-                          **CLC 95**

**Queen, Ellery**                                  **CLC 3, 11**
See also Dannay, Frederic; Davidson, Avram
(James); Lee, Manfred B(ennington);
Marlowe, Stephen; Sturgeon, Theodore
(Hamilton); Vance, John Holbrook

**Queen, Ellery, Jr.**
See Dannay, Frederic; Lee, Manfred
B(ennington)

**Queneau, Raymond** 1903-1976 **CLC 2, 5, 10,**
**42**
See also CA 77-80; 69-72; CANR 32; DLB 72;
MTCW 1, 2

**Quevedo, Francisco de** 1580-1645        **LC 23**

**Quiller-Couch, SirArthur (Thomas)** 1863-1944
**TCLC 53**
See also CA 118; 166; DLB 135, 153, 190

**Quin, Ann (Marie)** 1936-1973              **CLC 6**
See also CA 9-12R; 45-48; DLB 14

**Quinn, Martin**
See Smith, Martin Cruz

**Quinn, Peter** 1947-                            **CLC 91**

**Quinn, Simon**
See Smith, Martin Cruz

**Quiroga, Horacio (Sylvestre)** 1878-1937
**TCLC 20; DAM MULT; HLC**
See also CA 117; 131; HW 1; MTCW 1

**Quoirez, Francoise** 1935-                    **CLC 9**
See also Sagan, Francoise
See also CA 49-52; CANR 6, 39, 73; MTCW 1,
2

**Raabe, Wilhelm (Karl)** 1831-1910 **TCLC 45**
See also CA 167; DLB 129

**Rabe, David (William)** 1940-  **CLC 4, 8, 33;**
**DAM DRAM**
See also CA 85-88; CABS 3; CANR 59; DLB 7

**Rabelais, Francois** 1483-1553**LC 5; DA; DAB;**
**DAC; DAM MST; WLC**

**Rabinovitch, Sholem** 1859-1916
See Aleichem, Sholom
See also CA 104

**Rabinyan, Dorit** 1972-                        **CLC 119**
See also CA 170

**Rachilde** 1860-1953                            **TCLC 67**
See also DLB 123, 192

**Racine, Jean** 1639-1699 **LC 28; DAB; DAM**
**MST**

**Radcliffe, Ann (Ward)** 1764-1823**NCLC 6, 55**
See also DLB 39, 178

**Radiguet, Raymond** 1903-1923          **TCLC 29**
See also CA 162; DLB 65

**Radnoti, Miklos** 1909-1944                **TCLC 16**
See also CA 118

MTCW 1, 2

**Ribeiro, Darcy** 1922-1997　　　　**CLC 34**
　See also CA 33-36R; 156

**Ribeiro, Joao Ubaldo (Osorio Pimentel)** 1941-
　**CLC 10, 67**
　See also CA 81-84

**Ribman, Ronald (Burt)** 1932-　　　**CLC 7**
　See also CA 21-24R; CANR 46, 80

**Ricci, Nino** 1959-　　　　　　　**CLC 70**
　See also CA 137

**Rice, Anne** 1941-　　　**CLC 41; DAM POP**
　See also AAYA 9; BEST 89:2; CA 65-68; CANR
　12, 36, 53, 74; MTCW 2

**Rice, Elmer (Leopold)** 1892-1967 **CLC 7, 49;**
　**DAM DRAM**
　See also CA 21-22; 25-28R; CAP 2; DLB 4, 7;
　MTCW 1, 2

**Rice, Tim(othy Miles Bindon)** 1944- **CLC 21**
　See also CA 103; CANR 46

**Rich, Adrienne (Cecile)** 1929-**CLC 3, 6, 7, 11,**
　**18, 36, 73, 76; DAM POET; PC 5**
　See also CA 9-12R; CANR 20, 53, 74;
　CDALBS; DLB 5, 67; MTCW 1, 2

**Rich, Barbara**
　See Graves, Robert (von Ranke)

**Rich, Robert**
　See Trumbo, Dalton

**Richard, Keith**　　　　　　　　**CLC 17**
　See also Richards, Keith

**Richards, David Adams** 1950- **CLC 59; DAC**
　See also CA 93-96; CANR 60; DLB 53

**Richards, I(vor) A(rmstrong)** 1893-1979**C L C**
　**14, 24**
　See also CA 41-44R; 89-92; CANR 34, 74; DLB
　27; MTCW 2

**Richards, Keith** 1943-
　See Richard, Keith
　See also CA 107; CANR 77

**Richardson, Anne**
　See Roiphe, Anne (Richardson)

**Richardson, Dorothy Miller** 1873-1957**TCLC**
　**3**
　See also CA 104; DLB 36

**Richardson, Ethel Florence (Lindesay)** 1870-
　1946
　See Richardson, Henry Handel
　See also CA 105

**Richardson, Henry Handel**　　　**TCLC 4**
　See also Richardson, Ethel Florence (Lindesay)
　See also DLB 197

**Richardson, John** 1796-1852 **NCLC 55; DAC**
　See also DLB 99

**Richardson, Samuel** 1689-1761**LC 1, 44; DA;**
　**DAB; DAC; DAM MST, NOV; WLC**
　See also CDBLB 1660-1789; DLB 39

**Richler, Mordecai** 1931-**CLC 3, 5, 9, 13, 18, 46,**
　**70; DAC; DAM MST, NOV**
　See also AITN 1; CA 65-68; CANR 31, 62; CLR
　17; DLB 53; MAICYA; MTCW 1, 2; SATA
　44, 98; SATA-Brief 27

**Richter, Conrad (Michael)** 1890-1968**CLC 30**
　See also AAYA 21; CA 5-8R; 25-28R; CANR
　23; DLB 9, 212; MTCW 1, 2; SATA 3

**Ricostranza, Tom**
　See Ellis, Trey

**Riddell, Charlotte** 1832-1906　　　**TCLC 40**
　See also CA 165; DLB 156

**Ridgway, Keith** 1965-　　　　　**CLC 119**
　See also CA 172

**Riding, Laura**　　　　　　　　**CLC 3, 7**
　See also Jackson, Laura (Riding)

**Riefenstahl, Berta Helene Amalia** 1902-
　See Riefenstahl, Leni

See also CA 108

**Riefenstahl, Leni**　　　　　　　**CLC 16**
　See also Riefenstahl, Berta Helene Amalia

**Riffe, Ernest**
　See Bergman, (Ernst) Ingmar

**Riggs, (Rolla) Lynn** 1899-1954　　**TCLC 56;**
　**DAM MULT**
　See also CA 144; DLB 175; NNAL

**Riis, Jacob A(ugust)** 1849-1914　　**TCLC 80**
　See also CA 113; 168; DLB 23

**Riley, James Whitcomb** 1849-1916**TCLC 51;**
　**DAM POET**
　See also CA 118; 137; MAICYA; SATA 17

**Riley, Tex**
　See Creasey, John

**Rilke, Rainer Maria** 1875-1926**TCLC 1, 6, 19;**
　**DAM POET; PC 2**
　See also CA 104; 132; CANR 62; DLB 81;
　MTCW 1, 2

**Rimbaud, (Jean Nicolas) Arthur** 1854-1891
　**NCLC 4, 35; DA; DAB; DAC; DAM MST,**
　**POET; PC 3; WLC**

**Rinehart, Mary Roberts** 1876-1958**TCLC 52**
　See also CA 108; 166

**Ringmaster, The**
　See Mencken, H(enry) L(ouis)

**Ringwood, Gwen(dolyn Margaret) Pharis**
　1910-1984　　　　　　　　**CLC 48**
　See also CA 148; 112; DLB 88

**Rio, Michel** 19(?)-　　　　　　　**CLC 43**

**Ritsos, Giannes**
　See Ritsos, Yannis

**Ritsos, Yannis** 1909-1990　　**CLC 6, 13, 31**
　See also CA 77-80; 133; CANR 39, 61; MTCW
　1

**Ritter, Erika** 1948(?)-　　　　　**CLC 52**

**Rivera, Jose Eustasio** 1889-1928　**TCLC 35**
　See also CA 162; HW 1, 2

**Rivers, Conrad Kent** 1933-1968　　**CLC 1**
　See also BW 1; CA 85-88; DLB 41

**Rivers, Elfrida**
　See Bradley, Marion Zimmer

**Riverside, John**
　See Heinlein, Robert A(nson)

**Rizal, Jose** 1861-1896　　　　　**NCLC 27**

**Roa Bastos, Augusto (Antonio)** 1917-**CLC 45;**
　**DAM MULT; HLC**
　See also CA 131; DLB 113; HW 1

**Robbe-Grillet, Alain** 1922-**CLC 1, 2, 4, 6, 8, 10,**
　**14, 43**
　See also CA 9-12R; CANR 33, 65; DLB 83;
　MTCW 1, 2

**Robbins, Harold** 1916-1997　　**CLC 5; DAM**
　**NOV**
　See also CA 73-76; 162; CANR 26, 54; MTCW
　1, 2

**Robbins, Thomas Eugene** 1936-
　See Robbins, Tom
　See also CA 81-84; CANR 29, 59; DAM NOV,
　POP; MTCW 1, 2

**Robbins, Tom**　　　　　　**CLC 9, 32, 64**
　See also Robbins, Thomas Eugene
　See also BEST 90:3; DLBY 80; MTCW 2

**Robbins, Trina** 1938-　　　　　**CLC 21**
　See also CA 128

**Roberts, Charles G(eorge) D(ouglas)** 1860-1943
　**TCLC 8**
　See also CA 105; CLR 33; DLB 92; SATA 88;
　SATA-Brief 29

**Roberts, Elizabeth Madox** 1886-1941 **T C L C**
　**68**
　See also CA 111; 166; DLB 9, 54, 102; SATA
　33; SATA-Brief 27

**Roberts, Kate** 1891-1985　　　　**CLC 15**
　See also CA 107; 116

**Roberts, Keith (John Kingston)** 1935-**CLC 14**
　See also CA 25-28R; CANR 46

**Roberts, Kenneth (Lewis)** 1885-1957**TCLC 23**
　See also CA 109; DLB 9

**Roberts, Michele (B.)** 1949-　　　**CLC 48**
　See also CA 115; CANR 58

**Robertson, Ellis**
　See Ellison, Harlan (Jay); Silverberg, Robert

**Robertson, Thomas William** 1829-1871**NCLC**
　**35; DAM DRAM**

**Robeson, Kenneth**
　See Dent, Lester

**Robinson, Edwin Arlington** 1869-1935**T C L C**
　**5; DA; DAC; DAM MST, POET; PC 1**
　See also CA 104; 133; CDALB 1865-1917;
　DLB 54; MTCW 1, 2

**Robinson, Henry Crabb** 1775-1867**NCLC 15**
　See also DLB 107

**Robinson, Jill** 1936-　　　　　　**CLC 10**
　See also CA 102; INT 102

**Robinson, Kim Stanley** 1952-　　**CLC 34**
　See also AAYA 26; CA 126

**Robinson, Lloyd**
　See Silverberg, Robert

**Robinson, Marilynne** 1944-　　　**CLC 25**
　See also CA 116; CANR 80; DLB 206

**Robinson, Smokey**　　　　　　**CLC 21**
　See also Robinson, William, Jr.

**Robinson, William, Jr.** 1940-
　See Robinson, Smokey
　See also CA 116

**Robison, Mary** 1949-　　　　**CLC 42, 98**
　See also CA 113; 116; DLB 130; INT 116

**Rod, Edouard** 1857-1910　　　　**TCLC 52**

**Roddenberry, Eugene Wesley** 1921-1991
　See Roddenberry, Gene
　See also CA 110; 135; CANR 37; SATA 45;
　SATA-Obit 69

**Roddenberry, Gene**　　　　　　**CLC 17**
　See also Roddenberry, Eugene Wesley
　See also AAYA 5; SATA-Obit 69

**Rodgers, Mary** 1931-　　　　　**CLC 12**
　See also CA 49-52; CANR 8, 55; CLR 20; INT
　CANR-8; JRDA; MAICYA; SATA 8

**Rodgers, W(illiam) R(obert)** 1909-1969**CLC 7**
　See also CA 85-88; DLB 20

**Rodman, Eric**
　See Silverberg, Robert

**Rodman, Howard** 1920(?)-1985　　**CLC 65**
　See also CA 118

**Rodman, Maia**
　See Wojciechowska, Maia (Teresa)

**Rodriguez, Claudio** 1934-　　　**CLC 10**
　See also DLB 134

**Roelvaag, O(le) E(dvart)** 1876-1931**TCLC 17**
　See also CA 117; 171; DLB 9

**Roethke, Theodore (Huebner)** 1908-1963**CLC**
　**1, 3, 8, 11, 19, 46, 101; DAM POET; PC 15**
　See also CA 81-84; CABS 2; CDALB 1941-
　1968; DLB 5, 206; MTCW 1, 2

**Rogers, Samuel** 1763-1855　　　**NCLC 69**
　See also DLB 93

**Rogers, Thomas Hunton** 1927-　　**CLC 57**
　See also CA 89-92; INT 89-92

**Rogers, Will(iam Penn Adair)** 1879-1935
　**TCLC 8, 71; DAM MULT**
　See also CA 105; 144; DLB 11; MTCW 2;
　NNAL

**Rogin, Gilbert** 1929-　　　　　**CLC 18**
　See also CA 65-68; CANR 15

**Rohan, Koda**　　　　　　　　**TCLC 22**

3; DAM MULT, POET; PC 25
See also BW 2, 3; CA 116; 125; CANR 47, 74;
MTCW 1, 2

**Senna, Danzy** 1970-                                **CLC 119**
See also CA 169

**Serling, (Edward) Rod(man)** 1924-1975 **C L C
30**
See also AAYA 14; AITN 1; CA 162; 57-60;
DLB 26

**Serna, Ramon Gomez de la**
See Gomez de la Serna, Ramon

**Serpieres**
See Guillevic, (Eugene)

**Service, Robert**
See Service, Robert W(illiam)
See also DAB; DLB 92

**Service, Robert W(illiam)** 1874(?)-1958**TCLC
15; DA; DAC; DAM MST, POET; WLC**
See also Service, Robert
See also CA 115; 140; SATA 20

**Seth, Vikram** 1952-**CLC 43, 90; DAM MULT**
See also CA 121; 127; CANR 50, 74; DLB 120;
INT 127; MTCW 2

**Seton, Cynthia Propper** 1926-1982    **CLC 27**
See also CA 5-8R; 108; CANR 7

**Seton, Ernest (Evan) Thompson** 1860-1946
**TCLC 31**
See also CA 109; CLR 59; DLB 92; DLBD 13;
JRDA; SATA 18

**Seton-Thompson, Ernest**
See Seton, Ernest (Evan) Thompson

**Settle, Mary Lee** 1918-                        **CLC 19, 61**
See also CA 89-92; CAAS 1; CANR 44; DLB
6; INT 89-92

**Seuphor, Michel**
See Arp, Jean

**Sevigne, Marie (de Rabutin-Chantal) Marquise
de** 1626-1696                                        **LC 11**

**Sewall, Samuel** 1652-1730                        **LC 38**
See also DLB 24

**Sexton, Anne (Harvey)** 1928-1974**CLC 2, 4, 6,
8, 10, 15, 53; DA; DAB; DAC; DAM MST,
POET; PC 2; WLC**
See also CA 1-4R; 53-56; CABS 2; CANR 3,
36; CDALB 1941-1968; DLB 5, 169;
MTCW 1, 2; SATA 10

**Shaara, Jeff** 1952-                                **CLC 119**
See also CA 163

**Shaara, Michael (Joseph, Jr.)** 1929-1988**C L C
15; DAM POP**
See also AITN 1; CA 102; 125; CANR 52;
DLBY 83

**Shackleton, C. C.**
See Aldiss, Brian W(ilson)

**Shacochis, Bob**                                    **CLC 39**
See also Shacochis, Robert G.

**Shacochis, Robert G.** 1951-
See Shacochis, Bob
See also CA 119; 124; INT 124

**Shaffer, Anthony (Joshua)** 1926-            **CLC 19;
DAM DRAM**
See also CA 110; 116; DLB 13

**Shaffer, Peter (Levin)** 1926-**CLC 5, 14, 18, 37,
60; DAB; DAM DRAM, MST; DC 7**
See also CA 25-28R; CANR 25, 47, 74; CDBLB
1960 to Present; DLB 13; MTCW 1, 2

**Shakey, Bernard**
See Young, Neil

**Shalamov, Varlam (Tikhonovich)** 1907(?)-1982
**CLC 18**
See also CA 129; 105

**Shamlu, Ahmad** 1925-                            **CLC 10**

**Shammas, Anton** 1951-                            **CLC 55**

**Shange, Ntozake** 1948-**CLC 8, 25, 38, 74; BLC
3; DAM DRAM, MULT; DC 3**
See also AAYA 9; BW 2; CA 85-88; CABS 3;
CANR 27, 48, 74; DLB 38; MTCW 1, 2

**Shanley, John Patrick** 1950-                    **CLC 75**
See also CA 128; 133

**Shapcott, Thomas W(illiam)** 1935-            **CLC 38**
See also CA 69-72; CANR 49

**Shapiro, Jane**                                    **CLC 76**

**Shapiro, Karl (Jay)** 1913-**CLC 4, 8, 15, 53; PC
25**
See also CA 1-4R; CAAS 6; CANR 1, 36, 66;
DLB 48; MTCW 1, 2

**Sharp, William** 1855-1905                        **TCLC 39**
See also CA 160; DLB 156

**Sharpe, Thomas Ridley** 1928-
See Sharpe, Tom
See also CA 114; 122; INT 122

**Sharpe, Tom**                                        **CLC 36**
See also Sharpe, Thomas Ridley
See also DLB 14

**Shaw, Bernard**                                    **TCLC 45**
See also Shaw, George Bernard
See also BW 1; MTCW 2

**Shaw, G. Bernard**
See Shaw, George Bernard

**Shaw, George Bernard** 1856-1950**TCLC 3, 9,
21; DA; DAB; DAC; DAM DRAM, MST;
WLC**
See also Shaw, Bernard
See also CA 104; 128; CDBLB 1914-1945;
DLB 10, 57, 190; MTCW 1, 2

**Shaw, Henry Wheeler** 1818-1885    **NCLC 15**
See also DLB 11

**Shaw, Irwin** 1913-1984    **CLC 7, 23, 34; DAM
DRAM, POP**
See also AITN 1; CA 13-16R; 112; CANR 21;
CDALB 1941-1968; DLB 6, 102; DLBY 84;
MTCW 1, 21

**Shaw, Robert** 1927-1978                        **CLC 5**
See also AITN 1; CA 1-4R; 81-84; CANR 4;
DLB 13, 14

**Shaw, T. E.**
See Lawrence, T(homas) E(dward)

**Shawn, Wallace** 1943-                            **CLC 41**
See also CA 112

**Shea, Lisa** 1953-                                **CLC 86**
See also CA 147

**Sheed, Wilfrid (John Joseph)** 1930-**CLC 2, 4,
10, 53**
See also CA 65-68; CANR 30, 66; DLB 6;
MTCW 1, 2

**Sheldon, Alice Hastings Bradley** 1915(?)-1987
See Tiptree, James, Jr.
See also CA 108; 122; CANR 34; INT 108;
MTCW 1

**Sheldon, John**
See Bloch, Robert (Albert)

**Shelley, Mary Wollstonecraft (Godwin)** 1797-
1851**NCLC 14, 59; DA; DAB; DAC; DAM
MST, NOV; WLC**
See also AAYA 20; CDBLB 1789-1832; DLB
110, 116, 159, 178; SATA 29

**Shelley, Percy Bysshe** 1792-1822    **NCLC 18;
DA; DAB; DAC; DAM MST, POET; PC
14; WLC**
See also CDBLB 1789-1832; DLB 96, 110, 158

**Shepard, Jim** 1956-                                **CLC 36**
See also CA 137; CANR 59; SATA 90

**Shepard, Lucius** 1947-                            **CLC 34**
See also CA 128; 141

**Shepard, Sam** 1943- **CLC 4, 6, 17, 34, 41, 44;
DAM DRAM; DC 5**

See also AAYA 1; CA 69-72; CABS 3; CANR
22; DLB 7, 212; MTCW 1, 2

**Shepherd, Michael**
See Ludlum, Robert

**Sherburne, Zoa (Lillian Morin)** 1912-1995
**CLC 30**
See also AAYA 13; CA 1-4R; CANR 3, 37;
MAICYA; SAAS 18; SATA 3

**Sheridan, Frances** 1724-1766                    **LC 7**
See also DLB 39, 84

**Sheridan, Richard Brinsley** 1751-1816**N C L C
5; DA; DAB; DAC; DAM DRAM, MST;
DC 1; WLC**
See also CDBLB 1660-1789; DLB 89

**Sherman, Jonathan Marc**                        **CLC 55**

**Sherman, Martin** 1941(?)-                        **CLC 19**
See also CA 116; 123

**Sherwin, Judith Johnson**
See Johnson, Judith (Emlyn)

**Sherwood, Frances** 1940-                        **CLC 81**
See also CA 146

**Sherwood, Robert E(mmet)** 1896-1955**T C L C
3; DAM DRAM**
See also CA 104; 153; DLB 7, 26

**Shestov, Lev** 1866-1938                            **TCLC 56**

**Shevchenko, Taras** 1814-1861                    **NCLC 54**

**Shiel, M(atthew) P(hipps)** 1865-1947**TCLC 8**
See also Holmes, Gordon
See also CA 106; 160; DLB 153; MTCW 2

**Shields, Carol** 1935-        **CLC 91, 113; DAC**
See also CA 81-84; CANR 51, 74; MTCW 2

**Shields, David** 1956-                            **CLC 97**
See also CA 124; CANR 48

**Shiga, Naoya** 1883-1971        **CLC 33; SSC 23**
See also CA 101; 33-36R; DLB 180

**Shikibu, Murasaki** c. 978-c. 1014    **CMLC 1**

**Shilts, Randy** 1951-1994                        **CLC 85**
See also AAYA 19; CA 115; 127; 144; CANR
45; INT 127; MTCW 2

**Shimazaki, Haruki** 1872-1943
See Shimazaki Toson
See also CA 105; 134

**Shimazaki Toson** 1872-1943                    **TCLC 5**
See also Shimazaki, Haruki
See also DLB 180

**Sholokhov, Mikhail (Aleksandrovich)** 1905-
1984                                                **CLC 7, 15**
See also CA 101; 112; MTCW 1, 2; SATA-Obit
36

**Shone, Patric**
See Hanley, James

**Shreve, Susan Richards** 1939-                **CLC 23**
See also CA 49-52; CAAS 5; CANR 5, 38, 69;
MAICYA; SATA 46, 95; SATA-Brief 41

**Shue, Larry** 1946-1985**CLC 52; DAM DRAM**
See also CA 145; 117

**Shu-Jen, Chou** 1881-1936
See Lu Hsun
See also CA 104

**Shulman, Alix Kates** 1932-                    **CLC 2, 10**
See also CA 29-32R; CANR 43; SATA 7

**Shuster, Joe** 1914-                                **CLC 21**

**Shute, Nevil**                                      **CLC 30**
See also Norway, Nevil Shute
See also MTCW 2

**Shuttle, Penelope (Diane)** 1947-            **CLC 7**
See also CA 93-96; CANR 39; DLB 14, 40

**Sidney, Mary** 1561-1621                        **LC 19, 39**

**Sidney, Sir Philip** 1554-1586 **LC 19, 39; DA;
DAB; DAC; DAM MST, POET**
See also CDBLB Before 1660; DLB 167

**Siegel, Jerome** 1914-1996                        **CLC 21**
See also CA 116; 169; 151

Siegel, Jerry
   See Siegel, Jerome
Sienkiewicz, Henryk (Adam Alexander Pius)
   1846-1916          TCLC 3
   See also CA 104; 134
Sierra, Gregorio Martinez
   See Martinez Sierra, Gregorio
Sierra, Maria (de la O'LeJarraga) Martinez
   See Martinez Sierra, Maria (de la O'LeJarraga)
Sigal, Clancy 1926-          CLC 7
   See also CA 1-4R
Sigourney, Lydia Howard (Huntley) 1791-1865
   NCLC 21
   See also DLB 1, 42, 73
Siguenza y Gongora, Carlos de 1645-1700L C
   8; HLCS 1
Sigurjonsson, Johann 1880-1919    TCLC 27
   See also CA 170
Sikelianos, Angelos 1884-1951      TCLC 39
Silkin, Jon 1930-          CLC 2, 6, 43
   See also CA 5-8R; CAAS 5; DLB 27
Silko, Leslie (Marmon) 1948-CLC 23, 74, 114;
   DA; DAC; DAM MST, MULT, POP;
   WLCS
   See also AAYA 14; CA 115; 122; CANR 45,
   65; DLB 143, 175; MTCW 2; NNAL
Sillanpaa, Frans Eemil 1888-1964    CLC 19
   See also CA 129; 93-96; MTCW 1
Sillitoe, Alan 1928-    CLC 1, 3, 6, 10, 19, 57
   See also AITN 1; CA 9-12R; CAAS 2; CANR
   8, 26, 55; CDBLB 1960 to Present; DLB 14,
   139; MTCW 1, 2; SATA 61
Silone, Ignazio 1900-1978          CLC 4
   See also CA 25-28; 81-84; CANR 34; CAP 2;
   MTCW 1
Silver, Joan Micklin 1935-       CLC 20
   See also CA 114; 121; INT 121
Silver, Nicholas
   See Faust, Frederick (Schiller)
Silverberg, Robert 1935- CLC 7; DAM POP
   See also AAYA 24; CA 1-4R; CAAS 3; CANR
   1, 20, 36; CLR 58; DLB 8; INT CANR-20;
   MAICYA; MTCW 1, 2; SATA 13, 91; SATA-
   Essay 104
Silverstein, Alvin 1933-         CLC 17
   See also CA 49-52; CANR 2; CLR 25; JRDA;
   MAICYA; SATA 8, 69
Silverstein, Virginia B(arbara Opshelor) 1937-
   CLC 17
   See also CA 49-52; CANR 2; CLR 25; JRDA;
   MAICYA; SATA 8, 69
Sim, Georges
   See Simenon, Georges (Jacques Christian)
Simak, Clifford D(onald) 1904-1988CLC 1, 55
   See also CA 1-4R; 125; CANR 1, 35; DLB 8;
   MTCW 1; SATA-Obit 56
Simenon, Georges (Jacques Christian) 1903-
   1989   CLC 1, 2, 3, 8, 18, 47; DAM POP
   See also CA 85-88; 129; CANR 35; DLB 72;
   DLBY 89; MTCW 1, 2
Simic, Charles 1938-    CLC 6, 9, 22, 49, 68;
   DAM POET
   See also CA 29-32R; CAAS 4; CANR 12, 33,
   52, 61; DLB 105; MTCW 2
Simmel, Georg 1858-1918       TCLC 64
   See also CA 157
Simmons, Charles (Paul) 1924-    CLC 57
   See also CA 89-92; INT 89-92
Simmons, Dan 1948-    CLC 44; DAM POP
   See also AAYA 16; CA 138; CANR 53
Simmons, James (Stewart Alexander) 1933-
   CLC 43
   See also CA 105; CAAS 21; DLB 40

Simms, William Gilmore 1806-1870 NCLC 3
   See also DLB 3, 30, 59, 73
Simon, Carly 1945-          CLC 26
   See also CA 105
Simon, Claude 1913-1984    CLC 4, 9, 15, 39;
   DAM NOV
   See also CA 89-92; CANR 33; DLB 83; MTCW
Simon, (Marvin) Neil 1927-CLC 6, 11, 31, 39,
   70; DAM DRAM
   See also AITN 1; CA 21-24R; CANR 26, 54;
   DLB 7; MTCW 1, 2
Simon, Paul (Frederick) 1941(?)-    CLC 17
   See also CA 116; 153
Simonon, Paul 1956(?)-         CLC 30
Simpson, Harriette
   See Arnow, Harriette (Louisa) Simpson
Simpson, Louis (Aston Marantz) 1923-CLC 4,
   7, 9, 32; DAM POET
   See also CA 1-4R; CAAS 4; CANR 1, 61; DLB
   5; MTCW 1, 2
Simpson, Mona (Elizabeth) 1957-    CLC 44
   See also CA 122; 135; CANR 68
Simpson, N(orman) F(rederick) 1919-CLC 29
   See also CA 13-16R; DLB 13
Sinclair, Andrew (Annandale) 1935-    CLC 2,
   14
   See also CA 9-12R; CAAS 5; CANR 14, 38;
   DLB 14; MTCW 1
Sinclair, Emil
   See Hesse, Hermann
Sinclair, Iain 1943-          CLC 76
   See also CA 132
Sinclair, Iain MacGregor
   See Sinclair, Iain
Sinclair, Irene
   See Griffith, D(avid Lewelyn) W(ark)
Sinclair, Mary Amelia St. Clair 1865(?)-1946
   See Sinclair, May
   See also CA 104
Sinclair, May 1863-1946       TCLC 3, 11
   See also Sinclair, Mary Amelia St. Clair
   See also CA 166; DLB 36, 135
Sinclair, Roy
   See Griffith, D(avid Lewelyn) W(ark)
Sinclair, Upton (Beall) 1878-1968 CLC 1, 11,
   15, 63; DA; DAB; DAC; DAM MST, NOV;
   WLC
   See also CA 5-8R; 25-28R; CANR 7; CDALB
   1929-1941; DLB 9; INT CANR-7; MTCW
   1, 2; SATA 9
Singer, Isaac
   See Singer, Isaac Bashevis
Singer, Isaac Bashevis 1904-1991CLC 1, 3, 6,
   9, 11, 15, 23, 38, 69, 111; DA; DAB; DAC;
   DAM MST, NOV; SSC 3; WLC
   See also AITN 1, 2; CA 1-4R; 134; CANR 1,
   39; CDALB 1941-1968; CLR 1; DLB 6, 28,
   52; DLBY 91; JRDA; MAICYA; MTCW 1,
   2; SATA 3, 27; SATA-Obit 68
Singer, Israel Joshua 1893-1944    TCLC 33
   See also CA 169
Singh, Khushwant 1915-         CLC 11
   See also CA 9-12R; CAAS 9; CANR 6
Singleton, Ann
   See Benedict, Ruth (Fulton)
Sinjohn, John
   See Galsworthy, John
Sinyavsky, Andrei (Donatevich) 1925-1997
   CLC 8
   See also CA 85-88; 159
Sirin, V.
   See Nabokov, Vladimir (Vladimirovich)

Sissman, L(ouis) E(dward) 1928-1976CLC 9,
   18
   See also CA 21-24R; 65-68; CANR 13; DLB 5
Sisson, C(harles) H(ubert) 1914-    CLC 8
   See also CA 1-4R; CAAS 3; CANR 3, 48; DLB
   27
Sitwell, Dame Edith 1887-1964 CLC 2, 9, 67;
   DAM POET; PC 3
   See also CA 9-12R; CANR 35; CDBLB 1945-
   1960; DLB 20; MTCW 1, 2
Siwaarmill, H. P.
   See Sharp, William
Sjoewall, Maj 1935-          CLC 7
   See also CA 65-68; CANR 73
Sjowall, Maj
   See Sjoewall, Maj
Skelton, John 1463-1529         PC 25
Skelton, Robin 1925-1997       CLC 13
   See also AITN 2; CA 5-8R; 160; CAAS 5;
   CANR 28; DLB 27, 53
Skolimowski, Jerzy 1938-       CLC 20
   See also CA 128
Skram, Amalie (Bertha) 1847-1905 TCLC 25
   See also CA 165
Skvorecky, Josef (Vaclav) 1924-    CLC 15, 39,
   69; DAC; DAM NOV
   See also CA 61-64; CAAS 1; CANR 10, 34,
   63; MTCW 1, 2
Slade, Bernard          CLC 11, 46
   See also Newbound, Bernard Slade
   See also CAAS 9; DLB 53
Slaughter, Carolyn 1946-       CLC 56
   See also CA 85-88
Slaughter, Frank G(ill) 1908-      CLC 29
   See also AITN 2; CA 5-8R; CANR 5; INT
   CANR-5
Slavitt, David R(ytman) 1935-    CLC 5, 14
   See also CA 21-24R; CAAS 3; CANR 41; DLB
   5, 6
Slesinger, Tess 1905-1945       TCLC 10
   See also CA 107; DLB 102
Slessor, Kenneth 1901-1971      CLC 14
   See also CA 102; 89-92
Slowacki, Juliusz 1809-1849     NCLC 15
Smart, Christopher 1722-1771   LC 3; DAM
   POET; PC 13
   See also DLB 109
Smart, Elizabeth 1913-1986       CLC 54
   See also CA 81-84; 118; DLB 88
Smiley, Jane (Graves) 1949-CLC 53, 76; DAM
   POP
   See also CA 104; CANR 30, 50, 74; INT CANR-
   30
Smith, A(rthur) J(ames) M(arshall) 1902-1980
   CLC 15; DAC
   See also CA 1-4R; 102; CANR 4; DLB 88
Smith, Adam 1723-1790         LC 36
   See also DLB 104
Smith, Alexander 1829-1867     NCLC 59
   See also DLB 32, 55
Smith, Anna Deavere 1950-      CLC 86
   See also CA 133
Smith, Betty (Wehner) 1896-1972    CLC 19
   See also CA 5-8R; 33-36R; DLBY 82; SATA 6
Smith, Charlotte (Turner) 1749-1806 N C L C
   23
   See also DLB 39, 109
Smith, Clark Ashton 1893-1961     CLC 43
   See also CA 143; MTCW 2
Smith, Dave          CLC 22, 42
   See also Smith, David (Jeddie)
   See also CAAS 7; DLB 5
Smith, David (Jeddie) 1942-

See Smith, Dave
See also CA 49-52; CANR 1, 59; DAM POET
**Smith, Florence Margaret** 1902-1971
See Smith, Stevie
See also CA 17-18; 29-32R; CANR 35; CAP 2;
DAM POET; MTCW 1, 2
**Smith, Iain Crichton** 1928-1998    **CLC 64**
See also CA 21-24R; 171; DLB 40, 139
**Smith, John** 1580(?)-1631    **LC 9**
See also DLB 24, 30
**Smith, Johnston**
See Crane, Stephen (Townley)
**Smith, Joseph, Jr.** 1805-1844    **NCLC 53**
**Smith, Lee** 1944-    **CLC 25, 73**
See also CA 114; 119; CANR 46; DLB 143;
DLBY 83; INT 119
**Smith, Martin**
See Smith, Martin Cruz
**Smith, Martin Cruz** 1942-    **CLC 25; DAM
MULT, POP**
See also BEST 89:4; CA 85-88; CANR 6, 23,
43, 65; INT CANR-23; MTCW 2; NNAL
**Smith, Mary-Ann Tirone** 1944-    **CLC 39**
See also CA 118; 136
**Smith, Patti** 1946-    **CLC 12**
See also CA 93-96; CANR 63
**Smith, Pauline (Urmson)** 1882-1959 **TCLC 25**
**Smith, Rosamond**
See Oates, Joyce Carol
**Smith, Sheila Kaye**
See Kaye-Smith, Sheila
**Smith, Stevie**    **CLC 3, 8, 25, 44; PC 12**
See also Smith, Florence Margaret
See also DLB 20; MTCW 2
**Smith, Wilbur (Addison)** 1933-    **CLC 33**
See also CA 13-16R; CANR 7, 46, 66; MTCW
1, 2
**Smith, William Jay** 1918-    **CLC 6**
See also CA 5-8R; CANR 44; DLB 5; MAICYA;
SAAS 22; SATA 2, 68
**Smith, Woodrow Wilson**
See Kuttner, Henry
**Smolenskin, Peretz** 1842-1885    **NCLC 30**
**Smollett, Tobias (George)** 1721-1771 **LC 2, 46**
See also CDBLB 1660-1789; DLB 39, 104
**Snodgrass, W(illiam) D(e Witt)** 1926- **CLC 2,
6, 10, 18, 68; DAM POET**
See also CA 1-4R; CANR 6, 36, 65; DLB 5;
MTCW 1, 2
**Snow, C(harles) P(ercy)** 1905-1980 **CLC 1, 4,
6, 9, 13, 19; DAM NOV**
See also CA 5-8R; 101; CANR 28; CDBLB
1945-1960; DLB 15, 77; DLBD 17; MTCW
1, 2
**Snow, Frances Compton**
See Adams, Henry (Brooks)
**Snyder, Gary (Sherman)** 1930- **CLC 1, 2, 5, 9,
32, 120; DAM POET; PC 21**
See also CA 17-20R; CANR 30, 60; DLB 5,
16, 165, 212; MTCW 2
**Snyder, Zilpha Keatley** 1927-    **CLC 17**
See also AAYA 15; CA 9-12R; CANR 38; CLR
31; JRDA; MAICYA; SAAS 2; SATA 1, 28,
75
**Soares, Bernardo**
See Pessoa, Fernando (Antonio Nogueira)
**Sobh, A.**
See Shamlu, Ahmad
**Sobol, Joshua**    **CLC 60**
**Socrates** 469B.C.-399B.C.    **CMLC 27**
**Soderberg, Hjalmar** 1869-1941    **TCLC 39**
**Sodergran, Edith (Irene)**
See Soedergran, Edith (Irene)

**Soedergran, Edith (Irene)** 1892-1923  **TCLC
31**
**Softly, Edgar**
See Lovecraft, H(oward) P(hillips)
**Softly, Edward**
See Lovecraft, H(oward) P(hillips)
**Sokolov, Raymond** 1941-    **CLC 7**
See also CA 85-88
**Solo, Jay**
See Ellison, Harlan (Jay)
**Sologub, Fyodor**    **TCLC 9**
See also Teternikov, Fyodor Kuzmich
**Solomons, Ikey Esquir**
See Thackeray, William Makepeace
**Solomos, Dionysios** 1798-1857    **NCLC 15**
**Solwoska, Mara**
See French, Marilyn
**Solzhenitsyn, Aleksandr I(sayevich)** 1918-
**CLC 1, 2, 4, 7, 9, 10, 18, 26, 34, 78; DA;
DAB; DAC; DAM MST, NOV; SSC 32;
WLC**
See also AITN 1; CA 69-72; CANR 40, 65;
MTCW 1, 2
**Somers, Jane**
See Lessing, Doris (May)
**Somerville, Edith** 1858-1949    **TCLC 51**
See also DLB 135
**Somerville & Ross**
See Martin, Violet Florence; Somerville, Edith
**Sommer, Scott** 1951-    **CLC 25**
See also CA 106
**Sondheim, Stephen (Joshua)** 1930- **CLC 30,
39; DAM DRAM**
See also AAYA 11; CA 103; CANR 47, 68
**Song, Cathy** 1955-    **PC 21**
See also CA 154; DLB 169
**Sontag, Susan** 1933- **CLC 1, 2, 10, 13, 31, 105;
DAM POP**
See also CA 17-20R; CANR 25, 51, 74; DLB
2, 67; MTCW 1, 2
**Sophocles** 496(?)B.C.-406(?)B.C.    **CMLC 2;
DA; DAB; DAC; DAM DRAM, MST; DC
1; WLCS**
See also DLB 176
**Sordello** 1189-1269    **CMLC 15**
**Sorel, Georges** 1847-1922    **TCLC 91**
See also CA 118
**Sorel, Julia**
See Drexler, Rosalyn
**Sorrentino, Gilbert** 1929- **CLC 3, 7, 14, 22, 40**
See also CA 77-80; CANR 14, 33; DLB 5, 173;
DLBY 80; INT CANR-14
**Soto, Gary** 1952-  **CLC 32, 80; DAM MULT;
HLC**
See also AAYA 10; CA 119; 125; CANR 50,
74; CLR 38; DLB 82; HW 1, 2; INT 125;
JRDA; MTCW 2; SATA 80
**Soupault, Philippe** 1897-1990    **CLC 68**
See also CA 116; 147; 131
**Souster, (Holmes) Raymond** 1921- **CLC 5, 14;
DAC; DAM POET**
See also CA 13-16R; CAAS 14; CANR 13, 29,
53; DLB 88; SATA 63
**Southern, Terry** 1924(?)-1995    **CLC 7**
See also CA 1-4R; 150; CANR 1, 55; DLB 2
**Southey, Robert** 1774-1843    **NCLC 8**
See also DLB 93, 107, 142; SATA 54
**Southworth, Emma Dorothy Eliza Nevitte**
1819-1899    **NCLC 26**
**Souza, Ernest**
See Scott, Evelyn
**Soyinka, Wole** 1934- **CLC 3, 5, 14, 36, 44; BLC
3; DA; DAB; DAC; DAM DRAM, MST,**

MULT; DC 2; WLC
See also BW 2, 3; CA 13-16R; CANR 27, 39;
DLB 125; MTCW 1, 2
**Spackman, W(illiam) M(ode)** 1905-1990 **CLC
46**
See also CA 81-84; 132
**Spacks, Barry (Bernard)** 1931-    **CLC 14**
See also CA 154; CANR 33; DLB 105
**Spanidou, Irini** 1946-    **CLC 44**
**Spark, Muriel (Sarah)** 1918- **CLC 2, 3, 5, 8, 13,
18, 40, 94; DAB; DAC; DAM MST, NOV;
SSC 10**
See also CA 5-8R; CANR 12, 36, 76; CDBLB
1945-1960; DLB 15, 139; INT CANR-12;
MTCW 1, 2
**Spaulding, Douglas**
See Bradbury, Ray (Douglas)
**Spaulding, Leonard**
See Bradbury, Ray (Douglas)
**Spence, J. A. D.**
See Eliot, T(homas) S(tearns)
**Spencer, Elizabeth** 1921-    **CLC 22**
See also CA 13-16R; CANR 32, 65; DLB 6;
MTCW 1; SATA 14
**Spencer, Leonard G.**
See Silverberg, Robert
**Spencer, Scott** 1945-    **CLC 30**
See also CA 113; CANR 51; DLBY 86
**Spender, Stephen (Harold)** 1909-1995 **CLC 1,
2, 5, 10, 41, 91; DAM POET**
See also CA 9-12R; 149; CANR 31, 54; CDBLB
1945-1960; DLB 20; MTCW 1, 2
**Spengler, Oswald (Arnold Gottfried)** 1880-1936
**TCLC 25**
See also CA 118
**Spenser, Edmund** 1552(?)-1599 **LC 5, 39; DA;
DAB; DAC; DAM MST, POET; PC 8;
WLC**
See also CDBLB Before 1660; DLB 167
**Spicer, Jack** 1925-1965 **CLC 8, 18, 72; DAM
POET**
See also CA 85-88; DLB 5, 16, 193
**Spiegelman, Art** 1948-    **CLC 76**
See also AAYA 10; CA 125; CANR 41, 55, 74;
MTCW 2
**Spielberg, Peter** 1929-    **CLC 6**
See also CA 5-8R; CANR 4, 48; DLBY 81
**Spielberg, Steven** 1947-    **CLC 20**
See also AAYA 8, 24; CA 77-80; CANR 32;
SATA 32
**Spillane, Frank Morrison** 1918-
See Spillane, Mickey
See also CA 25-28R; CANR 28, 63; MTCW 1,
2; SATA 66
**Spillane, Mickey**    **CLC 3, 13**
See also Spillane, Frank Morrison
See also MTCW 2
**Spinoza, Benedictus de** 1632-1677    **LC 9**
**Spinrad, Norman (Richard)** 1940-    **CLC 46**
See also CA 37-40R; CAAS 19; CANR 20; DLB
8; INT CANR-20
**Spitteler, Carl (Friedrich Georg)** 1845-1924
**TCLC 12**
See also CA 109; DLB 129
**Spivack, Kathleen (Romola Drucker)** 1938-
**CLC 6**
See also CA 49-52
**Spoto, Donald** 1941-    **CLC 39**
See also CA 65-68; CANR 11, 57
**Springsteen, Bruce (F.)** 1949-    **CLC 17**
See also CA 111
**Spurling, Hilary** 1940-    **CLC 34**
See also CA 104; CANR 25, 52

**Stout, Rex (Todhunter)** 1886-1975  **CLC 3**
  See also AITN 2; CA 61-64; CANR 71

**Stow, (Julian) Randolph** 1935-  **CLC 23, 48**
  See also CA 13-16R; CANR 33; MTCW 1

**Stowe, Harriet (Elizabeth) Beecher** 1811-1896
  **NCLC 3, 50; DA; DAB; DAC; DAM MST,
  NOV; WLC**
  See also CDALB 1865-1917; DLB 1, 12, 42,
  74, 189; JRDA; MAICYA; YABC 1

**Strachey, (Giles) Lytton** 1880-1932 **TCLC 12**
  See also CA 110; DLB 149; DLBD 10; MTCW
  2

**Strand, Mark** 1934- **CLC 6, 18, 41, 71; DAM
  POET**
  See also CA 21-24R; CANR 40, 65; DLB 5;
  SATA 41

**Straub, Peter (Francis)** 1943-  **CLC 28, 107;
  DAM POP**
  See also BEST 89:1; CA 85-88; CANR 28, 65;
  DLBY 84; MTCW 1, 2

**Strauss, Botho** 1944-  **CLC 22**
  <indexSee also CA 157; DLB 124

**Streatfeild, (Mary) Noel** 1895(?)-1986**CLC 21**
  See also CA 81-84; 120; CANR 31; CLR 17;
  DLB 160; MAICYA; SATA 20; SATA-Obit
  48

**Stribling, T(homas) S(igismund)** 1881-1965
  **CLC 23**
  See also CA 107; DLB 9

**Strindberg, (Johan) August** 1849-1912**TCLC
  1, 8, 21, 47; DA; DAB; DAC; DAM DRAM,
  MST; WLC**
  See also CA 104; 135; MTCW 2

**Stringer, Arthur** 1874-1950  **TCLC 37**
  See also CA 161; DLB 92

**Stringer, David**
  See Roberts, Keith (John Kingston)

**Stroheim, Erich von** 1885-1957  **TCLC 71**

**Strugatskii, Arkadii (Natanovich)** 1925-1991
  **CLC 27**
  See also CA 106; 135

**Strugatskii, Boris (Natanovich)** 1933-**CLC 27**
  See also CA 106

**Strummer, Joe** 1953(?)-  **CLC 30**

**Strunk, William, Jr.** 1869-1946  **TCLC 92**
  See also CA 118; 164

**Stuart, Don A.**
  See Campbell, John W(ood, Jr.)

**Stuart, Ian**
  See MacLean, Alistair (Stuart)

**Stuart, Jesse (Hilton)** 1906-1984**CLC 1, 8, 11,
  14, 34; SSC 31**
  See also CA 5-8R; 112; CANR 31; DLB 9, 48,
  102; DLBY 84; SATA 2; SATA-Obit 36

**Sturgeon, Theodore (Hamilton)** 1918-1985
  **CLC 22, 39**
  See also Queen, Ellery
  See also CA 81-84; 116; CANR 32; DLB 8;
  DLBY 85; MTCW 1, 2

**Sturges, Preston** 1898-1959  **TCLC 48**
  See also CA 114; 149; DLB 26

**Styron, William** 1925-**CLC 1, 3, 5, 11, 15, 60;
  DAM NOV, POP; SSC 25**
  See also BEST 90:4; CA 5-8R; CANR 6, 33,
  74; CDALB 1968-1988; DLB 2, 143; DLBY
  80; INT CANR-6; MTCW 1, 2

**Su, Chien** 1884-1918
  See Su Man-shu
  See also CA 123

**Suarez Lynch, B.**
  See Bioy Casares, Adolfo; Borges, Jorge Luis

**Suckow, Ruth** 1892-1960  **SSC 18**
  See also CA 113; DLB 9, 102

**Sudermann, Hermann** 1857-1928  **TCLC 15**
  See also CA 107; DLB 118

**Sue, Eugene** 1804-1857  **NCLC 1**
  See also DLB 119

**Sueskind, Patrick** 1949-  **CLC 44**
  See also Suskind, Patrick

**Sukenick, Ronald** 1932-  **CLC 3, 4, 6, 48**
  See also CA 25-28R; CAAS 8; CANR 32; DLB
  173; DLBY 81

**Suknaski, Andrew** 1942-  **CLC 19**
  See also CA 101; DLB 53

**Sullivan, Vernon**
  See Vian, Boris

**Sully Prudhomme** 1839-1907  **TCLC 31**

**Su Man-shu**  **TCLC 24**
  See also Su, Chien

**Summerforest, Ivy B.**
  See Kirkup, James

**Summers, Andrew James** 1942-  **CLC 26**

**Summers, Andy**
  See Summers, Andrew James

**Summers, Hollis (Spurgeon, Jr.)** 1916-**CLC 10**
  See also CA 5-8R; CANR 3; DLB 6

**Summers, (Alphonsus Joseph-Mary Augustus)
  Montague** 1880-1948  **TCLC 16**
  See also CA 118; 163

**Sumner, Gordon Matthew**  **CLC 26**
  See also Sting

**Surtees, Robert Smith** 1803-1864  **NCLC 14**
  See also DLB 21

**Susann, Jacqueline** 1921-1974  **CLC 3**
  See also AITN 1; CA 65-68; 53-56; MTCW 1,
  2

**Su Shih** 1036-1101  **CMLC 15**

**Suskind, Patrick**
  See Sueskind, Patrick
  See also CA 145

**Sutcliff, Rosemary** 1920-1992 **CLC 26; DAB;
  DAC; DAM MST, POP**
  See also AAYA 10; CA 5-8R; 139; CANR 37;
  CLR 1, 37; JRDA; MAICYA; SATA 6, 44,
  78; SATA-Obit 73

**Sutro, Alfred** 1863-1933  **TCLC 6**
  See also CA 105; DLB 10

**Sutton, Henry**
  See Slavitt, David R(ytman)

**Svevo, Italo** 1861-1928  **TCLC 2, 35; SSC 25**
  See also Schmitz, Aron Hector

**Swados, Elizabeth (A.)** 1951-  **CLC 12**
  See also CA 97-100; CANR 49; INT 97-100

**Swados, Harvey** 1920-1972  **CLC 5**
  See also CA 5-8R; 37-40R; CANR 6; DLB 2

**Swan, Gladys** 1934-  **CLC 69**
  See also CA 101; CANR 17, 39

**Swarthout, Glendon (Fred)** 1918-1992**CLC 35**
  See also CA 1-4R; 139; CANR 1, 47; SATA 26

**Sweet, Sarah C.**
  See Jewett, (Theodora) Sarah Orne

**Swenson, May** 1919-1989**CLC 4, 14, 61, 106;
  DA; DAB; DAC; DAM MST, POET; PC
  14**
  See also CA 5-8R; 130; CANR 36, 61; DLB 5;
  MTCW 1, 2; SATA 15

**Swift, Augustus**
  See Lovecraft, H(oward) P(hillips)

**Swift, Graham (Colin)** 1949-  **CLC 41, 88**
  See also CA 117; 122; CANR 46, 71; DLB 194;
  MTCW 2

**Swift, Jonathan** 1667-1745  **LC 1, 42; DA;
  DAB; DAC; DAM MST, NOV, POET; PC
  9; WLC**
  See also CDBLB 1660-1789; CLR 53; DLB 39,
  95, 101; SATA 19

**Swinburne, Algernon Charles** 1837-1909
  **TCLC 8, 36; DA; DAB; DAC; DAM MST,
  POET; PC 24; WLC**
  See also CA 105; 140; CDBLB 1832-1890;
  DLB 35, 57

**Swinfen, Ann**  **CLC 34**

**Swinnerton, Frank Arthur** 1884-1982**CLC 31**
  See also CA 108; DLB 34

**Swithen, John**
  See King, Stephen (Edwin)

**Sylvia**
  See Ashton-Warner, Sylvia (Constance)

**Symmes, Robert Edward**
  See Duncan, Robert (Edward)

**Symonds, John Addington** 1840-1893 **N C L C
  34**
  See also DLB 57, 144

**Symons, Arthur** 1865-1945  **TCLC 11**
  See also CA 107; DLB 19, 57, 149

**Symons, Julian (Gustave)** 1912-1994 **CLC 2,
  14, 32**
  See also CA 49-52; 147; CAAS 3; CANR 3,
  33, 59; DLB 87, 155; DLBY 92; MTCW 1

**Synge, (Edmund) J(ohn) M(illington)** 1871-
  1909  **TCLC 6, 37; DAM DRAM; DC 2**
  See also CA 104; 141; CDBLB 1890-1914;
  DLB 10, 19

**Syruc, J.**
  See Milosz, Czeslaw

**Szirtes, George** 1948-  **CLC 46**
  See also CA 109; CANR 27, 61

**Szymborska, Wislawa** 1923-  **CLC 99**
  See also CA 154; DLBY 96; MTCW 2

**T. O., Nik**
  See Annensky, Innokenty (Fyodorovich)

**Tabori, George** 1914-  **CLC 19**
  See also CA 49-52; CANR 4, 69

**Tagore, Rabindranath** 1861-1941**TCLC 3, 53;
  DAM DRAM, POET; PC 8**
  See also CA 104; 120; MTCW 1, 2

**Taine, Hippolyte Adolphe** 1828-1893  **N C L C
  15**

**Talese, Gay** 1932-  **CLC 37**
  See also AITN 1; CA 1-4R; CANR 9, 58; DLB
  185; INT CANR-9; MTCW 1, 2

**Tallent, Elizabeth (Ann)** 1954-  **CLC 45**
  See also CA 117; CANR 72; DLB 130

**Tally, Ted** 1952-  **CLC 42**
  See also CA 120; 124; INT 124

**Talvik, Heiti** 1904-1947  **TCLC 87**

**Tamayo y Baus, Manuel** 1829-1898 **NCLC 1**

**Tammsaare, A(nton) H(ansen)** 1878-1940
  **TCLC 27**
  See also CA 164

**Tam'si, Tchicaya U**
  See Tchicaya, Gerald Felix

**Tan, Amy (Ruth)** 1952-  **CLC 59, 120; DAM
  MULT, NOV, POP**
  See also AAYA 9; BEST 89:3; CA 136; CANR
  54; CDALBS; DLB 173; MTCW 2; SATA
  75

**Tandem, Felix**
  See Spitteler, Carl (Friedrich Georg)

**Tanizaki, Jun'ichiro** 1886-1965**CLC 8, 14, 28;
  SSC 21**
  See also CA 93-96; 25-28R; DLB 180; MTCW
  2

**Tanner, William**
  See Amis, Kingsley (William)

**Tao Lao**
  See Storni, Alfonsina

**Tarassoff, Lev**
  See Troyat, Henri

**Very, Jones** 1813-1880      **NCLC 9**
See also DLB 1
**Vesaas, Tarjei** 1897-1970      **CLC 48**
See also CA 29-32R
**Vialis, Gaston**
See Simenon, Georges (Jacques Christian)
**Vian, Boris** 1920-1959      **TCLC 9**
See also CA 106; 164; DLB 72; MTCW 2
**Viaud, (Louis Marie) Julien** 1850-1923
See Loti, Pierre
See also CA 107
**Vicar, Henry**
See Felsen, Henry Gregor
**Vicker, Angus**
See Felsen, Henry Gregor
**Vidal, Gore** 1925-CLC 2, 4, 6, 8, 10, 22, 33, 72;
     **DAM NOV, POP**
See also AITN 1; BEST 90:2; CA 5-8R; CANR
13, 45, 65; CDALBS; DLB 6, 152; INT
CANR-13; MTCW 1, 2
**Viereck, Peter (Robert Edwin)** 1916- **CLC 4**
See also CA 1-4R; CANR 1, 47; DLB 5
**Vigny, Alfred (Victor) de** 1797-1863NCLC 7;
     **DAM POET; PC 26**
See also DLB 119, 192
**Vilakazi, Benedict Wallet** 1906-1947TCLC 37
See also CA 168
**Villa, Jose Garcia** 1904-1997      **PC 22**
See also CA 25-28R; CANR 12
**Villaurrutia, Xavier** 1903-1950      **TCLC 80**
See also HW 1
**Villiers de l'Isle Adam, Jean Marie Mathias**
     **Philippe Auguste, Comte de** 1838-1889
     **NCLC 3; SSC 14**
See also DLB 123
**Villon, Francois** 1431-1463(?)      **PC 13**
See also DLB 208
**Vinci, Leonardo da** 1452-1519      **LC 12**
**Vine, Barbara**      **CLC 50**
See also Rendell, Ruth (Barbara)
See also BEST 90:4
**Vinge, Joan (Carol) D(ennison)** 1948-CLC 30;
     **SSC 24**
See also CA 93-96; CANR 72; SATA 36
**Violis, G.**
See Simenon, Georges (Jacques Christian)
**Virgil** 70B.C.-19B.C.
See Vergil
See also DLB 211
**Visconti, Luchino** 1906-1976      **CLC 16**
See also CA 81-84; 65-68; CANR 39
**Vittorini, Elio** 1908-1966      **CLC 6, 9, 14**
See also CA 133; 25-28R
**Vivekananda, Swami** 1863-1902      **TCLC 88**
**Vizenor, Gerald Robert** 1934-CLC 103; **DAM**
     **MULT**
See also CA 13-16R; CAAS 22; CANR 5, 21,
44, 67; DLB 175; MTCW 2; NNAL
**Vizinczey, Stephen** 1933-      **CLC 40**
See also CA 128; INT 128
**Vliet, R(ussell) G(ordon)** 1929-1984 **CLC 22**
See also CA 37-40R; 112; CANR 18
**Vogau, Boris Andreyevich** 1894-1937(?)
See Pilnyak, Boris
See also CA 123
**Vogel, Paula A(nne)** 1951-      **CLC 76**
See also CA 108
**Voigt, Cynthia** 1942-      **CLC 30**
See also AAYA 3, 30; CA 106; CANR 18, 37,
40; CLR 13, 48; INT CANR-18; JRDA;
MAICYA; SATA 48, 79; SATA-Brief 33
**Voigt, Ellen Bryant** 1943-      **CLC 54**
See also CA 69-72; CANR 11, 29, 55; DLB 120

**Voinovich, Vladimir (Nikolaevich)** 1932-**CLC**
     **10, 49**
See also CA 81-84; CAAS 12; CANR 33, 67;
MTCW 1
**Vollmann, William T.** 1959-      **CLC 89; DAM**
     **NOV, POP**
See also CA 134; CANR 67; MTCW 2
**Voloshinov, V. N.**
See Bakhtin, Mikhail Mikhailovich
**Voltaire** 1694-1778      **LC 14; DA; DAB; DAC;**
     **DAM DRAM, MST; SSC 12; WLC**
**von Aschendrof, BaronIgnatz**
See Ford, Ford Madox
**von Daeniken, Erich** 1935-      **CLC 30**
See also AITN 1; CA 37-40R; CANR 17, 44
**von Daniken, Erich**
See von Daeniken, Erich
**von Heidenstam, (Carl Gustaf) Verner**
See Heidenstam, (Carl Gustaf) Verner von
**von Heyse, Paul (Johann Ludwig)**
See Heyse, Paul (Johann Ludwig von)
**von Hofmannsthal, Hugo**
See Hofmannsthal, Hugo von
**von Horvath, Odon**
See Horvath, Oedoen von
**von Horvath, Oedoen**
See Horvath, Oedoen von
**von Liliencron, (Friedrich Adolf Axel) Detlev**
See Liliencron, (Friedrich Adolf Axel) Detlev
     von
**Vonnegut, Kurt, Jr.** 1922-CLC 1, 2, 3, 4, 5, 8,
     **12, 22, 40, 60, 111; DA; DAB; DAC; DAM**
     **MST, NOV, POP; SSC 8; WLC**
See also AAYA 6; AITN 1; BEST 90:4; CA 1-
4R; CANR 1, 25, 49, 75; CDALB 1968-
1988; DLB 2, 8, 152; DLBD 3; DLBY 80;
MTCW 1, 2
**Von Rachen, Kurt**
See Hubbard, L(afayette) Ron(ald)
**von Rezzori (d'Arezzo), Gregor**
See Rezzori (d'Arezzo), Gregor von
**von Sternberg, Josef**
See Sternberg, Josef von
**Vorster, Gordon** 1924-      **CLC 34**
See also CA 133
**Vosce, Trudie**
See Ozick, Cynthia
**Voznesensky, Andrei (Andreievich)** 1933-
     **CLC 1, 15, 57; DAM POET**
See also CA 89-92; CANR 37; MTCW 1
**Waddington, Miriam** 1917-      **CLC 28**
See also CA 21-24R; CANR 12, 30; DLB 68
**Wagman, Fredrica** 1937-      **CLC 7**
See also CA 97-100; INT 97-100
**Wagner, Linda W.**
See Wagner-Martin, Linda (C.)
**Wagner, Linda Welshimer**
See Wagner-Martin, Linda (C.)
**Wagner, Richard** 1813-1883      **NCLC 9**
See also DLB 129
**Wagner-Martin, Linda (C.)** 1936-      **CLC 50**
See also CA 159
**Wagoner, David (Russell)** 1926- CLC 3, 5, 15
See also CA 1-4R; CAAS 3; CANR 2, 71; DLB
5; SATA 14
**Wah, Fred(erick James)** 1939-      **CLC 44**
See also CA 107; 141; DLB 60
**Wahloo, Per** 1926-1975      **CLC 7**
See also CA 61-64; CANR 73
**Wahloo, Peter**
See Wahloo, Per
**Wain, John (Barrington)** 1925-1994 **CLC 2,**
     **11, 15, 46**

See also CA 5-8R; 145; CAAS 4; CANR 23,
54; CDBLB 1960 to Present; DLB 15, 27,
139, 155; MTCW 1, 2
**Wajda, Andrzej** 1926-      **CLC 16**
See also CA 102
**Wakefield, Dan** 1932-      **CLC 7**
See also CA 21-24R; CAAS 7
**Wakoski, Diane** 1937- CLC 2, 4, 7, 9, 11, 40;
     **DAM POET; PC 15**
See also CA 13-16R; CAAS 1; CANR 9, 60;
DLB 5; INT CANR-9; MTCW 2
**Wakoski-Sherbell, Diane**
See Wakoski, Diane
**Walcott, Derek (Alton)** 1930-CLC 2, 4, 9, 14,
     **25, 42, 67, 76; BLC 3; DA; DAC; DAM**
     **MST, MULT, POET; DC 7**
See also BW 2; CA 89-92; CANR 26, 47, 75,
80; DLB 117; DLBY 81; MTCW 1, 2
**Waldman, Anne (Lesley)** 1945-      **CLC 7**
See also CA 37-40R; CAAS 17; CANR 34, 69;
DLB 16
**Waldo, E. Hunter**
See Sturgeon, Theodore (Hamilton)
**Waldo, Edward Hamilton**
See Sturgeon, Theodore (Hamilton)
**Walker, Alice (Malsenior)** 1944- CLC 5, 6, 9,
     **19, 27, 46, 58, 103; BLC 3; DA; DAB;**
     **DAC; DAM MST, MULT, NOV, POET,**
     **POP; SSC 5; WLCS**
See also AAYA 3; BEST 89:4; BW 2, 3; CA
37-40R; CANR 9, 27, 49, 66; CDALB 1968-
1988; DLB 6, 33, 143; INT CANR-27;
MTCW 1, 2; SATA 31
**Walker, David Harry** 1911-1992      **CLC 14**
See also CA 1-4R; 137; CANR 1; SATA 8;
SATA-Obit 71
**Walker, Edward Joseph** 1934-
See Walker, Ted
See also CA 21-24R; CANR 12, 28, 53
**Walker, George F.** 1947-      **CLC 44, 61; DAB;**
     **DAC; DAM MST**
See also CA 103; CANR 21, 43, 59; DLB 60
**Walker, Joseph A.** 1935-      **CLC 19; DAM**
     **DRAM, MST**
See also BW 1, 3; CA 89-92; CANR 26; DLB
38
**Walker, Margaret (Abigail)** 1915-1998CLC 1,
     **6; BLC; DAM MULT; PC 20**
See also BW 2, 3; CA 73-76; 172; CANR 26,
54, 76; DLB 76, 152; MTCW 1, 2
**Walker, Ted**      **CLC 13**
See also Walker, Edward Joseph
See also DLB 40
**Wallace, David Foster** 1962-      **CLC 50, 114**
See also CA 132; CANR 59; MTCW 2
**Wallace, Dexter**
See Masters, Edgar Lee
**Wallace, (Richard Horatio) Edgar** 1875-1932
     **TCLC 57**
See also CA 115; DLB 70
**Wallace, Irving** 1916-1990 CLC 7, 13; **DAM**
     **NOV, POP**
See also AITN 1; CA 1-4R; 132; CAAS 1;
CANR 1, 27; INT CANR-27; MTCW 1, 2
**Wallant, Edward Lewis** 1926-1962CLC 5, 10
See also CA 1-4R; CANR 22; DLB 2, 28, 143;
MTCW 1, 2
**Wallas, Graham** 1858-1932      **TCLC 91**
**Walley, Byron**
See Card, Orson Scott
**Walpole, Horace** 1717-1797      **LC 49**
See also DLB 39, 104
**Walpole, Hugh (Seymour)** 1884-1941TCLC 5

**Wergeland, Henrik Arnold** 1808-1845 N C L C
**5**
See also AAYA 2, 30; CA 29-32R; CANR 16,
38; CLR 3; DLB 52; JRDA; MAICYA; SAAS
2; SATA 1, 58; SATA-Essay 103
**Wersba, Barbara** 1932-                    **CLC 30**
See also CA 97-100; CANR 39, 78
**Wertmueller, Lina** 1928-                  **CLC 16**
See also CA 97-100; CANR 39, 78
**Wescott, Glenway** 1901-1987              **CLC 13**
See also CA 13-16R; 121; CANR 23, 70; DLB
4, 9, 102
**Wesker, Arnold** 1932-        **CLC 3, 5, 42; DAB;**
**DAM DRAM**
See also CA 1-4R; CAAS 7; CANR 1, 33;
CDBLB 1960 to Present; DLB 13; MTCW 1
**Wesley, Richard (Errol)** 1945-            **CLC 7**
See also BW 1; CA 57-60; CANR 27; DLB 38
**Wessel, Johan Herman** 1742-1785          **LC 7**
**West, Anthony (Panther)** 1914-1987      **CLC 50**
See also CA 45-48; 124; CANR 3, 19; DLB 15
**West, C. P.**
See Wodehouse, P(elham) G(renville)
**West, (Mary) Jessamyn** 1902-1984 **CLC 7, 17**
See also CA 9-12R; 112; CANR 27; DLB 6;
DLBY 84; MTCW 1, 2; SATA-Obit 37
**West, Morris L(anglo)** 1916-           **CLC 6, 33**
See also CA 5-8R; CANR 24, 49, 64; MTCW
1, 2
**West, Nathanael** 1903-1940 **TCLC 1, 14, 44;**
**SSC 16**
See also CA 104; 125; CDALB 1929-1941;
DLB 4, 9, 28; MTCW 1, 2
**West, Owen**
See Koontz, Dean R(ay)
**West, Paul** 1930-                    **CLC 7, 14, 96**
See also CA 13-16R; CAAS 7; CANR 22, 53,
76; DLB 14; INT CANR-22; MTCW 2
**West, Rebecca** 1892-1983        **CLC 7, 9, 31, 50**
See also CA 5-8R; 109; CANR 19; DLB 36;
DLBY 83; MTCW 1, 2
**Westall, Robert (Atkinson)** 1929-1993 **CLC 17**
See also AAYA 12; CA 69-72; 141; CANR 18,
68; CLR 13; JRDA; MAICYA; SAAS 2;
SATA 23, 69; SATA-Obit 75
**Westermarck, Edward** 1862-1939        **TCLC 87**
**Westlake, Donald E(dwin)** 1933-   **CLC 7, 33;**
**DAM POP**
See also CA 17-20R; CAAS 13; CANR 16, 44,
65; INT CANR-16; MTCW 2
**Westmacott, Mary**
See Christie, Agatha (Mary Clarissa)
**Weston, Allen**
See Norton, Andre
**Wetcheek, J. L.**
See Feuchtwanger, Lion
**Wetering, Janwillem van de**
See van de Wetering, Janwillem
**Wetherald, Agnes Ethelwyn** 1857-1940 **TCLC**
**81**
See also DLB 99
**Wetherell, Elizabeth**
See Warner, Susan (Bogert)
**Whale, James** 1889-1957                 **TCLC 63**
**Whalen, Philip** 1923-                   **CLC 6, 29**
See also CA 9-12R; CANR 5, 39; DLB 16
**Wharton, Edith (Newbold Jones)** 1862-1937
**TCLC 3, 9, 27, 53; DA; DAB; DAC; DAM**
**MST, NOV; SSC 6; WLC**
See also AAYA 25; CA 104; 132; CDALB 1865-
1917; DLB 4, 9, 12, 78, 189; DLBD 13;
MTCW 1, 2
**Wharton, James**
See Mencken, H(enry) L(ouis)

**Wharton, William (a pseudonym) CLC 18, 37**
See also CA 93-96; DLBY 80; INT 93-96
**Wheatley (Peters), Phillis** 1754(?)-1784 **LC 3,**
**50; BLC 3; DA; DAC; DAM MST, MULT,**
**POET; PC 3; WLC**
See also CDALB 1640-1865; DLB 31, 50
**Wheelock, John Hall** 1886-1978          **CLC 14**
See also CA 13-16R; 77-80; CANR 14; DLB
45
**White, E(lwyn) B(rooks)** 1899-1985 **CLC 10,**
**34, 39; DAM POP**
See also AITN 2; CA 13-16R; 116; CANR 16,
37; CDALBS; CLR 1, 21; DLB 11, 22;
MAICYA; MTCW 1, 2; SATA 2, 29, 100;
SATA-Obit 44
**White, Edmund (Valentine III)** 1940- **CLC 27,**
**110; DAM POP**
See also AAYA 7; CA 45-48; CANR 3, 19, 36,
62; MTCW 1, 2
**White, Patrick (Victor Martindale)** 1912-1990
**CLC 3, 4, 5, 7, 9, 18, 65, 69**
See also CA 81-84; 132; CANR 43; MTCW 1
**White, Phyllis Dorothy James** 1920-
See James, P. D.
See also CA 21-24R; CANR 17, 43, 65; DAM
POP; MTCW 1, 2
**White, T(erence) H(anbury)** 1906-1964 **C L C**
**30**
See also AAYA 22; CA 73-76; CANR 37; DLB
160; JRDA; MAICYA; SATA 12
**White, Terence de Vere** 1912-1994       **CLC 49**
See also CA 49-52; 145; CANR 3
**White, Walter**
See White, Walter F(rancis)
See also BLC; DAM MULT
**White, Walter F(rancis)** 1893-1955     **TCLC 15**
See also White, Walter
See also BW 1; CA 115; 124; DLB 51
**White, William Hale** 1831-1913
See Rutherford, Mark
See also CA 121
**Whitehead, E(dward) A(nthony)** 1933- **CLC 5**
See also CA 65-68; CANR 58
**Whitemore, Hugh (John)** 1936-           **CLC 37**
See also CA 132; CANR 77; INT 132
**Whitman, Sarah Helen (Power)** 1803-1878
**NCLC 19**
See also DLB 1
**Whitman, Walt(er)** 1819-1892   **NCLC 4, 31;**
**DA; DAB; DAC; DAM MST, POET; PC**
**3; WLC**
See also CDALB 1640-1865; DLB 3, 64; SATA
20
**Whitney, Phyllis A(yame)** 1903-    **CLC 42;**
**DAM POP**
See also AITN 2; BEST 90:3; CA 1-4R; CANR
3, 25, 38, 60; CLR 58; JRDA; MAICYA;
MTCW 2; SATA 1, 30
**Whittemore, (Edward) Reed (Jr.)** 1919- **CLC 4**
See also CA 9-12R; CAAS 8; CANR 4; DLB 5
**Whittier, John Greenleaf** 1807-1892 **NCLC 8,**
**59**
See also DLB 1
**Whittlebot, Hernia**
See Coward, Noel (Peirce)
**Wicker, Thomas Grey** 1926-
See Wicker, Tom
See also CA 65-68; CANR 21, 46
**Wicker, Tom**                            **CLC 7**
See also Wicker, Thomas Grey
**Wideman, John Edgar** 1941-  **CLC 5, 34, 36,**
**67; BLC 3; DAM MULT**
See also BW 2, 3; CA 85-88; CANR 14, 42,

67; DLB 33, 143; MTCW 2
**Wiebe, Rudy (Henry)** 1934-       **CLC 6, 11, 14;**
**DAC; DAM MST**
See also CA 37-40R; CANR 42, 67; DLB 60
**Wieland, Christoph Martin** 1733-1813 N C L C
**17**
See also DLB 97
**Wiene, Robert** 1881-1938                **TCLC 56**
**Wieners, John** 1934-                     **CLC 7**
See also CA 13-16R; DLB 16
**Wiesel, Elie(zer)** 1928- **CLC 3, 5, 11, 37; DA;**
**DAB; DAC; DAM MST, NOV; WLCS**
See also AAYA 7; AITN 1; CA 5-8R; CAAS 4;
CANR 8, 40, 65; CDALBS; DLB 83; DLBY
87; INT CANR-8; MTCW 1, 2; SATA 56
**Wiggins, Marianne** 1947-                 **CLC 57**
See also BEST 89:3; CA 130; CANR 60
**Wight, James Alfred** 1916-1995
See Herriot, James
See also CA 77-80; SATA 55; SATA-Brief 44
**Wilbur, Richard (Purdy)** 1921- **CLC 3, 6, 9, 14,**
**53, 110; DA; DAB; DAC; DAM MST,**
**POET**
See also CA 1-4R; CABS 2; CANR 2, 29, 76;
CDALBS; DLB 5, 169; INT CANR-29;
MTCW 1, 2; SATA 9
**Wild, Peter** 1940-                       **CLC 14**
See also CA 37-40R; DLB 5
**Wilde, Oscar** 1854(?)-1900 **TCLC 1, 8, 23, 41;**
**DA; DAB; DAC; DAM DRAM, MST,**
**NOV; SSC 11; WLC**
See also CA 104; 119; CDBLB 1890-1914;
DLB 10, 19, 34, 57, 141, 156, 190; SATA 24
**Wilder, Billy**                          **CLC 20**
See also Wilder, Samuel
See also DLB 26
**Wilder, Samuel** 1906-
See Wilder, Billy
See also CA 89-92
**Wilder, Thornton (Niven)** 1897-1975 **CLC 1, 5,**
**6, 10, 15, 35, 82; DA; DAB; DAC; DAM**
**DRAM, MST, NOV; DC 1; WLC**
See also AAYA 29; AITN 2; CA 13-16R; 61-
64; CANR 40; CDALBS; DLB 4, 7, 9; DLBY
97; MTCW 1, 2
**Wilding, Michael** 1942-                  **CLC 73**
See also CA 104; CANR 24, 49
**Wiley, Richard** 1944-                    **CLC 44**
See also CA 121; 129; CANR 71
**Wilhelm, Kate**                          **CLC 7**
See also Wilhelm, Katie Gertrude
See also AAYA 20; CAAS 5; DLB 8; INT
CANR-17
**Wilhelm, Katie Gertrude** 1928-
See Wilhelm, Kate
See also CA 37-40R; CANR 17, 36, 60; MTCW
1
**Wilkins, Mary**
See Freeman, Mary Eleanor Wilkins
**Willard, Nancy** 1936-                **CLC 7, 37**
See also CA 89-92; CANR 10, 39, 68; CLR 5;
DLB 5, 52; MAICYA; MTCW 1; SATA 37,
71; SATA-Brief 30
**William of Ockham** 1285-1347           **CMLC 32**
**Williams, Ben Ames** 1889-1953          **TCLC 89**
See also DLB 102
**Williams, C(harles) K(enneth)** 1936- **CLC 33,**
**56; DAM POET**
See also CA 37-40R; CAAS 26; CANR 57; DLB
5
**Williams, Charles**
See Collier, James L(incoln)
**Williams, Charles (Walter Stansby)** 1886-1945

TCLC 1, 11
See also CA 104; 163; DLB 100, 153
**Williams, (George) Emlyn** 1905-1987**CLC 15;
DAM DRAM**
See also CA 104; 123; CANR 36; DLB 10, 77;
MTCW 1
**Williams, Hank** 1923-1953        **TCLC 81**
**Williams, Hugo** 1942-            **CLC 42**
See also CA 17-20R; CANR 45; DLB 40
**Williams, J. Walker**
See Wodehouse, P(elham) G(renville)
**Williams, John A(lfred)** 1925-**CLC 5, 13; BLC
3; DAM MULT**
See also BW 2, 3; CA 53-56; CAAS 3; CANR
6, 26, 51; DLB 2, 33; INT CANR-6
**Williams, Jonathan (Chamberlain)** 1929-
**CLC 13**
See also CA 9-12R; CAAS 12; CANR 8; DLB
5
**Williams, Joy** 1944-            **CLC 31**
See also CA 41-44R; CANR 22, 48
**Williams, Norman** 1952-         **CLC 39**
See also CA 118
**Williams, Sherley Anne** 1944-**CLC 89; BLC 3;
DAM MULT, POET**
See also BW 2, 3; CA 73-76; CANR 25; DLB
41; INT CANR-25; SATA 78
**Williams, Shirley**
See Williams, Sherley Anne
**Williams, Tennessee** 1911-1983**CLC 1, 2, 5, 7,
8, 11, 15, 19, 30, 39, 45, 71, 111; DA; DAB;
DAC; DAM DRAM, MST; DC 4; WLC**
See also AITN 1, 2; CA 5-8R; 108; CABS 3;
CANR 31; CDALB 1941-1968; DLB 7;
DLBD 4; DLBY 83; MTCW 1, 2
**Williams, Thomas (Alonzo)** 1926-1990**CLC 14**
See also CA 1-4R; 132; CANR 2
**Williams, William C.**
See Williams, William Carlos
**Williams, William Carlos** 1883-1963**CLC 1, 2,
5, 9, 13, 22, 42, 67; DA; DAB; DAC; DAM
MST, POET; PC 7; SSC 31**
See also CA 89-92; CANR 34; CDALB 1917-
1929; DLB 4, 16, 54, 86; MTCW 1, 2
**Williamson, David (Keith)** 1942-    **CLC 56**
See also CA 103; CANR 41
**Williamson, Ellen Douglas** 1905-1984
See Douglas, Ellen
See also CA 17-20R; 114; CANR 39
**Williamson, Jack**              **CLC 29**
See also Williamson, John Stewart
See also CAAS 8; DLB 8
**Williamson, John Stewart** 1908-
See Williamson, Jack
See also CA 17-20R; CANR 23, 70
**Willie, Frederick**
See Lovecraft, H(oward) P(hillips)
**Willingham, Calder (Baynard, Jr.)** 1922-1995
**CLC 5, 51**
See also CA 5-8R; 147; CANR 3; DLB 2, 44;
MTCW 1
**Willis, Charles**
See Clarke, Arthur C(harles)
**Willis, Fingal O'Flahertie**
See Wilde, Oscar
**Willy**
See Colette, (Sidonie-Gabrielle)
**Willy, Colette**
See Colette, (Sidonie-Gabrielle)
**Wilson, A(ndrew) N(orman)** 1950-    **CLC 33**
See also CA 112; 122; DLB 14, 155, 194;
MTCW 2
**Wilson, Angus (Frank Johnstone)** 1913-1991

CLC 2, 3, 5, 25, 34; SSC 21
See also CA 5-8R; 134; CANR 21; DLB 15,
139, 155; MTCW 1, 2
**Wilson, August** 1945-    **CLC 39, 50, 63, 118;
BLC 3; DA; DAB; DAC; DAM DRAM,
MST, MULT; DC 2; WLCS**
See also AAYA 16; BW 2, 3; CA 115; 122;
CANR 42, 54, 76; MTCW 1, 2
**Wilson, Brian** 1942-            **CLC 12**
**Wilson, Colin** 1931-            **CLC 3, 14**
See also CA 1-4R; CAAS 5; CANR 1, 22, 33,
77; DLB 14, 194; MTCW 1
**Wilson, Dirk**
See Pohl, Frederik
**Wilson, Edmund** 1895-1972**CLC 1, 2, 3, 8, 24**
See also CA 1-4R; 37-40R; CANR 1, 46; DLB
63; MTCW 1, 2
**Wilson, Ethel Davis (Bryant)** 1888(?)-1980
**CLC 13; DAC; DAM POET**
See also CA 102; DLB 68; MTCW 1
**Wilson, John** 1785-1854          **NCLC 5**
**Wilson, John (Anthony) Burgess** 1917-1993
See Burgess, Anthony
See also CA 1-4R; 143; CANR 2, 46; DAC;
DAM NOV; MTCW 1, 2
**Wilson, Lanford** 1937- **CLC 7, 14, 36; DAM
DRAM**
See also CA 17-20R; CABS 3; CANR 45; DLB
7
**Wilson, Robert M.** 1944-         **CLC 7, 9**
See also CA 49-52; CANR 2, 41; MTCW 1
**Wilson, Robert McLiam** 1964-     **CLC 59**
See also CA 132
**Wilson, Sloan** 1920-            **CLC 32**
See also CA 1-4R; CANR 1, 44
**Wilson, Snoo** 1948-             **CLC 33**
See also CA 69-72
**Wilson, William S(mith)** 1932-    **CLC 49**
See also CA 81-84
**Wilson, (Thomas) Woodrow** 1856-1924**TCLC
79**
See also CA 166; DLB 47
**Winchilsea, Anne (Kingsmill) Finch Counte**
1661-1720
See Finch, Anne
**Windham, Basil**
See Wodehouse, P(elham) G(renville)
**Wingrove, David (John)** 1954-     **CLC 68**
See also CA 133
**Wintergreen, Jane**
See Duncan, Sara Jeannette
**Winters, Janet Lewis**            **CLC 41**
See also Lewis, Janet
See also DLBY 87
**Winters, (Arthur) Yvor** 1900-1968 **CLC 4, 8,
32**
See also CA 11-12; 25-28R; CAP 1; DLB 48;
MTCW 1
**Winterson, Jeanette** 1959-**CLC 64; DAM POP**
See also CA 136; CANR 58; DLB 207; MTCW
2
**Winthrop, John** 1588-1649         **LC 31**
See also DLB 24, 30
**Wirth, Louis** 1897-1952         **TCLC 92**
**Wiseman, Frederick** 1930-         **CLC 20**
See also CA 159
**Wister, Owen** 1860-1938          **TCLC 21**
See also CA 108; 162; DLB 9, 78, 186; SATA
62
**Witkacy**
See Witkiewicz, Stanislaw Ignacy
**Witkiewicz, Stanislaw Ignacy** 1885-1939
**TCLC 8**

See also CA 105; 162
**Wittgenstein, Ludwig (Josef Johann)** 1889-1951
**TCLC 59**
See also CA 113; 164; MTCW 2
**Wittig, Monique** 1935(?)-         **CLC 22**
See also CA 116; 135; DLB 83
**Wittlin, Jozef** 1896-1976        **CLC 25**
See also CA 49-52; 65-68; CANR 3
**Wodehouse, P(elham) G(renville)** 1881-1975
**CLC 1, 2, 5, 10, 22; DAB; DAC; DAM
NOV; SSC 2**
See also AITN 2; CA 45-48; 57-60; CANR 3,
33; CDBLB 1914-1945; DLB 34, 162;
MTCW 1, 2; SATA 22
**Woiwode, L.**
See Woiwode, Larry (Alfred)
**Woiwode, Larry (Alfred)** 1941-    **CLC 6, 10**
See also CA 73-76; CANR 16; DLB 6; INT
CANR-16
**Wojciechowska, Maia (Teresa)** 1927-**CLC 26**
See also AAYA 8; CA 9-12R; CANR 4, 41; CLR
1; JRDA; MAICYA; SAAS 1; SATA 1, 28,
83; SATA-Essay 104
**Wolf, Christa** 1929-            **CLC 14, 29, 58**
See also CA 85-88; CANR 45; DLB 75; MTCW
1
**Wolfe, Gene (Rodman)** 1931- **CLC 25; DAM
POP**
See also CA 57-60; CAAS 9; CANR 6, 32, 60;
DLB 8; MTCW 2
**Wolfe, George C.** 1954-      **CLC 49; BLCS**
See also CA 149
**Wolfe, Thomas (Clayton)** 1900-1938**TCLC 4,
13, 29, 61; DA; DAB; DAC; DAM MST,
NOV; SSC 33; WLC**
See also CA 104; 132; CDALB 1929-1941;
DLB 9, 102; DLBD 2, 16; DLBY 85, 97;
MTCW 1, 2
**Wolfe, Thomas Kennerly, Jr.** 1930-
See Wolfe, Tom
See also CA 13-16R; CANR 9, 33, 70; DAM
POP; DLB 185; INT CANR-9; MTCW 1, 2
**Wolfe, Tom**          **CLC 1, 2, 9, 15, 35, 51**
See also Wolfe, Thomas Kennerly, Jr.
See also AAYA 8; AITN 2; BEST 89:1; DLB
152
**Wolff, Geoffrey (Ansell)** 1937-    **CLC 41**
See also CA 29-32R; CANR 29, 43, 78
**Wolff, Sonia**
See Levitin, Sonia (Wolff)
**Wolff, Tobias (Jonathan Ansell)** 1945-  **C L C
39, 64**
See also AAYA 16; BEST 90:2; CA 114; 117;
CAAS 22; CANR 54, 76; DLB 130; INT 117;
MTCW 2
**Wolfram von Eschenbach** c. 1170-c. 1220
**CMLC 5**
See also DLB 138
**Wolitzer, Hilma** 1930-           **CLC 17**
See also CA 65-68; CANR 18, 40; INT CANR-
18; SATA 31
**Wollstonecraft, Mary** 1759-1797  **LC 5, 50**
See also CDBLB 1789-1832; DLB 39, 104, 158
**Wonder, Stevie**                 **CLC 12**
See also Morris, Steveland Judkins
**Wong, Jade Snow** 1922-           **CLC 17**
See also CA 109
**Woodberry, George Edward** 1855-1930
**TCLC 73**
See also CA 165; DLB 71, 103
**Woodcott, Keith**
See Brunner, John (Kilian Houston)
**Woodruff, Robert W.**

See Mencken, H(enry) L(ouis)
**Woolf, (Adeline) Virginia** 1882-1941**TCLC 1, 5, 20, 43, 56; DA; DAB; DAC; DAM MST, NOV; SSC 7; WLC**
See also Woolf, Virginia Adeline
See also CA 104; 130; CANR 64; CDBLB 1914-1945; DLB 36, 100, 162; DLBD 10; MTCW 1
**Woolf, Virginia Adeline**
See Woolf, (Adeline) Virginia
See also MTCW 2
**Woollcott, Alexander (Humphreys)** 1887-1943 **TCLC 5**
See also CA 105; 161; DLB 29
**Woolrich, Cornell** 1903-1968 **CLC 77**
See also Hopley-Woolrich, Cornell George
**Wordsworth, Dorothy** 1771-1855 **NCLC 25**
See also DLB 107
**Wordsworth, William** 1770-1850 **NCLC 12, 38; DA; DAB; DAC; DAM MST, POET; PC 4; WLC**
See also CDBLB 1789-1832; DLB 93, 107
**Wouk, Herman** 1915-**CLC 1, 9, 38; DAM NOV, POP**
See also CA 5-8R; CANR 6, 33, 67; CDALBS; DLBY 82; INT CANR-6; MTCW 1, 2
**Wright, Charles (Penzel, Jr.)** 1935-**CLC 6, 13, 28, 119**
See also CA 29-32R; CAAS 7; CANR 23, 36, 62; DLB 165; DLBY 82; MTCW 1, 2
**Wright, Charles Stevenson** 1932- **CLC 49; BLC 3; DAM MULT, POET**
See also BW 1; CA 9-12R; CANR 26; DLB 33
**Wright, Frances** 1795-1852 **NCLC 74**
See also DLB 73
**Wright, Jack R.**
See Harris, Mark
**Wright, James (Arlington)** 1927-1980**CLC 3, 5, 10, 28; DAM POET**
See also AITN 2; CA 49-52; 97-100; CANR 4, 34, 64; CDALBS; DLB 5, 169; MTCW 1, 2
**Wright, Judith (Arandell)** 1915- **CLC 11, 53; PC 14**
See also CA 13-16R; CANR 31, 76; MTCW 1, 2; SATA 14
**Wright, L(aurali) R.** 1939- **CLC 44**
See also CA 138
**Wright, Richard (Nathaniel)** 1908-1960 **C L C 1, 3, 4, 9, 14, 21, 48, 74; BLC 3; DA; DAB; DAC; DAM MST, MULT, NOV; SSC 2; WLC**
See also AAYA 5; BW 1; CA 108; CANR 64; CDALB 1929-1941; DLB 76, 102; DLBD 2; MTCW 1, 2
**Wright, Richard B(ruce)** 1937- **CLC 6**
See also CA 85-88; DLB 53
**Wright, Rick** 1945- **CLC 35**
**Wright, Rowland**
See Wells, Carolyn
**Wright, Stephen** 1946- **CLC 33**
**Wright, Willard Huntington** 1888-1939
See Van Dine, S. S.
See also CA 115; DLBD 16
**Wright, William** 1930- **CLC 44**
See also CA 53-56; CANR 7, 23
**Wroth, LadyMary** 1587-1653(?) **LC 30**
See also DLB 121
**Wu Ch'eng-en** 1500(?)-1582(?) **LC 7**
**Wu Ching-tzu** 1701-1754 **LC 2**
**Wurlitzer, Rudolph** 1938(?)- **CLC 2, 4, 15**
See also CA 85-88; DLB 173
**Wycherley, William** 1641-1715**LC 8, 21; DAM DRAM**

See also CDBLB 1660-1789; DLB 80
**Wylie, Elinor (Morton Hoyt)** 1885-1928 **TCLC 8; PC 23**
See also CA 105; 162; DLB 9, 45
**Wylie, Philip (Gordon)** 1902-1971 **CLC 43**
See also CA 21-22; 33-36R; CAP 2; DLB 9
**Wyndham, John** **CLC 19**
See also Harris, John (Wyndham Parkes Lucas) Beynon
**Wyss, Johann David Von** 1743-1818**NCLC 10**
See also JRDA; MAICYA; SATA 29; SATA-Brief 27
**Xenophon** c. 430B.C.-c. 354B.C. **CMLC 17**
See also DLB 176
**Yakumo Koizumi**
See Hearn, (Patricio) Lafcadio (Tessima Carlos)
**Yamamoto, Hisaye** 1921-**SSC 34; DAM MULT**
**Yanez, Jose Donoso**
See Donoso (Yanez), Jose
**Yanovsky, Basile S.**
See Yanovsky, V(assily) S(emenovich)
**Yanovsky, V(assily) S(emenovich)** 1906-1989 **CLC 2, 18**
See also CA 97-100; 129
**Yates, Richard** 1926-1992 **CLC 7, 8, 23**
See also CA 5-8R; 139; CANR 10, 43; DLB 2; DLBY 81, 92; INT CANR-10
**Yeats, W. B.**
See Yeats, William Butler
**Yeats, William Butler** 1865-1939**TCLC 1, 11, 18, 31, 93; DA; DAB; DAC; DAM DRAM, MST, POET; PC 20; WLC**
See also CA 104; 127; CANR 45; CDBLB 1890-1914; DLB 10, 19, 98, 156; MTCW 1, 2
**Yehoshua, A(braham) B.** 1936- **CLC 13, 31**
See also CA 33-36R; CANR 43
**Yep, Laurence Michael** 1948- **CLC 35**
See also AAYA 5; CA 49-52; CANR 1, 46; CLR 3, 17, 54; DLB 52; JRDA; MAICYA; SATA 7, 69
**Yerby, Frank G(arvin)** 1916-1991 **CLC 1, 7, 22; BLC 3; DAM MULT**
See also BW 1, 3; CA 9-12R; 136; CANR 16, 52; DLB 76; INT CANR-16; MTCW 1
**Yesenin, Sergei Alexandrovich**
See Esenin, Sergei (Alexandrovich)
**Yevtushenko, Yevgeny (Alexandrovich)** 1933-**CLC 1, 3, 13, 26, 51; DAM POET**
See also CA 81-84; CANR 33, 54; MTCW 1
**Yezierska, Anzia** 1885(?)-1970 **CLC 46**
See also CA 126; 89-92; DLB 28; MTCW 1
**Yglesias, Helen** 1915- **CLC 7, 22**
See also CA 37-40R; CAAS 20; CANR 15, 65; INT CANR-15; MTCW 1
**Yokomitsu Riichi** 1898-1947 **TCLC 47**
See also CA 170
**Yonge, Charlotte (Mary)** 1823-1901**TCLC 48**
See also CA 109; 163; DLB 18, 163; SATA 17
**York, Jeremy**
See Creasey, John
**York, Simon**
See Heinlein, Robert A(nson)
**Yorke, Henry Vincent** 1905-1974 **CLC 13**
See also Green, Henry
See also CA 85-88; 49-52
**Yosano Akiko** 1878-1942 **TCLC 59; PC 11**
See also CA 161
**Yoshimoto, Banana** **CLC 84**
See also Yoshimoto, Mahoko
**Yoshimoto, Mahoko** 1964-
See Yoshimoto, Banana
See also CA 144

**Young, Al(bert James)** 1939-**CLC 19; BLC 3; DAM MULT**
See also BW 2, 3; CA 29-32R; CANR 26, 65; DLB 33
**Young, Andrew (John)** 1885-1971 **CLC 5**
See also CA 5-8R; CANR 7, 29
**Young, Collier**
See Bloch, Robert (Albert)
**Young, Edward** 1683-1765 **LC 3, 40**
See also DLB 95
**Young, Marguerite (Vivian)** 1909-1995 **C L C 82**
See also CA 13-16; 150; CAP 1
**Young, Neil** 1945- **CLC 17**
See also CA 110
**Young Bear, Ray A.** 1950- **CLC 94; DAM MULT**
See also CA 146; DLB 175; NNAL
**Yourcenar, Marguerite** 1903-1987**CLC 19, 38, 50, 87; DAM NOV**
See also CA 69-72; CANR 23, 60; DLB 72; DLBY 88; MTCW 1, 2
**Yurick, Sol** 1925- **CLC 6**
See also CA 13-16R; CANR 25
**Zabolotsky, Nikolai Alekseevich** 1903-1958 **TCLC 52**
See also CA 116; 164
**Zamiatin, Yevgenii**
See Zamyatin, Evgeny Ivanovich
**Zamora, Bernice (B. Ortiz)** 1938- **CLC 89; DAM MULT; HLC**
See also CA 151; CANR 80; DLB 82; HW 1, 2
**Zamyatin, Evgeny Ivanovich** 1884-1937 **TCLC 8, 37**
See also CA 105; 166
**Zangwill, Israel** 1864-1926 **TCLC 16**
See also CA 109; 167; DLB 10, 135, 197
**Zappa, Francis Vincent, Jr.** 1940-1993
See Zappa, Frank
See also CA 108; 143; CANR 57
**Zappa, Frank** **CLC 17**
See also Zappa, Francis Vincent, Jr.
**Zaturenska, Marya** 1902-1982 **CLC 6, 11**
See also CA 13-16R; 105; CANR 22
**Zeami** 1363-1443 **DC 7**
**Zelazny, Roger (Joseph)** 1937-1995 **CLC 21**
See also AAYA 7; CA 21-24R; 148; CANR 26, 60; DLB 8; MTCW 1, 2; SATA 57; SATA-Brief 39
**Zhdanov, Andrei Alexandrovich** 1896-1948 **TCLC 18**
See also CA 117; 167
**Zhukovsky, Vasily (Andreevich)** 1783-1852 **NCLC 35**
See also DLB 205
**Ziegenhagen, Eric** **CLC 55**
**Zimmer, Jill Schary**
See Robinson, Jill
**Zimmerman, Robert**
See Dylan, Bob
**Zindel, Paul** 1936-**CLC 6, 26; DA; DAB; DAC; DAM DRAM, MST, NOV; DC 5**
See also AAYA 2; CA 73-76; CANR 31, 65; CDALBS; CLR 3, 45; DLB 7, 52; JRDA; MAICYA; MTCW 1, 2; SATA 16, 58, 102
**Zinov'Ev, A. A.**
See Zinoviev, Alexander (Aleksandrovich)
**Zinoviev, Alexander (Aleksandrovich)** 1922- **CLC 19**
See also CA 116; 133; CAAS 10
**Zoilus**
See Lovecraft, H(oward) P(hillips)
**Zola, Emile (Edouard Charles Antoine)** 1840-

1902**TCLC 1, 6, 21, 41; DA; DAB; DAC;
DAM MST, NOV; WLC**
See also CA 104; 138; DLB 123

**Zoline, Pamela** 1941-          **CLC 62**
See also CA 161

**Zorrilla y Moral, Jose** 1817-1893    **NCLC 6**

**Zoshchenko, Mikhail (Mikhailovich)** 1895-1958
     **TCLC 15; SSC 15**
See also CA 115; 160

**Zuckmayer, Carl** 1896-1977      **CLC 18**
See also CA 69-72; DLB 56, 124

**Zuk, Georges**
See Skelton, Robin

**Zukofsky, Louis** 1904-1978**CLC 1, 2, 4, 7, 11,
18; DAM POET; PC 11**
See also CA 9-12R; 77-80; CANR 39; DLB 5,
165; MTCW 1

**Zweig, Paul** 1935-1984      **CLC 34, 42**
See also CA 85-88; 113

**Zweig, Stefan** 1881-1942      **TCLC 17**
See also CA 112; 170; DLB 81, 118

**Zwingli, Huldreich** 1484-1531      **LC 37**
See also DLB 179

# Literary Criticism Series
# Cumulative Topic Index

This index lists all topic entries in Gale's *Classical and Medieval Literature Criticism, Contemporary Literary Criticism, Literature Criticism from 1400 to 1800, Nineteenth-Century Literature Criticism,* and *Twentieth-Century Literary Criticism.*

Topic Index

# *CMLC* Cumulative Nationality Index

# *CMLC* Cumulative Title Index

Title Index

Title Index

Title Index

Title Index

# *CMLC* Cumulative Critic Index

Terence **14**:305

**Cizevskij, Dmitrij**
*The Igor Tale* **1**:501

**Clark, Cyril Drummond Le Gros**
Su Shih **15**:381, 385

**Clark, David W.**
William of Ockham **32**:174

**Clark, Donald Lemen**
Hermogenes **6**:161

**Clark, George**
Aesop **24**:44

**Clark, James M.**
Meister Eckhart **9**:45, 54

**Clark, John**
*Poem of the Cid* **4**:230

**Clark, S. L.**
Hartmann von Aue **15**:228

**Clarke, H. Butler**
*Poem of the Cid* **4**:229

**Clarke, Howard W.**
*Odyssey* **16**:279

**Clauss, James J.**
Apollonius Rhodius **28**:71

**Cleary, Thomas**
The *Koran* **23**:305

**Clerk, Archibald**
Ossian **28**:294

**Clifton-Everest, J. M.**
Hartmann von Aue **15**:202

**Cline, Ruth Harwood**
Chretien de Troyes **10**:195

**Closs, August**
Gottfried von Strassburg **10**:255

**Cochrane, Charles Norris**
Thucydides **17**:243

**Coffin, Harrison Cadwallader**
St. Jerome **30**: 66

**Cohen, Shaye J. D.**
Josephus, Flavius **13**:263, 273

**Col, Pierre**
*Romance of the Rose* **8**:380

**Coleman, T. W.**
Rolle, Richard **21**:323

**Coleridge, H. N.**
Hesiod **5**:70

**Coleridge, Samuel Taylor**
*Arabian Nights* **2**:4
Aristophanes **4**:47
*Inferno* **3**:10
Pindar **12**:260

*Poem of the Cid* **4**:224

**Colgrave, Bertram**
Bede **20**:8, 82

**Colish, Marcia L.**
Augustine, St. **6**:123

**Colledge, Edmund**
Meister Eckhart **9**:68

**Collinder, Bjorn**
*Kalevala* **6**:247

**Collins, Christopher**
Longus **7**:25.

**Colton, Arthur W.**
Map, Walter **32**:76

**Colum, Padraic**
*Arabian Nights* **2**:26
*Mabinogion* **9**:165

**Comfort, W. W.**
Chretien de Troyes **10**:137

**Comparetti, Domenico**
*Kalevala* **6**:219

**Comper, Frances M. M.**
Rolle, Richard **21**:310

**Conant, Martha Pike**
*Arabian Nights* **2**:20

**Condren, Edward I.**
*Hrafnkel's Saga* **2**:112

**Congdon, Kirby**
Aesop **24**:39

**Congreve, William**
Pindar **12**:259

**Connor, W. Robert**
Thucydides **17**:307

**Cons, Louis**
Aesop **24**:18

**Conte, Gian Biagio**
Cato, Marcus Porcius **21**:54

**Conybeare, John Josias**
*Beowulf* **1**:55

**Cook, Albert S.**
Cynewulf **23**:27
Ovid **7**:412
*Poem of the Cid* **4**:270
Sophocles **2**:404

**Cook, Charles W.**
*Epic of Gilgamesh* **3**:352

**Cook, Robert G.**
Chretien de Troyes **10**:183

**Cooper, Arthur**
Li Po **2**:145

**Cooper, Lane**

*Poetics* **31**:120

**Copleston, Frederick C.**
Abelard **11**:14
Averroes **7**:16

**Copleston, Reginald S.**
Aeschylus **11**:95

**Copley, Frank O.**
Livy **11**:363
Terence **14**:349

**Corcoran, Thomas H.**
Seneca, Lucius Annaeus **6**:436

**Cornford, Francis Macdonald**
Aristophanes **4**:78
Plato **8**:272
Thucydides **17**:235

**Cornwallis, William**
Seneca, Lucius Annaeus **6**:334

**Cosman, Madeleine Pelner**
Gottfried von Strassburg **10**:292

**Costa, C. D. N.**
Seneca, Lucius Annaeus **6**:413

**Coulter, Cornelia C.**
Hroswitha of Gandersheim **29**:99

**Courthope, W. J.**
*Beowulf* **1**:59

**Courtney, W. L.**
Sappho **3**:394

**Cowell, Edward Byles**
Khayyam **11**:230

**Cowley, Abraham**
*The Book of Psalms* **4**:351
Pindar **12**:258

**Crabbe, Anna**
Boethius **15**:69

**Cracroft, Bernard**
*Arabian Nights* **2**:9

**Craigie, W. A.**
Barbour, John **33**:142
*Hrafnkel's Saga* **2**:78

**Cranston, Edwin A.**
Izumi, Shikibu **33**:264
Izumi, Shikibu **33**:303
*Kokinshu* **29**:295

**Crawford, John Martin**
*Kalevala* **6**:214

**Crawford, S. J.**
Cædmon **7**:92

**Creekmore, Hubert**
Juvenal **8**:64

**Creel, H. G.**
Lieh Tzu **27**:98

**Crem, Theresa M.**
Rhetoric **31**:238

**Croce, Benedetto**
*Inferno* **3**:58
Plato **8**:269
Terence **14**:326

**Croiset, Maurice**
Aristophanes **4**:70

**Crombie, A. C.**
Bacon, Roger **14**:79

**Cross, R. Nicol**
Socrates **27**:229

**Crossley-Holland, Kevin**
Norse Mythology **26**:337

**Crump, M. Marjorie**
Ovid **7**:314

**Crusemann, Frank**
*Torah* **30**:356

**Cruttwell, Charles Thomas**
Cato, Marcus Porcius **21**:22

**Cumming, William Patterson**
St. Birgitta **24**:89

**Cummings, Hubertis M.**
Boccaccio, Giovanni **13**:87

**Cunliffe, John W.**
Seneca, Lucius Annaeus **6**:339

**Cunningham, Stanley B.**
Albert the Great **16**:43, 65

**Curley III, Thomas F.**
Boethius **15**:97

**Curran, Leo C.**
Propertius, Sextus **32**:270

**Currie, H. MacL.**
Phaedrus **25**:366

**Curtius, Ernst Robert**
*Aeneid* **9**:345, 376
Augustine, St. **6**:56
Hermogenes **6**:158
*Inferno* **3**:98

**Dahlberg, Charles**
*Romance of the Rose* **8**:414

**Dall, Caroline H.**
Sordello **15**:328

**D'Alton, Rev. J. F.**
Cicero, Marcus Tullius **3**:207

**Dalven, Rae**
Anna Comnena **25**:58

**Damon, S. Foster**
Marie de France **8**:120

**Dandekar, R. N.**
*Mahabharata* **5**:227

Critic Index

Critic Index

**Critic Index**

Aristophanes **4**:155

**Pope, Alexander**
*Aeneid* **9**:313, 358
*Iliad* **1**:284
*Odyssey* **16**:192

**Pope, John C.**
Cædmon **7**:110

**Pope, Marvin H.**
*The Book of Job* **14**:181
*Song of Songs* **18**:266

**Popper, K. R.**
Plato **8**:348

**Portalie, Eugene**
Augustine, St. **6**:17

**Porter, Jean**
Aquinas, St. Thomas **33**:65

**Portor, Laura Spencer**
*Arabian Nights* **2**:23

**Poschl, Viktor**
*Aeneid* **9**:377

**Post, Chandler Rathfon**
*Razon de Amor* **16**:338

**Post, L. A.**
Menander **9**:218

**Pound, Ezra**
Bertran de Born **5**:22
*Inferno* **3**:99
*Odyssey* **16**:279
*Poem of the Cid* **4**:232
*The Song of Roland* **1**:173
Sordello **15**:347

**Powell, F. York**
*Hrafnkel's Saga* **2**:76

**Power, Eileen**
Polo, Marco **15**:291

**Powys, John Cowper**
*Iliad* **1**:358
*Inferno* **3**:88

**Powys, Llewelyn**
Khayyam **11**:275

**Prabhavananda, Swami**
*Bhagavad Gita* **12**:54

**Pratt, Norman T.**
Seneca, Lucius Annaeus **6**:429

**Preston, Keith**
Petronius **34**:266

**Prescott, Henry W.**
*Aeneid* **9**:335

**Press, Alan R.**
Bertran de Born **5**:48

**Pretor, Alfred**
Xenophon **17**:322

**Price, Arnold H.**
*Das Nibelungenlied* **12**:164

**Price, John Valdimir**
Ossian **28**:359

**Priest, George Madison**
Wolfram von Eschenbach **5**:301

**Priest, John F.**
Aesop **24**:73

**Pritchett, V. S.**
Murasaki, Lady **1**:452
*Poem of the Cid* **4**:263, 264

**Proclus Diadochus**
Euclid **25**:89
Plato **8**:209

**Prothero, Rowland E.**
*The Book of Psalms* **4**:373

**Proust, Marcel**
*Arabian Nights* **2**:25

**Prowett, C. G.**
Apuleius **1**:13

**Pruyser, Paul W.**
*Epic of Gilgamesh* **3**:343

**Pseudo-Longinus**
Demosthenes **13**:134, 175

**Puette, William J.**
Murasaki, Lady **1**:463

**Puhvel, Jaan**
Celtic Mythology **26**:13
Eastern Mythology **26**:179

**Purdon, Liam O.**
Barbour, John **33**:245

**Purser, Louis C.**
Ovid **7**:299

**Putnam, Edward Kirby**
Havelok **34**:145

**Putnam, Michael C. J.**
*Aeneid* **9**:428

**Quasimodo, Salvatore**
*Inferno* **3**:113
Sappho **3**:435

**Qudsi, Obaidullah**
Al-Biruni **28**:143

**Quennell, Peter**
Apuleius **1**:22

**Quiller-Couch, Sir Arthur**
*Beowulf* **1**:67

**Quinn, Kenneth**
*Aeneid* **9**:408
Catullus **18**:99, 116

**Quinones, Ricardo J.**

*Inferno* **3**:140

**Quintilian**
*Aeneid* **9**:294
Aristophanes **4**:40
Hesiod **5**:69
Menander **9**:203
Ovid **7**:286
Seneca, Lucius Annaeus **6**:403

**Rabin, Chaim**
*Song of Songs* **18**:259

**Radhakrishnan, Sarvepalli**
*Bhagavad Gita* **12**:14
*Mahabharata* **5**:195

**Radice, Betty**
Abelard **11**:56
Terence **14**:363

**Radner, Joan N.**
*Tain Bo Cualnge* **30**: 187

**Rahman, Fazlur**
Avicenna **16**:134

**Raleigh, Walter**
Boccaccio, Giovanni **13**:32

**Ralphs, Sheila**
*Inferno* **3**:135

**Ramanuja**
*Bhagavad Gita* **12**:3

**Rambachan, Anantanand**
Sankara **32**:365

**Ramsay, G. G.**
Juvenal **8**:38

**Rand, Edward Kennard**
*Aeneid* **9**:350
Boethius **15**:4
Cicero, Marcus Tullius **3**:210, 231

**Randall, Dale B. J.**
*Sir Gawain and the Green Knight* **2**:212

**Rankin, David**
Tertullian **29**:379

**Rankin, H. D.**
Petronius **34**:350

**Raphael, Frederic**
Catullus **18**:144

**Rapin, Rene**
*Iliad* **1**:276

**Rascoe, Burton**
Apuleius **1**:17
Boccaccio, Giovanni **13**:42

**Raven, J. E.**
Presocratic philosophy **22**:16
Parmenides **22**:234

**Rawlinson, Henry**
Polo, Marco **15**:267

**Raybin, David**
Bodel, Jean **28**:264

**Reckford, Kenneth J.**
Menander **9**:238

**Rees, D. A.**
Science **31**:353

**Regan, Mariann Sanders**
Petrarch **20**:293

**Rehder, Robert M.**
Rumi, Jalal al-Din **20**:367

**Reid, Margaret J. C.**
Arthurian Legend **10**:44, 62

**Reinhardt, Karl**
Sophocles **2**:351

**Reinstein, P. Gila**
Aesop **24**:52

**Reiss, Edmund**
Boethius **15**:88

**Rehder, Von R. M.**
Hafiz **34**:92

**Rejak, Tessa**
Josephus, Flavius **13**:278

**Renan, Ernest**
*The Book of Job* **14**:170
*Mabinogion* **9**:144

**Renard, John**
Rumi, Jalal al-Din **20**:389

**Renoir, Alain**
*The Song of Roland* **1**:199

**Rexroth, Kenneth**
Abelard **11**:55
Apuleius **1**:37
*Beowulf* **1**:118
*Bhagavad Gita* **12**:73
*Epic of Gilgamesh* **3**:323
*Kalevala* **6**:252
*Mahabharata* **5**:242
Murasaki, Lady **1**:441

**Rhodes, Jim**
*Pearl* **19**:393

**Rhys, John**
*Mabinogion* **9**:147

**Rice, Robert C.**
Cynewulf **23**:77

**Richards, Herbert**
Aristophanes **4**:75

**Richardson, Professor**
Ossian **28**:291

**Richardson, Samuel**
Aesop **24**:4

**Richardson, T. Wade**

*Critic Index*

Critic Index

**Critic Index**

Critic Index

ISBN 0-7876-3256-2

90000

9 780787 632564